EXPLANATORY NOTES

UPON

THE NEW TESTAMENT.

By JOHN WESLEY, M.A.,
LATE FELLOW OF LINCOLN COLLEGE, OXFORD.

Schmul Publishers
Rare Reprint Specialists
Salem, Ohio 44460
76

CARLTON & LANAHAN·
SAN FRANCISCO: E. THOMAS.
CINCINNATI: HITCHCOCK & WALDEN.

PREFACE.

1. For many years I have had a desire of setting down and laying together, what has occurred to my mind, either in reading, thinking, or conversation, which might assist serious. persons, who have not the advantage of learning, in understanding the New Testament. But I have been continually deterred from attempting any thing of this kind, by a deep sense of my own inability : of my want, not only of learning for such a work, but much more, of experience and wisdom. This has often occasioned my laying aside the thought. And when, by much importunity, I have been prevailed upon to resume it, still I determined to delay it as long as possible, that (if it should please God) I might finish my work and my life together.

2. But having lately had a loud call from God to arise and go hence, I am convinced that if I attempt any thing of this kind at all, I must not .delay any longer. My day is far spent, and (even in a natural way) the shadows of the evening come on apace. And I am the rather induced to do what little I can in this way, because I can do nothing else : being prevented, by my present weakness, from either travelling or preaching. But, blessed be God, I can still read, and write, and think. O that it may be to his glory !

3. It will be easily discerned, even from what I have said already, and much more from the *notes* themselves, that they were not principally designed for men of learning ; who are provided with many other helps : and much less for men of long and deep experience in the ways and word of God. I desire to sit at their feet, and to learn of them. But I write chiefly for plain unlettered men, who understand only their mother tongue, and yet reverence and love the word of God, and have a desire to save their souls.

4. In order to assist these in such a measure as I am able, I design first to set down the text itself, for the most part, in the common *English* translation, which is, in general, (so far as I can judge) abundantly the best that I have seen. Yet I do not say it is incapable of being brought, in several places, nearer to the original. Neither will I affirm, that the *Greek* copies from which this translation was made, are always the most correct. And therefore I shall take the liberty, as occasion may require, to make here and there a small alteration.

5. I am very sensible this will be liable to objections : nay, to objections of quite opposite kinds. Some will probably think, the text is altered too much ; and others, that it is altered too little. To the former I would observe, that I never knowingly, so much as in one place, altered it for altering sake : but there, and there only, where

first, the sense was made better, stronger, clearer, or more consistent with the context: secondly, where the sense being equally good, the phrase was better or nearer the original. To the latter, who think the alterations too few, and that the translation might have been nearer still, I answer, this is true: I acknowledge it might. But what valuable end would it have answered, to multiply such trivial alterations as add neither clearness nor strength to the text? This I could not prevail upon myself to do: so much the less because there is, to my apprehension, I know not what, peculiarly solemn and venerable in the old language of our translation. And suppose this a mistaken apprehension, and an instance of human infirmity; yet, is it not an excusable infirmity, to be unwilling to part with what we have been long accustomed to; and to love the very words by which God has often conveyed strength or comfort to our souls!

6. I have endeavoured to make the notes as short as possible that the comment may not obscure or swallow up the text: and as plain as possible, in pursuance of my main design, to assist the unlearned reader: for this reason I have studiously avoided, not only all curious and critical inquiries, and all use of the learned languages, but all such methods of reasoning and modes of expression as people in common life are unacquainted with: for the same reason, as I rather endeavour to obviate than to propose and answer questions, so I purposely decline going deep into many difficulties, lest I should leave the ordinary reader behind me.

7. I once designed to write down barely what occurred to my own mind, consulting none but the inspired writers. But no sooner was I acquainted with that great light of the Christian world, (lately gone to his reward,) Bengelius, than I entirely changed my design, being thoroughly convinced it might be of more service to the cause of religion, were I barely to translate his *Gnomon Novi Testamenti*, than to write many volumes upon it. Many of his excellent notes I have therefore translated. Many more I have abridged, omitting that part which was purely critical, and giving the substance of the rest. Those various readings likewise, which he has showed to have a vast majority of ancient copies and translations on their side, I have without scruple incorporated with the text; which, after his manner, I have divided all along (though not omitting the common division into chapters and verses, which is of use on various accounts) according to the matter it contains, making a larger or smaller pause, just as the sense requires. And even this is such a help in many places, as one who has not tried it can scarcely conceive.

8. I am likewise indebted for some useful observations to Dr. Heylin's *Theological Lectures:* and for many more to Dr. Guyse, and to the *Family Expositor* of the late pious and learned Dr. Doddridge

It was a doubt with me for some time, whether I should not subjoin to every note I received from them the name of the author from whom it was taken ; especially considering I had transcribed some, and abridged many more, almost in the words of the author. But upon farther consideration, I resolved to name none, that nothing might divert the mind of the reader from keeping close to the point in view, and receiving what was spoken only according to its own intrinsic value.

9. I cannot flatter myself so far (to use the words of one of the above-named writers) as to imagine that I have fallen into no mistakes in a work of so great difficulty. But my own conscience acquits me of having designedly misrepresented any single passage of Scripture, or of having written one line with a purpose of inflaming the hearts of Christians against each other. God forbid that I should make the words of the most gentle and benevolent Jesus a vehicle to convey such poison. Would to God that all the party names, and unscriptural phrases and forms, which have divided the Christian world, were forgot : and that we might all agree to sit down together, as humble, loving disciples, at the feet of our common Master, to hear his word, to imbibe his Spirit, and to transcribe his life in our own!

10. Concerning the Scriptures in general, it may be observed, the word of the living God, which directed the first patriarchs also, was, in the time of *Moses*, committed to writing. To this were added, in several succeeding generations, the inspired writings of the other prophets. Afterward, what the Son of God preached, and the Holy Ghost spake by the apostles, the apostles and evangelists wrote.— This is what we now style the *Holy Scripture :* this is that *word of God which remaineth for ever :* of which, though *heaven and earth pass away, one jot or tittle shall not pass away.* The Scripture therefore of the *Old and New Testament*, is a most solid and precious system of Divine truth. Every part thereof is worthy of God ; and all together are one entire body, wherein is no defect, no excess. It is the fountain of heavenly wisdom, which they who are able to taste, prefer to all writings of men, however wise, or learned, or holy.

11. An exact knowledge of the truth was accompanied in the inspired writers with an exactly regular series of arguments, a precise expression of their meaning, and a genuine vigour of suitable affections. The chain of argument in each book is briefly exhibited in the table prefixed to it, which contains also the sum thereof, and may be of more use than prefixing the argument to each chapter ; the division of the *New Testament* into chapters having been made in the dark ages, and very incorrectly ; often separating things that are closely joined, and joining those that are entirely distinct from each other.

12. In the language of the sacred writings, we may observe the utmost depth, together with the utmost ease All the elegancies of

human composures sink into nothing before it: God speaks not as man, but as God. His thoughts are very deep: and thence his words are of inexhaustible virtue. And the language of his messengers also is exact in the highest degree: for the words which were given them accurately answered the impression made upon their minds: and hence *Luther* says, " Divinity is nothing but a grammar of the language of the Holy Ghost." To understand this thoroughly, we should observe the *emphasis* which lies on every word; the holy *affections* expressed thereby, and the *tempers* shown by every writer. But how little are these, the latter especially, regarded? Though they are wonderfully diffused through the whole *New Testament*, and are in truth a continued commendation of him who acts, or speaks, or writes.

13. The *New Testament* is all those sacred writings in which the *New Testament* or covenant is described. The former part of this contains the writings of the evangelists and apostles: the latter, the revelation of Jesus Christ. In the former is, first, the history of Jesus Christ, from his coming in the flesh to his ascension into heaven; then the institution and history of the Christian Church, from the time of his ascension. The revelation delivers what is to be, with regard to Christ, the Church, and the universe, till the consummation of all things.

Bristol Hot-Wells, *January* 4, 1754.

NOTES

ON THE

GOSPEL ACCORDING TO ST. MATTHEW.

THE *Gospel* (that is, good tidings) means a book containing the good tidings of our salvation by Jesus Christ.

St. *Mark* in his Gospel presupposes that of St. *Matthew*, and supplies what is omitted therein. St. *Luke* supplies what is omitted by both the former: St. *John* what is omitted by all the three.

St. *Matthew* particularly points out the fulfilling of the prophecies for the con-viction of the Jews. St. *Mark* wrote a short compendium, and yet added many remarkable circumstances omitted by St. *Matthew*, particularly with regard to the apostles, immediately after they were called. St. *Luke* treated principally of the office of Christ, and mostly in a historical manner. St. *John* refuted those who denied his Godhead: each choosing to treat more largely on those things, which most suited the time when, and the persons to whom, he wrote.

The Gospel according to St. *Matthew* contains

ST. MATTHEW.

1 THE* book of the generation of Jesus Christ, the Son of Da-
2 vid, the son of Abraham. Abraham begat Isaac, and Isaac begat
3 Jacob, and Jacob begat Judah and his brethren; And Judah
  begat Pharez and Zarah of Thamar, and Pharez begat Esrom, and
4 Esrom begat Aram; and Aram begat Aminadab, and Aminadab
5 begat Naasson, and Naasson begat Salmon; and Salmon begat
6 Boaz of Rahab, and Boaz begat Obed of Ruth, and Obed begat Jesse;
  and Jesse begat David the king.
7 And David the king begat Solomon, of the *wife* of Uriah; and So-.
  lomon begat Rehoboam, and Rehoboam begat Abijah, and Abijah
8 begat Asa; and Asa begat Jehoshaphat, and Jehoshaphat begat
9 Jehoram, and Jehoram begat Uzziah: and Uzziah begat Jotham, and
10 Jotham begat Ahaz, and Ahaz begat Hezekiah, and Hezekiah begat
   Manasseth, and Manasseth begat Amon, and Amon begat Josiah.
11 and Josiah begat Jeconiah and his brethren, about the time they
12 were carried away to Babylon. And after they were brought to
   Babylon, Jeconiah begat Salathiel, and Salathiel begat Zerubbabel;
13 And Zerubbabel begat Abiud, and Abiud begat Eliakim, and Elia-

Verse 1. *The book of the generation of Jesus Christ*—That is, strictly speaking,
the account of his birth and genealogy. This title therefore properly relates to
the verses that immediately follow : but as it sometimes signifies the history of a
person, in that sense it may belong to the whole book. If there were any difficulties in this genealogy, or that given by St. Luke, which could not easily be
removed, they would rather affect the Jewish tables, than the credit of the evangelists : for they act only as historians setting down these genealogies, as they
stood in those public and allowed records. Therefore they were to take them as
they found them. Nor was it needful they should correct the mistakes, if there
were any. For these accounts sufficiently answer the end for which they are
recited. They unquestionably prove the grand point in view, that Jesus was of
the family from which the promised seed was to come. And they had more
weight with the Jews for this purpose, than if alterations had been made by
inspiration itself. For such alterations would have occasioned endless disputes
between them and the disciples of our Lord. *The son of David, the son of Abraham*—He is so called, because to these he was more peculiarly promised; and of
these it was often foretold the Messiah should spring.
  3. *Of Thamar*—St. Matthew adds the names of those women also, that were
remarkable in the sacred history.
  4. *Naasson*—Who was prince of the tribe of Judah, when the Israelites entered
into Canaan.
  5. *Obed begat Jesse*—The providence of God was peculiarly shown in this,
that Salmon, Boaz, and Obed, must each of them have been near a hundred
years old, at the birth of his son here recorded.
  6. *David the king*—Particularly mentioned under this character, because his
throne is given to the Messiah.
  8. *Jehoram begat Uzziah*—Jehoahaz, Joash, and Amaziah coming between. So
that he begat him mediately, as Christ is mediately the son of David and of Abraham. So the progeny of Hezekiah, after many generations, are called the sons
that should issue from him, which he should beget, Isaiah xxxix, 7.
  11. *Josiah begat Jeconiah*—Mediately, Jehoiakim coming between. *And his
brethren*—That is, his uncles. The Jews term all kinsmen brethren. *About the
time they were carried away*—Which was a little after the birth of Jeconiah.

* Luke iii, 31.

14 kim begat Azor; and Azor begat Zadock, and Zadock begat
15 Achim, and Achim begat Eliud; and Eliud begat Eleazar, and
16 Eleazar begat Matthan, and Matthan begat Jacob; and Jacob begat
Joseph, the husband of Mary, of whom was born Jesus, who is
called Christ.

17   So all the generations from Abraham to David *are* fourteen
generations : and from David to the carrying away to Babylon *are*
fourteen generations, and from the carrying away to Babylon to
Christ *are* fourteen generations.

18   Now the birth of Christ was on this wise : his mother Mary,
being espoused to Joseph, before they came together she was found
19 with child by the Holy Ghost.   Then Joseph, her husband, being
a just man, and yet not willing to make her a public example, pur-
20 posed to put her away privately.   But while he was thinking on
these things, behold, an angel of the Lord appeared to him in a
dream, saying, Joseph, *thou* son of David, fear not to take to thee
Mary thy wife; for that which is begotten in her is of the Holy
21 Ghost.   And she shall bring forth a son, and thou shalt call his name
22 Jesus; for he shall save his people from their sins.   (Now all this
was done, that it might be fulfilled which was spoken of the Lord

---

16. *The husband of Mary*—Jesus was generally believed to be the son of Joseph.
It was needful for all who believed this, to know, that Joseph was sprung from
David.   Otherwise they would not allow Jesus to be the Christ.   *Jesus, who is
called Christ*—The name Jesus respects chiefly the promise of blessing made to
Abraham : the name Christ, the promise of the Messiah's kingdom, which was
made to David.

It may be farther observed, that the word Christ in Greek, and Messiah in
Hebrew, signify anointed, and imply the prophetic, priestly, and royal characters,
which were to meet in the Messiah.   Among the Jews, anointing was the ceremony whereby prophets, priests, and kings were initiated into those offices.   And
if we look into ourselves, we shall find a want of Christ in all these respects.—
We are by nature at a distance from God, alienated from him, and incapable of a
free access to him.   Hence we want a mediator, an intercessor, in a word, a
Christ, in his priestly office.   This regards our state with respect to God.   And
with respect to ourselves, we find a total darkness, blindness, ignorance of God,
and the things of God.   Now here we want Christ in his prophetic office, to
enlighten our minds, and teach us the whole will of God.   We find also within
us a strange misrule of appetites and passions.   For these we want Christ in his
royal character, to reign in our hearts, and subdue all things to himself.

17. *So all the generations*—Observe, in order to complete the three fourteens,
David ends the first fourteen, and begins the second (which reaches to the
captivity) and Jesus ends the third fourteen.

When we survey such a series of generations, it is a natural and obvious
reflection, how *like the leaves of a tree one passeth away, and another cometh!* Yet
the earth still abideth.   And with it the goodness of the Lord which runs from
generation to generation, the common hope of parents and children.

Of those who formerly lived upon earth, and perhaps made the most conspicuous figure, how many are there whose names are perished with them? How
many, of whom only the names are remaining? Thus are we likewise passing
away! And thus shall we shortly be forgotten! Happy are we, if, while we are
forgotten by men, we are remembered by God! If our names, lost on earth, are
at length found written in the book of life!

19. *A just man*—A strict observer of the law : therefore not thinking it right
to keep her.

21. *Jesus*—That is, a Saviour.   It is the same name with Joshua (who was a
type of him) which properly signifies, *The Lord, Salvation.   His people*—Israel.
And all the Israel of God.

23 by the prophet, saying, *Behold, a virgin shall be with child, and
bring forth a Son, and they shall call his name Emmanuel,
24 (which is, being interpreted, God with us.) Then Joseph, being
raised from sleep, did as the angel of the Lord had commanded
25 him, and took unto him his wife : but he knew her not, till she
had † brought forth her Son, the first born. And he called his
name Jesus.

II. Now after Jesus was born in Bethlehem of Judea, in the days
of Herod the king, behold, wise men came from the east to Jerusa-
2 lem, saying, Where is he that is born King of the Jews ? For we
have seen his star in the east, and are come to do him homage.
3 When Herod the king had heard *these things*, he was troubled, and
4 all Jerusalem with him. And having assembled all the chief
priests and scribes of the people, he inquired of them, Where the
5 Christ was to be born ? And they said to him, in Bethlehem of

---

23. *They shall call his name Emmanuel*—To *be called*, only means, according
to the Hebrew manner of speaking, that the person spoken of shall really and
effectually be what he is called, and actually fulfil that title. Thus, *Unto us a
child is born—and his name shall be called Wonderful, Counsellor, the Mighty
God, the Prince of Peace*—That is, he shall be all these, though not so much
nominally, as really, and in effect. And thus was he called *Emmanuel;* which
was no common name of Christ, but points out his nature and office ; as he is God
incarnate, and dwells by his Spirit in the hearts of his people.

It is observable, the words in Isaiah are, *Thou* (namely, his mother) *shalt call;*
but here, *They*—that is, all his people, *shall call*—shall acknowledge *him* to be
Emmanuel, God with us. *Which being interpreted*—This is a clear proof that
St. Matthew wrote his Gospel in Greek, and not in Hebrew.

25. *He knew her not, till after she had brought forth*—It cannot be inferred from
hence, that he knew her afterward : no more than it can be inferred from that
expression, 2 Sam. vi, 23, *Michal had no child till the day of her death*, that she
had children afterward. Nor do the words that follow, *the first-born* son, alter
the case. For there are abundance of places, wherein the term *first born* is used,
though there were no subsequent children.

II. 1. *Bethlehem of Judea*—There was another Bethlehem in the tribe of Zebulon. *In the days of Herod*—commonly called Herod the Great, born at Ascalon.
The sceptre was now on the point of departing from Judah. Among his sons
were Archelaus, mentioned ver. 22 ; Herod Antipas, mentioned chap. xiv; and
Philip, mentioned Luke iii. Herod Agrippa, mentioned Acts xii, was his grandson.
Wise men—The first fruits of the Gentiles. Probably they were Gentile philosophers, who, through the Divine assistance, had improved their knowledge of
nature, as a means of leading to the knowledge of the one true God. Nor is it
unreasonable to suppose, that God had favoured them with some extraordinary
revelations of himself, as he did Melchisedec, Job, and several others, who were
not of the family of Abraham ; to which he never intended absolutely to confine
his favours. The title given them in the original was anciently given to all
philosophers, or men of learning; those particularly who were curious in examin-
ing the works of nature, and observing the motions of the heavenly bodies.

From the east—So Arabia is frequently called in Scripture. It lay to the east
of Judea, and was famous for gold, frankincense, and myrrh. *We have seen his
star*—Undoubtedly they had before heard Balaam's prophecy. And probably
when they saw this unusual star, it was revealed to them that this prophecy was
fulfilled. *In the east*—That is, while we were in the east.

2. *To do him homage*—To pay him that honour, by bowing to the earth before
him, which the eastern nations used to pay to their monarchs.

4. *The chief priests*—That is, not only the high priest and his deputy, with
those who formerly had borne that office : but also the chief man in each of those
twenty-four courses, into which the body of priests were divided, 1 Chron. xxiv,
10. The scribes were those whose peculiar business it was to explain the

---

* Isaiah vii, 14.　† Luke ii, 7.

6 Judea; for thus it is written by the prophet, * And thou, Bethlehem.
   in the land of Judah, art in nowise the least among the princes of
   Judah; · for out of thee shall come forth a Governor, who shall rule
7 my people Israel.   Then Herod, having privately called the wise
   men, inquired of them with great exactness, at what time the star
8 appeared: And sending them to Bethlehem, he said, Go, inquire
   exactly concerning the young child, and if ye find *him*, bring me
9 word again, that I also may come and do him homage.   And having heard the king, they departed; and lo, the star which they had
   seen in the east, moved on before them, till it came and stood over
10. where the young child was.   And seeing the star, they rejoiced
11 with exceeding great joy.   And being come into the house, they
   saw the young child, with Mary his mother; and falling down, they
   did him homage.   And opening their treasures, they presented to
12 him gifts, gold, frankincense, and myrrh.   And having been warned
   of God in a dream not to return to Herod, they retired into their
   own country another way.
13   And when they had retired, behold, an angel of the Lord
   appeareth to Joseph in a dream, saying, Arise, and take the young
   child and his mother, and flee into Egypt, and continue there till
   I shall tell thee: for Herod will seek the young child to destroy
14 him.   And he arose, and took the young child and his mother by
15 night, and retired into Egypt, And continued there till the death of
   Herod; that it might be fulfilled which was spoken of the Lord by
16 the prophet, saying, † Out of Egypt have I called my Son.   Then

---

Scriptures to the people.   They were the public preachers, or expounders of the
law of Moses.   Whence the chief of them were called doctors of the law.
   6. *Thou art in nowise the least among the princes of Judah*—That is, among the
cities belonging to the princes or heads of thousands in Judah.   When this and
several other quotations from the Old Testament are compared with the original,
it plainly appears, the apostles did not always think it necessary exactly to transcribe the passages they cited, but contented themselves with giving the general
sense, though with some diversity of language.   The words of Micah, which we
render, *Though thou be little*, may be rendered, *Art thou little?* And then the
difference which seems to be here between the prophet and the evangelist
vanishes away.
   8. *And if ye find* him, *bring me word*—Probably Herod did not believe he was
born; otherwise would not so suspicious a prince have tried to make sure work
at once?
   10. *Seeing the star*—Standing over where the child was.
   11. *They presented to him gifts*—It was customary to offer some present to any
eminent person whom they visited.   And so it is, as travellers observe, in the
eastern countries to this day.   *Gold, frankincense, and myrrh*—Probably these
were the best things their country afforded; and the presents ordinarily made to
great persons.
   This was a most seasonable, providential assistance for a long and expensive
journey into Egypt, a country where they were entirely strangers, and were to
stay for a considerable time.
   15. *That it might be fulfilled*—That is, whereby was fulfilled.   The original
word frequently signifies, not the design of an action, but barely the consequence
or event of it.   *Which was spoken of the Lord by the prophet*—on another occasion:
Out of Egypt have I called my Son—which was now fulfilled as it were anew.;
Christ being in a far higher sense the Son of God than *Israel*, of whom the words
were originally spoken.
   16. *Then Herod, seeing that he was deluded by the wise men*—So did his pride
teach him to regard this action, as if it were intended to expose him to the deri-

* Micah v, 2.   † Hosea xi, 1.

Herod, seeing he was deluded by the wise men, was exceeding wroth, and sending forth, slew all the male children that were in Bethlehem, and in all the confines thereof, from two years old and under ; according to the time which he had exactly inquired of the

17 wise men. Then was fulfilled that which was spoken by Jeremiah
18 the prophet, saying, * In Rama was there a voice heard, lamentation, and, weeping, and great mourning, Rachel weeping for her children, and would not be comforted, because they are not.
19 But when Herod was dead, behold, an angel of the Lord appeareth
20 in a dream to Joseph in Egypt, saying, Arise, and take the young child and his mother, and go into the land of Israel ; for they
21 are dead who sought the young child's life. And he arose, and took the young child and his mother, and came into the land of
22 Israel. But having heard, Archelaus reigneth over Judea in the room of his father Herod, he was afraid to go thither, and being warned of God in a dream, he turned aside into the region of
23 Galilee. And he came and dwelt in a city called Nazareth, that it might be fulfilled which was spoken by the prophets, He shall be called a Nazarene.

III. † In those days cometh John the Baptist preaching in the wilder-
2 derness of Judea, And saying, Repent ye ; for the kingdom of

sion of his subjects. *Sending forth*—a party of soldiers : *In all the confines thereof*—In all the neighbouring places, of which Rama was one.

17. *Then was fulfilled*—A passage of Scripture, whether prophetic, historical, or poetical, is in the language of the New Testament fulfilled, when an event happens to which it may with great propriety be accommodated.

18. *Rachel weeping for her children*—The Benjamites, who inhabited Rama, sprung from her. She was buried near this place; and is here beautifully represented risen, as it were out of her grave, and bewailing her lost children.— *Because they are not*—that is, are dead. The preservation of Jesus from this destruction, may be considered as a figure of God's care over his children in their greatest danger. God does not often, as he easily could, cut off their persecutors at a stroke. But he provides a hiding place for his people, and by methods not less effectual, though less pompous, preserves them from being swept away, even when the enemy comes in like a flood.

22. *He was afraid to go thither*—into Judea; and so *turned aside into the region of Galilee*—a part of the land of Israel not under the jurisdiction of Archelaus.

23. *He came and dwelt in Nazareth*—(where he had dwelt before he went tc Bethlehem) a place contemptible to a proverb. *So that* hereby was fulfilled what has been *spoken* in effect *by* several of *the prophets*, (though by none of them in express words,) *He shall be called a Nazarene*—that is, he shall be despised and rejected, shall be a mark of public contempt and reproach.

III. 1. *In those days*—that is, while Jesus dwelt there. *In the wilderness of Judea*—This was a wilderness properly so called, a wild, barren, desolate place as was that also where our Lord was tempted. But, generally speaking, a wilderness in the New Testament means only a common, or less cultivated place, in opposition to pasture and arable land.

2. *The kingdom of heaven*, and the kingdom of God, are but two phrases for the same thing. They mean, not barely a future happy state, in heaven, but a state to be enjoyed on earth : the proper disposition for the glory of heaven, rather than the possession of it. *Is at hand*—As if he had said, God is about to erect that kingdom, spoken of by Daniel (ch. ii, 44; and vii, 13, 14;) the kingdom of the God of heaven. It properly signifies here, the Gospel dispensation, in which subjects were to be gathered to God by his Son, and a society to be formed, which was to subsist first on earth, and afterward with God in glory. In some places of Scripture, the phrase more particularly denotes the state of it on earth : in others, it signifies only the state of glory : but it generally includes both. The

3 heaven is at hand. For this is he that was spoken of by the Pro
  phet Isaiah, saying, * The voice of one crying aloud in the wilderness, Prepare ye the way of the Lord, make his paths straight.
4 And this John had his raiment of camels' hair, and a leathern gir
  dle about his loins ; and his food was locusts and wild honey.
5   Then went out to him Jerusalem and all Judea, and all the region
6 round about Jordan, And were baptized of him in Jordan, confess
7 ing their sins. But seeing many of the Pharisees and Sadducees
  coming to his baptism, he said to them, Ye brood of vipers, who
8 hath showed you to flee from the wrath to come? Bring forth
9 therefore fruit worthy of repentance : And say not confidently

---

Jews understood it of a temporal kingdom, the seat of which they supposed would
be Jerusalem; and the expected sovereign of this kingdom they learned from
Daniel to call the Son of man.

Both John the Baptist and Christ took up that phrase, *the kingdom of heaven*,
as they found it, and gradually taught the Jews (though greatly unwilling to
learn) to understand it right. The very demand of repentance, as previous to it,
showed it was a spiritual kingdom, and that no wicked man, how politic, brave,
or learned soever, could possibly be a subject of it.

3. *The way of the Lord*—Of Christ. *Make his paths straight*—By removing
every thing which might prove a hinderance to his gracious appearance.

4. *John had his raiment of camels' hair*—Coarse and rough, suiting his character
and doctrine. *A leathern girdle*—Like Elijah, in whose spirit and power he came.
His food was locusts and wild honey—Locusts are ranked among clean meats,
Lev. xi, 22. But these were not always to be had. So in default of those, he
fed on wild honey.

6. *Confessing their sins*—Of their own accord; freely and openly.

Such prodigious numbers could hardly be baptized by immerging their whole
bodies under water : nor can we think they were provided with change of raiment
for it, which was scarcely practicable for such vast multitudes. And yet they
could not be immerged naked with modesty, nor in their wearing apparel with
safety. It seems, therefore, that they stood in ranks on the edge of the river, and
that John, passing along before them, cast water on their heads or faces, by
which means he might baptize many thousands in a day. And this way most
naturally signified Christ's baptizing them *with the Holy Ghost and with fire*,
which John spoke of, as prefigured by his baptizing with water, and which was
eminently fulfilled, when the Holy Ghost sat upon the disciples in the appearance
of tongues, or flames of fire.

7. *The Pharisees* were a very ancient sect among the Jews. They took their
name from a Hebrew word, which signifies to separate, because they separated
themselves from all other men. They were outwardly strict observers of the
law, fasted often, made long prayers, rigorously kept the Sabbath, and paid all
tithe, even of mint, anise, and cummin. Hence they were in high esteem among
the people. But inwardly, they were full of pride and hypocrisy.

The *Sadducees* were another sect among the Jews, only not so considerable as
the Pharisees. They denied the existence of angels, and the immortality of the
soul, and by consequence the resurrection of the dead. *Ye brood of vipers*—In
like manner, the crafty Herod is styled a fox, and persons of insidious, ravenous,
profane, or sensual dispositions, are named respectively by him who saw their
hearts, serpents, dogs, wolves, and swine; terms which are not the random
language of passion, but a judicious designation of the persons meant by them.
For it was fitting such men should be marked out, either for a caution to others,
or a warning to themselves.

8. *Repentance* is of two sorts; that which is termed legal, and that which is
styled evangelical repentance. The former (which is the same that is spoken of
here) is a thorough conviction of sin. The latter is a change of heart (and
consequently of life) from all sin to all holiness.

9. *And say not* confidently—The word in the original, vulgarly rendered,
Think not, seems here, and in many places, not to diminish, but rather add to

* Isaiah xl, 3.

within yourselves, We have Abraham to our Father; for I say
unto you, God is able of these stones to raise up children to Abra-
10 ham.   But the axe also already lieth at the root of the tree; therefore every tree that bringeth not forth good fruit, is hewn down
11 and cast into the fire.   I indeed baptize you with water unto repentance ; but he that cometh after me is mightier than I ; whose
shoes I am not worthy to bear ; he shall baptize you with the Holy
12 Ghost and with fire : Whose fan is in his hand, and he will
thoroughly cleanse his floor, and gather the wheat into the garner,
but will burn up the chaff with unquenchable fire.
13   * Then cometh Jesus from Galilee to Jordan unto John, to be
14 baptized by him.   But John forbad him, saying, I have need to be
15 baptized of thee, and comest thou to me ?   And Jesus answering
said to him, Suffer it now ; for thus it becometh us to fulfil all
16 righteousness.   Then he suffered him.   And Jesus being baptized,
went up straightway from the water, and, lo, the heavens were
opened to him, and he saw the Spirit of God descending like
17 a dove, and coming upon him.   And lo, a voice out of the heavens
saying, This is my beloved Son, in whom I delight.

the force of the word with which it is joined.   *We have Abraham to our father*—
It is almost incredible, how great the presumption of the Jews was on this their
relation to Abraham.   One of their famous sayings was, " Abraham sits near the
gates of hell, and suffers no Israelite to go down into it."   *I say unto you*—This
preface always denotes the importance of what follows.   *Of these stones*—Proba.
bly pointing to those which lay before them.

10. *But the axe also already lieth*—That is, there is no room for such idle preten-
ces.   Speedy execution is determined against all that do not repent.   The comparison seems to be taken from a woodman that has laid down his axe to put off his
coat, and then immediately goes to work to cut down the tree.   This refers to
the wrath to come in verse 7.   *Is hewn down*—Instantly, without farther delay.

11. *He shall baptize you with the Holy Ghost and with fire*—He shall fill you
with the Holy Ghost, inflaming your hearts with that fire of love, which many
waters cannot quench.   And this was done, even with a visible appearance as of
fire, on the day of pentecost.

12. *Whose fan*—That is, the word of the Gospel.   *His floor*—That is, his
Church, which is now covered with a mixture of wheat and chaff.   *He will gather
the wheat into the garner*—Will lay up those who are truly good in heaven.

15. *It becometh us to fulfil all righteousness.*—It becometh every messenger of
God to observe all his righteous ordinances.   But the particular meaning of our
Lord seems to be, that *it becometh us* to do (me to receive baptism, and you to
administer it) in order *to fulfil*, that is, that I may fully perform every part of the
righteous law of God, and the commission he hath given me.

16. *And Jesus being baptized*—Let our Lord's submitting to baptism teach us
a holy exactness in the observance of those institutions which owe their obliga.
tion merely to a Divine command.   Surely thus it becometh all his followers to
fulfil all righteousness.

Jesus had no sin to wash away.   And yet he was baptized.   And God owned
his ordinance, so as to make it the season of pouring forth the Holy Spirit upon
him.   And where can we expect this sacred effusion, but in an humble attendance
on Divine appointments ?   *Lo, the heavens were opened, and he saw the Spirit of
God*—St. Luke adds, *in a bodily form*—Probably in a glorious appearance of fire,
perhaps in the shape of a dove, *descending* with a hovering motion, till it rested
upon him.   This was a visible token of those secret operations of the blessed
Spirit, by which he was anointed in a peculiar manner ; and abundantly fitted
for his public work.

17. *And lo, a voice*—We have here a glorious manifestation of the ever-blessed
Trinity : the Father speaking from heaven, the Son spoken to, the Holy Ghost

* Mark i, 9   Luke iii, 21

IV. Then * was Jesus led up by the Spirit into the wilderness to
2 be tempted by the devil. And having fasted forty days and forty
3 nights, he was afterward hungry. And the. tempter coming to
him, said, If thou be the Son of God, command that these stones
4 be made bread. But he answering, said, It is written, † Man shall
not live by bread alone, but by every word that proceedeth out of
5 the mouth of God. Then the devil taketh him with him into
the holy city, and setteth him on the battlement of the temple,
6 And saith unto him, If thou be the Son of God, cast thyself down ;
for it is written, ‡ He shall charge his angels concerning thee, and
in their hands they shall bear thee up, lest at any time thou dash
7 thy foot against a stone. Jesus said to him, It is written again,
8 § Thou shalt not tempt the Lord thy God. Again, the devil taketh
him with him to an exceeding high mountain, and showeth him all
9 the kingdoms of the world and the glory of them. And saith to him,
All these things will I give thee, if thou wilt fall down and worship
10 me. Then Jesus saith to him, Get thee hence, Satan ; for it is
written, ‖ Thou shalt worship the Lord thy God, and him only shalt
11 thou serve. Then the devil leaveth him, and behold, angels came
and waited upon him.

descending upon him. *In whom I delight*—What an encomium is this! How
poor to this are all other kinds of praise ! To be the pleasure, the delight of God,
this is praise indeed: this is true glory: this is the highest, the brightest light,
that virtue can appear in.

IV. 1. *Then*—After this glorious evidence of his Father's love, he was completely armed for the combat. Thus after the clearest light and the strongest
consolation, let us expect the sharpest temptations. *By the Spirit*—Probably
through a strong inward impulse.

2. *Having fasted*—Whereby doubtless he received more abundant spiritual
strength from God. *Forty days and forty nights*—As did *Moses*, the giver of the
law, and *Elijah*, the great restorer of it. *He was afterward hungry*—And so
prepared for the first temptation.

3. *Coming to him*—In a visible form; probably in a human shape, as one that
desired to inquire farther into the evidences of his being the *Messiah*.

4. *It is written*—Thus Christ answered, and thus we may answer all the sug-
gestions of the devil. *By every word that proceedeth out of the mouth of God*—
That is, by whatever God commands to sustain him. Therefore it is not needful
I should work a miracle to procure bread, without any intimation of my
Father's will.

5. *The holy city*—So *Jerusalem* was commonly called, being the place God had
peculiarly chosen for himself. *On the battlement of the temple*—Probably over
the king's gallery, which was of such a prodigious height, that no one could look
down from the top of it without making himself giddy.

6. *In their hands*—That is, with great care.

7. *Thou shalt not tempt the Lord thy God*—By requiring farther evidence of
what he hath already made sufficiently plain.

8. *Showeth him all the kingdoms of the world*—In a kind of visionary representation.

9. *If thou wilt fall down and worship me*—Here Satan clearly shows who he
was. Accordingly Christ answering this suggestion, calls him by his own name,
which he had not done before.

10. *Get thee hence, Satan*—Not, get thee behind me, that is, into thy proper
place; as he said on a quite different occasion to Peter, speaking what was not
expedient.

11. *Angels came and waited upon him*—Both to supply him with food, and to
congratulate his victory.

* Mark i, 12 ; Luke iv, 1. † Deut. viii, 3. ‡ Psalm xci, 11, 12. § Deut. vi, 16
‖ Deut. vi, 13.

12   * But when he heard that John was cast into prison, he retired
13 into Galilee.   And leaving Nazareth, he came and dwelt at Caper-
     naum, which is on the sea coast, in the borders of Zebulon and
14 Naphthali : that it might be fulfilled which was spoken by Isaiah
15 the prophet, saying, † The land of Zebulon and the land of Naph-
     thali, by the way of the sea, beyond Jordan, Galilee of the Gentiles :
16 The people who walked in darkness saw a great light, and to them
     who sat in the region of the shadow of death, light is sprung up.
17   From that time Jesus began to preach and to say, Repent, for
18 the kingdom of heaven is at hand.   ‡ And walking by the sea of
     Galilee, he saw two brethren, Simon called Peter, and Andrew his
19 brother, casting a net into the sea, for they were fishers.   And he
     saith to them, Come after me, and I will make you fishers of men.
20 And straightway, leaving their nets, they followed him.   And going
21 on from thence, he saw two ·other brethren, James the *son* of
     Zebedee, and John his brother, in the vessel with Zebedee their
22 father, mending their nets ; and he called them.   And leaving the
     vessel and their father, they immediately followed him.
23   And Jesus went about all Galilee, teaching in their synagogues,
     and preaching the Gospel of the kingdom, and healing all manner
24 of disease and all manner of malady among the people.   And his
     fame went through all Syria : and they brought to him all sick
     people, that were held with divers diseases and tormenting pains ;
     and demoniacs, and lunatics, and paralytics ; and he healed them.

---

12. *He retired into Galilee*—This journey was not immediately after his
temptation.   He first went from Judea into Galilee, John i, 43 ; ii, 1.   Then into
Judea again, and celebrated the passover at Jerusalem, John ii, 13.   He baptized
in Judea while John was baptizing at Enon, John iii, 22, 23.   All this time John
was at liberty, ver. 24.   But the Pharisees being offended, chap. iv, 1 ; and John
put in prison, he then took this journey into Galilee.

13. *Leaving Nazareth*—Namely, when they had wholly rejected his word, and
even attempted to kill him, Luke iv, 29.

15. *Galilee of the Gentiles*—That part of Galilee which lay beyond Jordan was
so called, because it was in a great measure inhabited by Gentiles, that is,
heathens.

16. Here is a beautiful gradation, first, *they walked*, then they *sat in darkness*,
and lastly, *in the region of the shadow of death*.

17. *From that time Jesus began to preach*—He had preached before, both to
Jews and Samaritans, John iv, 41, 45.   But from this time began his solemn stated
preaching.   *Repent, for the kingdom of heaven is at hand*—Although it is the
peculiar business of Christ to establish the kingdom of heaven in the hearts of
men, yet it is observable, he begins his preaching in the same words with John
the Baptist : because the repentance which John taught still was, and ever will
be, the necessary preparation for that inward kingdom.   But that phrase is not
only used with regard to individuals in whom it is to be established, but also with
regard to the Christian Church, the whole body of believers.   In the former sense
it is opposed to repentance ; in the latter the Mosaic dispensation.

23. *The Gospel of the kingdom*—The Gospel, that is, the joyous message, is the
proper name of our religion : as will be amply verified in all who earnestly and
perseveringly embrace it.

24. *Through all Syria*—The whole province, of which the Jewish country was
only a small part.   *And demoniacs*—Men possessed with devils : *and lunatics,
and paralytics*—Men ill of the palsy, whose cases were of all others most deplo
rable and most helpless.

* Mark i, 14.   † Isaiah ix, 1, 2.   ‡ Mark i, 16 ; Luke v, 1.

25 And there followed him great multitudes from Galilee, and Decapolis, and Jerusalem, and Judea, and *from* beyond Jordan.

V.   And seeing the multitudes, he went up into the mountain ; and
2 when he was sat down his disciples came to him. And he opened
3 his mouth and taught them, saying, *Happy *are* the poor in spirit
4 for theirs is the kingdom of heaven. Happy *are* they that mourn,
5 for they shall be comforted. Happy *are* the meek ; for they shall
6 inherit the earth. Happy *are* they that hunger and thirst after
7 righteousness ; for they shall be satisfied. Happy *are* the merci-
8 ful ; for they shall obtain mercy. Happy *are* the pure in heart ;

25. *Decapolis*—A tract of land on the east side of the sea of Galilee, in which
were ten cities near each other.

V. 1. *And seeing the multitudes*—At some distance, as they were coming to
him from every quarter. *He went up into the mountain*—Which was near : where
there was room for them all. *His disciples*—not only his twelve disciples, but all
who desired to learn of him.

2. *And he opened his mouth*—A phrase which always denotes a set and solemn
discourse ; *and taught them*—To bless men; to make men happy, was the great
business for which our Lord came into the world. And accordingly he here
pronounces eight blessings together, annexing them to so many steps in Christianity. Knowing that happiness is our common aim, and that an innate instinct
continually urges us to the pursuit of it, he in the kindest manner applies to that
instinct, and directs it to its proper object.

Though all men desire, yet few attain, happiness, because they seek it where
it is not to be found. Our Lord therefore begins his Divine institution, which is
the complete art of happiness, by laying down before all that have ears to hear,
the true and only true method of acquiring it.

Observe the benevolent condescension of our Lord. He seems, as it were, to
lay aside his supreme authority as our legislator, that he may the better act the
part of our friend and Saviour. Instead of using the lofty style, in positive commands, he, in a more gentle and engaging way, insinuates his will and our duty,
by pronouncing those happy who comply with it.

3. *Happy are the poor*—In the following discourse there is, 1. A sweet invitation to true holiness and happiness, ver. 3-12. 2. A persuasive to impart it to
others, ver. 13-16. 3. A description of true Christian holiness, ver. 17 ; chap.
vii, 12, (in which it is easy to observe, the latter part exactly answers the former.) 4. The conclusion : giving a sure mark of the true way, warning against
false prophets, exhorting to follow after holiness. *The poor in spirit*—They who
are unfeignedly penitent, they who are truly convinced of sin ; who see and feel
the state they are in by nature, being deeply sensible of their sinfulness, guilti-
ness, helplessness. *For theirs is the kingdom of heaven*—The present inward
kingdom : righteousness, and peace, and joy in the Holy Ghost, as well as the
eternal kingdom, if they endure to the end.

4. *They that mourn*—Either for their own sins, or for other men's, and are
steadily and habitually serious. *They shall be comforted*—More solidly and deeply
even in this world, and eternally in heaven.

5. *Happy are the meek*—They that hold all their passions and affections evenly
balanced. *They shall inherit the earth*—They shall have all things really necessary for life and godliness. They shall *enjoy* whatever portion God hath given
them here, and shall hereafter *possess* the new earth, wherein dwelleth righteousness.

6. *They that hunger and thirst after righteousness*—After the holiness here
described. *They shall be satisfied* with it.

7. *The merciful*—The tender-hearted : they who love all men as themselves :
They shall obtain mercy—Whatever mercy therefore we desire from God, the
same let us show to our brethren. He will repay us a thousand fold, the love we
bear to any for his sake.

8. *The pure in heart*—The sanctified : they who love God with all their hearts.
They shall see God—In all things here ; hereafter in glory.

* Luke vi, 20.

9 for they shall see God. Happy *are* the peace makers; for they
10 shall be called the children of God. Happy *are* they who *are*
persecuted for righteousness' sake; for theirs is the kingdom of
11 heaven. Happy *are* ye when men shall revile and persecute you,
12 and say all manner of evil against you falsely for my sake: Rejoice
and be exceeding glad; for great is your reward in heaven; for so
persecuted they the prophets who were before you.
13 *Ye are the salt of the earth: but if the salt have lost its savour,
wherewith shall it be salted? It is thenceforth good for nothing,
14 but to be cast out and to be trodden under foot of men. Ye are
the light of the world. A city that is situated on a mountain cannot
15 be hid. † Neither do they light a candle and put it under a bushel,
but on a candlestick, and it giveth light to all that are in the house.
16 Let your light so shine before men, that they may see your good
works, and glorify your Father who is in heaven.
17 Think not that I am come to destroy the law or the prophets: I
18 am not come to destroy but to fulfil. ‡ For verily I say unto you,
Till heaven and earth pass away, one jot or one tittle shall in no-

9. *The peace makers*—They that out of love to God and man do all possible good to all men. *Peace* in the Scripture sense implies all blessings temporal and eternal. *They shall be called the children of God*—Shall be acknowledged such by God and man. One would imagine a person of this amiable temper and behaviour would be the darling of mankind. But our Lord well knew it would not be so, as long as Satan was the prince of this world. He therefore warns them before of the treatment all were to expect, who were determined thus to tread in his steps, by immediately subjoining, *Happy* are *they who* are *persecuted for righteousness' sake.*
Through this whole discourse we cannot but observe the most exact method which can possibly be conceived. Every paragraph, every sentence, is closely connected both with that which precedes, and that which follows it. And is not this the pattern for every Christian preacher? If any then are able to follow it without any premeditation, well: if not, let them not dare to preach without it. No rhapsody, no incoherency, whether the things spoken be true or false, comes of the Spirit of Christ.
10. *For righteousness' sake*—That is, because they have, or follow after, the righteousness here described. He that is truly a *righteous* man, he that *mourns*, and he that is *pure in heart*, yea, *all that will live godly in Christ Jesus, shall suffer persecution*, 2 Tim. iii, 12. The world will always say, Away with such fellows from the earth. *They are made to reprove our thoughts. They are grievous to us even to behold. Their lives are not like other men's; their ways are of another fashion.*
11. *Revile*—When present: *say all evil*—When you are absent.
12. *Your reward*—Even over and above the happiness that naturally and directly results from holiness.
13. *Ye*—Not the apostles, not ministers only; but all ye who are thus holy, *are the salt of the earth*—Are to season others.
14. *Ye are the light of the world*—If ye are thus holy, you can no more be hid than the sun in the firmament: no more than *a city on a mountain*—Probably pointing to that on the brow of the opposite hill.
15. Nay, the very design of God in giving you this light was, that it might shine.
16. *That they may see—and glorify*—That is, that seeing your good works, they may be moved to love and serve God likewise.
17. *Think not*—Do not imagine, fear, hope, *that I am come*—Like your teachers, *to destroy the law or the prophets. I am not come to destroy*—The moral law, *but to fulfil*—To establish, illustrate, and explain its highest meaning, both by my life and doctrine.

* Mark ix, 50; Luke xiii, 34.   † Mark iv, 21; Luke viii, 16; xi, 33.
‡ Luke xvi, 17; xxi, 33.

19 wise pass from the law till all things be effected. Whosoevei
therefore shall break one of the least of these commandments,
and teach men so, shall be the least in the kingdom of heaven;
but whosoever shall do and teach *them*, he shall be great in the
20 kingdom of heaven. For I say unto you, That unless your righteousness shall exceed *the righteousness* of the scribes and Phari-
21 sees, ye shall in nowise enter into the kingdom of heaven. Ye
have heard that it was said to them of old, * Thou shalt do no
murder, and whosoever shall do murder, shall be liable to the
22 judgment. But I say unto you, That whosoever is angry with
his brother shall be liable to the judgment; and whosoever shall
say to his brother, Raca, shall be liable to the council; but whoso-
23 ever shall say, Thou fool, shall be liable to hell fire. Therefore, if
thou bring thy gift to the altar, and shalt there remember, that thy
24 brother hath aught against thee, Leave there thy gift before the

18. *Till all things shall be effected*—Which it either requires or foretells. For
the law has its effect, when the rewards are given, and the punishments annexed
to it inflicted, as well as when its precepts are obeyed.
19. *One of the least*—So accounted by men; *and shall teach*—Either by word
or example; *shall be the least*—That is, shall have no part therein.
20. *The righteousness of the scribes and Pharisees*—Described in the sequel of
this discourse.
21. *Ye have heard*—From the scribes reciting the law; *Thou shalt do no murder*—And they interpreted this, as all the other commandments, barely of the
outward act. *The judgment*—The Jews had in every city a court of twenty-three
men, who could sentence a criminal to be strangled. But the sanhedrim only
(the great council which sat at Jerusalem, consisting of seventy-two men,) could
sentence to the more terrible death of stoning. That was called *the judgment*,
this *the council*.
22. *But I say unto you*—Which of the prophets ever spake thus? Their language is, Thus saith the Lord. Who hath authority to use this language, but
the one Lawgiver, who is able to save and to destroy. *Whosoever is angry
with his brother*—Some copies add, *without a cause*—But this is utterly foreign
to the whole scope and tenor of our Lord's discourse. If he had only forbidden
the being *angry without a cause*, there was no manner of need of that solemn
declaration, *I say unto you;* for the scribes and Pharisees themselves said as
much as this. Even they taught, men ought not to be angry *without a cause*.
So that this righteousness does not exceed theirs. But Christ teaches, that
we ought not, for any cause, to be so angry as to call any man *Raca*, or fool.
We ought not, for any cause, to be angry at the person of the sinner, but at his
sins only. Happy world, were this plain and necessary distinction thoroughly
understood, remembered, practised! *Raca* means, a silly man, a trifler. *Whosoever shall say, Thou fool*—Shall revile, or seriously reproach any man. Our
Lord specified three degrees of murder, each liable to a sorer punishment than
the other: not indeed from men, but from God. *Hell fire*—In the valley of Hin-
nom (whence the word in the original is taken) the children were used to be
burnt alive to Moloch. It was afterward made a receptacle for the filth of the
city, where continual fires were kept to consume it. And it is probable, if any
criminals were burnt alive, it was in this accursed and horrible place. Therefore both as to its former and latter state, it was a fit emblem of hell. It must
here signify a degree of future punishment, as much more dreadful than those
incurred in the two former cases, as burning alive is more dreadful than either
strangling or stoning.
23. *Thy brother hath aught against thee*—On any of the preceding accounts:
for any unkind thought or word: any that did not spring from love.
24. *Leaving thy gift, go*—For neither thy gift nor thy prayer will atone for
thy want of love: but this will make them both an abomination before God.

* Exod. xx, 13.

altar, and go, first be reconciled to thy brother, and then come
25 and offer thy gift.   * Agree with thine adversary quickly while
·   thou art in the way with him, lest at any time the adversary delivei
    thee to the judge, and the judge deliver thee to the officer, and
26 thou be cast into prison.   Verily I say unto thee, Thou shalt in no-
    wise come out thence, till thou hast paid the last farthing.
27   Ye have heard, that it was said, † Thou shalt not commit adul-
28 tery.   But I say unto you, That whosoever looketh upon a woman
    to lust after her, hath already committed adultery with her in his
29 heart.   ‡ But if thy right eye cause thee to offend, pluck it out,
    and cast *it* from thee ; for it is profitable for thee that one of thy
    members should perish, and not that thy whole body should be cast
30 into hell.   And if thy right hand cause thee to offend, cut it off, and
    cast it from thee ; for it is profitable for thee that one of thy mem-
    bers should perish, and not that thy whole body be cast into hell.
31   It hath been said, § Whosoever shall put away his wife, let him
32 give her a writing of divorce.   But I say unto you, Whosoever
    shall put away his wife, save for the cause of whoredom, causeth
    her to commit adultery : and whosoever shall marry her that is put
    away, committeth adultery.
33   Again, ye have heard that it was said to them of old, ‖ Thou
    shalt not forswear thyself, but shalt perform thine oaths unto the
34 Lord.   But I say unto you, Swear not at all, neither by heaven,
35 for it is God's throne : Nor by the earth, for it is his footstool :
36 neither by Jerusalem, for it is the city of the great King.   Neither

---

25. *Agree with thine adversary*—With any against whom thou hast thus
offended: *while thou art in the way*—Instantly, on the spot; before you part.
Lest the adversary deliver thee to the judge—Lest he commit his cause to God.

26. *Till thou hast paid the last farthing*—That is, for ever, since thou canst
never do this.

What has been hitherto said refers to meekness: what follows, to purity of
heart.

27. *Thou shalt not commit adultery*—And·this, as well as the sixth commandment, the scribes and Pharisees interpreted barely of the outward act.

29, 30. *If* a person as dear as a *right eye*, or as useful as a *right hand, cause
thee* thus *to offend*, though but in heart.

Perhaps here may be an instance of a kind of transposition which is frequently
found in the sacred writings : so that the 29th verse may refer to 27, 28 ; and
the 30th to ver. 21, 22.   As if he had said, Part with any thing, however dear to
you, or otherwise useful, if you cannot avoid sin while you keep it.   Even cut
off your right hand, if you are of so passionate a temper, that you cannot otherwise be restrained from hurting your brother.   Pull out your eyes, if you can no
otherwise be restrained from lusting after women.

31. *Let him give her a writing of divorce*—Which the scribes and Pharisees
allowed men to do on any trifling occasion.

32. *Causeth her to commit adultery*—If she marry again.

33. Our Lord here· refers to the promise made to the pure in heart of seeing
God in all things, and points out a false doctrine of the scribes, which arose from
their not thus seeing God.

What he forbids is, the swearing at all, 1, by any creature, 2, in our ordinary
conversation : both of which the scribes and Pharisees taught to be perfectly
innocent.

36. *For thou canst not make one hair white or black*—Whereby it appears, that
this also is not thine but God's.

* Luke xii, 58.   † Exod. xx, 14.   ‡ Chap. xviii, 8 ; Mark ix, 43.   § Deut xxiv 1
             Matt. xix, 7 ; Mark x, 2 ; Luke xvi, 18.   ‖ Exod. xx, 7

shalt thou swear by thy head; for thou canst not make one hair
37 white or black.   But let your conversation be yea, yea; nay, nay;
for whatsoever is more than these is of the evil one.
38   Ye have heard that it hath been said, * An eye for an eye,
39 and a tooth for a tooth.   But I say unto you, that ye resist not
the evil man : but whosoever shall smite thee on the right cheek,
40 turn to him the other also ; And if a man will sue thee, and take
41 away thy coat, let him have thy cloak also.   And whosoever shall
42 compel thee to go with him one mile, go with him twain.   † Give
to him that asketh thee, and from him that would borrow of thee,
turn not away.
43   Ye have heard that it hath been said, ‡ Thou shalt love thy
44 neighbour, and hate thine enemy.   But I say unto you, § Love
your enemies, bless them that curse you, do good to them that hate
you, and pray for them that despitefully use you and persecute
45 you : That ye may be the children of your Father, who is in
heaven ; for he maketh his sun to rise on the evil and on the good,
46 and sendeth rain on the just and the unjust.   For if ye love them
that love you, what reward have ye ?   Do not even the publicans

37. *Let your conversation be yea, yea ; nay, nay*—That is, in your common
discourse, barely affirm or deny.
38. *Ye have heard*—Our Lord proceeds to enforce such meekness and love on
those who are persecuted for righteousness' sake (which he pursues to the end
of the chapter) as were utterly unknown to the scribes and Pharisees.   *It hath
been said*—In the law, as a direction to judges, in case of violent and barbarous
assaults.   *An eye for an eye, and a tooth for a tooth*—And this has been interpreted,
as encouraging bitter and rigorous revenge.
39. *But I say unto you, that ye resist not the evil man*—Thus ; the Greek word
translated *resist* signifies standing in battle array, striving for victory.   If a man
smite thee on the right cheek—Return not evil for evil : yea, *turn to him the other*
—Rather than revenge thyself.
40, 41. Where the damage is not great, choose rather to suffer it, though
possibly it may on that account be repeated, than to demand *an eye for an eye*,
to enter into a rigorous prosecution of the offender.   The meaning of the whole
passage seems to be, rather than return evil for evil, when the wrong is purely
personal, submit to one bodily wrong after another, give up one part of your
goods after another, submit to one instance of compulsion after another.   That
the words are not literally to be understood, appears from the behaviour of our
Lord himself, John xviii, 22, 23.
42. Thus much for your behaviour toward the violent.   As for those who use
milder methods, *Give to him that asketh thee*—Give and lend to any so far, (but
no farther, for God never contradicts himself) as is consistent with thy engagements to thy creditors, thy family, and the household of faith.
43. *Thou shalt love thy neighbour ; and hate thy enemy*—God spoke the former
part ; the scribes added the latter.
44. *Bless them that curse you*—Speak all the good you can to and of them, who
speak all evil to and of you.   Repay love in thought, word, and deed, to those
who hate you, and show it both in word and deed.
45. *That ye may be the children*—That is, that ye may continue and appear
such before men and angels.   *For he maketh his sun to rise*—He gives them such
blessings as they will receive at his hands.   Spiritual blessings they will not
receive.
46. *The publicans*—were officers of the revenue, farmers, or receivers of the
public money : men employed by the Romans to gather the taxes and customs,
which they exacted of the nations they had conquered.   These were generally
odious for their extortion and oppression, and were reckoned by the Jews as the
very scum of the earth.

* Deut. xix, 21.   † Luke vi, 30.   ‡ Lev. xix, 18.   § Luke vi, 27 35

47 the same! And if ye salute your friends only, what do ye more
48 *than others;* do not even the heathens so? Therefore ye shall be
perfect, as your Father who is in heaven is perfect.
VI. Take heed that ye practise not your righteousness before
men, to be seen of them; otherwise ye have no reward from your
2 Father who is in heaven. Therefore when thou dost alms, do not
sound a trumpet before thee, as the hypocrites do, in the syna-
3 gogues, and in the streets, that they may have glory of men. Verily
I say unto you, they have their reward. But when thou dost
4 alms, let not thy left hand know what thy right hand doth: That
thy alms may be in secret, and thy Father who seeth in secret
5 will reward thee openly. And when thou prayest, thou shalt not
be as the hypocrites; for they love to pray standing in the syna-

47. *And if ye salute your friends only*—Our Lord probably glances at those
prejudices, which different sects had against each other, and intimates, that he
would not have his followers imbibe that narrow spirit. Would to God this
had been more attended to among the unhappy divisions and subdivisions, into
which his Church has been crumbled! And that we might at least advance so
far, as cordially to embrace our *brethren in Christ,* of whatever party or denomi-
nation they are!

48. *Therefore ye shall be perfect; as your Father who is in heaven is perfect*—
So the original runs, referring to all that holiness which is described in the foregoing verses, which our Lord in the beginning of the chapter recommends as
happiness, and in the close of it as perfection.

And how wise and gracious is this, to sum up, and, as it were, seal all his
commandments with a promise! Even the proper promise of the Gospel! That
he will *put those laws in our minds, and write them in our hearts!* He well knew
how ready our unbelief would be to cry out, this is impossible! And therefore
stakes upon it all the power, truth, and faithfulness of him to whom all things
are possible.

VI. 1. In the foregoing chapter our Lord particularly described the nature of
inward holiness. In this he describes that purity of intention without which
none of our outward actions are holy. This chapter contains four parts, 1. The
right intention and manner of giving alms, ver. 1-4. 2. The right intention,
manner, form, and prerequisites of prayer, ver. 5-15. 3. The right intention,
and manner of fasting, ver. 16-18. 4. The necessity of a pure intention in all
things, unmixed either with the desire of riches, or worldly care, and fear of
want, ver. 19-34.

This verse is a general caution against vain glory, in any of our good works:
All these are here summed up together, in the comprehensive word *righteousness.* This general caution our Lord applies in the sequel to the three principal
branches of it, relating to our neighbour, ver. 2-4: to God, ver. 5, 6: and to
ourselves, ver. 16-18.

To be seen—Barely the being seen, while we are doing any of these things, is
a circumstance purely indifferent. But the doing them with this view, to be seen
and admired, this is what our Lord condemns.

2. *As the hypocrites do*—Many of the scribes and Pharisees did this, under a
pretence of calling the poor together. *They have their reward*—All they will
have; for they shall have none from God.

3. *Let not thy left hand know what thy right hand doth*—A proverbial expression
for doing a thing secretly. Do it as secretly as is consistent, 1. With the doing
it at all. 2. With the doing it in the most effectual manner.

5. *The synagogues*—These were properly the places where the people assembled for public prayer, and hearing the Scriptures read and expounded. They
were in every city from the time of the Babylonish captivity, and had service in
them thrice a day on three days in the week. In every synagogue was a council
of grave and wise persons, over whom was a president, called the ruler of the
synagogue. But the word here, as well as in many other texts, signifies any
place of public concourse.

gogues, and in the corners of the streets, that they may appear
6 unto men: verily I say unto you, they have their reward. But
thou, when thou prayest, enter into thy closet, and having shut thy
door, pray to thy Father who is in secret, and thy Father who seeth
7 in secret shall reward thee. But when ye pray, use not vain repetitions, as the heathens; for they think they shall be heard for
8 their much speaking. Be not therefore like them; for your
Father knoweth what things ye have need of, before ye ask him.
9 * Thus therefore pray ye, Our Father, who art in heaven, hallowed
10 be thy name. Thy kingdom come; thy will be done on earth, as
11 it is in heaven. Give us this day our daily bread. And forgive
12 us our debts, as we forgive our debtors. And lead us not into

6 *Enter into thy closet*—That is, do it with as much secrecy as thou canst.

7. *Use not vain repetitions*—To repeat any words without meaning them, is
certainly a vain repetition. Therefore we should be extremely careful in all our
prayers to mean what we say; and to say only what we mean from the bottom
of our hearts. The vain and heathenish repetitions which we are here warned
against, are most dangerous, and yet very common; which is a principal cause
why so many, who still profess religion, are a disgrace to it. Indeed all the
words in the world are not equivalent to one holy desire. And the very best
prayers are but vain repetitions, if they are not the language of the heart.

8. *Your Father knoweth what things ye have need of*—We do not pray to inform
God of our wants. Omniscient as he is, he cannot be informed of any thing
which he knew not before: and he is always willing to relieve them. The chief
thing wanting is, a fit disposition on our part to receive his grace and blessing.
Consequently, one great office of prayer is, to produce such a disposition in us:
to exercise our dependence on God; to increase our desire of the things we ask
for; to make us so sensible of our wants, that we may never cease wrestling till
we have prevailed for the blessing.

9. *Thus therefore pray ye*—He who best knew what we ought to pray for, and
how we ought to pray, what matter of desire, what manner of address would
most please himself, would best become us, has here dictated to us a most perfect
and universal form of prayer, comprehending all our real wants, expressing all
our lawful desires; a complete directory and full exercise of all our devotions.

Thus—For these things; sometimes in these words, at least in this manner,
short, close, full.

This prayer consists of three parts, the preface, the petitions, and the conclusion. The preface, *Our Father, who art in heaven*, lays a general foundation
for prayer, comprising what we must first know of God, before we can pray in
confidence of being heard. It likewise points out to us that faith, humility, love
of God and man, with which we are to approach God in prayer.

I. *Our Father*—Who art good and gracious to all, our Creator, our Preserver;
the Father of our Lord, and of us in him, thy children by adoption and grace:
not my Father only, who now cry unto thee, but the Father of the universe, of
angels and men: *who art in heaven*—Beholding all things, both in heaven and
earth; knowing every creature, and all the works of every creature, and every
possible event from everlasting to everlasting: the almighty Lord and Ruler of
all, superintending and disposing all things; *in heaven*—Eminently there, but not
there alone, seeing thou fillest heaven and earth.

II. 1. *Hallowed be thy name*—Mayest thou, O Father, be truly known by all
intelligent beings, and with affections suitable to that knowledge: mayest thou be
duly honoured, loved, feared, by all in heaven and in earth, by all angels and
all men.

2. *Thy kingdom come*—May thy kingdom of grace come quickly, and swallow
up all the kingdoms of the earth: may all mankind, receiving thee, O Christ,
for their king, truly believing in thy name, be filled with righteousness, and
peace, and joy; with holiness and happiness, till they are removed hence into
thy kingdom of glory, to reign with thee for ever and ever.

* Luke xi, 2.

13 temptation, but deliver us from evil. For thine is the kingdom, and the power, and the glory, for ever and ever. Amen.
14 * For if ye forgive men their trespasses, your heavenly Father
15 will also forgive you. But if ye forgive not men their trespasses,
16 neither will your Father forgive your trespasses. Moreover, when ye fast, be not as the hypocrites, of a sad countenance ; for they disfigure their faces, that they may appear unto men to fast : verily
17 I say unto you, they have their reward. But thou, when thou
18 fastest, anoint thy head, and wash thy face : That thou appear not unto men to fast, but to thy Father who is in secret, and thy Father who seeth in secret shall reward thee.
19 † Lay not up for yourselves treasures on earth, where moth and
20 rust consume, and where thieves break through and steal : But lay

3. *Thy will be done on earth, as it is in heaven*—May all the inhabitants of the earth do thy will as willingly as the holy angels: 'may these do it continually even as they, without any interruption of their willing service ; yea, and perfectly as they: mayest thou, O Spirit of grace, through the blood of the everlasting covenant, make them perfect in every good work to do thy will, and work in them all that is well pleasing in thy sight.

4. *Give us*—O Father (for we claim nothing of right, but only of thy free mercy) *this day*—(for we take no thought for the morrow) *our daily bread*—All things needful for our souls and bodies: not only the meat that perisheth, but the sacramental bread, and thy grace, the food which endureth to everlasting life.

5. *And forgive us our debts, as we also forgive our debtors*—Give us, O Lord, redemption in thy blood, even the forgiveness of sins : as thou enablest us freely and fully to forgive every man, so do thou forgive all our trespasses.

6. *And lead us not into temptation, but deliver us from evil*—Whenever we are tempted, O thou that helpest our infirmities, suffer us not to *enter into temptation;* to be overcome or suffer loss thereby ; but make a way for us to escape, so that we may be more than conquerors, through thy love, over sin and all the consequences of it. Now the principal desire of a Christian's heart being the glory of God, (ver. 9, 10,) and all he wants for himself or his brethren being the daily bread of soul and body, (or the support of life, animal and spiritual,) pardon of sin, and deliverance from the power of it and of the devil, (ver. 11, 12, 13,) there is nothing beside that a Christian can wish for ; therefore this prayer comprehends all his desires. Eternal life is the certain consequence, or rather completion of holiness.

III. *For thine is the kingdom*—The sovereign right of all things that are or ever were created : *The power*—the executive power, whereby thou governest all things in thy everlasting kingdom : *And the glory*—The praise due from every creature, for thy power, and all thy wondrous works, and the mightiness of thy kingdom, which endureth through all ages, even for ever and ever. It is observable, that though the doxology, as well as the petitions of this prayer, is threefold, and is directed to the Father, Son, and Holy Ghost distinctly, yet is the whole fully applicable both to every person, and to the ever-blessed and undivided trinity.

16. *When ye fast*—Our Lord does not enjoin either fasting, alms-deeds, or prayer : all these being duties which were before fully established in the Church of God. *Disfigure*—By the dust and ashes which they put upon their heads, as was usual at the times of solemn humiliation.

17. *Anoint thy head*—So the Jews frequently did. Dress thyself as usual

19. *Lay not up for yourselves*—Our Lord here makes a transition from religious to common actions, and warns us of another snare, the love of money, as inconsistent with purity of intention as the love of praise. *Where rust and moth consume*—Where all things are perishable and transient.

He may likewise have a farther view in these words, even to guard us against

* Mark xi, 25. † Luke xii, 33

up for yourselves treasures in heaven, where neither moth nor rust
doth consume, and where thieves do not break through nor steal.
21 For where your treasure is, there will your heart be also. * The
22 eye is the lamp of the body : if therefore thine eye be single,
23 thy whole body shall be full of light. But if thine eye be evil, thy
whole body shall be full of darkness : if therefore the light that is
24 in thee be darkness, how great *is* that darkness ? † No man can
serve two masters : for either he will hate the one and love the
other, or he will cleave to the one and neglect the other. Ye can-
25 not serve God and mammon. ‡ Therefore I say unto you, Take
not thought for your life, what ye shall eat, or what ye shall drink,
nor for your body, what ye shall put on. Is not the life more than
26 meat, and the body than raiment ? Behold the birds of the air :
they sow not, neither do they reap, nor gather into barns ; yet your
27 heavenly Father feedeth them. Are ye not much better than
they ? And which of you, by taking thought, can add to his age
28 the smallest measure ? And why take ye thought for raiment ?
Consider the lilies of the field, how they grow ; they toil not, nei-
29 ther do they spin : And yet I say unto you, that even Solomon in
30 all his glory was not arrayed like one of these. Now if God so
clothe the grass of the field which to-day is, and to-morrow is cast
into the still, *will he* not much more *clothe* you, O ye of little faith !
31 Therefore take not thought, saying, What shall we eat, or what

---

making any thing on earth *our treasure*. For then a thing properly becomes our
treasure, when we set our affections upon it.
22. *The eye is the lamp of the body*—And what the eye is to the body, the
intention is to the soul. We may observe with what exact propriety our Lord
places purity of intention between worldly desires and worldly cares, either of
which directly tend to destroy. *If thine eye be single*—Singly fixed on God
and heaven, thy whole soul will be full of holiness and happiness. *If thine eye
be evil*—Not single, aiming at any thing else.
24. *Mammon*—Riches, money; any thing loved or sought, without reference to God.
25. And if you serve God, you need be careful for nothing. *Therefore take
not thought*—That is, be not anxiously careful. Beware of worldly cares;
for these are as inconsistent with the true service of God as worldly desires.
Is not the life more than meat ?—And if God give the greater gift, will he
deny the smaller ?
27. *And which of you*—If you are ever so careful, can even add a moment
to your own life thereby ? This seems to be far the most easy and natural
sense of the words.
29. *Solomon in all his glory was not arrayed like one of these*—Not in garments
of so pure a white. The eastern monarchs were often clothed in white robes.
30. *The grass of the field*—is a general expression, including both herbs and
flowers. *Into the still*—This is the natural sense of the passage. For it can
hardly be supposed that grass or flowers should be thrown into the oven the day
after they were cut down. Neither is it the custom in the hottest countries,
where they dry fastest, to heat ovens with them. *If God so clothe*—The word
properly implies, the putting on a complete dress, that surrounds the body on all
sides; and beautifully expresses that external membrane, which (like the skin in
a human body) at once adorns the tender fabric of the vegetable, and guards it
from the injuries of the weather. Every microscope in which a flower is viewed
gives a lively comment on this text.
31. *Therefore take not thought*—How kind are these precepts ! The substance
of which is only this, Do thyself no harm ! Let us not be so ungrateful to him,

* Luke xi, 34.　† Luke xvi, 13.　‡ Luke xii, 22.

32 shall we drink, or what shall we wear? (For after all these thing
   do the heathens seek) for your heavenly Father knoweth that ye
33 need all these things.   But seek ye first the kingdom of God and
   his righteousness, and all these things shall be added to you.
34 Take not therefore thought for the morrow : for the morrow shall
   take thought for itself : sufficient for the day is the evil thereof.
VII. * Judge not, that ye be not judged.   For with what judgment
 2 ye judge, ye shall be judged, and with what measure ye mete, it
 3 shall be measured to you.   † And why beholdest thou the mote
   in thy brother's eye, but observest not the beam in thine own eye?
 4 Or how sayest thou to thy brother, Let me pull out the mote from
 5 thine eye, and behold, a beam *is* in thine own eye?   Thou hypocrite, first cast out the beam out of thine own eye, and then shalt
 6 thou see clearly to cast the mote out of 'thy brother's eye.   Give
   not that which is holy to dogs, neither cast your pearls before
   swine, lest they trample them under their feet, and turning rend you.

---

nor so injurious to ourselves, as to harass and oppress our minds with that burden of anxiety, which he has so graciously taken off.   Every verse speaks at
once to the understanding, and to the heart.   We will not therefore indulge
these unnecessary, these useless, these mischievous cares.   We will not borrow
the anxieties and distresses of the morrow, to aggravate those of the present
day.   Rather we will cheerfully repose ourselves on that heavenly Father, who
knows we have need of these things; who has given us the life, which is more
than meat, and the body, which is more than raiment.   And thus instructed in
the philosophy of our heavenly Master, we will learn a lesson of faith and cheerfulness from every bird of the air, and every flower of the field.

33. *Seek the kingdom of God and his righteousness*—Singly aim at this, that
God, reigning in your heart, may fill it with the righteousness above described.
And indeed whosoever seeks this first, will soon come to seek this only.

34. *The morrow shall take thought for itself*—That is, be careful for the morrow when it comes.   *The evil thereof*—Speaking after the manner of men.   But
all trouble is, upon the whole, a real good.   It is good physic which God dispenses daily to his children, according to the need and the strength of each.

Chap. VII.   Our Lord now proceeds to warn us against the chief hinderances
of holiness.   And how wisely does he begin with judging? wherein all young
converts are so apt to spend that zeal which is given them for better purposes.

Ver. 1. *Judge not*—any man without full, clear, certain knowledge, without
absolute necessity, without tender love.

2. *With what measure ye mete, it shall be measured to you*—Awful words!   So
we may, as it were, choose for ourselves, whether God shall be severe or merciful
to us.   God and man will favour the candid and benevolent : but they must expect
judgment without mercy, who have showed no mercy.

3. In particular, why do you open your eyes to any fault of your brother,
while you yourself are guilty of a much greater?   *The mote*—The word properly
signifies a splinter or shiver of wood.   This and a beam, its opposite, were pro-
verbially used by the Jews, to denote, the one, small infirmities, the other, gross,
palpable faults.

4. *How sayest thou*—With what face?

5. *Thou hypocrite*—It is mere hypocrisy to pretend zeal for the amendment of
others while we have none for our own.   *Then*—When that which obstructed
thy sight is removed.

6. Here is another instance of that transposition, where of the two things proposed, the latter is first treated of.   *Give not—to dogs—lest turning they rend you :
Cast not—to swine—lest they trample them under foot.*

Yet even then, when *the beam is cast out of thine own eye, Give not*—That is,
talk not of the deep things of God to those whom you know to be wallowing in
sin · neither declare the great things God hath done for your soul to the profane,

* Luke vi, 37.   † Luke vi, 41.

7 * Ask, and it shall be given you; seek, and ye shall find; knock,
8 and it shall be opened to you. For every one that asketh, receiveth,
and he that seeketh, findeth, and to him that knocketh, it shall be
9 opened. What man is there of you, who if his son ask bread, will
10 give him a stone? And if he ask a fish, will he give him a ser-
11 pent? If ye then, being evil, know how to give good gifts to your
children, how much more will your Father who is in heaven give
12 good things to them that ask him? † Therefore all things whatsoever ye would that men should do to you, do ye even so to them:
for this is the law and the prophets.
13 ‡ Enter ye in through the strait gate: for wide is the gate and
broad is the way that leadeth to destruction, and many there are
14 that go in through it: Because strait is the gate and narrow is the
way that leadeth to life, and few there are that find it.
15 But beware of false prophets, who come to you in sheep's
clothing, but inwardly they are ravenous wolves. ◊ By their fruits
16 ye shall know them. Do men gather grapes from thorns, or figs
17 from thistles? So every good tree bringeth forth good fruit; but
18 the corrupt tree bringeth forth evil fruit. A good tree cannot
bring forth evil fruit, neither *can* a corrupt tree bring forth good

---

furious, persecuting wretches. Talk not of perfection, for instance, to the former; not of your experience to the latter. But our Lord does in nowise forbid
us to reprove, as occasion is, both the one and the other.

7. But *ask*—Pray for them, as well as for yourselves: in this there can be no
such danger. *Seek*—Add your own diligent endeavours to your asking: *and
knock*—Persevere importunately in that diligence.

8. *For every one, that asketh receiveth*—Provided he ask aright, and ask what is
agreeable to God's will.

11. *To them that ask him*—But on this condition, that ye follow the example
of his goodness, by doing to all as ye would they should do to you. *For this is
the law and the prophets*—This is the sum of all, exactly answering chap. v, 17.
The whole is comprised in one word, Imitate the God of love.
Thus far proceeds the doctrinal part of the sermon. In the next verse begins
the exhortation to practise it.

13. *The strait gate*—The holiness described in the foregoing chapters. And
this is the *narrow way*. *Wide is the gate, and many there are that go in through
it*—They need not seek for this; they come to it of course. *Many go in through
it, because strait is the other gate*—Therefore they do not care for it; they like a
wider gate.

15. *Beware of false prophets*—Who in their preaching describe a broad way
to heaven: it is their prophesying, their teaching the broad way, rather than
their walking in it themselves, that is here chiefly spoken of. All those are
false prophets, who teach any other way than that our Lord hath here marked
out. *In sheep's clothing*—With outside religion and fair professions of love:
Wolves—Not feeding, but destroying souls.

16. *By their fruits ye shall know them*—A short, plain, easy rule, whereby to
know true from false prophets: and one that may be applied by people of the
weakest capacity, who are not accustomed to deep reasoning. True prophets
convert sinners to God, or at least confirm and strengthen those that are converted. False prophets do not. They also are false prophets, who though
speaking the very truth, yet are not sent by the Spirit of God, but come in
their own name, to declare it: their grand mark is, " *Not turning men from the
power of Satan to God.*"

18. *A good tree cannot bring forth evil fruit, neither a corrupt tree good fruit*—
But it is certain, the goodness or badness here mentioned respects the doctrine,
rather than the personal character. For a bad man preaching the good doctrine

---

* Luke xi, 9.　† Luke vi, 31.　‡ Luke xiii, 24.　◊ Luke vi, 43, 44.

19 fruit.   Every tree that bringeth not forth good fruit is hewn down
20 and cast into the fire.   Wherefore by their fruits ye shall know
   them.
21   * Not every one that saith to me, Lord, Lord, shall enter into
   the kingdom of heaven, but he that doth the will of my Father who
22 is in heaven.   Many will say to me in that day, Lord, Lord, have
   we not prophesied in thy name, and in thy name have cast out
23 devils, and in thy name have done many wonderful works?   † And
   then will I declare unto them, I never knew you, depart from me,
24 ye that work iniquity.   ‡ Therefore whosoever heareth these my
   sayings, and doth them, I will liken him to a wise man, who built
25 his house on the rock.   And the rain descended, and the floods
   came, and the winds blew and beat on that house ; and it fell not ;
26 for it was founded on the rock.   But every one that heareth these
   my sayings, and doth them not, shall be likened to a foolish man,
27 who built his house on the sand.   And the rain descended, and
   the floods came, and the winds blew, and beat on that house ; and
28 it fell, and great was the fall of it.   And when Jesus had ended
29 these sayings, the multitudes were astonished at his teaching, For
   he taught them as one having authority, and not as the scribes.
VIII. And when he was come down from the mountain, great multi-
2 tudes followed him.   § And behold a leper came and worshipped
   him, saying, Lord, if thou wilt, thou canst make me clean.
3 And Jesus stretching forth his hand, touched him, saying, I will ;
   be thou made clean.   And immediately his leprosy was cleansed.
4 And Jesus saith to him, See thou tell no man, but go, show thyself

here delivered, is sometimes an instrument of converting sinners to God.   Yet I
do not aver, that all are true prophets who speak the truth, and thereby convert
sinners.   I only affirm, that none are such who do not.
   19. *Every tree that bringeth not forth good fruit is hewn down and cast into the
fire*—How dreadful then is the condition of that teacher who hath brought no sinners to God!
   21. *Not every one*—That is, no one *that saith, Lord, Lord*—That makes a mere
profession of me and my religion, *shall enter*—Whatever their false teachers may
assure them to the contrary : *He that doth the will of my Father*—as I have now
declared it.   Observe : every thing short of this is only saying, *Lord, Lord*.
   22. *We have prophesied*—We have declared the mysteries of thy kingdom,
wrote books ; preached excellent sermons : *In thy name done many wonderful
works*—So that even the working of miracles is no proof that a man has
saving faith.
   23. *I never knew you*—There never was a time that I approved of you : so that
as many souls as they had saved, they were themselves never saved from their
sins.   Lord, is it my case ?
   29. *He taught them*—The multitudes, *as one having authority*—With a dignity
and majesty peculiar to himself as the great Lawgiver, and with the demonstration and power of the Spirit : *and not as the scribes*—Who only expounded the
law of another ; and that in a lifeless, ineffectual manner.
   VIII. 2. *A leper came*—Leprosies in those countries were seldom curable by
natural means, any more than palsies or lunacy.   Probably this leper, though he
might not mix with the people, had heard our Lord at a distance.
   4. *See thou tell no man*—Perhaps our Lord only meant here, Not till thou hast
showed thyself to the priest,—who was appointed to inquire into the case of
leprosy.   But many others he commanded, absolutely, to tell none of the
miracles he had wrought upon them.   And this he seems to have done, chiefly

   * Luke vi, 46.   † Luke xiii, 27.   ‡ Luke vi, 47   § Mark i, 40 ; Luke v, 12.

to the priest, and offer the gift that * Moses commanded, for a testimony to them.

5 † And when he was entered into Capernaum, there came to him
6 a centurion, beseeching him, and saying, Lord, my servant lieth
7 in the house, ill of the palsy, grievously tormented. And Jesus
8 saith to him, I will come and heal him. The centurion answering said, Lord, I am not worthy that thou shouldst come under my roof : but speak in a word only, and my servant shall be
9 healed. For I am a man under authority, having soldiers under me : and I say unto this man, Go, and he goeth, and to another, Come, and he cometh, and to my servant, Do this, and he doth *it*.
10 When Jesus heard *it*, he marvelled, and said to them that followed, Verily I say unto you, I have not found so great faith, no,
11 not in Israel. ‡ And I say unto you, That many shall come from the east and west, and shall sit down with Abraham, and Isaac,
12 and Jacob in the kingdom of heaven. But the children of the kingdom shall be cast out into the outer darkness : § there shall
13 be the weeping and the gnashing of teeth. And Jesus said to ·the centurion, Go thy way, and as thou hast believed, be it unto thee. And his servant was healed in that hour.

---

for one or more of these reasons : 1. To prevent the multitude from thronging him, in the manner related Mark i, 45. 2. To fulfil the prophecy, Isaiah xlii, 1, that he would not be vain or ostentatious. This reason St. Matthew assigns, chap. xii, 17, &c. 3. To avoid the being taken by force and made a king, John vi, 15. And, 4. That he might not enrage the chief priests, scribes, and Pharisees, who were the most bitter against him, any more than was unavoidable, Matt. xvi, 20, 21. *For a testimony-* That I am the Messiah ; *to them*—The priests, who otherwise might have pleaded want of evidence.

5. *There came to him a centurion*—A captain of a hundred Roman soldiers. Probably he came a little way toward him, and then went back. He thought himself not worthy to come in person, and therefore spoke the words that follow by his messengers. As it is not unusual in all languages, so in the Hebrew it is peculiarly frequent, to ascribe to a person himself the thing which is done, and the words which are spoken by his order. And accordingly St. Matthew relates as said by the centurion himself, what others said by order from him. An instance of the same kind we have in the case of Zebedee's children. From St. Matthew, xx, 20, we learn it was their mother that spoke those words, which, Mark x, 35, 37, themselves are said to speak ; because she was only their mouth.

Yet from ver. 13, *Go thy way* home, it appears he at length came in person . probably on hearing that Jesus was nearer to his house than he apprehended when he sent the second message by his friends.

8. *The centurion answered*—By his second messengers.

9. *For I am a man under authority*—I am only an inferior officer : and what I command, is done even in my absence : how much more what thou commandest, · who art Lord of all !

10. *I have not found so great faith, no, not in Israel*—For the centurion was not an Israelite.

11. *Many* from the farthest parts of the earth shall embrace the terms and enjoy the rewards of the Gospel covenant established with *Abraham*. But the Jews, who have the first title to them, shall be shut out from the feast ; from grace here, and hereafter from glory.

12. *The outer darkness*—Our Lord here alludes to the custom the ancients had of making their feast in the night time. Probably while he was speaking this, the centurion came in person.

* Lev. xiv, 2.　† Luke vii, 1.　‡ Luke xiii, 29.　§ Matt. xiii, 42, 50 ; xxii, 13 · xxiv, 51 ; xxv, 30.

14 * And Jesus coming to Peter's house, saw his wife's mother
15 lying and sick of a fever. And he touched her hand, and the fever
left her; and she arose and waited upon them.
16 † When it was evening they brought to him many demoniacs:
and he cast out the spirits with a word, and healed all that were
17 ill: Whereby was fulfilled what was spoken by the Prophet Isaiah,
saying, ‡ Himself took our infirmities and bare our diseases.
18 And Jesus seeing great multitudes about him, commanded to
19 go to the other side. § And a certain scribe came and said to
20 him, Master, I will follow thee whithersoever thou goest. And
Jesus saith to him, The foxes have holes, and the birds of the air
have nests; but the Son of man hath not where to lay his head.
21 And another of his disciples said to him, Lord, suffer me first to
22 go and bury my father. But Jesus said to him, Follow me, and
23 leave the dead to bury their dead. ‖ And when he was come into
24 the vessel, his disciples followed him. And behold, there was a
great tempest in the sea, so that the vessel was covered with the
25 waves. But he was asleep. And his disciples coming to him
26 awoke him, saying, Lord, save us; we perish. And he saith unto
them, Why are ye fearful: O ye of little faith? Then arising, he
rebuked the winds and the sea, and there was a great calm. But
27 the men marvelled, saying, What manner of man is this, that even
the winds and the sea obey him?
28 ** And when he was come to the other side, into the country of
the Gergesenes, there met him two demoniacs, coming out of the

---

14. *Peter's wife's mother*—St. Peter was then a young man, as were all the apostles.

17. *Whereby was fulfilled what was spoken by the Prophet Isaiah*—He spoke it in a more exalted sense. The evangelist here only alludes to those words, as being capable of this lower meaning also. Such instances are frequent in the sacred writings, and are elegancies rather than imperfections. He fulfilled these words in the highest sense, by *bearing our sins in his own body on the tree:* in a lower sense, by sympathizing with us in our sorrows, and healing us of the diseases which were the fruit of sin.

18. *He commanded to go to the other side*—That both himself and the people might have a little rest.

20. *The Son of man*—The expression is borrowed from Daniel vii, 13, and is the appellation which Christ generally gives himself: which he seems to do out of humility, as having some relation to his mean appearance in this world. *Hath not where to lay his head*—Therefore do not follow me from any view of temporal advantage.

21. *Another said*—I will follow thee without any such view; but I must mind my business first. It is not certain that his father was already dead. Perhaps his son desired to stay with him, being very old, till his death.

22. *But Jesus said*—When God calls, leave the business of the world to them who are dead to God.

24. *The ship was covered*—So man's extremity is God's opportunity.

26. *Why are ye fearful*—Then *he rebuked the winds*—First, he composed their spirits, and then the sea.

28. *The country of the Gergesenes*—Or of *the Gadarenes*—Gergesa and Gadara were towns near each other. Hence the country between them took its name, sometimes from the one, sometimes from the other. *There met him two demoniacs*—St. Mark and St. Luke mention only one, who was probably the fiercer of the two, and the person who spoke to our Lord first. But this is no way incon-

---

* Mark i, 29; Luke iv, 38. † Mark i, 32; Luke iv, 40. ‡ Isaiah liii, 4. § Luke ix, 57.
‖ Mark iv, 35; Luke viii, 22. ** Mark v, 1; Luke viii, 26.

tombs, exceeding fierce, so that no one could pass by that way.
29 And behold they cried out, saying, What have we to do with thee
Jesus, thou Son of God? Art thou come hither to torment us
30 before the time? And there was at some distance from them a
31 herd of many swine feeding. So the devils besought him, saying,
If thou cast us out, suffer us to go into the herd of swine.
32 And he said to them, Go. And coming out, they went into the
swine, and behold the whole herd rushed down the precipice
33 into the sea, and perished in the waters. But they that kept them
fled, and going into the city, told every thing, and what had
34 befallen the demoniacs. And behold, the whole city came out to
meet Jesus; and seeing him, they besought him to depart out of
their coasts.
IX. And * going into the vessel, he passed over and came to his own
2 city. † And behold they brought to him a paralytic, lying on a
couch; and Jesus seeing their faith, said to the paralytic, Son, take
courage: thy sins are forgiven thee.
3 And behold certain of the scribes said within themselves, This
4 man blasphemeth. And Jesus knowing their thoughts, said,
5 Why think ye evil in your hearts? For which is easier, to say,
6 Thy sins are forgiven thee? Or to say, Arise and walk? But that
ye may know that the Son of man hath power on earth to forgive
sins, (then saith he to the paralytic,) Arise, take up thy couch,
7 and go to thy house. And he arose, and went to his own house.
8 And the multitude seeing it, marvelled and glorified God, who had
given such power to men.
9 ‡ And as Jesus passed along from thence, he saw a man named
Matthew, sitting at the receipt of custom, and saith to him, Follow

---

sistent with the account which St. Matthew gives. *The tombs*—Doubtless
those malevolent spirits love such tokens of death and destruction. Tombs
were usually in those days in desert places, at a distance from towns, and
were often made in the sides of caves, in the rocks and mountains. *No one
could pass*—Safely.

29. *What have we to do with thee*—This is a Hebrew phrase, which signifies
Why do you concern yourself about us? 2 Sam. xvi, 16. *Before the time*—The
great day.

30. *There was a herd of many swine*—Which it was not lawful for the Jews to
keep. Therefore our Lord both justly and mercifully permitted them to be
destroyed.

31. *He said, Go*—A word of permission only, not command.

34. *They besought him to depart out of their coasts*—They loved their swine so
much better than their souls! How many are of the same mind!

IX. 1. *His own city*—Capernaum, chap. iv, 13.

2. *Seeing their faith*—Both that of the paralytic, and of them that brought
him. *Son*—A title of tenderness and condescension.

3. *This man blasphemeth*—Attributing to himself a power (that of forgiving
sins) which belongs to God only.

5. *Which is easier*—Do not both of them argue a Divine power? Therefore
if I can heal his disease, I can forgive his sins: especially as his disease is the
consequence of his sins. Therefore these must be taken away, if that is.

6. *On earth*—Even in my state of humiliation.

8. So what was to the scribes an occasion of blaspheming, was to the people
an incitement to praise God.

9. *He saw a man named Matthew*—Modestly so called by himself. The other

* Mark v, 18; Luke viii, 37. † Mark ii, 3; Luke v, 18. ‡ Mark ii, 14; Luke v, 27.

10 me. And he arose and followed him. And as he sat at table in
the house, behold, many publicans and sinners came, and sat down
11 with him and his disciples. And the Pharisees seeing *it*, said to
his disciples, Why eateth your Master with publicans and sin-
12 ners. But Jesus hearing *it*, said to them, They that are whole
13 need not a physician, but they that are sick. But go ye and learn
what that meaneth, * I will have mercy and not sacrifice ; for I am
not come to call the righteous, but sinners.
14   † Then come to him the disciples of John, saying, Why do we
15 and the Pharisees fast often, but thy disciples fast not ? And Jesus
said to them, Can the children of the bride chamber mourn, as
long as the bridegroom is with them ? But the days will come,
when the bridegroom shall be taken away from them, and then
16 shall they fast. No man putteth a piece of new cloth on an old
garment: for that which is put in to fill it taketh from the gar-
17 ment, and the rent is made worse. Neither do men put new wine
into old leathern bottles, else the bottles burst, and the wine is
spilled, and the bottles are destroyed : but they put new wine into
new bottles, and both are preserved.
18   ‡ While he spake these things to them, behold, a certain ruler
coming, worshipped him, saying, My daughter is just dead: but
19 come and lay thine hand on her, and she shall live. And Jesus
20 arose and followed him. and *so did* his disciples. (And behold, a
woman who had had a flux of blood twelve years, coming behind

---

evangelists call him by his more honourable name, Levi. *Sitting*—In the very
height of his business, *at the receipt of custom*—The custom house, or place where
the customs were received.

10. *As Jesus sat at table in the house*—Of Matthew, who having invited many
of his old companions,' *made him a feast*, Mark ii, 15 ; and that a great one,
though he does not himself mention it. The *publicans*, or collectors of the taxes
which the Jews paid the Romans, were infamous for their illegal exactions:
Sinners—Open, notorious, sinners.

11. *The Pharisees said to his disciples, Why eateth your Master ?*—Thus they
commonly ask our Lord, Why do thy disciples this ? And his disciples, Why doth
your Master ?

13. *Go ye and learn*—Ye that take upon you to teach others. *I will have
mercy and not sacrifice*—That is, I will have mercy rather than sacrifice. I love
acts of mercy better than sacrifice itself.

14. *Then*—While he was at table.

15. *The children of the bride chamber*—The companions of the bridegroom.
Mourn—Mourning and fasting usually go together. As if he had said, While I
am with them, it is a festival time, a season of rejoicing, not mourning. But
after I am gone, all my disciples likewise shall be in fastings often.

16. This is one reason,—It is not a proper time for them to fast. Another is,
they are not ripe for it. *New cloth*—The words in the original properly signify
cloth that hath not passed through the fuller's hands, and which is consequently
much harsher than what has been washed and worn ; and therefore yielding less
than that, will tear away the edges to which it is sewed.

17. *New*—Fermenting *wine* will soon burst those *bottles*, the leather of which
is almost worn out. The word properly means vessels made of goats' skins,
wherein they formerly put wine, (and do in some countries to this day) to convey it from place to place. *Put new wine into new bottles*—Give harsh doctrines
to such as have strength to receive them.

18. *Just dead*—He had left her at the point of death, Mark v, 23. Probably a
messenger had now informed him she was dead.

20. *Coming behind*—Out of bashfulness and humility.

       * Hosea vi, 6.   † Mark ii, 18 ; Luke v, 33.   ‡ Mark v, 22 ; Luke viii, 41.

21 him, touched the hem of his garment. For she said within her-
22 self, If I but touch his garment I shall be made whole. And
Jesus turning and seeing her, said, Daughter, take courage ; thy
faith hath made thee whole. And the woman was made whole
23 from that hour.) And Jesus coming into the ruler's house, and
24 seeing the minstrels and the crowd making a noise, saith to them,
Withdraw ; for the maid is not dead, but sleepeth: and they de-
25 rided him. But when the crowd were put forth, he went in and
26 took her by the hand ; and the maid arose. And the fame of it
went abroad into all that country.
27   And as Jesus passed thence, two blind men followed him, crying aloud, and saying, Thou Son of David, have mercy on us.
28 And when he was come into the house, the blind men came to him ;
and Jesus saith to them, Believe ye that I am able to do this?
29 They say unto him, Yea, Lord. Then he touched their eyes, say-
30 ing, Be it unto you according to your faith. And their eyes were
opened ; and Jesus strictly charged them, saying, See that no man
31 know *it*. But when they were gone out, they spread his fame
abroad in all that country.
32   * As they were going out, behold they brought a dumb demoniac
33 to him. And when the devil was cast out, the dumb spake : and
the multitudes marvelled, saying, It was never seen thus, *even* in
34 Israel. But the Pharisees said, he casteth out the devils by the
prince of the devils.
35   And Jesus went about all the cities and villages, teaching in their
synagogues, and preaching the Gospel of the kingdom, and heal-
36 ing every disease and every malady. But seeing the multitudes
he was moved with tender compassion for them, because they
37 were faint and scattered, as sheep having no shepherd. † Then
saith he to his disciples, The harvest truly *is* great, but the labour-

---

22. *Take courage*—Probably she was struck with fear, when he turned and looked upon her, Mark v, 33 ; Luke viii, 47 ; lest she should have offended him, by touching his garment privately ; and the more so, because she was unclean according to the law, Lev. xv, 25.

23. *The minstrels*—The musicians. The original word means flute players. Musical instruments were used by the Jews as well as the heathens, in their lamentations for the dead, to soothe the melancholy of surviving friends, by soft and solemn notes. And there were persons who made it their business to perform this, while others sung to their music. Flutes were used especially on the death of children ; louder instruments on the death of grown persons.

24. *Withdraw*—There is no need of you now ; *for the maid is not dead*—Her life is not at an end ; *but sleepeth*—This is only a temporary suspension of sense and motion, which should rather be termed sleep than death.

25. *The maid arose*—Christ raised three dead persons to life ; this child, the widow's son, and Lazarus : one newly departed, another on the bier, the third smelling in the grave : to show us that no degree of death is so desperate as to be past his help.

33. Even *in Israel*—Where so many wonders have been seen.

36. *Because they were faint*—In soul rather than in body. *As sheep having no shepherd*—And yet they had many teachers ; they had scribes in every city. But they had none who cared for their souls, and none that were able, if they had been willing, to have wrought any deliverance. They had no pastors after God's own heart.

37. *The harvest truly is great*—When Christ came into the world, it was pro-

* Luke xi, 14.   † Luke x, 2.

38 ers *are* few.   Pray ye therefore the Lord of the harvest, that he
would thrust forth labourers into his harvest.

X.   And * having called to him his twelve disciples, he gave them
power over unclean spirits, to cast them out, and to heal every dis-
2 ease and every malady.   † Now the names of the twelve apostles
are these ; the first, Simon, who is called Peter, and Andrew his
brother ; James the *son* of Zebedee, and John his brother ;
3 Philip and Bartholomew, Thomas, and Matthew the publican ·
James the *son* of Alpheus, and Lebbeus, whose surname was
4 Thaddeus ; Simon the Canaanite, and Judas Iscariot, who also
5 betrayed him.   These twelve Jesus sent forth, having commanded
them, saying, Go not into the way of the Gentiles, and into a city
6 of the Samaritans enter not : But go rather to the lost sheep of
7 the house of Israel.   And as ye go, proclaim, saying, The king-
8 dom of heaven is at hand.   ‡ Heal the sick, cleanse the lepers,
raise the dead, cast out devils : freely ye have received, freely

perly the time of harvest ; till then it was the seed time only. *But the labourers
are few*—Those whom God sends ; who are holy, and convert sinners. Of others
there are many.

38. *The Lord of the harvest*—Whose peculiar work and office it is, and who
alone is able to do it : *that he would thrust forth*—for it is an employ not pleasing
to flesh and blood ; so full of reproach, labour, danger, temptation of every kind,
that nature may well be averse to it. Those who never felt this, never yet knew
what it is to be labourers in Christ's harvest. He sends them forth, when he
calls them by his Spirit, furnishes them with grace and gifts for the work, and
makes a way for them to be employed therein.

X. 1. *His twelve disciples*—Hence it appears that he had already chosen out
of his disciples, those whom he afterward termed apostles. The number seems
to have relation to the twelve patriarchs, and the twelve tribes of Israel.

2. *The first, Simon*—The first who was called to a constant attendance on
Christ ; although Andrew had seen him before Simon.

3. *Lebbeus*—Commonly called Judas, the brother of James.

4. *Iscariot*—So called from Iscarioth, (the place of his birth,) a town of the tribe
of Ephraim, near the city of Samaria.

5. *These twelve Jesus sent forth*—Herein exercising his supreme authority, as
God over all. None but God can give men authority to preach his word. *Go
not*—Their commission was thus confined now, because the calling of the Gentiles
was deferred till after the more plentiful effusion of the Holy Ghost on the day of
pentecost. *Enter not*—Not to preach ; but they might to buy what they wanted,
John iv, 9.

8. *Cast out devils*—It is a great relief to the spirits of an infidel, sinking under
a dread, that possibly the Gospel may be true, to find it observed by a learned
brother, that the diseases therein ascribed to the operation of the devil have the
very same symptoms with the natural diseases of lunacy, epilepsy, or convulsions ; whence he readily and very willingly concludes, that the devil had no
hand in them.

But it were well to stop and consider a little. Suppose God should suffer an
evil spirit to usurp the same power over a man's body, as the man himself has
naturally ; and suppose him actually to exercise that power ; could we conclude
the devil had no hand therein, because his body was bent in the very same manner wherein the man himself might have bent it naturally ?

And suppose God gives an evil spirit a greater power, to effect immediately the
organ of the nerves in the brain, by irritating them to produce violent motions,
or so relaxing them that they can produce little or no motion ; still the symptoms
will be those of over tense nerves, as in madness, epilepsies, convulsions ; or of
relaxed nerves, as in paralytic cases. But could we conclude thence that the
devil had no hand in them ? Will any man affirm that God cannot or will not,

* Mark iii, 14 ; vi, 7 ; Luke vi, 13 ; ix, 1.   † Acts i, 13.   ‡ Mark vi, 7 ; Luke ix, 2

9 give. Provide neither gold, nor silver, nor brass in your purses:
10 * Nor scrip for your journey, nor two coats, nor shoes, nor yet
   a staff : for the workman is worthy of his maintenance.
11 † And into whatsoever city or town ye shall enter, inquire who in
12 it is worthy, and there abide till ye go thence.᾿ And when ye
13 come into a house, salute it. And if the house be worthy, your
   peace shall come upon it; but if it be not worthy, your peace shall
14 return to you. And whosoever will not receive you, nor hear
   your words ; when you go out of that house or city, shake off the
15 dust from your feet. Verily I. say unto you, it shall be more
   tolerable for the land of Sodom and Gomorrah in the day of judgment, than for that city.
16 ‡ Behold I send you forth as sheep in the midst of wolves ; be
17 ye therefore wise as serpents, and harmless as doves. § But beware of men; for they will deliver you to the councils, and
18 scourge you in their synagogues. And ye shall be brought before
   governors and kings for my sake, for a testimony to them
19 and to the heathens. ‖ But when they deliver you, take no

---

on any occasion whatever, give such a power to an evil spirit ? Or that effects,.
the like of which may be produced by natural causes, cannot possibly be produced
by preternatural ? If this be possible, then he who affirms it was so, in any particular case, cannot be justly charged with falsehood, merely for affirming the
reality of a possible thing. Yet in this manner are the evangelists treated by
those unhappy men, who above all things dread the truth of the Gospel, because,
if it is true, they are of all men the most miserable.

Freely ye have received—All things ; in particular the power of working miracles ; *freely give*—Exert that power wherever you come.

9. *Provide not*—The stress seems to lie on this word : they might use what
they had ready ; but they might not stay a moment to provide any thing more,
neither take any thought about it. Nor indeed were they to take any thing with
them, more than was strictly necessary. 1. Lest it should retard them. 2. Because they were to learn hereby to trust to God in all future exigencies.

10. *Neither scrip*—That is, a wallet, or bag to hold provisions : *Nor yet a staff*—
We read, Mark vi, 8, Take nothing, save a staff only. He that had one might
take it ; they that had none, might not provide any. *For the workman is worthy
of his maintenance*—The word includes all that is mentioned in the 9th and 10th
verses ; all that they were forbidden to provide for themselves, so far as it was
needful for them.

11. *Inquire who is worthy*—That you should abide with him : who is disposed
to receive the Gospel. *There abide*—In that house, till ye leave the town.

12. *Salute it*—In the usual Jewish form, " Peace (that is, all blessings) be to
this house."

13. *If the house be worthy*—of it, God shall give them the peace you wish
them. If not, he shall give you what they refuse. The same will be the case,
when we pray for them that are not worthy.

14. *Shake off the dust from your feet*—The Jews thought the land of Israel so
peculiarly holy, that when they came home from any heathen country, they
stopped at the borders and shook or wiped off the dust of it from their feet, that
the holy land might not be polluted with it. Therefore the action here enjoined
was a lively intimation, that those Jews who had rejected the Gospel were holy
no longer, but were on a level with heathens and idolaters.

17. But think not that all your innocence and all your wisdom will screen you
from persecution. *They will scourge you in their synagogues*—In these the Jews
held their courts of judicature, about both civil and ecclesiastical affairs.

19. *Take no thought*—Neither at this time, on any sudden call, need we be
careful how or what to answer.

* Luke x, 7. † Mark vi, 10 ; Luke ix, 4. ‡ Luke x, 3. § Matt. xxiv 9. ‖ Luke xii, 11

thought, how or what ye shall speak; for it shall be given you
20 in that very hour what ye shall speak.   For it is not ye that
21 speak, but the Spirit of your Father who speaketh in you.   * But
the brother shall deliver up the brother to death, and the father
the child; and children shall rise up against their parents, and
22 kill them.   † And ye shall be hated of all men for my name's
sake : but he that endureth to the end, the same shall be saved.
23 But when they persecute you in this city, flee to another ; for
verily I say unto you, Ye shall not have gone over the cities
24 of Israel, till the Son of man be come.   ‡ The disciple is not above
25 his teacher, nor the servant above his lord.   It is enough for the
disciple that he be as his teacher, and the servant as his lord.   § If
they have called the Master of the house Beelzebub, how much
26 more them of his household?   ‖ Therefore fear them not; for
there is nothing covered, which shall not be made manifest ; nor
27 hid, that shall not be known.   ** What I tell you in the dark,
speak ye in the light, and what ye hear in the ear, proclaim on
28 the house tops.   And be not afraid of them who kill the body,
but are not able to kill the soul ; but rather be afraid of him who
29 is able to destroy both soul and body in hell.   Are not two sparrows sold for a farthing? and one of them shall not fall to the
30 ground without your Father.   †† Yea, even the hairs of your
31 head are all numbered.   Fear ye not, therefore ; ye are of more
32 value than many sparrows.   ‡‡ Whosoever therefore shall confess me before men, him will I confess before my Father who is

22. *Of all men*—That know not God.
23. *Ye shall not have gone over the cities of Israel*—Make what haste ye will;
till the Son of man be come—To destroy their temple and nation.
25. *How much more*—This cannot refer to the quantity of reproach and persecution : (for in this the servant cannot be above his lord :) but only to the certainty of it.
26. *Therefore fear them not*—For ye have only the same usage with your Lord.
There is nothing covered—So that however they may slander you now, your innocence will at length appear.
27. Even what I now tell you secretly is not to be kept secret long, but declared
publicly.   Therefore, *What ye hear in the ear, publish on the house top*—Two
customs of the Jews seem to be alluded to here.   Their doctors used to whisper
in the ear of their disciples what they were to pronounce aloud to others.   And
as their houses were low and flat roofed, they sometimes preached to the people
from thence.
28. *And be not afraid*—of any thing which ye may suffer for proclaiming it.
Be afraid of him who is able to destroy both body and soul in hell—It is remarkable, that our Lord commands those who love God, still to fear him, even on this
account, under this notion.
29, 30. The particular providence of God is another reason for your not fearing man.   For this extends to the very smallest things.   And if he has such care
over the most inconsiderable creatures, how much more will he take care of you,
(provided you confess him before men, before powerful enemies of the truth,) and
that not only in this life, but in the other also ?
32. *Whosoever shall confess me*—Publicly acknowledge me for the promised
Messiah.   But this confession implies the receiving his whole doctrine, Mark
viii, 38, and obeying all his commandments.

* Luke xxi, 16.   † Chap. xxiv, 13.   ‡ Luke vi, 30 ; John xv, 20.   § Chap. xii, 24
‖ Mark iv, 22; Luke viii, 17 ; xii, 2. .   ** Luke xii, 3   †† Luke xii, 7.   ‡‡ Mark
viii, 38; Luke ix, 26.

33 in neaven. But whosoever shall deny me before men, him will
34 I also deny before my Father who is in heaven. * Think not that
I am come to send peace on earth : I am not come to send peace,
35 but a sword. For I am come to set a man at variance with his
father, and the daughter with her mother, and the daughter-in-
36 law with her mother-in-law. † And the foes of a man *shall* be they
37 of his own household. He that loveth father or mother more
than me, is not worthy of me ; and he that loveth son or daughter
38 more than me, is not worthy of me ; ‡ And he that taketh not
39 his cross, and followeth after me, is not worthy of me. § He that
findeth his life shall lose it ; and he that loseth his life for my sake,
40 shall find it. ‖ He that entertaineth you, entertaineth me ; and he
41 that entertaineth me, entertaineth him that sent me. He that
entertaineth a prophet in the name of a prophet, shall receive a
prophet's reward : and he that entertaineth a righteous man in the
name of a righteous man, shall receive a righteous man's reward.
42 ** And whosoever shall give drink to one of these little ones a cup
of cold water only, in the name of a disciple, verily I say unto you,
he shall in nowise lose his reward.

XI.   And when Jesus had made an end of commanding his twelve
disciples, he departed thence, to teach and preach in their cities.
2   †† Now when John had heard in the prison the works of Christ,
3 he sent two of his disciples, And said to him, Art thou he that is to
4 come, or look we for another ?   And Jesus answering, said to them,
5 Go and tell John the things which ye hear and see. ‡‡ The blind
receive their sight, the lame walk ; the lepers are cleansed, and
the deaf hear; the dead are raised, and the poor have the Gospel

---

33, 34. *Whosoever shall deny me before men*—To which ye will be strongly
tempted. For *Think not that I am come*—That is, think not that universal peace
will be the immediate consequence of my coming. Just the contrary. Both public and private divisions will follow, wheresoever my Gospel comes with power.
Yet this is not the design, though it be the event of his coming, through the
opposition of devils and men.

36. *And the foes of a man*—That loves and follows me.

37. *He that loveth father or mother more than me*—He that is not ready to give
up all these, when they stand in competition with his duty.

38. *He that taketh not his cross*—That is, whatever pain or inconvenience cannot be avoided, but by doing some evil, or omitting some good.

39. *He that findeth his life shall lose it*—He that saves his life by denying me,
shall lose it eternally; and he that loseth his life by confessing me, shall save
it eternally. And as you shall be thus rewarded, so in proportion shall they who
entertain you for my sake.

41. *He that entertaineth a prophet*—That is, a preacher of the Gospel: *In the
name of a prophet*—That is, because he is such, shall share in his reward.

42. *One of these little ones*—The very least Christian.

XI. 1. *In their cities*—The other cities of Israel.

2. *He sent two of his disciples*—Not because he doubted himself; but to confirm their faith.

3. *He that is to come*—The *Messiah.*

4. *Go and tell John the things that ye hear and see*—Which are a stronger
proof of my being the *Messiah,* than any bare assertion can be.

5. *The poor have the Gospel preached to them*—The greatest mercy of all.

---

* Luke xii, 51.   † Micah vii, 6.   ‡ Chap. xvi, 24 ; Luke xiv, 27.   § Chap. xvi, 25 ;
John xii, 25.   ‖ Chap. xviii, 5 ; Luke x, 16 ; John xiii, 20.   ** Mark ix, 41.   †† Luke
vii, 18.   ‡‡ Isaiah xxix, 18 ; xxxv, 5.

6 preached to them : And happy is he whosoever shall not be
7 offended at me. And as they departed, Jesus said to the multitudes
concerning John, What went ye out into the wilderness to see !
8 A reed shaken with the wind? But what went ye out to see?
A man clothed in soft raiment? Behold, they that wear soft cloth-
9 ing are in kings' houses. But what went ye out to see? A pro-
10 phet? Yea, I say unto you, and more than a prophet. For this
is he of whom it is written, * Behold, I send my messenger before
11 thy face, who shall prepare thy way before thee. Verily I
say unto you, among them that are born of women, there hath
not risen a greater prophet than John the Baptist ; but he that is
12 least in the kingdom of heaven, is greater than he. And from
the days of John the Baptist till now the kingdom of heaven is
entered by force, and they who strive with all their might take it
13 by violence. † For all the prophets and the law prophesied until
14 John. And if ye are willing to receive *him*, he is ‡ Elijah, who
15 was to come. He that hath ears to hear, let him hear. But
16 whereto shall I liken this generation? It is like children sitting
17 in the markets, and calling to their fellows, And saying, We have

6. *Happy is he who shall not be offended at me*—Notwithstanding all these proofs that I am the Messiah.

7. *As they departed, he said concerning John*—Of whom probably he would not have said so much when they were present. *A reed shaken by the wind?*—No ; nothing could ever shake John in the testimony he gave to the truth. The expression is proverbial.

8. *A man clothed in soft, delicate raiment*—An effeminate courtier, accustomed to fawning and flattery? You may expect to find persons of such a character in palaces ; not in a wilderness.

9. *More than a prophet*—For the prophets only pointed me out afar off; but John was my immediate forerunner.

11. *But he that is least in the kingdom of heaven, is greater than he*—Which an ancient author explains thus :—" One perfect in the law, as John was, is inferior to one who is baptized into the death of Christ. For this is the kingdom of heaven, even to be buried with Christ, and to be raised up together with him. John was greater than all who had been then born of women, but he was cut off before the kingdom of heaven was given." [He seems to mean, that righteous-ness, peace, and joy, which constitute the present inward kingdom of heaven.] " He was blameless as to that righteousness which is by the law ; but he fell short of those who are perfected by the spirit of life which is in Christ. Whoso-ever, therefore, is least in the kingdom of heaven, by Christian regeneration, is greater than any who has attained only the righteousness of the law, because the law maketh nothing perfect." It may farther mean, the least true Chris-tian believer has a more perfect knowledge of Jesus Christ, of his redemption and kingdom, than John the Baptist had, who died before the full manifestation of the Gospel.

12. *And from the days of John*—That is, from the time that John had fulfilled his ministry, men rush into my kingdom with a violence like that of those who are taking a city by storm.

13. *For all the prophets and the law prophesied until John*—For all that is written in the law and the prophets only foretold as distant what is now fulfilled. In John the old dispensation expired, and the new began.

15. *He that hath ears to hear, let him hear*—A kind of proverbial expression ; requiring the deepest attention to what is spoken.

16. *This generation*—That is, the men of this age. They are like those froward children of whom their fellows complain, that they will be pleased no way

* Mal. iii, 1.   † Luke xvi, 16.   ‡ Mal. iv, 5.

piped unto you, and ye have not danced; we have mourned
18 unto you, and ye have not lamented. For John came neither eat-
19 ing nor drinking, and they say, He hath a devil. The Son of man
came eating and drinking, and they say, Behold a glutton and a
wine bibber, a friend of publicans and sinners; but wisdom is
20 justified by her children. Then began he to upbraid the cities
wherein the most of his mighty works had been done, because they
21 repented not. * Wo to thee, Chorazin; wo to thee, Bethsaida:
for if the mighty works which have been done in you, had been
done in Tyre and Sidon, they would have repented long ago in
22 sackcloth and ashes. Moreover I say to you, It shall be more
tolerable for Tyre and Sidon in the day of judgment than for you.
23 And thou, Capernaum, who hast been exalted to heaven, shalt be
brought down to hell: for if the mighty works which have been
done in thee, had been done in Sodom, it would have remained to
24 this day. Moreover I say unto you, It shall be more tolerable for
25 the land of Sodom in the day of judgment than for thee. † At that
time Jesus answering said, I thank thee, O Father, Lord of heaven
and earth, because thou hast hid these things from the wise and
26 prudent, and hast revealed them to babes. Even so, Father; for
27 so it seemed good in thy sight. All things are delivered to me by
my Father; and no one knoweth the Son but the Father; neither
knoweth any one the Father, save the Son, and he to whomsoever

18. *John came neither eating nor drinking*—In a rigorous austere way, like
Elijah. And they say, He hath a devil—Is melancholy, from the influence of an
evil spirit.

19. *The Son of man came eating and drinking*—Conversing in a free, familiar
way. *Wisdom is justified by her children*—That is, my wisdom herein is acknowledged by those who are truly wise.

20. *Then began he to upbraid the cities*—It is observable he had never upbraided
them before. Indeed at first they received him with all gladness, Capernaum in
particular.

21. *Wo to thee, Chorazin*—That is, miserable art thou. For these are not
curses or imprecations, as has been commonly supposed; but a solemn, compassionate declaration of the misery they were bringing on themselves. Chorazin
and Bethsaida were cities of Galilee, standing by the lake Gennesareth. Tyre
and Sidon were cities of Phenicia, lying on the sea shore. The inhabitants of
them were heathens.

22, 24. *Moreover I say unto you*—Beside the general denunciation of wo to
those stubborn unbelievers, the degree of their misery will be greater than even
that of Tyre and Sidon, yea, of Sodom.

23. *Thou Capernaum, who hast been exalted to heaven*—That is, highly honoured
by my presence and miracles.

25. *Jesus answering*—This word does not always imply, that something had
been spoken, to which an answer is now made. It often means no more than the
speaking in reference to some action or circumstance preceding. The following
words Christ speaks in reference to the case of the cities above mentioned: *I
thank thee*—That is, I acknowledge and joyfully adore the justice and mercy of
thy dispensations: *Because thou hast hid*—That is, because thou hast suffered
these things to be hid from men, who are in other respects wise and prudent,
while thou hast discovered them to those of the weakest understanding, to them
who are only wise to God-ward.

27. *All things are delivered to me*—Our Lord, here addressing himself to his
disciples, shows why men, wise in other things, do not know this: namely,
because none can know it by natural reason: none but those to whom he reveal-
eth it.

* Luke x, 13. † Luke x, 21.

28 the Son is pleased to reveal *him*. Come to me, all *ye* that labour
29 and are heavy laden, and I will give you rest. Take my yoke upon
   you, and learn of me; for I am meek and lowly in heart, and ye
30 shall find rest to your souls. For my yoke is easy and my burden
   is light.
XII. * At that time Jesus went on the Sabbath through the corn, and
   his disciples were hungry and plucked the ears of corn, and ate.
2 But the Pharisees seeing *it* said to him, Behold, thy disciples do
3 what is not lawful to do on the Sabbath. But he said to them, Have
   ye not read what David did when he was hungry, and they that
4 were with him? † How he entered into the house of God, and ate
   the show bread, which it was not lawful for him to eat, neither
5 for them who were with him, but only for the priests? Or have ye
   not read in the law, that on the Sabbath days the priests in the
6 temple profane the Sabbath and are blameless? But I say to you,
7 That a greater than the temple is here. ‡ And if ye had known
   what that meaneth, I will have mercy and not sacrifice, ye would
8 not have condemned the guiltless. For the Son of man is Lord
   even of the Sabbath.

---

28. *Come to me*—Here he shows to whom *he is pleased* to reveal these things ;
to the weary and heavy laden ; *ye that labour*—After rest in God : *and are heavy
laden*—With the guilt and power of sin : *and I will give you rest*—I alone (for
none else can) *will* freely *give you* (what ye cannot purchase) *rest* from the guilt
of sin by justification, and from the power of sin by sanctification.

29. *Take my yoke upon you*—Believe in me : receive me as your prophet, priest,
and king. *For I am meek and lowly in heart*—Meek toward all men, lowly
toward God : *and ye shall find rest*—Whoever therefore does not find rest of soul,
is not meek and lowly. The fault is not in the yoke of Christ : but in thee, who
hast not taken it upon thee. Nor is it possible for any one to be discontented,
but through want of meekness or lowliness.

30. *For my yoke is easy*—Or rather gracious, sweet, benign, delightful : *and
my burden*—Contrary to those of men, is ease, liberty, and honour.

XII. 1. *His disciples plucked the ears of corn, and ate*—Just what sufficed for
present necessity : dried corn was a common food among the Jews.

3. *Have ye not read what David did*—And necessity was a sufficient plea for
his transgressing the law in a higher instance.

4. *He entered into the house of God*—Into the tabernacle. The temple was not
yet built. *The show bread*—So they called the bread which the priest, who served
that week, put every Sabbath day on the golden table that was in the holy place,
before the Lord. The loaves were twelve in number, and represented the twelve
tribes of Israel : when the new were brought, the stale were taken away, but
were to be eaten by the priests only.

5. *The priests in the temple profane the Sabbath*—That is, do their ordinary
work on this, as on a common day, cleansing all things, and preparing the sacrifices. *A greater than the temple*—If therefore the Sabbath must give way to the
temple, much more must it give way to me.

7. *I will have mercy and not sacrifice*—That is, when they interfere with each
other, I always prefer acts of mercy, before matters of positive institution : yea,
before all ceremonial institutions whatever ; because these being only means of
religion, are suspended of course, if circumstances occur, wherein they clash with
love, which is the end of it.

8. *For the Son of man*—Therefore they are guiltless, were it only on this
account, that they act by my authority, and attend on me in my ministry, as the
priests attended on God in the temple : *is Lord even of the Sabbath*—This certainly
implies, that the Sabbath was an institution of great and distinguished importance ;
it may perhaps also refer to that signal act of authority which Christ afterward

* Mark ii, 23 ; Luke vi, 1.   † 1 Sam. xxi, 6.   ‡ Matt. ix, 13.

9 * And departing thence, he went into their synagogue. And
10 behold there was a man who had a withered hand. And they
asked him, saying, Is it lawful to heal on the Sabbath? that they
11 might accuse him. And he said to them, What man shall there
be among you, that shall have one sheep, who if he fall in a pit on
12 the Sabbath will not lay hold on it and lift *it* out? How much then
is a man better than a sheep? Wherefore it is lawful to do good
13 on the Sabbath day. Then saith he to the man, Stretch forth thy
hand. And he stretched *it* forth; and it was restored whole, as
14 the other. Then the Pharisees went out, and took counsel
15 together against him, how they might destroy him. And Jesus
knowing *it* withdrew from thence; and great multitudes followed
16 him, and he healed them all, And charged them not to make him
17 known: That it might be fulfilled which was spoken by the Pro-
18 phet Isaiah, saying, † Behold my servant, whom I have chosen, my
beloved in whom my soul delighteth; I will put my Spirit upon
19 him, and he shall show judgment to the heathens. He shall not
strive nor clamour, neither shall any man hear his voice in the
20 streets. He shall not break a bruised reed, and smoking flax he
21 shall not quench, till he send forth judgment unto victory. And in
his name shall the heathens trust.
22 ‡ Then was brought to him a demoniac, blind and dumb; and he
23 healed him, so that the blind and dumb both spake and saw. And
all the multitude were amazed and said, Is not this the Son of David?
24 § But the Pharisees hearing *it* said, This fellow casteth not out
25 devils but by Beelzebub the prince of the devils. And Jesus knowing their thoughts said to them, Every kingdom divided against
itself is brought to desolation, and every city or house divided
26 against itself shall not be established. And if Satan cast out Satan,

---

exerted over it, in changing it from the seventh to the first day of the week. If
we suppose here is a transposition of the 7th and 8th verses, then the 8th verse is
a proof of the 6th.

12. *It is lawful to do good on the Sabbath day*—To save a beast, much more
a man.

18. *He shall show judgment to the heathens*—That is, he shall publish the merciful Gospel to them also: the Hebrew word signifies either mercy or justice.

19. *He shall not strive, nor clamour; neither shall any man hear his voice in the
streets*—That is, he shall not be contentious, noisy, or ostentatious: but gentle,
quiet, and lowly. We may observe each word rises above the other, expressing
a still higher degree of humility and gentleness.

20. *A bruised reed*—A convinced sinner: one that is bruised with the weight
of sin : *smoking flax*—One that has the least good desire, the faintest spark of
grace : *till he send forth judgment unto victory*—That is, till he make righteous
ness completely victorious over all its enemies.

21. *In his name*—That is, in him.

22. *A demoniac, blind and dumb*—Many undoubtedly supposed these defects to
be merely natural. But the Spirit of God saw otherwise, and gives the true
account both of the disorder and the cure. How many disorders, seemingly
natural, may even now be owing to the same cause?

23. *Is not this the son of David*—That is, the *Messiah*.

25. *Jesus knowing their thoughts*—It seems, they had as yet only said it in their
hearts.

26. *How shall his kingdom be established*—Does not that subtle spirit know this
is not the way to establish his kingdom?

* Mark iii, 1 ; Luke vi, 6. † Isa. xlii, 1, &c. ‡ Luke xi, 14. § Mark iii, 22.

he is divided against himself : how then shall his kingdom be esta-
27 blished ? And if I by Beelzebub cast out devils, by whom do your
28 children cast them out? Therefore they shall be your judges. But
    if it be by the Spirit of God *that* I cast out devils, then the kingdom
29 of God is come upon you. How can one enter into the strong
    one's house, and plunder his goods, unless he first bind the strong
30 one ? And then will he plunder his house. He that is not with me,
    is against me, and he that gathereth not with me, scattereth.—
31 * Wherefore I say to you, All manner of sin and blasphemy shall
    be forgiven to men ; but the blasphemy against the Spirit shall not
32 be forgiven to men. And whosoever speaketh against the Son of
    man, it shall be forgiven him : but whosoever speaketh against the
    Holy Ghost, it shall not be forgiven him, neither in this world, nor
33 in that to come. † Either make the tree good and its fruit good,
    or make the tree corrupt and its fruit corrupt ; for the tree is
34 known by its fruit. Ye brood of vipers, how can ye, being evil,
    speak good things ? For out of the abundance of the heart the
35 mouth speaketh. A good man out of the good treasure of his heart
    bringeth forth good things : and an evil man out of the evil treasure
36 bringeth forth evil things. But I say to you, That every idle word

---

27. *By whom do your children*—That is, disciples, *cast them out*—It seems,
some of them really did this ; although the sons of Sceva could not. *Therefore
shall they be your judges*—Ask them, if Satan will cast out Satan : let even them
be judges in this matter. And they shall convict you of obstinacy and partiality,
who impute that in me to *Beelzebub*, which in them you impute to God. Beside, how can I rob him of his subjects, till I have conquered him? *The kingdom of God is come upon you*—Unawares ; before you expected : so the word
implies.

29. *How can one enter into the strong one's house, unless he first bind the strong
one*—So Christ coming into the world, which was then eminently the strong
one's, Satan's house, first bound him, and then took his spoils.

30. *He that is not with me is against me*—For there are no neuters in this war.
Every one must be either with Christ or against him ; either a loyal subject or a
rebel. And there are none upon earth, who neither promote nor obstruct his
kingdom. For he that does not gather souls to God, scatters them from him.

31. *The blasphemy against the Spirit*—How much stir has been made about
this ? How many sermons, yea, volumes, have been written concerning it ? And
yet there is nothing plainer in all the Bible. It is neither more nor less than the
ascribing those miracles to the power of the devil, which Christ wrought by the
power of the Holy Ghost.

32. *Whosoever speaketh against the Son of man*—In any other respects : *It shall
be forgiven him*—Upon his true repentance : *But whosoever speaketh* thus *against
the Holy Ghost, it shall not be forgiven, neither in this world nor in the world to
come*—This was a proverbial expression among the Jews, for a thing that would
never be done. It here means farther, He shall not escape the punishment of it,
either in this world, or in the world to come. The judgment of God shall overtake him, both here and hereafter.

33. *Either make the tree good and its fruit good : or make the tree corrupt and
its fruit corrupt*—That is, you must allow, they are both good, or both bad.—
For if the fruit is good, so is the tree ; if the fruit is evil, so is the tree also.
For the tree is known by its fruit—As if he had said, Ye may therefore know me
by my fruits. By my converting sinners to God, you may know that God hath
sent me.

34. In another kind likewise, *the tree is known by its fruit*—Namely, the heart
by the conversation.

36. Ye may perhaps think, God does not so much regard your words. *But I*

* Mark iii, 28 ; Luke xii, 10.   † Matt. vii, 16 ; Luke vi, 43.

which men shall speak, they shall give an account thereof in the
37 day of judgment.   For by thy words thou shalt be justified, or by
thy words thou shalt be condemned.

38 * Then certain of the scribes and Pharisees answered, saying,
39 Master, we would see a sign from thee.   And he answering said
to them An evil and adulterous generation seeketh a sign, and
there shall be no sign given it, but the sign of the Prophet *Jonah.*
40 † For as *Jonah* was three days and three nights in the belly of the
great fish, so shall the Son of man be three days and three nights
41 in the heart of the earth.   The men of Nineveh shall rise up in
the judgment with this generation and shall condemn it; for they
repented at the preaching of Jonah; and behold a greater than
Jonah is here.

42 ‡ The queen of the south shall rise up in the judgment with this
generation and shall condemn it; for she came from the uttermost parts of the earth, to hear the wisdom of Solomon; and
43 behold a greater than Solomon is here.   § When the unclean
spirit is gone out of a man, he walketh through dry places, seek-
44 ing rest, and findeth none.   Then he saith, I will return to my
house whence I came out, and when he is come, he findeth it

---

say to you—That not for blasphemous and profane words only, but *for every idle
word which men shall speak*—For want of seriousness or caution; for every discourse which is not conducive to the glory of God, *they shall give account in the
day of judgment.*

37. *For by thy words* (as well as thy tempers and works) *thou shalt* then *be*
either acquitted or condemned.   Your words as well as actions shall be produced
in evidence for or against you, to prove whether you was a true believer or not.
And according to that evidence you will either be acquitted or condemned in the
great day.

38. *We would see a sign*—Else we will not believe this.

39. *An adulterous generation*—Whose heart wanders from God, though they
profess him to be their husband.   Such adulterers are all those who love the
world, and all who seek the friendship of it.   *Seeketh a sign*—After all they have
had already, which were abundantly sufficient to convince them, had not their
hearts been estranged from God, and consequently averse to the truth.   *The sign
of Jonah*—Who was herein a type of Christ.

40. *Three days and three nights*—It was customary with the eastern nations
to reckon any part of a natural day of twenty-four hours, for the whole day.   Accordingly they used to say a thing was done after three or seven days, if it was
done on the third or seventh day, from that which was last mentioned.   Instances
of this may be seen, 1 Kings xx, 29; and in many other places.   And as the
Hebrews had no word to express a natural day, they used night and day, or day
and night for it.   So that to say a thing happened *after three days and three nights,*
was with them the very same, as to say, it happened after three days, or on the
third day.   See Esther iv, 16; v, 1; Gen. vii, 4, 12; Exod. xxiv, 18; xxxiv, 28.

42. *She came from the uttermost parts of the earth*—That part of Arabia from
which she came was the uttermost part of the earth that way, being bounded by
the sea.

43. But how dreadful will be the consequence of their rejecting me?   *When
the unclean spirit goeth out*—Not willingly, but being compelled by one that is
stronger than he.   *He walketh*—Wanders up and down; *through dry places*—
Barren, dreary, desolate; or places not yet watered with the Gospel: *Seeking rest,
and findeth none*—How can he, while he carries with him his own hell?   And is
it not the case of his children too?   Reader, is it thy case?

44. *Whence he came out*—He speaks as if he had come out of his own accord:
See his pride!   *He findeth it empty*—of God, of Christ, of his Spirit: *Swept*—from

* Matt. xvi, 1; Luke xi, 16, 29.   † Jonah ii, 1.   ‡ 1 Kings x, 1.   § Luke xi, 24.

45 empty, swept, and garnished. Then goeth he and taketh with him seven other spirits more wicked than himself, and they enter in and dwell there, and the last state of that man is worse than the first. So shall it be also to this wicked generation.

46 * While he yet talked to the multitude, behold his mother and his

47 brethren stood without, seeking to speak to him. And one said to him, Behold, thy mother and thy brethren stand without, seek-

48 ing to speak to thee. And he answering, said to him that told him,

49 Who is my mother, and who are my brethren? And stretching forth his hand toward his disciples, he said, Behold my mother and

50 my brethren. For whosoever shall do the will of my Father who is in heaven, the same is my brother, and sister, and mother.

XIII. † The same day went Jesus out of the house, and sat by the sea

2 side. And great multitudes were gathered together to him, so that he went into the vessel and sat, and the multitude stood on

3 the shore. And he spake many things to them in parables, saying,

4 Behold, the sower went forth to sow. And while he sowed, some *seeds* fell by the highway side, and the birds came and devoured

---

love, lowliness, meekness, and all the fruits of the Spirit : *And garnished*—With levity and security : so that there is nothing to keep him out, and much to invite him in.

45. *Seven other spirits*—That is, a great many ; a certain number being put for an uncertain : *More wicked than himself*—Whence it appears, that there are degrees of wickedness among the devils themselves : *They enter in and dwell*— For ever in him who is forsaken of God. *So shall it be to this wicked generation* —Yea, and to apostates in all ages.

46. *His brethren*—His kinsmen : they were the sons of Mary, the wife of Cleopas, or Alpheus, his mother's sister ; and came now *seeking to take him*, as one beside himself, Mark iii, 21.

48. *And he answering, said*—Our Lord's knowing why they came, sufficiently justifies his seeming disregard of them.

49, 50. See the highest severity, and the highest goodness ! Severity to his natural, goodness to his spiritual relations ! In a manner disclaiming the former, who opposed the will of his heavenly Father, and owning the latter, who obeyed it.

XIII. 2. *He went into the vessel*—Which constantly waited upon him, while he was on the sea coast.

3. *In parables*—The word is here taken in its proper sense, for apt similes or comparisons. This way of speaking, extremely common in the eastern countries, drew and fixed the attention of many, and occasioned the truths delivered to sink the deeper into humble and serious hearers. At the same time, by an awful mixture of justice and mercy, it hid them from the proud and careless.

In this chapter our Lord delivers seven parables ; directing the four former (as oeing of general concern) to all the people ; the three latter to his disciples.

Behold the sower—How exquisitely proper is this parable to be an introduction to all the rest ! In this our Lord answers a very obvious and a very important question. The same sower, Christ, and the same preachers sent by him, always sow the same seed : why has it not always the same effect ? He that hath ears to hear, let him hear !

4. *And while he sowed, some* seeds *fell by the highway side, and the birds came and devoured them*—It is observable, that our Lord points out the grand hinderances of our bearing fruit, in the same order as they occur. The first danger is, that the birds will devour the seed. If it escape this, there is then another danger, namely, lest it be scorched, and wither away. It is long after this that the thorns spring up and choke the good seed.

A vast majority of those who hear the word of God, receive the seed as by the *highway side*. Of those who do not lose it by the birds, yet many receive it as

* Mark iii, 31 ; Luke viii, 19.   † Mark iv, 1 ; Luke viii, 4.

5 them. Others fell upon stony *places*, where they had not much
earth; and they sprung up immediately, because they had not
6 depth of earth. And when the sun was up, they were scorched;
7 and because they had not root they withered away. And some fell
among thorns: and the thorns sprung up and choked them.
8 And others fell on the good ground, and brought forth fruit, some
9 a hundred*fold*, some sixty, some thirty. He that hath ears to
10 hear, let him hear. And the disciples came and said to him, Why
11 speakest thou to them in parables? He answering, said unto them,
Because to you it is given to know the mysteries of the kingdom
12 of heaven; but to them it is not given. For *whosoever hath, to
him shall be given; and he shall have abundance: but whosoever hath not, from him shall be taken away even what he hath.
13 Therefore I spake to them in parables, because seeing they see
not, and hearing they hear not, neither do they understand.
14 And in them is fulfilled the prophecy of *Isaiah*, who saith,
† Hearing, ye will hear, but in nowise understand, and seeing
15 ye will see, but in nowise perceive. For the heart of this people
is waxed fat, and *their* ears are dull of hearing, and their eyes have
they closed: lest at any time they should see with *their* eyes, and
hear with *their* ears, and understand with *their* hearts, and should
16 be converted, and I should heal them. ‡ But blessed are your eyes,
17 for they see, and your ears for they hear. For verily I say unto
you, That many prophets and righteous men have desired to see

---

on stony places. Many of them who receive it in a better soil, yet suffer *the thorns to grow up, and choke it:* so that few even of these endure to the end, and bear fruit unto perfection: yet in all these cases, it is not the will of God that hinders, but their own voluntary perverseness.

8. *Good ground*—Soft, not like that by the highway side; deep, not like the stony ground; purged, not full of thorns.

11. *To you,* who have, *it is given to know the mysteries of the kingdom of heaven*—The deep things which flesh and blood cannot reveal, pertaining to the inward, present kingdom of heaven. *But to them* who have not, *it is not given—Therefore speak I in parables*, that ye may understand, while they do not understand.

12. *Whosoever hath*—That is, improves what he hath, uses the grace given according to the design of the giver; *to him shall be given*—More and more, in proportion to that improvement. *But whosoever hath not*—Improves it not, *from him shall be taken even what he hath*—Here is the grand rule of God's dealing with the children of men: a rule fixed as the pillars of heaven. This is the key to all his providential dispensations; as will appear to men and angels in that day.

13. *Therefore I speak to them in parables, because seeing, they see not*—In pursuance of this general rule, I do not give more knowledge to this people, because they use not that which they have already: having all the means of seeing, hearing, and understanding, they use none of them: they do not effectually see, or hear, or understand any thing.

14. *Hearing ye will hear, but in nowise understand*—That is, Ye *will surely hear.* All possible means will be given you: yet they will profit you nothing; because your heart is sensual, stupid, and insensible; your spiritual senses are shut up; yea, you *have closed* your *eyes* against the light; as being unwilling to understand the things of God, and afraid, not desirous that he *should heal* you.

16. *But blessed are your eyes*—For you both see and understand. You know now to prize the light which is given you.

the things which ye see, and have not seen *them*, and to hear the
18 things which ye hear, and have not heard *them*. Hear ye there-
19 fore the parable of the sower. When any one heareth the word of
the kingdom, and considereth *it* not, the wicked one cometh, and
catcheth away what was sown in his heart. This is he who
20 received seed by the highway side. But he who received the seed
in stony *places*, is he that heareth the word and immediately
21 receiveth it with joy. Yet he hath not root in himself, and so
endureth but for a while : for when tribulation or persecution ariseth
22 because of the word, straightway he is offended. He that received
the seed among the thorns, is he that heareth the word ; and the
care of this world and the deceitfulness of riches choke the word,
23 and it becometh unfruitful. But he that receiveth seed on the good
ground, is he that heareth the word and considereth *it* : who also
beareth fruit and bringeth forth, some a hundred *fold*, some sixty,
some thirty.
24   He proposed to them another parable, saying, The kingdom of
25 heaven is like a man sowing good seed in his field. But while
men slept, his enemy came and sowed darnel amidst the wheat,

---

19. *When any one heareth the word, and considereth it not*—The first and most
general cause of unfruitfulness. *The wicked one cometh*—Either inwardly ; filling
the mind with thoughts of other things ; or by his agent. Such are all they that
introduce other subjects, when men should be considering what they have heard.

20. The seed sown *on stony places*, therefore *sprang up* soon, *because* it did not
sink deep, ver. 5. *He receiveth it with joy*—Perhaps with transport, with ecstacy :
struck with the beauty of truth, and drawn by the preventing grace of God.

21. *Yet hath he not root in himself*—No deep work of grace : no change in the
ground of his heart. Nay, he has no deep conviction ; and without this, good
desires soon wither away. *He is offended*—He finds a thousand plausible pre-
tences for leaving so narrow and rugged a way.

22. *He that received the seed among the thorns, is he that heareth the word and
considereth it*—In spite of Satan and his agents : yea, *hath root in himself*, is
deeply convinced, and in a great measure inwardly changed ; so that he will not
draw back, even *when tribulation or persecution ariseth*. And yet even in him,
together with the good seed, *the thorns spring up*, ver. 7, (perhaps unperceived
at first) till they gradually *choke* it, destroy all its life and power, *and it becometh
unfruitful*.
Cares are *thorns* to the poor : wealth to the rich ; the desire of other things to
all. *The deceitfulness of riches*—Deceitful indeed ! for they smile, and betray :
kiss, and smite into hell. They put out the eyes, harden the heart, steal away
all the life of God ; fill the soul with pride, anger, love of the world ; make men
enemies to the whole cross of Christ ! And all the while are eagerly desired, and
vehemently pursued, even by those who believe there is a God !

23. *Some a hundred fold, some sixty, some thirty*—That is, in various propor-
tions ; some abundantly more than others.

24. *He proposed another parable*—in which he farther explains the case of
unfruitful hearers. *The kingdom of heaven* (as has been observed before) sometimes signifies eternal glory : sometimes the way to it, inward religion ; sometimes, as here, the Gospel dispensation : the phrase is likewise used for a person
or thing relating to any one of those : so in this place it means, Christ preaching
the Gospel, who *is like a man sowing good seed*—The expression, *is like*, both
here and in several other places, only means, that the thing spoken of may be
illustrated by the following similitude. *Who sowed good seed in his field*—God
sowed nothing but good in his whole creation. Christ sowed only the good seed
of truth in his Church.

25. *But while men slept*—They ought to have watched : the Lord of the field
sleepeth not. *His enemy came and sowed darnel*—This is very like wheat, and

26 and went away. And when the blade **was** sprung up and brought
27 forth fruit, then appeared the darnel also. So the servants of the
householder came to him, and said, Sir, didst not thou sow good
seed in thy field? Whence then hath it darnel? He said to them,
28 An enemy hath done this. The servants said to him, Wilt thou
29 then, that we go and gather them up? But he said, No: lest gather-
30 ing up the darnel, ye root up the wheat with them. Suffer both
to grow together till the harvest; and at the time of the harvest I
will say to the reapers, Gather ye together first the darnel, and
bind it in bundles to burn it, but gather the wheat into my barn.
31 He proposed to them another parable, saying, * The kingdom of
heaven is like a grain of mustard seed, which a man took and sowed
32 in his field: Which indeed is the least of all seeds: but when it is
grown up, it is the greatest of herbs, and becometh a tree, so that
the birds of the air come and lodge in the branches of it.
33 He spake another parable to them: † The kingdom of heaven is
like leaven, which a woman taking, covered up in three measures
meal, till the whole was leavened.
34 All these things spake Jesus to the multitude in parables, and
35 without a parable spake he not unto them: Whereby was fulfilled
what was spoken by the prophet, saying, ‡ I will open my mouth

---

commonly grows among wheat rather than among other grain: but *tares* or
vetches are of the pulse kind, and bear no resemblance to wheat.

26. *When the blade was sprung up, then appeared the darnel*—It was not discerned before: it seldom appears, as soon as the good seed is sown: all at first
appears to be peace, and love, and joy.

27. *Didst not thou sow good seed in thy field? Whence then hath it darnel?*—
Not from the parent of good. Even the heathen could say,

> " No evil can from thee proceed:
> 'Tis only suffer'd, not decreed:
> As darkness is not from the sun,
> Nor mount the shades, till he is gone."

28. *He said, An enemy hath done this*—A plain answer to the great question
concerning the origin of evil. God made men (as he did angels) intelligent
creatures, and consequently free either to choose good or evil: but he implanted
no evil in the human soul: *An enemy* (with man's concurrence) *hath done this.*
Darnel, in the Church, is properly outside Christians, such as have the form of
godliness, without the power. Open sinners, such as have neither the form nor
the power, are not so properly darnel, as thistles and brambles: these ought to
be rooted up without delay, and not suffered in the Christian community. Whereas
should fallible men attempt to *gather up the darnel*, they would often *root up the
wheat with them.*

31. *He proposed to them another parable*—The former parables relate chiefly to
unfruitful hearers; these that follow, to those who bear good fruit. *The kingdom of heaven*—Both the Gospel dispensation, and the inward kingdom.

32. *The least*—That is, one of the least: a way of speaking extremely common among the Jews. *It becometh a tree*—In those countries it grows exceeding large and high. So will the Christian doctrine spread in the world, and the
life of Christ in the soul.

33. *Three measures*—This was the quantity which they usually baked at once:
till the whole was leavened—Thus will the Gospel leaven the world and grace the
Christian.

34. *Without a parable spake he not unto them*—That is, not at that time; at
other times he did.

* Mark iv, 30; Luke xiii, 18.   † Luke xiii, 20.   ‡ Psalm lxxviii, 2.

4

in parables ;· I will utter things hid from the foundation of the world.

36 Then Jesus having sent the multitude away, went into the house : and his disciples came to him, saying, Declare to us the
37 parable of the darnel of the field. He answering said to them, He
38 that soweth the good seed is the Son of man. The field is the world ; the good seed are the children of the kingdom, but the
39 darnel are the children of the wicked one. The enemy that sowed them is the devil : the harvest is the end of the world ; the
40 reapers are the angels. As therefore the darnel is gathered and
41 burnt with fire, so shall it be at the end of the world. The Son of man shall send forth his angels, and they shall gather out of his kingdom all things that offend, and them that do iniquity ;
42 And shall cast them into the furnace of fire : there shall be the
43 wailing and the gnashing of teeth. Then shall the righteous shine forth as the sun in the kingdom of their Father. He that hath ears to hear, let him hear.

44 Again, the kingdom of heaven is like treasure hid in a field, which a man having found hideth, and for joy thereof goeth and selleth all that he hath, and buyeth that field.

45 Again, the kingdom of heaven is like a merchant seeking goodly
46 pearls : Who having found one pearl of great value, went and sold all that he had, and bought it.

47 Again, the kingdom of heaven is like a net cast into the sea, and
48 gathering fishes of every kind : Which when it was full, they drew to the shore, and sitting down, gathered the good into vessels, but
49 cast the bad away. So shall it be at the end of the world. The angels shall come forth and sever the wicked from among the
50 just ; And shall cast them into the furnace of fire : there shall be
51 the wailing and the gnashing of teeth. Jesus saith to them, Have
52 ye understood all these things ? They say to him, Yea, Lord. Then saith he to them, Therefore every scribe instructed unto the

38. *The good seed are the children of the kingdom*—That is, the children of God, the righteous.

41. *They shall gather all things that offend*—Whatever had hindered or grieved the children of God ; whatever things or persons had hindered the good seed which Christ had sown from taking root or bearing fruit. The Greek word is, *All scandals.*

44. The three following parables are proposed, not to the multitude, but peculiarly to the apostles : the two former of them relate to those who receive the Gospel ; the third, both to those who receive, and those who preach it. *The kingdom of heaven is like treasure hid in a field*—The kingdom of God within us is a treasure indeed, but a treasure hid from the world, and from the most wise and prudent in it. He that *finds* this treasure, (perhaps when he thought it far from him,) hides it deep in his heart, and gives up all other happiness for it.

45. *The kingdom of heaven*—That is, one who earnestly seeks for it : in the 47th verse it means, the Gospel preached, which is *like a net* gathering of every kind : just so the Gospel, wherever it is preached, gathers at first both good and bad, who are for a season full of approbation and warm with good desires. But Christian discipline, and strong, close exhortation, begin that separation in this world, which shall be accomplished by the angels of God in the world to come.

52. *Every scribe instructed unto the kingdom of heaven*—That is, every duly prepared preacher of the Gospel has a treasure of Divine knowledge, out of

kingdom of heaven, is like a householder, who bringeth out of his treasure things new and old.

53 And when Jesus had finished these parables, he departed
54 thence : * And coming into his own country, he taught them in their synagogue, so that they were astonished, and said, Whence
55 hath HE this wisdom and these mighty works ? Is not this the carpenter's son ? Is not his mother called Mary ? And his brethren James and Joses and Simon and Jude ? And his sisters, are
56 they not all with us ? Whence then hath HE all these things ? † And
57 they were offended at him. But Jesus said to them, A prophet is not without honour save in his own country, and in his own house.
58 And he wrought not many mighty works there, because of their unbelief.

XIV. ‡ At that time Herod the tetrarch heard of the fame of Jesus,
2 And said to his servants, This is John the Baptist : he is risen from the dead, and therefore these mighty powers exert themselves
3 in him. § For Herod having apprehended John, had bound and put him in prison, for Herodias's sake, his brother Philip's wife.
4 For John had said to him, It is not lawful for thee to have her.
5 And when he would have put him to death, he feared the multitude,
6 because they accounted him a prophet. But when Herod's birthday was kept, the daughter of Herodias danced before them, and

---

which he is able to bring forth all sorts of instructions. The word *treasure* signifies any collection of things whatsoever, and the places where such collections are kept.

53. *He departed thence*—He crossed the lake from Capernaum : *and came* once more *into his own country*—*Nazareth :* but with no better success than he had had there before.

54. *Whence hath HE*—Many texts are not understood, for want of knowing the proper emphasis ; and others are utterly misunderstood, by placing the emphasis wrong. To prevent this in some measure, the emphatical words are here printed in capital letters.

55. *The carpenter's son*—The Greek word means, one that works either in wood, iron, or stone. *His brethren*—Our kinsmen. They were the sons of Mary, sister to the virgin, and wife of Cleophas or Alpheus. *James*—Styled by St. Paul also, *the Lord's brother*, Gal. i, 19. *Simon*—Surnamed the Canaanite.

57. *They were offended at him*—They looked on him as a mean, ignoble man, not worthy to be regarded.

58 *He wrought not many mighty works, because of their unbelief*—And the reason why many mighty works are not wrought now, is not, that the faith is not every where planted ; but, that unbelief every where prevails.

XIV. 1. *At that time*—When our Lord had spent about a year in his public ministry. *Tetrarch*—King of a fourth part of his father's dominions.

2. *He is risen from the dead*—Herod was a Sadducee : and the Sadducees denied the resurrection of the dead. But Sadduceeism staggers when conscience awakes.

3. *His brother Philip's wife*—Who was still alive.

4. *It is not lawful for thee to have her*—It was not lawful indeed for either of them to have her. For her father Aristobulus was their own brother. John's words were rough, like his raiment. He would not break the force of truth by using soft words, even to a king.

5. *He would have put him to death*—In his fit of passion ; but he was then restrained by fear of the multitude ; and afterward by the reverence he bore him

6. *The daughter of Herodias*—Afterward infamous for a life suitable to this beginning.

* Mark vi, 1 ; Luke iv, 16, 22.   † John iv, 44 ; Luke ix, 7.   ‡ Mark vi, 14.
§ Mark vi, 17.

7 pleased Herod. Whereupon he promised with an oath, to give
8 her whatever she should ask. And she, being before instructed by
her mother, said, Give me here John the Baptist's head in a
9 charger. And the king was sorry; yet for the oath's sake, and
them who sat with him at table, he commanded *it* to be given *her*.
10, 11. And he sent and beheaded John in the prison. And his head
was brought in a charger, and given to the damsel, and she carried
12 *it* to her mother. And his disciples came and took up the body,
13 and buried it, and went and told Jesus. * And Jesus hearing *it*,
withdrew thence by ship into a desert place apart: but when
the people heard *thereof*, they followed him by land out of
the cities.
14   And coming forth he saw a great multitude, and was moved
15 with tender compassion for them, and healed their sick. † And in
the evening his disciples came to him, saying, This is a desert
place, and the time is now past: send the multitude away, that
16 going into the villages, they may buy themselves victuals. But
17 Jesus said to them, They need not go: give ye them to eat. They
18 say to him, We have here but five loaves and two fishes. He
19 said, Bring them hither to me. And he commanded the multitude
to sit down on the grass; and taking the five loaves and the two
fishes, looking up to heaven he blessed and brake, and gave the
20 loaves to his disciples, and the disciples to the multitude. And
they all ate and were satisfied: and they took up of the fragments
21 that remained twelve baskets full. And they that had eaten were
22 about five thousand, beside women and children. ‡ And he constrained his disciples to go straightway into the vessel, and go
23 before him to the other side till he sent the multitude away. And
having sent the multitude away, he went up into a mountain apart
24 to pray. And in the evening he was there alone; but the vessel
was now in the midst of the sea, tossed by the waves; for the

8. *Being before instructed by her mother*—Both as to the matter and manner of her petition: *She said, Give me here*—Fearing if he had time to consider, he would not do it: *John the Baptist's head in a charger*—A large dish or bowl.

9. *And the king was sorry*—Knowing that John was a good man. *Yet for the oath's sake*—So he murdered an innocent man from mere tenderness of conscience.

10. *And he sent and beheaded John in the prison, and his head was given to the damsel*—How mysterious is the providence, which left the life of so holy a man in such infamous hands! which permitted it to be sacrificed to the malice of an abandoned harlot, the petulancy of a vain girl, and the rashness of a foolish, perhaps drunken prince, who made a prophet's head the reward of a dance! But we are sure the Almighty will repay his servants in another world for what ever they suffer in this.

13. *Jesus withdrew into a desert place*—1. To avoid Herod: 2. Because of the multitude pressing upon him, Mark vi, 32: and 3. To talk with his disciples, newly returned from their progress, Luke ix, 10: *apart*—From all but his disciples.

15. *The time is now past*—The usual meal time.

22. *He constrained his disciples*—Who were unwilling to leave him.

24. *In the evening*—Learned men say the Jews reckoned two evenings; the first beginning at three in the afternoon, the second, at sunset. If so, the latter is meant here.

* Mark vi, 32, 34; Luke ix, 10; John vi, 1. † Mark vi, 35; Luke ix, 12; John vi, 15.
‡ Mark vi, 45; John vi, 15.

25 wind was contrary. In the fourth watch of the night he went tc
26 them, walking on the sea. And the disciples seeing him walking
on the sea, were affrighted, saying, It is an apparition: and they
27 cried out for fear. But Jesus immediately spake to them, saying,
28 Take courage: it is I: be not afraid. And Peter answering, said,
29 Lord, if it be thou, bid me come to thee on the waters. And he
said, Come. And Peter going down from the vessel, walked on
30 the waters, to go to Jesus. But seeing the wind boisterous, he
31 was afraid; and beginning to sink, he cried, Lord, save me. And
immediately Jesus reaching forth his hand, caught him, and saith
32 to him, O thou of little faith, wherefore didst thou doubt? And
33 when they were come into the vessel, the wind ceased. Then they
that were in the vessel came and worshipped him, saying, Of a truth
thou art the Son of God.

34 And having crossed over, they came into the land of Gennesaret.
35 * And when the men of that place had knowledge of him, they
sent out into the country round about, and brought to him all that
36 were diseased; And besought him that they might touch but the
hem of his garment: and as many as touched were made perfectly
whole.

XV. † Then came to Jesus scribes and Pharisees who were at
2 Jerusalem, saying, Why do thy disciples transgress the tradition
of the elders? for they wash not their hands when they eat bread.
3 But he answering said, Why do ye also transgress the command-
4 ment of God through your tradition? For God said, ‡ Honour thy
father and mother: and he that revileth father or mother, let him
5 die the death. But ye say, Whosoever shall say to his father or
mother, *It is* a gift, by whatsoever thou mightest have been pro-
6 fited by me: He shall in nowise honour his father or his
mother. Thus have ye made void the command of God through
7 your tradition. Ye hypocrites, well did‾ Isaiah prophesy of you,
8 saying, § This people draweth nigh to me with their lips; but

---

25. *The fourth watch*—The Jews (as well as the Romans) usually divided the
night into four watches, of three hours each. The first watch began at six, the
second at nine, the third at twelve, the fourth at three in the morning. *If it be
thou*—It is the same as, Since it is thou. The particle *if* frequently bears this
meaning, both in ours and in all languages. So it means, John xiii, 14 and 17.
St. Peter was in no doubt, or he would not have quitted the ship.

30. *He was afraid*—Though he had been used to the sea, and was a skilful
swimmer. But so it frequently is. When grace begins to act, the natural courage and strength are withdrawn.

33. *Thou art the Son of God*—They mean, the Messiah.

XV. 2. *The elders*—The chief doctors or teachers among the Jews.

3. *They wash not their hands when they eat bread*—Food in general is termed
bread in Hebrew; so that to *eat bread* is the same as to make a meal.

4. *Honour thy father and mother*—Which implies all such relief as they stand
in need of.

5. *It is a gift by whatsoever thou mightest have been profited by me*—That is,
I have given, or at least, purpose to give to the treasury of the temple, what you
might otherwise have had from me.

7. *Well did Isaiah prophesy of you, saying*—That is, the description which
Isaiah gave of your fathers, is exactly applicable to you. The words therefore
which were a description of them, are a prophecy with regard to you.

* Mark vi, 45.   † Mark vii, 1.   ‡ Exod. xx, 12; xxi, 17.   § Isaiah xxix, 13.

9 their heart is far from me. But in vain do they worship me
10 teaching for doctrines the commandments of men. And calling
the multitude unto him, he said to them, Hear and understand.
11 Not that which goeth into the mouth defileth the man, but what
12 cometh out of the mouth, this defileth the man. Then came his
disciples and said to him, Knowest thou that the Pharisees,
13 hearing this saying, were offended? He answered and said, Every
plant which my heavenly Father hath not planted shall be rooted
14 up. * Let them alone; they are blind leaders of the blind: but
15 if the blind lead the blind, both will fall into a ditch. Then
16 answered Peter and said to him, Declare to us this parable. And
17 Jesus said, Are ye also yet without understanding? Do ye not
yet understand, that whatever entereth into the mouth, goeth into
18 the belly, and is cast out into the vault? But the things which proceed out of the mouth come out of the heart, and they defile the
19 man. For out of the heart proceed evil thoughts, murders, adul-
20 teries, fornications, thefts, false witness, railings. These are the
things which defile a man ; but to eat with unwashen hands defileth
not a man.
21 † And Jesus going thence, retired to the coast of Tyre and Si-
22 don. And behold, a woman of Canaan, coming out of those coasts,
cried to him, saying, Have mercy on me, O Lord, thou Son of
23 David: my daughter is grievously vexed with a devil. But he
answered her not a word. And his disciples came and besought
24 him, saying, Send her away, for she crieth after us. But he answering said, I am not sent but to the lost sheep of the house of
25 Israel. Then she came and worshipped him, saying, Lord, help
26 me. But he answering said, It is not good to take the children's
27 bread and cast it to the dogs. And she said, True, Lord: yet
the dogs eat of the crumbs which fall from their master's table.
28 And Jesus answering said to her, O woman, great is thy faith : be
it unto thee as thou wilt. And her daughter was healed from that
hour.

---

8. *Their heart is far from me*—And without this all outward worship is mere
mockery of God.
9. *Teaching the commandments of men*—As equal with, nay, superior to, those
of God. What can be a more heinous sin ?
13. *Every plant*—That is, every doctrine.
14. *Let them alone*—If they are indeed *blind leaders of the blind; let them alone :*
concern not yourselves about them : a plain direction how to behave with regard
to all such.
17. *Are ye also yet without understanding*—How fair and candid are the sacred
historians ? Never concealing or excusing their own blemishes.
19. First *evil thoughts*—then *murders*—and the rest. *Railings*—The Greek
word includes all reviling, backbiting, and evil speaking.
22. *A woman of Canaan*—Canaan was also called Syrophenicia, as lying between Syria properly so called, and Phenicia, by the sea side. *Cried to him*—
From afar, *Thou Son of David*—So she had some knowledge of the promised
Messiah.
23. *He answered her not a word*—He sometimes tries our faith in like manner.
24. *I am not sent*—Not primarily; not yet.
25. *Then came she*—Into the house where he now was.
28. *Thy faith*—Thy reliance on the power and goodness of God.

* Luke vi, 39.   † Mark vii, 24.

29   * And Jesus passing thence, came nigh the sea of Galilee ; and
30 going up into a mountain, he sat down there.   And great multi-
      tudes came to him, having with them the lame, blind, dumb, dis-
      abled, and many others ; and cast them at the feet of Jesus, and
31 he healed them : So that the multitudes wondered, seeing the
      dumb to speak, the disabled whole, the lame to walk, and the blind
32 to see : and they glorified the God of Israel. † Then Jesus calling
      his d sciples to him said, I have tender compassion on the multi-
      tude, because they continue with me now three days, and have
      nothing to eat : and I am not willing to send them away fasting,
33 lest they faint in the way.   And his disciples said to him, Whence
      should we have so many loaves in the wilderness, as to satisfy so
34 great a multitude ? And Jesus saith to them, How many loaves
35 have you ? They said, Seven, and a few small fishes.   And he
36 commanded the multitude to sit down on the ground.   And taking
      the seven loaves and the fishes, he gave thanks and brake *them*
37 and gave to his disciples, and the disciples to the multitude.   And
      they all ate and were satisfied, and they took up of the fragments
38 that remained seven baskets full.   And they that had eaten were
      four thousand men, beside women and children.
39   And having sent away the multitude, he took ship again, and
      came into the coasts of Magdala.
XVI. ‡ Then the Pharisees and Sadducees came to him and tempt-
  2 ing, desired him to show them a sign from heaven.   § He answer-
      ing said to them, In the evening ye say, *It will be* fair weather ;
  3 for the sky is red : And in the morning, *It will be* foul weather to-
      day ; for the sky is red and lowering.   O ye hypocrites, ye know
      to discern the face of the sky ; can ye not *discern* the signs of the
  4 times ? A wicked and adulterous generation seeketh after a sign ;
      but there shall no sign be given to it, but the sign of the Prophet
      Jonah.   And he left them and departed.
  5 || And when his disciples were come on the other side, they had
  6 forgotten to take bread.   ** And Jesus said to them. Take heed, and

---

29. *The sea of Galilee*—The Jews gave the name of seas to all large lakes.—
This was a hundred furlongs long, and forty broad. It was called also, *the sea
of Tiberias.* It lay on the borders of Galilee, and the city of Tiberias stood on
its western shore. It was likewise styled *the lake of Gennesareth :* perhaps a
corruption of Cinnereth, the name by which it was anciently called, Numbers
xxxiv, 11.
    32. *They continue with me now three days*—It was now the third day since
they came.
    36. *He gave thanks,* or *blessed* the food—That is, he praised God for it, and
prayed for a blessing upon it.
    XVI. 1. *A sign from heaven*—Such they imagined Satan could not counterfeit.
    3. *The signs of the times*—The signs which evidently show, that this is the
time of the Messiah.
    4. *A wicked and adulterous generation*—Ye would seek no farther sign, did not
your wickedness, your love of the world, which is spiritual adultery, blind your
understanding.
    6. *Beware of the leaven of the Pharisees*—That is, of their false doctrine : this
is elegantly so called ; for it spreads in the soul, or the Church, as leaven does
in meal.

* Mark vii, 31.   † Mark viii, 1.   ‡ Mark viii, 11 ; Matt. xii, 38.   § Luke xii. 54.
             || Mark viii, 14.   ** Luke xii, 1.

7 beware of the leaven of the Pharisees and Sadducees. And they
reasoned among themselves, saying, We have taken no bread.
8 Jesus knowing *it* said to them, O ye of little faith, why reason ye
9 among yourselves, because ye have taken no bread? Do ye not
understand nor remember the five loaves of the five thousand, and
10 how many baskets ye took up? Neither the seven loaves of the
11 four thousand, and how many baskets ye took up? How do ye not
understand, that I spake not to you concerning bread, to beware of
12 the leaven of the Pharisees and Sadducees? Then they understood,
that he did not bid *them* beware of the leaven of bread, but of the
doctrine of the Pharisees and Sadducees.
13   * And Jesus coming into the coasts of Cesarea Philippi, asked
his disciples saying, Whom do men say that the Son of man is?
14 And they said, Some *say*, John the Baptist; others Elijah; others
15 Jeremiah or one of the prophets. He saith to them, But whom
16 say ye that I am? And Simon Peter answering said, Thou art
17 the Christ, the Son of the living God. And Jesus answering said
to him, Happy art thou, Şimon Barjonah, for flesh and blood have
18 not revealed this to thee, but my Father who is in heaven. And
I say also to thee, Thou art Peter, and on this rock I will build my
19 Church, and the gates of hell shall not prevail against it. † And
I will give thee the keys of the kingdom of heaven: and whatsoever thou shalt bind on earth shall be bound in heaven, and whatso-

---

7. *They reasoned among themselves*—What must we do then for bread, since
we have taken no bread with us?

8. *Why reason ye*—Why are you troubled about this? Am I not able, if need so
require, to supply you by a word?

11. *How do ye not understand*—Beside, do you not understand, that I did not
mean *bread*, by the *leaven* of the Pharisees and Sadducees?

13. *And Jesus coming*—There was a large interval of time between what has
been related, and what follows. The passages that follow were but a short time
before our Lord suffered.

14. *Jeremiah, or one of the prophets*—There was at that time a current tradition
among the Jews, that either Jeremiah, or some other of the ancient prophets
would rise again before the Messiah came.

16. *Peter*—Who was generally the most forward to speak.

17. *Flesh and blood*—That is, thy own reason, or any natural power whatsoever.

18. *On this rock*—Alluding to his name, which signifies a rock, namely, the
faith which thou hast now professed; *I will build my Church*—But perhaps when
our Lord uttered these words, he pointed to himself, in like manner as when he
said, *Destroy this temple*, John ii, 19; meaning the temple of his body. And it
is certain, that as he is spoken of in Scripture, as the only foundation of the
Church, so this is that which the apostles and evangelists laid in their preaching.
It is in respect of laying this, that the names of the twelve apostles (not of St.
Peter only) were equally inscribed on the *twelve foundations* of the city of God,
Rev. xxi, 14. *The gates of hell*—As gates and walls were the strength of cities,
and as courts of judicature were held in their gates, this phrase properly signifies
the power and policy of Satan and his instruments. *Shall not prevail against it*
—Not against the Church universal, so as to destroy it. And they never did.
There hath been a small remnant in all ages.

19. *I will give thee the keys of the kingdom of heaven*—Indeed not to him alone,
(for they were equally given to all the apostles at the same time, John xx, 21.
22, 23,) but to him were first given the keys both of doctrine and discipline.
He first, after our Lord's resurrection, exercised the apostleship, Acts i, 15. And

* Mark viii, 27; Luke ix, 12.   † Matt. xviii, 18.

20 ever thou shalt loose on earth shall be loosed in heaven. Then charged he his disciples to tell no one that he was the Christ.

21 * From that time Jesus began to show his disciples, that he must go to Jerusalem and suffer many things from the elders and chief priests and scribes, and be killed, and be raised again the

22 third day. Then Peter taking hold of him, rebuked him, saying,

23 Favour thyself, Lord : this shall in nowise be unto thee. But he turning said to Peter, Get thee behind me, Satan ; thou art an offence to me : for thou savourest not the things of God, but the

24 things of men. † Then said Jesus to his disciples, If any man be willing to come after me, let him deny himself, and take up his

---

he first by preaching opened the kingdom of heaven, both to the Jews, Acts ii, and to the Gentiles, Acts x.

Under the term of *binding* and *loosing* are contained all those acts of discipline which Peter and his brethren performed as apostles : and undoubtedly what they thus performed on earth, God confirmed in heaven.

20. *Then charged he his disciples to tell no one that he was the Christ*—Jesus himself had not said it expressly even to his apostles, but left them to infer it from his doctrine and miracles. Neither was it proper the apostles should say this openly, before that grand proof of it, his resurrection. If they had, they who believed them would the more earnestly have sought to take and make him a king : and they who did not believe them would the more vehemently have rejected and opposed such a Messiah.

21. *From that time Jesus began to tell his disciples, that he must suffer many things*—Perhaps this expression, *began,* always implied his entering on a set and solemn discourse. Hitherto he had mainly taught them only one point, That he was the Christ. From this time he taught them another, That Christ must through sufferings and death enter into his glory. *From the elders*—The most honourable and experienced men ; *the chief priests*—Accounted the most reli. gious ; *and the scribes*—The most learned body of men in the nation. Would not one have expected,·that these should have been the very first to receive him ? But *not many wise, not many noble* were called. *Favour thyself*—The advice of the world, the flesh, and the devil, to every one of our Lord's followers.

23. *Get thee behind me*—Out of my sight. It is not improbable, Peter might step before him, to stop him. *Satan*—Our Lord is not recorded to have given so sharp a reproof to any other of his apostles on any occasion. He saw it was needful for the pride of Peter's heart, puffed up with the commendation lately given him. Perhaps the term *Satan* may not barely mean, Thou art my *enemy,* while thou fanciest thyself most my friend ; but also, Thou art acting the very part of Satan, both by endeavouring to hinder the redemption of mankind, and by giving me the most deadly advice that can ever spring from the pit of hell. *Thou savourest not*—Dost not relish or desire. We may learn from hence,— 1. That whosoever says to us in such a case, *Favour thyself,* is acting the part of the devil : 2. That the proper answer to such an adviser is, Get thee behind me : 3. That otherwise he will be *an offence* to us, an occasion of our stumbling, if not falling : 4. That this advice always proceeds from the not relishing the things of God, but the things of men. Yea, so far is this advice, *favour thyself,* from being fit for a Christian either to give or take, that *if any man will come after Christ,* his very first step is *to deny, or renounce himself :* in the room of his own will, to substitute the will of God, as his one principle of action.

24. *If any man be willing to come after me*—None is forced ; but if any will be a Christian, it must be on these terms, *Let him deny himself, and take up his cross*—A rule that can never be too much observed : let him in all things deny his own will, however pleasing, and do the will of God, however painful.

Should we not· consider all crosses, all things grievous to flesh and blood, as what they really are, as opportunities of embracing God's will at the expense of our own ? And consequently as so many steps by which we may advance toward perfection ? We should make a swift progress in the spiritual life, if we were

* Mark viii, 31 ; Luke ix, 22.   † Chap. x, 38.

25 cross and follow me. *For whosoever will save his life, shall lose it, and whosoever will lose his life for my sake, shall find it.
26 For what is a man profited, if he shall gain the whole world and lose his own soul? Or what shall a man give in exchange for his
27 soul? For the Son of man shall come in the glory of his Father, with his angels; and then shall he render to every man accord-
28 ing to his work. Verily I say to you, there are some standing here, who shall not taste of death, till they see the Son of man coming in his kingdom.

XVII. †And after six days, Jesus taketh Peter and James and John his brother, and bringeth them up into a high mountain apart,
2 And was transfigured before them; and his face shone as the sun,
3 And his raiment became white as the light. And behold there
4 appeared to them Moses and Elijah talking with him. Then Peter answering, said to Jesus, Lord, it is good for us to be here; if thou wilt, let us make here three tents, one for thee, and one for Moses,

---

faithful in this practice. Crosses are so frequent, that whoever makes advantage of them, will soon be a great gainer. Great crosses are occasions of great improvement: and the little ones, which come daily, and even hourly, make up in number what they want in weight. We may in these daily and hourly crosses make effectual oblations of our will to God; which oblations, so frequently repeated, will soon amount to a great sum. Let us remember then (what can never be sufficiently inculcated) that God is the author of all events: that none is so small or inconsiderable, as to escape his notice and direction. Every event therefore declares to us the will of God, to which thus declared we should heartily submit. We should renounce our own to embrace it; we should approve and choose what his choice warrants as best for us. Herein should we exercise ourselves continually; this should be our practice all the day long. We should in humility accept the little crosses that are dispensed to us, as those that best suit our weakness. Let us bear these little things, at least for God's sake, and prefer his will to our own in matters of so small importance. And his goodness will accept these mean oblations; for he despiseth not the day of small things.

25. *Whosoever will save his life*—At the expense of his conscience: whosoever, in the very highest instance, that of life itself, will not *renounce himself*, shall be lost eternally. But can any man hope he should be able *thus* to renounce himself, if he cannot do it in the smallest instances? *And whosoever will lose his life shall find it*—What he loses on earth he shall find in heaven.

27. *For the Son of man shall come*—For there is no way to escape the righteous judgment of God.

28. And as an emblem of this, there are some here who shall live to see the Messiah coming to set up his mediatorial kingdom, with great power and glory, by the increase of his Church, and the destruction of the temple, city, and polity of the Jews.

XVII. 1. *A high mountain*—Probably Mount Tabor.

2. *And was transfigured*—Or transformed. The indwelling Deity darted out its rays through the veil of the flesh; and that with such transcendent splendour, that he no longer bore the *form of a servant*. His face shone with Divine majesty, like the sun in its strength; and all his body was so irradiated by it, that his clothes could not conceal its glory, but became white and glittering as the very light, with which he covered himself as with a garment.

3. *There appeared Moses and Elijah*—Here for the full confirmation of their faith in Jesus, Moses, the giver of the law, Elijah, the most zealous of all the prophets, and God speaking from heaven, all bore witness to him.

4. *Let us make three tents*—The words of rapturous surprise. He says *three*, not six: because the apostles desired to be with their Master.

* Chap. x, 39; Mark viii, 35; Luke ix, 24; xvii, 33; John xii, 25.   † Mark ix, 2; Luke ix, 28.

5 and one for Elijah. While he was yet speaking, behold a bright cloud overshadowed them, and behold a voice out of the cloud saying, This is my beloved Son, in whom I delight: hear ye him.
6 And the disciples hearing *it*, fell on their face and were sore afraid.
7 And Jesus came and touched them, and said, Arise, and be not
8 afraid. And lifting up their eyes, they saw no man, but Jesus only.
9 And as they came down from the mountain, Jesus charged them, saying, Tell the vision to no man, till the Son of man be risen again
10 from the dead. And his disciples asked him, saying, Why then
11 say the scribes, That Elijah must come first? And Jesus answering said to them, Elijah truly doth come first, and will regulate all
12 things. But I say to you, That Elijah is come already, and they acknowledged him not, but have done to him whatever they listed.
13 So shall also the Son of man suffer from them. Then the disciples understood that he spoke to them of John the Baptist.
14 * And when they were come to the multitude, there came to
15 him a man, kneeling down to him, and saying, Lord, have mercy on my son, for he is lunatic, and suffereth grievously; for often he
16 falleth into the fire, and often into the water. And I brought him
17 to thy disciples, but they could not cure him. Then Jesus answering said, O unbelieving and perverse generation, how long shall I be with you? How long shall I suffer you? Bring him hither to
18 me. And Jesus rebuked the devil, and he went out of him, and the
19 child was cured from that hour. Then the disciples coming to
20 Jesus apart said, Why could not we cast him out? † And Jesus said to them, Because of your unbelief. For verily I say unto you, If ye have faith as a grain of mustard seed, ye shall say to this mountain, Remove hence to yonder place, and it shall remove, and

5. *Hear ye him*—As superior even to Moses and the prophets. See Deut. xviii, 17.

7. *Be not afraid*—And doubtless the same moment he gave them courage and strength.

9. *Tell the vision to no man*—Not to the rest of the disciples, lest they should be grieved and discouraged because they were not admitted to the sight: nor to any other persons, lest it should enrage some the more, and his approaching sufferings shall make others disbelieve it; *till the Son of man be risen again*—Till the resurrection should make it credible, and confirm their testimony about it.

10. *Why then say the scribes, that Elijah must come first*—Before the Messiah? If no man is to know of his coming? Should we not rather tell every man, that he is come, and that we have seen him, witnessing to thee as the Messiah?

11. *Regulate all things*—In order to the coming of Christ.

12. *Elijah is come already*—And yet when *the Jews asked John, Art thou Elijah? He said, I am not*, John i. His meaning was, I am not Elijah the Tishbite, come again into the world. But he was the person of whom Malachi prophesied under that name.

15. *He is lunatic*—This word might with great propriety be used, though the case was mostly preternatural; as the evil spirit would undoubtedly take advantage of the influence which the changes of the moon have on the brain and nerves.

17. *O unbelieving and perverse generation*—Our Lord speaks principally this to his disciples. *How long shall I be with you?*—Before you steadfastly believe?

20. *Because of your unbelief*—Because in this particular they had not faith. *If ye have faith as a grain of mustard seed*—That is, the least measure of it. But it is certain, the faith which is here spoken of does not always imply saving

* Mark ix, 14; Luke xi, 37   † Chap. xxi, 21; Luke xvii, 6

21 nothing shall be impossible to you.   Howbeit this kind goeth not
   out, but by prayer and fasting.
22   * And while they abode in Galilee, Jesus said to them, The Son
23 of man is about to be betrayed into the hands of men : And they
   will kill him, and the third day he will rise again; and they were
   exceedingly sorry.
24   And when they were come to Capernaum, they that received the
   tribute money came to Peter, and said, Doth not your Master pay
25 the tribute ?   He saith, Yes.   And when he came into the house,
   Jesus prevented him, saying, What thinkest thou, Simon ?   Of
26 whom do the kings of the earth take custom or tribute ?   Of their
27 own sons, or of strangers ?   He saith to him, Of strangers.   Jesus
   saith to him, Then are the sons free.   Yet that we may not
   offend them, go to the sea, and cast a hook, and take the fish
   that first cometh up.   And when thou hast opened his mouth,
   thou shalt find a piece of money.   That take, and give them
   for me and thee.
XVIII.   At that time came the disciples to Jesus, saying, Who is

---

faith.   Many have had it who thereby *cast out devils*, and yet will at last have
their portion with them.   It is only a supernatural persuasion given a man,
that God will work *thus* by him at that hour.   Now, *though I have all* this
faith, *so as to remove mountains*, yet *if I have not* the faith which worketh by
love, I am nothing.

To remove mountains was a proverbial phrase among the Jews, and is still
retained in their writings, to express a thing which is very difficult, and to
appearance impossible.

21. *This kind of devils—goeth not out but by prayer and fasting*—What a
testimony is here of the efficacy of fasting, when added to fervent prayer !   Some
kinds of devils the apostles had cast out before this, without fasting.

24. *When they were come to Capernaum*—Where our Lord now dwelt.   This
was the reason why they stayed till he came thither, to ask him for the tribute.
Doth not your Master pay tribute ?—This was a tribute or payment of a peculiar
kind, being half a shekel, (that is, about fifteen pence,) which every master of a
family used to pay yearly to the service of the temple, to buy salt, and little things
not otherwise provided for.   It seems to have been a voluntary thing, which
custom rather than any law had established.

25. *Jesus prevented him*—Just when St. Peter was going to ask him for it.
Of their own sons, or of strangers ?—That is, such as are not of their own family.

26. *Then are the sons free*—The sense is, This is paid for the use of the house
of God.   But I am the Son of God.   Therefore I am free from any obligation of
paying this to my own Father.

27. *Yet that we may not offend them*—Even those unjust, unreasonable men,
who claim what they have no manner of right to: do not contest it with them,
but rather yield to their demand, than violate peace or love.   O what would not
one of a loving spirit do for peace !   Any thing which is not expressly forbidden
in the word of God.   *A piece of money*—The original word is a *stater*, which
was in value two shillings and sixpence : just the sum that was wanted.   *Give
for me and thee*—Peter had a family of his own: the other apostles were the
family of Jesus.

How illustrious a degree of knowledge and power did our Lord here discover !
Knowledge, penetrating into this animal, though beneath the waters ; and power,
in directing this very fish to Peter's hook, though he himself was at a distance !
How must this have encouraged both him and his brethren in a firm dependence
on Divine Providence.

XVIII. 1. *Who is the greatest in the kingdom of heaven ?*—Which of us shall be
thy prime minister ?   They still dreamed of a temporal kingdom.

* Mark ix, 30 ; Luke ix, 44.

2 greatest in the kingdom of heaven? * And Jesus calling to him
3 a little child. set him in the midst of them, † And said, Verily I
say to you, Except ye be converted, and become as little chil-
4 dren, ye shall in nowise enter into the kingdom of heaven. Whosoever therefore shall humble himself as this little child, he is the
5 greatest in the kingdom of heaven. ‡ And whoso shall receive
6 one such little child in my name, receiveth me. § But whoso shall
offend one of these little ones that believe in me, it were better
for him that a millstone were hanged about his neck, and he were
7 drowned in the depth of the sea. Wo to the world because of
offences : for it must needs be that offences come ; but wo to that
8 man by whom the offence cometh. ‖ Wherefore if thy hand or
thy foot cause thee to offend, cut them off and cast *them* from thee ;
it is good for thee to enter into life halt or maimed, rather than
having two hands or two feet to be cast into the everlasting fire.
9 And if thine eye cause thee to offend, pluck it out, and cast *it* from
thee : it is good for thee to enter into life with one eye, rather
10 than having two eyes to be cast into hell fire. See that ye despise not one of these little ones ; for I say to you, that in heaven
their angels continually behold the face of my Father who is in
11 heaven. ** For the Son of man is come to save that which was

2. *And Jesus calling to him a little child*—This is supposed to have been the great Ignatius, whom Trajan, the wise, the good Emperor Trajan, condemned to be cast to the wild beasts at Rome!

3. *Except ye be converted*—The first step toward entering into the kingdom of grace, is to *become as little children :* lowly in heart, knowing yourselves utterly ignorant and helpless, and hanging wholly on your Father who is in heaven, for a supply of all your wants. We may farther assert, (though it is doubtful whether this text implies so much,) except ye be turned from darkness to light, and from the power of Satan to God : except ye be entirely, inwardly changed, renewed in the image of God, ye cannot enter into the kingdom of glory. Thus must every man be converted in this life, or he can never enter into life eternal. *Ye shall in nowise enter*—So far from being great in it.

5, 6. And all who are in this sense little children are unspeakably dear to me. Therefore help them all you can, as if it were myself in person, and see that ye offend them not; that is, that ye turn them not out of the right way, neither hinder them in it.

7. *Wo to the world because of offences*—That is, unspeakable misery will be in the world through them; *for it must needs be that offences come*—Such is the nature of things, and such the weakness, folly, and wickedness of mankind, that it cannot be but they will come; *but wo to that man*—That is, miserable is that man, *by whom the offence cometh. Offences* are, all things whereby any one is turned out of, or hindered in the way of God.

8, 9. *If thy hand, foot, eye, cause thee to offend*—If the most dear enjoyment, the most beloved and useful person, turn thee out of, or hinder thee in the way Is not this a hard saying? Yes; if thou take counsel with flesh and blood.

10. *See that ye despise not one of these little ones*—As if they were beneath your notice. Be careful to *receive* and not to *offend*, the very weakest believer in Christ : for as inconsiderable as some of these may appear to thee, the very angels of God have a peculiar charge over them : even those of the highest order, who continually appear at the throne of the Most High. *To behold the face of* God seems to signify the waiting near his throne ; and to be an allusion to the office of chief ministers in earthly courts, who daily converse with their princes.

11. Another, and yet a stronger reason for your not despising them is, that I myself came into the world to save them.

* Mark ix, 36 ; Luke x, 47.   † Chap. xix, 14.   ‡ Chap. x, 40 ; Luke x, 16 ; John xiii, 20.
§ Mark ix, 42 ; Luke i, 1.   ‖ Chap. v, 29 ; Mark ix, 43.   ** Luke xix, 10.

12 lost. *What think ye? If a man have a hundred sheep, and one
of them go astray, doth he not leave the ninety and nine, and go
13 into the mountains and seek that which was gone astray? And if
so be that he find it, verily I say to you, he rejoiceth more over
that *sheep*, than over the ninety and nine which went not astray.
14 So it is not the will of your Father who is in heaven, that one of
15 these little ones should perish. † But if thy brother shall sin
against thee, go and reprove him, between thee and him alone : if
16 he will hear thee, thou hast gained thy brother. But if he will not
hear, take with thee one or two more, that by the mouth of two or
17 three witnesses every word may be established. And if he will
not hear them, tell *it* to the Church ; but if he will not hear the
18 Church, let him be to thee as the heathen and the publican. Verily
I say to you, ‡ Whatsoever ye shall bind on earth shall be bound
in heaven, and whatsoever ye shall loose on earth shall be loosed
19 in heaven. Again I say to you, That if two of you shall agree on
earth, touching any thing that they shall ask, it shall be done for
20 them by my Father who is in heaven. For where two or three

14. *So it is not the will of your Father*—Neither doth my Father despise the
least of them. Observe the gradation. The angels, the Son, the Father.

15. But how can we avoid giving offence to some? or being offended at others!
Especially suppose they are quite in the wrong? Suppose they commit a known
sin? Our Lord here teaches us how : he lays down a sure method of avoiding all
offences. Whosoever closely observes this threefold rule, will seldom offend
others, and never be offended himself. If any do any thing amiss, of which thou
art an eye or ear witness, thus saith the Lord, *If thy brother*—Any who is a
member of the same religious community : *Sin against thee*, 1. *Go and reprove
him alone*—If it may be in person ; if that cannot so well be done, by thy messenger ; or in writing. Observe, our Lord gives no liberty to omit this ; or to
exchange it for either of the following steps. If this do not succeed, 2. *Take
with thee one or two more*—Men whom he esteems or loves, who may then con
firm and enforce what thou sayest ; and afterward, if need require, bear witness
of what was spoken. If even this does not succeed, then, and not before, 3. *Tell
it to the* elders of the *Church*—Lay the whole matter open before those who watch
over yours and his soul. If all this avail not, have no farther intercourse with
him, only such as thou hast with heathens.
Can any thing be plainer? Christ does here as expressly command all Christians who see a brother do evil, to take this way, not another, and to take these
steps, in this order, as he does to honour their father and mother.
But if so, in what land do the Christians live?
If we proceed from the private carriage of man to man, to proceedings of a
more public nature, in what Christian nation are Church censures conformed to
this rule? Is this the form in which ecclesiastical judgments appear, in the
popish, or even the Protestant world? Are these the methods used even by those
who boast the most loudly of the authority of Christ to confirm their sentences?
Let us earnestly pray, that this dishonour to the Christian name may be wiped
away, and that common humanity may not, with such solemn mockery, be
destroyed in the name of the Lord!
Let him be to thee as the heathen—To whom thou still owest earnest good will,
and all the offices of humanity.

18. *Whatsoever ye shall bind on earth*—By excommunication, pronounced in
the spirit and power of Christ. *Whatsoever ye shall loose*—By absolution from
that sentence. In the primitive Church, absolution meant no more than a discharge from Church censure. *Again I say*—And not only your intercession for
the penitent, but all your united prayers, shall be heard. How great then is the
power of joint prayer! *If two of you*—Suppose a man and his wife.

20. *Where two or three are gathered together in my name*—That is, to worship

are gathered together in my name, there am I in the midst of them.

21 Then came Peter to him and said, Lord, how often shall my brother sin against me, and I forgive him? Till seven times?
22 Jesus saith to him, I say not unto thee, till seven times, but till
23 seventy times seven. Therefore the kingdom of heaven is like a
24 king, who was minded to settle accounts with his servants. And when he had begun to settle, one was brought to him who owed him
25 ten thousand talents. But as he had not to pay, his lord commanded him to be sold, and his wife and children, and all that he had, and
26 payment to be made. Then the servant falling prostrate at his feet,
27 said, Lord, have patience with me, and I will pay thee all. And the lord of that servant, moved with tender compassion, loosed
28 him and forgave him the debt. But that servant going out, found one of his fellow servants who owed him a hundred pence, and
29 seized him by the throat, saying, Pay me what thou owest. And his fellow servant falling at his feet, besought him saying, Have
30 patience with me, and I will pay thee all. And he would not, but
31 went and cast him into prison, till he should pay the debt. But his fellow servants seeing what he had done, were very sorry, and came and gave their lord an exact account of all that was done.
32 Then his lord calling him, said to him, Thou wicked servant, I
33 forgave thee all that debt, because thou entreatedst me. Shouldst not thou also have had compassion on thy fellow servant, as I had
34 pity on thee? And his lord being wroth, delivered him to the tor-
35 mentors, till he should pay all that was due to him. So likewise will my heavenly Father do to you, if ye from your hearts forgive not every one his brother their trespasses.

---

me. *I am in the midst of them*—By my Spirit, to quicken their prayers, guide their counsels, and answer their petitions.

22. *Till seventy times seven*—That is, as often as there is occasion. A certain number is put for an uncertain.

23. *Therefore*—In this respect.

24. *One was brought who owed him ten thousand talents*—According to the usual computation, if these were talents of gold, this would amount to seventy-two millions sterling. If they were talents of silver, it must have been four millions, four hundred thousand pounds. Hereby our Lord intimates the vast number and weight of our offences against God, and our utter incapacity of making him any satisfaction.

25. *As he had not to pay, his lord commanded him to be sold*—Such was the power which creditors anciently had over their insolvent debtors in several countries.

30. *Went* with him before a magistrate, *and cast him into prison*, protesting he should lie there, *till he should pay the whole debt.*

34. *His lord delivered him to the tormentors*—Imprisonment is a much severer punishment in the eastern countries than in ours. State criminals, especially when condemned to it, are not only confined to a very mean and scanty allowance, but are frequently loaded with clogs or heavy yokes, so that they can neither lie nor sit at ease: and by frequent scourgings and sometimes rackings are brought to an untimely end. *Till he should pay all that was due to him*—That is, without all hope of release, for this he could never do.

How observable is this whole account; as well as the great inference our Lord draws from it! 1. The debtor was freely and fully forgiven; 2. He wilfully and grievously offended; 3. His pardon was retracted, the whole debt required, and the offender delivered to the tormentors for ever. And shall we still say, but when we are once freely and fully forgiven, our pardon can never be retracted?

XIX. * And Jesus when he had finished these sayings, departed
from Galilee, and came into the coasts of Judea beyond Jordan.
2 And great multitudes followed him, and he healed them there.
3 And the Pharisees came to him, tempting him and saying, Is it
4 lawful for a man to put away his wife for every cause ? And he
answering said to them, Have ye not read, that he who made
5 them, made them male and female from the beginning ? And said,
† For this cause a man shall leave father and mother and cleave to
6 his wife, and they twain. shall be one flesh ? Wherefore they are
no more twain, but one flesh. What therefore God hath joined
7 together let not man put asunder. They say to him, Why then
did Moses ‡ command to give a writing of divorce, and put her
8 away ? He saith to them, Because of the hardness of your hearts.
Moses permitted you to put away your wives ; but from the be-
9 ginning it was not so. And I say to you, Whosoever shall put
away his wife, except for whoredom, and marry another, committeth
adultery, and he that marrieth her that is put away, committeth
10 adultery. His disciples say to him, If the case of a man with *his*
11 wife be so, it is not expedient to marry. But he said to them,
All men do not receive this saying, but they to whom it is given.
12 For there are eunuchs, who- were born so from their mother's
womb, and there are eunuchs, who were made eunuchs by men ;
and there are eunuchs, who have made themselves eunuchs for the
kingdom of heaven's sake. He that is able to receive *it*, let him
receive *it*.

Verily, verily, I say unto you, *So likewise will my heavenly Father do to* you, *if
ye from your hearts forgive not every.one his brother their trespasses.*
XIX. 1. *He departed*—and from that.time *walked no more in Galilee.*
   2. *Multitudes followed him, and he healed them there*—That is, wheresoever
they followed him.
   3. *The Pharisees came tempting him*—Trying to make him contradict Moses.
For every cause—That is, for any thing which he dislikes in her. This the
scribes allowed.
   4. *He said, Have ye not read*—So instead of contradicting him, our Lord confutes them by the very words of Moses. *He who made them, made them male
and female from the beginning*—At least from the beginning of the Mosaic creation. And where do we read of any other ? Does it not follow, that God's
making Eve was part of his original design, and not a consequence of Adam's
beginning to fall ? By making them one man and one woman, he condemned
polygamy : by making them one flesh, he condemned divorce.
   5. *And said*—By the mouth of Adam, who uttered the words.
   7. *Why did Moses command*—Christ replies, *Moses permitted* (not commanded)
it, because of the hardness of your hearts—Because neither your fathers nor you
could bear the more excellent way.
   9. *And I say to you*—I revoke that indulgence from this day, so that from
henceforth, *Whosoever*, &c.
   11. *But he said to them*—This is not universally true ; it does not hold, with
regard to all men, but with regard to those only *to whom is given* this excellent
gift of God. Now this *is given* to three sorts of persons ; to some by natural
constitution, without their choice : to others by violence, against their choice ;
and to others by grace with their choice : who steadily withstand their natural
inclinations, that they may *wait upon God without distraction.*
   12. *There are eunuchs who have made themselves eunuchs for the kingdom of
heaven's sake*—Happy they ! who have abstained from marriage (though without
condemning or despising it) that they might walk more closely with God ! *He*

13   * Then were brought to him little children, that he might lay *his*
14   hands on them and pray : but his disciples rebuked them.   † But
Jesus said, Suffer the little children to come to me, and forbid
15   them not ; for of such is the kingdom of heaven.   And he laid his
hands on them and departed thence.
16   ‡ And behold one came and said to him, Good Master, what
17   good thing shall I do, that I may have eternal life ?   And he said
to him, Why callest thou me good ?   *There is* none good but one,
that is God : but if thou wilt enter into life, keep the command-
18   ments.   He saith to him, Which ?   Jesus said, § Thou shalt do no
murder : thou shalt not commit adultery : thou shalt not steal :
19   thou shalt not bear false witness : Honour *thy* father and mother,
20   and thou shalt love thy neighbour as thyself.   The young man
saith to him, All these things have. I kept from my childhood :
21   what lack I yet ?   Jesus saith to him, If thou desirest to be perfect, go, sell what thou hast, and give it to the poor, and thou shalt
22   have treasure in heaven : and come, follow me.   But the young
man hearing that saying, went away sorrowful ; for he had great
possessions.
23   Then said Jesus to his disciples, Verily I say to you, a rich
24   man shall with difficulty enter into the kingdom of heaven.   And
again I say to you, It is easier for a camel to go through the eye

that is able to receive it, let him receive it—This gracious command (for such it
is unquestionably, since to say, such a man may live single, is saying nothing.
Who ever doubted this ?) is not designed for all men : but only for those few who
are *able to receive it.*   O let these receive it joyfully !

13. *That he should lay his hands on them*—This was a rite which was very
early used, in praying for a blessing on young persons. See Gen. xlviii, 14, 20.
The disciples rebuked them—That is, them that brought them : probably thinking such an employ beneath the dignity of their Master.

14. *Of such is the kingdom of heaven*—Little children, either in a natural or
spiritual sense, have a right to enter into my kingdom.

16. *And behold one came*—Many of the poor had followed him from the beginning.   *One* rich man *came* at last.

17. *Why callest thou me good*—Whom thou supposest to be only a man. *There,
is none good*—Supremely, originally, essentially, *but God.   If thou wilt enter into
life, keep the commandments*—From a principle of loving faith.   Believe, and
thence love and obey.   And this undoubtedly is the way to eternal life.   Our Lord
therefore does not answer ironically, which had been utterly beneath his character, but gives a plain, direct, serious answer to a serious question.

20. *The young man saith, All these have I kept from my childhood*—So he
imagined ; and perhaps he had, as to the letter ; but not as to the spirit, which
our Lord immediately shows.

21. *If thou desirest to be perfect*—That is, to be a real Christian : *Sell what
thou hast*—He who reads the heart saw his bosom sin was love of the world ;
and knew he could not be saved from this, but by literally renouncing it.
To him therefore he gave this particular direction, which he never designed
for a general rule.   For him that was necessary to salvation : to us it is
not.   *To sell all* was an absolute duty to him ; to many of us it would be an
absolute sin.   *The young man went away*—Not being willing to have salvation
at so high a price.

24. *It is easier for a camel to go through the eye of a needle,* (a proverbial expression,) *than for a rich man to* go through the strait gate : that is, humanly
speaking, it is an absolute impossibility.   Rich man ! tremble ! feel this impossibility ; else thou art lost for ever !

* Mark x, 13 ; Luke xviii, 15.   † Chap. xviii, 3.   ‡ Mark x, 17 ; Luke xviii, 18.
§ Exod. xx, 12. &c

of a needle than for a rich man to enter into the kingdom of
25 God.   His disciples hearing *it*, were exceedingly amazed, saying,
26 Who then can be saved ?   But Jesus looking upon *them*, said to
them, With men this is impossible ; but with God all things are
possible.
27   Then Peter answering said to him, Behold we have forsaken
28 all, and followed thee.   What shall we have therefore ?   Jesus
said to them, Verily I say to you, that ye who have followed me,
in the renovation, when the Son of man shall sit on the throne of
his glory, ye also shall sit upon twelve thrones, judging the twelve
29 tribes of Israel.   And every one that hath forsaken house, or
brethren, or father, or mother, or wife, or children, or land,
for my name's sake, shall receive a hundred fold, and inherit
everlasting life.   * But many first *will* be last, and the last *will
be* first.

XX.   For the kingdom of heaven is like a householder, who went out
2 early in the morning to hire labourers into his vineyard.   And
having agreed with the labourers for a penny a day, he sent them

---

25. *His disciples were amazed, saying, Who then can be saved ?*—If rich men,
with all their advantages, cannot ?   Who ?   A poor man ; a peasant ; a beggar :
ten thousand of them, sooner than one that is rich.

26. *Jesus looking upon them*—To compose their hurried spirits.   O what a
speaking look was there !   *Said to them*—With the utmost sweetness : *With men
this is impossible*—It is observable, he does not retract what he had said : no, nor
soften it in the least degree, but rather strengthens it, by representing the salvation of a rich man as the utmost effort of Omnipotence.

28. *In the renovation*—In the final renovation of all things: *Ye shall sit*—In
the beginning of the judgment they shall *stand*, 2 Cor. v, 10.   Then being absolved, they *shall sit* with the Judge, 1 Cor. vi, 2 : *On twelve thrones*—So our
Lord promised, without expressing any condition : yet as absolute as the words
are, it is certain there is a condition implied, as in many scriptures, where none
is expressed.   In consequence of this, those twelve did not sit on *those twelve
thrones :* for the throne of Judas another took, so that he never sat thereon.

29. *And every one*—In every age and country; not you my apostles only ;
That hath forsaken houses, or brethren, or wife, or children—Either by giving
any of them up, when they could not be retained with a clear conscience ; or by
willingly refraining from acquiring them : *Shall receive a hundred fold*—In value,
though not in kind, even in the present world.

30. *But many first*—Many of those who were first called, *shall be last*—Shall
have the lowest reward : those who came after them being preferred before them :
and yet possibly both the first and the last may be saved, though with different
degrees of glory.

XX. 1. That some of those who were first called may yet be last, our Lord confirms by the following parable : of which the primary scope is, to show, That
many of the Jews would be rejected, and many of the Gentiles accepted ; the
secondary, That of the Gentiles, many who were first converted would be last
and lowest in the kingdom of glory ; and many of those who were last converted
would be first, and highest therein.   *The kingdom of heaven is like*—That is, the
manner of God's proceeding in his kingdom resembles that of *a householder*.   *In
the morning*—At six, called by the Romans and Jews, the first hour.   From
thence reckoning on to the evening, they called nine, the third hour ; twelve, the
sixth ; three in the afternoon, the ninth ; and five, the eleventh.   *To hire labourers into his vineyard*—All who profess to be Christians are in this sense labourers,
and are supposed during their life to be working in God's vineyard.

2. The Roman penny was about seven pence halfpenny.   [About thirteen and
three quarter cents, American.]   This was then the usual price of a day's labour

3 into his vineyard. And going out about the tnird hour he saw
4 others standing idle in the market place, and said to them, Go ye
   also into the vineyard, and whatsoever is right, I will give you.
5 And they went. Again·going out about the sixth and ninth hour,
6 he did likewise. And going out about the eleventh hour, he found
   others standing idle, and saith to them, Why stand ye here all the
7 day idle? They say to him, Because no man hath hired us. He
   saith to them, Go ye also into the vineyard, and whatsoever is
8 right ye shall receive. And in the evening the lord of the vineyard saith to the steward, Call the labourers, and pay them their
9 hire, beginning from the last to the first. And when they came
   who *were hired* about the eleventh hour, they received every one a
10 penny. But when the first came, they supposed that they should
   have received more; and they likewise received every one a penny.
11 And having received *it*, they murmured against the householder,
12 saying, These last have wrought one hour, and thou hast made
   them equal unto us, who have borne the burden and the heat of the
13 day. And he answering said to one of them, Friend, I do thee no
14 wrong. Didst not thou agree with me for a penny? Take what is
   thine, and go : it is my will to give to this last even as to thee.
15 Is it not lawful for me to do what I will with my own? Is thine
16 eye evil because I am good? * So the last shall be first, and the
   first last : for many are called, but few chosen.
17   † And Jesus going up to Jerusalem, took the twelve disciples
18 apart in the way, and said to them, Behold we go up to Jerusalem,

---

6. *About the eleventh hour*—That is, very late; long after the rest were called
8. *In the evening*—Of life; or of the world.
9. *Who were hired about the eleventh hour*—Either the Gentiles, who were
called long after the Jews into the vineyard of the Church of Christ; or those in
every age who did not hear, or at least understand the Gospel call, till their day
of life was drawing to a period. Some circumstances of the parable seem best to
suit the former, some the latter of these senses.
10. *The first supposed they should have received more*—Probably *the first* here
may mean the Jews, who supposed they should always be preferred before the
Gentiles.
12. *Thou hast made them equal to us*—So St. Peter expressly, Acts xv, 9.
God—*hath put no difference between us* (Jews) *and them,* (Gentiles,) *purifying
their hearts by faith.* And those who were equally holy here, whenever they
were called, will be equally happy hereafter.
14. *It is my will to give to this last* called among the heathens even *as to the first*
called among the Jews : yea, and to the late converted publicans and sinners,
even as to those who were called long before.
15. *Is it not lawful for me to do what I will with my own?*—Yea, doubtless, to
give either to Jew or Gentile a reward infinitely greater than he deserves. But
can it be inferred from hence, that it is lawful, or possible, for the merciful Father
of spirits to

" Consign an unborn soul to hell?
  Or damn him from his mother's womb ?"

Is thine eye evil because I am good—Art thou envious, because I am gracious?
Here is an evident reference to that malignant aspect, which is generally the
attendant of a selfish and envious temper.
16. *So the last shall be first, and the first last*—Not only with regard to the
Jews and Gentiles, but in a thousand other instances. *For many are called*--All
who hear the Gospel; *but few chosen*—Only those who obey it.

* Chap. xix, 30 ; xxii. 14.   † Mark x, 32; Luke xviii, 31.

and the Son of man will be betrayed to the chief priests and scribes
19 and they will condemn him to death, And will deliver him to the
Gentiles, to mock and scourge and crucify *him ;* and the third day
he shall rise again.
20   * Then came to him the mother of Zebedee's children with
her sons, worshipping *him*, and desiring a certain thing of him.
21 And he said to her, What wilt thou? She saith to him, Grant that
these my two sons may sit, the one on thy right hand, and the
22 other on thy left, in thy kingdom. But Jesus answering said, Ye
know not what ye ask. Are ye able to drink the cup that I am
about to drink, or to be baptized with the baptism that I am bap-
23 tized with? They say unto him, We are able.· And he saith to them,
Ye shall indeed drink my cup, and be baptized with the baptism
that I am baptized with; but to sit on my right hand and on my
left is not mine to give, save to them for whom it is prepared of
24 my Father. And the ten hearing *it*, were moved with indignation
25 against the two brethren. But Jesus calling them to him said,
Ye know that the princes of the Gentiles lord it over them, and
26 they that are great exercise authority upon them. † It shall
not be so among you ; but whosoever desireth to be great among
27 you, let him be your minister ; And whosoever desireth to be
28 chief among you, let him be your servant : Even as the Son of
man came not to be served, but to serve, and to give his life a
ransom for many.
29   ‡ And as they were going from Jericho, a great multitude fol-
30 lowed him. And behold two blind men sitting by the way side,
hearing that Jesus was passing by, cried out, saying, Have mercy
31 on us, O· Lord, thou Son of David. And the multitude charged
them to hold their peace : but they cried out the more, saying,
32 Have mercy on us, O Lord, thou Son of David. And Jesus stand-

20. *Then came to him the mother of Zebedee's children*—Considering what he
had been just speaking, was ever any thing more unreasonable? Perhaps Zebedee
himself was dead, or was not a follower of Christ.
21. *In thy kingdom*—Still they expected a temporal kingdom.
22. *Ye know not* what is implied in being advanced in my kingdom, and necessarily prerequired thereto. All who share in my kingdom must first share in
my sufferings. Are you able and willing to do this? Both these expressions,
The cup, the baptism, are to be understood of his sufferings and death. The like
expressions are common among the Jews.
23. *But to sit on my right hand*—Christ applies to the glories of heaven, what
his disciples were so stupid as to understand of the glories of earth. But he does
not deny that this is his to give. It is his to give in the strictest propriety, both
as God, and as the Son of man. He only asserts, that he gives it to none but
those for whom it is originally prepared; namely, those who endure to the end in
the *faith that worketh by love.*
25 *Ye know that the princes of the Gentiles lord it over them*—And hence you
imagine, the chief in my kingdom will do as they : ·but it will be quite otherwise.
26. *Your minister*—That is, your servant.
30. *Behold two blind men cried out*—St. Mark and St. Luke mention only one
of them, blind Bartimeus. He was far the more eminent of the two, and, as it
seems, spoke for both.
31. *The multitude charged them to hold their peace*—And so they will all who
begin to cry after the Son of David. But let those who feel their need of him
cry the more ; otherwise they will come short of a cure.

* Mark x, 35.   † Chap. xxiii, 11.   ‡ Mark x, 1 46; Luke xviii, 35.

ing still, called them, and said, What do ye desire that I should do
33 for you? They say to him, Lord, that our eyes may be opened.
34 So Jesus, moved with tender compassion, touched their eyes, and
immediately their eyes received sight, and they followed him.
XXI. *And when they drew nigh to Jerusalem, and came to Beth-
2 phage, at the mount of Olives, then sent Jesus two disciples, Saying
to them, Go into the village over against you, and straightway ye
shall find an ass tied and a colt with her; loose and bring *them*
3 to me. And if any man say aught to you, say, The Lord hath
4 need of them: and he will send them immediately. This was done
that it might be fulfilled which was spoken by the prophet, saying,
5 †Tell ye the daughter of Sion, Behold thy King cometh to thee
6 meek and sitting on an ass, even a colt the foal of an ass. And
7 the disciples went and did as Jesus had commanded them, And
brought the ass and the colt, and put on them their clothes and set
8 *him* thereon: And a very great multitude spread their garments in
the way; and others cut down branches from the trees and strewed
9 *them* in the way. And the multitudes that went before and that
followed after cried, saying, Hosanna to the Son of David; blessed
in the name of the Lord *is* he that cometh: Hosanna in the highest.
10 And as he came into Jerusalem, all the city was in a commotion,
11 saying, Who is this? And the multitude said, This is Jesus, the
prophet from Nazareth of Galilee.
12 ‡And Jesus went into the temple, and cast out all that sold and

---

XXI. 5. *The daughter of Sion*—That is, the inhabitants of Jerusalem: the
first words of the passage are cited from Isa. lxii, 11; the rest from Zech. ix, 9.
The ancient Jewish doctors were wont to apply these prophecies to the Messiah.
On an ass—The Prince of Peace did not take a horse, a warlike animal. But he
will ride on that by and by, Rev. xix, 11. In the patriarchal ages, illustrious
persons thought it no disgrace to make use of this animal: but it by no means
appears, that this opinion prevailed, or this custom continued, till the reign of
Tiberias. Was it a mean attitude wherein our Lord then appeared? Mean even
to contempt! I grant it: I glory in it: it is for the comfort of my soul; for the
honour of his humility, and for the utter confusion of all worldly pomp and
grandeur.
7. *They set him thereon*—That is, on the clothes.
8. *A great multitude spread their garments in the way*—A custom which was
usual at the creation of a king, 2 Kings ix, 13.
9. *The multitudes cried, saying*—Probably from a Divine impulse; for certainly
most of them understood not the words they uttered. *Hosanna*—(Lord save us)
was a solemn word in frequent use among the Jews. The meaning is, "We
sing hosanna to the Son of David. Blessed is he, the Messiah, of the Lord.
Save. Thou that art in the highest heavens." Our Lord restrained all public
tokens of honour from the people till now, lest the envy of his enemies should
interrupt his preaching before the time. But this reason now ceasing, he
suffered their acclamations, that they might be a public testimony against their
wickedness, who in four or five days after cried out, Crucify him, crucify him.
The expressions recorded by the other evangelists are somewhat different from
these: but all of them were undoubtedly used by some or others of the multitude.
11. *This is Jesus from Nazareth*—What a stumbling block was this! If he was
ot Nazareth, he could not be the Messiah. But they who earnestly desired to
know the truth would not stumble thereat: for upon inquiry (which such would
not fail to make) they would find, he was not of Nazareth, but Bethlehem.
12. *He cast out all that sold and bought*—Doves and oxen for sacrifice. He

* Mark xi, 1; Luke xix, 29; John xii, 12.   † Zech. ix, 9.   ‡ Mark xi, 11, 15;
Luke xix, 45.

bought in the temple, and overthrew the tables of the money chan-
13 gers, and the seats of them that were selling doves; And saith to
them, It is written, * My house shall be called the house of prayer,
14 but ye have made it a den of thieves. And the blind and lame
15 came to him in the temple, and he healed them. But the chief
priests and the scribes, seeing the wonders that he did, and the
children crying in the temple saying, Hosanna to the Son of David,
16 were sore displeased, And said to him, Hearest thou what these say?
And Jesus saith to them, Yea; have ye never read, † Out of the
17 mouth of babes and sucklings thou hast perfected praise? ‡ And
leaving them he went out of the city to Bethany, and lodged there.
18 Now in the morning, as he was returning to the city, he hungered.
19 And seeing a fig tree in the way, he came to it, and found nothing
thereon but leaves only. And he saith to it, Let no fruit grow on
thee henceforward for ever. And presently the fig tree withered
20 away. And the disciples seeing it marvelled, saying, How soon
21 is the fig tree withered away? Jesus answering said to them,
§ Verily I say to you, if ye have faith and doubt not, ye shall not
only do this *miracle* of the fig tree, but also if ye say to this mountain, Be thou lifted up, and be thou cast into the sea; it shall be
22 done. And all things whatsoever ye shall ask in prayer, believing,
ye shall receive.
23 ‖ And when he came into the temple, the chief priests and the
elders of the people came to him as he was teaching, and said, By
what authority dost thou these things? and who gave thee this
24 authority? And Jesus answering said to them, I will also ask you

had cast them out three years before, John ii, 14; bidding them *not make* that *house a house of merchandise.* Upon the repetition of the offence, he used sharper words. *In the temple*—That is, in the outer court of it, where the Gentiles used to worship. *The money changers*—The exchangers of foreign money into current coin, which those who came from distant parts might want to offer for the service of the temple.

13. *A den of thieves*—A proverbial expression, for a harbour of wicked men.
20. *The disciples seeing it*—As they went by, the next day.
21. *Jesus answering, said, If ye have faith*—Whence we may learn, that one great end of our Lord in this miracle was to confirm and increase their faith: another was, to warn them against unfruitfulness.
23. *When he was come into the temple, the chief priests came*—Who thought he violated their right: *and the elders of the people*—Probably, members of the sanhedrim, to whom that title most properly belonged: which is the more probable, as they were the persons under whose cognizance the late action of Christ, in purging the temple, would naturally fall These, with the chief priests, seem purposely to have appeared in a considerable company, to give the more weight to what they said, and if need were, to bear a united testimony against him. *As he was teaching*—Which also they supposed he had no authority to do, being neither priest, nor Levite, nor scribe. Some of the priests (though not as priests) and all the scribes were authorized teachers. *By what authority dost thou these things*—Publicly teach the people! And drive out those who had our commission to traffic in the outer court?
24. *I will ask you one thing*—Who have asked me many: *The baptism*, that is, the whole ministry *of John, was it from heaven or from men?*—By what authority did he act and teach? Did man or God give him that authority? Was it not God? But if so, the consequence was clear. For John testified that Jesus was the Christ.

* Isa. lvi, 7; Jer. vii, 11.   † Psalm viii, 2.   ‡ Mark xi, 11, 12.   § Chap. xvii, 20.
‖ Luke xx, 1; Mark xi, 27.

one thing, which if ye tell me, I will likewise tell you by
25 what authority I do these things. The baptism of John, whence
was it? from heaven or from men? And they reasoned among
themselves, saying, If we say from heaven, he will say, Why
26 then did ye not believe him? But if we say of men, we fear
27 the multitude; for all hold John as a prophet. And they answering said to Jesus, We cannot tell. And he said to them, Neither
28 tell I you by what authority I do these things. But what think
you? A man had two sons; and coming to the first, he said,
29 Son, go to work to-day in my vineyard. He answering said, I
30 will not; but afterward repenting he went. And coming to the
other he said likewise. And he answered, I *go*, sir: but went
31 not. Which of the two did the will of *his* father? They say to
him, The first. Jesus saith to them, Verily I say to you, the publicans and the harlots go into the kingdom of God before you
32 For John came to you in a way of righteousness, and ye believed
him not; but the publicans and the harlots believed him. And
ye seeing *it*, repented not afterward, that ye might believe him.
33 *Hear another parable. There was a certain householder, who
planted a vineyard, and hedged it round about, and digged a wine
press in it, and built a tower, and let it out to husbandmen, and
34 went into a far country. And when the season of fruit drew
near, he sent his servants to the husbandmen to receive the fruits
35 of it. And the husbandmen taking his servants beat one, and killed
36 another, and stoned another. Again he sent other servants more
37 than the former; and they did to them in like manner. Last of
all he sent to them his son, saying, They will reverence my son.
38 But the husbandmen seeing the son, said among themselves,
This is the heir; come, let us kill him and take possession of his
39 inheritance. And taking him they cast *him* out of the vineyard
40 and slew *him*. When therefore the lord of the vineyard cometh,
41 what will he do to those husbandmen? They say to him, He will.
miserably destroy those wicked men, and will let out the vineyard

---

25. *Why did ye not believe him*—Testifying this.
27. *Neither tell I you*—Not again, in express terms: he had often told them before, and they would not believe him.
30. *He answered, I go, sir: but went not*—Just so did the scribes and Phari-sees: they professed the greatest readiness and zeal in the service of God: but it was bare profession, contradicted by all their actions.
32. *John came in a way of righteousness*—Walking in it, as well as teaching it. *The publicans and harlots*—The most notorious sinners were reformed, though at first they said, *I will not. And ye seeing* the amazing change which was wrought in them, though at first ye said, *I go, sir, repented not afterward*—Were no more convinced than before. O how is this scripture fulfilled at this day!
33. *A certain householder planted a vineyard*—God planted the Church in Canaan; *and hedged it round about*—First with the law, then with his peculiar providence: *and digged a wine press*—Perhaps it may mean Jerusalem: *and built a tower*—The temple: *and went into a far country*—That is, left the keepers of his vineyard, in some measure, to behave as they should see good.
34. *He sent his servants*—His extraordinary messengers, the prophets: *to the husbandmen*—The ordinary preachers or ministers of the Jews.
41. *They say*—Perhaps some of the by-standers, not the chief priests or Phari-sees; who, as St. Luke relates, said, God forbid, Luke xx, 16.

* Mark xii, 1; Luke xx, 9.

to other husbandmen, who will render him the fruits in their
42 seasons. Jesus saith to them, Have you never read in the Scriptures, * The stone which the builders rejected is become the head
of the corner? This is the Lord's doing, and it is marvellous in our
43 eyes. Therefore I say to you, The kingdom of God shall be taken
from you, and given to a nation bringing forth the fruits thereof.
44 † And whosoever shall fall on this stone shall be broken : but on
45 whomsoever it shall fall, it will grind him to powder. And the
chief priests and the Pharisees hearing his parables, knew he spoke
46 of them. But when they sought to apprehend him, they feared the
multitude, because they took him for a prophet.

XXII. And Jesus answering, spake to them again in parables, say-
2 ing, The kingdom of heaven is like a king, who made a marriage
3 feast for his son. And sent forth his servants to call them that
4 were invited, to the marriage ; but thev would not come. Again
he sent forth other servants, saying, Tell them who were invited,
behold I have prepared my dinner, my oxen and fatlings are killed,
5 and all things are ready : come to the marriage. But they slight-
6 ing it, went one to his farm, another to his merchandise. And
the rest laying hold on his servants, treated them shamefully and
7 slew them. And the king hearing it was wroth, and sending forth
8 his troops, destroyed those murderers and burnt their city. Then
saith he to his servants, The marriage feast is prepared, but they
9 who were invited were not worthy. Go ye therefore into the
highways, and invite whomsoever ye find to the wedding banquet.
10 So those servants going out into the ways, gathered together all
whomsoever they found, both bad and good. And the feast was
11 abundantly supplied with guests. But the king coming in to see

42. *The builders*—The scribes and priests, whose office it was to build up the
Church. *Is become the head of the corner*—Or the chief corner stone: he is
become the foundation of the Church, on which the whole building rests, and is
the principal corner stone, for uniting the Gentiles to it, as the chief corner stone
of a house supports and links its two sides together.

43. *Therefore*—Because ye reject this corner stone. *The kingdom of God*—
That is, the Gospel.

44. *Whosoever shall fall on this stone shall be broken*—Stumblers at Christ
shall even then receive much hurt. He is said to fall on this stone, who hears
the Gospel and does not believe. *But on whomsoever it shall fall*—In vengeance,
it will utterly destroy him. It will fall on every unbeliever, when Christ cometh
in the clouds of heaven.

XXII. 1. *Jesus answering, spake*—That is, spake with reference to what had
just past.

2. *A king, who made a marriage feast for his son*—So did God, when he
brought his first-begotten into the world.

3. *Them that were invited*—Namely, the Jews.

4. *Fatlings*—Fatted beasts and fowls.

5. *One to his farm, another to his merchandise*—One must mind what he has ;
another, gain what he wants. How many perish by misusing lawful things !

7. *The king sending forth his troops*—The Roman armies employed of God
for that purpose. *Destroyed those murderers*—Primarily the Jews.

3. *Go into the highways*—The word properly signifies, the by-ways, or turnings
of the road.

10. *They gathered all*—By preaching every where.

11. *The guests*—The members of the visible Church.

* Psalm cxviii, 22. † Luke xx, 18.

the guests, saw there a man who had not on a wedding garment;
12 and saith to him, Friend, how camest thou in hither, not having
13 a wedding garment? And he was speechless. Then said the king
to his servants, Bind him hand and foot, and take him away, and
cast *him* into the outer darkness: there shall be the weeping and
14 the gnashing of teeth. * For many are called, but few chosen.
15 † Then went the Pharisees and consulted together how to
16 ensnare him in his talk. And they send to him their disciples with
the Herodians, saying, Master, we know that thou art true, and
teachest the way of God in truth; neither carest thou for any man;
17 for thou regardest not the person of men. Tell us therefore,
what thinkest thou? Is it lawful to give tribute to Cesar, .or not?
18 But Jesus knowing their wickedness, said, Why tempt ye me, ye
19 hypocrites? Show me the tribute money. And they brought to
20 him a penny. He said to them, Whose *is* this image and super-
21 scription? They say to him, Cesar's. Then said he to them, Render therefore to Cesar the things that are Cesar's, and to God the
22 things that are God's. And hearing it they marvelled. And they
left him and went away.
23 ‡ The same day came the Sadducees, who say there is no resur-
24 rection, and asked him, saying, Master, Moses said, § If a man
die having no children, his brother shall marry his wife and raise
25 up issue to his brother. Now there were with us seven brethren:
and the first having married a wife died, and having no issue, left
26 his wife to his brother. Likewise the second also, and the third,
27 unto the seventh. Last of all the woman died also. Therefore in
28 the resurrection, whose wife shall she be of the seven? For they
29 all had her. Jesus answering said to them, Ye err, not knowing

---

12. *A wedding garment*—The righteousness of Christ, first imputed, then implanted. It may easily be observed, this has no relation to the Lord's Supper,
but to God's proceeding at the last day.

14. *Many are called; few chosen*—Many hear; few believe. Yea, many are
members of the visible, but few of the invisible Church.

16. *The Herodians* were a set of men peculiarly attached to Herod, and consequently zealous for the interest of the Roman government, which was the main
support of the dignity and royalty of his family. *Thou regardest not the person
of men*—Thou favourest no man for his riches or greatness.

17. *Is it lawful to give tribute to Cesar?*—If he had said, Yes, the Pharisees
would have accused him to the people, as a betrayer of the liberties of his country. If he had said, No, the Herodians would have accused him to the Roman
governor.

18. *Ye hypocrites*—Pretending a scruple of conscience.

20. *The tribute money*—A Roman coin, stamped with the head of Cesar, which
was usually paid in tribute.

21. *They say to him, Cesar's*—Plainly acknowledging, by their having received
his coin, that they were under his government. And indeed this is a standing
rule. The current coin of every nation shows who is the supreme governor of
it. *Render therefore*, ye Pharisees, *to Cesar the things which* ye yourselves
acknowledge to be *Cesar's: and*, ye Herodians, while ye are zealous for Cesar,
see that ye *render to God the things that are God's.*

25. *Now there were with us seven brethren*—This story seems to have been a
kind of common-place objection, which no doubt they brought upon all occasions.

29. *Ye err, not knowing the Scriptures*—Which plainly assert a resurrection.
Nor the power of God—Which is well able to effect it. How many errors flow
from the same source?

* Chap. xx, 16.   † Mark xii, 13; Luke xx, 20.   ‡ Mark xii, 18.   § Deut. xxv, 5.

30 the Scriptures, nor the power of God. For in the resurrection
they neither marry nor are given in marriage, but aré as the angels
31 of God in heaven. But touching the resurrection of the dead, have
32 ye not read that which was spoken to you by God, saying, *I am
the God of Abraham, and the God of Isaac, and the God of Jacob.
33 He is not a God of the dead, but of the living. And the multitude
hearing *it*, were astonished at his doctrine.
34   † But the Pharisees having heard that he had silenced the Sad-
35 ducees, were gathered together. And one of them, a scribe, asked
36 *him* a question, trying him and saying, Master, which *is* the great
37 commandment in the law? Jesus said to him, ‡ Thou shalt love
the Lord thy God with all thy heart, and with all thy soul, and
38 with all thy mind. This is the first and great commandment. And
39 the second is like unto it, § Thou shalt love thy neighbour as thy-
40 self. On these two commandments hang all the law and the
prophets.
41   ‖ While the Pharisees were gathered together, Jesus asked
42 them, saying, What think ye of Christ? Whose son is he? They
43 say to him, David's. He saith to them, How doth David then by
44 the Spirit call him Lord? Saying, ** The Lord said to my Lord,
Sit thou on my right hand, till I make thine enemies thy footstool.
45 If David then call him Lord, how is he his son? And no man
46 was able to answer him a word ; neither durst any from that day
question him any more.
XXIII. Then spake Jesus to the multitudes and to his disciples, say-
2 ing, The scribes and Pharisees sit in the chair of Moses : All
3 things therefore whatsoever they bid you observe, observe and do :

---

30. *They are as the angels*—Incorruptible and immortal. So is the *power* of
God shown in them! So little need had they of marriage!
31. *Have ye not read*—The Sadducees had a peculiar value for the books of
Moses. Out of these therefore our Lord argues with them.
32. *I am the God of Abraham*—The argument runs thus : God is not the God
of the dead, but of the living : (for that expression, *Thy God*, implies both benefit
from God to man, and duty from man to God) but he is the God of Abraham,
Isaac, and Jacob: therefore, Abraham, Isaac, and Jacob are not dead, but living.
Therefore, the soul does not die with the body. So indeed the Sadducees supposed, and it was on this ground that they denied the resurrection.
33. *At his doctrine*—At the clearness and solidity of his answers.
35. *A scribe asking him a question, trying him*—Not, as it seems, with any ill
design : but barely to make a farther trial of that wisdom, which he had shown
in silencing the Sadducees.
43. *How doth David then by the Spirit*—By inspiration, *call him Lord ?* If he
be merely the son (or descendant) of David? If he be, as you suppose, a mere
man, the son of a man?
44. *The Lord said to my Lord*—This his dominion, to which David himself
was subject, shows both the heavenly majesty of the king, and the nature of his
kingdom. *Sit thou on my right hand*—That is, remain in the highest authority
and power.
46. *Neither durst any question him any more*—Not by way of ensnaring or
tempting him.
XXIII. 1. *Then*—Leaving all converse with his adversaries, whom he now
left to the hardness of their hearts.
2. *The scribes sit in the chair of Moses*—That is, read and expound the law of
Moses, and are their appointed teachers.

* Exod. iii, 6.   † Mark xii, 28; Luke x, 25.   ‡ Deut. vi, 5.   § Lev. xix, 18.
‖ Luke xx, 41.   ** Psalm cx, 1.

4 but do not ye after their works ; for they say and do not. * For
they bind heavy burdens and grievous to be borne, and lay *them*
on men's shoulders, but they will not move them with their finger.
5 † But all their works they do, to be seen of men : they make broad
6 their phylacteries, and enlarge the fringes of their garments. And
love the uppermost places at feasts, and the chief seats in the syna-
7 gogues, And salutations in the markets, and to be called by men,
8 Rabbi, rabbi. But be not ye called rabbi ; for one is your teacher,
9 and all are your brethren. And call no man your father on earth ;
10 for one is your Father, who is in heaven. Neither be ye called
11 masters ; for one is your Master, *even* Christ. ‡ But he that is
12 greatest among you shall be your servant. § Whosoever shall
exalt himself, shall be humbled, and he that shall humble himself,
shall be exalted.
13 But wo to you, scribes and Pharisees, hypocrites ; for ye shut
the kingdom of heaven against men: ye go not in, neither suffer
14 ye them that are entering to go in. ‖ Wo to you, scribes and
Pharisees, hypocrites : for ye devour widows' houses, and for a
pretence make long prayers ; therefore ye shall receive the greater
15 damnation. Wo to you, scribes and Pharisees, hypocrites ; for
ye compass sea and land to make one proselyte, and when he is
become so, ye make him two-fold more the child of hell than your-
16 selves. Wo to you, ye blind guides ; who say, Whosoever shall

---

3. *All things therefore*—Which they read out of the law, and enforce
therefrom.

5. *Their phylacteries*—The Jews, understanding those words literally, *It shall
be as a token upon thy hand, and as frontlets between thine eyes*, Exod. xiii, 16.
*And thou shalt bind these words for a sign upon thine hand, and they shall be as
frontlets between thine eyes*, Deut. vi, 8 ; used to wear little scrolls of paper or
parchment, bound on their wrist and foreheads, on which several texts of Scripture were writ. These they supposed, as a kind of charm, would preserve them
from danger. And hence they seem to have been called phylacteries, or pre-
servatives.
The fringes of their garments—Which God had enjoined them to wear, to
remind them of doing all the commandments, Num. xv, 38. These, as well as
their phylacteries, the Pharisees affected to wear broader and larger than
other men.

8, 9, 10. The Jewish *rabbis* were also called *father* and *master*, by their several
disciples, whom they required, 1. To believe implicitly what they affirmed, without asking any farther reason ; 2. To obey implicitly what they enjoined, without seeking farther authority. Our Lord, therefore, by forbidding us either to
give or receive the title of rabbi, master, or father, forbids us either to receive
any such reverence, or to pay any such to any but God.

12. *Whosoever shall exalt himself shall be humbled, and he that shall humble
himself shall be exalted*—It is observable that no one sentence of our Lord's is so
often repeated as this : it occurs, with scarce any variation, at least ten times in
the evangelists.

13. *Wo to you*—Our Lord pronounced eight blessings upon the mount : he
pronounces eight woes here ; not as imprecations, but solemn, compassionate
declarations of the misery, which these stubborn sinners were bringing upon
themselves. *Ye go not in*—For ye are not poor in spirit ; and ye hinder those
that would be so.

16. *Wo to you, ye blind guides*—Before he had styled them *hypocrites*, from
their personal character: now he gives them another title, respecting their
influence upon others. Both these appellations are severely put together in the

* Luke xv, 46.   + Mark xii, 38.   ‡ Chap. xx, 26.   § Luke xiv, 11 ; xviii, 14.
‖ Mark xii, 40 ; Luke xx, 47.

swear by the temple, it is nothing; but whosoever shall swear by
17 the gold of the temple he is bound.   Ye fools and blind: for which
is greater, the gold, or the temple that sanctifieth the gold?
18 And whosoever shall swear by the altar, *ye say*, it is nothing: but
19 whosoever shall swear by the gift that is upon it, is bound.   Ye
fools and blind; for which *is* greater, the gift, or the altar that
20 sanctifieth the gift? He therefore that sweareth by the altar, sweareth
21 by it and by all things thereon.   And he that sweareth by the tem-
22 ple, sweareth by it and by him that dwelleth therein.   And he
that sweareth by heaven, sweareth by the throne of God, and by
23 him that sitteth thereon.   Wo to you, scribes and Pharisees, hypocrites; for ye pay tithe of mint, and anise, and cummin, and have
neglected the weightier matters of the law, judgment, mercy, and
faith: these ought ye to have done, and not to have neglected the
24 others.   Ye blind guides, who strain out a gnat, and swallow a
25 camel.   Wo to you, scribes and Pharisees, hypocrites; for ye
cleanse the outside of the cup and the dish; but within they are
26 full of rapine and intemperance.   Thou blind Pharisee, cleanse first
the inside of the cup and of the dish, that the outside of them may
27 be clean also.   Wo to you, scribes and Pharisees, hypocrites; for
ye are like whited sepulchres, which outwardly indeed appear beautiful, but within are full of dead men's bones and of all uncleanness.
28 So ye likewise outwardly appear righteous to men; but within are
29 full of hypocrisy and iniquity.   Wo to you, scribes and Pharisees,
hypocrites; for ye build the tombs of the prophets, and adorn the
30 sepulchres of the righteous, and say, If we had been in the days
of our fathers, we would not have been partakers with them in the
31 blood of the prophets.   Wherefore ye testify against yourselves,

23d and 25th verses; and this severity rises to the height in the 33d verse. *The gold of the temple*—The treasure kept there. *He is bound*—To keep his oath.
20. *He that sweareth by the altar, sweareth by it, and by all things thereon*—Not only by the gift, but by the holy fire, and the sacrifice; and above all, by that God to whom they belong; inasmuch as every oath by a creature is an implicit appeal to God.
23. *Judgment*—That is, justice: *Faith*—The word here means fidelity.
24. *Ye blind guides, who* teach others to do as you do yourselves, to *strain out a gnat*—From the liquor they are going to drink! *and swallow a camel*—It is strange, that glaring false print, *strain at* a gnat, which quite alters the sense, should run through all the editions of our English Bibles.
25. *Full of rapine and intemperance*—The censure is double (taking intemperance in the vulgar sense.)   These miserable men procured unjustly what they used intemperately.   No wonder tables so furnished prove a snare, as many find by sad experience.   Thus luxury punishes fraud while it feeds disease with the fruits of injustice.   But intemperance in the full sense takes in not only all kinds of outward intemperance, particularly in eating and drinking, but all intemperate or immoderate desires, whether of honour, gain, or sensual pleasure.
26. *Ye build the tombs of the prophets*—And that is all, for ye neither observe their sayings, nor imitate their actions.
30. *We would not have been partakers*—So ye make fair professions, as did your fathers.
31. *Wherefore ye testify against yourselves*—By your smooth words as well as devilish actions: *that ye are* the genuine *sons of them who killed the prophets* of their own times, while they professed the utmost veneration for those of past ages.
From the 3d to the 30th verse is exposed every thing that commonly passes in the world for religion, whereby the pretenders to it keep both themselve

32 that ye are the sons of them who killed the prophets. Fill ye up
33 then the measure of your fathers. Ye serpents, ye brood of vipers,
34 how can ye escape the damnation of hell? *Wherefore behold I
send to you prophets, and wise men, and scribes; and *some* of them
ye will kill and crucify, and *some* of them ye will scourge in your
35 synagogues, and persecute from city to city: That upon you may
come all the righteous blood shed on the earth, from the blood of
Abel the righteous, to the blood of Zechariah the son of Barachiah,
36 whom ye slew between the temple and the altar. Verily I say to
37 you, all these things shall come upon this generation. †O Jerusalem, Jerusalem, that killest the prophets, and stonest them who
were sent unto thee, how often would I have gathered thy children
together even as a bird gathereth her young under *her* wings;
38 and ye would not! Behold your house is left unto you desolate.
39 For I say to you, ye shall not see me from this time, till ye say
Blessed *is* he that cometh in the name of the Lord.

and others from entering into the kingdom of God; from attaining, or
even seeking after those tempers, in which alone true Christianity consists. As,
1. Punctuality in attending on public and private prayer, ver. 4–14. 2. Zeal to
make proselytes to our opinion or communion, though they have less of the
spirit of religion than before, ver. 15. 3. A superstitious reverence for consecrated places or things, without any for Him to whom they are consecrated,
ver. 16–22. 4. A scrupulous exactness in little observances, though with the
neglect of justice, mercy, and faith, ver. 23, 24. 5. A nice cautiousness to
cleanse the outward behaviour, but without any regard to inward purity, ver.
25, 26. 6. A specious face of virtue and piety, covering the deepest hypocrisy
and villany, ver. 27, 28. 7. A professed veneration for all good men, except
those among whom they live.

32. *Fill ye up*—A word of permission, not of command: as if he had said, I
contend with you no longer: I leave you to yourselves: you have conquered:
now ye may follow the devices of your own hearts. *The measure of your fathers*
—Wickedness: ye may now be as wicked as they.

33. *Ye serpents*—Our Lord having now lost all hope of reclaiming these, speaks
so as to affright others from the like sins.

34. *Wherefore*—That it may appear you are the true children of those murderers, and have a right to have their iniquities visited on you: *Behold, I send*—Is
not this speaking as one having authority? *Prophets*—Men with supernatural
credentials: *Wise men*—Such as have both natural abilities and experience; *and
scribes*—Men of learning: but all will not avail.

35. *That upon you may come*—The consequence of which will be, that upon
you will come the vengeance of all *the righteous blood shed on the earth*—
Zechariah the son of Barachiah—Termed Jehoiada, 2 Chron. xxiv, 20, where
the story is related: *Ye slew*—Ye make that murder also of your fathers your
own, by imitating it: *Between the temple*—That is, the inner temple, *and the
altar*—Which stood in the outer court. Our Lord seems to refer to this
instance, rather than any other, because he was the last of the prophets on
record that were slain by the Jews for reproving their wickedness: and because
God's *requiring* this blood as well as that of Abel, is particularly taken notice of
in Scripture.

38. *Behold your house*—The temple, which is now your house, not God's:
Is left unto you—Our Lord spake this as he was going out of it for the last
time: *Desolate*—Forsaken of God and his Christ, and sentenced to utter
destruction.

39. *Ye*—Jews in general; men of Jerusalem in particular: *shall not see me
from this time*—Which includes the short space till his death, *till*, after a long
interval of desolation and misery, *ye say, Blessed is he that cometh in the name of*

* Luke xi, 49.   † Luke xiii, 34.

XXIV. *And Jesus going out of the temple departed: and his disciples came to *him* to show him the buildings of the temple.
2 And Jesus said to them, Do ye see all these things? Verily I say to you, There shall not be left here one stone upon another,
3 which shall not be thrown down. And as he sat on the mount of Olives, his disciples came to him privately, saying, Tell us when shall these things be? And what *shall be* the sign of thy
4 coming, and of the end of the world? And Jesus answering said,
5 Take heed that no man deceive you. For many will come in my name, saying, I am the Christ, and will deceive many.
6 And ye shall hear of wars and rumours of wars; see that ye be not troubled: for all these things must come to pass: but the
7 end is not yet. For nation shall rise against nation, and kingdom against kingdom: and there shall be famines and pestilences and
8 earthquakes in divers places: All these *are* the beginning of
9 sorrows. †Then will they deliver you up to affliction, and will kill you; and ye shall be hated of all nations for my name's
10 sake. And then will many be offended, and will betray one

the Lord—Ye receive me with joyful and thankful hearts. This also shall be accomplished in its season.

XXIV. 2. *There shall not be left one stone upon another*—This was most punctually fulfilled; for after the temple was burnt, Titus, the Roman general, ordered the very foundations of it to be dug up; after which the ground on which it stood was ploughed up by Turnus Rufus.

3. *As he sat on the mount of Olives*—Whence they had a full view of the temple. *When shall these things be? And what shall be the sign of thy coming, and of the end of the world?*—The disciples inquire confusedly, 1. Concerning the time of the destruction of the temple; 2. Concerning the signs of Christ's coming, and of the end of the world, as if they imagined these two were the same thing.

Our Lord answers distinctly concerning, 1. The destruction of the temple and city, with the signs preceding, ver. 4, &c, 15, &c. 2. His own coming, and the end of the world, with the signs thereof, ver. 29-31. 3. The time of the destruction of the temple, ver. 32, &c. 4. The time of the end of the world, ver. 36.

4. *Take heed that no man deceive you*—The caution is more particularly designed for the succeeding Christians, whom the apostles then represented. The first sign of my coming is, the rise of false prophets. But it is highly probable, many of these things refer to more important events, which are yet to come.

5. *Many shall come in my name*—First, false Christs, next, false prophets, ver. 11. At length, both together, ver. 24. And indeed never did so many impostors appear in the world as a few years before the destruction of Jerusalem; undoubtedly because that was the time wherein the Jews in general expected the Messiah.

6. *Wars*—Near: *Rumours of wars*—At a distance. *All these things must come to pass*—As a foundation for lasting tranquillity. *But the end*—Concerning which ye inquire, *is not yet*—So far from it, that this is but *the beginning of sorrows.*

9. *Then shall they deliver you up to affliction*—As if ye were the cause of all these evils. *And ye shall be hated of all nations*—Even of those who tolerate all other sects and parties; but in no nation will the children of the devil tolerate the children of God.

10. *Then shall many be offended*—So as utterly to make shipwreck of faith and a pure conscience. But hold ye fast faith, ver. 11, in spite of false prophets: love, even when iniquity and offences abound, ver. 12. And hope, unto the end, ver. 13. He that does so, shall be snatched out of the burning. *The love of many will wax cold*—The generality of those who love God will (like the Church at Ephesus, Rev. ii, 4,) leave their first love.

* Mark xiii, 1; Luke xxi, 5. † Matt. x, 17.

11 another, and hate one another.   And many false prophets will rise
12 and will deceive many.   And because iniquity shall abound, the
love of many will wax cold.
13   * But he that shall endure to the end, the same shall be saved.
14 † And this Gospel of the kingdom shall be preached in all the
world, for a testimony to all nations : and then shall the end come
15 ‡ When therefore ye see the abomination of desolation spoken of
by Daniel the prophet standing in the holy place, (he that readeth,
16 let him understand,) Then let them who are in Judea flee to the
17 mountains : Let not him that is on the house top, come down to
18 take any thing out of his house : Neither let him who is in the
19 field return back to take his clothes.   But wo to them that are
20 with child, and to them that give suck in those days.   And pray
ye that your flight be not in the winter, neither on the Sabbath.
21 For then shall be great tribulation, such as was not from the
22 beginning of the world to this time, nor ever shall be.   And unless
those days were shortened, no flesh would be saved; but for the

14. *This Gospel shall be preached in all the world*—Not universally : this is
not done yet : but in general through the several parts of the world, and not only
in Judea   And this was done by St. Paul and the other apostles, before Jerusalem was destroyed.   *And then shall the end come*—Of the city and temple.
Josephus's History of the Jewish War is the best commentary on this chapter.
It is a wonderful instance of God's providence, that he, an eye witness, and one
who lived and died a Jew, should, especially in so extraordinary a manner, be
preserved, to transmit to us a collection of important facts, which so exactly
illustrate this glorious prophecy, in almost every circumstance.
15. *When ye see the abomination of desolation*—Daniel's term is, *The abomination that maketh desolate*, chap. xi, 31; that is, the standards of the desolating
legions, on which they bear the abominable images of their idols: *Standing in
the holy place*—Not only the temple and the mountain on which it stood, but the
whole city of Jerusalem, and several furlongs of land round about it, were accounted holy; particularly the mount on which our Lord now sat, and on which
the Romans afterward planted their ensigns.   *He that readeth let him understand*—
Whoever reads that prophecy of Daniel, let him deeply consider it.
16. *Then let them who are in Judea flee to the mountains*—So the Christians
did, and were preserved.   It is remarkable that after the Romans under Cestus
Gallus made their first advances toward Jerusalem, they suddenly withdrew
again, in a most unexpected and indeed impolitic manner.   This the Christians took as a signal to retire, which they did, some to Pella, and others to
Mount Libanus.
17. *Let not him that is on the house top come down to take any thing out of his
house*—It may be remembered that their stairs used to be on the outside of their
houses.
19. *Wo to them that are with child, and to them that give suck*—Because they
cannot so readily make their escape.
20. *Pray ye that your flight be not in the winter*—They did so; and their
flight was in the spring.   *Neither on the Sabbath*—Being on many accounts
inconvenient; beside that many would have scrupled to travel far on that day.
For the Jews thought it unlawful to walk above two thousand paces (two miles)
on the Sabbath day.
21. *Then shall be great tribulation*—Have not many things spoken in the
chapter, as well as in Mark xiii, and Luke xxi, a farther and much more extensive
meaning than has been yet fulfilled ?
22. *And unless those days were shortened*—By the taking of Jerusalem sooner
than could be expected: *No flesh would be saved*—The whole nation would be
destroyed.   *But for the elect's sake*—That is, for the sake of the Christians.

* Matt x, 22; Mark xiv, 13; Luke xxi, 17.   † Mark xiii, 10.   ‡ Mark xiii, 14;
Luke xxi, 20; Dan. ix, 27.

23 elect's sake, those days shall be shortened. * Then if any say to
24 you, Lo here *is* Christ, or there ; believe *it* not. For false Christs
    and false prophets will arise and show great signs and wonders,
25 so that they would deceive (if possible) even the elect. Behold I
26 have told you before. Therefore if they say to you, Behold he is
    in the desert, go not forth : Behold *he is* in the secret chambers,
27 believe *it* not. For as the lightning goeth from the east, and
    shineth even to the west, so shall also the coming of the Son of
28 man be. † For wheresoever the carcass is, there will the eagles
29 be gathered together. ‡ Immediately after the tribulation of those
    days, the sun shall be darkened, and the moon shall not give her
    light ; and the stars shall fall from heaven, and the powers of the
30 heavens shall be shaken. And then shall appear the sign of the
    Son of man in heaven ; and then shall all the tribes of the earth
    mourn, and shall see the Son of man coming in the clouds of
31 heaven, with power and great glory. And he will send forth his
    angels with a lound-sounding trumpet, and they shall gather
    together his elect from the four winds, from one end of heaven
    to the other.
32   § Learn a parable from the fig tree : when its branch is now
    tender and shooteth forth leaves, ye know that the summer *is* nigh.
33 So likewise when ye see all these things, know that it is nigh, *even*
34 at the doors. Verily I say to you, This generation shall not pass

---

24. *They would deceive, if possible, the very elect*—But it is not possible that
God should suffer the body of Christians to be thus deceived.

27. *For as the lightning goeth forth*—For the next coming of Christ will be as
quick as lightning ; so that there will not be time for any such previous warning.

28. *For wheresoever the carcass is, there will the eagles be gathered together*—
Our Lord gives this, as a farther reason, why they should not hearken to any
pretended deliverer. As if he had said, Expect not any deliverer of the Jewish
nation ; for it is devoted to destruction. It is already before God a dead carcass,
which the Roman eagles will soon devour.

29. *Immediately after the tribulation of those days*—Here our Lord begins to
speak of his last coming. But he speaks not so much in the language of man as
of God, with whom a thousand years are as one day, one moment. Many of the
primitive Christians not observing this, thought he would come immediately, in
the common sense of the word : a mistake which St. Paul labours to remove, in
his Second Epistle to the Thessalonians. *The powers of the heavens*—Probably the
influences of the heavenly bodies.

30. *Then shall appear the sign of the Son of man in heaven*—It seems a little
before he himself descends. The sun, moon, and stars being extinguished, (probably not those of our system only,) the sign of the Son of man (perhaps the cross)
will appear in the glory of the Lord.

31. *They shall gather together his elect*—That is, all that have endured to the
end in the faith which worketh by love.

32. *Learn a parable*—Our Lord having spoken of the signs preceding the two
grand events, concerning which the apostles had inquired, begins here to speak
of the time of them. And to the question proposed, ver. 3, concerning the time
of the destruction of Jerusalem, he answers ver. 34. Concerning the time of the
end of the world, he answers ver. 36.

34. *This generation* of men now living *shall not pass till all these things be done*—
The expression implies, that great part of that generation would be passed away,
but not the whole. Just so it was. For the city and temple were destroyed
thirty-nine or forty years after.

* Mark xiii, 21 ; Luke xvii, 23.   † Luke xvii, 37.   ‡ Mark xiii, 24 ; Luke xxi, 25.
§ Mark xiii, 28 ; Luke xxi, 29.

35 away till all things be done   Heaven and earth shall pass away,
36 but my words shall not pass away.   But of that day and hour
knoweth no man, neither the angels of heaven, but my Father
only.
37   * But as the days of Noah, so shall also the coming of the Son of
38 man be.   For as in the days that were before the flood, they were
eating and drinking, marrying and giving in marriage, till the day
39 that Noah entered into the ark, And knew not till the flood came
and took them all away ; so shall also the coming of the Son of
man be.
40   Then shall two men be in the field : one is taken and one is
41 left.   Two women *shall* be grinding in the mill ; one is taken, and
one is left.
42   † Watch therefore ; for ye know not what hour your Lord
43 cometh.   But ye know this, that if the householder had known in
what watch the thief would have come, he would have watched,
44 and not have suffered his house to be broken open.   Therefore
be ye also ready : for at an hour ye think not, the Son of man com-
45 eth.   Who then is the faithful and wise servant, whom his Lord
hath appointed ruler over his household, to give them food in due
46 season ? Happy *is* that servant, whom his Lord coming shall find
47 so doing.   Verily I say to you, he will appoint him ruler over all
48 his goods.   But if that evil servant say in his heart, My lord
49 delays his coming : And shall begin to smite his fellow servant,
50 and shall eat and drink with the drunken : The lord of that servant shall come in a day that he expecteth *him* not, and in an hour
51 that he is not aware of, And shall cut him asunder, and allot him
his portion with the hypocrites : there shall be the weeping and
the gnashing of teeth.

---

36. *But of that day*—The day of judgment ; *Knoweth no man*—Not while our
Lord was on earth.   Yet it might be afterward revealed to St. John consistently
with this.

40. *One is taken*—Into God's immediate protection ; *and one is left*—To share
the common calamities.   Our Lord speaks as having the whole transaction present before his eyes.

41. *Two women shall be grinding*—Which was then a common employment
of women.

42. *Ye know not what hour your Lord cometh*—Either to require your soul of
you, or to avenge himself of this nation.

45. *Who then is the faithful and wise servant*—Which of you aspires after this
character ? *Wise*—Every moment retaining the clearest conviction, that all he
now has is only intrusted to him as a steward : *Faithful*—Thinking, speaking,
and acting continually, in a manner suitable to that conviction.

48. *But if that evil servant*—Now evil, having *put away faith and a good
conscience.*

51. *And allot him his portion with the hypocrites*—The worst of sinners, as
upright and sincere as he was once.

If ministers are the persons here primarily intended, there is a peculiar propriety in the expression.   For no hypocrisy can be baser, than to call ourselves
ministers of Christ, while we are the slaves of avarice, ambition, or sensuality.
Wherever such are found, may God reform them by his grace, or disarm them of
that power and influence, which they continually abuse to his dishonour, and to
their own aggravated damnation !

* Luke xvii, 26.   † Mark xiii, 33 ; Luke xii, 35 ; xxi, 34

XXV. Then shall the kingdom of heaven be like ten virgins who
2 taking their lamps, went forth to meet the bridegroom. But five
3 of them were wise, and five *were* foolish. They that were foolish
4 taking their lamps, took no oil with them. But the wise took oil
5 in their vessels with their lamps. While the bridegroom delayed,
6 they all slumbered and slept. But at midnight there was a cry,
   Behold the bridegroom cometh: come ye forth to meet him.
7 Then all those virgins arose and trimmed their lamps. And the
8 foolish said to the wise, Give us of your oil; for our lamps are
9 gone out. But the wise answered, Lest there be not enough for
   us and you: go ye rather to them that sell, and buy for your-
10 selves. And while they went to buy, the bridegroom came ; and
   they that were ready went in with him to the marriage ; and the
11 door was shut. Afterward come also the other virgins, saying,
12 Lord, Lord, open to us. But he answering said, Verily I say to
13 you, I know you not. Watch therefore ; for ye know not the day
   nor the hour.
14   * For *the kingdom of heaven is* as a man travelling into a far country, *who* called his own servants, and delivered to them his goods.

XXV. This chapter contains the last public discourse which our Lord
uttered before he was offered up. He had before frequently declared what would
be the portion of all the workers of iniquity. But what will become of those
who do no harm ? Honest, inoffensive, *good sort* of people ? We have here a
clear and full answer to this important question.

1. *Then shall the kingdom of heaven*—That is, the candidates for it, *be like
ten virgins*—The bridemaids on the wedding night were wont to go to the
house where the bride was, with burning lamps or torches in their hands, to wait
for the bridegroom's coming. When he drew near, they went to meet him with
their lamps, and to conduct him to the bride.

3. *The foolish took no oil with them*—No more than kept them burning just for
the present. None to supply their future want, to recruit their lamp's decay.
The lamp is faith. A *lamp and oil with it*, is faith working by love.

4. *The wise took oil in their vessels*—Love in their hearts. And they daily
sought a fresh supply of spiritual strength, till their faith was made perfect.

5. *While the bridegroom delayed*—That is, before they were called to attend
him, *they all slumbered and slept*—Were easy and quiet, the wise enjoying a true,
the foolish a false peace.

6. *At midnight*—In an hour quite unthought of.

7. *They trimmed their lamps*—They examined themselves and prepared to
meet their God.

8. *Give us of your oil, for our lamps are gone out*—Our faith is dead. What a time
to discover this ! Whether it mean the time of death, or of judgment. *Unto which
of the saints wilt thou* then *turn ?* Who can help thee at such a season ?

9. *But the wise answered, Lest there be not enough for us and you !*—Beginning
the sentence with a beautiful abruptness; such as showed their surprise at the
state of those poor wretches, who had so long deceived them, as well as their
own souls. *Lest there be not enough*—It is sure there is not ; for no man has
more than holiness enough for himself. *Go ye rather to them that sell*—Without
money and without price : that is, to God, to Christ. *And buy*—If ye can. O
no ! The time is past and returns no more !

13. *Watch therefore*—He that watches has not only a burning lamp, but likewise oil in his vessel. And even when he sleepeth, his heart waketh. He is
quiet ; but not secure.

14. Our Lord proceeds by a parable still plainer (if that can be) to declare the
final reward of a *harmless man.* May God give all such in this their day, ears
to hear and hearts to understand it ! *The kingdom of heaven*—That is, the King
of heaven, Christ.

15 And to one he gave five talents, to another two, and to another one, to each according to his own ability, and immediately took his
16 journey.   Then he who had received the five talents, went and
17 traded with them, and gained other five talents.   And likewise he
18 that *had received* the two, he also gained other two.   But he that had received the one, went and digged in the earth, and hid his
19 master's money.   After a long time the master of those servants
20 cometh and reckoneth with them.   And he that had received the five talents came and brought other five talents, saying, Sir, thou deliveredst to me five talents, behold, I have gained to them five
21 talents more.   His master said to him, Well done, good and faithful servant : thou hast been faithful over a few things ; I will set
22 thee over many things : enter thou into the joy of thy lord.   He also that had received the two talents, came and said, Sir, thou deliveredst to me two talents ; behold, I have gained to them two
23 other talents.   His master said to him, Well done, good and faithful servant ; thou hast been faithful over a few things ; I will set
24 thee over many things : enter thou into the joy of thy lord.   Then he that had received the one talent came and said, Sir, I knew that thou art a hard man, reaping where thou hast not sown, and gather-
25 ing whence thou hast not scattered.   And being afraid, I went and
26 hid thy talent in the earth ; lo, thou hast what is thine.   His master answering said to him, Thou wicked and slothful servant, thou knewest that I reap where I sowed not, and gather whence I had
27 not scattered.   Thou oughtest therefore to have put my money to the bankers, and at my coming I should have received my own with
28 interest.   Take therefore the talent from him, and give *it* to him
29 who hath ten talents.   * For to every one that hath shall be given, and he shall have abundance : but from him that hath not shall be
30 taken away even what he hath.   And cast ye the unprofitable ser-

---

15. *To one he gave five talents, to another two, and to another one*—And who knows whether (all circumstances considered) there be a greater disproportion than this, in the talents of those who have received the most, and those who have received the fewest ? *According to his own ability*—The words may be translated more literally, *according to his own mighty power.   And immediately took his journey*—To heaven.

18. *He that had received one*—Made his having fewer talents than others a pretence for not improving any.   *Went and hid his master's money*—Reader, art thou doing the same? Art thou hiding the talent God hath lent thee ?

24. *I knew thou art a hard man*—No.   Thou knowest him not.   He never knew God, who thinks him a hard master.   *Reaping where thou hast not sown*—That is, requiring more of us than thou hast given us power to perform.   So does every obstinate sinner, in one kind or other, lay the blame of his own sins on God.

25. *And I was afraid*—Lest if I had improved my talent, I should have had the more to answer for.   So from this fear, one will not learn to read, another will not hear sermons !

26. *Thou knewest*—That I require impossibilities ! This is not an allowing, but a strong denial of the charge.

27. *Thou oughtest therefore*—On that very account, on thy own supposition, to have improved my talent, as far as was possible.

29. *To every one that hath shall be given*—So close does God keep to this stated rule, from the beginning to the end of the world.

30. *Cast ye the unprofitable servant into the outer darkness*—For what ? what

* Matt. xiii, 12

vant into the outer darkness: there shall be the weeping and the gnashing of teeth.

31 When the Son of man shall come in his glory, and all the holy angels with him, then shall he sit upon the throne of his glory.
32 And all the nations shall be gathered before him, and he will separate them one from another, as a shepherd separateth the sheep
33 from the goats. And he will set the sheep on his right hand, and
34 the goats on his left. Then will the king say to them on his right hand, Come, ye blessed of my Father, inherit the kingdom prepared
35 for you from the foundation of the world. For I was hungry, and ye gave me meat; I was thirsty, and ye gave me drink; I was
36 a stranger, and ye took me in: Naked, and ye clothed me: I was sick, and ye visited me; I was in prison, and ye came to me.
37 Then will the righteous answer him, saying, Lord, when saw we thee hungry, and fed *thee?* Or thirsty, and gave *thee* drink?
38 When saw we thee a stranger, and took *thee* in? Or naked, and
39 clothed *thee?* Or when saw we thee sick or in prison, and came
40 to *thee?* And the king will answer and say to them, Verily I say to you, inasmuch as ye did *it* to one of the least of these my bre-
41 thren, ye did *it* to me. Then will he say to them on his left hand,

had he done? It is true he had not done good. But neither is he charged with doing any harm. Why, for this reason, for *barely doing no harm,* he is consigned to outer darkness. He is pronounced a *wicked,* because he was a *slothful,* an *unprofitable servant.* So *mere harmlessness,* on which many build their hope of salvation, was the cause of his damnation! *There shall be the weeping*—Of the careless thoughtless sinner; *and the gnashing of teeth*—Of the proud and stubborn

The same great truth, that there is no such thing as negative goodness, is in this chapter shown three times: 1. In the parable of the virgins; 2. In the still plainer parable of the servants, who had received the talents; and 3. In a direct unparabolical declaration of the manner wherein our Lord will proceed at the last day. The several parts of each of these exactly answers each other, only each rises above the preceding.

31. *When the Son of man shall come in his glory, and all the holy angels with him*—With what majesty and grandeur does our Lord here speak of himself Giving us one of the noblest instances of the true sublime. Indeed not man, descriptions in the sacred writings themselves seem to equal this. Methinks we˙ can hardly read it without imagining ourselves before the awful tribunal it describes.

34. *Inherit the kingdom*—Purchased by my blood, for all who have believed in me with the faith which wrought by love. *Prepared for you*—On purpose for you. May it not be probably inferred from hence, that man was not created merely to fill up the places of the fallen angels?

35. *I was hungry, and ye gave me meat; I was thirsty, and ye gave me drink*—All these works of outward mercy suppose faith and love, and must needs be accompanied with works of spiritual mercy. But works of this kind the Judge could not mention in the same manner. He could not say, I was in error, and ye recalled me to the truth; I was in sin, and ye brought me to repentance. *In prison*—Prisoners need to be visited above all others, as they are commonly solitary and forsaken by the rest of the world.

37. *Then shall the righteous answer*—It cannot be, that either the righteous or the wicked should answer in these very words. What we learn herefrom is, that neither of them have the same estimation of their own works as the Judge hath.

40. *Inasmuch as ye did it to one of the least of these my brethren, ye did it to me*—What encouragement is here to assist the household of faith? But let us likewise remember to *do good to all men.*

41. *Depart into the everlasting fire, which was prepared for the devil and his angels*—Not originally for you: you are intruders into everlasting fire.

Depart from me, ye cursed, into the everlasting fire, which was
42 prepared for the devil and his angels. For I was hungry, and ye
43 gave me no meat; I was thirsty, and ye gave me no drink: I was
a stranger, and ye took me not in; naked, and ye clothed me not;
44 sick and in prison, and ye visited me not. Then will they also
answer him, saying, Lord, when saw we thee hungry, or athirst, or
a stranger, or naked, or sick, or in prison, and did not minister unto
45 thee? Then will he answer them, saying, Verily I say to you, inasmuch as ye did it not unto one of the least of these, ye did it not
46 to me. And these shall go away into everlasting punishment; but
the righteous into life everlasting.
XXVI. * And when Jesus had finished all these discourses, he said
2 to his disciples, Ye know that after two days is the passover,
3 and the Son of man is betrayed to be crucified. Then the chief
priests and the scribes, and the elders of the people, assembled
together at the palace of the high priest, who was called Caiaphas,
4 And consulted together how they might apprehend Jesus by subtilty
5 and kill him. But they said, Not at the feast, lest there be a tumult
among the people.
6 † Now when Jesus was in Bethany, in the house of Simon the
7 leper, There came to him a woman, having an alabaster box of
very costly ointment, and poured it on his head, as he sat at table.

---

44. *Then will they answer*—So the endeavour to justify themselves, will remain
with the wicked even to that day!

46. *And these shall go away into everlasting punishment, but the righteous into
life everlasting*—Either therefore the punishment is strictly eternal, or the reward
is not: the very same expression being applied to the former as to the latter. The
Judge will speak first to the righteous, in the audience of the wicked. The wicked
shall then go away into everlasting fire, in the view of the righteous. Thus the
damned shall see nothing of the everlasting life; but the just will see the punishment of the ungodly. It is not only particularly observable here, 1. That the
punishment lasts as long as the reward; but, 2. That this punishment is so far
from ceasing at the end of the world, that it does not begin till then.

XXVI. 1. *When Jesus had finished all these discourses*—When he had spoken
all he had to speak. Till then he would not enter upon his passion: then he
would delay it no longer.

2. *After two days is the passover*—The manner wherein this was celebrated
gives much light to several circumstances that follow. The master of the family
began the feast with a cup of wine, which having solemnly blessed, he divided
among the guests, Luke xxii, 17. Then the supper began with the unleavened
bread and bitter herbs; which when they had all tasted, one of the young persons
present (according to Exod. xii, 26) asked the reason of the solemnity. This
introduced *the showing forth*, or declaration of it: in allusion to which we read
of showing forth the Lord's death, 1 Cor. xi, 26. Then the master rose up and
took another cup, before the lamb was tasted. After supper, he took a thin loaf
or cake, which he broke and divided to all at the table, and likewise the cup,
usually called the cup of thanksgiving, of which he drank first, and then all the
guests. It was this bread and this cup which our Lord consecrated to be a standing memorial of his death.

3. *The chief priests and the scribes and the elders of the people*—(Heads of families.) These together constituted the sanhedrim, or great council, which had
the supreme authority, both in civil and ecclesiastical affairs.

5. *But they said, Not at the feast*—This was the result of human wisdom.
But when Judas came they changed their purpose. So the counsel of God took
place, and the true paschal Lamb was offered up on the great day of the paschal
solemnity.

* Mark xiv, 1 · Luke xxii, 1.   † Mark xiv, 3.

8 But his disciples seeing *it*, had indignation, saying, To what pur-
9 pose *is* this waste? For this might have been sold for much, and
10 given to the poor. Jesus knowing it, said to them, Why trouble
11 ye the woman? She hath wrought a good work on me. For ye
12 have the poor always with you; but me ye have not always. For
   in pouring this ointment on my body, she hath done it for my burial.
13 Verily I say to you, wheresoever this Gospel shall be preached in
   the whole world, this also which she hath done shall be spoken for
   a memorial of her.
14   * Then one of the twelve, called Judas Iscariot, going to the
15 chief priests, said, What will ye give me, and I will deliver him
   to you? And they bargained with him for thirty pieces of silver
16 And from that time he sought opportunity to deliver him.
17   † On the first day of unleavened bread, the disciples came to
   Jesus, saying to him, Where wilt thou that we prepare for thee to
18 eat the passover? And he said, Go into the city to such a man,
   and say to him, The Master saith, My time is at hand: I keep
19 the passover at thy house with my disciples. And the disciples
   did as Jesus had appointed them; and they made ready the
   passover.
20   ‡ When the evening was come, he sat down with the twelve.
21 And as they ate he said, Verily I say to you, one of you will
22 betray me. And they were exceeding sorrowful and began each
23 of them to say to him, Lord, is it I? And he answering, said, He
   that dippeth *his* hand with me in the dish, the same will betray me.
24 The Son of man indeed goeth as it is written of him: but wo to
   that man by whom the Son of man is betrayed: it had been good
25 for that man if he had never been born. Then Judas who be-

---

8. *His disciples seeing* it, *had indignation, saying*—It seems several of them
were angry, and spoke, though none so warmly as Judas Iscariot.
    11. *Ye have the poor always with you*—Such is the wise and gracious provi-
dence of God, that we may have always opportunities of relieving their wants,
and so laying up for ourselves treasures in heaven.
    12. *She hath done it for my burial*—As it were for the embalming of my body.
Indeed this was not her design : but our Lord puts this construction upon it, to
confirm thereby what he had before said to his disciples, concerning his approaching death.
    13. *This Gospel*—That is, this part of the Gospel history.
    15. *They bargained with him for thirty pieces of silver*—(About three pounds
fifteen shillings sterling; or sixteen dollars sixty-seven cents,) the price of a slave,
Exod. xxi, 32.
    17. *On the first day of unleavened bread*—Being Thursday, the fourteenth day
of the first month, Exod. xii, 6, 15.
    18. *The Master saith, My time is at hand*—That is, the time of my suffering.
    23. *He that dippeth his hand with me in the dish*—Which it seems Judas was
doing at that very time. This *dish* was a vessel full of vinegar, wherein they
dipped their bitter herbs.
    24. *The Son of man goeth* through sufferings to glory, *as it is written of him*—
Yet this is no excuse for him that betrayeth him: miserable will that man be :
it had been good for that man if he had not been born—May not the same be said
of every man that finally perishes? But who can reconcile this, if it were true
of Judas alone, with the doctrine of universal salvation?

* Mark xiv, 10; Luke xxii, 3.   † Mark xiv, 12; Luke xxii, 7.   ‡ Mark xiv, 17;
                                        Luke xxii, 14.

trayed him answering said, Master, is it I ? He saith to him, Thou
hast said.

26   And after°they had eaten, Jesus took the bread, and blessed and
brake and gave *it* to his disciples, and said, Take, eat; this is my
27   body. And he took the cup, and having given thanks, gave *it* to
28   them, saying, Drink ye all of it. For this is my blood of the new
29   testament, which is shed for many, for the remission of sins. I say
to you, I will not drink henceforth of this fruit of the vine till that
day when I drink it new with you in my Father's kingdom.

30   * And when they had sung the hymn, they went out into the
31   mount of Olives. Then saith Jesus to them, All ye will be
offended at me this night, for it is written, † I will smite the Shep-
32   herd, and the sheep of the flock shall be scattered. But after I am
33   risen, I will go before you into Galilee. Peter answering said
to him, Though all should be offended at thee, I will never be
34   offended. Jesus said to him, Verily I say to thee, That in this very
35   night before cock crowing thou wilt deny me thrice. Peter saith
to him, If I must die with thee, yet I will in nowise deny thee. In
like manner also said all the disciples.

36   ‡ Then cometh Jesus with them to a place called Gethsemane,

---

25. *Thou hast said*—That is, it is as thou hast said.

26. *Jesus took the bread*—*the bread* or cake, which the master of the family
used to divide among them, after they had eaten the passover. The custom
our Lord now transferred to a nobler use. *This* bread *is*, that is, signifies or
represents *my body*, according to the style of the sacred writers. Thus Gen.
xl, 12, The three branches are three days. Thus Gal. iv, 24, St. Paul speaking of
Sarah and Hagar, says, These are the two covenants. Thus in the grand type of
our Lord, Exod. xii, 11, God says of the paschal lamb, This is the Lord's
passover. Now Christ substituting the holy communion for the passover, follows
the style of the Old Testament, and uses the same expressions the Jews were
wont to use in celebrating the passover.

27. *And he took the cup*—Called by the Jews the cup of thanksgiving; which
the master of the family used likewise to give to each after supper.

28. *This* is the sign of *my blood*, whereby the new testament or covenant is
confirmed. *Which is shed for many*—As many as spring from Adam.

29. *I will not drink henceforth of this fruit of the vine, till I drink it new
with you in my Father's kingdom*—That is, I shall taste no more wine, till I
drink wine of quite another kind in the glorious kingdom of my Father. And
of this you shall also partake with me.

30. *And when they had sung the hymn*—Which was constantly sung at the
close of the passover. It consisteth of six psalms, from the 113th to the 118th
The mount of Olives—Was over against the temple, about two miles from
Jerusalem.

31. *All ye will be offended at me*—Something will happen to me, which will
occasion your falling into sin by forsaking me.

32. *But* notwithstanding this, *after I am risen I will go before you* (as a shepherd before his sheep) *into Galilee* Though you forsake me, I will not for this
forsake you.

34. *Before cock crowing thou wilt deny me thrice*—That is, before three in the
morning, the usual time of cock crowing: although one cock was heard to crow
once, after Peter's first denial of his Lord.

35. *In like manner also said all the disciples*—But such was the tenderness of
our Lord, that he would not aggravate their sin by making any reply.

36. *Then cometh Jesus to a place called Gethsemane*—That is, the valley of
fatness. The garden probably had its name from its soil and situation, laying in

* Mark xiv, 26; Luke xxii, 39; John xviii, 1.   † Zech. xiii, 7.   ‡ Mark xiv, 32;
Luke xxii, 40.

and saith to the disciples, Sit ye here, while I go and pray yonder
37 And taking with him Peter and the two sons of Zebedee, he began
38 to be sorrowful and in deep anguish.   Then saith he to them
My soul is exceeding sorrowful, even unto death; tarry ye here,
39 and watch with me.   And going a little farther he fell on his face
and prayed, saying, O my Father, if it be possible, let this cup pass
40 from me; yet not as I will, but as thou *wilt*.   And he cometh to
the disciples, and findeth them asleep, and saith to Peter, What.
41 Could not ye watch with me one hour ?   Watch and pray, that ye
enter not into temptation :   the spirit indeed *is* willing, but the
42 flesh *is* weak.   Again going away the second time he prayed, saying, O my Father, if this cup cannot pass from me, unless I drink
43 it, thy will be done.   And coming, he findeth them asleep again ;
44 for their eyes were weighed down.   And leaving them, he went
away again, and prayed the third time, saying the same words.
45 Then cometh he to his disciples, and saith to them, Sleep on now
and take *your* rest : behold the hour is come, and the Son of man
46 is betrayed into the hand of sinners.   Rise ; let us be going :
behold he that betrayeth me is at hand.
47   * And while he was yet speaking, lo, Judas one of the twelve
came, and with him a great multitude with swords and clubs from
48 the chief priests and elders of the people.   Now he that betrayed
him had given them a signal, saying, Whomsoever I shall kiss,
49 is he ; seize him.   And forthwith coming to Jesus, he said, Hail,
50 Master, and kissed him.   And Jesus said to him, Friend, wherefore art thou come ?   Then came they up and laid hands on Jesus,

---

some little valley between two of those many hills, the range of which constitutes
the mount of Olives.

37. *And taking with him Peter and the two sons of Zebedee*—To be witnesses
of all ; *he began to be sorrowful and in deep anguish*—Probably from feeling the
arrows of the Almighty stick fast in his soul, while God laid on him the iniquities
of us all.   Who can tell what painful and dreadful sensations were then impressed
on him by the immediate hand of God ?   The former word in the original properly
signifies, to be penetrated with the most exquisite sorrow ; the latter to be quite
depressed, and almost overwhelmed with the load.

39. *And going a little farther*—*About a stone's cast*, Luke xxii, 41—So that
the apostles could both see and hear him still.   *If it be possible, let this cup pass
from me*—And it did pass from him quickly.   When he cried unto God with
strong cries and tears, he was heard in that which he feared.   God did take
away the terror and severity of that inward conflict.

41. *The spirit*—Your spirit : ye yourselves.   *The flesh*—Your nature.   How
gentle a rebuke was this, and how kind an apology ! especially at a time when
our Lord's own mind was so weighed down with sorrow.

45. *Sleep on now*, if you can, *and take your rest*—For any farther service you
can be of to me.

50. The heroic behaviour of the blessed Jesus, in the whole period of his
sufferings, will be observed by every attentive eye, and felt by every pious
heart : although the sacred historians, according to their usual but wonderful
simplicity, make no encomiums upon it.   With what composure does he go forth
to meet the traitor !   With what calmness receive that malignant kiss !   With
what dignity does he deliver himself into the hands of his enemies !   Yet plainly
showing his superiority over them, and even then leading as it were captivity
captive !

51. *And one of them striking the servant of the high priest*—Probably the per-

* Mark xiv, 43 ; Luke xxii, 47 ; John xviii, 2.

51 and took him. *And behold one of them that were with Jesus,
stretching out *his* hand, drew his sword, and striking the servant of
52 the high priest, cut off his ear.   Then said Jesus to him, Put up
again thy sword into its place ; for all they that take the sword shall
53 perish by the sword.   Thinkest thou that I cannot ask my Father,
and he will presently send me more than twelve legions of angels?
54 But how then shall the Scriptures be fulfilled, that thus it must be
done?
55   † In that hour Jesus said to the multitudes, Are ye come out as
against a robber, with swords and clubs to take me?   I sat daily
with you teaching in the temple and ye apprehended me not.   But
56 all this is done, that the Scriptures might be fulfilled.   Then all
the disciples forsook him and fled.
57   ‡ And they that had apprehended Jesus, led *him* away to Caiaphas
the high priest, where the scribes and the elders were assembled.
58 But Peter followed him afar off to the high priest's palace, and
59 going in, sat with the servants to see the end.   Now the chief
priests, and elders, and all the council sought false witness against
60 Jesus, to put him to death, But found none ; yea, though many false
witnesses came, *yet* found they none.   At last came two false wit-
61 nesses, and said, This *fellow* said, I am able to destroy the temple
62 of God, and to build it in three days.   And the high priest rising
up said to him, Answerest thou nothing?   What do these witness
63 against thee?   But Jesus held his peace.   And the high priest
answering said to him, I adjure thee by the living God, to tell us,
if thou art the Christ, the Son of God?   Jesus saith to him, Thou
64 hast said.   Moreover I say to you, Hereafter shall ye see the Son
of man sitting on the right hand of power, and coming upon the
65 clouds of heaven.   Then the high priest rent his clothes, saying,

son that seized Jesus first ; *Cut off his ear*—Aiming, it seems, to cleave his head,
but that by a secret providence interposing, he declined the blow.
   52. *All they that take the sword*—Without God's giving it them : without sufficient authority.
   53. *He will presently give me more than twelve legions of angels*—The least
of whom, it is probable, could overturn the earth and destroy all the inhabitants
of it.
   57. *They led him away to Caiaphas*—From the house of Annas, the father-in-
law of Caiaphas, to whom they had carried him first.
   58. *But Peter followed him afar off*—Variously agitated by conflicting pas
sions ; love constrained him to *follow* his Master ; fear made him follow *afar off.*
And going in, sat with the servants—Unfit companions as the event showed.
   60. *Yet found they none*—On whose evidence they could condemn him to die
At last came two false witnesses—Such they were, although part of what they
said was true ; because our Lord did not speak some of those words at all ; nor
any of them in this sense.
   64. *Hereafter shall ye see the Son of man*—He speaks in the third person,
modestly, and yet plainly ; *Sitting on the right hand of power*—That is, the right
hand of God: *And coming upon the clouds of heaven*—As he is represented by
Daniel, chap. vii, 13, 14.   Our Lord looked very unlike that person now ! But
nothing could be more awful, more majestic and becoming, than such an admonition in such circumstances !
   65. *Then the high priest rent his clothes*—Though the high priest was forbidden
to rend his clothes (that is, his upper garment) in some cases where others were

* Mark xiv, 47 ; Luke xxii, 49 ; John xxviii, 10.   † Mark xiv, 48 ; Luke xxii, 52.
‡ Mark xiv, 53 ; Luke xxii, 54 ; John xviii, 12.

He hath spoken blasphemy : what farther need have we of wit-
66 nesses ? Behold now ye have heard his blasphemy. What think
67 ye ? They answering said, He is worthy of death. Then did they
68 spit in his face and buffet him, and others smote *him*, Saying,
Prophesy to us, thou Christ, who is he that smote thee ?
69 Now Peter sat without in the hall. And a maid servant came to
70 him, saying, Thou also wast with Jesus of Galilee. But he denied
71 before all, saying, I know not what thou sayest. And when he
was gone out into the porch, another *maid* saw him, and said to
them that were there, This *fellow* also was with Jesus of Nazareth.
72 And again he denied with an oath, I know not the man. And after
awhile they that stood by came and said to Peter, Surely thou art
73 also *one* of them ; for thy speech discovereth thee. Then began
74 he to curse and to swear, I know not the man. And immediately
75 the cock crew. And Peter remembered the word of Jesus, who
said to him, Before cock crowing thou wilt deny me thrice. And
going out he wept bitterly.
XXVII. * In the morning, all the chief priests and elders of the peo-
2 ple consulted together against Jesus, to put him to death. And
having bound *him*, they led him away and delivered him to Pontius
Pilate the governor.
3 Then Judas who had betrayed him, seeing that he was con
demned, repenting himself, brought back the thirty pieces of silver
4 to the chief priests and elders, Saying, I have sinned in betraying
5 innocent blood. And they said, What *is that* to us ? See thou *to*
it. And having thrown down the pieces of silver in the temple,
6 he withdrew, and going away hanged himself. And the chief
priests taking the pieces of silver, said, It is not lawful to put them

allowed to do it, Lev. xxi, 10; yet in case of blasphemy or any public calamity,
it was thought allowable. Caiaphas hereby expressed, in the most artful manner,
his horror at hearing such grievous blasphemy.

67. *Then*—After he had declared he was the Son of God, the sanhedrim doubtless ordered him to be carried out, while they were consulting what to do. And
then it was that the soldiers who kept him began these insults upon him.

72. *He denied with an oath*—To which possibly he was not unaccustomed,
before our Lord called him.

73. *Surely thou art also one of them, for thy speech discovereth thee*—Malchus
might have brought a stronger proof than this. But such is the overruling providence of God, that the world, in the height of their zeal, commonly catch hold
of the very weakest of all arguments against the children of God.

74. *Then began he to curse and to swear*—Having now quite lost the reins, the
government of himself.

XXVII. 1. *In the morning*—As the sanhedrim used to meet in one of the courts
of the temple, which was never opened in the night, they were forced to stay till
the morning before they could proceed regularly, in the resolution they had taken
to put him to death.

2. *Having bound him*—They had bound him when he was first apprehended.
But they did it now afresh, to secure him from any danger of an escape, as he
passed through the streets of Jerusalem.

3. *Then Judas, seeing that he was condemned*—Which probably he thought
Christ would have prevented by a miracle.

4. *They said, what is that to us?*—How easily could they digest innocent
blood ! And yet they had a conscience ! *It is not lawful* (say they) *to put it into*
the treasury—But very lawful to slay the innocent !

5. *In that part of the temple* where the sanhedrim met.

* Mark xv, 1 ; Luke xxii, 66 ; xxiii, 1 ; John xviii, 28.

7 in the treasury, because it is the price of blood.   And having consulted together, they bought with them the potter's field, to bury
8 foreigners in.   Wherefore that field was called the field of blood
9 unto this day.   Then was fulfilled what was spoken by the
   prophet, saying, * And they took the thirty pieces of silver, the
   price of him that was valued, whom they of the children of Israel
10 did value, And gave them for the potter's field, as the Lord commanded me.
11   And Jesus stood before the governor.   And the governor ques
   tioned him, saying, Art thou the king of the Jews ?   And Jesus
12 said to him, Thou sayest.   But while he was accused by the chief
13 priests and elders, he answered nothing.   Then said Pilate to him,
   Hearest thou not how many things they witness against thee ?
14 And he answered him to never a word, so that the •governor marvelled greatly.
15   † Now at every feast the governor was wont to release to the
16 people a prisoner, whom they would.   And they had then a noto-
17 rious prisoner, named Barabbas.   Therefore when they were
   gathered together, Pilate said to them, Whom will ye that I release
18 to you ?   Barabbas, or Jesus who is called Christ ?   For he knew
   that for envy they had delivered him.
19   While he sat on the judgment seat, his wife sent to him, saying,
   Have thou nothing to do with that just man ; for I have suffered
20 many things to-day in a dream because of him.   But the chief
   priests and elders persuaded the multitude to ask Barabbas, and
21 destroy Jesus.   The governor answering, said to them, Which of
22 the two will ye that I release to you ?   They said, Barabbas.   Pilate
   said to them, What shall I do then with Jesus who is called
23 Christ ?   They say to him, Let him be crucified.   And the
   governor said, Why, what evil hath he done ?   But they cried out
24 the more vehemently, saying, Let him be crucified.   Then Pilate,

---

7. *They bought with them the potter's field*—Well known, it seems, by that
name.   This was a small price for a field so near Jerusalem.   But the earth had
probably been digged for potters' vessels, so that it was now neither fit for tillage
nor pasture, and consequently of small value.   *Foreigners*—Heathens especially,
of whom there were then great numbers in Jerusalem.
9. *Then was fulfilled*—What was figuratively represented of old, was now
really accomplished.   *What was spoken by the prophet*—The word Jeremy, which
was added to the text in latter copies, and thence received into many translations, is evidently a mistake: for he who spoke what St. Matthew here cites (or
rather paraphrases) was not Jeremy, but Zechariah.
10. *As the Lord commanded me*—To write, to record.
11. *Art thou the king of the Jews?*—Jesus before Caiaphas avows himself to be
the Christ, before Pilate to be a king; clearly showing thereby, that his answering no more, was not owing to any fear.
15. *At every feast*—Every year, at the feast of the passover.
18. *He knew that for envy they had delivered him*—As well as from malice and
revenge ; they envied him, because the people magnified him.
22. *They all say, Let him be crucified*—The punishment which Barabbas had
deserved : and this probably made them think of it.   But in their malice they
forgot with how dangerous a precedent they furnished the Roman governor.
And indeed within the compass of a few years it turned dreadfully upon
themselves.

* Zech. xi, 12.   † Mark xv, 6 ; Luke xxiii, 17 ; John xviii, 39.

seeing that he could prevail nothing, but rather a tumult was made,
taking water washed *his* hands before the multitude, saying, I am
25 innocent of the blood of this just man : see ye *to it.* Then all the
26 people answering said, His blood *be* on us, and on our children.
Then released he Barabbas to them, and having scourged Jesus,
he delivered him to be crucified.
27   * Then the soldiers of the governor taking Jesus into the common
28 hall gathered to him the whole troop. And stripping him they put
29 on him a scarlet robe, And platting a crown of thorns, they put it
upon his head, and a cane in his right hand ; and kneeling before
30 him, they mocked him, saying, Hail, king of the Jews. And
spitting on him, they took the cane and smote him on the head.
31 And after they had mocked him, they stripped him of the robe,
and put his own raiment on him, and led him away to crucify *him.*
32 And coming out they found a man of Cyrene, Simon by name :
him they compelled to bear his cross.
33   † And coming to a place called Golgotha, that is, the place of a
34 skull, They gave him vinegar mingled with gall to drink, and
35 when he had tasted *thereof*, he would not drink. And having crucified him they parted his garments, casting lots, that it might be

---

24. *Then Pilate took water and washed his hands*—This was a custom frequently
used among the heathens as well as among the Jews, in token of innocency.

25. *His blood be on us and on our children*—As this imprecation was dreadfully answered in the ruin so quickly brought on the Jewish nation, and the
calamities which have ever since pursued that wretched people, so it was peculiarly fulfilled by Titus the Roman general, on the Jews whom he took during the
siege of Jerusalem. So many, after having been scourged in a terrible manner,
were crucified all round the city, that in a while there was not room near the
wall for the crosses to stand by each other. Probably this befell some of those
who now joined in this cry, as it certainly did many of their children : the very
finger of God thus pointing out their crime in crucifying his Son.

26. *He delivered him to be crucified*—The person crucified was nailed to the
cross as it lay on the ground, through each hand extended to the utmost stretch,
and through both the feet together. Then the cross was raised up, and the foot
of it thrust with a violent shock into a hole in the ground prepared for it. This
shock disjointed the body, whose whole weight hung upon the nails, till the
persons expired through mere dint of pain. This kind of death was used only by
the Romans, and by them inflicted only on slaves and the vilest criminals.

27. *The whole troop—or cohort.* This was a body of foot commanded by the
governor, which was appointed to prevent disorders and tumults, especially on
solemn occasions.

28. *They put on him a scarlet robe*—Such as kings and generals wore ; probably an old tattered one.

32. *Him they compelled to bear his cross*—He bore it himself, till he sunk
under it, John xix, 17.

33. *A place called Golgotha, that is, the place of a skull*—Golgotha in Syriac
signifies a skull or head : it was probably called so from this time ; being an
eminence upon Mount Calvary, not far from the king's gardens.

34. *They gave him vinegar mingled with gall*—Out of derision : which, however nauseous, he received and tasted of. St. Mark mentions also a different
mixture which was given him, *Wine mingled with myrrh:* such as it was customary to give to dying criminals, to make them less sensible of their sufferings :
but this our Lord refused to taste, determining to bear the full force of his pains

35. *They parted his garments*—This was the custom of the Romans. The soldiers performed the office of executioners, and divided among them the spoils of
the criminals. *My vesture*—That is, my inner garment.

---

* Mark xv, 16 · John xix, 2.   † Mark xv, 22 ; Luke xxiii, 33 ; John xix, 17

fulfilled which was spoken by the prophet * They parted my gar-
36 ments among them, and for my vesture they cast lots. And sitting
37 down they guarded him there, And set up over his head his accusation written, THIS IS JESUS, THE KING OF THE JEWS.
38 † Then were two robbers crucified with him, one on the right hand
and one on the left.
39   And they that were passing by reviled him, wagging their heads
40 and saying, Thou that destroyest the temple, and buildest *it* in
three days, save thyself. If thou be the Son of God, come down
41 from the cross. In like manner the chief priests also with the
42 scribes and elders mocking *him*, said, He saved others : Cannot
he save himself ? If he be the King of Israel, let him now come
43 down from the cross, and we will believe him. He trusted in God :
let him deliver him now if he will have him ; for he said, I am the
44 Son of God. ‡ And even the robbers that were crucified with him,
cast the same reproach upon him.
45   Now from the sixth hour there was darkness over all the earth,
46 unto the ninth hour. And about the ninth hour, Jesus cried with a
loud voice, saying, § Eli, Eli, lama sabachthani ? That is, My
47 God, my God, why hast thou forsaken me ? Some of them that
48 stood there hearing *it*, said, He calleth Elijah. ‖ And immediately
one of them running and taking a sponge filled *it* with vinegar, and
49 putting *it* on a cane, gave him to drink. The rest said, Let be : let
us see whether Elijah will come to save him.
50   Jesus having cried again with a loud voice, dismissed *his* spirit.

---

45. *From the sixth hour, there was darkness over all the earth unto the ninth hour*
—Insomuch, that even a heathen philosopher seeing it, and knowing it could not
be a natural eclipse, because it was at the time of the full moon, and continued
three hours together, cried out, " Either the God of nature suffers, or the frame
of the world is dissolved."
By this darkness God testified his abhorrence of the wickedness which was then
committing. It likewise intimated Christ's sore conflicts with the Divine justice,
and with all the powers of darkness.
46. *About the ninth hour, Jesus cried with a loud voice*—Our Lord's great agony
probably continued these three whole hours, at the conclusion of which he thus
cried out, while he suffered from God himself what was unutterable. *My God,
my God, why hast thou forsaken me?*—Our Lord hereby at once expresses his trust
in God, and a most distressing sense of his letting loose the powers of darkness
upon him, withdrawing the comfortable discoveries of his presence, and filling his soul with a terrible sense of the wrath due to the sins which he was
bearing.
48. *One taking a sponge, filled it with vinegar*—Vinegar and water was the
usual drink of the Roman soldiers. It does not appear, that this was given him
in derision, but rather with a friendly design, that he might not die before Elijah
came.
50. *After he had cried with a loud voice*—To show that his life was still whole
in him *He dismissed his spirit*—So the original expression may be literally
translated : an expression admirably suited to our Lord's words, John x, 18 : *No
man taketh my life from me, but I lay it down of myself.* He died by a voluntary
act of his own, and in a way peculiar to himself. He alone of all men that ever
were, could have continued alive even in the greatest tortures, as long as he
pleased, or have retired from the body whenever he had thought fit. And how
does it illustrate that love which he manifested in his death ? Insomuch as he
did not use his power to quit his body, as soon as it was fastened to the cross,

* Psalm xxii, 18.   † Mark xv, 27 ; Luke xxiii, 32.   ‡ Mark xv, 32 ; Luke xxiii, 33.
§ Psalm xxii, 1.   ‖ John xix, 28.

51   And behold the veil of the temple was rent in twain from the top
to the bottom, and the earth was shaken and the rocks were torn
52 asunder: And the tombs were opened, and many bodies of holy
53 men that slept were raised, And coming out of the tombs after his
resurrection, went into the holy city and appeared to many.
54   And the centurion and they that were with him, guarding Jesus,
seeing the earthquake and the things that were done, feared greatly,
saying, Truly this was the Son of God.
55   And many women were there, beholding afar off, who had fol-
56 lowed Jesus from Galilee, serving him. Among whom were Mary
Magdalene, and Mary the mother of James and Joses, and the
mother of Zebedee's children.
57   * In the evening, there came a rich man of Arimathea, named
58 Joseph, who also himself was a disciple of Jesus. He going to
Pilate, asked the body of Jesus: then Pilate commanded the body
59 to be delivered. And Joseph taking the body wrapped it in clean
60 linen, And laid it in his own new tomb, which he had hewn out in
the rock, and having rolled a great stone to the door of the tomb,
61 departed. And Mary Magdalene was there and the other Mary,
sitting over against the sepulchre.
62   Now on the morrow, the *day* after the day of preparation, the

---

leaving only an insensible corpse, to the cruelty of his murderers: but continued
his abode in it, with a steady resolution, as long as it was proper. He then retired from it, with a majesty and dignity never known or to be known in any
other death: *dying*, if one may so express it, *like the Prince of life.*

51. Immediately upon his death, while the sun was still darkened, *the veil of
the temple,* which separated the holy of holies from the court of the priests, though
made of the richest and strongest tapestry, was rent in two from the top to the
bottom: so that while the priest was ministering at the golden altar (it being the
time of the sacrifice) the sacred oracle, by an invisible power was laid open to
full view: God thereby signifying the speedy removal of the veil of the Jewish
ceremonies, the casting down the partition wall, so that the Jews and Gentiles
were now admitted to equal privileges, and the opening a way through the veil
of his flesh for all believers into the most holy place. *And the earth was shaken—*
There was a general earthquake through the whole globe, though chiefly near
Jerusalem: God testifying thereby his wrath against the Jewish nation, for the
horrid impiety they were committing.

52. Some of the tombs were shattered and laid open by the earthquake, and
while they continued unclosed (and they must have stood open all the Sabbath,
seeing the law would not allow any attempt to close them) *many bodies of holy
men were raised,* (perhaps Simeon, Zacharias, John the Baptist, and others who
had believed in Christ, and were known to many in Jerusalem,) *And coming out
of the tombs after his resurrection, went into the holy city* (Jerusalem) *and appeared
to many*—Who had probably known them before: God hereby signifying, that
Christ had conquered death, and would raise all his saints in due season

54. *The centurion*—The officer who commanded the guard; *and they that were
with him feared, saying, Truly this was the Son of God*—Referring to the words
of the chief priests and scribes, ver. 43: *He said, I am the Son of God.*

56. *James*—The less: he was so called, to distinguish him from the other James,
the brother of John; probably because he was less in stature.

57. *When the evening was come*—That is, after three o'clock; the time from
three to six they termed the evening.

62. *On the morrow, the day that followed the day of the preparation*—The day
of preparation was the day before the Sabbath, whereon they were to prepare for
the celebration of it. The next day then was the Sabbath according to the Jews.

* Mark xv, 42; Luke xxiii, 50; John xix, 38.

63 chief priests and Pharisees were gathered together to Pilate, Saying, Sir, we remember that impostor said while he was yet alive,
64 After three days I will rise again. Command therefore that the sepulchre be secured till the third day, lest his disciples coming steal him away, and say to the people, He is risen from the dead;
65 so the last imposture shall be worse than the first. Pilate said to
66 them, Ye have a guard; go make *it* as secure as you can. So they went and secured the sepulchre, sealing the stone, and setting a guard.

XXVIII. * Now after the Sabbath, as it began to dawn toward the first *day* of the week, came Mary Magdalene and the other Mary,
2 to see the sepulchre. And behold there had been a great earthquake, and an angel of the Lord descending from heaven, had come and rolled away the stone from the door and sat upon it.
3 His countenance was like lightning, and his raiment white as
4 snow. And for fear of him the guards trembled, and became as
5 dead *men*. But the angel answering said to the women, Fear not
6 ye; for I know ye seek Jesus who was crucified. He is not here; for he is risen, as he said : come, see the place where the Lord
7 lay. And going quickly tell his disciples that he is risen from the dead. And behold he goeth before you into Galilee : there
8 shall ye see him. Lo, I have told you. And departing quickly from the sepulchre with fear and great joy, they ran to tell his
9 disciples. And behold Jesus met them and said, Hail. And they

But the evangelist seems to express it by this circumlocution, to show the Jewish Sabbath was then abolished.

63. *That impostor said, while he was yet alive, After three days I will rise again*—We do not find that he had ever said this to *them*, unless when *he spoke of the temple of his body*, John ii, 19, 21. And if they here refer to what he then said, how perverse and iniquitous was their construction on these words, when he was on his trial before the council? Chap. xxvi, 61. Then they seemed not to understand them!

65. *Ye have a guard*—Of your own, in the tower of Antonia, which was stationed there for the service of the temple.

66. *They went and secured the sepulchre, sealing the stone, and setting a guard*—They set Pilate's signet, or the public seal of the sanhedrim upon a fastening which they had put on the stone. And all this uncommon caution was overruled by the providence of God, to give the strongest proofs of Christ's ensuing resurrection; since there could be no room for the least suspicion of deceit, when it should be found, that his body was raised out of a new tomb, where there was no other corpse, and this tomb hewn out of a rock, the mouth of which was secured by a great stone, under a seal, and a guard of soldiers.

XXVIII. 2. *An angel of the Lord had rolled away the stone and sat upon it*—St. Luke and St. John speak of two angels that appeared : but it seems as if only one of them had appeared sitting on the stone without the sepulchre, and then going into it, was seen with another angel, sitting, one where the head, the other where the feet of the body had lain.

6. *Come, see the place where the Lord lay*—Probably in speaking he rose up, and going before the women into the sepulchre, said, Come, see the place. This clearly reconciles what St. John relates, xx, 12, this being one of the two angels there mentioned.

7. *There shall ye see him*—In his solemn appearance to them all together. But their gracious Lord would not be absent so long: he appeared to them several times before then. *Lo, I have told you*—A solemn confirmation of what he had said.

* Mark xvi, 1; Luke xxiv, 1; John xx, 1

coming to him took hold of his feet and worshipped him. Then
10 said Jesus to them, Fear not. Go, tell my brethren to go into
Galilee, and there shall they see me.
11 While they were going, behold some of the guard coming into
the city, told the chief priests all the things that had been done.
12 And having met together with the elders and consulted, they gave
13 much money to the soldiers, Saying, Say, his disciples came by
14 night, and stole him while we slept. And if the governor hear this
15 we will persuade him and secure you. So they taking the money
did as they were taught, and this saying is commonly reported
among the Jews till this day.
16 Then the eleven disciples went into Galilee to the mountain
17 where Jesus had appointed them. And when they saw him they
18 worshipped him, though some had doubted. And Jesus coming
spake to them, saying, All power is given me in heaven and in
19 earth: * Go ye and disciple all nations, baptizing them in the
name of the Father, and of the Son, and of the Holy Ghost:
20 Teaching them to observe all things whatsoever I have commanded
you; and lo, I am with you always, even to the end of the world.

9. *Hail*—The word in its primary sense means, "Rejoice:" in its secondary and more usual meaning, "Happiness attend you."

10. *Go tell my brethren*—I still own them as such, though they so lately disowned and forsook me.

13. *Say, his disciples came by night, and stole him while we slept*—Is it possible, that any man of sense should digest this poor, shallow inconsistency? If ye were awake, why did you let the disciples steal him? If asleep, how do you know they did?

16. *To the mountain where Jesus had appointed them*—This was probably Mount Tabor, where, (it is commonly supposed,) he had been before transfigured. It seems to have been here also, that he appeared to above five hundred brethren at once.

18. *All power is given to me*—Even as man. As God, he had all power from eternity.

19. *Disciple all nations*—Make them my disciples. This includes the whole design of Christ's commission. Baptizing and teaching are the two great branches of that general design. And these were to be determined by the circumstances of things; which made it necessary in baptizing adult Jews or heathens, to teach them before they were baptized; in discipling their children, to baptize them before they were taught; as the Jewish children in all ages were first circumcised, and after taught to do all God had commanded them.

* Mark xvi, 15.

NOTES

GOSPEL ACCORDING TO ST. MARK.

7

ST. MARK.

1 THE* beginning of the Gospel of Jesus Christ, the Son of God:
2 As it is written in the prophets, † Behold, I send my messenger
3 before thy face, who shall prepare thy way before thee. ‡ The
voice of one crying aloud in the wilderness, Prepare ye the way
4 of the Lord, make his paths straight. John was baptizing in the
wilderness and preaching the baptism of repentance, for the
5 remission of sins. And there went out to him all the country of
Judea, and all they of Jerusalem, and were baptized of him in the
6 river Jordan, confessing their sins. And John was clothed with
camels' hair, and with a leathern girdle about his loins, and ate
7 locusts and wild honey, And proclaimed, saying, There cometh after
me one mightier than I, the latchet of whose shoes I am not worthy
8 to stoop down and unloose. I indeed have baptized you with
9 water; but he will baptize you with the Holy Ghost. § And in
those days, Jesus came from Nazareth of Galilee, and was bap-
10 tized by John at Jordan. And coming up from the water, straightway he saw the heavens opened, and the Spirit as a dove descend-
11 ing upon him. And a voice came from heaven, saying, Thou art
12 my beloved Son, in whom I delight. ‖ And immediately the Spirit
13 thrusteth him out into the wilderness. And he was there in the
wilderness forty days, tempted by Satan; and was with the wild
beasts: and the angels served him.

Verse 1. *The beginning of the Gospel of Jesus Christ*—The evangelist speaks with strict propriety: for the beginning of the Gospel is in the account of John the Baptist, contained in the first paragraph; the Gospel itself in the rest of the book.

4. *Preaching the baptism of repentance*—That is, preaching repentance, and baptizing as a sign and means of it.

7. *The latchet of whose shoes I am not worthy to unloose*—That is, to do him the very meanest service.

12. *And immediately the Spirit thrusteth him out into the wilderness*—So in all the children of God, extraordinary manifestations of his favour are wont to be followed by extraordinary temptations.

13. *And he was there forty days, tempted by Satan*—Invisibly. ,After this followed the temptation by him in a visible shape, related by St. Matthew. *And he was with the wild beasts*—Though they had no power to hurt him. St. Mark not only gives us a compendium of St. Matthew's Gospel, but likewise several valuable particulars, which the other evangelists have omitted.

* Matt. iii, 1; Luke iii, 1.   † Mal. iii, 1.   ‡ Isa. xl, 3.   § Matt. iii, 13. Luke iii, 21.
  ‖ Matt. iv, 1; Luke iv, 1.

14 * Now after John was put in prison, Jesus came into Galilee,
15 preaching the Gospel of the kingdom of God, Saying, The time
    is fulfilled, and the kingdom of God is at hand: repent ye, and be-
16 lieve the Gospel. † And walking by the sea of Galilee, he saw
    Simon and Andrew his brother casting a net into the sea, (for they
17 were fishermen.) And Jesus said to them, Come ye after me, and
18 I will make you fishers of men. And straightway leaving their
19 nets, they followed him. And having gone thence a little farther,
    he saw James *the son* of Zebedee, and John his brother, who were
20 also in the vessel mending their nets: And he called them; and
    immediately leaving their father Zebedee in the vessel with the
    hired servants, they went after him.
21 ‡ And they go into Capernaum. And straightway on the Sab-
22 bath, he went into the synagogue and taught. And they were
    astonished at his teaching; for he taught them as one having au-
23 thority, and not as the scribes. And there was in their synagogue
24 a man having an unclean spirit, and he cried out, Saying, Let us
    alone: what have we to do with thee, Jesus of Nazareth? Art thou
25 come to destroy us? I know thee who thou art, the Holy One of
    God. And Jesus rebuked him, saying, Hold thy peace and come
26 out of him. And the unclean spirit having torn him, and cried with
27 a loud noise, came out of him. And they were all amazed, so that
    they questioned among themselves, saying, What is this? What
    new teaching *is* this? For with authority he commandeth even
28 the unclean spirits, and they obey him. And immediately his fame
    went forth into all the country of Galilee round about.
29 § And coming out of the synagogue, they entered forthwith into
30 the house of Simon and Andrew, with James and John. And
    Simon's wife's mother lay ill of a fever, and immediately they tell
31 him of her. And he came, and taking her by the hand, lifted her
    up; and straightway the fever left her, and she waited on them.
32 And in the evening, when the sun was set, they brought to him all
33 that were diseased, and them that were possessed with devils. And
34 the whole city was gathered together at the door. And he healed
    many that were ill of divers diseases, and cast out many devils, and
    suffered not the devils to say that they knew him.

---

15. *The time is fulfilled*—*The time* of my kingdom, foretold by Daniel, expected by you, *is fully come*.

18. *Straightway leaving their nets, they followed him*—From this time they for-sook their employ, and constantly attended him. Happy they who follow Christ at the first call!

26. *A loud noise*—For he was forbidden to speak. Christ would neither suffer those evil spirits to speak in opposition, nor yet in favour of him. He needed not their testimony, nor would encourage it, lest any should infer that he acted in concert with them.

32. *When the sun was set*—And, consequently, the Sabbath was ended, which they reckoned from sunset to sunset.

33. *And the whole city was gathered together at the door*—O what a fair pros-pect was here! Who could then have imagined that all these blossoms would die away without fruit?

34. *He suffered not the devils to say that they knew him*—That is, according to

35 * And·in the morning, rising a great while before day, he went
36 out and departed into a desert place, and prayed there. And Simon
37 and they that were with him followed after him. And having found
38 him, they say to him, All men seek thee. And he saith to them,
    Let us go to the neighbouring towns, that I may preach there also :
39 for therefore am I come. And he preached in their synagogues
    throughout all Galilee, and cast out devils.
40 † And there came to him a leper beseeching him, and kneeling
    down to him, and saying to him, If thou wilt thou canst make me
41 clean. And Jesus, moved with tender compassion, stretching out
    his hand, touched him, and saith to him, I will : be thou clean.
42 And when he had spoken, immediately the leprosy departed from
43 him, and he was made clean. And having straitly charged him,
44 he forthwith sent him away, And saith to him, See thou say
    nothing to any man : but go, show thyself to the priest, and offer
    for thy cleansing what Moses commanded for a testimony to them
45 But he going out published *it* much, and blazed abroad the matter,
    so he could no more openly enter into the city; but he was without
    in desert places : and they came to him from every quarter.
II. And again he entered into Capernaum after some days : and it
2   was heard that he was in the house. And many were gathered
    together, so that there was no room for *them*, no, not even about
3   the door. And he spake the word to them. ‡ And they came to
4   him, bringing a paralytic, borne of four. And not being able to
    come nigh him for the crowd, they uncovered the roof where he
    was, and having broken *it* up, they let down the couch whereon

Dr. Mead's hypothesis, (that the Scriptural demoniacs were only diseased persons,)
He suffered not the diseases to say that they knew him!
35. *Rising a great while before day*—So did he labour for us, both day
and night.
44. *See thou say nothing to any man*—But our blessed Lord gives no such
charge to *us*. If he has made us clean from our leprosy of sin, we are not commanded to conceal it. On the contrary, it is our duty to publish it abroad, both
for the honour of our Benefactor, and that others who are sick of sin may be encouraged to ask and hope for the same benefit. *But go, show thyself to the priest,*
and offer for thy cleansing what Moses commanded for a testimony to them—The
priests seeing him, pronouncing him clean, Lev. xiii, 17, 23, 28, 37, and accordingly allowing him to offer as Moses commanded, Lev. xiv, 2, 7, was such a proof
against them, that they durst never say the leper was not cleansed; which out
of envy or malice against our Saviour they might have been ready to say, upon
his presenting himself to be viewed, according to the law, if by the cleansed
person's talking much about his cure, the account of it had reached their ears
before he came in person. This is one great reason why our Lord commanded
this man to *say nothing*.
45. *So that Jesus could no more openly enter into the city*—It was also to prevent this inconvenience that our Lord had enjoined him silence.
II. 1. *And again*—After having been in desert places for some time, he
returned privately to the city. *In the house*—In Peter's house.
2. *And immediately many were gathered together*—Hitherto continued the
general impression on their hearts. Hitherto, even at Capernaum, all who heard
received the word with joy.
4. *They uncovered the roof*—Or, *took up the covering*, the lattice or trap door,
which was on all their houses, (being flat roofed.) And finding it not wide
enough, broke the passage wider, to let down the couch.

* Luke iv, 42.　† Matt. viii, 2 ; Luke v, 12.　‡ Matt. ix, 2 ; Luke v, 18.

5 the paralytic lay. Jesus seeing their faith, said to the paralytic,
6 Son, thy sins are forgiven thee. But certain of the scribes were
7 sitting there, and reasoning in their hearts, Why doth this *man*
8 thus speak blasphemies? Who can forgive sins, but God only?
And Jesus immediately knowing in his spirit that they so reasoned
in themselves, said to them, Why reason ye thus in your hearts?
9 Which is easier? To say to the paralytic, *Thy* sins are forgiven
10 thee? Or to say, Arise, and take up thy couch, and walk? But
that ye may know that the Son of man hath authority on earth to
11 forgive sins: (He saith to the paralytic) I say to thee, Arise,
12 take up thy couch, and go to thine house. And immediately he
arose, and taking up his couch, went forth before them all; so that
they were all amazed, and glorified God, saying, We never saw
it thus.
13   And he went forth again by the sea side, and all the multitude
14 came to him, and he taught them. * And passing by he saw Levi,
the *son* of Alpheus, sitting at the receipt of custom, and saith to
15 him, Follow me. And he arose and followed him. And as Jesus
sat at meat in his house, many publicans also and sinners sat together with Jesus and his disciples; for there were many, and they
16 followed him. And the scribes and Pharisees seeing him eating
with publicans and sinners, said to his disciples, How is it that
17 he eateth and drinketh with publicans and sinners? And Jesus
hearing *it* saith to them, They that are whole need not a physician
but they that are sick: I came not to call the righteous but sin
18 ners. † Now the disciples of John and the Pharisees used to fast:
and they come and say to him, Why do the disciples of John and
19 of the Pharisees fast, but thy disciples fast not? And Jesus said to
them, Can the children of the bride chamber fast while the bride-'
groom is with them? As long as they have the bridegroom with
20 them they cannot fast. But•the days will come, when the bridegroom shall be taken away from them; and then shall they fast in

---

6. *But certain of the scribes*—See whence the first offence cometh! As yet
not one of the plain unlettered people were offended. They all rejoiced in the
light, till these *men* of *learning* came, to put darkness for light, and light for
darkness. Wo to all such blind guides! Good had it been for these if they had
never been born. O God, let me never offend one of thy simple ones! Sooner
let my tongue cleave to the roof of my mouth!
    12. *They were all amazed*—Even the scribes themselves for a time.
    13. *All the multitude came to him*—Namely, *by the sea side*. And he as rea-
dily taught them there as if they had been in a' synagogue.
    15. *Many publicans and* notorious *sinners sat with Jesus*—Some of them
doubtless invited by Matthew, moved with compassion for his old companions in
sin. But the next words, *For there were many, and they followed him*, seem to imply,
that the greater part, encouraged by his gracious words and the tenderness of his
behaviour, and impatient to hear more, stayed for no invitation, but pressed in after
him, and kept as close to him as they could.
    16. *And the scribes and Pharisees said*—So now the wise men being joined by
the saints of the world, went a little farther in raising prejudices against our
Lord. In his answer he uses as yet no harshness, but only calm, dispassionate
reasoning.
    17. *I came not to call the righteous*—Therefore if these were righteous I should
not call them. But now, they are the very persons I came to save.

* Matt. ix, 9; Luke v, 27.   † Matt. ix, 14; Luke v, 33.

21 those days. No man seweth a piece of new cloth on an old garment: else the new piece that filleth it up taketh away from the
22 old, and the rent is made worse. And no man putteth new wine
into old leathern bottles; else the new wine bursteth the bottles,
and the wine is spilt, and the bottles are lost: but new wine must
be put into new bottles.
23 * And he went through the corn fields on the Sabbath day ·
24 and his disciples as they went plucked the ears of corn. And
the Pharisees said to him, Behold, why do they on the Sabbath
25 that which is not lawful? And he said to them, Have ye never
read what David did, when he had need and was hungry, he and
26 they that were with him? † How he went into the house of God
in *the days* of Abiathar the high priest, and ate the show bread,
which is not lawful for any but the priests to eat, and gave also to
27 them who were with him? And he said to them, The Sabbath was
28 made for man, and not man for the Sabbath. Moreover the Son of
man is Lord even of the Sabbath.
III.   ‡ And he entered again into the synagogue: and there was
2 a man there who had a withered hand. And they watched him
whether he would heal him on the Sabbath, that they might accuse
3 him. And he saith to the man that had the withered hand, Stand
4 up in the midst. And he saith to them, Is it lawful to do good on
the Sabbath, or to do evil? To save life, or to kill? But they held
5 their peace. And looking round upon them with anger, being
grieved for the hardness of their hearts, he saith to the man,
Stretch forth thine hand. And he stretched *it* forth: and his
6 hand was restored. And the Pharisees going out, straightway took
counsel with the Herodians against him, that they might destroy him.
7   Then Jesus withdrew with his disciples to the sea; and a great

---

26. *In the days of Abiathar the high priest*—Abimelech, the father of Abiathar, was high priest then; Abiathar himself not till some time after. This
phrase therefore only means, In the time of Abiathar, who was afterward the
high priest.
27. *The Sabbath was made for man*—And therefore must give way to man's
necessity.
28. *Moreover the Son of man is Lord even of the Sabbath*—Being the supreme
Lawgiver, he hath power to dispense with his own laws; and with this in particular.
III. *He entered again into the synagogue*—At Capernaum on the same day.
2. *And they*—The scribes and Pharisees, *watched him, that they might accuse
him*—Pride, anger, and shame, after being so often put to silence, began now to
ripen into malice.
4. *Is it lawful to save life or to kill?*—Which he knew they were seeking
occasion to do. *But they held their peace*—Being confounded, though not
convinced.
5. *Looking round upon them with anger, being grieved*—Angry at the sin,
grieved at the sinner; the true standard of Christian anger. But who can
separate anger at sin from anger at the sinner? None but a true believer
in Christ.
6. *The Pharisees going out*—Probably leaving the scribes to watch him still:
took counsel with the Herodians—as bitter as they usually were against each
other.

* Matt. xii, 1; Luke vi, 1.   † 1 Sam. xxi, 6.   ‡ Matt. xii, 9; Luke vi, 6.

8 multitude from Galilee followed him, and from Judea, And from
Jerusalem, and from Idumea, and from beyond Jordan; and they
about Tyre and Sidon, a great multitude, having heard what great
9 ·things he did, came to him. And he spake to his disciples, that a
vessel should wait on him, because of the multitude, lest they
10 should throng him. For he had healed many, so that they rushed
11 in upon him, as many as had plagues. And the unclean spirits,
when they saw him, fell down before him and cried, saying, Thou
12 art the Son of God. And he strictly charged them not to make
13 him known. * And he goeth up into the mountain, and calleth to
14 him whom he would, and they came to him. † And he ordained
twelve, that they might be with him, and that he might send them
15 forth to preach, And to have power to heal diseases and cast out
16 devils. And Simon he surnamed Peter: And James the *son* of
17 Zebedee, and John the brother of James (and he surnamed them
18 Boanerges, that ıs, sons of thunder) and Andrew and Philip, and
Bartholomew, and Matthew, and Thomas, and James the *son* of
19 Alpheus, and Thaddeus, and Simon the Canaanite, And Judas
Iscariot, who also betrayed him.
20   And they come into a house : and the multitude cometh toge-
21 ther again, so that they could not so much as eat bread. And his
relations hearing *of it*, came out to lay hold on him ; for they said,
22 He is beside himself. ‡ But the scribes who had come down
from Jerusalem said, He hath Beelzebub, and by the prince of the
23 devils casteth he out devils. And calling them to him, he said to
24 them in parables, How can Satan cast out Satan? If a kingdom
25 be divided against itself, that kingdom cannot stand. And if a
26 house be divided against itself, that house cannot stand. If Satan
then be risen up and divided against himself, he cannot stand, but
27 hath an end. None can enter into the strong one's house and

8. *From Idumea*—The natives of which had now professed the Jewish religion
above a hundred and fifty yeers. *They about Tyre and Sidon*—The Israelites
who lived in those coasts.
10. *Plagues* or *scourges* (so the Greek word properly means) seem to be those
very painful or afflictive disorders which were frequently sent, or at least permitted of God, as a scourge or punishment of sin.
12. *He charged them not to make him known*—It was not the time : nor were
they fit preachers.
13. *He calleth whom he would*—With regard to the eternal states of men, God
always acts as just and merciful. But with regard to numberless other things,
he seems to us to act as a mere sovereign.
16. *He surnamed them sons of thunder*—Both with respect to the warmth and
impetuosity of their spirit, their fervent manner of preaching, and the power of
their word.
20. *To eat bread*—That is, to take any subsistence.
21. *His relations*—His mother and his brethren, ver. 31. But it was some time
before they could come near him.
22. *The scribes* and Pharisees, Matt. xii, 22 ; *who had come down from Jerusalem*
—Purposely on the devil's errand. And not without success. For the common
people now began to drink in the poison, from these learned, good, honourable
men ! *He hath Beelzebub*—at command, is in league with him : *And by the prince
of the devils casteth he out devils*—How easily may a man of learning elude the
strongest proof of a work of God ! How readily can he account for every incident
without ever taking God into the question.

* Luke vi, 12.   † Matt. x, 2 ; Luke vi, 13 ; Acts i, 13.   ‡ Matt. xii, 24 ; Luke xi, 15.

plunder his goods, unless he first bind the strong one, and then he
28 will plunder his house. * Verily I say to you, All sins shall be
forgiven the sons of men, and blasphemies wherewith soever they
29 shall blaspheme, But he that shall blaspheme against the Holy
Ghost hath never forgiveness, but is liable to eternal damnation :
30 Because they said, He hath an unclean spirit. † Then come his
31 brethren and his mother, and standing without, sent to him, calling
32 him. And the multitude sat about him : and they say to him,
33 Behold, thy mother and thy brethren without seek for thee. And
he answered them, saying, Who is my mother or my brethren ?
34 And looking round on them who sat about him, he said. Behold my
35 mother and my brethren. For whosoever shall do the will of God,
the same is my brother and sister and mother.
IV. ‡ And again he taught by the sea side, and a great multitude
was gathered to him, so that going into the vessel, he sat in the
2 sea, and the whole multitude was by the sea on the land. And he
taught them many things by parables, and said to them in his
3 teaching, Hearken : Behold, a sower went out to sow. And as he
4 sowed, some fell by the highway side, and the birds came and
5 devoured it. And some fell on stony ground, where it had not
much earth : and immediately it sprung up, because it had no
6 depth of earth. But when the sun was up, it was scorched, and
7 because it had no root, it withered away. And some fell among
thorns, and the thorns grew up and choked it, and it yielded no
8 fruit. And other fell on good ground, and yielded fruit springing
up and increasing, and brought forth some thirty, and some sixty,
9 and some a hundred. And he said, he that hath ears to hear, let
him hear.

30. *Because they said, He hath an unclean spirit*—Is it not astonishing, that
men who have ever read these words, should doubt, what is the blasphemy
against the Holy Ghost ? Can any words declare more plainly, that it is "the
ascribing those miracles to the power of the devil which Christ wrought by the
power of the Holy Ghost ?"

31. *Then come his brethren and his mother*—Having at length made their way
through the crowd, so as to come to the door. His brethren are here named
first, as being first and most earnest in the design of taking him : for neither did
these of his brethren believe on him. They *sent to him, calling him*—They sent
one into the house, who called him aloud, by name.

34. *Looking round on them who sat about him*—With the utmost sweetness ;
He said, Behold my mother and my brethren—In this preference of his true disciples even to the Virgin Mary, considered merely as his mother after the flesh,
he not only shows his high and tender affection for them, but seems designedly
to guard against those excessive and idolatrous honours, which he foresaw would
in after ages be paid to her.

IV. 2. *He taught them many things by parables*—After the usual manner of
the eastern nations, to make his instructions more agreeable to them, and to impress them the more upon attentive hearers. A parable signifies not only a simile
or comparison, and sometimes a proverb, but any kind of instructive speech,
wherein spiritual things are explained and illustrated by natural, Prov. i, 6. *To
understand a proverb and the interpretation*—The proverb is the literal sense, the
interpretation is the spiritual ; resting in the literal sense killeth, but the spiritual
giveth life.

3. *Heark n*—This word he probably spoke with a loud voice, to stop the noise
and hurry of the people.

* Matt. xii, 31 ; Luke xii, 10.   † Matt. xii, 46 ; Luke viii, 19.   ‡ Matt. xiii, 1 ;
Luke viii, 4.

10 And when he was alone, they that were about him, with the
1 twelve, asked him of the parable. And he said to them, To you
it is given to know the mystery of the kingdom of God: but to
12 them that are without all things are in parables; So that seeing
they see, and do not perceive, and hearing they hear, and do not
understand; lest at any time they should be converted, and *their*
sins should be forgiven them.
13 And he saith to them, Know ye not this parable? How then
14 will ye know all parables? The sower soweth the word. And
15 these are they by the highway side, where the word is sown: but
when they have heard, Satan cometh immediately, and taketh
16 away the word sown in their hearts. And these are they likewise who have received the seed on stony ground, who when they
17 have heard the word immediately receive it with joy: But have
not root in themselves, but are only for a time, afterward, when
affliction or persecution ariseth because of the word, they are pre-
18 sently offended. And these are they that have received it among
19 thorns, who hear the word, And the cares of this world, and the
deceitfulness of riches, and the desire of other things entering in,
20 choke the word, and it becometh unfruitful. And these are they
that have received it on the good ground, who hear the word and
receive *it*, and bring forth fruit, some thirty *fold*, some sixty, and
21 some a hundred. * And he said to them, Is a candle brought to
be put under a bushel or under a bed, and not to be set on a candle-
22 stick? † For there is nothing hid, which shall not be made
manifest, neither was any thing kept secret, but that it might
23 come abroad. If any man hath ears to hear, let him hear. And
24 he said to them, Take heed what ye hear. With what measure
ye mete, it shall be measured to you, and to you that hear, shall
25 more be given. ‡ For he that hath, to him shall be given; and

---

10. *When he was alone*—That is, retired apart from the multitude.
11. *To them that are without*—So the Jews termed the heathens: so our Lord
terms all obstinate unbelievers: for they shall not enter into his kingdom: they
shall abide in outer darkness.
12. *So that seeing they see and do not perceive*—They would not see before
now they could not, God having given them up to the blindness which they
had chosen.
13. *Know ye not this parable?*—Which is as it were the foundation of all those
that I shall speak hereafter; and is so easy to be understood?
19. *The desire of other things choke the word*—A deep and important truth!
The desire of any thing, otherwise than as it leads to happiness in God, directly
tends to barrenness of soul. *Entering in*—Where they were not before. Let
him therefore who has received and retained the word, see that no other desire
then enter in, such as perhaps till then he never knew. *It becometh unfruitful*
—After the fruit had grown almost to perfection.
21. *And he said, Is a candle*—As if he had said, I explain these things to you,
I give you this light, not to conceal, but to impart it to others. And if I conceal any thing from you now, it is only that it may be more effectually manifested
hereafter.
24. *Take heed what ye hear*—That is, attend to what you hear, that it may
have its due influence upon you. *With what measure you mete*—That is, according to the improvement you make of what you have heard, still farther assistance
shall be given. *And to you that hear*—That is, with improvement.

* Matt. v, 15; Luke viii, 16; xi, 33.　† Matt. x, 26; Luke viii, 17.　‡ Matt. xiii, 12;
Luke viii, 18.

he that hath not, from him shall be taken even that which he hath.

26 And he said, So is the kingdom of God, as if a man should cast
27 seed into the ground, And should sleep and rise night and day,
28 and the seed should spring and grow up he knoweth not how. For the earth bringeth forth fruit of itself, first the ·blade, then the ear,
29 after that the corn in the ear. But when the fruit is brought forth, immediately he putteth in the sickle, because· the harvest is come.
30 *And he said, Whereto shall we liken the kingdom of God?
31 Or with what comparison shall we compare it? *It is* like a grain of mustard seed, which when it is sown in the earth, it is one of
32 the least seeds that is in the earth. But when it is sown it grow-eth up and becometh greater than all herbs, and putteth forth great branches, so that the birds of the air may lodge under the
33 shadow of it. And with many such parables spake he the word to
34 them, as they were able to hear. But without a parable spake he not to them : and in private he expounded all things to his disciples.
35 †And the same day in the evening he saith to them, Let us
36 go over to the other side. And having sent away the multitude, they take him as he was in the vessel. And there were with him
37 other little vessels. And there ariseth a great storm of wind, and
38 the waves beat into the vessel, so that it was now full. But he was asleep on the pillow, in the stern. And they awake him and
39 say to him, Master, carest thou not that we perish? And he arose and rebuked the wind, and said to the sea, Peace ; be still.
40 And the wind ceased, and there was a great calm. And he saith to them, Why are ye so fearful? How is it, that ye have not faith?
41 And they feared exceedingly, and said one to another, Who is this, that even the wind and the sea obey him?

25. *He that hath*—That improves whatever he has received, to the good of others, as well as of his own soul.

26. *So is the kingdom of God*—The inward kingdom is like seed *which a man casts into the ground*—This a preacher of the Gospel casts into the heart. And he *sleeps and rises night and day*—That is, he has it continually in his thoughts. Meantime *it springs and grows up he knows not how*—Even he that sowed it can-not explain how it grows. For as the earth by a curious kind of mechanism, which the greatest philosophers cannot comprehend, does as it were spontane-ously bring forth first the blade, then the ear, then the full corn in the ear : so the soul, in an inexplicable manner, brings forth, first weak graces, then stronger, then full holiness : and all this of itself, as a machine, whose spring of motion is within itself. Yet observe the amazing exactness of the comparison. The earth brings forth no corn (as the soul no holiness) without both the care and toil of man, and the benign influence of heaven.

29. *He putteth in the sickle*—God cutteth down and gathereth the corn into his garner.

33. *He spake the word as they were able to hear it*—Adapting it to the capacity of his hearers, and speaking as plain as he could without offending them. A rule never to be forgotten by those who instruct others.

36. *They take him as he was in the vessel*—They carried him immediately in the same vessel from which he had been preaching to the people.

38. *On the pillow*—So we translate it, for want of a proper English expression, for that particular part of the vessel near the rudder, on which he lay.

39. *Peace*—Cease thy tossing : *Be still*—Cease thy roaring ; literally, *Be thou gagged.*

* Matt. xiii, 31 ; Luke xiii, 18.   † Matt. viii, 23 ; Luke viii, 22.

V.   * And they came to the other side of the sea, into the country of
2 the Gadarenes. And as he came out of the vessel, there met him
3 immediately out of the tombs a man with an unclean spirit, Who
   had *his* dwelling in the tombs, and no man could bind him, no, not
4 with chains. For he had often been bound with fetters and chains,
   and the chains had been plucked asunder by him, and the fetters
5 broken in pieces ; and no man could tame him. And always, night
   and day, he was in the tombs and in the mountains, crying and cut-
6 ting himself with stones. But seeing Jesus afar off, he ran and
7 worshipped him, And crying with a loud voice, said, What have I
   to do with thee, Jesus, thou Son of the most high God ? I adjure
8 thee by God, that thou torment me not. (For he had said to
9 him, Come out of the man, thou unclean spirit.) And he asked
   him, What *is* thy name ? And he saith to him, My name is
10 Legion ; for we are many. And he earnestly besought him, that he
11 would not send them away out of the country. Now there was
12 there at the mountain a great herd of swine feeding. And all the
   devils besought him, saying, Send us to the swine, that we may go
13 into them, And Jesus forthwith gave them leave. And the unclean spirits going out, entered into the swine, and the herd rushed
   down the steep into the sea, (they were about two thousand,) and
14 were stifled in the sea. And they that fed the swine fled, and
   told *it* in the city and in the country. And they went out to see
15 what it was that was done. And they come to Jesus, and see the
   demoniac who had had the Legion, sitting and clothed and in his
16 right mind : and they were afraid. And they that saw *it* told them
17 how it befell the demoniac, and concerning the swine. And they
18 prayed him to depart out of their coasts. † And as he went into
   the vessel, he that had been possessed with the devils, besought
19 him that he might be with him. But he suffered him not, but said
   to him, Go home to thy friends, and tell them how great things the
20 .Lord hath done for thee, and hath had compassion on thee. And
   he departed and published in Decapolis, how great things Jesus
   had done for him. And all men marvelled.
21   ‡ And when Jesus was passed over again in the vessel to the
   other side, a great multitude was gathered to him, and he was
22 near the sea. § And there cometh one of the rulers of the syna-

---

V. 2. *There met him a man with an unclean spirit*—St. Matthew mentions two.
Probably this, so particularly spoken of here, was the most remarkably fierce
and ungovernable.
   9. *My name is Legion! for we are many*—But all these seem to have been
under one commander, who accordingly speaks all along, both for them and
himself.
   15. *And they were afraid*—It is not improbable they might otherwise have
offered some rudeness, if not violence.
   19. *Tell them how great things the Lord hath done for thee*—This was peculiarly needful there, where Christ did not go in person.
   20. *He published in Decapolis*—Not only at home, but in all that country
where Jesus himself did not come.
   22. *One of the rulers of the synagogue*—To regulate the affairs of every synagogue, there was a council of grave men. Over these was a president, who was

* Matt viii, 28 ; Luke viii, 26.   † Matt. ix, 1 ; Luke viii, 37.   ‡ Luke viii, 40.
§ Matt. ix, 18 ; Luke viii, 41.

23 gogue, Jairus by name, and seeing him, falleth at his feet, And
besought him greatly, saying, My little daughter is at the point cf
death: come and lay thy hands on her that she may be healed,
24 and she shall live. And he went with him, and a great multitude
25 followed him and thronged him. *And a certain woman who had
26 had a flux of blood twelve years, And had suffered many things
of many physicians, and had spent all that she had, and was
27 nothing bettered, but rather grown worse, Having heard of Jesus,
28 came in the crowd behind, and touched his garment. For she
29 said, If I but touch his clothes, I shall be whole. And the fountain
of her blood was straightway dried up, and she perceived in *her*
30 body that she was healed of that plague. And Jesus immediately
knowing in himself the virtue which had gone out of him, turning
31 about in the crowd said, Who touched my clothes? And his disciples said to him, Thou seest the multitude thronging thee, and
32 sayest thou, Who touched me? And he looked round to see
33 her that had done this. And the woman fearing and trembling,
knowing what was done in her, came and fell down before him,
34 and told him all the truth. And he said to her, Daughter, thy
faith hath made thee whole: go in peace, and continue whole of
35 thy plague. While he was yet speaking, they came from the ruler
of the synagogue's *house*, saying, Thy daughter is dead: why
36 troublest thou the Master farther? When Jesus heard the word
spoken, he saith to the ruler of the synagogue, Fear not; only
37 believe. And he suffered no man to follow him, save Peter, and
38 James, and John the brother of James. And he cometh to the
house of the ruler of the synagogue, and seeth a tumult, and them
39 that wept and wailed greatly. And coming in, he saith to them,
Why make ye this tumult and weep? The damsel is not dead,
40 but sleepeth. And they laughed him to scorn. But having put
them all out, he taketh the father and the mother of the damsel,
and them that were with him, and goeth in where the damsel was
41 lying. And taking the damsel by the hand, he said to her, Tali-
tha cumi, which is, being interpreted, Damsel (I say to thee) arise.
42 And straightway the damsel arose and walked: for she was twelve
years old. And they were astonished with a great astonishment.
43 And he charged them straitly, that no man should know it, and
commanded that something should be given her to eat.
VI.   † And he went out from thence, and came into his own coun-

termed *the ruler of the synagogue*. Sometimes there was no more than one
ruler in a synagogue.
37. *John, the brother of James*—When St. Mark wrote, not long after our
Lord's ascension, the memory of St. James, lately beheaded, was so fresh, that
his name was more known than that of John himself.
40. *Them that were with him*—Peter, James, and John.
43. *He charged them that no man should know it*—That he might avoid every
appearance of vain glory, might prevent too great a concourse of people, and
might not farther enrage the scribes and Pharisees against him; the time for his
death, and for the full manifestation of his glory, being not yet come. *He commanded something should be given her to eat*—So that when either natural or
spiritual life is restored, even by immediate miracle, all proper means are to be
used in order to preserve it.

* Matt. ix, 20; Luke viii, 43.   † Matt. xiii, 54; Luke iv, 16.

2 try, and his disciples follow him. And on the Sabbath he taught
in the synagogue, and many hearing were astonished, saying,
Whence hath this man these things? And what wisdom is this
that is given him, and such mighty works as are wrought by his
3 hands? Is not this the carpenter? The son of Mary, the brother
of James and Joses, and of Jude and Simon! Are not his sisters
4 here with us? And they were offended at him. And Jesus said to
them, A prophet is not without honour, but in his own country, and
5 among his own kindred, and in his own house. And he could do
no miracle there, save that he laid his hands on a few sick, and
6 healed them. And he marvelled because of their unbelief. And he
went round about through the villages teaching.
7 * And he called to him the twelve, and sent them forth by two
8 and two, and gave them power over unclean spirits; † And commanded them to take nothing for their journey, save a staff only;
9 no scrip, no bread, no money in their purse; But be shod with
10 sandals, and put not on two coats. ‡ And he said to them, Wheresoever ye enter into a house, there abide till ye depart from that
11 place. And whosoever shall not receive you, nor hear you, departing thence shake off the dust under your feet for a testimony
against them. Verily I say to you, it shall be more tolerable for
Sodom and Gomorrah in the day of judgment than for that city.
12 § And they went out and preached that men should repent. And
13 they cast out many devils, and ‖ anointed with oil many that were
sick, and healed *them.*
14 ** And King Herod heard (for his name was spread abroad) and

VI. 3. *Is not this the carpenter?*—There can be no doubt, but in his youth he
wrought with his supposed father Joseph.
5. *He could do no miracle there*—Not consistently with his wisdom and goodness. It being inconsistent with his wisdom to work them there, where it
could not promote his great end; and with his goodness, seeing he well knew
his countrymen would reject whatever evidence could be given them. And
therefore to have given them more evidence, would only have increased their
damnation.
6. *He marvelled*—As man. As he was God, nothing was strange to him.
8. *He commanded them to take nothing for their journey*—That they might be
always unincumbered, free, ready for motion. *Save a staff only*—He that had
one might take it; but he that had not was not to provide one, Matt. x, 9.
9. *Be shod with sandals*—As you usually are. Sandals were pieces of strong
leather or wood, tied under the sole of the foot by strings, something resembling
modern clogs. *The shoes* which they are in St. Matthew forbidden to take, were
a kind of short boots, reaching a little above the mid-leg, which were then com
monly used in journeys. Our Lord intended by this mission to initiate them into
their apostolic work. And it was doubtless an encouragement to them all their
life after, to recollect the care which God took of them, when they had left all
they had, and went out quite unfurnished for such an expedition. In this view
our Lord himself leads them to consider it, Luke xxii, 35: *When I sent you
forth without purse or scrip, lacked ye any thing?*
13. *They anointed with oil many that were sick*—Which St. James gives as a
general direction, (ch. v, 11, 15,) adding those peremptory words, *And the Lord
shall heal him*—He shall be restored to health: not by the natural efficacy of the
oil, but by the supernatural blessing of God. And it seems this was the great
standing means of healing desperate diseases in the Christian Church, long before *extreme unction* was used or heard of, which bears scarce any resemblance

* Matt. x, 1; Luke ix, 1.   † Matt. x, 9; Luke ix, 3.   ‡ Matt. x, 11; Luke ix, 4.
§ Luke ix, 6.   ‖ James v, 14, 15.   ** Matt. xiv, 1; Luke ix, 7.

he said, John the Baptist is risen from the dead, and therefore
15 these mighty powers exert themselves in him. Others say, It is
Elijah : and others said, It is a prophet, as one of the prophets.
16 But Herod hearing *thereof*, said, This is John whom I beheaded :
17 he is risen from the dead. For Herod himself had sent and apprehended John, and bound him in prison, for Herodias's sake, his
18 brother Philip's wife, for he had married her. For John had said
to Herod, It is not lawful for thee to have thy brother's wife.
19 Therefore Herodias was incensed against him, and was desirous to
20 have killed him ; but she could not : For Herod reverenced John,
knowing that he was a just and holy man, and preserved him :
and when he heard him he did many things, and heard him glad-
21 ly. And a convenient day being come, when Herod on his birthday made a feast for his lords, captains, and principal men of
22 Galilee : When the daughter of Herodias had come in and danced
and pleased Herod and his guests, the king said to the damsel,
23 Ask of me whatsoever thou wilt, and I will give *it* thee. And he
swore to her, Whatsoever thou shalt ask me, I will give thee,
24 to the half of my kingdom. And going out, she said to her mother, What shall I ask ? And she said, The head of John the Bap-
25 tist. And coming in quickly with haste to the king, she asked,
saying, I will that thou give me immediately in a charger the head
26 of John the Baptist. And the king was exceeding sorry : *yet*
for his oath's sake, and for the sake of his guests, he would not re-
27 ject her. And immediately the king sent one of his guard, and
28 commanded his head to be brought. And he went and beheaded
him in the prison, and brought his head in a charger, and gave it
29 to the damsel, and the damsel gave it to her mother. And the
disciples hearing *it*, came and took up his corpse and laid it in a
tomb.
30   * And the apostles gathered themselves together to Jesus, and
told him all things, both what they had done and what they had
31 taught. † And he said to them, Come ye yourselves apart into a
desert place, and rest a little. For there were many coming and
32 going, and they had no leisure so much as to eat. And they de-
33 parted into a desert place by boat privately. And many saw them

---

to it ; the former being used only as a means of health ; the latter only when life
is despaired of.
15. *A prophet, as one of the prophets*—Not inferior to one of the ancient
prophets.
16. *But Herod hearing thereof*—Of their various judgments concerning him,
still *said, It is John.*
20. *And preserved him*—Against all the malice and contrivances of Herodias.
And when he heard him—Probably sending for him, at times, during his imprisonment, which continued a year and a half. *He heard him gladly*—Delusive joy !
While Herodias lay in his bosom.
21. *A convenient day*—Convenient for her purpose. *His lords, captains, and
principal men of Galilee*—The great men of the court, the army, and the province.
23. *To the half of my kingdom*—A proverbial expression.
26. *Yet for his oath's sake, and for the sake of his guests*—Herod's honour was
like the conscience of the chief priests, Matt. xxvii, 6. To shed innocent blood
wounded neither one nor the other.
32. *They departed*—Across a creek or corner of the lake.

ᵉ Luke ix, 10.   † Matt. xiv, 13 ; John vi, 1.

departing and knew him, and ran on foot thither from all the cities,
34 and outwent them, and came together to him. And Jesus coming out saw a great multitude, and was moved with tender compassion for them: because they were as sheep having no shep-
35 herd, and he taught them many things. And when the day was now far spent, the disciples coming to him said, This is a desert
36 place, and it is now late, Send them away, that they may go into the country and villages round about, and buy themselves bread, for
37 they have nothing to eat. He answering said to them, Give ye them to eat. And they say to him, Shall we go and buy two hun-
38 dred pennyworth of bread, and give them to eat? He saith to them, How many loaves have ye? Go and see. And when they
39 knew, they said, Five, and two fishes. And he commanded them
40 to make all sit down by companies on the green grass. And they
41 sat down in ranks by hundreds and by fifties. And taking the five loaves and the two fishes, looking up to heaven he blessed, and brake the loaves, and gave *them* to his disciples to set before them ;
42 and he divided the two fishes among them all. And they all ate
43 and were satisfied. And they took up twelve baskets full of the
44 fragments and of the fishes. And they that had eaten of the loaves were about five thousand men.
45 　* And straightway he constrained his disciples to go into the vessel, and go before to the other side toward Bethsaida, while he sent
46 away the people. † And having sent them away, he went to the
47 mountain to pray, And in the evening the vessel was in the midst
48 of the sea, and he alone on the land. And he saw them toiling in .rowing; (for the wind was contrary to them;) and about the fourth watch of the night he cometh to them, walking on the sea, and
49 would have passed by them. But they seeing him walking on the
50 sea, supposed it to be an apparition, and cried out. (For they all saw him and were troubled.) And immediately he spoke with them,
51 and saith to them, Take courage: it is I ; be not afraid. And he went up to them into the vessel, and the wind ceased : and they
52 were amazed in themselves above measure and wondered. For they considered not *the miracle* of the loaves ; for their heart was hardened.
53 　‡ And having passed over, they came to the land of Gennesaret,
54 and drew to shore. And when they were come out of the vessel
55 they knew him, And ran through that whole country round about, and brought about in beds them that were ill, where they heard he
56 was. And wheresoever he entered into villages, cities, or country

---

34. *Coming out*—of the vessel.
40. *They sat down in ranks*—The word properly signifies a parterre or bed in a garden; by a metaphor, a company of men ranged in order, *by hundreds and by fifties*—That is, fifty in rank, and a hundred in file. So a hundred multiplied by fifty, make just five thousand.
43. *Full of the fragments*—of the bread.
45. *He constrained his disciples*—Who did not care to go without him.
48. *And he saw them*—For the darkness could veil nothing from him. *And would have passed by them*—That is, walked, as if he was passing by.
52. *Their heart was hardened*—And yet they were not reprobates. It means only, they were slow and dull of apprehension.

　* Matt. xiv, 22.　　† Matt. xiv, 23 ; John vi, 15.　　‡ Matt. xiv, 34 ; John vi, 21.

places, they laid the sick in the public places, and besought him that they might touch if it were but the hem of his garment; and as many as touched him were made whole.

VII. * Then assembled together to him the Pharisees and certain of
2 the scribes coming from Jerusalem. And they saw some of his
3 disciples eat bread with defiled, that is, unwashen hands. Now the Pharisees and all the Jews, except they wash *their* hands to the
4 wrist, eat not, holding the tradition of the elders. And *coming* from the market, unless they wash, they eat not: and many other things there are which they have received to hold, the washing of
5 cups and pots and brazen vessels and couches. Then the Pharisees and the scribes ask him, Why walk not thy disciples according to the tradition of the elders, but eat bread with defiled hands?
6 He answering said to them, Well hath Isaiah prophesied of you, hypocrites, as it is written, † This people honoureth me with their
7 lips, but their heart is far from me. But in vain do they worship
8 me, teaching for doctrines the commandments of men. For leaving the commandment of God, ye hold the tradition of men, the washing of pots and cups: and many other such like things ye do.
9 And he said to them, Full well ye abolish the commandments of
10 God, that ye may keep your own tradition. For Moses said,
‡ Honour thy father and thy mother, and, § Whoso revileth father
11 or mother, he shall surely die. But ye say, If a man shall say to his father or mother, *It is* Corban, that is, a gift, by whatsoever
12 thou mightest have been profited by me; *he shall be free.* And ye
13 suffer him no more to do aught for his father or his mother; Abrogating the word of God by your tradition which ye have delivered;
14 and many such like things ye do. And calling together all the multitude he said to them, Hearken to me every one of you and
15 consider. There is nothing entering into a man from without which can defile him; but the things which come out of him, these
16 are they that defile the man. If any man have ears to hear, let him
17 hear. And when he was come from the multitude into the house,
18 his disciples asked him concerning the parable. And he saith to them, Are even ye so without understanding? Do ye not perceive, that whatsoever entereth into a man from without cannot defile him,
19 Because it entereth not into his heart, but into the belly, and goeth
20 into the vault, purging all meats? And he said, That which com-
21 eth out of the man, that defileth the man. For from within, out of

---

VII. 1. *Coming from Jerusalem*—Probably on purpose to find occasion against him.
4. *Washing of cups and pots and brazen vessels and couches*—The Greek word (*baptisms*) means indifferently either washing or sprinkling. The cups, pots, and vessels were washed; the couches sprinkled.
5. *The tradition of the elders*—The rule delivered down from your forefathers.
15. *There is nothing entering into a man from without which can defile him*—Though it is very true, a man may bring guilt, which is moral defilement, upon himself, by eating what hurts his health, or by excess either in meat or drink; yet even here the pollution arises from the wickedness of the heart, and is just proportionable to it. And this is all that our Lord asserts.
19. *Purging all meats*—Probably the seat was usually placed over running water.

* Matt. xv, 1. † Isaiah xxix, 13. ‡ Exod. xx, 12. § Exod. xxi, 17.

ST. MARK.

the heart of man proceed evil thoughts, adulteries, fornications
22 murders, Thefts, covetousness, wickedness, deceit, lasciviousness
23 envy, evil speaking, pride, foolishness. All these evil things come
from within, and defile the man.
24 * And he arose and went thence into the borders of Tyre and
Sidon. And entering into a house he would have had no man
25 know *it ;* but he could not be hid. For a woman, whose young
daughter had an unclean spirit, having heard of him, came and fell
26 at his feet, (The woman was a Greek, a Syrophenician by nation,)
27 and besought him to cast the devil out of her daughter. But Jesus said to her, Let the children first be satisfied ; for it is not
28 right to take the children's bread and cast it to the dogs. She answered and said to him, True, Lord : yet the dogs under the table
29 eat of the children's crumbs. And he said to her, For this saying,
30 go : the devil is gone out of thy daughter. And going to her
house, she found her daughter lying on the bed, and the devil
gone out.
31 † And departing again from the borders of Tyre and Sidon, he
came to the sea of Galilee, through the midst of the country of De-
32 capolis. And they bring to him one that was deaf and dumb, and
33 beseech him to put his hand upon him. And taking him aside
from the multitude, he put his fingers into his ears, and spitting,
34 touched his tongue. And looking up to heaven, he groaned and
35 saith to him, Ephphatha, that is, Be opened. And straightway his
ears were opened, and the string of his tongue was loosed, and
36 he spake plain. And he charged them to tell no man ; but the
more he charged them, so much the more a great deal they pub-
37 lished *it.* And were beyond measure astonished, saying, He hath
done all things well : he maketh both the deaf to hear and the
dumb to speak.
VIII. ‡ In those days the multitude being very great, and having
2 nothing to eat, calling to him his disciples, he saith to them, I have
compassion on the multitude, because they continue with me now
3 three days and have nothing to eat. And if I send them away
fasting to their own home, they will faint by the way ; for divers
4 of them came from far. And his disciples answered him, Whence
can one satisfy these men with bread here in the wilderness ?

---

22. *Wickedness*—The word means ill natured, cruelty, inhumanity, and all
malevolent affections. *Foolishness*—Directly contrary to sobriety of thought and
discourse : all kind of wild imaginations and extravagant passions.
26. *The woman was a Greek* (that is, a Gentile, not a Jew) a Syrophenician
or Canaanite. Canaan was also called Syrophenicia, as lying between Syria,
properly so called, and Phenicia.
33. *He put his fingers into his ears*—Perhaps intending to teach us, that we are
not to prescribe to him (as they who brought this man attempted to do) but to
expect his blessing by whatsoever means he pleases : even though there should
be no proportion or resemblance between the means used, and the benefit to be
conveyed thereby.
34. *Ephphatha*—This was a word of SOVEREIGN AUTHORITY, not an
address to God for power to heal : such an address was needless ; for Christ had
a perpetual fund of power residing in himself, to work all miracles whenever he
pleased, even to the raising the dead, John v, 21, 26.
36. *Them*—The blind man and those that brought him.

* Matt. xv, 21.   † Matt. xv, 29.   ‡ Matt. xv, 32.

5 And he asked them. How many loaves have ɣe ?   And they said,
6 Seven.   And he commanded the multitude to sit down on the
ground ; and taking the seven loaves, having given thanks, he
brake and gave to his disciples to set before *them ;* and they did
7 set *them* before the people.   And they had a few small fishes : and
having blessed *them,* he commanded to set them also before *them.*
8 So they did eat and were satisfied ; and they took up fragments
9 that were left, seven baskets.   And they that had eaten were about
four thousand : and he sent them away.
10   And straightway going into the vessel with his disciples, he came
into the parts of Dalmanutha.
11   * And the Pharisees came forth and questioned with him, seeking
12 of him a sign from heaven, tempting him.   And sighing deeply in
his spirit, he said, Why doth this generation seek a sign ?   Verily
I say to you, There shall no sign be given to this generation
13 † And he left them ; and going into the vessel again, went to the
other side.
14   Now they had forgotten to take bread ; nor had they in the vessel
15 with them any more than one loaf.   And he charged them, saying,
Take heed, beware of the leaven of the Pharisees and the leaven
16 of Herod.   And they reasoned among themselves, saying, We
17 have no bread.   And Jesus knowing *it,* said to them, Why reason
ye because ye have no bread ?   Perceive ye not yet, neither con-
18 sider ?   Have ye your heart yet hardened ?   Having eyes, see ye
19 not ?   And having ears, hear ye not ?   And do not ye remember ?
When I brake the five loaves among the five thousand, how many
baskets full of fragments took ye up ?   They say to him, Twelve.
20 And when the seven among the four thousand, how many baskets
21 full of fragments took ye up ?   And they said, Seven.   And he said
to them, How is it that ye do not understand ?
22   And he cometh to Bethsaida.   And they bring to him a blind
23 man, and beseech him to touch him.   And taking the blind man
by the hand, he led him out of the town, and having spit on his

---

VIII. 8. *So they did eat*—This miracle was intended to demonstrate, that
Christ was the true bread which cometh down from heaven ; for he who was almighty to create bread without means to support natural life, could not want
power to create bread without means to support spiritual life.   And this heavenly
bread we stand so much in need of every moment, that we ought to be always
praying, Lord, evermore give us this bread.
11. *Tempting him*—That is, trying to ensnare him.
12. *Why doth this generation*—(that is, these scribes and Pharisees) *seek a sign ?*
Not out of sincerity but out of hypocrisy.
15. *Beware of the leaven of the Pharisees and of Herod,* or of the Sadducees ;
two opposite extremes.
17, 18. Our Lord here affirms of all the apostles, (for the question is equivalent to an affirmation,) That their *hearts were hardened ; that having eyes they
saw not, having ears they heard not ; that they did not consider, neither understand :* the very same expressions that occur in the thirteenth of Matthew.   And
yet it is certain they were not judicially hardened.   Therefore all these strong
expressions do not necessarily import any thing more than the present want of
spiritual understanding.
23. *He led him out of the town*—It was in just displeasure against the inhabit
ants of Bethsaida for their obstinate infidelity, that our Lord would work no more

* Matt. xvi, 1.   † Matt. xvi, 4.

eves, and put *his* hands upon him, he asked him if he saw aught?
24 And looking up he said, I see men as trees walking. Then he
25 put his hands again on his eyes, and made him look up, and
°6 he was restored, and saw all men clearly. And he sent him away
to his house, saying, Neither go into the town, nor tell *it* to any in
the town.
27   * And Jesus went out and his disciples into the towns of Cesarea, Philippi. And in the way he asked his disciples, saying to
28. them, Whom do men say that I am? And they answered, John the
Baptist; but some *say* Elijah; and others, one of the prophets.
29 And he saith to them, But whom say ye that I am? And Peter
30 answering, saith to him, Thou art the Christ. And he charged
them that they should tell no man of him.
31   † And he began to teach them, that the Son of man must suffer
many things, and be rejected by the elders and the chief priests
32 and scribes, and be killed, and after three days rise again. And
33 he spake that saying openly. And Peter taking hold of him,
rebuked him. But he turning about, and looking on his disciples,
rebuked Peter, saying, Get thee behind me, Satan; for thou savourest not the things of God, but the things of men.
34   And when he had called the people to him, with his disciples
also, he said to them, Whosoever is willing to come after me, let
him deny himself, and take up his cross and follow me.
35   ‡ For whosoever desireth to save his life shall lose it; but
whosoever shall lose his life, for my sake and the Gospel's, shall
36 save it. For what shall it profit a man, if he shall gain the whole
37 world, and lose his own soul? Or what shall a man give in exchange
38 for his soul? § For whosoever shall be ashamed of me and of
my words in this adulterous and sinful generation, of him shall also
the Son of man be ashamed, when he cometh in the glory of his
Father, with the holy angels.

miracles among them, nor even suffer the person he had cured, either to go into
the town, or to tell it to any therein.
    24. *I see men as trees walking*—He distinguished men from trees only by
their motion.
    30. He enjoined them silence for the present, 1. That he might not encourage
the people to set him up for a temporal king; 2. That he might not provoke the
scribes and Pharisees to destroy him before the time; and, 3. That he might not
forestall the bright evidence which was to be given of his Divine character after
his resurrection.
    32. *He spake that saying openly*—Or in express terms. Till now he had only
intimated it to them. *And Peter taking hold of him*—Perhaps by the arms
or clothes.
    33. *Looking on his disciples*—That they might the more observe what he said
to Peter.
    34. *And when he called the people*—To hear a truth of the last importance, and
one that equally concerned them all. *Let him deny himself*—His own will, in
all things small and great, however pleasing, and that continually: *And take up
his cross*—Embrace the will of God, however painful, daily, hourly, continually.
Thus only can he follow me in holiness to glory.
    38. *Whosoever shall be ashamed of me and of my words*—That is, avowing
whatever I have said (particularly of self denial and the daily cross) both by
word and action.

IX.   And he said to them, Verily I say unto you, there are some of
them that stand here, who shall not taste of death till they see the
kingdom of God coming with power.

2   * And after six days Jesus taketh with him Peter and James
and John, and carrieth them up into a high mountain, by them-
3 selves apart, and was transfigured before them.   And his garments
became shining exceeding white, as snow, such as no fuller on
4 earth can whiten.   And there appeared to them Elijah with Moses,
5 and they were talking with Jesus.   And Peter answering, saith to
Jesus, Master, it is good for us to be here ; and let us make three
6 tents, one for thee, and one for Moses, and one for Elijah.   For
7 he knew not what to say ; for they were sore afraid.   And there
came a cloud overshadowing them, and a voice came out of the
8 cloud, saying, This is my beloved Son; hear ye him.   And suddenly
looking round, they saw no man any more, save Jesus only, with
9 themselves.   And as they came down from the mountain, he
charged them to tell no man the things they had seen, till the
10 Son of man were risen from the dead.   And they laid hold on that
saying, questioning one with another, What meaneth, Till he were
11 risen from the dead?   And they asked him, saying, Why say the
12 scribes that Elijah must come first?   And he answering, told
them, Elijah verily coming first, restoreth all things ; and how it
is written of the Son of man that he must suffer many things,
13 and be set at nought.   But I say to you, Elijah is come, as it
is written of him: and they have done to him whatsoever they
listed.

14   † And coming to *his* disciples, he saw a great multitude about
15 them, and scribes questioning with them.   And straightway all
the multitude seeing him, were greatly amazed, and running to

IX. 1. *Till they see the kingdom of God coming with power*—So it began
to do at the day of pentecost, when three thousand were converted to God
at once.

2. *By themselves*—That is, separate from the multitude : *Apart*—From the
other apostles : *and was transfigured*—The Greek word seems to refer to the
form of God, and the form of a servant, (mentioned by St. Paul, Phil. ii, 6, 7,)
and may intimate, that the Divine rays, which the indwelling God let out on this
occasion, made the glorious change from one of these forms into the other.

3. *White as snow, such as no fuller can whiten*—Such as could not be equalled
either by nature or art.

4. *Elijah*—Whom they expected : *Moses, whom they did not.*

7. *There came a* (bright, luminous) *cloud, overshadowing them*—This seems
to have been such a cloud of glory as accompanied Israel in the wilderness,
which, as the Jewish writers observe, departed at the death of Moses.   But
it now appeared again, in honour of our Lord, as the great Prophet of the
Church, who was prefigured by Moses. *Hear ye him*—Even preferably to Moses
and Elijah.

12. *Elijah verily coming first restoreth all things : and how it is written*—That
is, *And* he told them *how it is written*—As if he had said, Elijah's coming is not
inconsistent with my suffering.   He is come : yet I shall suffer.   The first part
of the verse answers their question concerning Elijah ; the second refutes their
error concerning the Messiah's continuing for ever.

15. *All the multitude seeing him were greatly amazed*—At his coming so suddenly, so seasonably, so unexpectedly : perhaps also at some unusual rays of
majesty and glory, which yet remained on his countenance.

* Matt. xvii 1 ; Luke ix, 28.   † Matt. xvii, 14 ; Luke ix, 37.

118   ST. MARK.

16 him, saluted him. And he asked the scribes, What question ye
17 with them? And one of the multitude answering said, Master, I
18 have brought to thee my son, who hath a dumb spirit. And where
   soever he taketh him, he teareth him, and he foameth and gnasheth
   with his teeth, and pineth away. And I spake to thy disciples
19 to cast him out, and they could not. He answering them, saith,
   O faithless generation, how long shall I be with you? How long
20 shall I suffer you? Bring him to me. And they brought him to
   him. And when he saw him, immediately the spirit tore him,
21 and he fell on the ground, and wallowed, foaming. And he asked
   his father, How long is it since this came to him? And he said,
22 From a little child. And it hath often cast him both into the fire
   and into the waters to destroy him; but if thou canst do any thing,
23 have compassion on us and help us. Jesus saith to him, If thou
24 canst believe, all things are possible to him that believeth. And
   straightway the father of the child crying out, said with tears,
25 Lord, I do believe: help thou mine unbelief. And Jesus seeing
   that the multitude came running together, rebuked the unclean
   spirit, saying to him, Thou deaf and dumb spirit, I command thee,
26 come out of him, and enter no more into him. And having cried
   and rent him sore, he came out; and he was as dead, so that many
27 said, He is dead. But Jesus taking him by the hand, lifted him up,
   and he arose.
28   And when he was come into a house, his disciples asked him
29 privately, Why could not we cast him out? And he said to them,
   This kind can come forth by nothing but by prayer and fasting.
30   * And departing thence, they passed through Galilee, and he
31 was not willing that any should know it. For he taught his disciples, and said to them, The Son of man is delivered into the hands
   of men; and they will kill him, and after he hath been killed,

17. *And one of the multitude answering*—The scribes gave no answer to our
Lord's question. They did not care to repeat what they had said to his disciples.
A dumb spirit—A spirit that takes his speech from him.
20. *When he saw him*—When the child saw Christ; when his deliverance was
at hand. *Immediately the spirit tore him*—Made his last grand effort to destroy
him. Is it not generally so, before Satan is cast out of a soul, of which he has
long had possession?
22. *If thou canst do any thing*—In so desperate a case: *Have compassion on
us*—Me as well as him.
23. *If thou canst believe*—As if he had said, The thing does not turn on my
power, but on thy faith. *I* can do all things: canst *thou* believe?
24. *Help thou mine unbelief*—Although my faith be so small, that it might
rather be termed unbelief, yet help me.
25. *Thou deaf and dumb spirit*—So termed, because he made the child so.
When Jesus spake, the devil heard, though the child could not. *I command
thee*—I myself now; not my disciples.
26. *Having rent him sore*—So does even the body sometimes suffer, when God
comes to deliver the soul from Satan.
30. *They passed through Galilee*—Though not through the cities, but by them,
in the most private ways. *He was not willing that any should know it: for he
taught his disciples*—He wanted to be alone with them some time, in order to
instruct them fully concerning his sufferings. *The Son of man is delivered*—It
is as sure as if it were done already.

* Matt. xvii, 22; Luke ix, 44.

32 he shall rise the third day. But they understood not the word, and were afraid to ask him.
33 * And he came to Capernaum. And being in the house, he asked them, What was it ye disputed among yourselves by the
34 way? But they held their peace; for they had been debating
35 among themselves in the way, who *should* be greatest. And sitting down, he called the twelve, and saith to them, If any man desire to be the first, let him be least of all, and the servant of
36 all. † And taking a little child, he set him in the midst· of
37 them, and taking him up in his arms, he said to them, Whosoever shall receive one such little child in my name, receiveth me; and whosoever shall receive me, receiveth not *only* me, but him that sent me.
38 ‡ And John answered him, saying, Master, we saw one casting out devils in thy name, who followeth not us, and we forbad him,
39 because he followeth not us. And Jesus said, Forbid him not; for there is no one who shall do a miracle in my name, that can readily
40 speak evil of me. For he that is not against you is for you,
41 § For whosoever shall give you a cup of cold water to drink in my name, because ye belong to Christ, verily I say to you, he shall in nowise lose his reward.

---

32. *They understood not the word*—They did not understand how to reconcile the death of our Saviour (nor consequently his resurrection, which supposed his death) with their notions of his temporal kingdom.
34. *Who should be greatest*—Prime minister in his kingdom.
35. *Let him be the least of all*—Let him abase himself the most.
37. *One such little child*—Either in years or in heart.
38. *And John answered him*—As if he had said, But ought we to receive those who *follow not us?* *Master, we saw one casting out devils in thy name*—Probably this was one of John the Baptist's disciples, who believed in Jesus, though he did not yet associate with our Lord's disciples. *And we forbad him, because he followeth not us*—How often is the same temper found in *us?* How readily do we also *lust to envy?* But how does that spirit become a disciple, much more a minister of the benevolent Jesus! St. Paul had learnt a better temper, when he *rejoiced that Christ was preached*, even by those who were his personal enemies. But to confine religion to them that follow us, is a narrowness of spirit which we should avoid and abhor.
39. *Jesus said*—Christ here gives us a lovely example of candour and moderation. He was willing to put the best construction on doubtful cases, and to treat as friends those who were not avowed enemies. Perhaps in this instance it was a means of conquering the remainder of prejudice, and perfecting what was wanting in the faith and obedience of these persons. *Forbid him not*—Neither directly nor indirectly discourage or hinder any man who brings sinners from the power of Satan to God, *because he followeth not us*, in opinions, modes of worship, or any thing else which does not affect the essence of religion.
40. *For he that is not against you, is for you*—Our Lord had formerly said, He that is not with me, is against me: thereby admonishing his hearers, that the war between him and Satan admitted of no neutrality, and that those who were indifferent to him now, would finally be treated as enemies. But here in another view, he uses a very different proverb; directing his followers to judge of men's characters in the most candid manner; and charitably to hope that those who did not oppose his cause wished well to it. Upon the whole, we are to be rigorous in judging ourselves, and candid in judging each other.
41. *For whosoever shall give you a cup*—Having answered St. John, our Lord here resumes the discourse which was broken off at the 37th verse.

* Luke ix, 46.   † Matt. xviii 2; Luke ix, 47.   ‡ Luke ix, 49.   § Matt. x, 42.

42   *And whosoever shall offend one of the little ones that believe in me, it were better for him that a millstone were hanged about
43 his neck, and he were cast into the sea. †And if thy hand cause thee to offend, cut it off: it is good for thee to enter into life maimed, rather than having two hands, to go into hell, into the fire that
44 never shall be quenched: ‡Where their worm dieth not, and the
45 fire is not quenched. And if thy foot cause thee to offend, cut it off: it is good for thee to enter halt into life, rather than having two feet to be cast into hell, into the fire that never shall be quench-
46 ed: Where their worm dieth not, and the fire is not quenched.
47 And if thine eye cause thee to offend, pluck it out: it is good for thee to enter into the kingdom of God having one eye, rather
48 than having two eyes to be cast into hell fire: Where their worm
49 dieth not, and the fire is not quenched. For every one shall be
50 salted with fire, and every sacrifice shall be salted with salt. § Salt *is* good: but if the salt have lost its saltness, wherewith will ye season it? Have salt in yourselves, and have peace one with another.

X. ‖And he arose and cometh thence into the coasts of Judea, through the country beyond Jordan: and the multitudes resort to
2 him again, and as he was wont, he taught them again. **And the Pharisees coming, asked him, Is it lawful for a man to put away

42. On the contrary, *whosoever shall offend* the very least Christian.
43. *And if* a person *cause thee to offend*—(The discourse passes from the case of offending, to that of being offended) if one who is as useful or dear to thee as a hand or eye, hinder or slacken thee in the ways of God, renounce all intercourse with him. This primarily relates to persons, secondarily to things.
44. *Where their worm*—That gnaweth the soul, (pride, self will, desire, malice, envy, shame, sorrow, despair,) *dieth not*—No more than the soul itself: *and the fire* (either material, or infinitely worse!) that tormenteth the body, *is not quenched* for ever.
49. *Every one*—Who does not cut off the offending member, and consequently is cast into hell, *shall be*, as it were, *salted with fire*, preserved, not consumed thereby; *whereas every* acceptable *sacrifice shall be salted with* another kind of *salt*, even that of Divine grace, which purifies the soul, (though frequently with pain) and preserves it from corruption.
50. Such *salt is good* indeed; highly beneficial to the world, in respect of which I have termed you the *salt of the earth. But if the salt* which should season others, *have lost its own saltness, wherewith will ye season it?*—Beware of this; see that ye retain your savour; and as a proof of it, *have peace one with another.*
   More largely this obscure text might be paraphrased thus :—
   As every burnt offering was salted with salt, in order to its being cast into the fire of the altar, so every one who will not part with his hand or eye, shall fall a sacrifice to Divine justice, and be cast into hell fire, which will not consume, but preserve him from a cessation of being. And on the other hand, every one, who, denying himself and taking up his cross, offers up himself as a living sacrifice to God, shall be seasoned with grace, which like salt will make him savoury, and preserve him from destruction for ever.
   As *salt is good* for preserving meats, and making them savoury, so it is good that ye be seasoned with grace, for the purifying your hearts and lives, and for spreading the savour of my knowledge, both in your own souls, and wherever ye go. But as salt if it loses its saltness is fit for nothing, so ye, if ye lose your faith and love, are fit for nothing but to be utterly destroyed. See therefore that grace abide in you, and that ye no more contend, *Who shall be greatest.*
   X. 1. *He cometh thence*—From Galilee.

  * Matt. xviii, 6; Luke xvii, 1. † Matt. v, 29; xviii, 8. ‡ Isa. lxvi, 24. § Matt. v, 13; Luke xiv, 34. ‖ Matt xix, 1. ** Ma t. v, 31; xix, 7; Luke xvi, 18

3 his wife? tempting him. And he answering, said to them,
4 What did Moses command you? They said, * Moses suffered to
5 write a bill of divorce, and to put *her* away. And Jesus answering, said to them, For your hardness of heart he wrote you this
6 precept. But from the beginning of the creation God made them
7 male and female. † For this cause shall a man leave his father
8 and mother, and cleave to his wife; And they twain shall be one
9 flesh; so then they are no more twain but one flesh. What there-
10 fore God hath joined together, let not man put asunder. And in the
11 house his disciples asked him again of the same matter. And he
saith to them, Whosoever shall put away his wife and marry an-
12 other, committeth adultery against her. And if a woman shall put
away her husband, and be married to another, she committeth
adultery.
13 ‡ And they brought little children to him that he might touch
14 them; but the disciples rebuked those that brought *them*. But Jesus
seeing *it*, was much displeased, and said to them, Suffer the little
children to come to me, and forbid them not; for of such is the
15 kingdom of God. Verily I say to you, Whosoever shall not receive
the kingdom of God as a little child, he shall in nowise enter
16 therein. And taking them up in his arms, he put his hands upon
them, and blessed them.
17 § And as he was going out into the way, one running and kneeling to him, asked him, Good Master, what shall I do that I may
18 inherit eternal life? But Jesus saith to him, Why callest thou me
19 good? *There is* none good but one, *that is* God. Thou knowest
the commandments, Do not commit adultery, Do not murder, Do
not steal, Do not bear false witness, Defraud not, Honour thy
20 father and mother. And he answering, said to him, Master, all
21 these have I kept from my childhood. Then Jesus looking upon
him, loved him, and said to him, One thing thou lackest: Go, sell
whatsoever thou hast, and give to the poor, and thou shalt have
treasure in heaven : and come, follow me, taking up thy cross.

6. *From the beginning of the creation*—Therefore Moses in the first of Genesis
gives us an account of things from *the beginning of the creation.* Does it not
clearly follow, that there was no creation previous to that which Moses describes?
God made them male and female—Therefore Adam did not at first contain both
sexes in himself: but God made Adam, when first created, male only; and Eve
female only. And this man and woman he joined together, in a state of innocence, as husband and wife.
11, 12. All polygamy is here totally condemned.
14. *Jesus seeing it was much displeased*—At their blaming those who were not'
blame worthy : and endeavouring to hinder the children from receiving a blessing. *Of such is the kingdom of God*—The members of the kingdom which I am
come to set up in the world are such as these, as well as grown persons, of a
child-like temper.
15. *Whosoever shall not receive the kingdom of God as a little child*—As totally
disclaiming all worthiness and fitness, as if he were but a week old.
20. *He answering, said to him, Master*—He stands reproved now, and drops the
epithet *good.*
21. *Jesus looking upon him*—And looking into his heart, *loved him*—Doubtless
for the dawnings of good which he saw in him : *and said to him*—Out of tender
love, *One thing thou lackest*—The love of God, without which all religion is a

* Deut. xxiv. 1. † Gen. ii, 24. ‡ Matt. xix, 13. § Matt. xix, 16; Luke xviii, 18

122   ST. MARK.

22 But he was sad at that saying, and went away grieved; for he had
23 great possessions. And Jesus looking round said to his disciples, How hardly shall they that have riches enter into the kingdom of
24 God? And the disciples were astonished at his words. But Jesus answering again saith to them, Children, how hard is it for
25 them that trust in riches to enter into the kingdom of God? It is easier for a camel to go through the eye of a needle, than for a
26 rich man to enter into the kingdom of God. And they were astonished out of measure, saying to each other, Who then can be
27 saved? And Jesus looking upon them, said, With men *it is* impos-
28 sible, but not with God, for with God all things are possible. And
29 Peter said to him, Lo, we have left all and followed thee. And Jesus answering said, Verily I say to you, there is none that hath left house, or brethren, or sisters, or father, or mother, or wife, or
30 children, or lands, for my sake and the Gospel's, But he shall receive a hundred fold now in this time, houses and brethren and sisters and mothers and children and lands with persecutions, and
31 in the world to come eternal life. But many *that are* first shall be last, and the last first.
32   * And they were in the way going up to Jerusalem, and Jesus went before them. And they were amazed, and as they followed, they were afraid. And taking the twelve again he told them what
33 things were to befall him: Behold, we go up to Jerusalem, and the Son of man shall be betrayed to the chief priests, and the scribes: and they will condemn him to death, and deliver him to the Gen-
34 tiles. And they will mock him and scourge him and spit upon him and kill him. And the third day he will rise again.
35   † And James and John the sons of Zebedee come to him, saying, Master, we would that thou shouldest do for us whatever we shall
36 ask. And he said to them, What would ye that I should do for
37 you? They said to him, Grant us to sit one on thy right hand,
38 and one on thy left hand, in thy glory. But Jesus said to them,

---

dead carcass. In order to this, throw away what is to thee the grand hinderance of it. Give up thy great idol, riches. *Go, sell whatsoever thou hast.*

24. *Jesus saith to them, Children*—See how he softens the harsh truth, by the manner of delivering it! And yet without retracting or abating one tittle: *How hard is it for them that trust in riches*—Either for defence, or happiness, or deliverance from the thousand dangers that life is continually exposed to. That these cannot enter into God's glorious kingdom, is clear and undeniable: but *it is easier for a camel to go through a needle's eye,* than for a man to have riches, and not trust in them. Therefore, *it is easier for a camel to go through the eye of a needle, than for a rich man to enter the kingdom.*

28. *Lo, we have left all*—Though the young man would not.

30. *He shall receive a hundred fold, houses, &c.*—Not in the same kind: for it will generally be *with persecutions:* but in value: a hundred fold more happiness than any or all of these did or could afford. But let it be observed, none is entitled to this happiness, but he that will accept it *with persecutions.*

32. *They were in the way to Jerusalem, and Jesus went before them: and they were amazed*—At his courage and intrepidity, considering the treatment which he had himself told them he should meet with there: *and as they followed, they were afraid*—Both for him and themselves: nevertheless he judged it best to prepare them, by telling them more particularly what was to ensue.

35. *Saying*—By their mother. It was she, not they that uttered the words.

* Matt. xx, 17; Luke xviii, 31.   † Matt. xx, 20.

Ye know not what ye ask. Can ye dri ık of the cup that I drink
39 of, and be baptized with the baptism that I am baptized with ? And
they said to him, We can. And Jesus said to them, Ye shall indeed drink of the cup that I drink of, and be baptized with the
40 baptism that I am baptized with. But to sit on my right hand
and on my left, is not mine to give, save to them for whom it is
41 prepared. And the ten hearing *it* were much displeased concern-
42 ing James and John. But Jesus calling them to him, saith unto
them, Ye know that they who rule over the Gentiles, lord it over
43 them, and their great ones exercise authority upon them. But it
shall not be so among you ; but whosoever desireth to be great
44 among you, shall be your servant. And whosoever desireth to be
45 the chief, shall be the servant of all. For the Son of man came
not to be served, but to serve, and to give his life a ransom for
many.
46 * And they come to Jericho. And as he went out of Jericho
with his disciples and a great multitude, blind Bartimeus, the son
47 of Timeus, sat by the way side begging. And hearing, It is Jesus
of Nazareth, he cried out and said, Jesus, thou Son of David, have
48 mercy on me. And many charged him to hold his peace ; but
he cried so much the more a great deal, Thou Son of David, have
49 mercy on me. And Jesus standing still, commanded him to be
called. And they call the blind man, saying to him, Take courage ;
50 rise ; he calleth thee. And casting away his garment, he rose
51 and came to Jesus. And Jesus answering said to him, What wilt
thou that I should do for thee ? The blind man said to him, Lord,
52 that I may receive my sight. And Jesus said, Go ; thy faith hath
saved thee. And immediately he received his sight, and followed
him in the way.

XI. † And when they were come nigh to Jerusalem to Bethphage and
Bethany, at the mount of Olives, he sendeth two of his disciples,
2 And saith to them, Go ye into the village over against you, and as
soon as ye enter it, ye shall find a colt tied, whereon never man
3 sat : loose and bring him. And if any say to you, Why do ye this ?
say, The Lord hath need of him ; and straightway he will send
4 him hither. And they went and found the colt tied at the door,

---

38. *Ye know not what ye ask*—Ye know not that ye ask for sufferings, which
must needs pave the way to glory. *The cup*—Of inward ; *the baptism*—Of out.
ward sufferings. Our Lord was *filled* with sufferings within, and *covered* with
them without.

40. *Save to them for whom it is prepared*—Them *who by patient continuance in
well doing, seek for glory, and honour, and immortality.* For these only eternal
life *is prepared.* To these only he will *give it* in that day ; and to every man his
own reward, according to his own labour.

45. *A ransom for many*—Even for as many souls as needed such a ransom,
2 Cor. v, 15.

50. *Casting away his garment*—Through joy and eagerness.

XI. 1. *To Bethphage and Bethany, at the mount of Olives*—The limits of Be.
thany reached to the mount of Olives, and joined to those of Bethphage. Bethphage was part of the suburbs of Jerusalem, and reached from the mount of
Olives to the walls of the city. Our Lord was now come to the place where the
boundaries of Bethany and Bethphage met.

* Matt. xx, 29 ; Luke xviii, 35. † Matt. xxi, 1 ; Luke xix, 29 ; John xii, 12.

5 without, in the street, and they loose him.   And some of them that
6 stood there said, What do ye, loosing the colt ? And they said to
7 them as Jesus had commanded ; and they let him go.   And they
   brought the colt to Jesus, and cast their garments on him, and he
8 sat on him.   And many spread their garments in the way : and
   others cut down branches from the trees, and strewed *them* in the
9 way.   And they that went before, and they that followed after cried,
   saying, Hosanna : blessed in the name of the Lord *is* he that
10 cometh.   Blessed *be* the kingdom of our father David that cometh :
   hosanna in the highest.
11   * And Jesus entered into Jerusalem, *and* into the temple, and
   having looked round about upon all things, it being now evening,
   he went out to Bethany with the twelve.
12   † And on the morrow, as they were coming from Bethany, he
13 was hungry.   And seeing a fig tree afar off, having leaves, he
   came, if haply he might find any thing thereon : and coming to it,
   he found nothing but leaves ; for it was not a season of figs.
14 And he answering said to it, No man eat fruit of thee hereafter for
15 ever ; and his disciples heard.   ‡ And they come to Jerusalem.
   And Jesus going into the temple, drove out them that bought and
   sold in the temple, and overthrew the tables of the money chan-
16 gers, and the seats of them that sold doves, And suffered not that
17 any one should carry a vessel through the temple.   And he taught,
   saying to them, Is it not written, § My house shall be called of all
   nations a house of prayer ? But ye have made it a den of thieves.
18 And the scribes and the chief priests heard *it*, and sought how they
   might destroy him : for they feared him, because the whole multitude was astonished at his teaching.
19   ‖ And when evening was · come he went out of the city.   And
20 passing by in the morning, they saw the fig tree dried up from
21 the roots.   And Peter remembering, saith to him, Master, behold,
22 the fig tree which thou cursedst is withered away.   And Jesus

---

13. *For it was not a season of figs*—It was not (as we say) a good year for
figs ; at least not for that early sort, which alone was ripe so soon in the spring.
  If we render the words, *It was not the season of figs*, that is, the time of
gathering them in, it may mean, *The season was not yet :* and so (inclosing the
words in a parenthesis, *And coming to it, he found nothing but leaves*) it may refer
to the former part of the sentence, and may be considered as the reason of
Christ's going to see whether there were any figs on this tree.   Some who also
read that clause in a parenthesis, translate the following words, *for where he was,
it was the season of figs*.   And it is certain, this meaning of the words suits best
with the great design of the parable, which was to reprove the Jewish Church
for its unfruitfulness at that very season, when fruit might best be expected
from them.
  16. *He suffered not that any should carry a vessel through the temple*—So
strong notions had our Lord, of even relative holiness ! And of the regard due to
those places (as well as times) that are peculiarly dedicated to God.
  18. *They feared him*—That is, they were afraid to take him by violence, lest
it should raise a tumult ; *because all the people was astonished at his teaching*—
Both at the excellence of his discourse, and at the majesty and authority with
which he taught.
  22. *Have faith in God*—And who could find fault, if the Creator and Proprietor of all things were to destroy, by a single word of his mouth, a thousand of his

* Matt. xxi, 10, 17.   † Matt. xxi, 18.   ‡ Matt. xxii, 12 ; Luke xix, 45.
            § Isaiah lvi, 7 ; Jer. vii, 11.   ‖ Matt. xxi, 20.

23 answering saith to them, Have faith in God.   For verily I say to
you, Whosoever shall say to this mountain, Be thou removed and
cast into the sea, and not doubt in his heart, but believe that the
things which he saith shall come to pass, he shall have whatso-
24 ever he saith.   Therefore I say to you, All things whatsoever ye
ask in prayer, believe that ye shall receive, and ye shall have *them*.
25 * But when ye stand praying, forgive, if ye have aught against
any, that your Father who is in heaven may forgive you also your
26 trespasses.   But if ye do not forgive, neither will your Father
who is in heaven forgive your trespasses.
27   † And they come again to Jerusalem.   And as he was walking in
the temple, the chief priests and the scribes and the elders come
28 to him, and say to him, By what authority dost thou these things ?
29 And who gave thee authority to do these things ? Jesus answering
said to them, I also will ask you one question, and answer me,
30 and I will tell you by what authority I do these things.   Was the
31 baptism of John from heaven or from men ? Answer me.   And
they reasoned among themselves, saying, If we say from heaven,
32 he will say, Why then did ye not believe him ? But if we say from
men : they feared the people ; for all accounted John, that he was
33 indeed a prophet.   And they answering say to Jesus, We cannot
tell.   And Jesus answering saith to them, Neither tell I you by
what authority I do these things.
XII.   ‡ And he said to them in parables, A man planted a vineyard,
and set a hedge about it, and digged a wine fat, and built a tower,
2 and let it out to husbandmen, and went into a far country.   And
at the season he sent a servant to the husbandmen to receive from
3 the husbandmen of the fruit of the vineyard.   But they took him,
4 and beat *him*, and sent *him* away empty.   And again he sent to
them another servant ; and at him they cast stones, and wounded
5 *him* in the head, and sent *him* away shamefully handled.   And
again he sent another, and him they killed ; and many others,
6 beating some and killing some.   Having yet therefore one son, his
well beloved, he sent him also last to them, saying, They will re-
7 verence my son.   But those husbandmen said among themselves,
This is the heir : come, let us kill him, and the inheritance will
8 be ours.   And they took him and killed *him*, and cast *him* out of
9 the vineyard.   What therefore will the lord of the vineyard do ?
He will come and destroy the husbandmen, and will give the vine-
10 yard to others.   And have ye not read even this scripture ? § The
stone which the builders rejected, this is become the head of the
11 corner ? This was the Lord's doing, and it is marvellous in our
12 eyes.   And they sought to seize him, but feared the multitude ;

---

inanimate creatures, were it only to imprint this important lesson more deeply
on one immortal spirit ?
   25. *When ye stand praying*—Standing was their usual posture when they
prayed.   *Forgive*—And on this condition, ye shall have whatever you ask, without wrath or doubting.
   XII. 12. *They feared the multitude*—How wonderful is the providence of God,
using all things for the good of his children ! Generally the multitude is restrained

* Matt. vi, 14.   † Matt. xxi, 23 ; Luke xx, 1.   ‡ Matt. xxi, 43 ; Luke xx, 9.
§ Psalm cxviii, 22.

for they knew he had spoken the parable against them ; and leaving him, they went away.

13 * And they send to him certain of the Pharisees, and of the He-
14 rodians, to catch him in *his* discourse. And they coming say to him, Master, we know that thou art true, and carest for no man ; for thou regardest not the person of men, but teachest the way of
15 God in truth. Is it lawful to give tribute to Cesar, or not ? Shall we give, or shall we not give ? But he, knowing their hypocrisy, said to them, Why tempt ye me ? Bring me a penny, that I may
16 see *it ;* and they brought *it.* And he saith to them. Whose *is* this
17 image and inscription ? They say to him, Cesar's. And Jesus answering said to them, Render to Cesar the things that are Cesar's, and to God the things that are God's. And they marvelled at him.
18 † Then come to him the Sadducees, who say there is no resur-
19 rection, and they asked him, saying, Master, Moses wrote to us, ‡ If a man's brother die, and leave a wife, and leave no children, that his brother should take his wife, and raise up issue to his bro-
20 ther. There were seven brethren, and the first took a wife, and
21 dying left no issue. And the second took her and died, neither
22 left he any issue ; and the third likewise. And the seven took
23 her and left no issue. Last of all died the woman also. In the resurrection, therefore, when they shall rise, whose wife shall she
24 be of them ? For the seven had her to wife. And Jesus answering, said to them, Do ye not therefore err, because ye know not
25 the Scriptures, neither the power of God ? For when they rise from the dead, they neither marry nor are given in marriage, but are
26 as the angels who are in heaven. And touching the dead that they rise, Have ye not read in the book of Moses, § how in the bush God spake to him, saying, I *am* the God of Abraham, and the
27 God of Isaac, and the God of Jacob ? He is not the God of the dead, but the God of the living. Ye therefore greatly err.
28 || And one of the scribes coming to him, having heard them disputing together, *and* perceiving that he had answered them well,
29 asked him, Which is the first commandment of all ? And Jesus answered him, The first commandment of all *is,* ** Hear, O Israel ; the

---

from tearing them in pieces only by the fear of their rulers. And here the rulers themselves are restrained, through fear of the multitude !

17. *They marvelled at him*—At the wisdom of his answer.

25. *When they rise from the dead, neither* men *marry nor* women *are given in marriage.*

27. *He is not the God of the dead, but the God of the living*—That is, (if the argument be proposed at length,) since the character of his being the God of any persons, plainly intimates a relation to them, not as dead, but as living ; and since he cannot be said to be at present their God at all, iᶠ they are utterly dead ; nor to be the God of human persons, such as Abraham, Isaac, and Jacob, consisting of souls and bodies, if their bodies were to abide in everlasting death ; there must needs be a future state of blessedness, and a resurrection of the body to share with the soul in it.

28. *Which is the first commandment ?*—The principal, and most necessary to be observed.

29. *The Lord our God is one Lord*—This is the foundation of the first commandment, yea, of all the commandments. The Lord our God, the Lord, the

* Matt. xxii, 15 ; Luke xx, 20.   † Matt. xxi, 23 ; Luke xx, 27.   ‡ Deut. xxv, 5
§ Exol. iii, 6. || Matt. xxvii, 34 ; Luke x, 25.   ** Deut. vi, 4.

30 Lord our God is one Lord. And thou shalt love the Lord thy
God with all thy heart, and with all thy soul, and with all thy
31 mind, and with all thy strength. This *is* the first commandment.
And the second *is* like unto it, * Thou shalt love thy neighbour
32 as thyself. There is no other commandment greater than these.
And the scribes said to him, Excellently well, Master! Thou hast
33 said the truth; for he is one: and there is no other but he. And
to love him with all the heart, and with all the understanding,
and with all the mind, and with all the strength, and to love his
neighbour as himself, is more than all whole burnt offerings and
34 sacrifices. And Jesus, seeing that he answered discreetly, said
to him, Thou art not far from the kingdom of God. And no
man after that durst question him any more.
35 † And Jesus answering as he taught in the temple, said, How
36 say the scribes, that Christ is the Son of David? For David himself said by the Holy Ghost, ‡ The Lord saith to my Lord, Sit
thou on my right hand, till I make thine enemies thy footstool.
37 David therefore himself calleth him Lord: how is he then his
son? And a great multitude heard him gladly.
38 § And he said to them in his teaching, Beware of the scribes,
who love to walk in long robes, and to be saluted in the market
39 places, And the chief seats in the synagogues, and the uppermost
40 places at feasts; Who devour widows' houses, and for a pretence
make long prayers: these shall receive the greater damnation.
41 ‖ And Jesus sitting over against the treasury, beheld how the
people cast money into the treasury: and many that were rich
42 cast in much. And a poor widow coming, cast in two mites,

God of all men, is one God, essentially, though three persons. From this unity
of God it follows, that we owe all our love to him alone.

30. *With all thy strength*—That is, the whole strength and capacity of thy
understanding, will, and affections.

31. *The second is like unto it*—Of a like comprehensive nature: comprising
our whole duty to man. *There is no other* moral, much less ceremonial *commandment, greater than these.*

33. *To love him with all the heart*—To love and serve him, with all the united
powers of the soul in their utmost vigour; *and to love his neighbour as himself*—
To maintain the same equitable and charitable temper and behaviour toward all
men, as we, in like circumstances, would wish for from them toward ourselves,
is a more necessary and important duty, than the offering the most noble and
costly sacrifices.

34. *Jesus said to him, Thou art not far from the kingdom of God*—Reader, art
not thou? then go on: be a real Christian: else it had been better for thee to
have been afar off.

38. *Beware of the scribes*—There was an absolute necessity for these repeated
cautions. For, considering their inveterate prejudices against Christ, it could
never be supposed the common people would receive the Gospel till these incor-
rigible blasphemers of it were brought to just disgrace.

Yet he delayed speaking in this manner till a little before his passion, as knowing what effect it would quickly produce. Nor is this any precedent for us: we
are not invested with the same authority.

41. *He beheld how people cast money into the treasury*—This treasury received
the voluntary contributions of the worshippers who came up to the feast; which
were given to buy wood for the altar, and other necessaries not provided for in
any other way.

* Lev. xix, 18.   † Matt. xxii, 41; Luke xx, 41.   ‡ Psa. cx, 1.   § Matt. xxiii, 5;
Luke xx, 46.   ‖ Luke xx, 1.

43 which make a farthing. And calling to him his disciples, he saith
to them, Verily I say unto you, that this poor widow hath cast in
44 more than they all who have cast into the treasury. For they all
did cast in of their abundance : but she of her penury did cast in
all that she had, even her whole living.

XIII. * And as he was going out of the temple, one of his disciples
saith to him, Master, see what manner of stones, and what man-
2 ner of buildings! And Jesus answering said to him, Seest thou
these great buildings ? There shall not be left one stone upon
3 another that shall not be thrown down. And as he sat on the
mount of Olives, over against the temple, Peter and James and
4 John and Andrew asked him privately, Tell us when shall these
things be ? And what *shall be* the sign when all these things shall
5 be fulfilled? And Jesus answering said, Take heed lest any de-
6 ceive you. For many will come in my name saying, I am *He*,
7 and will deceive many. But when ye shall hear of wars and rumours of wars, be not troubled ; for *it* must be : but the end *is* not
8 yet. For nation shall rise against nation, and kingdom against
kingdom : and there shall be earthquakes in divers places, and
there shall be famines and troubles : these *are* the beginning of
9 sorrows. † But take heed to yourselves, for they will deliver you
to councils, and ye shall be beaten in synagogues, and shall stand
before rulers and kings for my sake, for a testimony to them.
10 ‡ And the Gospel must first be published among all nations. But
11 when they shall hale you and deliver *you* up, take no thought beforehand what ye shall speak, neither do ye premeditate ; but whatsoever shall be given you in that hour, that speak ; for it is not ye
12 that speak, but the Holy Ghost. Now the brother shall betray the
brother to death, and the father the son : and the children shall rise
13 up against their parents, and cause them to be put to death. And
ye shall be hated of all men for my name's sake ; but he that endureth to the end, he shall be saved.
14 § But when ye shall see the abomination of desolation spoken
of by Daniel the prophet standing where it ought not, (let him that
readeth understand,) then let them that are in Judea flee to the
15 mountains : And let not him that is on the house top go down into
the house, neither enter in, to take any thing out of his house.
16 And let not him that is in the field turn back to take up his gar-
17 ment. But wo to them that are with child, and to them that give
18 suck in those days. And pray ye that your flight be not in the
19 winter. For in those days shall be affliction, such as was not from

---

43. *I say to you, that this poor widow hath cast in more than they all*—See
what judgment is cast on the most specious, outward actions by the Judge of all !
And how acceptable to him is the smallest, which springs from self-denying love !

XIII. 4. Two questions are here asked ; the one concerning the destruction
of Jerusalem : the other concerning the end of the world.

11. *The Holy Ghost* will help you. But do not depend upon any other help
For all the nearest ties will be broken.

14. *Where it ought not*—That place being set apart for sacred uses.

19. *In those days shall be affliction, such as was not from the beginning of the*

* Matt. xxiv, 1 ; Luke xxi, 5. † Luke xxi, 12. ‡ Matt. xxiv, 14. § Matt. xxiv, 15;
Luke xxi, 20 ; Dan. ix, 27.

the beginning of the creation, which God .created until now, neithei
20 shall be. And unless the Lord had shortened those days, no flesh
should be saved : but for the elect's sake whom he hath chosen.
21 he hath shortened those days * Then if any man say to you, Lo,
22 here *is* Christ, or lo, *he is* there, believe *it* not. For false Christs
and false prophets shall rise, and shall show signs and wonders, to
23 seduce, if possible, even the elect. But take ye heed : Behold, I
have foretold you all things.
24 But in those days, after that tribulation, the sun shall be darken-
25 ed, and the moon shall not give her light, And the stars of heaven
shall be falling, and the powers that are in the heavens shall be
26 shaken. And then shall they see the Son of man coming in the
27 clouds, with great power and glory. And then shall he send his
angels, and gather together his elect, from the four winds, from the
uttermost part of the earth, to the uttermost part of heaven.
28 † Now learn a parable from the fig tree. When its branch is
now tender and putteth forth leaves, ye know that summer is nigh.
29 So likewise when ye see these things come to pass, know that he
30 is nigh, *even* at the door. Verily I say to you, this generation shall
31 in nowise pass, till all these things be done. Heaven and earth
shall pass away, but my words shall in nowise pass away.
32 But of that day or that hour knoweth no one, no, not the angels
that are in heaven, neither the Son, but the Father.
33 ‡ Take heed ; watch and pray : for ye know not when the time
34 is. *For the Son of man is* § as a man taking a far journey, who
left his house, and gave authority to his servants, and to éach his
35 work, and commanded the porter to watch. Watch ye therefore ;
for ye know not when the master of the house cometh ; at evening,
36 or at midnight, at cock crowing, or in the morning : Lest coming
37 suddenly he find you sleeping. And what I say to you, I say to
all, Watcʰ.
XIV. ‖ And after two days was the feast of the passover and of unleavened bread ; and the chief priests and the scribes sought how
they might apprehend him by subtlety, and put him to death.
2 But they said, Not at the feast, lest there be a tumult of the peo-

creation—May it not be doubted, whether this be yet fully accomplished ? Is not
much of this affliction still to come ?
20. *The elect*--The Christians : *whom he hath chosen*—That is, hath taken out
of, or separated from, the world, *through sanctification of the Spirit and belief
of the truth. He hath shortened*—That is, will surely shorten.
24. *But in those days*—Which immediately precede the end of the world : *after
that tribulation*—Above described.
29. *He is nigh*—The Son of man.
30. *All these things*—Relating to the temple and the city.
32. *Of that day*—The day of judgment is often in the Scriptures emphatically
called *that day. Neither the Son*—Not as man : as man he was no more omniscient than omnipresent. But as God he knows all the circumstances of it.
34. The Son of man is *as a man taking a far journey*—Being about to leave
this world and go to the Father, he appoints the services that are to be perform
ed by all his servants, in their several stations. This seems chiefly to respect
ministers at the day of judgment : but it may be applied to all men, and to the
time of death.

* Matt. xxiv, 23. † Matt. xxiv, 32 ; Luke xxi, 28. ‡ Matt. xxiv, 42 ; Luke xxi, 34.
§ Matt. xxv, 14 ; Luke xix, 12. ‖ Matt. xxvi, 1 ; Luke xxii, 1.
9

3 ple.   * And he being in Bethany ın the house of Simon the leper
as he sat at table, there came a woman having an alabaster box of
ointment, of spikenard, very costly ; and shaking the box, she
4 poured it on his head.   But there were some that had indignation
within themselves, and said, Why was this waste of the ointment
5 made ?   For this ointment might have been sold for more than three
6 hundred pence and given to the poor.   And they murmured at her.
But Jesus said, Let her alone : why trouble ye her?   She hath
7 wrought a good work on me.   For the poor ye have always with
you, and when ye will ye may do them good ; but me ye have not
8 always.   She hath done what she could: she hath beforehand
9 embalmed my body for the burial.   Verily I say to you, wheresoever this Gospel shall be preached throughout the whole world,
what she hath done shall be spoken of also, for a memorial of her.
10   † And Judas Iscariot, one of the twelve, went to the chief priests,
11 to betray him unto them.   And hearing it they were glad, and promised to give him money.   And he sought how he might conveniently betray him.
12   ‡ And on the first day of unleavened bread, when they killed the
passover, his disciples say to him, Where wilt thou that we go and
13 prepare, that thou mayest eat the passover?   And he sendeth two
of his disciples, and saith to them, Go ye into the city, and there
shall meet you a man carrying a pitcher of water: follow him.
14 And wheresoever he shall go in, say ye to the man of the house,
The Master saith, Where is the guest chamber, where I shall eat
15 the passover with my disciples?   And he will show you a large
16 upper room furnished: there make ready for us.   And his disciples went forth, and came into the city, and found as he had said
to them.   And they made ready the passover.
17   § And in the evening he cometh with the twelve.   And as they
18 sat and ate, Jesus said, Verily I say to you, one of you that eat
19 with me will betray me.   And they were sorrowful, and said to
20 him one by one, Is it I ?   And another said, Is it I ?   And he answering said to them, It is one of the twelve that dippeth with me in
21 the dish.   The Son of man indeed goeth as it is written of him :
but wo to that man by whom the Son of man is betrayed : it had
been good for that man if he had not been born.
22   And as they ate, Jesus took bread, and blessed, and brake it,
23 and gave to them, and said, Take, eat : this is my body.   And he
took the cup, and having given thanks, gave it them, and they all
24 drank of it.   And he said to them, This is my blood of the New

XIV. 4. *Some had indignation*—Being incited thereto by Judas : *and said*—
Probably to the women.
10. *Judas went to the chief priests*—Immediately after this reproof, having
anger now added to his covetousness.
13. *Go into the city, and there shall meet you a man*—-It was highly seasonable
for our Lord to give them this additional proof both of his knowing all things,
and of his influence over the minds of men.
15. *Furnished*—The word properly means, *spread* with carpets.
24. *This is my blood of the New Testament*—That is, this I appoint to be a

* Matt. xxvi, 6.   † Matt. xxvi, 14; Luke xxii, 3.   ‡ Matt. xxvi, 17; Luke xxii. 7.
§ Matt. xxvi, 20; Luke xxii, 14.

25 Testament, which is shed for many. Verily I say to you, I will drink no more of the fruit of the vine, till that day that I drink it new in the kingdom of God.

26 * And having sung the hymn, they went out toward the mount
27 of Olives. And Jesus saith to them, Ye will all be offended at me this night; for it is written, † I will smite the shepherd, and the
28 sheep shall be scattered. But after I am risen, I will go before
29 you into Galilee. But Peter said to him, Though all men shall
30 be offended, *yet will* not I. Jesus saith to him, Verily I say to thee, That thou to-day, this night before the cock crow twice, wilt
31 deny me thrice. But he said the more vehemently, If I must die with thee I will in nowise deny thee. In like manner also said they all.

32 ‡ And they come to a place named Gethsemane; and he saith
33 to his disciples, Sit here while I shall pray. And he taketh with him Peter and James and John; and he began to be sore amazed
34 and in deep anguish, And saith to them, My soul is exceeding sor-
35 rowful *even* to death: tarry ye here and watch. And going for- ward a little, he fell on the ground, and prayed, that if it were
36 possible, the hour might pass from him. And he said Abba, Fa- ther, all things *are* possible to thee: take away this cup from me:
37 yet not what I will, but what thou wilt. And he cometh and find- eth them sleeping, and saith to Peter, Simon, sleepest thou?—
38 Couldest thou not watch one hour? Watch and pray lest ye enter into temptation; the spirit indeed *is* willing, but the flesh *is* weak.
39 And going away again he prayed, speaking the same words. And
40 returning, he found them asleep again (for their eyes were heavy)
41 and they knew not what to answer him. And he cometh the third time, and saith to them, Sleep on now, and take *your* rest. It is enough. The hour is come: behold, the Son of man is betrayed

---

perpetual sign and memorial of my blood, as shed for establishing the new covenant, that all who shall believe in me may receive all its gracious promises.

25. *I will drink no more of the fruit of the vine, till I drink it new in the king- dom of God*—That is, I shall drink no more before I die: the next wine I drink will not be earthly, but heavenly.

27. *This night*—The Jews in reckoning their days began with the evening, according to the Mosaic computation, which called the evening and the morning the first day, Gen. i, 5. And so that which after sunset is here called this night, is, ver. 30, called to-day. The expression there is peculiarly significant. *Verily I say to thee, that thou* thyself, confident as thou art, *to-day*, even within four and twenty hours; yea, *this night*, or ever the sun be risen, nay, *before the cock crow twice*, before three in the morning, *wilt deny me thrice.* Our Lord doubt- less spoke so determinately, as knowing a cock would crow once before the usual time of cock crowing. By chap. xiii, 35, it appears, that the third watch of the night, ending at three in the morning, was commonly styled the *cock crowing.*

33. *Sore amazed*—The original word imports the most shocking amazement, mingled with grief: and that word in the next verse which we render *sorrowful*, intimates, that he was *surrounded with sorrow* on every side, breaking in upon him with such violence, as was ready to separate his soul from his body.

36. *Abba, Father*—St. Mark seems to add the word *Father*, by way of expli- cation.

37. *Saith to Peter*—The zealous, the confident Peter.

* Matt. xxvi, 30; Luke xxii, 39; John xviii, 1.   † Zech. xiii, 7.   ‡ Matt. xxvi, 36

42 into the hands of sinners.   Rise up; let us go : lo, he that betray
     eth me is at hand.
43   * And immediately, while he yet spake, cometh up Judas, one
     of the twelve, and with him a great multitude, with swords and
44 clubs from the chief priests, and the scribes, and the elders.   Now
     he that betrayed him had given them a signal, saying, Whomso-
45 ever I shall kiss, is he : seize and lead him away safely.   And
     when he was come, he goeth straightway to him, and saith, Mas-
46 ter, Master! and kissed him.   And they laid their hands on him,
47 and took him.   † And one of them that stood by, drawing a sword,
48 smote the servant of the high priest, and cut off his ear.   And
     Jesus answering said to them, Are ye come out as against a rob
49 ber, with swords and clubs to take me ?   I was daily with you in
     the temple teaching, and ye took me not; but that the Scriptures
50 may be fulfilled.   Then they all forsook him and fled.   And a
51 certain young man followed him, having a linen cloth cast about
52 his naked body; and the young men laid hold on him.   And he
     left the linen cloth, and fled from them naked.
53   ‡ And they led Jesus away to the high priest, and with him
     assembled all the chief priests, and the elders, and the scribes.
54 And Peter followed him afar off, even into the palace of the high
     priest, and sat with the servants, and warmed himself at the fire.
55   § Then the chief priests and all the council sought for evidence
56 against Jesus, to put him to death, and found none.   For many
     bore false witness against him; but their evidences were not suf-
57 ficient.   And certain men arising bore false witness against him,
58 saying, We heard him say, I will destroy this temple made with
     hands, and in three days I will build another made without hands.
59 And neither so was their evidence sufficient.   Then the high priest
60 rising up in the midst, asked Jesus, saying, Answerest thou no-
61 thing ?   What is it that these witness against thee ?   ‖ But he held
     his peace, and answered nothing.   Again the high priest asked

---

· 44. *Whomsoever I shall kiss*—Probably our Lord, in great condescension, had
used (according to the Jewish custom) to permit his disciples to do this, after
they had been some time absent.
51. *A young man*—It does not appear, that he was one of Christ's disciples.
Probably hearing an unusual noise, he started up out of his bed, not far from
the garden, and ran out with only the sheet about him, to see what was the
matter.   *And the young men laid hold on him*—Who was only suspected to be
Christ's disciple : but could not touch them who really were so.
55 *All the council sought for witness and found none*—What an amazing proof
of the overruling providence of God, considering both their authority, and the
rewards they could offer, that no two consistent witnesses could be procured, to
charge him with any gross crime.
56. *Their evidences were not sufficient*—The Greek words literally rendered are,
Were not equal : not equal to the charge of a capital crime : it is the same word
in the 59th verse.
58. *We heard him say*—It is observable, that the words which they thus misrepresented, were spoken by Christ at least three years before, John ii, 19.—
Their going back so far to find matter for the charge, was a glorious, though
silent attestation of the unexceptionable manner wherein he had behaved, through
the whole course of his public ministry.

* Matt. xxvi, 47 ; Luke xxii, 47 ; John xviii, 2.   † Matt. xxvi, 51 ; Luke xxii, 49
John xviii, 10.   ‡ Matt. xxvi, 57 ; Luke xxii, 54 ; John xviii, 12.   § Matt. xxvi, 59
‖ Matt. xxvi, 63 : Luke xxii, 67.

him and said to him, Art thou the Christ, the Son of the Blessed?
62 And Jesus said, I am; and ye shall see the Son of man sitting
at the right hand of power, and coming with the clouds of heaven.
63 Then the high priest rent his clothes, and saith, What farther need
64 have we of witnesses? Ye have heard the blasphemy: what think
65 ye? And they all condemned him to be worthy of death. And
some began to spit on him, and to cover his face, and to buffet
him, and say to him, Prophesy   And the servants smote him with
the palms of their hands.
66   * And as Peter was in the hall below, there cometh one of the
67 maids of the high priest. And seeing Peter warming himself,
she looked on him, and said, Thou wast also with Jesus of Naza-
68 reth. But he denied, saying, I know not, neither understand I
what thou meanest. And he went out into the porch and the
69 cock crew. And the maid seeing him again, said to them that
70 stood by, This is *one* of them. And he denied it again. And a
little after those that stood by said again to Peter, Surely thou
art *one* of them; for thou art a Galilean, and thy speech agreeth
71 *thereto.* Then began he to curse and to swear, I know not this man
72 of whom ye speak. And the second time the cock crew. And
Peter called to mind the word that Jesus had said to him, Before
the cock crow twice, thou wilt deny me thrice. And he covered
his head and wept.
XV. † And straightway in the morning the chief priests having
consulted with the elders and scribes, and the whole council, having bound Jesus, carried *him* away and delivered *him* to Pilate.
2 And Pilate asked him, Art thou the king of the Jews? And he
3 answering said to him, Thou sayest *it.* ‡ And the chief priests
4 accused him of many things. And Pilate asked him again, saying,
Answerest thou nothing? Behold how many things they witness
5 against thee. But Jesus answered nothing any more, so that
6 Pilate marvelled. Now at every feast he released to them one
7 prisoner, whomsoever they would. And there *was* one named
Barabbas, who lay bound with them that had made insurrection
8 with him, who had committed murder in the insurrection. And
the multitude crying aloud, asked *him to do* as he had ever done
9 for them. And Pilate answered them, saying, Will ye that I
10 release to you the king of the Jews? (For he knew that the chief
11 priests had delivered him for envy.) But the chief priests stirred
up the people *to ask,* that he would rather release Barabbas to them.
12 And Pilate answering said to them again, What will ye then that
I do to *him* whom ye call the king of the Jews? And they cried

---

72. *And he covered his head*—Which was a usual custom with mourners, and
was fitly expressive both of grief and shame.
XV. 7. *Insurrection*—A crime which the Roman governors, and Pilate in particular, were more especially concerned and careful to punish.
9. *Will ye that I release to you the king of the Jews*—Which does this wretched
man discover most? Want of justice, or courage, or common sense? The poor
coward sacrifices justice to popular clamour, and enrages those whom he seeks to
appease, by so unseasonably repeating that title, *The king of the Jews,* which he
could not but know was so highly offensive to them.

* Matt. xxvi, 69; Luke xxii, 56; John xviii, 25.   † Matt. xxvii, 1, 2; Luke xxii, 66;
xxiii, 1; John xviii, 28.   ‡ Matt. xxvii, 12.

13 out again, Crucify him. Then Pilate said to them, Why, what
14 evil hath he done? But they cried out the more exceedingly,
15 Crucify him. And Pilate, willing to satisfy the people, released
Barabbas to them, and having scourged Jesus, delivered *him* to be
crucified.

16 * And the soldiers led him away to the hall called Prætorium,
17 and call together the whole troop. And they clothe him with
purple, and having platted a crown of thorns, put it about his *head.*
18 And they saluted him, Hail, king of the Jews. And they smote
19 him on the head with a cane, and spit upon him, and bowing their
20 knees, did him homage. † And when they had mocked him, they
took the purple robe from him, and put his own clothes on him, and
21 led him out to crucify him. And they compel one Simon a Cyrenian, who was passing by, coming out of the country, the father of
Alexander and Rufus, to bear his cross.
22 ‡ And they bring him to the place, Golgotha, which is, being
23 interpreted, the place of a skull. And they gave him to drink
24 wine mingled with myrrh; but he received *it* not. And when they
had crucified him, they parted his garments, casting lots upon
25 them, what every man should take. And it was the third hour
26 when they crucified him. And there was an inscription of his
27 accusation written over, THE KING OF THE JEWS. And
with him they crucify two thieves, one on his right hand, and
28 one on his left. And the scripture was fulfilled, which saith, § And
29 he was numbered with the transgressors. ‖ And they that passed
by, reviled him, wagging their heads and saying, Ah, thou that
30 destroyest the temple, and buildest it in three days, Save thyself,
31 and come down from the cross. In like manner also the chief
priests mocking said to one another, with the scribes, He saved
32 others; cannot he save himself? Let the Christ, the king of
Israel, come down now from the cross, that we may see and believe.
33 They also that were crucified with him reviled him. ** And when
the sixth hour was come, there was darkness over all the earth
34 until the ninth hour. And at the ninth hour Jesus cried with a
loud voice, Eloi, Eloi, lama sabacthani? Which is, being inter-
35 preted, My God, my God, why hast thou forsaken me? And
some of them that stood by hearing *it* said, Behold, he calleth
36 Elijah. And one ran, and filling a sponge with vinegar, put *it* on a

---

16. *Prætorium*—The inner hall, where the prætor, a Roman magistrate, used
to give judgment. But St. John calls the whole palace by this name.
17. *Purple*—As royal robes were usually purple and scarlet, St. Mark and John
term this a purple robe, St. Matthew a scarlet one. The Tyrian purple is said
not to have been very different from scarlet.
21. *The father of Alexander and Rufus*—These were afterward two eminent
Christians, and must have been well known when St. Mark wrote.
24, 25. St. Mark seems to intimate, that they first nailed him to the cross,
then parted his garments, and afterward reared up the cross.
34. *My God, my God, why hast thou forsaken me*—Thereby claiming God as
his God; and yet lamenting his Father's withdrawing the tokens of his love, and
treating him as an enemy, while he bare our sins.

* Matt. xxvii, 27; John xix, 2.   † Matt. xxvii, 31; John xix, 16.   ‡ Matt. xxvii, 33
Luke xxiii, 33; John xix, 17.   § Isaiah liii, 12.   ‖ Matt. xxvii, 39.   ** Matt
xxvii, 45; Luke xxiii, 44.

cane, and gave him to drink, saying, Let alone ; let us see if Elijah
will come to take him down.

37   * And Jesus cried with a loud voice, and expired.

38   And the veil of the temple was rent in twain, from the top to
39 the bottom. And the centurion, who stood over against him, seeing
that having so cried he expired, said, Truly this man was the
40 Son of God. There were also women, beholding from afar, among
whom was Mary Magdalene and Mary the mother of James the
41 less, and of Joses, and Salome : Who also when he' was in Galilee,
followed him and served him, and many other women who had
come up with him to Jerusalem.

42   † And the evening being now come, (because it was the prepa-
43 ration, that is, the day before the Sabbath,) Joseph of Arimathea,
an honourable counsellor, who also himself waited for the kingdom
of God, came and went in boldly to Pilate, and asked the body of
44 Jesus. And Pilate marvelled that he was dead already : and calling to him the centurion, he asked if he had been any while dead ?
45 And when he knew it of the centurion, he gave the body to Joseph
46 And having bought fine linen, he took him down and wrapped *him*
in the linen, and laid him in a sepulchre, which was hewn out of a
47 rock, and rolled a stone to the door of the sepulchre. And Mary
Magdalene and Mary the mother of Joses beheld where he was laid.

XVI. ‡ And when the Sabbath was over, Mary Magdalene, and
Mary *the mother* of James and Salome, had bought spices, that
2 they might come and embalm him. And very early in the morning, the first day of the week, they came to the sepulchre, at the
3 rising of the sun. And they said one to another, Who shall roll us
4 away the stone from the door of the sepulchre ? (For it was very
great.) And looking up, they saw that the stone was rolled away.
5 And entering into the sepulchre, they saw a young man sitting on
the right side, clothed in a white robe ; and they were affrighted.
6 He saith to them, Be not affrighted : ye seek Jesus of Nazareth,
who was crucified. He is risen : he is not here. Behold the place
7 where they laid him. But go, tell his disciples, and Peter, He
goeth before you into Galilee : there shall ye see him, as he said

41. *Who served him*—Provided him with necessaries.

42. *Because it was the day before the Sabbath*—And the bodies might not hang
on the Sabbath day : therefore they were in haste to have them taken down.

43. *Honourable*—A man of character and reputation : *A counsellor*—A member
of the sanhedrim. *Who waited for the kingdom of God*—Who expected to see it
set up on earth.

46. *He rolled a stone*—By his servants. It was too large for him to roll himself.

XVI. 2. *At the rising of the sun*—They set out *while it was yet dark*, and
came within sight of the sepulchre, for the first time, just as it grew light enough
to discern that the stone was rolled away, Matt. xxviii, 1 ; Luke xxiv, 1 ; John
xx, 1. But by the time Mary had called Peter and John, and they had viewed
the sepulchre, the sun was rising.

3. *Who shall roll us away the stone*—This seems to have been the only difficulty they apprehended. So they knew nothing of Pilate's having sealed the
stone, and placed a guard of soldiers there.

7. *And Peter*—Though he so oft denied his Lord. What amazing goodness
was this !

* Matt. xxvii, 50 ; Luke xxiii, 46 ; John xix, 30. † Matt. xxvii, 57 ; Luke xxiii, 50 ;
John xix, 38. ‡ Matt. xxviii, 1 ; Luke xxiv, 1 ; John xx, 1.

8 to you. And going out they fled from the sepulchre; for they
   trembled and were amazed : and they said nothing to any, for they
9 were afraid. * Now when *Jesus* was risen early, the first day of
   the week, he appeared first to Mary Magdalene, out of whom he
10 had cast seven devils. † She went and told them that had been
11 with him, as they mourned and wept. But they hearing that he
12 was alive, and had been seen of her, believed not. ‡ After that he
   appeared in another form unto two of them, as they were walking,
13 going into the country. And they went and told *it* to the rest,
14 neither believed they them. § Afterward he appeared to the
   eleven sitting at meat, and upbraided them with their unbelief and
   hardness of heart, because they believed not them who had seen
   him when he was risen.
15   And he said to them, ‖ Go ye into all the world, and preach the
16 Gospel to every creature. He that believeth and is baptized, shall
17 be saved ; but he that believeth not shall be condemned. And these
   signs shall follow them that believe: in my name they shall cast out
18 devils: they shall speak with new tongues: They shall take up serpents, and if they drink any deadly thing, it shall in nowise hurt
   them: they shall lay hands on the sick, and they shall recover.
19   ** So then the Lord after he had spoken to them, was received up
20 into heaven, and sat on the right hand of God. And they went
   forth, and preached every where, the Lord working with them
   and confirming the word with signs following.

---

13. *Neither believed they them*—They were moved a little by the testimony of
these, added to that of St. Peter, Luke xxiv, 34; but they did not yet fully believe it.
   15. *Go ye into all the world, and preach the Gospel to every creature*—Our
Lord speaks without any limitation or restriction. If therefore every creature
in every age hath not heard it, either those who should have preached, or those
who should have heard it, or both, *made void the counsel of* God herein.
   16. *And is baptized*—In token thereof. Every one that believed was baptized. ' *But he that believeth not*—Whether baptized or unbaptized, shall perish
everlastingly.
   17. *And these signs shall follow them that believe*—An eminent author subjoins, " That believe with that very faith mentioned in the preceding verse."
(Though it is certain that a man may work miracles, and not have saving faith,
Matt. vii, 22, 23.) " It was not one faith by which St. Paul was saved, another
by which he wrought miracles. Even at this day in every believer faith has a
latent miraculous power ; (every effect of prayer being really miraculous ;)
although in many, both because of their own littleness of faith, and because the
world is unworthy, that power is not exerted. Miracles, in the beginning, were
helps to faith ; now also they are the object of it. At Leonberg, in the memory
of our fathers, a cripple that could hardly move with crutches, while the dean
was preaching on this very text, was in a moment made whole." *Shall follow*—
The word and faith must go before. *In my name*—By my authority committed
to them. Raising the dead is not mentioned. So our Lord performed even more
than he promised.
   18. *If they drink any deadly thing*—But not by their own choice. God never
calls us to try any such experiments.
   19. *The Lord*—How seasonable is he called by this title! *After he had spoken
to them*—For forty days.
   20. *They preached every where*—At the time St. Mark wrote, the apostles had
already gone into all the known world, Rom. x, 18; and each of them was there
known where he preached : the name of Christ only was known throughout
the world.

* John xx, 11   † Luke xxiv, 9 ; John xx, 18.   ‡ Luke xxiv, 13.   § Luke xxiv 36;
               John xx. 19.   ‖ Matt. xxviii, 19.   ** Luke xxiv, 50.

NOTES

GOSPEL ACCORDING TO ST. LUKE.

———

1   FORASMUCH as many have undertaken to compose a narrative of
2   the facts which have been fully confirmed among us, Even as they
who were eye witnesses and ministers of the word from the begin-
3   ning, delivered *them* to us : It seemed good to me also, having
accurately traced all things from their first rise, to write unto thee
4   in order, most excellent Theophilus, That thou mayest know the
certainty of those things wherein thou hast been instructed.

====

Verses 1, 2. This short, weighty, artless, candid dedication, belongs to the
Acts, as well as the Gospel of St. Luke.
Many have undertaken—He does not mean St. Matthew or Mark ; and St. John
did not write so early. For these were *eye witnesses* themselves and *ministers
of the word.*
3. *To write in order*—St. Luke describes in order of time ; first, *The Acts of
Christ ;* his conception, birth, childhood, baptism, miracles, preaching, passion,
resurrection, ascension: then, *The Acts of the Apostles.* But in many smaller
circumstances he does not observe the order of time. *Most excellent Theophilus*—This was the appellation usually given to Roman governors. Theophilus
(as the ancients inform us) was a person of eminent quality at Alexandria.
In Acts i, 1, St. Luke does not give him that title. He was then probably
a private man.
After the preface St. Luke gives us the history of Christ, from his coming
into the world to his ascension into heaven.

5   There was in the days of Herod, the king of Judea, a certain priest named Zacharias, of the course of Abia : and his wife *was*
6 of the daughters of Aaron, and her name *was* Elisabeth. And they were both righteous before God, walking in all the command-
7 ments and ordinances of the Lord blameless. And they had no child, because Elisabeth was barren, and they were both advanced
8 in years. And while he executed the priest's office before God
9 in the order of his course, According to the custom of the priest's office, his lot was to burn the incense, going into the temple of
10 the Lord. And the whole multitude of the people were praying
11 without, at the time of the incense, And there appeared to him an angel of the Lord, standing on the right side of the altar of incense.
12 And Zacharias seeing *him* was troubled, and fear fell upon him.
13 But the angel said to him, Fear not, Zacharias ; for thy prayer is heard, and thy wife Elisabeth shall bear thee a son, and thou shalt
14 call his name John. And thou shalt have joy and exultation, and
15 many shall rejoice at his birth. For he shall be great before the Lord, and shall drink neither wine nor strong drink ; and he shall

---

5. *The course of Abia*—The priests were divided into twenty-four courses, of which that of Abia was the eighth, 1 Chron. xxiv, 10. Each course ministered in its turn, for seven days, from Sabbath to Sabbath. And each priest of the course or set in waiting, had his part in the temple service assigned him by lot.

6. *Walking in all the* moral *commandments, and* ceremonial *ordinances, blameless*—How admirable a character ! May our behaviour be thus unblamable, and our obedience thus sincere and universal !

10. *The people were praying without, at the time of the incense*—So the pious Jews constantly did. And this was the foundation of that elegant figure, by which prayer is in Scripture so often compared to incense. Perhaps one reason of ordaining incense might be, to intimate the acceptableness of the prayer that accompanied it ; as well as to remind the worshippers of that sacrifice of a sweet-smelling savour, which was once to be offered to God for them, and of that incense, which is continually *offered with the prayers of the saints, upon the golden altar that is before the throne,* Rev. viii, 3, 4.

12. *Zacharias was troubled*—Although he was accustomed to converse with God, yet we see he was thrown into a great consternation, at the appearance of his angelical messenger, nature not being able to sustain the sight. Is it not then an instance of the goodness as well as of the wisdom of God, that the services, which these heavenly spirits render us, are generally invisible ?

13. *Thy prayer is heard*—Let us observe with pleasure, that the prayers of pious worshippers come up with acceptance before God ; to whom no costly perfume is so sweet, as the fragrancy of an upright heart. An answer of peace was here returned, when the case seemed to be most helpless. Let us wait patiently for the Lord, and leave to his own wisdom the time and manner wherein he will appear for us. *Thou shalt call his name John*—John signifies the grace or favour of Jehovah. A name well suiting the person, who was afterward so highly in favour with God, and endued with abundance of grace ; and who opened a way to the most glorious dispensation of grace in the Messiah's kingdom. And so Zacharias's former prayers for a child, and the prayer which he, as the repre sentative of the people, was probably offering at this very time, for the appearing of the Messiah, were remarkably answered in the birth of his forerunner.

15. *He shall be great before the Lord*—God the Father : of the Holy Ghost and the Son of God mention is made immediately after. *And shall drink neither wine*

be filled with the Holy Ghost, even from his mother's womb.
16 And many of the children of Israel shall he turn to the Lord their
17 God. And he shall go before him in the spirit and power of
Elijah, to turn the hearts of the fathers to the children, and the
disobedient to the wisdom of the just; to make ready a people
18 prepared for the Lord. And Zacharias said to the angel,
Whereby shall I know this? For I am an old man, and my wife
19 advanced in years. And the angel answering, said to him, I am
Gabriel, that stand in the presence of God, and am sent to speak
20 to thee, and to show thee these glad tidings. And behold, thou
shalt be dumb, and not able to speak, till the day that these things
are done, because thou believedst not my words, which shall be
21 fulfilled in their season. And the people were waiting for Zacha-
22 rias, and marvelled that he tarried so long in the temple. And
coming out, he could not speak to them; and they perceived that
he had seen a vision in the temple; for he beckoned to them, and
23 remained speechless. And when the days of his ministration
24 were accomplished, he went to his own house. And after these
days, his wife Elisabeth conceived, and hid herself five months,
25 saying, Thus hath the Lord done to me, in the days wherein he
looked upon me, to take away my reproach among men.
26 And in the sixth month, the Angel Gabriel was sent from God,
27 to a city of Galilee, named Nazareth. To a virgin of the house of
David, espoused to a man whose name was Joseph, and the vir-

---

nor strong drink—Shall be exemplary for abstemiousness and self denial; and so
much the more filled with the Holy Ghost.

16. *And many of the children of Israel shall he turn*—None therefore need be
ashamed of "preaching like John the Baptist." *To the Lord their God*—To
Christ.

17. *He shall go before him,* Christ, *in the power and spirit of Elijah*—With the
same integrity, courage, austerity, and fervour, and the same power attending
his word: *to turn the hearts of the fathers to the children*—To reconcile those
that are at variance, to put an end to the most bitter quarrels, such as are very
frequently those between the nearest relations: *and the hearts of the disobedient
to the wisdom of the just*—And the most obstinate sinners to true wisdom, which
is only found among them that are righteous before God.

18. *Zacharias said, Whereby shall I know this?*—In how different a spirit did
he blessed virgin say, *How shall this be?* Zacharias disbelieved the fact: Mary
had no doubt of the thing; but only inquired concerning the manner of it.

19. *I am Gabriel, that stand in the presence of God*—Seven angels thus stand
before God, Rev. viii, 2; who seem the highest of all. There seems to be a
remarkable gradation in the words, enhancing the guilt of Zacharias's unbelief.
As if he had said, I am Gabriel, a holy angel of God: yea, one of the highest
order. Not only so, but am now peculiarly sent from God; and that with a message to thee in particular. Nay, *and to show thee glad tidings,* such as ought to
be received with the greatest joy and readiness.

20. *Thou shalt be dumb*—The Greek word signifies deaf, as well as dumb: and
it seems plain, that he was as unable to hear, as he was to speak; for his friends
were obliged to make signs to him, that he might understand them, ver. 62.

21. *The people were waiting*—For him to come and dismiss them (as usual)
with the blessing.

24. *Hid herself*—She retired from company, that she might have the more
leisure to rejoice and bless God for his wonderful mercy.

25. *He looked upon me to take away my reproach*—Barrenness was a great
reproach among the Jews. Because fruitfulness was promised to the righteous.

26. *In the sixth month*—After Elisabeth had conceived.

27. *Espoused*—It was customary among the Jews, for persons that married,

28 gin's name *was* Mary. And the angel coming in to her, said, Hail, thou highly favoured; the Lord *is* with thee: blessed *art*
29 thou among women. But she seeing *him*, was troubled at his saying, and reasoned, what manner of salutation this should be.
30 And the angel said to her, Fear not, Mary: for thou hast found
31 favour with God. And behold, thou shalt conceive in thy womb,
32 and bring forth a son, and shalt call his name Jesus. He shall be great, and shall be called the Son of the Highest; and the Lord
33 God shall give him the throne of his father David. And he shall reign over the house of Jacob for ever, and of his kingdom there
34 shall be no end. Then said Mary to the angel, How shall this be,
35 seeing I know not a man? And the angel answering said to her, The Holy Ghost shall come upon thee, and the power of the Highest shall overshadow thee; therefore also that holy thing which
36 shall be born, shall be called the Son of God. And behold, thy cousin Elisabeth, she hath also conceived a son in her old age:
37 and this is the sixth month with her who was called barren. For
38 with God nothing shall be impossible. And Mary said, Behold the handmaid of the Lord: be it unto me according to thy word. And the angel departed from her.
39 And Mary arose in those days, and went with haste into the hill
40 country, into a city of Judah, And entered into the house of Za-
41 charias, and saluted Elisabeth. And when Elisabeth heard the

to contract before witnesses some time before. And as Christ was to be born of a pure virgin, so the wisdom of God ordered it to be of one espoused, that to prevent reproach he might have a reputed father, according to the flesh.

28. *Hail, thou highly favoured; the Lord is with thee; blessed art thou among women*—Hail is the salutation used by our Lord to the women after his resurrection: *thou art highly favoured*, or *hast found favour with God*, ver. 30, is nc more than was said of Noah, Moses, and David. *The Lord is with thee*, was said to Gideon, Judg. vi, 12 ; *and blessed shall she be above women*, of Jael, Judg. v, 24. This salutation gives no room for any pretence of paying adoration to the virgin ; as having no appearance of a prayer, or of worship offered to her.

32. *He shall be called the Son of the Highest*—In this respect also : and that in a more eminent sense than any, either man or angel, can be called so. *The Lord shall give him the throne of his father David*—That is, the spiritual kingdom, of which David's was a type.

33. *He shall reign over the house of Jacob*—In which all true believers are included.

35. *The Holy Ghost shall come upon thee, and the power of the Highest shall overshadow thee*—The power of God was put forth by the Holy Ghost, as the immediate Divine agent in this work : and so he exerted the power of the Highest as his own power, who together with the Father and the Son is the most high God. *Therefore also*—Not only as he is God from eternity, but on this account likewise he *shall be called the Son of God*.

36. *And behold, thy cousin Elisabeth*—Though Elisabeth was of the house of Aaron, and Mary of the house of David, by the father's side, they might be related by their mothers. For the law only forbad heiresses marrying into another tribe. And so other persons continually intermarried; particularly the families of David and of Levi.

38. *And Mary said, Behold the handmaid of the Lord*—It is not improbable, that this time of the virgin's humble faith, consent, and expectation, might be the very time of her conceiving.

39. *A city of Judah*—Probably Hebron, which was situated in the hill country of Judea, and belonged to the house of Aaron.

41. *When Elisabeth heard the salutation of Mary*—The discourse with which she saluted her, giving an account of what the angel had said, the joy of her

salutation of Mary, the babe leaped in her womb : and Elisabeth
42 was filled with the Holy Ghost, And cried with a loud voice and
said, Blessed *art* thou among women, and blessed *is* the fruit of
43 thy womb. And whence *is* this to me, that the mother of my
44 Lord should come to me ? For lo ! when the voice of thy salutation sounded in my ears, the babe leaped in my womb for joy.
45 And happy *is* she that believed ; for there shall be a performance
46 of those things which were told her from the Lord. And Mary
47 said, My soul doth magnify the Lord, and my spirit hath rejoiced
48 in God my Saviour. For he hath regarded the low estate of his
handmaid : for behold, from henceforth all generations shall call
49 me blessed. For he that is mighty hath done to me great things,
50 and holy *is* his name. And his mercy is on them that fear him,
51 from generation to generation. He hath wrought strength with
his arm ; he hath scattered the proud in the imagination of their
52 hearts. He hath put down the mighty from *their* thrones, and
53 exalted them of low degree. He hath filled the hungry with good
54 things, but sent the rich empty away. He hath helped his servant
55 Israel, in remembrance of *his* mercy, As he spoke to our fathers,
56 to Abraham and to his seed for ever. And Mary abode with her
about three months, and returned to her own house.
57 　Now Elisabeth's- full time came, that she should be delivered,
58 and she brought forth a son. And her neighbours and relations
heard that the Lord had showed great mercy upon her, and they
59 rejoiced with her. And on the eighth day they came to circumcise the child, and they called him Zacharias, after the name of
60 his father. But his mother answering, said, Nay, but he shall be
61 called John. And they said to her, There is none of thy kindred
62 that is called by that name. And they made signs to his father,
63 what he would have him called. And asking for a writing tablet,

---

soul so affected her body, that the very child in her womb was moved in an uncommon manner, as if it leaped for joy.

45. *Happy is she that believed*—Probably she had in her mind the unbelief of
Zacharias.

46. *And Mary said*—Under a prophetic impulse, several things, which perhaps
she herself did not then fully understand.

47. *My spirit hath rejoiced in God my Saviour*—She seems to turn her thoughts
here to Christ himself, who was to be born of her, as the angel had told her, he
should be the Son of the Highest, whose name should be Jesus, the Saviour.
And she rejoiced in hope of salvation through faith in him, which is a blessing
common to all true believers, more than in being his mother after the flesh,
which was an honour peculiar to her. And certainly she had the same reason
to rejoice in God her Saviour that we have : because he had *regarded the low
estate of his handmaid*, in like manner as he regarded our low estate ; and vouchsafed to come and save her and us, when we were reduced to the lowest estate
of sin and misery.

51. *He hath wrought strength with his arm*—That is, he hath shown the exceeding greatness of his power. She speaks prophetically of those things as already done, which God was about to do by the Messiah. *He hath scattered the
proud*—Visible and invisible.

52. *He hath put down the mighty*—Both angels and men.

54. *He hath helped his servant Israel*—By sending the Messiah.

55. *To his seed*—His spiritual seed : all true believers.

56. *Mary returned to her own house*—And thence soon atter to Bethlehem

60. *His mother said*—Doubtless by revelation, or a particular impulse from God.

he wrote saying, His name is John. And they marvelled all.
64 And immediately his mouth was opened, and his tongue *loosed*, and
65 he spake, blessing God. And fear came on all that dwelt round
about them, and all these things were noised abroad, in all the
66 hill country of Judea. And all that heard *them*, laid *them* up in their
hearts, saying, What manner of child shall this be? And the hand·
67 of the Lord was with him. And his father Zacharias was filled
68 with the Holy Ghost, and prophesied, saying, Blessed be the Lord
69 God of Israel; for he hath visited and redeemed his people, And
hath raised up a horn of salvation for us, in the house of his ser-
70 vant David: As he spake by the mouth of his holy prophets, who
71 have been since the world began: That we should be saved from
72 our enemies, and from the hand of all that hate us; To perform
the mercy *promised* to our fathers, and to remember his holy cove-
73 nant, The oath which he sware to our father Abraham, That he
74 would grant us, being delivered out of the hand of his enemies, to
75 serve him without, fear, In holiness and righteousness before him,
76 all the days of our life. And thou, child, shalt be a prophet of the
Highest: for thou shalt go before the face of the Lord, to prepare
77 his ways, To give knowledge of salvation to his people, by the
78 remission of their sins, Through the tender mercy of our God,
79 whereby the day spring from on high hath visited us, To shine on
them that sit in darkness and in the shadow of death, to direct our
80 feet into the way of peace. And the child grew, and waxed strong
in spirit, and was in the deserts, till the day of his being shown to
Israel.
II. And in those days there went out a decree from Augustus Ce-
2 sar, that all the world should be enrolled. (Now this first enrol
3 ment was made when Cyrenius was governor of Syria.) And all
4 went to be enrolled, every one to his own city. And Joseph also
went up from Galilee, out of the city of Nazareth into Judea, to the
city of David, which is called Bethlehem, (because he was of the

---

66. *The hand of the Lord*—The peculiar power and blessing of God.
67. *And Zacharias prophesied*—Of things immediately to follow. But it is observable, he speaks of Christ chiefly; of John only, as it were, incidentally.
69. *A horn*—Signifies honour, plenty, and strength. *A horn of salvation*—That is, a glorious and mighty Saviour.
70. *His prophets, who have been since the world began*—For there were prophets from the very beginning.
74. *To serve him without fear*—Without any slavish fear. Here is the substance of the great promise. That we shall be always holy, always happy: that being delivered from Satan and sin, from every uneasy and unholy temper, we shall joyfully love and serve God, in every thought, word, and work.
76. *And thou, child*—He now speaks to John; yet not as a parent, but as a prophet.
77. *To give knowledge of salvation by the remission of sins*—The knowledge of the remission of our sins being the grand instrument of present and eternal salvation, Heb. viii, 11, 12. But the immediate sense of the words seems to be, to preach to them the Gospel doctrine of salvation by the remission of their sins.
78. *The day spring*—Or the rising sun; that is, Christ.
II. 1. *That all the world should be enrolled*—That all the inhabitants, male and female, of every town in the Roman empire, with their families and estates, should be registered.
2. *When Cyrenius was governor of Syria*—When Publius Sulpicius Quirinus governed the province of Syria, in which Judea was then included.

5 family and household of David,) To be enrolled with Mary, his
6 espoused wife, being with child. And while they were there, the
7 days were fulfilled, that she should be delivered. * And she
brought forth her son, the first born, and swathed him, and laid
him in a manger, because there was no room for them in the inn.
8 And there were in the same country, shepherds lying out in the
9 field, and keeping watch over their flock by night. And lo, an angel of the Lord came upon them, and the glory of the Lord shone
10 round about them : and they were sore afraid. And the angel
said to them, Fear not; for behold I bring you glad tidings of
11 great joy, which shall be to all people. For to you is born this
12 day in the city of David, a Saviour, who is Christ the Lord. And
this *shall be* a sign to you ; ye shall find the babe, wrapped in swad-
13 dling clothes, lying in a manger. And suddenly there was with
the angel a multitude of the heavenly host, praising God and say-
14 ing, Glory to God in the highest ; and on earth peace ; good will
toward men.
15 And when the angels were gone away from them into heaven,
the shepherds said one to another, Let us go to Bethlehem, and see
this thing which is done, which the Lord hath made known to us.
16 And they came with haste, and found Mary and Joseph, and the
17 babe lying in the manger. And having seen *it*, they made known
abroad the saying which was told them concerning the child.
18 And all that heard wondered at the things which were told them
19 by the shepherds. But Mary kept all these things, comparing them
20 together in her heart. And the shepherds returned, glorifying and
praising God for all the things that they had heard and seen, as it
was told them.
21 And when eight days were fulfilled, to circumcise the child, his
name was called Jesus, which was named of the angel, before he
was conceived in the womb.
22 And when the days of purification were fulfilled according to the

---

6. *And while they were there, the days were fulfilled that she should be delivered*—Mary seems not to have known that the child must have been born in Bethlehem, agreeably to the prophecy. But the providence of God took care for it.
7. *She laid him in the manger*—Perhaps it might rather be translated *in the
stall*. . They were lodged in the ox stall, fitted up on occasion of the great concourse, for poor guests. *There was no room for them in the inn*—Now also, there
is seldom room for Christ in an inn.
11. *To you*—Shepherds ; Israel ; mankind.
14. *Glory be to God in the highest ; on earth peace ; good will toward men*—
The shouts of the multitude are generally broken into short sentences. This rejoicing acclamation strongly represents the piety and benevolence of these heavenly spirits : as if they had said, *Glory be to God in the highest heavens :* let all
the angelic legions resound his praises. For with the Redeemer's birth, *peace*,
and all kind of happiness, come down to dwell *on earth :* yea, the overflowings
of Divine *good will* and favour are now exercised *toward men.*
20. *For all the things that they had heard*—From Mary ; *as it was told them*—
By the angels.
21. *To circumcise the child*—That he might visibly be *made under the law* by a
sacred rite, which obliged him to keep the whole law ; as also that he might be
owned to be the seed of Abraham, and might put an honour on the solemn dedication of children to God.
22. *The days*—The forty days prescribed, Lev. xii, 2, 4.

law of Moses, they brought him up to Jerusalem, to present him to
23 the Lord: (As it is written in the law of the Lord, * Every male
24 that openeth the womb shall be holy to the Lord,) And to offer a
sacrifice according to that which is said in the law of the Lord,
† A pair of turtle doves, or two young pigeons.
25 And behold, there was a man in Jerusalem whose name was
Simeon, and this man was just and devout, waiting for the consola-
26 tion of Israel : and the Holy Ghost was upon him. And it had
been revealed to him by the Holy Ghost, that he should not see
27 death before he had seen the Lord's Christ. And he came by
the Spirit into the temple. And when his parents brought in the
28 child Jesus, to do for him after the custom of the law, He took him
29 up in his arms, and blessed God, and said, Lord, now lettest thou
30 thy servant depart in peace, according to thy word : For mine
31 eyes have seen thy salvation ; Which thou hast prepared before
32 the face of all people. A light revealed to the Gentiles, and the
glory of thy people Israel. And Joseph and his mother marvelled
33 at those things which were spoken of him. And Simeon blessed
34 them, and said to Mary his mother, Behold, this child is set for
the fall and rising again of many in Israel, and for a sign which
35 shall be spoken against, (Yea, and a sword shall pierce through
thy own soul also,) that the thoughts of many hearts may be revealed.
36 And there was *one* Anna, a prophetess, the daughter of Pha-
nuel, of the tribe of Asher : she was far advanced in years, having
37 lived with a husband seven years *from* her virginity. And she
was a widow of about four-score and four years, who departed not
from the temple, but served *God* with fastings and prayers, night
38 and day. And she coming in at that hour, gave thanks to the Lord,

---

24. *A pair of turtle doves, or two young pigeons*—This offering sufficed for the
poor.
25. *The consolation of Israel*—A common phrase for the Messiah, who was to
be the everlasting consolation of the Israel of God. *The Holy Ghost was upon
him*—That is, he was a prophet.
27. *By the Spirit*—By a particular revelation or impulse from him.
30. *Thy salvation*—Thy Christ, thy Saviour.
32. *And the glory of thy people Israel*—For after the Gentiles are enlightened,
all Israel shall be saved.
33. *Joseph and his mother marvelled at those things which were spoken*—For
they did not thoroughly understand them.
34. *Simeon blessed them*—Joseph and Mary. *This child is set for the fall and
rising again of many*—That is, he will be a savour of death to some, to unbelievers : a savour of life to others, to believers : *and for a sign which shall be spoken
against*—A sign from God, yet rejected of men : but the time for declaring this
at large was not yet come : *that the thoughts of many hearts may be revealed*—
The event will be, that by means of that contradiction, the inmost thoughts of
many, whether good or bad, will be made manifest.
35. *A sword shall pierce through thy own soul*—So it did, when he suffered :
particularly at his crucifixion.
37. *Fourscore and four years*—These were the years of her life, not her
widowhood only. *Who departed not from the temple*—Who attended there at all
the stated hours of prayer. *But served God with fastings and prayers*—Even at
hat age. *Night and day*—That is, spending therein a considerable part of the
night, as well as of the day.

* Exod. xiii. 2.   † Lev xii, 8.

and spake of him to all that were waiting for redemption in Jeru-
39 salem.   And when they had performed all things, according to the
law of the Lord, they returned into Galilee, to their own city Na-
40 zareth.   And the child grew, and waxed strong in spirit, filled with
wisdom ; and the grace of God was upon him.
41   Now his parents went to Jerusalem every year at the feast of
42 the passover.   And when he was twelve years old, they went up
43 to Jerusalem, after the custom of the feast.   And when they had
fulfilled the days, as they returned, the child Jesus tarried behind
44 in Jerusalem ; and Joseph and his mother knew *it* not, But supposing him to be ·in the company, they went a day's journey ; and
sought him among *their* kinsfolk and among *their* acquaintance.
45 And not finding him, they went back to Jerusalem, seeking him.
46 And after three days, they found him in the temple, sitting in the
midst of the doctors, both hearing them and asking them ques-
47 tions.   And all that heard him were astonished at his understand-
48 ing and answers.   And seeing him they were amazed.   And his
mother said to him, Son, why hast thou done thus to us ?   Behold,
49 thy father and I have sought thee sorrowing.   And he said to
them, Why sought ye me ?   Knew ye not that I must be about
50 my Father's business ?   And they understood not the saying which

38. *To all that were waiting for redemption*—The sceptre now appeared to be
departing from Judah, though it was not actually gone : Daniel's weeks were
plainly near their period.   And the revival of the spirit of prophecy, together
with the memorable occurrences relating to the birth of John the Baptist, and
of Jesus, could not but encourage and quicken the expectation of pious persons
at this time.
Let the example of these aged saints animate those, whose hoary heads, like
theirs, are a crown of glory, being found in the way of righteousness.   Let those
venerable lips, so soon to be silent in the grave, be now employed in the praises
of their Redeemer.   Let them labour to leave those behind, to whom Christ will
be as precious as he has been to them ; and who will be waiting for God's salvation, when they are gone to enjoy it.
40. *And the child grew*—In bodily strength and stature ; *and waxed strong in
spirit*—The powers of his human mind daily improved ; *filled with wisdom*—By
the light of the indwelling Spirit, which gradually opened itself in his soul ; *and
the grace of God was upon him*—That is, the peculiar favour of God rested upon
him, even as man.
43. *The child Jesus*—St. Luke describes *in order* Jesus *the fruit of the womb*,
chap. i, 42 ; *an infant*, chap. ii, 12 ; *a little child*, ver. 40 ; *a child* here, and afterward *a man*.   So our Lord passed through and sanctified every stage of human
life.   Old age only did not become him.
44. *Supposing him to have been in the company*—As the men and women
usually travelled in distinct companies.
46. *After three days*—The first day was spent in their journey, the second, in
their return to Jerusalem : and the third, in searching for him there : *they found
him in the temple*—In an apartment of it : *sitting in the midst of the doctors*—
Not one word is said of his disputing with them, but only of his *asking* and
answering questions, which was a very usual thing in these assemblies, and
indeed the very end of them.   And if he was, with others, at the feet of these
teachers (where learners generally sat) he might be said to be in the midst of
them, as they sat on benches of a semi-circular form, raised above their hearers
and disciples.
49. *Why sought ye me ?*—He does not blame them for losing, but for thinking
it needful to seek him : and intimates, that he could not be lost, nor found any
where, but doing the will of a higher parent.
50. It is observable that Joseph is not mentioned after this time ; whence it is
probable, he did not live long after.

51 he spake to them. And he went down with them, and came to
    Nazareth, and was subject to them ; but his mother kept all these
52 things in her heart. And Jesus increased in wisdom and in stature,
    and in favour with God and man.
III. * Now in the fifteenth year of the reign of Tiberius ·Cesar,
    Pontius Pilate being governor of Judea, and Herod being tetrarch
    of Galilee, and his brother Philip tetrarch of Iturea and of the re-
2   gion of Trachonitis, and Lysanias tetrarch of Abilene, Annas being
    the high priest and Caiaphas, the word of God came to John, the
3   son of Zacharias, in the wilderness. And he came into all the
    country about Jordan, preaching the baptism of repentance, for the
4   remission of sins : As it is written in the book of the words of the
    Prophet Isaiah, saying, † The voice of one crying aloud in the
    wilderness, Prepare ye the way of the Lord, make his paths straight.
5   Every valley shall be filled, and every mountain and hill shall be
    brought low ; and the crooked shall be made straight, and the rough
6   ways smooth : And all flesh shall see the salvation of God. Then
7   said he to the multitude that came forth to be baptized of him, Ye
    brood of vipers, who hath warned you to flee from the wrath to come ?
8   Bring forth therefore fruits worthy of repentance ; and begin not
    to say within yourselves, We have Abraham to our father ; for I
    say to you, that God is able of these stones to raise up children
9   to Abraham. And now also the axe lieth at the root of the trees :
    every tree therefore which bringeth not forth good fruit, is hewn
    down and cast into the fire.
10   And the multitude asked him, saying, What then shall we do ?

52. *Jesus increased in wisdom*—As to his human nature, *and in favour with
God*—In proportion to that increase. It plainly follows, that though a man
were pure, even as Christ was pure, still he would have room to increase in holiness, and in consequence thereof to increase in the favour, as well as in the
love of God.
III. 1. *The fifteenth year of Tiberius*—Reckoning from the time when Augustus made him his colleague in the empire. *Herod being tetrarch of Galilee*—The
dominions of Herod the Great were, after his death, divided into four parts or
tetrarchies. This Herod his son was tetrarch of Galilee, reigning over that
fourth part of his dominions. His brother reigned over two other fourth parts,
the region of Iturea, and that of Trachonitis (that tract of land on the other side
Jordan, which had formerly belonged to the tribe of Manasseh.) *And Lysanias*
(probably descended from a prince of that name, who was some years before
governor of that country) *was tetrarch* of the remaining part of Abilene, which
was a large city of Syria, whose territories reached to Lebanon and Damascus,
and contained great numbers of Jews.
2. *Annas being high priest, and Caiaphas*—There could be but one high priest,
strictly speaking, at once. Annas was the high priest at that time, and Caiaphas
his sagan or deputy.
5. *Every valley shall be filled,* &c—That is, every hinderance shall be removed.
6. *The salvation of God*—The Saviour, the Messiah.
8. *Say not within yourselves, We have Abraham to our father*—That is, trust
not in your being members of the visible Church, or in any external privileges
whatsoever : for God now requires a change of heart ; and that without delay.
10. *He answereth*—It is not properly John, but the Holy Ghost, who teaches
us in the following answers, how to come ourselves, and how to instruct other
penitent sinners to come to Christ, that he may give them rest. The sum of all
this is, *Cease to do evil, learn to do well.* These are the *fruits worthy of
repentance.*

* Matt. iii, 1 ; Mark i, 1.   † Isaiah xl, 3.

11 He answering saith to them, He that hath two coats, let him impart to him that hath none; and he that hath meat, let him do
12 likewise. And publicans also came to be baptized, and said to
13 him, Master, what shall we do? And he said to them, Exact no
14 more than what is appointed you. And soldiers likewise asked
him, saying, And what shall we do? And he said to them, Do
violence to no man, neither accuse *any* falsely; and be conten
with your pay.
15   And as the people were in expectation, and all mused in their
16 hearts of John, whether he was not the Christ, John answered,
saying to them all, I indeed baptize you with water, but one mightier than I cometh, the latchet of whose shoes I am not worthy to
unloose: he shall baptize you with the Holy Ghost and with fire:
17 Whose fan *is* in his hand, and he will thoroughly purge his floor,
and will gather the wheat into his garner, but the chaff he will
18 burn with unquenchable fire. And many other things in *his* ex-
19 hortation preached he to the people. But Herod the tetrarch being reproved by him concerning Herodias, his brother Philip's
20 wife, and concerning all the evils which Herod had done, Added
also this above all, that he shut up John in prison.
21   * Now when all the people were baptized, it came to pass, that
Jesus also being baptized, and praying, the heaven was opened,
22 And the Holy Ghost descended in a bodily form, as a dove, upon
him, and a voice came from heaven, saying, Thou art my beloved
Son, in thee I delight.
23   And Jesus was about thirty years of age, when he began *his
ministry*, being, as was supposed, the son of Joseph, *who was the son*
24 of Heli, *The son* of Matthat, *the son* of Levi, *the son* of Melchi, *the*
25 *son* of Janna, *the son* of Joseph, *The son* of Mattathias, *the son* of
26 Amos, *the son* of Nahum, *the son* of Esli, *the son* of Nagge, *The son*
of Maath, *the son* of Mattathias, *the son* of Shimei, *the son* of Jo-
27 seph, *the son* of Judah, *The son* of Johanan, *the son* of Rhesa, *the son*

20. *He shut up John*—This circumstance, though it happened after, is here mentioned before our Lord's baptism, that his history (that of John being concluded) may then follow without any interruption.

21. *Jesus praying, the heaven was opened*—It is observable, that the three voices from heaven, see chap. ix, 29, 35; John xii, 28; by which the Father bore witness to Christ, were pronounced either while he was praying, or quickly after it.

23. *And Jesus was*—John's beginning was computed by the years of princes: our Saviour's by the years of his own life, as a more august era. *About thirty years of age*—He did not now enter upon his thirtieth year (as the common translation would induce one to think) but he now entered on his public ministry: being of such an age as the Mosaic law required. Our great Master attained not, as it seems, to the conclusion of his thirty-fourth year. Yet what glorious achievements did he accomplish within those narrow limits of time! Happy that servant, who, with any proportionable zeal, despatches the great business of life; and so much the more happy, if his sun go down at noon. For the space that is taken from the labours of time, shall be added to the rewards of eternity. *The son of Heli*—That is, the son-in-law: for Heli was the father of Mary. So St. Matthew writes the genealogy of Joseph, descended from David by Solomon; St. Luke that of Mary, descended from David by Nathan. In the genealogy of Joseph (recited by St. Matthew) that of Mary is implied, the Jews being accustomed to marry into their own families.

* Matt. iii, 13; Mark i. 9.

28 of Zerubbabel, *the son* of Salathiel, *the son* of Neri, *The son* of
Melchi, *the son* of Addi, *the son* of Cosam, *the son* of Elmodam, *the*
29 *son* of Er, *The son* of Jose, *the son* of Eleazar, *the son* of Jorim, *the*
30 *son* of Matthat, *the son* of Levi, *The son* of Simeon, *the son* of Judah
31 *the son* of Joseph, *the son* of Johanan, *the son* of Eliakim, *The son* of
Melea, *the son* of Menan, *the son* of Mattatha, *the son* of Nathan, *the*
32 *son* of David, *The son* of Jesse, *the son* of Obed, *the son* of Booz,
33 *the son* of Salmon, *the son* of Naasson, *The son* of Aminadab, *the son*
34 of Aaron, *the son* of Esrom, *the son* of Phares, *the son* of Judah, *The*
son of Jacob, *the son* of Isaac, *the son* of Abraham, *the son* of Terah,
35 *the son* of Nahor, *The son* of Saruch, *the son* of Ragau, *the son* of
36 Phalec, *the son* of Heber, *the son* of Sala, *The son* of Cainan, *the son*
of Arphaxad, *the son* of Shem, *the son* of Noah, *the son* of Lamech,
37 *The son* of Methuselah, *the son* of Enoch, *the son* of Jared, *the son*
38 of Maleleel, *the son* of Cainan, *The son* of Enos, *the son* of Seth,
the son of Adam, *the son* of God.

IV.   * And Jesus being full of the Holy Ghost, returned from Jor-
2 dan, and was led by the Spirit into the wilderness, Being forty
days tempted by the devil. And in those days he ate nothing, and
3 when they were ended, he hungered. And the devil said to him,
If thou be the Son of God, command this stone that it be made
4 bread. And Jesus answered him, saying, It is written, † Man
5 shall not live by bread alone, but by every word of God. And
the devil leading him up into a high mountain, showed him all
6 the kingdoms of the world in a moment. And the devil said to
him, All this power will I give thee, and the glory of them ; for
7 it is delivered to me, and I give it to whomsoever I will. If
8 thou therefore wilt worship me, all shall be thine. And Jesus
answering said to him, It is written, ‡ Thou shalt worship the
9 Lord thy God, and him only shalt thou serve. And he brought
him to Jerusalem, and set him on the battlement of the temple,
and said to him, If thou be the Son of God, cast thyself down from
10 hence : For it is written, § He shall charge his angels concerning
11 thee, to keep thee : And in their hands they shall bear thee up,
12 lest at any time thou dash thy foot against a stone. And Jesus
answering said to him, It is said, ‖ Thou shalt not tempt the Lord
13 thy God. And the devil having ended all the temptation, departed
from him till a convenient season.
14   And Jesus returned in the power of the Spirit into Galilee, and

---

38. *Adam* the son *of God*—That is, whatever the sons of Adam receive from
their human parents, Adam received immediately from God, except sin and
misery.
IV. 1. *The wilderness*—Supposed by some to have been in Judea ; by others to
have been that great desert of Horeb or Sinai, where the children of Israel were
tried for forty years, and Moses and Elijah fasted forty days.
6. *I give it to whomsoever I will*—Not so, Satan. It is God, not thou, that
putteth down one, and setteth up another : although sometimes Satan, by God's
permission, may occasion great revolutions in the world.
13. *A convenient season*—In the garden of Gethsemane, chap. xxii, 53.
14. *Jesus returned in the power of the Spirit*—Being more abundantly strengthened after his conflict.

* Matt. iv, 1 ; Mark i, 12.   † Deut. viii, 3.   ‡ Deut. vi, 13.   § Psa. xci, 11.
‖ Deut. vi, 16.

there went out a fame of him through all the region round
15 about   And he taught in their synagogues, being glorified of all.
16 * And he came to Nazareth, where he was brought up; and as
   his custom was, he went into the synagogue on the Sabbath, and
17 stood up to read.   And there was delivered to him the book of
   the Prophet Isaiah, and having opened the book, he found the
18 place where it was written, † The Spirit of the Lord is upon me,
   because he hath anointed me to preach the Gospel to the poor; he
   hath sent me to heal the broken hearted; to proclaim deliverance
   to the captives, and recovery of sight to the blind, to set at liberty
   them that are bruised, to publish the acceptable year of the Lord.
19 And having closed the book, he gave *it* again to the servant, and
20 sat down.   And the eyes of all in the synagogue were fastened
21 on him.   And he said to them, To-day is this scripture fulfilled in
22 your ears.   And they all bare him witness, and wondered at the
   gracious words which proceeded out of his mouth.   And they said,
23 Is not this Joseph's son?   And he said to them, Ye will surely say
   to me this proverb, Physician, heal thyself.   Whatsoever we have
24 heard done in Capernaum, do also here in thy own country.   And
   he said, Verily I say to you, No prophet is acceptable in his own

15. *Being glorified of all*—So God usually gives strong cordials after strong temptations. But neither their approbation continued long, nor the outward calm which he now enjoyed.

16. *He stood up*—Showing thereby that he had a desire to read the Scripture to the congregation: on which the book was given to him. It was the Jewish custom to read standing, but to preach sitting.

17. *He found*—It seems, opening upon it, by the particular providence of God.

18. *He hath anointed me*—With the Spirit. He hath, by the power of his Spirit which dwelleth in me, set me apart for these offices. *To preach the Gospel to the poor*—Literally and spiritually.

How is the doctrine of the ever-blessed trinity interwoven, even in those scriptures where one would least expect it? How clear a declaration of the great Three-One is there in those very words, *The Spirit—of the Lord is upon me! To proclaim deliverance to the captives, and recovery of sight to the blind, to set at liberty them that are bruised*—Here is a beautiful gradation, in comparing the spiritual state of men to the miserable state of those captives, who are not only cast into prison, but, like Zedekiah, had their eyes put out, and were laden and bruised with chains of iron.

19. *The acceptable year*—Plainly alluding to the year of jubilee, when all, both debtors and servants, were set free.

21. *To-day is this scripture fulfilled in your ears*—By what you hear me speak.

22. *The gracious words which proceeded out of his mouth*—A person of spiritual discernment may find in all the discourses of our Lord a peculiar sweetness, gravity, and becomingness, such as is not to be found in the same degree, not even in those of the apostles.

23. *Ye will surely say*—That is, your approbation now outweighs your prejudices. But it will not be so long. You will soon ask, why my love does not begin at home? Why I do not work miracles here, rather than at Capernaum? It is because of your unbelief. Nor is it any new thing for me to be despised in my own country. So were both Elijah and Elisha, and thereby driven to work miracles among heathens, rather than in Israel.

24. *No prophet is acceptable in his own country*—That is, in his own neighbourhood. It generally holds, that a teacher sent from God is not so acceptable to his neighbours as he is to strangers. The meanness of his family, or lowness of his circumstances, bring his office into contempt: nor can they suffer that

25 country. I tell you of a truth, Many widows were in Israel in the days of Elijah, * when the heaven was shut up three years and six months, while a great famine was through all the land. 26 Yet to none of these was Elijah sent, but to Sarepta, *a city* of 27 Sidon, to a widow. And many lepers were in Israel in the time of Elisha the prophet, yet none of them were cleansed, but 28 † Naaman the Syrian. And all in the synagogue hearing these 29 things, were filled with fury, And rising up, thrust him out of the city, and brought him to the brow of the hill whereon their city 30 was built, to cast him down headlong. But he passing through the midst of them, went away.

31 ‡ And he came down to Capernaum, a city of Galilee, and 32 taught them on the Sabbath days. And they were astonished at 33 his teaching, for his word was with authority. And there was in the synagogue a man who had a spirit of an unclean devil: and he 34 cried out with a loud voice, saying, Let us alone: What have we to do with thee, Jesus of Nazareth? Art thou come to destroy us? 35 I know thee who thou art; the Holy One of God. And Jesus rebuked him, saying, Hold thy peace, and come out of him. And the devil having thrown him in the midst, came out of him, and 36 hurt him not. And they were all amazed, and spake among themselves, saying, What word is this, that with authority and power he commandeth the unclean spirits, and they come out! 37 And the fame of him went forth into every place of the country round about.

38 § And rising up out of the synagogue, he entered into Simon's house. And Simon's wife's mother was ill of a great fever, and

he, who was before equal with, or below themselves, should now bear a superior character.

25. *When the heaven was shut up three years and six months*—Such a proof had they that God had sent him. In 1 Kings xviii, 1, it is said, *The word of the Lord came to Elijah in the third year :* namely, reckoning not from the beginning of the drought, but from the time when he began to sojourn with the widow of Sarepta. A year of drought had preceded this, while he dwelt at the brook Cherith. So that the whole time of the drought was (as St. James likewise observes) three years and six months.

28. *And all in the synagogue were filled with fury*—Perceiving the purport of his discourse, namely, that the blessing which they despised, would be offered to, and accepted by, the Gentiles. So changeable are the hearts of wicked men! So little are their starts of love to be depended on! So unable are they to bear the close application, even of a discourse which they most admire!

30. *Passing through the midst of them*—Perhaps invisibly; or perhaps they were overawed; so that though they saw, they could not touch him.

31. *He came down to Capernaum*—And dwelt there, entirely quitting his abode at Nazareth.

34. *What have we to do with thee*—Thy present business is with men, not with devils. *I know thee who thou art*—But surely he did not know a little before, that he was God over all, blessed for ever; or he would not have dared to tell him, *All this power is delivered to me, and I give it to whomsoever I will. The Holy One of God*—Either this confession was extorted from him by terror, (for the devils believe and tremble,) or he made it with a design to render the character of Christ suspected. Possibly it was from hence the Pharisees took occasion to say, *He casteth out devils by the prince of the devils.*

* 1 Kings xvii 19 · xviii, 44.   † 2 Kings v, 14.   ‡ Mark i, 21.   § Matt. viii, 14; Mark i, 29.

39 they besought him for her. And standing over her, he rebuked
the fever, and it left her: and immediately she arose and served
40 them. * Now when the sun was set, all that had any sick of
divers diseases brought them to him; and he laid his hands on
41 every one of them, and healed them. And devils also came out
of many, crying out and saying, Thou art Christ, the Son of
God. And he rebuking them, suffered them not to say that they
42 knew he was the Christ. † And when it was day, going out he
went into a desert place : and the multitude sought him, and came
43 to him, and detained him, that he might not depart from them. And
he said to them, I must preach the kingdom of God to other cities
44 also, for therefore am I sent. And he preached in the synagogues
of Galilee.
V.   ‡ And as the multitude pressed on him to hear the word of
2 God, · he stood by the lake Gennesareth, And saw two vessels
standing by the lake ; but the fishermen were gone out of them,
3 and were washing *their* nets. And going into one of the vessels,
which was Simon's, he desired him to thrust out a little from the
4 land. And sitting down, he taught the multitude out of the vessel.
When he had ceased speaking, he said to Simon, Launch out into
5 the deep, and let down your nets for a draught. · But Simon answering said to him, Master, having toiled all night, we have taken
6 nothing : nevertheless at thy word I will let down the net. And
having done this they enclosed a great multitude of fishes, and the
7 net brake. And they beckoned to their partners, who were in the
other vessel to come and help them ; and they came and filled
8 both the vessels so that they began to sink. Simon Peter seeing
it, fell down at Jesus's knees, saying, Depart from me ; for I am a
9 sinful man, O Lord. For astonishment seized him, and all that
were with him, at the draught of fishes which they had taken.
10 And in like manner also James and John, the sons of Zebedee,
11 who were partners with Simon. And Jesus said to Simon, Fear
not : from henceforth thou shalt catch men. And when they had
brought their vessels to land, they forsook all and followed him.
12   § And when he was in a certain city, behold, a man full of
leprosy, who seeing Jesus, fell on *his* face, and besought him, say-
13 ing, Lord, if thou wilt, thou canst make me clean. And stretching
forth *his* hand he touched him, saying, I will ; be thou clean.
14 And immediately the leprosy departed from him. And he charged
him to tell no man : but go, show thyself to the priest, and offer
for thy cleansing, ‖ as Moses commanded, for a testimony to them.
15 But the fame of him went abroad the more, and great multitudes

---

40. *When the sun was set*—And consequently ʿne Sabbath ended, which they
reckoned from sunset to sunset.
V. 6. *Their net brake*—Began to tear.
8. *Depart from me, for I am a sinful man*—And therefore not worthy to be in
thy presence.
11. *They forsook all and followed him*—They had followed him before, John
ı, 43, but not so as to forsake all. Till now, they wrought at their ordinary
calling.

＊ Matt. viii, 16 ; Mark i, 32.   † Mark i, 35.   ‡ Matt. iv, 18 ; Mark i, 16.
§ Matt. viii, 2 ; Mark i, 40.   ‖ Lev. xiv, 2.

came together, to hear and to be healed by him of their infirmities
16 But he withdrew into the deserts and prayed.
17 And on a certain day as he was teaching, there were Phari
sees and doctors of the law sitting by, who were come out of every
town of Galilee, and *out of* Judea and Jerusalem : and the power
18 of the Lord was *present* to heal them. * And behold men bringing
on a couch a man that was ill of the palsy ; and they sought to
19 bring him in and lay *him* before him. And, not finding by what
way they might bring him in through the multitude, they went up
on the house, and let him down through the tiling with *his* couch
20 into the midst, before Jesus. And seeing their faith, he said to
21 him, Man, thy sins are forgiven thee. And the scribes and the
Pharisees reasoned, saying, Who is this that speaketh blasphemies ?
22 Who can forgive sins but God only ? And Jesus knowing their
thoughts, answered and said to them, Why reason ye ·in your
23 hearts ? Which is easier ? To say, Thy sins are forgiven thee ?
24 Or to say, Arise and walk ? But that ye may know that the Son
of man hath authority on earth to forgive sins (he said to the paralytic) I say to thee, Arise, take up thy couch, and go to thine house.
25 And immediately rising up before them, and taking up that on
26 which he lay, he went to his house, glorifying God. And they
were all amazed, and glorified God, and were filled with fear, saying, We have seen strange things to-day.
27 † And after these things he went forth, and saw a publican, named
Levi, sitting at the receipt of custom, and said to him, Follow me.
28 And leaving all, he rose up and followed him. And Levi made
29 him a great entertainment in his own house ; And there was a
great company of publicans and of others that sat down with them.
30 But the scribes and Pharisees murmured against his disciples,
saying, Why do ye eat and drink with publicans and sinners ?
31 And Jesus answering said to them, They that are whole need not
32 a physician, but they that are sick. I came not to call the right-
33 eous, but sinners to repentance. ‡ And they said to him, Why do
the disciples of John, and likewise of the Pharisees, fast often and
34 make prayers ; but thine eat and drink ? And he said to them,

---

16. *He withdrew*—The expression in the original implies, that he did so
frequently.
17. *Sitting by*—As being more honourable than the bulk of the congregation,
who stood. *And the power of the Lord was present to heal them*—To heal the
sickness of their souls, as well as all bodily diseases.
19. Not being able to *bring him in through the multitude, they went* round
about by a back passage, and going up the stairs on the outside, they came *upon
the* flat-roofed *house*, and *let him down* through the trap door, such as was on the
top of most of the Jewish houses : doubtless, with such circumspection as the
circumstances plainly required.
26. *We have seen strange things to-day*—Sins forgiven, miracles wrought.
28. *Leaving all*—His business and gain.
29. *And Levi made him a great entertainment*—It was necessarily great, because of the great number of guests.
33. *Make prayers*—Long and solemn.
34. *Can ye make*—That is, is it proper to make men fast and mourn, during a
festival solemnity ?

* Matt. ix, 2 ; Mark ii, 3.　　† Matt. ix, 9 ; Mark ii, 14.　　‡ Matt. ix, 14 ; Mark ii, 18.

Can ye make the children of the bride chamber fast, while the
35 bridegroom is with them? But the days will come, when the
bridegroom shall be taken away from them: and then shall they
36 fast in those days. He spake also a parable to them, No man
putteth a piece of a new garment upon an old; otherwise both the
new maketh a rent, and the piece out of the new agreeth not with
37 the old. And no man putteth new wine into old leathern bottles:
else the new wine will burst the bottles, and be spilled, and the
38 bottles will perish. But new wine must be put into new bottles, and
39 both are preserved. And no man having drunk old wine, straightway desireth new; for he saith, The old is better.
VI.   * And on the first Sabbath after the second *day* of unleavened
bread, he went through the corn fields, and his disciples plucked
2 the ears of corn, and ate, rubbing *them* in *their* hands. And certain of the Pharisees said to them, Why do ye what it is not law-
3 ful to do on the Sabbath day? And Jesus answering them said,
Have ye not read even this, what David did, when himself hun-
4 gered, and they that were with him? † How he went into the
house of God, and took and ate the show bread, and gave also to
them that were with him, which it is not lawful to eat, but for the
5 priests only? And he said to them, The Son of man is Lord even
of the Sabbath.
.6   ‡ And on another Sabbath also he went into the synagogue and
taught. And there was a man whose right hand was withered.·
7 And the scribes and the Pharisees watched, whether he would
heal on the Sabbath, that they might find an accusation against
8 him. But he knew their thoughts, and said to the man that had
the withered hand, Rise and stand forth in the midst. And he
9 arose and stood forth. Then said Jesus to them, I will ask you,
Which is lawful on the Sabbath, To do good, or to do evil? To save
10 life, or to kill? And looking round upon them all, he said to him,
Stretch forth thy hand; and he did so: and his hand was restored
11 as the other. And they were filled with madness, and talked one
with another what they should do to Jesus.
12   § And in those days he went out into the mountain to pray, and
13 continued all night in the prayer of God. ‖ And when it was day
he called to him his disciples, and chose twelve of them, whom

---

36. *He spake also a parable*—Taken from clothes and wine; therefore peculiarly proper at a feast.
39. *And no man having drunk old wine*—And beside, men are not wont to be
immediately freed from old prejudices.
VI. 1. *The first Sabbath*—So the Jews reckoned their Sabbaths, from the
passover to pentecost; the first, second, third, and so on, till the seventh Sabbath (after the second day.) This immediately preceded pentecost, which was
the fiftieth day after the second day of unleavened bread.
2. *Why do ye*—St. Matthew and Mark represent the Pharisees as proposing
the question to our Lord himself. It was afterward, probably, they proposed it
to his disciples.
9. *To save life or to kill*—He just then probably saw the design to kill him
rising in their hearts.
12. *In the prayer of God*—The phrase is singular and emphatical, to imply an
extraordinary and sublime devotion.

* Matt. xii, 1; Mark ii, 23.   † 1 Sam. xxi, 6.   ‡ Matt. xii, 9; Mark iii, 1.
        § Mark iii, 13.   ‖ Matt. x, 2; Mark iii, 14; Acts i, 13.

14 also he named apostles : Simon (whom also he named Peter)
and Andrew his brother, James and John, Philip and Bartholo-
15 mew, Matthew and Thomas, James the *son* of Alpheus, and
16 Simon called Zelotes, Jude *the brother* of James, and Judas Iscariot,
17 who also became a traitor. And coming down with them, he stood
on a plain, and the company of his disciples, and a great multitude of people from all Judea and Jerusalem, and the sea coast of
Tyre and Sidon, who were come to hear him, and to be healed of
18 their diseases ; And they that were vexed with unclean spirits : and
19 they were healed. And the whole multitude sought to touch him ;
for virtue went out of him, and healed them all.
20   * And lifting up his eyes on his disciples he said, Happy *are*
21 ye poor; for yours is the kingdom of God. Happy *are* ye that
hunger now ; for ye shall be satisfied : happy *are* ye that weep now ;
22 for ye shall laugh. Happy *are* ye when men shall hate you, and
shall separate you *from their company*, and shall revile you, and
23 cast out your name as evil, for the Son of man's sake. Rejoice in
that day and leap for joy : for behold your reward *is* great in hea
24 ven ; for in like manner did their fathers to the prophets. But
25 wo to you that are rich ; for ye have your consolation. Wo to you
that are full ; for ye shall hunger ; wo to you that laugh now ; for
26 ye shall mourn and weep. Wo *to you*, when all men shall speak
well of you ; for so did their fathers to the false prophets.
27   † But I say to you that hear, Love your enemies ; do good to
28 them that hate you. Bless them that curse you, pray for them
29 that despitefully use you. ‡ And to him that smiteth thee on the
cheek, offer also the other : and to him that taketh away thy cloak,
30 forbid not *to take* thy coat also. § Give to every man that asketh
thee, and of him that taketh away thy goods, ask *them* not again.

15. *Simon called Zelotes*—Full of zeal ; otherwise called Simon the Canaanite.
17. *On a plain*—At the foot of the mountain.
20. In the following verses our Lord, in the audience of his newly-chosen disciples, and of the multitude, repeats, *standing on the plain*, many remarkable
passages of the sermon he had before delivered, *sitting on the mount.*
He here again pronounces the *poor* and the *hungry*, the *mourners*, and the *per
secuted*, happy; and represents as miserable those who are *rich*, and *full*, and
joyous, and *applauded :* because generally prosperity is a sweet poison, and
affliction a healing, though bitter medicine. Let the thought reconcile us to
adversity, and awaken our caution when the world smiles upon us; when a
plentiful table is spread before us, and our cup is running over; when our spirits
are gay ; and we hear (what nature loves) our own praise from men. *Happy
are ye poor*—The word seems here to be taken literally : ye who have left all
for me.
24. Miserable are *ye rich*—If ye have received or sought your consolation or
happiness therein.
25. *Full*—Of meat and drink, and worldly goods. *That laugh*—That are of a
light trifling spirit.
26. *Wo to you when all men shall speak well of you*—But who will believe this ?
27. *But I say to you that hear*—Hitherto our Lord had spoken only to particu
lar sorts of persons : now he begins speaking to all in general.
29. *To him that smiteth thee on the cheek*—*Taketh away thy cloak*—These seem
to be proverbial expressions, to signify an invasion of the tenderest points of
honour and property. *Offer the other*—*Forbid not thy coat*—That is, rather yield
to his repeating the affront or injury, than gratify resentment in righting your
self, in any method not becoming Christian love.

* Matt. v, 3   † Matt. v, 44.   ‡ Matt. v, 39.   § Matt. v, 42.

31   * And as ye would that men should do to you, do ye also to them
32 likewise.   For if ye love them that love you, what thank have ye ?
33 For sinners also love those that love them.   And if ye do good to
   them that do good to you, what thank have ye ?   For even sinners
34 do the same.   And if ye lend to them of whom ye hope to receive,
   what thank have ye ?   For even sinners lend to sinners, to receive
35 as much again.   But love ye your enemies, and do good and lend,
   hoping for nothing again ; and your reward shall be great, and ye
   shall be sons of the Highest ; for he is kind to the unthankful
36 and the evil.   Be ye therefore merciful, as your Father also is
37 merciful.   † Judge not, and ye shall not be judged : condemn not
   and ye shall not be condemned : forgive, and ye shall be forgiven :
38 G.ve and it shall be given to you ; good measure, pressed down,
   and shaken together, and running over, shall they give into your
   bosom.   For with the same measure that ye mete with, it shall
39 be measured to you again.   And he spoke a parable to them,
   ‡ Can the blind lead the blind ?   Will they not both fall into the
40 ditch ?   § The disciple is not above his master, but every one that
41 is perfected, shall be as his master.   ‖ And why beholdest thou the
   mote that is in thy brother's eye, but perceivest not the beam that
42 is in thine own eye ?   Or how canst thou say to thy brother, Brother, let me pull out the mote that is in thine eye, thou thyself not
   seeing the beam that is in thine own eye.   Thou hypocrite, cast
   first the beam out of thine own eye, and then shalt thou see clearly
43 to pull out the mote that is in thy brother's eye.   For there is no
   good tree which bringeth forth corrupt fruit, neither a corrupt tree
44 which bringeth forth good fruit.   For every tree is known by its
   own fruit ; for they do not gather figs from thorns, nor from a bram-
45 ble do they gather grapes.   A good man, out of the good treasure
   of his heart, bringeth forth that which is good ; and an evil man, out

30. *Give to every one*—Friend or enemy, what thou canst spare, and he really
wants : *and of him that taketh away thy goods*—By borrowing, if he be insolvent,
ask them not again.

32. It is greatly observable, our Lord has so little regard for one of the highest
instances of *natural* virtue, namely, the returning love for love, that he does not
account it even to deserve thanks.   *For even sinners,* saith he, *do the same :* men
who do not regard God at all.   Therefore he may do this, who has not taken
one step in Christianity.

38. *Into your bosom*—Alluding to the mantles the Jews wore, into which a large
quantity of corn might be received.   *With the same measure that ye mete with,
it shall be measured to you again*—Amazing goodness! So we are permitted
even to carve for ourselves !   We ourselves are, as it were, to tell God *how much*
mercy he shall show us !   And can we be content with less than the very *largest
measure ?*   Give then to man, what thou designest to receive of God.

39 *He spake a parable*—Our Lord sometimes used parables when he knew
plain and open declarations would too much inflame the passions of his hearers.
It is for this reason he uses this parable, *Can the blind lead the blind ?*—Can the
scribes teach this way, which they know not themselves ?   Will not they and
their scholars per sh together ?   Can they make their disciples any better than
themselves ?   But as for those who will be my disciples, *they shall be all taught
of God ;* who wil enable them to *come to the measure of the stature of the fulness
of their Master.*   Be not ye like their disciples, censuring others, and not amend
mg yourselves.

* Matt. vii, 12   † Matt. vii, 1.   ‡ Matt. xv, 14.   § Matt. x, 24 ; John xv, 20.
‖ Matt. vii, 3.

of the evil treasure of his heart, bringeth forth that which is evil:
46 for out of the abundance of the heart his mouth speaketh.   * And
why call ye me Lord, Lord, and do not the things which I say?
47 † Whosoever cometh to me, and heareth my sayings, and doth
48 them, I will show you to whom he is like.   He is like a man
who built a house, and digged deep, and laid the foundation on a
rock : and when a flood arose, the stream broke vehemently upon
that house, but could not shake it; for it was founded on a rock.
49 But he that heareth, and doth not, is like a man that built a house
without a foundation upon the earth : against which the stream
broke vehemently, and immediately it fell; and the breach of that
house was great.

VII.   ‡ Now when he had ended all his sayings in the hearing of
2 the people, he entered into Capernaum.   And a certain centurion's
3 servant who was dear to him, was sick and ready to die.   And
hearing of Jesus, he sent to him elders of the Jews, beseeching
4 him to come and heal his servant.   And coming to Jesus, they besought him earnestly, saying, he is worthy for whom thou shouldest
5 do this.   For he loveth our nation, and hath himself built us a
6 synagogue.   Then Jesus went with them.   And when he was now
not far from the house, the centurion sent friends to him, saying
to him, Lord, trouble not thyself; for I am not worthy that thou
7 shouldest enter under my roof.   Wherefore neither thought I myself worthy to come to thee ; but speak in a word, and my servant
8 shall be healed.   For I am a man set under authority, having soldiers under me : and I say to one, Go, and he goeth, and to ano-
other, Come, and he cometh, and to my servant, Do this, and he
9 doth it.   Jesus hearing these things, marvelled at him, and turning, said to the people that followed him, I say to you, I have
10 not found so great faith in Israel.   And they that had been
sent, returning to the house, found the servant whole that had
been sick.

11   And he went afterward to a city called Nain, and many of his
12 disciples went with him and a great multitude.   And as he drew
nigh the gate of the city, behold a dead man was carried out, the
only son of his mother, and she was a widow ; and a great multi-
13 tude of the city was with her.   And the Lord seeing her, was
14 moved with tender compassion for her, and said, Weep not.   And
15 coming near, he touched the bier, and the bearers stood still.   And
he said, Young man, I say to thee, Arise.   And the dead man sat
16 up, and began to speak : and he delivered him to his mother.ᐟ   And
fear seized all, and they glorified God, saying, A great prophet is
17 risen up among us ; and God hath visited his people.   And this
rumour of him went forth through all Judea, and all the country
round about.

18   ◊ And the disciples of John informed him of all these things.
19 And John, calling to him two of his disciples, sent *them* to Jesus,

---

46. *And why call ye me Lord, Lord*—What will fair professions avail, without
a life answerable thereto ?

VII. 3. *Hearing of Jesus*—Of his miracles, and of his arrival at Capernaum

* Matt. vii 21   † Matt. v ·, 24.   ‡ Matt. viii, 5.   ◊ Matt. xi, 2.

20 saying, Art thou he that is to come, or look we for another? And
the men being come to him, said, John the Baptist hath sent us to
thee, saying, Art thou he that is to come, or look we for another?
21 And in that hour he cured many of diseases and plagues, and of
22 evil spirits, and to many that were blind he gave sight. And he
answering said to them, Go and relate to John the things ye have
seen and heard: the blind see; the lame walk; the lepers are
cleansed; the deaf hear; the dead are raised; to the poor the Gos-
23 pel is preached. And happy is he, whosoever shall not be offend-
24 ed at me. And when the messengers of John were departed, he
said to the people concerning John, What went ye out into the
25 wilderness to see? A reed shaken by the wind? But what went
ye out to see? A man clothed in soft garments? Behold, they
that are splendidly apparelled, and live delicately, are in kings' pa-
26 laces. But what went ye out to see? A prophet? Yea, I say
27 to you, and much more than a prophet. This is he of whom it is
written, * Behold, I send my messenger before thy face, who shall
28 prepare thy way before thee. For I say to you, Among those that
are born of women, there is not a greater prophet than John the
Baptist; but he that is least in the kingdom of God is greater than
29 he. And all the people that heard him, and the publicans, justified
30 God, being baptized with the baptism of John. But the Pharisees
and the scribes made void the counsel of God toward themselves,
31 being not baptized of him. To whom then shall I liken the men
32 of this generation, and to what are they like? They are like children sitting in the market place, and calling one to another, and
saying, We have piped to you, and ye have not danced; we have
33 mourned to you, and ye have not wept. For John the Baptist came
neither eating bread, nor drinking wine; and ye say he hath a
34 devil. The Son of man is come eating and drinking; and ye say,

22. *To the poor the Gospel is preached*—Which is the greatest mercy, and the greatest miracle of all.

24. *When the messengers were departed*—He did not speak the following things in the hearing of John's disciples, lest he should seem to flatter John, or to compliment him into an adherence to his former testimony. To avoid all suspicion of this kind, he deferred his commendation of him, till the messengers were gone; and then delivered it to the people, to prevent all imaginations, as if John were wavering in his judgment, and had sent the two disciples for his own, rather than their satisfaction.

28. *There is not a greater prophet than John*—A greater teacher. *But he that is least in the kingdom of God*—The least teacher whom I send forth.

29. *And all the people*—Our Lord continues his discourse: *justified God*—Owned his wisdom and mercy in thus calling them to repentance, and preparing them for Him that was to come.

30. *But the Pharisees and scribes*—The good, learned, honourable men: *made void the counsel*, the gracious design, *of God toward them*—They disappointed all these methods of his love, and would receive no benefit from them.

32. *They are like children sitting in the market place*—So froward and perverse, that no contrivance can be found to please them. It is plain our Lord means, that they were like the children complained of, not like those that made the complaint.

34. *But wisdom is justified by all her children*—The children of wisdom are those who are truly wise unto salvation. The wisdom of God in all these dispensations, these various methods of calling sinners to repentance, is owned and heartily approved by all these.

* Mal. iii. 1.

Behold a gluttonous man, and a wine bibber, a friend of publicans
35 and sinners.   But wisdom is justified by all her children.
36   And one of the Pharisees asked him to eat with him.   And go-
37 ing into the Pharisee's house, he sat down to table.   And behold,
a woman in the city, who had been a sinner, when she knew
that Jesus sat at table in the Pharisee's house, brought an alabaster
38 box of ointment, And standing at his feet behind *him* weeping
watered his feet with a shower of tears, and wiped *them* with the
hairs of her head, and kissed his feet, and anointed them with the
39 ointment.   But the Pharisee, who had invited him, seeing *it*, spake
within himself, saying, This man, if he were a prophet, would have
known who and what manner of woman *this is* that toucheth him;
40 for she is a sinner.   And Jesus answering said to him, Simon, I
41 have somewhat to say to thee.   And he saith, Master, say on.   A
certain creditor had two debtors : the one owed five hundred pence,
42 and the other fifty.   But they having nothing to pay, he frankly
43 forgave them both.   Which therefore will love him most?   Simon
answering said, I suppose he to whom he forgave most.   He said
44 to him, Thou hast rightly judged.   And turning to the woman, he
said to Simon, Seest thou this woman?   I entered into thy house,
thou gavest me no water for my feet : but she hath watered my
45 feet with tears, and wiped *them* with the hairs of her head.   Thou
gavest me no kiss ; but she, from the time I came in, hath not
46 ceased to kiss my feet.   Thou didst not anoint my head with oil :
47 but she hath anointed my feet with ointment.   Wherefore I say to
thee, those many sins of hers are forgiven ; therefore she loveth
48 much : but he to whom little is forgiven, loveth little.   And he saith
49 to her, Thy sins are forgiven thee.   And they that sat at table with
50 him said within themselves, Who is this that forgiveth sins also?
And he said to the woman, Thy faith hath saved thee : go in peace.
VIII.   And afterward he went through every city and village preaching and publishing the glad tidings of the kingdom of God : and the
2 twelve *were* with him.   And certain women who had been healed

---

36. *And one of the Pharisees asked him to eat with him*—Let the candour with
which our Lord accepted this invitation, and his gentleness and prudence at this
ensnaring entertainment, teach us to mingle the wisdom of the serpent, with the
innocence and sweetness of the dove.   Let us neither absolutely refuse all
favours, nor resent all neglects, from those whose friendship is at best very
doubtful, and their intimacy by no means safe.

37. *A woman*—Not the same with Mary of Bethany, who anointed him six
days before his last passover.

40. *And Jesus said, Simon, I have somewhat to say to thee*—So tender and courteous an address does our Lord use even to a proud, censorious Pharisee !

43. *Which of them will love him most ?*—Neither of them will love him at all,
before he has forgiven them.   An insolvent debtor, till he is forgiven, does not
love, but *fly* his creditor.

44. *Thou gavest me no water*—It was customary with the Jews to show respect and kindness to their welcome guests, by saluting them with a kiss,
washing their feet, and anointing their heads with oil, or some fine ointment.

47. *Those many sins of hers are forgiven; therefore she loveth much*—The fruit
of her having had much forgiven.   It should carefully be observed here, that her
love is mentioned as the *effect* and *evidence*, not the *cause* of her pardon.   She
knew that much had been forgiven her, and therefore she loved much.

50. *Thy faith hath saved thee*—Not thy love.   Love is salvation.

of evil spirits and infirmities, Mary, called Magdalene, out of whom
3 had gone seven devils, And Joanna, the wife of Chuza, Herod's
steward, and Susanna, and many others, who ministered to him of
their substance.
4 * And a great multitude being gathered together, coming to him
5 out of every city, he spake by a parable, A sower went forth to
sow his seed: and while he sowed, some fell by the high-way side;
and it was trodden down, and the birds of the air devoured it.
6 And some fell upon the rock, and springing up, it withered away,
7 because it lacked moisture. And some fell among thorns, and the
8 thorns sprang up with it, and choked it. And other fell on good
ground, and sprang up, and yielded fruit a hundred fold. And
saying these things, he cried aloud, He that hath ears to hear, let
9 him hear. And his disciples asked him, What is the parable?
10 And he said, To you it is given to know the mysteries of the kingdom of God, but to others in parables, so that seeing they do not
11 see, and hearing they do not understand. Now the parable is
12 this: the seed is the word of God. Those by the high-way side
are they that hear; then cometh the devil and taketh away the
word out of their hearts, lest they should believe and be saved.
13 Those on the rock *are they* who, when they hear, receive the word
with joy. But they have no root, who for a while believe; but in
14 time of temptation fall away. That which fell among the thorns
are they who, having heard, go forth, and are choked with cares,
and riches, and pleasures of *this* life, and bring no fruit to perfec-
15 tion. But that on the good ground are they who, having heard
the word, keep it in an honest and good heart, and bring forth fruit
16 with perseverance. † No man having lighted a candle, covereth it
with a vessel, or putteth it under a bed; but setteth *it* on a can-
17 dlestick, that they who come in may see the light. ‡ For there is
nothing hid that shall not be discovered, neither any thing con-
18 cealed, that shall not be known and come to light. § Take heed
therefore, how ye hear: for whosoever hath, to him shall be given;
and whosoever hath not, from him shall be taken away even what
he most assuredly hath.
19 ‖ Then came toward him his mother and his brethren, but could
20 not come to him for the crowd. And it was told him *by some* who
said, Thy mother and thy brethren stand without, desiring to speak
21 with thee. And he answering said to them, My mother and my
brethren are these who hear the word of God and do it.

VIII. 2. *Mary Magdalene*—Or Mary of Magdala, a town in Galilee: probably
the person mentioned in the last chapter.
15. *Who—keep it*—Not like the high-way side: *And bring forth fruit*—Not
like the thorny ground: *With perseverance*—Not like the stony.
16. *No man having lighted a candle*—As if he had said, And let your good fruit
appear openly.
17. *For nothing is hid*—Strive not to conceal it at all; for you can conceal
nothing long.
18. The word commonly translated *seemeth*, wherever it occurs, does not
weaken, but greatly strengthens the sense.

* Matt. xiii, 1; Mark iv, 1.   † Matt. v, 15; Mark iv, 21; Chap. xi, 33.   ‡ Matt. x, 26;
Mark iv, 22; Chap. xii, 2.   § Matt. xiii, 12; Mark iv, 25; Chap. xix, 26.   ‖ Matt. xii,
46; Mark iii, 31.

22   * And on a certain day he went into a vessel with his disciples : and he said to them, Let us go over to the other side of the lake.
23 And they put to sea. And as they sailed, he fell asleep. And there came down a storm of wind on the lake, and they were filled
24 *with water*, and were in danger. And coming to him, they awoke him, saying, Master, master, we perish ! And rising he rebuked the wind and the raging of the water, and they ceased, and there
25 was a calm. And he said to them, Where is your faith ? But they were afraid and wondered, saying one to another, What manner of man is this ? For he commandeth even the winds and the water, and they obey him.
26   † And they sailed to the country of the Gadarenes, which is
27 over against Galilee. And as he went forth to land, there met him out of the city, a certain man that had had devils a long time, and
28 wore no clothes neither abode in a house, but in the tombs. But seeing Jesus, he cried out and fell down before him, and said with a loud voice, What have I to do with thee, Jesus, thou Son of the
29 most high God ? I beseech thee torment me not. (For he had commanded the unclean spirit to come out of the man : for many times it had caught him, and he had been kept bound with chains and fetters, and breaking the bands asunder, he had been driven by
30 the devil into the deserts.) And Jesus asked him, saying, What is thy name ? And he said, Legion ; because many devils had
31 entered into him. And they besought him that he would not com-
32 mand them to go away into the abyss. And there was a herd of many swine feeding on the mountain : and they besought him, that he would suffer them to enter into them : and he suffered
33 them. Then the devils going out of the man, entered into the swine : and the herd rushed down the steep into the lake, and were
34 stifled. And they that fed them, seeing what was done, fled, and
35 went and told *it* in the city and in the country. Then they went out to see what was done, and came to Jesus, and found the man out of whom the devils were departed, sitting at the feet of Jesus,
36 clothed, and in his right mind · and they were afraid. They also that had seen *it* related to them, how he that was possessed by the
37 devils, was healed. ‡ Then the whole multitude of the country of the Gadarenes round about, besought him to depart from them ; for they were taken with great fear, and he went into the vessel and
38 returned. And the man out of whom the devils were departed, besought him that he might be with him. But Jesus sent him
39 away, saying, Return home, and tell how great things God hath done for thee. And he went and published through the whole city, how great things Jesus had done for him.

---

29. *For many times it had caught him*—Therefore our compassionate Lord made the more haste to cast him out.
31. *The abyss*—That is, the bottomless pit.
32. *To enter into the swine*—Not that they were any easier in the swine than out of them. Had it been so, they would not so soon have dislodged themselves, by destroying the herd.

* Matt. viii, 23 ; Mark iv, 35.   † Matt. viii, 28 ; Mark v, 1.   ‡ Matt. ix, 1 ; Mark v, 18.

40 *And when Jesus returned, the multitude gladly received him ;
41 for they were all waiting for him. And behold, there came a man
    named Jairus, and he was a ruler of the synagogue ; and falling
    down at the feet of Jesus, he besought him to come to his house
42 For he had an only daughter, about twelve years of age, and she
43 lay dying. But as he went, the multitude thronged him. And a
    woman who had had a flux of blood twelve years, and had spent
    all her living upon physicians, neither could be healed by any,
44 Coming behind him, touched the border of his garment, and imme-
45 diately her flux of blood stanched. And Jesus said, Who touched
    me ; when all denied, Peter and they that were with him, said,
    Master, the multitude throng thee, and press *thee*, and sayest thou,
46 Who *is it* that touched me ? And Jesus said, Some one hath
47 touched me ; for I know that virtue is gone out of me. And the
    woman, seeing that she was not hid, came trembling, and falling
    down before him, declared to him before all the people, for what
    cause she had touched him, and how she had been healed imme-
48 diately. And he said to her, Daughter, take courage : thy faith
49 hath saved thee ; go in peace. While he yet spake, there cometh
    one from the ruler of the synagogue's, saying to him, Thy daugh-
50 ter is dead, trouble not the Master. Jesus hearing *it*, answered
    him, saying, Fear not; only believe, and she shall be made
51 whole. And coming into the house, he suffered none to go in,
    save Peter and John and James, and the father and the mother of
52 the maiden. And all wept and bewailed her. But he said, Weep
53 not; she is not dead ; but sleepeth. And they laughed him to
54 scorn, knowing that she was dead. And he put them all out, and
55 taking her by the hand, called, saying, Maid, arise. And her
    spirit returned, and she arose straightway, and he commanded to
56 give her to eat. And her parents were astonished ; but he charged
    them to tell no man what had been done.
IX. †And calling together the twelve, he gave them power and
2   authority over all devils and to cure diseases. And he sent them
3   to preach the kingdom of God, and to heal the sick. And said to
    them, Take nothing for your journey, neither staves, nor scrip,
4   nor bread, nor money : neither have two coats apiece. And into
5   whatsoever house ye enter there abide and thence depart. And
    whosoever will not receive you, when ye go out of that city shake
    off the very dust from your feet for a testimony against them.
6   And they departed, and went through the towns preaching the
    Gospel, and healing every where.
7   ‡Now Herod the tetrarch heard of all the things that were done
8   by him. And he was perplexed, because it was said by some,
    that John was risen from the dead ; and by some, that Elijah had
    appeared : by others, that one of the old prophets was risen again.

52. *She is not dead but sleepeth*—Her soul is not separated finally from the
body; and this short separation is rather to be called sleep than death.
IX. 4. *There abide and thence depart*—That is, stay in that house till ye leave
the city.
7. *It was said by some*—And soon after by Herod himself.
8. *That Elijah had appeared*—He could not rise again, because he did not die.
* Mark v. 21.   † Matt. x, 1 ; Mark vi, 7.   ‡ Matt. xiv, 1 ; Mark vi, 14.

9 And Herod said, John have I beheaded ; but who is this of whom I hear such things ? And he sought to see him.

10 * And the apostles returning, told him whatsoever they had done And he took them and went aside privately into the desert of Beth-

11 saida. And when the multitudes knew *it*, they followed him, and he received them, and spake to them of the kingdom of God, and

12 healed them that had need of healing. † And the day began to decline : and the twelve coming to him said, Send the multitude away, that they may go into the towns and country round about, and lodge, and find victuals : for we are here in a desert place.

13 But he said to them, Give ye them to eat. And they said, We have no more than five loaves and two fishes, except we should go and

14 buy meat for all this people. For they were about five thousand men. And he said to his disciples, Make them sit down by fifties

15 in a company. And they did so, and made them all sit down.

16 Then taking the five loaves and the two fishes, and looking up to heaven, he blessed them and brake, and gave to the disciples to set

17 before the multitude. And they all ate and were satisfied, and there were taken up of fragments that remained twelve baskets.

18 ‡ And as he was praying apart, his disciples were with him. And he asked them saying, Whom say the people that I am ? They

19 answering said, John the Baptist ; but some *say*, Elijah ; and

20 others, that one of the old prophets is risen again. He said to

21 them, But whom say ye that I am ? Peter answering said, The Christ of God. But he straitly charged and commanded them,

22 to tell this to no man, saying, The Son of man must suffer many things, and be rejected of the elders and chief priests and scribes, and be killed, and be raised the third day.

23 And he said to all, If any *man* be willing to come after me, let him deny himself, and take up his cross daily, and follow me.

24 § For whosoever desireth to save his life shall lose it; but whoso-

25 ever shall lose his life for my sake, he shall save it : For what is a man profited, if he gain the whole world, and lose himself or be

26 cast away ? For whosoever shall be ashamed of me and of my words, of him shall the Son of man be ashamed, when he shall come in his own glory, and *in his* Father's, and that of the holy angels.

27 And I tell you of a truth there are some standing here, who shall not taste of death till they see the kingdom of God.

28 ‖ And about eight days after these sayings, he took Peter and

29 John and James, and went up into the mountain to pray. And as he prayed the fashion of his countenance was altered, and his rai-

30 ment became white and glistering. And behold, two men talked

31 with him, who were Moses and Elijah, Who appearing in glory,

---

18. *Apart*—From the multitude. *And he asked them*—When he had done praying, during which they probably stayed at a distance.
22. *Saying*—Ye must prepare for a scene far different from this.
23. *Let him deny himself, and take up his cross*—The necessity of this duty has been shown in many places : the extent of it is specified here, *daily*—Therefore that day is lost wherein no cross is taken up.
31. *In glory*—Like Christ with whom they talked.

* Mark vi, 30.   † Matt. xiv, 15 ; Mark vi, 35 ; John vi, 3.   ‡ Matt. xiv, 13 ; Mark viii, 27.
§ Matt. xvi, 25 · Mark viii, 35 ; John xii, 25.   ‖ Matt. xvii, 1 ; Mark ix, 2.

spake of his decease, which he was about to accomplish at Jeru-
32 salem. But Peter and those with him were weighed down with
sleep; and awaking they saw his glory, and the two men that
33 stood with him. And just as they were parting from him, Peter
said to Jesus, Master, it is good for us to be here : and let us make
three tents, one for thee, and one for Moses, and one for Elijah,
34 not knowing what he said. While he spake thus, a cloud came
and overshadowed them, and they feared while they entered into
35 the cloud. And there came a voice out of the cloud, saying, This
36 is my beloved Son ; hear ye him. And when the voice was past,
Jesus was found alone : and they held their peace, and told no man
in those days any of those things which they had seen.
37 * And the next day, as they came down from the mountain, a
38 great multitude met him. And behold, a man from the multitude
cried aloud, saying, Master, I beseech thee, look upon my son ; for
39 he is my only child. And lo, a spirit taketh him, and he suddenly
crieth out, and it teareth him that he foameth, and bruising him
40 hardly departeth from him, And I besought thy disciples to cast
41 him out, and they could not. And Jesus answering, said, O faithless and perverse generation, how long shall I be with you and
42 suffer you ? Bring thy son hither. And as he was yet coming, the
devil threw him down and tore *him :* and Jesus rebuked the un
clean spirit, healed the child, and delivered him again to his father.
43 And they were all amazed at the mighty power of God. And
while they all wondered at all things which Jesus did, he said to
44 his disciples, Let these sayings sink down into your ears ; † for the
45 Son of man shall be delivered into the hands of men. But they
understood not this saying, and it was hid from them, so that they
46 perceived it not; and they feared to ask him of this saying. And
there arose a reasoning among them, which of them was the great-
47 est ? ‡ And Jesus seeing the reasoning of their heart, took a
48 little child, and set him by him, And said to them, Whosoever
shall receive this child, in my name, receiveth me ; and whosoever shall receive me, receiveth him that sent me : for he that is
49 least among you all, the same shall be great. § And John answering, said, Master, we saw one casting out devils in thy name, and
50 we forbad him ; because he followeth not us. And Jesus said to
him, Forbid *him* not, for he that is not against you is for you.
51 And when the days were fulfilled, that he should be received

32. *They saw his glory*—The very same expression in which it is described by St. John, chap. i, 14; and by St. Peter, 2 Pet. i, 16.
34. *A cloud came and overshadowed them* all. *And they*, the apostles, *feared, while they (Moses and Elijah) entered into the cloud*, which took them away.
44. *Let these sayings sink down into your ears*—That is, consider them deeply. In joy remember the cross. So wisely does our Lord balance praise with sufferings.
46. *And there arose a reasoning among them*—This kind of reasoning always arose at the most improper times that could be imagined.
48. *And said to them*—If ye would be truly great, humble yourselves to the meanest offices. He that is least in his own eyes shall be great indeed.
51. *The days are fulfilled that he should be received up*—That is, the time of

* Matt. xvii, 14 ; Mark ix, 14.   † Matt. xvii, 22 ; Mark ix, 20.   ‡ Matt. xviii, 2 ·
Mark ix, 37.   § Mark ix, 38.

52 up, he steadfastly set his face to go to Jerusalem. And sent messengers before his face, and they went and entered into a village
53 of the Samaritans, to make ready for him. But they did not re
ceive him, because his face was as though he would go to Jerusa-
54 lem. And his disciples James and John seeing *it*, said, Lord, wilt
thou that we bid fire come from heaven and consume them, even as
55 Elijah did? But he turning, rebuked them, and said, Ye know not
56 what manner of spirit ye are of: For the Son of man is not come
to destroy men's lives, but to save *them*. And they went to another
village.
57 * And as they went in the way, one said to him, Lord, I will
58 follow thee whithersoever thou goest. But Jesus said to him, The
foxes have holes, and the birds of the air *have* nests : but the Son
59 of man hath not where to lay his head. And he said to another,
Follow me. But he said, Lord, suffer me first to go and bury my
60 father. Jesus said to him, Let the dead bury their dead, but go
61 thou and preach the kingdom of God. And another also said,
Lord, I will follow thee ; but suffer me first to bid them farewell
62 that are in my house. Jesus said to him, No man having put his
hand to the plough, and looking back, is fit for the kingdom of
God.
X. After these things the Lord appointed other seventy also, and
sent them two by two before his face into every city and place,
2 whither he himself intended to come. And he said to them, † The
harvest truly *is* plenteous, but the labourers *are* few : pray ye
therefore the Lord of the harvest, that he would thrust forth la-
3 bourers into his harvest. ‡ Go : behold I send you forth as lambs
4 in the midst of wolves. Carry not purse, or scrip, or shoes, and
5 salute no man by the way. And into whatsoever house ye enter,

his passion was now at hand. St. Luke looks through this, to the glory which
was to follow. *He steadfastly set his face*—Without fear of his enemies, or
shame of the cross, Heb. xii, 2.

52. *He sent messengers to make ready*—A lodging and needful entertainment for
him and those with him.

53. *His face was as though he would go to Jerusalem*—It plainly appeared, he
was going to worship at the temple, and thereby, in effect, to condemn the Samaritan worship at Mount Gerizim.

54. *As Elisha did*—At or near this very place, which might put it into the
minds of the apostles to make the motion now, rather than at any other time or
place, where Christ had received the like affront.

55. *Ye know not what manner of spirit*—The spirit of Christianity is. It is
not a spirit of wrath and vengeance, but of peace, and gentleness, and love.

58. *But Jesus said to him*—First understand the terms : consider on what conditions thou art to follow me.

61. *Suffer me first to bid them farewell that are in my house*—As Elisha did
after Elijah had called him from the plough, 1 Kings xix, 19 ; to which our
Lord's answer seems to allude.

62. *Is fit for the kingdom of God*—Either to propagate or to receive it.

X. 2. *Pray ye the Lord of the harvest, that he would thrust forth labourers*—
For God alone can do this : he alone can qualify and commission men for
this work.

4. *Salute no man by the way*—The salutations usual among the Jews took up
much time. But these had so much work to do in so short a space, that they
had not a moment to spare.

* Matt. viii, 19.　　† Matt. ix, 37.　　‡ Matt. x, 16.

6 first say, Peace *be* to this house. And if a son of peace be there, your peace shall rest upon it: if not, it shall turn to you again.
7 * And remain in the same house eating and drinking such things as they have; for the labourer is worthy of his hire: remove
8 not from house to house. And into whatsoever city ye enter, and they receive you, eat such things as are set before you.—
9 And heal the sick that are therein, and say to them, The kingdom
10 of God is come nigh to you. But into whatsoever city ye enter
11 and they receive you not, going out into the street of it, say, Even the dust of your city which cleaveth to our feet do we wipe off against you; yet know this that the kingdom of God is at hand.
12 I say to you it shall be more tolerable for Sodom in that day than
13 for that city. † Wo to thee, Chorazin, wo to thee, Bethsaida; for if the mighty works which have been done in you, had been done in Tyre and Sidon, they would have repented long ago, sitting in
14 sackcloth and ashes. But it shall be more tolerable for Tyre and
15 Sidon in the judgment than for you. And thou Capernaum, which
16 hast been exalted to heaven, shalt be thrust down to hell. ‡ He that heareth you, heareth me; and he that rejecteth you, rejecteth me;
17 and he that rejecteth me, rejecteth him that sent me. And the se- venty returned with joy, saying, Lord, even the devils are subject to
18 us through thy name. And he said to them, I beheld Satan falling
19 as lightning from heaven. Behold, I give you power to tread on serpents and scorpions, and over all the power of the enemy, and
20 nothing shall in any wise hurt you. Yet in this rejoice not, that the spirits are subject to you; but rather rejoice, that your names
21 are written in heaven. § In that hour Jesus rejoiced in spirit and said, I thank thee, O Father, Lord of heaven and earth, that thou hast hid these things from the wise and prudent, and hast revealed them to babes; even so, Father, for so it seemeth good in thy sight.
22 All things are delivered to me of my Father; and no one know- eth who the Son is, but the Father, and who the Father is, but the
23 Son, and *he* to whom the Son is pleased to reveal *him*. ‖ And

---

6. *A son of peace*—That is, one worthy of it.
11. *The kingdom of God is at hand*—Though ye will not receive it.
13. *Wo to thee, Chorazin*—The same declaration Christ had made some time before. By repeating it now, he warns the seventy not to lose time by going to those cities.
18. *I beheld Satan*—That is, when ye went forth, I saw the kingdom of Satan, which was highly exalted, swiftly and suddenly cast down.
19. *I give you power*—That is, I continue it to you: *and nothing shall hurt you*—Neither the power, nor the subtilty of Satan.
20. *Rejoice not* so much *that the devils are subject to you, as that your names are written in heaven*—Reader, so is thine, if thou art a true believer. God grant it may never be blotted out!
21. *Lord of heaven and earth*—In both of which thy kingdom stands, and that of Satan is destroyed. *That thou hast hid these things*—He rejoiced not in the destruction of the wise and prudent, but in the display of the riches of God's grace to others, in such a manner as reserves to Him the entire glory of our salvation, and hides pride from man.
22. *Who the Son is*—Essentially one with the Father: *who the Father is*— How great, how wise, how good!

* Matt. x, 11. † Matt. xi, 21. ‡ Matt. x, 40; John xiii, 20. § Matt xi, 25.
‖ Matt. xiii, 16.

turning to the disciples apart, he said, Blessed *are* the eyes which
24 see the things that ye see. For I tell you, many prophets and
kings have desired to see the things which ye see, and have not
seen *them*, and to hear the things which ye hear, and have not
heard *them*.
25 * And behold, a certain scribe stood up, and trying him, said,
26 Master, what shall I do to inherit eternal life? He said to him,
27 What is written in the law? How readest thou? And he answering, said, † Thou shalt love the Lord thy God with all thy
heart, and with all thy soul, and with all thy strength, and with all
28 thy mind; and thy neighbour as thyself. And he said to him,
29 Thou hast answered right; ‡ this do and thou shalt live. But he
willing to justify himself, said to Jesus, And who is my neighbour?
30 And Jesus answering, said, A certain man went down from Jerusalem to Jericho, and fell among robbers, who having stripped and
31 wounded *him*, departed, leaving *him* half dead. And it came to
pass that a certain priest came down that way, and seeing him,
32 passed by on the other side. And likewise a Levite, when he was
33 at the place, came and looked, and passed by on the other side. But
a certain Samaritan journeying, came where he was, and seeing him,
34 was moved with tender compassion, And going to him, bound up

27. *Thou shalt love the Lord thy God*—That is, thou shalt unite all the faculties
of thy soul to render him the most intelligent and sincere, the most affectionate
and resolute service. We may safely rest in this general sense of these important words, if we are not able to fix the particular meaning of every single word.
If we desire to do this, perhaps the heart, which is a general expression, may be
explained by the three following, With all thy soul, with the warmest affection,
with all thy strength, the most vigorous efforts of thy will, and with all thy mind
or understanding, in the most wise and reasonable manner thou canst; thy understanding guiding thy will and affections.
28. *Thou hast answered right; this do, and thou shalt live*—Here is no irony,
but a deep and weighty truth. He, and he alone, shall live for ever, who thus
loves God and his neighbour in the present life.
29. *To justify himself*—That is, to show he had done this.
30. *From Jerusalem to Jericho*—The road from Jerusalem to Jericho (about
eighteen miles from it) lay through desert and rocky places : so many robberies
and murders were committed therein, that it was called *the bloody way*. Jericho was
situated in the valley : hence the phrase of *going down* to it. About twelve thousand priests and Levites dwelt there, who all attended the service of the temple.
31. The common translation is, *by chance*—Which is full of gross improprieties. For if we speak strictly, there is no such thing in the universe as either
chance or fortune. *A certain priest came down that way, and passed by on the
other side*—And both he and the Levite no doubt could find an excuse for passing over on the other side, and might perhaps gravely thank God for their own
deliverance, while they left their brother bleeding to death. Is it not an emblem
of many living characters, perhaps of some who bear the sacred office? O house
of Levi and of Aaron, is not the day coming, when the virtues of heathens and
Samaritans will rise up in judgment against you?
33. *But a certain Samaritan came where he was*—It was admirably well
judged to represent the distress on the side of the Jew, and the mercy on that of
the Samaritan. For the case being thus proposed, self interest would make the
very scribe sensible, how amiable such a conduct was, and would lay him open
to our Lord's inference. Had it been put the other way, prejudice might more
easily have interposed, before the heart could have been affected.
34. *Pouring in oil and wine*—Which when well beaten together are one of the
best balsams that can be applied to a fresh wound.

* Matt. xxii, 35; Mark xii, 28. † Deat. vi, 5; Lev. xix, 18 ‡ Lev. xviii, 5.

his wounds, pouring in oil and wine, and setting him on his own
35 beast, brought him to an inn, and took care of him. And on the
morrow departing, he took out two pieces of money, and gave *them*
to the host, and said to him, Take care of him; and whatsoever
36 thou spendest more, as I come back I will repay thee. Which now
of these three, thinkest thou, was the neighbour to him that fell
37 among the robbers? And he said, He that showed mercy on him.
Then said Jesus to him, Go and do thou in like manner.
38 And as they went, he entered into a certain village, and a cer-
39 tain woman named Martha received him into her house. And she
had a sister called Mary, who also sitting at the feet of Jesus, heard
40 his discourse. But Martha was encumbered with much serving;
and coming to him she said, Lord, dost thou not care, that my sis-
41 ter hath left me to serve alone? Bid her therefore help me. But
Jesus answering, said to her, Martha, Martha! Thou art careful
42 and hurried about many things: But one thing is needful; and
Mary hath chosen the good part, which shall not be taken from
her.
XI. And as he was praying in a certain place, when he ceased, one
of his disciples said to him, Lord, teach us to pray, as John also
2 taught his disciples. * And he said to them, when ye pray, say,

36. *Which of these was the neighbour to him that fell among the robbers*—
Which acted the part of a neighbour?
37. *And he said, He that showed mercy on him*—He could not for shame say
otherwise, though he thereby condemned himself and overthrew his own false
notion of the neighbour to whom our love is due. *Go and do thou in like manner*
—Let us *go and do likewise*, regarding every man as our neighbour who needs
our assistance. Let us renounce that bigotry and party zeal which would contract our hearts into an insensibility for all the human race, but a small number
whose sentiments and practices are so much our own, that our love to them is
but self love reflected. With an honest openness of mind let us always remember that kindred between man and man, and cultivate that happy instinct
whereby, in the original constitution of our nature, God has strongly bound us to
each other.
40. *Martha was encumbered*—The Greek word properly signifies *to be drawn*
different ways at the same time, and admirably expresses the situation of a mind,
surrounded (as Martha's then was) with so many objects of care, that it hardly
knows which to attend to first.
41. *Martha, Martha!*—There is a peculiar spirit and tenderness in the repetition of the word: *thou art careful*, inwardly, and *hurried*, outwardly.
42. *Mary hath chosen the good part*—To save her soul. Reader, hast thou?
XI. 1. *Lord, teach us to pray, as John also taught his disciples*—The Jewish
masters used to give their followers some short form of prayer, as a peculiar badge
of their relation to them. This it is probable John the Baptist had done. And
in this sense it seems to be that the disciples now asked Jesus, to *teach them to
pray*. Accordingly he here repeats that form, which he had before given them
in his sermon on the mount, and likewise enlarges on the same head, though still
speaking the same things in substance. And this prayer uttered from the heart,
and in its true and full meaning, is indeed the badge of a real Christian: for is
not such whose first and most ardent desire is the glory of God, and the happiness of man by the coming of his kingdom? Who asks for no more of this
world than his daily bread, longing meantime for the bread that came down from
heaven? And whose only desires for himself are forgiveness of sins, (as he
heartily forgives others,) and sanctification.
2. *When ye pray, say*—And what he said to them is undoubtedly said to us
also. We are therefore here directed, not only to imitate this in all our prayers,
but to use this very form of prayer.
* Matt. vi, 9.

3 Our Father who art in heaven, hallowed be thy name.   Thy
  kingdom come : thy will be done as in heaven, so on earth.—
4 Give us day by day our daily bread.   And forgive us our sins ; for
  we also forgive every one that is indebted to us.   And lead us not
5 into temptation, but deliver us from evil.   And he saith to them,
  Which of you shall have a friend, and shall go to him at midnight,
6 and say to him, Friend, lend me three loaves : For a friend of mine
  on his journey is come to me, and I have nothing to set before
7 him : And he from within shall answer, Trouble me not : the door
8 is now shut, and my children are with me in bed : I cannot rise
  and give thee ?   I tell you, though he will not rise and give him
  because he is his friend, yet because of his importunity, he will
9 rise and give him as many as he needeth.   * And I say to you,
  Ask and it shall be given you, seek and ye shall find, knock and
10 it shall be opened to you.   For every one that asketh receiveth,
   and he that seeketh findeth, and to him that knocketh it shall be
11 opened.   If a son shall ask bread of any of you that is a father,
12 will he give him a stone ?   Or if he ask a fish, will he for a fish
   give him a serpent ?   Or if he shall ask an egg, will he give him a
13 scorpion ?   If ye then being evil know how to give good gifts to
   your children, how much more will your heavenly Father give the
   Holy Spirit to them that ask him ?
14   † And he was casting out a devil, and it was dumb : and when
   the devil was gone out, the dumb spake, and the multitude wonder-
15 ed.   ‡ But some of them said, He casteth out devils by Beelzebub
16 the prince of the devils : § And others tempting him, sought of him
17 a sign from heaven.   But he knowing their thoughts, said to them,
   Every kingdom divided against itself is brought to desolation, and
18 a house divided against a house falleth.   If Satan then be divided
   against himself, how shall his kingdom stand ?   Because ye say
19 that I cast out devils by Beelzebub.   And if I cast out devils by
   Beelzebub, by whom do your sons cast them out ?   Therefore they
20 shall be your judges.   But if I cast out devils by the finger of

---

4. Forgive us ; for we forgive them—Not once, but continually. This does
not denote the meritorious cause of our pardon ; but the removal of that hinderance which otherwise would render it impossible.
  5. At midnight—The most unseasonable time : but no time is unseasonable
with God, either for hearing or answering prayer.
  13. How much more shall your heavenly Father—How beautiful is the gradation ! A friend : a father : God ! Give the Holy Spirit—The best of gifts, and that
which includes every good gift.
  14. It was dumb—That is, it made the man so.
  15. But some said, He casteth out devils by Beelzebub—These he answers, ver.
17.   Others, to try whether it were so or no, sought a sign from heaven. These
he reproves in the 29th and following verses.   Beelzebub signifies the lord of
flies, a title which the heathens gave to Jupiter, whom they accounted the chief
of their gods, and yet supposed him to be employed in driving away flies from
their temple and sacrifices.   The Philistines worshipped a deity under this name,
as the god of Ekron : from hence the Jews took the name, and applied it to the
chief of the devils.
  17. A house—That is, a family.
  20. If I cast out devils by the finger of God—That is, by a power manifestly
Divine.   Perhaps the expression intimates farther, that it was done without any

* Matt vii 7   † Matt. xii, 22.   ‡ Mark iii, 22.   § Matt. xii, 38.

21 God, then the kingdom of God is come upon you. While the
22 strong one armed guardeth his palace, his goods are in peace, But
when he that is stronger than him cometh upon him and overcometh him, he taketh from him his complete armour wherein he
23 trusted and divideth his spoils. He that is not with me is against
24 me, and he that gathereth not with me scattereth. When the unclean spirit is gone out of a man, he walketh through dry places,
seeking rest; and finding none, he saith, I will return to my house
25 whence I came out. And coming he findeth *it* swept and garnished.
26 Then goeth he and taketh to him seven other spirits more wicked
than himself; and entering in they dwell there; and the last state
of that man becometh worse than the first.
27　As he spake these things, a certain woman lifting up her voice
out of the multitude said to him, Blessed is the womb that bare
28 thee, and the paps which thou hast sucked! But he said, Yea,
rather blessed are they that hear the word of God and keep it.
29　And the multitudes being gathered thick together, he said, This
is an evil generation: it seeketh a sign; but no sign shall be given
30 it, save the sign of Jonah. For as Jonah was a sign to the Ninevites,
31 so shall also the Son of man be to this generation. The queen of
the south shall rise up in the judgment with the men of this generation and condemn them; for she came from the utmost parts of
the earth to hear the wisdom of Solomon; and behold, a greater
32 than Solomon *is* here. The Ninevites shall rise up in judgment
with this generation and condemn it; for they repented at the
preaching of Jonah; and behold, a greater than Jonah *is* here.
33　* No man having lighted a candle, putteth *it* in a secret place,
neither under a bushel, but on a candlestick, that they who come

---

labour: *then the kingdom of God is come upon you*—Unawares, unexpected: so
the Greek word implies.

21. *The strong one armed*—The devil, strong in himself, and armed with the
pride, obstinacy, and security of him in whom he dwells.

26. *The last state of that man becometh worse than the first*—Whoever reads
the sad account Josephus gives of the temple and conduct of the Jews, after the
ascension of Christ and before their final destruction by the Romans, must acknowledge that no emblem could have been more proper to describe them.
Their characters were the vilest that can be conceived, and they pressed on to
their own ruin, as if they had been possessed by legions of devils, and wrought
up to the last degree of madness. But this also is fulfilled in all who totally and
finally apostatize from true faith.

27. *Blessed is the womb that bare thee, and the paps which thou hast sucked!*—
How natural was the thought for a woman! And how gently does our Lord reprove her!

28. *Yea, rather blessed are they that hear the word of God and keep it*—For if
even she that bare him had not done this, she would have forfeited all her blessedness.

29. *It seeketh*—The original word implies seeking more, or over and above
what one has already.

32. *They repented at the preaching of Jonah*—But it was only for a season.
Afterward they relapsed into wickedness, till (after about forty years) they were
destroyed. It is remarkable, that in this also the comparison held. God re-
prieved the Jews for about forty years; but they still advanced in wickedness,
till having filled up their measure, they were destroyed with an utter destruction.

33. The meaning is, God gives you this Gospel light, that you may repent.

* Matt. v, 15; Mark iv, 21; Chap. viii, 16.

34 in may see the light.   * The eye is the lamp of the body; there
    fore when thine eye is single, thy whole body is full of light, bu'
35 when *thine eye* is evil, thy body also *is* full of darkness.   Take
36 heed therefore, lest the light that is in thee be darkness.   If then
    thy whole body *be* full of light, not having any part dark, the whole
    shall be *as* full of light, as when a lamp enlighteneth thee with its
    bright shining.
37   And as he spake, a certain Pharisee asked him to dine with
38 him.   And he went in and sat down to table.   But the Pharisee
    seeing *it,* marvelled that he had not first washed himself before
39 dinner.   And the Lord said to him, † Now ye Pharisees cleanse
    the outside of the cup and dish : but your inward part is full of
40 rapine and wickedness.   Ye unthinking men, did not he that made
41 the outside make the inside also ?   But give what is in *them* in
42 alms, and behold all things are clean to you.   But wo to you, Pha-
    risees ; for ye tithe mint and rue and all herbs, and pass by justice
    and the love of God : these ought ye to have done, and not to leave
43 the other undone.   Wo to you, Pharisees ; for ye love the upper-
44 most seats in the synagogues, and salutations in the markets.   Wo
    to you ; for ye are as graves which appear not, and men that walk
45 over them are not aware.   And one of the lawyers answering said
46 to him, Master, thus saying thou reproachest us also.   And he said,
    Wo to you lawyers also ; for ye load men with burthens grievous to
    be borne, and ye yourselves touch not the burthens with one of your
47 fingers.   Wo to you ; for ye build the sepulchres of the prophets,
48 and your fathers killed them.   Truly ye bare witness that ye ap-
    prove the deeds of your fathers ; for whom they killed, ye build

Let your eye be singly fixed on him, aim only at pleasing God; and while you
do this, your whole soul will be full of wisdom, holiness, and happiness.

34. *But when thine eye is evil*—When thou aimest at any thing else, thou wilt
be full of folly, sin, and misery.   On the contrary,

36. *If thy whole body be full of light*—If thou art filled with holy wisdom, having no part dark, giving way to no sin or folly, then that heavenly principle
will, like the clear flame of a lamp in a room that was dark before, shed its light
into all thy powers and faculties.

39. *Now ye Pharisees*—Probably many of them were present at the Pharisee's
house.

41. *Give what is in them*—The vessels which ye clean, *in alms, and all things
are clean to you.*   As if he had said, By acts directly contrary to rapine and
wickedness, show that your hearts are cleansed, and these outward washings are
needless.

42. *Wo to you*—That is, miserable are you.   In the same manner is the phrase
to be understood throughout the chapter.

44. *For ye are as graves which appear not*—Probably in speaking this our Lord
fixed his eyes on the scribes.   *As graves which appear not*, being overgrown
with grass, so that men are not aware, till they stumble upon them, and either
hurt themselves, or at least are defiled by touching them.   On another occasion
Christ compared them to whited sepulchres, fair without, but foul within ; Matthew xxiii, 27.

45. *One of the lawyers*—That is scribes ; expounders of the law.

48. *Whom they killed, ye build their sepulchres*—Just like them pretending
great reverence for the ancient prophets, while ye destroy those whom God sends
to yourselves.   Ye therefore *bear witness* by this deep hypocrisy that ye are of the
very same spirit with them.

* Matt. vi, 22.   † Matt. xxiii, 25.

49 their sepulchres. * Therefore also the wisdom of God hath said,
I will send them prophets and apostles, and *some* of them they will
50 kill, and persecute *the rest.* So that the blood of all the prophets
shed from the foundation of the world, shall be required of this
51 generation. From the blood of Abel to the blood of Zachariah,
who was destroyed between the temple and the altar : verily I say
52 to you, it shall be required of this generation. Wo to you, lawyers ;
for ye have taken away the key of knowledge : ye have not entered
in yourselves ; and them that were entering in, ye have hindered.
53 And as he said these things to them, the scribes and the Pharisees
began fiercely to fasten upon *him*, and to urge him to speak of
54 many things, Laying wait for him, and seeking to catch something
out of his mouth, that they might accuse him.
XII.   † In the meantime an innumerable multitude being gathered
together, so that they trod one upon another, he said to his disci-
2 ples first, Beware of the leaven of the Pharisees, which is hypocrisy. For there is nothing covered that shall not be uncovered,
3 neither hid, that shall not be made known : ‡ So that whatsoever
ye have spoken in darkness shall be heard in the light, and what
ye have whispered in closets shall be proclaimed on the house-
4 tops. But I say to you, my friends, Fear not them that kill the
5 body, and after that can do no more : But I will show you whom
ye shall fear : fear him, who after he hath killed, hath power to
6 cast into hell : yea, I say to you, fear him. Are not five sparrows
sold for two farthings ? Yet not one of them is forgotten before
7 God. But § even the hairs of your head are all numbered. Fear
8 not therefore : ye are of more value than many sparrows. || And
I say to you, Whosoever shall confess me before men, him shall
9 the Son of man also confess before the angels of God. But he
that denieth me before men, shall be denied before the angels of
10 God. ** And whosoever shall speak against the Son of man, it

49. *The wisdom of God*, agreeably to this, *hath said*—In many places of Scripture, though not in these very words, *I will send them prophets*—Chiefly under the
Old Testament : *and apostles*—Under the New.
50. *The blood of all shall be required of this generation*—That is, shall be visibly and terribly punished upon it.
51. And so it was within forty years, in a most astonishing manner, by the
dreadful destruction of the temple, the city, and the whole nation. *Between the
temple and the altar*—In the court of the temple.
52. *Ye have taken away the key of knowledge*—Ye have obscured and destroyed
the knowledge of the Messiah, which is the key of both the present and the
future kingdom of heaven ; the kingdom of grace and glory. *Ye have not entered
in*—Into the present kingdom of heaven.
XII. 1. *He said to his disciples first*—But afterward (ver. 54) to all the people.
4. *But I say to you, Fear not*—Let not the fear of man make you act the hypocrite, or conceal any thing which I have commissioned you to publish.
5. *Fear him who hath power to cast into hell*—Even to his peculiar friends,
Christ gives this direction. Therefore the fearing of God as having power to
cast into hell, is to be pressed even on true believers.
6. *Are not five sparrows*—But trust as well as fear him.
8. *And I say to you*—If you avoid all hypocrisy, and openly avow my Gospel :
The Son of man shall confess you—*before the angels*—At the last day.
10 *And whosoever*—As if he had said, Yet the denying me in some degree, may,

shall be forgiven him: but to him who blasphemeth against the
11 Holy Ghost, it shall not be forgiven. *But when they bring you
to the synagogues and to magistrates and powers, take no thought
12 how or what ye shall answer, or what ye shall say. For the Holy
Ghost shall teach you in that hour what ye ought to say.
13 And one of the multitude said to him, Master, speak to my
14 brother, that he divide the inheritance with me. But he said to
15 him, Man, who made me a judge or a divider over you? And he
said to them, Take heed and beware of covetousness : for a man's
life consisteth not in the abundance of the things which he pos-
16 sesseth. And he spake a parable to them, saying, The land of a
17 certain rich man brought forth plentifully. And he reasoned in
himself, saying, What shall I do? For I have no room where to
18 stow my fruits. And he said, This I will do : I will pull down my
barns and build greater; and there will I stow all my fruits and
19 goods. And I will say to my soul, Soul, thou hast much goods
laid up for many years : take thine ease ; eat, drink, be merry.
20 But God said to him, Thou fool, this night they require thy soul of
21 thee : and whose shall the things be that thou hast provided? So is
he that layeth up treasure for himself, and is not rich toward God.
22 †And he said to his disciples, therefore I say to you, Take no
thought for your life what ye shall eat, neither for the body what
23 ye shall put on. The life is more than meat, and the body than
24 raiment. Consider the ravens ; for they neither sow nor reap ;
neither have storehouse nor barn : yet God feedeth them. How
25 much better are ye than the birds? And which of you by taking
26 thought, can add the least measure to his age? If ye then be not
able to do even that which is least, why take ye thought for the
27 rest? Consider the lilies, how they grow ; they toil not, neither
do they spin ; and yet I say to you, that Solomon in all his glory
28 was not arrayed like one of these. If then God so clothe the grass
which is to-day in the field, and to-morrow is cast into the still,
29 how much more will he clothe you, O ye of little faith? And seek

upon true repentance, be forgiven ; but if it rise so high as that of the blasphemy against the Holy Ghost, it shall never be forgiven, neither is there place
for repentance.
11. *Take no thought*—Be not solicitous about the matter or manner of your
defence ; nor how to express yourselves.
14. *Who made me a judge?*—In worldly things. His kingdom is not of this
world.
15. *He said to them*—Perhaps to the two brothers, and through them to the
people. *A man's life*—That is, the comfort or happiness of it.
17. *What shall I do?*—The very language of want! Do? Why, lay up treasure in heaven.
20. *Thou fool*—To think of satisfying thy soul with earthly goods ! To depend
on living many years! Yea, one day! *They*—The messengers of death, commissioned by God, *require thy soul of thee !*
21. *Rich toward God*—Namely, in faith, and love, and good works.
25. *Which of you can add the least measure*—It seems, to add one cubit to a
thing (which is the phrase in the original) was a kind of proverbial expression for
making the least addition to it.
28. *The grass*—The Greek word means all sorts of herbs and flowers.
29. *Neither be ye of a doubtful mind*—The word in the original signifies, any

* Matt. x, 19 ; Mark iii, 28 ; Chap. xxi, 12   † Matt. vi, 25

not ye what ye shall eat or what ye shall drink, neither be ye of a
30 doubtful mind. For the nations of the world seek all these things ;
31 and your Father knoweth that ye need these things. But seek ye
the kingdom of God, and all these things shall be added to you.
32 Fear not, little flock, for it is your Father's good pleasure to give
33 you the kingdom. * Sell what ye have and give alms : provide
yourselves purses which wax not old, a treasure in the heavens
that faileth not, where no thief approacheth, neither moth corrupt-
34 eth. For where your treasure is, there will your heart be also.
35 Let your loins be girt, and your lamps burning, And ye like men
36 that wait for their Lord, when he will return from the wedding,
that, when he cometh and knocketh, they may open to him imme-
37 diately. Happy those servants, whom the Lord, when he cometh,
shall find watching ; verily I say to you, that he will gird himself, and make them sit down to table, and will come and serve
38 them. And if he shall come in the second watch, or come in the
39 third watch, and find *them* so, happy are those servants. And this
ye know, that if the master of the house had known what hour the
thief would have come, he would have watched, and not have suf-
40 fered his house to be broke open. Therefore be ye also ready ; for
41 the Son of man cometh in an hour when ye think not. Then Peter
said to him, Lord, speakest thou this parable to us, or also to all ?
42 And the Lord said, Who is that faithful and wise steward, whom
his Lord shall make ruler over his household, to give the allowance
43 of food in due season? Happy that servant, whom his Lord, when
44 he cometh, shall find so doing. Verily I say to you, he will set
45 him over all that he hath. But if that servant say in his heart,
My Lord delayeth his coming, and shall begin to beat the men

---

speculations or musings in which the mind fluctuates, or is suspended (like meteors in the air) in an uneasy hesitation.

32. *It is your Father's good pleasure to give you the kingdom*—How much
more food and raiment? And since ye have such an inheritance, regard not
your earthly possessions.

33. *Sell what ye have*—This is a direction, not given to all the multitude:
(much less is it a standing rule for all Christians:) neither to the apostles; for
they had nothing to sell, having left all before : but to his other disciples, (mentioned ver. 22, and Acts i, 15,) especially to the seventy, that they might be free
from all worldly entanglements.

35. *Let your loins be girt*—An allusion to the long garments, worn by the
eastern nations, which they girded or tucked up about their loins, when they
journeyed or were employed in any labour: as also to the lights that servants
used to carry at weddings, which were generally in the night.

37. *He will come and serve them*—The meaning is, he will show them his love,
in the most condescending and tender manner.

38. The Jews frequently divided the night into three watches, to which our
Lord seems here to allude.

41. *Speakest thou this parable to us*—Apostles and disciples: *Or to all*—The
people ? Does it concern us alone ? Or all men ?

42. *Who is that faithful and wise steward*—Our Lord's answer manifestly implies, that he had spoken this parable primarily (though not wholly) to the
ministers of his word: *Whom his lord shall make ruler over his household*—For
his wisdom and faithfulness.

43. *Happy is that servant*—God himself pronounces him wise, faithful, happy !
Yet we see, he might fall from all, and perish for ever.

* Matt. vi, 19.

servants and maidens, and to eat, and drink, and be drunken:
46 The Lord of that servant will come in a day when he expecteth not, and at an hour when he knoweth not, and will cut
him in sunder, and appoint *him* his portion with the unfaithful.
47 And that servant who knew his Lord's will, and prepared not,
neither did according to his will, shall be beaten with many
48 *stripes.* But he that knew not, and did things worthy of stripes,
shall be beaten with few. For to whomsoever much is given,
of him much shall be required; and to whom they have com-
49 mitted much, of him they will ask the more. I am come to send
50 fire on the earth. And what do I desire? That it were already
kindled! I have a baptism to be baptized with: and how am I
51 straitened till it be accomplished! * Suppose ye that I am come
to give peace upon earth? I tell you, Nay, but rather division:
52 For from henceforth there shall be five in one house divided,
53 three against two, and two against three. The father shall be
divided against the son, and the son against the father; the mother
against the daughter, and the daughter against the mother; the
mother-in-law against her daughter-in-law, and the daughter-in-law
against her mother-in-law.
54 † And he said to the people also, When ye see a cloud rising
out of the west, straightway ye say, There cometh a heavy shower,
55 and so it is. And when *ye find* the south wind blowing, ye say,
56 There will be sultry heat; and it is *so.* Ye hypocrites, ye know
to discern the face of the earth and of the sky: how do ye not
57 discern this season? Yea, and why even of yourselves judge ye
58 not what is right? ‡ When thou art going with thine adversary

46. *The Lord will appoint him his portion*—His everlasting portion, *with the unfaithful*—As faithful as he was once, God himself being the Judge!
47. *And that servant who knew his Lord's will shall be beaten with many stripes*—And his having much knowledge will increase, not lessen, his punishment.
49. *I am come to send fire*—To spread the fire of heavenly love over all the earth.
50. *But I have a baptism to be baptized with*—I must suffer first, before I can set up my kingdom. And how I long to fight my way through all!
51. *Suppose ye that I am come to send peace upon earth*—That universal peace will be the immediate effect of my coming? Not so, but quite the contrary.
52. *There shall be five in one house, three against two, and two against three*—There being an irreconcilable enmity between the Spirit of Christ and the spirit of the world.
53. *The father against the son*—For those who reject me will be implacable toward their very nearest relations who receive me. At this day also is this scripture fulfilled. Now likewise there is no concord between Christ and Belial.
54. *And he said to the people also*—In the preceding verses he speaks only to his disciples. *From the west*—In Judea, the west wind, blowing from the sea, usually brought rain: the south wind, blowing from the deserts of Arabia, occasioned sultry heat.
56. *How do ye not discern this season*—Of the Messiah's coming, distinguishable by so many surer signs.
57. *Why even of yourselves*, without any external sign, *judge ye not what is right?*—Why do ye not discern and acknowledge the intrinsic excellence of my doctrine?
58. *When thou art going*—As if he had said, And ye have not a moment to

* Mark x, 34.   † Matt. xvi, 2.   ‡ Matt v, 25.

to the magistrate, give diligence in the way to be delivered
from him, lest he hale thee to the judge, and the judge deliver
59 thee to the officer, and the officer cast thee into prison. I tell
thee, thou shalt in nowise come out thence till thou hast paid the
last mite.
XIII. And there were present at that season some that told him of
the Galileans, whose blood Pilate had mingled with their sacrifices.
2 And Jesus answering said to them, Suppose ye that those Galileans were sinners above all the Galileans, because they suffered
3 such things? I tell you, Nay; but except ye repent, ye shall all
4 likewise perish. Or those eighteen on whom the tower in Siloam
fell and slew them, suppose ye that they were sinners above all
5 men that dwelt at Jerusalem? I tell you, Nay; but except ye
6 repent, ye shall all likewise perish. He spake also this parable
A man had a fig tree* planted in his vineyard; and he came seek-
7 ing fruit thereon, and found none. Then said he to the keeper of
the vineyard, Behold, three years I come seeking fruit from this
fig tree, and find none; cut it down: why doth it also cumber the
8 ground? And he answering said to him, Lord, let it alone this
9 year also, till I shall dig about it and dung it. Perhaps it may bear
fruit; but if not, after that thou shalt cut it down.
10   And he was teaching in one of the synagogues on the Sabbath.
11 And behold, there was a woman who had had a spirit of infirmity
eighteen years, and was bowed together, and utterly unable to lift
12 up herself. And Jesus seeing her, called her to him, and said
13 to her, Woman, thou art loosed from thy infirmity. And he laid
his hands on her, and immediately she was made straight, and
14 glorified God. And the ruler of the synagogue being much displeased, because Jesus had healed on the Sabbath day, answered

---

lose. For the executioners of God's vengeance are at hand. And when he hath
once delivered you over to them, ye are undone for ever.
    59. *A mite*—was about the third part of a farthing sterling.
    XIII. 1. *The Galileans, whose blood Pilate had mingled with their sacrifices*—
Some of the followers of Judas Gaulonites. They absolutely refused to own the
Roman authority. Pilate surrounded and slew them, while they were worshipping in the temple, at a public feast.
    3. *Ye shall all likewise perish*—All ye of Galilee and of Jerusalem shall perish
in the very same manner. So the Greek word implies. And so they did. There
was a remarkable resemblance between the fate of these Galileans and of the.
main body of the Jewish nation; the flower of which was slain at Jerusalem by
the Roman sword, while they were assembled at one of their great festivals.
And many thousands of them perished in the temple itself, and were literally
buried under its ruins.
    6. *A man had a fig tree*—Either we may understand God the Father by him
that had the vineyard, and Christ by him that kept it: or Christ himself is he
that hath it, and his ministers they that keep it.
    7. *Three years*—Christ was then in the third year of his ministry. But it may
mean only several years; a certain number being put for an uncertain. *Why
doth it also cumber the ground?*—That is, not only bear no fruit itself, but take
up the ground of another tree that would.
    11. *She was bowed together, and utterly unable to lift up herself*—The evil
spirit which possessed her afflicted her in this manner. To many doubtless it
appeared a natural distemper. Would not a modern physician have termed it a
nervous case?

* Psalm lxxx, 8, &c.

and said to the multitude, There are six days, in which *men* ought
to work : on these therefore come and be healed, and not on the
15 Sabbath. , The Lord answered him and said, Thou hypocrite, doth
not each of you loose his ox or his ass from the stall on the Sabbath,
16 and lead him away to watering ?   And ought not this woman, being
a daughter of Abraham, whom Satan hath bound, lo *these* eighteen
17 years, to be loosed from this bond on the Sabbath ?   And when he
had said these things, all his adversaries were ashamed : and all
the multitude rejoiced for all the glorious things that were done
by him.
18   * Then said he, To what is the kingdom of God like, and to
19 what shall I resemble it ?   It is like a grain of mustard seed which
a man took and cast into his garden ; and it grew and became a
great tree, and the birds of the air lodged in the branches of it.
20 † Again he said, Whereto shall I liken the kingdom of God ?   It is
21 like leaven, which a woman took and covered up in three measures
of meal, till the whole was leavened.
22   And he went through all the cities and villages, teaching and
23 journeying toward Jerusalem.   Then said one to him, Lord, are
24 there few that are saved ?   And he said to him, ‡ Strive to enter in
through the strait gate ; for many, I say to you, will seek to en-
25 ter in, and shall not be able.   When once the master of the house
is risen up, and hath shut the door, and ye begin to stand without,
and knock at the door, saying, Lord, Lord, open to us : he shall
26 answer and say to you, I know ye not whence ye are.   Then
shall ye say, We have eaten and drunk in thy presence, and thou
27 hast taught in our streets.   § But he shall say, I tell you I know
not whence ye are : depart from me, all ye workers of iniquity.
28 ‖ There shall be weeping and gnashing of teeth, when ye shall
see Abraham, and Isaac, and Jacob, and all the prophets in the
29 kingdom of God, and yourselves thrust out.   And they shall come
from the east and the west, and the north and the south, and shall
30 sit down in the kingdom of God.   ** But behold there are last who
shall be first, and there are first who shall be last.

15. *Thou hypocrite*—For the real motive of his speaking was envy, not (as he
pretended) pure zeal for the glory of God.
16. *And ought not this woman?*—*Ought not* any human creature, which is so
far better than an ox or an ass ?   Much more, *this daughter of Abraham*—pro
bably in a spiritual as well as natural sense, *to be loosed?*
21. *Covered up*—So that, for a time, nothing of it appeared.
24. *Strive to enter in*—Agonize.   Strive as in an agony.   So the word signifies
Otherwise none shall enter in.   Barely *seeking* will not avail.
25. And even *agonizing* will not avail, after the door is shut.   Agonize, therefore, now by faith, prayer, holiness, patience.   *And ye begin to stand without*—
Till then they had not thought of it !   O how new will that sense of their misery
be ? How late ? How lasting ? *I know not whence ye are*—I know not, that is, I
approve not of your ways.
29. *They shall sit down in the kingdom of God*—Both the kingdom of grace
and of glory.
30. *But there are last*—Many of the Gentiles who were latest called, shall be
most highly rewarded ; and many of the Jews who were first called, shall have
no reward at all.

* Matt. xiii, 31 ; Mark iv, 30.   † Matt. xiii, 33.   ‡ Matt. vii, 13.   § Matt. vii 23,
                    ‖ Matt. viii, 11.   ** Matt. xix, 30.

CHAPTER XIV. 179

31 The same day came certain Pharisees saying to him, Go out
32 and depart from hence; for Herod is minded to kill thee. And
he said to them, Go and tell that fox, Behold, I cast out devils,
and I perform cures to-day and to-morrow; and the third day I am
33 perfected. But I must go on to-day and to-morrow, and the day
following; for it cannot be that a prophet perish out of Jerusalem.
34 * O Jerusalem, Jerusalem, that killest the prophets, and stonest
them that are sent to thee, how often would I have gathered thy
children together, as a bird *gathereth* her brood under *her* wings.
35 and ye would not! Behold, your house is left to you desolate: and
I say to you, Ye shall not see me, till *the time* come when ye shall
say, Blessed is he that cometh in the name of the Lord.
XIV. And as he went into the house of one of the chief Pharisees on
2 the Sabbath, to eat bread, they were watching him. And behold,
3 there was a certain man before him, who had the dropsy. And
Jesus answering spake to the scribes and Pharisees, saying, Is it
lawful to heal on the Sabbath day? But they held their peace.
4 And he took him and healed him, and let *him* go, And answered
5 them, saying, Which of you shall have an ass or an ox fallen into
a pit, and will not straightway pull him out on the Sabbath day?
6 And they could not answer him again to these things.
7 And he spake a parable to them that were invited, when he

31. *Herod is minded to kill thee*—Possibly they gave him the caution out of
good will.
32. *And he said, Go and tell that fox*—With great propriety so called, for his
subtilty and cowardice. The meaning of our Lord's answer is, Notwithstanding
all that he can do, I shall for the short time I have left, do the works of him that
sent me. When that time is fulfilled, I shall be offered up. Yet not here, but
in the bloody city. *Behold, I cast out devils*—With what majesty does he speak
to his enemies! With what tenderness to his friends! *The third day I am perfected*—On the third day he left Galilee, and set out for Jerusalem, to die there.
But let us carefully distinguish between those things wherein Christ is our
pattern, and those which were peculiar to his office. His extraordinary office
justified him in using that *severity of language*, when speaking of *wicked princes,
and corrupt teachers*, to which we have no call; and by which we should only
bring scandal on religion, and ruin on ourselves, while we irritated rather than
convinced or reformed those whom we so indecently rebuked.
33. *It cannot be, that a prophet perish out of Jerusalem*—Which claims prescription for murdering the messengers of God. Such cruelty and malice cannot
be found elsewhere.
34. *How often would I have gathered thy children together*—Three solemn
visits he had made to Jerusalem since his baptism for this very purpose.
35. *Your house is left to you desolate*—Is now irrecoverably consigned to desolation and destruction: *And verily I say to you*, after a very short space, *ye shall
not see me till the time come, when* taught by your calamities, *ye shall* be ready
and disposed to *say, Blessed is he that cometh in the name of the Lord*. It does
not imply, that they should then see Jesus at all; but only that they would earnestly wish for the Messiah, and in their extremity be ready to entertain any
who should assume that character.
XIV. 2. *There was a certain man before him*—It does not appear that he was
come thither with any insidious design. Probably he came, hoping for a cure,
or perhaps was one of the family.
3. *And Jesus answering, spake*—Answering the thoughts which he saw rising
in their hearts.
7 *He spake a parable*—The ensuing discourse is so termed, because several

* Matt. xxiii, 37.

8 marked how they chose the chief seats, saying to them, When thou
art invited by any man to a marriage feast, sit not down in the
highest place, lest a more honourable man than thou be invited by
9 him; And he that invited thee and him come and say to thee,
Give this man place.   And then thou shalt begin with shame to
10 take the lowest place.   But when thou art invited, go and sit down
in the lowest place, that when he who invited thee cometh, he may
say, Friend, go up higher: then shalt thou have honour in the
11 presence of them that sit at table with thee.   * For every one that
exalteth himself shall be humbled, and he that humbleth himself
shall be exalted.
12 ·   Then said he also to him that had invited him, When thou makest
a dinner or a supper, call not thy friends, nor thy brethren, nor
thy kinsmen, nor *thy* rich neighbours, lest they also invite thee
13 again, and a recompense be made thee.   But when thou makest
an entertainment, invite the poor, the disabled, the lame, the blind:
14 And thou shalt be blessed; for they cannot recompense thee; but
thou shalt be recompensed at the resurrection of the just.
5   And one of them that sat at table with him hearing these things,
said to him, Happy is he that shall eat bread in the kingdom of
16 God.   Then said he to him, A certain man made a great supper,
17 and invited many, And he sent his servant at supper time to say
to them that were invited, Come, for all things are now ready.—
18 And they all with one *consent* began to make excuse.   The first
said to him, I have bought a field, and I must needs go and see it:
19 I pray thee have me excused.   And another said, I have bought
five yoke of oxen, and I go to prove them: I pray thee have me
20 excused.   And another said, I have married a wife, and therefore
21 I cannot come.   So the servant came, and showed his lord these

---

parts are not to be understood literally.   The general scope of it is, Not only at
a marriage feast, but on every occasion, *he that exalteth himself shall be abased,
and he that abaseth himself shall be exalted.*
   12. *Call not thy friends*—That is, I do not bid thee call thy friends or thy
neighbours.   Our Lord leaves these offices of humanity and courtesy as they
were, and teaches a higher duty.   But is it not implied herein, that we should
be sparing in entertaining those that need it not, in order to assist those that
do need, with all that is saved from those needless entertainments?   *Lest a
recompense be made*—This fear is as much unknown to the world, as even the
fear of riches.
   14. *One of them that sat at table hearing these things*—And being touched
therewith, *said, Happy is he that shall eat bread in the kingdom of God*—Alluding
to what had just been spoken.   It means, he that shall have a part in the resurrection of the just.
   16. *Then said he*—Continuing the allusion.   *A certain man made a great supper*—As if he had said, All men are not sensible of this happiness.   Many might
have a part in it, and will not.
   18. *They all began to make excuse*—One of them pleads only his own will, *I
go:* another, a pretended necessity, *I must needs go:* the third, impossibility,
I cannot come: all of them want the holy hatred mentioned ver. 26.   All of
them perish by things in themselves lawful.   *I must needs go*—The most urgent
worldly affairs frequently fall out just at the time when God makes the freest
offers of salvation.
   21. *The servant came and showed his lord these things*—So ministers ought to
lay before the Lord in prayer the obedience or disobedience of their hearers.

* Matt xxiii, 12.

things.   Then the master of the house being angry, said to his
servants, Go out quickly into the streets and lanes of the city, and
bring in hither the poor, and the disabled, and the lame, and the
22 blind.   And the servant said, Sir, it is done as thou hast commanded;
23 and yet there is room.   And the lord said to the servant, Go out into
the highways and hedges, and compel *them* to come in, that my
24 house may be filled.   For I say to you, that none of those men who
were invited shall taste of my supper.
25   And great multitudes went with him.   And he turned and said
26 to them, * If any man come to me, and hate not his father, and
mother, and wife, and children, and brethren, and sisters, yea, and
27 his own life also, he cannot be my disciple.   And whosoever doth
not bear his cross, and come after me, cannot be my disciple.
28 And which of you intending to build a tower sitteth not down
first, and computeth the cost, whether he hath sufficient to finish
29 it?   Lest haply after he hath laid the foundation, and is not able
30 to finish *it*, all that behold mock him, saying, This man began to
31 build, and was not able to finish.   Or what king marching to en-
counter another king in war, sitteth not down first, and consulteth
whether he be able with ten thousand, to meet him that cometh
32 against him with twenty thousand?   If not, while the other is yet
a great way off, he sendeth an embassage, and desireth conditions
33 of peace.   So every one of you, who forsaketh not all that he hath,
34 cannot be my disciple.   † Salt *is* good; but if the salt have lost its
35 savour, wherewith shall it be seasoned?   It is neither fit for the
land nor yet for dung; they cast it out.   He that hath ears to hear,
let him hear.
XV.   Then drew near to him all the publicans and sinners, to hear
2 him.   And the Pharisees and scribes murmured, saying, This
3 man receiveth sinners, and eateth with them.   And he spake a

---

23. *Compel them to come in*—With all the violence of love, and the force of
God's word.   Such compulsion, and such only, in matters of religion, was used
by Christ and his apostles.

24. *For* refers to *Go out*, ver. 23.

26. *If any man come to me, and hate not his father*—Comparatively to Christ:
yea, so as actually to renounce his field, oxen, wife, all things, and act as if he
hated them, when they stand in competition with him.

28. *And which of you intending to build a tower*—That is, and whoever of you
intends to follow me, let him first seriously weigh these things.

31. *Another king*—Does this mean, the prince of this world?   Certainly he
has greater numbers on his side.   How numerous are his children and servants!

33. *So*—Like this man, who, being afraid to face his enemy, sends to make
peace with him, *every one who forsaketh not all that he hath*—1. By withdrawing
his affections from all the creatures; 2. By enjoying them only in and for God,
only in such a measure and manner as leads to him; 3. By hating them all, in
the sense above mentioned, *cannot be my disciple*—But will surely desist from
building that tower, neither can he persevere in fighting the good fight of faith.

34. *Salt*—Every Christian, but more eminently every minister.

XV. 1. *All the publicans*—That is, all who were in that place.   It seems our
Lord was in some town of Galilee of the Gentiles, from whence he afterward
went to Jerusalem, ch. xvii, 11.

3. *He spake*—Three parables of the same import: for the sheep, the piece of
silver, and the lost son, all declare (in direct contrariety to the Pharisees and
scribes) in what manner God receiveth sinners.

* Matt x, 37.   † Matt. v, 13; Mark ix, 50.

4 parable to them, saying, * Who of you having a hundred sheep, and losing one of them, doth not leave the ninety and nine in the
5 wilderness, and go after that which is lost, till he find it? And
6 having found *it*, he layeth *it* on his shoulders rejoicing. And coming home, he calleth together his friends and neighbours, saying to
7 them, Rejoice with me; for I have found my sheep which was lost. I say to you, Thus joy shall be in heaven over one sinner that repenteth, more than over ninety and nine just persons, who do not
8 need repentance. Or what woman having ten pieces of silver, if she lose one piece, doth not light a candle and sweep the house,
9 and seek diligently till she find *it*? And having found it, she calleth *her* friends and neighbours together, saying, Rejoice with
10 me, for I have found the piece which I had lost. Thus I say to you, There is joy in the presence of the angels of God over one sinner that repenteth.
11 And he said, A certain man had two sons. And the younger
12 of them said to his father, Father, give me the portion of goods
13 that falleth *to me*. And he divided to them *his* substance. And not many days after, the younger son having gathered all together, took a journey into a far country, and there squandered away
14 his substance, living riotously: And when he had spent all, there arose a mighty famine in that country; and he began to be in
15 want. And he went and joined himself to a citizen of that country;
16 and he sent him into his fields to feed swine. And he would fain

---

4. *Leave the ninety and nine in the wilderness*—Where they used to feed: all uncultivated ground, like our commons, was by the Jews termed wilderness or desert. *And go after*—In recovering a lost soul, God as it were labours. May we not learn hence, that to let them alone who are in sin, is both unchristian and inhuman!

7. *Joy shall be*—Solemn and festal joy, *in heaven*—First, in our blessed Lord himself, and then among the angels and spirits of just men, perhaps informed thereof by God himself, or by the angels who ministered to them. *Over one sinner*—One gross, open, notorious sinner, *that repenteth*—That is, thoroughly changed in heart and life; *more than over ninety and nine just persons*—Comparatively just, outwardly blameless: *that need not such a repentance*—For they need not, cannot repent of the sins which they never committed.

The sum is, as a father peculiarly rejoices when an extravagant child, supposed to be utterly lost, comes to a thorough sense of his duty; or as any other person who has recovered what he had given up for gone, has a more sensible satisfaction in it, than in several other things equally valuable, but not in such danger: so do the angels in heaven peculiarly rejoice in the conversion of the most abandoned sinners. Yea, and God himself so readily forgives and receives them, that he may be represented as having part in the joy.

12. *Give me the part of goods that falleth to me*—See the root of all sin! A desire of disposing of ourselves; of independency on God!

13. *He took a journey into a far country*—Far from God: God was not in all his thoughts: *And squandered away his substance*—All the grace he had received.

14. *He began to be in want*—All his worldly pleasures failing, he grew conscious of his want of real good.

15. *And he joined himself to a citizen of that country*—Either the devil or one of his children, the genuine citizens of that country which is far from God. *He sent him to feed swine*—He employed him in the base drudgery of sin.

16. *He would fain have filled his belly with the husks*—He would fain have satisfied himself with worldly comforts. Vain, fruitless endeavour!

* Matt. xviii. 12.

have filled his belly with the husks that the swiné ate : and no
17 man gave to him. And coming to himself he said, How many hired
servants of my father have bread enough and to spare, and I am
18 perishing with hunger ? I will arise and go to my father, and will
say to him, Father, I have sinned against Heaven and before thee :
19 I am no more worthy to be called thy son; make me as one of thy
20 hired servants. And he arose and came to his father : but while
he was yet a great way off, his father saw him, and his bowels
21 yearned, and he ran, and fell on his neck, and kissed him. And
the son said unto him, Father, I have sinned against Heaven and
22 before thee, and am no more worthy to be called thy son. But the
father said to his servants, Bring forth the best robe and put *it* on
23 him, and put a ring on his hand, and shoes on *his* feet. And bring
24 hither the fatted calf, and kill *it*, and let us eat and be merry. For
this my son was dead, and is alive again: he was lost, and is found.
25 And they began to be merry. Now his eldest son was in the field.
And as he came and drew nigh to the house, he heard music and
26 dancing. And calling one of the servants, he asked what these
27 things meant ? And he told him, Thy brother is come, and thy
father hath killed the fatted calf, because he hath received him in
28 good health. But he was angry, and would not go in : therefore
29 his father coming out, entreated him. And he answering, said to
his father, Lo, so many years do I serve thee, neither transgressed
I thy commandment at any time ; yet thou never gavest me a kid,
30 that I might make merry with my friends. But as soon as this
thy son was come, who hath devoured thy substance with harlots,
31 thou hast killed for him the fatted calf. And he said to him,
32 Son, thou art always with me, and all that I have is thine. But it

17. *And coming to himself*—For till then he was beside himself, as all men are, so long as they are without God in the world.

18. *I will arise and go to my father*—How accurately are the first steps of true repentance here pointed out ! *Against Heaven*—Against God.

20. *And he arose and came to his father*—The moment he had resolved, he began to execute his resolution. *While he was yet a great way off, his father saw him*—Returning, starved, naked.

22. *But the father said*—Interrupting him before he had finished what he intended to say. So does God frequently cut an earnest confession short by a display of his pardoning love.

23. *Let us be merry*—Both here, and wherever else this word occurs, whether in the Old or New Testament, it implies nothing of levity, but a solid, serious, religious, heartfelt joy : indeed this was the ordinary meaning of the word two hundred years ago, when our translation was made.

25. *The elder son* seems to represent the Pharisees and scribes, mentioned verse 2.

27. *Thy father hath killed the fatted calf*—Perhaps he mentions this rather than the robe or ring, as having a nearer connection with the music and dancing.

28. *He was angry, and would not go in*—How natural to us is this kind of resentment !

29. *Lo, so many years do I serve thee*—So he was one of the instances mentioned ver. 7. How admirably therefore does this parable confirm that assertion ! *Yet thou never gavest me a kid, that I might make merry with my friends*—Perhaps God does not usually give much joy to those who never felt the sorrows of repentance.

31. *Thou art ever with me, and all that I have is thine*—This suggests a strong reason against murmuring at the indulgence shown to the greatest of sinners. As the father's receiving the younger son did not cause him to disinherit the

was meet to make merry and be glad ; for this thy brother was
dead, and is alive again ; and was lost, and is found.
XVI. And he said also to his disciples, There was a certain rich
man who had a steward ; and he was accused to him as wasting
2 his goods. And calling him, he said to him, Why hear I this of
thee ? Give an account of thy stewardship, for thou canst be no
3 longer steward. And the steward said in himself, What shall I do ?
For my lord taketh away the stewardship from me. I cannot dig ;
4 to beg I am ashamed. I know what to do, that when I am removed

---

elder ; so God's receiving notorious sinners will be no loss to those who have
always served him ; neither will he raise these to a state of glory equal to that
of those who have always served him, if they have, upon the whole, made a
greater progress in inward as well as outward holiness.

32. *This thy brother was dead, and is alive*—A thousand of these delicate
touches in the inspired writings escape an inattentive reader. In the 30th verse,
the elder son had unkindly and indecently said, *This thy son.* The father in
his reply mildly reproves him, and tenderly says, *This thy brother*—Amazing
intimation, that the best of men ought to account the worst sinners their bre
thren still ; and should especially remember this relation, when they show any
inclination to return.

Our Lord in this whole parable shows, not only that the Jews had no cause to
murmur at the reception of the Gentiles, (a point which did not at that time so
directly fall under consideration,) but that if the Pharisees were indeed as good as
they fancied themselves to be, still they had no reason to murmur at the kind
treatment of any sincere penitent. Thus does he condemn them, even on their
own principles, and so leaves them without excuse.

We have in this parable a lively emblem of the condition and behaviour of sinners in their natural state. Thus, when enriched by the bounty of the great
common Father, do they ungratefully run from him, ver. 12. Sensual pleasures
are eagerly pursued, till they have squandered away all the grace of God, ver. 13.
And while these continue, not a serious thought of God can find a place in their
minds. And even when afflictions come upon them, ver. 14, still they will make
hard shifts before they will let the grace of God, concurring with his providence,
persuade them to think of a return, ver. 15, 16.

When they see themselves naked, indigent, and undone, then they recover the
exercise of their reason, ver. 17. Then they remember the blessings they have
thrown away, and attend to the misery they have incurred. And hereupon they
resolve to return to their father, and put the resolution immediately in practice,
ver. 18, 19.

Behold with wonder and pleasure the gracious reception they find from Divine,
injured goodness ! When such a prodigal comes to his father, he sees him afar
off, ver. 20. He pities, meets, embraces him, and interrupts his acknowledg.
ments with the tokens of his returning favour, ver. 21. He arrays him with the
robe of a Redeemer's righteousness, with inward and outward holiness ; adorns
him with all his sanctifying graces, and honours him with the tokens of adopting
love, ver. 22. And all this he does with unutterable delight, in that he who was
lost is now found, ver. 23, 24.

Let no elder brother murmur at this indulgence, but rather welcome the prodigal back into the family. And let those who have been thus received, wander
no more, but emulate the strictest piety of those who for many years have served
their heavenly Father, and not transgressed his commandments.

XVI. *And he said also to his disciples*—Not only to the scribes and Pharisees
to whom he had hitherto been speaking, but to all the *younger* as well as the
elder brethren : to the returning prodigals who were now *his disciples. A certain rich man had a steward*—Christ here teaches all that are now in favour
with God, particularly pardoned penitents, to behave wisely in what is committed to them.

3. *To beg I am ashamed*—But not ashamed to cheat ! This was likewise a
sense of honour ! " By men called honour, but by angels pride."

4. *I know*—That is, I am resolved, *what* to do.

from the stewardship, they may receive me into their houses.
5 So having called to him every one of his lord's debtors, he said to
6 the first, How much owest thou to my lord? And he said, A
hundred measures of oil. He said to him, Take thy bill, and sit
7 down quickly, and write fifty. Then said he to another, And how
much owest thou? He said, A hundred measures of wheat. He
8 saith, Take thy bill, and write four-score. And the lord commended the unjust steward, because he had done wisely; for the
children of this world are wiser in their generation than the chil-
9 dren of light. And I say to you, Make to yourselves friends of the
mammon of unrighteousness, that, when ye fail, they may receive
10 you into the everlasting habitations. He that is faithful in the least,
is faithful also in much; and he that is unjust in the least, is unjust
11 also in much. If therefore ye have not been faithful in the unrighteous mammon, who will intrust you with the true *riches?*
12 And if ye have not been faithful in that which is another's, who
13 will give you that which is your own? * No servant can serve two
masters; for either he will hate the one, and love the other, or he
will cleave to the one, and despise the other. Ye cannot serve
God and mammon.

8. *And the lord commended the unjust steward*—Namely, in this respect, because he had used timely precaution : so that though the dishonesty of such a
servant be detestable, yet his foresight, care, and contrivance, about the interests
of this life, deserve our imitation, with regard to the more important affairs of
another. *The children of this world*—Those who seek no other portion than this
world : *Are wiser*—Not absolutely, for they are, one and all, egregious fools; but
they are more consistent with themselves ; they are truer to their principles;
they more steadily pursue their end ; they are wiser *in their generation*—That is,
in their own way, *than the children of light*—The children of God, whose light
shines on their hearts.
9. *And I say to you*—Be good stewards even of the lowest talents wherewith
God hath intrusted you. *Mammon* means riches or money It is termed the
mammon of unrighteousness, because of the manner wherein it is commonly
either procured or employed. Make yourselves friends of this, by doing all
possible good, particularly to the children of God : that when ye fail, when your
flesh and your heart faileth, when this earthly tabernacle is dissolved, those of
them who have gone before may receive, may welcome you into the everlasting
habitations.
10. And whether ye have more or less, see that ye be faithful as well as wise
stewards. He that is faithful in what is meanest of all, worldly substance, is also
faithful in things of a higher nature ; and he that uses these lowest gifts unfaith-
fully, is likewise unfaithful in spiritual things.
11. *Who will intrust you with the true riches?*—How should God intrust you
with spiritual and eternal, which alone are true riches?
12. *If ye have not been faithful in that which was another's*—None of these
temporal things are yours : you are only stewards of them, not proprietors :
God is the proprietor of all; he lodges them in your hands for a season : but
still they are his property. Rich men, understand and consider this. If your
steward uses any part of your estate (so called in the language of men) any
farther or any otherwise than you direct, he is a knave : he has neither conscience nor honour. Neither have you either one or the other, if you use any
part of that estate, which is in truth God's, not yours, any otherwise than he
directs. *That which is your own*—Heaven, which when you have it, will be your
own for ever.
13. And you cannot be faithful to God, if you trim between God and the
world, if you do not serve him alone.

* Matt. vi, 24.

14   And the Pharisees, who were covetous, heard all these things,
15 and they derided him.   And he said to them, Ye are they who
justify yourselves before men : but God knoweth your hearts ;
and that which is highly esteemed among men, is an abominaticn
16 before God.   * The law and the prophets *were* until John : from
that time the kingdom of God is preached, and every man forceth
17 into it.   † Yet it is easier for heaven and earth to pass, than for one
18 tittle of the law to fail.   ‡ Whosoever putteth away his wife and
marrieth another, committeth adultery ; and. whosoever marrieth
her that is put away from *her* husband, committeth adultery.
19 There was a certain rich man, who was clothed in purple and fine
20 linen, and feasted splendidly every day.   And there was a certain
beggar, named Lazarus, who was laid at his gate full of sores ;
21 And desiring to be fed with the crumbs that fell from the rich
22 man's table : yea, the dogs also came and licked his sores.   And
the beggar died, and was carried by angels into Abraham's bosom :
23 the rich man also died, and was buried : And in hell lifting up his
eyes, being in torments, he seeth Abraham afar off and Lazarus in
24 his bosom ; And crying out, he said, Father Abraham, have mercy
on me, and send Lazarus to dip the tip of his finger in water and
25 cool my tongue ; for I am tormented in this flame.   But Abraham

15. *And he said to them, Ye are they who justify yourselves before men*—The
sense of the whole passage is, that pride, wherewith you justify yourselves, feeds
covetousness, derides the Gospel, ver. 14, and destroys the law, ver. 18.   All
which is illustrated by a terrible example.   *Ye justify yourselves before men*—Ye
think yourselves righteous, and persuade others to think you so.
16. *The law and the prophets were* in force *until John : from that time* the Gospel
takes place ; and humble upright men receive it with inexpressible earnestness.
17. Not that the Gospel at all destroys the law.
18. But ye do ; particularly in this notorious instance.
19. *There was a certain rich man*—Very probably a Pharisee, and one that *justified himself before men ;* a very honest, as well as honourable gentleman : though
it was not proper to mention his name on this occasion : *who was clothed in purple and fine linen*—and doubtless esteemed on this account, (perhaps not only by
those who sold it, but by most that knew him,) as encouraging trade, and acting
according to his quality : *And feasted splendidly every day*—And consequently
was esteemed yet more, for his generosity and hospitality in keeping so good a
table.
20. *And there was a certain beggar named Lazarus*, (according to the Greek
pronunciation) or Eleazer.   By his name it may be conjectured, he was of no
mean family, though it was thus reduced.   There was no reason for our Lord to
conceal his name, which probably was then well known.   Theophylact observes,
from the tradition of the Hebrews, that he lived at Jerusalem.   *Yea, the dogs
also came and licked his sores*—It seems this circumstance is recorded to show
that all his ulcers lay bare, and were not closed or bound up.
22. *And the beggar*—Worn out with hunger, and pain, and want of all things,
died : and was carried by angels (amazing change of the scene !) *into Abraham's
bosom*—So the Jews styled paradise ; the place where the souls of good men remain from death to the resurrection.   *The rich man also died, and was buried*—
Doubtless with pomp enough, though we do not read of his lying in state ; that
stupid, senseless pageantry, that shocking insult on a poor, putrefying carcass, was
reserved for our enlightened age !
23. *He seeth Abraham afar off*—And yet knew him at that distance : and shall
not Abraham's children, when they are together in paradise, know each other !
24. *Father Abraham, have mercy on me*—It cannot be denied, but here is one

* Matt. xi, 13.   † Matt. v, 18.   ‡ Matt. v, 31 ; xix, 7.

said, Son, remember that thou in thy lifetime receivedst thy good
things, and likewise Lazarus evil things : but now he is comforted,
26 and thou art tormented. And beside all this, between us and you
there is a great gulf fixed; so that they who would pass from
hence to you, cannot, neither can they pass that *would come* to us
27 from thence. Then he said, I pray thee, therefore, father, that thou
28 wouldst send him to my father's house : For I have five brethren ;
that he may testify to them, lest they also come into this place of
29 torment. Abraham saith to him, They have Moses and the pro-
30 phets ; let them hear them. And he said, Nay, father Abraham ;
31 but if one go to them from the dead, they will repent. And he said
to him, If they hear not Moses and the prophets, neither will they
be persuaded though one rose from the dead.
XVII. Then said he to the disciples, * It is impossible but offences
2 will come ; but wo *to him* through whom they come. It were better for him that a millstone were hanged about his neck, and he
cast into the sea, than that he should offend one of these little ones.
3 † Take heed to yourselves ; if thy brother sin, rebuke him, and if
4 he repent, forgive him. And if he sin against thee seven times
in a day, and seven times in a day return to thee, saying, I repent,
5 thou shalt forgive him. ‡ And the apostles said to the Lord, In-
6 crease our faith. And the Lord said, If ye had faith as a grain of
mustard seed, ye might say to this sycamine tree, Be thou rooted

precedent in Scripture of praying to departed saints : but who is it that prays,
and with what success ?   Will any, who considers this, be fond of copying after
him ?
25. *But Abraham said, Son*—According to the flesh. Is it not worthy of observation, that Abraham will not revile even a damned soul ? and shall living men
revile one another ? *Thou in thy lifetime receivedst thy good things*—Thou didst
choose and accept of worldly things as thy good, thy happiness. And can any
be at a loss to know why he was in torments ? This damnable idolatry, had there
been nothing more, was enough to sink him to the nethermost hell.
26. *Beside this there is a great gulf fixed*—Reader, to which side of it wilt
thou go ?
28. *Lest they also come into this place*—He might justly fear lest their reproaches should add to his own torment.
31. *Neither will they be persuaded*—Truly to repent : for this implies an entire
change of heart : but a thousand apparitions cannot effect this. God only can,
applying his word.
XVII. 1. *It is impossible but offences will come*—And they ever did and do
come chiefly by Pharisees, that is, men who trust in themselves that they are
righteous, and despise others.
2. *Little ones*—Weak believers.
3. *Take heed to yourselves*—That ye neither offend others, nor be offended by
others.
4. *If he sin against thee seven times in a day, and seven times in a day return,
saying, I repent*—That is, if he give sufficient proof that he does really repent,
after having sinned ever so often, receive him just as if he had never sinned
against thee. But this forgiveness is due only to real penitents. In a lower
sense we are to forgive all, penitent or impenitent ; (so as to bear them the sin-
cerest good will, and to do them all the good we can ;) and that not seven times
only, but seventy times seven.
5. *Lord, increase our faith*—That we may thus forgive, and may neither offend
nor be offended.
6. *And he said, If ye had faith as a grain of mustard seed*—If ye had the least

* Matt. xviii, 6 ; Mark ix, 42.   † Matt. xviii, 15.   ‡ Matt. xvii, 20.

7 up, and be thou planted in the sea ; and it should obey you. But which of you having a servant ploughing or feeding cattle, will say
8 to him as soon as he cometh from the field, Come and sit down to table? And will not rather say to him, Make ready wherewith I may sup, and gird thyself and serve me till I have eaten, and after-
9 ward thou shalt eat and drink? Doth he thank that servant because
10 he did the things that were commanded him? I think not. So likewise ye, when ye have done all the things that are commanded you, say, We are unprofitable servants : we have done what was our duty to do.
11   And as he went to Jerusalem, he passed through the midst of
12 Samaria and Galilee. And as he entered into a certain village,
13 there met him ten lepers, who stood afar off: And they lifted up
14 *their* voice and said, Jesus. Master, have mercy on us. And seeing *them*, he said to them, Go, show yourselves to the priests. And as they went, they were cleansed.
15   And one of them, when he saw that he was healed, turned back,
16 and with a loud voice glorified God. And fell down on *his* face
17 at his feet, giving him thanks ; and he was a Samaritan. And
18 Jesus answering said, Were there not ten cleansed? But where are the nine ? There are not found returning to give glory to God,
19 save this stranger. And he said to him, Arise and go, thy faith hath saved thee.
20   And being asked by the Pharisees, When cometh the kingdom of God, he answered them and said, The kingdom of God cometh
21 not with observation. Neither shall they say, Lo here, or lo there ;
22 for behold, the kingdom of God is within you. And he said to the disciples, The days will come, when ye shall desire to see one of
23 the days of the Son of man, and shall not see *it.* * And when they shall say to you, See here ; or see there ; go not, nor follow *them.*

---

measure of true faith, no instance of duty would be too hard for you. *Ye would say to this sycamine tree*—This seems to have been a kind of proverbial expression.

7. *But which of you*—But is it not meet that you should first obey, and then triumph? Though still with a deep sense of your utter unprofitableness.

9. *Doth he thank that servant*—Does he account himself obliged to him?

10. *When ye have done all, say, We are unprofitable servants*—For a man cannot profit God. Happy is he who judges himself an unprofitable servant : miserable is he whom God pronounces such. But though we are unprofitable to him, our serving him is not unprofitable to us. For he is pleased to give by his grace a value to our good works, which in consequence of his promise entitles us to an eternal reward.

20. *The kingdom of God cometh not with observation*—With such outward pomp as draws the observation of every one.

21. *Neither shall they say, Lo here, or lo there*—This shall not be the language of those who are, or shall be sent by me, to declare the coming of my kingdom. *For behold the kingdom of God is within* or *among you*—Look not for it in distant times or remote places : it is now in the midst of you : it is come : it is present in the soul of every true believer : it is a spiritual kingdom, an internal principle. Wherever it exists, it exists in the heart.

22. *Ye shall desire to see one of the days of the Son of man*—One day of mercy, or one day wherein you might converse with me, as you do now.

23. *They shall say, See, Christ is here, or there*—Limiting his presence to this or that place.

* Matt. xxiv, 28.

24 For as the lightning that lighteneth out of the cne *part* under heaven, shineth to the other *part* under heaven, so shall the Son of
25 man be in his day.   But first he must suffer many things, and be
26 rejected by this generation.   * And as it was in the days of Noah,
27 so shall it be also in the days of the Son of man.   They ate, they
drank, they married, they were given in marriage, till the day that
Noah entered into the ark, and the flood came and destroyed them
28 all.   Likewise also as it was in the days of Lot : they ate, they
29 drank, they bought, they sold, they planted, they builded : But
the day that Lot went out of Sodom, it rained fire and brimstone
30 from heaven and destroyed them all.   Even thus shall it be in the
31 day that the Son of man is revealed.   In that day, he that shall be
on the house top and his goods in the house, let him not go down
to take them away : and he that is in the field, let him likewise not
32 return back.   Remember Lot's wife.   † Whosoever shall seek to
33 save his life, shall lose it, and whosoever shall lose *his life*, shall
34 preserve it.   I tell you, in that night there shall be two men in
35 one bed ; one shall be taken and the other left.   Two women
shall be grinding together ; one shall be taken and the other left.
36 Two men shall be in the field : one shall be taken and the other
37 left.   ‡ And they answering said to him, Where, Lord ?   And he
said to them, Wheresoever the body *is*, there will the eagles be
gathered together.
XVIII.   And he spake a parable to them to this end, that men
2 ought always to pray, and not to faint, Saying, There was in a
certain çity a judge who feared not God nor reverenced man.
3 And there was a widow in that city, and she came to him, saying,
4 Do me justice on mine adversary.   And he would not for a while,
but afterward he said in himself, Though I fear not God nor
5 reverence man, Yet because this widow giveth me trouble, I will
do her justice, lest by her continual coming she weary me out.
6 And the Lord said, Hear what the unjust judge saith !   And shall
7 not God vindicate his own elect, who cry aloud to him day and

---

24. *So shall also the Son of man be*—So swift, so wide, shall his appearing be :
In his day—The last day.

26. *The days of the Son of man*—Those which immediately follow that which
is eminently styled *his day*.

31. *In that day*—(Which will be the grand type of the last day) when ye shall
see Jerusalem encompassed with armies.

32. *Remember Lot's wife*—And escape with all speed, without ever looking behind you.

33. The sense of this and the following verses is, Yet as great as the danger
will be, do not seek to save your life by violating your conscience : if you do, you
will surely lose it : whereas if you should lose it for my sake, you shall be paid
with life everlasting.   But the most probable way of preserving it now, is to be
always ready to give it up : a peculiar Providence shall then watch over you, and
put a difference between you and other men.

XVIII. 1. *He spake a parable to them*—This and the following parable warn us
against two fatal extremes, with regard to prayer : the former against faintness
and weariness, the latter against self confidence.

7. *And shall not God*—The most just Judge, *vindicate his own elect*—Preserve
the Christians from all their adversaries, and in particular save them out of the
eneral destruction, and avenge them of the Jews ? *Though he bear long with*

* Matt. xxiv, 37.   † Luke ix, 24 ; John xii, 25.   ‡ Matt. xxiv, 28.

8 night, though he bear long with them? I tell you he will vindicate
them speedily. Yet when the Son of man cometh, will he find
faith upon earth?

9 And he spake this parable to certain who trusted in themselves
10 that they were righteous, and despised others. Two men went
up into the temple to pray, the one a Pharisee, and the other a
11 publican. The Pharisee stood by himself and prayed thus, God,
I thank thee, that I am not as other men *are*, rapacious, unjust,
12 adulterers, or even as this publican. I fast twice in the week: 1
13 give tithes of all that I possess. And the publican standing afar
off, would not so much as lift up his eyes to heaven, but smote
14 upon his breast, saying, God be merciful to me a sinner. I tell
you this man went down to his house justified rather than the
other; for every one that exalteth himself shall be humbled, and
he that humbleth himself shall be exalted.

15 * And they brought to him also infants, that he might touch
16 them; but the disciples seeing it, rebuked them. But Jesus calling them to him, said, Suffer little children to come to me and for-
17 bid them not: for of such is the kingdom of God. Verily I say to
you, Whosoever shall not receive the kingdom of God as a little
child, shall, in nowise enter therein.

18 † And a certain ruler asked him, saying, Good Master, what
19 shall I do to inherit eternal life? But Jesus said to him, Why
callest thou me good? *There is* none good save one, *that is,* God.
20 Thou knowest the commandments, ‡ Do not commit adultery.
21 Do not murder. Do not steal Do not bear false witness. Honour thy father and thy mother. And he said, All these have I
22 kept from my childhood. Jesus hearing these things said to him,
Yet lackest thou one thing: sell all that thou hast. and distribute
to the poor, and thou shalt have treasure in heaven; and come,

---

them—Though he does not immediately put an end, either to the wrongs of the
wicked, or the sufferings of good men.

8. *Yet when the Son of man cometh, will he find faith upon earth*—Yet notwithstanding all the instances both of his long suffering and of his justice,
whenever he shall remarkably appear, against their enemies in this age or in
after ages, how few true believers will be found upon earth!

9. *He spake this parable*—Not to hypocrites; the Pharisee here mentioned
was no hypocrite, no more than an outward adulterer: but he *sincerely trusted
in himself that he was righteous*, and accordingly told God so, in the prayer which
none but God heard.

12. *I fast twice in the week*—So did all the strict Pharisees: every Monday
and Thursday. *I give tithes of all that I possess*—Many of them gave one full
tenth of their income in tithes, and another tenth in alms. the sum of this plea
is, I do no harm: I use all the means of grace: I do all the good I can.

13. *The publican standing afar off*—From the holy of holies, *would not so much
as lift up his eyes to heaven*—Touched with shame, which is more ingenuous
than fear.

14. *This man went down*—From the hill on which the temple stood, *justified
rather than the other*—That is, and not the other.

16. *Calling them*—Those that brought the children: *of such is the kingdom of
God*—Such are subjects of the Messiah's kingdom. And such as these it properly belongs to.

22. *Yet lackest thou one thing*—Namely, to love God more than mammon.
Our Saviour knew his heart, and presently put him upon a trial which laid it open

* Matt. xix, 13; Mark x, 13.　† Matt. xix, 16; Mark x, 17.　‡ Exod. xx, 1", &c

23 follow me. And when he heard this, he was very sorrowful ; for
24 he was very rich. And Jesus seeing that he was very sorrowful,
   said, How hardly shall they that have riches enter into the king-
25 dom of God ? It is easier for a camel to go through a needle's eye,
26 than for a rich man to enter into the kingdom of God. And they
27 that heard it said, Who then can be saved ? And he said, The
28 things impossible with men, are possible with God. Then Peter
29 said, Lo, we have left all and followed thee. And he said to them,
   Verily I say unto you, There is no man that hath left house, or
   parents, or brethren, or wife, or children, for the kingdom of God's
30 sake, Who shall not receive manifold more in the present time, and
   in the world to come life everlasting.
31   * Then he took to him the twelve, and said to them, Behold,
   we go up to Jerusalem, and all things that are written by the pro-
32 phets will be accomplished on the Son of man. For he will be
   delivered to the Gentiles, and will be mocked, and spitefully
33 entreated, and spitted on : And they will scourge him, and put him
34 to death : and the third day he will rise again. And they understood none of these things ; and this saying was hid from them,
   neither knew they the things which were spoken.
35   † And while he was yet nigh to Jericho, a certain blind man sat
36 by the way side begging. And hearing the multitude pass by, he
37 asked what it meant ? And they told him,' Jesus of Nazareth pass-
38 eth by. And he cried aloud, saying, Jesus, thou Son of David,
39 have mercy on me. And they that went before charged him to
   hold his peace ; but he cried so much the more, Thou Son of David,
40 have mercy on me. And Jesus standing still, commanded him to
41 be brought to him : and when he was come near, he asked him, Say-
42 ing, What wilt thou that I should do for thee ? He said, Lord, that
   I may receive my sight. And Jesus said to him, Receive thy
43 sight, thy faith hath saved thee. And immediately he received his
   sight, and followed him, glorifying God : and all the people seeing
   it, gave praise to God.
XIX. And he entered and passed through Jericho. And behold a
2 man named Zaccheus, who was the chief of the publicans, and he
3 was rich. And he sought to see Jesus who he was, and could not
4 for the crowd, because he was little of stature. And running be-

fore, he climbed up into a sycamore tree to see him ; for he was to
5 pass by that way.   And Jesus, when he came to the place, looking
up saw him, and said to him, Zaccheus, make haste and come
6 down ; for to-day I must abide at thy house.   And he made haste
7 and came down, and received him joyfully.   And seeing *it*, they
all murmured, saying, He is gone in to be a guest with a sinner.
8 And Zaccheus stood and said to·the Lord, Behold, Lord, the half
of my goods I give to the poor, and if I have wronged any man of
9 any thing, I restore *him* four-fold.   And Jesus said to him, To-day
is salvation come to this house ; forasmuch as he also is a son of
10 Abraham.   * For the Son of man is come to seek and to save that
which was lost.
11   And as they were hearing these things, he added and spake a
parable, because he was nigh Jerusalem, and because they thought
12 the kingdom of God would immediately appear.   He said therefore, † A certain nobleman went into a far country, to receive for
13, himself a kingdom, and to return.   And having called ten of his
servants, he gave them ten pounds, and said unto them, Trade till
14 I come.   But his citizens hated him, and sent an embassy after
15 him, saying, We will not have this man to reign over us.   And
when he was returned, having received the kingdom, he command
ed those servants to be called to him, to whom he had given the
16 money, to know what each had gained by trading.   Then came
17 the first, saying, Lord, thy pound hath gained ten pounds.   And he
said to him, Well done, good servant; because thou hast been
18 faithful in a very little, be thou governor over ten cities.   And the
19 second came, saying, Lord, thy pound hath gained five pounds.   And
20 he said to him likewise, Be thou also over five cities.   And another
came, saying,   Lord, behold thy pound, which I have kept laid up
21 in a napkin.   For I feared thee, because thou art an austere man :
thou takest up what thou layedst not down, and reapest what thou

4. *And running before*—With great earnestness.   *He climbed up*—Notwith·
standing his quality : desire conquering honour and shame.
5. *Jesus said, Zaccheus, make haste and come down*—What a strange mixture
of passions must Zaccheus have now felt, hearing one speak, as knowing both
his name and his heart !
7. *They all murmured*—All who were near : though most of them rather out
of surprise than indignation.
8. *And Zaccheus stood*—Showing by his posture, his deliberate purpose and
ready mind, *and said, Behold, Lord, I give*—I determine to do it immediately.
9. *He also is a son of Abraham*—A Jew born, and as such has a right to the
first offer of salvation.
11. *They thought the kingdom of God*—A glorious temporal kingdom, *would
immediately appear.*
12. *He went into a far country to receive a kingdom*—Christ went to heaven,
to receive his sovereign power as man, even all authority in heaven and earth.
13. *Trade till I come*—To visit the nation, to destroy Jerusalem, to judge the
world : or, in a more particular sense, to require thy soul of thee.
14. *But his citizens*—Such were those of Jerusalem, *hated him, and sent an
embassy after him*—The word seems to imply, their sending ambassadors to a
superior court, to enter their protest against his being admitted to the regal
power.   In such a solemn manner did the Jews protest, as it were, before God,
that Christ should not reign over them : *this man*—So they call him in contempt.
15. *When he was returned*—In his glory.

* Matt. xviii, 11.   † Matt. xxv, 14 ; Mark xiii, 34:

22 didst not sow. And he saith to him, Out of thy own mouth will I
judge thee, thou wicked servant. Thou knowest that I am an
austere man, taking up what I laid not down, and reaping what I
23 did not sow. Wherefore then gavest thou not my money into the
bank, and at my coming I should have received it with interest?
24 And he said to them that stood by, Take the pound from him, and
25 give it to him that hath ten pounds. (And they said to him, Lord,
26 he hath ten pounds!) * For I say unto you, To every one that hath
shall be given: but from him that hath not, even what he hath
27 shall be taken away from him. Moreover, those my enemies, who
would not that I should reign over them, bring hither and slay be-
28 fore me. And having said these things, he went before going up
to Jerusalem.
29 † And as he drew nigh to Bethphage and Bethany, at the mount
called *the mount* of Olives, he sent two of his disciples, saying,
30 Go ye into the village over against *you*, in which entering, ye shall
find a colt tied, whereon never man yet sat, loose him and bring
31 *him* hither. And if any man ask you, Why do ye loose *him*, thus
32 shall ye say to him, The Lord hath need of him. And they that
33 were sent went, and found even as he had said to them. And as
they were loosing the colt, the owners thereof said to them, Why
34 loose ye the colt? And they said, The Lord hath need of him. And
35 they brought him to Jesus, and they cast their garments on the
36 colt, and set Jesus thereon. And as he went, they spread their
37 clothes in the way. And when he was now come nigh, at the descent of the mount of Olives, the whole multitude of the disciples
began to rejoice and praise God with a loud voice, for all the mighty
38 works that they had seen, Saying, Blessed *be* the king that cometh in the name of the Lord: peace be in heaven, and glory in the
39 highest. And some of the Pharisees from among the multitude
40 said to him, Master, rebuke thy disciples. And he answering said
to them, I tell you, that if these should hold their peace, the stones
41 would immediately cry out. And as he drew near, he beheld the
42 city, and wept over it, Saying, O that thou hadst known, even thou,
43 at least in this thy day, the things *that are* for thy peace! But
now they are hid from thine eyes. For the days shall come upon

23. *With interest*—Which does not appear to be contrary to any law of God
or man. But this is no plea for *usury*, that is, the taking such interest as implies
any degree of oppression or extortion.
25. *They said*—With admiration, not envy.
27. *He went before*—The foremost of the company, showing his readiness to
suffer.
29. *He drew nigh to* the place where the borders of Bethphage and Bethany
met, which was *at the* foot of the *mount of Olives.*
37. *The whole multitude began to praise God*—Speaking at once, as it seems,
from a Divine impulse, words which most of them did not understand.
38. *Peace in heaven*—God being reconciled to man.
39. *Rebuke thy disciples*—Paying thee this immoderate honour.
40. *If these should hold their peace, the stones*, which lie before you, *would cry
out*—That is, God would raise up some still more unlikely instruments to declare
his praise. For the power of God will not return empty.
42. *O that thou hadst known, at least in this thy day*—After thou hast
neglected so many. *Thy day*—The day wherein God still offers thee his blessings.

thee, that thine enemies shall cast a trench about thee, and com-
44 pass thee round, and straiten thee on every side, And shall cast
thee to the ground, and thy children *that are* in thee; and they
shall not leave in thee one stone upon another: because thou knewest not the time of thy visitation.

45   * And going into the temple, he drove out them that sold, and
46 them that bought therein, Saying to them, It is written, † My house
is the house of prayer, but ye have made it a den of thieves.

47   And he was daily teaching in the temple. But the chief priests
and the scribes, and the chief of the people, sought to destroy him,
48 And found not what they might do; for all the people hung upon
him to hear him.

XX.   ‡ And on one of those days, as he taught the people in the
temple and preached the Gospel, the chief priests and the scribes
2 came upon him, with the elders. And spake to him, saying, Tell
us. By what authority dost thou these things, and who is he that
3 gave thee this authority? And he answering, said, I will also ask
you one thing, and tell me, Was the baptism of John from hea-
4 ven, or of men? And they reasoned among themselves, saying,
5 If we say from heaven, he will say, Why then did ye not believe
6 him? But if we say of men, all the people will stone us; for they
7 are persuaded that John was a prophet. And they answered,
8 They could not tell whence. Jesus said to them, Neither tell I
you by what authority I do these things.

9   § Then he spake this parable to the people: A certain man
planted a vineyard, and let it out to husbandmen and went into a
10 far country for a long time. And at the season he sent a servant
to the husbandmen, that they might give him of the fruit of the
11 vineyard; but the husbandmen beat and sent him away empty. And
again he sent another servant: and they beat him also, and treated
12 *him* shamefully, and sent *him* away empty. And again he sent
13 a third, and they wounded him also, and cast *him* out. Then
said the lord of the vineyard, What shall I do? I will send my
14 beloved son; perhaps seeing him they will reverence *him*. But
the husbandmen seeing him, reasoned among themselves, saying,
This is the heir: come, let us kill him, that the inheritance may
15 be ours. So they cast him out of the vineyard and killed *him*.
16 What therefore will the lord of the vineyard do to them? He will
come and destroy these husbandmen, and give the vineyard to

---

43. *Thine enemies shall cast a trench about thee, and compass thee around*—
All this was exactly performed by Titus, the Roman general.

44. *And thy children within thee*—All the Jews were at that time gathered
together, it being the time of the passover. *They shall not leave in thee one stone
upon another*—Only three towers were left standing for a time, to show the former strength and magnificence of the place. But these likewise were afterward
levelled with the ground.

XX. 9. *A long time*—It was a long time from the entrance of the Israelites
into Canaan to the birth of Christ.

16. *He will destroy these husbandmen*—Probably he pointed to the scribes,
chief priests, and elders: who allowed, *he will miserably destroy those wicked
men,* Matt. xxi, 41; but could not bear that this should be applied to themselves.

* Matt. xxi, 12; Mark xi, 11.   † Isa. lvi, 7.   ‡ Matt. xxi, 23; Mark xi, 27.
§ Matt. xxi, 33; Mark xii, 1.

17 others. And hearing *it* they said, God forbid. And he looked on them and said, What is this then that is written, * The stone which the builders rejected, this is become the head of the corner?
18 † Whosoever shall fall on that stone shall be broken; but on
19 whomsoever it shall fall, it will grind him to powder. And the chief priests and scribes sought to lay hands on him the same hour; but they feared the people, for they knew he had spoken this parable against them.
20 ‡ And watching *him*, they sent forth spies, feigning themselves to be just men, to take hold of his discourse, that they might deli-
21 ver him to the power and authority of the governor. And they asked him, saying, Master, we know that thou speakest and teachest rightly, neither acceptest thou persons, but teachest the way of
22 God in truth: Is it lawful for us to give tribute to Cesar or no?
23 But he, observing their craftiness, said to them, Why tempt ye me?
24 Show me a penny. Whose image and inscription hath it? They
25 answering said, Cesar's. He said, Render therefore to Cesar the things which are Cesar's, and to God the things which are God's.
26 And they could not take hold of his words before the people; and marvelling at his answer, they held their peace.
27 § Then certain of the Sadducees (who deny there is any resurrection) coming to him, asked him, saying, Master, Moses
28 wrote to us, ‖ If a man's brother die, having a wife, and he die without children, that his brother should take his wife, and raise
29 up seed to his brother. Now there were seven brethren, and the
30 first taking a wife, died without children. And the second took
31 her to wife, and he died childless. And the third took her, and in like manner the seven also; and they died and left no children.
32 Last of all the woman died also. Therefore in the resurrection
33 whose wife of them is she? For seven had her to wife. And Jesus
34 answering said to them, The children of this world marry, and
35 are given in marriage. But they who are counted worthy to obtain that world, and the resurrection from the dead, neither marry
36 nor are given in marriage. For neither can they die any more;

They might also mean, *God forbid* that we should be guilty of such a crime as your parable seems to charge us with, namely, rejecting and killing the heir. Our Saviour answers, But yet will ye do it, as is prophesied of you.

17. *He looked on them*—To sharpen their attention.

20. *Just men*—Men of a tender conscience. *To take hold of his discourse*—If he answered as they hoped he would.

21. *Thou speakest*—In private, *and teachest*—In public.

24. *Show me a penny*—A Roman penny, which was the money that was usually paid on that occasion.

26. *They could not take hold of his words before the people*—As they did after ward before the sanhedrim, in the absence of the people, chap. xxii, 67, &c.

34. *The children of this world*—The inhabitants of earth, *marry and are given in marriage*—As being all subject to the law of mortality; so that the species is in need of being continually repaired.

35. *But they who obtain that world*—Which they enter into, before *the resun rection of the dead.*

36. *They are the children of God*—In a more eminent sense when they rise again.

* Psa. cxviii, 22.   † Matt. xxi, 45.   ‡ Matt. xxii, 16; Mark xii, 12.   § Matt. xxii, 23; Mark xii, 18.   ‖ Deut. xxv, 5.

for they are equal to angels, and are the children of God, being the
37 children of the resurrection. But that the dead are raised, even
Moses showed at the bush, * when he calleth the Lord, The God
38 of Abraham, and the God of Isaac, and the God of Jacob   For he
is not a God of the dead, but of the living ; so that all live to him.
39 And some of the scribes answering said, Master, thou hast spoken
40 excellently well. And after that, they durst not ask him any question at all.
41   † And he said to them, How say they that Christ is David's
42 son ? And David himself saith in the book of Psalms, ‡ The
43 Lord said unto my Lord, Sit thou on my right hand, Till I make
44 thine enemies thy footstool. David therefore calleth him Lord :
45 how is he then his son ? Then in the hearing of all the people, he
46 said to his disciples, § Beware of the scribes, who desire to walk
in long robes, and love salutations in the markets, and the highest
47 seats in the synagogues, and the chief places at feasts, ‖ Who
devour widows' houses, and for a pretence make long prayers ; these
shall receive greater damnation.
XXI.   ** And looking up he saw the rich casting their gifts into the
2 treasury. And he saw also a certain poor widow casting in thither
3 two mites. , And he said, Of a truth I say to you, This poor widow
4 hath cast in more than they all. For all of these have of their
abundance cast into the offerings of God : but she of her penury
hath cast in all the living that she had.
5   †† And as some spake of the temple, that it was adorned with
6 goodly stones and gifts, he said, *As for* these things which ye behold,

---

37. *That the dead are raised*, even Moses, as well as the other prophets showed,
when he calleth—That is, when he recites the words which God spoke of himself, *I am the God of Abraham, &c.* It cannot properly be said, that God is the
God of any who are totally perished.

38. *He is not a God of the dead*, or, *there is no God of the dead*—That is, the
term God implies such a relation, as cannot possibly subsist between him and the
dead ; who in the Sadducees' sense are extinguished spirits ; who could neither
worship him, nor receive good from him. *So that all live to him*—All who have
him for their God, live to and enjoy him. This sentence is not an argument for
what went before ; but the proposition which was to be proved. And the consequence is apparently just. For as all the faithful are the children of Abraham, and the Divine promise of being *a God to him and his seed* is entailed upon
them, it implies their continued existence and happiness in a future state as
much as Abraham's. And as the body is an essential part of man, it implies
both his resurrection and theirs ; and so overthrows the entire scheme of the
Sadducean doctrine.

40. *They durst not ask him any question*—The Sadducees durst not. One of
the scribes did, presently after.

XXI. 1. *He looked up*—From those on whom his eyes were fixed before.

5. *Goodly stones*—Such as no engines now in use could have brought, or even
set upon each other. Some of them (as an eye witness who lately measured
them writes) were forty-five cubits long, five high, and six broad ; yet brought
thither from another country. *And gifts*—Which persons delivered from imminent dangers had, in accomplishment of their vows, hung on the walls
and pillars.

The marble of the temple was so white, that it appeared like a mountain of
snow at a distance. And the gilding of many parts made it, especially when the
sun shone, a most splendid and beautiful spectacle.

* Exod. iii, 6.   † Matt. xxii, 41 ; Mark xii, 35.   ‡ Psalm cx, 1. *   § Matt. xxiii, 5.
‖ Matt. xxiii, 14   ** Mark xii, 41   †† Matt. xxiv, 1 ; Mark xiii, 1.

the days will come, in which there shall not be left one stone upon
7 another, that shall not be thrown down. And they asked him,
saying, Master, when shall these things be? And what *is* the sign,
8 when these things shall come to pass? And he said, Take heed
that ye be not deceived: for many shall come in my name, saying,
9 I am *the Christ;* and the time is near. Go ye not after them. And
when ye shall hear of wars and commotions, be not terrified; for
10 these things must be first; but the end is not immediately. Then
said he to them, Nation shall rise against nation, and kingdom
11 against kingdom. And great earthquakes shall be in divers places,
and famines and pestilences, and there shall be fearful sights and
12 great signs from heaven. * But before all these things they shall
lay their hands on you and persecute *you,* delivering *you* up to the
synagogues and into prisons, being brought before kings and rulers
13 for my name's sake. And it shall turn to you for a testimony.
14 Settle it therefore in your hearts, not to premeditate what to
15 answer. For I will give you a mouth and wisdom, which all your
16 adversaries shall not be able to gainsay or resist. † But ye shall
be betrayed both by parents, and brethren, and kinsfolk, and
17 friends : and *some* of you they will cause to be put to death. ‡ And
18 ye shall be hated by all men for my name's sake. But there
19 shall not a hair of your head perish. In your patience possess
20 ye your souls. And when ye see Jerusalem compassed with
21 armies, then know that the desolation thereof is nigh. Then let
them that are in Judea flee to the mountains, and let them that are
in the midst of it depart out, and let not them that are in the coun-
22 tries enter into it. For these are the days of vengeance, that all
23 things which are written may be fulfilled. But wo to them that
are with child, and to them that give suck in those days; for there
24 shall be great distress in the land, and wrath on this people. And
they shall fall by the edge of the sword, and shall be led away cap-

8. *I am the Christ; and the time is near*—When I will deliver you from all
your enemies. They are the words of the seducers.
9. *Commotions*—Intestine broils ; civil wars.
11. *Fearful sights and signs from heaven*—Of which Josephus gives a circum‑
stantial account.
13. *It shall turn to you for a testimony*—Of your having delivered your own
souls, and of their being without excuse.
18. *Not a hair of your head*—A proverbial expression, *shall perish*—Without
the special providence of God. And then, not before the time, nor without a
full reward.
19. *In your patience possess ye your souls*—Be calm and serene, masters of
yourselves, and superior to all irrational and disquieting passions. By keeping
the government of your spirits, you will both avoid much misery, and guard the
better against all dangers.
21. *Let them that are in the midst of it*—Where Jerusalem stands (that is, they
that are in Jerusalem) *depart out of it,* before their retreat is cut off by the uniting
of the forces near the city, *and let not them that are in the* adjacent *countries* by
any means *enter into it.*
22. *All things which are written*—Particularly in Daniel.
24. *They shall fall by the edge of the sword, and shall be led away captive*—
Eleven hundred thousand perished in the siege of Jerusalem, and above ninety
thousand were sold for slaves. So terribly was this prophecy fulfilled ! *And Jeru‑
salem shall be trodden by the Gentiles*—That is, inhabited. So it was indeed.

* Mark xiii, 9.   † Matt. x, 21   ‡ Matt xxi , 13 ; Mark xiii, 13.

tive into all nations; and Jerusalem shall be trodden by the Gen-
25 tiles, till the times of the Gentiles are fulfilled. * And there shall
be signs in the sun, and moon, and stars; and upon the earth dis-
26 tress of nations, with perplexity, the sea roaring and tossing : Men
fainting away for fear, and expectation of the things coming upon
27 the world ; for the powers of the heavens shall be shaken. And
then shall they see the Son of man coming in a cloud, with power
and great glory.
28   Now when these things begin to come to pass, look up and lift
up your heads ; for your redemption draweth nigh.
29   And he spake a parable to them, Behold the fig tree and all the
30 trees. When they now shoot forth, ye see and know of your-
31 selves, that summer is now nigh. So likewise when ye see these
32 things come to pass, know that the kingdom of God is nigh. Verily I say unto you, this generation shall not pass away, till all
33 things be effected. Heaven and earth shall pass away, but my
34 words shall in nowise pass away. † But take heed to yourselves,
lest at any time your hearts be overloaded with gluttony and
drunkenness, and the cares of this life, and so that day come upon
35 you unawares. For as a snare shall it come on all them that sit
36 on the face of the whole earth. Watch ye therefore and pray
always, that ye may be counted worthy to escape all these things
which will come to pass, and to stand before the Son of man.

The land was sold, and no Jew suffered even to come within sight of Jerusalem.
The very foundations of the city were ploughed up, and a heathen temple built
where the temple of God had stood. The times of the Gentiles—That is, the
times limited for their treading the city ; which shall terminate in the full conversion of the Gentiles.

25. And there shall be—Before the great day, which was typified by the destruction of Jerusalem : signs—Different from those mentioned ver. 11, &c.

28. Now when these things—Mentioned ver. 8, and ver. 10, &c, begin to come
to pass, look up with firm faith, and lift up your heads with joy : for your redemption out of many troubles draweth nigh, by God's destroying your implacable
enemies.

29. Behold the fig tree and all the trees—Christ spake this in the spring, just
before the passover ; when all the trees were budding on the mount of Olives,
where they then were.

30. Ye know of yourselves—Though none teach you.

31. The kingdom of God is nigh—The destruction of the Jewish city, temple,
and religion, to make way for the advancement of my kingdom.

32. Till all things be effected—All that has been spoken of the destruction of
Jerusalem, to which the question, ver. 7, relates : and which is treated of from
the 8th to the 24th verse.

34. Take heed, lest at any time your hearts be overloaded with gluttony and
drunkenness—And was there need to warn the apostles themselves against such
sins as these ? Then surely there is reason to warn even strong Christians against
the very grossest sins. Neither are we wise, if we think ourselves out of the
reach of any sin : and so that day—Of judgment or of death, come upon you, even
you that are not of this world—Unawares.

35. That sit—Careless and at ease.

36. Watch ye therefore—This is the general conclusion of all that precedes.
That ye may be counted worthy—This word sometimes signifies an honour conferred on a person, as when the apostles are said to be counted worthy to suffer
shame for Christ, Acts v, 41. Sometimes meet or becoming : as when John
the Baptist exhorts, to bring fruits worthy of repentance, Luke iii, 8. And so to

* Matt. xxiv, 29 ; Mark xiii, 24.   † Matt. xxiv, 42 ; Mark xiii, 33; Chap. xii, 35

37 Now by day he was teaching in the temple ; and at night going
38 out he lodged at the mount called *the mount* of Olives. And all
the people came early in the morning to him in the temple to
hear him.

XXII. * Now the feast of unleavened bread drew nigh, which is called
2 the passover. And the chief priests and scribes sought how they
might kill him ; but they feared the people.
3 Then entered Satan into Judas, surnamed Iscariot, being of the
4 number of the twelve. And he went and talked with the chief
5 priests and captains, how he might betray him to them. And they
6 were glad, and agreed to give him money. And he promised and
sought opportunity to betray him to them, in the absence of the
multitude.
7 † And the *first* day of unleavened bread was come, when the pass-
8 over was to be killed. And he sent Peter and John, saying, Go
9 and make ready the passover for us, that we may eat *it*. And they
10 said to him, Where wilt thou that we make *it* ready ? And he said
to them, Behold, when ye are entered into the city, a man will
meet you bearing a pitcher of water ; follow him into the house
11 where he entereth. And say to the master of the house, The Master saith to thee, Where is the guest chamber, where I shall eat
12 the passover with my disciples ? And he will show you a large
13 upper room furnished ; there make ready. And they went, and
found as he had said to them. And they made ready the passover
14 ‡ And when the hour was come, he sat down, and the twelve
15 apostles with him. And he said to them, With desire have I de-
16 sired to eat this passover with you, before I suffer. For I say to
you, I will not eat thereof any more, till it be fulfilled in the king-

---

be counted worthy to escape, is to have the honour of it, and to be fitted or prepared for it. *To stand*—With joy and triumph : not to fall before him as his
enemies.
37. *Now by day*—In the day time, *he was teaching in the temple*—This shows
how our Lord employed his time after coming to Jerusalem : but it is not said,
he was this day in the temple, and next morning the people came. It does not
therefore by any means imply, that he came any more after this into the temple.
38. *And all the people came early in the morning to hear him*—How much happier were his disciples in these early lectures, than the slumbers of the morning
could have made them on their beds ! Let us not scruple to deny ourselves the
indulgence of unnecessary sleep, that we may morning after morning place
ourselves at his feet, receiving the instructions of his word, and seeking those of
his Spirit.
XXII. 3. *Then entered Satan*—Who is never wanting to assist those whose
heart is bent upon mischief.
4. *Captains*—Called *captains of the temple*, ver. 52. They were Jewish
officers, who presided over the guards which kept watch every night in the
temple.
15. *With desire have I desired*—That is, I have earnestly desired it. He desired it, both for the sake of his disciples, to whom he desired to manifest himself farther, at this solemn parting : and for the sake of his whole Church, that
he might institute the grand memorial of his death.
16. *For I will not eat thereof any more*—That is, it will be the last I shall eat
with you before I die. *The kingdom of God* did not properly commence till his
resurrection. Then was *fulfilled* what was typified by the passover.

* Matt. xxvi, 1 ; Mark xiv, 1. † Matt. xxvi, 17 ; Mark xiv, 12. ‡ Matt. xxvi, 20
Mark xiv, 17

17 dom of God. And he took the cup, and gave thanks, and said, Take
18 this and divide *it* among yourselves. For I say to you, I will not
   drink of the fruit of the vine till the kingdom of God shall come.
19 And he took bread, and gave thanks, and brake *it*, and gave to them
   saying, This is my body which is given for you; do this in re-
20 membrance of me. Likewise also the cup after supper, saying,
   This cup *is* the New Testament in my blood, which is shed for
21 you. But behold, the hand of him that betrayeth me *is* with me
22 on the table. And truly the Son of man goeth as it was determined;
23 but wo to that man by whom the Son of man is betrayed. And they
   inquired among themselves, which of them it was, that would do
24 this? There was also a contention among them, which of them
25 was greatest. And he said to them, The kings of the Gentiles
   lord it over them, and they that exercise authority upon them, have
26 the title of benefactors. But ye *shall* not *be* so; but he that *is*
   greatest among you, let him be as the least, and he that *is* chief as
27 he that serveth. For which *is* greater, he that sitteth at table, or
   he that serveth? *Is* not he that sitteth at table? But I am in the
28 midst of you as he that serveth. Ye are they who have continued
29 with me in my temptations. And I appoint to you a kingdom, as

17. *And he took the cup*—That cup which used to be brought at the beginning of the paschal solemnity, *and said, Take this and divide it among yourselves; for I will not drink*—As if he had said, Do not expect me to drink of it : I will drink no more before I die.

19. *And he took bread*—Namely, some time after, when supper was ended, wherein they had eaten the paschal lamb. *This is my body*—As he had just now celebrated the paschal supper, which was called the passover, so in like figurative language, he calls this bread his body. And this circumstance of itself was suffi. cient to prevent any mistake, as if this bread was his real body, any more than the paschal lamb was really the passover.

20. *This cup is the New Testament*—Here is an undeniable figure, whereby the cup is put for the wine in the cup. And this is called, *The New Testament in Christ's blood*, which could not possibly mean, that it was the New Testament itself, but only the seal of it, and the sign of that blood which was shed to con firm it.

21. *The hand of him that betrayeth me is with me on the table*—It is evident Christ spake these words before he instituted the Lord's Supper : for all the other evangelists mention the sop, *immediately after receiving* which *he went out*: John xiii, 30. Nor did he return any more, till he came into the garden to betray his Master. Now this could not be dipped or given, but while the meat was on the table. But this was all removed before that bread and cup were brought.

24. *There was also a contention among them*—It is highly probable, this was the same dispute which is mentioned by St. Matthew and St. Mark : and conse. quently, though it is related here, it happened some time before.

25. *They that exercise* the most arbitrary *authority over them, have* from their flatterers *the* vain *title of benefactors.*

26. *But* ye are to be benefactors to mankind, not by governing, but by serving.

27. *For*—This he proves by his own example. *I am in the midst of you*—Just now : see with your eyes. I take no state upon me, but *sit in the midst*, on a level with the lowest of you.

28. *Ye have continued with me in my temptations*—And all his life was nothing else, particularly from his entering on his public ministry.

29. *And I*—Will preserve you in all your temptations, till ye enter into the kingdom of glory : *appoint to you*—By these very words. Not a primacy to one, but a kingdom to every one : on the same terms : *as my Father hath appointed to me*—Who have fought and conquered.

30 my Father has appointed to me, That ye may eat and drink at my table in my kingdom, and sit on thrones, judging the twelve tribes
31 of Israel. And the Lord said, Simon, Simon, behold, Satan hath
32 desired *to have* you, that he might sift *you* as wheat. But I have prayed for thee that thy faith fail not; and when thou art returned,
33 strengthen thy brethren. And he said to him, Lord, I am ready to
34 go with thee both to prison and to death. And he said, I tell thee, Peter, it shall not be *the time of* cock crowing this day, before thou
35 wilt thrice deny that thou knowest me. And he said to them, When I sent you without purse, and scrip, and shoes, lacked ye any
36 thing? And they said, Nothing. Then said he to them, But now he that hath a purse, let him take *it*, and likewise *his* scrip; and he
37 that hath no sword, let him sell his garment and buy one.* For I say to you, That this which is written must yet be accomplished in me, * And he was numbered with the transgressors. For the
38 things concerning me have an end. And they said, Lord, behold, here *are* two swords. And he said to them, It is enough.
39 † And going out, he went, according to *his* custom, to the mount
40 of Olives, and his disciples also followed him. And when he was at the place he said to them, Pray that ye enter not into temptation.
41 And as he was withdrawing from them about a stone's cast, and
42 kneeling down, he prayed, Saying, Father, if thou art willing, remove this cup from me: nevertheless, not my will but thine be done.
43 And there appeared to him an angel from heaven strengthening
44 him. And being in an agony he prayed more earnestly: and his

30. *That ye may eat and drink at my table*—That is, that ye may enjoy the highest happiness, as guests, not as servants. These expressions seem to be primarily applicable to the twelve apostles, and secondarily, to all Christ's servants and disciples, whose spiritual powers, honours, and delights, are here represented in figurative terms, with respect to their advancement both in the kingdom of grace and of glory.

31. *Satan hath desired to have you*—My apostles, *that he might sift you as wheat*—Try you to the uttermost.

32. *But I have prayed for thee*—Who wilt be in the greatest danger of all: *that thy faith fail not*—Altogether: *and when thou art returned*—From thy flight, *strengthen thy brethren*—All that are weak in faith; perhaps scandalized at thy fall.

34. *It shall not be the time of cock crowing this day*—The common time of cock crowing (which is usually about three in the morning) probably did not come till after the cock which Peter heard had crowed twice, if not oftener.

35. *When I sent you—lacked ye any thing*—Were ye not borne above all want and danger?

36. *But now*—You will be quite in another situation. You will want every thing. *He that hath no sword, let him sell his garment and buy one*—It is plain, this is not to be taken literally. It only means, This will be a time of extreme danger.

37. *The things which are written concerning me have an end*—Are now drawing to a period; are upon the point of being accomplished.

38. *Here are two swords*—Many of Galilee carried them when they travelled, to defend themselves against robbers and assassins, who much infested their roads. But did the apostles need to seek such defence? *And he said, It is enough*—I did not mean literally, that every one of you must have a sword.

40. *The place*—The garden of Gethsemane.

43. *Strengthening him*—Lest his body should sink and die before the time.

44. *And being in an agony*—Probably just now grappling with the powers of

sweat was as it were great drops of blood falling down on the
45 ground. And rising up from prayer, he came to his disciples, and
46 found them sleeping for sorrow, And he said to them, Why sleep
ye? Rise and pray, lest ye enter into temptation.
47 And while he yet spake, behold a multitude, and he that was
called Judas, one of the twelve, went before them, and drew near
48 to Jesus to kiss him. And Jesus said to him, Judas, betrayest
49 thou the Son of man with a kiss? * And they who were about
him seeing what would follow, said to him, Lord, shall we smite
50 with the sword? And one of them smote the servant of the high
51 priest, and cut off his right ear. And Jesus answering, said,
52 Suffer ye thus far. And touching his ear he healed him. Then
Jesus said to the chief priests, and captains of the temple, and the
elders, who were come to him, Are ye come out as against a
53 robber with swords and clubs? When I was daily with you in the
temple, ye stretched not forth your hands against me: but this is
your hour and the power of darkness.
54 † Then taking him, they led him, and brought him to the high
55 priest's house: and Peter followed afar off. And when they had
kindled a fire in the midst of the hall, and were sat down together,
56 Peter sat down among them. But a certain maid seeing him as
he sat by the light, and looking earnestly upon him, said, This
57 man also was with him. But he denied him, saying, Woman, I
know him not. And after a while another saw him and said,
58 Thou also art of them. And Peter said, Man, I am not. And about
59 one hour after, another confidently affirmed, saying, Of a truth
60 this man also was with him, for he is a Galilean. And Peter said,
61 Man, I know not what thou meanest. And immediately, while he

darkness: feeling the weight of the wrath of God, and at the same time surrounded with a mighty host of devils, who exercised all their force and malice
to persecute and distract his wounded spirit. *He prayed more earnestly*—Even
with stronger cries and tears: *and his sweat*—As cold as the weather was, *was
as it were great drops of blood*—Which, by the vehement distress of his soul, were
forced out of the pores, in so great a quantity as afterward united in large, thick,
grumous drops, and even *fell to the ground.*
48. *Betrayest thou the Son of man*—He whom thou knowest to be the Son of
man, the Christ?
49. *Seeing what would follow*—That they were just going to seize him.
51. *Suffer* me at least to have my hands at liberty *thus far*, while I do one more
act of mercy.
52. *Jesus said to the chief priests, and captains, and the elders who were come*
—And all these came of their own accord: the soldiers and servants were sent.
53. *This is your hour*—Before which ye could not take me: *and the power of
darkness*—The time when Satan has power.
58. *Another* man *saw him and said*—Observe here, in order to reconcile the
four evangelists, that divers persons concurred in charging Peter with belonging
to Christ. 1. The maid that led him in, afterward seeing him at the fire, first
put the question to him, and then positively affirmed, that he was with Christ.
2. Another maid accused him to the standers by, and gave occasion to the man
here mentioned, to renew the charge against him, which caused the second denial. 3. Others of the company took notice of his being a Galilean, and were
seconded by the kinsman of Malchus, who affirmed he had seen him in the gar
den. And this drew on the third denial.
59. *And about one hour after*—So he did not recollect himself in all that time

* Matt. xxvi, 51; Mark xiv, 47. † Matt. xxvi, 57; Mark xiv. 53; John xviii, 12.

yet spake, the cock crew. And the Lord turning looked upon
Peter. And Peter remembered the word of the Lord, how he had
62 said to him, Before cock crowing thou wilt deny me thrice. And
Peter went out, and wept bitterly.
63 　* And the men that held Jesus mocked and smote him. And
64 having blindfolded him, they struck him on the face, and asked him,
65 saying, Prophesy, who is it that smote thee? And many other
things blasphemously spake they against him.
66 　† And when it was day, the elders of the people and the chief
priests and the scribes came together, and led him into their
67 council, saying, Art thou the Christ? Tell us. And he said to
68 them, If I tell you, ye will not believe. And if I also ask *you*, ye
69 will not answer me, nor let *me* go. Hereafter shall the Son of man
70 sit on the right hand of the power of God. And they all said, Art
71 thou then the Son of God? He said, Ye say *it :* I am. And they
said, What farther need have we of evidence? For we ourselves
have heard from his own mouth.
XXIII. ‡ And the whole multitude of them arose, and led him to
2 Pilate. And they accused him, saying, We found this *fellow* perverting our nation, and forbidding to give tribute to Cesar, saying
3 that he himself is Christ a king. And Pilate asked him, saying,
Art thou the king of the Jews? And he answering him said, Thou
4 sayest. Then said Pilate to the chief priests and the multitude, I
find no fault in this man.
5 　But they were the more violent, saying, He stirreth up the
people, teaching through all Judea, beginning from Galilee, to this
6 place. Pilate hearing of Galilee asked if the man was a Galilean?
7 And when he knew that he belonged to Herod's jurisdiction, he
sent him to Herod, who himself was also in Jerusalem at that time.
8 And Herod seeing Jesus was exceeding glad; for he had been
long desirous to see him, because he had heard many things of
9 him, and hoped to see some miracle done by him. And he ques-

---

64. *And having blindfolded him, they struck him on the face*—This is placed by
St. Matthew and Mark, after the council's condemning him. Probably he was
abused in the same manner, both before and after his condemnation.

65. *Many other things blasphemously spake they against him*--The expression
is remarkable. They charged' him with blasphemy, because he said he was the
Son of God : but the evangelist fixes that charge on them, because he really
was so.

70. *They all said, Art thou then the Son of God?*—Both these, the Son of God,
and the Son of man, were known titles of the Messiah; the one taken from his
Divine, and the other from his human nature.

XXIII. 4. *Then said Pilate*—After having heard his defence—*I find no fault
in this man*—I do not find that he either asserts or attempts any thing seditious
or injurious to Cesar.

5. *He stirreth up the people, beginning from Galilee*—Probably they mentioned Galilee to alarm Pilate, because the Galileans were notorious for sedition
and rebellion.

7. *He sent him to Herod*—As his proper judge.

8. *He had been long desirous to see him*—Out of mere curiosity.

9. *He questioned him*—Probably concerning the miracles which were reported
to have been wrought by him.

* Matt xxvi, 67; Mark xiv, 65. 　† Matt. xxvi, 63; Mark xiv, 61. 　‡ Matt. xxvii, 1 ·
Mark xv, 1 ; John xviii, 28.

10 tioned him in many words, but he answered him nothing. And the chief priests and scribes stood and vehemently accused him.

11 And Herod having with his soldiers set him at nought, and mocked *him*, and arrayed him in a splendid robe, sent him back to Pilate.

12 And the same day Pilate and Herod were made friends together: for before they were at enmity between themselves.

13 And Pilate having called together the chief priests, and the
14 rulers, and the people, said to them, Ye have brought this man to me, as perverting the people; and behold, I having examined *him* before you, have found no fault in this man, touching the things
15 whereof ye accuse him. Nor yet Herod; for I sent you to him; and lo, he hath done nothing worthy of death. I will therefore
16 chastise and release him. *For he was under a necessity of
17 releasing one to them at the feast. And they cried all at once,
18 saying, Away with this *man*, and release to us Barabbas: (Who
19 for an insurrection made in the city, and for murder, had been cast
20 into prison.) Pilate desiring to release Jesus, spake again to them.
21 But they cried out, saying, Crucify him, crucify him. He said to
22 them the third time, Why, what evil hath he done? I have found no cause of death in him: I will therefore chastise and release
23 him. But they were instant with loud voices, requiring that he should be crucified. And the voices of them and of the chief
24 priests prevailed. And Pilate gave sentence, that what they desired
25 should be done. And he released to them him, that for insurrection and murder had been cast into prison, whom they desired; but he delivered Jesus to their will.

26 †And as they led him away, they laid hold on one Simon, a Cyrenian, coming out of the country; and on him they laid the
27 cross, that he might bear *it* after Jesus. And there followed him a great company of people and of women, who also bewailed and
28 lamented him. But Jesus turning to them, said, Daughters of Jerusalem, weep not for me, but weep for yourselves, and for your
29 children. For behold, the days are coming in which they will say, Happy *are* the barren, and the wombs that never bare, and the
30 breasts that never gave suck. ‡Then shall they say to the
31 mountains, Fall on us; and to the hills, Cover us. For if they do these things in the green tree, what shall be done in the dry?

11. *Herod set him at nought*—Probably judging him to be a fool, because he answered nothing. *In a splendid robe*—In royal apparel; intimating that he feared nothing from this king.

15. *He hath done nothing worthy of death*—According to the judgment of Herod also.

16. *I will therefore chastise him*—Here Pilate began to give ground, which only encouraged them to press on.

22. *He said to them the third time, Why, what evil hath he done?*—As Peter, a disciple of Christ, dishonoured him by denying him thrice, so Pilate, a heathen, honoured Christ, by thrice owning him to be innocent.

31. *If they do these things in the green tree, what shall be done in the dry?*— Our Lord makes use of a proverbial expression, frequent among the Jews, who compare a good man to a green tree, and a bad man to a dead one: as if he had said, If an innocent person suffer thus, what will become of the wicked? Of those who are as ready for destruction as dry wood for the fire?

* Matt. xxvii, 15; Mark xv, 6; John xviii, 39. † Matt. xxvii, 31; Mark xv, 21; John xix, 16. ‡ Hos. x, 8.

32 And there were also led two other *men*, malefactors, to be put to death with him.
33   And when they were come to the place, called *the place* of a skull, there they crucified him, and the two malefactors, one on
34 the right hand, and one on the left.   Then said Jesus, Father, forgive them; for they know not what they do.   And they parted
35 his garments and cast lots.   And the people stood beholding.   And the rulers also with them derided *him*, saying, He saved others;
36 let him save himself, if he be the Christ, the chosen of God.   And the soldiers also mocked him, coming to him, and offering him
37 vinegar, And saying, If thou be the king of the Jews, save thyself.
38 * And an inscription also was written over him in Greek, and Latin, and Hebrew letters, THIS IS THE KING OF THE JEWS.
39   And one of the malefactors, who were hanging, reviled him, say-
40 ing, If thou be the Christ, save thyself and us.   But the other answering, rebuked him, saying, Dost thou not fear God, seeing thou
41 art in the same condemnation?   And we indeed justly; for we receive the due reward of our deeds: but this *person* hath done
42 nothing amiss.   And he said to Jesus, Lord, remember me, when
43 thou comest in thy kingdom.   And Jesus said to him, Verily I say unto thee, To-day shalt thou be with me in paradise.

---

34. *Then said Jesus*—Our Lord passed most of the time on the cross in silence: yet seven sentences which he spoke thereon are recorded by the four evangelists, though no one evangelist has recorded them all.   Hence it appears that the four Gospels are, as it were, four parts, which, joined together, make one symphony.   Sometimes one of these only, sometimes two or three, sometimes all sound together.   *Father*—So he speaks both in the beginning and at the end of his sufferings on the cross: *Forgive them*—How striking is this passage! While they are actually nailing him to the cross, he seems to feel the injury they did to their own souls more than the wounds they gave him; and as it were to forget his own anguish out of a concern for their own salvation.

And how eminently was his prayer heard! It procured forgiveness for all that were penitent, and a suspension of vengeance even for the impenitent.

35. *If thou be the Christ;* v. 37.   *If thou be the king*—The priests deride the name of Messiah: the soldiers the name of king.

39. *And one of the malefactors reviled him*—St. Matthew says, the robbers: St. Mark, they that were crucified with him, reviled him.   Either therefore St. Matthew and Mark put the plural for the singular (as the best authors sometimes do) or both reviled him at the first, till one of them felt "the overwhelming power of saving grace."

40. *The other rebuked him*—What a surprising degree was here of repentance, faith, and other graces! And what abundance of good works, in his public confession of his sin, reproof of his fellow criminal, his honourable testimony to Christ, and profession of faith in him, while he was in so disgraceful circumstances as were stumbling even to his disciples! This shows the power of Divine grace.   But it encourages none to put off their repentance to the last hour; since, as far as appears, this was the first time this criminal had an opportunity of knowing any thing of Christ, and his conversion was designed to put a peculiar glory on our Saviour in his lowest state, while his enemies derided him, and his own disciples either denied or forsook him.

42. *Remember me when thou comest*—From heaven, *in thy kingdom*—He acknowledges him a king, and such a king, as after he is dead, can profit the dead.   The apostles themselves had not then so clear conceptions of the kingdom of Christ.

43. *In paradise*—The place where the souls of the righteous remain from death till the resurrection.   As if he had said, I will not only remember thee then, but this very day

* Matt. xxvii, 37; Mark xv, 26; John xix, 19.

44 *And it was about the sixth hour; and there was darkness over
45 all the earth till the ninth hour. And the sun was darkened, and
46 the veil of the temple was rent in the midst. And Jesus crying
with a loud voice, said, Father, into thy hands I commend my
47 spirit. And having said thus, he expired. And the centurion
seeing what was done, glorified God, saying, Certainly this was a
48 righteous man. And all the people who had come together to
that sight, beholding the things which were done, returned, smiting
49 their breasts.· And all his acquaintance, and the women who had
followed him from Galilee, stood afar off, beholding these things.
50 †And behold a man named Joseph, a counsellor, a good man and
51 a just: (He had not consented to the counsel and deed of them,)
of Arimathea, a city of the Jews, who also himself waited for the
52 kingdom of God: This *man* going to Pilate, asked the body of
53 Jesus. And taking it down, he wrapped it in fine linen, and laid it
in a sepulchre that was hewn in stone, wherein never man before
54 was laid. And that day was the preparation; the Sabbath drew on.
55 And the women who had come with him from Galilee, following
56 after, beheld the sepulchre, and how his body was laid. And returning, they prepared spices and ointments, and rested on the Sabbath, according to the commandment.

XXIV. ‡And on the first day of the week, very early in the morning,
they came to the sepulchre, bringing the spices which they had
prepared, and certain *others* with them.
2 And they found the stone rolled away from the sepulchre; And
3 entering, they found not the body of the Lord Jesus. And while
4 they were perplexed concerning it, behold, two men stood by them
5 in shining garments. And as they were afraid and bowed *their*
face to the earth, they said to them, Why seek ye the living among
6 the dead? He is not here, but is risen. Remember how he
7 spake to you being yet in Galilee, Saying, the Son of man must
be delivered into the hands of sinful men, and be crucified, and
8 rise again the third day. And they remembered his words, And
9 returning from the sepulchre, told all these things to the eleven,

---

44. *There was darkness over all the earth*—The noon-tide darkness, covering
the sun, obscured all the upper hemisphere. And the lower was equally darkened, the moon being in opposition to the sun, and so receiving no light from it.

46. *Father, into thy hands*—The Father receives the Spirit of Jesus: Jesus
himself the spirits of the faithful.

47. *Certainly this was a righteous man*—Which implies an approbation of all
he had done and taught.

48. *All the people*—Who had not been actors therein, *returned smiting their
breasts*—In testimony of sorrow.

XXIV. 1. *Certain others with them*—Who had not come from Galilee.

4. *Behold two*—Angels in the form of *men*. Mary had seen them a little before. They had disappeared on these women's coming to the sepulchre, but now
appeared again. St. Matthew and Mark mention only one of them, appearing
like a young man.

6. *Remember how he spake to you, saying, The Son of man must be delivered*—
This is only a repetition of the words which our Lord had spoken to them before
his passion But it is observable, he never styles himself the Son of man after
his resurrection.

* Matt. xxvii, 45 ; Mark xv, 38. † Matt. xxvii, 57; Mark xv, 43 ; John xix, 38.
‡ Matt. xxviii, 1 ; Mark xvi, 1; John xx, 1.

10 and to all the rest. It was Mary Magdalene, and Joanna, and Mary
the mother of James, and the other women with them, who told
11 these things to the apostles. And their words seemed to them
12 as idle tales, and they believed them not. But Peter rising up, ran
to the sepulchre ; and stooping down, he seeth the linen clothes
laid by themselves : and he went home, wondering at what was
come to pass.
13 * And behold two of them were going that day to a village called
14 Emmaus, which was sixty furlongs from Jerusalem. And they
15 talked together of all these things which had happened. And as
they talked and argued together, Jesus himself drew near, and
16 went with them. But their eyes were holden so that they did not
17 know him. And he said to them, What discourses are these that
ye have one with another as ye walk, and are sad ? And one of
18 them, whose name was Cleopas, answering said to him, Dost thou
alone *even* sojourn at Jerusalem, and hast not known the things
19 which are come to pass there in these days ? And he said to
them, What things ? And they said to him, Those concerning
Jesus of Nazareth, (who was a prophet mighty in deed and word
20 before God and all the people ;) How our chief priests and rulers
delivered him to be condemned to death, and have crucified him.
21 But we trusted that it had been he who should have redeemed
Israel. And beside all this, to-day is the third day since these
22 things were done. Yea, and certain women of our company have
23 astonished us, who were early at the sepulchre, And not finding
his body, they came, saying, That they had seen also a vision of
24 angels, who say, He is alive. And some of the men who were
with us went to the sepulchre, and found *it* so as the women had
25 said ; but him they saw not. Then he said to them, O foolish,
and slow of heart to believe all that the prophets have spoken !
26 Ought not Christ to have suffered these things, and to enter into
27 his glory ? And beginning at Moses and all the prophets, he explained to them the things in all the Scriptures, concerning him-
28 self. And they drew nigh the village whither they were going,
29 and he made as though he would go farther. But they constrained
him, saying, Abide with us ; for it is going toward evening, and
30 the day declines. And he went in to abide with them. And as
he sat at table with them, he took the bread, and blessed *it*, and
31 brake and gave to them. And their eyes were opened, and they

21. *To-day is the third day*—The day he should have risen again, if at all.
25. *O foolish*—Not understanding the designs and works of God : *And slow of heart*—Unready to believe what the prophets have so largely spoken.
26. *Ought not Christ*—If he would redeem man, and fulfil the prophecies con-cerning him, *to have suffered these things ?*—These very sufferings which occa-sion your doubts, are the proofs of his being the Messiah. *And to enter into his glory*—Which could be done no other way.
28. *He made as though he would go farther*—Walking forward, as if he was going on ; and he would have done it, had they not pressed him to stay.
29. *They constrained him*—By their importunate entreaties.
30. *He took the bread, and blessed, and brake*—Just in the same manner as when he instituted his last supper.
31. *Their eyes were opened*—That is, the supernatural cloud was removed : *And he vanished*—Went away insensibly.
* Mark xvi, 12

32 knew him, and he vanished out of their sight. And they said one
to another, Was not our heart burning within us, while he was
33 talking to us in the way, and opening the Scriptures to us? And
rising up the same hour, they returned to Jerusalem, and found
34 the eleven met together, and them that were with them, Saying,
35 The Lord is risen indeed, and hath appeared to Simon. And they
told the things *done* in the way, and how he was known by them in
he breaking of bread.
36   * And as they spake thus, Jesus himself stood in the midst of
37 them, and said to them, Peace *be* unto you. But being terrified
38 and affrighted, they thought they saw a spirit. And he said to
them, Why are ye troubled? And why do reasonings arise in
39 your hearts? Behold my hands and my feet, that it is I myself.
Handle me and see : for a spirit hath not flesh and bones, as you
40 see me have. And having spoken this, he showed them *his* hands
41 and *his* feet. And while they yet believed not for joy, and won-
42 dered, he said to them, Have ye here any meat? And they gave
43 him a piece of a broiled fish and of a honeycomb. And he took *it*,
and ate before them.
44   And he said to them, These *are* the words which I spake to
you, being yet with you, that all things written in the law of
Moses, and the prophets, and the psalms concerning me, must be
45 fulfilled. Then opened he their understanding, to understand the
46 Scriptures, And said to them, Thus it is written, and thus it be-
hoved Christ to suffer, and to rise from the dead the third day :
47 And that repentance and remission of sins should be preached in

32. *Did not our heart burn within us*—Did not we feel an unusual warmth of
love! Was not our heart burning, &c.
33. *The same hour*—Late as it was.
34. *The Lord hath appeared to Simon*—Before he *was seen of the twelve* apostles, 1 Cor. xv, 5.
He had, in his wonderful condescension and grace, taken an opportunity on
the former part of that day (though where, or in what manner, is not recorded)
to show himself to Peter, that he might early relieve his distresses and fears, on
account of having so shamefully denied his Master.
35. *In the breaking of bread*—The Lord's Supper
36. *Jesus stood in the midst of them*—It was just as easy to his Divine power
to open a door undiscernibly, as it was to come in at a door opened by some
other hand.
40. *He showed them his hands and his feet*—That they might either see or feel
the prints of the nails.
41. *While they believed not for joy*—They did in some sense believe : otherwise they would not have rejoiced. But their excess of joy prevented a clear,
rational belief.
43. *He took it and ate before them*—Not that he had any need of food ; but to
give them still farther evidence.
44. *And he said*—On the day of his ascension. *In the law, and the prophets,
and the psalms*—The prophecies as well as types, relating to the Messiah, are
contained either in the books of Moses (usually called the law) in the Psalms,
or in the writings of the prophets ; little being said directly concerning him in
the historical books.
45. *Then opened he their understanding, to understand the Scriptures*—He had
explained them before to the two as they went to Emmaus. But still they understood them not, till he took off the veil from their hearts, by the illumination
of his Spirit.

* Mark xvi, 14, 19 ; John xx, 19.

48 his name to all nations, beginning at Jerusalem. And ye are
49 witnesses of these things. And behold I send the promise of my
Father upon you: but tarry in the city of Jerusalem, till ye be
clothed with power from on high.
50   And he led them out as far as Bethany; and lifting up his hands,
51 he blessed them. And while he was blessing them, he was parted
52 from them, and carried up into heaven. And they worshipped him,
53 and returned to Jerusalem with great joy, And were continually in
the temple, praising and blessing God.

47. *Beginning at Jerusalem*—This was appointed most graciously and wisely:
graciously, as it encouraged the greatest sinners to repent, when they saw that
even the murderers of Christ were not excepted from mercy: and wisely, as
hereby Christianity was more abundantly attested; the facts being published first
on the very spot where they happened.

49. *Behold I send the promise*—Emphatically so called; the Holy Ghost.

50. *He led them out as far as Bethany*—Not the town, but the district: to the
mount of Olives, Acts i, 12, which stood within the boundaries of Bethany.

51. *And while he was blessing them, he was parted from them*—It was much
more proper that our Lord should ascend into heaven, than that he should rise
from the dead, in the sight of the apostles. For his resurrection was proved when
they *saw him alive after his passion:* but they could not see him in heaven while
they continued on earth.

14

NOTES

ON THE

GOSPEL ACCORDING TO ST. JOHN.

In this book is set down the history of the Son of God dwelling among men; that,

ST. JOHN.

1 IN the beginning existed the Word, and the Word was with **God,**
2 and the Word was God. The same was in the beginning with
3 God. All things were made by him, and without him was not one
4 single thing made that was made. In him was life, and the life
5 was the light of men. And the light shineth in darkness, but the
darkness perceived it not.
6 There was a man sent from God whose name *was* John. The
7 same came for a testimony to testify of the light, that all through

---

Verse 1. *In the beginning*—(Referring to Gen. i, 1, and Prov. viii, 23.) When all
things began to be made by the Word: in the beginning of heaven and earth,
and this whole frame of created beings, the Word existed, without any beginning. He was when all things began to be, whatsoever had a beginning. *The
Word*—So termed Psa. xxxiii, 6, and frequently by the seventy, and in the Chal-
dee paraphrase. So that St. John did not borrow this expression from Philo, or
any heathen writer. He was not yet named Jesus, or Christ. He is *the Word*
whom the Father begat or *spoke* from eternity; by whom the Father *speaking*,
maketh all things; who speaketh the Father to us. We have, in the 18th verse,
both a real description of the Word, and the reason why he is so called. *He is
the only-begotten Son of the Father, who is in the bosom of the Father, and hath
declared him. And the Word was with God*—Therefore distinct from God the
Father. The word rendered *with*, denotes a perpetual tendency as it were of the
Son to the Father, in unity of essence. He was *with* God alone; because
nothing beside God had then any being. *And the Word was God*—Supreme,
eternal, independent. There was no creature, in respect of which he could be
styled God in a relative sense. Therefore he is styled so in the absolute sense.
The Godhead of the Messiah being clearly revealed in the Old Testament, (Jer
xxiii, 7; Hos. i, 6; Psa. xxiii, 1,) the other evangelists aim at this, to prove
that Jesus, a true man, was the Messiah. But when, at length, some from hence
began to doubt of his Godhead, then St. John expressly asserted it, and wrote in
this book as it were a supplement to the Gospels, as in the Revelation to the
prophets.
2. *The same was in the beginning with God*—This verse repeats and contracts
into one the three points mentioned before. As if he had said, This Word, who
was God, was in the beginning, and was with God.
3. *All things* beside God were made, and all things which were made, were
made by the Word. In the first and second verse is described the state of things
before the creation: ver. 3, In the creation: ver. 4, In the time of man's innocency: ver. 5, In the time of man's corruption.
4. *In him was life*—He was the foundation of life to every living thing, as well
as of being to all that is. *And the life was the light of men*—He who is essential
life, and the giver of life to all that liveth, was also the light of men; the fountain
of wisdom, holiness, and happiness, to man in his original state.
5. *And the light shineth in darkness*—Shines even on fallen man; *but the
darkness*—Dark, sinful man, *perceiveth it not.*
6. *There was a man*—The evangelist now proceeds to him who testified of *the
light*, which he had spoken of in the five preceding verses.
7. *The same came for* (that is, in order to give) *a testimony*—The evangelist,
with the most strong and tender affection, interweaves his own testimony with
that of John, by noble digressions, wherein he explains the office of the Baptist;
partly premises and partly subjoins a farther explication to his short sentences.
What St. Matthew, Mark, and Luke term the Gospel, in respect of the promise
going before, St. John usually terms the testimony, intimating the certain know
ledge of the relator; *to testify of the light*—Of Christ.

8 it might believe. He was not the light, but *was sent* to testify of
9 the light. *This* was the true light, who lighteth every man that
10 cometh into the world. He was in the world, and the world was
11 made by him ; yet the world knew him not. He came to his own,
12 and his own received him not. But as many as received him, to
them gave he privilege to become the sons of God, to them that
13 believe in his name : Who were born, not of blood, nor by the will
of the flesh, nor by the will of man, but of God.
14 And the Word was made flesh, and tabernacled among us (and
we beheld his glory, the glory as of the only begotten of the Father) full of grace and truth.
15 John testified of him and cried, saying, This is he of whom I
said, He that cometh after me is preferred before me, for he was
16 before me. And out of his fulness have we all received, even grace
17 upon grace. For the law was given by Moses, *but* grace and truth

---

9. *Who lighteth every man*—By what is vulgarly termed natural conscience,
pointing out at least the general lines of good and evil. And this light, if man
did not hinder, would shine more and more to the perfect day.

10. *He was in the world*—Even from the creation.

11. *He came*—In the fulness of time, *to his own*—Country, city, temple : *And
his own*—People, *received him not.*

12. *But as many as received him*—Jews or Gentiles ; *that believe on his name*—
That is, on him. The moment they believe, they are sons ; and because they
are sons, *God sendeth forth the Spirit of his Son into their hearts, crying, Abba,
Father.*

13. *Who were born*—Who became the sons of God, *not of blood*—Not by descent
from *Abraham, nor by the will of the flesh*—By natural generation, *nor by the will
of man*—Adopting them, *but of God*—By his Spirit.

14. *Flesh* sometimes signifies corrupt nature ; sometimes the body ; sometimes,
as here, the whole man. *We beheld his glory*—We his apostles, particularly
Peter, James, and John, Luke ix, 32. *Grace and truth*—We are all by nature liars
and children of wrath, to whom both grace and truth are unknown. But we are
made partakers of them, when we are accepted *through the Beloved.*

The whole verse might be paraphrased thus : *And* in order to raise us to this
dignity and happiness, *the* eternal *Word*, by a most amazing condescension, *was
made flesh*, united himself to our miserable nature, with all its innocent infirmities. *And* he did not make us a transient visit, but *tabernacled among us* on
earth, displaying his glory in a more eminent manner, than even of old in the
tabernacle of Moses. *And we* who are now recording these things *beheld his
glory* with so strict an attention, that we can testify, it was in every respect
such a glory as became the *only begotten of the Father.* For it shone forth not
only in his transfiguration, and in his continual miracles, but in all his tempers,
ministrations, and conduct through the whole series of his life. In all he appeared *full of grace and truth :* he was himself most benevolent and upright ;
made those ample discoveries of pardon to sinners, which the Mosaic dispensation
could not do : and really exhibited the most substantial blessings, whereas that
was but *a shadow of good things to come.*

15. *John cried*—With joy and confidence ; *This is he of whom I said*—John
had said this before our Lord's baptism, although he *then* knew him not in person : he knew him first at his baptism, and afterward cried, *This is he of whom I
said.* &c. *He is preferred before me*—in his office : *for he was before me*—in his
nature.

16. *And*—Here the apostle confirms the Baptist's words : as if he had said, He
is indeed preferred before thee : so we have experienced : *We all*—That believe.
have received—All that we enjoy *out of his fulness :* and in the particular, *grace
upon grace*—One blessing upon another, immeasurable grace and love.

17. *The law*—Working wrath and containing shadows : *was given*—No philo
sopher, poet, or orator, ever chose his words so accurately as St. John. *The law,*

18 were by Jesus Christ. No man hath seen God at any time ; the
only-begotten Son, who is in the bosom of the Father, he hath de-
19 clared *him*. And this is the testimony of John, when the Jews sen
priests and Levites from Jerusalem to ask him, Who art thou
20 And he confessed and denied not, but confessed, I am not the
21 Christ. And they asked him, What then ? Art thou Elijah ? And
22 he saith, I am not. Art thou the prophet? And he answered,
No. Then said they to him, Who art thou ? That we may give
23 an answer to them that sent us. What sayest thou of thyself ?
He said, * I *am* the voice of one crying aloud in the wilderness,
Make straight the way of the Lord, as said the Prophet Isaiah.
24 And they who were sent were of the Pharisees. And they asked
25 him and said to him, Why baptizest thou then, if thou art not the
26 Christ, nor Elijah, neither the prophet? John answered them saying, I baptize with water, but there standeth one among you whom
27 ye know not. He it is, who coming after me, is preferred before
28 me, whose shoes latchet I am not worthy to unloose. These
things were done in Bethabara, beyond Jordan, where John was
b'aptizing.
29 The next day he seeth Jesus coming toward him, and saith,
Behold the Lamb of God, who taketh away the sin of the world,
30 This is he of whom I said, After me cometh a man who is prefer-
31 red before me ; for he was before me. And I knew him not, but

---

saith he, was given *by Moses : grace* was *by Jesus Christ*. Observe the reason
for placing each word thus : *"The law* of Moses was not his own. *The grace* of
Christ was. His *grace* was opposite to the *wrath*, his *truth* to the *shadowy* ceremonies of the law. *Jesus*—St. John having once mentioned the incarnation
(ver. 14,) no more uses that name, *the Word*, in all his book.
18. *No man hath seen God*—With bodily eyes : yet believers see him with the
eye of faith. *Who is in the bosom of the Father*—The expression denotes the
highest unity, and the most intimate knowledge.
19. *The Jews*—Probably the great council *sent*.
20. *I am not the Christ*—For many supposed he was.
21. *Art thou Elijah ?*—He was not that Elijah (the Tishbite) of whom they
spoke. *Art thou the prophet*—Of whom Moses speaks, Deut. xviii, 15.
23. *He said*—I am that forerunner of Christ of whom Isaiah speaks. *I am the
voice*—As if he had said, Far from being Christ, or even Elijah, I am nothing but
a voice : a sound that so soon as it has expressed the thought of which it is the
sign, dies into air, and is known no more.
24. *They who were sent were of the Pharisees*—Who were peculiarly tenacious of
old customs, and jealous of any innovation (except those brought in by their own
scribes) unless the innovator had unquestionable proofs of Divine authority.
25. *They asked him, Why baptizest thou then ?*—Without any commission from
the sanhedrim ? And not only heathens (who were always baptized before they
were admitted to circumcision) but Jews also ?
26. *John answered, I baptize*—To prepare for the Messiah ; and indeed to show
that Jews, as well as Gentiles, must be proselytes to Christ, and that these as
well as those stand in need of being washed from their sins.
28. *Where John was baptizing*—That is, used to baptize.
29. *He seeth Jesus coming and saith, Behold the Lamb*—Innocent ; to be offered
up; prophesied of by Isaiah, chap. liii, 7, typified by the paschal lamb, and by
the daily sacrifice : *The Lamb of God*—Whom God gave, approves, accepts of ;
who taketh away—Atoneth for ; *the sin*—That is, all the sins : *of the world*—Of
all mankind. Sin and the world are of equal extent.
31. *I knew him not*—Till he came to be baptized. How surprising is this !

* Isaiah xl, 3.

that he might be manifested to Israel, therefore am I come baptiz-
32 ing with water. And John testified, saying, I saw the Spirit de-
33 scending from heaven as a dove, and it abode upon him. And I
knew him not, but he that sent me to baptize with water, he had
said to me, On whom thou shalt see the Spirit descending and
34 abiding on him, this is he who baptizeth with the Holy Ghost. And
I saw *it*, and testified, that this is the Son of God.

35 Again, the next day, John was standing, and two of his disciples,
36 And looking upon Jesus walking, he saith, Behold the Lamb of
37 God. And the two disciples heard him speak, and they followed
Jesus. And Jesus turning and seeing them following, saith to them,
38 What seek ye? They said to him, Rabbi, (that is, being interpreted, Master,) where dwellest thou? He saith to them, Come and
39 see. They came and saw where he dwelt, and abode with him
40 that day; for it was about the tenth hour. Andrew, Simon Peter's
brother, was one of the two who heard John *speak*, and followed
41 him. He first findeth his own brother Simon, and saith to him,
We have found the Messiah (which is being interpreted the Christ.)
42 And he brought him to Jesus. And Jesus looking upon him, said,
Thou art Simon, the son of Jonah; thou shalt be called Cephas,
which is by interpretation, Peter.

43 The day following he was minded to depart into Galilee, and
44 findeth Philip, and saith to him, Follow me. Now Philip was of
45 Bethsaida, the city of Andrew and Peter. Philip findeth Nathanael
and saith to him, We have found him, whom Moses in the law
and the prophets described, Jesus of Nazareth, the son of Jo-
46 seph. And Nathanael saith to him, Can any good thing come out

considering how nearly they were related, and how remarkable the conception
and birth of both had been. But there was a peculiar providence visible in our
Saviour's living, from his infancy to his baptism, at Nazareth: John all the time
living the life of a hermit in the deserts of Judea, Luke i, 80, ninety or more
miles from Nazareth: hereby that acquaintance was prevented which might have
made John's testimony of Christ suspected.

34. *I saw it*—That is, the Spirit so descending and abiding on him. *And testified*—From that time.

37. *They followed Jesus*—They walked after him, but had not the courage to
speak to him.

41. *He first findeth his own brother Simon*—Probably both of them sought him:
Which is, being interpreted, the Christ—This the evangelist adds, as likewise those
words in the 38th verse, *that is, being interpreted, Master*.

42. *Jesus said, Thou art Simon, the son of Jonah*—As none had told our Lord
these names, this could not but strike Peter. *Cephas, which is Peter*—Meaning
the same in Syriac which *Peter* does in Greek, namely, a rock.

45. *Jesus of Nazareth*—So Philip thought, not knowing he was born in Bethlehem. Nathanael was probably the same with Bartholomew, that is, the son of
Tholomew. St. Matthew joins Bartholomew with Philip, chap. x, 3, and St.
John places Nathanael in the midst of the apostles, immediately after Thomas,
chap. xxi, 2, just as Bartholomew is placed, Acts i, 13.

46. *Can any good thing come out of Nazareth?*—How cautiously should we
guard against popular prejudices? When these had once possessed so honest a
heart as that of Nathanael, they led him to suspect the blessed Jesus himself for
an impostor, because he had been brought up at Nazareth. But his integrity
prevailed over that foolish bias, and laid him open to the force of evidence, which
a candid inquirer will always be glad to admit, even when it brings the most
unexpected discoveries. *Can any good thing*—That is, have we ground from
Scripture to expect the Messiah, or any eminent prophet from Nazareth? *Philip*

47 of Nazareth? Philip saith to him, Come and see. Jesus saw Nathanael coming toward him, and saith of him, Behold an Israelite
48 indeed, in whom is no guile. Nathanael saith to him, Whence knowest thou me? Jesus answered and said to him, Before Philip
49 called thee, when thou wast under the fig tree, I saw thee. Nathanael answered and said to him, Rabbi, thou art the Son of God,
50 thou art the King of Israel. Jesus answered and said to him, Because I said to thee, I saw thee under the fig tree, believest thou?
51 Thou shalt see greater things than these. And he saith to him, Verily, verily I say to you, Hereafter ye shall see the heaven opened, and the angels of God ascending and descending on the Son of man.

II. And the third day there was a marriage in Cana of Galilee, and
2 the mother of Jesus was there. And both Jesus and his disciples
3 were invited to the marriage. And wine falling short, the mother
4 of Jesus saith to him, They have not wine. Jesus saith to her, Woman, what *is it* to me and thee? Mine hour is not yet come.
5 His mother saith to the servants, Whatsoever he saith to you, do.
6 And there were set there six water pots of stone, after the manner

---

saith, Come and see—The same answer which he had received himself from our Lord the day before.

48. *Under the fig tree I saw thee*—Perhaps at prayer.

49. *Nathanael answered*—Happy are they that are ready to believe, swift to receive the truth and grace of God. *Thou art the Son of God*—So he acknowledges now more than he had heard from Philip: *The Son of God, the king of Israel*—A confession both of the person and office of Christ.

51. *Hereafter ye shall see*—All of these, as well as thou, who believe on me now in my state of humiliation, shall hereafter see me come in my glory, and all the angels of God with me. This seems the most natural sense of the words, though they may also refer to his ascension.

II. 1. *And the third day*—After he had said this. *In Cana of Galilee*—There were two other towns of the same name, one in the tribe of Ephraim, the other in Cælosyria.

2. *Jesus and his disciples were invited to the marriage*—Christ does not take away human society, but sanctifies it. Water might have quenched thirst; yet our Lord allows wine; especially at a festival solemnity. Such was his facility in drawing his disciples at first, who were afterward to go through rougher ways.

3. *And wine falling short*—How many days the solemnity had lasted, and on which day our Lord came, or how many disciples might follow him, does not appear. *His mother saith to him, They have not wine*—Either she might mean, supply them by miracle; or, Go away, that others may go also, before the want appears.

4. *Jesus saith to her, Woman*—So our Lord speaks also, chap. xix, 26. It is probable this was the constant appellation which he used to her. He regarded his Father above all, not *knowing* even his mother *after the flesh*. *What is it to me and thee?* A mild reproof of her inordinate concern and untimely interposal. *Mine hour is not yet come*—The time of *my* working this miracle, or of my going away.

May we not learn hence, if his mother was rebuked for attempting to direct him in the days of his flesh, how absurd it is to address her as if she had a right to command him, on the throne of his glory? Likewise how indecent it is for us to direct his supreme wisdom, as to the time or manner in which he shall appear for us in any of the exigencies of life!

5. *His mother saith to the servants*—Gathering from his answer he was about to do something extraordinary.

6. *The purifying of the Jews*—Who purified themselves by frequent washings particularly before eating.

of the purifying of the Jews, containing two or three measures
7 apiece. Jesus saith to them, Fill the water pots with water. And
8 they filled them up to the brim. And he saith to them, Draw out
now, and carry to the governor of the feast. And they carried *it*.
9 When the governor of the feast had tasted the water that was
made wine, (he knew not whence it was, but the servants who had
drawn the water knew,) the governor of the feast called the bride-
10 groom, And saith to him, Every man doth set out good wine first,
and when men have well drunk, then that which is worse: *but*
11 thou hast kept the good wine till now. Jesus wrought this beginning of miracles in Cana of Galilee, and manifested his glory, and
his disciples believed on him.
12 After this he went down to Capernaum, he and his mother, and his
brethren, and his disciples: and they tarried there not many days.
13 For the passover of the Jews was nigh. And Jesus went up
14 to Jerusalem, And found in the temple them that sold oxen,
15 and sheep, and doves, and the changers of money sitting. And
having made a scourge of rushes, he drove all out of the temple,
both the sheep, and the oxen, and poured out the changers' money,
16 and overthrew the tables, And said to them that sold doves, Take
these things hence: make not my Father's house a house of traffic.
17 And his disciples remembered that it is written, * The zeal of
18 thine house eateth me up. Then answered the Jews, and said to
him, What sign showest thou us, seeing thou dost these things?
19 Jesus answered and said to them, Destroy this temple, and I will
20 raise it up in three days. Then said the Jews, Forty and six years
was this temple in building, and wilt thou raise it up in three days?
21 But he spake of the temple of his body. When therefore he was
22 risen from the dead, his disciples remembered that he had said this;
and they believed the scripture, and the word which Jesus had

---

9. *The governor of the feast*—The bridegroom generally procured some friend
to order all things at the entertainment.

10. *And saith*—St. John barely relates the words he spoke, which does not
imply his approving them. *When they have well drunk*—does not mean any
more than toward the close of the entertainment.

11. *And his disciples believed*—More steadfastly.

14. *Oxen, and sheep, and doves*—Used for sacrifice: *And the changers of money*—Those who changed foreign money for that which was current at Jerusalem, for the convenience of them that came from distant countries.

15. *Having made a scourge of rushes*—(Which were strewed on the ground,)
he drove all out of the temple, (that is, the court of it,) *both the sheep and the
oxen*—Though it does not appear that he struck even them; and much less, any
of the men. But a terror from God, it is evident, fell upon them.

18. *Then answered the Jews*—Either some of those whom he had just driven
out, or their friends: *What sign showest thou?*—So they require a miracle, to
confirm a miracle!

19. *This temple*—Doubtless pointing, while he spoke, to his body, the temple
and habitation of the Godhead.

20. *Forty and six years*—Just so many years before the time of this conversation, Herod the Great had begun his most magnificent reparation of the temple,
(one part after another,) which he continued all his life, and which was now
going on, and was continued thirty-six years longer, till within six or seven years
of the destruction of the state, city, and temple by the Romans.

* Psa. xlix, 9.

23 said. Now when he was in Jerusalem at the passover, on the feast
   day, many believed in his name, beholding the miracles which he
24 did. But Jesus did not trust himself to them, because he knew all
25 men, And needed not that any should testify of man; for he knew
   what was in man.
III. Now there was a man of the Pharisees, named Nicodemus, a
2 ruler of the Jews. The same came to him by night, and said to
   him, Rabbi, we know that thou art a teacher come from God: for
   no man can do these miracles which thou dost, except God be with
3 him. Jesus answered and said to him, Verily, verily I say unto
   thee, Except a man be born again, he cannot see the kingdom of
4 God. Nicodemus saith to him, How can a man be born when he
   is old? Can he enter a second time into his mother's womb, and
5 be born? Jesus answered, Verily, verily I say unto thee, Except
   a man be born of water and the Spirit, he cannot enter into the
6 kingdom of God. That which is born of the flesh is flesh; and
7 that which is born of the Spirit is spirit. Marvel not that I said
8 unto thee, Ye must be born again. The wind bloweth where it

---

22. *They believed the scripture, and the word which Jesus had said*—Concerning his resurrection.
23. *Many believed*—That he was a teacher sent from God.
24. *He did not trust himself to them*—Let us learn hence not rashly to put ourselves into the power of others. Let us study a wise and happy medium between
universal suspiciousness and that easiness which would make us the property of
every pretender to kindness and respect.
25. *He*—To whom all things are naked, *knew what was in man*—Namely, a
desperately deceitful heart.
III. 1. *A ruler*—One of the great council.
2. *The same came*—Through desire; but *by night*—Through shame: *We
know*—Even we rulers and Pharisees.
3. *Jesus answered*—That knowledge will not avail thee unless thou *be born
again*—Otherwise thou canst not see, that is, experience and enjoy, either the
inward or the glorious kingdom of God.
In this solemn discourse our Lord shows, that no external profession, no ceremonial ordinances or privileges of birth, could entitle any to the blessings of
the Messiah's kingdom: that an entire change of heart as well as of life was
necessary for that purpose: that this could only be wrought in man by the
almighty power of God: that every man born into the world was by nature in a
state of sin, condemnation, and misery: that the free mercy of God had given
his Son to deliver them from it, and to raise them to a blessed immortality:
that all mankind, Gentiles as well as Jews, might share in these benefits, procured by his being lifted up on the cross, and to be received by faith in him:
but that if they rejected him, their eternal, aggravated condemnation, would
be the certain consequence. *Except a man be born again*—If our Lord by
being *born again* means only reformation of life, instead of making any new
discovery, he has only thrown a great deal of obscurity on what was before plain
and obvious.
4. *When he is old*—As Nicodemus himself was.
5. *Except a man be born of water and of the Spirit*—Except he experience
that great inward change by the Spirit, and be baptized (wherever baptism can
be had) as the outward sign and means of it.
6. *That which is born of the flesh is flesh*—Mere flesh, void of the Spirit, yea,
at enmity with it; *And that which is born of the Spirit is spirit*—Is spiritual,
heavenly, divine, like its Author.
7. *Ye must be born again*—To be born again, is to be inwardly changed from
all sinfulness to all holiness. It is fitly so called, because as great a change then
passes on the soul as passes on the body when it is born into the world.
8. *The wind bloweth*—According to its own nature, not thy will, *and thou*

listeth, and thou hearest the sound thereof, but canst not tell whence
it cometh, and whither it goeth : so is every one that is born of the
9 Spirit. Nicodemus answered and said to him, How can these
10 things be ? Jesus answered and said to him, Art thou a teacher of
11 Israel, and knowest not these things ? Verily, verily I say to thee,
We speak what we know, and testify what we have seen ; yet ye
12 receive not our testimony. If I have told you earthly things, and
ye believe not, how would ye believe if I told you heavenly things ?
13 For no one hath gone up to heaven, but he that came down from
14 heaven, the Son of man, who is in heaven. And as * Moses lifted
up the serpent in the wilderness, so must the Son of man be lifted
15 up, That whosoever believeth on him may not perish, but have
16 everlasting life. For God so loved the world, that he gave his
only-begotten Son, that whosoever believeth on him may not perish,
17 but have everlasting life. For God sent not his Son into the world,
to condemn the world, but that the world might be saved through
18 him. He that believeth on him, is not condemned ; but he that
believeth not is condemned already, because he hath not believed
19 on the name of the only-begotten Son of God. And this is the
condemnation, that light is come into the world, and men loved

hearest the sound thereof—Thou art sure it doth blow, *but canst not* explain the
particular manner of its acting. *So is every one that is born of the Spirit*—The
fact is plain, the manner of his operations inexplicable.

11. *We speak what we know*—I and all that believe in me.

12. *Earthly things*—Things done on earth ; such as the new birth, and the
present privileges of the children of God. *Heavenly things*—Such as the eternity
of the Son, and the unity of the Father, Son, and Spirit.

13. *For no one*—For here you must rely on my single testimony, whereas
there you have a cloud of witnesses : *Hath gone up to heaven, but he that came
down from heaven. Who is in heaven*—Therefore he is omnipresent ; else he
could not be in heaven and on earth at once. This is a plain instance of what
is usually termed the communication of properties between the Divine and human
nature ; whereby what is proper to the Divine nature is spoken concerning the
human, and what is proper to the human is, as here, spoken of the Divine.

14. *And as Moses*—And even this single witness will soon be taken from you ;
yea, and in a most ignominious manner.

15. *That whosoever*—He must be *lifted up*, that hereby he may purchase salvation for all believers : all those who look to him by faith recover spiritual health,
even as all that looked at that *serpent* recovered bodily health.

16. Yea, and this was the very design of God's love in sending him into the
world. *Whosoever believeth on him*—With that faith which worketh by love,
and hold fast the beginning of his confidence steadfast to the end. *God so
loved the world*—That is, all men under heaven ; even those that despise his
love, and will *for that cause* finally perish. Otherwise not to believe would be
no sin to them. For what should they believe ? Ought they to believe that
Christ was given for them ? Then he was given for them. *He gave his only
Son*—Truly and seriously. And *the Son of God gave himself*, Gal. iv, 4, truly
and seriously.

17. *God sent not his Son into the world to condemn the world*—Although many
accuse him of it.

18. *He that believeth on him is not condemned*—Is acquitted, is justified before
God. *The name of the only-begotten Son of God*—The name of a person is often
put for the person himself. But perhaps it is farther intimated in that expression, that the person spoken of is great and magnificent. And therefore it is
generally used to express either God the Father or the Son.

19 *This is the condemnation*—That is, the cause of it. So God is clear.

* Num. xxi, 8, 9.

20 darkness rather than light, because their deeds were evil. For
   every one that doth evil, hateth the light, neither cometh to the
21 light, lest his deeds should be reproved. But he that practiseth
   the truth, cometh to the light, that his deeds may be made manifest, that they are wrought in God.
22   After these things Jesus and his disciples went into the land of
23 Judea, and there he tarried with them and baptized. And John also
   was baptizing in Enon, near Salim, because there was much water
24 there ; and they came and were baptized. For John was not yet
   cast into prison.
25   Then there arose a dispute between some of John's disciples
26 and the Jews about purifying. And they came to John, and said
   to him, Rabbi, he that was with thee beyond Jordan, to whom
   thou gavest testimony, behold he baptizeth, and all men come to
27 him. John answered and said, A man can receive nothing, unless
28 it be given him from heaven. Ye yourselves bear me witness that
29 I said, I am not the Christ, but I am sent before him. He that
   hath the bride is the bridegroom ; but the friend of the bridegroom
   who standeth and heareth him, rejoiceth greatly because of the
30 bridegroom's voice : this my joy therefore is fulfilled. He must
31 increase, but I *must* decrease. He that cometh from above is
   above all : he that is of the earth is earthly, and speaketh of the
32 earth : he that cometh from heaven is above all. And what he
   hath seen and heard, that he testifieth : yet no man receiveth his
33 testimony. He that hath received his testimony, hath set to his

---

21. *He that practiseth the truth* (that is, true religion) *cometh to the light*—So
even Nicodemus afterward did. *Are wrought in God*—That is, in the light,
power, and love of God.

22. *Jesus went*—From the capital city, *Jerusalem, into the land of Judea*—That
is, into the country. *There he baptized*—Not himself; but his disciples by his
order, chap. iv, 2.

23. *John also was baptizing*—He did not repel them that offered, but he more
willingly referred them to Jesus.

25. *The Jews*—Those men of Judea, who now went to be baptized by Jesus;
and John's disciples, who were mostly of Galilee : *about purifying*—That is, baptism. They disputed, which they should be baptized by.

27. *A man can receive nothing*—Neither he nor I. Neither could he do this,
unless God had sent him : nor can I receive the title of Christ, or any honour comparable to that which he hath received from heaven. They seem to
have spoken with jealousy and resentment ; John answers with sweet composure
of spirit.

29. *He that hath the bride is the bridegroom*—He whom the bride follows.
But all men now come to Jesus. Hence it is plain he is the bridegroom. *The
friend who heareth him*—Talk with the bride ; *rejoiceth greatly*—So far from
envying or resenting it.

30. *He must increase, but* I must *decrease*—So they who are now, like John,
burning and shining lights, must (if not suddenly eclipsed) like him gradually
decrease, while others are *increasing* about them ; as they in their turns grew
up, amidst the decays of the former generation. Let us know how to set, as
well as how to rise ; and let it comfort our declining days to trace, in those who
are likely to succeed us in our work, the openings of yet greater usefulness.

31. It is not improbable, that what is added, to the end of the chapter, are the
words of the evangelist, not the Baptist. *He that is of the earth*—A mere man ;
of earthly original, has a spirit and speech answerable to it.

32. *No man*—None comparatively, exceeding few ; *receiveth his testimony*—
With true faith.

34 seal, that God is true. For he whom God hath sent, speaketh the words of God; for God giveth not *him* the Spirit by measure
35 The Father loveth the Son, and hath given all things into his hand.
36 He that believeth on the Son, hath everlasting life : but he that obeyeth not the Son, shall not see life ; but the wrath of God abideth on him.
IV. When therefore the Lord knew that the Pharisees had heard,
2 Jesus maketh and baptizeth more disciples than John, (Though
3 Jesus himself baptized not; but his disciples,) He left Judea, and
4 departed again into Galilee. And he must needs go through Samaria.
5 Then cometh he to a city of Samaria, called Sychar, near the field
6 that Jacob gave to his son Joseph. Now Jacob's well was there. Jesus therefore being wearied with the journey, sat thus by the
7 well. It was about the sixth hour. There cometh a woman of Samaria to draw water. Jesus saith to her, Give me to drink.
8 (For his disciples were gone to the city to buy meat.) Then saith
9 the Samaritan woman to him, How dost thou, being a Jew, ask drink of me, who am a Samaritan woman ? For the Jews have no deal-
10 ings with the Samaritans. Jesus answered and said unto her, If thou hadst known the gift of God, and who it is that saith to thee, Give me to drink, thou wouldst have asked of him, and he would
11 have given thee living water. The woman saith to him, Sir, thou hast nothing to draw with, and the well is deep ; whence then hast
12 thou that living water ? Art thou greater than our father Jacob, who gave us the well, and himself drank thereof, and his children,
13 and his cattle ? Jesus answered and said to her, Whosoever drink-

---

33. *Hath set to his seal*—It was customary among the Jews for the witness to set his seal to the testimony he had given. *That God is true*—Whose words the Messiah speaks.

34. *God giveth not him the Spirit by measure*—As he did to the prophets, but immeasurably. Hence he speaketh the words of God in the most perfect manner.

36. *He that believeth on the Son hath everlasting life*—He hath it already. For he loves God. And love is the essence of heaven. *He that obeyeth not*—A consequence of not believing.

IV. 1. *The Lord knew*—Though none informed him of it.

3. *He left Judea*—To shun the effects of their resentment.

4. *And he must needs go through Samaria*—The road lying directly through it.

5. *Sychar*—Formerly called Sichem or Shechem. *Jacob gave*—On his death bed, Gen. xlviii, 22.

6. *Jesus sat down*—Weary as he was. *It was the sixth hour*—Noon ; the heat of the day.

7. *Give me to drink*—In this one conversation he brought her to that knowledge which the apostles were so long in attaining.

8. *For his disciples were gone*—Else he needed not have asked her.

9. *How dost thou*—Her open simplicity appears from her very first words. *The Jews have no dealings*—None by way of friendship. They would receive no kind of favour from them.

10. *If thou hadst known the gift*—The living water ; *and who it is*—He who alone is able to give it : *thou wouldst have asked of him*—On those words the stress lies. *Water*—In like manner he draws the allegory from bread, chap. vi, 27, and from light, chap. viii, 12 ; the first, the most simple, necessary, common, and salutary things in nature. *Living water*—The Spirit and its fruits. But she might the more easily mistake his meaning, because living water was a common phrase among the Jews for spring water.

12. *Our father Jacob*—So they fancied he was ; whereas they were, in truth, a mixture of many nations, placed there by the king of Assyria, in the room of

14 eth of this water, will thirst again. But whosoever drinketh of the
water that I shall give him, will never thirst, but the water that I
shall give him, will become in him a fountain of water springing
15 up into everlasting life. The woman saith to him, Sir, give me
16 this water, that I thirst not, neither come hither to draw. Jesus
17 saith to her, Go, call thy husband, and come hither. The woman
answered and said, I have no husband. Jesus said to her, Thou
18 hast well said, I have no husband : For thou hast had five husbands, and he whom thou now hast, is not thy husband : this thou
19 saidst truly. The woman saith to him, Sir, I perceive that thou
20 art a prophet. Our fathers worshipped in this mountain : but ye
say, that at Jerusalem is the place where men ought to worship.
21 Jesus saith to her, Woman, believe me, the hour cometh, when ye
shall neither in this mountain, nor at Jerusalem, worship the Fa-
22 ther. Ye worship ye know not what ; we know what we worship ;
23 for salvation is from the Jews. But the hour cometh, and now is,

the Israelites whom he had carried away captive, 2 Kings xvii, 24. *Who gave
us the well*—In Joseph their supposed forefather : *and drank thereof*—So even
he had no better water than this.

14. *Will never thirst*—Will never (provided he continue to drink thereof) be
miserable, dissatisfied, without refreshment. If ever that thirst returns, it will
be the fault of the man, not the water *But the water that I shall give him*—The
spirit of faith working by love, *shall become in him*—An inward living principle,
a fountain—Not barely a well, which is soon exhausted, *springing up into everlasting life*—Which is a confluence, or rather an ocean of streams arising from
this fountain.

15. *That I thirst not*—She takes him still in a gross sense.

16. *Jesus saith to her*—He now clears the way that he might give her a better
kind of water than she asked for. *Go, call thy husband*—He strikes directly at
her bosom sin.

17. *Thou hast well said*—We may observe in all our Lord's discourses the utmost weightiness, and yet the utmost courtesy.

18. *Thou hast had five husbands*—Whether they were all dead or not, her own
conscience now awakened would tell her.

19. *Sir, I perceive*—So soon was her heart touched.

20. The instant she perceived this, she proposes what she thought the most
important of all questions. *This mountain*—Pointing to Mount Gerizim. Sanballat, by the permission of Alexander the Great, had built a temple upon Mount
Gerizim, for Manasseh, who for marrying Sanballat's daughter had been expelled from the priesthood and from Jerusalem, Neh. xiii, 28. This was the
place where the Samaritans used to worship in opposition to Jerusalem. And it
was so near Sychar, that a man's voice might be heard from the one to the
other. *Our fathers worshipped*—This plainly refers to Abraham and Jacob (from
whom the Samaritans pretended to deduce their genealogy) who erected altars in
this place : Gen. xii, 6, 7, and xxxiii, 18, 20. And possibly to the whole congregation, who were directed when they came into the land of Canaan to put
the blessing upon Mount Gerizim, Deut. xi, 29. *Ye Jews say, In Jerusalem is
the place*—Namely, the temple.

21. *Believe me*—Our Lord uses this expression in this manner but once ; and
that to a Samaritan. To his own people, the Jews, his usual language is, *I say
unto you.* *The hour cometh when ye*—Both Samaritans and Jews, *shall worship
neither in this mountain, nor at Jerusalem*—As preferable to any other place.
True worship shall be no longer confined to any one place or nation.

22. *Ye worship ye know not what*—Ye Samaritans are ignorant, not only of the
place, but of the very object of worship. Indeed, *they feared the Lord* after a
fashion ; but at the same time served their own gods, 2 Kings xvii, 33. *Salvation is from the Jews*—So spake all the prophets, that the Saviour should arise out
of the Jewish nation : and that from thence the knowledge of him should spread
to all nations under heaven.

when the true worshippers shall worship the Father in spirit and
24 in truth: for the Father seeketh such to worship him. God *is* a
Spirit, and they that worship him must worship in spirit and *in*
25 truth. The woman saith to him, I' know that the Messiah is coming who is called Christ: when he is come, he will tell us all
26 things. Jesus saith to her, I that speak to thee am *He.* And upon
27 this came his disciples, and marvelled that he talked with a woman. Yet none said, What seekest thou? Or, Why talkest thou
with her?
28   The woman then left her water pot, and went to the city, and
29 saith to the men, Come, see a man who told me all things that ever
30 I did: Is not this the Christ? Then they went out of the city,
and came to him.
31   In the meantime his disciples prayed him, saying, Master, eat.
32 But he said to them, I have meat to eat that ye know not of. The
33 disciples said one to another, Hath any man brought him to eat?
34 Jesus saith to them, My meat is, to do the will of him that sent
35 me, and to finish his work. Say ye not, There are yet four
months, and the harvest cometh? Lo, I say to you, lift up' your
eyes and survey the fields, for they are white already to the har-
36 vest. And he that reapeth receiveth wages, and gathereth fruit
to life eternal, that both he that soweth and he that reapeth may

---

23. *The true worshippers shall worship the Father*—Not here or there only, but
at all times and in all places.

24. *God is a Spirit*—Not only remote from the body, and all the properties of
it, but likewise full of all spiritual perfections, power, wisdom, love, holiness.
And our worship should be suitable to his nature. We should worship him with
the truly spiritual worship of faith, love, and holiness, animating all our tempers,
thoughts, words, and actions.

25. *The woman saith*—With joy for what she had already learned, and desire
of fuller instruction.

26. *Jesus saith*—Hasting to satisfy her desire before his disciples came. *I am
He*—Our Lord did not speak this so plainly to the Jews who were so full of the
Messiah's temporal kingdom. If he had, many would doubtless have taken up
arms in his favour, and others have accused him to the Roman governor. Yet he
did in effect declare the thing, though he denied the particular title. For in a
multitude of places he represented himself, both as the Son of man, and as the
Son of God: both which expressions were generally understood by the Jews as
peculiarly applicable to the Messiah.

27. *His disciples marvelled that he talked with a woman*—Which the Jewish
rabbis reckoned scandalous for a man of distinction to do. They marvelled likewise at his talking with a woman of that nation, which was so peculiarly hateful
to the Jews. *Yet none said*—To the woman, *What seekest thou?*—Or to Christ,
Why talkest thou with her?

28. *The woman left her water pot*—Forgetting smaller things.

29. *A man who told me all things that ever I did*—Our Lord had told her but a
few things. But his words awakened her conscience, which soon told her all the
rest. *Is not this the Christ?*—She does not doubt of it herself, but incites them
to make the inquiry.

31. *In the meantime*—Before the people came.

34. *My meat*—That which satisfies the strongest appetite of my soul.

35. *The fields are white already*—As if he had said, The spiritual harvest is
ripe already. The Samaritans, ripe for the Gospel, covered the ground round
about them.

36. *He that reapeth*—Whoever saves souls, *receiveth wages*—A peculiar blessing to himself, *and gathereth fruit*—Many souls: *that he that soweth*—Christ the
reat sower of the seed, *and he that reapeth may rejoice together*—In heaven.

37 rejoice together. And herein is the saying true, One soweth, and
38 another reapeth. I have sent you to reap that whereon you have
bestowed no labour : others have laboured, and ye are entered into
their labour.
39 And many of the Samaritans out of the city believed on him,
for the saying of the woman testifying, He told me all that ever I
40 did. So when the Samaritans were come to him, they besought
41 him to tarry with them. And he abode there two days. And
42 many more believed, because of his word, And said to the woman,
We no longer believe, because of thy saying; for we have heard
him ourselves, and know that this is indeed the Christ, the Saviour
of the world.
43 After the two days, he departed thence, and went into Galilee.
44 (Now Jesus himself had testified, * That a prophet hath not honour
45 in his own country.) And when he was come into Galilee, the
Galileans received him, having seen all the things that he did in
Jerusalem at the feast. For they also had come to the feast.
46 So he came again to Cana of Galilee, where he had made the
water wine. And there was a certain nobleman, whose son was
47 sick at Capernaum. When he heard that Jesus was come out of
Judea into Galilee, he went to him, and besought him to come down
48 and heal his son, for he was at the point of death. Jesus said to
him, Unless ye see signs and wonders, ye will in nowise believe.
49 The nobleman said to him, Sir, come down, ere my child die. Je-
50 sus said to him, Go: thy son liveth. And the man believed the
51 word that Jesus spake to him, and he went. And as he was now
going down his servants met him, and told him, saying, Thy son
52 liveth. Then he asked of them the hour when he amended. And
they said to him, Yesterday at the seventh hour the fever left him.
53 So the father knew it was at the same hour, in which Jesus had
said to him, Thy son liveth. And himself believed, and his whole
54 house. This second miracle again Jesus wrought, being come out
of Judea into Galilee.
V. After this there was a feast of the Jews, and Jesus went up to
2 Jerusalem. Now there is in Jerusalem by the sheep gate, a bath
which is called in the Hebrew tongue, Bethesda, having five por-

37. *That saying*—A common proverb; *One soweth*—The prophets and Christ; *another reapeth*—The apostles and succeeding ministers.
38. *I*—The Lord of the whole harvest, *have sent you*—He had employed them already in baptizing, ver. 2.
42. *We know that this is the Saviour of the world*—And not of the Jews only.
43. *He went into Galilee*—That is, into the country of Galilee : but not to Nazareth. It was at that town only that he *had no honour.* Therefore he went to other towns.
47. *To come down*—For Cana stood much higher than Capernaum.
48. *Unless ye see signs and wonders*—Although the Samaritans believed without them.
52. *He asked the hour when he amended*—The more exactly the works of God are considered, the more faith is increased.
V. 1. *A feast*—Pentecost.
2. *There is in Jerusalem*—Hence it appears, that St. John wrote his Gospel before Jerusalem was destroyed : it is supposed about thirty years after the

* Matt. xiii, 57.

3 ticos. In these lay a great multitude of diseased, of blind, halt,
4 withered, waiting for the moving of the water. For an angel went
down at certain times into the bath, and the water was troubled:
and whosoever went in first, after the troubling of the water, was
5 made whole, whatsoever disease he had. And a certain man was
6 there, who had been diseased eight and thirty years. Jesus seeing him lie, and knowing that he had now been diseased a long
7 time, saith to him, Desirest thou to be made whole? The infirm
man answered him, Sir, I have no man to put me into the bath,
when the water is troubled; and the while I am coming, another
8 steppeth down before me. Jesus saith to him, Rise, take up thy
9 bed and walk. And immediately the man was made whole, and
took up his bed and walked: and the same day was the Sabbath.
10 Then said the Jews to him that was healed, It is the Sabbath; it
11 is not lawful for thee to take up thy bed. He answered, He that
12 made me whole, said to me, Take up thy bed and walk. Then
asked they him, Who is the man that said to thee, Take up thy
13 bed and walk? And he that was healed knew not who he was;
14 for Jesus had retired, a multitude being in the place. Afterward
Jesus findeth him in the temple, and said to him, Lo, thou art made
15 whole: sin no more, lest a worse thing come to thee. The man
departed and told the Jews, that it was Jesus who had made him
whole.
16 And therefore the Jews persecuted Jesus, because he had done
17 these things on the Sabbath. But Jesus answered them, My Father
18 worketh until now, and I work. Therefore the Jews sought the

ascension. *Having five porticos*—Built for the use of the sick. Probably the basin had five sides! *Bethesda* signifies *the house of mercy.*
4. *An angel*—Yet many undoubtedly thought the whole thing to be purely natural. *At certain times*—Perhaps at a certain hour of the day, during this paschal week, *went down*—The Greek word implies that he had ceased going down, before the time of St. John's writing this. God might design this to raise expectation of the acceptable time approaching, to add a greater lustre to his Son's miracles, and to show that his ancient people were not entirely forgotten of him. *The first*—Whereas the Son of God healed every day not one only, but whole multitudes that resorted to him.
7. *The sick man answered*—Giving the reason why he was not made whole, notwithstanding his desire.
14. *Sin no more*—It seems his former illness was the effect or punishment of sin.
15. *The man went and told the Jews, that it was Jesus who had made him whole*—One might have expected, that when he had published the name of his benefactor, crowds would have thronged about Jesus, to have heard the words of his mouth, and to have received the blessings of the Gospel. Instead of this, they surround him with a hostile intent: they even conspire against his life, and for an imagined transgression in point of ceremony, would have put out this light of Israel. Let us not wonder then, if our good be evil spoken of: if even candour, benevolence, and usefulness, do not disarm the enmity of those who have been taught to prefer sacrifice to mercy; and who, disrelishing the genuine Gospel, naturally seek to slander and persecute the professors, but especially the defenders of it.
17. *My Father worketh until now, and I work*—From the creation till now he hath been working without intermission. I do likewise. This is the proposition which is explained from ver. 19, to ver. 30, confirmed and vindicated in the 31st and following verses.
18. *His own Father*—The Greek word means *his own Father* in such a sense as no creature can speak. *Making himself equal with God*—It is evident all the

more to kill him, because he not only broke the Sabbath, but also
said that God was his own Father, making himself equal with God.
19 Then answered Jesus and said to them, Verily, verily I say unto
you, the Son can do nothing of himself, but what he seeth the Father do : but what things soever he doth, these also doth the Son
20 likewise. For the Father loveth the Son, and showeth him all
things that himself doth : and he will show him greater works than
21 these, so that ye will marvel. For as the Father quickeneth the
22 dead, so the Son also quickeneth whom he will. For neither doth
the Father judge any one, but hath given all judgment to the Son ;
23 That all men may honour the Son, even as they honour the Fa
ther. He that honoureth not the Son, honoureth not the Father
24 that sent him. Verily, verily I say unto you, he that heareth my
word, and believeth on him that sent me, hath everlasting life, and
cometh not into condemnation, but is passed from death to life.
25 Verily, verily I say to you, The hour is coming, and now is, when
the dead shall hear the voice of the Son of God, and they that hear
26 shall live. For as the Father hath life in himself, so hath he
27 given to the Son also to have life in himself, And hath given him

---

hearers so understood him, and that our Lord never contradicted. but con.
firmed it.

19. *The Son can do nothing of himself*—This is not his imperfection, but his
glory, resulting from his eternal, intimate, indissoluble unity with the Father.
Hence it is absolutely impossible, that the Son should *judge, will, testify, or teach*
any thing without the Father, ver. 30, &c ; chap. vi, 38 ; chap. vii, 16 ; or that
he should be known or believed on, separately from the Father. And he here
defends his doing good every day, without intermission, by the example of his
Father, from which he cannot depart : *these doth the Son likewise*—All *these*,
and only these ; seeing he and the Father are one.

20. *The Father showeth him all things that himself doth*—A proof of the most
intimate unity. *And he will show him*—By doing them. At the same time (not
at different times) the Father showeth and doth, and the Son seeth and doth.
Greater works—Jesus oftener terms them works, than signs or wonders, because
they were not wonders in his eyes. *Ye will marvel*—So they did, when he raised
Lazarus.

21. *For*—He declares which are those greater works, raising the dead, and
judging the world. The power of *quickening whom he will* follows from the
power of *judging*. These two, *quickening* and *judging*, are proposed ver. 21, 22.
The acquittal of believers, which presupposes *judgment*, is treated of in the 24th
verse : the *quickening* some of the dead, ver. 25; and the general resurrection, ver. 28.

22. *For neither doth the Father judge*—Not without the Son : but he doth *judge*
by that man whom he hath ordained, Acts xvii, 31.

23. *That all men may honour the Son, even as they honour the Father*—Either
willingly, and so escaping condemnation, by faith : or unwillingly, when feeling
the wrath of the Judge. This *demonstrates* the EQUALITY of the Son with the
Father. If our Lord were God only by office or investiture, and not in the unity
of the Divine essence, and in all respects equal in Godhead with the Father, he
could not be honoured *even as*, that is, with the *same* honour that they honoured
the Father. *He that honoureth not the Son*—With the *same* equal honour, greatly
dishonoureth *the Father that sent him*.

24. *And cometh not into condemnation*—Unless he make shipwreck of the faith

25. *The dead shall hear the voice of the Son of God*—So did Jairus's daughter,
the widow's son, Lazarus.

26. *He hath given to the Son*—By eternal generation, *to have life in himself*—
Absolute, independent.

27. *Because he is the Son of man*—He is appointed to judge mankind because
he was made man.

authority to execute judgment likewise, because he is the Son of
28 man. Marvel not at this : for the time is coming in which all that
29 are in the graves shall hear his voice, And shall come forth, they
that have done good to the resurrection of life, and they that have
30 done evil to the resurrection of damnation. I can do nothing of
myself: as I hear, I judge, and my judgment is just; because I
31 seek not my own will, but the will of him that sent me. If I tes-
32 tify of myself, my testimony is not valid. There is another that
testifieth of me, and I know that the testimony which he testifieth
of me is valid.
33 Ye sent to John, and he bare testimony to the truth. But I
34 receive not testimony from man ; but these things I say, that ye
35 may be saved. He was a burning and a shining light, and ye
36 were willing for a season to rejoice in his light. But I have a
greater testimony than *that* of John: for the works which the
Father hath given me to fulfil, the very works that I do testify of
37 me, that the Father hath sent me. And the Father who hath
sent me, he hath testified of me : ye have neither heard his voice
38 at any time, nor seen his form. And ye have not his word abid-
39 ing in you; for whom he hath sent, ye believe not. Search the
Scriptures : in them ye are assured ye have eternal life : and it
40 is they that testify of me. Yet ye will not come to me, that ye
41 may have life. I receive not honour from men, But I know you,
42 that ye have not the love of God in you. For I am come in my
43 Father's name, and ye receive me not: if another shall come in

28. *The time is coming-* —When not two or three, but all shall rise.
29. *The resurrection of life*—That resurrection which leads to life everlasting.
30. *I can do nothing of myself*—It is impossible I should do any thing separately from my Father. *As I hear*—Of the Father, and see, so I judge and do ;
because I am essentially united to him. See ver. 19.
31. *If I testify of myself*—That is, if I alone, (which indeed is impossible,) *my
testimony is not valid.*
32. *There is another* —The Father, ver. 37, *and I know that,* even in your judgment, his testimony is beyond exception.
33. *He bare testimony*—That I am the Christ.
34. *But I* have no need to *receive, &c. But these things*—Concerning John,
whom ye yourselves reverence, *I say, that ye may be saved*—So really and
seriously did he will their salvation. Yet they were not saved. Most, if not all
of them, died in their sins.
35. *He was a burning and a shining light*—Inwardly burning with love and
zeal, outwardly shining in all holiness. *And* even *ye were willing for a season*—
A short time only.
37. *He hath testified of me*—Namely at my baptism. I speak not of my supposed father Joseph. Ye are utter strangers to him of whom I speak.
38. *Ye have not his word*—All who believe have the word of the Father (the
same with the word of the Son) abiding in them, that is, deeply ingrafted in
their hearts.
39. *Search the Scriptures*—A plain command to all men. *In them ye are
assured ye have eternal life*—Ye know they show you the way to eternal life
And these very Scriptures testify of me.
40. *Yet ye will not come unto me*—As they direct you.
41. *I receive not honour from men*—I need it not. I seek it not from you for
my own sake.
42. *But I know you*—With this ray he pierces the hearts of the hearers. And
this doubtless he spake with the tenderest compassion.
43. *If another shall come*—Any false Christ.

44 his own name, him will ye receive. How can ye believe, while
ye receive honour one of another, and seek not the honour that is
45 from God only? Think not that I will accuse you to the Father:
there is one that accuseth you, *even* Moses, in whom ye trust.
46 For had ye believed Moses, ye would have believed me: for he
47 wrote of me. But if ye believe not his writings, how shall ye believe my words.

VI.   * After these things, Jesus went over the sea of Galilee, *the*
2 *sea* of Tiberias, And a great multitude followed him, because they
3 had seen the miracles which he did on the diseased. But Jesus
4 went up into the mountain, and sat there with his disciples. And
5 the passover, a feast of the Jews, was nigh. Jesus then lifting up
his eyes, and seeing a great multitude coming to him, saith to Phi-
6 lip, Whence shall we buy bread, that these may eat? (But this
he said trying him: for he himself knew what he intended to do.)
7 Philip answered him, Two hundred penny worth of bread is not
8 sufficient for them, that each of them may take a little. One of
9 his disciples, Andrew, Simon Peter's brother, saith to him, Here is
a lad, who hath five barley loaves and two small fishes: but what
10 are they among so many? Jesus said, Make the men sit down.
(Now there was much grass in the place.) So the men sat down,
11 in number about five thousand. Then Jesus took the loaves, and
having given thanks, distributed to the disciples, and the disciples
to them that were sat down, and likewise of the fishes as much as
12 they would. When they were filled, he saith to his disciples,
13 Gather up the fragments which remain, that nothing be lost. They
therefore gathered *them*, and filled twelve baskets with the fragments of the five barley loaves, which remained over and above to
14 them that had eaten. Then those men having seen the miracle
which Jesus did, said, Of a truth this is the prophet that was to
15 come into the world. Jesus therefore knowing that they were
about to come and take him by force to make him a king, again
retired to the mountain all alone.
16   † In the evening, his disciples went down to the sea, and entering into the vessel, they went over the sea toward Capernaum:
17 And it was now dark, and Jesus was not come to them. And the

---

44. *While ye receive honour*—That is, while ye seek the praise of men rather
than the praise of God. At the feast of pentecost, kept in commemoration of
the giving the law from Mount Sinai, their sermons used to be full of the praises
of the law, and of the people to whom it was given. How mortifying then must
the following words of our Lord be to them, while they were thus exulting in
Moses and his law!
45. *There is one that accuseth you*—By his writings.
46. *He wrote of me*—Every where; in all his writings; particularly Deut.
xviii, 15, 18.
VI. 1. *After these things*—The history of between ten and eleven months is to
be supplied here from the other evangelists.
3. *Jesus went up*—Before the people overtook him.
5. *Jesus saith to Philip*—Perhaps he had the care of providing victuals for the
family of the apostles.
15. *He retired to the mountain alone*—Having ordered his disciples to cross
over the lake.

* Matt. xiv. 13; Mark vi, 32; Luke ix, 10.   † Matt. xiv, 22; Mark vi, 45.

18 sea ran high, a great wind blowing. And having rowed about five
19 and twenty or thirty furlongs, they see Jesus walking on the sea,
20 and drawing nigh to the vessel: and they were afraid. But he
21 saith to them, It is I; be not afraid. Then they willingly received
   him into the vessel; and immediately the vessel was at the land to
   which they were bound.
22 The day following, the multitude who had stood on the other side
   of the sea, because they saw there was no other vessel there, save
   that one into which his disciples went, and that Jesus went not into
   the vessel with his disciples, but *that* his disciples were gone away
23 alone: (But there came other little vessels from Tiberias, near the
   place where they had eaten bread, after the Lord had given thanks.)
24 When they saw that Jesus was not there, neither his disciples,
   they also went aboard the vessels, and came to Capernaum seek
   ing Jesus.
25 And having found him on the other side of the sea, they said to
26 him, Rabbi, when comest thou hither? Jesus answered them and
   said, Verily, verily I say to you, ye seek me, not because ye saw
   the miracles, but because ye did eat of the loaves and were
27 satisfied. Labour not for the meat which perisheth, but for that
   which endureth to everlasting life, which the Son of man will-give
28 you; for him hath God the Father sealed. Then said they to him,
29 What shall we do, that we may work the works of God? Jesus
   answered and said to them, This is the work of God, that ye believe
30 on him whom he hath sent. They said therefore to him, What sign
   dost thou then, that we may see and believe thee? What dost thou
31 work? Our fathers ate manna, in the wilderness, as it is written,
32 * He gave them bread from heaven to eat. Then said Jesus to them,

---

22. *Who had stood on the other side*—They were forced to stay a while, because
there were then no other vessels; and they stayed the less unwillingly, because
they saw that Jesus was not embarked.
26. Our Lord does not satisfy their curiosity, but corrects the wrong motive
they had in seeking him: *because ye did eat*—Merely for temporal advantage.
Hitherto Christ had been gathering hearers: he now begins to try their sincerity,
by a figurative discourse concerning his passion, and the fruit of it, to be received
by faith.
27. *Labour not for the meat which perisheth*—For bodily food: not for that
only, not chiefly: not at all, but in subordination to grace, faith, love, the *meat
which endureth to everlasting life*. Labour, *work* for this; *for everlasting life.*
So our Lord expressly commands, *work for life*, as well as *from life :* from a principle of faith and love. *Him hath the Father sealed*—By this very miracle, as well
as by his whole testimony concerning him. See chap. iii, 33. *Sealing* is a mark
of the authenticity of a writing.
28. *The works of God*—Works pleasing to God.
29. *This is the work of God*—The work most pleasing to God, and the foundation of all others: *that ye believe*—He expresses it first properly, afterward figuratively.
30. *What sign dost thou?*—Amazing, after what they had just seen!
31. *Our fathers ate manna*—This sign Moses gave them. *He gave them bread
from heaven*—From the lower sublunary heaven; to which Jesus opposes the
highest heaven: in which sense he says seven times, ver. 32, 33, 38, 50, 58, 62,
that he himself *came down from heaven.*
32. *Moses gave you not bread from heaven*—It was not Moses who gave the
manna to your fathers; but *my Father* who now *giveth the true bread from heaven.*

* Psalm lxxviii, 24.

Verily, verily I say unto you, Moses gave you not the bread from
33 heaven ; but my Father giveth you the true bread from heaven. For
the bread of God is he that cometh down from heaven, and giveth
34 life to the world. Then said they to him, Lord, ever give us this
35 bread. And Jesus said to them, I am the bread of life. He that
cometh to me shall never hunger, and he that believeth on me shall
36 never thirst. But I told you, that though ye have seen me, ye be-
37 lieve not. All that the Father giveth me, will come to me, and him
38 that cometh to me, I will in nowise cast out. For I came down
from heaven, not to do my own will, but the will of him that sent
39 me. And this is the will of him that sent me, That of all which
he hath given me, I should lose nothing, but should raise it up at
40 the last day. And this is the will of him that sent me, that every
one who seeth the Son, and believeth on him, should have everlasting life : and I will raise him up at the last day.
41   The Jews then murmured about him, because he said, I am the
42 bread which came down from heaven. And they said, Is not this
Jesus, the son of Joseph, whose father and mother we know ?
43 How then saith he, I came down from heaven ? Jesus answered
44 and said to them, Murmur not among yourselves. No man can
come unto me, unless the Father who hath sent me, draw him ;
45 and I will raise him up at the last day. It is written in the prophets, * And they shall be all taught of God. Every man therefore that hath heard and learned of the Father cometh to me.
46 Not that any man hath seen the Father, save he who is from God;

33. *He that—giveth life to the world*—Not (like the manna) to one people only :
and that from generation to generation. Our Lord does not yet say, I am that
bread ; else the Jews would not have given him so respectful an answer, ver. 34.
34. *Give us this bread*—Meaning it still, in a literal sense : yet they seem now
to be not far from believing.
35. *I am the bread of life*—Having and giving life : *he that cometh—he that
believeth*—Equivalent expressions : *shall never hunger, thirst*—Shall be satisfied,
happy, for ever.
36. *I have told you*—Namely, ver. 26.
37. *All that the Father giveth me*—All that feel themselves lost, and follow
the drawings of the Father, he in a peculiar manner giveth to the Son : *will come
to me*—By faith. *And him that* thus *cometh to me, I will in nowise cast out*—I
will give him pardon, holiness, and heaven, if he endure to the end—*to rejoice
in his light.*
39. *Of all which he hath* already *given me*—See chap. xvii, 6, 12. If they
endure to the end. But Judas did not.
40. Here is the sum of the three foregoing verses. *This is the will of him that
sent me*—This is the whole of what I have said : this is the eternal, unchangeable will of God. Every one who truly believeth, shall have everlasting life.
Every one that seeth and believeth—The Jews saw, and yet believed not. *And I
will raise him up*—As this is the will of him that sent me, I will perform it
effectually.
44. *Christ* having checked their murmuring, continues what he was saying,
ver. 40. *No man comes to me, unless my Father draw him*—No man can believe
in Christ, unless God give him power : he draws us first, by good desires. Not
by compulsion, not by laying the will under any necessity ; but by the strong and
sweet, yet still resistible, motions of his heavenly grace.
45. *Every man that hath heard*—The secret voice of God, he, and he only
believeth.
46. *Not that any one*—Must expect him to appear in a visible shape. *He who
is from or with God*—In a more eminent manner than any creature.

* Isaiah liv, 13.

47 he hath seen the Father.   Verily, verily I say unto you, he that
48 believeth on me hath everlasting life.   I am the bread of life.
49 Your fathers ate manna in the wilderness, and *yet* died.   This is
    the bread which cometh down from heaven, that a man may eat
50 of it, and not die.   I am the living bread which came down from
51 heaven: If any man eat of this bread, he shall live for ever, and
    the bread that I will give is my flesh, which I will give for the life
    of the world.
52   The Jews then debated among themselves, saying, How can this
53 man give us *his* flesh to eat?   But Jesus said to them, Verily,
    verily I say unto you, unless ye eat the flesh of the Son of man,
54 and drink his blood, ye have no life in you.   He that eateth my
    flesh, and drinketh my blood, hath eternal life, and I will raise him
55 up at the last day.   For my flesh is meat indeed, and my blood is
56 drink indeed.   He that eateth my flesh and drinketh my blood,
57 abideth in me, and I in him.   As the living Father hath sent me,
    and I live by the Father, so he that eateth me, even he shall live
58 by me.   This is the bread which came down from heaven ; not as
    your fathers ate manna, and died : he that eateth of this bread, shall
59 live for ever.   These things he said in the synagogue, teaching at
    Capernaum.
60   Many of his disciples hearing *it*, said, This is a hard saying :
61 who can hear it ?   Jesus knowing in himself that his disciples
62 murmured about this, said to them, Doth this offend you ?   *What*
63 if ye shall see the Son of man ascend where he was before ?   It is
    the Spirit that quickeneth : the flesh profiteth nothing : the words
64 that I have spoken, *they* are Spirit and *they* are life.   But there

---

50. *Not die*—Not spiritually ; not eternally.

51. *If any eat of this bread*—That is, believe in me : *he shall live for ever*—
In other words, he that believeth to the end shall be saved.   *My flesh which I
will give you*—This whole discourse concerning his flesh and blood refers directly
to his passion, and but remotely, if at all, to the Lord's Supper.

52. Observe the degrees : the Jews are tried here ; the disciples, ver. 60–66
the apostles, ver. 67.

53. *Unless ye eat the flesh of the Son of man*—Spiritually : unless ye draw continual virtue from him by faith.   Eating his flesh is only another expression for
believing.

55. *Meat—drink indeed*—With which the soul of a believer is as truly fed, as
his body with meat and drink.

57. *I live by the Father*—Being one with him.   *He shall live by me*—Being
one with me.   Amazing union !

58. *This is*—That is, I am *the bread*—Which is not like the manna your fathers
ate, who died notwithstanding.

60. *This is a hard saying*—Hard to the children of the world, but sweet to
the children of God.   Scarce ever did our Lord speak more sublimely, even to
the apostles in private.   *Who can hear*—Endure *it ?*

62. *What if ye shall see the Son of man ascend where he was before ?*—How
much more incredible will it then appear to you, that he should give you his flesh
to eat ?

63. *It is the Spirit*—The spiritual meaning of these words, by which God
giveth life.   *The flesh*—The bare, carnal, literal meaning, *profiteth nothing*.   *The
words which I have spoken, they are spirit*—Are to be taken in a spiritual sense ·
and, when they are so understood, *they are life*—That is, a means of spiritual
life to the hearers.

64. *But there are some of you who believe not*—And so receive no life by them,
because you take them in a gross literal sense.   *For Jesus knew from the begin*

are some of you who believe not. (For Jesus had known from the
beginning who they were that believed not, and who would betray
65 him.) And he said, Therefore said I to you, That no man can
come to me, unless it be given him by my Father.
66   From this *time* many of his disciples went back and walked no
67 more with him. Then said Jesus to the twelve, Are ye also
68 minded to go away? Then Simon Peter answered him, saying,
Lord, to whom shall we go? Thou hast the words of eternal life.
69 And we have believed and known, that thou art the Christ, the
70 Son of the living God. Jesus answered them, Have not I chosen
71 you twelve? Yet one of you is a devil. He spake of Judas Iscariot, *the son* of Simon; for he it was that would betray him, being
one of the twelve.
VII.   After these things Jesus walked in Galilee: for he would not
2 walk in Judea, because the Jews sought to kill him. Now the
3 Jews' feast of tabernacles was nigh. His brethren therefore said
to him, Depart hence and go into Judea, that thy disciples *there*
4 also may see the works which thou dost. For no man doth any
thing in secret, but desireth to be publicly known: if thou dost
5 these things, show thyself to the world. (For neither did his bre-
6 thren believe on him.) Jesus saith to them, My time is not yet
7 come: your time is always ready. The world cannot hate you,
but me it hateth; because I testify of it, that its works are evil.
8 Go ye up to the feast: I go not up to this feast yet; because my

---

ning—Of his ministry: *who would betray him*—Therefore it is plain, God does
foresee future contingencies:—

" But his foreknowledge causes not the fault,
  Which had no less proved certain unforeknown."

65. *Unless it be given*—And it is given to those only who will receive it on
God's own terms.

66. *From this time many of his disciples went back*—So our Lord now began
to purge his floor: the proud and careless were driven away, and those remained
who were meet for the Master's use.

68. *Thou hast the words of eternal life*—Thou, and thou alone, speakest the
words which show the way to life everlasting.

69. *And we*—Who have been with thee from the beginning, whatever others
do, *have known*—Are absolutely assured, *that thou art the Christ.*

70. *Jesus answered them*—And yet even ye have not all acted suitable to this
knowledge. *Have I not chosen* or *elected you twelve?*—But they might fall even
from that election. *Yet one of you*—On this gracious warning, Judas ought to
have repented; *is a devil*—Is now influenced by one.

VII. 1. *After these things Jesus walked in Galilee*—That is, continued there,
for some months after the second passover. *For he would not walk*—Continue in
Judea; *because the Jews*—Those of them who did not believe; and in particular
the chief priests, scribes, and Pharisees, *sought* an opportunity *to kill him.*

2. *The feast of tabernacles*—The time, manner, and reason of this feast may
be seen, Lev. xxiii, 34, &c.

3. *His brethren*—So called according to the Jewish way of speaking. They
were his cousins, the sons of his mother's sister. *Depart hence*—From this obscure place.

4. *For no man doth any thing*—Of this kind, *in secret; but rather desireth to
be* of public use. *If thou* really *dost these things*—These miracles which are reported; *show thyself to the world*—To all men.

6. *Jesus saith, Your time is always ready*—This or any time will suit you.

7. *The world cannot hate you*—Because ye are of the world. *But me it hateth*
—And all that bear the same testimony.

9 time is not yet fully come. Having said these things to them, he
abode in Galilee.

10   But when his brethren were gone up, then he·also went up to
11 the feast, not openly, but as it were privately. Then the Jews
12 sought him at the feast, and said, Where is he? And there was
much murmuring among the multitude concerning him : for some
13 said, He is a good man, others said, Nay ; but he seduceth the
people. However no man spake openly of him, for fear of the
Jews.

14   Now at the middle of the feast, Jesus went up into the temple
15 and taught. And the Jews marvelled, saying, How doth this man
16 know letters, having never learned? Jesus answered them and
17 said, My doctrine is not mine, but his that sent me. If any man
be willing to do his will, he shall know of the doctrine, whether it
18 be of God, or whether I speak of myself. He that speaketh of
himself, seeketh his own glory; but he that seeketh the glory of
him that sent him, the same is true, and there is no unrighteous-
19 ness in him. Did not Moses give you the law? Yet none of you
20 keepeth the law. Why seek ye to kill me? The people answered
21 and said, Thou hast a devil. Who seeketh to kill thee? Jesus
answered and said to them, I did one work, and ye all marvelled at
22 it. Moses gave you circumcision, (not that it is of Moses, but of
23 the fathers,) and ye circumcise a man on the Sabbath. If a man

10. *He also went up to the feast*—This was his last journey but one to Jerusa
lem. The next time he went up he suffered.
11. *The Jews*—The men of Judea, particularly of Jerusalem.
12. *There was much murmuring among the multitude*—Much whispering;
many private debates with each other, among those who were come from distant
parts.
13. *However no man spake openly of him*—Not in favour of him : *for fear of the
Jews*—Those that were in authority.
14. *Now at the middle of the feast*—Which lasted eight days. It is probable
this was on the Sabbath day. *Jesus went up into the temple*—Directly, without
stopping any where else.
15. *How does this man know letters, having never learned?*—How comes he to
be so well acquainted with sacred literature as to be able thus to expound the
Scripture, with such propriety and gracefulness, seeing he has never learned this,
at any place of education?
16. *My doctrine is not mine*—Acquired by any labour of learning ; *but his that
sent me*—Immediately infused by him.
17. *If any man be willing to do his will, he shall know of the doctrine, whether
it be of God*—This is a universal rule, with regard to all persons and doctrines.
He that is thoroughly willing to do it, shall certainly know what the will of
God is.
18. *There is no unrighteousness in him*—No deceit or falsehood.
19. But ye are unrighteous; for ye violate the very law which ye profess so
much zeal for.
20 *The people answered, Thou hast a devil*—A lying spirit. *Who seeketh to
kill thee?*—These, coming from distant parts, probably did not know the design
of the priests and rulers.
21. *I did*—At the pool of Bethesda : *one work*—Out of many : *and ye all
marvelled at it*—Are amazed, because I did it on the Sabbath day.
22. *Moses gave you circumcision*—The sense is, because Moses enjoined you
circumcision (though indeed it was far more ancient than him) you think it no
harm to circumcise a man on the Sabbath : and are ye angry at me (which anger
had now continued sixteen months) for doing so much greater a good, for healing
a man, body and soul, on the Sabbath?

receive circumcision on the Sabbath, that the law of Moses may
not be broken; are ye angry at me, because I entirely healed a
24 man on the Sabbath? Judge not according to appearance, but judge
righteous judgment.
25 Then said some of them of Jerusalem, Is not this he whom they
seek to kill? And lo he speaketh boldly, and they say nothing to
26 him. Do the rulers know indeed that this is the Christ? Howbeit,
27 we know this man, whence he is: but when Christ cometh none
28 knoweth whence he is: Then cried Jesus in the temple as he taught
saying, Do you both know me, and know whence I am? And yet I
am not come of myself, but he that sent me is true, whom ye know
29 not. But I know him; for I am from him, and he hath sent me.
30 Then they sought to seize him; but no man laid hands on him, be-
31 cause his hour was not yet come. And many of the multitude believed on him, and said, When Christ cometh, will he do more
32 miracles than these which this man hath done! The Pharisees
heard the multitude whispering such things concerning him, and
33 the Pharisees and the chief priests sent officers to seize him. Then
said Jesus to them, Yet a little time I am with you, and then I go
34 to him that sent me. Ye shall seek, and shall not find me, and
35 where I am ye cannot come. Then said the Jews among themselves, Whither will he go, that we shall not find him? Will he go
36 to the dispersed among the Greeks, and teach the Greeks? What
saying is this that he said, Ye shall seek me, and shall not find
me ; and where I am ye cannot come?
37 On the last, the great *day* of the feast, Jesus stood and cried,
38 saying, If any man thirst, let him come to me and drink. * He

27. *When Christ cometh, none knoweth whence he is*—This Jewish tradition was
true, with regard to his Divine nature: in that respect none could *declare his
generation.* But it was not true with regard to his human nature, for both his
family and the place of his birth were plainly foretold.
28. *Then cried Jesus*—With a loud and earnest voice. *Do ye both know me,
and know whence I am ?*—Ye do indeed know whence I am as a man. But ye
know not my Divine nature, nor that I am sent from God.
29. *I am from him*—By eternal generation : *and he hath sent me*—His mission
follows from his generation. These two points answer those : Do ye *know me ?*
Do ye *know whence I am ?*
30. *His hour*—The time of his suffering.
33. *Then said Jesus*—Continuing his discourse (from the 29th verse) which
they had interrupted.
34. *Ye shall seek me*—Whom ye now despise. These words are, as it were,
the text which is commented upon in this and the following chapter. *Where I
am*—Christ's so frequently saying while on earth, *where I am,* when he spake
of his being in heaven, intimates his perpetual presence there in his Divine nature: though his going thither was a future thing, with regard to his human
nature.
35. *Will he go to the dispersed among the Greeks*—The Jews scattered abroad
in heathen nations, Greece particularly. Or, *Will he teach the Greeks ?*—The
heathens themselves.
37. *On the last, the great day of the feast*—On this day there was the greatest
concourse of people, and they were then wont to fetch water from the fountain
of Siloam, which the priests poured out on the great altar, singing one to an
other, *With joy shall ye draw water from the wells of salvation.* On this day
likewise they commemorated God's miraculously giving water out of the rock,
and offered up solemn prayers for seasoanable rains.
* Zech. xiv, 3.

that believeth on me, out of his belly (as the Scriptuıe hath said)
39 shall flow rivers of living water. This he spake of the Spirit,
which they who believed on him were to receive : for the Holy
Ghost was not yet *given*, because Jesus was not yet glorified.
40 Many of the multitude therefore, hearing this discourse, said, Cer-
41 tainly this is the prophet. Others said, This is the Christ. But
42 some said, Doth Christ come out of Galilee ? Hath not the Scripture said, that Christ cometh of the seed of David, and from
43 * Bethlehem, the town where David was ? So there was a division
44 among the people concerning him. And some of them would
45 have seized him : but ro man laid hands on him. So the officers
came to the chief priests and Pharisees ; and they said to them,
46 Why have ye not brought him ? The officers answered, Never man
47 spake like this man. The Pharisees answered, Are ye also de-
48 ceived ? Hath any of the rulers believed on him, or of the Pha-
49 risees ? But this populace, who know not the law, are accursed.
50 Nicodemus (he that came to him by night, being one of them)
51 saith to them, Doth our law judge a man before it hear him, and
52 know what he doth ? They answered and said to him, Art thou also
a Galilean ? Search and see, that out of Galilee ariseth no prophet.
53 And every man went to his own house. But Jesus went to the
mount of Olives.
VIII. And early in the morning he returned to the temple; and all the
2 people came to him, and sitting down he taught them. And the

---

38. *He that believeth*—This answers to *let him come* to me. And whosoever
doth come to him by faith, his inmost soul shall be filled with *living water*, with
abundance of peace, joy, and love, which shall likewise flow from him to others. *As
the Scripture hath said*—Not expressly in any one particular place. But here is
a general reference to all those scriptures which speak of the *effusion of the Spirit* by the Messiah, under the similitude of *pouring out water.*

39. *The Holy Ghost was not yet given*—That is, those fruits of the Spirit were
not yet given even to true believers, in that full measure.

40. *The prophet*—Whom we expect to be the forerunner of the Messiah.

42. *From Bethlehem*—And how could they forget that Jesus was born there ?
Had not Herod given them terrible reason to remember it ?

48. *Hath any of the rulers*—Men of rank or eminence, *or of the Pharisees*—
Men of learning or religion, *believed on him ?*

49. *But this populace, who know not the law*—This ignorant rabble ; *are accursed*
—Are by that ignorance exposed to the curse of being thus seduced.

50. *Nicodemus, he that came to him by night*—Having now a little more courage,
being one of them—Being present as a member of the great council, *saith to them*
—Do not we ourselves act as if we *knew not the law*, if we pass sentence on a
man before we hear him ?

52. *They answered*—By personal reflection ; the argument they could not answer, and therefore did not attempt it. *Art thou also a Galilean ?*—One of his
party ? *Out of Galilee ariseth no prophet*—They could not but know the contrary.
They knew Jonah arose out of Gethhepher ; and Nahum from another village
in Galilee. Yea, and Thisbe, the town of Elijah, the Tishbite, was in Galilee
alʒ. They might likewise have known that Jesus was not born in Galilee, but
at Bethlehem, even from the public register there, and from the genealogies of
the family of David. They were conscious this poor answer would not bear examination, and so took care to prevent a reply.

53. *And every man went to his own house*—So that short plain question of Nicodemus spoiled all their measures, and broke up the council ! *A word spoken
in season, how good it is !* Especially when God gives it his blessing.

* Micah v. 2.

3 scribes and Pharisees brought in a woman taken in adultery, anu
4 having set her in the midst, They say to him, Master, this woman
5 was taken actually committing adultery. Now * Moses hath commanded us in the law to stone such. What therefore sayest thou?
6 This they spoke tempting him, that they might have to accuse
him. But Jesus stooping down, wrote with his finger on the
7 ground. And as they continued asking him, he raised himself,
and said to them, He that is without sin among you, let him cast
8 the first stone at her. Then stooping down again, he wrote on the
9 ground. But they who heard *it* went out one by one, beginning
at the eldest; and Jesus was left alone, and the woman in the
10 midst. Then Jesus raising himself up, said to her, Woman,
where are thine accusers? Hath no man condemned thee? She
11 saith, No man, sir. And Jesus saith unto her, Neither do I condemn thee. Go, and sin no more. .
12 Then spake Jesus again to them, I am the light of the world;
he that followeth me shall in nowise walk in darkness, but shall·
13 have the light of life. The Pharisees therefore said to him, Thou
14 testifiest of thyself: thy testimony is not valid. Jesus answered

VIII. 5. *Moses hath commanded us to stone such*—If they spoke accurately, this must have been a.woman, who, having been *betrothed to a husband*, had been guilty of this crime before the marriage was completed; for such only Moses commanded to be stoned. He commanded indeed that other adulteresses should be put to death; but the manner of death was not specified.

6. *That they might have to accuse him*—Either of usurping the office of a judge, if he condemned her, or of being an enemy to the law, if he acquitted her. *Jesus stooping down, wrote with his finger on the grouna*—God wrote once in the Old Testament; Christ once in the New: perhaps the words which he after-ward spoke, when they continued asking him. By this silent action, he, 1, fixed their wandering, hurrying thoughts, in order to awaken their consciences: and, 2, signified that he was not then come to condemn but to save the world.

7. *He that is without sin*—He that is not guilty (his own conscience being the judge) either of the same sin, or of some nearly resembling it; *let him*—as a wit-ness, *cast the first stone at her.*

9. *Beginning at the eldest*—Or the elders. *Jesus was left alone*—By all those scribes and Pharisees who proposed the question. But many others remained, to whom our Lord directed his discourse presently after.

10. *Hath no man condemned thee?*—Hath no judicial sentence been passed upon thee?

11. *Neither do I condemn thee*—Neither do I take upon me to pass any such sentence. Let this deliverance lead thee to repentance.

12. *He that followeth me shall in nowise walk in darkness*—In ignorance, wickedness, misery: *but shall have the light of life*—He that closely, humbly, steadily follows me, shall have the Divine light continually shining upon him, diffusing over his soul knowledge, holiness, joy, till he is guided by it to life everlasting.

13. *Thou testifiest of thyself; thy testimony is not valid*—They retort upon our Lord his own words, chap. v, 31; *if I testify of myself, my testimony is not valid.* He had then added, *There is another who testifieth of me.* To the same effect he replies here, ver. 14, *Though I testify of myself, yet my testimony is valid;* for I am inseparably united to the Father. *I know*—And from firm and certain knowledge proceeds the most unexceptionable testimony: *whence I came, and whither I go*—To these two heads may be referred all the doctrine concern-ing Christ. The former is treated of ver. 16, &c, the latter ver. 21, &c. *For I know whence I came*—That is, For I came from God, both as God and as man. And *I know it,* though ye do not.

* Deut. xxii, 23.

and said to them, Though I testify of myself, *yet* my testimony is
valid : for I know whence I came, and whither I go : but ye know
15 not whence I came, or whither I go. Ye judge after the flesh : I
16 judge no man. And yet if I judge, my judgment is valid ; for I am
17 not alone : but I and the Father that sent me. Even in your law
18 it is written, * The testimony of two men is valid. I am one that
testify of myself, and the Father that sent me testifieth of me.
19 Then said they to him, Where is thy Father? Jesus answered,
Ye neither know me nor my Father. If ye had known me, ye
20 would have known my Father also. These words spake he in the
treasury, as he taught in the temple. . And no man seized him ; for
his hour was not yet come.
21   Then said Jesus again to them, I go, and ye shall seek me, and
22 shall die in your sin. Whither I go, ye cannot come. The Jews
said therefore, Will he kill himself? Because he saith, Whither
23 I go, ye cannot come. And he said to them, Ye are of them that
are beneath ; I am of them that are above : ye are of this world ;
24 I am not of this world. Therefore I said, Ye shall die in your
sins ; for if ye believe not that I AM, ye shall die in your sins.
25 Then said they to him, Who art thou? And Jesus saith to them,
26 Even what I say to you from the beginning. I have many things
to say and to judge of you ; but he that sent me is true ; and I
27 speak to the world the things which I have heard from him. They

15. *Ye judge after the flesh*—As the flesh, that is, corrupt nature dictates. *I judge no man*—Not thus ; not now ; not at my first coming.

16. *I am not alone*—No more in judging, than in testifying : *but I and the Father that sent me*—His Father *is in him, and he is in the Father,* chap. xiv, 10, 11 ; and so the Father is no more alone without the Son, than the Son is without the Father, Prov. viii, 22, 23, 30. His Father and he are not one and another God, one God, (though distinct persons,) and so inseparable from each other. And though the Son came from the Father, to assume human nature, and perform his office as the Messiah upon earth, as God is sometimes said to come from heaven, for particular manifestations of himself; yet Christ did not leave the Father, nor the Father leave him, any more than God leaves heaven when he is said to come down to the earth.

19. *Then said they to him, Where is thy Father? Jesus answered*—Showing the perverseness of their question ; and teaching that they ought first to know the Son, if they would know the Father. *Where the Father is*—he shows, ver. 23. Meantime he plainly intimates that the Father and he were distinct persons, as they were two witnesses ; and yet one in essence, as the knowledge of him includes the knowledge of the Father.

23. *Ye are*—Again he passes over their interruption, and proves what he advanced, ver. 21. *Of them that are beneath*—From the earth. *I am of them that are above*—Here he directly shows whence he came, even from heaven, and whither he goes.

24. *If ye believe not that I* AM—Here (as in the 58th verse) our Lord claims the Divine name, I AM, Exod. iii, 14. But the Jews, as if he had stopped short, and not finished the sentence, answered, *Who art thou?*

25. *Even what I say to you from the beginning*—The same which *I say to you,* as it were in one discourse, with one even tenor from the time I first spake to you.

26. *I have many things to say and to judge of you*—I have much to say concerning your inexcusable unbelief : *but he that sent me is true*—Whether ye believe or no. *And I speak the things which I have heard from him*—I deliver truly what he hath given me in charge.

* Deut. xix, 15.

28 understood not that he spake to them of the Father. Jesus therefore said to them, When ye shall have lifted up the Son of man,
then shall ye know that I AM, and *that* I do nothing of myself, but
29 as my Father hath taught me, I speak these things. And he that
sent me is with me; the Father hath not left me alone; for I dc
30 always the things that please him. As he spake these words, many
believed on him.
31   Then said Jesus to the Jews who believed on him, If ye con-
32 tinue in my word, ye are my disciples indeed: And ye shall know
33 the truth, and the truth shall make you free. They answered him,
We are Abraham's offspring, and were never enslaved to any man:
34 how sayest thou, Ye shall be made free? Jesus answered them,
Verily, verily I say unto you, He that committeth sin is the slave
35 of sin: And the slave abideth not in the house for ever: *but* the Son
36 abideth for ever. If therefore the Son shall make you free, you will
37 be free indeed. I know that ye are Abraham's offspring; yet ye seek
38 to kill me, because my word hath no place in you. I speak that which
I have seen with my Father, and ye do that which ye have heard
39 from your father. They answered and said to him, Abraham is our
father. Jesus saith to them, If ye were the children of Abraham
40 ye would do the works of Abraham. But now ye seek to kill me,
41 a man who have told you the truth which I have heard from God.
Abraham did not thus. Ye do the deeds of your father. They said
to him, We were not born of fornication; we have one Father, *even*
42 God. Jesus said to them, If God were your Father, ye would
love me; for I proceeded forth, and come from God. I am come
43 not of myself, but he hath sent me. Why do ye not understand

---

27. *They understood not*—That by him that sent him he meant God the Father.
Therefore in the 28th and 29th verses he speaks plainly of the Father, and again
claims the Divine name, I AM.

28. *When ye shall have lifted up*—On the cross, *ye shall know*—And so many
of them did, *that I* AM—God over all; *and that I do nothing of myself*—Being
one with the Father.

29. *The Father hath not left me alone*—Never from the moment I came into
the world.

32. *The truth*—Written in your hearts by the Spirit of God, *shall make you
free*—From guilt, sin, misery, Satan.

33. *They*—The other Jews that were by, (not those that believed,) as appears
by the whole tenor of the conversation. *We were never enslaved to any man*—A
bold, notorious untruth. At that very time they were enslaved to the Romans.

34. *Jesus answered*—Each branch of their objection, first concerning freedom,
then concerning their being Abraham's offspring, ver. 37, &c. *He that committeth sin, is*, in fact, *the slave of sin.*

35. *And the slave abideth not in the house*—All sinners shall be cast out of
God's house, as the slave was out of Abraham's: *but I, the Son, abide* therein
for ever.

36. *If I therefore make you free, ye*—shall partake of the same privilege: being
made free from all guilt and sin, ye shall abide in the house of God for ever.

37. *I know that ye are Abraham's offspring*—As to the other branch of your
objection, *I know that ye are Abraham's offspring*, after the flesh; but not in a
spiritual sense. Ye are not followers of the faith of Abraham: my word hath
no place in your hearts.

41. *Ye do the deeds of your father*—He is not named yet. But when they
presumed to call God their Father, then he is expressly called the devil, ver. 44.

42. *I proceeded forth*—As God, *and come*—As Christ.

43. *Ye cannot*—Such is your stubbornness and pride, *hear*—Receive, obey

44 my discourse? *Even* because ye cannot hear my word. Ye are
of *your* father the devil, and your will is to do the desires of your
father. He was a murderer from the beginning, and abode not in
the truth; for there is no truth in him. When he speaketh a lie,
45 he speaketh of his own; for he is a liar, and the father of it. But
46 because I speak the truth, ye believe me not. Which of you convicteth me of sin? And if I speak the truth, why do ye not believe
47 me? He that is of God heareth God's words; ye therefore hear
48 *them* not, because ye are not of God. Then answered the Jews,
and said to him, Say we not well that thou art a Samaritan, and
49 hast a devil? Jesus answered, I have not a devil; but I honour
50 my Father, and ye dishonour me. I seek not my own glory;
51 there is one that seeketh *it* and judgeth. Verily, verily I say unto
52 you, If a man keep my word, he shall never see death. Then
said the Jews to him, Now we know that thou hast a devil. Abraham is dead and the prophets: yet thou sayest, If a man keep my
53 word, he shall never taste of death. Art thou greater than our
54 father Abraham, who is dead? The prophets also are dead.
Whom makest thou thyself? Jesus answered, If I honour myself,
my honour is nothing; it is my Father that honoureth me, of
55 whom ye say, He is our God. Yet ye have not known him: but
I know him. And if I should say I know him not, I should be a
56 liar like you: but I know him, and keep his word. Your father
Abraham longed to see my day; and he saw *it* and was glad.

---

my word. Not being desirous to do my will, ye cannot understand my doctrine, chap. vii, 17.

44. *He was a murderer*—In inclination, *from the beginning*—Of his becoming a devil; *and abode not in the truth*—Commencing murderer and liar at the same time. And certainly *he was a killer of men* (as the Greek word properly signifies) *from the beginning* of the world: for from the very creation he designed and con- trived the ruin of men. *When he speaketh a lie, he speaketh of his own*—For he is the proper parent, and, as it were, creator of it. See the origin not only of lies, but of evil in general!

45. *Because I speak the truth*—Which liars hate.

46. *Which of you convicteth me of sin?*—And is not my life as unreprovable as my doctrine? Does not my whole behaviour confirm the truth of what I teach?

47. *He that is of God*—That either loves or fears him, *heareth*—With joy and reverence, *God's words*—Which I preach.

48. *Say we not well*—Have we not just cause to say, *Thou art a Samaritan*— An enemy to our Church and nation; *and hast a devil?*—Art possessed by a proud and lying spirit?

49. *I honour my Father*—I seek his honour only.

50. *I seek not my own glory*—That is, as I am the Messiah, I consult not my own glory. I need not. For my Father consulteth it, and will pass sentence on you accordingly.

51. *If a man keep my word*—So will my Father consult my glory. We keep his doctrine by believing, his promises by hoping. his command by obeying. *He shall never see death*—That is, death eternal. He shall live for ever. Hereby he proves that he was no Samaritan; for the Samaritans in general were Sadducees.

54. *If I honour myself*—Referring to their words, *Whom makest thou thyself?*

56. *He saw it*—By faith in types, figures, and promises; as particularly in Melchisedec; in the appearance of Jehovah to him in the plains of Mamre, Gen. xviii, 1; and in the promise that *in his seed all the nations of the earth shall be blessed.* Possibly he had likewise a peculiar revelation either of Christ's first or second coming.

57 Then said the Jews to him, Thou art not yet fifty years old, and hast
58 thou seen Abraham? Jesus said to them, Verily, verily I say unto
59 you, Before Abraham was, I AM. Then they took up stones to cast at
him; but Jesus concealed himself, and went out of the temple,
going through the midst of them, and so passed on.
IX. And as he passed on, he saw a man blind from his birth:
2 And his disciples asked him, saying, Master, who sinned, this
3 man, or his parents, that he was born blind? Jesus answered,
Neither hath this man sinned, nor his parents; but that the works
4 of God might be made manifest through him. I must work the
works of him that sent me, while it is day; the night is coming
5 when no man can work. While I am in the world, I am the light
6 of the world. Having said this, he spat on the ground, and made
clay with the spittle, and anointed the eyes of the blind man with
the clay, and said to him, Go, wash at the pool of Siloam (which
7 is by interpretation, Sent.) He went therefore, and washed, and
came seeing.

---

57. *Thou art not yet fifty years old*—At the most. Perhaps the gravity of our Lord's countenance, together with his afflictions and labours, might make him appear older than he really was. *Hast thou seen Abraham*—Which they justly supposed must have been, if Abraham had seen him.

58. *Before Abraham was I* AM—Even from everlasting to everlasting. This is a direct answer to the objection of the Jews, and shows how much *greater* he was than Abraham.

59. *Then they took up stones*—To stone him as a blasphemer; *but Jesus concealed himself*—Probably by becoming invisible; *and so passed on*—With the same ease as if none had been there.

IX. 2. *Who sinned, this man or his parents, that he was born blind?*—That is, was it for his own sins, or the sins of his parents? They suppose (as many of the Jews did, though without any ground from Scripture) that he might have sinned in a pre-existent state, before he came into the world.

3. *Jesus answered, Neither hath this man sinned, nor his parents*—It was not the manner of our Lord to answer any questions that were of no use, but to gratify an idle curiosity. Therefore he determines nothing concerning this. The scope of his answer is, It was neither for any sins of his own, nor yet of his parents; but that the power of God might be displayed.

4. *The night is coming*—Christ is the light. When the light is withdrawn night comes, *when no man can work*—No man can do any thing toward working out his salvation after this life is ended. Yet Christ can work always. But he was not to work upon earth, only during the day, or season which was appointed for him.

5. *I am the light of the world*—I teach men inwardly by my Spirit, and outwardly by my preaching, what is the will of God; and I show them, by my example, how they must do it.

6. *He anointed the eyes of the blind man with the clay*—This might almost have blinded a man that had sight. But what could it do toward curing the blind? It reminds us that God is no farther from the event, when he works either with, or without means, and that all the creatures are only that which his almighty operation makes them.

7. *Go, wash at the pool of Siloam*—Perhaps our Lord intended to make the miracle more taken notice of. For a crowd of people would naturally gather round him to observe the event of so strange a prescription, and it is exceeding probable, the guide who must have led him in traversing a great part of the city, would mention the errand he was going upon, and so call all those who saw him to a greater attention.

From the fountain of Siloam, which was without the walls of Jerusalem, a little stream flowed into the city, and was received in a kind of basin, near the temple, and called the pool of Siloam. *Which is, by interpretation, Sent*—And

8   Then the neighbours and they who had seen him before, when
9   he was blind, said, Is not this he who used to sit begging? Some
said, This is he: others, He is like him: *but* he said, I am *he*.
10 They said to him, How were thine eyes opened? He answered
11 and said, A man called Jesus made clay and anointed my eyes,
12 and said to me, Go to the pool of Siloam and wash. And I went,
and washed, and received sight. Then said they to him, Where
is he? He said, I know not.
13 They bring to the Pharisees the man who had aforetime been
14 blind. (It was the Sabbath, when Jesus made the clay and opened
15 his eyes.) Again the Pharisees also asked him how he had
received his sight? He said to them, He put clay on my eyes, and
16 I washed, and see. Therefore said some of the Pharisees, This
man is not of God because he keepeth not the Sabbath. Others
17 said, How can a man that is a sinner do such miracles? And there
was a division among them. They say to the blind man again,
What sayest thou of him, for that he hath opened thine eyes?
18 He said, He is a prophet. But the Jews did not believe concerning him, that he had been blind and received his sight, till they had
19 called the parents of him who had received his sight. And they
asked them, saying, Is this your son, who ye say was born blind?
20 How then doth he now see? His parents answered them, and said
21 We know that this is our son, and that he was born blind. But
how he now seeth, we know not, or who hath opened his eyes we
know not. He is of age: ask him; he will speak concerning
22 himself. His parents said this because they feared the Jews; for
the Jews had already agreed, That if any man should own him *to
23 be* Christ, he should be put out of the synagogue. Therefore said
his parents, He is of age; ask him.
24 Therefore they called a second time the man that had been
blind, and said to him, Give glory to God; we know that this man
25 is a sinner. He answered and said, That he is a sinner I know
26 not: one thing I know, that I was blind and now see. They said
to him again, What did he to thee? How opened he thine eyes?
27 He answered them, I have told you already, and ye did not
hearken: why would you hear *it* again? Are ye also willing to be
28 his disciples? Then they reviled him and said, Thou art a disci-

---

so was a type of the Messiah, who was sent of God. *He went and washed, and
came seeing*—He believed, and obeyed, and found a blessing. Had he been wise
in his own eyes, and reasoned, like Naaman, on the impropriety of the means,
he had justly been left in darkness. Lord, may our proud hearts be subdued to
the methods of thy recovering grace! May we leave thee to choose how thou
wilt bestow favours, which it is our highest interest to receive on any terms.

11. *A man called Jesus*—He seems to have been before totally ignorant of him.

14. *Anointing the eyes*—With any kind of medicine on the Sabbath, was
particularly forbidden by the tradition of the elders.

16. *This man is not of God*—Not sent of God. *How can a man that is a sinner*—That is, one living in wilful sin, *do such miracles?*

17. *What sayest thou of him, for that he hath opened thine eyes?*—What inference dost thou draw herefrom?

22. *He should be put out of the synagogue*—That is, be excommunicated.

27. *Are ye also*—As well as I, at length convinced and *willing to be his disciples?*

29 ple of that *fellow;* but we are disciples of Moses.   We know that
God spake to Moses ; but we know not this *fellow,* whence he is.
30 The man answered and said to them, Why, herein is a marvellous
thing, that ye know not whence he is : although he hath opened
my eyes ! We know that God heareth not sinners ; but if a
man be a worshipper of God, and do his will, him he heareth.
32 Since the world began it was not heard that any man opened the
33 eyes of one that was born blind.   If this man were not of God, he
34 could do nothing.   They answered and said to him, Thou wast
altogether born in sin, and dost thou teach us ? And they cast
him out.
35   Jesus heard that they had cast him out ; and having found him,
36 he said to him, Dost thou believe on the Son of God ? He an-
37 swered and said, Sir, who is he, that I may believe on him ? Jesus
said to him, Thou hast both seen him, and he that talketh with
38 thee is he.   And he said, Lord, I believe.   And he worshipped
39 him.   Jesus said, For judgment am I come into the world, that they
40 who see not may see, and that they who see may become blind.
And some of the Pharisees that were with him heard this, and said to
41 him, Are we blind also ? Jesus said to them, If ye had been blind
ye would have no sin.   But now ye say, We see : therefore your
sin remaineth.
X.   Verily, verily I say to you, he that entereth not by the door
into the sheepfold, but climbeth up some other way, he is a thief

29. *We know not whence he is*—By what power and authority he does these
things.
30. *The man answered*—Utterly illiterate as he was.   And with what strength
and clearness of reason ! So had God opened the eyes of his understanding, as
well as his bodily eyes. *Why, herein is a marvellous thing, that ye*—The teachers
and guides of the people, should not know, that a man who has wrought a
miracle, the like of which was never heard of before, must be from heaven, sent
by God.
31. *We*—Even we of the populace, *know that God heareth not sinners*—Not
impenitent sinners, so as to answer their prayers in this manner.   The honest
courage of this man in adhering to the truth, though he knew the consequence,
ver. 22, gives him claim to the title of a confessor.
33. *He could do nothing*—Of this kind ; nothing miraculous.
34. *Born in sin*—And therefore, they supposed, born blind.   *They cast him
out*—Of the synagogue ; excommunicated him.
35. *Having found him*—For he had sought him.
36. *Who is he, that I may believe?*—This implies some degree of faith already.
He was ready to receive whatever Jesus said.
37. *Lord, I believe*—What an excellent spirit was this man of ! Of so deep and
strong an understanding ; (as he had just shown to the confusion of the Pharisees,) and yet of so teachable a temper !
39. *For judgment am I come into the world*—That is, the consequence of my
coming will be, that by the just judgment of God, while the blind in body and
soul receive their sight, they who boast they see, will be given up to still greater
blindness than before.
41. *If ye had been blind*—Invincibly ignorant ; if ye had not had so many
means of knowing : *ye would have had no sin*—Comparatively to what ye have
now. *But now ye say*—Ye yourselves acknowledge, *Ye see, therefore your sin
remaineth*—Without excuse, without remedy.
X. 1. *He that entereth not by the door*—By Christ.   He is the only lawful entrance. *Into the sheepfold*—The Church. *He is a thief and a robber*—In God's
account.   Such were all those teachers, to whom our Lord had just been
speaking.

2 and a robber. But he that entereth in by the door is the shepherd
3 of the sheep. To him the door keeper openeth, and the sheep
   hear his voice, and he calleth his own sheep by name, and leadeth
4 them out. And when he hath led forth his own sheep, he goeth
   before them, and the sheep follow him: for they know his voice
5 They will not follow a stranger, but will flee from him; for they
6 know not the voice of strangers. This parable spake Jesus to
   them; but they understood not what things they were which he
   spake to them.
7   Therefore Jesus said to them again, Verily, verily I say unto you,
8 I am the door of the sheep. Whosoever are come before me, are
9 thieves and robbers; but the sheep did not hear them. I am the
   door; if any one enter in by me, he shall be safe, and shall go in and
10 out, and find pasture. The thief cometh not, but to steal, and to kill,
   and to destroy: I am come, that they may have life, and that they
11 may have it abundantly: I am the good shepherd: the good shep-
12 herd layeth down his life for the sheep. But the hireling, who is

---

3. *To him the door keeper openeth*—Christ is considered as the shepherd, ver. 11. *As the door* in the first and following verses. And as it is not unworthy of Christ to be styled *the door*, by which both the sheep and the true pastor enter, so neither is it unworthy of God the Father to be styled *the door keeper.* See Acts xiv, 27; Col. iv, 3; Rev. iii, 8; Acts xvi, 14. *And the sheep hear his voice* —The circumstances that follow, exactly agree with the customs of the ancient eastern shepherds. They *called their sheep by name, went before them* and the sheep *followed* them. So real Christians hear, listen to, understand, and obey the voice of the shepherd whom Christ hath sent. And he counteth them *his own,* dearer than any friend or brother: *calleth,* advises, directs each *by name,* and *leadeth them out,* in the paths of righteousness, beside the waters of comfort.

4. *He goeth before them*—In all the ways of God, teaching them in every point, by example as well as by precept; *and the sheep follow him*—They tread in his steps: *for they know his voice*—Having the witness in themselves that his words are *the wisdom and the power of God.* Reader, art thou a shepherd of souls? Then answer to God. Is it thus with thee and thy flock?

5. *They will not follow a stranger*—One whom Christ hath not sent, who doth not answer the preceding description. Him *they will not follow*—And who can constrain them to it? *But will flee from him*—As from the plague. *For they know not the voice of strangers*—They cannot relish it; it is harsh and grating to them. They find nothing of God therein.

6. *They*—The Pharisees, to whom our Lord more immediately spake, as ap pears from the close of the foregoing chapter.

7. *I am the door*—Christ is both the Door and the Shepherd, and all things.

8. *Whosoever are come*—Independently of me, assuming any part of my cha-racter, pretending, like your elders and rabbis, to a power over the consciences of men, attempting to make laws in the Church, and to teach their own traditions as the way of salvation: all those prophets and expounders of God's word, that enter not by the door of the sheepfold, but run before I have sent them by my Spirit. Our Lord seems in particular to speak of those that had undertaken this office since he began his ministry, *are thieves*—Stealing temporal profit to them-selves, *and robbers*—Plundering and murdering the sheep.

9. *If any one*—As a sheep, *enter in by me*—Through faith, *he shall be safe*— From the wolf, and from those murdering shepherds. *And shall go in and out* —Shall continually attend on the shepherds whom I have sent; *and shall find pasture*—Food for his soul in all circumstances.

10. *The thief cometh not but to steal, and to kill, and to destroy*—That is, no-thing else can be the consequence of a shepherd's coming, who does not *enter in by me.*

12. *But the hireling*—It is not the bare *receiving* hire, which denominates a man a hireling: (for *the labourer is worthy of his hire;* Jesus Christ himself

not the shepherd, whose own the sheep are not, seeth the wolf
coming, and leaveth the sheep, and fleeth : so the wolf seizeth them,
13 and scattereth the sheep.   The hireling fleeth, because he is a
14 hireling, and careth not for the sheep.   I am the good shepherd,
15 and know my *sheep,* and am known of mine : (As the Father knoweth me, and I know the Father) and I lay down my life for the
16 sheep.   I have also other sheep which are not of this fold : I must
bring them likewise, and they will hear my voice, and there shall
17 be one flock, *and* one shepherd.   Therefore doth my Father love
18 me, because I lay down my life, that I may take it again.   No one
taketh it from me, but I lay it down of myself.   I have power to lay
it down, and I have power to take it again.   This commission have
19 I received of my Father.   There was again a division among
20 the Jews because of these sayings.   Many of them said, He hath a
devil, and is mad : why hear ye him ?   Others said, These are not
21 the words of one that hath a devil.   Can a devil open the eyes of
the blind ?

22   Now the feast of the dedication came on at Jerusalem : and it

being the Judge : yea, and the *Lord hath ordained, that they who preach the Gospel, should live of the Gospel :*) but the *loving* hire : the loving the hire more than
the work : the working *for the sake* of the hire.   He is a hireling, who would
not work, were it not for the hire ; to whom this is the great (if not only) motive of working.   O God! If a man who works only *for hire* is such a wretch,
a mere *thief and a robber,* what is he who continually takes the hire, and yet
does not work at all ? *The wolf*—signifies any enemy who, by force or fraud,
attacks the Christian's faith, liberty, or life.   *So the wolf seizeth and scattereth
the flock*—He seizeth some, and scattereth the rest ; the two ways of hurting the
flock of Christ.

13. *The hireling fleeth because he is a hireling*—Because he loves the hire, not
the sheep.

14. *I know my sheep*—With a tender regard and special care : *and am known
of mine*—With a holy confidence and affection.

15. *As the Father knoweth me, and I know the Father*—With such a knowledge
as implies an inexpressible union : *and I lay down my life*—Speaking of the
present time.   For his whole life was only a going unto death.

16. *I have also other sheep*—Which he foreknew ; *which are not of this fold*—
Not of the Jewish Church or nation, but Gentiles.   *I must bring them likewise*—
Into my Church, the general assembly of those whose names are written in heaven.   *And there shall be one flock*—(Not one *fold,* a plain false print) no corrupt
or divided flocks remaining.   *And one shepherd*—Who laid down his life for the
sheep, and will leave no hireling among them.   The unity both of the flock and
the shepherd shall be completed in its season.   The shepherd shall bring all into
one flock : and the whole flock *shall hear* the *one shepherd.*

17. *I lay down my life that I may take it again*—I cheerfully die to expiate the
sins of men, to the end I may rise again for their justification.

18. *I lay it down of myself*—By my own free act and deed.   *I have power to
lay it down, and I have power to take it again*—I have an original power and
right of myself, both to lay it down as a ransom, and to take it again, after full
satisfaction is made, for the sins of the whole world.   *This commission have I received of my Father*—Which I readily execute.

He chiefly spoke of the Father, before his suffering : of his own glory, after it.
Our Lord's receiving this commission as mediator is not to be considered as the
ground of his power to lay down and resume his life.   For this he had in him
self, as having an original right to dispose thereof, antecedent to the Father's
commission.   But this commission was the reason why he thus used his power
in laying down his life.   He did it in obedience to his Father.

21. *These are not the words*—The word in the original takes in actions too.

22. *I was the feast of the dedication*—Instituted by Judas Maccabeus, 1 Macc

23 was winter. And Jesus was walking in the temple, in Solomon's
24 portico. Then came the Jews round about him, and said to him,
How long dost thou keep us in suspense? If thou be the Christ,
25 tell us plainly. Jesus answered them, I have told you; yet ye do
not believe.; the works that I do in my Father's name, they testify
26 of me. But as I have told you, ye do not believe, because ye are
27 not of my sheep. My sheep hear my voice, and I know them, and
28 they follow me. And I give them eternal life, and they shall never
29 perish, neither shall any pluck them out of my hand. My Father,
who gave *them* me, is greater than all; and none shall pluck *them*
30 out of my Father's hand. I and the Father are one.
31   Then the Jews again took up stones to stone him. Jesus an-
32 swered them, Many good works have I showed you from my Fa-
33 ther; for which of those works do ye stone me? The Jews
answered him, We stone thee not for a good work, but for blas-
34 phemy, and because thou being a man, makest thyself God. Jesus answered them, Is it not written in your law, *I said ye are
35 gods? If he call them gods to whom the word of God came (and
36 the Scripture cannot be broken) say ye of him whom God hath
sanctified and sent into the world, Thou blasphemest, because I

---

iv, 59, when he purged and dedicated the altar and temple after they had been
polluted.   So our Lord observed festivals even of human appointment.   Is it not,
at least, innocent for us to do the same?

23. *In Solomon's portico*—Josephus informs us, that when Solomon built the
temple, he filled up a part of the adjacent valley, and built a portico over it toward the east. This was a noble structure, supported by a wall four hundred
cubits high : and continued even to the time of Albinus and Agrippa, which was
several years after the death of Christ.

26. *Ye do not believe, because ye are not of my sheep*—Because ye do not, will
not *follow me :* because ye are proud, unholy, lovers of praise, lovers of the
world, lovers of pleasure, not of God.

27, 28, 29. *My sheep hear my voice, and I know them, and they follow me,* &c.
—Our Lord still alludes to the discourse he had before this festival. As if he
had said, My sheep are they who, 1. *Hear my voice* by faith ; 2. Are *known* (that
is, approved) by me, as loving me ; and 3. *Follow* me, keep my commandments,
with a believing, loving heart.   And to those who, 1. *Truly believe* (observe three
promises annexed to three conditions) I give eternal life. He does not say,
I *will*, but I *give. For he that believeth* hath *everlasting life.* Those whom, 2. *I
know* truly to love me, *shall never perish,* provided they abide in my love. 3. Those
who *follow me,* neither men nor devils can pluck out of my hand. *My Father
who hath,* by an unchangeable decree, *given me* all that believe, love, and obey, *is
greater than all* in heaven or earth, *and none is able to pluck them out of his hand.*

30. *I and the Father are one*—Not by consent of will only, but by unity of
power, and consequently of nature. *Are*—This word confutes Sabellius, proving
the plurality of persons : *one*—This word confutes Arius, proving the unity of
nature in God.   Never did any prophet before, from the beginning of the world,
use any one expression of himself, which could possibly be so interpreted as this
and other expressions were, by all that heard our Lord speak.   Therefore if he
was not God he must have been the vilest of men.

35. *If he* (God) *called them gods unto whom the word of God came,* (that is, to
whom God was then speaking,) *and the Scripture cannot be broken*—That is, nothing which is written therein can be censured or rejected.

36. *Say ye of him whom the Father hath sanctified, and sent into the world*—
This sanctification (whereby he is essentially the Holy One of God) is mentioned
as prior to his mission, and together with it implies, Christ was God in the highest sense, infinitely superior to that wherein those judges were so called.

* Psalm lxxxii, 6.

37 said, I am the Son of God? If I do not the works of my Father,
38 believe me not. But if I do, though ye believe not me, believe the
    works, that ye may know and believe, that the Father *is* in me,
39 and I in him. Therefore they sought again to seize him; but he
    escaped out of their hands.
40   And he went away again beyond Jordan, to the place where John
41 baptized at first, and there he abode. And many came to him and
    said, John did no miracle: but all things that John spake of this
42 man were true. And many believed on him there.
XI.   Now one Lazarus, of Bethany, the town of Mary, and her sis-
2   ter Martha, was sick. (It was *that* Mary who anointed the Lord
    with ointment, and wiped his feet with her hair, whose brother
3   Lazarus was sick.) Therefore *his* sisters sent to him, saying,
4   Lord, behold he whom thou lovest is sick. Jesus hearing *it*, said,
    This sickness is not to death, but for the glory of God, that the
5   Son of God may be glorified thereby. Now Jesus loved Martha,
6   and her sister, and Lazarus. So after he had heard that he was
7   sick, he abode still two days in the place where he was. Then
    after this he saith to the disciples, Let us go into Judea again.
8   The disciples say to him, Master, the Jews but now sought to
9   stone thee, and goest thou thither again? Jesus answered, Are
    there not twelve hours in the day? If any man walk in the day
10 he stumbleth not, because he seeth the light of this world. But if
11 any man walk in the night, he stumbleth, because the light is not
12 in him. Thus he spake, and after that he saith to them, Our friend

---

38. *That ye may know and believe*—In some a more exact knowledge precedes,
in others it follows faith. *I am in the Father and the Father in me. I and the
Father are one*—These two sentences illustrate each other.

40. *To the* desert *place where John baptized*, and gave so honourable a testimony of him.

41. *John did no miracle*—An honour reserved for him, whose forerunner he was
XI. 1. *One Lazarus*—It is probable, Lazarus was younger than his sisters.
Bethany is named, the town of Mary and Martha, and Lazarus is mentioned
after them, ver. 5. Ecclesiastical history informs us, that Lazarus was now
thirty years old, and that he lived thirty years after Christ's ascension.

2. *It was that Mary who* afterward *anointed*, &c. She was more known than
her elder sister Martha, and as such is named before her.

4. *This sickness is not to death, but for the glory of God*—The event of this
sickness will not be death, in the usual sense of the word, a final separation of
his soul and body; but a manifestation of the glorious power of God.

7. *Let us go into Judea*—From the country east of Jordan, whither he had retired some time before, when the Jews sought to stone him, chap. x, 39, 40.

9. *Are there not twelve hours in the day?*—The Jews always divided the space
from sunrise to sunset, were the days longer or shorter, into twelve parts: so
that the hours of their day were all the year the same in number, though much
shorter in winter than in summer. *If any man walk in the day he stumbleth not*—
As if he had said, So there is such a space, a determined time, which God has
allotted me. *During that time I stumble not*, amidst all the snares that are laid
for me. *Because he seeth the light of this world*—And so I see the light of God
surrounding me.

10. *But if a man walk in the night*—If he have not light from God; if his providence does no longer protect him.

11. *Our friend Lazarus sleepeth*—This he spoke, just when he died. *Sleepeth*—Such is the death of good men in the language of heaven. But the disciples did not yet understand this language. And the slowness of our understand
ing makes the Scripture often descend to our barbarous manner of speaking.

13 Lazarus sleepeth; but I go to awake him. Then the disciples
said, Lord, if he sleep, he will recover. Jesus spake of his death ;
14 but they thought he had spoken of the natural rest in sleep. Then
15 said Jesus to them plainly, Lazarus is dead. And I am glad for
your sake I was not there, that ye may believe : but let us go to
16 him. Then said Thomas, called Didymus, to his fellow disciples
Let us also go, that we may die with him.
17 When Jesus came, he found he had been now four days in the
18 tomb. (Now Bethany was near Jerusalem, about fifteen furlongs
19 off.) And many of the Jews were come to Martha and Mary, to
20 comfort them concerning their brother. When Martha heard that
Jesus was coming, she went and met him ; but Mary sat in the
21 house. Then said Martha to Jesus, Lord, if thou hadst been here,
22 my brother had not died. But I know even now, that whatsoever
23 thou wilt ask of God, God will give it thee. Jesus saith to her,
24 Thy brother shall rise again. Martha said to him, I know that he
25 shall rise again in the resurrection at the last day. Jesus said to
her, I am the resurrection and the life ; he that believeth in me,
26 though he die, yet shall he live ; and whosoever liveth and be-
27 lieveth in me, shall not die for ever. Believest thou this ? She
saith to him, Yea, Lord, I believe thou art the Christ, the Son of
28 God, who was to come into the world. Having said this, she went
and privately called Mary her sister, saying, The Master is come,
29 and calleth for thee. As soon as she heard it, she arose quickly
30 and came to him. Jesus was not yet come into the town, but was
31 at the place where Martha had met him. The Jews then who
were with her in the house and comforted her, seeing Mary, that
she arose up quickly and went out, followed her, saying, She is
32 going to the tomb to weep there. When Mary was come where
Jesus was, and saw him, she fell at his feet, saying to him, Lord, if
33 thou hadst been here, my brother had not died. When Jesus therefore saw her weeping, and the Jews weeping who came with her,
34 he groaned deeply, and troubled himself and said, Where have ye
35 laid him ? They say to him, Lord, come and see. Jesus wept.
36 Then said the Jews, Behold how he loved him ! And some of

---

16. *Thomas* in Hebrew, as *Didymus* in Greek, signifies a twin. *With him*—
With Jesus, whom he supposed the Jews would kill. It seems to be the language
of despair.

20. *Mary sat in the house*—Probably not hearing what was said.

22. *Whatsoever thou wilt ask, God will give it thee*—So that she already believed he could raise him from the dead.

25. *I am the resurrection*—Of the dead. *And the life*—Of the living. *He that
believeth in me, though he die, yet shall he live*—In life everlasting.

32. *She fell at his feet*—This Martha had not done. So she makes amends
for her slowness in coming.

33. *He groaned*—So he restrained his tears. So he stopped them soon after,
ver. 38. *He troubled himself*—An expression amazingly elegant, and full of the
highest propriety. For the affections of Jesus were not properly passions, but
voluntary emotions, which were wholly in his own power. And this tender
trouble which he now voluntarily sustained, was full of the highest order and
reason.

35. *Jesus wept*—Out of sympathy with those who were in tears all around
him, as well as from a deep sense of the misery sin had brought upon human
nature.

37 them said, Could not this person, who opened the eyes of the blind,
38 have even caused that this man should not have died? Jesus again
39 groaning in himself, cometh to the tomb. It was a cave, and a
   stone lay upon it. Jesus saith, Take away the stone. Martha,
   the sister of the deceased, saith to him, Lord, by this time he stink-
40 eth; for he had been *buried* four days. Jesus saith to her, Said I
   not to thee, if thou wouldest believe, thou shouldest see the glory
   of God? Then they took away the stone *from* where the dead lay.
41 And Jesus lifted up his eyes and said, Father, I thank thee that
42 thou hast heard me. And I knew that thou hearest me always:
   but I spake this because of the people who stand by, that they
43 may believe that thou hast sent me. And having spoken thus, he
44 cried with a loud voice, Lazarus, come forth. And he that had
   been dead came forth, bound hand and foot with grave clothes, and
   his face was wrapt about with a napkin. Jesus saith to them, Loose
   him, and let him go.
45   Many therefore of the Jews who were come to Mary, and had
46 seen the things which Jesus had done, believed on him. But
   some of them went to the Pharisees, and told them what things
47 Jesus had done. Then the chief priests and elders assembled a
   council and said, What do we? For this man doth many miracles.
48 If we let him thus alone, all men will believe on him, and the

---

37. *Could not this person have even caused, that this man should not have died?*—Yet they never dreamed that he could raise him again! What a strange mixture of faith and unbelief.

38. *It was a cave*—So Abraham, Isaac, and Jacob, and their wives, except Rachel, were buried in the cave of Machpelah, Gen. xlix, 29, 30, 31. These caves were commonly in rocks, which abounded in that country, either hollowed by nature or hewn by art. And the entrance was shut up with a great stone, which sometimes had a monumental inscription.

39. *Lord, by this time he stinketh*—Thus did reason and faith struggle together.

40. *Said I not*—It appears by this, that Christ had said more to Martha than is before recorded.

41. *Jesus lifted up his eyes*—Not as if he applied to his Father for assistance. There is not the least show of this. He wrought the miracle with an air of absolute sovereignty, as the Lord of life and death. But it was as if he had said, I thank thee, that by the disposal of thy providence, thou hast granted my desire, in this remarkable opportunity of exerting my power, and showing forth thy praise.

43. *He cried with a loud voice*—That all who were present might hear. *Lazarus, come forth!*—Jesus called him out of the tomb as easily as if he had been not only alive, but awake also.

44. *And he came forth bound hand and foot with grave clothes*—Which were wrapt round each hand and each foot, *and his face was wrapt about with a napkin*—If the Jews buried as the Egyptians did, the face was not covered with it, but it only went round the forehead, and under the chin; so that he might easily see his way.

45. *Many believed on him*—And so the Son of God was glorified, according to what our Lord had said, ver. 4.

46. *But some of them went to the Pharisees*—What a dreadful confirmation of that weighty truth, If they hear not Moses and the prophets, neither will they be persuaded though one rose from the dead!

47. *What do we?*—What? Believe. Yea, but death yields to the power of Christ sooner than infidelity.

48. *All men will believe*—And receive him as the Messiah. And this will give such umbrage to the Romans that they *will come and subvert both our place*—Temple; *and nation*—Both our Church and state. Were they really afraid of

49 Romans will come and subvert both our place and nation. And one
of them, Caiaphas, being the high priest that year, said to them,
50 Ye know nothing, Nor consider it as expedient for us, that one
man should die for the people, and that the whole nation perish not.
51 He spake not this of himself, but being high priest that year, he
52 prophesied, that Jesus should die for the nation : And not for that
nation only, but that he might also gather into one all the children
53 of God that were scattered abroad. Therefore from that day they
consulted together to put him to death.
54   Jesus therefore walked no longer openly among the Jews, but
went thence into the country, near the wilderness, to a city called
55 Ephraim, and there continued with his disciples. And the passover
of the Jews was nigh ; and many went up to Jerusalem, to purify
56 themselves. Then sought they for Jesus, and said one to another,
standing in the temple, What think ye ? That he will not come to
57 the feast? Now both the chief priests and Pharisees had given
order, That if any man knew where he was, he should show *it*,
that they might apprehend him.
XII. Then Jesus, six days before the passover, came to Bethany,
where Lazarus was, who had been dead, whom he had raised from
2 the dead. There they made him a supper, and Martha served ;
3 but Lazarus was one of them who sat at table with him. Then
Mary, taking a pound of ointment, of very costly spikenard, anointed the feet of Jesus, and wiped his feet with her hair ; and the
4 house was filled with the odour of the ointment. But one of his
5 disciples, Judas Iscariot, who was about to betray him, saith, Why
was not this ointment sold for three hundred pence, and given to

this ? Or was it a fair colour only ? Certainly it was no more. For they could
not but know, that he that raised the dead was able to conquer the Romans.

49. *That year*—That memorable year, in which Christ was to die. It was the
last and chief of Daniel's seventy weeks, the fortieth year before the destruction
of Jerusalem, and was celebrated for various causes, in the Jewish history.
Therefore that year is so peculiarly mentioned: Caiaphas was the high priest
both before and after it. *Ye know nothing*—He reproves their slow deliberations
in so clear a case.

50. *It is expedient that one man should die for the people*—So God overruled
his tongue, for *he spake not of himself*, by his own spirit only, but by the spirit
of prophecy.' And thus he gave unawares as clear a testimony to the priestly,
as Pilate did to the kingly office of Christ.

52. *But that he might gather into one*—Church, *all the children of God that
were scattered abroad*—Through all ages and nations.

55. *Many went up to purify themselves*—That they might remove all hinderances to their eating the passover.

XII. 1. *Six days before the passover*—Namely, on the Sabbath : that which
was called by the Jews, The Great Sabbath. This whole week was anciently
termed The great and holy week. *Jesus came*—From Ephraim, chap. ix, 54.

2. It seems Martha was a person of some figure, from the great respect which
was paid to her and her sister, in visits and condolences on Lazarus's death, as
well as from the costly ointment mentioned in the next verse. And probably it
was at their house our Lord and his disciples lodged, when he returned from Jerusalem to Bethany, every evening of the last week of his life, upon which he
was now entered.

3. *Then Mary, taking a pound of ointment*—There were two persons who poured
ointment on Christ. One toward the beginning of his ministry, at or near Nain,
Luke vii, 37, &c. The other six days before his last passover, at Bethany ; the
account of whom is given here, as well as by St. Matthew and Mark.

6 the poor? This he said, not because he cared for the poor, but because he was a thief and had the purse, and bare what was put
7 therein.   Then Jesus said, Let her alone; against the day of my
8 burial hath she kept this.   Ye have the poor always with you : but
me ye have not always.
9 Now much people of the Jews knew that he was there, and came
not only for the sake of Jesus, but also to see Lazarus, whom he
10 had raised from the dead.   But the chief priests consulted, how
11 to kill Lazarus also, Because on his account, many of the Jews
went away, and believed on Jesus.
12 * The next day, a great multitude who were come to the feast,
13 having heard that Jesus was coming to Jerusalem, † Took branches,
of palm trees, and went out to meet him, and cried, Hosanna :
blessed in the name of the Lord *is* he that cometh, the King of
14 Israel.   And Jesus having found a young ass, rode thereon, as it
15 is written, ‡ Fear not, daughter of Sion ; behold thy King cometh,
16 sitting on an ass's colt.   These things his disciples understood not
at first : but when Jesus had been glorified, then they remembered
that these things were written of him, and *that* they had done these
17 things to him.   And the multitude who were with him, when he
called Lazarus out of the tomb, and raised him from the dead, bare
18 witness.   For this cause also the multitude went to meet him, be-
19 cause they heard he had done this miracle.   The Pharisees therefore said to each other, Perceive ye how ye prevail nothing ?
Behold, the world is gone after him.
20 Now among those who came up to worship at the feast, there
21 were certain Greeks.   These came to Philip of Bethsaida in Gali-

---

7. *Against the day of my burial*—Which now draws nigh.
10. *The chief priests consulted, how to kill Lazarus also*—Here is the plain
reason why the other evangelists, who wrote while Lazarus was living, did not
relate his story.
12. *The next day*—On Sunday.   *Who were come to the feast*—So that this
multitude consisted chiefly of Galileans, not men of Jerusalem.
15. *Fear not*—For his meekness forbids fear, as well as the end of his coming.
16. *These things his disciples understood not at first*—The design of God's providential dispensations is seldom understood at first.   We ought therefore to
believe, though we understand not, and to give ourselves up to the Divine disposal.   The great work of faith is, to embrace those things which we know not
now, but shall know hereafter.   *When he had been glorified*—At his ascension.
17. *When he called Lazarus out of the tomb*—How admirably does the apostle
express, as well the greatness of the miracle, as the facility with which it was
wrought! The easiness of the Scripture style on the most grand occurrences, is
more sublime than all the pomp of orators.
18. *The multitude went to meet him, because they heard*—From those who had
seen the miracle.   So in a little time both joined together, to *go before* and to
follow him.
20. *Certain Greeks*—A prelude of the Gentile Church.   That these were circumcised does not appear.   But they *came up* on purpose *to worship* the God
of Israel.
21. *These came to Philip of Bethsaida in Galilee*—Perhaps they used to lodge
there, in their journey to Jerusalem.   Or they might believe, a Galilean would
be more ready to serve them herein, than a Jew.   *Sir*—They spake to him, as
to one they were little acquainted with.   *We would see Jesus*—A modest request.
They could scarce expect that he would now have time to talk with them.

* Matt. ix, 8; Mark xi, 8; Luke xix, 36.   † Psalm cxviii, 26.   ‡ Zech. ix, 9

22 lee, and asked him, saying, Sir, we desire to see Jesus. Philip
   cometh and telleth Andrew ; and again Andrew and Philip tell Je-
23 sus. And Jesus answered them, saying, The hour is come, that
24 the Son of man should be glorified. Verily, verily I say unto you,
   Unless a grain of wheat that falleth into the ground die, it remain-
25 eth alone; but if it die, it bringeth forth much fruit. *He that
   loveth his life shall lose it: and he that hateth his life in this world
26 shall preserve it to life eternal. If any man serve me, let him follow me, and where I am, there shall also my servant be : if any
   man serve me, him will the Father honour.
27   Now is my soul troubled. And what shall I say ? Father, save
28 me from this hour? But for this cause I came, for this hour.
   Father, glorify thy name. Then a voice came from heaven, I have
29 both glorified it, and I will glorify it again. The multitude who
   stood and heard it, said, It thundered ; others said, An angel spake
30 to him. Jesus answered and said, This voice came not because
31 of me, but for your sakes. Now is the judgment of this world :
32 now shall the prince of this world be cast out. And I, when I am
   lifted up from the earth, will draw all men to me. (He spake this,
33 signifying what death he should die.) The multitude answered

23. *The hour is come that the Son of man should be glorified*—With the Father
and in the sight of every creature. But he must suffer first.
24. *Unless a grain of wheat die*—The late resurrection of Lazarus gave our
Lord a natural occasion of speaking on this subject. And agreeable to his infinite knowledge, he singles out, from among so many thousands of seeds, almost
the only one that dies in the earth : and which therefore was an exceeding
proper similitude, peculiarly adapted to the purpose for which he uses it. The
like is not to be found in any other grain, except millet, and the large bean.
25. *He that loveth his life*—More than the will of God ; *shall lose it* eternally :
and *he that hateth his life*—In comparison of the will of God, shall *preserve it.*
26. *Let him follow me*—By hating his life : *and where I am*—In heaven. *If
any man serve me*—Thus, *him will the Father honour.*
27. *Now is my soul troubled*—He had various foretastes of his passion. *And
what shall I say?*—Not what shall I *choose ?* For his heart was fixed in choosing
the will of his Father : but he laboured for utterance. The two following clauses,
Save me from this hour—For *this cause I came*—Into the world ; *for* the sake
of *this hour* (of suffering) seem to have glanced through his mind in one moment.
But human language could not so express it.
28. *Father, glorify thy name*—Whatever I suffer. Now the trouble was over.
I have glorified it—By thy entrance into *this hour. And I will glorify it*—By
thy passing through it.
29. *The multitude who stood and heard*—A sound, but not the distinct words.
In the most glorious revelations there may remain something obscure, to exercise
our faith. *Said, It thundered*—Thunder did frequently attend a voice from
heaven. Perhaps it did so now.
31. *Now*—This moment. And from this moment Christ thirsted more than
ever, till his baptism was accomplished. *Is the judgment of this world*—That is,
now is the judgment given concerning it, whose it shall be. *Now shall the prince
of this world*—Satan, who had gained possession of it by sin and death, *be cast
out*—That is, judged, condemned, *cast out* of his possession, and out of the bounds
of Christ's kingdom.
32. *Lifted up from the earth*—This is a Hebraism which signifies dying.
Death in general is all that is usually imported. But our Lord made use of this
phrase, rather than others that were equivalent, because it so well suited the
particular manner of his death. *I will draw all men*—Gentiles as well as Jews.
And those who follow my drawings, Satan shall not be able to keep.

* Matt. x, 39

34 him, We have heard * out of the law, that the Christ abideth for
ever: and how sayest thou, The Son of man must be lifted up
35 Who is this Son of man? Then Jesus said to them, Yet a little
while is the light with you. Walk while ye have the light, lest
darkness overtake you; for he that walketh in darkness, knoweth
36 not whither he goeth. While ye have the light, believe in the
light, that ye may become children of light. These things spake
Jesus, and retiring concealed himself from them.
37 But though he had done so many miracles before them, *yet* they
38 believed not on him ; So that the word of the Prophet Isaiah was
fulfilled, which he said, † Lord, who hath believed our report?
39 And to whom hath the arm of the Lord been revealed? Therefore
40 they could not believe, according to what Isaiah said again, ‡ He
hath blinded their eyes, and hardened their heart, that they might
not see with *their* eyes, and understand with their heart, and be
41 converted, that I might heal them. These things said Isaiah, when
42 he saw his glory, and spake of him. Nevertheless many even of
the rulers believed on him, but they did not confess *him*, because
of the Pharisees, lest they should be put out of the synagogue.
43 For they loved the praise of man more than the praise of God.
44 Jesus said with a loud voice, He that believeth on me, believeth
45 not on me, but on him that sent me. And he that seeth me, seeth
46 him that sent me. I am come a light into the world, that whoso-
47 ever believeth on me, may not continue in darkness. If any man
hear my words, and believe not, I judge him not ; for I am not
48 come to judge the world, but to save the world. He that rejecteth
me, and receiveth not my words, hath one that judgeth him ; the
word which I have spoken, that shall judge him at the last day.
49 For I have not spoken of myself, but the Father who sent me, he

34. *How sayest thou, The Son of man must be lifted up ?*—How can these things be reconciled? Very easily. He first dies, and then *abideth for ever*. *Who is this Son of man ?*
35. *Then Jesus said to them*—Not answering them directly, but exhorting them to improve what they had heard already. *The light*—I and my doctrine.
36. *The children of light*—The children of God, wise, holy, happy.
37. *Though he had done so many miracles·before them*—So that they could not but see them.
38. *The arm of the Lord*—The power of God manifested by Christ, in his preaching, miracles, and work of redemption.
39. *Therefore* now *they could not believe*—That is, by the just judgment of God, for their obstinacy and wilful resistance of the truth, they were at length so left to the hardness of their hearts, that neither the miracles nor doctrines of our Lord could make any impression upon them.
41. *When he saw his glory*—Christ's, Isa. vi, 1, &c. And it is there expressly said to be the glory of the Lord, Jehovah, the Supreme God.
44. *Jesus said with a loud voice*—This which follows to the end of the chapter, is with St. John the epilogue of our Lord's public discourses, and a kind of re-capitulation of them. *Believeth not on me*—Not on me alone, *but* also *on him that sent me :* because the Father hath *sent* the Son, and because he and the Father *are one.*
45. *And he that seeth me*—By the eye of faith.
47. *I judge him not*—Not now: *for I am not come to judge the world.* See, Christ *came to save* even them that finally perish! Even these are a part of that world, which he lived and died to save.

* Psa. cx, 4.   † Isaiah liii, 1.   ‡ Isaiah vi, 10; Matt. xiii, 14; Acts xxviii, 26.

gave me commandment, what I should say, and how I should
50 speak. And I know that his commandment is life everlasting;
what therefore I speak to you, as the Father hath said to me, so I
speak.
XIII. Now before the feast of the passover, Jesus knowing his hour
was come, to pass out of this world to the Father, having loveo
2 his own who were in the world, he loved them to the end. And
while they were at supper (the devil having now put it into the
3 heart of Judas Iscariot, *the son* of Simon, to betray him) Jesus
knowing the Father had given all things into his hands, and that he
4 was come forth from God, and going to God, Riseth from supper,
and layeth aside his garments, and taking a towel, girdeth himself.
5 After that, he poured water into the basin, and began to wash the
feet of the disciples, and to wipe *them* with the towel wherewith
6 he was girded. Then cometh he to Simon Peter, who saith to him,
7 Lord, dost thou wash my feet? Jesus answered and said to him,
8 What I do, thou knowest not now; but thou shalt know hereafter.
Peter saith to him, Thou shalt never wash my feet. Jesus an-
9 swered him, If I wash thee not, thou hast no part with me. Simon
Peter saith to him, Lord, not my feet only, but also *my* hands and
10 *my* head. Jesus saith to him, He who hath been bathed, needeth
only to wash *his* feet, and is clean all over: and ye are clean;
11 but not all. For he knew who would betray him: therefore he
said, Ye are not all clean.
12 So after he had washed their feet, and taken his garments, sitting down again, he said to them, Know ye what I have done to
13 you? Ye call me Master and Lord; and ye say well; for *so* I am.
14 If I then, your Lord and Master, have washed your feet, ye ought

50. *His commandment*—Kept, *is life everlasting*—That is the way to it, and
t! e beginning of it.
XIII. 1. *Before the feast*—Namely, on Wednesday, in the paschal week. *Having loved his own*—His apostles, *he loved them to the end*—Of his life.
2. *Having now*—Probably now first.
3. *Jesus knowing*—Though conscious of his own greatness, thus humbled
himself.
4. *Layeth aside his garments*—That part of them which would have hindered
him.
5. *Into the basin*—A large vessel was usually placed for this very purpose,
wherever the Jews supped.
7. *What I do thou knowest not now; but thou shalt know hereafter*—We do not
now know perfectly any of his works, either of creation, providence, or grace. It
is enough that we can love and obey now, and that we shall *know hereafter*.
8. *If I wash thee not*—If thou dost not submit to my will, *thou hast no part
with me*—Thou art not my disciple. In a more general sense it may mean, If I
do not wash thee in my blood, and purify thee by my Spirit, thou canst have no
communion with me, nor any share in the blessings of my kingdom.
9. *Lord, not my feet only*—How fain would man be wiser than God! Yet this
was well meant, though ignorant earnestness.
10. And so ye, having been already cleansed, need only *to wash your feet*—
That is, to walk holy and undefiled.
14. *Ye ought also to wash one another's feet*—And why did they not? Why do
we not read of any one apostle ever washing the feet of any other? Because
they understood the Lord better. They knew he never designed that this should
be literally taken. He designed to teach them the great lesson of humble love,
as well as to confer inward purity upon them. And hereby he teaches us, 1. In
every possible way to assist each other in attaining that purity; 2. To wash each

15 also to wash one another's feet. For I have given you an exam
16 ple, that ye also may do as I have done to you. Verily, verily I
say unto you, the servant is not greater than his Lord, neither he
17 that is sent greater than he that sent him. If ye know these
18 things, happy are ye, if ye do them. I speak not of you all : I
know whom I have chosen, that the scripture may be fulfilled, * He
19 that eateth bread with me, hath lifted up his heel against me. Now
I tell you before it is done, that when it is done, ye may believe
20 that I am *he*. † Verily, verily I say unto you, he that receiveth
whomsoever I send, receiveth me, and he that receiveth me, receiveth him that sent me.

21 Jesus having said this, was troubled in spirit, and testified, and
said, Verily, verily I say unto you, one of you will betray me.
22 Then the disciples looked one on another doubting of whom he
23 spake. Now there was lying in the bosom of Jesus one of the
24 disciples whom Jesus loved. Simon Peter therefore beckoned to
25 him, to ask who it was of whom he spake. He then, leaning on
26 the breast of Jesus, saith to him, Lord, who is it? Jesus answered,
It is he to whom I shall give the sop when I have dipped it.
And having dipped the sop, he giveth it to Judas Iscariot, *the son*
27 of Simon. And after the sop, then Satan entered into him. Then
28 said Jesus to him, What thou doest, do quickly. Now none at the
29 table knew why he said this to him. But some thought, as Judas
had the purse, that Jesus had said to him, Buy what we have need of
30 against the feast, or, Give something to the poor. He then having
received the sop, went out immediately. And it was night when
he went out.

---

other's feet, by performing all sorts of good offices to each other, even those of
the lowest kind, when opportunity serves, and the necessity of any calls for them.

16. *The servant is not greater than his lord*—Nor therefore ought to think much
of either doing or suffering the same things.

18. *I speak not of you all*—When I call you happy, *I know* one of *you twelve
whom I have chosen*, will betray me ; whereby that scripture will be fulfilled.

20. And I put my own honour upon you, my ambassadors.

21. *One of you*—The speaking thus indefinitely at first was profitable to them all.

23. *There was lying in the bosom of Jesus*—That is, sitting next to him at table.
This phrase only expresses the then customary posture at meals, where the guests
all leaned sidewise on couches. And each was said to *lie in the bosom* of him
who was placed next above him. *One of the disciples whom Jesus loved*—St. John
avoids with great care the expressly naming himself. Perhaps our Lord now
gave him the first proof of his peculiar love, by disclosing this secret to him.

24. *Simon Peter*—Behind Jesus, who lay between them.

25. *Leaning* down, and so asking him privately.

26. *Jesus answered*—In his ear. So careful was he not to offend (if it had been
possible) even Judas himself. *The sop*—Which he took up while he was speaking. *He giveth it to Judas*—And probably the other disciples thought Judas peculiarly happy! But when even this instance of our Lord's tenderness could not
move him, then Satan took full possession.

27. *What thou doest, do quickly*—This is not a permission, much less a command.
It is only as if he had said, If thou art determined to do it, why dost thou delay?
Hereby showing Judas, that he could not be hid, and expressing his own readi-
ness to suffer.

28. *None knew why he said this*—Save John and Judas.

30. *He went out*—To the chief priests. But he returned afterward, and was with
them when they ate the passover, Matt. xxvi, 20, though not at the Lord's Supper

* Psalm xli, 9. † Matt. x, 4(

31   Jesus saith, Now is the Son of man glorified, and. God is glori-
32 fied by him.   If God be glorified by him, God will also glorify him
33 with himself, and will shortly glorify him.   Beloved children, yet
   a little while I am with you: ye shall seek me, and as I said to the
34 Jews, * Whither I go ye cannot come, so now I say to you.   A new
   commandment I give you, that ye love one another: as I have
35 loved you, that ye also love one another.   By this shall all men
36 know that ye are my disciples, if ye have love one to another.   Simon Peter said to him, Lord, whither goest thou?   Jesus answered
   him, Whither I go, thou canst not follow me now; but thou wilt
37 follow me hereafter.   Peter saith to him, Lord, why cannot I fol-
38 low thee now?   I will lay down my life for thy sake.   Jesus answered him, Wilt thou lay down thy life for my sake?   Verily, verily I
   say unto thee, the cock shall not have crowed, till thou hast denied
   me thrice.
XIV.   Let not your heart be troubled: believe in God: be-
2 lieve also in me.   In my Father's house are many mansions;
   if not, I would have told you.   I go to prepare a place for
3 you.   And if I go and prepare a place for you, I will come again
   and receive you to myself, that where I am, ye may be also.
4 And whither I go ye know, and the way ye know.   Thomas saith
5 to him, Lord, we know not whither thou goest, and how can we
6 know the way?   Jesus saith, l am the way, and the truth, and the
7 life; no man cometh to the Father but by me.   If ye had known

---

31. *Jesus saith*—Namely, the next day; on Thursday, in the morning.   Here
the scene, as it were, is opened, for the discourse which is continued in the following chapters.   *Now*—While I speak this, *the Son of man is glorified*—Being
fully entered into his glorious work of redemption.   This evidently relates to the
glory which belongs to his suffering in so holy and victorious a manner.
   33. *Ye cannot come*—Not yet; being not yet ripe for it.
   34. *A new commandment*—Not new in itself; but new in the school of Christ:
for he had never before taught it them expressly.   Likewise new, as to the degree
of it, *as I have loved you.*
   36. *Peter saith, Lord, whither goest thou?*—St. Peter seems to have thought,
that Christ, being rejected by the Jews, would go to some other part of the earth
to erect his throne, where he might reign without disturbance, according to the
gross notions he had of Christ's kingdom.   *Thou canst not follow me now*—But
Peter would not believe him.   And he did follow him, chap. xviii, 15.   But it
was *afar off.*   And not without great loss.
   38. *The cock shall not have crowed*—That is, cock crowing shall not be over,
till thou hast denied me thrice—His three-fold denial was thrice foretold; first, at
the time mentioned here; secondly, at that mentioned by St. Luke; lastly, at
that recorded by St. Matthew and Mark.
   XIV. 1. *Let not your heart be troubled*—At my departure.   *Believe*—This is the
sum of all his discourse, which is urged till they did believe, chap. xvi, 30.   And
then our Lord prays and departs.
   2. *In my Father's house are many mansions*—Enough to receive both the holy
angels, and your predecessors in the faith, and all that now believe, and a great
multitude, which no man can number.
   4. *The way*—Of faith, holiness, sufferings.
   5. *Thomas saith*—Taking him in a gross sense.
   6. To the question concerning the way, he answers, *I am the way.*   To the
question concerning knowledge, he answers, *I am the truth.*   To the question
whither, *I am the life.*   The first is treated of in this verse; the second, ver.
7-17; the third, ver. 18, &c.

* Chap. vii 34.

me, ye would have known my Father also : from henceforth ye
8 have known him, and have seen him. Philip saith to him, Lord
9 show us the Father, and it sufficeth us. Jesus saith to him,
Have I been so long with you, and hast thou not known me,
Philip? He that hath seen me, hath seen the Father; and how
10 sayest thou, Show us the Father? Believest thou not that I *am*
in the Father, and the Father in me? The words that I speak
to you, I speak not of myself; and the Father that dwelleth in me,
11 he doth the works. Believe me, because I *am* in the Father, and
the Father in me ; but if not, believe me for the sake of the works.
12 Verily, verily I say unto you, He that believeth on me, the works
which I do shall he do also ; and greater than these shall he do,
13 because I go to my Father. And whatsoever ye shall ask in my
name, I will do it, that the Father may be glorified through the Son.
14 If ye shall ask any thing in my name, I will do *it*.
15 　If ye love me, keep my commandments. And I will ask the
16 Father, and he will give you another Comforter, to remain with
you for ever, *even* the Spirit of truth, whom the world cannot
17 receive, because it seeth him not, neither knoweth him. But ye
18 know him, for he remaineth with you, and shall be in you. I
19 will not leave you orphans : I come to you. Yet a little while,
and the world seeth me no more : but ye see me : because I live,
20 ye shall live also. At that day ye shall know that I am in my
21 Father, and you in me, and I in you. He that hath my command-

---

7. *Ye have known*—Ye have begun to know him.

10. *I am in the Father—The words that I speak*, &c.—That is, I am one with
the Father, in essence, in speaking, and in acting.

11. *Believe me*—On my own word, *because I am* God. *The works*—This
respects not merely the miracles themselves, but his sovereign, Godlike way of
performing them.

12. *Greater works than these shall he do*—So one apostle wrought miracles
merely by his shadow, Acts v, 15 ; another by *handkerchiefs carried from his
body*, Acts xix, 12 ; and all spake with various tongues. But the converting one
sinner is a greater work than all these. *Because I go to my Father*—To send
you the Holy Ghost.

15. *If ye love me, keep my commandments*—Immediately after faith he exhorts
to love and good works.

16. *And I will ask the Father*—The 21st verse shows the connection between
this and the preceding verses. *And he will give you another Comforter*—The
Greek word signifies also an advocate, instructer, or encourager. *Another*—For
Christ himself was one. *To remain with you for ever*—With you, and your followers in faith, to the end of the world.

17. *The Spirit of truth*—Who has, reveals, testifies, and defends the truth as it
is in Jesus. *Whom the world*—All who do not love or fear God, *cannot receive,
because it seeth him not*—Having no spiritual senses, no internal eye to discern
him ; nor consequently knoweth him. *He shall be in you*—As a constant guest.
Your bodies and souls shall be temples of the Holy Ghost dwelling in you.

18. *I will not leave you orphans*—A word that is elegantly applied to those who
have lost any dear friend. *I come to you*—What was certainly and speedily to be,
our Lord speaks of as if it were already.

19. *But ye see me*—That is, ye shall certainly see me. *Because I live, ye shall
live also*—Because I am the living One in my Divine nature, and shall rise again
in my human nature, and live for ever in heaven : therefore ye shall live the life
of faith and love on earth, and hereafter the life of glory.

20. *At that day*—When ye see me after my resurrection ; but more eminently
at the day of pentecost.

ments, and keepeth them, he it is that loveth me : and he that loveth me, shall be loved by my Father, and I will love him, and will manifest myself to him.

22 Judas (not Iscariot) saith to him, Lord, how is it that thou art
23 about to manifest thyself to us, and not to the world? Jesus answered and said to him, If any man love me, he will keep my words; and my Father will love him, and we will come to him, and
24 make our abode with him. He that loveth me not, keepeth not my words ; and the word which ye hear is not mine, but the Father's who sent me.

25 These things have I spoken to you, while I remained with you.
26 But the Comforter, the Holy Ghost, whom the Father will send in my name, he will teach you all things, and will bring all things
27 to your remembrance, whatsoever I have said to you. Peace I will leave with you; my peace I will give unto you; not as the world giveth, give I unto you. Let not your heart be troubled,
28 neither let it be afraid. Ye heard me say to you, I go, and come *again* to you. If ye loved me, ye would have rejoiced, because I
29 go to the Father; for the Father is greater than I. And now I have told you, before it cometh to pass, that when it is come to
30 pass ye may believe. Hereafter I shall not talk much with you; for the prince of this world is coming ; but he hath nothing in me :
31 But that the world may know that I love the Father, and as the Father commanded me, so I do. Arise, and let us go hence.

---

21. *He that hath my commandments*—Written in his heart. *I will manifest myself to him*—More abundantly.

23. *Jesus answered*—Because ye love and obey me, and they do not, therefore I will reveal myself to you, and not to them. *My Father will love him*—The more any man loves and obeys, the more God will love him. *And we will come to him, and make our abode with him*—Which implies such a large manifestation of the Divine presence and love, that the former in justification is as nothing in comparison of it.

26. *In my name*—For my sake, in my room, and as my agent. *He will teach you all things*—Necessary for you to know. Here is a clear promise to the apostles, and their successors in the faith, that the Holy Ghost will teach them all that truth which is needful for their salvation.

27. *Peace I leave with you*—Peace in general ; peace with God and with your own consciences. *My peace*—In particular; that peace which I enjoy, and which I create, *I give*—At this instant. *Not as the world giveth*—Unsatisfying, unsettled, transient; but filling the soul with constant, even tranquillity. Lord, evermore give us this peace ! How serenely may we pass through the most turbulent scenes of life, when all is quiet and harmonious within ! Thou hast made peace through the blood of thy cross. May we give all diligence to preserve the inestimable gift inviolate, till it issue in everlasting peace !

28. GOD *the Father is greater than I*—As he was man. As God, neither is greater nor less than the other.

29. *I have told you*—Of my going and return.

30. *The prince of this world is coming*—To make his grand assault. *But he hath nothing in me*—No right, no claim, or power. There is no guilt in me, to give him power over me ; no corruption to take part with his temptation.

31. *But* I suffer him thus to assault me, 1. Because it is the Father's commission to me, chap. x, 18. 2. To convince the world of my love to the Father, in being *obedient unto death*, Phil. ii, 8. *Arise, let us go hence*—Into the city, to the passover. All that has been related from chap. xii, 31, was done and said on Thursday, without the city. But what follows in the fifteenth, sixteenth, and seventeenth chapters, was said in the city, on the very evening of the passover just before he went over the brook Kedron.

XV.　I am the true vine, and my Father is the husbandman.　Every
2 branch in me that beareth not fruit, he taketh away; and every
one that beareth fruit, he purifieth it, that it may bear more fruit.
3 Now ye are clean through the word which I have spoken to you.
4 Abide in me, and I in you.　As the branch cannot bear fruit of
itself, unless it abide in the vine, so neither *can* ye, unless ye
5 abide in me.　I am the vine, ye *are* the branches.　He that abideth
in me, and I in him, he beareth much fruit; but separate from me
6 ye can do nothing.　If any one abide not in me, he is cast out as a
branch, and is withered: and they gather and cast them into the
7 fire, and they are burned.　If ye abide in me, and my words abide
in you, ye shall ask whatsoever ye will, and it shall be done for
8 you.　Hereby is my Father glorified, that ye bear much fruit: so
9 shall ye be my disciples.　As the Father hath loved me, so have 1
10 also loved you.　Abide ye in my love.　If ye keep my commandments, ye shall abide in my love, even as I have kept my Father's
11 commandments, and abide in his love.　I have spoken these
things to you, that my joy might remain in you, and your joy
12 might be full.　This is my commandment, That ye love one an-
13 other, as I have loved you.　No one hath greater love than this,
14 that a man lay down his life for his friends.　Ye are my friends,
15 if ye do whatsoever I command you.　I no longer call you servants, for the servant knoweth not what his lord doth: but I have

---

XV. 1. *I am the true vine*—So *the true bread*, chap. vi, 32; that is, the most
excellent.

2. *Every one that beareth fruit, he purifieth*—*by obeying the truth*, 1 Pet. i, 22;
and by inward or outward sufferings, Heb. xii, 10, 11.　So purity and fruitfulness
help each other.　*That it may bear more fruit*—For this is one of the noblest
rewards God can bestow on former acts of obedience, to make us yet more holy,
and fit for farther and more eminent service.

3. *Ye are clean*—All of you, to whom I now speak, are purged from the guilt
and power of sin; *by the word*—Which, applied by the Spirit, is the grand instrument of purifying the soul.

4. *Abide in me*—Ye who are now pure by living faith, producing all holiness;
by which alone ye can be in me.

5. *I am the vine, ye are the branches*—Our Lord in this whole passage speaks
of no branches but such as are, or at least were once, united to him by living faith.

6. *If any one abide not in me*—By living faith; not by Church communion
only.　He may thus abide in Christ, and be *withered* all the time, and *cast into
the fire* at last.　*He is cast out*—Of the vineyard, the invisible Church. Therefore
he was in it once.

7. *If ye abide in me, ye shall ask*—Prayers themselves are a fruit of faith, and
they produce more fruit.

8. *So shall ye be my disciples*—Worthy of the name.　To be a disciple of Christ
is both the foundation and height of Christianity.

9. *Abide ye in my love*—Keep your place in my affection.　See that ye do not
forfeit that invaluable blessing.　How needless a caution, if it were impossible
for them not to abide therein?

10. *If ye keep my commandments, ye shall abide in my love*—On these terms,
and no other, ye shall remain the objects of my special affection.

11. *That my joy might remain in you*—The same joy which I feel in loving the
Father, and keeping his commandments.

12. *Your joy* will *be full, if ye* so *love one another*.

13. *Greater love*—To his friends.　He here speaks of them only.

14. *Ye are my friends, if ye do whatsoever I command you*—On this condition,
not otherwise.　A thunderbolt for Antinomianism!　Who then dares assert that
God's love does not at all depend on man's works?

called you friends : for all things that I have heard from my
16 Father, I have made known to you. Ye have not chosen me, but
I have chosen you, and appointed you that ye may go and bear
fruit, and that your fruit may remain; that whatsoever ye shall ask
17 of the Father in my name, he may give it you. This I command
you, That ye love one another.
18   If the world hate you, ye know it hated me before *it hated* you.
19 If ye were of the world, the world would love its own; but because
ye are not of the world, but I have chosen you out of the world,
20 therefore the world hateth you. Remember the word that I said
to you, * The servant is not greater than his lord. If they have
persecuted me, they will also persecute you : if they have kept my
21 saying, they will keep yours also. But all these things will they
do to you, for my name's sake, because they know not him that sent
22 me. If I had not come and spoken to them, they had not had sin ;
23 but now they have no excuse for their sin. He that hateth me,
24 hateth my Father also. If I had not done among them the works
which no other did, they had not had sin : but now have they seen
25 *them*, and yet hated both me and my Father. So that the word
which is written in their law is fulfilled, † They hated me without
26 a cause. But when the Comforter is come, whom I will send to
you from the Father, the Spirit of truth, who proceedeth from the
27 Father, he shall testify of me. Ye also shall testify, because ye
have been with me from the beginning.
XVI.   I have told you these things, that ye may not be offended.
2 They will put you out of the synagogues ; yea, the time cometh,

---

15. *All things*—Which might be of service to you.
16. *Ye*—My apostles, *have not chosen me, but I have chosen you*—As clearly
appears from the sacred history : *and appointed you, that ye may go and bear
fruit*—I have chosen and appointed you for this end, that ye may go and convert sinners : *and that your fruit may remain*—That the fruit of your labours
may remain to the end of the world ; yea, to eternity ; *that whatsoever ye shall
·ask*—The consequence of your going and bearing fruit will be, that all your
prayers will be heard.
19. *Because ye are not of the world, therefore the world hateth you*—Because
your maxims, tempers, actions, are quite opposite to theirs. For the very same
reason must the world in all ages hate those who are not of the world.
21. *All these things will they do to you, because they know not him that sent
me*—And in all ages and nations they who know not God will, *for this cause*,
hate and persecute those that do.
22. *They had not had sin*—Not in this respect.
23. *He that hateth me*—As every unbeliever doth. For as the love of God is
inseparable from faith, so is the hatred of God from unbelief.
26. *When the Comforter is come, whom I will send from the Father, the Spirit
of truth, who proceedeth from the Father, he shall testify of me*—The Spirit's
coming, and being *sent* by our Lord *from the Father, to testify of him*, are personal characters, and plainly distinguish him from the Father and the Son ; and
his title *as the Spirit of truth*, together with his *proceeding from the Father*, can
agree to none but a Divine person. And that he proceeds from the Son, as well
as from the Father, may be fairly argued from his being called *the Spirit of Christ*,
1 Pet. i, 11 ; and from his being here said to be *sent by Christ from the Father*, as
well as sent by the Father *in his name*.
XVI. 2. *The time cometh, that whosoever killeth you will think he doth God
service*—But, blessed be God, the time is so far past, that those who bear the name

* Chap. xiii, 16; Matt. x, 24 ; Luke vi, 40.   † Psa lxix, 4.

3 that whosoever killeth you will think he doth God service. These
things will they do, because they have not known the Father nor
4 me. But I have told you these things, that when the time shall
come, ye may remember I told you them. I did not tell you these
5 things at the beginning, because I was with you. But now i go
to him that sent me, and none of you asketh me, Whither goest
6 thou? But because I have told you these things, sorrow hath filled
7 your heart. But I tell you the truth; it is expedient for you that
I go: for if I go not, the Comforter will not come to you; but if I
8 depart, I will send him to you. And he coming will convince the
9 world of sin, and of righteousness, and of judgment: Of sin, be-
10 cause they believe not on me: Of righteousness, because I go to
11 my Father, and ye see me no more: Of judgment, because the
prince of this world is judged.
12   I have yet many things to say to you: but ye cannot bear them
13 now. But when he, the Spirit of truth, is come, he will guide you
into all the truth; for he will not speak of himself: but whatsoever he shall hear, he will speak; and he will show you the things
14 which are to come. He will glorify me; for he will take of mine,
15 and show it you. All things that the Father hath are mine: there-
16 fore I said, He will take of mine, and show it you. A little while

of Christ do not now generally suppose they do him service by killing each other
for a difference in opinion or mode of worship.

3. *They have not known the Father nor me*—This is the true root of persecution
in all its forms.

4. *I did not tell you these things at the beginning, because I was with you*—
To bear the chief shock in my own person, and to screen you from it.

5. *None of you asketh me*—Now when it is most seasonable. Peter did ask
this before, chap. xiii, 36.

7. *It is expedient for you*—In respect of the Comforter, ver. 7, &c, and of me,
ver. 16, &c, and of the Father, ver. 23, &c.

8. *He*—Observe his twofold office; toward the world, ver. 8, &c; toward believers, ver. 12, &c: *will convince*—All of *the world*—Who do not obstinately
resist, by your preaching and miracles, *of sin, and of righteousness, and of judgment*—He who is convinced *of sin* either accepts the *righteousness* of Christ, or
is *judged* with Satan. An abundant accomplishment of this we find in the *Acts
of the Apostles.*

9. *Of sin*—Particularly of unbelief, which is the confluence of all sins, and
binds them all down upon us.

10. *Of righteousness, because I go to my Father*—Which the Spirit will
testify, though ye do not then see me. But I could not go to him if I were
not righteous.

11. *The prince of this world is judged*—And in consequence thereof dethroned,
deprived of the power he had so long usurped over men. Yet those who reject
the deliverance offered them will remain slaves of Satan still.

12. *I have yet many things to say*—Concerning my passion, death, resurrection, and the consequences of it. These things we have, not in uncertain traditions, but in the Acts, the Epistles, and the Revelation. *But ye cannot bear them
now*—Both because of your littleness of faith, and your immoderate sorrow.

13. *When he is come*—It is universally allowed that the Father, Son, and Holy
Ghost dwell in all believers. And the internal agency of the Holy Ghost is generally admitted. That of the Father and the Son, as represented in this Gospel,
deserves our deepest consideration.

15. *All things that the Father hath are mine*—Could any creature say this?

16. *A little while and ye shall not see me*—When I am buried: *and again, a
little while, and ye shall see me*—When I am risen: *because I go to my Father*—
I die and rise again, in order to ascend to my Father.

and ye shall not see me ; and again, a little while and ye shall see
17 me, because I go to the Father. Then *some* of his disciples said
to each other, What is this that he saith to us ? A little while
and ye shall not see me ; and again, a little while and ye shall see
18 me ? And, Because I go to the Father ? They said therefore,
What is this that he saith, A little while ? We understand not
19 what he saith. Jesus knew they were desirous to ask him, and
said to them, Ye inquire among you of this, that I said, A little
while and ye shall not see me : and again, A little while and ye
20 shall see me. Verily, verily I say unto you, Ye will weep and
lament ; but the world will rejoice : ye will be sorrowful ; but your
21 sorrow shall be turned into joy. A woman when she is in travail
hath sorrow, because her hour is come : but when she hath
brought forth the child, she no longer remembereth the anguish,
22 for joy that a man is born into the world. And ye now therefore
have sorrow ; but I will see you again, and your heart shall rejoice,
23 and your joy no one taketh from you. And in that day ye shall
not question me about any thing. Verily, verily I say unto you,
Whatsoever ye shall ask the Father in my name, he will give you.
24 Hitherto ye have asked nothing in my name : ask, and ye shall
25 receive, that your joy may be full. I have spoken these things to
you in parables : but the time is coming when I will no longer
speak to you in parables, but will show you plainly the Father
26 At that day ye shall ask in my name : and I say not to you, that I
27 will pray the Father for you. For the Father himself loveth you,
because ye have loved me, and have believed that I came forth from
28 God. I came forth from the Father, and am come into the world :
again, I leave the world, and go to the Father.
29 His disciples say to him, Lo, now speakest thou plainly, and
30 speakest no parable. Now we are sure that thou knowest all
things, and needest not that any should question thee : by this we
31 believe that thou camest forth from God. Jesus answered, Ye

19. *Jesus said to them*—Preventing their question.

20. *Ye will weep and lament*—When ye see me dead ; *but your sorrow will be turned into joy*—When ye see me risen.

22. *Ye now therefore have sorrow*—This gives us no manner of authority to assert all believers *must* come into a state of darkness They never *need* lose either their peace, or love, or the witness that they are the children of God. They never *can* lose these, but either through sin, or ignorance, or vehement temptation, or bodily disorder.

23. *Ye shall not question me about any thing*—Which you do not now understand. You will not need to inquire of me ; for you will know all things clearly. *Whatsoever ye shall ask*—Knowledge, love, or any thing else, *he will give it*—Our Lord here gives us a charte blanche. Believer, write down what thou wilt. He had said, chap. xiv, 13, *I will do it,* where the discourse was of *glorifying the Father through the Son.* Here, speaking of the love of the Father to believers, he saith, *He will give* it.

24. *Hitherto ye have asked nothing in my name*—For they had asked him directly for all they wanted.

26. *At that day ye shall ask*—For true knowledge begets prayer. *And I say not that I will pray*—This in nowise implies that he will not : it means only, The Father himself now loves you, not only because of my intercession, but also because of the faith and love which he hath wrought in you.

30. *Thou knowest all things*—Even our hearts. Although no question is asked thee, yet thou answerest the thoughts of every one. *By this we believe that thou*

32 do now believe. *But* lo, the hour is coming, yea, is already come,
that ye will be scattered every one to his own, and shall leave me
33 alone: and yet I am not alone, for the Father is with me. I have
spoken these things to you, that ye may have peace in me. In the
world ye shall have tribulation; but take courage, I have overcome
the world.

XVII. These things spake Jesus, and lifted up his eyes to heaven,
and said, Father, the hour is come: glorify thy Son, that thy Son
2 also may glorify thee: As thou hast given him power over all
flesh, that he may give eternal life to all whom thou hast given
3 him. And this is life eternal, to know thee, the only true God,
4 and Jesus Christ, whom thou hast sent. I have glorified thee on
5 earth. I have finished the work which thou gavest me to do. And
now, Father, glorify thou me with thyself, with the glory which I
had with thee before the world was.

6 I have manifested thy name to the men whom thou hast given
7 me out of the world. Thine they were, and thou hast given them
me, and they have kept thy word. Now they know, that all
8 things whatsoever thou hast given me are of thee. For I have
given them the words which thou gavest me, and they have received

camest forth from God—They as it were echo back the words which he had spoken
in the 27th verse, implying, *We believe in God; we believe also in thee.*

Chap. xvii. In this chapter our Lord prays, 1. For himself, ver. 1-5. 2. For
the apostles, ver. 6-19; and again, ver. 24-26. 3. For all believers, ver. 20-23.
And 4. For the world, ver. 21-23. In his prayer he comprises all he had said
from chap. xiii, 31, and seals, as it were, all he had hitherto done, beholding things
past, present, and to come. This chapter contains the easiest words, and the
deepest sense of any in all the Scripture: yet is here no incoherent rhapsody,
but the whole is closely and exactly connected.

XVII. 1. *Father*—This simplicity of appellation highly became the only-begotten Son of God; to which a believer then makes the nearest approach, when he
is fullest of love and humble confidence. *The hour is come*—The appointed time
for it; *glorify thy Son*—The Son glorified the Father, both before and after his
own glorification. When he speaks to the Father he does not style himself the
Son of man.

2. *As thou hast given him power over all flesh*—This answers to *glorify thy
Son. That he may give eternal life,* &c.—This answers to *that thy Son may
glorify thee. To all whom thou hast given him*—To all believers. This is a clear
proof that Christ designed his sacrifice should avail for all: yea, that *all flesh,*
every man, should partake of everlasting life. For as the Father had *given him
power over all flesh,* so he *gave himself a ransom for all.*

3. *To know*—By loving, holy faith, *thee the only true God*—The only cause and
end of all things; not excluding the Son and the Holy Ghost, no more than the
Father is excluded from being Lord, 1 Cor. viii, 6; but the false gods of the heathens; *and Jesus Christ*—As their prophet, priest, and king: *this is life eternal*—It is both the way to, and the essence of, everlasting happiness.

4. *I have finished the work*—Thus have I glorified thee, laying the foundation
of thy kingdom on earth.

5. *The glory which I had*—He does not say *received*—He always had it, till he
emptied himself of it in the days of his flesh.

6. *I have manifested thy name*—All thy attributes; and in particular thy
paternal relation to believers; *to the men whom thou hast given me*—The apostles, and so ver. 12. *They were thine*—By creation, and by descent from Abraham. *And thou hast given them me*—By giving them faith in what I have
spoken. So ver. 9.

7. *Now they know that all things*—Which I have done and spoken, *are of
thee*—And consequently right and true.

8. *They have received them*—By faith.

them, and have known surely, that I came forth fiom thee, and
9 they have believed that thou hast sent me. I pray for them: I
pray not for the world, but for them whom thou hast given me;
10 for they are thine. And all things that are mine are thine, and
11 that are thine are mine; and I am glorified by them. And I
am no longer in the world, but these are in the world, and I come
to thee. Holy Father, keep through thy name them whom thou
12 hast given me, that they may be one, as we *are.* While I was with
them in the world I kept them through thy name. Those whom
thou hast given me I have guarded, and none of them is lost,
but the son of perdition,* that the Scripture might be fulfilled
13 And now I am coming to thee, and I speak these things in the
14 world, that they may have my joy fulfilled in them. I have given
them thy word, and the world hath hated them, because they are
15 not of the world, even as I am not of the world. I do not pray
that thou wouldest take them out of the world, but that thou wouldest
16 keep them from the evil one. They are not of the world, as I am
17 not of the world. Sanctify them through the truth: thy word is
18 truth. As thou hast sent me into the world, I also have sent them
19 into the world. And for their sakes I sanctify myself, that they
also may be sanctified through the truth.
20   Neither pray I for these alone, but for them also who will believe
21 on me through their word: That they all may be one; as thou,

---

9. *I pray not for the world*—Not in these petitions, which are adapted to the
state of believers only. (He prays for the world at the 21st and 23d verses, *that
they may believe—That they may know God hath sent him.*) This no more proves
that our Lord did not pray for the *world,* both before and afterward, than his
praying for the apostles alone, ver. 6–19, proves that he did not pray for *them
also which shall believe through their word,* ver. 20.

10. *All things that are mine are thine, and that are thine are mine*—These are
very high and strong expressions, too grand for any mere creature to use; as
implying that all things whatsoever, inclusive of the Divine nature, perfections,
and operations, are the common property of the Father and the Son. And this
is the original ground of that peculiar property, which both the Father and the
Son have in the persons who were given to Christ as Mediator; according to what
is said in the close of the verse, of his being *glorified by them;* namely, believing
in him, and so acknowledging his glory.

11. *Keep them through thy name*—Thy power, mercy, wisdom, *that they may
be one*—with us and with each other; one body, separate from the world: *as we
are*—By resemblance to us, though not equality.

12. *Those whom thou hast given me I have guarded, and none of them is lost,
but the son of perdition*—So one even of them whom God *had given him is lost.*
So far was even that decree from being unchangeable! *That the Scripture might
be fulfilled*—That is, whereby the Scripture was fulfilled. *The son of perdition*
signifies one that deservedly perishes; as *a son of death,* 2 Sam. xii, 5; *children
of hell,* Matt. xxiii, 15, and *children of wrath,* Eph. ii, 3, signify persons justly
obnoxious to death, hell, wrath.

13. *In the world*—That is, before I leave the world. *My joy*—The joy I feel
at going to the Father.

15. *That thou wouldest take them out of the world*—Not yet: *but that thou
wouldest keep them from the evil one*—Who reigns therein.

17. *Sanctify*—Consecrate them by the anointing of thy Spirit to their office,
and perfect them in holiness, by means of thy word.

19. *I sanctify myself*—I devote myself as a victim, to be sacrificed.

20. *For them who will believe*—In all ages.

21. *As thou art in me*—This also is to be understood in a way of similitude,

* Psalm cix, 8.

Father, *art* in me, and I in thee, that they also may be one in us ;
22 that the world may believe that thou hast sent me. And the glory
which thou hast given me, I have given them, that they may be one
23 as we are one : I in them, and thou in me, that they may be perfected in one ; and that the world may know, that thou hast sent
me, and hast loved them as thou hast loved me.
24 Father, I will that these also whom thou hast given me, be with
me where I am, that they may behold my glory which thou hast
given me ; for thou lovedst me before the foundation of the world.
25 Righteous Father, though the world hath not known thee, yet I
have known thee, and these have known that thou hast sent me.
26 And I have declared to them thy name, and will declare *it*, that
the love wherewith thou hast loved me may be in them, and I in
them.
XVIII. * Jesus having spoken these words, went forth with his disciples over the brook Kedron, where was a garden, into which he
2 entered and his disciples. † And Judas also, who betrayed him,
knew the place : for Jesus had often met there with his disciples.
3 Judas then having received a troop of soldiers, and officers from
the chief priests and Pharisees, cometh thither with lanterns, and
4 torches, and arms. Then Jesus knowing all things that were
coming upon him, going forth said to them, Whom seek ye ?
5 They answered him, Jesus of Nazareth. Jesus saith to them, I
6 am *he*. And Judas also, who betrayed him, stood with them. As

---

and not of sameness or equality. *That the world may believe*—Here Christ prays
for the world. Observe the sum of his whole prayer, 1. Receive me into thy own
and my glory ; 2. Let my apostles share therein ; 3. And all other believers :
4. And let all the world believe.

22. *The glory which thou hast given me, I have given them*—The glory of the
only begotten shines in all the sons of God. How great is the majesty of
Christians.

24. Here he returns to the apostles. *I will*—He asks, as having a right to be
heard, and prays, not as a servant, but a Son : *that they may behold my glory*—
Herein is the happiness of heaven, 1 John iii, 2.

25. *Righteous Father*—The admission of believers to God through Christ,
flows even from the justice of God.

26. *I have declared to them thy name*—Thy new, best name of love ; *that the
love wherewith thou hast loved me*—That thou and *thy love, and I* and my love,
may be in them—That they may love me with that love.

XVIII. 1. *A garden*—Probably belonging to one of his friends. He might
retire to this private place, not only for the advantage of secret devotion, but also
that the people might not be alarmed at his apprehension, nor attempt, in the
first sallies of their zeal, to rescue him in a tumultuous manner. Kedron was
(as the name signifies) a dark shady valley, on the east side of Jerusalem, between the city and the mount of Olives, through which a little brook ran, which
took its name from it. It was this brook, which David, a type of Christ, went
over with the people, weeping in his flight from Absalom.

3. *A troop of soldiers*—A cohort of Roman foot.

6. *As soon as he said, I am he, they went backward and fell to the ground*—
How amazing is it, that they should renew the assault, after so sensible an experience both of his power and mercy ! But probably the priests among them
might persuade themselves and their attendants, that this also was done by Beelzebub ; and that it was through the providence of God, not the indulgence of Jesus, that they received no farther damage.

* Matt. xxvi, 30 ; Mark xiv, 26 ; Luke xxii, 39.   † Matt. xxvi, 30 ; Mark xiv, 43 ;
Luke xxii, 47.

7 soon as he said to them, I am *he*, they went backward and fell to
8 the ground. He asked them again, Whom seek ye? And they
said, Jesus of Nazareth. Jesus answered, I have told you, I am *he*:
9 if therefore ye seek me, let these go : That the * saying might be
fulfilled which he had spoken, Of them whom thou hast given me,
10 I have lost none. Then Simon Peter, having a sword, drew it, and
smote the high priest's servant, and cut off his right ear. The
11 servant's name was Malchus. Then said Jesus to Peter, Put up
the sword into its scabbard. The cup which my Father hath given
me, shall I not drink it?
12 † Then the soldiers and the captain, and officers of the Jews
13 took Jesus and bound him. And led him away to Annas first, (for
he was father-in-law to Caiaphas, who was high priest that year.)
14 Caiaphas was he who had counselled the Jews, that it was expe-
15 dient one man should die for the people. Now Simon Peter followed Jesus, and another disciple. That disciple was known to
the high priest, and went with Jesus into the palace of the high
16 priest. But Peter stood at the door without : therefore the other
disciple, who was known to the high priest, went out and spake to
17 her that kept the door, and brought in Peter. Then saith the maid
who kept the door to Peter, Art not thou also *one* of this man's dis-
18 ciples? He saith, I am not. And the servants and officers having
made a fire of coals (for it was cold) stood and warmed themselves :
19 and Peter stood with them and warmed himself. Then the high
20 priest asked Jesus of his disciples and of his doctrine. Jesus answered him, I spake openly to the world ; I was continually teaching in the synagogue and in the temple, whither all the Jews
21 resort, and in secret have I said nothing. Why askest thou me?
Ask them that heard me, what I said to them : behold they know
22 what I said. When he had said thus, one of the officers, who stood
by, gave Jesus a blow, saying, Answerest thou the high priest so?
23 Jesus answered, If I have spoken evil, bear witness of the evil :
24 but if well, why smitest thou me? (Now Annas had sent him
bound to Caiaphas the high priest.)

8. *If ye seek me, let these* (my disciples) *go*—It was an eminent instance of his
power over the spirits of men, that they so far obeyed this word, as not to seize
even Peter, when he had cut off the ear of Malchus.
10. *Then Simon Peter*—No other evangelist names him. Nor could they
safely. But St. John, writing after his death, might do it without any such inconvenience.
13. Annas had been high priest before his son-in-law Caiaphas. And though
he had for some time resigned that office, yet they paid so much regard to his
age and experience, that they brought Christ to Annas first. But we do not read
of any thing remarkable which passed at the house of Annas ; for which reason
his being carried thither is omitted by the other evangelists.
17. *Art thou also*—As well as the others, *one of this man's disciples*—She does
not appear to have asked with any design to hurt him.
20. *I spake openly*—As to the manner : *continually*—As to the time : *in the
synagogue and temple*—As to the place. *In secret have I said nothing*—No
point of doctrine which I have not taught in public.
21. *Why askest thou me*—Whom thou wilt not believe?
22. *Answerest thou the high priest so?*—With so little reverence?
24. *Now Annas had sent him to Caiaphas*—As is implied ver. 13. *Bound*—Being still bound, ver. 12.
* Chap. xxii, 12.   † Matt. xxvi, 57 ; Mark xiv, 53 ; Luke xxii, 54

25 And Simon Peter was standing and warming himself. They
said to him, Art not thou also one of his disciples? He denied and
26 said, I am not. One of the servants of the high priest (being kins-
27 man to him whose ear Peter had cut off) said, Did not I see thee
in the garden with him? Peter denied again, and immediately the
cock crew.
28 * Then they led Jesus from Caiaphas to the governor's palace,
and it was early: and they went not into the palace themselves,
29 that they might not be defiled, but might eat the passover. Pilate
therefore went out to them, and said, What accusation do ye bring
30 against this man? They answered and said to him, If he were not
31 a malefactor, we should not have delivered him to thee. Then said
Pilate to them, Take ye him, and judge him according to your law.
The Jews said to him, It is not lawful for us to put any man to death:
32 So the † saying of Jesus was fulfilled which he spake, signifying
33 what death he should die. Then Pilate returned into the palace,
and called Jesus, and said to him, Art thou the king of the Jews?
34 Jesus answered him, Sayest thou this of thyself? or did others tell
35 it thee of me? Pilate answered, Am I a Jew? thy own nation, even
36 the chief priests, have delivered thee to me. What hast thou done?
Jesus answered, My kingdom is not of this world: if my kingdom
were of this world, my servants would have fought, that I might
not be delivered to the Jews: but my kingdom is not from hence.
37 Pilate said to him, Art thou a king then? Jesus answered, Thou
sayest. I am a king. To this end was I born, and for this cause
came I into the world, that I might bear witness to the truth.
38 Every one that is of the truth, heareth my voice. Pilate saith to
him, What is truth? And having said this, he went out again to
39 the Jews, and saith to them, I find no fault in him. But ye have
a custom that I should release to you one at the passover: will ye
40 therefore that I release to you the king of the Jews? Then cried
they all again, saying, Not this man, but Barabbas. Now Barabbas
was a robber.

28. *They went not into the palace themselves, lest they should be defiled*—By
going into a house which was not purged from leaven, Deut. xvi, 4.
31. *It is not lawful for us to put any man to death*—The power of inflicting
capital punishment had been taken from them that very year. So *the sceptre* was
departed from Judah, and transferred to the Romans.
32. *Signifying what death he should die*—For crucifixion was not a Jewish,
but a Roman punishment. So that had he not been condemned by the Roman
governor, he could not have been crucified.
36. *My kingdom is not of this world*—Is not an external, but a spiritual kingdom; *that I might not be delivered to the Jews*—Which Pilate had already attempted to do, ver. 31, and afterward actually did, chap. xix, 16.
37. *Thou sayest*—The truth. *To this end was I born*—Speaking of his human
origin: his Divine was above Pilate's comprehension. Yet it is intimated in the
following words, *I came into the world, that I might witness to the truth*—Which
was both declared to the Jews, and in the process of his passion to the princes
of the Gentiles also. *Every one that is of the truth*—That is, a lover of it, *heareth
my voice*—A universal maxim. Every sincere lover of truth will hear him, so as
to understand and practise what he saith.
38. *What is truth?*—Said Pilate, a courtier; perhaps meaning what signifies
truth? Is that a thing worth hazarding your life for? So he left him presently,
to plead with the Jews for him, looking upon him as an innocent but weak man

* Matt. xxvii, 2; Mark xv, 1; Luke xxiii, 1. † Chap. iii, 14.

XIX. * Then Pilate therefore took Jesus and scourged *him*. And
2 the soldiers having platted a crown of thorns, put *it* on his head,
3 and put on him a purple robe, And said, Hail, king of the Jews.
4 And they smote him on the cheeks. Pilate went out again, and
saith to them, Lo, I bring him forth to you, that ye may know I
5 find no fault in him. Then Jesus came forth, wearing the crown
of thorns, and the purple robe. And he saith to them, Behold the
6 man. But when the chief priests and the officers saw him, they
7 cried out saying, Crucify, crucify him. Pilate saith to them, Take
ye him and crucify *him*; for I find no fault in him. The Jews answered him, We have a law, and by our law he ought to die, be-
8 cause he made himself the Son of God. When Pilate heard that
9 saying, he was the more afraid, And returned into the palace, and
saith to Jesus, Whence art thou? But Jesus gave him no answer.
10 Then Pilate saith to him, Speakest thou not to me? Knowest thou
not that I have power to crucify thee, and have power to release
11 thee? Jesus answered, Thou couldst have no power over me, unless it were given thee from above: therefore he that delivered me
12 to thee hath the greater sin. Upon this Pilate sought to release
him: but the Jews cried out saying, If thou release this man, thou
art not a friend to Cesar. Whosoever maketh himself a king,
13 speaketh against Cesar. Pilate hearing this saying, brought Jesus forth, and sat on the judgment seat, in a place called the pave-
14 ment, but in Hebrew, Gabbatha; (it was the preparation of the
passover, and about the third hour;) and saith to the Jews, Behold
15 your king. But they cried out, Away *with him*, away *with him*, crucify him. Pilate saith to them, Shall I crucify your king? The
16 chief priests answered, We have no king but Cesar. Then delivered he him to them to be crucified.
17 † And they took Jesus and led him away. And he bearing his
cross, went forth to the place called *the place* of a skull, which is
18 called in Hebrew, Golgotha; Where they crucified him, and two
19 others with him, one on each side, and Jesus in the midst. And

---

XIX. 7. *By our law he ought to die, because he made himself the Son of God—*
Which they understood in the highest sense, and therefore accounted blasphemy.

8. *He was the more afraid*—He seems to have been afraid before of shedding
innocent blood.

9. *Whence art thou?*—That is, whose son art thou?

11. *Thou couldst have no power over me*—For I have done nothing to expose
me to the power of any magistrate. *Therefore he that delivered me to thee,*
namely, Caiaphas, knowing this, is more blamable than thou.

13. *Pilate sat down on the judgment seat*—Which was then without the palace,
in a place called, in Greek, *the pavement,* on account of a beautiful piece of
Mosaic work, with which the floor was adorned: *but in Hebrew, Gabbatha*—Or
the high place, because it stood on an eminence, so that the judge sitting on his
throne might be seen and heard by a considerable number of people.

14. *It was the preparation of the passover*—For this reason both the Jews and
Pilate were desirous to bring the matter to a conclusion. Every Friday was
called the preparation, (namely, for the Sabbath.) And as often as the passover
fell on a Friday, that day was called the preparation of the passover.

17. *Bearing his cross*—Not the whole cross, (for that was too large and heavy,)
but the transverse beam of it, to which his hands were afterward fastened.
This they used to make the person to be executed carry.

* Matt. xxvii, 26; Mark xv, 15.   † Matt. xxvii, 31; Mark xv, 20; Luke xxiii, 26.

Pilate wrote an inscription also, and put it on the cross: and the writing was, JESUS OF NAZARETH THE KING OF THE
20 JEWS. Many of the Jews read this inscription ; for the place where Jesus was crucified was near the city : and it was written in
21 Hebrew, *and* Greek, *and* Latin. Then said the chief priests to Pilate, Write not, The king of the Jews; but that he said I am the
22 king of the Jews. Pilate answered, What I have written, I have
23 written. And the soldiers, when they had crucified Jesus, took his garments and made four parts, to every soldier a part, and also *his* vesture : now the vesture was without seam, woven from the
24 top throughout. They said therefore one to another, Let us not rend it, but cast lots for it, whose it shall be ; that the scripture might be fulfilled which saith, * They parted my garments among them, and cast lots for my vesture. These things therefore the soldiers did.
25 Now there stood by the cross of Jesus, his mother, and his mother's sister, Mary *the wife* of Cleopas, and Mary Magdalene.
26 Jesus therefore seeing his mother, and the disciple standing by
27 whom he loved, saith to his mother, Woman, behold thy son. Then saith he to the disciple, Behold thy mother. And from that hour the disciple took her to his own home.
28 After this, Jesus knowing that all things were now accomplished,
29 that the scripture might be fulfilled, saith, I thirst. Now there was set a vessel full of vinegar. And filling a sponge with † vinegar,
30 and putting it on *a stalk of* hyssop, they put it to his mouth. When Jesus had taken the vinegar, he said, It is finished, and bowing the head, he delivered up *his* spirit.
31 Now because it was the preparation, lest the bodies should remain upon the cross on the Sabbath (for that Sabbath was a great

<hr>

19. *Jesus of Nazareth, the king of the Jews*—Undoubtedly these were the very words, although the other evangelists do not express them at large.

20. *It was written in Latin*—For the majesty of the Roman empire ; in *Hebrew* —Because it was the language of the nation ; *and in Greek*—For the information of the Hellenists, who spoke that language, and came in great numbers to the feast.

22. *What I have written, I have written*—That shall stand.

23. *The vesture*—The upper garment.

24. *They parted my garments among them*—No circumstance of David's life bore any resemblance to this, or to several other passages in the 22d Psalm. So that in this scripture, as in some others, the prophet seems to have been thrown into a preternatural ecstacy, wherein, personating the Messiah, he spoke barely what the Spirit dictated, without any regard to himself.

25. *His mother's sister*—But we do not read she had any brother. She was her father's heir, and as such transmitted the right of the kingdom of David to Jesus : *Mary, the wife of Cleopas*—Called likewise Alpheus, the father, as Mary was the mother of James, and Joses, and Simon, and Judas

27. *Behold thy mother*—To whom thou art now to perform the part of a son in my place, a peculiar honour which Christ conferred on him. *From that hour* —From the time of our Lord's death.

29. *A stalk of hyssop*—Which in those countries grows exceeding large and strong.

30. *It is finished*—My suffering: the purchase of man's redemption. *He delivered up his spirit*—To God, Matt. xxvii, 50.

31. *Lest the bodies should remain on the cross on the Sabbath*—Which they

* Psalm xxii. 28.   † Psalm lxix, 21.

day) the Jews besought Pilate, that their legs might be broken, and
32 they might be taken away.   Then came the soldiers, and brake
the legs of the first, and of the other, who was crucified with him.
33 But coming to Jesus, when they saw he was dead already, they
34 brake not his legs.   But one of the soldiers pierced his side with a
35 spear, and forthwith there came out blood and water.   And he
that saw hath testified *it*, and his testimony is true, and he know-
36 eth that he saith true, that ye also may believe.   For these things
37 were done that the scripture might be fulfilled, * A bone of it shall
not be broken.   And again another scripture saith, † They shall
look on him whom they have pierced.

38   And after these things, Joseph of Arimathea (being a disciple of
Jesus, but secretly, for fear of the Jews) asked Pilate leave to take
away the body of Jesus.   And Pilate gave him leave.   He came
39 therefore and took the body of Jesus.   And Nicodemus also
came (who at first had come to Jesus by night) bringing a mixture
40 of myrrh and aloes, about a hundred pounds.   So they took the
body of Jesus, and wrapped it in linen clothes with the spices, as
41 the manner of the Jews is to bury.   Now in the place where he
was crucified, there was a garden, and in the garden a new sepul-
42 chre, in which no man had ever been laid.   There therefore they
laid Jesus, because of the preparation day of the Jews ; for the
sepulchre was nigh.

XX.   ‡ The first day of the week cometh Mary Magdalene early,
while it was yet dark, to the sepulchre, and seeth the stone taken
2 away from the sepulchre.   Then she runneth and cometh to Simon Peter, and to the other disciple whom Jesus loved, and saith

---

would have accounted a profanation of any Sabbath, but of that in particular
For that Sabbath was a great day—Being not only a Sabbath, but the second day
of the feast of unleavened bread (from whence they reckoned the weeks to pentecost :) and also the day for presenting and offering the sheaf of new corn; so
that it was a treble solemnity.

34. *Forthwith there came out blood and water*—It was strange, seeing he was
dead, that blood should come out ; more strange, that water also ; and most
strange of all, that both should come out immediately, at one time, and yet distinctly.   It was pure and true water, as well as pure and true blood.   The as-
severation of the beholder and testifier of it, shows both the truth and greatness
of the miracle and mystery.

35. *His testimony is true*—Valid, unexceptionable.   *And he knoweth*—And his
conscience beareth him witness, that he testifieth this for no other end, than
that ye may believe.

36. *A bone of it shall not be broken*—This was originally spoken of the paschal
lamb, an eminent type of Christ.

37. *They shall look on him whom they have pierced*—He was pierced by the soldier's spear.   They who have occasioned his sufferings by their sins (and who
has not ?) *shall* either *look upon him* in this world with penitential sorrow : or
with terror, when he cometh in the clouds of heaven, Rev. i, 7.

38. *Joseph of Arimathea asked Pilate—And Nicodemus also came*—Acknow
ledging Christ, when even his chosen disciples forsook him.   In that extremity
Joseph was no longer afraid, Nicodemus no longer ashamed.

41. *In the place where he was crucified*—There was a garden in the same tract
of land : but the cross did not stand in the garden.

42. *Because of the preparation*—That is, they chose the rather to lay him in
that *sepulchre* which was *nigh*, because it was the day before the Sabbath, which
also was drawing to an end, so that they had no time to carry him far.

* Exod. xii, 46.   † Zech. xii, 10.   ‡ Matt. xxviii, 1 ; Mark xvi, 1 ; Luke xxiv, 1.

to them They have taken away the Lord out of the sepulchre, and
3 we know not where they have laid him. Then Peter went out and
4 the other disciple, and came to the sepulchre. They both ran together, but the other disciple outran Peter, and came first to the
5 sepulchre. And stooping down, he seeth the linen clothes lying :
6 yet went he not in. Then cometh Simon Peter following him, and
7 went into the sepulchre, and seeth the linen clothes lie, And the
napkin that had been about his head, not lying with the linen
8 clothes, but folded up in a place by itself. Then the other disciple
who came first to the sepulchre, went in ; and he saw and be-
9 lieved. For as yet they knew not the scripture, that he must
10 rise again from the dead. Then the disciples went home again.
11 * But Mary stood without at the sepulchre weeping. And as
12 she wept, she stooped down into the sepulchre, and seeth two angels in white sitting, where the body of Jesus had laid, one at the
13 head, and one at the feet. And they say to her, Woman, why
weepest thou ? She saith to them, They have taken away my Lord,
14 and I know not where they have laid him. And having said this
she turned herself back, and seeth Jesus standing, but knew not
15 that it was Jesus. Jesus saith to her, Woman, why weepest thou ?
Whom seekest thou ? She supposing him to be the gardener, saith
to him, Sir, if thou hast borne him hence, tell me where thou hast
16 laid him, and I will take him away. Jesus saith to her, Mary!
17 She turning, saith to him, Rabboni ; that is, Master. Jesus saith
to her; Touch me not ; for I am not yet ascended to my Father.
But go to my brethren, and say to them, I ascend to my Father
8 and your Father, and to my God, and your God. Mary Magdalene
cometh and telleth the disciples that she had seen the Lord, and
that he had spoken these things to her.
9 † The same day, the first day of the week, at evening, the doors
being shut, where the disciples were assembled for fear of the Jews,
Jesus came and stood in the midst, and saith to them, Peace be

XX. 3. *Peter went out*—Of the city.
6. *Peter seeth the linen clothes lie—and the napkin folded up*—The angels who
ministered to him when he rose, undoubtedly folded up the napkin and linen
clothes.
8. *He saw*—That the body was not there, *and believed*—That they had taken
it away as Mary said.
9. *For as yet*—They had no thought of his rising again.
10. *They went home*—Not seeing what they could do farther.
11. *But Mary stood*—With more constancy.
16. *Jesus saith to her, Mary !*—With his usual voice and accent.
17. *Touch me not*—Or rather, *Do not cling to me* (for she held him by the feet,)
Matt. xxviii, 9. Detain me not now. You will have other opportunities of conversing with me. For *I am not ascended to my Father*—I have not yet left the
world. *But go* immediately *to my brethren*—Thus does he intimate in the strongest manner the forgiveness of their fault, even without ever mentioning it.
These exquisite touches, which every where abound in the evangelical writings,
show how perfectly Christ knew our frame. *I ascend*—He anticipates it in his
thoughts, and so speaks of it as a thing already present. To *my Father and your
Father, to my God and your God*—This uncommon expression shows that the
only-begotten Son has all kind of fellowship with God. And a fellowship with
God the Father, some way resembling his own, he bestows upon his brethren.
Yet he does not say, *Our God:* for no creature can be raised to an equality with

20 unto you. And having said this he showed them his hands and his side. Then were the disciples glad, when they saw the Lord

21 The said Jesus to them again, Peace be unto you. As the Father

22 hath sent me, even so send I you. And having said this, he breathed on *them*, and saith to them, Receive ye the Holy Ghost.

23 Whose soever sins ye remit, they are remitted to them ; and whose soever sins ye retain, they are retained.

24 But Thomas called Didymus, one of the twelve, was not with

25 them when Jesus came. The other disciples therefore said to him, We have seen the Lord. But he said to them, Unless I see the print of the nails in his hands, and put my finger into the place of the nails, and my hand into his side, I will not believe.

26 And after eight days his disciples were again within, and Thomas with them. Jesus cometh, the doors being shut, and stood in

27 the midst, and said, Peace be unto you. Then said he to Thomas, Reach hither thy finger, and behold my hands, and reach hither thy hand, and put it upon my side, and be not faithless, but believ-

28 ing. And Thomas answered and said to him, My Lord, and my

29 God. Jesus saith to him, Thomas, because thou hast seen me, thou hast believed: happy *are* they that have not seen, and yet have believed.

30 And Jesus wrought many other miracles also, in the presence

31 of his disciples, which are not written in this book. But these are

him : but *my God and your God :* intimating that the Father is his in a singular and incommunicable manner ; and ours through him, in such a kind as a creature is capable of.

21. *Peace be unto you*—This is the foundation of the mission of a true Gospel minister, peace in his own soul, 2 Cor. iv, 1. *As the Father hath sent me, so send I you*—Christ was the apostle of the Father, Heb. iii, 1. Peter and the rest, the apostles of Christ.

22. *He breathed on them*—New life and vigour, *and saith*, as ye receive this breath out of my mouth, so *receive ye* the Spirit out of my fulness : the *Holy Ghost* influencing you in a peculiar manner, to fit you for your great embassy. This was an earnest of pentecost.

23. *Whose soever sins ye remit*—(According to the tenor of the Gospel, that is, supposing them to repent and believe) *they are remitted, and whose soever sins ye retain* (supposing them to remain impenitent) *they are retained.* So far is plain. But here arises a difficulty. Are not the sins of one who truly repents, and unfeignedly believes in Christ, *remitted*, without sacerdotal absolution ? And are not the sins of one who does not repent or believe, *retained* even with it ? What then does this commission imply ? Can it imply any more than, 1. A power of *declaring* with authority the Christian terms of pardon ; whose sins are *remitted* and whose *retained* ? As in our daily form of absolution ; and 2. A power of inflicting and remitting ecclesiastical censures ? That is, of excluding from, and re-admitting into, a Christian congregation.

26. *After eight days*—On the next *Sunday.*

28. *And Thomas said, My Lord and my God*—The disciples had said, We have seen the Lord. *Thomas* now not only acknowledges him to be the Lord, as he had done before, and to be risen, as his fellow disciples had affirmed, but also confesses his Godhead, and that more explicitly than any other had yet done. And all this he did without putting his hand upon his side.

30. *Jesus wrought many miracles, which are not written in this book*—Of St. John, nor indeed of the other evangelists

31. *But these things are written that ye may believe*—That ye may be confirmed in believing. Faith cometh sometimes by reading ; though ordinarily by *hearing*.

written, that ye may believe that Jesus is the Christ, the Son of
God, and that believing ye may have life through his name

XXI. After these things Jesus manifested himself again to the
2 disciples at the sea of Tiberias; he manifested *himself* thus ; There
were together Simon Peter, and Thomas called Didymus, and Nathanael of Cana in Galilee, and the *sons* of Zebedee, and two other
3 of his disciples. Simon Peter saith to them, I go a fishing. They
say to him, We also go with thee. They went out and entered
4 into the vessel, but caught nothing that night. When the morning
was come, Jesus stood on the shore ; but the disciples knew not
5 that it was Jesus. Then said Jesus to them, Children, have ye
6 any meat? They answered him, No. And he said to them, Cast
your net on the right side of the vessel, and ye shall find. They
cast, therefore, and now they were not able to draw it, for the mul-
7 titude of fishes. Then the disciple whom Jesus loved saith to
Peter, It is the Lord. Simon Peter hearing that it was the Lord,
girt on his upper coat (for he was stript) and threw himself into the
8 sea. And the other disciples came in the vessel (for they were not
far from land, about two hundred cubits) drawing the net *full* of fishes
9 When they came to land they see a fire of coals there, and fish laid
10 thereon, and bread. Jesus saith to them, Bring of the fishes which
11 ye have taken now. Simon Peter went on board, and drew the
net to land, full of great fishes, a hundred and fifty and three : and
12 though there were so many, the net was not broken. Jesus saith
to them, Come ye *and* dine. And none of the disciples presumed
13 to ask him, Who art thou? knowing that it was the Lord. Jesus
then cometh and taketh bread, and giveth to them, and fish likewise.
14 This was the third time that Jesus showed himself to his disciples,
after he was risen from the dead.
15 When they had dined, Jesus saith to Simon Peter, Simon, *son*
of Jonah, lovest thou me more than these *do?* He saith to him,
Yea, Lord, thou knowest that I love thee. He saith to him, Feed
16 my lambs. He saith to him again, the second time, Simon, *son* of

XXI. 2. *There were together*—At home, in one house.
4. *They knew not that it was Jesus*—Probably their eyes were holden.
6. *They were not able to draw it for the multitude of fishes*—This was not only
a demonstration of the power of our Lord, but a kind supply for them and their
families, and such as might be of service to them, when they waited afterward
in Jerusalem. It was likewise an emblem of the great success which should
attend them as *fishers of men.*
7. *Peter girt on his upper coat (for he was stript* of it before)—Reverencing the
presence of his Lord: *and threw himself into the sea*—To swim to him immediately. The love of Christ draws men through fire and water.
12. *Come ye and dine*—Our Lord needed not food. *And none presumed*—To
ask a needless question.
14. *The third time*—That he appeared to so many of the apostles together.
15. *Simon, son of Jonah*—The appellation Christ had given him, when he made
that glorious confession, Matt. xvi, the remembrance of which might make him
more deeply sensible of his late denial of him whom he had so confessed. *Lovest
thou me?*—Thrice our Lord asks him, who had denied him thrice : *more than
these*—Thy fellow disciples *do?*—Peter thought so once, Matt. xxvi, 33, but he
now answers only—*I love thee*, without adding *more than these. Thou knowest*—
He had now learnt by sad experience that Jesus knew his heart. *My lambs*—
The weakest and tenderest of the flock.

Jonah, lovest thou me? He saith to him, Yea, Lord, thou knowest
17 that I love thee. He saith to him, Feed my sheep   He saith to
him the third time, Simon, *son* of Jonah, lovest thou me? Peter was
grieved, because he said to him the third time, Lovest thou me?
And he said to him, Lord, thou knowest all things ; thou knowest
18 that I love thee. Jesus saith to him, Feed my sheep: Verily, verily I say unto thee, when thou wast young, thou didst gird thyself,
and walk whither thou wouldest: but when thou shalt be old,
thou shalt stretch out thy hands, and another shall gird thee, and
19 carry *thee* whither thou wouldest not. This he said, signifying by
20 what death he should glorify God. And having said this, he saith
to him, Follow me. Peter turning about, seeth the disciple
whom Jesus loved following, who also leaned on his breast at
21 supper, and said, Lord, who is he that betrayeth thee? Peter
22 seeing him, saith to Jesus, Lord, and what *shall* this man *do?*
Jesus saith to him, If I will that he tarry till I come, what *is it* to
23 thee? Follow thou me. Then went this saying abroad among
the brethren, that that disciple should not die. Yet Jesus did
not say to him, That he should not die: but, If I will that he tarry
till I come, what *is it* to thee?
24   This is the disciple who testifieth of these things, and wrote these
25 things: and we know that his testimony is true. And there are also
many other things which Jesus did, which, if they were to be writ
ten particularly, I suppose that even the world itself would not
contain the books that were written.

17. *Because he said the third time*—As if he did not believe him.
18. *When thou art old*—He lived about thirty-six years after this : *another shall
gird thee*—They were tied to the cross till the nails were driven in ; *and shall
carry thee*—With the cross: *whither thou wouldest not*—According to nature ; to
the place where the cross was set up.
19. *By what death he should glorify God*—It is not only by acting, but chiefly
by suffering, that the saints glorify God. *Follow me*—Showing hereby likewise
what death he should die.
20. *Peter turning*—As he was walking after Christ. *Seeth the disciple whom
Jesus loved following him*—There is a peculiar spirit and tenderness in this plain
passage. Christ orders St. Peter to follow him in token of his readiness to be
crucified in his cause. St. John stays not for the call ; he rises and follows him
too ; but says not one word of his own love or zeal. He chose that the action
only should speak this ; and even when he records the circumstance, he tells us
not what that action meant, but with great simplicity relates the fact only. If
here and there a generous heart sees and emulates it, be it so ; but he is not
solicitous that men should admire it. It was addressed to his beloved Master,
and it was enough that he understood it.
22. *If I will that he tarry*—Without dying, *till I come*—To judgment. Certainly he did tarry, till Christ came to destroy Jerusalem. And who can tell,
when or how he died? *What is that to thee?*—Who art to follow me long before.
23. *The brethren*—That is, the Christians. Our Lord himself taught them
that appellation, chap. xx, 17. *Yet Jesus did not say to him, that he should not
die*—Not expressly. And St. John himself, at the time of writing his Gospel,
seems not to have known clearly, whether he should die or not.
24. *This is the disciple who testifieth*—Being still alive after he had *wrote. And
we know that his testimony is true*—The Church added these words to St. John's
Gospel, as Tertius did those to St. Paul's Epistle to the Romans, chap. xvi, 22.
25. *If they were to be written particularly*—Every fact, and all the circumstances of it. *I suppose*—This expression, which softens the hyperbole, shows
that St. John wrote this verse.

NOTES

ON

THE ACTS OF THE APOSTLES.

This book, in which St. Luke records the actions of the apostles, particularly of St. Peter and St. Paul, (whose companion in travel he was,) is as it were the centre between the Gospel and the Epistles. It contains, after a very brief recapitulation of the evangelical history, a continuation of the history of Christ, the event of his predictions, and a kind of supplement to what he had before spoken to his disciples, by the Holy Ghost now given unto them. It contains also the seeds, and first stamina of all those things, which are enlarged upon in the epistles.

The Gospels treat of Christ the head. The Acts show that the same things befell his body; which is animated by his Spirit, persecuted by the world, defended and exalted by God.

In this book is shown the Christian doctrine, and the method of applying it to Jews, heathens, and believers; that is, to those who are to be converted, and those who are converted: the hinderances of it in particular men, in several kinds of men, in different ranks and nations: the propagation of the Gospel, and that grand revolution among both Jews and heathens: the victory thereof, in spite of all opposition, from all the power, malice, and wisdom of the whole world, spreading from one chamber into temples, houses, streets, markets, fields, inns, prisons, camps, courts, chariots, ships, villages, cities, islands: to Jews, heathens, magistrates, generals, soldiers, eunuchs, captives, slaves, women, children, sailors: to Athens, and at length to Rome.

THE PARTS OF IT ARE SEVEN:

THE ACTS.

1 THE former treatise have I composed, O Theophilus, of all things
2 which Jesus began both to do and to teach, Until the day he was
taken up, after having through the Holy Ghost given command-
3 ment to the apostles whom he had chosen : To whom also he presented himself alive, after his passion, by many infallible proofs,
being seen by them forty days, and speaking of the things pertain-
4 ing to the kingdom of God. And having assembled *them* together,
he commanded them not to depart from Jerusalem, but to wait for
the promise of the Father, which, *saith he*, ye have heard from me.
5 For John indeed baptized with water; but ye shall be baptized with
6 the Holy Ghost not many days hence. And when they were come
together, they asked him, saying, Lord, dost thou at this time
7 restore the kingdom to Israel? But he said to them, It is not for
you to know the times or the seasons which the Father hath put in
8 his own power. But ye shall receive power, the Holy Ghost being
come upon you, and shall be witnesses to me, both in Jerusalem,
and in all Judea, and Samaria, and to the uttermost part of the earth.
9 And having spoken these things, while they beheld, he was taken
10 up, and a cloud received him from their sight. And while they
were steadfastly looking up to heaven, as he went up, behold two
11 men, in white apparel, stood by them, Who also said, Ye men of

---

Verse 1. *The former treatise*—In that important season which reached from
the resurrection of Christ to his ascension, *the former treatise* ends, and this
begins : this describing the Acts of the Holy Ghost, (by the apostles,) as that does
the acts of Jesus Christ. *Of all things*—In a summary manner: *which Jesus
began to do—until the day*—That is, of all things which Jesus did from the beginning till that day.

2. *After having given commandment*—In the 3d verse St. Luke expresses in
general terms what Christ said to his apostles during those *forty days.* But in
the 4th and following verses he declares what he said on the day of his ascension.
He had brought his former account down to that day ; and from that day begins
the Acts of the Apostles.

3. *Being seen by them forty days*—That is, many times during that space.
And speaking of the things pertaining to the kingdom of God—Which was the
sum of all his discourses with them before his passion also.

4. *Wait for the promise of the Father, which ye have heard from me*—When he
was with them a little before, as it is recorded, Luke xxiv, 49.

5. *Ye shall be baptized with the Holy Ghost*—And so are all true believers to
the end of the world. But the extraordinary gifts of the Holy Ghost also are
here promised.

6. *Dost thou at this time*—At the time thou now speakest of? *not many days
hence? restore the kingdom to Israel?*—They still seemed to dream of an outward,
temporal kingdom, in which the Jews should have dominion over all nations. It
seems they came in a body, having before concerted the design, to ask when this
kingdom would come.

7. *The times or the seasons—Times*, in the language of the Scriptures, denote
a longer ; *seasons*, a shorter space. *Which the Father hath put in his own power*—
To be revealed when and to whom it pleaseth him.

8. *But ye shall receive power—and shall be witnesses to me*—That is, ye shall
be empowered to witness my Gospel. both by your preaching and suffering.

Gaiilçe, why stand ye gazing into heaven? This Jesus who is taken up from you into heaven, shall come as ye have seen him

12 going into heaven. Then they returned to Jerusalem from the mount called Olivet, which is from Jerusalem a Sabbath-day's journey.

13 *And when they were come in, they went up into the upper room, where both Peter and James, and John and Andrew, Philip and Thomas, Bartholomew and Matthew, James the son of Alpheus,

14 and Simon Zelotes, and Jude the brother of James, tarried. These all continued with one accord in prayer and supplication with the women, and Mary the mother of Jesus, and his brethren.

15 And in these days, Peter standing up in the midst of the disciples, (the number of persons together was about a hundred and

16 twenty,) said, Men, brethren, this † scripture must needs have been fulfilled, which the Holy Ghost spake before, by the mouth of David, concerning Judas, who was guide to them that appre-

17 hended Jesus. For he was numbered with us, and had obtained

18 part of this ministry. Now this man purchased a field with the reward of iniquity, and falling down on his face, he burst asunder

19 in the middle, and all his bowels gushed out. And it was known to all that dwell at Jerusalem, so that that field is called, in their

20 own tongue, Akeldama, that is, The field of blood. For it is writ-ten in the book of Psalms, ‡ Let his habitation be desolate, and le

21 no man dwell therein: and, § His bishopric let another take. Where-fore of these men who have been with us all the time that the Lord

22 Jesus was going in and out over us, Beginning from the baptism of John, till the day he was taken up from us, one must be a witness

23 with us of his resurrection. And they appointed two, Joseph called

12. *A Sabbath-day's journey*—The Jews generally fix this to two thousand cubits, which is not a mile.

13. *They went up into the upper room*—The upper rooms, so frequently men-tioned in Scripture, were chambers in the highest part of the house, set apart by the Jews for private prayer. These, on account of their being so retired and con venient, the apostles now used for all the offices of religion.

14. *His brethren*—His near kinsmen, who for some time did not believe; it seems not till near his death.

15. *The number of persons together*—Who were together in the upper room. *were a hundred and twenty*—But he had undoubtedly many more in other places; of whom more than five hundred saw him at once after his resurrec-tion, 1 Cor. xv, 6.

18. *This man purchased a field with the reward of iniquity*—That is, a field was purchased with the reward of his iniquity; though very possibly Judas might design the purchase. *And falling down on his face*—It seems the rope broke before, or as he died.

19. *In their own tongue*—This expression, *That is, the field of blood*, St. Luke seems to have added to the words of St. Peter, for the use of Theophilus and other readers who did not understand Hebrew.

20. *His bishopric*—That is, his apostleship.

21. *All the time that the Lord Jesus was going in and out*—That is, conversing familiarly: *over us*—as our Master.

22. *To be a witness with us of his resurrection*—And of the circumstances which preceded and followed it.

23. *And they appointed two*—So far the faithful could go by consulting together,

* Matt. x, 2; Mark iii, 14; Luke vi, 13.   † Psa. xli, 9.   ‡ Psa. lxix, 25.
§ Psa. cix, 8.

24 Barsabas, who was surnamed Justus, and Matthias. And they
prayed and said, Thou, Lord, who knowest the hearts of all, show
25 which of these two thou hast chosen, To take part of this ministry
and apostleship, from which Judas by transgression fell, to go to
26 his own place. And they gave forth their lots, and the lot fell upon
Matthias ; and he was numbered with the eleven apostles.

II. And when the day of pentecost was come, they were all with
2 one accord in one place. And suddenly there came a sound from
heaven, as of a rushing violent wind, and it filled all the house
3 where they were sitting. And there appeared to them distinct
4 tongues, as of fire ; and it sat upon each of them. And they were
all filled with the Holy Ghost, and began to speak with other
5 tongues, as the Spirit gave them utterance. And there were
dwelling in Jerusalem Jews, devout men, out of every nation
6 under heaven. And when this was noised abroad, the multitude
came together, and were confounded, because every man heard
7 them speaking in his own language. And they were amazed, and
marvelled, saying one to another, Behold, are not all these who are
8 speaking Galileans ? And how hear we every one, in our own
9 native language, Parthians, and Medes, and Elamites, and dwell-
ers in Mesopotamia, and Judea, and Cappadocia, Pontus and Asia,
10 Phrygia and Pamphylia, Egypt, and the parts of Africa about

---

but no farther. Therefore here commenced the proper use of the lot, whereby a
matter of importance, which cannot be determined by any ordinary method, is
committed to the Divine decision.

25. *Fell*—By his *transgression*—Some time before his death : *to go to his own
place*—That which his crimes had deserved, and which he had chosen for himself,
far from the other apostles, in the region of death.

II. At the pentecost of Sinai, in the Old Testament, and the pentecost of
Jerusalem, in the New, where the two grand manifestations of God, the legal
and the evangelical ; the one from the mountain, and the other from heaven ;
the terrible, and the merciful one. *They were all with one accord in one place*—
So here was a conjunction of company, minds, and place ; the whole hundred and
twenty being present.

2. *And suddenly there came a sound from heaven*—So will the Son of man come
to judgment. *And it filled all the house*—That is, all that part of the temple
where they were sitting.

3. *And there appeared distinct tongues, as of fire*—That is, small flames of fire.
This is all which the phrase, *tongues of fire*, means in the language of the seventy.
Yet it might intimate God's touching their tongues as it were (together with their
hearts) with Divine fire : his giving them such words as were active and penetrating,
even as flaming fire.

4. *And they began to speak with other tongues*—The miracle was not in the ears
of the hearers, (as some have unaccountably supposed,) but in the mouth of the
speakers. And this family praising God together, with the tongues of all the
world, was an earnest that the whole world should in due time praise God in
their various tongues. *As the Spirit gave them utterance*—Moses, the type of
the law, was of a slow tongue ; but the Gospel speaks with a fiery and flaming one.

5. *And there were dwelling in Jerusalem Jews*—Gathered from all parts by the
peculiar providence of God.

6. *The multitude came together, and were confounded*—The motions of their
minds were swift and various.

9. *Judea*—The dialect of which greatly differed from that of Galilee. *Asia*—
The country strictly so called.

10. *Roman sojourners*—Born at Rome, but now living at Jerusalem. These
seem to have come to Jerusalem after those who are above mentioned. All of
hem were partly Jews by birth, and partly proselytes.

11 Cyrene, and Roman sojourners, (Jews and proselytes,) Cretans and
   Arabians, we hear them speaking in our tongues the wonderfu.
12 works of God? And they were all amazed, and were in doubt,
13 saying one to another, What can this mean? But others mocking,
   said, They are full of sweet wine.
14 Then Peter standing up with the eleven, lifted up his voice,
   and said to them, Men of Judea, and all ye that dwell at Jerusalem,
15 be this known to you, and hearken to my words. These are not
   drunken, as ye suppose : for it is *but* the third hour of the day.
 6 But this is that which was spoken by the Prophet Joel, * And it
17 shall come to pass in the last days, saith God, I will pour out of my
   Spirit upon all flesh : and your sons and your daughters shall
   prophesy, and your young men shall see visions, and your old men
18 shall dream dreams : And in those days I will pour out of my Spirit upon my servants and upon my handmaids, and they shall pro-
19 phesy. And I will show prodigies in heaven above, and signs on

11. *Cretans*—One island seems to be mentioned for all. *The wonderful works
of God*—Probably those which related to the miracles, death, resurrection, and
ascension of Christ, together with the effusion of his Spirit, as a fulfilment of his
promises, and the glorious dispensations of Gospel grace.

12. *They were all amazed*—All the devout men.

13. *But others mocking*—The world begins with *mocking*, thence proceeds to
cavilling, chap. iv, 7 ; to threats, ver. 17 ; to imprisoning, chap. v, 18 ; blows,
ver. 40 ; to slaughter, chap. vii, 58. These mockers appear to have been some of
the natives of Judea, and inhabitants of Jerusalem, (who understood only the
dialect of the country,) by the apostle's immediately directing his discourse to
them in the next verse. *They are full of sweet wine*—So the Greek word properly signifies. There was no new wine so early in the year as pentecost. Thus
natural men are wont to ascribe supernatural things to mere natural causes ; and
many times as impudently and unskilfully as in the present case.

14. *Then Peter standing up*—All the gestures, all the words of Peter,. show
the utmost sobriety ; *lifted up his voice*—With cheerfulness and boldness ; *and
said to them*—This discourse has three parts ; each of which, ver. 14, 22, 29,
begins with the same appellation, *men :* only to the last part he prefixes with
more familiarity the additional word *brethren*. *Men of Judea*—That is, ye that
are born in Judea. St. Peter spoke in Hebrew, which they all understood.

15. *It is but the third hour of the day*—That is, nine in the morning. And on
the solemn festivals the Jews rarely ate or drank any thing till noon.

16. *But this is that which was spoken of by the prophet*—But there is another
and better way of accounting for this.

17. The times of the Messiah are frequently called the last days, the Gospel
being the last dispensation of Divine grace. *I will pour out of my Spirit*—Not
on the day of pentecost only, *upon all flesh*—On persons of every age, sex, and
rank. *And your young men shall see visions*—In young men the outward senses
are most vigorous, and the bodily strength is entire, whereby they are best qualified
to sustain the shock which usually attends the visions of God. In old men the
internal senses are most vigorous, suited to divine dreams. Not that the old are
wholly excluded from the former, nor the young from the latter.

18. *And upon my servants*—On those who are literally in a state of servitude.

19. *And I will show prodigies in heaven above, and signs on earth beneath*—
Great revelations of grace are usually attended with great judgments on those who
reject it. *In heaven*—Treated of, ver. 20. *On earth*—Described in this verse.
Such signs were those mentioned, ver. 22, before the passion of Christ ; which are so
mentioned as to include also those at the very time of the passion and resurrection, at the destruction of Jerusalem, and at the end of the world.

   Terrible indeed were those prodigies in particular which preceded the destruction of Jerusalem : such as the flaming sword hanging over the city, and the fiery

* Joel ii, 28

20 earth beneath, blood, and fire, and vapour of smoke. The sun
shall be turned into darkness, and the moon into blood, before the
21 day of the Lord, the great and illustrious *day*, come. But it shall
come to pass, that whosoever shall call on the name of the Lord,
22 shall be saved. Men of Israel, hear these words: Jesus of Nazareth, a man pointed out to you of God, by miracles, and wonders,
and signs, which God wrought by him in the midst of you, as
23 yourselves also know; Him, being delivered by the determinate
counsel and foreknowledge of God, ye have taken, and by wicked
24 hands have crucified and slain: whom God hath raised up,
having loosed the pains of death, as it was not possible that he
25 should be held under it. For David speaketh concerning him,
* I have seen the Lord always before my face, for he is on my
26 right hand, that I may not be moved. Therefore my heart
is glad, and my tongue exulteth; yea, and my flesh shall rest
27 in hope. For thou wilt not leave my soul in hades, neither wilt
28 thou suffer thy Holy One to see corruption. Thou hast made
known to me the ways of life; thou wilt fill me with joy by thy
29 countenance. Men *and* brethren, I may say to you freely of the

comet pointing down upon it for a year; the light that shone upon the temple
and the altar in the night, as if it had been noon-day; the opening of the great
and heavy gate of the temple without hands; the voice heard from the most holy
place, *Let us depart hence;* the admonition of Jesus the son of Ananus, crying
for seven years together, *Wo, wo, wo;* the vision of contending armies in the
air, and of entrenchments thrown up against a city there represented; the terrible thunders and lightnings, and dreadful earthquakes, which every one considered as portending some great evil: all which, through the singular providence
of God, are particularly recorded by Josephus. *Blood*—War and slaughter.
Fire—Burnings of houses and towns, involving all in clouds of *smoke.*

20. *The moon shall be turned into blood*—A bloody colour: *before the day of
the Lord*—Eminently the last day; though not excluding any other day or
season, wherein the Lord shall manifest his glory, in taking vengeance of his
adversaries.

21. *But—whosoever shall call on the name of the Lord*—This expression implies the whole of religion, and particularly prayer uttered in faith; *shall be saved*
—From all those plagues; from sin and hell.

23. *Him, being delivered by the determinate counsel and foreknowledge of God*—
The apostle here anticipates an objection, Why did God suffer such a person to
be so treated? Did he not know what wicked men intended to do? And had he
not power to prevent it? Yea. He knew all that those wicked men intended to
do. And he had power to blast all their designs in a moment. But he did not
exert that power, because he *so loved the world!* Because it was the determined
counsel of his love, to redeem mankind from eternal death, by the death of his
only-begotten Son.

24. *Having loosed the pains of death*—The word properly means, the pains of
a woman in travail. *As it was not possible that he should be held under it*—Because the Scripture must needs be fulfilled.

27. *Thou wilt not leave my soul in hades*—The invisible world. But it does
not appear, that ever our Lord went into hell. His soul, when it was separated
from the body, did not go thither, but to paradise, Luke xxiii, 43. The meaning
is, Thou wilt not leave my soul in its separate state, nor suffer my body to be
corrupted.

28. *Thou hast made known to me the ways of life*—That is, Thou hast raised
me from the dead. *Thou wilt fill me with joy by thy countenance*—When I
ascend to thy right hand.

29. *The patriarch*—A more honourable title than king.

* Psalm xvi, 8.

patriarch David, that he is both dead and buried, and his sepulchre
30 is among us to this day.   Therefore being a prophet, and knowing
that God had sworn with an oath to him, that of the fruit * of
31 his loins *one* should sit on his throne ; he foreseeing *this*, spake of
the resurrection of Christ, That his soul was not left in hades,
32 neither did his flesh see corruption.   This Jesus God hàth raised
33 up, whereof all we are witnesses.   Being therefore exalted by the
right hand of God, and having received from the Father the promise
of the Holy Ghost, he hath shed forth this, which ye now see and
34 hear.   For David is not ascended into the heavens ; but he saith
himself, † The Lord said to my Lord, Sit thou on my right hand,
35 Until I make thine enemies thy footstool.   Therefore let all the
36 house of Israel know assuredly, that God hath made this Jesus
whom ye crucified both Lord and Christ.
37   And hearing *this*, they were pierced to the heart, and said
to Peter and the rest of the apostles, Brethren, what shall
38 we do ?   And Peter said, Repent, and be baptized every one
of you, in the name of Jesus, for the remission of sins, and
39 ye shall receive the gift of the Holy Ghost.   For the promise
is to you and to your children, and to all that are afar off, whom-
40 soever the Lord our God shall call.   And with many other words
did he testify and exhort, saying, Save yourselves from this per-

---

32. *He foreseeing this, spake of the resurrection of Christ*—St. Peter argues
thus : It is plain, David did not speak this of himself.   Therefore he spake of
Christ's rising.   But how does that promise of a kingdom imply his resurrection ?
Because he did not receive it before he died, and because his kingdom was to endure for ever, 2 Sam. vii, 13.

33. *Being exalted by the right hand of God*—By the right hand; that is, the
mighty power of God.   Our Lord was exalted at his ascension to God's right
hand in heaven.

34. *Sit thou on my right hand*—In this and the following verse is an allusion
to two ancient customs ; one, to the highest honour that used to be paid to persons by placing them on the right hand, as Solomon did Bathsheba, when sitting
on his throne, 1 Kings ii, 19 ; and the other, to the custom of conquerors, who
used to tread on the necks of their vanquished enemies, as a token of their entire
victory and triumph over them.

35. *Until I make thine enemies thy footstool*—This text is here quoted with the
greatest address, as suggesting in the words of David, their great prophetic
monarch, how certain their own ruin must be, if they went on to oppose Christ.

36. *Lord*—Jesus, after his exaltation, is constantly meant by this word in the
New Testament, unless sometimes where it occurs, in a text quoted from the
Old Testament.

37. *They said to the apostles, Brethren*—They did not style them so before.

38. *Repent*—And hereby return to God: *be baptized*—Believing *in the name
of Jesus*—And ye shall receive the gift of the Holy Ghost*—See the three-one
God clearly proved.   See chap. xxvi, 20.   *The gift of the Holy Ghost* does not
mean in this place the power of speaking with tongues.   For the promise of
this was not given *to all that were afar off*, in distant ages and nations.   But
rather the constant fruits of faith, even righteousness, and peace, and joy in the
Holy Ghost.   *Whomsoever the Lord our God shall call*—(Whether they are Jews
or Gentiles) by his word and by his Spirit : and who are not disobedient to the
heavenly calling.   But it is observable St. Peter did not yet understand the very
words he spoke.

40. *And with many other words did he testify and exhort*—In such an accepted
time we should add line upon line, and not leave off, till the thing is done.

* Psalm lxxxix, 4, &c.   † Psalm cx, 1.

41 verse generation. Then they, gladly receiving his word, were baptized; and there were added *to them* that day about three thou-
42 sand souls. And they continued steadfast in the teaching of the apostles, and the fellowship, and the breaking of bread, and the
43 prayers. And fear came upon every soul, and many wonders and
44 signs were wrought by the apostles. And all that believed were
45 together, and had all things common, And sold their possessions
46 and goods, and divided them to all, as any one had need. And continuing daily with one accord in the temple, and breaking the bread at home, they partook of their food with gladness and single-
47 ness of heart: Praising God, and having favour with all the people. And the Lord added daily to the Church those who were saved.

III. Now Peter and John went up together into the temple, at the
2 hour of prayer, the ninth *hour.* And a certain man, lame from his mother's womb, was carried, whom they laid daily at the gate of the temple, called Beautiful, to ask alms of them that were enter-

---

Save yourselves from this perverse generation—Many of whom were probably mocking still.

41. *And there were added*—To the hundred and twenty.

42. *And they continued steadfast*—So their daily Church communion consisted in these four particulars: 1. Hearing the word; 2. Having all things common; 3. Receiving the Lord's Supper; 4. Prayer.

> Ye diff'rent sects, who all declare,
> Lo here is Christ, and Christ is there;
> Your stronger proofs divinely give,
> And *show* me where *the Christians* live!

43. *And fear came upon every soul*—Of those who did not join with them: whereby persecution was prevented, till it was needful for them.

45. *And sold their possessions*—Their lands and houses; *and goods*—Their movables. *And parted them to all as any one had need*—To say the Christians did this only till the destruction of Jerusalem, is not true; for many did it long after. Not that there was any positive command for so doing: it needed not; for love constrained them. It was a natural fruit of that love wherewith each member of the community loved every other as his own soul. And if the whole Christian Church had continued in this spirit, this usage must have continued through all ages. To affirm therefore that Christ did not *design it should continue,* is neither more nor less than to affirm, that Christ did not design this measure of *love should continue.* I see no proof of this.

46. *Continuing daily—breaking the bread*—In the Lord's Supper, as did many Churches for some ages. *They partook of their food with gladness and singleness of heart*—They carried the same happy and holy temper through all their common actions: eating and working with the same spirit wherewith they prayed and received the Lord's Supper.

47. *The Lord added daily such as were saved*—From their sins: from the guilt and power of them.

III. .. *The ninth hour*—The Jews divided the time from sunrise to sunset into twelve hours; which were consequently of unequal length at different times of the year, as the days were longer or shorter. The third hour therefore was nine in the morning; the ninth three in the afternoon; but not exactly. For the third hour was the middle space between sunrise and noon; which, if the sun rose at five, (the earliest hour of its rising in that climate,) was half an hour after eight: if at seven (the latest hour of its rising there) was half an hour after nine. The chief hours of prayer were the third and ninth; at which seasons the morning and evening sacrifices were offered, and incense (a kind of emblem representing prayer) burnt on the golden altar.

2. *At the gate of the temple, called Beautiful*—This gate was added by Herod the Great, between the court of the Gentiles and that of Israel. It was thirty cubits high, and fifteen broad, and made of Corinthian brass, more pompous in

3 ing into the temple. Who seeing Peter and John about to go into
4 the temple, asked an alms. And Peter looking steadfastly upon
5 him, with John, said, Look on us. And he gave heed to them, ex-
6 pecting to receive something of them. Then said Peter, Silver and
gold have I none; but what I have, I give thee : in the name of
7 Jesus Christ of Nazareth, rise up and walk. And taking him by
the right hand he lifted *him* up, and immediately his feet and ankle
8 bones were strengthened, And leaping up, he stood and walked,
and went with them into the temple, walking, and leaping, and
9 praising God. And all the people saw him walking and praising
10 God. And they knew him, that this was he who had sat for alms
at the Beautiful gate of the temple, and were filled with wonder and
amazement at that which had befallen him.
11 And as he held Peter and John, all the people ran together to
them, in the portico that is called Solomon's, greatly wondering.
12 And Peter seeing *it*, answered the people, Ye men of Israel, why
marvel ye at this ? Or why do ye fix your eyes on us as if by our
13 own power or piety we had made this man to walk ? The God of
Abraham, and Isaac, and Jacob, the God of our fathers, hath
glorified his Son Jesus, whom ye delivered up, and renounced him
in the presence of Pilate, when he was determined to release *him*.
14 But ye renounced the Holy One and the Just, and desired a mur-
15 derer to be granted you, and killed the Prince of life, whom God
16 hath raised from the dead, whereof we are witnesses. And his
name, through faith in his name, hath strengthened this man, whom
ye see and know : yea, the faith which is by him, hath given him
17 this perfect soundness, in the presence of you all. And now, bre-
18 thren, I know that through ignorance ye did *it*, as did also your rulers.
But God hath thus fulfilled the things which he foretold by the mouth

---

its workmanship and splendour than those that were covered with silver
and gold.

6. *Then said Peter, Silver and gold have I none*—How unlike his supposed
successor ! Can the bishop of *Rome* either say or do the same ?

12. *Peter answered the people*—Who were running together, and inquiring
into the circumstances of the fact.

13. *The God of our fathers*—This was wisely introduced in the beginning of
his discourse, that it might appear they taught no new religion, inconsistent with
that of Moses, and were far from having the least design to divert their regards
from the God of *Israel*. *Hath glorified his Son*—By this miracle, *whom ye
delivered up*—When God had given him to you, and when ye ought to have
received him as a most precious treasure, and to have preserved him with all
your power.

14. *Ye renounced the Holy One*—Whom God had marked out as such ; *and the
Just One*—Even in the judgment of Pilate.

16. *His name*—Himself : his power and love. *The faith which is by him*— Of
which he is the giver, as well as the object.

17. *And now, brethren*—A word full of courtesy and compassion, *I know*—He
speaks to their heart, *that through ignorance ye did it*—which lessened, though it
could not take away, the guilt. *As did also your rulers*—The prejudice lying
from the authority of the chief priests and elders, he here removes, but with
great tenderness. He does not call them our, but your rulers. For as the Jewish dispensation ceased at the death of Christ, consequently so did the authority
of its rulers

18. *But God*—Who was not ignorant, permitted this which he had foretold,
to bring good out of it.

19 of all the prophets, that his Christ should sufler. Repent ye therefore and be· converted, that your sins may be blotted out, that the
20 times of refreshing may come from the presence of the Lord, And
21 he may send to you Jesus Christ, who was before appointed, Whom
heaven must receive, till the times of the restitution of all things,
22 which God hath spoken by the mouth of his holy prophets. For
Moses truly said to the fathers, * The Lord your God shall raise
you up a prophet of your brethren, like unto me ; him shall ye
23 hear in all things, whatsoever he shall say to you. And it shall
come to pass that every soul who will not hear that prophet, shall
24 be destroyed from among the people. Yea, and all the prophets
from Samuel and them that followed, whosoever have spoken
25 have also foretold these days. Ye are the sons of the prophets and
of the covenant which God made with our fathers, saying to Abraham, †And in thy seed shall all the families of the earth be bless
26 ed. God having raised up his Son, hath sent him to you first, to
bless you, by turning every one of you from your iniquities.
IV. And as they were speaking to the people, the priests, and the

---

19. *Be converted*—Be turned from sin and Satan unto God. See chap. xxvi,
20. But this term, so common in modern writings, very rarely occurs in Scripture : perhaps not once in the sense we now use it, for an entire change from
vice to holiness. *That the times of refreshing*—Wherein God largely bestows
his refreshing grace, *may come*—To you also. To others they will assuredly
come, whether ye repent or no.
20. *And he may send*—The apostles generally speak of our Lord's second
coming, as being just at hand. *Who was before appointed*—Before the foundation
of the world.
21. *Till the times of the restitution of all things*—The apostle here comprises
at once the whole course of the times of the New Testament, between our Lord's
ascension and his coming in glory. The most eminent of these are the apostolic age, and that of the spotless Church, which will consist of all the Jews and
Gentiles united, after all persecutions and apostacies are at an end.
22. *The Lord shall raise you up a prophet like unto me*—And that in many
particulars. Moses instituted the Jewish Church : Christ instituted the Christian. With the prophesying of Moses was soon joined the effect, the deliverance
of Israel from Egypt : with the prophesying of Christ that grand effect, the deliverance of his people from sin and death. Those who could not bear the voice
of God, yet desired to hear that of Moses. Much more do those who are wearied with the law, desire to hear the voice of·Christ. Moses spake to the people all, and only those things, which God had commanded him : so did Christ.
But though he was like Moses, yet he was infinitely superior to him, in person,
as well as in office.
23. *Every soul who will not hear that prophet, shall be destroyed from among
the people*—One cannot imagine a more masterly address than this, to warn the
Jews of the dreadful consequence of their infidelity, in the very words of their
favourite prophet, out of a pretended zeal for whom they rejected Christ.
24. *These days*—The days of the *Messiah*.
25. *Ye are the sons of the prophets and of the covenant*—That is, heirs of the
prophecies. To you properly, as the first heirs, belong the prophecies and the
covenant.
26. *To bless you, by turning you from your iniquities*—Which is the great
Gospel blessing.
IV. 1. *And as they were speaking to the people, the priests*—*came upon them*—So
wisely did God order, that they should first bear a full testimony to the truth in
the temple, and then in the great council ; to which they could have had no access, had they not been brought before it as criminals.

* Deut. xviii, 15.   † Gen. xii, 3.

2 captain of the temple, and the Sadducees came upon them, Being grieved that they taught the people, and preached through Jesus
3 the resurrection from the dead. And they laid hands on them, and
4 put them in hold till the next day for it was now evening. But many' of them who had heard the word, believed: and the number
5 of the men was about five thousand. And on the morrow were gathered together at Jerusalem their rulers, and elders, and scribes,
6 And Annas the high priest, and Caiaphas, and John, and Alexander,
7 and as many as were of the kindred of the high priest. And having set them in the midst, they asked, By what power, or by wha
8 name, have ye done this? Then Peter, filled with the Holy Ghost,
9 said to them, Ye rulers of the people, and elders of Israel, If we are examined this day of the benefit done to the impotent man, by
10 what means he is healed, Be it known to you all, and to all the people of Israel, that by the name of Jesus Christ of Nazareth, whom ye crucified, whom God hath raised from the dead, by him
11 doth this man stand before you whole. * This is the stone which was set at nought by you builders, which is become the head of
12 the corner. And there is salvation in no other; for there is no other name under heaven given among men, whereby we must be saved.
13 And seeing the boldness of Peter and John, and understanding that they were illiterate and uneducated men, they marvelled, and

2. *The priests being grieved*—That the name of Jesus was preached to the people; especially they were offended at the doctrine of his resurrection; for as they had put him to death, his rising again proved him to be the Just One, and so brought *his blood upon their heads.* The priests were grieved, lest their office and temple services should decline, and Christianity take root, through the preaching of the apostles, and their power of working miracles: *the captain of the temple*—Being concerned to prevent all sedition and disorder, *the Sadducees*—Being displeased at the overturning of all their doctrines, particularly with regard to the resurrection.

4. *The number of the men*—Beside women and children, *were about five thousand*—So many did our Lord now feed at once with the bread from heaven!

5. *Rulers, and elders, and scribes*—Who were eminent for power, for wisdom, and for learning.

6. *Annas*, who had been *the high priest, and Caiaphas*, who was so then.

7. *By what name*—By what authority, *have ye done this?*—They seem to speak ambiguously on purpose.

8. *Then Peter, filled with the Holy Ghost*—That moment. God moves his instruments, not when they please, but just when he sees it needful. *Ye rulers*—He gives them the honour due to their office.

10. *Be it known to you all*—Probably the herald of God proclaimed this with a loud voice. *Whom God hath raised from the dead*—They knew in their own consciences that it was so. And though they had hired the soldiers to tell a most senseless and incredible tale to the contrary, Matt. xxviii, 12, 15, yet it is observable, they did not, so far as we can learn, dare to plead it before Peter and John.

12. *There is no other name whereby we must be saved*—The apostle uses a beautiful gradation, from the temporal deliverance which had been wrought for the poor cripple, by the power of Christ, to that of a much nobler and more important kind, which is wrought by Christ for impotent and sinful souls. He therein follows the admirable custom of his great Lord and Master, who continually took occasion from earthly to speak of spiritual things.

13. *Illiterate and uneducated men*—Even by such men (though not by such only) hath God in all ages caused his word to be preached before the world.

* Psalm cxviii, 22.

14 took knowledge of them, that they had been with Jesus. And beholding the man who had been healed standing with them, they
15 had nothing to say against *it*. But having ordered them to go out
of the council, they conferred among themselves, saying, What
16 shall we do to these men? For that indeed a signal miracle hath
been wrought by them, *is* manifest to all that dwell in Jerusalem,
17 and we cannot deny *it*. Yet that it spread no farther among the
people, let us severely threaten them, that they speak no more to
18 any man in this name. And having called them, they charged
19 them, not to speak at all, nor teach in the name of Jesus. But
Peter and John answering, said to them, Whether it be just in the
20 sight of God, to obey you rather than God, judge ye. For we can-
21 not but speak the things which we have seen and heard. And having threatened them again, they let *them* go, finding nothing how
they might punish them, because of the people : for they all glori-
22 fied God for that which was done. For the man on whom this
miracle of healing had been wrought, was above forty years old.
23 And being let go, they went to their own company, and related
24 all that the chief priests and elders had said to them, And having
heard *it*, they lifted up their voice to God with one accord, and
said, Lord, thou *art* the God who madest heaven and earth, and
the sea, and all that in them is : who saidst by the mouth of thy
25 servant David, * Why did the heathen rage, and the people imagine
26 vain things ? The kings of the earth set themselves in array,
and the rulers were gathered together against the Lord and
27 against his Christ. For of a truth, both Herod and Pontius Pilate,
with the Gentiles and the people of Israel, were gathered together
28 against thy holy child Jesus, whom thou hast anointed. To do
whatsoever thy hand and thy counsel before determined to be done.
29 And now, Lord, behold their threatenings, and give thy servants to
30 speak thy word with all boldness, While thou stretchest forth thy
hand to heal, and signs and wonders are done through the name
31 of thy holy child Jesus. And while they were praying, the

17. *Yet that it spread no farther*—For they look upon it as a mere gangrene.
So do all the world upon genuine Christianity. *Let us severely threaten them*—
Great men, ye do nothing. They have a greater than you to flee to.
18. *They charged them not to speak*—Privately ; *nor teach*—Publicly.
19. *Whether it be just to obey you rather than God, judge ye*—Was it not by
the same spirit, that Socrates, when they were condemning him to death, for
teaching the people, said, " O ye Athenians, I embrace and love you ; but I will
obey God rather than you. And if you would spare my life on condition I should
cease to teach my fellow citizens, I would die a thousand times rather than accept the proposal."
21. *They all glorified God*—So much wiser were the people than those who
were over them.
34. The sense is, Lord, thou hast all power. And thy word is fulfilled. Men
do rage against thee: but it is in vain.
27. *Whom thou hast anointed*—To be king of Israel.
28. The sense is, but they could do no more than thou wast pleased to permit,
according to thy *determinate counsel*, to save mankind by the sufferings of thy
Son. And what was needful for this end, thou didst *before determine* to permit
to be done.
30. *Thou stretchest forth thy hand*—Exertest thy power.

* Psalm ii, 1.

place in which they were assembled was shaken, and they were all filled with the Holy Ghost, and spake the word of God with boldness.

32 And the multitude of them that believed were of one heart, and of one soul: and not so much as one said that aught of the things
33 which he had was his own, but they had all things common. And the apostles gave forth their testimony of the resurrection of the Lord Jesus with great power, and great grace was upon them all:
34 For neither was there any one among them that wanted: for whosoever were possessors of houses or lands sold them, and brought
35 the prices of the things that were sold, And laid them down at the feet of the apostles, and distribution was made to every one according as any had need.
36 And Joses, by the apostles surnamed Barnabas, which is, being interpreted a son of consolation, a Levite, a Cyprian by birth,
37 Having an estate, sold *it*, and brought the money, and laid it at the feet of the apostles.
V. But a certain man named Ananias, with Sapphira his wife, sold
2 a possession, And kept back *part* of the price, his wife also being privy *to it*, and bringing a certain part, laid it at the feet of the apos-
3 tles. But Peter said, Ananias, why hath Satan filled thy heart, to lie to the Holy Ghost? And to keep back *part* of the price of the
4 land? While it remained, did it not remain thine? And when it was

31. *They were all filled*—Afresh; *and spake the word with boldness*—So their petition was granted.

32. *And the multitude of them that believed*—Every individual person *were of one heart and one soul*—Their love, their hopes, their passions joined: *and not so much as one*—In so great a multitude: this was a necessary consequence of that union of heart; *said that aught of the things which he had was his own*—It is impossible any one should, while all *were of one soul.* So long as that truly Christian love continued, they could not but *have all things common.*

33. *And great grace*—A large measure of the inward power of the Holy Ghost, *was upon them all*—Directing all their thoughts, words, and actions.

34. *For neither was there any one among them that wanted*—We may observe, this is added as the proof that *great grace was upon them all.* And it was the immediate, necessary consequence of it: yea, and must be to the end of the world. In all ages and nations, the same cause, the same degree of grace, could not but in like circumstances produce the same effect. *For whosoever were possessors of houses and lands sold them*—Not that there was any particular command for this; but there was great grace and great love: of which this was the natural fruit.

35. *And distribution was made*—At first by the apostles themselves, afterward by them whom they appointed.

36. *A son of consolation*—Not only on account of his so largely assisting the poor with his fortune; but also of those peculiar gifts of the Spirit, whereby he · was so well qualified both to comfort and to exhort.

37. *Having an estate*—Probably of considerable value. It is not unlikely that it was in Cyprus. Being a Levite, he had no portion, no distinct inheritance in Israel.

V. 1. *But a certain man named Ananias*—It is certain, not a believer, for all that believed *were of one heart and of one soul:* probably not baptized; but intending now to offer himself for baptism.

2. *And bringing a certain part*—As if it had been the whole: perhaps saying it was so.

3. *To lie to the Holy Ghost*—Who is in us. *And to keep back*—Here was the first instance of it. This was the first attempt to bring propriety of goods into the Christian Church.

sold, was it not in thy power? Why hast thou conceived this thing
5 in thy heart? Thou hast not lied to men but to God. And Ananias hearing these words, fell down and expired; and great fear
6 came on all that heard these things. And the young men rising
7 up, wound him up, and carrying *him* out, buried him. And it was
about the space of three hours after, when his wife, not knowing
8 what was done, came in. And Peter said to her, Tell me, if ye
9 sold the land for so much? And she said, Yea, for so much. And
Peter said to her, Why have ye agreed together to tempt the
Spirit of the Lord? Behold, the feet of them that have buried thy
10 husband *are* at the door, and shall carry thee out. And immediately she fell at his feet and expired; and the young men coming
in, found her dead, and carrying *her* out, buried her by her husband.
11 And great fear came upon all the Church, and upon all that heard
these things.
12   And many signs and wonders were wrought among the people
by the hands of the apostles: (and they were all with one accord
13 in Solomon's portico: And none of the rest durst join themselves
14 to them; but the people magnified them, And the more were multitudes, both of men and women believing, added to the Lord:)
15 So that they brought out the sick along the streets, and laid *them*
on beds and couches, that even the shadow of Peter ʻcoming by,
16 might overshadow some of them. And multitudes also of the cities
round about came together to Jerusalem, bringing persons sick and
troubled by unclean spirits, and they were all healed.

4. *While it remained, did it not remain thine?*—It is true, whosoever among
the Christians (not one excepted) had houses or lands, sold them, and laid the
price at the feet of the apostles. But it was in his own choice to be a Christian
or not: and consequently either to sell his land, or keep it. *And when it was
sold, was it not in thy power?*—For it does not appear that he professed himself a
Christian when he sold it. *Why hast thou conceived this thing in thy heart?*—
So profanely to dissemble on so solemn an occasion? *Thou hast not lied to men
only, but to God* also. Hence the Godhead of the Holy Ghost evidently appears:
since lying to him, ver. 3, is lying to God.
5. *And Ananias fell down and expired*—And this severity was not only just,
considering that complication of vain glory, covetousness, fraud, and impiety,
which this action contained: but it was also wise and gracious, as it would effectually deter any others from following his example. It was likewise a convincing proof of the upright conduct of the apostles, in managing the sums with
which they were intrusted; and in general of their Divine mission. For none
can imagine that Peter would have had the assurance to pronounce, and much
less the power to execute such a sentence, if he had been guilty himself of a fraud
of the same kind; or had been belying the Holy Ghost in the whole of his pre-
tensions to be under his immediate direction.
7. *About the space of three hours*—How precious a space! The woman had a
longer time for repentance.
8. *If ye sold the land for so much*—Naming the sum.
10. *The Church*—This is the first time it is mentioned: and here is a native
specimen of a New-Testament Church; which is a company of men, called by
the Gospel, grafted into Christ by baptism, animated by love, united by all kind
of fellowship, and disciplined by the death of Ananias and Sapphira.
12. *And they were all*—All the believers.
13. *None of the rest*—No formalists or hypocrites, *durst join themselves*—In an
outward show only, like Ananias and Sapphira.
14. But so much *the more were* true believers *added*, because unbelievers kept
at a distance.

17 But the high priest arising, and all that were with him, which
18 was the sect of the Sadducees, were filled with zeal, And laid their
hands on the apostles, and put them into the common prison.
19 But an angel of the Lord opened the prison doors by night, and
20 leading them out, said, Go, stand and speak in the temple the
21 words of this life. And hearing this, they went into the temple
early in the morning and taught. But the high priest being come,
and they that were with him, called together the council, even the
whole senate of the children of Israel, and sent to the prison, to
22 have them brought. But when the officers came, they found them
23 not in the prison; and returning they said, Truly we found the
prison shut with all safety, and the keepers standing before the
24 doors; but having opened them, we found no man within. When
the captain of the temple and the chief priests heard these things,
25 they doubted of them, what this should be. Then came one and
told them, Behold, the men whom ye put in prison are standing
26 in the temple, and teaching the people. Then the captain going
with the officers brought them, not with violence, for they feared
27 the people lest they should be stoned. And having brought them,
28 they set them before the council. And the high priest asked them,
Did not we strictly command you, not to teach in this name? And
lo, ye have filled Jerusalem with your doctrine, and would bring
29 the blood of this man upon us. Then Peter and the other apostles answering said, We ought to obey God rather than men.
30 The God of our fathers hath raised up Jesus, whom ye slew, hang-
31 ing him on a tree. Him hath God exalted, a Prince and a Saviour,
with his right hand, to give repentance to Israel, and forgiveness
32 of sins. And we are witnesses of these things, and also the Holy

17. *The high priest—and the sect of the Sadducees*—A goodly company for the priest! He, and these deniers of any angel or resurrection, *were filled with zeal* —Angry, bitter, persecuting zeal.

20. *The words of this*—That is, these words of life : words which show the way to life everlasting.

23. *We found the prison shut*—The angel probably had shut the doors again.

24. *They doubted what this should be*—They were even at their wits' end. The world, in persecuting the children of God, entangle themselves in number-less difficulties.

28. *Did not we strictly command you, not to teach?*—See the poor cunning of the enemies of the Gospel. They make laws and interdicts at their pleasure, which those who obey God cannot but break ; and then take occasion thereby to censure and punish the innocent, as guilty. *Ye would bring the blood of this man upon us*—An artful and invidious word. The apostles did not desire to accuse any man. They simply declared the naked truth.

29. *Then Peter*—In the name of all the apostles, *said*—He does not now give them the titles of honour, which he did before, chap. iv, 8; but enters directly upon the subject, and justifies what he had done. This is, as it were, a continua-tion of that discourse, but with an increase of severity.

30. *Hath raised up Jesus*—Of the seed of David, according to the promises made to our fathers.

31. *Him hath God exalted*—From the grave to heaven ; *to give repentance*— Whereby Jesus is received as a Prince ; *and forgiveness of sins*—Whereby he is received as a Saviour. Hence some infer, that repentance and faith are as mere gifts as remission of sins. Not so: for man co-operates in the former, but not in the latter. God alone forgives sins.

32. *And also the Holy Ghost*—A much greater witness.

33 Ghost, whom God hath given to them that obey him   When they
heard this, they were *rut to the heart*, and took counsel to slay
34 them.   But a certain Pharisee, named Gamaliel, a doctor of the
law, had in honour by all the people, rising up in the council,
35 ordered to put the men out a little space : And said to them, Ye
men of Israel, take heed to yourselves, what ye are about to do,
36 touching these men.   For before these days rose up Theudas,
boasting himself to be somebody, to whom was joined a number
of men, about four hundred, who was slain, and all who hearkened
37 to him were scattered and came to nothing.   After this man rose
up Judas of Galilee, in the days of the enrolment, and drew away
much people after him ;   he also perished, and all who had hear-
38 kened unto him were dispersed.   And now I say to you, Refrain
from these men, and let them alone ; for if this counsel or this
39 work be of men, it will come to nought, But if it be of God, ye
cannot overthrow it, *and take heed* lest ye be found even fighting
40 against God.   And to him they agreed.   And having called the
apostles, and scourged *them*, they charged *them* not to speak in the
41 name of Jesus, and dismissed them.   And they departed from the
presence of the council, rejoicing that they were counted worthy
42 to suffer shame for his name.   And they ceased not to teach
and preach Jesus Christ daily, in the temple, and from house to
house.
VI   Now in these days, the disciples multiplying, there arose a
murmuring of the Hellenists against the Hebrews, because their

---

34. *But a certain Pharisee*—And as such believing the resurrection of the
dead ; *a doctor*, or teacher *of the law*—That is, a scribe, and indeed one of the
highest rank ; *had in honour by all the people*—Except the Sadducees ; *rising up
in the council*—So God can raise defenders of his servants, whensoever and wheresoever he pleases.

36. *Before these days*—He prudently mentions the facts first, and then makes
the inference.

38. *Let them alone*—In a cause which is manifestly good, we should immediately join.   In a cause, on the other hand, which is manifestly evil, we should
immediately oppose.   But in a sudden, new, doubtful occurrence, this advice is
eminently useful.   *If this counsel or this work*—He seems to correct himself, as
if it were some sudden *work*, rather than a *counsel* or design.   And so it was.
For the apostles had no counsel, plan, or design of their own ; but were mere
instruments in the hand of God, working just as he led them from day to day.

41. *Rejoicing—to suffer shame*—This is a sure mark of the truth, joy in affliction, such is true, deep, pure.

VI. 1. *There arose a murmuring*—Here was the first breach made on those
who were before *of one heart and of one soul*.   Partiality crept in unawares on
some ; and murmuring on others.   Ah Lord ! how short a time did pure, genuine, undefiled Christianity remain in the world !   O the depth !   How unsearchable
are thy counsels !   Marvellous are thy ways, O King of saints !   The Hellenists
were Jews born out of Palestine.   They were so called, because they used the
Greek as their mother tongue.

In this partiality of the Hebrews, and murmuring of the Hellenists, were the
seeds of a general persecution sown.   Did God ever, in any age or country,
withdraw his restraining providence, and let loose the world upon the Christians, till there was a cause among themselves ?   Is not an open, general persecution, always both penal and medicinal ?   A punishment of those that will not
accept of milder reproofs, as well as a medicine to heal their sickness ?   And at
the same time a means both of purifying and strengthening those whose heart is
still right with God.

2 widows were neglected in the daily ministration. Then the
twelve calling the multitude of the disciples together, said, It is
not right that we should leave the word of God, and serve tables.
3 Therefore, brethren, look out from among you seven men of good
report, full of the Holy Ghost and wisdom, whom we will set over
4 this business. But we will constantly attend to prayer, and to the
5 ministry of the word. And the saying pleased the whole multitude : and they chose Stephen, a man full of faith and of the Holy
Ghost, and Philip, and Prochorus, and Nicanor, and Timon, and
6 Parmenas, and Nicholas, a proselyte of Antioch ; Whom they set
before the apostles, and having prayed, they laid their hands upon
7 them. And the word of God grew, and the number of disciples
was multiplied in Jerusalem greatly : and a great company of the
priests were obedient to the faith.
8   And Stephen, full of grace and power, did great wonders and
9 miracles among the people. But there arose certain of the synagogue, which is called *that* of the Libertines, and Cyrenians, and
Alexandrians, and of them of Cilicia and Asia, disputing with Ste-
10 phen. And they were not able to withstand the wisdom and the
11 spirit by which he spake. Then they suborned men who said, We
have heard him speaking blasphemous words against Moses and
12 against God. And they stirred up the people, and the elders, and
the scribes, and coming upon *him*, dragged him away, and brought
13 *him* to the council, And set up false witnesses, who said, This man

---

2. *It is not right that we should leave the word of God and serve tables*—In
the first Church, the primary business of apostles, evangelists, and bishops, was to
preach the word of God ; the secondary, to take a kind of paternal care (the
Church being then like a family,) for the food, especially of the poor, the strangers, and the widows. Afterward, the deacons of both sexes were constituted
for this latter business. And whatever time they had to spare from this, they
employed in works of spiritual mercy. But their proper office was, to take care
of the poor. And when some of them afterward preached the Gospel, they did
this not by virtue of their deaconship, but of another commission, that of evangelists, which they probably received, not before, but after they were appointed
deacons. And it is not unlikely that others were chosen deacons, or stewards,
in their room, when any of these commenced evangelists.
3. *Of good report*—That there may be no room to suspect them of partiality
or injustice. *Full of the Holy Ghost and wisdom*—For it is not a light matter
to dispense even the temporal goods of the Church. To do even this well, a large
measure both of the gifts and grace of God is requisite. *Whom we will set over
this business*—It would have been happy for the Church, had its ordinary ministers in every age taken the same care to act in concert with the people committed to their charge, which the apostles themselves, extraordinary as their office
was, did on this and other occasions.
4. *We will constantly attend to prayer, and to the ministry of the word*—This
is doubtless the proper business of a Christian bishop : to speak to God in prayer ;
to men in preaching his word, as an ambassador for Christ.
5. *And they chose*—It seems seven Hellenists, as their names show. *And Nicholas a proselyte*—To whom the proselytes would the more readily apply.
7. *And the word of God grew*—The hinderances being removed.
9. *There arose certain of the synagogue which is called*—It was one and the same
synagogue which consisted of these several nations. Saul of Cilicia was doubtless a member of it ; whence it is not at all improbable, that Gamaliel presided
over it. *Libertines*—So they were styled, whose fathers were once slaves, and
afterward made free. This was the case of many Jews who had been taken cap
tive by the Romans.

ceaseth not to speak words against this holy place and the law.
14 For we have heard him say, that this Jesus of Nazareth will destroy this place, and change the rites which Moses delivered us.
15 And all that were sitting in the council, looking steadfastly on him,
saw his face as the face of an angel.
VII.   Then said the high priest, Are these things so? And he said.
2 Men, brethren, and fathers, hearken. The God of glory appeared
to our father Abraham, * being in Mesopotamia, before he dwelt
3 in Haran, And said to him, Come out of thy country, and from
4 thy kindred, and come into a land which I will show thee.   And

---

14. *We have heard him say*—So they might. But yet the consequence they
drew would not follow.

15. *As the face of an angel*—Covered with supernatural lustre. They reckoned
his preaching of Jesus to be the Christ was destroying Moses and the law; and
God bears witness to him, with the same glory as he did to Moses, when he gave
the law by him.

VII. 2. *And he said*—St. Stephen had been accused of blasphemy against Moses, and even against God; and of speaking against the temple and the law,
threatening that Jesus would destroy the one, and change the other. In answer
to this accusation, rehearsing as it were the articles of his historical creed, he
speaks of God with high reverence, and a grateful sense of a long series of acts
of goodness to the Israelites, and of Moses with great respect, on account of his
important and honourable employments under God : of the temple with regard,
as being built to the honour of God ; yet not with such superstition as the Jews ;
putting them in mind, that no temple could comprehend God. And he was going
on, no doubt, when he was interrupted by their clamour, to speak to the last
point, the destruction of the temple, and the change of the law by Christ. *Men,
brethren, and fathers, hearken*—The sum of his discourse is this : I acknowledge
the glory of God revealed to the fathers, ver. 2 ; the calling of Moses, ver. 34,
&c ; the dignity of the law, verses 8, 38, 44 ; the holiness of *this place*, verses
7, 45, 47. And indeed the law is more ancient than the temple ; the promise
more ancient than the law. For God showed himself the God of Abraham,
Isaac, Jacob, and their children freely, ver. 2, &c ; 9, &c ; 17, &c ; 32, 34, 35 ;
and they showed faith and obedience to God, ver. 4, 20, &c, 23, particularly by
their regard for the law, ver. 8, and the promised land, ver. 16. Meantime, God
never confined his presence to this one place or to the observers of the law. For
he hath been acceptably worshipped before the law was given, or the temple
built, and out of this land, ver. 2, 9, 33, 44. And that our fathers and their posterity were not tied down to this land, their various sojournings, ver. 4, &c ; 14,
29, 44, and exile, ver. 43, show. But you and your fathers have always been
evil, ver. 9 ; have withstood Moses, ver. 25, &c, 39, &c ; have despised the land,
ver. 39, forsaken God, ver. 40, &c, superstitiously honoured the temple, ver. 48,
resisted God and his Spirit, ver 50, killed the prophets and the Messiah himself,
ver. 51, and kept not the law for which ye contend, ver. 53. Therefore God is
not bound to you ; much less to you alone. And truly this solemn testimony of
Stephen is most worthy of his character, as *a man full of the Holy Ghost, and
of faith and power :* in which, though he does not advance so many regular propositions, contradictory to those of his adversaries, yet he closely and nervously
answers them all. Nor can we doubt but he would, from these premises, have
drawn inferences touching the destruction of the temple, the abrogation of the
Mosaic law, the punishment of that rebellious people ; and above all, touching
Jesus of Nazareth, the true Messiah, had not his discourse been interrupted by
the clamours of the multitude, stopping their ears, and rushing upon him. *Men,
brethren, and fathers*—All who are here present, whether ye are my equals in
years, or of more advanced age. The word which in this and in many other
places is rendered *men* is a mere expletive. *The God of glory*—The glorious God,
appeared to Abraham before he dwelt in Haran—Therefore Abraham knew God,
long before he was in this land.

3. *Which I will show thee*—Abraham knew not where he went.

* Gen. xii, 1.

coming out of the land of the Chaldeans, he dwelt in Haran. And from thence, after his father was dead, he removed him into this
5 land, wherein ye now dwell. And he gave him no inheritance in it, no not to set his foot on; yet he promised to give it him for a
6 possession, even to his seed after him, when he had no child. And God spake thus : That * his seed should sojourn in a strange land (and they will enslave them and treat *them* evil) four hundred years,
7 And the nation to whom they shall be in bondage will I judge, said God. And after that, they shall come forth, and serve me in this
8 place. † And he gave him the covenant of circumcision, and so he begat Isaac, and circumcised him the eighth day, and Isaac Ja-
9 cob, and Jacob the twelve patriarchs. ‡ And the patriarchs moved with envy, sold Joseph into Egypt; but God was with him,
10 And delivered him out of all his afflictions, and gave him favour and wisdom in the sight of Pharaoh king of Egypt, and he appoint-
11 ed him governor over Egypt and all his house. Now there came a famine over all the land of Egypt and Canaan, and great affliction,
12 and our fathers found no sustenance. But Jacob hearing there was
13 corn in Egypt, sent our fathers first. And the second *time*, Joseph was made known to his brethren, and Joseph's kindred was made
14 known to Pharaoh. Then Joseph sending, called thither his father
15 Jacob and all his kindred, seventy-five souls. So Jacob went down
16 into Egypt, and died, he and our fathers, and were carried over to Shechem, and laid in the sepulchre that Abraham bought for a

4. *After his father was dead*—While Terah lived, Abraham lived partly with him, partly in Canaan : but after he died, altogether in Canaan.

5. *No, not to set his foot on*—For the field mentioned, ver. 16, he did not receive by a Divine donation, but bought it ; even thereby showing that he was a stranger in the land.

7. *They shall serve me*—Not the Egyptians.

8. *And so he begat Isaac*—After the covenant was given, of which circumcision was the seal.

9. *But God was with him*—Though he was not in this land.

12. *Sent our fathers first*—Without Benjamin.

14. *Seventy-five souls*—So the seventy interpreters, (whom St. Stephen follows,) one son and a grandson of Manasseh, and three children of Ephraim, being added to the seventy persons mentioned Gen. xlvi, 27.

16. *And were carried over to Shechem*—It seems that St. Stephen, rapidly running over so many circumstances of history, has not leisure (nor was it needful where they were so well known) to recite them all distinctly. Therefore he here contracts into one, two different sepulchres, places, and purchases, so as in the former history, to name the buyer, omitting the seller, in the latter, to name the seller, omitting the buyer. Abraham bought a burying place of the children of Heth, Gen. xxiii. There Jacob was buried. Jacob bought a field of the children of Hamor. There Joseph was buried. You see here, how St. Stephen contracts these two purchases into one. This concise manner of speaking, strange as it seems to us, was common among the Hebrews ; particularly, when in a case notoriously known, the speaker mentioned but part of the story, and left the rest, which would have interrupted the current of his discourse, to be supplied in the mind of the hearer. *And laid in the sepulchre that Abraham bought*—The first land which these strangers bought was for a sepulchre. They sought for a country in heaven. Perhaps the whole sentence might be rendered thus : *So Jacob went down into Egypt and died, he and our fathers, and were carried over to Shechem, and laid by the sons* (that is, descendants) *of Hamor, the father of Shechem, in the sepulchre that Abraham bought for a sum of money.*

× Gen. xv, 13.   † Gen. xvii, 10.   ‡ Gen. xxxvii, 28.

17 sum of money, of the sons of Hamor, *the father* of Shechem.
* And when the time of the promise which God had sworn to Abra-
18 ham drew near, the people increased and multiplied in Egypt. Till
19 another king arose, who had not known Joseph. He dealing sub-
tilly with our kindred, evil entreated our fathers, by causing their
20 *male* infants to be exposed, that they might not live. † In which
time Moses was born, and was exceeding beautiful, who was nursed
21 three months in his father's house. And when he was exposed,
Pharaoh's daughter took him up, and brought him up for her own
22 son. And Moses was educated in all the wisdom of the Egyptians,
23 and was mighty in words and in deeds. But when he was full forty
years old, it came into his heart to visit his brethren the children
24 of Israel. And seeing one wronged, he defended and avenged him
25 that was oppressed, smiting the Egyptian. For he supposed his
brethren would have understood, that God would deliver them by
26 his hand; but they understood *it* not. And the next day he showed
himself to them as they were quarrelling, and would have per-
27 suaded them to peace, saying, Men, ye are brethren : why do ye
wrong one another ? But he that wronged his neighbour thrust him
away, saying, Who appointed thee a prince and a judge over us ?
28 Wilt thou kill me, as thou didst the Egyptian yesterday ? And
29 Moses fled at that saying, and was a sojourner in the land of Midian,
30 where he begat two sons. ‡ And forty years being expired, the
angel of the Lord appeared to him in the wilderness, in a flame
31 of fire in a bush. And Moses seeing *it*, wondered at the sight.
But as he drew near to behold it, the voice of the Lord came to
32 him, I *am* the God of thy fathers, the God of Abraham, and the God
of Isaac, and the God of Jacob. And Moses trembled, and durst
33 not behold. Then said the Lord to him, Loose thy shoes from
34 thy feet: for the place where thou standest is holy ground. I have
surely seen the evil treatment of my people which is in Egypt, and
have heard their groaning, and am come down to deliver them.

18. *Another king*—Probably of another family.
19. *Exposed*—Cast out to perish by hunger or wild beasts.
20. *In which time*—A sad but a seasonable time.
21. *Pharaoh's daughter took him up*—By which means, being designed for a ùingdom, he had all those advantages of education, which he could not have had, ìf he had not been exposed.
22. *In all the wisdom of the Egyptians*—Which was then celebrated in all the ƴorld, and for many ages after. *And mighty in words*—Deep, solid, weighty, ᴕhough not of a ready utterance.
23. *It came into his heart*—Probably by an impulse from God.
24. *Seeing one wronged*—Probably by one of the task masters.
25. *They understood it not*—Such was their stupidity and sloth; which made him aᶠerward unwilling to go to them.
26. *He showed himself*—Of his own accord, unexpectedly.
27. *Who appointed thee*—" Under the presence of the want of a call by man, the instruments of God are often rejected."
30. *The angel*—The Son of God ; as appears from his styling himself Jehovah. *In a flame of fire*—Signifying the majesty of God then present.
33. *Then said the Lord, Loose thy shoes*—An ancient token of reverence ; *for the place is holy ground*—The holiness of places depends on the peculiar presence of God there.

* Exod. i, 7.   † Exod. ii, 2.   ‡ Exod. iii, 2

35 And now come, I will send thee into Egypt. This Moses, whom
   they refused, saying, Who appointed thee a prince and a judge,
   the same did God send *to be* a ruler and a deliverer, by the hand
36 of the angel, who appeared to him in the bush. He brought them
   out, doing wonders and signs in the land of Egypt, and in the Red
   Sea, and in the wilderness forty years.
37   This is that Moses who said to the children of Israel, * The
   Lord your God will raise you up out of your brethren, a prophet
38 like me : him shall ye hear. † This is he that was in the Church
   in the wilderness, with the angel who spoke to him in Mount Sinai
   and *with* our fathers ; who received the living oracles to give to
39 us : ‡ Whom our fathers would not obey, but thrust *him* from
40 them, and in their hearts turned back into Egypt, Saying to Aaron,
   Make us gods to go before us ; for this Moses, who brought us out
41 of the land of Egypt, we know not what is become of him. And
   they made a calf in those days, and offered sacrifice to the idol, and
42 rejoiced in the works of their hands. And God turned and gave
   them up, to worship the host of heaven ; as it is written in the
   book of the prophets, § Have ye offered victims and sacrifices to
43 me for forty years in the wilderness, O house of Israel ? Yea, ye
   took up the shrine of Moloch, and the star of your god Remphan,

---

35. *This Moses whom they refused*—Namely, forty years before. Probably,
not they, but their fathers did it, and God imputes it to them. So God frequently
imputes the sins of the fathers to those of their children who are of the same
spirit. *Him did God send to be a deliverer*—Which is much more than a judge ;
by the hand of—That is, by means of *the angel*—This angel who spoke to Moses
on Mount Sinai expressly called himself Jehovah, a name which cannot, without
the highest presumption, be assumed by any created angel, since *he whose name
alone is Jehovah, is the Most High over all the earth*, Psalm lxxxiii, 18. It was
therefore the Son of God who delivered the law to Moses, under the character of
Jehovah, and who is here spoken of as the angel of the covenant, in respect of
his mediatorial office.
   37. *The Lord will raise you up a prophet*—St. Stephen here shows that there
is no opposition between Moses and Christ.
   38. *This is he*—Moses. *With the angel, and with our fathers*—As a mediator
between them. *Who received the living oracles*—Every period beginning with,
And the Lord said unto Moses, is properly an oracle. But the oracles here
intended are chiefly the ten commandments. These are termed living, because
all the word of God, applied by his Spirit, is living and powerful, Heb. iv, 12,
enlightening the eyes, rejoicing the heart, converting the soul, raising the dead.
   40. *Make us gods to go before us*—Back into Egypt.
   41. *And they made a calf*—In imitation of Apis, the Egyptian god : *and
rejoiced in the works of their hands*—In the god they had made.
   42. *God turned*—From them in anger ; *and gave them up*—Frequently, from
the time of the golden calf, to the time of Amos, and afterward. *The host of
heaven*—The stars are called an army or host, because of their number, order,
and powerful influence. *In the book of the prophets*—Of the twelve prophets,
which the Jews always wrote together in one book. *Have ye offered*—The passage of Amos referred to, chap. v, 25, &c, consists of two parts ; of which the
former confirms ver. 41, of the sin of the people ; the latter the beginning of ver.
42, concerning their punishment. *Have ye offered to me*—They had offered many
sacrifices ; but God did not accept them as offered to him, because they sacrificed
to idols also ; and did not sacrifice to him with an upright heart.
   43. *Ye took up*—Probably not long after the golden calf : but secretly ; else
Moses would have mentioned it. *The shrine*—A small, portable chapel, in
which was the image of their god. Moloch was the planet Mars, which they

* Deut xviii, 15   † Exod. xix, 3.   ‡ Exod. xxxiii, 1   § Amos v, 25.

figures which ye made to worship them: and I will carry you
44 away beyond Babylon. Our fathers had the tabernacle of the testimony in the wilderness, as he had appointed who spake to Moses,
45 to make it according to the model which he had seen: * Which
also our fathers having received, brought in with Joshua into the
possession of the Gentiles, whom God drove out from the face of
46 our fathers, till the days of David: Who found favour in the sight
of God, and petitioned to find a habitation for the God of Jacob.
47 But Solomon built him a house. Yet the Most High dwelleth
48 not in temples made with hands, as saith the prophet, † Heaven is
49 my throne, and earth my footstool. What house will ye build me,
50 saith the Lord; or what is the place of my rest? Hath not my
51 hand made all these things? Ye stiff necked and uncircumcised in
heart and ears, ye always resist the Holy Ghost: as your fathers,'
52 so do ye. Which of the prophets have not your fathers persecuted? And they have slain them that foretold the coming of the
Just One, of whom ye have now been the betrayers and murderers:
53 Who have received the law by the administration of angels, and
54 have not kept it. And hearing these things, they were cut to the
55 heart, and gnashed their teeth upon him. But he being full of the
Holy Ghost, looking steadfastly up to heaven, saw the glory of

worshipped under a human shape. Remphan, that is, Saturn, they represented
by a star. *And I will carry you beyond Babylon*—That is, beyond Damascus
(which is the word in Amos) and Babylon. This was fulfilled by the king of
Assyria, 2 Kings xvii, 6.
44. *Our fathers had the tabernacle of the testimony*—The testimony was properly
the two tables of stone, on which the ten commandments were written. Hence
the ark which contained them is frequently called the ark of the testimony;
and the whole tabernacle in this place. *The tabernacle of the testimony—according to the model which he had seen*—When he was caught up in the visions of
God on the mount.
45. *Which our fathers having received*—From their ancestors ; *brought into the
possession of the Gentiles*—Into the land which the Gentiles possessed before.
So that God's favour is not a necessary consequence of inhabiting this land. All
along St. Stephen intimates two things: 1. That God always loved good men in
every land : 2. That he never loved bad men even in this.
46. *Who petitioned to find a habitation for the God of Jacob*—But he did not
obtain his petition: for God remained without any temple till Solomon built
him a house. Observe how wisely the word is chosen with respect to what
follows.
48. *Yet the Most High inhabiteth not temples made with hands*—As Solomon
declared at the very dedication of the temple, 1 Kings viii, 27. *The Most High*
—Whom as such no building can contain.
49. *What is the place of my rest?*—Have I need to rest?
51. *Ye stiff necked*—Not bowing the neck to God's yoke ; *and uncircumcised
in heart*—So they showed themselves, ver. 54 ; *and ears*—As they showed,
ver. 57. So far were they from receiving the word of God into their hearts,
that they would not hear it even with their ears. *Ye*—And your fathers, *always*—As often as ever ye are called, *resist the Holy Ghost*—Testifying by the
prophets of Jesus, and the whole truth. This is the sum of what he had shown
at large.
53. *Who have received the law by the administration of angels*—God, when he
gave the law on Mount Sinai, was attended with thousands of his angels, Gal. iii,
19 ; Psa. lxviii, 17.
55. *But he looking steadfastly up to heaven, saw the glory of God*—Doubtless
he saw such a glorious representation, God miraculously operating on his ima-

* Josh. iii, 14.   † Isaiah lxvi, 1.

56 God, and Jesus standing on the right hand of God : And said, Behold, I see the heavens opened, and the Son of man standing on
57 the right hand of God. The‭ they cried with a loud voice, and
58 stopped their ears, and rushed upon him with one accord ; And
casting *him* out of the city, stoned *him :* and the witnesses laid
down their clothes at the feet of a young man, whose name was
59 Saul. And they stoned Stephen, invoking and saying, Lord Jesus,
60 receive my spirit. And kneeling down he cried with a loud voice,
Lord, lay not this sin to their charge. And having said this, he fell
asleep ; and Saul was consenting to his death.

VIII. And at that time there arose a great persecution against the
Church which was in Jerusalem. And they were all dispersed
through the countries of Judea and Samaria, except the apostles.
2 And devout men buried Stephen, and made lamentation over
3 him. But Saul made havoc of the Church, entering into every
4 house, and hauling men and women, committed *them* to prison.
Therefore they that were dispersed went every where, preaching
the word.
5 And Philip coming down to a city of Samaria, preached Christ
6 to them. And the people with one accord gave heed to the things
which Philip spoke, hearing and seeing the miracles which he did.
7 For unclean spirits, crying with a loud voice, came out of many

---

gination, as on Ezekiel's, when he sat in his house at Babylon, and saw
Jerusalem, and seemed to himself transported thither, chap. viii, 1-4. And probably other martyrs, when called to suffer the last extremity, have had extraordinary assistance of some similar kind.

56. *I see the Son of man standing*—As if it were just ready to receive him.
Otherwise he is said to sit at the right hand of God.

57. *They rushed upon him*—Before any sentence passed.

58. *The witnesses laid down their clothes at the feet of a young man, whose
name was Saul—O Saul,* couldst thou have believed, if one had told thee, that
thou thyself shouldst be stoned in the same cause ? and shouldst triumph in committing thy soul likewise to that Jesus whom thou art now blaspheming ? His
dying prayer reached thee, as well as many others. And the martyr Stephen,
and Saul the persecutor, (afterward his brother both in faith and martyrdom,)
are now joined in everlasting friendship, and dwell together in the happy company of those who *have made their robes white in the blood of the Lamb.*

59. *And they stoned Stephen, invoking and saying, Lord Jesus, receive my
spirit*—This is the literal translation of the words, the name of God not being in
the original. Nevertheless such a solemn prayer to Christ, in which a departing
soul is thus committed into his hands, is such an act of worship, as no good man
could have paid to a mere creature ; Stephen here worshipping Christ in the very
same manner in which Christ worshipped the Father on the cross.

VIII. *At that time there was great persecution against the Church*—Their adversaries having tasted blood, were the more eager. *And they were all dispersed*
—Not all the Church : if so, who would have remained for the apostles to teach,
or Saul to persecute ? But *all* the teachers *except the apostles,* who, though in
the most danger, stayed with the flock.

2. *Devout men*—Who feared God more than persecution. And yet were they
not of little faith ? Else they would not have *made so great lamentation.*

3. *Saul made havoc of the Church*—Like some furious beast of prey. So the
Greek word properly signifies. *Men and women*—Regarding neither age nor sex.

4. *Therefore they that were dispersed went every where*—These very words are
reassumed, after as it were a long parenthesis, chap. xi, 19, and the thread of the
story continued.

5. *Stephen*—Being taken away, Philip, his next colleague, (not the apostle,)
rises in his place.

that had them, and many sick of the palsy and lame were healed.
8 And there was great joy in that city. But a certain man, named
9 Simon, had been before in the city, using magic, and astonishing
10 the Samaritans, saying that he was some great one. To whom
they all gave heed, from the least to the greatest, saying, This man
11 is the great power of God. They gave heed to him, because he
12 had a long time astonished them with witchcraft. But when they
believed Philip, preaching the things of the kingdom of God,
and the name of Jesus Christ, they were baptized, both men and
13 women. And Simon himself believed also: and being baptized,
he continued with Philip, and was astonished, beholding the signs
14 and mighty miracles which were done. And the apostles who
were at Jerusalem, hearing that Samaria had received the word of
15 God, sent to them Peter and John: Who being come down, prayed
16 for them, that they might receive the Holy Ghost. For as yet
he was fallen upon none of them: only they had been baptized in
17 the name of the Lord Jesus. Then they laid hands on them, and
18 they received the Holy Ghost. And Simon seeing that through
laying on of the hands of the apostles the Holy Ghost was given,
19 offered them money, Saying, Give me also this power, that on
20 whomsoever I lay hands, he may receive the Holy Ghost. But
Peter said to him, Thy money perish with thee, because thou hast
21 thought to purchase the gift of God with money, Thou hast
neither part nor lot in this matter: for thy heart is not right in
22 the sight of God. Repent therefore of this thy wickedness, and
pray God, if perhaps the thought of thy heart may be forgiven thee.
23 For I see thou art in the gall of bitterness, and the bond of iniquity.
24 And Simon answering said, Pray ye to the Lord for me, that none

9. *A certain man—using magic*—So there was such a thing as witchcraft
once! In Asia at least, if not in Europe or America.
12. *But when they believed*—What Philip preached, then they saw and felt the
real power of God, and submitted thereto.
13. *And Simon believed*—That is, was convinced of the truth.
14. *And the apostles hearing that Samaria*—The inhabitants of that country,
had received the word of God—By faith, *sent Peter and John*—He that sends must
be either superior, or at least equal, to him that is sent. It follows that the college of the apostles was equal if not superior to Peter.
15. *The Holy Ghost*—In his miraculous gifts? Or his sanctifying graces?
Probably in both.
18. *Simon offered them money*—And hence the procuring any ministerial func-
tion, or ecclesiastical benefice by money, is termed Simony.
21. *Thou hast neither part*—By purchase, *nor lot*—Given gratis, *in this matter*—This gift of God. *For thy heart is not right before God*—Probably St. Peter
discerned this long before he had declared it; although it does not appear that
God gave to any of the apostles a universal power of discerning the hearts
of all they conversed with; any more than a universal power of healing all the
sick they came near. This we are sure St. Paul had not; though he was not
inferior to the chief of the apostles. Otherwise he would not have suffered the
illness of Epaphroditus to have brought him *so near to death*, Phil. ii, 25–27;
nor have left so useful a fellow labourer as *Trophimus sick at Miletus*, 2 Tim.
iv, 20.
22. *Repent—if perhaps the thought of thy heart may be forgiven thee*—Without
all doubt if he had repented, he would have been forgiven. The doubt was, whether he would repent. *Thou art in the gall of bitterness*—In the highest degree
of wickedness, which is bitterness, that is, misery to the soul; *and in the bond
of iniquity*—Fast bound therewith.

25 of these things which ye have spoken may come upon me. They
then having testified and spoken the word of the Lord, returned
toward Jerusalem, and preached the Gospel in many villages of
the Samaritans.
26 And an angel of the Lord spake to Philip, saying, Arise, and go
toward the south by the way leading down from Jerusalem to Gaza,
27 which is desert. And he arose and went. And lo! an Ethiopian,
an eunuch of great authority under Candace, queen of the Ethio
pians, who was over all her treasure, and had come to Jerusalem
28 to worship, Was returning, and sitting in his chariot, read the
29 Prophet Isaiah. Then the Spirit said to Philip, Go near and join
30 thyself to this chariot. And Philip running to him, heard him
read the Prophet Isaiah, and said, Understandest thou what
31 thou readest? And he said, How can I, unless some one guide
32 me? And he desired Philip to come up, and sit with him. The
portion of Scripture which he was reading was this, * He was led
as a sheep to the slaughter, and like a lamb dumb before his
33 shearer, so he opened not his mouth. In his humiliation his judgment was taken away; and who shall declare his generation? For
34 his life is taken from the earth. And the eunuch answering Philip,
said, I pray thee, of whom speaketh the prophet this? Of himself,
35 or of some other man? Then Philip opening his mouth, and begin-
36 ning from this scripture, preached Jesus to him. And as they went
on the way, they came to a certain water. And the eunuch said,
37 Behold water: what hindereth me to be baptized? And Philip
said, If thou believest with all thy heart thou mayest. And he an-

---

26. *The way which is desert*—There were two ways from Jerusalem to Gaza,
one desert, the other through a more populous country.

27. *An eunuch*—Chief officers were anciently called eunuchs, though not
always literally such; because such used to be chief ministers in the eastern
courts. *Candace, queen of the Ethiopians*—So all the queens of Ethiopia were
called.

28. *Sitting in his chariot, he read the Prophet Isaiah*—God meeteth those
that remember him in his ways. It is good to read, hear, seek information
even in a journey. Why should we not redeem all our time?

30. *And Philip running to him, said, Understandest thou what thou readest?*—
He did not begin about the weather, news, or the like. In speaking for God, we
may frequently come to the point at once, without circumlocution.

31. *He desired Philip to come up and sit with him*—Such was his modesty, and
thirst after instruction.

32. *The portion of Scripture*—By reading that very chapter, the fifty-third of
Isaiah, many Jews, yea, and atheists, have been converted. Some of them history records. God knoweth them all.

33. *In his humiliation his judgment was taken away*—That is, when he was a
man, he had no justice shown him. To *take away* a person's *judgment*, is a proverbial phrase for oppressing him. *And who shall declare*, or count *his generation*—That is, who can number *his seed*, Isa. liii, 10; which he hath purchased
by laying down his life?

36. *And as they went on the way they came to a certain water*—Thus, even the
circumstances of the journey were under the direction of God. The kingdom
of God suits itself to external circumstances, without any violence, as air yields
to all bodies, and yet pervades all. *What hindereth me to be baptized?*—Probably
he had been circumcised: otherwise Cornelius would not have been the first fruits
of the Gentiles.

38 swered and said, I believe that Jesus is the Son of God. And he
   commanded the chariot to stop, and they both went down into the
39 water, both Philip and the eunuch; and he baptized him. And
   when they were come up out of the water, the Spirit of the Lord
   caught away Philip, that the eunuch saw him no more; and he
40 went on his way rejoicing. But Philip was found at Azotus; and
   passing through, he preached in all the cities till he came to
   Cesarea.
IX. But * Saul, still breathing threatening and slaughter against the
2 disciples of the Lord, going to the high priest, desired of him
   letters to Damascus to the synagogues, that if he found any of this
   way, he might bring both men and women bound to Jerusalem.
3 And as he journeyed, he drew near Damascus; and suddenly there
4 shone about him a light from heaven. And falling to the earth he
   heard a voice saying to him, Saul, Saul, why persecutest thou
5 me? And he said, Who art thou, Lord? And the Lord said, I am
   Jesus whom thou persecutest. *It is* hard for thee to kick against
6 the goads. And he trembling and astonished, said, Lord, what
   wilt thou have me to do? And the Lord *said* to him, Arise, and go
7 into the city, and it shall be told thee what thou must do. And the
   men that journeyed with him stood astonished, hearing the noise,
8 but seeing no man. And Saul arose from the earth; and his eyes
   being opened, he saw no man; but they led him by the hand, and
9 brought *him* into Damascus. And he was three days without sight,

38. *And they both went down*—Out of the chariot. It does not follow that he
was baptized by immersion. The text neither affirms nor intimates any thing
concerning it.
39. *The Spirit of the Lord caught away Philip*—Carried him away with a
miraculous swiftness, without any action or labour of his own. This had befallen
several of the prophets.
40. *But Philip was found at Azotus*—Probably none saw him, from his leaving
the eunuch, till he was there.
IX. 2. *Bound*—By the connivance, if not authority, of the governor, under
Aretas the king. See ver. 14, 24.
3. *And suddenly*—When God suddenly and vehemently attacks a sinner, it is
the highest act of mercy. So Saul, when his rage was come to the height, is
taught not to *breathe slaughter*. And what was wanting in time to confirm him
in his discipleship, is compensated by the inexpressible terror he sustained. By
his also the suddenly constituted apostle was guarded against the grand snare
into which novices are apt to fall.
4. *He heard a voice*—Severe, yet full of grace.
5. *To kick against the goads*—is a Syriac proverb, expressing an attempt that
brings nothing but pain.
6. *It shall be told thee*—So God himself sends Saul to be taught by a man, as
the angel does Cornelius, chap. x, 5. Admirable condescension! that the Lord
deals with us by men, like ourselves.
7. *The men—stood*—Having risen before Saul; for they also fell to the ground,
chap. xxvi, 14. It is probable they all journeyed on foot. *Hearing the noise*—
But not an articulate voice. And seeing the light, but not Jesus himself, chap.
xxvi, 13, &c.
9. *And he was three days*—An important season! So long he seems to have
been in the pangs of the new birth. *Without sight*—By scales growing over his
eyes, to intimate to him the blindness of the state he had been in, to impress him
with a deeper sense of the almighty power of Christ, and to turn his thoughts
inward, while he was less capable of conversing with outward objects. This was

* Chap. xxii, 3, &c; chap. xxvi, 9, &c.

10 and neither ate nor drank. And there was a certain disciple at
Damascus, named Ananias. And the Lord said to him in a vision,
11 Ananias. And he said, Behold, I *am here*, Lord. And the Lord
said to him, Arise, go into the street called Straight, and inquire
in the house of Judas for *one* named Saul of Tarsus; for behold,
12 he is praying. And he hath seen in a vision a man named Ananias,
coming in, and putting his hand on him, that he may recover his
13 sight. But Ananias answered, Lord, I have heard by many of this
man, how much evil he hath done to thy saints at Jerusalem.
14 And here also he hath authority from the chief priests to bind all
15 that call on thy name. But the Lord said unto him, Go: for he
is a chosen vessel to me, to bear my name before nations and kings,
16 and the children of Israel. For I will show him how great things
17 he must suffer for my name's sake. And Ananias went and entered
into the house, and putting his hands on him, said, Brother Saul,
the Lord hath sent me, Jesus who appeared to thee in the way thou
camest, that thou mayest recover thy sight, and be filled with the
18 Holy Ghost. And immediately as it were scales fell from his eyes,
19 and he recovered his sight, and arose and was baptized. And having received food he was strengthened.
20 And he was certain days with the disciples in Damascus: and
straightway he preached Jesus in the synagogues, that he is the
21 Son of God. But all that heard were amazed, and said, Is not this
he who destroyed those that call on this name in Jerusalem? And
came hither for this intent, that he might bring them bound to the
22 chief priests? But Saul increased the more in strength, and confounded the Jews who dwelt at Damascus, proving that this is the
23 Christ. And when many days were fulfilled, the Jews consulted
24 together to kill him. But their lying in wait was known by Saul:
25 and they guarded the gates day and night to kill him. Then the
disciples taking him by night, let *him* down the wall in a basket.
26 And coming to Jerusalem, he endeavoured to join himself to the
disciples; but they were all afraid of him, not believing that he
27 was a disciple. But Barnabas taking him, brought *him* to the apos-

---

likewise a manifest token to others, of what had happened to him in his journey,
and ought to have humbled and convinced those bigoted Jews, to whom he had
been sent from the sanhedrim.

11. *Behold he is praying*—He was shown thus to Ananias.

12. *A man called Ananias*—His name also was revealed to Saul.

13. *But he answered*—How natural it is to *reason* against God

14. *All that call on thy name*—That is, all Christians.

15. *He is a chosen vessel to bear my name*—That is, to testify of me. It is
undeniable, that some men are unconditionally chosen or elected, to do some
works for God

16. *For I*—Do thou as thou art commanded. I will take care of the rest;
will show him—In fact, through the whole course of his ministry. *How great
things he must suffer*—So far will he be now from persecuting others.

17. *The Lord hath sent me*—Ananias does not tell Saul all which Christ had
said concerning him. It was not expedient that he should know yet to how great
a dignity he was called.

24. *They guarded the gates day and night*—That is, the governor did, at their
request, 2 Cor. xi, 32.

26. *And coming to Jerusalem*—Three years after, Gal. i, 18. These three
years St. Paul passes over, chap. xxii, 17, likewise.

tles, and declared to them, how he had seen the Lord in the way,
and that he had spoken to him, and how he had preached boldly
28 at Damascus in the name of Jesus: And he was with them, com-
29 ing in and going out at Jerusalem. And preaching boldly in the
name of the Lord Jesus, he spake and disputed with the Hellenists:
30 but they attempted to kill him: *Which* the brethren knowing,
31 brought him down to Cesarea, and sent him forth to Tarsus. Then
the Church through all Judea, and Galilee, and Samaria had peace:
and being built up, and walking in the fear of God, and the comfort of the Holy Ghost, *was* multiplied.
32 And as Peter passed through all *parts*, he came down also to the
33 saints that dwelt at Lydda. And he found there a certain man
named Eneas, who had kept his bed eight years, being ill of a
34 palsy. And Peter said to him, Eneas, Jesus Christ healeth thee.
35 Arise and make thy bed. And he arose immediately: And all that
dwelt in Lydda and Sharon saw *him*, and turned to the Lord.
36 Now there was at Joppa a certain disciple named Tabitha,
which is by interpretation Dorcas; this woman was full of good
37 works and alms deeds which she did. And in those days she was
sick and died; whom having washed, they laid in an upper cham-
38 ber. And Lydda being near Joppa, the disciples hearing Peter
was there, sent to him two men, desiring that he would not delay
39 to come to them. Then Peter arose and went with them; whom
being come, they brought into the upper chamber: and all the
widows stood by him weeping, and showing the coats and gar-
40 ments which Dorcas had made, while she was with them. But
Peter having put them all out, kneeled down and prayed; and

27. *To the apostles*—Peter and James, Gal. i, 18, 19. *And declared*—He who
has been an enemy to the truth ought not to be trusted till he gives proof that
he is changed.
31. *Then the Church*—The whole body of Christian believers, *had peace*—
Their bitterest persecutor being converted. *And being built up*—In holy, loving
faith, continually increasing, *and walking in*—That is, speaking and acting only
from this principle, *the fear of God and the comfort of the Holy Ghost*—An excellent mixture of inward and outward peace, tempered with filial fear.
35. *Lydda* was a large town, one day's journey from Jerusalem. It stood in
the plain or valley of Sharon, which extended from Cesarea to Joppa, and was
noted for its fruitfulness.
36. *Tabitha, which is by interpretation Dorcas*—She was probably a Hellenist
Jew, known among the Hebrews by the Syriac name Tabitha, while the Greeks
called her in their own language, Dorcas. They are both words of the same
import, and signify a roe or fawn.
38. *The disciples sent to him*—Probably none of those at Joppa had the gift
of miracles. Nor is it certain that they expected a miracle from him.
39. *While she was with them*—That is, before she died.
40. *Peter having put them all out*—That he might have the better opportunity
of wrestling with God in prayer, *said, Tabitha, arise. And she opened her eyes,
and seeing Peter, sat up*—Who can imagine the surprise of Dorcas, when called
back to life? Or of her friends, when they saw her alive? For the sake of themselves, and of the poor, there was cause of rejoicing, and much more, for such
a confirmation of the Gospel. Yet to herself it was matter of resignation, not
joy, to be called back to these scenes of vanity: but doubtless, her remaining
days were still more zealously spent in the service of her Saviour and her God.
Thus was a richer treasure laid up for her in heaven, and she afterward returned
to a more exceeding weight of glory, than that from which so astonishing a providence had recalled her for a season.

41 turning to the body, said, Tabitha, arise. And she opened her
eyes, and seeing Peter, sat up. And giving her his hand, he lifted
her up, and having called the saints and widows, he presented her
42 alive. And it was known through all Joppa, and many believed on
43 the Lord. And he tarried many days in Joppa, with one Simon,
a tanner.
X.   And there was a certain man in Cesarea, named Cornelius, a
2 centurion of that called the Italian band, A devout *man*, and fearing God with all his house, who gave much alms to the people,
3 and prayed to God always. He saw plainly in a vision, about the
ninth hour of the day, an angel of God coming in to him, and say-
4 ing to him, Cornelius. And looking steadfastly on him, and being
affrighted, he said, What is it, sir? And he said to him, Thy
prayers and thine alms are come up for a memorial before God.
5 And now send men to Joppa, and call hither Simon, who is sur-
6 named Peter. He lodgeth with one Simon, a tanner, whose house
7 is by the sea. And when the angel who spake to him was departed, he called two of his household servants, and a devout soldier
8 of them that waited on him continually: And having declared all
9 things to them, he sent them to Joppa. On the morrow, as they
journeyed and drew nigh to the city, Peter went up on the house-
10 top to pray, about the sixth hour. And he became very hungry,
and would have eaten; but while they made ready, he fell into a
11 trance, And saw heaven opened, and a certain vessel like a great
sheet, tied at the four corners, descending and let down on the
12 earth: Wherein were all four-footed creatures, and creeping things
13 of the earth, and fowls of the air. And a voice came to him, Rise,
14 Peter, kill and eat. But Peter said, In nowise, Lord: for I have

X. *And there was a certain man*—The first fruits of the *Gentiles, in Cesarea*—
Where Philip had been before, chap. viii, 40; so that the doctrine of salvation
by faith in Jesus was not unknown there. Cesarea was the seat of the civil
government, as Jerusalem was of the ecclesiastical. It is observable, that the
Gospel made its way first through the metropolitan cities. So it first seized
Jerusalem and Cesarea: afterward *Philippi, Athens, Corinth, Ephesus, Rome*
itself. *A centurion,* or captain, *of that called the Italian band*—That is, troop
or company.
    2. *Who gave much alms to the people*—That is, to the Jews, many of whom
were at that time extremely poor.
    3. *He saw in a vision*—Not in a trance, like Peter : *plainly,* so as to leave one
not accustomed to things of this kind no room to suspect any imposition.
    4. *Thy prayers and thine alms are come up for a memorial before God*—Dare any
man say, These were only *splendid sins?* Or that they were an abomination before God? And yet it is certain, in the Christian sense Cornelius was then an
unbeliever. He had not then faith in Christ. So certain it is, that every one
who seeks faith in Christ, should seek it in prayer, and doing good to all men :
though in strictness what is not exactly according to the Divine rule must stand
in need of Divine favour and indulgence.
    . 8. *A devout soldier*—How many such attendants have our modern officers? *A
devout soldier* would now be looked upon as little better than a deserter from his
colours.
    10. *And he became very hungry*—At the usual meal time. The symbols in
visions and trances, it is easy to observe, are generally suited to the state of the
natural faculties.
    11. *Tied at the corners*—Not all in one knot, but each fastened as it were up
to heaven.
    4 *But Peter said, In nowise, Lord*—When God commands a strange or

15 never eaten any thing common or unclean   And the voice *came*
to him again, the second time, What God hat purified, call not
16 thou common.   This was done thrice, and the vessel was taken
17 up again to heaven.   Now while Peter doubted in himself what
the vision he had seen should mean, behold the men sent by Cornelius, having inquired out Simon's house, stood at the gate,
18 And calling asked, whether Simon, surnamed Peter, lodged there?
19 While Peter was musing on the vision, the Spirit said to him, Be-
20 hold, three men seek thee.   Arise therefore and go down, and go
21 with them, doubting nothing; for I have sent them.   Then Peter
going down to the men, said, Behold, I am he whom ye seek:
22 for what cause are ye come?   And they said, Cornelius, a centurion, a just man, and fearing God, and of good report among all the
nation of the Jews, was warned of God by a holy angel, to send
23 for thee to his house, and to hear words from thee.   And he invited them in and lodged *them.*   And the next day, rising up, he
went away with them ; and certain brethren from Joppa went with
24 him.   And the day following they entered into Cesarea : and Cornelius was waiting for them, having called together his kinsmen
25 and near friends : And as Peter was coming in, Cornelius met
26 him, and falling down at his feet, worshipped *him :* But Peter
27 raised him up, saying, Arise : I myself also am a man : And as
he talked with him, he went in and found many come together :
28 And he said to them, Ye know it is unlawful for a Jew to join with
or come to one of another nation ; but God hath showed me to
29 call no man common or unclean : Therefore being sent for, I came
without gainsaying : I ask, therefore, for what intent ye have sent
30 for me?   And Cornelius said, Four days ago I was fasting till this

seemingly improper thing, the first objection frequently finds pardon.   But it
ought not to be repeated.   This doubt and delay of St. Peter had several good
effects.   Hereby the will of God in this important point was made more evident
and incontestable.   And Peter also, having been so slow of belief himself, could
the more easily bear the doubting of his brethren, chap. xi, 2, &c.
    15. *What God hath purified*—Hath made and declared clean.   Nothing but
what is clean can come down from heaven.   St. Peter well remembered this saying in the council at Jerusalem, chap. xv, 9.
    16. *This was done thrice*—To make the deeper impression.
    17. *While Peter doubted in himself, behold the men*—Frequently the things
which befall us *within* and from *without* at the same time, are a key to each
other.   The things which thus concur and agree together, ought to be diligently
attended to.
    19. *Behold three men seek thee, arise therefore and go down, and go with them,
doubting nothing*—How gradually was St. Peter prepared to receive this new
admonition of the Spirit !   Thus God is wont to lead on his children by degrees,
always giving them light for the present hour.
    24. *Cornelius was waiting for them*—Not engaging himself in any secular busi-
ness during that solemn time, but being altogether intent on this one thing.
    26. *I myself also am a man*—And not God, who alone ought to be worshipped,
Matt. iv, 10.   Have all his pretended successors attended to this ?
    28. *But God hath showed me*—He speaks sparingly to *them* of his former doubt,
and his late vision.
    29. *I ask for what intent ye have sent for me?*—St. Peter knew this already.
But he puts Cornelius on telling the story, both that the rest might be informed,
and Cornelius himself more impressed by the narration : the repetition of which,
even as we read it, gives a new dignity and spirit to Peter's succeeding discourse.
    30. *Four days ago I was fasting*—The first of these days he had the vision ;

hour, and at the ninth hour I was praying in my house, and
31 behold a man stood before me in bright clothing, And said, Cornelius, thy prayer is heard, and thine alms are remembered be-
32 fore God. Send therefore to Joppa, and call hither Simon, who is
surnamed Peter; he lodgeth in the house of Simon a tanner by
33 the sea, who being come shall speak to thee. Immediately therefore I sent to thee, and thou hast done well in coming : now therefore we are all present before God, to hear all things that are
commanded thee by God.
34   Then Peter opening *his* mouth, said, I perceive of a truth that
35 God is not a respecter of persons : But in every nation, he that
36 feareth him, and worketh righteousness, is accepted by him. *This
is* the word which he sent to the children of Israel, preaching the
glad tidings of peace through Jesus Christ: he is Lord of all.
37 Ye know the word which was published through all Judea, begin-
38 ning from Galilee, after the baptism which John preached : How
God anointed Jesus of Nazareth with the Holy Ghost and with
power, who went about doing good, and healing all that were op-
39 pressed by the devil ; for God was with him. And we are witnesses of all things which he did, both in the land of the Jews and
in Jerusalem : whom yet they slew, having hanged *him* on a tree.
40 Him God raised up the third day, and showed him openly ; (Not

the second his messengers came to Joppa; on the third, St. Peter set out ; and on
the fourth, came to Cesarea.
31. *Thy prayer is heard*—Doubtless he had been praying for instruction, how
to worship God in the most acceptable manner.
33. *Now therefore we are all present before God*—The language of every truly
Christian congregation.
34. *I perceive of a truth*—More clearly than ever, from such a concurrence of
circumstances. *That God is not a respecter of persons*—Is not partial in his love.
The words mean, in a particular sense, that he does not confine his love to one
nation ; in a general, that he is loving to every man, and willeth all men should
be saved.
35. *But in every nation he that feareth God and worketh righteousness*—He that,
first, reverences God, as great, wise, good, the cause, end, and governor of all
things ; and secondly, from this awful regard to him, not only avoids all known
evil, but endeavours, according to the best light he has, to do all things well ;
is accepted of him—Through Christ, though he knows him not. The assertion
is express, and admits of no exception. He is in the favour of God, whether
enjoying his written word and ordinances or not. Nevertheless the addition of
these is an unspeakable blessing to those who were before in some measure accepted. Otherwise God would never have sent an angel from heaven to direct
Cornelius to St. Peter.
36. *This is the word which God sent*—When he sent his Son into the world,
preaching—Proclaiming by him—*peace* between God and man, whether Jew or
Gentile, by the God-man. *He is Lord of* both ; yea, Lord of and over all.
37. *Ye know the word which was published*—You know the facts in general,
the meaning of which I shall now more particularly explain and confirm to you.
The baptism which John preached—To which he invited them by his preaching,
in token of their repentance. This began in Galilee, which is near Cesarea.
38. *How God anointed Jesus*—Particularly at his baptism, thereby inaugurating
him to his office : *with the Holy Ghost and with power*—It is worthy our remark,
that frequently when the Holy Ghost is mentioned there is added a word particularly adapted to the present circumstance. So the deacons were to be full
of the Holy Ghost and wisdom, chap. vi, 3. Barnabas was full of the Holy Ghost
and faith, chap. xi, 24. The disciples were filled with joy, and with the Holy
Ghost, chap xiii, 52. And here, where his mighty works are mentioned, Christ

41 to all the people, but to witnesses, chosen before of God, *even* to us,
who did eat and drink with him,) after he rose from the dead.
42 And he commanded us to proclaim to the people, and to testify,
that it is he who is ordained by God the Judge of the living, and the
43 dead. To him give all the prophets witness, that every one who
believeth in him, receiveth forgiveness of sins through his name.
44   While Peter was yet speaking these words, the Holy Ghost fell
45 on all that were hearing the word. And the believers of the circumcision, as many as came with Peter, were amazed, that the
46 gift of the Holy Ghost was poured out on the Gentiles also.   For
they heard them speaking with tongues and magnifying God.
47 Then Peter answered, Can any man forbid water, that these should
not be baptized, who have received the Holy Ghost, even as we?
48 And he commanded them to be baptized in the name of the Lord.
Then they prayed him to tarry certain days.
XI.   Now the apostles and brethren who were in Judea heard that
2 the Gentiles also had received the word of God.   And when Peter
was come up to Jerusalem, they of the circumcision debated with
3 him saying, Thou wentest in to men uncircumcised, and didst eat
4 with them.   Then Peter beginning, laid *all things* before them in

---

himself is said to be anointed with the Holy Ghost and with power. *For God
was with him*—He speaks sparingly here of the majesty of Christ, as considering
the state of his hearers.

41. *Not* now *to all the people*—As before his death ; *to us who did eat and
drink with him*—That is, conversed familiarly and continually with him, in the
time of his ministry.

42. *It is he who is ordained by God the Judge of the living and the dead*—Of
all men, whether they are alive at his coming, or had died before it. This was
declaring to them, in the strongest terms, how entirely their happiness depended
on a timely and humble subjection to him who was to be their final Judge.

43. *To him give all the prophets witness*—Speaking to heathens he does not
quote any in particular ; *that every one who believeth in him*—Whether he be Jew
or Gentile ; *receiveth remission of sins*—Though he had not before either feared
God, or worked righteousness.

44. *The Holy Ghost fell on all that were hearing the word*—Thus were they
consecrated to God, as the first fruits of the Gentiles. And thus did God give a
clear and satisfactory evidence, that he had accepted them as well as the Jews.

45. *The believers of the circumcision*—The believing Jews.

47. *Can any man forbid water, that these should not be baptized, who have received the Holy Ghost?*—He does not say they have the baptism of the Spirit ;
therefore they do not need baptism with water. But just the contrary : if they
have received the Spirit, then baptize them with water.

How easily is this question decided, if we will take the word of God for our
rule ! Either men have received the Holy Ghost or not. If they have not, *Repent*, saith God, *and be baptized, and ye shall receive the gift of the Holy Ghost.*
If they have, if they are already baptized with the Holy Ghost, then *who can
forbid water ?*

48. *In the name of the Lord*—Which implies the Father who anointed him, and
the Spirit with which he was anointed to his office. But as the Gentiles had before believed in God the Father, and could not but now believe in the Holy Ghost,
under whose powerful influence they were at this very time, there was the less
need of taking notice, that they were baptized into the belief and profession of
the sacred Three : though doubtless the apostle administered the ordinances in
that very form which Christ himself had prescribed.

XI. 4. *Peter laid all things before them*—So he did not take it ill to be ques
tioned, nor desire to be treated as infallible. And he answers the more mildly
because it related to a point which he had not readily believed himself.

5 order, saying, I was praying in the city of Joppa, and *being* in a
trance, I saw a vision, a certain vessel descending, as it were a
great sheet, let down from heaven by the four corners, and it
6 came even to me : On which looking steadfastly, I observed and
saw four-footed creatures of the earth, and creeping things, and
7 fowls of the air. And I heard a voice saying to me, Rise, Peter,
8 kill and eat. But I said, In nowise Lord ; for nothing common
9 or unclean hath ever entered into my mouth. And the voice from
heaven answered me again, What God hath purified, call not thou
10 common. This was done thrice, and all were drawn up again
11 into heaven. And behold immediately three men stood at the
12 house where I was, sent from Cesarea to me. And the Spirit
bade me go with them, doubting nothing : these six brethren also
13 went with me, and we entered into the man's house. And he told
us how he had seen an angel standing in his house, and saying to
him, Send men to Joppa, and call hither Simon, surnamed Peter,
14 Who shall tell thee words, whereby thou and all thy family may
15 be saved. And as I began to speak, the Holy Ghost fell on them,
16 even as on us at the beginning. Then I remembered the word of
the Lord, how he said, John indeed baptized with water, but ye
17 shall be baptized with the Holy Ghost. If then God gave to them
the same gift as even to us, when we believed on the Lord Jesus
18 Christ, who was I that could withstand God ? When they heard
these things, they were quiet, and glorified God, saying, Then
God hath given to the Gentiles also repentance unto life.
19   Now they who had been dispersed by the distress which arose
about Stephen, travelled as far as Phenicia, and Cyprus, and An-
20 tioch, speaking the word to none but Jews only. And some of them
were men of Cyprus and Cyrene, who coming into Antioch, spake

---

5. *Being in a trance*—Which suspends the use of the outward senses.
14. *Saved*—With the full Christian salvation, in this world and the world to
come.
17. *To us, when we believed*—The sense is, because we believed, not because
we were circumcised, was the Holy Ghost given to us. *What was I*—A mere
instrument in God's hand. They had inquired only concerning his *eating with
the Gentiles.* He satisfies them likewise concerning his baptizing them, and shows
that he had done right in going to Cornelius, not only by the command of God,
but also by the event, the descent of the Holy Ghost.
And *who are* we *that* we *should withstand God ?* Particularly by laying down
rules of Christian communion which exclude any whom he has admitted into
the Church of the first born, from worshipping God together. O that all
Church governors would consider how bold an usurpation this is on the
authority of the supreme Lord of the Church! O that the sin of thus withstanding God may not be laid to the charge of those, who perhaps with a
good intention, but in an over fondness for their own forms, have done it, and
are continually doing it.
18. *They glorified God*—Being thoroughly satisfied. *Repentance unto life*—
True repentance is a change from spiritual death to spiritual life, and leads to
life everlasting.
19. *They who had been dispersed*—St. Luke here resumes the thread of his
narration, in the very words wherewith he broke it off, chap. viii, 6. As far as
Phenicia to the north, Cyprus to the west, and Antioch to the east.
20. *Some of them were men of Cyprus and Cyrene*—Who were more accustomed to converse with the Gentiles. *Who coming into Antioch*—Then the
capital of Syria, and, next to Rome and Alexandria, the most considerable city of

21 to the Greeks, preaching the Lord Jesus. And the hand of the
Lord was with them; and a great number believed and turned to
22 the Lord. And tidings of these things came to the ears of the
Church that was in Jerusalem, and they sent forth Barnabas to go
23 as far as Antioch: Who coming and seeing the grace of God, was
glad, and exhorted *them* all to cleave unto the Lord with full purpose
24 of heart. For he was a good man, and full of the Holy Ghost and
25 faith. And a considerable multitude was added to the Lord. Then
went he to Tarsus to seek Saul, and having found him, he brought
26 him to Antioch. And a whole year they assembled themselves with
the Church, and taught a considerable multitude: and the disciples
were first called Christians at Antioch.
27 In those days prophets came from Jerusalem to Antioch. And
28 one of them, named Agabus, rising up, signified by the Spirit that
there would be a great famine through all the world; which also
29 came to pass under Claudius Cesar. Then the disciples determined to send relief, every one according to his ability, to the
30 brethren who dwelt in Judea: Which also they did, sending *it* to
the elders by the hand of Barnabas and Saul.
XII. About that time Herod the king stretched forth his hands to
2 afflict certain of the Church. And he slew James the brother of
3 John with the sword. And perceiving it pleased the Jews, he
proceeded to take Peter also: (Then were the days of unleavened
4 bread.) Whom having apprehended, he put him in prison, delivering him to four quaternions of soldiers to keep him, intending to
5 bring him forth to the people after the passover. So Peter was

the empire. *Spake to the Greeks*—As the Greeks were the most celebrated of
the Gentile nations near Judea, the Jews called all the Gentiles by that name.
Here we have the first account of the preaching the Gospel to the idolatrous
Gentiles. All those to whom it had been preached before, did at least worship
one God, the God of Israel.
  21. *And the hand of the Lord*—That is, the power of his Spirit.
  26. *And the disciples were first called Christians at Antioch*—Here it was that
they first received this standing appellation. They were before termed Nazarenes
and Galileans.
  28. *Agabus rising up*—In the congregation. *All the world*—The word frequently signifies all the Roman empire. And so it is doubtless to be taken here.
  29. *Then*—Understanding the distress they would otherwise be in on that account, *the disciples determined to send relief to the brethren in Judea*—Who
herein received a manifest proof of the reality of their conversion.
  30. *Sending it to the elders*—Who gave it to the deacons, to be distributed by
them, as every one had need.
  XII. *About that time*—So wisely did God mix rest and persecution in due time
and measure succeeding each other. *Herod*—Agrippa; the latter was his Roman, the former his Syrian name. He was the grandson of Herod the Great,
nephew to Herod Antipas, who beheaded John the Baptist; brother to Herodias,
and father to that Agrippa before whom St. Paul afterward made his defence.
Caligula made him king of the tetrarchy of his uncle Philip, to which he afterward
added the territories of Antipas. Claudius made him also king of Judea, and added
thereto the dominions of Lysanias.
  2. *James the brother of John*—So one of the brothers went to God the first, the
other the last of the apostles.
  3. *Then were the days of unleavened bread*—At which the Jews came together
from all parts.
  4. *Four quaternions*—Sixteen men, who watched by turns day and night.
  5. *Continual prayer was made for him*—Yet when their prayer was answered,

kept in the prison; but continual prayer was made to God by the Church for him.

6 And when Herod was about to bring him forth, the same night Peter was sleeping between two soldiers, bound with two chains,
7 and the guards before the door were keeping the prison. And behold, an angel of the Lord stood over him, and light shined in the house: and smiting Peter on the side he waked him, saying, Rise
8 up quickly. And his chains fell off from his hands. And the angel said to him, Gird thyself, and bind on thy sandals; and he did so. And he said to him, Throw thy garment about thee, and follow me.
9 And going out, he followed him. And he knew not that it was real which was done by the angel, but thought he saw a vision.
10 When they had passed through the first and the second ward, they came to the iron gate that leadeth to the city, which opened to them of its own accord: and going out, they went on through one
11 street; and immediately the angel departed from him. And Peter coming to himself, said, Now I know of a truth, that the Lord hath sent his angel, and delivered me out of the hand of Herod, and
12 *from* all the expectation of the people of the Jews. And having considered, he went to the house of Mary, the mother of John, sur-
13 named Mark, where many were gathered together praying. And as he knocked at the door of the gate, a damsel came to hearken,
14 named Rhoda. And knowing Peter's voice, she opened not the gate for joy, but running in, told *them* that Peter stood before the
15 gate. And they said to her, Thou art mad. But she constantly
16 affirmed it was so. Then they said, It is his angel. But Peter continued knocking. And opening *the door* they saw him, and
17 were astonished. But he beckoning to them with his hand to be silent, declared to them how the Lord had brought him out of the prison. And he said, Show these things to James and to the bre-

they could scarce believe it, ver. 15. But why had they not prayed for St. James also? Because he was put to death as soon as apprehended.

6. *Peter was sleeping*—Easy and void of fear; *between two soldiers*—Sufficiently secured to human appearance.

7. *His chains*—With which his right arm was bound to one of the soldiers, and his left arm to the other.

8. *Gird thyself*—Probably he had put off his girdle, sandals, and upper garment, before he lay down to sleep.

10. *The first and second ward*—At each of which doubtless was a guard of soldiers. *The gate opened of its own accord*—Without either Peter or the angel touching it. *And they went on through one street*—That Peter might know which way to go. *And the angel departed from him*—Being himself sufficient for what remained to be done.

11. *Now I know of a truth*—That this is not a vision, ver. 9.

12. *And having considered*—What was best to be done. *Many were gathered together*—At midnight.

13. *The gate*—At some distance from the house; *to hearken*—If any knocked.

14. *And knowing Peter's voice*—Bidding her open the door.

15. *They said, Thou art mad*—As we say, Sure you are not in your senses to talk so. *It is his angel*—It was a common opinion among the Jews, that every man had his particular guardian angel, who frequently assumed both his shape and voice. But this is a point on which the Scriptures are silent.

17. *Beckoning to them*—Many of whom being amazed, were talking together *And he said, Show these things to James*—The brother or kinsman of our Lord, and author of the epistle which bears his name. He appears to have been a per

18 thren. And going out he went to another place. Now when it was day, there was no small stir among the soldiers, what was
19 become of Peter. And Herod having sought for him, and not found *him*, examined the keepers, and commanded *them* to be put
20 to death. And going down from Judea to Cesarea, he abode *there*. And he was highly incensed against them of Tyre and Sidon: but they came with one accord to him, and having gained Blastus, the king's chamberlain, sued for peace; because their country was nourished by the king's country.
21 And on a set day, Herod, arrayed in royal apparel, and sitting
22 on his throne, made an oration to them. And the people shouted,
23 *It is* the voice of a god, and not of a man. And immediately an angel of the Lord smote him, because he gave not glory to God;
24 and being eaten by worms, he expired. But the word of God grew and multiplied.
25 And Barnabas and Saul, having fulfilled their service, returned from Jerusalem, taking with them John, surnamed Mark.
XIII. Now there were in the 'Church that was at Antioch, prophets and teachers, Barnabas, and Simeon called Niger, and Lucius of Cyrene, and Manaen, who had been brought up with Herod the
2 tetrarch, and Saul. And as they were ministering to the Lord and fasting, the Holy Ghost said, Separate me Barnabas and Saul for

son of considerable weight and importance, probably the chief overseer of that province, and of the Church in Jerusalem in particular. *He went into another place*—Where he might be better concealed till the storm was over.

19. *Herod commanded them to be put to death*—And thus the wicked suffered in the room of the righteous. *And going down from Judea*—With shame, for not having brought forth Peter, according to his promise.

20. *Having gained Blastus*—To their side, *they sued for*, and obtained *peace*—Reconciliation with Herod. And so the Christians of those parts were, by the providence of God, delivered from scarcity. *Their country was nourished*—Was provided with corn, *by the king's country*—Thus Hiram also, king of Tyre, desired of Solomon food or corn for his household, 1 Kings v, 9.

21. *And on a set day*—Which was solemnized yearly, in honour of Claudius Cesar; *Herod, arrayed in royal apparel*—In a garment so wrought with silver, that the rays of the rising sun striking upon, and being reflected from it, dazzled the eyes of the beholders. *The people shouted, It is the voice of a god*—Such profane flattery they frequently paid to princes. But the commonness of a wicked custom rather increases than lessens the guilt of it.

23. *And immediately*—God does not delay to vindicate his injured honour; *an angel of the Lord smote him*—Of this other historians say nothing: so wide a difference there is between Divine and human history! An angel of the Lord brought out Peter; an angel smote Herod. Men did not see the instruments in either case. These were only known to the people of God. *Because he gave not glory to God*—He willingly received it to himself, and by this sacrilege filled up the measure of his iniquities. So then vengeance tarried not. *And he was eaten by worms*, or vermin—How changed! And on the fifth day expired in exquisite torture. Such was the event! The persecutor perished, and the Gospel *grew and multiplied*.

25. *Saul returned*—To Antioch; *taking John, surnamed Mark*—The son of Mary, (at whose house the disciples met, to pray for Peter,) who was sister to Barnabas.

XIII. *Manaen, who had been brought up with Herod*—His foster brother, now freed from the temptations of a court.

2. *Separate me Barnabas and Saul for the work to which I have called them*—This was not ordaining them. St. Paul was ordained long before, and that *not of men, neither by man:* it was only inducting him to the province for which ou.

3 the work to which I have called them. Then having fasted and
4 prayed, and laid their hands on them, they sent *them* away. So
being sent forth by the Holy Ghost, they went down to Seleucia, and
5 from thence sailed to Cyprus. And being at Salamis, they preached
the word of God in the synagogues of the Jews; and they had
6 also John for *their* attendant. And having gone through the whole
isle as far as Paphos, they found a certain magician, a false prophet,
7 a Jew, whose name *was* Bar-jesus, Who was with the proconsul,
Sergius Paulus, a prudent man. He calling to him Barnabas and
8 Saul, desired to hear the word of God. But Elymas the magician
(so is his name by interpretation) withstood them, seeking to turn
9 away the proconsul from the faith. Then Saul, (who *is* also *called*
Paul,) filled with the Holy Ghost, fixing his eyes upon him, said,
10 O full of all guile and of all mischief, thou son of the devil, thou
enemy of all righteousness, wilt thou not cease to pervert the right
11 ways of the Lord? And now behold the hand of the Lord *is* upon
thee; and thou shalt be blind, not seeing the sun for a season.
And immediately a mist and darkness fell upon him, and going
12 about, he sought some to lead him. Then the proconsul, seeing
what was done, believed, being astonished at the doctrine of the
Lord.
13 And Paul and those with him loosing from Paphos, came to
Perga in Pamphylia; but John withdrawing from them, returned
14 to Jerusalem. And departing from Perga, they came to Antioch
in Pisidia; and going into the synagogue on the Sabbath day, they
15 sat down. And after the reading of the law and the prophets, the
chief of the synagogue sent to them, saying, Brethren, if ye have

Lord had appointed him from the beginning, and which was now revealed to the
prophets and teachers. In consequence of this they fasted, prayed, and laid their
hands on them, a rite which was used not in ordination only, but in blessing, and
on many other occasions.

3. *Then having fasted*—Again. Thus they did also, chap. xiv, 23.

5. *In the synagogues*—Using all opportunities that offered.

6. *Paphos* was on the western, *Salamis* on the eastern part of the island.

7. *The proconsul*—The Roman governor of Cyprus, *a prudent man*—And therefore not overswayed by Elymas, but desirous to inquire farther.

9. *Then Saul, who was also called Paul*—It is not improbable, that coming
now among the Romans, they would naturally adapt his name to their own language, and so called him Paul instead of Saul. Perhaps the family of the proconsul might be the first who addressed to or spoke of him by this name. And
from this time, being the apostle of the Gentiles, he himself used the name which
was more familiar to them.

10. *O full of all guile*—As a false prophet, *and all mischief*—As a magician.
Thou son of the devil—A title well suited to a magician; and one who not only
was himself unrighteous, but laboured to keep others from all goodness. *Wilt
thou not cease to pervert the right ways of the Lord?*—Even now thou hast heard
the truth of the Gospel.

11. *And immediately a mist*—Or dimness within, *and darkness* without, *fell
upon him.*

12. *Being astonished at the doctrine of the Lord*—Confirmed by such a miracle

13. *John withdrawing from them returned*—Tired with the fatigue, or shrink
ing from danger.

14. *Antioch in Pisidia*—Different from the Antioch mentioned ver. 1.

15. *And after the reading of the law and the prophets, the chief of the synagogue sent to them*—The law was read over once every year, a portion of it every
Sabbath : to which was added a lesson taken out of the prophets. After this was

16 any word of exhortation to the people, speak. Then Paul standing, and waving his hand, said, Ye men of Israel, and ye that fear
17 God, hearken. * The God of this people chose our fathers, and
raised. the people, while sojourning in the land of Egypt, and
18 brought them out of it with an uplifted arm. † And he suffered
their manners in the wilderness about the space of forty years.
9 And having destroyed seven nations in the land of Canaan, he
divided their land to them by lot, about four hundred and fifty years.
20 And after that, he gave *them* judges ; until Samuel the prophet.
21 And afterward they desired a king : and God gave them Saul the
22 son of Kish, a man of the tribe of Benjamin, forty years. And
having removed him, ‡ he raised up to them David for their king,
to whom also bearing witness he said, I have found David, the *son*
of Jesse, a man after my own heart, who will do all my will.
23 Of this man's seed hath God, according to *his* promise, raised
24 unto Israel a Saviour, Jesus ; John having first preached before his
coming, the baptism of repentance to all the people of Israel.
25 § And as John was fulfilling his course, he said, Whom think ye
that I am ? I am not *he.* But behold one cometh after me, the
shoes of whose feet I am not worthy to loose.
26 Men, brethren, children of the stock of Abraham, and those

over, any one might speak to the people, on any subject he thought convenient.
Yet it was a circumstance of decency which Paul and Barnabas would hardly
omit, to acquaint the rulers with their desire of doing it : probably by some message before the service began.
16. *Ye that fear God*—Whether proselytes or heathens.
17. *The God*—By such a commemoration of God's favours to their fathers, at
once their minds were conciliated to the speaker, they were convinced of their
duty to God, and invited to believe his promise, and the accomplishment of it.—
The six verses, 17–22, contain the whole sum of the Old Testament. *Of this
people*—Paul here chiefly addresses himself to those whom he styles, *Ye that fear
God :* he speaks of Israel first ; and ver. 26, speaks more directly to the Israelites
themselves. *Chose*—And this exalted the people ; not any merit or goodness of
their own, Ezek. xx, 5. *Our fathers—Abraham* and his posterity.
19. *Seven nations*—Enumerated Deut. vii, 1 ; *about four hundred and fifty
years*—That is, from the choice of the fathers to the dividing of the land ; it was
about four hundred and fifty years.
21. *He gave them Saul forty years*—Including the time wherein *Samuel* judged
Israel.
22. *Having removed him*—Hence they might understand that the dispensations
of God admit of various changes. *I have found David, a man after my own heart*
—This expression is to be taken in a limited sense. David was such at that
time, but not at all times. And he was so, in that respect, as he performed all
God's will, in the particulars there mentioned: But he was not a *man after God's
own heart,* in other respects, wherein he performed his own will. In the matter
of Uriah, for instance, he was as far from being a *man after God's own heart* as
Saul himself was. It is therefore a very gross, as well as dangerous mistake, to
suppose this is the character of David in every part of his behaviour. We must
beware of this, unless we would recommend adultery and murder as *things after
God's own heart.*
24. *John having first preached*—He mentions this, as a thing already known
to them. And so doubtless it was. For it gave so loud an alarm to the whole
Jewish nation, as could not but be heard of in foreign countries, at least as
remote as Pisidia.
25. *His course*—His work was quickly finished, and might therefore well be
termed a course or race.

* Isaiah i, 2.　† Deut. i, 31.　‡ 1 Sam. xvi, 12, 13.　§ Luke iii, 16.

among you who fear God, to you is the word of this salvation sent.
27 For they that dwell at Jerusalem, and their rulers, neither knowing him, nor the sayings of the prophets, which are read every
28 Sabbath day, have fulfilled *them*, in condemning *him*.   And though
they found no cause of death *in him*, yet desired they Pilate, that
29 he might be put to death.   And when they had fulfilled all things
that were written of him, taking *him* down from the tree, they laid
30 *him* in a sepulchre.   But God raised him from the dead.   And he
31 was seen many days by them who came up with him from Galilee
to Jerusalem, who are his witnesses to the people.
32 And we declare to you glad tidings, that the promise which was
33 made to the fathers, God hath fulfilled this to us their children, in
raising up Jesus : as it was written also in the second Psalm,
34 * Thou art my Son, this day have I begotten thee.   And because
he raised him up from the dead, no more to return to corruption,
35 he spake thus, † I will give you the sure mercies of David.   Wherefore he saith also in another Psalm, ‡ Thou wilt not suffer thy
36 Holy One to see corruption.   Now David having served the will
of God in his generation, fell asleep, and was added to his fathers,
37 and saw corruption.   But he whom God raised did not see cor-
38 ruption.   Be it known unto you therefore, men *and* brethren, that
39 through this man is preached to you the forgiveness of sins.   And
by him every one that believeth is justified from all things, from

27. *For they that dwell at Jerusalem, and their rulers*—He here anticipates a
strong objection, " Why did not they at Jerusalem, and especially their rulers,
believe?" They know not him, because they understood not those very prophets
whom they read or heard continually.   Their very condemning him, innocent
as he was, proves that they understood not the prophecies concerning him.

29. *They fulfilled all things that were written of him*—So far could they go,
but no farther.

31. *He was seen many days by them who came up with him from Galilee to
Jerusalem*—This last journey both presupposes all the rest, and was the most
important of all.

33. *Thou art my Son, this day have I begotten thee*—It is true, he was the Son
of God from eternity.   The meaning therefore is, I have this day declared thee
to be my Son.   As St. Paul elsewhere, *declared to be the Son of God with power,
by the resurrection from the dead*, Rom. i, 4.   And it is with peculiar propriety
and beauty that God is said to *have begotten him*, on the day when he raised him
from the dead, as he seemed then to be born out of the earth anew.

34. *No more to return to corruption*—That is, to die no more.   *I will give you
the sure mercies of David*—The blessings promised to David in Christ.   These
are sure, certain, firm, solid, to every true believer in him.   And hence the resur
rection of Christ necessarily follows; for without this, those blessings could not
be given.

35. *He saith*—David in the name of the Messiah.

36. *David, having served the will of God in his generation, fell asleep*—So his
service extended not itself beyond the bounds of the common age of man : but
the service of the Messiah to all generations, as his kingdom to all ages.   *Served
the will of God*—Why art thou here, thou who art yet in the world ? Is it not
that thou also mayest *serve the will of God ?*   Art thou serving it now ? Doing
all his will ? And was added to his fathers—Not only in body.   This expression
refers to the soul also, and supposes the immortality of it.

39. *Every one that believeth is justified from all things*—Has the actual forgiveness of all his sins, at the very time of his believing ; *from which ye could
not be justified*—Not only ye cannot now ; but ye never could.   For it afforded
no expiation for presumptuous sins.   *By the law of Moses*—The whole Mosaic

* Psalm ii, 7.   † Isaiah lv, 3.   ‡ Psalm xvi, 10.

40 which ye could not be justified by the law of Moses. Beware
therefore, lest that come upon you, which is spoken in the pro-
41 phets, * Behold, ye despisers, and wonder and perish, for I work
a work in your days, a work which ye will in nowise believe,
though a man declare it unto you.
42   And when the Jews were going out of the synagogue, the Gentiles besought *them*, that these words might be spoken on the Sab-
43 bath between. And when the congregation was broken up, many
of the Jews and religious proselytes followed Paul and Barnabas,
who speaking to them, persuaded them to continue in the grace of
God.
44   And the next Sabbath almost the whole city was gathered to-
45 gether to hear the word of God. But the Jews seeing the multitudes, were filled with zeal, and spake against the things spoken
46 by Paul, contradicting and blaspheming. Then Paul and Barnabas
speaking boldly, said, It was necessary that the word of God should
be spoken to you first ; but seeing ye thrust it from you, and judge
yourselves unworthy of eternal life, behold ! we turn to the Gen-
47 tiles. For so hath the Lord commanded us, *saying*, † I have set
thee for a light of the Gentiles, so that thou mightest be for salva-
48 tion to the ends of the earth. And the Gentiles hearing *it* were
glad, and glorified the word of the Lord : and as many as were

institution ! The division of the law into moral and ceremonial was not so common among the Jews, as it is among us. Nor does the apostle here consider it
at all : but Moses and Christ are opposed to each other.
40. *Beware*—A weighty and seasonable admonition. No reproof is as yet
added to it.
41. *I work a work which ye will in nowise believe*—This was originally spoken
to those, who would not believe that God would ever deliver them from the
power of the Chaldeans. But it is applicable to any who will not believe the
promises, or the works of God.
42. *When the Jews were going out*—Probably many of them, not bearing to
hear him, went out before he had done. *The Sabbath between*—So the Jews call
to this day the Sabbath between the first day of the month Tisri (on which the
civil year begins) and the tenth of the same month, which is the solemn day of
expiation.
43. *Who speaking to them*—More familiarly, *persuaded them to continue*—For
trials were at hand, *in the grace of God*—That is, to adhere to the Gospel or
Christian faith.
46. *Then Paul and Barnabas speaking boldly, said*—Those who hinder others
must be publicly reproved. *It was necessary*—Though ye are not worthy : he
shows that he had not preached to them, from any confidence of their believing,
but seeing ye judge yourselves unworthy of eternal life—They indeed judged none
but themselves worthy of it. Yet their rejecting of the Gospel was the same as
saying, "We are unworthy of eternal life." *Behold !*—A thing now present !
An astonishing revolution ! *We turn to the Gentiles*—Not that they left off
preaching to the Jews in other places. But they now determined to lose no
more time at Antioch on their ungrateful countrymen, but to employ themselves
wholly in doing what they could for the conversion of the Gentiles there.
47. *For so hath the Lord commanded us*—By sending us forth, and giving us
an opportunity of fulfilling what he had foretold. *I have set thee*—The Father
speaks to Christ.
48. *As many as were ordained to eternal life*—St. Luke does not say foreordained. He is not speaking of what was done from eternity, but of what was
then done, through the preaching of the Gospel. He is describing that ordination, and that only, which was at the very time of hearing it. During this ser-

* Hab. i, 5.   † Isaiah xlix, 6.

49 ordained to eternal life believed. And the word of the Lord was
50 published through all that country. But the Jews stirred up the
devout honourable women, and the chief men of the city, and raised
a persecution against Paul and Barnabas, and cast them out of
51 their coasts. And they shook off the dust of their feet against
52 them, and went to Iconium. And the disciples were filled with joy
and with the Holy Ghost.
XIV. And in Iconium they went together into the synagogue of the
Jews, and so spake that a great multitude both of the Jews and
2 Greeks believed. But the unbelieving Jews stirred up the Gentiles,
3 and made their minds evil affected against the brethren. Yet they
abode a long time speaking boldly in the Lord, who bare witness
to the word of his grace, and granted signs and wonders to be done
4 by their hands. But the multitude of the city was divided: and
5 part held with the Jews, and part with the apostles. And when
there was an assault both of the Gentiles and Jews with their
6 rulers, to use them despitefully, and to stone them, Being aware
of it, they fled to Lystra and Derbe, cities of Lycaonia, and the
7 country round about, And preached the Gospel there.
8 And there sat a certain man at Lystra, impotent in his feet,
having been a cripple from his mother's womb, who had never
9 walked. This man heard Paul speaking; who fixing his eyes
10 upon him, and perceiving that he had faith to be healed, Said with
11 a loud voice, Stand upright on thy feet. And he leaped and walked. But the multitude, seeing what Paul had done, lifted up their
voices, saying, in the Lycaonian language, The gods are come
12 down to us in the likeness of men. And they called Barnabas
Jupiter, and Paul Mercurius, because he was the chief speaker.
13 Then the priest of Jupiter, which was before their city, brought
bulls and garlands to the gates, and with the multitude would have
14 sacrificed. But when the apostles Barnabas and Paul heard it,

---

mon those believed, says the apostle, to whom God then gave power to believe.
It is as if he had said, "They believed, whose *hearts the Lord opened;*" as he
expresses it in a clearly parallel place, speaking of the same kind of ordination,
Acts xvi, 14, &c. It is observable, the original word is not once used in Scripture to express eternal predestination of any kind. The sum is, all those and
those only, who were now ordained, now believed. Not that God rejected the
rest: it was his will that they also should have been saved: but they thrust salvation from them. Nor were they who then believed constrained to believe.
But grace was then first copiously offered them. And they did not thrust it
away, so that a great multitude even of Gentiles were converted. In a word,
the expression properly implies, a present operation of Divine grace working
faith in the hearers.

XIV. 1. *They so spake*—Persecution having increased their strength.
9. *He had faith to be healed*—He felt the power of God in his soul; and thence
knew it was sufficient to heal his body also.
11. *The gods are come down*—Which the heathens supposed they frequently
did; Jupiter especially. But how amazingly does the prince of darkness blind
the minds of them that believe not! The Jews would not own Christ's Godhead, though they saw him work numberless miracles. On the other hand, the
heathens seeing mere men work one miracle, were for deifying them immediately.
13. *The priest of Jupiter*—Whose temple and image were just without the
gate of the city, *brought garlands*—To put on the victims, *and bulls*—The usual
offerings to Jupiter.

they rent their clothes, and sprang in among the people, crying
15 out and saying, Men, why do ye these things ? We also are men
of like passions with you, and preach to you, to turn from these
vanities unto the living God, who made the heaven and the earth,
16 the sea, and all things that are therein : Who in times past suffer-
17 ed all nations to walk in their own ways : Yet he left not himself
without witness, in that he did good, giving rain from heaven and
18 fruitful seasons, filling our hearts with food and gladness. And
with these sayings scarce restrained they the multitude from sacrificing to them.
19   But there came thither Jews from Antioch and Iconium, who
persuaded the multitude, and having stoned Paul, dragged *him* out
20 of the city, supposing he had been dead. But as the disciples
stood round about him, he rose and went into the city ; and the
21 next day he departed with Barnabas to Derbe. And having preached the Gospel to that city, and made many disciples, they returned
22 to Lystra, and Iconium, and Antioch : Confirming the souls of the
disciples, and exhorting them to continue in the faith ; and that we
23 must through many tribulations enter into the kingdom of God. And
when they had ordained them presbyters in every Church, and had
prayed with fasting, they commended them to the Lord, on whom
24 they had believed. And having passed through Pisidia, they came
25 to Pamphylia, And having spoken the word in Perga, they went
26 down to Attalia, And thence sailed back to Antioch, from whence

---

14. *They sprang in among the people, crying out*—As in a fire, or other sudden and great danger.
15. *To turn from these vanities*—From worshipping any but the true God. He
does not deign to call them gods ; *unto the living God*—Not like these dead idols ;
who made the heaven and the earth, the sea—Each of which they supposed to
have its own gods.
16. *Who in times past*—He prevents their objection, " But if these things are
so, we should have heard them from our fathers." *Suffered*—An awful judgment, *all nations*—The multitude of them that err does not turn error into truth,
to walk in their own ways—The idolatries which they had chosen.
17. *He left not himself without witness*—For the heathens had always from
God himself a testimony both of his existence and of his providence ; *in that he
did good*—Even by punishments he testifies of himself ; but more peculiarly by
benefits ; *giving rain*—By which air, earth, and sea, are, as it were, all joined
together ; *from heaven*—The seat of God ; to which St. Paul probably pointed
while he spoke, filling the body with food, the soul with gladness.
19. *Who persuaded the multitude*—Moved with equal ease either to adore or
murder him.
20. *But as the disciples stood round*—Probably after sunset. The enraged
multitude would scarce have suffered it in the day time : *he rose and went into
the city*—That he should be able to do this, just after he had been left for dead, was
a miracle little less than a resurrection from the dead. Especially considering
the manner wherein the Jewish malefactors were stoned. The witnesses first
threw as large a stone as they could lift, with all possible violence upon his head,
which alone was sufficient to dash the skull in pieces. All the people then joined, as long as any motion or token of life remained.
23. *When they had ordained them presbyters in every Church*—Out of those who
were themselves but newly converted. So soon can God enable even a babe in
Christ to build up others in the common faith : *they commended them to the
Lord*—An expression implying faith in Christ, as well as love to the brethren.
25. Perga and Attalia were cities of Pamphylia.
26. *Recommended to the grace*—Or favour, *of God, for the work which they had*

they had been recommended to the grace of God, for the work
27 which they had fulfilled. And being come, and having gathered
the Church together, they related all that God had done with them
28 and that he had opened the door of faith to the Gentiles. And they
abode there a long time with the disciples.

XV. But certain men coming down from Judea taught the brethren
Except ye be circumcised after the manner of Moses, ye cannot
2 be saved. When therefore Paul and Barnabas had had no small
contention and debate with them, they determined that Paul and
Barnabas, and certain others of them, should go up to the apostles
3 and elders at Jerusalem about this question. And being brought
on their way by the Church, they passed through Phenicia and
Samaria, declaring the conversion of the Gentiles ; and they caused
4 great joy to all the brethren. And being come to Jerusalem, they
were received by the Church, and the apostles and elders ; and
5 they declared all things which God had done with them. But
there rose up, *said they*, certain of the sect of the Pharisees, who
believed, saying, That we ought to circumcise them, and com-
6 mand them to keep the law of Moses. And the apostles and elders
came together to consider of this matter.
7 And after much debate, Peter rose up and said to them, Brethren, ye know that God long ago made choice among us, that the
Gentiles should by my mouth hear the word of the Gospel and
8 believe. And God who knoweth the heart bare them witness,
9 giving the Holy Ghost to them also, even as to us ; And put no

---

fulfilled—This shows the nature and design of that laying on of hands, which
was mentioned chap. xiii, 3.

XV. 1. *Coming down from Judea*—Perhaps to supply what they thought Paul
and Barnabas had omitted.

2. *They* (the brethren) *determined that Paul and Barnabas, and certain others
should go up to Jerusalem about this question*—This is the journey to which St.
Paul refers, Gal. ii, 1, 2, when he says he went up by revelation : which is very
consistent with this ; for the Church in sending them might be directed by a revelation made either immediately to St. Paul, or to some other person, relating
to so important an affair. Important indeed it was, that these Jewish imposi-
tions should be solemnly opposed in time ; because multitudes of converts were
still zealous for the law, and ready to contend for the observance of it. Indeed
many of the Christians of Antioch would have acquiesced in the determination
of Paul alone. But as many others might have prejudices against him, for his
having been so much concerned for the Gentiles, it was highly expedient to take
the concurrent judgment of all the apostles on this occasion.

4. *They were received*—That is solemnly welcomed.

5. *But certain Pharisees*—For even believers are apt to retain their former
turn of mind, and prejudices derived therefrom. *The law of Moses*—The whole
law, both moral and ritual.

7. *After much debate*—It does not appear that this was among the apostles
themselves. But if it had, if they themselves had debated at first, yet might their
final decision be from an unerring direction. For how really soever they were
inspired, we need not suppose their inspiration was always so instantaneous and
express, as to supersede any deliberation in their own minds, or any consultation
with each other. *Peter rose up*—This is the last time he is mentioned in the Acts.

8. *God bare them witness*—That he had accepted them, by giving them the
Holy Ghost.

9. *Purifying*—This word is repeated from chap. x, 15 ; *their hearts*—The heart
is the proper seat of purity ; *by faith*—Without concerning themselves with the
Mosaic law.

difference between us and them, purifying their hearts by faith.
10 Now therefore why tempt ye God to put a yoke on the neck of the
disciples, which neither our fathers nor we were able to bear?
11 But we believe, that through the grace of the Lord Jesus, we shall
be saved even as they.
12   Then all the multitude kept silence, and hearkened to Barnabas
and Paul, declaring what miracles and wonders God had wrought
13 by them among the Gentiles.   And when they held their peace,
14 James answered, saying, Brethren, hearken to me.   Simon hath
declared, how God at first visited the Gentiles, to take out of them
15 a people for his name.   And to this agree the words of the pro-
16 phets, as it is written, * After this I will return and build again the
fallen tabernacle of David; I will build again the ruins thereof,
17 and will set it up, That the residue of men may seek the Lord, and
all the Gentiles on whom my name is called, saith the Lord, who
18 doth these things.   Known unto God are all his works from eter-
19 nity.   Wherefore I judge, that we trouble not them who from
20 among the Gentiles turn to God.   But that we write to them, to

10. *Now therefore*—Seeing these things are so : *why tempt ye God?*—Why do
ye provoke him to anger, by putting so heavy *a yoke on* their neck ?
11. *The Lord Jesus*—He does not here say our Lord ; because in this solemn
place he means the Lord of all, *we*—Jews, *shall be saved even as they*—Gentiles,
namely, *through the grace of the Lord Jesus*, not by our observance of the ceremonial law.
12. *Miracles and wonders*—By which also what St. Peter had said was confirmed.
14. *Simon hath declared*—James, the apostle of the Hebrews, calls Peter by his
Hebrew name.   *To take out of them a people for his name*—That is to believe in
him, to be called by his name.
15. *To this agree*—St. Peter had urged the plain fact, which St. James confirms by Scripture prophecy.   *The words of the prophets*—One of whom is immediately cited.
16. *After this*—After the Jewish dispensation expires.   *I will build again the
fallen tabernacle of David*—By raising from his seed the Christ, who shall build
on the ruins of his fallen tabernacle a spiritual and eternal kingdom.
17. *The Gentiles on whom my name is called*—That is, who are called by my
name ; who are my people.
18. *Known unto God are all his works from eternity*—Which the apostle infers
from the prophecy itself, and the accomplishment of it.   And this conversion of
the Gentiles being known to him from eternity, we ought not to think a new or
strange thing.
It is observable, he does not speak of God's works in the natural world, (which
had been nothing to his present purpose,) but of his dealing with the children of
men.   Now he could not know these, without knowing the characters and actions of particular persons, on a correspondence with which the wisdom and
goodness of his providential dispensations is founded.   For instance, he could not
know how he would deal with heathen idolaters (whom he was now calling into
his Church) without knowing there would be heathen idolaters : and yet this was
a thing purely contingent, a thing as dependent on the freedom of the human
mind, as any we can imagine.   This text, therefore, among a thousand more, is
an unanswerable proof, that God foreknows future contingencies, though there
are difficulties relating hereto which men cannot solve.
20. *To abstain from fornication*—Which even the philosophers among the heathens did not account any fault.   It was particularly frequent in the worship of
their idols, on which account they are here named together.   *And from things
strangled*—That is, from whatever had been killed, without pouring out the blood.
When God first permitted man to eat flesh, he commanded Noah, and in him all

* Amos ix, 11.

abstain from things offered to idols, and fornication, and things
21 strangled, and blood. For Moses hath of old time them that preach
him in every city, being read in the synagogues every Sabbath day.
22 Then it seemed good to the apostles and elders with the whole
Church, to send chosen men from among them to Antioch with
Paul and Barnabas, Judas, surnamed Barsabas, and Silas, chief
23 men among the brethren, writing thus by their hand: The apostles, and elders, and the brethren, salute the brethren who are of
24 the Gentiles, in Antioch, and Syria, and Cilicia. Forasmuch as we
have heard that some who came from us have troubled you with
words, unsettling your minds, saying, Ye must be circumcised, and
25 keep the law, whom we commanded not; It seemed good to us,
being assembled with one accord, to send to you chosen men, with
26 our beloved Barnabas and Paul; Men that have hazarded their
27 lives for the name of our Lord Jesus Christ. We have sent
therefore Judas and Silas, who will also tell you the same things
28 by mouth. For it seemed good to the Holy Ghost and to us, that
no farther burden be laid upon you than these necessary things,
29 To abstain from meats offered to idols, and blood, and things
strangled, and fornication; from which keeping yourselves ye will
do well. Fare ye well.

---

his posterity, whenever they killed any creature for food, to abstain from the blood thereof. It was to be poured upon the ground as water: doubtless in honour of that blood which was in due time poured out for the sin of the world.

21. Perhaps the connection is, To the Jews we need write nothing on these heads; for they hear the law continually.

22. *With the whole Church*—Which therefore had a part therein; *to send cho-sen men*—Who might put it beyond all dispute, that this was the judgment of the apostles and all the brethren.

23. *Writing thus*, and sending *it by their hand*—The whole conduct of this affair plainly shows that the Church in those days had no conception of St. Peter's primacy, or of his being the chief judge in controversies. For the decree is drawn up, not according to his, but the Apostle James's proposal and direction: and that in the name, not of St. Peter, but of all the apostles and elders, and of the whole Church. Nay, St. Peter's name is not mentioned at all, either in the order for sending to Jerusalem on the question, ver. 2, or in the address of the messengers concerning it, ver. 4, or in the letter which was written in answer.

24. *Forasmuch as*, &c.—The simplicity, weightiness, and conciseness of this letter are highly observable.

26. *Men that have hazarded their lives*—This is spoken of Paul and Barnabas.

27. *Who will tell you the same things*—Which we have written.

28. *These necessary things*—All of these were necessary tor that time. But the first of them was not necessary long; and the direction concerning it was therefore repealed by the same Spirit, as we read in the former Epistle to the Corinthians.

29. *Blood*—The eating which was never permitted the children of God from the beginning of the world. Nothing can be clearer than this. For, 1. From Adam to Noah no man ate flesh at all; consequently no man then ate blood. 2. When God allowed Noah and his posterity to eat flesh, he absolutely forbade them to eat blood; and accordingly this, with the other six precepts of Noah, was delivered down from Noah to Moses. 3. God renewed this prohibition by Moses, which was not repealed from the time of Moses till Christ came. 4. Neither after his coming did any presume to repeal this decree of the Holy Ghost, till it seemed good to the bishop of Rome so to do, about the middle of the eighth century. 5. From that time those Churches which acknowledged his authority held the eating of blood to be an indifferent thing. But, 6. In all

30 So being dismissed, they came to Antioch, and having assembled
31 the multitude, they delivered the epistle : *Which* having read, they
32 rejoiced for the consolation. And Judas and Silas, being themselves also prophets, exhorted and confirmed the brethren with
33 many words. And after they had tarried a space, they were dis-
34 missed with peace by the brethren to the apostles. But it seemed
35 good to Silas to remain there. Paul also and Barnabas abode in
Antioch, teaching and preaching with many others also the word
of the Lord.
36 And after certain days Paul said to Barnabas, Let us go again
and visit the brethren in every city where we have preached the
·37 word of the Lord, *and see* how they do. And Barnabas counselled
38 to take with them John, surnamed Mark. But Paul thought it
not right to take with them him who had departed from them
39 from Pamphylia, and went not with them to the work. And there
was a sharp contention, so that they parted from each other ; and
40 Barnabas taking Mark with him, sailed away to Cyprus ; But Paul
having chosen Silas, departed ; being recommended by the bre-
41 thren to the grace of God. And he went through Syria and Cilicia
confirming the Churches.

those Churches which never did acknowledge the bishop of Rome's authority, it
never was allowed to eat blood; nor is it allowed at this day. This is the plain
fact ; let men reason as plausibly as they please on one side or the other. *From
which keeping yourselves ye will do well*—That is, ye will find a blessing. This
gentle manner of concluding was worthy the apostolical wisdom and goodness.
But how soon did succeeding councils of inferior authority change it into the
style of anathemas ! Forms which have proved an occasion of consecrating
some of the most devilish passions under the most sacred names ; and like some
ill-adjusted weapons of war, are most likely to hurt the hand from which they
are thrown.

35. *Paul and Barnabas abode in Antioch*—And it was during this time that
Peter came down from Jerusalem, and that St. Paul withstood him to the face,
for separating himself from the Gentiles, Gal. ii, 11, &c.

36. *Let us go and visit the brethren in every city where we have preached*—
This was all that St. Paul designed at first ; but it was not all that God designed
by his journey, whose providence carried him much farther than he intended
And see how they do—How their souls prosper : how they grow in faith, hope
love : what else ought to be the grand and constant inquiry in every ecclesiastical visitation ? Reader, how dost thou do ?

37. *Barnabas counselled to take John*—His kinsman.

38. *But Paul thought it not right*—To trust him again, who had deserted them
before : who had shrunk from the labour and danger of converting those they were
now going to confirm.

39. *And there was a sharp contention*—Literally, a paroxysm, or fit of a fever.
But nothing in the text implies that the sharpness was on both sides. It is far
more probable that it was not ; that St. Paul, who had the right on his side, (as
he undoubtedly had,) maintained it with love. *And Barnabas taking Mark with
him, sailed away to Cyprus*—Forsaking the work in which he was engaged, he
went away to his own country.

40. *But Paul departed*—Held on his intended course : *being recommended by
the brethren to the grace of God*—We do not find that Barnabas stayed for this.
O how mighty is the grace of God ! which in the midst of the world, in the
midst of sin, among so many snares of Satan, and in spite of the incredible weakness and depravity of nature, yet overcomes all opposition, sanctifies, sustains, and
preserves us to the end!

It appears not only that Paul and Barnabas were afterward thoroughly reconciled, 1 Cor. ix, 6 ; Gal. ii, 9 ; but also that John was again admitted by St. Paul
as a companion in his labours, Col. iv, 10 ; Phil. ver. 24 ; 2 Tim. iv, 1

XVI. And he came down to Derbe and Lystra. And behold a cer
tain disciple was there, named Timotheus, the son of a certain
2 Jewess that believed ; but his father *was* a Greek : Who was well
3 reported of by the brethren in Lystra and Iconium. Him Paul
would have to go forth with him ; and he took and circumcised
him, because of the Jews who were in those places ; for they all
4 knew his father that he was a Greek. And as they went through
the cities they gave them the decrees, which were made by the
5 apostles and elders that were at Jerusalem, to keep. And the
Churches were established in the faith, and increased in number
daily.
6   And having gone through Phrygia and the region of Galatia,
7 being forbid by the Holy Ghost to preach the word in Asia, Coming
to Mysia, they attempted to go to Bithynia ; but the Spirit suffered
8 them not. And passing by Mysia, they came down to Troas.
9 And a vision appeared to Paul by night : a man of Macedonia stood
and entreated him, saying, Come over into Macedonia, and help us.
10 And as soon as he had seen the vision, immediately we sought to go
into Macedonia, assuredly inferring that the Lord called us to preach
11 the Gospel to them. Sailing therefore from Troas, we ran with a
12 straight course to Samothracia, and the next day to Neapolis : And
from thence to Philippi, which is the first city of that part of Macedonia, *and* a colony.
13   And we abode in that city certain days. And on the Sabbath we
went out of the gate, by a river side, where prayer was wont to be

XVI. 3. *He took and circumcised him because of the Jews*—The unbelieving
Jews, to whom he designed he should preach. For they would not have conversed with him at all, so long as he was uncircumcised.
6. *And having gone through Phrygia*—And spoken there what was sufficient,
as well as in *the region of Galatia, being forbid by the Spirit* (probably by an
inward dictate) to speak as yet in the proconsular Asia, the time for it not
being come.
7. *Coming to Mysia, and passing* it *by,* as being a part of *Asia, they attempted
to go into Bithynia ; but the Spirit suffered them not*—Forbidding them as before.
Sometimes a strong impression, for which we are not able to give any account, is
not altogether to be despised.
9. *A vision appeared to Paul by night*—It was not a dream, though it was by
night. No other dream is mentioned in the New Testament than that of Joseph
and of Pilate's wife. *A man of Macedonia*—Probably an angel clothed in the
Macedonian habit, or using the language of the country, and representing the
inhabitants of it. *Help us*—Against Satan, ignorance, and sin.
10. *We sought to go into Macedonia*—This is the first place in which St. Luke
intimates his attendance on the apostle. And here he does it only in an oblique
manner. Nor does he throughout the history once mention his own name, or
any one thing which he did or said for the service of Christianity ; though Paul
speaks of him in the most honourable terms, Col. iv, 14 ; 2 Tim. iv, 11 ; and probably as the brother whose praise in the Gospel went through all the Churches,
2 Cor. viii 18. The same remark may be made on the rest of the sacred historians, who every one of them show the like amiable modesty.
11. *We ran with a straight course*—Which increased their confidence that God
had called them.
12. *The first city*—*Neapolis* was the first city they came to in that part of
Macedonia which was nearest to Asia : in that part which was farthest from it,
Philippi. The river Strymon ran between them. Philippi was a Roman colony.
13. *We went out of the gate*—The Jews usually held their religious assemblies
(either by choice or constraint) at a distance from the heathens : *by a river side*—

made; and sitting down, we spake to the women who were come
14 together. And a certain woman named Lydia, a seller of purple,
of the city of Thyatira, a worshipper of God, heard; whose heart
the Lord opened to attend to the things which were spoken by Paul.
15 And when she was baptized and her family, she entreated *us*, saying,
Since ye have judged me to be faithful to the Lord, come into my
6 house and abide *there*. And she constrained us. And as we were
going to prayer, a certain damsel possessed by a spirit of divination
17 met us, who brought her masters much gain by divining. She
following after Paul and us, cried out, saying, These men are servants of the most high God, who declare to you the way of salva-
18 tion. And this she did for many days. But Paul being grieved,
turned and said to the spirit, I command thee in the name of Jesus
19 Christ, to come out of her. And he came out the same hour. But
when her masters saw that the hope of their gain was gone, laying
hold of Paul and Silas, they dragged *them* into the market place to
20 the magistrates. And having brought them to the pretors, they
21 said, These men, being Jews, exceedingly trouble our city, And
teach customs, which it is not lawful for us, being Romans, to
22 receive, neither to observe. And the multitude rose up together
against them; and the pretors tearing off their garments, com-
23 manded to beat *them* with rods. And when they had laid many stripes
upon them they cast *them* into prison, charging the jailer to keep
24 them safely; Who having received such a charge, thrust them
25 into the inner prison, and secured their feet in the stocks. But at

Which was also convenient for purifying themselves. *Where prayer was wont
to be made*—Though it does not appear there was any house built there. *We
spake*—At first in a familiar manner. Paul did not immediately begin to preach

14. *A worshipper of God*—Probably acquainted with the prophetic writings
whose heart the Lord opened—The Greek word properly refers to the opening of
the eyes: and the heart has its eyes, Eph. i, 18. These are closed by nature
and to open them is the peculiar work of God.

15. *She was baptized and her family*—Who can believe that in so many fami
lies there was no infant? Or that the Jews, who were so long accustomed to
circumcise their children, would not now devote them to God by baptism? *She
entreated us*—The souls of the faithful cleave to those by whom they were
gained to God. *She constrained us*—By her importunity. They did not imme.
diately comply, lest any should imagine they sought their own profit by coming
into Macedonia.

17. *These men are*—A great truth: but St. Paul did not need, nor would accept,
of such testimony.

19. *The magistrates*—The supreme magistrates of the city. In the next verse
they are called by a title which often signifies pretors. These officers exercised
both the military and civil authority.

20. *Being Jews*—A nation peculiarly despised by the Romans.

21. *And teach customs which it is not lawful for us to receive*—The world has
received all the rules and doctrines of all the philosophers that ever were. But
this is a property of Gospel truth: it has something in it peculiarly intolerable to
the world.

23. *They laid many stripes upon them*—Either they did not immediately say
they were Romans, or in the tumult it was not regarded. *Charging the jailer*
—Perhaps rather to quiet the people than because they thought them criminal.

24. *Secured their feet in the stocks*—These were probably those large pieces of
wood, in use among the Romans, which not only loaded the legs of the prisoner,
but also kept them extended in a very painful manner.

25. *Paul and Silas sung a hymn to God*—Notwithstanding weariness, hunger

midnight Paul and Silas having prayed, sung a hymn to God. and
26 the prisoner's heard them. And suddenly there was a great earthquake, so that the foundations of the prison were shaken: and
immediately all the doors were opened, and every one's bands were
27 loosed. And the jailer awaking out of his sleep, and seeing the
doors of the prison opened, drew his sword, and was going to kill
28 himself, supposing the prisoners were fled. But Paul cried with
a loud voice, saying, Do thyself no harm; for we are all here.
29 Then he called for lights, and sprang in, and trembling, fell down
30 before Paul and Silas. And having brought them out he said, Sirs,
31 what must I do to be saved? And they said, Believe in the Lord
32 Jesus Christ, and thou shalt be saved and thy household. And they
spake the word of the Lord to him and to all that were in his house.
33 And taking them that very hour of the night, he washed their
stripes, and was immediately baptized, he and all his household
34 And having brought them up into his house, he set a table before
them, and rejoiced, believing in God with his whole family.
35   And when it was day, the pretors sent the sergeant, saying, Let
36 those men go. And the jailer told Paul, The magistrates have sent
37 to let you go: now therefore depart, and go in peace. But Paul
said to them, They have beaten us publicly uncondemned, and
have cast us into prison, who are Romans: and do they now thrust
us out privately? Nay verily: but let them come themselves and
38 conduct us out. And the sergeants reported these words to the
pretors; and they were afraid when they heard that they were
39 Romans. And they came and comforted them: and conducting
40 *them* out, requested that they would depart from the city. And

stripes, and blood. *And the prisoners heard*—A song to which they were not
accustomed.

28. *But Paul cried*—As they were all then in the dark, it is not easy to say,
how Paul knew of the jailer's purpose; unless it were by some immediate notice
from God, which is by no means incredible. *With a loud voice*—Through
earnestness, and because he was at some distance. *Do thyself no harm*—Although
the Christian faith opens the prospect into another life, yet it absolutely forbids
and effectually prevents a man's discharging himself from this.

20. *Sirs*—He did not style them so the day before. *What must I do to be
saved?*—From the guilt I feel and the vengeance I fear? Undoubtedly God then
set his sins in array before him, and convinced him in the clearest and strongest
manner that the wrath of God abode upon him.

31. *Thou shalt be saved and thy household*—If ye believe. They did so, and
were saved.

33. *He washed their stripes*—It should not be forgot, that the apostles had not
the power of working miraculous cures when they pleased, either on themselves,
or their dearest friends. Nor was it expedient they should, since it would
have frustrated many wise designs of God, which were answered by their
sufferings.

34. *He set a table before them and rejoiced*—Faith makes a man joyful, prudent, liberal.

35. *The pretors sent*—Being probably terrified by the earthquake; *saying, Let
those men go*—How different from the charge given a few hours before! And how
great an ease of mind to the jailer!

37. *They have beaten us publicly, being Romans*—St. Paul does not always
plead this privilege. But in a country where they were entire strangers, such
treatment might have brought upon them a suspicion of having been guilty of
some uncommon crime, and so have hindered the course of the Gospel.

40. *When they had seen the brethren, they comforted them and departed*—

coming out of the prison, they entered into *the house of* Lydia : and when they had seen the brethren, they comforted them and departed.

XVII. And having journeyed through Amphipolis and Apollonia, they came to Thessalonica, where there was a synagogue of the
2 Jews. And Paul, according to his custom, went in to them, and three Sabbath days discoursed with them from the Scriptures;
3 Opening *them* and evincing, That Christ ought to suffer, and to rise from the dead, and that this is the Christ, *even* Jesus, whom I
4 declare unto you. And some of them believed, and were joined to Paul and Silas, and a great number of the devout Greeks, and not
5 a few of the principal women. But the Jews who believed not, filled with zeal, taking to them some of the mean and profligate fellows, and making a mob, set all the city in an uproar; and assaulting the house of Jason, sought to bring them out to the people.
6 But not finding them, they dragged Jason and certain brethren to the rulers of the city, crying aloud, These men, that have turned
7 the world upside down, are come hither also : Whom Jason hath privately received : and all these men act contrary to the decrees
8 of Cesar, saying, That there is another king, *one* Jesus. And they alarmed the multitude and the rulers of the city, when they heard
9 these things. However, having taken security of Jason, and of the rest, they let them go.
10 But the brethren immediately sent away Paul and Silas by night to Berea, who coming *thither*, went into the synagogue of
11 the Jews. These were more ingenuous than those of Thessalo-

---

Though many circumstances now invited their stay, yet they wisely complied with the request of the magistrates, that they might not seem to express any degree of obstinacy or revenge, or give any suspicion of a design to stir up the people.

XVII. 1. *And taking their journey through Amphipolis and Apollonia*—St. Luke seems to have been left at Philippi; and to have continued in those parts, travelling from place to place among the Churches, till St. Paul returned thither. For here he leaves off speaking of himself as one of St. Paul's company; neither does he resume that style, till we find them together there, chap. xx, 5, 6. After this he constantly uses it to the end of the history. Amphipolis and Apollonia were cities of Macedonia.

2. *And Paul, according to his custom*—Of doing all things, as far as might be, in a regular manner, *went in to them three Sabbath days*—Not excluding the days between.

4. *Of the principal women, not a few*—Our free thinkers pique themselves upon observing, that women are more religious than men; and this, in compliment both to religion and good manners, they impute to the weakness of their understandings. And indeed as far as nature can go, in imitating religion by performing the outward acts of it, this picture of religion may make a fairer show in women than in men, both by reason of their more tender passions, and their modesty, which will make those actions appear to more advantage. But in the case of true religion, which always implies taking up the cross, especially in time of persecution, women lie naturally under a great disadvantage, as having less courage than men. So that their embracing the Gospel was a stronger evidence of the power of him whose strength is perfected in weakness, as a stronger assistance of the Holy Spirit was needful for them to overcome their natural fearfulness.

11. *These were more ingenuous*—Or generous. To be teachable in the things of God is true generosity of soul. The *receiving the word with all readiness of mind*, and the most accurate search into the truth, are well consistent.

THE ACTS.

nica, receiving the word with all readiness of mind, *and* daily
12 searching the Scriptures, whether those things were so. Therefore many of them believed, and of the Grecian women of con-
13 siderable rank, and of the men not a few. But when the Jews of
Thessalonica knew that the word of God was preached by Paul at
Berea also, they came thither likewise, and stirred up the multi-
14 tude. Then the brethren sent away Paul immediately, to go as it
15 were to the sea; but Silas and Timothy continued there. And
they that conducted Paul, brought him as far as Athens, and having received an order to Silas and Timothy, to come to him with
all speed, they departed.
16 Now, while Paul was waiting for them at Athens, his spirit was
provoked within him, seeing the city wholly given to idolatry.
17 He therefore discoursed in the synagogue to the Jews and the
devout persons, and in the market place daily to those whom he
18 met with. Then some of the Epicurean and Stoic philosophers
encountered him: and some said, What would this babbler say?
Others, He seemeth to be a proclaimer of strange gods; because
19 he preached to them Jesus, and the resurrection. And they took
him and brought him to the Areopagus, saying, May we know
20 what this new doctrine *is*, which is spoken by thee? For thou
bringest certain strange things to our ears; we would therefore
21 know what these things mean: (For all the Athenians, and the
strangers sojourning there, spent their time in nothing else but
telling or hearing some new thing.)

12. *Many of them*—Of the Jews. *And of the Grecian women*—Who were
followed by their husbands.
16. *While Paul was waiting for them*—Having no design, as it seems, to preach
at Athens, but his zeal for God drew him into it unawares, without staying till
his companions came.
18. *Some of the Epicurean and Stoic philosophers*—The Epicureans entirely
denied a providence, and held the world to be the effect of mere chance; asserting sensual pleasure to be man's chief good, and that the soul and body died together. The Stoics held, that matter was eternal; that all things were governed
by irresistible fate; that virtue was its own sufficient reward, and vice its own
sufficient punishment. It is easy to see, how happily the apostle levels his discourse at some of the most important errors of each, while, without expressly
attacking either, he gives a plain summary of his own religious principles. *What
would this babbler say?*—Such is the language of natural reason, full of, and
satisfied with itself. Yet even here St. Paul had some fruit; though nowhere
less than at Athens. And no wonder, since this city was a seminary of philosophers, who have ever been the pest of true religion. *He seemeth to be a proclaimer*—This he returns upon them at the 23d verse; *of strange gods*—Such as
are not known even at Athens. *Because he preached to them Jesus and the resurrection*—A god and a goddess. And as stupid as this mistake was, it is the less
to be wondered at, since the Athenians might as well count the resurrection a
deity, as shame, famine, and many others.
19. *The Areopagus*, or hill of Mars, (dedicated to Mars, the heathen god of
war,) was the place where the Athenians held their supreme court of judicature
But it does not appear he was carried thither as a criminal. The original number of its judges was twelve; but afterward it increased to three hundred. These
were generally men of the greatest families in Athens, and were famed for
justice and integrity.
21. *And the strangers sojourning there*—And catching the distemper of them.
Some new thing—The Greek word signifies some newer thing. New things
quickly grew cheap, and they wanted those that were newer still.

22   Then Paul standing in the midst of the Areopagus, said, Ye men
of Athens, I perceive that ye are greatly addicted to the worship
23 of invisible powers.   For as I passed along and beheld the objects
of your worship, I found an altar, on which was inscribed, TO
THE UNKNOWN GOD: him therefore whom ye worship
24 without knowing him, I proclaim unto you.   God who made the
world and all things therein, being the Lord of heaven and earth,
25 dwelleth not in temples made with hands : Neither is he served
by men's hands, as though he needed any thing, he himself
26 giving to all life, and breath, and all things.   And he hath made
of one blood the whole nation of men, to dwell on all the face
of the earth, having determined the times before appointed, and
27 the bounds of their habitation : That they might seek God, if
haply they might feel after him and find him, though he be not far
28 from every one of us.   For in him we live, and move, and have
our being ; as certain likewise of your own poets have said, For

---

22. *Then Paul standing in the midst of the Areopagus*—An ample theatre ;
said—Giving them a lecture of natural divinity, with admirable wisdom, acuteness, fulness, and courtesy.   They inquire after new things: *Paul* in his divinely
philosophical discourse, begins with the first, and goes on to the last things, both
which were new things to them.   He points out the origin and the end of all
things, concerning which they had so many disputes, and equally refutes both
the Epicurean and Stoic.   *I perceive*—With what clearness and freedom does
he speak ! Paul against Athens !

23. *I found an altar*—Some suppose this was set up by Socrates, to express
in a covert way his devotion to the only true God, while he derided the plurality
of the heathen gods, for which he was condemned to death : and others, that
whoever erected this altar, did it in honour to the God of Israel, of whom there
was no image, and whose name Jehovah was never made known to the idolatrous
Gentiles.   *Him proclaim I unto you*—Thus he fixes the wandering attention of
these blind philosophers ; proclaiming to them an unknown, and yet not a new
God.

24. *God who made the world*—Thus is demonstrated even to reason, the one
true, good God; absolutely different from the creatures, from every part of the
visible creation.

25. *Neither is he served as though he needed any thing,* or person—The Greek
word equally takes in both.   *To all*—That live and breathe ;—in him we live ;
and breathe—In him we move.   By breathing life is continued.   I breathe this
moment : the next is not in my power : *and all things*—For in him we are.   So
exactly do the parts of this discourse answer each other.

26. *He hath made of one blood the whole nation of men*—By this expression the
apostle showed them in the most unaffected manner, that though he was a Jew,
he was not enslaved to any narrow views, but looked on all mankind as his brethren: *having determined the times*—That it is God who gave men the earth to
inhabit, Paul proves from the order of times and places, showing the highest
wisdom of the Disposer, superior to all human counsels.   *And the bounds of their
habitation*—By mountains, seas, rivers, and the like.

27. *If haply*—The way is open; God is ready to be found.   But he will lay
no force upon man ; *they might feel after him*—This is in the midst between
seeking and finding.   Feeling being the lowest and grossest of all our senses, is
fitly applied to the low knowledge of God ; *though he be not far from every one
of us*—We need not go far to seek or find him.   He is very near us ; in us.   It
is only perverse reason which thinks he is afar off.

28. *In him*—Not in ourselves, *we live, and move, and have our being*—This denotes his necessary, intimate, and most efficacious presence.   No words can better express the continual and necessary dependence of all created beings, in their
existence and all their operations, on the first and almighty cause, which the
truest philosophy as well as divinity teaches.   *As certain also of your own poets*

29 we are also his offspring. Being then the offspring of God, **we**
ought not to think the Godhead is like gold or silver, or stone,
30 graven by art and contrivance of man.   The times of ignorance,
indeed, God overlooked; but he now commandeth all men every
31 where to repent.   Because he hath appointed a day in which he
will judge the world righteously, by the man whom he hath ordained, *whereof* he hath given assurance to all *men*, in that he hath
32 raised him from the dead.   And when they heard of the resurrection from the dead, some mocked; but others said, We will hear
33 thee again concerning this.   So Paul departed from among them.
34 Howbeit some clave to him and believed; among whom *was* even
Dionysius the Areopagite, and a woman named Damaris, and others
with them.

XVIII.   After these things, Paul departing from Athens, came to
2 Corinth.   And finding a certain Jew named Aquila, born in Pontus, lately come from Italy with Priscilla his wife, (because Claudius had commanded all the Jews to depart from Rome,) he went to

---

have said—Aratus, whose words these are, was an Athenian, who lived almost
three hundred years before this time.   They are likewise to be found, with the
alteration of one letter only, in the hymn of Cleanthes to Jupiter or the supreme
being, one of the purest and finest pieces of natural religion in the whole world
of Pagan antiquity.

29. *We ought not to think*—A tender expression; especially in the first person plural.   As if he had said, Can God himself be a less noble being than we who
are his offspring?   Nor does he only here deny, that these are like God, but that
they have any analogy to him at all, so as to be capable of representing him.

30. *The times of ignorance*—What! does he object ignorance to the knowing
Athenians?   Yes, and they acknowledge it by this very altar.   God *overlooked*—
As one paraphrases, "The beams of his eye did in a manner shoot over it."   He
did not appear to take notice of them, by sending express messages to them as
he did to the Jews.   *But now*—This day, this hour, saith Paul, puts an end to
the Divine forbearance, and brings either greater mercy or punishment.   Now
he commandeth all men every where to repent—There is a dignity and grandeur
in this expression, becoming an ambassador from the King of heaven.   And this
universal demand of repentance declared universal guilt in the strongest manner, and admirably confronted the pride of the haughtiest Stoic of them all.   At
the same time it bore down the idle plea of fatality.   For how could any one
repent of doing what he could not but have done?

31. *He hath appointed a day in which he will judge the world*—How fitly does
he speak this, in their supreme court of justice?   *By the man*—So he speaks,
suiting himself to the capacity of his hearers.   *Whereof he hath given assurance
to all men, in that he hath raised him from the dead*—God raising Jesus demonstrated hereby, that he was to be the glorious Judge of all.   We are by no means
to imagine that this was all which the apostle intended to have said, but the indolence of some of his hearers and the petulancy of others cut him short.

32. *Some mocked*—Interrupting him thereby.   They took offence at that which
is the principal motive of faith, from the pride of reason.   And having once
stumbled at this, they rejected all the rest.

33. *So Paul departed*—Leaving his hearers divided in their judgment.

34. *Among whom was even Dionysius the Areopagite*—One of the judges of that
court : on whom some spurious writings have been fathered in later ages, by
those who are fond of high-sounding nonsense.

XVIII. 1. *Paul departing from Athens*—He did not stay there long.   The philosophers there were too easy, too indolent, and too wise in their own eyes to
receive the Gospel.

2. *Claudius*, the Roman emperor, *had commanded all the Jews to depart from
Rome*—All who were Jews by birth.   Whether they were Jews or Christians by
religion, the Romans were too stately to regard.

3 them.   And as he was of the same trade, he abode with them and
4 wrought, for they were tent makers by trade.   And he discoursed
  in the synagogue every Sabbath, and persuaded the Jews and
  Greeks.
5   And when Silas and Timotheus were come from Macedonia,
  Paul was pressed in spirit, and testified to the Jews that Jesus
6 was the Christ.   But when they set themselves in opposition and
  blasphemed, he shook his raiment and said to them, Your blood *is*
  upon your own head ; I am pure : from henceforth I will go to the
7 Gentiles.   And going thence he went into the house of one named
  Justus, *one* that worshipped God, whose house was adjoining to
8 the synagogue.   And Crispus, the ruler of the synagogue, believed
  on the Lord with all his house, and many of the Corinthians hear-
9 ing, believed and were baptized.   Then the Lord said to Paul by
  a vision, in the night, Fear not, but speak and hold not thy peace :
10 For I am with thee, and no man shall set on thee to hurt thee ;
11 for I have much people in this city.   And he continued there a
  year and six months, teaching the word of God among them.
12   But when Gallio was proconsul of Achaia, the Jews made an
  assault with one consent upon Paul, and brought him to the judg-
13 ment seat, saying, This *fellow* persuadeth men to worship God
14 contrary to the law.   And when Paul was about to open his
  mouth, Gallio / said to the Jews, If it were an act of injustice, or
  wicked licentiousness, O ye Jews, reason would that I should bear

3. *They were tent makers by trade*—For it was a rule among the Jews (and
why is it not among the Christians ?) to bring up all their children to some trade,
were they ever so rich or noble.   •
    5. *And when Silas and Timotheus were come from Macedonia*—Silas seems to
have stayed a considerable time at Berea : but Timotheus had come to the apostle
while he was at Athens, and been sent by him to comfort and confirm the Church
at Thessalonica, 1 Thess. iii, 1–5.   But now at length both Silas and Timotheus
came to the apostle at Corinth.   *Paul was pressed in spirit*—The more probably
from what Silas and Timotheus related.   Every Christian ought diligently to observe any such pressure in his own spirit, and if it agree with Scripture, to follow it : if he does not he will feel great heaviness.
    6. *He shook his raiment*—To signify he would from that time refrain from
them : and to intimate, that God would soon shake them off as unworthy to be
numbered among his people.   *I am pure*—None can say this but he that has
borne a full testimony against sin.   *From henceforth I will go to the. Gentiles*—
But not to them altogether.   He did not break off all intercourse with the Jews
even at Corinth.   Only he preached no more in their synagogue.
    7. *He went into the house of one named Justus*—A Gentile, and preached there,
though probably he still lodged with Aquila.
    8. *And many hearing*—The conversation of Crispus, and the preaching of
Paul.
    10. *I am with thee :* therefore *fear not* all the learning, politeness, grandeur,
or power of the inhabitants of this city.   *Speak and hold not thy peace*—For thy
labour shall not be in vain.   *For I have much people in this city*—So he prophetically calls them that afterward believed.
    11. *He continued there a year and six months*—A long time !   But how few
souls are now gained in a longer time than this ?   Who is in the fault ?   Generally both teachers and hearers.
    12. *When Gallio was proconsul of Achaia*—Of which Corinth was the chief
city.   This Gallio, the brother of the famous Seneca, is much commended both
by him and by other writers, for the sweetness and generosity of his temper,
and easiness of his behaviour.   Yet one thing he lacked !   But he knew it not
and had no concern about it.

15 with you. But if it be a question of words and names, and of
   your law, look ye *to it;* for I will be no judge of these matters.
16 And he drove them away from the judgment seat. Then they all
17 took Sosthenes, the ruler of the synagogue, and beat him before
   the judgment seat. And Gallio cared for none of these things.
18 And Paul still continued many days ; and *then* taking leave of
   the brethren, sailed thence for Syria, and with him Priscilla and
   Aquila, having shaved his head at Cenchrea ; for he had a vow.
19 And he came to Ephesus and left them there ; but he himself
20 going into the synagogue, reasoned with the Jews. But though
   they entreated *him* to tarry longer with them, he consented not :
21 But took his leave of them, saying, I must by all means keep the
   approaching feast at Jerusalem, but I will return to you again, if
22 God will. And he set sail from Ephesus. And landing at Cesarea, he went up and saluted the Church, and went down to Antioch.
23 And having spent some time *there*, he departed and went through
   the country of Galatia and Phrygia in order, confirming all the
   disciples.
24   Now a certain Jew, Apollos by name, born at Alexandria, an
25 eloquent man, mighty in the Scriptures, came to Ephesus. This
   man had been instructed in the way of the Lord, and being fervent
   in spirit he spake and taught diligently the things of Jesus, know

---

15. *But if it be*—He speaks with the utmost coolness and contempt, *a question
of names*—The names of the heathen gods were fables and shadows. But the
question concerning the name of Jesus is of more importance than all things
else under heaven. Yet there is this singularity (among a thousand others) in
the Christian religion, that human reason, curious as it is in all other things,
abhors to inquire into it.

17. *Then they all took Sosthenes*—The successor of Crispus, and probably
Paul's chief accuser, *and beat him*—It seems because he had occasioned them so
much trouble to no purpose, *before the judgment seat*—One can hardly think in
the sight of Gallio, though at no great distance from him. And it seems to
have had a happy effect. For Sosthenes himself was afterward a Christian,
1 Cor. i, 1.

18. *Paul continued many days*—After the year and six months, to confirm
the brethren. *Aquila having shaved his head*—As was the custom in a vow, chap.
xxi, 24 ; Num. vi, 18. *At Cenchrea*—A seaport town, at a small distance from
Corinth.

21. *I must by all means keep the feast at Jerusalem*—This was not from any
apprehension that he was obliged in conscience to keep the Jewish feasts ; but
to take the opportunity of meeting a great number of his countrymen to whom
he might preach Christ, or whom he might farther instruct, or free from the
prejudices they had imbibed against him. *But I will return to you*—So he did,
chap. xix, 1.

22. *And landing at Cesarea, he went up*—Immediately to Jerusalem ; *and
saluted the Church*—Eminently so called, being the mother Church of Christian
believers : and having kept the feast there, he went down from thence to
Antioch.

23. *He went over the country of Galatia and Phrygia*—It is supposed, spending about four years therein, including the time he stayed at Ephesus.

24. *An eloquent man, mighty in the Scriptures*—Of the Old Testament. Every
talent may be of use in the kingdom of God, if joined with the knowledge of the
Scriptures and fervour of spirit.

25. *This man had been instructed*—Though not perfectly, *in the way of the
Lord*—In the doctrine of Christ. *Knowing only the baptism of John*—Only what
John taught those whom he baptized, namely, to repent and believe in a Messiah
shortly to appear.

26 ing only the baptism of John. And he spake boldly in the synagogue. And Aquila and Priscilla hearing him, took him to their
27 house, and explained to him the way of God more perfectly. And
  when he was desirous to go over to Achaia, the brethren wrote,
  exhorting the disciples to receive him; who being come thither,
28 greatly helped through grace them that had believed. For he earnestly debated with the Jews in public, showing by the Scriptures
  that Jesus was the Christ.
XIX. Now while Apollos was at Corinth, Paul having passed through
  the upper parts, came to Ephesus; and finding certain disciples,
2 He said to them, Have ye received the Holy Ghost since ye
  believed? And they said to him, Nay, we have not so much as
3 heard, whether there be any Holy Ghost. He said to them, Into
  what then were ye baptized? And they said, Into John's baptism.
4 And Paul said, John baptized with the baptism of repentance, telling the people to believe on him that was to come after him, that
5 is, on Jesus. And hearing *this*, they were baptized in the name
6 of the Lord Jesus. And Paul laying *his* hands on them, the Holy
  Ghost came upon them, and they spake with tongues and prophe-
7 sied. And they were in all about twelve men. And going into
8 the synagogue, he spake boldly, for three months discoursing and
9 persuading the things concerning the kingdom of God. But when
  some were hardened and believed not, but spake reproachfully of
  the way before the multitude, he departed from them, and separated
  the disciples, discoursing daily in the school of one Tyrannus.
10 And this was done for the space of two years, so that all the

26. *He spake*—Privately; and taught publicly. Probably he returned to live
at Alexandria, soon after he had been baptized by John; and so had no opportunity of being fully acquainted with the doctrines of the Gospel, as delivered
by Christ and his apostles. *And explained to him the way of God more perfectly*
—He who knows Christ, is able to instruct even those that are mighty in the
Scriptures.
27. *Who greatly helped through grace*—It is through grace only that any gift
of any one is profitable to another. *Them that had believed*—Apollos did not
plant, but water. This was the peculiar gift which he had received. And he was
better able to convince the Jews, than to convert the heathens.
XIX. 1. *Having passed through*—Galatia and Phrygia, which were termed *the
upper parts of Asia Minor*. *Certain disciples*—Who had been formerly baptized
by John the Baptist, and since imperfectly instructed in Christianity.
2. *Have ye received the Holy Ghost?*—The extraordinary gifts of the Spirit, as
well as his sanctifying graces? *We have not so much as heard*—Whether there
be any such gifts.
3. *Into what were ye baptized*—Into what dispensation? To the sealing of
what doctrine? *Into John's baptism*—We were baptized by John and believe
what he taught.
4. *John baptized*—That is, the whole baptism and preaching of John pointed
at Christ. After this John is mentioned no more in the New Testament. Here
he gives way to Christ altogether.
5. *And hearing this, they were baptized*—By some other. Paul only *laid his
hands upon them*. *They were baptized*—They were baptized twice; but not with
the same baptism. John did not administer that baptism which Christ afterward
commanded, that is, in the name of the Father, Son, and Holy Ghost.
9. *The way*—The Christian way of worshipping God. *He departed*—Leaving
them their synagogue to themselves. *Discoursing daily*—Not on the Sabbath
only, *in the school of one Tyrannus*—Which we do not find was any otherwise
consecrated, than by preaching the Gospel there.
10 *All* who desired it among *the inhabitants of* the proconsular *Asia*, now

inhabitants of Asia, both Jews and Greeks, heard the word of he Lord.

11 And God wrought special miracles by the hands of Paul, So
12 that handkerchiefs or aprons were carried from his body to the sick, and the diseases departed from them, and the evil spirits came
13 out of them. And some of the vagabond Jews, exorcists, undertook to name the name of the Lord Jesus over those who had evil spirits, saying, We adjure you by Jesus, whom Paul preacheth.
14 And there were seven sons of one Sceva a Jewish chief priest, who
15 did this. But the evil spirit answering said, Jesus I know, and
16 Paul I know ; but who are ye ? And the man in whom the evil spirit was, leaping upon them, and getting the mastery of them, prevailed against them, so that they fled out of that house naked and wounded.
17 And this was known to all, both Jews and Greeks, dwelling at Ephesus, and fear fell on them all, and the name of the Lord Jesus was
18 magnified. And many of those who believed came confessing
19 and openly declaring their deeds. Many also of those who had practised curious arts, bringing their books together, burned them before all men, and they computed the value of them, and found it
20 fifty thousand *pieces* of silver. So powerfully did the word of God grow and prevail.
21 After these things were ended, Paul purposed in spirit, having passed through Macedonia and Achaia, to go to Jerusalem, saying,

heard the word: St. Paul had been forbidden to preach it in Asia before, chap. xvi, 6. But now the time was come.

11. *Special miracles*—Wrought in a very uncommon manner.

12. *Evil spirits*—Who also occasioned many of those diseases, which yet might appear to be purely natural.

13. *Exorcists*—Several of the Jews about this time pretended to a power of casting out devils, particularly by certain arts or charms, supposed to be derived from Solomon. *Undertook to name*—Vain undertaking ! Satan laughs at all those who attempt to expel him either out of the bodies or the souls of men but by Divine faith. All the light of reason is nothing to the craft or strength of that subtle spirit. His craft cannot be known but by the Spirit of God ; nor can his strength be conquered but by the power of faith.

17. *And the name of the Lord Jesus was magnified*—So that even the malice of the devil wrought for the furtherance of the Gospel.

18. *Many came confessing*—Of their own accord, *and openly declaring their deeds*—The efficacy of God's word, penetrating the inmost recesses of their soul, wrought that free and open confession to which perhaps even torments, would not have compelled them.

19. *Curious arts*—Magical arts, to which that soft appellation was given by those who practised them. Ephesus was peculiarly famous for these. And as these practices were of so much reputation there, it is no wonder the books which taught them should bear a great price. *Bringing their books together*—As it were by common consent, *burnt them*—Which was far better than selling them, even though the money had been given to the poor. *Fifty thousand pieces of silver* —If these pieces of silver be taken for Jewish shekels, the sum will amount to six thousand two hundred and fifty pounds.

20. *So powerfully did the word of God grow*—In extent, *and prevail*—In power and efficacy.

21. *After these things were ended*—Paul sought not to rest, but pressed on, as if he had yet done nothing. He is already possessed of Ephesus and Asia. He purposes for Macedonia and Achaia. He has his eye upon Jerusalem, then upon Rome ; afterward on Spain, Rom. xv, 27. No Cesar, no Alexander the Great, no other hero, comes up to the magnanimity of this little Benjamite. Faith and love to God and man had enlarged his heart, even as the sand of the sea.

CHAPTER XIX. 331

22 After I have been there, I must see Rome also. And having sent
two of those who ministered to him, Timotheus and Erastus to
23 Macedonia, he himself stayed in Asia for a season. And about
24 that time there arose no small tumult concerning the way. For a
man named Demetrius, a silversmith, who made silver shrines for
25 Diana, procured no small gain to the artificers: Whom having
gathered together with the workmen employed in such things,
he said, Sirs, ye know that our maintenance arises from this
26 occupation. But ye see and hear, that not at Ephesus only, but
almost through all Asia, this Paul hath persuaded and turned aside
much people : saying, that they are not gods which are made with
27 hands : So that there is danger not only that this our craft should
come into disgrace, but also that the temple of the great goddess
Diana should be despised, and her majesty destroyed, whom
28 all Asia and the world worshippeth. And hearing *this,* they were
filled with rage, and cried out, saying, Great *is* Diana of the
29 Ephesians, And the whole city was filled with confusion : and
they rushed with one accord into the theatre, dragging with them
Gaius and Aristarchus, men of Macedonia, Paul's fellow travel-
30 lers. And when Paul would have gone in to the people, the dis-
31 ciples would not suffer him. And some also of the principal
officers of Asia, being his friends, sent to him, and desired that
32 he would not venture himself into the theatre. Some therefore
cried one thing, and some another ; for the assembly was confused,
and the greater part did not know for what they were come to-
33 gether. And they thrust Alexander forward from among the mul-

24. *Silver shrines*—Silver models of that famous temple, which were bought
not only by the citizens, but by strangers from all parts. *The artificers*—The
other silversmiths.
25. *The workmen*—Employed by him and them.
26. *Saying, that they are not gods which are made with hands*—This manifestly
shows, that the contrary opinion did then generally prevail, namely, that there
was a real Divinity in their sacred images. Though some of the later heathens
spoke of them just as the Romanists do now.
27. *There is danger, not only that this our craft* [trade] *should come into disgrace, but also that the temple of the great goddess Diana should be despised*—
No wonder a discourse should make so deep an impression, which was edged both
by interest and superstition. The great goddess was one of the standing titles
of Diana. *Her majesty destroyed*—Miserable majesty, which was capable of
being thus destroyed ! *Whom all Asia and the world*—That is, the Roman empire,
worshippeth—Although under a great variety of titles and characters. But the
multitude of those that err does not turn error into truth.
29. *They rushed with one accord*—Demetrius and his company, *into the theatre*
—Where criminals were wont to be thrown to the wild beasts, *dragging with
them Gaius and Aristarchus*—When they could not find Paul. Probably they
hoped to oblige them to fight with the wild beasts, as some think St. Paul had
done before.
30. *When Paul would have gone in to the people*—Being above all fear, to
plead the cause of his companions, and prove they are not gods which are made
with hands.
31. *The principal officers of Asia*—The Asian priests, who presided over the
public games, which they were then celebrating in honour of Diana.
32. *The greater part did not know for what they were come together*—Which
is commonly the case in such an assembly.
33. *And they thrust forward*—Namely, the artificers and workmen, *Alexander*
—Probably some well-known Christian whom they saw in the crowd : *the Jews*

titude, the Jews pushing him on; and Alexander waving with his
34 hand, would have made a defence to the people : But when they
knew that he was a Jew, one voice arose from them all, crying out
35 for about two hours, Great *is* Diana of the Ephesians. But the
register, having pacified the people, said, Ye men of Ephesus,
what man is there who knoweth not, that the city of the Ephesians
is a worshipper of the great Diana, and of the *image* which fell
36 down from Jupiter ? Seeing then these things cannot be denied, ye
37 ought to be quiet, and to do nothing rashly. For ye have brought
these men, who are neither robbers of temples, nor blasphemers
38 of your goddess. If then Demetrius and the artificers that are
with him have a charge against any one, the courts are held, and
39 there are proconsuls ; let them implead one another. But if ye
inquire any thing concerning other matters, it shall be determined
40 in a lawful assembly. And indeed we are in danger to be questioned for sedition concerning this day ; there being no cause,
41 whereby we can account for this concourse. And having said these
things, he dismissed the assembly.
XX. And after the tumult was ceased, Paul having called the disciples to him, and exhorted *them*, departed to go into Macedonia.
2 And having gone through those parts, and exhorted them with
3 much discourse, he came into Greece. And having abode *there*
three months, an ambush being laid for him by the Jews, as he
was about to sail into Syria, he determined to return through Ma-
4 cedonia. And there accompanied him to Asia, Sopater of Berea ;
and of the Thessalonians, Aristarchus and Secundus ; and Gaius of
Derbe and Timotheus ; and of Asia, Tychicus and Trophimus.
5 These going before, stayed for us at Troas. And we set sail for
6 Philippi after the days of unleavened bread, and came to them at

---

pushing him on—To expose him to the more danger. *And Alexander waving
with his hand*—In token of desiring silence, *would have made a defence*—For
himself and his brethren.

34. *But when they knew that he was a Jew*—And consequently an enemy to
their worship of images ; they prevented him, by *crying, Great is Diana of the
Ephesians*.

35. *The register*—Probably the chief governor of the public games. *The image
which fell down from Jupiter*—They believed that very image of Diana, which
stood in her temple, fell down from Jupiter in heaven. Perhaps he designed to
insinuate, as if falling down from Jupiter, it was not made with hands, and so
was not that sort of idols which Paul had said were no gods.

37. *Nor blasphemers of your goddess*—They simply declared the one God, and
the vanity of idols in general.

38. *There are proconsuls*—One in every province. There was one at Ephesus.

39. *In a lawful assembly*—In such a regular assembly as has authority to judge
of religious and political affairs.

40. *This concourse*—He wisely calls it by an inoffensive name.

XX. 1. *After the tumult was ceased*—So Demetrius gained nothing. Paul
remained there till all was quiet.

2. *He came into Greece*—That part of it which lay between Macedonia and
Achaia.

3. *An ambush being laid for him*—In his way to the ship.

4. *To Asia*—There some of them left him. But Trophimus went with him to
Jerusalem, chap. xxi, 29. Aristarchus, even to Rome, chap. xxvii, 2.

6. *We set sail*—St. Luke was now with St. Paul again, as we learn from his
manner of expressing himself.

7 Troas in five days, where we abode seven days. And on the first
day of the week, when we were met together to break bread, Paul
being to depart on the morrow, preached to them, and continued
8 his discourse till midnight. And there were many lamps in the
9 upper room where they were assembled. And a certain young
man, named Eutychus, sitting in the window fell into a deep sleep:
and as Paul still continued his discourse, being overpowered with
sleep, he fell down from the third story, and was taken up dead.
10 And Paul went down and fell on him; and taking *him* in his arms,
11 said, Be not troubled; for his life is in him. And going up again,
and having broken bread, he conversed long with them, even till
12 break of day, and so departed. And they brought the young man
13 alive, and were not a little comforted. But we going before into
the ship sailed to Assos, where we were to take up Paul; for so
14 he had appointed, being himself to go on foot. And when he met
15 us at Assos, we took him up and came to Mitylene. And sailing
thence, we came the following day over against Chios, and the next
day we touched at Samos, and having tarried at Trogyllium the
16 day after came to Miletus. For Paul had determined to sail by
Ephesus, that he might not spend any time in Asia; for he hasted,
if it were possible, to be at Jerusalem on the day of pentecost.
17   And sending to Ephesus from Miletus, he called thither the
18 elders of the Church. And when they were come to him, he said
to them, Ye know in what manner I have conversed among you
19 all the time from the first day I came into Asia, serving the Lord
with all humility, and with tears, and trials, which befell me through

7. *To break bread*—That is, to celebrate the Lord's Supper; *continued his discourse*—Through uncommon fervour of spirit.
8. *There were many lamps in the room where they were assembled*—To prevent
any possible scandal.
9. *In the window*—Doubtless kept open, to prevent heat, both from the lamps
and the number of people.
10. *Paul fell on him*—It is observable, our Lord never used this gesture. Bu
Elijah and Elisha did as well as Paul. *His life is in him*—He is alive again.
11. *So departed*—Without taking any rest at all.
12. *And they brought the young man alive*—But alas! How many of those
who have allowed themselves to sleep under sermons, or as it were to dream
awake, have slept the sleep of eternal death, and fallen to rise no more!
13. *Being himself to go on foot*—That he might enjoy the company of his
Christian brethren a little longer, although he had passed the night without
sleep, and though Assos was of difficult and dangerous access by land.
14. *Mitylene*—Was a city and part of the isle of Lesbos, about seven miles distant from the Asiatic coast.
16. *For Paul had determined to sail by Ephesus*—Which lay on the other side
of the bay. *He hasted to be at Jerusalem on the day of pentecost*—Because then
was the greatest concourse of people.
17. *Sending to Ephesus, he called the elders of the Church*—These are called
bishops in the 28th verse, (rendered *overseers* in our translation.) Perhaps elders
and bishops were then the same; or no otherwise different than are the rector of
a parish and his curates.
18. *Ye know*—Happy is he who can thus appeal to the conscience of his
hearers.
19. *Serving*—See the picture of a faithful servant! *The Lord*—Whose the
Church is, *with all humility, and with tears, and trials*—These are the concomi-
ants of it. The service itself is described more particularly in the following
verse. This humility he recommends to the Ephesians themselves, Eph. iv 2.

20 the ambushes of the Jews: *And* that I have withheld nothing
   which was profitable, but have preached to you, and taught you,
21 publicly and from house to house: Testifying both to Jews and
   Greeks repentance toward God and faith in the Lord Jesus Christ.
22   And now being bound by the Spirit, I go to Jerusalem, not
23 knowing the things that shall befall me there: Save that the Holy
   Ghost testifieth to me in every city, saying that bonds and afflic-
24 tions await me.   But none of these things move me; nor do I
   count my life precious to myself, so I may finish my course with
   joy, and the ministry which I have received of the Lord Jesus, to
25 testify the Gospel of the grace of God.   And now I know that ye
   all among whom I have conversed, proclaiming the kingdom of God,
26 shall see my face no more.   Wherefore I take you to record this
27 day, that I *am* pure from the blood of all *men:* For I have not
28 shunned to declare unto you all the counsel of God.   Take heed
   therefore to yourselves, and to the whole flock over which the Holy
   Ghost hath made you overseers, to feed the Church of God, which
29 he hath purchased with his own blood.   For I know this, that after
   my departure, grievous wolves will enter in among you, not sparing
30 the flock.   Yea, from among yourselves men will arise, speaking

---

His tears are mentioned again, ver. 31, as also 2 Cor. ii, 4; Phil. iii, 18. These
passages laid together supply us with the genuine character of St. Paul. Holy
tears, from those who seldom weep on account of natural occurrences, are no
mean specimen of the efficacy and proof of the truth of Christianity. Yet joy
is well consistent therewith, ver. 24. The same person may be *sorrowful, yet
always rejoicing.*

20. *I have preached*—Publicly; *and taught*—From house *to house.* Else he had
not been pure from their blood. For even an apostle could not discharge his duty
by public preaching only. How much less can an ordinary pastor!

21. *Repentance toward God*—The very first motion of the soul toward God is
a kind of repentance.

22. *Bound by the Spirit*—Strongly impelled by him.

23. *Save that*—Only this I know in general; *the Holy Ghost witnesseth*—By
other persons. Such was God's good pleasure to reveal these things to him, not
immediately, but by the ministry of others.

24. *Nor do I count my life precious*—It adds great force to this and all the other
passages of Scripture, in which the apostles express their contempt of the world,
that they were not uttered by persons like Seneca and Antoninus, who talked
elegantly of despising the world in the full affluence of all its enjoyments; but
by men who daily underwent the greatest calamities, and exposed their lives in
proof of their assertions.

25. *Ye shall see my face no more*—He wisely inserts this, that what follows
might make the deeper impression.

27. *For I have not shunned*—Otherwise if any had perished, their blood would
have been on his head.

28. *Take heed therefore*—I now devolve my care upon you; first *to yourselves;*
then *to the flock over which the Holy Ghost hath made you overseers*—For no man,
or number of men upon earth, can constitute an *overseer*, bishop, or any other
Christian minister. To do this is the peculiar work of the Holy Ghost: *to feed
the Church of God*—That is, the believing, loving, holy children of God; *which
he hath purchased*—How precious is it then in his sight! *with his own blood*—
For it is the blood of the only-begotten Son of God, 1 John i, 7.

29. *Grievous wolves*—From without, namely, false apostles. They had not yet
broke in on the Church at Ephesus.

30. *Yea, from among yourselves men will arise*—Such were the Nicolaitans,
of whom Christ complains, Rev. ii, 6; *to draw away disciples*—From the purity
of the Gospel and the unity of the body.

31 perverse things, to draw away disciples after them. Therefore watch, remembering that for three years I ceased not to warn every one, night and day, with tears.

32 And now, brethren, I commend you to God, and to the word of his grace, who is able to build you up, and to give you an inherit-
33 ance among all them that are sanctified. I have coveted no man's
34 silver, or gold, or apparel. Yea, you yourselves know that these hands' have ministered to my necessities and to them that were
35 with me. I have showed you all things, that thus labouring ye ought to help the weak, and to remember the word of the Lord Jesus, that he himself said, It is happier to give than to receive.
36 And having said these things, he kneeled down, and prayed with
37 them all. And they all wept sore, and falling on Paul's neck,
38 kissed him; Sorrowing most for that word which he spake, that they should see his face no more. And they conducted him to the ship.

XXI. And when we were torn away from them, and had set sail, we ran with a straight course to Coos, next day to Rhodes, and
2 from thence to Patara. And finding a ship passing over to Phe-
3 nicia, we went aboard and set sail. And coming within sight of Cyprus, and leaving it on the left hand, we set sail to Syria, and
4 landed at Tyre; for there the ship was to unload her burden. And finding disciples, we tarried there seven days, who told Paul by the

---

31. *I ceased not to warn every one night and day*- -This was watching indeed! Who copies after this example?

32. *The word of his grace*—It is the grand channel of it, to believers as well as unbelievers. *Who is able to build you up*—To confirm and increase your faith, love, holiness. God can thus build us up, without any instrument. But he does build us up by them. O beware of dreaming that you have less need of human teachers after you know Christ than before! *And to give you an inherit ance*—Of eternal glory, *among them that are sanctified*—And so made meet for it A large number of these Paul doubtless knew, and remembered before God.

33. *I have coveted*—Here the apostle begins the other branch of his farewell discourse, like old Samuel, 1 Sam. xii, 3, taking his leave of the children of Israel.

34. *These hands*—Callous, as you see, with labour. Who is he that envies such a bishop or archbishop as this?

35. *I have showed you*—Bishops, by my example, *all things*—And this among the rest; *that thus labouring*—So far as the labours of your office allow you time; *ye ought to help the weak*—Those who are disabled by sickness, or any bodily infirmity, from maintaining themselves by their own labour. *And to remember*—Effectually, so as to follow it; *the word which he himself said*—Without doubt his disciples remembered many of his words which are not recorded. *It is happier to give*—To imitate God, and have him, as it were, indebted to us.

37. *They all wept*—Of old, men, yea, the best and bravest of men, were easily melted into tears; a thousand instances of which might be produced from profane as well as sacred writers. But now, notwithstanding the effeminacy which almost universally prevails, we leave those tears to women and children.

38. *Sorrowing most for that word which he spake, that they should see his face no more*—What sorrow will be in the great day, when God shall speak that word to all who are found on the left hand, that they shall see his face no more!

XXI. 1. *And when we were torn away from them*—Not without doing violence both to ourselves and them.

3. *We landed at Tyre*—That there should be Christians there was foretold, Psa. lxxxvii, 4. What we read in that psalm of the Philistines and Ethiopians also may be compared with Acts viii, 40; xxvii, 4.

4. *And finding disciples, we tarried there seven days*—In order to spend a

5 Spirit not to go up to Jerusalem. But when we had finished these
days, we departed and went our way ; and they all attended us out
of the city, with their wives and children : and kneeling down on
6 the sea shore we prayed. And having embraced each other, we
7 took ship, and they returned home. And having finished *our* voyage, we came from Tyre to Ptolemais, and saluting the brethren,
8 we abode with them one day. And the next day we departed and
came to Cesarea ; and entering into the house of Philip the evan-
9 gelist, who was *one* of the seven, we abode with him. And he had
10 four daughters, virgins, who were prophetesses. And as we tarried
many days, a certain prophet named Agabus came down from
11 Judea. And coming to us, he took up Paul's girdle, and binding
his own feet and hands, said, Thus saith the Holy Ghost, So shall
the Jews at Jerusalem bind the man whose girdle this is, and
12 deliver *him* into the hands of the Gentiles. And when we heard
these things, both we, and they of the place, besought him not to
13 go up to Jerusalem. But Paul answered, What mean ye, weeping
and breaking my heart ? I am ready not only to be bound, but also
14 to die at Jerusalem, for the name of the Lord Jesus. And when
he would not be persuaded, we ceased, saying, The will of the
Lord be done.
15   And after these days we took up our carriages, and went up to

---

Sabbath with them. *Who told Paul by the Spirit*—That afflictions awaited him
at Jerusalem. This was properly what they said by the Spirit. They themselves
advised him not to go up. The disciples seemed to understand their prophetic
impulse to be an intimation from the Spirit, that Paul, if he were so minded, might
avoid the danger, by not going to Jerusalem.

7. *Having finished our voyage*—From Macedonia, chap. xx, 6, *we came to
Ptolemais*—A celebrated city on the sea coast, anciently called Accos. It is now,
like many other once noble cities, only a heap of ruins.

8. *We came to Cesarea*—So called from a stately temple which Herod the Great
dedicated there to Augustus Cesar. It was the place where the Roman governor
of Judea generally resided and kept his court. *The evangelist, who was one of
the seven* deacons—An evangelist is a preacher of the Gospel to those who had
never heard it, as Philip had done to the Samaritans, to the Ethiopian eunuch,
and to all the towns from Azotus to Cesarea, chap. viii, 5, 26, 40. It is not unlikely he spent the following years preaching in Tyre and Sidon, and the other
heathen cities in the neighbourhood of Galilee, his house being at Cesarea, a convenient situation for that purpose. *We abode with him*—We lodged at his house
during our stay at Cesarea.

10. *A certain prophet came*—The nearer the event was, the more express were
the predictions which prepared Paul for it.

11. *Binding his own feet and hands*—In the manner that malefactors were wont
to be bound when apprehended. *So shall the Jews bind the man whose girdle
this is*—St. Paul's bonds were first particularly foretold at Cesarea, to which he
afterward came in bonds, chap. xxiii, 33.

12. *Both we,* (his fellow travellers,) *and they of the place, besought him not to go
up to Jerusalem*—St. Paul knew that this prediction had the force of a command.
They did not know this.

13. *Breaking my heart*—For the apostles themselves were not void of human
affections. *I am ready not only to be bound, but to die*—And to him that is ready
for it, the burden is light.

14. *And when he would not be persuaded*—This was not obstinacy, but true
Christian resolution. We should never be persuaded, either to do evil, or to omit
doing any good which is in our power ; saying, *the will of the Lord be done*—
Which they were satisfied Paul knew.

15. *We took up our carriages*—Our baggage ; which probably went by sea before.

16 Jerusalem, and *some* of the disciples also from Cesarea went with us, and brought us to one Mnason, a Cyprian, an old disciple, with whom we should lodge.

17 And when we were come up to Jerusalem, the brethren received
18 us gladly. And the next day Paul went in with us to James, and
19 all the elders were present. And having saluted them, he gave them a particular account of those things which God had done
20 among the Gentiles by his ministry. And having heard *it*, they glorified God, and said to him, Thou seest, brother, how many thousands of believing Jews there are, and they are all zealous
21 for the law. But they have been informed concerning thee, that thou teachest the Jews who are among the Gentiles, to apostatize from Moses, telling them not to circumcise *their* children, nor to
22 walk after the customs. What is it therefore? The multitude must needs come together; for they will hear that thou art come.
23 Therefore do this that we say to thee : there are with us four men,
24 who have a vow on them : Take them and purify thyself with them, and be at charges with them, that they may shave their heads : and all will know, that there is nothing of those things which they have heard of thee ; but *that* thou thyself walkest orderly, keeping the
25 law. As touching the Gentiles that believe, we have written and determined, that they should observe no such thing ; save only that they keep themselves from what is offered to idols, and from
26 blood, and from what is strangled, and from fornication. Then

---

What they took with them now in particular was the alms they were carrying to Jerusalem, chap. xxiv, 17.

16. *The disciples brought us to one Mnason, a Cyprian, an old disciple*—He was a native of Cyprus, but an inhabitant of Jerusalem, and probably one of the first converts there.

18. *Paul went in with us*—That it might appear we are all of one mind, *to James*—Commonly called the Lord's brother; the only apostle then presiding over the Churches in Judea.

20. *They are all zealous for the law*—For the whole Mosaic dispensation. How astonishing is this! Did none of the apostles, beside St. Paul, know that this dispensation was now abolished? And if they did both know and testify this, how came their hearers not to believe them?

21. *They have been informed concerning thee, that thou teachest the Jews*—not *to circumcise their children, nor to walk after the customs*—Of the Mosaic law. And so undoubtedly he did. And so he wrote to all the Churches in Galatia, among whom were many Jews. Yea, and James himself had long before assented to Peter, affirming before all the apostles and all the brethren, chap. xv, 10, That this very law was *a yoke which* (said he) *neither our fathers nor we were able to hear*—Amazing! that they did not know this! Or, that if they did, they did not openly testify it at all hazards, to every Jewish convert in Jerusalem!

22. *What is it therefore*—What is to be done? *The multitude must needs come together*—They will certainly gather together in a tumultuous manner, unless they be some way pacified.

23. *Therefore*—To obviate their prejudice against thee : *do this that we say to thee*—Doubtless they *meant* this advice *well :* but could Paul follow it in godly sincerity? Was not the yielding so far to the judgment of others too great a deference to be paid to any mere men?

24. *And all will know—that thou thyself walkest orderly, keeping the law*—Ought he not, without any reverence to man, where the truth of God was so deeply concerned, to have answered plainly, I do not keep the Mosaic law ; neither need any of you. Yea, Peter doth not keep the law. And God himself expressly commanded him not to keep it ; ordering him to *go in to men uncircumcised, and to eat with them*, chap. xi, 3, which the law utterly forbids.

22

Paul took the men, and the next day purifying himself with them, entered into the temple, declaring the accomplishment of the days of purification, till the offering should be offered for every one of
27 them. And when the seven days were about to be accomplished, the Jews that were from Asia seeing him in the temple, stirred up
28 all the multitude; and laid hands on him, Crying out, Men of Israel, help! This is the man that teacheth all men every where against the people, and the law, and this place: yea, and hath even
29 brought Greeks into the temple, and polluted this holy place. For they had before seen Trophimus the Ephesian with him in the city,
30 whom they supposed Paul had brought into the temple. And the whole city was moved, and the people ran together: and laying hold on Paul, they dragged him out of the temple : and immediately the gates were shut.
31 And as they went about to kill him, word came to the tribune of
32 the cohort, that all Jerusalem was in an uproar. Who immediately took soldiers and centurions, and ran down to him ; and when they saw the tribune and soldiers, they ceased from beating Paul.
33 Then the tribune came near, and took him, and commanded *him* to be bound with two chains, and inquired who he was, and what
34 he had done? But some among the multitude cried out one

---

26. *Then Paul took the men*—Yielding his own judgment to their advice, which seemed to flow not out of spiritual but carnal wisdom; *seeming* to be what he really was *not :* making *as if* he believed the law still in force. *Declaring*— Giving notice to the priests in waiting, that he designed to accomplish *the days of purification*, till all the sacrifice should be offered, as the Mosaic law required, Num. vi, 13.

27. *And when the seven days were about to be accomplished*—When after giving notice to the priests, they were entering upon the accomplishment of those days. It was toward the beginning of them that Paul was seized. *The Jews that were from Asia*—Some of those Jews who came from Asia to the feast.

28. *Against the people*—The Jewish nation ; *and the law*—Of Moses ; *and this place*—The temple. *Yea, and hath even brought Greeks into the temple*—They might come into the outer court. But they imagined Paul had brought them into the inner temple, and had thereby polluted it.

30. *And immediately the gates were shut*—Both to prevent any farther viola- tion of the temple; and to prevent Paul's taking sanctuary at the horns of the altar.

31. *And as they went about to kill him*—It was a rule among the Jews, that any uncircumcised person who came into the inner temple, might be stoned without farther process. And they seemed to think Paul, who brought such in thither, deserved no better treatment. *Word came to the tribune*—A cohort or detachment of soldiers, belonging to the Roman legion, which lodged in the ad- jacent castle of Antonia, were stationed on feast days near the temple, to pre- vent disorders. It is evident, Lysias himself was not present, when the tumult began. Probably he was the oldest Roman tribune (or colonel) then at Jerusa lem. And as such he was the commanding officer of the legion quartered at the castle.

33. *Then the tribune*—Having made his way through the multitude, *came near and took him*—And how many great ends of providence were answered by this imprisonment? This was not only a means of preserving his life, (after he had suffered severely for worldly prudence,) but gave him an opportunity of preach- ing the Gospel safely, in spite of all tumult, chap. xxii, 22, yea, and that in those places to which otherwise he could have had no access, ver. 40. *And com- manded him to be bound with two chains*—Taking it for granted he was some notorious offender. And thus the prophecy of Agabus was fulfilled, though by the hands of a Roman.

thing, some another; and when he could not know the certainty
for the tumult, he commanded him to be carried into the castle
35 But when he came upon the stairs, he was borne of the soldiers,
36 through the violence of the multitude. For the throng of people
37 followed after, crying, Away with him. And as Paul was about
to be brought into the castle, he said to the tribune, May I speak
38 to thee? Who said, Canst thou speak Greek? Art not thou that
Egyptian, who before these days madest an uproar, and leddest out
39 four thousand murderers into the wilderness? But Paul said, I am
a man who am a Jew of Tarsus in Cilicia, a citizen of no mean
city: and I beseech thee give me leave to speak to the people.
40 And when he had given him leave, Paul standing on the stairs waved
his hand to the people: and a great silence being made, he spake
to them in the Hebrew tongue, saying,
XXII. Brethren, and fathers, hear ye now my defence unto you.
2 (And when they heard that he addressed them in the Hebrew tongue,
3 they kept the more silence: and he saith) I am verily a Jew, born
at Tarsus in Cilicia, but brought up in this city at the feet of
Gamaliel, accurately instructed in the law of our fathers, and was
4 zealous toward God, as ye are all this day. And I persecuted this
way to the death, binding and delivering into prisons both men and
5 women: As likewise the high priest is my witness, and all the
estate of the elders: from whom also I received letters to the bre

---

35. *When he came upon the stairs*—The castle of Antonia was situate on a
rock fifty cubits high, at that corner of the outward temple, where the western
and northern porticos joined, to each of which there were stairs descending
from it.

37. *As Paul was about to be brought into the castle*—The wisdom of God taught
him to make use of that very time and place.

38. *Art not thou that Egyptian*—Who came into Judea when Felix had been
some years governor there! Calling himself a prophet, he drew much people after
him; and having brought them through the wilderness, led them to Mount Olivet,
promising that the walls of the city should fall down before them. But Felix
marching out of Jerusalem against him, his followers quickly dispersed, many
of whom were taken or slain; but he himself made his escape.

40. *In the Hebrew tongue*—That dialect of it, which was then commonly spoken
at Jerusalem.

XXII. 1. *Hear ye now my defence*—Which they could not hear before for the
tumult.

3. *I am verily*—This defence answers all that is objected, chap. xxi, 28. As
there, so here also mention is made of the person of Paul, ver. 3, of *the people*
and *the law*, ver. 3, 5, 12; of *the temple*, ver. 17; of *teaching all men*, ver. 15-17,
21; and of the truth of his doctrine, ver. 6. But he speaks closely and nervously,
in few words, because the time was short. *But brought up at the feet of Gamaliel*—The scholars usually sat on low seats, or upon mats on the floor, at the feet
of their masters, whose seats were raised to a considerable height. *Accurately
instructed*—The learned education which Paul had received was once no doubt
the matter of his boasting and confidence. Unsanctified learning *made his bonds
strong*, and furnished him with numerous arguments against the Gospel. Yet
when the grace of God had changed his heart, and turned his accomplishments
into another channel, he was the fitter instrument to serve God's wise and merciful purposes, in the defence and propagation of Christianity.

4. *And persecuted this way*—With the same zeal that you do now. *Binding
both men and women*—How much better was his condition, now he was bound
himself.

5. *The high priest is my witness*—Is able to testify. *The brethren*—Jews: so
this title was not peculiar to the Christians.

thren, and went to Damascus; to bring them who were there
5 bound to Jerusalem to be punished. But as I journeyed and drew
near to Damascus, about noon suddenly there shone from heaven
7 a great light round about me. And I fell to the ground, and heard
8 a voice saying to me, Saul, Saul, why persecutest thou me? And
I answered, Who art thou, Lord? And he said to me, I am Jesus
9 of Nazareth, whom thou persecutest. And they that were with me
saw the light, and were terrified; but they did not hear the voice
10 of him that spake to me. And I said, What shall I do, Lord? And
the Lord said to me, Rise and go into Damascus, and there it
shall be told thee of all things which are appointed thee to do.
11 And as I could not see for the glory of that light, being led by the
12 hand by them that were with me, I came into Damascus. And
one Ananias, a devout man according to the law, well reported of
13 by all the Jews that dwelt there, Coming to me, stood and said to
me, Brother Saul, receive thy sight. And the same hour I looked
14 up upon him: And he said, The God of our fathers hath chosen thee,
to know his will, and see that Just One, and hear the voice of his
15 mouth. For thou shalt be his witness to all men, of what thou hast
16 seen and heard. And now why tarriest thou? Arise and be baptized, and wash away thy sins, calling on the name of the Lord.
17 And when I was returned to Jerusalem, and was praying in the
18 temple, I was in a trance; And saw him saying to me, Make haste,
and depart quickly out of Jerusalem; for they will not receive thy
19 testimony concerning me. And I said, Lord, they know that I
imprisoned, and beat in every synagogue them that believed on
20 thee. And when the blood of thy martyr Stephen was shed, I also
was standing by, and consenting, and kept the garments of them
21 that slew him. But he said to me, Depart: for I will send thee
far off to the Gentiles.

---

6. *About noon*—All was done in the face of the sun. *A great light shone*—By
whatever method God reveals himself to us, we shall have everlasting cause to
recollect it with pleasure. Especially·when he has gone in any remarkable
manner out of his common way for this gracious purpose. If so, we should
often dwell on the particular circumstances, and be ready, on every proper occasion, to recount those wonders of power and love, for the encouragement and
instruction of others.

9. *They did not hear the voice*—Distinctly; but only a confused noise.

12. *A devout man according to the law*—A truly religious person, and though
a believer in Christ, yet a strict observer of the law of Moses.

16. *Be baptized, and wash away thy sins*—Baptism administered to real penitents, is both a means and seal of pardon. Nor did God ordinarily in the primitive Church bestow this on any, unless through this means.

17. *When I was returned to Jerusalem*—From *Damascus, and was praying in
the temple*—Whereby he shows that he still·paid the temple its due honour, as
the house of prayer. *I was in a trance*—Perhaps he might continue standing all
the while, so that any who were near him would hardly discern it.

18. *And I saw him*—Jesus, *saying to me, Depart quickly out of Jerusalem*—
Because of the snares laid for thee: and in order to preach where they will hear.

19. *And I said*—It is not easy for a servant of Christ, who is himself deeply
impressed with Divine truths, to imagine to what a degree men are capable of
hardening their hearts against thee. He is often ready to think with Paul, It is·
impossible for any to resist such evidence. But experience makes him wiser
and shows that wilful unbelief is proof against all truth and reason.

20. *When the blood of thy martyr Stephen was shed, I also was standing by*—A

22   And they heard him to this word, and *then* lifted up their voice
and said, Away with such a fellow from the earth; for it is not fit
23 that he should live.   And as they cried out, and rent their gar-
24 ments, and cast dust into the air, The tribune commanded him to
be brought into the castle, and ordered him to be examined by
scourging, that he might know for what cause they cried so against
25 him.   And as they were binding him with thongs, Paul said to
the centurion that stood by, Is it lawful for you to scourge a Ro-
26 man even uncondemned?   The centurion hearing *it*, went and told
the tribune, saying, Consider what thou art about to do; for this
27 man is a Roman.   Then the tribune came and said to him, Tell
28 me, art thou a Roman?   He said, Yea.   And the tribune answered,
I purchased this freedom with a great sum of money.   And Paul
29 said, But I was *free* born.   Then they who were going to examine him, immediately departed from him: and the tribune was
afraid, after he knew he was a Roman, because he had bound him.
30   And on the morrow, desiring to know the certainty, what he was
accused of by the Jews, he loosed him from *his* bonds, and commanded the chief priests and all the council to come; and bringing
Paul down, set him before them.
XXIII.   And Paul earnestly beholding the council, said, Brethren, I
2 have lived in all good conscience before God till this day.   And
3 Ananias the high priest commanded them that stood by to smite
him on the mouth.   Then said Paul to him, God is about to smite

real convert still retains the remembrance of his former sins. He confesses them
and is humbled for them, all the days of his life.
   22. *And they heard him to this word*—Till he began to speak of his mission to
the Gentiles, and this too in such a manner as implied that the Jews were in
danger of being cast off.
   23. *They rent their garments*—In token of indignation and horror at this pretended blasphemy, *and cast dust into the air*—Through vehemence of rage, which
they knew not how to vent.
   25. *And as they*—The soldiers ordered by the tribune, *were binding him with
thongs*—A freeman of Rome might be bound with a chain and beaten with a
staff: but he might not be bound with thongs, neither scourged, or beaten with
rods: *Paul said to the centurion*—The captain, who stood by to see the orders
of the tribune executed.
   26. *Consider what thou art about to do; for this man is a Roman*—Yea, there
was a stronger reason to consider. For this man was a servant of God.
   28. *But I was free born*—Not barely as being born at Tarsus; for this was not
a Roman colony. But probably either his father, or some of his ancestors, had
been made free of Rome, for some military service.
   We learn hence, that we are under no obligation as Christians to give up our
civil privileges (which we are to receive and prize as the gift of God) to every
insolent invader. In a thousand circumstances, gratitude to God, and duty to
men, will oblige us to insist upon them; and engage us to strive to transmit
them improved, rather than impaired to posterity.
   XXIII. 1. *And Paul earnestly beholding the council*—Professing a clear conscience by his very countenance; and likewise waiting to see whether any of
them was minded to ask him any question, *said, I have lived in all good conscience before God till this day*—He speaks chiefly of the time since he became a
Christian. For none questioned him concerning what he had been before. And
yet even in his unconverted state, although he was in an error, yet he had acted
from conscience, *before God*—Whatever men may think or say of me.
   3. *Then said Paul*—Being carried away by a sudden and prophetic impulse
God is about to smite thee, thou whited wall—Fair without; full of dirt and rub-
bish within. And he might well be so termed, not only as he committed this

thee, thou whited wall. , For sittest thou to judge me according to the law, and commandest me to be smitten contrary to the law?

4 But they that stood by, said, Revilest thou God's high priest?
5 Then said Paul, I was not aware, brethren, that it was the high priest; for it is written, * Thou shalt not revile the ruler of thy
6 people. But Paul perceiving that the one part were Sadducees, and the other Pharisees, cried out in the council, Brethren, I am a Pharisee, the son of a Pharisee; for the hope of the resurrection
7 of the dead am I called in question. And when he had said this, there arose a contention between the Pharisees and the Sadducees;
8 and the multitude was divided. For the Sadducees say there is no resurrection, neither angel nor spirit; but the Pharisees confess
9 both. And there was a great clamour: and the scribes of the Pharisees' side arising, contended, saying, We find no evil in this man: but if a spirit or an angel hath spoken to him, let us not fight
10 against God. And as a great disturbance arose, the tribune fearing lest Paul should be torn in pieces by them, commanded the soldiers to go down, and pluck him from among them, and bring him into the castle.
11 And the night following, the Lord standing by him, said, Be of good courage, Paul: for as thou hast testified the things concern-

---

outrage, while gravely sitting on the tribunal of justice ; but also as, at the same time that he stood high in the esteem of the citizens, he cruelly defrauded the priests of their legal subsistence, so that some of them even perished for want. And God did remarkably smite him; for about five years after this, his house being reduced to ashes, in a tumult begun by his own son, he was besieged in the royal palace ; where having hid himself in an old aqueduct, he was dragged out and miserably slain.

5. *I was not aware, brethren, that it was the high priest*—He seems to mean, I did not advert to it, in the prophetic transport of my mind : but he does not add, that his not adverting to it proceeded from the power of the Spirit coming upon him; as knowing they were not able to bear it. This answer admirably shows the situation of mind he was then in, partly with regard to the bystanders, whom he thus softens, adding also the title of brethren, and justifying their reproof by the prohibition of Moses ; partly with regard to himself, who, after that singular transport subsided, was again under the direction of the general command.

6. *I am a Pharisee, the son of a Pharisee : for the hope of the resurrection of the dead am I called in question*—So he was in effect; although not formally, or explicitly.

8. *The Pharisees confess both*—Both the resurrection, and the existence of angels and separate spirits.

9. *And the scribes of the Pharisees' side arising*—Every sect contains both learned and unlearned. The former used to be the mouth of the party. *If a spirit*—St. Paul in his speech from the stairs had affirmed, that Jesus, whom they knew to have been dead, was alive, and that he had spoken to him from heaven, and again in a vision. So they add nothing, only they construe it in their own way, putting an angel or spirit for Jesus.

11. *And the night following, the Lord Jesus*—What Paul had before purposed in spirit, chap. xix, 21, God now in due time confirms. Another declaration to the same effect is made by an angel of God, chap. xxvii, 23. And from the 23d chapter the sum of this book turns on the testimony of Paul to the Romans. How would the defenders of St. Peter's supremacy triumph, could they find out half as much ascribed to him ! *Be of good courage, Paul*—As he laboured under singular distresses and persecutions, so he was favoured with extraordinary assurances of the Divine assistance. *Thou must testify*—Particular promises

* Exod. xxii, 28.

12 ing me at Jerusalem, so thou must testify at Rome also. And
   when it was day, some of the Jews entering into a conspiracy
   bound themselves by a curse, saying, that they would neither eat
13 nor drink till they had killed Paul. And they were more than
14 forty who had made this confederacy. And they came to the chief
   priests and elders, and said, We have bound ourselves by a solemn
15 curse, not to taste any thing till we have killed Paul. Now therefore ye with the council signify to the tribune, that he bring him
   down to you to-morrow, as though ye would more accurately know
   the things concerning him : and we, before he come near, are
16 ready to kill him. But Paul's sister's son, hearing of *their* lying
17 in wait, came, and entering into the castle, told Paul. And Paul
   calling to him one of the centurions, said, Conduct this young man
18 to the tribune ; for he hath something to tell him. So he took and
   brought him to the tribune, and said, Paul the prisoner calling me
   to him, desired me to bring this young man to thee, who hath
19 something to tell thee. And the tribune taking him by the hand,
   and going aside privately, asked, What is it that thou hast to tell
20 me ? And he said, The Jews have agreed to ask thee to bring
   down Paul to-morrow to the council, as if they would inquire some-
21 thing concerning him more accurately. But do not yield to them ;
   for there are more than forty of them lie in wait, who have bound
   themselves with a curse, neither to eat nor drink till they have
   killed him : and now are they ready, expecting a promise from
22 thee. So the tribune dismissed the young man, having charged
   him, Tell no man that thou hast discovered these things to me.
23 And having called to him two of the centurions, he said, Prepare
   two hundred soldiers to go to Cesarea, and seventy horsemen, and
24 two hundred spearmen, by the third hour of the night. And provide beasts, to set Paul upon, and conduct *him* safe to Felix the
25 governor. And he wrote a letter after this manner, Claudius Ly-
26 sias to the most excellent Governor Felix, greeting. As this man
27 was seized by the Jews, and about to be killed by them, I came
   with the soldiery and rescued him, having learned that he was a

---

are usually given when all things appear desperate. *At Rome* also—Danger is
nothing in the eyes of God : all hinderances farther his work. A promise of
what is afar off, implies all that necessarily lies between. Paul shall testify at
Rome : therefore he shall come to Rome ; therefore he shall escape the Jews, the
sea, the viper.

12. *Some of the Jews bound themselves*—Such execrable vows were not uncommon among the Jews. And if they were prevented from accomplishing
what they had vowed, it was an easy matter to obtain absolution from their
rabbis.

15. *Now therefore ye*—Which they never scrupled at all, as not doubting but
they were doing God service.

17. *And Paul*—Though he had an express promise of it from Christ, was not
to neglect any proper means of safety.

19. *And the tribune taking him by the hand*—In a mild, condescending way.
Lysias seems to have conducted this whole affair with great integrity, humanity,
and prudence.

24. *Provide beasts*—If a change should be necessary, *to set Paul* on—So we
read of his riding once ; but not by choice.

27. *Having learned that he was a Roman*—True ; but not before he rescued
him. Here he uses art.

28 Roman. And desiring to know the crime of which they accused
29 him, I brought him before their council: Whom I found to be
accused concerning questions of their law, but to be charged with
30 nothing worthy of death or of bonds. And when it was shown
me, that an ambush was about to be laid for the man by the Jews,
I immediately sent *him* to thee, commanding his accusers also to
say before thee what they have against him. Farewell.
31 The soldiers therefore taking Paul, as it was commanded them,
32 brought *him* by night to Antipatris. On the morrow they returned
33 to the castle, leaving the horsemen to go with him: Who entering
into Cesarea, and delivering the letter to the governor, presented
34 Paul also before him, And having read *it*, he asked of what pro-
35 vince he was? And being informed that he was of Cilicia, I will
give thee, said he, a thorough hearing, when thy accusers also are
come. And he commanded him to be kept in Herod's palace.
XXIV. And after five days, Ananias the high priest came down with
the elders, and a certain orator, *named* Tertullus; who appeared
2 before the governor against Paul. And he being called, Tertullus
began to accuse *him*, saying, Seeing we enjoy great peace through
thee, and that very worthy deeds are done to this nation by thy
3 prudence always, and in all places, We accept *it*, most excellent
4 Felix, with all thankfulness. But that I may not trouble thee far-
5 ther, I beseech thee of thy clemency to hear us a few words. For
we have found this man a pestilent fellow, and a mover of sedition
among all the Jews throughout the world, and a ringleader of the
6 sect of the Nazarenes: Who hath also attempted to profane the
temple ; whom we seized and would have judged according to our
7 law. But Lysias the tribune coming upon us, with great violence
8 took him away out of our hands, Commanding his accusers to come
to thee, whereby thou mayest thyself, on examination, take know-
9 ledge of all these things, of which we accuse him. And the Jews
also assented, saying that these things were so.
10 Then Paul, after the governor had made a sign to him to speak,

---

31. *The soldiers brought him by night to Antipatris*—But not the same night
they set out. For Antipatris was about thirty-eight of our miles northwest of
Jerusalem. Herod the Great rebuilt it, and gave it this name in honour of his
father Antipater : Cesarea was near seventy miles from Jerusalem, and about
thirty from Antipatris.
35. *In Herod's palace*—This was a palace and a court built by Herod the
Great. Probably some tower belonging to it might be used for a kind of state
prison.
XXIV. 1. *Ananias*—Who would spare no trouble on the occasion, with several of the elders, members of the sanhedrim.
2. *Tertullus began*—A speech how different from St. Paul's ; which is true,
modest, solid, and without paint. Felix was a man of the most infamous cha
racter, and a plague to all the provinces over which he presided.
4. *But that I may not trouble thee any farther*—By trespassing either on thy
patience or modesty. The eloquence of Tertullus was as bad as his cause : a
lame introduction, a lame transition, and a lame conclusion. Did not God confound the orator's language ?
10. *Knowing—for several years thou hast been a judge over this nation*—And
so not unacquainted with our religious rites and customs, and consequently more
capable of understanding and deciding a cause of this nature. There was no
flattery in this. It was a plain fact. He governed Judea six or seven years.
I answer for myself—As it may be observed, his answer exactly corresponds

answered, Knowing thou hast been for several years a judge to
11 this nation, I cheerfully answer for myself: As thou mayest know
that 'it is but twelve days since I went up to worship at Jerusalem.
12 And they neither found me disputing with any man in the temple,
nor making any insurrection among the multitude either in the
13 synagogues or in the city. Nor can they prove the things whereof
14 they now accuse me. But this I confess unto thee, that after the
way which they call heresy, so worship I the God of my fathers,
believing all things which are written in the law and in the pro-
15 phets : Having hope in God that there shall be a resurrection of
the dead, both of the just and of the unjust, which they themselves
16 also expect. And for this cause do I also exercise myself to have
always a conscience void of offence toward God and toward men.
17 Now after several years I came to bring alms to my nation and
18 offerings. Whereupon certain Jews from Asia found me purifying
19 in the temple, neither with multitude, nor with tumult : Who ought
to have been present before thee, and to accuse *me*, if they had
20 any thing against me. Or let these themselves say what crime
21 they found in me when I stood before the council. Unless *it be*
concerning this one word, that I cried, standing among them,
Touching the resurrection of the dead, * I am called in question by
you this day.
22   And when Felix heard these things, he put them off, saying,
After I have been more accurately informed concerning this way,

with the three articles of Tertullus's charge: sedition, heresy, and profanation
of the temple. As to the first, he suggests, that he had not been long enough
at Jerusalem to form a party and attempt an insurrection: (for it was about
twelve days since he came up thither; five of which he had been at Cesarea,
ver. 1; one or two were spent in his journey thither, and most of the rest he
had been confined at Jerusalem.) And he challenges them, in fact, to produce
any evidence of such practices, ver. 11-13. As to the second, he confesses
himself to be a Christian; but maintains this to be a religion perfectly agreeable to the law and the prophets, and therefore deserving a fair reception, ver.
14, 16. And as for profaning the temple, he observes that he behaved there in
a most peaceful and regular manner, so that his innocence had been manifest
even before the sanhedrim, where the authors of the tumult did not dare to
appear against him.
    14. *After the way which they call heresy*—This appellation St. Paul corrects.
Not that it was then an odious word; but it was not honourable enough. A
party or sect (so that word signifies) is formed by men. This way was prescribed by God. The apostle had now said what was sufficient for his defence;
but having a fair occasion, he makes an ingenuous confession of his faith in this
verse, his hope in the next, his love in the 17th. *So worship I the God of my
fathers*—This was a very proper plea before a Roman magistrate; as it proved
that he was under the protection of the Roman laws, since the Jews were so:
whereas had he introduced the worship of new gods he would have forfeited that
protection. *Believing all things which are written*—Concerning the Messiah.
    15. *Both of the just and of the unjust*—In a public court this was peculiarly
proper to be observed.
    16. *For this cause*—With a view to this, *I also exercise myself*—As well as
they.
    19. *Who ought to have been present before thee*—But the world never commit
greater blunders, even against its own laws, than when it is persecuting the children of God.
    21. *Unless* they think me blamable for *this one word*—Which nevertheless was
the real truth.
                              * Chap. xxiii, 6.

when Lysias the tribune cometh down, I will take full cognizance
23 of your ·affair. And he commanded the centurion to keep him,
and let *him* have liberty, and to hinder none of his friends from
ministering to him.
24 And after some days, Felix coming with Drusilla, his wife, who
was a Jewess, sent for Paul, and heard him concerning the faith in
25 Christ. And as he reasoned concerning justice, temperance, and
the judgment to come, Felix being terrified, answered, Go thy way
for this 'ime : when I have a convenient season I will afterward
26 call for thee. And he hoped also that money would have been
given him by Paul : therefore he sent for him the oftener, and
27 discoursed with him. And after two years Felix was succeeded
by Portius Festus : and Felix desiring to gratify the Jews, left
Paul bound.
XXV. Now when Festus was come into the province, after three
2 days he went up from Cesarea to Jerusalem. Then the high priest

22. *After I have been more accurately informed*—Which he afterward was ; and
he doubtless (as well as Festus and Agrippa) transmitted a full account of these
things to Rome.
23. *He commanded the centurion to let him have liberty*—To be only a prisoner
at large. Hereby the Gospel was spread more and more ; not to the satisfaction
of the Jews. But they could not hinder it.
24. *And after Paul* had been kept *some days* in this gentle confinement at
Cesarea, Felix, who had been absent for a short time, coming thither again, *with
Drusilla, his wife*—The daughter of Herod Agrippa, one of the finest women of
that age. Felix persuaded her to forsake her husband, Azizus, king of Emessa,
and to be married to himself, though a heathen. She was afterward, with a son
she had by Felix, consumed in an eruption of Mount Vesuvius. *Concerning the
faith in Christ*—That is, the doctrine of Christ.
25. *And as he reasoned of justice, temperance, and judgment to come*—This
was the only effectual way of preaching Christ to an unjust, lewd judge. *Felix
being terrified*—How happily might this conviction have ended, had he been careful to pursue the views which were then opening upon his mind ! But, like
thousands, he deferred the consideration of these things to a more convenient
season. A season which, alas ! never came. For though he heard again, he was
terrified no more.
In the meantime we do not find Drusilla, though a Jewess, was thus alarmed.
She had been used to hear of a future judgment : perhaps too she trusted to the
being a daughter of Abraham, or to the expiation of the law, and so was proof
against the convictions which seized on her husband, though a heathen. Let
this teach us to guard against all such false dependencies as tend to elude those
convictions that might otherwise be produced in us by the faithful preaching
of the word of God. Let us stop our ears against those messengers of Satan,
who appear as angels of light ; who would teach us to reconcile the hope of
salvation with a corrupt heart or an unholy life. *Go thy way for this time*—
O how will every damned soul one day lament his having neglected such a time
as this !
26. *He hoped also*—An evil hope : so when he heard his eye was not single.
No marvel then that he profited nothing by all St. Paul's discourses : *that money
would be given*—By the Christians for the liberty of so able a minister. And
waiting for this, unhappy Felix fell short of the treasure of the Gospel.
27. *But after two years*—After St. Paul had been two years a prisoner, *Felix
desiring to gratify the Jews, left Paul bound*—Thus men of the world, to gratify
one another, stretch forth their hands to the things of God ! Yet the wisdom of
Felix did not profit him, did not satisfy the Jews at all. Their accusations followed him to Rome, and had utterly ruined him, but for the interest which his
brother Pallas had with Nero.
XXV. 2. *Then the high priest and the chief of the Jews appeared against*

and the chief of the Jews appeared before him against Paul, and
3 besought him, Begging favour against him, that he would send for
4 him to Jerusalem, lying in wait to kill him by the way. But Festus
answered, That Paul was kept at Cesarea, and that he himself
5 would depart *thither* shortly. Therefore let those of you, said he,
who are able, go down with me and accuse the man, if there be
6 any *wickedness* in him. And having tarried among them not more
than eight or ten days, he went down to Cesarea; and the next
day, sitting on the judgment seat, he commanded Paul to be
7 brought. And when he was come, the Jews who had come down
from Jerusalem stood round about *him*, bringing many and heavy
8 accusations against Paul, which they were not able to prove : While
he answered for himself, Neither against the law of the Jews, nor
9 against the temple, nor against Cesar, have I offended at all. But
Festus, desiring to gratify the Jews, answered Paul, and said, Art
thou willing to go up to Jerusalem, and there be judged before me
10 concerning these things ? Then said Paul, I am standing at Cesar's judgment seat, where I ought to be judged : I have done no
11 wrong to the Jews, as thou also very well knowest. For if indeed
I have done wrong, and have committed any thing worthy of death,
I refuse not to die ; but if there is nothing of the things whereof
these accuse me, no man can give me up to them. I appeal to
12 Cesar. Then Festus, having conferred with the council, answered
Hast thou appealed to Cesar ? To Cesar shalt thou go.
13 And after certain days, King Agrippa and Bernice came to Ce-
14 sarea, to salute Festus. And when they had been there many
days, Festus declared the cause of Paul to the king, saying, There

---

Paul—In so long a time their rage was not cooled. So much louder a call had
Paul to the Gentiles.

4. *But Festus answered*—So Festus's care to preserve the imperial privileges
was the means of preserving Paul's life. By what invisible springs does God
govern the world! With what silence, and yet with what wisdom and energy!

5. *Let those of you who are able*—Who are best able to undertake the journey,
and to manage the cause. *If there be any wickedness in him*—So he does not
pass sentence before he hears the cause.

6. *Not more than ten days*—A short space for a new governor to stay at such
a city as Jerusalem. He could not with any convenience have heard and decided
the cause of Paul within that time.

7. *Bringing many accusations*—When many accusations are heaped together,
frequently not one of them is true.

8. *While he answered*—To a general charge a general answer was sufficient.

9. *Art thou willing to go up to Jerusalem*—Festus could have ordered this without asking Paul. But God secretly overruled the whole, that he might have an
occasion of appealing to Rome.

10. *I am standing at Cesar's judgment seat*—For all the courts of the Roman
governors were held in the name of the emperor, and by commission from him.
No man can give me up—He expresses it modestly : the meaning is, Thou canst
not. *I appeal to Cesar*—Which any Roman citizen might do before sentence
was passed.

12. *The council*—It was customary for a considerable number of persons of
distinction to attend the Roman governors. These constituted a kind of council,
with whom they frequently advised.

13. *Agrippa*—The son of Herod Agrippa, chap. xii, 1; *and Bernice*—His
sister, with whom he lived in a scandalous familiarity. This was the person
whom Titus Vespasian so passionately loved, that he would have made her empress, had not the clamours of the Romans prevented it.

15 is a certain man left prisoner by Felix: About whom when I was
at Jerusalem, the chief priests and elders of the Jews appeared
16 before *me*, desiring judgment against him. To whom I answered,
It is not the custom of the Romans to give up any man, till he that
is accused have the accusers face to face, and liberty to make
17 his defence touching the crime laid to his charge. When therefore they were come hither, I without any delay sat on the judgment seat the next day, and commanded the man to be brought
18 forth. Against whom when the accusers stood up, they brought
19 no accusation of such things as I supposed; But had certain questions against him, relating to their own religious worship, and
about one Jesus that was dead, whom Paul affirmed to be alive.
20 And as I doubted of such manner of questions, I asked if he would
go to Jerusalem, and there be judged concerning these matters.
21 But Paul appealing to be kept for the hearing of Augustus, I com-
22 manded him to be kept till I could send him to Cesar. Then
Agrippa said to Festus, I would also hear the man myself. And
he said, To-morrow thou shalt hear him.
23   And on the morrow, when Agrippa was come and Bernice with
great pomp, and were entered into the place of audience with the
tribunes and principal men of the city, at the command of Festus,
24 Paul was brought forth. And Festus said, King Agrippa, and all
ye who are present with us, ye see this man, about whom all the
multitude of the Jews have pleaded with me, both at Jerusalem and
25 here, crying out, that he ought not to live any longer. But when I
found that he had committed nothing worthy-of death, and he had
26 himself appealed to the emperor, I determined to send him: Of
whom I have nothing certain to write to *my* lord: therefore I have
brought him before you, and especially before thee, O King Agrippa,
27 that after examination taken, I may have somewhat to write. For
it seemeth to me unreasonable to send a prisoner, and not to signify
also the crimes *alleged* against him.
XXVI.   Then Agrippa said to Paul, It is permitted thee to speak
for thyself. And Paul, stretching forth his hand, made his defence.

15. *Desiring judgment against him*—As upon a previous conviction, which they falsely pretended.
16. *It is not the custom of the Romans*—How excellent a rule, to condemn no one unheard! A rule, which as it is common to all nations, (courts of inquisition only excepted,) so it ought to direct our proceedings in all affairs, not only in public, but private life.
18. *Such things as I supposed*—From their passion and vehemence.
19. *But had certain questions*—How coldly does he mention the things of the last importance! *And about one Jesus*—Thus does Festus speak of Him, to whom every knee shall bow! *Whom Paul affirmed to be alive*—And was this a doubtful question? But why, O Festus, didst thou doubt concerning it? Only because thou didst not search into the evidence of it. Otherwise that evidence might have opened to thee, till it had grown up into full conviction; and thy illustrious prisoner have led thee into the glorious liberty of the children of God.
23. *With the tribunes and principal men of the city*—The chief officers, both military and civil.
XXVI. *And Paul stretching forth his hand*—Chained as it was: a decent expression of his own earnestness, and proper to engage the attention of his hearers; *answered for himself*—Not only refuting the accusations of the Jews, but enlarging upon the faith of the Gospel.

2 I think myself happy, King Agrippa, that I am this day to make my
defence before thee, concerning all those things whereof I am ac-
3 cused by the Jews,'Who art accurately acquainted with all the
customs and questions which are among the Jews : wherefore I
beseech thee to hear me patiently.
4   The manner of my life from my youth, which was from the beginning among my own nation at Jerusalem, all the Jews know,
5 Who knew me from the first, (if they would testify,) that I lived a
6 Pharisee, after the striestst sect of our religion. And now I stand
in judgment for the hope of the promise made by God to our
7 fathers : To which our twelve tribes, worshipping continually night
and day, hope to attain : concerning which hope, King Agrippa, I
8 am accused by the Jews. What ! Is it judged by you an incredible
9 thing, that God should raise the dead ? I indeed thought myself,
that I ought to do many things contrary to the name of Jesus of
10 Nazareth : Which also I did in Jerusalem ; and having received
authority from the chief priests, I shut up many of the saints in
prisons, and when they were killed, I gave my vote against *them*.
11 And frequently punishing them in all the synagogues, I compelled
them to blaspheme ; and being exceedingly mad against them, I

2. *King Agrippa*—There is a peculiar force in thus addressing a person by
name. Agrippa felt this.
3. *Who art accurately acquainted*—Which Festus was not; *with the customs*—
In practical matters ; *and questions*—In speculative. This word Festus had used
in the absence of Paul, chap. xxv, 19, who, by the Divine leading, repeats and
explains it. Agrippa had had peculiar advantages for an accurate knowledge
of the Jewish customs and questions, from his education under his father Herod,
and his long abode at Jerusalem.
  Nothing can be imagined more suitable or more graceful, than this whole dis
course of Paul before Agrippa ; in which the seriousness of the Christian, the
boldness of the apostle, and the politeness of the gentleman and the scholar, appear in a most beautiful contrast, or rather a most happy union.
4. *From my youth, which was from the beginning*—That is, which was from
the beginning of my youth.
5. *If they would testify*—But they would not, for they well knew what weight
his former life must add to his present testimony.
6. *And now*--This and the two following verses are in a kind of parenthesis,
and show that what the Pharisees rightly taught concerning the resurrection,
Paul likewise asserted at this day. The ninth verse is connected with the fifth.
For Pharisaism impelled him to persecute. *I stand in judgment for the hope of
the promise*—Of the resurrection. So it was in effect. For unless Christ had
risen, there could have been no resurrection of the dead. And it was chiefly for
testifying the resurrection of Christ, that the Jews still persecuted him.
7. *Our twelve tribes*—For a great part of the ten tribes also had at various times
returned from the east to their own country, James i, 1 ; 1 Pet. i, 1. *Worshipping
continually night and day*—That is, this is what they aim at in all their public
and private worship.
8. *Is it judged by you an incredible thing*—It was by Festus, chap. xxv, 19, to
whom Paul answers as if he had heard him discourse.
9. *I thought*—When I was a Pharisee : *that I ought to do many things*—Which
ne now enumerates.
10. *I shut up many of the saints*—Men not only innocent, but good, just, holy.
I gave my vote against them—That is, I joined with those who condemned them.
Perhaps the chief priests did also give him power to vote on these occasions.
11. *I compelled them*—That is, some of them ; *to blaspheme*—This is the most
dreadful of all ! Repent, ye enemies of the Gospel. If Spira, who was compelled, suffered so terribly, what will become of those who compel, like Saul, but do
not repent like him.

12 persecuted *them* even to foreign cities. *Whereupon as I was
going to Damascus, with authority and commission from the chief
13 priests, At mid day, O king, I saw in the way a light from heaven, above the brightness of the sun shining round me and them
14 that journeyed with me. And when we were all fallen down to
the earth, I heard a voice saying to me in the Hebrew tongue
Saul, Saul, why persecutest thou me? *It is* hard for thee to kick
15 against the goads. And I said, Who art thou, Lord? And he said,
16 I am Jesus whom thou persecutest. But rise and stand upon thy
feet; for I have appeared to thee for this purpose, to ordain thee
a minister and a witness, both of the things which thou hast seen,
17 and of those in which I will appear to thee, Delivering thee from
18 the people, and the Gentiles, to whom I now send thee, To open
their eyes, that they may turn from darkness to light, and from the
power of Satan to God; that they may receive through faith which
is in me, forgiveness of sins, and an inheritance among them that
19 are sanctified. From that time, O King Agrippa, I was not disobe-
20 dient to the heavenly vision, But first to them at Damascus and a
Jerusalem, and through all the country of Judea, and *then* to the
Gentiles, I declared, that they should repent and turn to God,
21 doing works worthy of repentance. For these things the Jews
seizing me in the temple, attempted to kill me with their own hands.
22 But having obtained help from God, I continue till this day, testifying both to small and great, saying nothing but what both the pro-
23 phets and Moses have declared should be, That Christ having
suffered, and being the first who rose from the dead, should show

13. *O King*—Most seasonably, in the height of the narration, does he thus fix
the king's attention. *Above the brightness of the sun*—And no marvel. For what
is the brightness of this created sun, to the Sun of righteousness, the brightness
of the Father's glory?
14. *In the Hebrew tongue*—St. Paul was not now speaking in Hebrew: when
he was, chap. xxiii, 7, he did not add, *In the Hebrew tongue.* Christ used this
tongue both on earth and from heaven.
17. *Delivering thee from the people*—The Jews *and the Gentiles, to whom,* both
Jews and Gentiles, *I now send thee*—Paul gives them to know, that the liberty
he enjoys even in bonds, was promised to him, as well as his preaching to the
Gentiles. *I,* denotes the authority of the sender. *Now,* the time whence his
mission was dated. For his apostleship, as well as his conversion, commenced
at this moment.
18. *To open*—He opens them, who sends Paul; and he does it by Paul who is
sent; *their eyes*—Both of the Jews and Gentiles: *that they may turn*—Through
the power of the Almighty, from the spiritual darkness wherein they were involved, to the light of Divine knowledge and holiness, *and from the power of
Satan,* who now holds them in sin, guilt, and misery, to the love and happy service of God: *that they may receive through faith*—(He seems to place the same
blessings in a fuller light,) pardon, holiness, and glory.
19. *From that time*—Having received power to obey, *I was not disobedient*—
I did obey, I used that power, Gal. i, 16. So that even this grace whereby St
Paul was influenced, was not irresistible.
20. *I declared*—From that hour to this, both to Jew and Gentile, *that they
should repent*—This repentance, we may observe, is previous both to inward and
outward holiness.
21. *For these things*—The apostle now applies all that he had said.
22. *Having obtained help from God*—When all other help failed, God sent the
Romans from the castle, and so fulfilled the promise he had made, ver. 17.
* Acts ix, 2.

24 light to the people and to the Gentiles. And as ne was thus making his defence, Festus said with a loud voice, Paul, thou art beside
25 thyself, much learning doth make thee mad. But he said, I am not mad, most excellent Festus, but utter the words of truth and sobrie-
26 ty. For the king knoweth of these things ; to whom also I speak with freedom ; for I am persuaded none of these things are hidden
27 from him, for this was not done in a corner. King Agrippa, bᵉ
28 lievest thou the prophets ? I know that thou believest. Then Agrippa said unto Paul, Almost thou persuadest me to be a Chris-
29 tian. And Paul said, I would to God, that not only thou, but like-wise all that hear me, were this day both almost and altogether such as I am, except these bonds.
30 And as he said this, the king rose up, and the governor, and Ber-
31 nice, and they that sat with them. And as they were going away, they spake one to another, saying, This man doth nothing worthy
32 of death, or of bonds. And Agrippa said unto Festus, This man might have been set at liberty if he had not appealed unto Cesar.
XXVII. And when it was determined to sail into Italy, they deliver-

---

24. *Festus said, Paul, thou art beside thyself*—To talk of men's rising from the dead ! And of a Jew's enlightening not only his own nation, but the polite and learned Greeks and Romans ! Nay, Festus, it is thou that *art beside thyself.* That strikest quite wide of the mark. And no wonder : he saw that nature did not act in Paul ; but the grace that acted in him he did not see. And therefore he took all this ardour which animated the apostle for a mere start of learned phrensy.

25. *I am not mad, most excellent Festus*—The style properly belonging to a Roman propretor. How inexpressibly beautiful is this reply ! How strong ! yet how decent and respectful ! Madmen seldom call men by their names, and titles of honour. Thus also St. Paul refutes the charge. *But utter the words of truth* (confirmed in the next verse) *and sobriety*—The very reverse of madness. And both these remain, even when the men of God act with the utmost vehemence.

26. *For the king knoweth of these things*—St. Paul having refuted Festus, pursues his purpose, returning naturally, and as it were, step by step, from Festus to Agrippa. *To whom I speak with freedom*—This freedom was probably one circumstance which Festus accounted madness.

27. *King Agrippa, believest thou the prophets ?*—He that believes these, believes Paul, yea, and Christ. The apostle now comes close to his heart. What did Agrippa feel when he heard this ? *I know that thou believest !*—Here Paul lays so fast hold on the king that he can scarce make any resistance.

28. *Then Agrippa said unto Paul, Almost thou persuadest me to be a Christian !*—See here, Festus altogether a heathen, Paul alogether a Christian, Agrippa halting between both. Poor Agrippa ! But almost persuaded ! So near the mark, and yet fall short ! Another step, and thou art within the vail. Reader, stop not with Agrippa ; but go on with Paul.

29. *I would to God*—Agrippa had spoke of being a Christian, as a thing wholly in his own power. Paul gently corrects this mistake ; intimating, it is the gift and the work of God ; *that all that hear me*—It was modesty in St. Paul, not to apply directly to them all ; yet he looks upon them and observes them ; *were such as I am*—Christians indeed ; full of righteousness, peace, and joy in the Holy Ghost. He speaks from a full sense of his own happiness, and an over-flowing love to all.

30. *And as he said this, the king rose up*—An unspeakably precious moment to Agrippa. Whether he duly improved it or no, we shall see in that day.

31. *This man doth nothing worthy of death or of bonds*—They speak of his whole life, not of one action only. And could ye learn nothing more than this from that discourse ? A favourable judgment of such a preacher, is not all that God requires.

XXVII. 1. *As soon as it was determined to sail*—As being a shorter and less expensive passage to Rome.

ed Paul, and certain other prisoners, to a centurion named Julius,
2 of the Augustan cohort. And going aboard a ship of Adramyttium, that was to sail by the coasts of Asia, we set sail, Aristarchus,
a Macedonian of Thessalonica, being with us. And the next day
3 we reached Sidon. And Julius treating Paul courteously, per-
4 mitted *him* to go to *his* friends to take refreshment. And setting
sail from thence, we sailed under Cyprus, because the winds were
5 contrary. And having sailed through the sea of Cilicia, and Pam-
6 phylia, we came to Myra, *a city* of Lycia. And the centurion finding a ship of Alexandria there, bound for Italy, put us on board of it.
7 And when we had sailed slowly many days, and were scarce come
over against Cnidus, the wind not suffering us, we sailed under
8 Crete, over against Salmone. And passing it with difficulty, we
came to a certain place called the Fair Havens, near which was
9 the city Lasea. And as much time was spent, and sailing was now
dangerous, because the fast was already past, Paul exhorted *them*,
10 Saying to them, Sirs, I perceive that this voyage will be with injury and much damage, not only to the lading and the ship, but also
11 to our lives. But the centurion regarded the master and the owner
of the vessel more than the things which were spoken by Paul
12 And as the haven was not convenient to winter in, the greater part
advised to set sail from thence also, if by any means they might
reach Phenice, to winter *there*, *which is* a haven of Crete looking
to the southwest and northwest.
13 And as the south wind blew gently, supposing they had obtained
their purpose, they weighed anchor, and sailed on close by Crete.
14 But not long after there arose against it a tempestuous wind named
15 Euroclydon. And the ship being caught, and not able to bear up
16 against the wind, we let *her* drive. And running under a certain

2. *Adramyttium*—was a sea port of Mysia. Aristarchus and Luke went with
Paul by choice, not being ashamed of his bonds.
3. *Julius treating Paul courteously*—Perhaps he had heard him make his
defence.
4. *We sailed under Cyprus*—Leaving it on the left hand.
7. *Cnidus*—was a cape and city of Caria.
8. *The Fair Havens* still retain the name. But the city of Lasea is now utterly lost, together with many more of the hundred cities for which Crete was
once so renowned.
9. *The fast*, or day of atonement, was kept on the tenth of Tisri, that is, the
25th of September. This was to them an ill time of sailing; not only because
winter was approaching, but also because of the sudden storms, which are still
common in the Mediterranean at that time of the year. *Paul exhorted them*—
Not to leave Crete. Even in external things, faith exerts itself with the greatest
presence of mind, and readiness of advice.
10. *Saying to them*—To the centurion and other officers.
11. *The centurion regarded the master*—And indeed it is a general rule, believe
an artificer in his own art. Yet when there is the greatest need, a real Christian
will often advise even better than him.
12. *Which is a haven*—Having a double opening, one to the southwest, the
other to the northwest.
14. *There arose against it*—The south wind; *a tempestuous wind*, called in
those parts Euroclydon. This was a kind of hurricane, not carrying them any
one way, but tossing them backward and forward. These furious winds are now
called levanters, and blow in all directions from the northeast to the southeast.
16. *We were hardly able to get masters of the boat*—To prevent its being
staved

island called Clauda, we were hardly able to get master of the
17 boat: Which having taken up, they used helps, undergirding the
ship, and fearing lest they should fall into the quicksands, they
18 struck sail, and so were driven.   And as we were in an exceeding
great storm, the next day they lightened the ship.   And the third
19 day we cast out with our own hands the tackling of the ship.   And
20 as neither sun nor stars appeared for many days, and no small
tempest lay on *us*, all hope of our being saved was now taken
away.
21   But after long abstinence, Paul standing in the midst of them,
said, Sirs, ye should have hearkened to me, and not have loosed
22 from Crete, and *so* have avoided this injury and loss.   Yet now I
exhort you to be of good courage; for there shall be no loss of
23 *any* life among you, but of the ship *only*.   For there stood by me
this night an angel of the God whose I am, and whom I serve,
24 Saying, Fear not, Paul; thou must be presented before Cesar: and
25 lo, God hath given thee all them that sail with thee.   Wherefore,
sirs, take courage : for I trust in God, that it shall be even as it
26 hath been spoken to me.   But we must be cast on a certain island.
27 And when the fourteenth night was come, as we were driven up
and down in the Adriatic sea, about midnight the sailors suspected
28 that they drew nigh some land.   And sounding, they found twenty
fathoms; and having gone a little farther, sounding again, they
29 found fifteen fathoms.   And fearing lest we should fall upon rough
places, they cast four anchors out of the stern, and wished for the
30 day.   But when the sailors were attempting to flee out of the ship,
and had let down the boat into the sea, under pretence that they
31 were going to carry out anchors out of the foreship, Paul said to

18. *They lightened the ship*—Casting the heavy goods into the sea.
19. *We cast out the tackling of the ship*—Cutting away even those masts that
were not absolutely necessary.
20. *Neither sun nor stars appeared for many days*—Which they could the less
spare, before the compass was found out.
21. *This loss*—Which is before your eyes.
23. *The God whose I am, and whom I serve*—How short a compendium of
religion! Yet how full! Comprehending both faith, hope, and love.
24. *God hath given*—Paul had prayed for them. And God gave him their
lives; perhaps their souls also. And the centurion, subserving the providence
of God, gave to Paul the lives of the prisoners. How wonderfully does his providence reign in the most contingent things! And rather will many bad men
be preserved with a few good, (so it frequently happens,) than one good man
perish with many bad. So it was in this ship: so it is in the world. *Thee*—At
such a time as this, there was not the same danger, which might otherwise have
been, of St. Paul's seeming to speak out of vanity, what he really spoke out of
necessity. *All the souls*—Not only all the prisoners, as Julius afterward did,
ver. 43; ask for souls, they shall be given thee: yea, more than thou hopest
for, *that sail with thee*—So that Paul, in the sight of God, was the master and
pilot of the ship.
27. *The fourteenth night*—Since they left Crete, ver. 18, 19. *In the Adriatic
sea*—So the ancients called all that part of the Mediterranean, which lay south
of Italy.
30. *The sailors were attempting to flee out of the ship*—Supposing the boat
would go more safely over the shallows.
31. *Unless these* mariners *abide in the ship*—Without them ye know not how
to manage her, *ye cannot be saved*—He does not say *we*. That they would not

the centurion and the soldiers, Unless these abide in the ship, ye
32 cannot be saved. Then the soldiers cut off the ropes of the boat,
33 and let it fall off. And while the day was coming on, Paul exhorted
them all to take food, saying, This day is the fourteenth that ye
34 have tarried and continued fasting, having taken nothing. Therefore I exhort you to take food: for this is for your preservation;
35 for there shall not a hair fall from the head of any of you. And
having spoken thus, he took bread, and gave thanks to God before
36 them all· and having broken it, he began to eat. Then were they
37 all encouraged, and they also took meat. And we were in the ship,
38 in all two hundred and seventy-six souls. And when they were
satisfied with food, they lightened the ship, casting out the wheat
39 into the sea. And when it was day, they did not know the land:
but they observed a certain creek having a shore, into which they
40 were minded if possible to thrust the ship: And having taken up
the anchors, they committed it to the sea, at the same time loosing
the rudder bands, and hoisting up the stay sail to the wind, they
41 made for the shore. But falling into a place where two seas met,
they ran the ship aground; and the fore part sticking fast, remained
immovable, but the hinder part was broken by the force of the
42 waves. And the counsel of the soldiers was to kill the prisoners,
43 lest any one should swim away and escape. But the centurion,
being desirous to save Paul, hindered them from their purpose, and
commanded those that could swim, throwing themselves *into the*
44 *sea,* first to get away to land. And the rest, some on boards, and

---

have regarded. The soldiers were not careful for the lives of the prisoners : nor
was Paul careful for his own.

We may learn hence, to use the most proper means for security and success,
even while we depend on Divine Providence, and wait for the accomplishment
of God's own promise. He never designed any promise should encourage rational creatures to act in an irrational manner ; or to remain inactive, when he
has given them natural capacities of doing something, at least, for their own
benefit. To expect the accomplishment of any promise, without exerting these,
is at best vain and dangerous presumption, if all pretence of relying upon it be
not profane hypocrisy.

33. *Ye continue fasting, having taken nothing*—No regular meal , through a
deep sense of their extreme danger. Let us not wonder then, if men who have
a deep sense of their extreme danger of everlasting death, for a time forget even
to eat their bread, or to attend to their worldly affairs. Much less let us censure
that as madness, which may be the beginning of true wisdom.

34. *This is for your preservation*—That ye may be the better able to swim to
shore.

36. *Then they were all encouraged*—By his example, as well as words.

38. *Casting out the wheat*—So firmly did they now depend on what St. Paul
had said.

39. *They did not know the land*—Which they saw near them : *having a level
shore.*

40. *Loosing the rudder bands*—Their ships had frequently two rudders, one on
each side. These were fastened while they let the ship drive ; but were now
loosened, when they had need of them to steer her into the creek.

41. *A place where two seas met*—Probably by reason of a sand bank running
parallel with the shore.

42. *The counsel*—Cruel, unjust, ungrateful.

44. *They all escaped safe to land*—And some of them doubtless received the
apostle as a teacher sent from God. These would find their deliverance from
the fury of the sea, but an earnest of an infinitely greater deliverance, and are

some on *broken pieces* of the ship ; and so it came to pass, that they all escaped safe to land.

XXVIII. And being escaped, we then knew, that the island was
2 called Melita. And the barbarians showed us uncommon kindness ; for having kindled a fire, they brought us all to *it*, because
3 of the present rain, and because of the cold. Now as Paul was gathering a bundle of sticks, and laying them on the fire, a viper
4 coming from the heat fastened upon his hand. And when the barbarians saw the venomous animal hanging on his hand, they said one to another, Doubtless this man is a murderer, whom, though
5 he hath escaped the sea, vengeance hath not suffered to live. But having shaken off the venomous animal into the fire, he suffered no
6 harm. However, they expected that he would have swollen, or suddenly fallen down dead : but after having waited a considerable time, seeing no mischief befall him, they changed their minds, and said he was a god.
7 And near that place was the estate of a chief man of the island, named Publius, who receiving us into his house, entertained us
8 courteously three days. Now the father of Publius lay sick of a fever and bloody flux ; to whom Paul went in, and having prayed
9 laid his hands on him and healed him. And when this was done, the rest also in the island, who had disorders, came and were healed,

---

long ere this lodged with him in a more peaceful harbour than Malta, or than the earth could afford.

XXVIII. 1. *Melita* or Malta, is about twelve miles broad, twenty long, and sixty distant from Sicily to the south. It yields abundance of honey, (whence its name was taken,) with much cotton, and is very fruitful, though it has only three feet depth of earth above the solid rock. The Emperor Charles the Fifth gave it, in 1530, to the knights of Rhodes, driven out of Rhodes by the Turks. They are a thousand in number, of whom five hundred always reside on the island.

2. *And the barbarians*—So the Romans and Greeks termed all nations but their own. But surely the generosity shown by these uncultivated inhabitants of Malta, was far more valuable than all the varnish which the politest education could give, where it taught not humanity and compassion.

4. *And when the barbarians saw—they said*—Seeing also his chains, *Doubtless this man is a murderer*—Such rarely go unpunished even in this life ; *whom vengeance hath not suffered to live*—They look upon him as a dead man already.

It is with pleasure that we trace among these barbarians the force of conscience, and the belief of a particular providence : which some people of more learning have stupidly thought it philosophy to despise. But they erred in imagining, that calamities must always be interpreted as judgments. Let us guard against this, lest, like them, we condemn not only the innocent, but the excellent of the earth.

5. *Having shaken off the venomous animal, he suffered no harm*—The words of an eminent modern historian are, " No venomous kind of serpent now breeds in Malta, neither hurts if it be brought thither from another place. Children are seen there handling and playing even with scorpions ; I have seen one eating them." If this be so, it seems to be fixed by the wisdom of God, as an eternal memorial of what he once wrought there.

6. *They changed their minds, and said he was a god*—Such is the stability of human reason ! A little before he was a murderer ; and presently he is a god : (just as the people of Lystra ; one hour sacrificing, and the next stoning :) nay, but there is a medium. He is neither a murderer nor a god, but a man of God. But natural men never run into greater mistakes, than in judging of the children of God.

7. *The chief man of the island*—In wealth if not in power also. *Three days*—The first three days of our stay on the island.

10 Who likewise honoured us with many honours, and when we de
parted, put on board such things as were necessary.
11   And after three months we sailed in a ship of Alexandria, which
had wintered in the island, whose sign was Castor and Pollux.
12 And arriving at Syracuse, we tarried *there* three days, Whence
13 coasting round, we came to Rhegium, and the south wind rising
14 after one day, we came the next to Puteoli · Where finding brethren, we were entreated to tarry with them seven days, and so we
15 went toward Rome.   And the brethren having heard of us, came
out thence to meet us, *some* as far as Appii-Forum, and *others* to
the Three Taverns, whom, when Paul saw, he thanked God and
took courage.
16 ' And when we were come to Rome, the centurion delivered the
prisoners to the captain of the guard : but Paul was suffered to
17 dwell by himself, with the soldier that kept him.   And after three
days he called the chief of the Jews together.   And when they
were come together, he said to them, Brethren, though I have done
nothing against the people, or the customs of our fathers, yet have
I been delivered a prisoner from Jerusalem into the hands of the
18 Romans : Who having examined me, were willing to have released
19 *me*, because there was no cause of death in me.   But when the Jews
opposed *it*, I was constrained to appeal to Cesar ; not that I had any
20 thing to accuse my nation of.   For this cause therefore have I
entreated to see and speak with you : for *it is* on account of the
21 hope of Israel, *that* I am bound with this chain.   And they said to
him, We have neither received letters from Judea concerning thee,
nor hath any of the brethren coming hither, related or spoken any
22 evil of thee.   But we desire to hear of thee what thou thinkest ;

---

11. *Whose sign was*—It was the custom of the ancients to have images on
the head of their ships, from which they took their names. *Castor and Pollux*
—Two heathen gods who were thought favourable to mariners.

15. *The brethren*—That is, the Christians, *came out thence to meet us*—It is
remarkable that there is no certain account by whom Christianity was planted at
Rome. Probably some inhabitants of that city were at Jerusalem on the day of
pentecost, Acts ii, 10 ; and being then converted themselves, carried the Gospel
thither at their return. Appii-Forum was a town fifty-one miles from Rome ;
the Three Taverns about thirty. *He took courage*—He saw Christ was at Rome
also, and now forgot all the troubles of his journey.

16. *With the soldier*—To whom he was chained, as the Roman custom was.

17. *And after three days*—Given to rest and prayer, *Paul called the chief of
the Jews together*—He always sought the Jews first ; but being now bound, he
could not so conveniently go round to them. *Though I have done nothing*—
Seeing him chained, they might have suspected he had. Therefore he first
obviates this suspicion.

19. *When the Jews opposed it*—He speaks tenderly of them, not mentioning
their repeated attempts to murder him. *Not that I had any thing to accuse my
nation of*—Not that I had any design to accuse others, but merely to defend
myself.

20. *The hope of Israel*—What Israel hopes for, namely, the Messiah and the
resurrection.

21. *We have neither received letters concerning thee*—There must have been a
peculiar providence in this, *nor has any of the brethren*—The Jews, *related*—Pro-
fessedly, in a set discourse, *or spoke*—Occasionally, in conversation, *any evil of
thee*—How must the bridle then have been in their mouth !

22. *This sect we know is every where spoken against*—This is no proof at all
of a bad cause, but a very probable mark of a good one.

for concerning this sect, we know that it is every where spoken against.

23 And having appointed him a day, many came to him at his lodging, to whom he expounded, testifying the kingdom of God, and persuading them concerning Jesus, both from the law of Moses
24 and the prophets, from morning till evening. And some believed
25 the things that were spoken, and some believed not. And not agreeing with each other, they brake up the assembly, after Paul had spoken one word, Well spake the Holy Ghost by the Prophet
26 Isaiah to your fathers, Saying, * Go to this people and say, Hearing ye shall hear, and shall not understand, and seeing ye shall see,
27 and shall not perceive. For the heart of this people is waxed gross, and with their ears they hear heavily, and their eyes have they closed ; lest they should see with *their* eyes, and hear with *their* ears, and understand with *their* hearts, and should be con-
28 verted, and I should heal them. Be it known therefore unto you, that the salvation of God is sent to the Gentiles, and they will
29 hear. And when he had said these things, the Jews departed, having great debating with each other.
30 And he continued two whole years in his own hired house, and
31 received all that came to him, Preaching the kingdom of God, and teaching the things that relate to the Lord Jesus Christ, with all freedom of speech, no man forbidding him.

23. *To whom he expounded, testifying the kingdom of God, and persuading them concerning Jesus*—These were his two grand topics, 1. That the kingdom of the Messiah was of a spiritual, not temporal nature : 2. That Jesus of Nazareth was the very person foretold, as the Lord of that kingdom. On this head he had as much need to persuade as to convince, their will making as strong a resistance as their understanding.
24. *And some believed the things that were spoken*—With the heart, as well as understanding.
25. *Well spake the Holy Ghost to your fathers*—Which is equally applicable to you.
26. *Hearing ye shall hear*—That is, ye shall most surely hear, *and shall not understand*—The words manifestly denote a judicial blindness, consequent upon a wilful and obstinate resistance of the truth. First they would not, afterward they could not, believe.
28. *The salvation of God is sent to the Gentiles*—Namely, from this time. Before this no apostle had been at Rome. St. Paul was the first.
30. *And Paul continued two whole years*—After which this book was written, long before St. Paul's death, and was undoubtedly published with his approbation by St. Luke, who continued with him to the last, 2 Tim. iv, 11. *And received all that came to him*—Whether they were Jews or Gentiles. These two years completed twenty-five years after our Saviour's passion. Such progress had the Gospel made by that time, in the parts of the world which lay west of Jerusalem, by the ministry of St. Paul among the Gentiles. How far eastward the other apostles had carried it in the same time, history does not inform us.
31. *No man forbidding him*—Such was the victory of the word of God. While Paul was preaching at Rome, the Gospel shone with its highest lustre. Here therefore the Acts of the Apostles end; and end with great advantage. Otherwise St Luke could easily have continued his narrative to the apostle's death.

* Isaiah vi, 9, &c; Matt. xiii, 14; John xii, 40.

NOTES

ST. PAUL'S EPISTLE TO THE ROMANS.

MANY of the writings of the New Testament are written in the form of epistles. Such are not only those of St. Paul, James, Peter, Jude, but also both the treatises of St. Luke, and all the writings of St. John. Nay, we have seven epistles herein, which the Lord Jesus himself sent by the hand of John to the seven Churches: yea, the whole Revelation is no other than an epistle from him.

Concerning the epistles of Paul, we may observe, he writes in a very different manner to those Churches which he had planted himself, and to those who had not seen his face in the flesh. In his letters to the former, a loving or sharp familiarity appears, as their behaviour was more or less suitable to the Gospel: to the latter, he proposes his pure, unmixed Gospel, in a more general and abstract manner.

As to the time wherein he wrote his epistles, it is probable he wrote about the year of Christ according to the common reckoning,

48	from Corinth	the epistle to the Thessalonians ;
49	from Phrygia	to the Galatians ;
52	from Ephesus	the first to the Corinthians ;
	from Troas	the first epistle to Timothy ;
	from Macedonia	the second to the Corinthians, and that to Titus ;
	from Corinth	to the Romans ;
57	from Rome	to the Philippians, to Philemon, to the Ephesians and Colossians ;
58	from Italy	to the Hebrews ;
66	from Rome	the second to Timothy.

As to the general epistles, it seems St. James wrote a little before his death, which was A. D. 63. St. Peter, who was martyred in the year 67, wrote his latter epistle a little before his death, and not long after his former. St. Jude wrote after him, when the mystery of iniquity was gaining ground swiftly. St. John is believed to have wrote all his epistles a little before his departure. The Revelation he wrote A. D. 96.

That St. Paul wrote this epistle from Corinth, we may learn from his commending to the Romans Phebe, a servant of the Church of Cenchrea, chap. xvi, 1, a port of Corinth, and from his mentioning the salutations of Gaius and Erastus, chap. xvi, 23, who were both Corinthians. Those to whom he wrote seem to have been chiefly foreigners, both Jews and Gentiles, whom business drew from other provinces ; as appears, both by his writing in Greek, and by his salutations of several former acquaintance.

His chief design herein is to show, 1. That neither the Gentiles by the law of nature, nor the Jews by the law of Moses, could obtain justification before God · and that therefore it was necessary for both to seek it from the free mercy of God by faith. 2. That God has an absolute right to show mercy on what terms he pleases and to withhold it from those who will not accept of it on his own terms.

THIS EPISTLE CONSISTS OF FIVE PARTS.

To express the design and contents of this epistle a little more at large, the apostle labours throughout, to fix in those to whom he writes, a deep sense of the excellency of the Gospel, and to engage them to act suitably to it. For this purpose, after a general salutation, chap. i, 1–7, and profession of his affection for them, ver. 8–15, he declares he shall not be ashamed openly to maintain the Gospel at Rome, seeing it is the powerful instrument of salvation, both to Jews and Gentiles, by means of faith, ver. 16, 17. And in order to demonstrate this, he shows,

1. That the world greatly needed such a dispensation, the Gentiles being in a most abandoned state, ver. 18–32; and the Jews, though condemning others, being themselves no better, chap. ii, 1–29. As notwithstanding some cavils, which he obviates, chap. iii, 1–8, their own Scriptures testify, 9–19. So that all were under a necessity of seeking justification by this method, 20–31.

2. That Abraham and David themselves sought justification by faith, and not by works, chap. iv, 1–25.

3. That all who believe are brought into so happy a state, as turns the greatest afflictions into matter of joy, chap. v, 1–11.

4. That the evils brought on mankind by Adam, are abundantly recompensed to all that believe in Christ, 12–21.

5. That far from dissolving the obligations to practical holiness, the Gospel increases them by peculiar obligations, chap. vi, 1–23.

In order to convince them of these things the more deeply, and to remove their fondness for the Mosaic law, now they were married to Christ by faith in him, chap. vii, 1–6, he shows how unable the motives of the law were to produce that holiness which believers obtain by a living faith in the Gospel, chap. vii, 7–25; viii, 1, 2; and then gives a more particular view of those things which rendered the Gospel effectual to this great end, ver. 3–39.

That even the Gentiles, if they believed, should have a share in these blessings; and that the Jews, if they believed not, should be excluded from them; being a point of great importance, the apostle bestows the 9th, 10th, and 11th chapters in settling it. He begins the 9th chapter by expressing his tender love and high esteem for the Jewish nation, ver. 1–5; and then shows,

1. That God's rejecting great part of the seed of Abraham, yea, and of Isaac too, was an undeniable fact, 6–13.

2. That God had not chosen them to such peculiar privileges for any kind of goodness either in them or their fathers, 14–24.

3. That his accepting the Gentiles, and rejecting many of the Jews, had been foretold both by Hosea and Isaiah, ver. 25–33.

4. That God had offered salvation to Jews and Gentiles on the same terms, though the Jews rejected it, chap. x, 1–21.

5. That though the rejection of Israel for their obstinacy was general, yet it was not total: there being still a remnant among them who did embrace the Gospel, chap. xi, 1–10.

6. That the rejection of the rest was not final, but in the end *all Israel should be saved*, ver. 11–31.

7. That meantime even their obstinacy and rejection served to display the unsearchable wisdom and love of God, ver. 32–36.

The rest of the epistle contains practical instructions and exhortations. He particularly urges, 1. An entire consecration of themselves to God, and a care to glorify him by a faithful improvement of their several talents, chap. xii, 1–11. 2. Devotion, patience, hospitality, mutual sympathy, humility, peace, and meekness, ver. 12–21. 3. Obedience to magistrates, justice in all its branches, love the fulfilling of the law, and universal holiness, chap. xiii, 1–14. 4. Mutual candour between those who differed in judgment touching the observance of the Mosaic law, chap. xiv, 1–23; xv, 1–17; in enforcing which he is led to mention the extent of his own labours, and his purpose of visiting the Romans; in the meantime recommending himself to their prayers, ver. 18–33. And after many salutations, chap. xvi, 1–16, and a caution against those who cause divisions, he concludes with a suitable blessing and doxology, ver. 17–27.

ROMANS

1 PAUL, a servant of Jesus Christ, called *to be* an apostle, sepa-
2 rated to the Gospel of God, * Which he had promised before,
3 by his prophets in the holy Scriptures; Concerning his Son, Jesus
  Christ our Lord, who was of the seed of David according to the
4 flesh. *But* declared the Son of God with power, according to the
5 Spirit of holiness, by the resurrection from the dead; By whom we

Verse 1. *Paul, a servant of Jesus Christ*—To this introduction the conclusion answers, chap. xv, 15, &c. *Called to be an apostle*—And made an apostle by that calling. While God calls, he makes what he calls. As the Judaizing teachers disputed his claim to the apostolical office, it is with great propriety that he asserts it in the very entrance of an epistle, wherein their principles are entirely overthrown. And various other proper and important thoughts are suggested in this short introduction; particularly the prophecies concerning the Gospel, the descent of Jesus from David, the great doctrines of his Godhead and resurrection, the sending the Gospel to the Gentiles, the privileges of Christians, and the obedience and holiness to which they were obliged, in virtue of their profession. *Separated*—By God, not only from the bulk of other men, from other Jews, from other disciples, but even from other Christian teachers, to be a peculiar instrument of God in spreading the Gospel.

2. *Which he promised before*—Of old time, frequently, solemnly. And the promise and accomplishment confirm each other.

3. *Who was of the seed of David according to the flesh*—That is, with regard to his human nature. Both the natures of our Saviour are here mentioned; but the human is mentioned first, because the Divine was not manifested in its full evidence till after his resurrection.

4. *But* powerfully declared *to be the Son of God, according to the Spirit of holiness*—That is, according to his Divine nature. *By the resurrection from the dead*—For this is both the fountain and the object of our faith; and the preaching of the apostles was the consequence of Christ's resurrection.

5. *By whom we have received*—I and the other apostles, *grace and apostleship*

* Deut xviii, 18; Isa. ix, 6, 7; Chap. liii, and lxi; Jer. xxii, 15.

have received grace and apostleship, for obedience to the faith in
6 all nations for his name, Among whom are ye also the called of
7 Jesus Christ: To all that are in Rome, *who are* beloved of· God,
called *and* holy, Grace to you, and peace from God our Father, and
the Lord Jesus Christ.
8   First, I thank my God, through Jesus Christ, for you all, that
9 your faith is spoken of through the whole world. For God, whom
I serve with my spirit in the Gospel of his Son, is my witness,
10 how incessantly I make mention of you, Always requesting in my
prayers to come unto you, if by any means now at length I may
11 have a prosperous journey by the will of God. For I long to see
you, that I may impart to you some spiritual gift, that ye may be

—The favour to be an apostle, and the qualifications for it. *For obedience to
the faith in all nations*—That is, that all nations may embrace the faith of Christ.
For his name—For his sake, out of regard to him.
    6. *Among whom*—The nations brought to the obedience of faith, *are ye also*—
But St. Paul gives them no pre-eminence above others.
    7. *To all that are in Rome*—Most of these were heathens by birth, ver. 13,
though with Jews mixed among them. They were scattered up and down in
that large city, and not yet reduced into the form of a Church. Only some had
begun to meet in the house of Aquila and Priscilla. *Beloved of God*—And from
his free love, not from any merit of yours, called by his word and his Spirit to
believe in him, and now, through faith, holy, as he is holy. *Grace*—The peculiar favour of God, *and peace*—All manner of blessings, temporal, spiritual, and
eternal. This is both a Christian salutation and an apostolic benediction; *from
God our Father, and the Lord Jesus Christ*—This is the usual way wherein the
apostles speak, "God the Father, God our Father." Nor do they often, in
speaking of him, use the word Lord, as it implies the proper name of God, Jehovah. In the Old Testament indeed, the holy men generally said, The Lord
our God. For they were then as it were servants, whereas now they are sons.
And sons so well know their father, that they need not frequently mention his
proper name. It is one and the same peace, and one and the same grace, which
is from God and from Jesus Christ. Our trust and prayer fix on God, as he is the
Father of Christ, and on Christ, as he presents us to the Father.
    8. *I thank*—In the very entrance of this one epistle are the traces of all spi
ritual affections; but of thankfulness above all; with the expression of which
almost all St. Paul's epistles begin. He here particularly thanks God, that what
otherwise himself should have done, was done at Rome already. *My God*—This
very word expresses faith, hope, love, and consequently all true religion: *through
Jesus Christ*—The gifts of God all pass through Christ to us, and all our petitions and thanksgivings pass through Christ to God: *that your faith is spoken
of*—In this kind of congratulations, St. Paul describes either the whole of Christianity, as Col. i, 3, &c, or some part of it, as 1 Cor. i, 5. Accordingly here he
mentions the faith of the Romans, suitably to his design, ver. 12, 17. *Through
the whole world*—This joyful news spreading every where, that there were Christians also in the imperial city. And the goodness and wisdom of God established
faith in the chief cities; in Jerusalem and Rome particularly, that from thence it
might be diffused to all nations.
    9. *God, whom I serve*—As an apostle, *in my spirit*—Not only with my body,
but with my inmost soul, *in the Gospel*—By preaching it.
    10. *Always*—In my solemn addresses to God, *if by any means now at length*—
This accumulation of particles declares the strength of his desire.
    11. *That I may impart to you*—Face to face, by laying on of hands, prayer,
preaching the Gospel, private conversation, *some spiritual gift*—With such gifts
the Corinthians, who had enjoyed the presence of St. Paul, abounded, 1 Cor. i, 7;
xii, 1; xiv, 1. So did the Galatians likewise, Gal. iii, 5. And indeed all those
Churches which had had the presence of any of the apostles, had peculiar advantages in this kind, from the laying on of their hands, Acts xix, 6; viii, 17, &c·
2 Tim. i, 6. But as yet the Romans were greatly inferior to them in this respect,

362 ROMANS.

12 established, That is, to be comforted together with you, by the
13 mutual faith both of you and me. Now I would not have you ignorant, brethren, that I have often purposed to come to you, (though
I have been hindered hitherto,) that I might have some fruit
14 among you also, even as among the other Gentiles. I am a debtor
both to the Greeks and the Barbarians, both to the wise and to the
15 unwise. Therefore, as much as in me is, I am ready to preach
16 the Gospel to you also who are at Rome. For I am not ashamed
of the Gospel of Christ ; for it is the power of God unto salvation
to every one that believeth, both to the Jew and to the Gentile.
17 For the righteousness of God is revealed therein from faith to
faith ; as it is written, * The just shall live by faith.

for which reason the apostle in the 12th chapter also says little, if any thing, of
their spiritual gifts. He therefore desires to impart some, *that they may be
established;* for by these was the testimony of Christ confirmed among them.
That St. Peter had no more been at Rome than St. Paul at the time when this
epistle was written, appears from the general tenor thereof, and from this place
in particular. For otherwise what St. Paul wishes to impart to the Romans,
would have been imparted already by St. Peter.

12. *That is, I long to be comforted—by the mutual faith both of you and me—*
He not only associates the Romans with, but even prefers them before himself.
How different is this style of the apostle from that of the modern court of
Rome !

13. *Brethren*—A frequent, holy, simple, sweet, and yet grand appellation. The
apostles but rarely address persons by their names, as, O ye Corinthians : O Ti
motheus. St. Paul generally uses this appellation, brethren ; sometimes in exhortation, My beloved ; or, My beloved brethren : St. James, Brethren, My brethren, My beloved brethren. St. Peter and Jude always, Beloved ; St. John,
frequently, Beloved ; once, Brethren ; oftener than once, My little children.
Though I have been hindered hitherto—Either by business, see chap. xv, 22, or
persecution, 1 Thess. ii, 2, or the Spirit, Acts xvi, 7. *That I might have some
fruit*—Of my ministerial labours ; even as I have already had from the many
Churches I have planted and watered *among the other Gentiles.*

14. *To the Greeks and the Barbarians*—He includes the Romans under the
Greeks ; so that this division comprises all nations. *Both to the wise and the
unwise*—For there were unwise even among the Greeks, and wise even among
the Barbarians. *I am a debtor* to all—I am bound by my Divine mission to preach
the Gospel to them.

16. *For I am not ashamed of the Gospel*—To the world indeed it is folly and
weakness, 1 Cor. i, 18. Therefore in the judgment of the world he ought to be
ashamed of it ; especially at Rome, the head and theatre of the world. But
Paul is not ashamed ; *knowing it is the power of God unto salvation, to every one
that believeth*—The great and gloriously powerful means of saving all who
accept salvation in God's own way. As St. Paul comprises the sum of the
Gospel in this epistle, so he does the sum of the epistle in this and the following verse. *Both to the Jew and the Gentile*—There is a noble frankness, as well
as a comprehensive sense, in these words ; by which he on the one hand shows
the Jews their absolute need of the Gospel, and on the other, tells the politest
and greatest nation in the world, both that their salvation depended on receiving
it, and that the first offers of it were in every place always to be made to the
despised Jews.

17. *The righteousness of God*—This expression sometimes means, God's eternal, essential righteousness, which includes both justice and mercy, and is
eminently shown in condemning sin, and yet justifying the sinner. Sometimes
it means that righteousness by which a man, through the gift of God, is made
and is righteous, and that both by receiving Christ through faith, and by a conformity to the essential righteousness of God. St. Paul, when treating of justification, means hereby the righteousness of faith : therefore called *the righteous-*

* Hab. ii. 4.

18   For the wrath of God is revealed from heaven against all un-
     godliness and unrighteousness of men, who detain the truth in un-
19   righteousness.   For what is to be known of God is manifest in them ;
20   for God hath showed *it* to them.   For those things of him which
     are invisible, both his eternal power and Godhead, are clearly seen
     from the creation of the world, being understood by the things
21   which are made, so that they are without excuse : Because know-
     ing God, they did not glorify *him* as God, neither were thankful,
     but became vain in their reasonings, and their foolish heart was dark-
22   ened.   Professing to be wise, they became fools, and changed the
23   glory of the incorruptible God into an image in the likeness of cor-
     ruptible man, and of birds, and of four-footed creatures, and reptiles.

---

ness of God, because God found out and prepared, reveals and gives, approves
and crowns it.   In this verse the expression means, The whole benefit of God
through Christ for the salvation of a sinner.   *Is revealed*—Mention is made
here, and ver. 18, of a twofold revelation, of wrath and of righteousness : the
former, little known to nature, is revealed by the law : the latter, wholly unknown to nature, by the Gospel.   That goes before, and prepares the way ; this
follows : each, the apostle says, *is revealed*, at the present time, in opposition to
the times of ignorance.   *From faith to faith*—By a gradual series of still clearer
and clearer promises.   *As it is written*—St. Paul had just laid down three propositions : 1. Righteousness is by faith, ver. 17.   2. Salvation is by righteousness,
ver. 16.   3. Both to the Jews and to the Gentiles, ver. 16.   Now all these are
confirmed by that single sentence, *The just shall live by faith*—Which was primarily spoken of those who preserved their lives when the Chaldeans besieged
Jerusalem, by believing the declarations of God, and acting according to them.
Here it means, He shall obtain the favour of God, and continue therein, by
believing.

     18. *For*—There is no other way of obtaining life and salvation.   Having laid
down his proposition, the apostle now enters upon the proof of it.   His first
argument is, The law condemns all men, as being under sin.   None therefore is
justified by the works of the law.   This is treated of to chap. iii, 20.   And
hence he infers, Therefore justification is by faith.   *The wrath of God is revealed*—Not only by frequent and signal interpositions of Divine Providence,
but likewise in the sacred oracles, and by us, his messengers.   *From heaven*—
This speaks the majesty of Him whose wrath is revealed, his all-seeing eye, and
the extent of his wrath: whatever is under heaven is under the effects of his
wrath, believers in Christ excepted.   *Against all ungodliness and unrighteousness*—These two are treated of in ver. 23, &c : *of men*—He is speaking here of
the Gentiles, and chiefly the wisest of them ; *who detain the truth*—For it strug-
gles against their wickedness, *in unrighteousness*—The word here includes ungodliness also.

     19. *For what is to be known of God*—Those great principles which are indis-
pensably necessary to be known, *is manifest in them ; for God hath showed it to
them*—By the light which enlightens every man that cometh into the world.

     20. *For those things of him which are invisible, are seen*—By the eye of the
mind ; *being understood*—They are seen by them, and them only, who use their
understanding.

     21. *Because knowing God*—For the wiser heathens did know, that there was
one supreme God : yet from low and base considerations, they conformed to the
idolatry of the vulgar.   *They did not glorify him as God, neither were thankful*—
They neither thanked him for his benefits, nor glorified him for his Divine perfections ; *but became vain*—Like the idols they worshipped, *in their reasonings*—
Various, uncertain, foolish.   What a terrible instance have we of this, in the
writings of Lucretius !   What vain reasonings, and how dark a heart amidst so
pompous professions of wisdom !

     23. *And changed*—With the utmost folly !   Here are three degrees of ungod
liness and of punishment.   The first is described, ver 21–24.   The second, ver.
25–27   The third in the 28th and following verses.   The punishment in each

24 Wherefore God also gave them up to uncleanness through the de
sires of their hearts, to dishonour their bodies among themselves,
25 Who changed the truth of God into a lie, and worshipped and
served the creature above the Creator, who is blessed for ever!
26 Amen. Therefore God gave them up to vile affections; for even
their women changed the natural use to that which is against na-
27 ture; And likewise also men, leaving the natural use of the women,
burned in their lust toward each other, men with men working
filthiness, and receiving in themselves the just recompense of their
28 error. And as they did not like to retain God in *their* knowledge,
God gave them up to an undiscerning mind, to do the things
29 which were not expedient, Filled with all injustice, fornication,
maliciousness, covetousness, wickedness: full of envy, murder, con-
30 tention, deceit, malignity: Whisperers, backbiters; haters of God,
violent, proud: boasters, inventors of evil things: disobedient to
31 parents, Without understanding, covenant breakers, without natu-
32 ral affection, implacable, unmerciful. Who knowing the righteous
judgment of God, that they who practise such things are worthy of

---

case is expressed by *God gave them up.* If a man will not worship God as God,
he is so left to himself, that he throws away his very manhood. *Reptiles*—Or
creeping things: as beetles, and various kinds of serpents.

24. *Wherefore*—One punishment of sin is from the very nature of it, as ver. 27
Another, as here, is from vindictive justice. *Uncleanness*—Ungodliness and un
cleanness are frequently joined, 1 Thess. iv, v, as are the knowledge of God and
purity. *God gave them up*—By withdrawing his restraining grace.

25. *Who changed the truth*—The true worship of God, *into a lie*—False, abominable adolatries, *and worshipped*—Inwardly, *and served*—Outwardly.

26. *Therefore God gave them up to vile affections*—To which the heathen Romans were then abandoned to the last degree; and none more than the emperors
themselves.

27. *Receiving the just recompense of their error*—Their idolatry; being punished
with that unnatural lust, which was as horrible a dishonour to the body, as their
idolatry was to God.

28. *God gave them up to an undiscerning mind*—Treated of ver. 32, *to do things
not expedient*—(Even the vilest abominations) treated of ver. 29–31.

29. *Filled with all injustice*—This stands in the first place, *unmercifulness* in
the last. *Fornication*—includes here every species of uncleanness. *Maliciousness*—The Greek word properly implies a temper, which delights in hurting
another even without any advantage to itself.

30. *Whisperers*—Such as secretly defame others. *Backbiters*—Such as speak
against others behind their back. *Haters of God*—That is, rebels against him;
deniers of his providence, or accusers of his justice in their adversities. Yea,
having an inward heart enmity to his justice and holiness. *Inventors of evil
things*—Of new pleasures, new ways of gain, new arts of hurting, particularly
in war.

31. *Covenant breakers*—It is well known, the Romans, as a nation, from the
very beginning of their commonwealth, never made any scruple of vacating altogether the most solemn engagement, if they did not like it, though made by their
supreme magistrate, in the name of the whole people. They only gave up the
general who had made it, and then supposed themselves to be at full liberty!
Without natural affection—The custom of exposing their own new-born children
to perish by cold, hunger, or wild beasts, which so generally prevailed in the
heathen world, particularly among the Greeks and Romans, was an amazing instance of this; as is also that of killing their aged and helpless parents, now common among the American heathens.

32. *Not only do the same, but have pleasure in those that practise them*—This is
the highest degree of wickedness. A man may be hurried by his passions to do
the thing he hates. But he that has pleasure in those that do evil, loves wicked-

death, not only do the same, but have pleasure in those that practise them.

.I.   Therefore thou art inexcusable, O man, whosoever thou art
that judgest; for in that thou judgest the other, thou condemnest
2 thyself; for thou that judgest practisest the same things.   For we
know that the judgment of God is according to truth, against them
3 who practise such things.   And thinkest thou this, O man, who
judgest them that practise such things, and dost the same, that
4 thou shalt escape the judgment of God?   Or despisest thou the
riches of his goodness, and forbearance, and long suffering, not
5 knowing that the goodness of God leadeth thee to repentance?   But
after thy hardness and impenitent heart treasurest up to thyself
wrath in the day of wrath, and revelation, and righteous judgment
6 of God?   Who will * render to every one according to his works:
7 To them that by patient continuance in well-doing seek for glory,
8 and honour, and immortality, eternal life.   But to them that are
contentious, and do not obey the truth, but obey unrighteousness,
9 *shall be* indignation, and wrath, tribulation and anguish, *Even*

---

ness for wickedness' sake. And hereby he encourages them in sin, and heaps the
guilt of others upon his own head.

II. 1. *Therefore*—The apostle now makes a transition from the Gentiles to the
Jews, till at ver. 6 he comprises both.   *Thou art inexcusable*—Seeing knowledge without practice only increases guilt.   *O man*—Having before spoken of
the Gentile in the third person, he addresses the Jew in the second person.   But
he calls him by a common appellation, as not acknowledging him to be a Jew.
See ver. 17, 28.   *Whosoever thou art that judgest*—Censurest, condemnest: *for
in that thou judgest the other*—The heathen: *thou condemnest thyself, for thou
dost the same things*—In effect ; in many instances.

2. *For we know*—Without any teaching; *that the judgment of God*—Not
thine, who exceptest thyself from its sentence, *is according to truth*—Is just,
making no exception, ver. 5, 6, 11, and reaches the heart as well as the life,
ver. 16.

3. *That thou shalt escape*—Rather than the Gentile.

4. *Or despisest thou*—Dost thou go farther still, from hoping to escape his
wrath, to the abuse of his love ?   *The riches*—The abundance *of his goodness, for
bearance, and long suffering*—Seeing thou both hast sinned, dost sin, and wilt sin.
All these are afterward comprised in the single word goodness; *leadeth thee*—
That is, is designed of God to lead or encourage thee to it.

5. *Treasurest up wrath*—Although thou thinkest thou art treasuring up all
good things.   O what a treasure may a man lay up either way, in this short day
of life : *to thyself*—Not to him whom thou judgest; *in the day of wrath, and
revelation, and righteous judgment of God*—Just opposite to *the goodness, and
forbearance, and long suffering of God.*   When God shall be revealed ; then shall
also be revealed the secrets of men's hearts, ver. 16.   *Forbearance* and *revelation*
respect God, and are opposed to each other ; long suffering and righteous judgment respect the sinner ; goodness and wrath are words of a more general
import.

7. *To them that seek for glory*—For pure love does not exclude faith, hope,
desire, 1 Cor. xv, 58.

8. *But to them that are contentious*—Like thee, O Jew, who thus fightest
against God.   The character of a false Jew is disobedience, stubbornness, impatience.   *Indignation and wrath, tribulation and anguish,* alluding to Psalm lxxviii,
49.   *He cast upon them*—The Egyptians, *the fierceness of his anger, wrath, and
indignation, and trouble ;* and finally intimating, that the Jews would in the day
of vengeance be more severely punished, than even the Egyptians were when
God made their plagues so wonderful.

9. *Of the Jew first*—Here we have the first express mention of the Jews in

* Prov. xxiv, 12.

upon every soul of man who worketh evil, of the Jew first, and
10 also the Gentile : But glory, and honour, and peace *shall be* to
every one who worketh good, to the Jew first. and also to the
Gentile.
11 For there is no respect of persons with God. For as many as have
12 sinned without the law, shall also perish without the law ; and as many
13 as have sinned under the law, shall be judged by the law. For not
the hearers of the law *are* just with God, but the doers of the
14 law shall be justified. For when the Gentiles, who have not the
law, do by nature the things contained in the law, these not having
15 the law, are a law to themselves ; Who show the work of the law
written upon their hearts, their conscience also bearing witness,
and their thoughts among themselves, accusing or even defending
16 *them*, In the day when God will judge the secrets of men by
Christ Jesus, according to my Gospel.

this chapter. And it is introduced with great propriety. Their having been
trained up in the true religion, and having had Christ and his apostles first sent
to them, will place them in the foremost rank of the criminals that obey not the
truth.

10. *But glory*—Just opposite to *wrath*, from the Divine approbation, *honour*,
opposite to *indignation*, by the Divine appointment, and *peace* now and for ever,
opposed to *tribulation* and *anguish*.

11. *For there is no respect of persons with God*—He will reward every one
according to his works. But this is well consistent with his distributing advantages and opportunities of improvement, according to his own good pleasure.

12. *For as many as have sinned*—He speaks as of the time past, for all time
will be past at the day of judgment. *Without the law*—Without having any written law ; *shall also perish without the law*—Without regard had to any outward
law ; being condemned by the law written in their hearts. The word *also* shows
the agreement of the manner of sinning with the manner of suffering. *Perish*—
He could not so properly say, shall be judged without the law.

13. *For not the hearers of the law are* even now *just before God ; but the doers
of the law shall be justified*—Finally acquitted and rewarded. A most sure and
important truth ; which respects the Gentiles also, though principally the Jews.
But St. Paul speaks of the former, ver. 14, &c, of the latter, ver. 17, &c. Here
is therefore no parenthesis : for the 16th verse also depends on the 15th, not on
the 12th.

14. *For when the Gentiles*—That is, any of them. St. Paul having refuted
the perverse judgment of the Jews concerning the heathens, proceeds to show
the just judgment of God against them. He now speaks directly of the heathens, in order to convince the heathens. Yet the concession he makes to these,
serves more strongly to convince the Jews. *Do by nature*—That is, without an
outward rule ; though this also, strictly speaking, is by preventing grace. *The
things contained in the law*—The ten commandments being only the substance of
the law of nature. *These not having the* written *law, are a law unto themselves*
—That is, what the law is to the Jews, they are, by the grace of God, to themselves; namely, a rule of life.

15. *Who show*—To themselves, to other men, and in a sense, to God himself;
the work of the law—The substance, though not the letter of it ; *written on their
hearts*—By the same hand which wrote the commandments on the tables of
stone ; *their conscience*—There is none of all its faculties which the soul has less
in its power than this; *bearing witness*—In a trial, there are the plaintiff, the
defendant, and the witnesses. Conscience, and sin itself, are witnesses against
the heathens. *Their thoughts* sometimes excuse, sometimes condemn them.
Among themselves—Alternately, like plaintiff and defendant. *Accusing, or even
defending them*—The very manner of speaking shows that they have far more
room to accuse than to defend.

16. *In the day*—That is, *who show* this *in the day*—Every thing will then be
shown to be what it really is. In that day will appear the law written in their

17 But if thou art called a Jew, and restest in the law, and gloriest in
18 God, And knowest *his* will, and discernest the things that differ,
19 being instructed out of the law : And art confident that thyself art
20 a guide to the blind, a light of them that are in darkness, An
   instructer of the ignorant, a teacher of babes, having the form of
21 knowledge and truth in the law : Thou that teachest another, dost
   not teach thyself : thou that proclaimest, a man should not steal,
22 dost steal : Thou that sayest, A man should not commit adultery,
   dost commit adultery : thou that abhorrest idols, committest sa-
23 crilege. Thou that gloriest in the law, by transgressing the law
24 dishonourest thou God ? For the name of God is blasphemed among
25 the Gentiles through you, * as it is written, Circumcision indeed
   profiteth, if thou keepest the law ; but if thou art a transgressor of
26 the law, thy circumcision is become uncircumcision. Therefore
   if the uncircumcision keep the righteousness of the law, shall not
27 his uncircumcision be counted for circumcision ? Yea, the uncir-

---

hearts, as it often does in the present life ; *when God shall judge the secrets of men*—On secret circumstances depends the real quality of actions, frequently unknown to the actors themselves, ver. 29. Men generally form their judgments even of themselves, merely from what is apparent. *According to my Gospel*—According to the tenor of that Gospel which is committed to my care. Hence it appears that the Gospel also is a law.

17. *But if thou art called a Jew*—This highest point of Jewish glorying, (after a farther description of it interposed, ver. 17-20, and refuted, ver. 21-24,) is itself refuted, ver. 25, &c. The description consists of twice five articles ; of which the former five, ver. 17, 18, show what he boasts of in himself ; the other five, ver. 19, 20, what he glories in, with respect to others. The first particular of the former five answers to the first of the latter ; the second to the second, and so on. *And restest in the law*—Dependest on it, though it can only condemn thee ; *and gloriest in God*—As thy God : and that too, to the exclusion of others.

19. *Blind—in darkness—ignorant—babes*—These were the titles which the Jews generally gave the Gentiles.

20. *Having the form of knowledge and truth*—That is, the most accurate knowledge of the truth.

21. *Thou dost not teach thyself*—He does not teach himself, who does not practise what he teaches. *Dost thou steal—commit adultery—commit sacrilege*—Sin grievously against thy neighbour, thyself, God. St. Paul had shown the Gentiles, first their sins against God, then against themselves, then against their neighbours. He now inverts the order. For sins against God are the most glaring in a heathen, but not in a Jew. *Thou that abhorrest idols*—Which all the Jews did, from the time of the Babylonish captivity ; *thou committest sacrilege*—Dost what is still worse, robbing him, *who is God over all*, of the glory which is due to him.

None of these charges were rashly advanced against the Jews of that age. For as their own historian relates, some even of the priests lived by rapine, and others in gross uncleanness. And as for sacrilegiously robbing God and his altar, it had been complained of ever since Malachi. So that the instances are given with great propriety and judgment.

25. *Circumcision indeed profiteth*—He does not say justifies. How far it profitted is shown in the 3d and 4th chapters ; *thy circumcision is become uncircumcision*—Is so already in effect. Thou wilt have no more benefit by it, than if thou hadst never received it. The very same observation holds with regard to baptism.

26. *If the uncircumcision*—That is, a person uncircumcised, *keep the law*—Walk agreeably to it ; *shall not his uncircumcision be counted for circumcision*—In the sight of God ?

27. *Yea, the uncircumcision that is by nature*—Those who are, literally speaking,

* Isaiah lii, 5.

cumcision that is by nature, fulfilling the law, shall judge thee, who
28 by the letter and circumcision transgressest the law. For he is no
a Jew, who is an outward Jew, neither *is that* circumcision which
29 is apparent in the flesh. But he *is* a Jew, who is one inwardly,
and circumcision *is that* of the heart, in the spirit, not in the etter;
whose praise is not from men, but from God.
III. What then *is* the advantage of the Jew, or what the profit of
2 the circumcision?   Much every way; chiefly in that they were
3 entrusted with the oracles of God.   For what if some believed
4 not?   Shall their unbelief disannul the faithfulness of God?   God
forbid: let God be true, and every man a liar; as it is written,
* That thou mightest be justified in the saying, and mightest over-
5 come when thou art judged.   But if our unrighteousness commend the righteousness of God, what shall we say?   *Is* not God
6 unjust, who taketh vengeance?   I speak as a man. * God forbid;
7 otherwise how should God judge the world?   But if the truth of
God hath abounded to his glory through my lie, why am I still
8 judged as a sinner?   And why may we not (as we are slandered,
and as some affirm us to say) do evil, that good may come?
Whose condemnation is just.

---

uncircumcised, *fulfilling the law*—As to the substance of it, *shall judge thee*—
Shall condemn thee in that day: *who by the letter and circumcision*—Who having
the bare, literal, external circumcision, *transgresseth the law.*

28. *For he is not a Jew*—In the most important sense, that is, one of God's
beloved people, *who is one in outward show* only; *neither is that* the true acceptable *circumcision which is apparent in the flesh.*

29. *But he is a Jew*—That is, one of God's people, *who is one inwardly*—In
the secret recesses of his soul; *and* the acceptable *circumcision is that of the
heart,* [referring to Deut. xxx, 6,] the putting away all inward impurity.   This is
seated *in the spirit,* the inmost soul renewed by the Spirit of God, *and not in the
letter,* not in the external ceremony: *whose praise is not from men; but from
God*—The only Searcher of the heart.

III. 1. *What then,* may some say, *is the advantage of the Jew,* or *of the cir
cumcision*—That is, those that are circumcised, above the Gentiles?

2. *Chiefly in that they were entrusted with the oracles of God*—The Scriptures,
in which are so great and precious promises; other prerogatives will follow, chap.
ix, 4, 5.   St. Paul here singles out this, by which, after removing the objection,
he vill convict them so much the more.

3. *Shall their unbelief disannul the faithfulness of God?*—Will he not still make
good his promises to them that do believe?

5. *But,* it may be farther objected, if *our unrighteousness* be subservient to God's
glory, is it not unjust in him to punish us for it?   *I speak as a man*—As human
weakness would be apt to speak.

6 *God forbid*—By no means.   If it were unjust in God to punish that unrighteousness, which is subservient to his own glory; *how should God judge the
world?*—Since all the unrighteousness in the world will then *commend the righteousness of God.*

7. *But,* may the objector reply, *if the truth of God hath abounded*—Has been
more abundantly shown, *through my lie*—If my lie, that is, practice contrary to
truth, conduces to the glory of God, by making his truth shine with superior
advantage, *why am I still judged as a sinner?*—Can this be said to be any sin at
all?   Ought I not to do what would otherwise be evil, that so much *good may
come?*   To this the apostle does not deign to give a direct answer, but cuts the
objector short with a severe reproof.

8. *Whose condemnation is just*—The condemnation of all who either speak or
act in this manner.   So the apostle absolutely denies the lawfulness of *doing
evil,* any evil, *that good may come.*
* Psalm li, 4.

9   What then ? Are we better *than they ?* In no wise : for we have
10 before proved all, both Jews and Gentiles, to be under sin. As it
11 is written, * There is none righteous, no not one. There is none
12 that understandeth ; there is none that seeketh after God. They
     have all turned aside, they are together become unprofitable ;
13 there is none that doeth good, no not one. † Their throat *is* an
     open sepulchre ; with their tongues they have used deceit ; the
14 ‡ poison of asps *is* under their lips. § Whose mouth is full of
15 cursing and bitterness ; ‖ Their feet *are* swift to shed blood ;
16 Destruction and misery are their ways, And they have not
17 known the way of peace ; ** The fear of God is not before their
18 eyes. Now we know that whatsoever the law saith, it saith to
19 them that are under the law ; that every mouth may be stopped,
20 and all the world become guilty before God. Therefore no flesh
     shall be justified in his sight by the works of the law ; for by the
     law is the knowledge of sin.
21.   But now the righteousness of God is manifested without the law,

---

9. *What then ?*—Here he resumes what he said, ver. 1. *Under sin*—Under the guilt and power of it : the Jews by transgressing the written law : the Gentiles by transgressing the law of nature.

10. *As it is written*—That all men are under sin, appears from the vices which have raged in all ages. St. Paul therefore rightly cites David and Isaiah, though they spoke primarily of their own age, and expressed what manner of men God sees when he *looks down from heaven*, not what he makes them by his grace. *There is none righteous*—That is the general proposition. The particulars follow ; their dispositions and designs, ver. 11, 12, their discourse, ver. 13, 14, their actions, ver. 16–18.

11. *There is none that understandeth*—The things of God.

12. *They have all turned aside*—From the good way. *They are become unprofitable*—Helpless, impotent, unable to profit either themselves or others.

13. *Their throat*—Is noisome and dangerous *as an open sepulchre.* Observe the progress of evil discourse, proceeding out of the heart, through the throat, tongue, lips, till the whole mouth is filled therewith. *The poison of asps*—Infectious, deadly, backbiting, tale bearing, evil speaking, *is under* (for honey is *on*) *their lips.* An asp is a venomous kind of serpent.

14. *Cursing*—Against God : *bitterness*—Against their neighbour.

17. *Of peace*—Which can only spring from righteousness.

18. *The fear of God is not before their eyes*—Much less is the love of God in their heart.

19. *Whatsoever the law*—The Old Testament, *saith, it saith to them that are under the law*—That is, to those who own its authority ; to the Jews, and not the Gentiles. St. Paul quoted no scripture against them, but pleaded with them only from the light of nature. *Every mouth*—Full of bitterness, ver. 14, and yet of boasting, ver. 27, *may become guilty*—May be fully convicted, and apparently liable to most just condemnation. These things were written of old, and were quoted by St. Paul, *not to make* men criminal, but to *prove* them so.

20. *No flesh shall be justified*—None shall be forgiven and accepted of God, *by the works of the law*—On this ground, that he hath kept the law. St. Paul means chiefly the moral part of it, ver. 19, chap. ii, 21, &c, 26, which alone is not abolished, ver. 31. And it is not without reason, that he so often mentions *the works of the law,* whether ceremonial or moral. For it was on these only the Jews relied, being wholly ignorant of those that spring from faith. *For by the law is only the knowledge of sin*—But no deliverance either from the guilt or power of it.

21. *But now the righteousness of God*—That is, the manner of becoming righteous which God hath appointed, *without the law*—Without that previous obedience

* Psalm xiv, 1, &c   † Psalm v 9.   ‡ Psalm cxl, 3.   § Psalm x, 7.
‖ Isaiah lix. 7, 8.   ** Psalm xxxvi, 1.

22 being attested by the law and the prophets, Even the righteousness of God, by the faith of Jesus Christ, to all and upon all that
23 believe : for there is no difference : For all have sinned, and are
24 fallen short of the glory of God, And are justified freely by his
25 grace, through the redemption which is in Christ Jesus : Whom
God hath set forth a propitiation, through faith in his blood, for a
demonstration of his righteousness, by the remission of past sins,
26 through the forbearance of God : For a demonstration, *I say*, of
his righteousness in this present time, that he might be just, and
yet the justifier of him that believeth in Jesus.
27　Where *is* boasting then ? It is excluded. By what law ? Of
28 works ? Nay, but by the law of faith. We conclude then, that a
29 man is justified by faith, without the works of the law. *Is* God *the*
God of the Jews only, and not also of the Gentiles ? Surely of the
30 Gentiles also : Seeing *it is* one God who will justify the circum-

which the law requires : without reference to the law, or dependence on it ; *is*
manifested—In the Gospel ; *being attested by the law* itself, *and by the prophets*
—By all the promises in the Old Testament.

22. *To all*—The Jews, *and upon all*—The Gentiles, *that believe ; for there is*
no difference—Either as to the need of justification, or the manner of it.

23. *For all have sinned*—In Adam, and in their own persons ; by a sinful nature, sinful tempers, and sinful actions ; *and are fallen short of the glory of*
God—The supreme end of man ; short of his image on earth, and the enjoyment
of him in heaven.

24. *And are justified*—Pardoned and accepted, *freely*—Without any merit of
their own, *by his grace*—Not their own righteousness or works, *through the re-*
demption—The price Christ has paid. *Freely by his grace*—One of these expressions might have served to convey the apostle's meaning ; but he doubles his
assertion, in order to give us the *fullest conviction* of the truth, and to impress
us with a sense of its *peculiar importance*. It is not possible to find words that
should more *absolutely* exclude all consideration of our own works and obedience ; or more emphatically ascribe the whole of our justification to free unmerited goodness.

25. *Whom God hath set forth*—Before angels and men, *a propitiation*—To
appease an offended God. But if, as some teach, God never was offended, there
was no need of this propitiation. And if so, Christ died in vain. *To declare*
his righteousness—To demonstrate not only his clemency, but his justice : even
that vindictive justice, whose essential character and principal office is, to punish
sin : *by the remission of past sins*—All the sins antecedent to their believing.

26. *For a demonstration of his righteousness*—Both of his justice and mercy,
that he might be just—Showing his justice on his own Son ; *and yet the* merciful
justifier of every one *that believeth in Jesus. That he might be just*—Might
evidence himself to be strictly and inviolably righteous in the administration of
his government, even while he is the merciful *justifier* of the sinner *that believeth*
in Jesus. The attribute of justice must be preserved inviolate. And inviolate it
is preserved, if there was a real infliction of punishment on our Saviour. On
this plan, all the attributes harmonize. Every attribute is glorified : and not one
superseded, no, nor so much as clouded.

27. *Where is the boasting then of the Jew against the Gentile ? It is excluded.*
By what law ? Of works ? Nay—This would have left room for boasting ; *but*
by the law of faith—Since this requires all, without distinction, to apply as guilty
and helpless sinners, to the free mercy of God in Christ. *The law of faith* is
that Divine constitution which makes faith, not works, the condition of acceptance.

28. *We conclude then, that a man is justified by faith*—And even by this, not
as it is a work, but as it receives Christ, and consequently has something essen
tially different from all our works whatsoever.

29. *Surely of the Gentiles also*—As both nature and the Scriptures show.

30. *Seeing it is one God who*—Shows mercy to both, and by the very same
means.

31 cision by faith, and the uncircumcision through *the same* faith.   Do
   we then make void the law through faith?   God forbid: yea, we
   establish the law.
IV.   What shall we say then, That our father Abraham hath found justi-
2 fication according to the flesh?   If Abraham was justified by works,
3 he hath whereof to glory: but *he hath* not in the sight of God.   For
   what saith the Scripture?   * Abraham believed God, and it was
4 imputed to him for righteousness.   Now to him that worketh, the
5 reward is not reckoned of grace, but of debt.   But to him that
   worketh not, but believeth on him that justifieth the ungodly, his
6 faith is imputed to him for righteousness.   So David also affirmeth the happiness of the man to whom God imputeth righteous-
7 ness without works: † Happy *are* they whose iniquities are for-

---

31. *We establish the law*—Both the authority, purity, and the end of it; by
defending that which the law attests: by pointing out Christ, the end of it, and
by showing how it may be fulfilled in its purity.

IV. Having proved it by argument, he now proves by example, and such example as must have greater weight with the Jews than any other. 1. That justification is by faith; 2. That it is free for the Gentiles.

1. *That our father Abraham hath found*—Acceptance with God; *according to
the flesh*—That is, by works.

2. The meaning is; if Abraham had been justified by works, he would have
had room to glory. But he had not room to glory. Therefore he was not justified y works.

3. *Abraham believed God*—That promise of God concerning the numerousness
of his seed, Gen. xv, 5, 7; but especially the promise concerning Christ, Gen.
xii, 3; through whom all nations should be blessed: *and it was imputed to him
for righteousness*—God accepted him, as if he had been altogether righteous.

4. *Now to him that worketh*—All that the law requires, the reward is no favour,
but an absolute debt.

These two examples are selected and applied with the utmost judgment and
propriety. Abraham was the most illustrious pattern of piety among the Jewish
patriarchs; David was the most eminent of their kings. If then neither of these
was justified by his own obedience; if they both obtained acceptance with God,
not as upright beings who might claim it, but as sinful creatures who must implore
it, the consequence is glaring. It is such as must strike every attentive understanding, and must affect every individual person.

5. *But to him that worketh not*—It being impossible he should without faith,
but believeth—his faith is imputed to him for righteousness—Therefore God's
affirming of Abraham, that faith was imputed to him for righteousness, plainly
shows that he worked not; or, in other words, that he was not justified by works,
but by faith only. Hence we see plainly how groundless that opinion is, that
holiness or sanctification is previous to our justification. For the sinner being
first convinced of his sin and danger by the Spirt of God, stands trembling before
the awful tribunal of Divine justice; and has nothing to plead but his own guilt
and the merits of a Mediator. Christ here interposes; justice is satisfied; the sin
is remitted, and pardon is applied to the soul, by a Divine faith, wrought by the
Holy Ghost, who then begins the great work of inward sanctification. Thus God
justifies the ungodly, and yet remains just and true to all his attributes! But
let none hence presume to continue in sin; for to the impenitent God is a consuming fire. *On him that justifieth the ungodly*—If a man could possibly be made
holy before he was justified, it would entirely set his justification aside; seeing he
could not in the very nature of the thing be justified, if he were not at that very
time ungodly.

6. *So David also*—David is fitly introduced after Abraham, because he also
received and delivered down the promise; *affirmeth*—A man is justified by faith
alone, and not by works. *Without works*—That is, without regard to any former
good works supposed to have been done by him.

8 given, and whose sins are covered; Happy *is* the man to whom the
9 Lord will not impute sin. *Cometh* this happiness then on the circumcision *only*, or on the uncircumcision also? For we say that faith was
10 imputed to Abraham for righteousness. How was it then imputed? When he was in circumcision or in uncircumcision? Not
11 in circumcision, but in uncircumcision. And he received the sign
of circumcision, a seal of the righteousness of the faith, which *he
had* in uncircumcision, that he might be the father of all who
believe in uncircumcision, that righteousness may be imputed to
12 them also. And the father of the circumcision to them, who not
only are of the circumcision, but also walk in the footsteps of that
13 faith of our father Abraham, which he had in uncircumcision. For
the promise, that he should be the heir of the world, *was* not
to Abraham or his seed by the law, but by the righteousness of
14 faith. For if they who are of the law *are* heirs, faith is made void,
15 and the promise of no effect. Because the law worketh wrath
16 for where no law is, *there is* no transgression. Therefore *it is* of

---

7. *Happy are they whose sins are covered*—With the veil of Divine mercy. If
there be indeed such a thing as happiness on earth, it is the portion of that man
whose iniquities are forgiven, and who enjoys the manifestation of that pardon.
Well may he endure all the afflictions of life with cheerfulness, and look upon
death with comfort. O let us not contend against it, but earnestly pray that this
happiness may be ours.

9. *Cometh this happiness*—Mentioned by Abraham and David, *on the circumcision*—Those that are circumcised only. *Faith was imputed to Abraham for
righteousness*—This is fully consistent with our being justified, that is, pardoned
and accepted by God upon our believing, for the sake of what Christ hath done
and suffered. For though this and this alone be the meritorious cause of our acceptance with God, yet faith may be said to be *imputed to us for righteousness*,
as it is the sole condition of our acceptance. We may observe here, *Forgiveness*,
not imputing sin, and *imputing righteousness*, are all one.

10. *Not in circumcision*—Not after he was circumcised: for he was justified
before Ishmael was born, Gen. xv; but he was not circumcised till Ishmael was
thirteen years old, Gen. xvii, 25.

11. *And*—After he was justified, *he received the sign of circumcision*—Circumcision, which was a sign or token of his being in covenant with God: *a seal*—
An assurance on God's part, that he accounted him righteous, upon his believing,
before he was circumcised; *who believe in uncircumcision*—That is, though they
are not circumcised.

12. *And the father of the circumcision*—Of those who are circumcised, and
believe as Abraham did. To those who believe not, Abraham is not a father,
neither are they his *seed*.

13. *The promise that he should be the heir of the world*—Is the same as that he
should be *the father of all nations;* namely, of those in all nations who received
the blessing. The whole world was promised to him and them conjointly. Christ
is the heir of the world, and of all things; and so are all Abraham's seed, all that
believe in him with the faith of Abraham.

14. *If they* only *who are of the law*, who have kept the whole law, *are heirs,
faith is made void;* no blessing being to be obtained by it; *and* so *the promise*
is *of no effect.*

15. *Because the law*—Considered apart from that grace, which though it was
in fact mingled with it, yet is no part of the legal dispensation, is so difficult,
and we so weak and sinful, that instead of bringing us a blessing it only
worketh wrath; it becomes to us an occasion of wrath, and exposes us to punishment as transgressors. *Where there is no law*—In force, there can be *no transgression* of it.

16. *Therefore it*—The blessing, *is of faith, that it might be of grace*—That it
might appear to flow from the free love of God, and *that the promise might be*

faith, that *it might be* of grace, that the promise might be firm to all
the seed; not only to that also which is of the law, but to that also
17 which is of the faith of Abraham, who is the father of us all, (As it is
written, * I have appointed thee a father of many nations) before
God in whom he believed, as quickening the dead, and calling the
18 things that are not, as though they were : Who against hope believed in hope, that he should be the father of many nations, ac-
19 cording to that which was spoken, † So shall thy seed be. And
not being weak in faith, he considered not his own body now dead,
being about a hundred years old, nor the deadness of Sarah's
20 womb. He staggered not at the promise of God through unbe-
21 lief, but was strengthened in faith, giving glory to God, And being fully assured, that what he had promised he was able also to
22 perform. And therefore it was imputed to him for righteousness.
23 Now it was not written on his account only, that it was imputed
24 unto him, But on ours also, to whom it will be imputed, if we be-
25 lieve on him who raised up Jesus our Lord from the dead, Who
was delivered for our offences, and was raised for our justification.
V. Therefore being justified by faith, we have peace with God,
2 through our Lord Jesus Christ : By whom also we have had ac-

---

firm, sure, and effectual, to *all the* spiritual seed of Abraham ; not only Jews, but
Gentiles also, if they follow his faith.

17. *Before God*—Though before men nothing of this appeared, those nations
being then unborn : *as quickening the dead*—The dead are not dead to him. And
even the things that are not, are *before God*—*And calling the things that are not*
—Summoning them to rise into being, and appear before him. The seed of Abraham did not then exist ; yet God said, *So shall thy seed be*. A man can say to
his servant actually existing, *Do this;* and he doth it. But God saith to the light,
while it does not exist, *Go forth;* and it goeth.

18–21. The apostle shows the power and excellence of that faith, to which he
ascribes justification. *Who against hope*—Against all probability, *believed* and
hoped in the promise. The same thing is apprehended both by faith and hope ;
by faith, as a thing which God hath spoken ; by hope, as a good thing which
God hath promised to us. *So shall thy seed be*—Both natural and spiritual, as
the stars of heaven for multitude.

20. *Giving* God the *glory* of his truth and power.

23. *On his account only*—To do personal honour to him.

24. *But on ours also*—To establish us in seeking justification by faith, and not
by works ; and to afford a full answer to those who say that " to be justified *by
works* means only by Judaism : to be justified *by faith* means by embracing
Christianity, that is, the system of doctrines so called." Sure it is that Abraham could not in this sense be justified either by faith or by works ; and equally
sure, that David (taking the words thus) was justified by works, not by faith.
Who raised up Jesus from the dead—As he did in a manner both Abraham and
Sarah. *If we believe on him who raised up Jesus*—God the Father therefore is
the proper object of justifying faith. It is observable, that St. Paul here, in
speaking both of our faith and of the faith of Abraham, puts a part for the whole.
And he mentions that part, with regard to Abraham, which would naturally affect
the Jews most.

25. *Who was delivered*—To death, *for our offences*—As an atonement for
them ; *and raised for our justification*—To empower us to receive that atonement
by faith.

V. 1. *Being justified by faith*—This is the sum of the preceding chapters, *we
have peace with God*—Being enemies to God no longer, ver. 10, neither fearing
his wrath, ver. 9 : we have peace ; hope, love, and power over sin, the sum of the
5th, 6th, 7th, and 8th chapters. These are the fruits of justifying faith : where
these are not, that faith is not.

* Gen. xvii, 5. † Gen. xv, 5.

cess through faith into this grace wherein we stand, and rejoice in
3 hope of the glory of God.   And not only *so*, but we glory in tribu-
4 lations also, knowing that tribulation worketh patience, And patience
5 experience, and experience hope ; And hope shameth us not, because the love of God is shed abroad in our hearts by the Holy
6 Ghost which is given unto us.   For when we were yet without
7 strength, in due time Christ died for the ungodly.   Now one will
scarce die for a just man ; yet perhaps for the good man one would
8 even dare to die.   But God recommendeth his love toward us, in
9 that, while we were yet sinners, Christ died for us.   Much more
then being now justified by his blood, we shall be saved from wrath
10 through him.   For if, being enemies, we were reconciled to God
by the death of his Son, much more being reconciled, we shall
11 be saved through his life.   And not only *so*, but we also glory in

---

2. *Into this grace*—This state of favour.

3. *We glory in tribulations also*—Which we are so far from esteeming a mark
of God's displeasure, that we receive them as tokens of his fatherly love, whereby
we are prepared for a more exalted happiness.   The Jews objected to the perse
cuted state of the Christians as inconsistent with the people of the Messiah.   It
is therefore with great propriety that the apostle so often mentions the blessings
arising from this very thing.

4. *And patience* works more *experience* of the sincerity of our grace, and of
God's power and faithfulness.

5. *Hope shameth us not*—That is, gives us the highest glorying.   We glory in
this our hope, *because the love of God is shed abroad in our hearts*—The Divine
conviction of God's love to us, and that love to God, which is both the earnest
and the beginning of heaven : *by the Holy Ghost*—The efficient cause of all these
present blessings, and the earnest of those to come.

6. How can we now doubt of God's love ? *for when we were without strength*
—Either to think, will, or do any thing good, *in due time*—Neither too soon nor
too late; but in that very point of time which the wisdom of God knew to be
more proper than any other, *Christ died for the ungodly*—Not only to set them
a pattern, or to procure them power to follow it.   It does not appear that this
expression of dying for any one, has any other signification, than that of rescuing
the life of another, by laying down our own.

7. *A just man*—One that gives to all what is strictly their due ; *the good man*—
One who is eminently holy, full of love, of compassion, kindness, mildness, of
every heavenly and amiable temper.   *Perhaps—one—would—even—dare to die*—
Every word increases the strangeness of the thing, and declares even this to be
something great and unusual.

8. *But God recommendeth*—A most elegant expression.   Those are wont to be
recommended to us, who were before either unknown to, or alienated from us,
while we were sinners—So far from being *good*, that we were not even *just*.

9. *By his blood*—By his blood shedding *we shall be saved from wrath through
him*—That is, from all the effects of the wrath of God.   But is there then
wrath in God ?   Is not wrath a human passion ?   And how can this human
passion be in God ?   We may answer this by another question : is not love a
human passion ?   And how can this human passion be in God ?   But to answer
directly : wrath in man, and so love in man, is a human passion.   But wrath
in God is not a human passion ; nor is love, as it is in God.   Therefore the
inspired writers ascribe both the one and the other to God, only in an ana-
logical sense.

10. *If*—As sure as.   So the word frequently signifies ; particularly in this and
the 8th chapter.   *We shall be saved*—Sanctified and glorified, *through his life*—
Who *ever liveth to make intercession for us*.

11. *And not only so, but we also glory*—The whole sentence, from the 3d to the
11th verse, may be taken together thus : We not only *rejoice in hope of the glory
of God, but also* in the midst of tribulations, *we glory in* God himself, *through our
Lord Jesus Christ*, by whom we have now received the reconciliation.

God, through our Lord Jesus Christ, by whom we have now re
ceived the reconciliation.

12   Therefore as by one man sin entered into the world, and death
13 by sin, even so death passed upon all men, in that all sinned.   For
until the law, sin was in the world : but sin is not imputed, where
14 there is no law.   Nevertheless death reigned from Adam to Moses,
even over them that had not sinned after the likeness of Adam's
15 transgression, who is the figure of him that was to come.   Yet not
as the offence, so also *is* the free gift.   For if by the offence of one
many died, much more the grace of God, and the gift by grace,
16 that of one man, Jesus Christ, hath abounded unto many.   And not
as *the loss* by one that sinned, *so is* the gift ; for the sentence was

12. *Therefore*—This refers to all the preceding discourse ; from which the
apostle infers what follows : he does not therefore properly make a digression,
but returns to speak again of sin and of righteousness. *As by one man*—Adam ;
who is mentioned, and not Eve, as being the representative of mankind ; *sin
entered into the world*—Actual sin, and its consequence, a sinful nature ; *and
death*—With all its attendants. *It entered into the world*, when it entered into
being ; or till then it did not exist, *by sin*—Therefore it could not enter before
sin. *Even so death passed upon all men*—Namely, by one man, *in that*—So the
word is used also, 2 Cor. v. 4 : *all sinned*—In Adam. These words assign the
reason why death came upon *all men ;* infants themselves not excepted, *in that
all sinned.*

13. *For until the law, sin was in the world*—All, I say, had sinned, for sin was
in the world long before the written law ; *but,* I grant, *sin is not* so much *imputed,*
nor so severely punished by God, *where there is no* express *law* to convince men
of it. Yet that all had sinned even then appears, in that all died.

14. *Death reigned*—And how vast is his kingdom ! Scarce can we find any
king, who has as many subjects, as are the kings whom he hath conquered ! *Even
over them that had not sinned after the likeness of Adam's transgression*—Even
over infants who had never sinned, as Adam did, in their own persons ; and over
others, who had not, like him, sinned against an express law. *Who is the figure
of him that was to come*—Each of them being a public person, and a federal head
of mankind. The one, the fountain of sin and death to mankind by his offence ;
the other, of righteousness and life by his free gift.

Thus far the apostle shows the agreement between the first and second Adam ;
afterward he shows the difference between them. The agreement may be summed up thus : as by one man sin entered into the world, and death by sin ; so
by one man righteousness entered into the world, and life by righteousness. As
death passed upon all men, in that all had sinned ; so life passed upon all men,
(who are in the second Adam by faith,) in that all are justified. And as death
through the sin of the first Adam, reigned *even over them who had not sinned
after the likeness of Adam's transgression : so* through the righteousness of Christ,
even those who have not obeyed, after the likeness of his obedience, shall reign
in life. We may add, as the sin of Adam, without the sins which we afterward
committed, brought us death ; so the righteousness of Christ, without the good
works which we afterward performed, brings us life ; although still every good,
as well as evil work, will receive its due reward.

15. *Yet not*—St. Paul now describes the difference between Adam and Christ ;
and that much more directly and expressly than the agreement between them.
Now the fall and the free gift differ, 1. In amplitude, ver. 15.   2. He from whom
sin came, and he from whom the free gift came, (termed also *the gift of righteousness,*) differ in power, ver. 16.   3. The reason of both is subjoined, ver. 17.
4. This premised, the offence and the free gift are compared, with regard to their
effect, ver. 18, and with regard to their cause, ver. 19.

16. *The sentence was by one offence to* Adam's *condemnation*—Occasioning the
sentence of death to pass upon him, which by consequence overwhelmed his
posterity : *but the free gift is of many offences unto justification*—Unto the pur
chasing it for all men, notwithstanding many offences.

by one *offence* to condemnation ; but the free gift *is* of many offences
17 unto justification.　For if through one man's offence, death reigned
by one, they who receive the abundance of grace and the gift of
righteousness, shall much more reign in life by one, *even* Jesus
18 Christ.　As therefore by one offence *the sentence of death came*
upon all men to condemnation, so also by one righteousness, *the*
19 *free gift came* upon all men to justification of life.　For as by
the disobedience of one man, many were constituted sinners, so by
20 the obedience of one, many shall be constituted righteous.　But
the law came in between, that the offence might abound : yet
21 where sin abounded, grace did much more abound : That as sin
had reigned through death, so grace also might reign through
righteousness to eternal life, by Jesus Christ our Lord.

VI.　What shall we say, then ?　We will continue in sin, that grace
2 may abound ?　God forbid.　How shall we who are dead to sin live
3 any longer therein ?　Know ye not, that as many of us as have been
baptized into Jesus Christ, have been baptized into his death ?
4 Therefore we are buried with him through baptism into death, that
as Christ was raised from the dead by the glory of the Father, so ·
5 we also should walk in newness of life.　For if we have been planted

---

17. There is a difference between *grace* and the *gift*.　*Grace* is opposed to the *offence*, the *gift* to *death*, being the *gift of life*.

18. *Justification of life* is that sentence of God, by which a sinner under sentence of death is adjudged to life.

19. *As by the disobedience of one man, many*, that is, all men, *were constituted sinners*—Being then in the loins of their first parent, the common head and representative of them all ; *so by the obedience of one*—By his obedience unto death : by his dying for us ; *many*—All that believe, *shall be constituted righteous*—Justified, pardoned.

20. *The law came in between*—The offence and the free gift, *that the offence might abound*—That is, the consequence, (not the design,) of the law's coming in, was, not the taking away of sin, but the increase of it ; *yet where sin abounded grace did much more abound*—Not only in the remission of that sin which Adam brought on us, but of all our own ; not only in remission of sins, but infusion of holiness : not only in deliverance from death, but admission to everlasting life ; a far more noble and excellent life than that which we lost by Adam's fall.

21. *That as sin had reigned—so grace also might reign*—Which could not reign before the fall ; before man had sinned.　*Through righteousness to eternal life, through Jesus Christ our Lord*—Here is pointed out the source of all our blessings, the rich and free grace of God.　The *meritorious cause ;* not any works of righteousness of man, but the alone merits of our Lord Jesus Christ.　The *effect* or *end* of all ; not only pardon, but life ; Divine life, leading to glory.

VI. The apostle here sets himself more fully to vindicate his doctrine from the consequence above suggested, chap. iii, 7, 8.　He had then only in strong terms denied and renounced it.　Here he removes the very foundation thereof.

2 *Dead to sin*—Free both from the guilt and from the power of it.

3. *As many as have been baptized into Jesus Christ, have been baptized into his death*—In baptism we, through faith, are ingrafted into Christ, and we draw new spiritual life from this new root, through his Spirit, who fashions us like unto him, and particularly with regard to his death and resurrection.

4. *We are buried with him*—Alluding to the ancient manner of baptizing by immersion : *that as Christ was raised from the dead by the glory*—Glorious power *of the Father, so we also* by the same power should rise again : and as he lives a new life in heaven, so we *should walk in newness of life.*　This, says the apostle, our very baptism represents to us.

5. *For*—Surely these two must go together ; so that if we are indeed made conformable to his death, we shall also know the power of his resurrection.

together in the likeness of his death, we shall be also *in the likeness*
6 of his resurrection : Knowing this, that our old man is crucified
with *him*, that the body of sin might be destroyed, that we might
7 no longer serve sin.   For he that is dead is freed from sin.   And
8 we believe, that if we are dead with Christ, we shall also live with
9 him : Knowing that Christ being raised from the dead, dieth no
10 more ; death no more hath dominion over him.   For in that he
died, he died to sin once for all ; but in that he liveth, he liveth
11 unto God.   So reckon ye yourselves to be dead indeed to sin, but
12 alive to God, through Jesus Christ our Lord.   Therefore let not
sin reign in your mortal body, to obey it in the desires thereof.
13 Neither present your members to sin *as* instruments of unrighteousness ; but present yourselves to God, as alive from the dead, and
14 your members to God, *as* instruments of righteousness : For sin
shall not have dominion over you ; for ye are not under the law,
but under grace.
15   What then ? Shall we sin, because we are not under the law,
16 but under grace ? God forbid.   Know ye not, that to whom ye present yourselves servants to obey, his servants ye are whom ye
obey ? Whether of sin unto death, or of obedience unto righteous-
17 ness ? But thanks *be* to God, that whereas ye were the servants
of sin, ye have *now* obeyed from the heart the form of doctrine
18 into which ye have been delivered.   Being then set free from sin,

---

6. *Our old man*—Coeval with our being, and as old as the fall, our evil nature ; a strong and beautiful expression for that entire depravity and corruption,
which by nature spreads itself over the whole man, leaving no part uninfected.
This in a believer is *crucified with Christ*, mortified, gradually killed, by virtue
of our union with him : *that the body of sin*—All evil tempers, words, and actions, which are the *members of the old man*, Col. iii, 5, *might be destroyed.*
  7. *For he that is dead*—With Christ, *is freed from* the guilt of past, and from
the power of present *sin*, as dead men from the commands of their former
masters.
  8. *Dead with Christ*—Conformed to his death, by dying to sin.
  10. *He died to sin*—To atone for and abolish it : *he liveth unto God*—A glorious eternal life, such as we shall live also.
  12. *Let not sin reign even in your mortal body*—It must be subject to death,
but it need not be subject to sin.
  13. *Neither present your members to sin*—To corrupt nature, a mere tyrant :
but to God—Your lawful king.
  14. *Sin shall not have dominion over you*—It has neither right nor power. *For
ye are not under the law*—A dispensation of terror and bondage, which only
shows sin, without enabling you to conquer it ; *but under grace*—Under the merciful dispensation of the Gospel, which brings complete victory over it ; to every
one who is under the powerful influences of the spirit of Christ.
  17. *The form of doctrine into which ye have been delivered*—Literally it is, *the
mould into which ye have been delivered*—Which, as it contains a beautiful allusion, conveys also a very instructive admonition : intimating that our minds, all
pliant and ductile, should be conformed to the Gospel precepts, as liquid metals
take the figure of the mould into which they are cast.
  18. *Being then set free from sin*—We may see the apostle's method thus far at
one view.

19 ye are become the servants of righteousness.• I speak after the
manner of men, because of the weakness of your flesh. As ye
have presented your members servants to uncleanness and iniquity unto iniquity, so now present your members servants of
20 righteousness unto holiness. For when ye were the servants of
21 sin, ye were free from righteousness. What fruit had ye then
from those things whereof ye are now ashamed? For the end of
22 those things *is* death. But now being made free from sin, and
become servants to God, ye have your fruit unto holiness, and the
23 end everlasting life. For death *is* the wages of sin; but eternal
life *is* the gift of God through Jesus Christ our Lord.
VII. Know ye not, brethren, (for I speak to them that know the law,)
2 that the law hath dominion over a man as long as he liveth! For
the married woman is bound to *her* husband while he is alive; but
if *her* husband be dead, she is freed from the law of her husband.
3 Therefore if she marry another man while her husband liveth, she
will be called an adulteress: but if her husband be dead, she is
free from that law, so as to be no adulteress, though she marry
4 another man. Therefore ye also, my brethren, are become dead
to the law by the body of Christ; that ye might be married to another, *even* to him who was raised from the dead, that we may

---

5. Justification, whereby God forgives all past sin, and freely accepts the sinner,   Chap. iii, 24
6. The gift of the Holy Ghost : a sense of God's love : new, inward life,   v, 5 ; vi, 4
7. The free service of righteousness,   vi, 12

19. *I speak after the manner of men*—Thus it is necessary that the Scripture
should let itself down to the language of men; *because of the weakness of your
flesh.* Slowness of understanding flows from the weakness of the flesh, that is,
of human nature. *As ye have presented your members servants to uncleanness
and iniquity unto iniquity, so now present your members servants of righteousness,
unto holiness*—Iniquity (whereof uncleanness is an eminent part) is here opposed
to *righteousness.* And *unto iniquity* is the opposite of *unto holiness. Righteousness* here, is a conformity to the Divine will; *holiness*, to the whole Divine nature. Observe! they who are *servants of righteousness* go on to *holiness*, but they
who are *servants to iniquity* get no farther. Righteousness is *service*, because we
live according to the will of another ; but *liberty*, because of our inclination to
it and delight in it.
20. *When ye were the servants of sin, ye were free from righteousness*—In all
reason therefore ye ought now to be free from unrighteousness ; to be as uniform
and zealous in serving God, as ye were in serving the devil.
21. *Those things*—He speaks of them as afar off.
23. *Death*—Temporal, spiritual, and eternal, *is the* due *wages of sin. But
eternal life is the gift of God*—The difference is remarkable. Evil works *merit*
the reward they receive ; good works do not. The former demand wages, the
latter accept a free gift.
VII. The apostle continues the comparison between the former and the present state of a believer, and at the same time endeavours to wean the Jewish believers from their fondness for the Mosaic law. *I speak to them that know the
law*—To the Jews chiefly here. *As long*—So long, and no longer, *as it liveth*—
The law is here spoken of (by a common figure) as a person, to which as to a
husband, life and death are ascribed. But he speaks indifferently of the law
being dead to us, or we to it, the sense being the same.
2. *She is freed from the law of her husband*—From that law which gave him
a peculiar property in her.
4. *Thus ye also*—Are now as free from the Mosaic law, as a husband is, when
his wife is dead. *By the body of Christ*—Offered up ; that is, by the merits of his
death, that law expiring with him.

5 bring forth fruit to God. For when we were in the flesh, the motions of sins, which were by the law, wrought in our members, so
6 as to bring forth fruit unto death. But now we are freed from the
law, being dead unto that whereby we were held, so that we serve
in newness of spirit, and not in the oldness of the letter.
7 What shall we say then? That the law is sin? God forbid.
Yea, I should not have known sin, but for the law. I had not
8 known lust, unless the law had said, Thou shalt not covet. But
sin taking occasion by the commandment, wrought in me all man-
9 ner of desire: for without the law sin *was* dead. And I was once
alive without the law; but when the commandment came, sin re-
10 vived, and I died. And the commandment which *was intended*
11 for life, this I found unto death. For sin taking occasion by the
12 commandment, deceived me, and by it slew me. So that the law
is holy, and the commandment holy, and just, and good.
13 Was then that which is good made death to me? God forbid.

5. *When ye were in the flesh*—Carnally minded, in a state of nature: before
we believed in Christ. *Our sins which were by the law,* accidentally occasioned,
or irritated thereby; *wrought in our members*—Spread themselves all over the
whole man.

6. *Being dead to that whereby we were held*—To our old husband, the law,
that we might serve in newness of spirit—In a new, spiritual manner, *and not
in the oldness of the letter*—Not in a bare literal, external way, as we did before.

7. *What shall we say then?*—This is a kind of digression, (to the beginning of
the next chapter,) wherein the apostle, in order to show, in the most lively manner, the weakness and inefficacy of the law, changes the person, and speaks as
of himself, concerning the misery of one under the law. This St. Paul frequently does when he is not speaking of his own person, but only assuming
another character, Rom. iii, 6; 1 Cor. x, 30; chap. iv, 6. The character here
assumed, is that of a man, first, ignorant of the law, then under it, and sincerely
but ineffectually striving to serve God. To have spoken this of himself, or any
true believer, would have been foreign to the whole scope of his discourse;
nay, utterly contrary thereto; as well as to what is expressly asserted, chap.
viii, 2. *Is the law sin?*—Sinful in itself, or a promoter of sin? *I had not known
lust*—That is, evil desire. I had not known it to be a sin. Nay, perhaps I should
not have known that any such desire was in me. It did not appear till it was
stirred up by the prohibition.

8. *But sin*—My inbred corruption, *taking occasion by the commandment*—Forbidding, but not subduing it, was only fretted, and *wrought in me* so much the
more *all manner of* evil *desire. For* while I was *without the* knowledge of *the
law, sin was dead;* neither so apparent, nor so active; nor was I under the least
apprehensions of any danger from it.

9. *And I was once alive without the law*—Without the close application of it.
I had much life, wisdom, virtue, strength. So I thought. But when the commandment (that is, the law, a part put for the whole: but this expression parti
cularly intimates its compulsive force, which restrains, enjoins, urges, forbids,
threatens) came in its spiritual meaning to my heart, with the power of God, *sin
revived, and I died*—My inbred sin took fire, and all my virtue and strength died
away. And I then saw myself to be dead in sin, and liable to death eternal.

10. *The commandment which was intended for life*—Doubtless it was originally
intended by God as a grand means of preserving and increasing spiritual life, and
leading to life everlasting.

11. *Deceived me*—While I expected life by the law, sin came upon me unawares,
and slew all my hopes.

12. *The commandment*—That is, every branch of the law, *is holy, just, and
good*—It springs from, and partakes of, the holy nature of God: it is every way
just and right in itself. It is designed wholly for the good of man.

13. *Was then that which is good made the* cause of evil *to me?*—Yea, of

But sin; that it might appear sin, working death in me by that which is good: so that sin might by the 'commandment become
14 exceeding sinful. We know that the law is spiritual; but I am
15 carnal, sold under sin. For that which I do, I approve not; for
16 I do not practise what I would, but what I hate, that I do. If then
17 I do what I would not, I consent to the law that *it is* good. Now
18 then it is no more I that do it, but sin that dwelleth in me. For
I know that in me, that is, in my flesh, dwelleth no good thing: for to will is present with me, but *how* to perform what is good, I find
19 not. For the good that I would, I do not; but the evil which I
20 would not, that I do. Now, if I do that which I would not, it is no
21 more I that do it, but sin that dwelleth in me. I find then a
22 law, that when I would do good evil is present with me. For I
23 delight in the law of God after the inward man. But I see another law in my members, warring against the law of my mind, and captivating me to the law of sin, which is in my members.
24 O wretched man that I am! Who shall deliver me from the body
25 of this death? I thank God, through Jesus Christ our Lord. So

death, which is the greatest of evils? Not so. But it was sin which was made death to me, inasmuch as it wrought death in me even *by that which is good*— By the good law, *so that sin by the commandment became exceeding sinful*—The consequence of which was, that inbred sin, thus driving furiously in spite of the commandment, became exceeding sinful; the guilt thereof being greatly aggravated.

14. *I am carnal*—St. Paul having compared together the past and present state of believers, that in the flesh, ver. 5, and that in the spirit, ver. 6; in answering two objections, (*is then the law sin?* ver. 7, and *is the law death?* ver. 13,) interweaves the whole process of a man reasoning, groaning, striving, and escaping from the legal to the evangelical state. This he does from ver. 7 to the end of this chapter. *Sold under sin*—Totally enslaved: slaves bought with money were absolutely at their masters' disposal.

16. *It is good*—This single word implies all the three that were used before, ver. 12, holy, just, and good.

17. *It is no more I that* can properly be said to do it, but rather sin that dwelleth in me: that makes, as it were, another person, and tyrannizes over me.

18. *In my flesh*—The flesh here signifies the whole man as he is by nature

21. *I find then a law*—An inward, constraining power, flowing from the dictate of corrupt nature.

22. *For I delight in the law of God*—This is more than I consent to, ver. 16. The day of liberty draws near; *the inward man*—Called the mind, ver. 23 and 25.

23. *But I see another law in my members*—Another inward constraining power of evil inclinations and bodily appetites, *warring against the law of my mind*— The dictate of my mind, which delights in the law of God, *and captivating me*— In spite of all my resistance.

24. *O wretched man that I am!*—The struggle is now come to the height; and the man finding there is no help in himself, begins almost unawares to pray, *Who shall deliver me?*—He then seeks and looks for deliverance, till God in Christ appears to answer his question. The word which we translate deliver, implies force; and indeed without this there can be no deliverance. The *body of this death*—That is, this body of death; this mass of sin, leading to death eternal, and cleaving as close to me as my body to my soul. We may observe, the deliverance is not wrought yet.

25. *I thank God through Jesus Christ our Lord*—That is, God will deliver me through Christ. But the apostle (as his frequent manner is) beautifully interweaves his assertion with thanksgiving: the hymn of praise answering in a manner to the voice of sorrow. *O wretched man that I am! So then*—He here sums up the whole, and concludes what he began, ver. 7. *I myself*—Or rather,

then I myself with my mind serve the law of God, but with my flesh the law of sin.

VIII.   Therefore *there is* now no condemnation to those that are in
2 Christ Jesus, who walk not after the flesh but after the Spirit.   For the law of the Spirit of life in Christ Jesus hath freed me from the
3 law of sin and death.   For what the law could not do in that it was weak through the flesh, God *hath done:* sending his own Son in the likeness of sinful flesh, *to be a sacrifice* for sin, he hath
4 condemned sin in the flesh: That the righteousness of the law might be fulfilled in us, who walk not after the flesh, but after the
5 Spirit.   They that are after the flesh, mind the things of the flesh;
6 but they that are after the Spirit, the things of the Spirit.   Now to be carnally-minded *is* death; but to be spiritually-minded *is* life
7 and peace :   Because to be carnally minded *is* enmity against God; for it is not subject to the law of God, neither indeed can be.
8 So then they who are in the flesh cannot please God.   But ye are not in the flesh, but in the Spirit, if the Spirit of God dwell in

that I (the person whom I am personating till his deliverance is wrought) *serve the law of God with my mind*—My reason and conscience declare for God; *but with my flesh the law of sin*—But my corrupt passions and appetites still rebel. The man is now utterly weary of his bondage, and upon the brink of liberty.

VIII. 1. *There is therefore now no condemnation*—Either for things present or past.   Now he comes to deliverance and liberty.   The apostle here resumes the thread of his discourse, which was interrupted, chap. vii, 7.

2. *The law of the Spirit*—That is, the Gospel, *hath freed me from the law of sin and death*—That is, the Mosaic dispensation.

3. *For what the law*—Of Moses, *could not do, (in that it was weak through the flesh*—Incapable of conquering our evil nature,) if it could, God needed not to have sent *his own Son in the likeness of sinful flesh*—We with our sinful flesh were devoted to death.   But God sending his own Son in the likeness of that flesh, though pure from sin, he condemned that sin which was in our flesh: gave sentence that sin should be destroyed, and the believer wholly delivered from it.

4. *That the righteousness of the law*—The holiness it required, described, ver. 5–11, *might be fulfilled in us, who walk not after the flesh, but after the Spirit*— Who are guided in all our thoughts, words, and actions, not by corrupt nature, but by the Spirit of God.   From this place St. Paul describes primarily the state of believers, and that of unbelievers, only to illustrate this.

5. *They that are after the flesh*—Who remain under the guidance of corrupt nature, *mind the things of the flesh*—Have their thoughts and affections fixed on such things as gratify corrupt nature; namely, on things visible and temporal; on things of the earth, on pleasure, (of sense or imagination,) praise, or riches; *but they who are after the Spirit*—Who are under his guidance, *mind the things of the Spirit*—Think of, relish, love things invisible, eternal; the things which the Spirit hath revealed, which he works in us, moves us to, and promises to give us.

6. *For to be carnally minded*—That is, to mind the things of the flesh, *is death*—The sure mark of spiritual death, and the way to death everlasting: *but to be spiritually minded* That is, to mind the things of the Spirit, *is life*—A sure mark of spiritual life, and the way to life everlasting; and attended with *peace*— The peace of God, which is the foretaste of life everlasting, and peace with God, opposite to the enmity mentioned in the next verse.

7. *Enmity against God*—His existence, power, and providence.

8. *They who are in the flesh*—Under the government of it.

9. *In the Spirit*—Under his government.   *If any man have not the Spirit of Christ*—Dwelling and governing in him, *he is none of his*—He is not a member of Christ; not a Christian; not in a state of salvation.   A plain, express declaration, which admits of no exception.   He that hath ears to hear, let him hear.

9 yòu.   And ıf any man have not the Spirit of Christ, he is none of
10 his.   Now if Christ *be* in you, the body indeed *is* dead because
11 of sin, but the Spirit *is* life because of righteoushess.   And if the
Spirit of him that raised up Jesus from the dead dwell in you, he
that raised up Christ from the dead, will also quicken your mortal
bọdies by his Spirit that dwelleth in you.
12   Therefore, brethren, we are not debtors to the flesh, to live
13 after the flesh.   For if ye live after the flesh, ye shall die ; but if
ye through the Spirit mortify the deeds of the flesh, ye shall live.
14 For as many as are led by the Spirit of God, they are the sons of
15 God.   For ye have not received the spırıt of bondage again unto
fear, but ye have received the Spirit of adoption, whereby we cry
16 Abba, Father.   The same Spirit beareth witness with our spirits,
17 that we are the children of God.   And if children, then heirs, heirs
of God, and joint heirs with Christ : if we suffer with *him*, that we
18 may also be glorified with *him*.   For I reckon that the sufferings
of the present time *are* not worthy *to be compared* with the glory
19 which shall be revealed in us.   For the earnest expectation of the

---

10. *Now if Christ be in you*—Where the Spirit of Christ is, there is Christ :
the body indeed is dead—Devoted to death, *because of sin*—Heretofore committed ; *but the Spirit is life*—Already truly alive ; *because of righteousness*—Now
attained. From ver. 10, St. Paul having finished what he had begun, chap. vi, 1,
describes purely the state of believers.
12. *We are not debtors to the flesh*—We ought not to follow it.
13. *The deeds of the flesh*—Not only evil actions, but evil desires, tempers,
thoughts. *If ye mortify*—Kill, destroy these, *ye shall live*—The life of faith more
abundantly here, and hereafter the life of glory.
14. *For as many as are led by the Spirit of God*—In all the ways of righteousness, *they are the sons of God*—Here St. Paul enters upon the description of those
blessings, which he comprises, ver. 30, in the word glorified : though indeed he
does not describe mere glory, but that which is still mingled with the cross. The
sum is, through sufferings to glory.
15. *For ye*—Who are real Christians, *have not received the spirit of bondage*—
The Holy Ghost was not properly a spirit of bondage, even in the time of the
Old Testament. Yet there was something of bondage remaining even in those
who then had received the Spirit : *again*—As the Jews did before : *we*—All and
every believer, *cry*—The word denotes a vehement speaking, with desire, confidence, constancy ; *Abba, Father*—The latter word explains the former. By using
both the Syriac and the Greek word, St. Paul seems to point out the joint cry
both of the Jewish and Gentile believers. The spirit of bondage here seems
directly to mean those operations of the Holy Spirit, by which the soul, on its
first conviction, feels itself in bondage to sin, to the world, to Satan, and
obnoxious to the wrath of God. This therefore and the Spirit of adoption are
one and the same Spirit, only manifesting itself in various operations, according
to the various circumstances of the persons.
16. *The same Spirit beareth witness with our spirit*—With the spirit of every
true believer, by a testimony distinct from that of his own spirit, or the testimony
of a good conscience. Happy they who enjoy this clear and constant.
17. *Joint heirs*—That we may know it is a great inheritance which God will
give us ; for he hath given a great one to his Son. *If we suffer with him*—Willingly and cheerfully, for righteousness' sake. This is a new proposition, referring
to what follows.
18. *For I reckon*—This verse gives the reason, why he but now mentioned
sufferings and glory. When that glory shall be revealed in us, then the sons of
God will be revealed also.
19. *For the earnest expectatiŏn*—The word denotes a lively hope of something
diawing near, and a vehement longing after it ; *of the creation*—Of all visible
creatures, (believers excepted, who are spoken of apart.) Each kınd, according

20 creation waiteth for the revelation of the sons of God. For the
　creation was made subject to vanity, not willingly, but by him
21 who subjected *it*, In hope that the creation itself shall be delivered
　from the bondage of corruption, into the glorious liberty of the
22 children of God. For we know that the whole creation groaneth
23 together and travaileth together until now. And not only *they*,
　but even we ourselves, who have the first fruits of the Spirit,
　even we ourselves groan within ourselves, waiting for the adop-
24 tion, the redemption of our body. For we are saved by hope;
　but hope that is seen is not hope: for what a man seeth, how
25 does he yet hope for? But if we hope for what we see not, we
26 patiently wait for it. Likewise the Spirit also helpeth our in-
　firmities; for we know not what we should pray for as we ought;
　but the Spirit itself maketh intercession for us, with groanings
27 which cannot be uttered. But he who searcheth the hearts,
　knoweth what *is* the mind of the Spirit: for he maketh inter-
　cession for the saints according to God.
28　And we know, that all things work together for good to them

---

as it is capable. All these have been sufferers through sin. And to all these
(the finally impenitent excepted) shall refreshment redound from the glory of the
children of God. Upright heathens are by no means to be excluded from this
earnest expectation. Nay, perhaps something of it may at some times be found
even in the vainest of men; who (although in the hurry of life they mistake
vanity for liberty, and partly stifle, partly dissemble their groans, yet) in their
sober, quiet, sleepless, afflicted hours, pour forth many sighs in the ear of God.
　20. *The creation was made subject to vanity*—Abuse, misery, and corruption,
by him who subjected it—Namely, God, Gen. iii, 17; v, 29. Adam only made it
liable to the sentence which God pronounced; yet not without hope.
　21. *The creation itself shall be delivered*—Destruction is not deliverance. Therefore whatsoever is destroyed, or ceases to be, is not delivered at all. Will then
any part of the creation be destroyed? *Into the glorious liberty*—The excellent
state wherein they were created.
　22. *For the whole creation groaneth together*—With joint groans, as it were
with one voice. *And travaileth*—Literally, is in the pain of childbirth; to be
delivered of the burden of the curse: *until now*—To this very hour, and so on
till the time of deliverance.
　23. *And even we, who have the first fruits of the Spirit*—That is, the Spiri.
who is the first fruits of our inheritance. *The adoption*—Persons who had been
privately adopted among the Romans, were often brought forth into the forum,
and there publicly owned as their sons, by those who adopted them. So at the
general resurrection, when the body itself is redeemed from death, the sons of
God shall be publicly owned by him in the great assembly of men and angels.
The redemption of our body—From corruption to glory and immortality.
　24. *For we are saved by hope*—Our salvation is now only in hope. We do not
yet possess this full salvation.
　26. *Likewise the Spirit*—Nay, not only the universe, not only the children of
God, but also the Spirit of God himself, as it were, groaneth while he helpeth
oui infirmities or weaknesses. Our understandings are weak, particularly in
the things of God; our desires are weak; our prayers are weak. *We know not*
—Many times, *what we should pray for*—Much less are we able to pray for it
as we ought: *but the Spirit maketh intercession for us*—In our hearts, even as
Christ does in heaven; *with groanings*—The matter of which is from ourselves;
but the Spirit forms them; and they are frequently inexpressible, even by the
faithful themselves.
　27. *But he who searcheth the hearts*—Wherein the Spirit dwells and intercedes;
knoweth—Though man cannot utter it, *what is the mind of the Spirit: for he
maketh intercession for the saints*—Who are near to God, *according to God*—
According to his will, as is worthy of God, and acceptable to him.

that love God, to them that are called according to *his* purpose
29 For whom he foreknew, he also predestinated, conformable to the
image of his Son, that*he might be the first born among many
30 brethren. And whom he predestinated, them he also called ; and
whom he called, them he also justified : and whom he justified,

---

28. *And we know*—This in general ; though we do not always know particularly what to pray for ; *that all things*—Ease or pain, poverty or riches, and the ten thousand changes of life, *work together for good*—Strongly and sweetly for spiritual and eternal good ; *to them that are called according to his purpose*—His gracious design to save a lost world by the death of his Son. This is a new proposition. St. Paul being about to recapitulate the whole blessing contained in justification, (termed glorification, ver. 30,) first goes back to the purpose or de cree of God, which is frequently mentioned in holy writ.

To explain this (nearly in the words of an eminent writer) a little more at large. When a man has a work of time and importance before him, he pauses, consults, and contrives ; and when he has laid a plan, resolves or decrees to proceed accordingly. Having observed this in ourselves, we are ready to apply it to God also : and he in condescension to us has applied it to himself.

The works of providence and redemption are vast and stupendous, and therefore we are apt to conceive of God, as deliberating and consulting on them, and then decreeing to act, according to the counsels of his own will. As if, long before the world was made, he had been concerting measures, both as to the making and governing of it, and had then writ down his decrees, which altered not, any more than the laws of the Medes and Persians. Whereas to take this consulting and decreeing in a literal sense would be the same absurdity, as to ascribe a real, human body, and human passions to the ever-blessed God.

This is only a popular representation of his infallible knowledge and un changeable wisdom ; that is, he does all things as wisely as a man can possibly do, after the deepest consultation, and as steadily pursues the most proper method, as one can do, who has laid a scheme beforehand. But then, though the effects be such as would argue consultation and consequent decrees in man, yet what need of a moment's consultation in Him, who sees all things at one view ?

Nor had God any more occasion to pause, and deliberate, and lay down rules for his own conduct, from all eternity, than he has now. What! was there any fear of his mistaking afterward, if he had not beforehand prepared decrees to direct him what he was to do ? Will any man say, he was wiser before the creation than since ? Or had he then more leisure ? That he should take that opportunity to settle his affairs, and make rules for himself, from which he was never to vary ?

He has doubtless the same wisdom and all other perfections at this day which he had from eternity ; and is now as capable of making decrees, or rather has no more occasion for them now than formerly : his understanding being always equally clear and bright, his wisdom equally infallible.

29. *Whom he foreknew he also predestinated, conformable to the image of his Son*—Here the apostle declares who those are whom he foreknew and predestinated to glory, namely, those who are conformable to the image of his Son. This is the mark of those who are foreknown and will be glorified, 2 Tim. ii, 9 ; Phil. iii, 10, 21.

30. *Them he*—In due time, called by his Gospel and his Spirit : and whom he called, when obedient to the heavenly calling, Acts xxvi, 19, *he also justified*—Forgave and accepted : *and whom he justified*—Provided they continued in his goodness, chap. xi, 22, he in the end *glorified*—St. Paul does not affirm, either here, or in any other part of his writings, that precisely the same number of men are called, justified, and glorified. He does not deny that a believer may fall away and be cut off, between his special calling and his glorification, chap. xi, 22. Neither does he deny, that many are called, who never are justified. He only affirms, that this is the method whereby God leads us step by step toward heaven. *He glorified*—He speaks as one looking back from the goal, upon the race of faith. Indeed grace, as it is glory begun, is both an earnest and a fore taste of eternal glory.

31 them he also glorified. What shall we say then to these things?
32 if God *be* for us, who *can be* against us? He that spared not his
own Son, but delivered him up for us all, how shall he not with
33 him also freely give us all things? Who shall lay any thing to the
charge of God's elect? *It is* God that justifieth, Who *is* he that
34 condemneth? *It is* Christ that died, yea rather, that is risen again,
who is also at the right hand of God, who likewise maketh inter-
35 cession for us. Who shall separate us from the love of Christ?
Shall affliction, or distress, or persecution, or hunger, or nakedness

---

31. *What shall wĕ say then to these things?*—Related in the 3d, 5th, and 8th
chapters? As if he had said, We cannot go, think, or wish any thing farther. *If
God be for us*—Here follow four periods, one general, and three particular. Each
begins with glorying in the grace of God, which is followed by a question suitable to it, challenging all opponents; to all which I am persuaded, &c, is a general answer. The general period is, If God be for us, who can be against us?
The first particular period, relating to the past time is, He that spared not his
own Son, how shall he not freely give us all things? The second, relating to the
present, is, It is God that justifieth: who is he that condemneth? The third, relating to the future, is, *It is Christ that died*—Who shall separate us from the
love of Christ?
32. *He that*—This period contains four sentences. He spared not his own
Son, therefore he will freely give us all things. He delivered him up for us;
therefore none can lay any thing to our charge. *Freely*—For all that follows
justification is a free gift also. *All things*—Needful or profitable for us.
33. *God's elect*—The above-cited author observes, that long before the coming
of Christ the heathen world revolted from the true God, and were therefore reprobated or rejected.
But the nation of the Jews were chosen to be the people of God, and were
therefore styled, * The children or sons of God, † Holy people, ‡ Chosen seed,
§ The elect, ‖ The called of God. And these titles were given to all the nation
of Israel, including both good and bad.
Now the Gospel having the most strict connection with the books of the Old
Testament, where these phrases frequently occur; and our Lord and his apostles
being native Jews, and beginning to preach in the land of Israel, the language in
which they preached would of course abound with the phrases of the Jewish nation. And hence it is easy to see, why such of them as would not receive him
were styled *reprobated.* For they no longer continued to be the people of God.
Whereas this and those other honourable titles were continued to all such Jews
as embraced Christianity. And the same appellations which once belonged to
the Jewish nation, were now given to the Gentile Christians also; together with
which they were invested with all the privileges of *the chosen people of* God; and
nothing could cut them off from these, but their own wilful apostasy.
It does not appear that even good men were ever termed God's elect, till above
two thousand years from the creation. God's electing or choosing the nation of
Israel, and separating them from the other nations, who were sunk in idolatry
and all wickedness, gave the first occasion to this sort of language. And as the
separating the Christians from the Jews was a like event, no wonder it was expressed in like words and phrases: only with this difference, the term elect was
of old applied to all the members of the visible Church; whereas in the New
Testament it is applied only to the members of the invisible.
34. *Yea rather, that is risen*—Our faith should not stop at his death, but be
exercised farther on his resurrection, kingdom, second coming. *Who maketh intercession for us*—Presenting there his obedience, his sufferings, his prayers, and
our prayers sanctified through him.
35. *Who shall separate us from the love of Christ* toward us? *Shall affliction
or distress*—He proceeds in order, from less troubles to greater: can any of
these separate us from his protection in it; and (if he sees good) deliverance
from it?

* Deut. xiv, 1.   † Chap. vii, 6; Chap. xiv, 2.   ‡ Deut. iv, 37   § Isaiah lxi, 8, 9;
Chap. xliii, 20.   ‖ Isa. xlviii, 12
25

36 or peril, or sword ? (As it is written, * For thy sake we are killed
   all the day long, we are accounted as sheep for the slaughter.)
37 Nay, in all these things we more than conquer, through him who
38 hath loved us. For I am persuaded, that neither death, nor life,
   nor angels, nor principalities, nor powers, nor things present, nor
39 things to come, Nor height, nor depth, nor any other creature
   shall be able to separate us from the love of God, which is in
   Christ Jesus our Lord.
IX.   I say the truth in Christ, I lie not; my conscience also bearing
2 me witness in the Holy Ghost, That I have great sorrow and
3 continual anguish in my heart. For I could wish that I myself

36. *All the day*—That is, every day, continually. *We are accounted*—By our
enemies ; by ourselves.
   37. *We more than conquer*—We are not only no losers, but abundant gainers
by all these trials. This period seems to describe the full assurance of hope.
   38. *I am persuaded*—This is inferred from the 34th ver. in an admirable order,
Neither death shall hurt us ;   For Christ is dead :
Nor life ;   is risen :
Nor angels, nor principalities, nor powers ; nor things } is at the right hand of
   present, nor things to come ;   {   God :
Nor height, nor depth ; nor any other   } maketh intercession for
   creature ;   {   us.
   Neither death—Terrible as it is to natural men ; a violent death in particular,
ver. 36 : *nor life*—With all the affliction and distress it can bring, ver. 35 : or a
long, easy life ; or all living men : *nor angels*—Whether good (if it were possible
they should attempt it) or bad, with all their wisdom and strength ; *nor principalities, nor powers*—Not even those of the highest rank, or the most eminent
power ; *nor things present*—Which may befall us, during our pilgrimage, or the
whole world, till it passeth away : *nor things to come*—Which may occur either
when our time on earth is past, or when time itself is at an end, as the final judgment, the general conflagration, the everlasting fire : *nor height, nor depth*—The
former sentence respected the differences of times, this, the differences of places.
How many great and various things are contained in these words we do not,
need not, cannot know yet. *The height*—In St. Paul's sublime style is put for
heaven : *the depth*—For the great abyss : that is, neither the heights, I will not
say of walls, mountains, seas, but of heaven itself, can move us ; nor the abyss
itself, the very thought of which might astonish the boldest creature. *Nor any
creature*—Nothing beneath the Almighty ; visible enemies he does not even deign
to name ; *shall be able*—Either by force, ver. 35, or by any legal claim, ver. 33,
&c, *to separate us from the love of God in Christ*—Which will surely save, protect,
deliver us who believe, in, and through, and from them all.
   Chapter ix. In this chapter St. Paul, after strongly declaring his love and
esteem for them, sets himself to answer the grand objection of his countrymen,
namely, that the rejection of the Jews, and reception of the Gentiles, was con
trary to the word of God. That he had not here the least thought of personal
election or reprobation, is manifest : 1. Because it lay quite wide of his design,
which was this : to show that God's rejecting the Jews, and receiving the Gentiles, was consistent with his word : 2. Because such a doctrine would not only
have had no tendency to convince, but would have evidently tended to harden the
Jews : 3. Because when he sums up his argument in the close of the chapter, he
has not one word, or the least intimation about it.
   IX. 1. *In Christ*—This seems to imply an appeal to him. *In the Holy Ghost*—
Through his grace.
   2. *I have great sorrow*—A high degree of spiritual sorrow and of spiritual joy
may consist together, chap. viii, 39. By declaring his sorrow for the unbelieving
Jews, who excluded themselves from all the blessings he had enumerated, he
snows that what he was now about to speak, he did not speak from any prejudice
to them.
   3. *I could wish*—Human words cannot fully describe the motions of souls that
                              * Psalm lxiv, 22.

were accursed from Christ, for my brethren, my kinsmen after the
4 flesh: Who are Israelites, whose *is* the adoption, and the glory,
and the covenants, and the giving of the law, and the worship *of*
5 God, and the promises: Whose *are* the fathers, and from whom,
according to the flesh, Christ *came*, who is over all, God blessed
6 for ever. Not as if the word of God had fallen to the ground; for
7 all *are* not Israel, who are of Israel. Neither because they are the
seed of Abraham, *are they* all children, but, *In Isaac shall thy seed
8 be called: That is, not the children of the flesh *are* the children

---

ar3 full of God. As if he had said, I could wish to suffer in their stead; yea, to
be an anathema from Christ in their place. In how high a sense he wished this,
who can tell, unless himself had been asked, and had resolved the question? Cer
tainly he did not then consider himself at all, but only others, and the glory of
God. The thing could not be; yet the wish was pious and solid; though with a
tacit condition, if it were right and possible.

4. *Whose is the adoption,* &c.—He enumerates six prerogatives, of which the
first pair respect God the Father, the second Christ, the third the Holy Ghost.
The adoption and the glory—That is, Israel is the first-born child of God, and the
God of glory is their God, Deut. iv, 7; Psa. cvi, 20. These are relative to each
other. At once God is the Father of Israel, and Israel are the people of God.
He speaks not here of the ark, or any corporeal thing. God himself is the glory
of his people Israel. *And the covenants, and the giving of the law*—The covenant
was given long before the law. It is termed covenants, (in the plural,) because it
was so often and so variously repeated; and because there were two dispositions
of it, Gal. iv, 24, frequently called two covenants: the one promising, the other
exhibiting the promise. *And the worship and the promises*—The true way of
worshipping God; and all the promises made to the fathers.

5. To the preceding St. Paul now adds two more prerogatives: theirs *are*
the fathers—The patriarchs and holy men of old, yea, the Messiah himself.
Who is over all, God blessed for ever—The original words imply, the self-exist-
ent, independent Being, who was, is, and is to come: over all, the Supreme; as
being God, and, consequently, blessed for ever. No words can more clearly
express his Divine, supreme majesty, and his gracious sovereignty both over
Jews and Gentiles.

6. *Not as if*—The Jews imagined that the word of God must fail if all their
nation were not saved. This St. Paul now refutes, and proves that the word
itself had foretold their falling away; *the word of God*—The promises of God to
Israel, *had fallen to the ground*—This could not be. Even now, says the apostle,
some enjoy the promises; and hereafter all Israel shall be saved. This is the
sum of the 9th, 10th, and 11th chapters. *For*—Here he enters upon the proof
of it, all are not Israel, *who are of Israel*—The Jews vehemently maintained
the contrary; namely, that all who were born Israelites, and they only, were
the people of God. The former part of this assertion is refuted here, the latter,
ver. 24, &c. The sum is, God accepts all believers, and them only; and this is
no way contrary to his word. Nay, he hath declared in his word, both by
types and by express testimonies, that believers are accepted as the children of
the promise, while unbelievers are rejected, though they are children after the
flesh. *All are not Israel*—Not in the favour of God, who are lineally descended
of Israel.

7. *Neither because they are* lineally *the seed of Abraham*, will it follow that *they*
are all the children of God—This did not hold even in Abraham's own family; and
much less in his remote descendants. But God then said, *In Isaac shall thy seed*
be called—That is, Isaac, not Ishmael, shall be called thy seed; that seed to which
the promise is made.

8. *That is, not the children,* &c.—As if he had said, This is a clear type of
things to come; showing us, that in all succeeding generations, not the children
of the flesh, the lineal descendants of Abraham, *but the children of the pro*
mise—They to whom the promise is made, that is, believers, are the children
of God.

* Gen. xxi, 12.

9 of God, but the children of promise are counted for the seed. For
this *is* the word of the promise, * At this time I will come, and
10 Sarah shall have a son. And not only *this*, but when Rebecca
11 also had conceived by one man, our. father Isaac, *The children*
being not yet born, neither having done any good or evil, (that
the purpose of God according to election might stand, not of works,
12 but of him that called,) It was said to her, † The elder shall serve
13 the younger. As it is written, ‡ I have loved Jacob, and hated
Esau.
14   What shall we say then? *Is there* injustice with God? God
15 forbid. For he saith to Moses, § I will have mercy on whom I
will have mercy, and I will have compassion on whom I will have
16 compassion. *It is* not therefore of him that willeth, nor of him
17 that runneth, but of God that showeth mercy. Moreover, the

---

9. *For this is the word of promise*—By the power of which Isaac was conceived, and not by the power of nature. Not whosoever is born of thee shall be
blessed, but *at this time*—Which I now appoint, *I will come, and Sarah shall have
a son*—And he shall inherit the blessing.
    10. *And* that God's blessing does not belong to all the descendants of Abraham,
appears not only by this instance, but by that of Esau and Jacob, who was chosen
to inherit the blessing before either of them had done good or evil. The apostle
mentions this to show that neither were their ancestors accepted through any
merit of their own. *That the purpose of God according to election might stand*—
Whose purpose was to elect or choose the promised seed, not of works, not for
any preceding merit in him he chose; but of him that called of his own good
pleasure, who called to that privilege whom he saw good.
    12. *The elder*—Esau, *shall serve the younger*—Not in person, for he never did,
but in his posterity. Accordingly the Edomites were often brought into subjection
by the Israelites.
    13. *As it is written*—With which word in Genesis, spoken so long before, that
of Malachi agrees; I have loved Jacob with a peculiar love; that is, the Israelites, the posterity of Jacob; and I have comparatively hated Esau, that is, the
Edomites, the posterity of Esau. But observe, 1. This does not relate to the
person of Jacob or Esau. 2. Nor does it relate to the eternal state either of
them or their posterity. Thus far the apostle has been proving his proposition,
namely, that the exclusion of a great part of the seed of Abraham, yea, and of
Isaac, from the special promises of God, was so far from being impossible, that,
according to the Scriptures themselves, it had actually happened. He now introduces and refutes an objection.
    14. *Is there injustice with God?*—Is it unjust in God to give Jacob the blessing
rather than Esau? Or to accept believers, and them only? *God forbid*—In nowise: this is well consistent with justice; for he has a right to fix the terms
on which he will show mercy, according to his declaration to Moses, petitioning
for all the people, after they had committed idolatry with the golden calf, *I will
have mercy on whom I will have mercy*—According to the terms I myself have
fixed; and I will have compassion on whom I will have compassion; namely
on those only who submit to my terms, who accept of it in the way that I have
appointed.
    16. *It*—The blessing, *therefore, is not of him that willeth, nor of him that run-
neth*—It is not the effect either of the will or the works of man, but of the grace
and power of God. The will of man is here opposed to the grace of God, and
man's running, to the Divine operation. And this general declaration respects
not only Isaac and Jacob, and the Israelites in the time of Moses, but likewise
all the spiritual children of Abraham, even to the end of the world.
    17. *Moreover*—God has an indisputable right to reject those who will not
accept the blessings on his own terms. And this he exercised in the case of
Pharaoh: to whom, after many instances of stubbornness and rebellion, he said

* Gen. xviii, 10.   † Gen. xxv, 23   ‡ Mal. i, 2, 3.   § Exod. xxxiii, 19.

Scripture saith to Pharaoh, * For this very thing have I raised thee up, that I may show my power in thee, and that my name may 18 be declared through all the earth. So then he hath mercy on 19 whom he willeth, and whom he willeth he hardeneth. But thou wilt say to me, Why doth he still find fault? For who hath resist- 20 ed his will? Nay, but who art thou, O man, that repliest against God! Shall the thing formed say to him that formed it, Why 21 hast thou made me thus? † Hath not the potter power over the clay, out of the same mass to make one vessel to honour, and

---

(as it is recorded in Scripture,) *For this very thing have I raised thee up*—That is, unless thou repent, this will surely be the consequence of my raising thee up, making thee a great and glorious king, that my power will be shown upon thee, (as indeed it was by overwhelming him and his army in the sea,) *and my name declared through all the earth*—As it is at this day. Perhaps this may have a still farther meaning. It seems that God was resolved to show his power over the river, the insects, other animals, (with the natural causes of their health, diseases, life, and death,) over meteors, the air, the sun, all of which were worshipped by the Egyptians, from whom other nations learned their idolatry, and at once over all their gods, by that terrible stroke, of slaying all their priests, and their choicest victims, the first born of man and beast: and all this with a design not only to deliver his people Israel, for which a single act of Omnipotence would have sufficed, but to convince the Egyptians, that the objects of their worship were but the creatures of Jehovah, and entirely in his power, and to draw them and the neighbouring nations, who should hear of all these wonders, from their idolatry, to worship the one God. For the execution of this design, in order to the display of the Divine power over the various objects of their worship, in a variety of wonderful acts, which were at the same time just punishments for their cruel oppression of the Israelites, God was pleased to raise to the throne of an absolute monarchy a man, not whom he had *made* wicked on purpose, but whom he found so, the proudest, the most daring and obstinate of all the Egyptian princes; and who, being incor- .igible, well deserved to be set up in that situation where the Divine judgments fell the heaviest.

18. *So then*—That is, accordingly he does show mercy on his own terms; namely, on them that believe: *and whom he willeth*—Namely, them that believe not, *he hardeneth*—Leaves to the hardness of their hearts.

19. *Why doth he still find fault*—The particle *still* is strongly expressive of the objector's sour, morose murmuring: *for who hath resisted his will?*—The word *his* likewise expresses his surliness and aversion to God, whom he does not even deign to name.

20. *Nay, but who art thou, O man!*—Little, impotent, ignorant *man, that repliest against God?*—That accusest God of injustice, for himself fixing the terms on which *he will show mercy? Shall the thing formed say to him that formed it, Why hast thou made me thus?*—Why hast thou made me capable of honour and immortality only by believing?

21. *Hath not the potter power over the clay*—And much more hath not God power over his creatures, to appoint one vessel, namely, the believer, *to honour*, and another, the unbeliever, *to dishonour.*

If we survey the right which God has over us in a more general way, with regard to his intelligent creatures, God may be considered in two different views, as Creator, Proprietor, and Lord of all, or as their moral Governor and Judge.

God, as sovereign Lord and Proprietor of all, dispenses his gifts or favours to his creatures with perfect wisdom; but by no rules or methods of proceeding that we are acquainted with. The time when we shall exist, the country where we shall live, our parents, our constitution of body and turn of mind: these, and numberless other circumstances, are doubtless ordered with perfect wisdom, but by rules that lie quite out of our sight.

* Exod. ix, 16.   † Jer. xviii, 6, 7.

22 another to dishonour? What if God being willing to show *his*
wrath, and to make his power known, *yet* endured with much long
23 suffering the vessels of wrath fitted for destruction? And that
he might make known the riches of his glory on the vessels of
24 mercy, whom he had before prepared for glory? Even us whom
25 he hath called, not only of the Jews, but also of the Gentiles: As
he saith also in Hosea, * I will call them my people, who were
26 not my people, and her beloved who was not beloved. † And it
shall come to pass, in the place where it was said to them, Ye *are*
not my people, there shall they be called the sons of the living God.
27 But Isaiah crieth concerning Israel, ‡ Though the number of the
children of Israel be as the sand of the sea, the remnant *only* shall
28 be saved. For he is finishing and cutting short *his* account in
righteousness; for the Lord will make a short account upon earth.
29 And as Isaiah had said before, Unless the Lord of hosts had left us
a seed, we had been as Sodom, and had been made like Gomorrah.

But God's methods of dealing with us, as our Governor and Judge, are clearly
revealed and perfectly known; namely, that he will finally reward every man
according to his works: *he that believeth shall be saved, and he that believeth not
shall be damned.*

Therefore, though *he hath mercy on whom he willeth, and whom he willeth he
hardeneth,* (that is, suffers to be hardened in consequence of their obstinate
wickedness,) yet his is not the will of an arbitrary, capricious, or tyrannical
being. He wills nothing but what is infinitely wise and good; and therefore his
will is a most proper rule of judgment. He *will* show mercy, as he hath assured
us, to none but true believers, nor harden any but such as obstinately refuse
his mercy.

22. *What if God being willing*—(referring to ver. 18, 19.) That is, although
t was now his will, because of their obstinate unbelief, *to show his wrath*, which
necessarily presupposes sin, *and to make his power known*—this is repeated from
the 17th verse; *yet endured*—As he did *Pharaoh with much long suffering*—Which
should have led them to repentance; *the vessels of wrath*—Those who had moved
his wrath by still rejecting his mercy; *fitted for destruction*—By their own wilful
and final impenitence: is there any injustice in this?

23. *That he might make known*—What if by showing such long suffering even
to the vessels of wrath, he did more abundantly show the greatness of his glorious
goodness, wisdom, and power, on the vessels of mercy; on those whom he had
himself by his grace prepared for glory: is this any injustice?

24. *Even us*—Here the apostle comes to another proposition; of grace free
for all, whether Jew or Gentile: *of the Jews*—This he treats of, ver. 25. *Of the
Gentiles*—Treated of in the same verse.

25. *Beloved*—As a spouse; *who once was not beloved*—Consequently, not unconditionally elected. This relates directly to the final restoration of the Jews.

26. *There they shall be called the sons of God*—So that they need not leave
their own country and come to Judea.

27. *But Isaiah* testifies, That, (as many Gentiles will be accepted, so) many
Jews will be rejected: that out of all the thousands of Israel, *a remnant* only
shall be saved. This was spoken originally of the few that were saved from the
ravage of Sennacherib's army.

28. *For he is finishing* or *cutting short the account*—In rigorous justice, will
leave but a small remnant. There will be so general a destruction, that but a
small number will escape.

29. *As Isaiah had said before,* (namely, chap. i, 9, concerning those who were
besieged in Jerusalem by Rezin and Pekah,) *Unless the Lord had left us a seed*—
Which denotes, 1. The present paucity; 2. The future abundance: *we had been
as Sodom*, so that it is no unexampled thing for the main body of the Jewish
nation to revolt from God, and perish in their sin.

* Hosea ii, 22.   † Hosea i, 10.   ‡ Isaiah x, 22, 23.

30 What shall we say then? That the Gentiles who followed not after
righteousness, have attained to righteousness, even the righteous-
31 ness which is by faith: But Israel, following after the law of right-
32 eousness, hath not attained to the law of righteousness. Wherefore? because they *sought it* not by faith but as it were by works.
33 for they stumbled at the stumbling-stone; As it is written, * Behold,
I lay in Sion a stone of stumbling, and a rock of offence: and
† every one that believeth shall not be ashamed.

X. Brethren, the desire of my heart, and my prayer to God for
2 Israel is, that they may be saved. For I bear them record, that
they have a zeal for God, but not according to knowledge,
3 for they being ignorant of the righteousness of God, and seeking
to establish their own righteousness, have not submitted to the
4 righteousness of God. For Christ *is* the end of the law for right-
5 eousness to every one that believeth. For Moses describeth the
righteousness which is by the law, ‡ The man who doth these
6 things shall live by them. But the righteousness which is by faith
speaketh thus; § Say not in thy heart, who shall ascend into

30. *What shall we say then?*—What is to be concluded from all that has been
said, but this, *that the Gentiles who followed not after righteousness*—Who a while
ago had no knowledge of, no care or thought about it, *have attained to righteousness,* (or justification,) *even the righteousness which is by faith.* This is the first
conclusion we may draw from the preceding observations. The second is, That
Israel, the Jews, although *following after the law of righteousness*—The law
which, duly used, would have led them to faith, and thereby to righteousness, *have
not attained to the law of righteousness*—To that righteousness or justification
which is one great end of the law.

32. And *wherefore* have they not? Is it because God eternally decreed they
should not? there is nothing like this to be met with; but agreeable to his argument, the apostle gives us this good reason for it, Because they sought it not by
faith, whereby alone it could be attained; but as it were, in effect, if not pro-
fessedly, by works. For they stumbled at that stumbling-stone, Christ crucified.

33. *As it is written*—Foretold by their own prophet, *Behold, I lay in Sion*—I
exhibit in my Church, what, though it was in truth the only sure foundation of
happiness, yet will be in fact a *stumbling-stone and rock of offence*—An occasion
of ruin to many, through their obstinate unbelief.

X. *My prayer to God is, that they may be saved*—He would not have prayed
for this, had they been absolutely reprobated.

2. *They have a zeal, but not according to knowledge*—They had zeal without
knowledge. We have knowledge without zeal.

3. *For they being ignorant of the righteousness of God*—Of the method God has
established for the justification of a sinner, *and seeking to establish their own
righteousness*—Their own method of acceptance with God, *have not submitted to
the righteousness of God*—The way of justification which he hath fixed.

4. *For Christ is the end of the law*—The scope and aim of it. It is the very
design of the law to bring men to believe in Christ for justification and salvation
And he alone gives that pardon and life which the law shows the want of, but
cannot give. To every one, whether Jew or Gentile, treated of ver. 11, &c.
that believeth, treated of ver. 5, &c.

5. *For Moses describeth the* only *righteousness* which is attainable *by the law,*
when he saith, *The man who doeth these things shall live by them*—That is, he
that perfectly keeps all these precepts in *every* point, he alone may claim life and
salvation by them. But this way of justification is impossible to any, who have
ever transgressed any one law in *any* point.

6. *But the righteousness which is by faith*—The method of becoming righteous
by believing, speaketh a very different language, and may be considerd as ex-

7 heaven? (that is, to bring Christ down:) Or who shall descend into
8 the abyss? (that is, to bring Christ again from the dead.)   But
   what saith he?   The word is nigh thee, *even* in thy mouth, and in
9 thy heart; that is, the word of faith which we preach: That if thou
   confess with thy mouth the Lord Jesus, and believe in thy heart
10 that God raised him from the dead, thou shalt be saved.   For
   with the heart man believeth to righteousness, and with the mouth
   confession is made to salvation.
11   For the Scripture saith, * Every one that believeth on him shall
12 not be ashamed.   For there is no difference between the Jew and
    the Greek: for the same Lord of all is rich to all that call upon
13 him.   For † whosoever shall call upon the name of the Lord
14 shall be saved.   But how shall they call on him, in whom they
    have not believed?   And how shall they believe in him, of whom
    they have not heard?   And how shall they hear without a preacher?
15 But how shall they preach, unless they be sent?   As it is written,
    ‡ How beautiful *are* the feet of them who bring the good tidings of
    peace, who bring the glad tidings of good things!
16   But all have not obeyed the Gospel.   For Isaiah saith, § Lord,
17 who hath believed our report?   Faith then *cometh* by hearing, and
18 hearing by the word of God.   But I say, Have they not heard?
    Yes, verily; ‖ their voice is gone into all the earth, and their words
19 to the ends of the world.   But I say, Hath not Israel known? First,

pressing itself thus: (to accommodate to our present subject the words which
Moses spake, touching the plainness of his law:) *Say not in thy heart, Who shall
ascend into heaven,* as if it were, *to bring Christ down: or, who shall descend into
the grave,* as if it were, *to bring him again from the dead.*   Do not imagine that
these things are to be done *now,* in order to procure thy pardon and salvation.

8. *But what saith he?* (*Moses*)—Even these words, so remarkably applicable
to the subject before us.   All is done ready to thy hand.   *The word is nigh thee*—
Within thy reach; easy to be understood, remembered, practised.   This is emi
nently true of the word of faith, the Gospel, which we preach: the sum of which
is, If thy heart believe in Christ, and thy life confess him, thou shalt be saved.

9. *If thou confess with thy mouth*—Even in time of persecution, when such a
confession may send thee to the lions.

10. *For with the heart*—Not the understanding only, *man believeth to righteousness*—So as to obtain justification: *and with the mouth confession is made,* so as
to obtain final salvation.   Confession here implies the whole of outward, as believing does the root of all inward religion.

12. *The same Lord of all is rich*—So that his blessings are never to be exhausted, nor is he ever constrained to hold his hand.   The great truth proposed
in the 11th verse, is so repeated here, and in the 13th, and farther confirmed
ver. 14, 15, as not only to imply, that whosoever calleth upon him shall be saved;
but also that the will of God is, that all should savingly call upon him.

15. *But how shall they preach unless they be sent?*—Thus by a chain of reasoning, from God's will, that the Gentiles also should call upon him, St. Paul infers,
that the apostles were sent by God to preach to the Gentiles also.   *The feet*—
Their very footsteps, their coming.

17. *Faith*—indeed ordinarily cometh by hearing, even by hearing the word of
God.

18. *But* their unbelief was not owing to the want of hearing.   For they *have
heard.   Yes verily*—So many nations have already heard the preachers of the Gospel, that I may in some sense say of them as David did of the lights of heaven.

19. *But hath not Israel known?*—They might have known, even from Moses

        * Isaiah xxviii, 16.   † Joel ii, 32   ‡ Isaiah lii, 7.   § Isaiah liii, 1.
                              ‖ Psalm xix, 4.

Moses saith, *I will provoke you to jealousy by *them that are* not
20 a nation; by a foolish nation I will anger you. But Isaiah is very
bold, and saith, †I was found by them that sought me not: I was
21 made manifest to them that asked not after me. Whereas with
regard to Israel he saith, All the day have I stretched forth my
hands to an unbelieving and gainsaying people.

XI. I say then, Hath God rejected his people? God forbid. For
I also am an Israelite, of the seed of Abraham, of the tribe of
2 Benjamin. God hath not rejected his people whom he foreknew.
Know ye not what the Scripture saith of Elijah? how he pleadeth
3 with God against Israel: ‡Lord, they have killed thy prophets,
and digged down thy altars; and I am left alone, and they seek
4 my life. But what saith the answer of God to him? I have reserved to myself seven thousand men who have not bowed the
5 knee to Baal. And so likewise at the present time, there is a
6 remnant, according to the election of grace. But if by grace, then
it is no more of works: else grace is no longer grace. And if *it
be* of works, then it is no more grace; else work is no longer work.
7 What then? Israel hath not obtained that which he seeketh, but
8 the election hath obtained, and the rest were blinded: According
as it is written, §God hath given them a spirit of slumber, eyes
that they should not see, and ears that they should not hear, unto

and Isaiah, that many of the Gentiles would be received, and many of the
Jews rejected. *I will provoke you to jealousy by them that are not a nation*—As
they followed gods that were not gods, so he accepted in their stead a nation
that was not a nation, that is, a nation that was not in covenant with God. *A
foolish nation*—Such are all who know not God.

20. *But Isaiah is very bold*—And speaks plainly what Moses but intimated.

21. *An unbelieving and gainsaying people*—Just opposite to those, who believed
with their hearts, and made confession with their mouths.

XI. 1. *Hath God rejected his* whole *people*—All Israel! In no wise. Now
there is a remnant who believe, ver. 5. And hereafter all Israel will be
saved, ver. 26.

2. *God hath not rejected* that part of *his people whom he foreknew*—Speaking
after the manner of men. For in fact knowing and foreknowing are the same
thing with God, who knows or sees all things at once from everlasting to everlasting. *Know ye not*—That in a parallel case, amidst a general apostasy, when
Elijah thought the whole nation was fallen into idolatry, God knew there was a
remnant of true worshippers?

4. *To Baal*—Nor to the golden calves.

5. *According to the election of grace*—According to that gracious purpose of
God, He that believeth shall be saved.

6. *And if by grace, then it is no more of works*—Whether ceremonial or moral
else grace is no longer grace—The very nature of grace is lost. *And if it be of
works, then it is no more grace : else work is no longer work*—But the very nature
of it is destroyed. There is something so absolutely inconsistent, between the
being justified by grace, and the being justified by works, that if you suppose
either, you of necessity exclude the other. For what is given to works is the
payment of a debt; whereas grace implies an unmerited favour. So that the same
benefit cannot, in the very nature of things, be derived from both.

7. *What then?*—What is the conclusion from the whole? It is this: That
Israel in general hath not attained justification: but those of them only who be
lieve; *and the rest were blinded*—By their own wilful prejudice.

8. *God hath* at length withdrawn his Spirit, and so given them up to a spirit of
slumber; which is fulfilled unto this day.

* Deut. xxxii, 21.   † Isaiah lxv, 1, 2.   ‡ 1 Kings xix, 10.   § Isaiah xxix, 10.

9 this day.   And David saith, * Let their table become a snare, and a
10 trap, and a stumbling block, and a recompense to them., Let their
   eyes be darkened that they may not see, and bow down their back
11 alway.   I say then, Have they stumbled so as to fall ? God forbid.
   But by their fall salvation *is come* to the Gentiles, to provoke them
12 to jealousy.   But if their fall *be* the riches of the world, and their
   loss the riches of the Gentiles, how much more their fulness ?
13 For I speak to you Gentiles, as I am the apostle of the Gentiles :
14 I magnify my office : If by any means I may provoke to jealousy
15 *those who are* my flesh, and save some of them.   For if the casting away of them *be* the reconciling of the world, what *will* the
16 receiving *of them be*, but life from the dead ?   For if the first fruits
   be holy, so *is* the lump : and if the root *be* holy, so *are* the branches.
17 And if some of the branches were broken off, and thou being a
   wild olive tree wert grafted in among them, and with them par-
18 takest of the root and fatness of the olive tree, Boast not against
   the branches, but if thou boast, thou bearest not the root, but the
19 root thee.   Wilt thou say then, The branches were broken off, that I
20 might be grafted in ?   Well ; they were broken off for unbelief,

---

9. *And David saith*—In that prophetic imprecation, which is applicable to
them, as well as to Judas ; *a recompense*—Of their preceding wickedness.   So sin
is punished by sin.   And thus the Gospel, which should have fed and strengthened
their souls, is become a means of destroying them.

11. *Have they stumbled so as to fall*—Totally or finally ?   No, but by their fall
(or slip ; it is a very soft word in the original) salvation is come to the Gentiles.
See an instance of this, Acts xiii, 46.   *To provoke them*—The Jews themselves,
to jealousy.

12. The first part of this verse is treated of ver. 13, &c, the latter, how much
more their fulness, that is, their full conversion, ver. 23, &c.

So many prophecies refer to this grand event, that it is surprising any
Christian can doubt of it.   And these are greatly confirmed by the wonderful
preservation of the Jews as a distinct people to this day.   When it is accomplished, it will be so strong a demonstration, both of the Old and New Testament revelation, as will doubtless convince many thousand deists, in countries
nominally Christian ; of whom there will of course be increasing multitudes
among merely nominal Christians.   And this will be a means of swiftly propagating the Gospel among Mohammedans and pagans : who would probably have
received it long ago, had they conversed only with real Christians.

13. *I magnify my office*—Far from being ashamed of ministering to the Gentiles, I glory therein : the rather, as it may be a means of provoking my brethren
to jealousy.

14. *My flesh--*My kinsmen.

15. *Life from the dead*—Overflowing life to the world, which was dead.

16. And this will surely come to pass.   *For if the first fruits be holy, so is the
lump*—The consecration of them was esteemed the consecration of all.   And so
the conversion of a few Jews is an earnest of the conversion of all the rest.
And if the root be holy—The patriarchs from whom they spring, surely God will
at length make their descendants also holy.

17. *Thou*—O Gentile, *being a wild olive tree*—Had the graft been nobler than
the stock, yet its dependence on it for life and nourishment would leave it no
room to boast against it.   How much less, when, contrary to what is practised
among men, the wild olive tree is ingrafted on the good.

18. *Boast not against the branches*—Do not they do this, who despise the Jews ?
or deny their future conversion ?

20. *They were broken off for unbelief and thou standest by faith*—Both conditionally, not absolutely ; if absolutely, there might have been room to boast ; *by
faith--*The free gift of God, which therefore ought to humble thee.

* Psalm lxix, 22, 23.

21 and thou standeth by faith : Be not high minded, but fear. For if
God spared not the natural branches, *take heed* lest he also spare
22 not thee. Behold therefore the goodness and the severity of God!
Toward them that fell, severity ; but toward thee, goodness, if thou
23 continue in his goodness ; else shalt thou also be cut off. And
they, if they do not continue in unbelief, shall be grafted in ; for
24 God is able to graft them in again. For if thou wert cut off from
the natural wild olive tree, and grafted contrary to nature into a
good olive tree ; how much more shall these, who are natural
25 *branches*, be grafted into their own olive tree ? Brethren, I would
not that ye should be ignorant of this mystery, (lest ye should be
wise in your own conceits,) that hardness is in part happened to
26 Israel, till the fulness of the Gentiles be come in ; And so all Israel
shall be saved, as it is written, * The Deliverer shall come out of
27 Sion, and shall turn away iniquity from Jacob. And this *is* my
28 covenant with them, when I shall take away their sins. With regard to the Gospel, *they are* enemies for your sake ; but as for the
29 election, *they are* beloved, for the sake of their fathers. For the
30 gifts and the calling of God *are* without repentance. As then ye
were once disobedient to God, but have now obtained mercy through
31 their disobedience : So these also have now been disobedient, that
32 through your mercy they may likewise find mercy. For God hath
shut up all together in disobedience, that he might have mercy
33 upon all. O the depth of the riches, and wisdom, and knowledge

---

21. *Be not high minded, but fear*—We may observe, this fear is not opposed
to trust, but to pride and security.

22. *Else shalt thou*—Also, who now standest by faith, be both totally and
finally cut off.

24. *Contrary to nature*—For according to nature, we graft the fruitful branch
into the wild stock; but here the wild branch is grafted into the fruitful stock.

25. St. Paul calls any truth, known but to a few, a mystery. Such had been
the calling of the Gentiles. Such was now the conversion of the Jews. *Lest
ye should be wise in your own conceits*—Puffed up with your present advantages:
dreaming that ye are the only Church; or that the Church of Rome cannot fail.
Hardness in part has happened to Israel, till—Israel therefore is neither totally
nor finally rejected : *the fulness of the Gentiles be come in*—Till there be a vast
harvest among the heathens.

26. *And so all Israel shall be saved*—Being convinced by the coming in of the
Gentiles. But there will be a still larger harvest among the Gentiles, when all
Israel is come in. *The Deliverer shall come*—Yea, the Deliverer is come ; but
not the full fruit of his coming.

28. *They are now enemies*—To the Gospel, to God, and to themselves, which
God permits for your sake : *but as for the election*—That part of them who believe, they are beloved.

29. *For the gifts and the calling of God are without repentance*—God does not
repent of his gifts to the Jews, or his calling of the Gentiles.

32. *For God hath shut up all together in disobedience*—Suffering each in their
turn to revolt from him. First, God suffered the Gentiles in the early age to
revolt, and took the family of Abraham as a peculiar seed to himself. Afterward
he permitted them to fall through unbelief, and took in the believing Gentiles
And he did even this to provoke the Jews to jealousy, and so bring them also in
the end to faith. This was truly a mystery in the Divine conduct, which the
apostle adores with such holy astonishment.

33. *O the depth of the riches, and wisdom, and knowledge of God!*—In the 9th
chapter St. Paul had sailed but in a narrow sea ; now he is in the ocean. The

* Isaiah lix, 20.

of God! How unsearchable *are* his judgments and his ways past
34 tracing out! For * who hath known the mind of the Lord? Or who
35 hath been his counsellor? Who hath first given to him, and it
36 shall be repaid him again? For of him, and through him, and to him
are all things: to him *be* glory for ever! Amen.

XII. I exhort you therefore, brethren, by the tender mercies of
God, to present your bodies unto God, a living sacrifice, holy,
2 acceptable, *which is* your reasonable service. And be not conformed to this world, but be ye transformed by the renewing of
your mind, that ye may prove what *is* that good, and acceptable,
3 and perfect will of God. And I say, through the grace which is
given to me, to every one that is among you, not to think *of himself* above what he ought to think, but to think soberly, according
4 as God hath distributed to every one the measure of faith. For as

depth of the riches is described, ver. 35, the depth of wisdom, ver. 34, the depth
of knowledge in the latter part of this verse. Wisdom directs all things to the
best end; knowledge sees that end. *How unsearchable are his judgments*—
With regard to unbelievers, *his ways*—With regard to believers! His ways are
more upon a level, his judgments a great deep. But even his ways we cannot
trace.

34. *Who hath known the mind of the Lord*—Before or any farther than he has
revealed it.

35. *Given to him*—Either wisdom or power?

36. *Of him*—as the Creator; *through him*, as the Preserver: *to him*, as the ultimate End, are all things. To him be the glory of his riches, wisdom, knowledge.
Amen! A concluding word in which the affection of the apostle when it is
come to the height shuts up all.

XII. 1. *I exhort you*—St. Paul uses to suit his exhortations to the doctrines
he has been delivering. So here the general use from the whole is contained in
the first and second verses. The particular uses follow, from the third verse to
the end of the epistle. *By the tender mercies of God*—The whole sentiment is
derived from chapters i–v. The expression itself is particularly opposed to the
wrath of God, chap. i, 18. It has a reference here to the entire Gospel, to the
whole economy of grace or mercy, delivering us from the wrath of God, and ex-
citing us to all duty. *To present*—(So chap. vi, 13; xvi, 19;) now actually to
exhibit before God, *your bodies*—That is, yourselves; a part is put for the whole;
the rather, as in the ancient sacrifices, of beasts, the body was the whole. These
also are particularly named, in opposition to that vile abuse of their bodies, mentioned chap. i, 24. Several expressions follow, which have likewise a direct reference to other expressions in the same chapter; *a sacrifice*—Dead to sin, and
living—By that life, which is mentioned chap. i, 17, chap. vi, 4, &c. *Holy*—
Such as the holy law requires, chap. vii, 12. Acceptable, chap. viii, 8, *which is
your reasonable service*—The worship of the heathens was utterly unreasonable,
chap. i, 18, &c; so was the glorying of the Jews, chap. ii, 3, &c. But a Christian
acts in all things by the highest reason, from the mercy of God inferring his
own duty.

2. *And be not conformed*—Neither in judgment, spirit, nor behaviour; *to this
world*—Which neglecting the will of God, entirely follows its own; *that ye may
prove*—Know by sure trial: which is easily done by him who has thus presented
himself to God, *what is that good, and acceptable, and perfect will of God*—The
will of God is here to be understood of all the preceptive part of Christianity,
which is in itself so excellently good, so acceptable to God, and so perfective of
our natures.

3. *And I say*—He now proceeds to show what that will of God is: *through
the grace which is given to me*—He modestly adds this, lest he should seem to
forget his own direction; *to every one that is among you*—Believers at Rome.
Happy, had they always remembered this! *The measure of faith*—(Treated of in
the first and following chapters) from which all other gifts and graces flow.

* Isaiah xl. 13.

ın one body we have many members, and all members have not
5 the same office, So we being many are one body in Christ, and
6 every one members of each other.   Having then gifts differing according to the grace that is given us, whether *it be* prophecy, *let*
7 *us prophesy* according to the analogy of faith : Or ministry, *let us
wait* on our ministering ; or he that teacheth on teaching ; or he
8 that exhorteth, on exhortation.   He that imparteth, *let him do it*
with simplicity ; he that presideth, with diligence ; he that showeth
mercy, with cheerfulness.
9   *Let* love *be* without dissimulation.   Abhor that which is evil,
10 cleave to that which is good.   In brotherly love be full of tender
affection toward each other, in honour preferring one another :
11 Not slothful in business, fervent in spirit, serving the Lord : R٤
12 joice in hope, be patient in tribulation, continue instant in prayer.
13 Communicate to the necessities of the saints, pursue hospitality.
14 Bless them who persecute you ; bless and curse not.   Rejoice
15 with them that rejoice, and weep with them that weep.   Agree

5. *So we*—All believers, *are one body*—Closely connected together in Christ,
and consequently ought to be helpful to each other.
6. *Having then gifts differing according to the grace which is given us*—Gifts
are various : grace is one : *whether it be prophecy*—This, considered as an extraordinary gift, is that whereby heavenly mysteries are declared to men, or things
to come foretold.   But it seems here to mean the ordinary gift of expounding
Scripture : *let us prophesy according to the analogy of faith*—St. Peter expresses
it, as the oracles of God : according to the general tenor of them ; according to
that grand scheme of doctrine which is delivered therein, touching original sin,
justification by faith, and present, inward salvation.   There is a wonderful analogy between all these ; and a close and intimate connection between the chief
heads of that faith which was once delivered to the saints.   Every article therefore, concerning which there is any question, should be determined by this rule :
every doubtful scripture interpreted, according to the grand truths which run
through the whole.
7. *Ministering*—As deacons.   He that teacheth catechumens, for whom particular instructers were appoined.   *He that exhorteth*—Whose peculiar business
it was to urge Christians to duty, and to comfort them in trials.
8. *He that presideth*—That hath the care of a flock.   *He that showeth mercy*—
In any instance, *with cheerfulness*—Rejoicing that he hath such an opportunity.
9. Having spoken of faith and its fruit, ver. 3, &c, he comes now to love.
The 9th, 10th, and 11th verses refer to chapter the seventh ; the 12th verse to
chapter the eighth : the 13th verse, of communicating to the saints, whether Jews
or Gentiles, to chapter the ninth, &c.   Part of the 16th verse is repeated from
chap. xi, 25.   *Abhor that which is evil ; cleave to that which is good*—Both inwardly and outwardly, whatever ill will or danger may follow.
10. *In honour preferring one another*—Which you will do, if you habitually
consider what is good in others, and what is evil in yourselves.
11. Whatsoever ye do, do it with your might.   In every business, diligently
and fervently serving the Lord ; doing all to God, not to man.
12. *Rejoicing in hope*—Of perfect holiness and everlasting happiness.   Hitherto
the apostle has been treating of faith and love ; now of hope also.   (See the 5th
and 8th chapters.)   Afterward, of duties toward others ; saints, ver. 13.   Persecutors, ver. 14.   Friends, strangers, enemies, ver. 15, &c.
13. *Communicate to the necessities of the saints*—Relieve all Christians that are
in want.   It is remarkable, that the apostle, treating expressly of the duties flowing from the communion of saints, yet never says one word about the dead.
Pursue hospitality—Not only embracing those that offer, but seeking opportunities to exercise it.
14. *Curse not*—No, not in your heart.
15. *Rejoice*—The direct opposite to weeping is laughter : but this does not se
well suit a Christian.

16 in the same affection toward each other. Mind not high, but con
17 descend to low things. Be not wise in your own conceit. Render to no man evil for evil. Provide things honest in the sight of
18 all men. If it be possible, as much as lieth in you, live peacea-
19 bly with all men. Dearly beloved, revenge not yourselves, but
rather give place unto wrath; for it is written, * Vengeance *is*
20 mine; I will repay, saith the Lord. Therefore if † thy enemy
hunger, feed him; if he thirst, give him drink; for in so doing
21 thou shalt heap coals of fire upon his head. Be not overcome
with evil, but overcome evil with good.
XIII. Let every soul be subject to the supreme powers, for there
is no power but from God; the powers that be are appointed by
2 God. Whosoever therefore resisteth the power, resisteth the
appointment of God; and they that resist shall receive to them-
3 selves condemnation. For rulers are not a terror to good works,
but to evil. Wouldst thou then not be afraid of the power? Do
that which is good, and thou shalt have praise from it; for he is
4 the servant of God to thee for good. But if thou dost that which
is evil, be afraid; for he beareth not the sword in vain; for he

16. *Mind not high things*—Desire not riches, honour, or the company of the great.
17. *Provide*—Think beforehand; contrive to give as little offence as may be to any.
19. *Dearly beloved*—So he softens the rugged spirit, *revenge not yourselves,* but leave that to God. Perhaps it might more properly be rendered, *Leave room for wrath*—That is, the wrath of God, to whom vengeance properly belongs.
20. *Feed him*—With your own hand: if it be needful, even put bread into his mouth. *Heap coals of fire upon his head*—That part which is most sensible.

" So artists melt the sullen ore of lead,
By heaping coals of fire upon its head:
In the kind warmth the metal learns to glow,
And pure from dross, the silver runs below."

21. And if you see no present fruit, yet persevere. *Be not overcome with evil*—As all are who avenge themselves. *But overcome evil with good*—Conquer your enemies by kindness and patience.
XIII. St. Paul writing to the Romans, whose city was the seat of the empire, speaks largely of obedience to magistrates. And this was also in effect a public apology for the Christian religion. *Let every soul be subject to the supreme pow-ers*—An admonition peculiarly needful for the Jews. Power, in the singular number, is the supreme authority; powers are they who are invested with it. That is more readily acknowledged to be from God than these. The apostle affirms it of both. They are all from God, who constituted all in general, and permits each in particular by his providence. *The powers that be are appointed by God*—It might be rendered, are subordinate to, or orderly disposed under God: implying that they are God's deputies or vicegerents; and, consequently, their authority being in effect his, demands our conscientious obedience.
2. *Whoever resisteth the power*—In any other manner than the laws of the community direct, *shall receive condemnation*—Not only from the magistrate, but from God also.
3. *For rulers are* in the general, notwithstanding some particular excep-tions, a terror to evil works only. *Wouldst thou then not be afraid?*—There is one fear which precedes evil actions, and deters from them: this should always remain. There is another fear which follows evil actions: they who do well a free from this.
4. *The sword*—The instrument of capital punishment which God authorizes um to inflict.

* Deut. xxxii, 35.   † Prov. xxv, 21, &c.

is the servant of God, an avenger for wrath against him that doth
5 evil. Wherefore *ye* must needs be subject, not only for wrath, but
6 also for conscience' sake. For this cause ye pay tribute also :· for
they are the ministers of God, attending continually on this very
7 thing. Render therefore to all their dues : tribute to whom
tribute *is due*, custom to whom custom, fear to whom fear, honour
8 to whom honour. Owe no man any thing, but love one another ;
9 for he that loveth another, hath fulfilled the law. For this, Thou
shalt not commit adultery, thou shalt not kill, thou shalt not steal,
thou shalt not bear false witness, thou shalt not covet, and if *there
be* any other commandment, it is summed up in this saying, Thou
10 shalt love thy neighbour as thyself. Love worketh no evil to *his*
neighbour : therefore love *is* the fulfilling of the law.
11   And *do* this, knowing the season, that *it is* high time now to
awake out of sleep ; for salvation is nearer to us now than when
12 we *first* believed. The night is far spent ; the day is at hand ;
let us therefore put off the works of darkness, and put on the
13 armour of light. Let us walk decently as in the day ; not in banqueting and drunken entertainments ; not in uncleannesses and
14 wantonness, not in strife and envy. But put ye on the Lord Jesus
Christ, and make not provision for the flesh, *to fulfil* the desires
thereof.

5. *Not only for* fear of *wrath*—That is, punishment from man ; *but for conscience' sake*—Out of obedience to God.
6. *For this cause*—Because they are the ministers (officers) of God, for the public good. *This very thing*—The public good.
7. *To all* magistrates ; *tribute*—Taxes on your persons or estates ; *custom*—
For the goods exported or imported ; *fear*—Obedience ; *honour*—Reverence. All
these are due to the supreme power.
8. *From* our duty to magistrates he passes on to general duties. *To love one
another*—An eternal debt which can never be sufficiently discharged. But yet if
this be rightly performed, it discharges all the rest. *For he that loveth another*—
As he ought, *hath fulfilled the* whole *law*—Toward his neighbour.
9. *If there be any other* more particular commandment toward our neighbour,
as there are many in the law, *it is summed up in this*—So that if you was not
thinking of it, yet if your heart was full of love, you would fulfil it.
10. *Therefore love is the fulfilling of the law*—For the same love which restrains
from all evil, incites us to all good.
11. *And do this*—Fulfil the law of love in all the instances above mentioned ;
knowing the season—Full of grace, but hasting away : *that it is high time to awake
out of sleep*—How beautifully is the metaphor carried on ! This life, a night : the
resurrection, the day : the Gospel shining on the heart, the dawn of this day: we
are to awake out of sleep ; to rise up and throw away our night clothes, fit only
for darkness, and put on new. And being soldiers, we are to arm, and prepare
for fight, who are encompassed with so many enemies.
The day dawns, when we receive faith, and then sleep gives place. Then it
is time to rise, to arm, to walk, to work, lest sleep steal upon us again. Final
salvation, glory, is nearer to us now than when we first believed. It is continually advancing, flying forward upon the swiftest wings of time. And that
which remains between the present hour and eternity, is comparatively but a
moment.
13. *Banqueting*—Luxurious, elegant feasts.
14. *But put ye on the Lord Jesus Christ*—Herein is contained the whole of
our salvation. It is a strong and beautiful expression for the most intimate union
with nim, and being clothed with all the graces which were in him. The apostle
does not say, Put on purity and sobriety, peacefulness and benevolence. But he
says all this, and a thousand times more at once, in saying, Put on Christ. *And*

XIV. Him that is weak in the faith, receive; *but* not to doubtful
2 disputations. For one believeth that he may eat all things;
3 'another who is weak, eateth herbs. Let not him that eateth
despise him that eateth not : and let not him that eateth not judge
4 him that eateth; for God hath received him. Who art thou
that judgest another's servant? To his own master he standeth
or falleth. Yea, he shall be upheld; for God is able to uphold
5 him. One man esteemeth one day above another; another esteemeth every day *alike;* let every man be fully persuaded in his
6 own mind. He that regardeth the day, regardeth *it* to the
Lord; and he that regardeth not the day, to the Lord he
doth not regard *it.* He that eateth, eateth to the Lord; for he
giveth God thanks; and he that eateth not, to the Lord he eateth
7 not, and giveth God thanks. For none of us liveth to himself,
and none dieth to himself. But if we live, we live unto the Lord;
8 and if we die, we die unto the Lord. Whether therefore we live
9 or die, we are the Lord's. For to this end Christ both died and
lived, that he might be the Lord both of the dead and of the living.
10 But why dost thou judge thy brother? or why dost thou despise
thy brother? for we shall all stand before the judgment seat of
11 Christ. For it is written, * As I live, saith the Lord, every knee
12 shall bow to me, and every tongue shall confess to God. So then
13 every one of us shall give an account of himself to God. Let us
therefore no longer judge one another; but judge this rather, not
14 to lay a stumbling block or a scandal before a brother. I know,

───────────────

make not provision—To raise foolish desires; or when they are raised already, to
satisfy them.
 XIV. 1. *Him that is weak*—Through needless scruples, *receive*—With all love
and courtesy into Christian fellowship: *but not to doubtful disputations*—About
questionable points.
 2. *All things*—All sorts of food, though forbidden by the law.
 3. *Despise him that edteth not*—As over scrupulous or superstitious. *Judge
him that eateth*—As profane, or taking undue liberties: *for God hath received
him*—Into the number of his children, notwithstanding this.
 5. *One day above another*—As new moons and other Jewish festivals. *Let every
man be fully persuaded*—That a thing is lawful before he does it.
 6. *Regardeth it to the Lord*—That is, out of a principle of conscience toward
God. *To the Lord he doth not regard it*—He also acts from a principle of con.
science. *He that eateth not*—Flesh, *giveth God thanks*—For his herbs.
 7. *None of us*—Christians, in the things we do, *liveth to himself*—Is at his own
disposal; doth his own will.
 10. *Or why dost thou despise thy brother?*—Hitherto the apostle has addressed
the weak brother. Now he speaks to the stronger.
 11. *As I live*—An oath proper to him, because he only possesseth life infinite
and independent. It is Christ who is here termed both Lord and God; as it is
he to whom we live, and to whom we die. *Every tongue shall confess to God*—
Shall own him as their rightful Lord; which shall then only be accomplished in
its full extent. The Lord grant we may find mercy in that day! And may i'
also be imparted to those who have differed from us! Yea, to those who have
censured and condemned us for things which we have done from a desire to please
him, or refused to do, from a fear of offending him.
 13. *But judge this rather* concerning ourselves, *not to lay a stumbling block*—
By moving him to do as thou dost, though against his conscience; *or a scandal*—
Moving him to hate or judge thee.
 4. *I am assured by the Lord Jesus*—Perhaps by a particular revelation, *that*

* Isaiah xlv, 23.

and am assured bv the Lord Jesus, that nothing *is* unclean of itself; but to him that accounteth any thing to be unclean, *it is*
15 unclean. But if thy brother *is* grieved by *thy* meat, thou no longer walkest charitably. Destroy not him by thy meat, for whom
16 Christ died. Therefore let not your good be evil spoken of.
17 For the kingdom of God is not meat and drink, but righteous-
18 ness, and peace, and joy in the Holy Ghost. And he that in these
19 serveth Christ, *is* acceptable to God, and approved by men. Let us therefore pursue the things that tend to peace, and to mutual
20 edification. For meat destroy not the work of God. All things indeed *are* pure : but *it is* evil to that man who eateth with offence
21 *It is* good not to eat flesh, neither to drink wine, nor *to do any* thing whereby thy brother stumbleth, or is offended, or made weak.
22 Hast thou faith? have it to thyself before God. Happy *is* he that
23 condemneth not himself in that thing which he alloweth. But he that doubteth is condemned if he eat, because *it is* not of faith; for whatsoever *is* not of faith is sin.
XV. Therefore we who are strong ought to bear the infirmities
2 of the weak, and not to please ourselves. Let every one of us
3 please *his* neighbour, for *his* good to edification. For Christ pleased not himself; but as it is written, * The reproaches of

---

there is nothing—Neither flesh nor herbs, *unclean of itself*—Unlawful under the Gospel.

15. *If thy brother is grieved*—That is, wounded, led into sin, *destroy not him for whom Christ died*—So we see he for whom Christ died may be destroyed! *with thy meat*—Do not value thy meat more than Christ valued his life.

16. *Let not then your good* and lawful liberty *be evil spoken of*—By being offensive to others.

17. *For the kingdom of God*—That is, true religion, does not consist in external observances; but in righteousness, the image of God stamped on the heart, the love of God and man, accompanied with the peace that passeth all understanding, and joy in the Holy Ghost.

18. *In these*—Righteousness, peace, and joy. *Men*—Wise and good men.

19. *Peace* and *edification* are closely joined. Practical divinity tends equally to peace and to edification. Controversial divinity less directly tends to edification; although sometimes, as they of old, we cannot build without it, Neh. iv, 17.

20. *The work of God*—Which he builds in the soul by faith, and in the Church by concord. *It is evil to that man who eateth with offence*—So as to offend another thereby.

21. *Thy brother stumbleth*—By imitating thee against his conscience, contrary to righteousness; or is offended at what thou dost, to the loss of his peace; or made weak; hesitating between imitation and abhorrence, to the loss of that joy in the Lord which was his strength.

22. *Hast thou faith?*—That all things are pure, *have it to thyself before God*—In circumstances like these, keep it to thyself, and do not offend others by it. *Happy is he that condemneth not himself*—By an improper use of even innocent things. And happy is he who is free from a doubting conscience: he that hath this may allow the thing, yet condemn himself for it.

23. *Because it is not of faith*—He does not believe it lawful. And in all these cases, *whatsoever is not of faith is sin*—Whatever a man does, without a full persuasion of its lawfulness, it is sin to him.

XV. 1. *We who are strong*—Of a clearer judgment, and free from these scruples. *And not to please ourselves*—Without any regard to others.

2. *For his good*—This is a general word; edification is one species of good.

* Psalm lxix. 9
26

4 them that reproached thee, fell upon me. For whatsoever things were written aforetime, were written for our instruction, that we, through patience and consolation of the Scriptures, may have
5 hope. Now the God of patience and consolation give you to think the same thing, *one with another*, according to Christ Jesus,
6 That ye may with one mind *and* one mouth glorify the God and
7 Father of our Lord Jesus Christ. Wherefore receive ye one another, as Christ also hath received you, to the glory of God
8 Now I say, Christ Jesus was a servant of the circumcision, for the truth of God, to confirm the promises *made* to the fathers:
9 And that the Gentiles might glorify God for *his* mercy, as it is written, * For this cause I will confess to thee among the Gen-
10 tiles, and sing unto thy name. And again he saith, † Rejoice, ye
11 Gentiles, with his people. And again, ‡ Praise the Lord, all ye
12 Gentiles, and laud him, all ye people. And again Isaiah saith, § There shall be the root of Jesse, and he that ariseth to rule over
13 the Gentiles: in him shall the Gentiles hope. Now the God of hope fill you with all joy and peace in believing, that ye may abound in hope by the power of the Holy Ghost.
14 And I myself also am persuaded of you, my brethren, that ye likewise are full of goodness, being filled with all knowledge, and
15 able to admonish one another. Nevertheless, brethren, I have written the more boldly to you in some respect, as putting you in
16 mind, because of the grace which is given to me of God, That I

---

3. *But* bore not only the infirmities, but reproaches of his brethren, and so fulfilled that scripture.

4. *Aforetime*—In the Old Testament: *that we through patience and consolation of the Scriptures might have hope*—That through the consolation which God gives us by these, we may have patience and a joyful hope.

5. *According* to the power of Jesus Christ.

6. *That ye*—Both Jews and Gentiles, believing with one mind, and confessing with one mouth.

7. *Receive ye one another*—Weak and strong, with mutual love.

8. *Now I say*—The apostle here shows how Christ received us: *Christ Jesus*—Jesus is the name, Christ the surname. The latter was first known to the Jews, the former to the Gentiles. Therefore he is styled Jesus Christ, when the words stand in the common natural order. When the order is inverted, as here, the office of Christ is more solemnly considered: *was a servant*—Of his Father; *of the circumcision*—For the salvation of the circumcised, the Jews. *For the truth of God*—To manifest the truth and fidelity of God.

9. *As it is written*—In the 18th Psalm, where the Gentiles and Jews are spo. ken of, as joining in the worship o˜ the God of Israel.

12. *There shall be the root of Jesse*—That kings and the Messiah should spring from his house was promised to Jesse before it was to David. *In him shall the Gentiles hope*—Who before had been without hope, Eph. ii, 12.

13. *Now the God of hope*—A glorious title of God; but till now unknown to the heathens, for their goddess *Hope*, like their other idols, was nothing; whose temple at Rome was burnt by lightning. It was indeed built again not long after, but was again burnt to the ground.

14. There are several conclusions of this epistle. The first begins at this verse, the second, chap. xvi, 1; the third, ver. 17; the fourth, ver. 21; and the 5th, ver. 25. *Ye are full of goodness*—By being created anew, *and filled with all knowledge*—By long experience of the things of God: *To admonish*—To in struct, and confirm.

15. *Because of the grace*—That is, because I am an apostle of the Gentiles.

* Psalm xviii, 49.   † Deut. xxxii, 43.   ‡ Psalm cxvii, 1.   § Isaiah xi, 10.

should be the servant of Jesus Christ to the Gentiles, ministering the Gospel of God, that the offering up of the Gentiles may be
17 acceptable, being sanctified by the Holy Ghost. I have therefore whereof to glory, through Jesus Christ, in the things pertaining to
18 God. For I will not dare to speak of any thing which Christ hath not wrought by me, to make the Gentiles obedient, by word and
19 deed, through mighty signs and wonders, by the power of the Spirit of God, so that I have fully preached the Gospel of Christ,
20 from Jerusalem round about, as far as Illyricum : Striving so to preach the Gospel, not where Christ had been named, lest I should
21 build upon another man's foundation. But as it is written, * They to whom he was not spoken of, shall see ; and they that have not
22 heard shall understand. Therefore I was also long hindered from
23 coming to you. But now, having no longer place in these countries, and having had a great desire for many years to come to you,
24 Whenever I go into Spain, I hope to see you as I pass by, and to be brought forward by you in my way thither, if first I may be somewhat satisfied with your *company*.
25 But I am now going to Jerusalem, serving the saints. For it
26 hath pleased them of Macedonia and Achaia to make a contribu
27 tion for the poor of the saints that are in Jerusalem. It hath pleased them, and they are their debtors. For if the Gentiles

---

16. *The offering up of the Gentiles*—As living sacrifices.

17. *I have whereof to glory through Jesus Christ*—All my glorying is in and through him.

18. *By word—by the power of the Spirit, by deed*—Namely, through mighty signs and wonders.

20. *Not where Christ had been named*—These places he generally declined, (though not altogether,) having a holy ambition (so the Greek word means) to make the first proclamation of the Gospel, in places where it was quite unheard of, in spite of all the difficulty and dangers that attended it. *Lest I should build upon another man's foundation*—The providence of God seemed in a special manner, generally, to prevent this, (though not entirely,) lest the enemies of the apostle, who sought every occasion to set light by him, should have had room to say, that he was behind other apostles, not being sufficient for planting of Churches himself, but only for preaching where others had been already ; or that he declined the more difficult part of the ministry.

22. *Therefore I have been long hindered from coming to you*—Among whom Christ had been named.

23. *Having no longer place in these parts*—Where Christ has now been preached in every city.

24. *Into Spain*—Where the Gospel had not yet been preached. *If first I may be somewhat satisfied with your company*—How remarkable is the modesty with which he speaks ? They might rather desire to be satisfied with his. Somewhat satisfied, intimating the shortness of his stay. Or perhaps, that Christ alone can thoroughly satisfy the soul.

26. *The poor of the saints that are in Jerusalem*—It can by no means be inferred from this expression, that the community of goods among the Christians was then ceased. All that can be gathered from it is, that in this time of extreme dearth, (Acts xi, 28, 29,) some of the Church in Jerusalem were in want, the rest being barely able to subsist themselves, but not to supply the necessities of their brethren.

27. *It hath pleased them, and they are their debtors*—That is, they are bound to it, in justice as well as mercy. *Spiritual things*—By the preaching of the Gospel : *carnal things*—Things needful for the body.

* Isaiah liii, 15.

have partaken of their spiritual things, they ought to minister to
28 them in carnal things. When therefore I have performed this, and
29 sealed to them this fruit, I will go by you into Spain. And I know
that when I come to you I shall come in the fulness of the bless-
30 ing of the Gospel of Christ. Now I beseech you, brethren, by
our Lord Jesus Christ, and by the love of the Spirit, to strive to-
31 gether with me, in *your* prayers to God for me, That I may be delivered from the unbelievers in Judea, and that my service at Jeru-
32 salem may be acceptable to the saints: That I may come to you
with joy by the will of God, and may be refreshed together with
33 you. Now the God of peace *be* with you all.
XVI. I commend unto you Phebe our sister, who is a servant of
2 the Church in Cenchrea. That ye may receive her in the Lord, as
becometh saints, and help her in whatsoever business she needeth
you: for she hath been a helper of many, and of myself *also*.
3 Salute Priscilla and Aquila, my fellow labourers in Christ Jesus:
4 Who for my life have laid down their own necks; to whom
not I alone owe my thanks, but likewise all the Churches of the
5 Gentiles. *Salute* also the Church that is in their house. Salute
my beloved Epenetus, who is the first fruits of Asia unto Christ.

---

28. *When I have sealed to them this fruit*—When I have safely delivered to them, as under seal, this fruit of their brethren's love. *I will go by you into Spain* —Such was his design. But it does not appear, that Paul went into Spain. There are often holy purposes in the minds of good men, which are overruled by the providence of God, so as never to take effect. And yet they are precious in the sight of God.

30. *I beseech you—by the love of the Spirit*—That is, by the love which is the genuine fruit of the Spirit. *To strive together with me in your prayers*—He must pray himself, who would have others strive together with him in prayer. Of all the apostles, St. Paul alone is recorded to desire the prayers of the faithful for himself. And this he generally does in the conclusions of his epistles: yet not without making a difference. For he speaks in one manner to them whom he treats as his children, with the gravity or even severity of a father, (such as Timothy, Titus, the Corinthians, and Galatians,) in another, to them whom he treats rather like equals, such as the Romans, Ephesians, Thessalonians, Colossians, Hebrews.

31. 1. *That I may be delivered*—He is thus urgent from a sense of the importance of his life to the Church. Otherwise he would have rejoiced to depart, and to be with Christ. *And that my service may be acceptable*—In spite of all their prejudices; to the end the Jewish and Gentile believers may be knit together in tender love.

32. *That I may come to you*—This refers to the former, *with joy*—To the latter part of the preceding verse.

XVI. *I commend unto you Phebe*—The bearer of this letter. *A servant*—The Greek word is a deaconess, *of the Church in Cenchrea*—In the apostolic age, some grave and pious women were appointed deaconesses in every Church. It was their office not to teach publicly, but to visit the sick, the women in particular, and to minister to them both in their temporal and spiritual necessities.

2. *In the Lord*—That is, for the Lord's sake, and in a Christian manner. St Paul seems fond of this expression.

4. *Who have for my life*, as it were laid down their own necks, that is, exposed themselves to the utmost danger, *but likewise all the Churches of the Gentiles*— Even that at Rome, for preserving so valuable a life.

5. *Salute the Church that is in their house*—Aquila had been driven from Rome in the reign of Claudius, but was now returned, and performed the same part there, which Gaius did at Corinth, chap. xvi, 23. Where any Christian had a large house, there they all assembled together; though as yet the Christians at

6 Salute Mary; who hath bestowed much labour on us. Salute
7 Andronicus and Junius, my kinsmen, and my fellow prisoners,
who are of note among the apostles, who also were in Christ be-
8 fore me. Salute Amplias, my beloved in the Lord. Salute Urba-
9 nus, our fellow labourer in Christ, and my beloved Stachys.
10 Salute Apelles, approved in Christ. Salute those *of the family* of
11 Aristobulus. Salute my kinsman Herodion. Salute those *of the*
12 *family* of Narcissus, who are in the Lord. Salute Tryphena and
Tryphosa, who labour in the Lord. Salute the beloved Persis,
13 who hath laboured much in the Lord. Salute Rufus, chosen in
14 the Lord, and his mother and mine. Salute Asyncritus, Phlegon,
Hermes, Patrobus, Hermas, and the brethren who are with them.
15 Salute Philologus and Julias, Nereus and his sister, and Olympas,
16 and all the saints that are with them. Salute one another with a
holy kiss. The Churches of Christ salute you.
17   Now I beseech you, brethren, mark them who cause divisions
and offences, contrary to the doctrine which ye have learned, and
18 avoid them. For such serve not the Lord Jesus Christ, but their
own belly, and by good words and fair speeches deceive the hearts

Rome had neither bishops nor deacons. So far were they from any shadow of papal power. Nay, there does not appear to have been then in the whole city any more than one of these domestic Churches. Otherwise there can be no doubt, but St. Paul would have saluted them also. *Epenetus*—Although the apostle had never been at Rome, yet had he many acquaintance there. But here is no mention of Linus or Clemens, whence it appears, they did not come to Rome till after this. *The first fruits of Asia*—The first convert in the Proconsular Asia.

7. *Who are of note among the apostles*—They seem to have been some of the most early converts. *Fellow prisoners*—For the Gospel's sake.

9. *Our fellow labourer*—Mine and Timothy's, ver. 21.

10. *Those of the family of Aristobulus and Narcissus, who are in the Lord*—It seems only part of their families were converted. Probably some of them were not known to St. Paul by face, but only by character. Faith does not create mo roseness but courtesy, which even the gravity of an apostle did not hinder.

12. *Salute Tryphena and Tryphosa*—Probably they were two sisters.

13. *Salute Rufus*—Perhaps the same that is mentioned, Mark xv, 21; *and his mother and mine*—This expression may only denote the tender care which Rufus's mother had taken of him.

14. *Salute Asyncritus, Phlegon, &c.*—He seems to join those together, who were joined by kindred, nearness of habitation, or any other circumstance. It could not but encourage the poor, especially to be saluted by name, who perhaps did not know that the apostle had ever heard of them. It is observable, that while the apostle forgets none who are worthy, yet he adjusts the nature of his salutation to the degrees of worth in those whom he salutes.

15. *Salute all the saints*—Had St. Peter been then at Rome, St. Paul would doubtless have saluted him by name; since no one in this numerous catalogue was of an eminence comparable to his. But if he was not then at Rome, the whole Roman tradition, with regard to the succession of their bishops, fails in the most fundamental article.

16. *Salute one another with a holy kiss*—Termed, by St. Peter, the kiss of love, Pet. v, 15. So the ancient Christians concluded all their solemn offices, the men saluting the men, and the women the women. And this apostolical custom seems to have continued for some ages in all Christian Churches.

17. *Mark them who cause divisions*—Such there were therefore at Rome also. *Avoid them*—Avoid all unnecessary intercourse with them.

18. *By good words*—Concerning themselves, making great promises, *and fair speeches*—Concerning you, praising and flattering you. *The harmless*—Who doing no ill themselves, are not upon their guard against them that do.

19 of the harmless. For your obedience is come abroad unto all men.
I rejoice therefore on your behalf; but I would have you wise with
regard to that which is good, and simple with regard to that which
20 is evil. And the God of peace shall bruise Satan under your feet
shortly. The grace of our Lord Jesus Christ *be* with you.
21 Timotheus my fellow labourer, and Lucius, and Jason, and Sosi-
22 pater my kinsmen, salute you. I, Tertius, who wrote this epistle,
salute you in the Lord. Gaius, my host, and of the whole Church,
23 saluteth you. Erastus, the chamberlain of the city, saluteth you,
24 and Quartus, a brother. The grace of our Lord Jesus Christ *be*
with you all.
25 Now to him who is able to stablish you according to my Gospel,
and the preaching of Jesus Christ, (according to the revelation of the
26 mystery kept secret since the world began, But now made manifest,
and by the Scriptures of the prophets, according to the commandment of the eternal God, made known to all nations for the obedi-
27 ence of faith:) To the only wise God, to him *be* glory through
Jesus Christ for ever. Amen!

19. *But I would have you*—Not only obedient, but discreet also, *wise with regard to that which is good*—As knowing in this as possible, *and simple with regard
to that which is evil*—As ignorant of this as possible.

20. *The God of peace*—The author and lover of it, giving a blessing to
your discretion, *shall bruise Satan under your feet*—Shall defeat all the artifices
of that sower of tares, and unite you more and more together in love.

21. *Timotheus my fellow labourer*—Here he is named even before St. Paul's
kinsmen. But as he had never been at Rome, he is not named in the beginning
of the epistle.

22. *I, Tertius, who wrote this epistle, salute you*—Tertius, who wrote what the
apostle dictated, inserted this, either by St. Paul's exhortation, or ready permission. *Gaius*—The Corinthian, 1 Cor. i, 14, *my host, and of the whole Church*—
Who probably met for some time in his house.

23. *The chamberlain of the city*—Of Corinth.

25. *Now to him who is able*—The last words of this epistle exactly answer the
first, chap. i, 1-5: in particular, concerning the power of God, the Gospel, Jesus Christ, the Scriptures, the obedience of faith, all nations, *to stablish you*—
Both Jews and *Gentiles, according to my Gospel, and the preaching of Jesus Christ*
—That is, according to the tenor of the Gospel of Jesus Christ, which I preach.
According to the revelation of the mystery—Of the calling of the Gentiles, which
as plainly as it was foretold in the prophets, was still hid from many even of the
believing Jews.

26. *According to the commandment*—The foundation of the apostolical office, *of
the eternal God*—A more proper epithet could not be. A new dispensation infers
no change in God. Known unto him are all his works, and every variation of
them, from eternity, *made known to all nations*—Not barely that they might know,
but enjoy it also, through obeying the faith.

27. *To the only wise God*—Whose manifold wisdom is known in the Church
through the Gospel, Eph. iii, 10. To him who is able, and to the wise God are
joined, as 1 Cor. i, 24, where Christ is styled the wisdom of God, and the power
of God. To him be glory through Christ Jesus for ever. And let every believer
say, Amen!

NOTES

ST. PAUL'S FIRST EPISTLE TO THE CORINTHIANS

Corinth was a city of Achaia, situate on the isthmus which joins Peloponne-
ous, now called *the Morea*, to the rest of Greece.   Being so advantageously situated for trade, the inhabitants of it abounded in riches, which by too natural a
consequence led them into luxury, lewdness, and all manner of vice.
Yet even here St. Paul planted a numerous Church, chiefly of heathen converts : to whom, about three years after he had left Corinth, he wrote this epistle
from Ephesus: as well to correct various disorders of which they were guilty,
as to answer some questions which they had proposed to him

THE EPISTLE CONSISTS OF

I. The inscription . . . . Chap. i, 1–3
II. The treatise itself, in which is,
  1. An exhortation to concord, beating down all glorying in the
      flesh 4–iv, 21
  2. A reproof,
    1. For not excommunicating the incestuous person . . . v, 1–13
    2. For going to law before heathen judges . . . . vi, 1–11
    3. A dissuasive from fornication 12–20
    4. An answer to the questions they had proposed concerning
        marriage . . . . vii, 1, 10, 25, 36, 39
    5. Concerning things sacrificed to idols . . . . viii, 1–ix, 1
    6. Concerning the veiling of women 2–16
    7. Concerning the Lord's Supper 17–34
    8. Concerning spiritual gifts . . . . . xii, xiii, xiv
    9. Concerning the resurrection . . . . . . xv, 1–58
    10. Concerning the collection for the poor; the coming of
        himself; of Timothy ; of Apollos; the sum of all . xvi, 1, 5, 10
                                                                12, 13, 14
III. The conclusion 15, 17 19-24

I. CORINTHIANS.

1   Paul, called *to be* an apostle of Jesus Christ, through the will of
2 God, and Sosthenes the brother, To the Church of God, which is in

Ver. 1. *Paul, called* to be *an apostle*—There is great propriety in every clause of
the salutation, particularly in this, as there were some in the Church of Corinth,
who called the authority of his mission in question : *through the will of God*—
Called the commandment of God, 1 Tim. i, 1.   This was to the Churches the
ground of his authority ; to Paul himself, of an humble and ready mind.   By the
mention of God, the authority of man is excluded, Gal. i, 1, by the mention of
the will of God, the merit of Paul, chap. xv, 8, &c.   *And Sosthenes*—A Corinthian, St. Paul's companion in travel.   It was both humility and prudence in
the apostle, thus to join his name with his own, in an epistle wherein he was to
reprove so many irregularities.   *Sosthenes the brother*—Probably this word is

Corinth, to them who are sanctified through Christ Jesus, called *and* holy, with all that in every place call upon the name of our Lord
3 Jesus Christ, both theirs and ours : Grace *be* unto you, and peace from God our Father, and the Lord Jesus Christ.
4 I thank my God always on your behalf, for the grace of God
5 which is given to you by Christ Jesus : That in every thing ye are
6 enriched through him, in all utterance and *in* all knowledge, As
7 the testimony of Christ was confirmed among you : So that ye are wanting in no good gift, waiting for the revelation of our Lord Je-
8 sus Christ, Who will also confirm you to the end, *that ye may be*
9 blameless in the day of our Lord Jesus Christ. God *is* faithful by whom ye were called into the fellowship of his Son Jesus Christ our Lord.
10 Now I exhort you, brethren, by the name of our Lord Jesus Christ, that ye all speak the same thing, and *that* there be no schisms among you, but *that* ye be perfectly joined together, in the same mind and
11 in the same judgment. For it hath been declared to me of you, my

---

emphatical ; as if he had said, Who from a Jewish opposer of the Gospel became a faithful brother.

2. *To the Church of God which is in Corinth*—St. Paul, writing in a familiar manner to the Corinthians, as also to the Thessalonians and Galatians, uses this plain appellation. To the other Churches he uses a more solemn address. *Sanctified through Jesus Christ*—And so undoubtedly they were in general, notwithstanding some exceptions : *called*—Of Jesus Christ, Rom. i, 6, *and*—As the fruit of that calling, made holy. *With all that in every place*—Nothing could better suit that catholic love which St. Paul labours to promote in this epistle, than such a declaration of his good wishes for every true Christian upon earth. *Call upon the name of our Lord Jesus Christ*—This plainly implies that all Christians pray to Christ as well as to the Father through him.

4. *Always*—Whenever I mention you to God in prayer.

5. *In all utterance and knowledge*—Of Divine things. These gifts the Corinthians particularly admired. Therefore this congratulation naturally tended to soften their spirits, and make way for the reproofs which follow.

6. *The testimony of Christ*—The Gospel, *was confirmed among you*—By these gifts attending it. They knew they had received these by the hand of Paul : and this consideration was highly proper, to revive in them their former reverence and affection for their spiritual father.

7. *Waiting* with earnest desire *for the* glorious *revelation of our Lord Jesus Christ*—A sure mark of a true or false Christian. To long for, or dread this revelation.

8. *Who will also*, if you faithfully apply to him, *confirm you to the end—in the day of Christ*—Now it is our day, wherein we are to work out our salvation. Then it will be eminently the day of Christ, and of his glory in the saints.

9. *God is faithful*—To all his promises : and therefore *to him that hath shall be given : by whom ye are called*—A pledge of his willingness to save you unto the uttermost.

10. *Now I exhort you*—Ye have faith and hope : secure love also by the endearing *name of our Lord Jesus Christ*—Infinitely preferable to all the human names in which we glory, *that ye all speak the same thing*—They now spoke different things, ver. 12 : *and that there be no schisms among you*—No alienation of affection from each other. Is this word ever taken in any other sense in Scripture ? *But that ye be joined in the same mind*—Affections, desires, *and judgment*—Touching all the grand truths of the Gospel.

11. *It hath been declared to me—by them of the family of Chloe*—Which some suppose to have been the wife of Stephanas, and the mother of Fortunatus, and Achaicus. By these three the Corinthians had sent their letter to St. Paul, chap. xvi, 17. *That there are contentions*—A word equivalent with schisms in the preceding verse.

brethren, by them *of the family* of Chloe, that there are contentions
12 among you. Now this I say, every one of you saith, 1 am of Paul,
13 and I of Apollos, and I of Cephas, and I of Christ. Is Christ
divided? Was Paul crucified for you? Or were you baptized
14 into the name of Paul? I thank God that I baptized none of you
15 but Crispus and Gaius : Lest any should say that I had baptized
16 in my own name. I baptized also the house of Stephanas. I
know not that I baptized any other.
17 For Christ did not send me to baptize, but to preach the Gospel; *but* not with wisdom of speech, lest the cross of Christ
18 should be made of none effect. For the doctrine of the cross is
indeed to them that perish foolishness : but to us who are saved,
19 it is the power of God. For it is written, *I will destroy the
wisdom of the wise, and abolish the understanding of the prudent
20 † Where *is* the wise? Where *is* the scribe? Where *is* the dis-
puter of this world? Hath not God made foolish the wisdom of this
21 world? For since, in the wisdom of God, the world by wisdom

12. *Now this I say*—That is, what I mean is this : There are various parties
among you, who set themselves one against another, in behalf of the several
teachers they admire. *And I of Christ*—They spoke well; if they had not on
this pretence despised their teachers, chap. iv, 8 : perhaps they valued themselves
on having heard Christ preach in his own person.

13. *Is Christ divided?*—Are not all his members still under one head? Was
not he alone crucified for you all? And were ye not all baptized in his name?
The glory of Christ then is not to be divided between him and his servants;
neither is the unity of the body to be torn asunder, seeing Christ is one still.

14. *I thank God*, (a pious phrase for the common one, *I rejoice*,) that in the
course of his providence, I baptized none of you, but Crispus (once the ruler of
the synagogue) and Gaius.

15. *Lest any should say that I baptized in my own name*—In order to attach
them to myself.

16. *I know not*—That is, it does not at present occur to my memory, that I
baptized any other.

17. *For God did not send me to baptize*—That was not my chief errand : those
of inferior rank and abilities could do it : (though all the apostles were sent to
baptize also, Matt. xxviii, 19 :) *but to preach the Gospel*—So the apostle slides
into his general proposition : *but not with wisdom of speech*—With the arti-
ficial ornaments of discourse, invented by human wisdom, *lest the cross of Christ
should be made of none effect*—The whole effect of St. Paul's preaching was owing
to the power of God accompanying. the plain declaration of this great truth,
Christ bore our sins upon the cross. But this effect might have been imputed to
another cause, had he come with that wisdom of speech which they admired.

18. *To them that perish*—By obstinately rejecting the only name whereby they
can be saved. *But to us who are saved*—Now saved from our sins, and in the
way of everlasting salvation, it is the great instrument of the power of God.

19. *For it is written*—And the words are remarkably applicable to this great
event.

20. *Where is the wise? &c.*—The deliverance of Judea from Sennacherib, is
what Isaiah refers to in these words ; in a bold and beautiful allusion to which
the apostle, in the clause that follows, triumphs over all the opposition of human
wisdom to the victorious Gospel of Christ. What could the *wise* men of the
Gentiles do against this? or the Jewish scribes? or the disputers of this world?
those among both, who, proud of their acuteness, were fond of controversy, and
thought they could confute all opponents? *Hath not God made foolish the wisdom of this world?*—That is, shown it to be very foolishness.

21. *For since in the wisdom of God*—According to his wise disposals, leaving
them to make the trial, *the world*, whether Jewish or Gentile, by all its boasted

* Isaiah xxix, 14. † Isaiah xxxiii, 16.

knew not God, it pleased God by the foolishness of preaching to
22 save them that believe. For whereas the Jews demand signs
23 and the Greeks seek wisdom, We preach Christ crucified, to the
24 Jews a stumbling block, and to the Greeks foolishness: But to
them that are called, both Jews and Greeks, Christ the power of
25 God, and the wisdom of God. Because the foolishness of God is
wiser than men, and the weakness of God is stronger than men
26 Behold your calling, brethren: that not many wise men after the
27 flesh, not many mighty, not many noble, *are called:* But God
hath chosen the foolish things of the world to shame the wise, and
the weak things of the world hath God chosen to shame the
28 things that are mighty: And the base things of the world, and
things that are despised, hath God chosen; yea, things that are
29 not, to bring to nought the things that are; That no flesh may
30 glory before God. But of him are ye in Christ Jesus, who is made
by God unto us wisdom, and righteousness, and sanctification, and
31 redemption: That as it is written, * He that glorieth, let him glory
in the Lord.
II.   And I, brethren, when I came to you, came not with loftiness
of speech or of wisdom, declaring to you the testimony of God.

wisdom, knew not God—Though the whole creation declared its Creator, and
though he declared himself by all the prophets; it pleased God by a way which
those who perish count mere foolishness, to save them that believe.

22. *For whereas the Jews demand* of the apostles, as they did of their Lord,
more signs still, after all they have seen already; and the Greeks or Gentiles
seek wisdom—The depths of philosophy, and the charms of eloquence.

23. *We* go on to *preach*, in a plain, and historical, not rhetorical or philosophical manner, *Christ crucified, to the Jews a stumbling block*, just opposite to
the *signs* they demand, *and to the Greeks foolishness*, a silly tale, just opposite to
the *wisdom* they seek.

24. *But to them that are called*—And obey the heavenly calling, Christ, with
his cross, his death, his life, his kingdom. And they experience, first, that he is
the power, then that he is the wisdom of God.

25. *Because the foolishness of God*—The Gospel scheme, which the world judge
to be mere foolishness, is wiser than the wisdom of men; and weak as they account it, stronger than all the strength of men.

26. *Behold your calling*—What manner of men they are whom God calls; *that
not many wise men after the flesh*—In the account of the world, *not many mighty*
—Men of power and authority.

28. *Things that are not*—The Jews frequently called the Gentiles *them that
are not*, Esdras vi, 56, 57; in so supreme contempt did they hold them. *The
things that are*—In high esteem.

29. *That no flesh*—A fit appellation. Flesh is fair, but withering as grass:
may glory before God—In God we ought to glory.

30. *Of him*—Out of his free grace and mercy, *are ye*—Ingrafted into Christ
Jesus, *who is made unto us* that believe *wisdom*, who were before utterly foolish
and ignorant; *righteousness*, the sole ground of our justification, who were
before under the wrath and curse of God; *sanctification*, a principle of universal holiness, whereas before we were altogether dead in sin; and *redemption*, that is, complete deliverance from all evil, and eternal bliss both of soul
and body.

31. *Let him glory in the Lord*—Not in himself, not in the flesh, not in the
world.

II. 1. *And I* accordingly came to you, *not with loftiness of speech or of wisdom*—I did not affect either deep wisdom or eloquence; *declaring the testimony
of God*—What God gave me to testify concerning his Son.

* Jeremiah ix, 23, 24.

2 For I determined not to know any thing among you save Jesus
3 Christ and him crucified. And I was with you in weakness, and
4 in fear, and in much trembling. And my speech and my preaching
was not with the persuasive words of human wisdom, but with the
5 demonstration of the Spirit and of power; That your faith might
not stand in the wisdom of men, but in the power of God.
6 Yet we speak wisdom among the perfect: but not the wisdom
of this world, nor of the rulers of this world, that come to nought:
7 But we speak the hidden wisdom of God in a mystery, which God
8 ordained before the world for our glory; Which none of the rulers
of this world knew; for had they known *it*, they would not have
9 crucified the Lord of glory. But as it is written, * Eye hath not
seen, nor hath ear heard, neither hath it entered into the heart of
0 man, what things God hath prepared for them that love him. But
God hath revealed *them* to us by his Spirit; for the Spirit search-
1 eth all things, even the deep things of God. For what man knoweth the things of a man, but the spirit of a man which is in him?

2. *I determined not to know any thing*—To waive all my other knowledge, and
not to preach any thing, *save Jesus Christ and him crucified*—That is, what he
did, suffered, taught. A part is put for the whole.
3. *And I was with you*—At my first entrance, *in weakness* of body, 2 Cor. xii,
7; *and in fear*—Lest I should offend any; *and in much trembling*—The emotion
of my mind affecting my very body.
4. *And my speech* in private, as well as *my* public *preaching, was not with the
persuasive words of human wisdom*, such as the wise men of the world use; *but
with the demonstration of the Spirit and of power*—With that powerful kind of
demonstration which flows from the Holy Spirit; which works on the conscience
with the most convincing light and the most persuasive evidence.
5. *That your faith might not* be built on *the wisdom* or power *of man, but on*
the wisdom and *power of God.*
6. *Yet we speak wisdom*—Yea, the truest and most excellent wisdom, *among*
the perfect—Adult, experienced Christians. By wisdom here he seems to mean,
not the whole Christian doctrine, but the most sublime and abstruse parts of it.
But not the wisdom admired and taught by the men *of this world, nor of the rulers*
of this world, Jewish or heathen, *that come to nought*—Both they and their wisdom, and the world itself.
7. *But we speak the* mysterious *wisdom of* God, which was *hidden* for many
ages from all the world; and is still hidden even from *babes in Christ;* much
more from all unbelievers. *Which God ordained before the world*—So far is this
from *coming to nought*, like worldly wisdom: *for our glory*—Arising from the
glory of our Lord, and then to be revealed, when all worldly glory vanishes.
8. *Had they known it*—That wisdom, *they would not have crucified*—Punished
as a slave, *the Lord of glory*—The giving Christ this august title, peculiar to the
great Jehovah, plainly shows him to be the supreme God. In like manner the
Father is styled, *the Father of glory*, Eph. i, 17; and the Holy Ghost, *the Spirit*
of glory, 1 Pet. iv, 14. The application of this title to all the three shows that
the Father, Son, and Holy Ghost, are *the God of glory;* as the only true God is
called, Psa. xxix, 3, and vii, 2.
9. *But* this ignorance of theirs fulfils what *is written* concerning the blessings
of the Messiah's kingdom. No natural man hath either *seen, heard*, or known,
the things which God hath prepared, for them that love him.
10. *But God hath revealed* (yea, and freely given, ver. 12,) *them to us;* even
inconceivable peace and joy unspeakable, *by his Spirit*—Who intimately and fully
knows them: *for the Spirit searcheth even the deep things of God*—Be they ever
so hidden and mysterious: the depths both of his nature and his kingdom.
11. *For what man knoweth the things of a man*—All the inmost recesses of his
mind; although men are all of one nature, and so may the more easily know one

* Isaiah lxiv, 4

So the'things of God also knoweth no one, but the Spirit cf God.
12 Now we have received, not the spirit of the world, but the Spirit
which is of God, that we may know the things which are freely
13 given to us of God. Which also we speak, not in words taught by
human ,wisdom, but in those taught by the Spirit, explaining spi-
14 ritual things by spiritual *words*. But the natural man receiveth
not the things of the Spirit of God; for they are foolishness to
him : neither can he know them, because they are spiritually
15 discerned. But the spiritual man discerneth indeed all things,
16 yet ne himself is discerned by no man. * For who hath known
the mind of the Lord, that he may instruct him? But we have the
mind of Christ.
III.   And I, brethren, could not speak to you as unto spiritual, but as
2 unto carnal, as unto babes in Christ. I fed you with milk, not with
3 meat; for ye were not able *to bear it :* nor are ye now able. For
ye are still carnal: for while *there is* among you emulation, and
strife, and divisions, are ye not carnal, and walk according to man ?
4 For while one saith, I am of Paul, and another, I *am* of Apollos ;
are ye not carnal ?

---

another. *So the things of God knoweth no one but the Spirit*—Who consequently
is God.

12. *Now we have received not the spirit of the world*—This spirit is not properly
received; for the men of the world always had it. But Christians *receive* the
Spirit of God, which before they had not.

13. *Which also we speak,* as well as know, *in words taught by the Holy Spirit*
—Such are all the words of Scripture. How high a regard ought we then to
retain for them ! *Explaining spiritual things by spiritual words*—Or *adapting
spiritual words to spiritual things*—Being taught of the Spirit to express the things
of the Spirit.

14. *But the natural man*—That is, every man who hath not the Spirit, who
has no other way of obtaining knowledge but by his senses and natural understanding, *receiveth not*—Does not understand or conceive, *the things of the
Spirit*—The things revealed by the Spirit of God, whether relating to his nature
or his kingdom; *for they are foolishness to him*—He is so far from understanding, that he utterly despises them. *Neither can he know them*—As he has not the
will, so neither has he the power; *because they are spiritually discerned*—They
can only be discerned by the aid of that Spirit, and by those spiritual senses which
he has not.

15. *But the spiritual man*—He that hath the Spirit, *discerneth all* the *things
of* God, whereof we have been speaking, *yet he himself is discerned by no man*—
No natural men. They neither understand what he is, nor what he says.

16. *Who*—What natural men. *We*—Spiritual men, apostles in particular, *have*
—Know, understand, *the mind of Christ*—Concerning the whole plan of Gospel
salvation.

III. 1. *And I, brethren*—He spoke before, chap. ii, 1, of his entrance, now of
his progress among them ; *could not speak to you as unto spiritual*—Adult, experienced Christians ; *but as unto* men who were still in a great measure *carnal;
as unto babes in Christ*—Still weak in grace, though eminent in gifts, chap. i, 5.

2. *I fed you* as babes *with milk*—The first and plainest truths of the Gospel.
So should every preacher suit his doctrine to his hearers.

3. *For while there is among you emulation* in your hearts, *strife* in your words,
and actual *divisions, are ye not carnal, and walk according to man ?*—As mere
men ? not as Christians, according to God.

4. *I am of Apollos*—St. Paul named himself and Apollos, to show that he would
condemn any division among them, even though it were in favour of himself, or

* Isaiah xl, 13.

5 Who then is Paul, and who *is* Apollos, but ministers by whom
6 ye believed, even as the Lord gave to every man? I planted, Apol-
7 los watered; but God gave the increase. So then, neither is he
that planteth any thing, nor he that watereth; but God that giveth
8 the increase. But he that planteth and he that watereth are one;
and every one shall receive his own reward, according to his
9 own labour. For we are fellow labourers of God: ye are God's
10 husbandry, ye are God's building. According to the grace of God
given to me, as a wise master builder I have laid the foundation,
and another buildeth thereon; but let every one take heed how he
11 buildeth thereon. For other foundation can no man lay than what
12 is laid, which is Jesus Christ: And if any one build on this founda-
13 tion, gold, silver, costly stones; wood, hay, stubble; Every one's
work shall be made manifest; for the day shall declare *it*: for it
is revealed by fire; yea, the fire shall try every one's work, of

---

the dearest friend he had in the world. *Are ye not carnal?*—For the Spirit of
God allows no party zeal.

5. *Ministers*, or servants, by whom ye believed, as the Lord, the Master of those
servants, gave to every man.

7. *God that giveth the increase* is all in all; without him neither planting nor
watering avails.

8. *But he that planteth and he that watereth are one*—Which is another argument against division. Though their labours are different, they are all employed
in one general work, the saving souls. Hence he takes occasion to speak of the
reward of them that labour faithfully, and the awful account to be given by all.
Every one shall receive his own peculiar *reward, according to his own* peculiar
labour—Not only according to his success. But he who labours much, though
with small success, shall have a great reward.

Has not all this reasoning the same force still? Ministers are still barely
instruments in God's hand, and depend as entirely as ever on his blessing, to give
the increase to their labours. Without this they are nothing; with it, their part
is so small, that they hardly deserve to be mentioned. May their hearts and hands
be more united! And retaining a due sense of the honour God doth them in em-
ploying them, may they faithfully labour, not as for themselves, but for the great
Proprietor of all, till the day come when he will reward them in full proportion
to their fidelity and diligence.

9. *For we are all fellow labourers*—God's labourers, and fellow labourers with
each other. *Ye are God's husbandry*—This is the sum of what went before; it is
a comprehensive word, taking in both a field, a garden, and a vineyard. *Ye are
God's building*—This is the sum of what follows.

10. *According to the grace of God given to me*—This he premises, lest he should
seem to ascribe it to himself. *Let every one take heed how he buildeth thereon*—
That all his doctrines may be consistent with the foundation.

11. *For other foundation*—On which the whole Church, and all its doctrines,
duties, and blessings may be built; *can no man lay than what is laid*—In the
counsels of Divine wisdom, in the promises and prophecies of the Old Testament,
in the preaching of the apostles, St. Paul in particular; *which is Jesus Christ*—
Who, in his person and offices, is the firm, immovable rock of ages, every way
sufficient to bear all the weight that God himself, or the sinner, when he believes,
can lay upon him.

12. *If any one build gold, silver, costly stones*—Three sorts of materials which
will bear the fire; true and solid doctrines; *wood, hay, stubble*—Three which
will not bear the fire. Such are all the doctrines, ceremonies, and forms of human invention, all but the substantial, vital truths of Christianity.

13. The time is coming, when every one's work shall be made manifest; for
the day of the Lord, that great and final day, shall declare it to all the world.
For it is revealed—What faith beholds as so certain and so near, is spoken of as
already present; *by fire: yea, the fire shall try every man's work of what sort it is*—

14 what sort it is. If any one's work which he hath built thereon
15 shall remain, hè shall receive a reward. If any one's work shall
be burnt, he shall suffer loss, but himself shall be saved, yet so as
16 through the fire. Know ye not that ye are the temple of God,
17 and the Spirit of God dwelleth in you? If any man destroy the
temple of God, him shall God destroy: for the temple of God is
18 holy; which *temple* ye are. Let none deceive himself: if any one
among you thinketh himself to be wise, let him become a fool in
19 this world, that he may become wise. For the wisdom of this
world is foolishness with God; as it is written, * He taketh the wise
20 in their own craftiness. And again, † The Lord knoweth the rea-
21 sonings of the wise, that they are vain. Therefore let none glory
22 in men; for all things are yours: Whether Paul, or Apollos, or Cephas; or the world, or life, or death, or things present, or things
23 to come, all are yours, And ye *are* Christ's, and Christ *is* God's.

The strict process of that day will try every man's doctrines, whether they came up to the Scripture standard or not. Here is a plain allusion to the flaming light and consuming heat of the general conflagration. But the expression, when ap plied to the trying of doctrines, and consuming those that are wrong, is evidently figurative; because no material fire can have such an effect on what is of a moral nature. And therefore it is added, he who builds wood, hay, or stubble, shall be saved as through the fire; or, as narrowly as a man escapes through the fire, when his house is all in flames about him.

This text then is so far from establishing the Romish purgatory, that it utterly overthrows it. For the fire here mentioned does not exist, till the day of judg- ment; therefore if this be the fire of purgatory, it follows, that purgatory does not exist before the day of judgment.

14. *He shall receive a reward*—A peculiar degree of glory. Some degree even the other will receive; seeing he held the foundation; though through ignorance he built thereon what would not abide the fire.

15. *He shall suffer loss*—The loss of that peculiar degree of glory.

16. *Ye*—All Christians, *are the temple of God*—The most noble kind of build- ing, ver. 9.

17. *If any man destroy the temple of God*—Destroy a real Christian, by schisms, or doctrines fundamentally wrong, *him shall God destroy*—He shall not be saved at all; not even as through the fire.

18. *Let him become a fool in this world*—Such as the world accounts so; *that he may become wise*—In God's account.

19. *For* all the boasted wisdom of the world is mere foolishness in the sight of God. *He taketh the wise in their own craftiness*—Not only while they think they are acting wisely; but by their very wisdom, which itself is their snare and the occasion of their destruction.

20. *That they are but vain*—Empty, foolish; they and all their thoughts.

21. *Therefore*—Upon the whole, *let none glory in men*—So as to divide into parties on their account. *For all things are yours*—And we in particular. We are not your lords, but rather your servants.

22. *Whether Paul, or Apollos, or Cephas*—We are all equally yours to serve you for Christ's sake, *or the world*—This leap from Peter to the world greatly enlarges the thought, and argues a kind of impatience of enumerating the rest Peter and every one in the whole world, however excellent in gifts, or grace, or office, are also your servants for Christ's sake; *or life, or death*—These, with all their various circumstances, are disposed as will be most for your advantage: or things present on earth, or things to come in heaven. Contend therefore no more about these little things, but be ye united in love, as ye are in blessings.

23. *And ye are Christ's*—His property, his subjects, his members, *and Christ is God's*—As Mediator he refers all his services to his Father's glory.

* Job v, 13   † Psalm xciv, 11.

IV. Let a man so account us, as servants of Christ, and stewards of
2 the mysteries of God. Moreover, it is required in stewards, that a
3 man be found faithful. But it is a very small thing with me to be
judged by you, or by any man's judgment: yea, I judge not myself.
4 For I am not conscious to myself of any thing, yet am I not hereby
5 justified; but he that judgeth me is the Lord. Therefore judge
nothing before the time, until the Lord come, who both will bring
to light the hidden things of darkness, and manifest the counsels of
the hearts. And then shall every man have praise from God.
6   These things, brethren, I have by a figure transferred to myself and Apollos, for your sakes; that ye may learn by us not to
think *of men* above * what is *here* written, that ye may not be
7 puffed up for one against another. For who maketh thee to differ *from another?* And what hast thou which thou hast not received? But if thou hast received *it*, why dost thou boast, as if
8 thou hadst not received *it?* Now ye are full: now ye are rich:
9 ye have reigned as kings without us. And I would ye did reign,
that we also might reign with you. For I know assuredly, God
hath set forth us, the apostles, last, as appointed to death; for we

---

IV. 1. *Let a man account us as servants of Christ*—The original word properly
signifies, such servants as laboured at the oar in rowing vessels; and accordingly intimates the pains which every faithful minister takes in his Lord's work.
O God, where are these ministers to be found? Lord, thou knowest. *And stewards of the mysteries of God*—Dispensers of the mysterious truths of the Gospel.
3. *Yea, I judge not myself*—My final state is not to be determined by my own
judgment.
4. *I am not conscious to myself of any thing* evil: *yet am I not hereby justified*—
I depend not on this, as a sufficient justification of myself in God's account: *but
he that judgeth me is the Lord*—By his sentence I am to stand or fall.
5. *Therefore judge nothing before the time*—Appointed for judging all men;
until the Lord come, who in order to pass a righteous judgment, which otherwise would be impossible, will both bring to light the things which are now
covered with impenetrable darkness, and manifest the most secret springs of action, the principles and intention of every heart. *And then shall every one*, every
faithful steward, *have praise of God.*
6. *These things*—Mentioned chap. i, 10, &c, I have by a very obvious figure
transferred to myself, and Apollos, and Cephas, instead of naming those particular preachers at Corinth, to whom ye are so fondly attached, *that ye may learn
by us*—From what has been said concerning us, (who, however eminent we are,
are mere instruments in God's hand,) not to think of any man above what is here
written, or above what Scripture warrants.
7. *Who maketh thee to differ*—Either in gifts or graces? *As if thou hadst not
received it*—As if thou hadst it originally from thyself.
8. *Now ye are full*—The Corinthians abounded with spiritual gifts. And so
did the apostles. But the apostles, by continual want and sufferings, were
kept from self complacency. The Corinthians suffering nothing, and having
plenty of all things, were pleased with and applauded themselves. And they
were like children, who being raised in the world, disregarded their poor parents. *Now ye are full*, (says the apostle, in a beautiful gradation,) *ye are rich,
ye have reigned as kings*—A proverbial expression, denoting the most splendid
and plentiful circumstances, without any thought of us. *And I would ye did
reign*—In the best sense: I would ye had attained the height of holiness: *that
we might reign with you*—Having no more sorrow on your account, but sharing
in your happiness.
9. *God hath set forth us last, as appointed to death*—Alluding to the Roman
custom, of bringing forth those persons last on the stage, either to fight with

* Chap. iii, 7.

10 are made a spectacle to the world, both to angels and to men. We *are* fools for Christ's sake ; but ye *are* wise in Christ : we *are* weak ; but ye *are* strong ; ye *are* honourable ; but we without

11 honour.   Even to this present hour we both hunger and thirst,

12 and are naked, and are buffeted, and have no certain abode, And labour, working with our own hands : being reviled, we bless :

13 being persecuted we suffer it : Being defamed, we entreat : we are made as the filth of the world, and offscouring of all things

14 to this day.   I do not write these things to shame you, but as my

15 beloved children, I warn *you*.   For if ye have ten thousand instructers in Christ, yet *have ye* not many fathers ; for I have be-

16 gotten you in Christ Jesus through the Gospel.   I beseech you

17 therefore, be ye followers of me.   For this cause I have sent to you Timotheus, who is my beloved son, and faithful in the Lord, who shall remind you of my ways in Christ, as I teach every

18 where in every church.   Now some are puffed up, as if I would

19 not come to you.   But I will come to you shortly, if the Lord permit, and will know, not the speech of them who are puffed up, but

20 the power.   For the kingdom of God *is* not in speech, but in power.

21 What will ye ?   That I come to you with a rod ?   Or in love, and the spirit of meekness ?

each other, or with wild beasts, who were devoted to death : so that if they escaped one day, they were brought out again and again, till they were killed.

10. *We are fools*, in the account of the world, *for Christ's sake : but ye are wise in Christ*—Though ye are Christians, ye think yourselves wise ; and ye have found means to make the world think you so too. *We are weak*—In presence, in infirmities, in sufferings : *but ye are strong*—In just opposite circumstances.

11. *And are naked*—Who can imagine a more glorious triumph of the truth, than that which is gained in these circumstances ?   When St. Paul, with an impediment in his speech, and a person rather contemptible than graceful, appeared in a mean, perhaps tattered dress, before persons of the highest distinction, and yet commanded such attention, and made such deep impressions upon them

12. *We bless*—*suffer it*—*entreat*—We do not return revilings, persecution, defamation : nothing but blessing.

13. *We are made as the filth of the world, and offscouring of all things*—Such were those poor wretches among the heathens, who were taken from the dregs of the people, to be offered as expiatory sacrifices to the infernal gods.   They were loaded with curses, affronts, and injuries all the way they went to the altars. And when the ashes of those unhappy men were thrown into the sea, these very names were given them in the ceremony.

14. *I do not write these things to shame you, but as my beloved children, I warn you*—It is with admirable prudence and sweetness the apostle adds this, to prevent any unkind construction of his words.

15. *I have begotten you*—This excludes not only Apollos, his successor, but also Silas and Timothy, his companions.   And a relation between a spiritual father and his children brings with it an inexpressible nearness and affection.

16. *Be ye followers of me*—In that spirit and behaviour, which I have so largely declared.

17. *My beloved son*—Elsewhere he styles him brother, 2 Cor. i, 1 ; but here paternal affection takes place. *As I teach*—No less by example than precept.

18. *Now some are puffed up*—St. Paul saw by a Divine light the thoughts which would arise in their hearts. *As if I would not come*—Because I send Timothy.

19. *I will know*—He here shows his fatherly authority ; *not the* big empty speech of these vain boasters, but how much of the power of God attends them

20. *For the kingdom of God*—Real religion, does not consist in words, but in the power of God ruling the heart.

21. *With a rod*—That is, with severity.

CHAPTER V. 417

V. It is commonly reported *that there* is fornication among you, and such fornication as *is* not even heard of among the heathens, that
2 one should have his father's wife. And are ye puffed up? Have ye not rather mourned, that he who hath done this deed might be
3 taken from among you? For I verily as absent in body, but present in spirit, have already, as if I were present, judged him who
4 hath so done this, In the name of our Lord Jesus Christ, when ye are gathered together, and my spirit, with the power of our Lord
5 Jesus Christ, To deliver such a one to Satan, for the destruction of the flesh, that the spirit may be saved in the day of the Lord
6 Jesus. Your glorying *is* not good: know ye not, that a lit
7 tle leaven leaveneth the whole lump? Purge out the old leaven, that ye may be a new lump, as ye are unleavened; for our pass-
8 over is slain for us, *even* Christ: Therefore let us keep the feast; not with the old leaven, nor with the leaven of wickedness and malignity, but with the unleavened bread of sincerity and truth.
9 I wrote to you in an epistle, Not to converse with lewd persons,
10 But not altogether with the lewd persons of this world, or the cove-

---

V. 1. Fornication—The original word implies criminal conversation of any kind whatever. *His father's wife*—While his father was alive.

2. *Are ye puffed up?*—Should ye not rather have mourned, have solemnly humbled yourselves, and at that time of solemn mourning have expelled that notorious sinner from your communion?

3. *I verily as present in spirit*—Having a full (it seems a miraculous) view of the whole fact, have already, as if I were actually present, judged him who hath so scandalously done this.

4. *And my spirit*—Present with you, *with the power of the Lord Jesus Christ*—To confirm my sentence.

5. *To deliver such a one*—This was the highest degree of punishment in the Christian Church. And we may observe, the passing this sentence was the act of the apostle, not of the Corinthians: *to Satan*—Who was usually permitted, in such cases, to inflict pain or sickness on the offender: *for the destruction*—Though slowly and gradually, *of the flesh*—Unless prevented by speedy re pentance.

6. *Your glorying*—Either in your gifts or prosperity, at such a time as this, is not good. *Know ye not, that a little leaven*—One sin, or one sinner, *leaveneth the whole lump*—Diffuses guilt and infection through the whole congregation?

7. *Purge out therefore the old leaven*—Both of sinners and of sin, *that ye may be a new lump, as ye are unleavened*—That is, that being unleavened ye may be a new lump holy unto the Lord. *For our passover is slain for us*—The Jewish passover, about the time of which this epistle was wrote, (chap. v, 11,) was only a type of this. What exquisite skill both here and every where conducts the zeal of the inspired writer? How surprising a transition is here? And yet how perfectly natural; the apostle, speaking of the incestuous criminal, slides into his darling topic, a crucified Saviour. Who would have expected it on such an occasion? Yet when it is thus brought in, who does not see and admire both the propriety of the subject, and the delicacy of its introduction?

8. *Therefore let us keep the feast*—Let us feed on him by faith. Here is a plain allusion to the Lord's Supper, which was instituted in the room of the passover; *not with the old leaven*—Of heathenism or Judaism. Malignity is stubbornness in evil. Sincerity and truth seem to be put here for the whole of true inward religion.

9. *I wrote to you in a* former *epistle*—And doubtless both St. Paul and the other apostles wrote many things which are not extant now. *Not to converse*—Familiarly; not to contract any intimacy or acquaintance with them, more than is absolutely necessary.

10. *But* I did not mean that ye should altogether refrain from conversing with heathens, though they are guilty in some of these respects. *Covetous* ra-

27

tous, or the rapacious, or idolaters, for then ye must go out of the
11 world. But I have now written unto you, if any who is named a
brother be a lewd person, or covetous, or an idolater, or a railer,
or a drunkard, or rapacious, not to converse with such a one, no,
12 not to eat with him. For what have I to do to judge them that are
13 without? Do not ye judge them that are within? (But them that
are without God will judge:) And ye will take away from among
yourselves the wicked person.
VI. Dare any of you, having a matter against another, refer it to
2 the unjust, and not to the saints? Know ye not, that the saints
shall judge the world? And if the world is judged by you, are ye
3 unworthy to judge the smallest matters? Know ye not that we
shall judge angels? How much more things pertaining to this
4 life? If then ye have any controversies of things pertaining to
this life, do ye set them to judge who are of no esteem in the
5 Church? I speak to your shame. What, is there not so much as
one wise man among you, that shall be able to judge between his
6 brethren? But brother goeth to law with brother, and this before
7 the infidels. Indeed there is altogether a fault among you, that ye
have contests with each other. Why do ye not rather suffer wrong?
Why do ye not rather suffer yourselves to be defrauded? Nay, ye
8 do wrong, and defraud even *your* brethren. Know ye not that the
9 unjust shall not inherit the kingdom of God? Be not deceived,
neither fornicators, nor idolaters, nor adulterers, nor the effeminate,

---

pacious, idolaters—Sinners against themselves, their neighbour, God. *For then
ye must go out of the world*—Then all civil commerce must cease. So that going
out of the world, which some account a perfection, St. Paul accounts an utter
absurdity.

11. *Who is named a brother*—That is, a Christian, especially if a member of
the same congregation; *rapacious*—Guilty of oppression, extortion, or any open
injustice. *No, not to eat with him*—Which is the lowest degree of familiarity.

12. I speak of Christians only. For what have I to do to judge heathens? But
ye, as well as I, judge those of your own community.

13. *Them that are without, God will judge*—The passing sentence on these he
hath reserved to himself. *And ye will take away—that wicked person*—This
properly belongs to you.

VI. 1. *The unjust*—The heathens. A Christian could expect no justice from
these. *The saints*—Who might easily decide these smaller differences, in a private and friendly manner.

2. *Know ye not*—This expression occurs six times in this single chapter. And
that with a peculiar force. For the Corinthians knew, and gloried in it: but
they did not practise; *that the saints*—After having been judged themselves,
shall judge the world—Shall be assessors with Christ in the judgment wherein he
shall condemn all the wicked, as well angels as men, Matt. xix, 28; Rev. xx, 4

4. *Them who are of no esteem in the Church*—That is, heathens, who, as such,
could be in no esteem with the Christians.

5. *Is there not one among you*, who are such admirers of wisdom, that is wise
enough to decide such causes?

7. *Indeed there is a fault*, that ye quarrel with each other at all, whether ye go
to law or no. *Why do ye not rather suffer wrong?*—All men cannot, or will not
receive this saying. Many aim only at this, "I will neither do wrong nor suffer
it." These are honest heathens, but no Christians.

8. *Nay, ye do wrong*—Openly, *and defraud*—Privately. O how powerfully did
the mystery of iniquity already work!

9. *Idolatry* is here placed between fornication and adultery, because they generally accompanied it. *Nor the effeminate*—Who live in an easy, indolent way,
taking up no cross, enduring no hardship.

10 nor Sodomites, Nor thieves, nor the covetous, nor revilers, nor the
11 rapacious, shall inherit the kingdom of God.   And such were some
of you : but ye are washed, but ye are sanctified, but ye are justified in the name of the Lord Jesus, and by the Spirit of our God.
12   All things are lawful for me ; but all things are not expedient :
all things are lawful for me ; but I will not be brought under the
13 power of any.   Meats *are* for the belly, and the belly for meats ;
yet God will destroy both it and them.   But the body *is* not for
14 fornication, but for the Lord, and the Lord for the body.   And
God hath both raised up the Lord, and will also raise us up by his
15 power.   Know ye not, that your bodies are members of Christ ?
Shall I then take the members of Christ, and make them the mem-
16 bers of a harlot ?   God forbid.   Know ye not, that he who is joined
to a harlot is one body ?   * For they two, saith he, shall be one
17 flesh.   But he that is joined to the Lord is one spirit.   Flee for-
18 nication.   Every sin that a man doth, is without the body ; but he
19 that committeth fornication, sinneth against his own body.   Know
ye not, that your body is the temple of the Holy Ghost, who is in
20 you, whom ye have from God ?   And ye are not your own : for ye

---

But how is this ?   These good-natured, harmless people are ranked with idolaters and Sodomites !   We may learn hence, that we are never secure from the
greatest sins, till we guard against those which are thought the least, nor indeed,
till we think no sin is little ; since every one is a step toward hell.

11. *And such were some of you : but ye are washed*—From those gross abominations ; yea, and ye are inwardly sanctified, not before, but in consequence of
your being justified, *in the name*—That is, by the merits of the Lord Jesus, through
which your sins are forgiven, and by the Spirit of our God, by whom ye are
thus washed and sanctified.

12. *All things,* which are lawful for you, *are lawful for me : but all things are
not always expedient*—Particularly when any thing would offend my weak brother ; or when it would enslave my own soul.   For though *all things are lawful
for me, yet I will not be brought under the power of any*—So as to be uneasy when
I abstain from it.   For if so, then I am under the power of it.

13. As if he had said, I speak this chiefly with regard to meats ; (and would
to God all Christians would consider it !) particularly with regard to those offered to idols, and those forbidden in the Mosaic law.   These, I grant, are all indifferent, and have their use ; though it is only for a time ; then meats and the
organs which receive them, will together moulder into dust.   But the case is
quite otherwise with fornication.   This is not indifferent, but at all times evil.
For the body is for the Lord—Designed only for his service : and the Lord, in an
important sense, for the body, being the Saviour of this as well as of the soul ;
in proof of which God hath already raised him from the dead.

17. *But he that is joined to the Lord*—By faith, *is one spirit with him*—And
shall he make himself one flesh with a harlot ?

18. *Flee fornication*—All unlawful commerce with women, with speed, with
abhorrence, with all your might.   Every sin that a man commits against his
neighbour terminates upon an object out of himself, and does not so immediately
pollute his body, though it does his soul : *but he that committeth fornication sinneth against his own body*—Pollutes, dishonours, and degrades it to a level with
brute beasts.

19. And even your body is not, strictly speaking, your own.   Even this *is the
temple of the Holy Ghost*—Dedicated to him, and inhabited by him.   What the
apostle calls elsewhere the temple of God, chap. iii, 16, 17, and the temple of the
living God, 2 Cor. vi, 16, he here styles the temple of the Holy Ghost ; plainly
showing, that the Holy Ghost is the living God.

20. *Glorify God with your body and your spirit*—Yield your bodies and all thei

* Genesis ii, 24.

are bought with a price : therefore glorify God with your body and
your spirit, which are God's.
VII.   Now concerning the things whereof ye wrote to me, *it is* good
2 for a man not to touch a woman.   Yet *to avoid* fornication, let
every man have his own wife : and let every woman have her own
3 husband.   Let the husband render the debt to the wife ; and in
4 like manner the wife to the husband.   The wife hath not power
over her own body, but the husband : and in like manner the hus-
5 band also hath not power over his own body, but the wife.   Withdraw not from each other, unless *it be* by consent for a time, that
ye may give yourselves up to fasting and prayer, and may come
6 together again, lest Satan tempt you through your incontinence.   But
7 I say this by permission, not by way of precept.   For I would that
all men were even as myself : but every one hath his proper gift
from God, one after this manner, and another after that.
8   But to the unmarried and the widows I say, It is good for them
9 if they remain even as I.   But if they have not power over themselves, let them marry ; for it is better to marry than to burn.
10   The married I command, *yet* not I, but the Lord, * That the
11 wife depart not from her husband.   But if she depart let her remain unmarried, or be reconciled to her husband.   And let not the
12 husband put away his wife.   To the rest speak I, not the Lord.
If any brother hath an unbelieving wife, and she consent to dwell

members, as well as your souls and all their faculties, as instruments of righteousness to God.   Devote and employ all ye have, and all ye are, entirely, unre-
servedly, and for ever to his glory.
    VII. 1. *It is good for a man*—Who is master of himself, *not to touch a woman*
—That is, not to marry.   So great and many are the advantages of a single life.
    2. *Yet* when it is needful in order to avoid fornication, *let every man have his
own wife;* his own; for Christianity allows no polygamy.
    3. *Let* not married persons fancy that there is any perfection in living with
each other as if they were unmarried.   *The debt*—This ancient reading seems
far more natural than the common one.
    4. *The wife—the husband*—Let no one forget this, on pretence of greater
purity.
    5. *Unless it be by consent, for a time*—That on those special and solemn occa-
sions, ye may entirely give yourselves up to the exercises of devotion ; *lest*—If
ye should long remain separate, *Satan tempt you*—To unclean thoughts, if not
actions too.
    6. *But I say this*—Concerning your separating for a time, and coming together
again.   Perhaps he refers also to ver. 2.
    7. *For I would that all men were* herein *even as I*—I would that all believers
who are now unmarried would remain eunuchs for the kingdom of heaven's
sake.   St. Paul having tasted the sweetness of this liberty, wished others to enjoy
it, as well as himself, *but every one has his proper gift from God*—According to
our Lord's declaration, All men cannot receive this saying, save they, the happy
few, to whom it is given, Matt. xix, 11.
    8. *It is good for them if they remain even as I*—That St. Paul was then single is
certain.   And from Acts vii, 58, compared with the following parts of the history, it seems probable that he always was so.   It does not appear that this declaration (any more than ver. 1) hath any reference at all to a state of persecution.
    10. *Not I*—Only ; *but the Lord—Christ*—By his express command, Matt. v, 32.
    11. *But if she depart*—Contrary to this express prohibition.   *And let not the
husband put away his wife*—Except for the cause of adultery.
    12. *To the rest*—Who are married to unbelievers, *speak I*—By revelation from
God, though our Lord hath not left any commandment concerning it.   *Let him*
                              * Matthew v, 32.

3 with him, let him not put her away.   And the wife who hath an
unbelieving husband, that consenteth to live with her, let her not
14 put him away. For the unbelieving husband hath been sanctified by
the wife ; and the unbelieving wife hath been sanctified by the husband.   Else were your children unclean; but now they are holy.
15 But if the unbeliever depart, let him depart: a brother or a sister
16 is not enslaved in such *cases;* but God hath called us to peace. For
how knowest thou, O wife, but thou mayest save thy husband ? Or
17 how knowest thou, O husband, but thou mayest save thy wife ? But
as God hath distributed to every one, as the Lord hath called every
18 one, so let him walk.   And thus I ordain in all the Churches.   Is
any one called being circumcised ? let him not become uncircumcised : is any one called in uncircumcision ? let him not be cir-
19 cumcised.   Circumcision is nothing, and uncircumcision is no-
20 thing, but keeping the commandments of God.   Let every one in
21 the calling wherein he is called, therein abide.   Wast thou called,
being a bond man ? care not for it : but if thou canst be made free,
22 use *it* rather.   For he that is called by the Lord, *being* a bond man,
is the Lord's free man ; and in the like manner, he that is called
23 *being* free, is the bond man of Christ.   Ye are bought with a price ;
24 do not become the bond slaves of men.   Brethren, let every one
wherein he is called, therein abide with God.
25   Now concerning virgins, I have no commandment from the
Lord ; but I give my judgment as one who hath obtained mercy

not put her away—The Jews indeed were obliged of old to put away their idolatrous wives, Ezra x, 3.   But their case was quite different.   They were absolutely
forbid to marry idolatrous women.   But the persons here spoken of were married, while they were both in a state of heathenism.

14. *For the unbelieving husband hath,* in many instances, *been sanctified by the
wife—Else your children* would have been brought up heathens, whereas now
they are Christians.   As if he had said, Ye see the proof of it before your eyes.

15. *A brother or a sister*—A Christian man or woman, *is not enslaved*—Is at
full liberty in such cases.   *But God hath called us to peace*—To live peaceably
with them, if it be possible.

17. *But as God hath distributed*—The various stations of life, and various rela
tions to every one, let him take care to discharge his duty therein.   The Gospel
disannuls none of these : *and thus I ordain in all the Churches*—As a point of
the highest concern.

19. *Circumcision is nothing, and uncircumcision is nothing*—Will neither promote nor obstruct our salvation.   The one point is keeping the commandments
of God ; faith working by love.

20. *In the calling*—The outward state wherein he is when God calls him.
Let him not seek to change this without a clear direction from Providence.

21. *Care not for it*—Do not anxiously seek liberty, *but if thou canst be free,
use it rather*—Embrace the opportunity.

22. *Is the Lord's free man*—Is free in this respect.   The Greek word implies
one that was a slave, but now is free; *is the bond man of Christ*—Not free in this
respect, not at liberty to do his own will.

23. *Ye are bought with a price*—Ye belong to God: therefore, where it can be
avoided, *do not become the bond slaves of men*—Which may expose you to many
temptations.

24. *Therein abide with God*—Doing all things as unto God, and as in his immediate presence.   They who thus abide with God preserve a holy indifference with
regard to outward things.

25. *Now concerning virgins,* of either sex, *I have no commandment from the
Lord*—By a particular revelation : nor was it necessary he should ; for the

26 of the Lord to be faithful. I apprehend, therefore, that this is good
for the present distress, that *it is* good for a man to continue as
27 he is. Art thou bound to a wife? seek not to be loosed: art thou
28 loosed from a wife? seek not a wife. Yet if thou dost marry, thou
hast not sinned; and if a virgin marry, she hath not sinned. Never-
29 theless, such will have trouble in the flesh; but I spare you. But
this I say, brethren, the time is short: it remaineth, that even they
30 that have wives, be as if they had none: And they that weep, as
if they wept not; and they that rejoice, as if they rejoiced not;
31 and they that buy, as if they possessed not; And they that use this
world, as not abusing it; for the fashion of this world passeth
32 away: Now I would have you without carefulness. The unmarried man careth for the things of the Lord, how he may please
33 the Lord. But the married careth for the things of the world,
34 how he may please his wife. There is a difference also between
a wife and a virgin. The unmarried woman careth for the things
of the Lord, that she may be holy both in body and spirit: but the
married careth for the things of the world, how she may please

apostles wrote nothing which was not divinely inspired: but with this difference; sometimes they had a particular revelation, and a special commandment:
at other times they wrote from the Divine light which abode with them, the
standing treasure of the Spirit of God. And this also was not their private
opinion, but a Divine rule of faith and practice. As one whom God hath made
faithful in my apostolic office; who therefore faithfully deliver what I receive
from him.

26, 27. *This is good for the present distress*—While any Church is under persecution, *for a man to continue as he is*—Whether married or unmarried. St. Paul
does not here urge the present distress, as a reason for celibacy, any more than
for marriage; but for a man's not seeking to alter his state, whatever it be, but
making the best of it.

28. *Such will have trouble in the flesh*—Many outward troubles; *but I spare
you*—I speak as little and as tenderly as possible.

29. *But this I say, brethren*—With great confidence: the time of our abode
here is short. It plainly follows, that even those who have wives, be as serious,
zealous, active, dead to the world, as devoted to God, as holy in all manner of
conversation, as if they had none. By so easy a transition does the apostle slide
from every thing else to the one thing needful; and forgetting whatever is temporal, is swallowed up in eternity.

30. *And they that weep, as if they wept not*—Though sorrowful, yet always
rejoicing; *they that rejoice, as if they rejoiced not*—Tempering their joy with
godly fear; *they that buy, as if they possessed not*—Knowing themselves to be
only stewards, not proprietors.

31. *And they that use this world, as not abusing it*—Not seeking happiness in
it, but in God: using every thing therein only in such a manner and degree as
most tends to the knowledge and love of God; *for the* whole scheme and *fashion
of this world*—This marrying, weeping, rejoicing, and all the rest, not only will
pass, but now passeth away; is this moment flying off like a shadow.

32. *Now I would have you*, for this flying moment, *without carefulness*, without any incumbrance of your thoughts. The unmarried man, if he understand
and use the advantage he enjoys, careth only for the things of the Lord, how he
may please the Lord.

33. *But the married careth for the things of the world*, (and it is duty so to do,
so far as becomes a Christian,) how he may please his wife, and provide all things
needful for her and his family.

34. *There is a difference also between a wife and a virgin*—Whether the
Church be under persecution or not. *The unmarried woman*—If she know and
use her privilege, careth only for the things of the Lord. All her time, care, and
thoughts centre in this, How *she may be holy both in body and spirit* This is the

35 her husband.   And this I say for your own profit, not that I may
   cast a snare upon you, but that ye may decently wait upon the
36 Lord, and without distraction.   But if any think that he acteth indecently toward his virgin, if she be above age, and need so require,
37 let him do what he will, he sinneth not : let them marry.   Nevertheless, he that standeth steadfast in his heart, having no necessity,
   but having power over his own will, and hath determined this in
38 his heart, to keep his virgin, doth well.   So then he also that
   'giveth in marriage, doth well, but he that giveth not in marriage,
   doth better.
39   The wife is bound as long as her husband liveth; but if her
   husband be dead, she is at liberty to marry whom she will; only
40 in the Lord.   But she is happier if she continue as she is, in my
   judgment; and I think that I also have the Spirit of God.
VIII.   Now as to things sacrificed to idols, we know : for all of us
2 have knowledge.   Knowledge puffeth up, but love edifieth.   And
   if any one think he knoweth any thing, he knoweth nothing yet
3 as he ought to know.   But if any one love God, he is known by
4 him.   I say, as to the eating of things, sacrificed to idols, we know
   that an idol *is* nothing in the world, and that *there is* no God but
5 one.   For though there be that are called gods, whether in hea-

---

standing advantage of a single life in all ages and nations.   But who makes a
suitable use of it ?

35. *Not that I may cast a snare upon you*—Who are not able to receive this
saying; *but for your profit*—Who are able, that ye may resolutely and perseveringly *wait upon the Lord*—The word translated *wait* signifies sitting close by
a person in a good posture to hear.   So Mary sat at the feet of Jesus, Luke
x, 39; *without distraction*—Without having the mind drawn any way from its
centre, from its close attention to God, by any person, or thing, or care, or
incumbrance whatsoever.

36. *But if any* parent *think he* should otherwise *act indecently*, unbecoming his
character *toward his* virgin daughter, *if she be above age*, (or of full age,) *and
need so require*, ver. 9, *let them marry*—Her suitor and she.

37. *Having no necessity*—Where there is no such need; *but having power over
his own will*—Which would incline him to desire the increase of his family, and
the strengthening it by new relations.

38. *Doth better*—If there be no necessity.

39. *Only in the Lord*—That is, only let Christians marry Christians; a standing direction, and one of the utmost importance.

40. *I also*—As well as any of you, *have the Spirit of God*—Teaching me all
things.   This does not imply any doubt; but the strongest certainty of it, together with a reproof of them for calling it in question.   Whoever therefore would
conclude from hence that St. Paul was not certain he had the Spirit of Christ,
neither understands the true import of the words, nor considers how expressly
he lays claim to the Spirit, both in this epistle, chap. ii, 16; xiv, 37; and the
other, chap. xiii, 3.   Indeed it may be doubted whether the word here and elsewhere translated *think*, does not always imply the fullest and strongest assurance;
see chap. x, 12.

VIII. 1. *Now concerning* the next question you proposed, *all of us have knowledge*—A gentle reproof of their self conceit : knowledge without love always
puffeth up.   *Love* alone *edifies*—Builds us up in holiness.

2. *If any man think he knoweth any thing*—Aright, unless so far as he is taught
by God, *he knoweth nothing yet as he ought to know*—Seeing there is no true knowledge without Divine love.

3. *He is known*—That is, approved *by him*, Psa. i, 6.

4. *We know that an idol is nothing*—A mere nominal god, having no divinity
virtue, or power.

6 ven or on earth, (as there are many gods and many lords,) Yet to
us *there is but* one God, the Father, from whom *are* all things,
and we for him; and one Lord Jesus Christ, by whom *are* all
7 things, and we by him. But *there is* not in all men this knowledge; for some do even until now, with consciousness of the idol,
eat *it* as sacrificed to the idol; and their conscience, being weak,
is defiled.

8   But meat commendeth us not to God; for neither if we eat,
9 are we the better, nor if we eat not, are we the worse   But take
heed, lest by any means this your liberty become a stumbling
10 block to the weak.   For if any one see thee, who hast knowledge,
sitting at meat in an idol temple, will not the conscience of him
that is weak be encouraged to eat of the things sacrificed to the
11 idol?   And through thy knowledge shall the weak brother perish,
12 for whom Christ died.   But when ye sin thus against your brethren, and wound their weak conscience, ye sin against Christ.
13 Wherefore if meat make my brother to offend, I will eat no flesh
while the world standeth, lest I make my brother to offend.
IX.   Am I not free?   Am I not an apostle?   Have I not seen Jesus
2 Christ our Lord?   Are not ye my work in the Lord?   If I am not

---

5. *For though there be that are called gods*—By the heathens, both celestial,
(as they term them,) terrestrial, and infernal deities.

6. *Yet to us*, Christians, *there is but one God*—This is exclusive, not of the
one Lord, as if he were an inferior Deity; but only of the idols, to which the
one God is opposed: *from whom are all things*—By creation, providence, and
grace: *and we for him*—The end of all we are, have, and do: *and one Lord*—
Equally the object of Divine worship; *by whom are all things*—Created, sustained, and governed; *and we by him*—Have access to the Father, and all
spiritual blessings.

7. *Some eat with consciousness of the idol*—That is, fancying it is something,
and that it makes the meat unlawful to be eaten; *and their conscience being
weak*—Not rightly informed, *is defiled*—Contracts guilt by doing it.

8. *But meat commendeth us not to God*—Neither by eating, nor by refraining
from it.   Eating and not eating are in themselves things merely indifferent.

10. *For if any one see thee who hast knowledge*—Whom he believes to have
more knowledge than himself, and who really hast this knowledge, that *an idol
is nothing: sitting* down to an entertainment *in an idol temple*—The heathens
frequently made entertainments in their temples on what had been sacrificed to
their idols: *will not the conscience of him that is weak*—Scrupulous, *be encouraged*—By thy example, *to eat*—Though with a doubting conscience.

11. *And through thy knowledge shall the weak brother perish, for whom Christ
died*—And for whom thou wilt not lose a meal's meat, so far from dying for him!
We see Christ died even for them that perish.

12. *Ye sin against Christ*—Whose members they are. .

13. *If meat*—Of any kind.   Who will follow this example?   What preacher
or private Christian will abstain from any thing lawful in itself, when it offends
a weak brother?

IX. 1. *Am I not free?   Am I not an apostle?*—That is, Have not I the liberty
of a common Christian?   Yea, that of an apostle?   He vindicates his apostleship, ver. 3; his apostolical liberty, ver. 4–19.   *Have I not seen Jesus Christ?*—
Without this he could not have been one of those first grand witnesses.   *Are not
ye my work in the Lord?*—A full evidence that God hath sent me?   And yet
some, it seems, objected to his being an apostle, because he had not asserted his
privilege in demanding and receiving such maintenance from the Churches as was
due to that office.

2. *Ye are the seal of my apostleship*—Who have received not only faith by my
mouth, but all the gifts of the Spirit by my hands.

an apostle to others, yet I am to you; for ye are the seal of my
3 apostleship.   My answer to them who examine me is this :
4 Have we not power to eat and to drink? Have we not power
5 to lead about a sister, a wife, as well as the other apostles, and
6 brethren of the Lord, and Peter?   Or I only and Barnabas, have
7 we not power to forbear working?   Who ever serveth as a soldier
   at his own charge?   Who planteth a vineyard, and doth not eat its
   fruit?   Or who feedeth a flock, and doth not eat of the milk of the
8 flock? Do I speak these things as a man?   Doth not the law also
9 speak the same?   For it is written in the law of Moses, * Thou
   shalt not muzzle the ox that treadeth out the corn.   Doth God
10 take care for oxen?   Or speaketh he altogether for our sakes? for
   our sakes it was written : for he who plougheth ought to plough
   in hope, and he that thresheth in hope *ought* to be a partaker of
11 his hope.   If we have sown unto you spiritual things, *is it* a great
12 matter, if we shall reap your carnal things?   If others partake of
   this power over you, *do* not we rather?   Yet we have not used this
   power : but we suffer all things, lest we should give any hinderance
13 to the Gospel of Christ.   Know ye not that they who are employed
   about holy things, are fed out of the temple?   And they who wait
14 at the altar, are partakers with the altar?   So also hath the Lord
   † ordained, that they who preach the Gospel should live of the
15 Gospel.   But I have used none of these things ; nor have I written thus, that it might be done so unto me : for *it were* better for

---

3. *My answer to them who examine me*—Concerning my apostleship, *is this*—
Which I have now given.
   4. *Have we not power*—I and my fellow labourers, *to eat and to drink*—At the
expense of those among whom we labour ?
   5. *Have we not power to lead about with us a sister*, or *a wife*, and to demand
sustenance for her also ? as well as the other apostles, (who therefore it is plain
did this,) and Peter ?   Hence we learn, 1. That St. Peter continued to live with
his wife after he became an apostle :- 2. That he had no rights as an apostle which
were not common to St. Paul.
   6. *To forbear working*—With our hands.
   8. *Do I speak as a man?*—Barely on the authority of human reason?   Does
not God also say, in effect, the same thing ?   *The ox that treadeth out the corn*—
This was the custom in Judea, and many eastern nations : in several of them
it is retained still.   And at this day horses tread out the corn in some parts
of Germany.
   9. *Doth God* in this direction *take care for oxen* only ? Hath he not a farther
meaning ?   And so undoubtedly he hath, in all the other Mosaic laws of this
kind.
   10. *He who plougheth* ought *to plough in hope*—Of reaping.   This seems to be
a proverbial expression ; *and he that thresheth in hope*—Ought not to be disappointed, ought to eat the fruit of his labours.   And so ought they who labour in
God's husbandry.
   11. *Is it a great matter, if we shall reap* as much of your carnal things as is
needful for our sustenance ?   Do ye give us things of greater value than those
you receive from us ?
   12. *If others*—Whether true or false apostles, *partake of this power*—Have a
right to be maintained, do not we rather, on account of our having laboured so
much more ? *lest we should give any hinderance to the Gospel*—By giving an occasion of cavil or reproach.
   15. *It were better for me to die, than*—To give occasion to them that seek occasion against me, 2 Cor. xi, 12.

* Deut. xxv, 4   † Matt. x, 10.

me to die, than that any man should make *this* my glorying void
16 For if I preach the Gospel, I have nothing to glory of: for a necessity lieth upon me, and wo to me if I preach not the Gospel.
17 If indeed I do this willingly, I have a reward; but if unwillingly,
18 *yet* a dispensation is entrusted to me. What then *is* my reward?
that when I preach the Gospel, I may make the Gospel without
19 charge, that I abuse not my power in the Gospel. For though I
am free from all men, I made myself the servant of all, that I
20 might gain the more. To the Jews I became as a Jew, that I
might gain the Jews: to them that are under the law, as under the
21 law, that I might gain them that are under the law: To them that
are without the law, as without the law, (being not without the
law to God, but under the law to Christ,) that I might gain them
22 that are without the law. To the weak I became as weak, that I
might gain the weak: I became all things to all men, that by all
23 means I might save some. And this I do for the Gospel's sake,
24 that I may be partaker thereof with *you*. Know ye not, that they
who run in the race, all run: but one receiveth the prize? So run
25 that ye may obtain. And every one that contendeth, is temperate
in all things: and they indeed, to obtain a corruptible crown, but

---

17. *Willingly*—He seems to mean without receiving any thing. St. Paul here
speaks in a manner peculiar to himself. Another might have preached willingly,
and yet have received a maintenance from the Corinthians. But if he had received any thing from them, he would have termed it preaching unwillingly.
And so in the next verse; another might have used that power without abusing
it. But his own *using* it at all, he would have termed *abusing* it. *A dispensation is entrusted to me*—Therefore I dare not refrain.

18. *What then is my reward*—That circumstance in my conduct, for which I
expect a peculiar reward from my great Master? *That I abuse not*—Make not an
unseasonable use of my power which I have in preaching the Gospel.

19. *I made myself the servant of all*—I acted with as self-denying a regard to
their interest, and as much caution not to offend them, as if I had been literally
their servant, or slave. Where is the preacher of the Gospel who treads in the
same steps?

20. *To the Jews I became as a Jew*—Conforming myself in all things to their
manner of thinking and living, so far as I could with innocence. *To them that
are under the law*—Who apprehend themselves to be still bound by the Mosaic
law, *as under the law*—Observing it myself while I am among them. Not that
he declared this to be necessary, or refused to converse with those who did
not observe it. This was the very thing which he condemned in St. Peter,
Gal. ii, 14.

21. *To them that are without the law*—The heathens, *as without the law*—
Neglecting its ceremonies. *Being not without the law to God*—But as much as
ever under its moral precepts, *under the law to Christ*—And in this sense all
Christians will be under the law for ever.

22. *I became as weak*—As if I had been scrupulous too. *I became all things
to all men*—Accommodating myself to all, so far as I could consistent with truth
and sincerity.

24. *Know ye not that*—In those famous games which are kept at the isthmus
near your city, *they who run in the* foot *race all run*, though *but one receiveth the
prize?* How much greater encouragement have you to run, since ye may all
receive the prize of your high calling?

25. *And every one that* there *contendeth is temperate in all things*—To an almost incredible degree; using the most rigorous self denial in food, sleep, and
every other sensual indulgence. *A corruptible crown*—A garland of leaves, which
must soon wither. The moderns only have discovered that it is legal to do all
this, and more for an eternal crown, than they did for a corruptible!

26 we an incorruptible.   I therefore so run, not є s uncertainly ; I so
27 fight, not as one that beateth the air.   But I keep under my body,
    and bring *it* into subjection, lest by any means, after having preach-
    ed to others, I myself should become a reprobate.
X.   Now I would not have you ignorant, brethren, that our fathers
2 were all * under the cloud, and all † passed through the sea.   And
3 were all baptized unto Moses, in the cloud and in the sea, And
4 ‡ all ate the same spiritual meat, And § all drank the same spi-
    ritual drink (for they drank out of the spiritual rock which follow-
5 ed them ; and that rock was Christ.)   Yet with the most of them
    God was not well pleased ; for they were overthrown in the wil-
6 derness.   Now these things were our examples, that we might

---

26. *I so run, not as uncertainly*—I look straight to the goal ; I run straight toward it.   I cast away every weight, regard not any that stand by.   *I fight not
as one that beateth the air*—This is a proverbial expression for a man's missing
his blow, and spending his strength, not on his enemy, but on empty air.

27. *But I keep under my body*—By all kinds of self denial, *and bring it into
subjection*—To my spirit and to God.   The words are strongly figurative, and
signify the mortification of the body of sin, by an allusion to the natural bodies
of those who were bruised or subdued in combat.   *Lest by any means after having preached*—The Greek word means, after having discharged the office of a
herald (still carrying on the allusion) whose office it was to proclaim the conditions, and to display the prizes.   *I myself should become a reprobate*—Disapproved
by the Judge, and so falling short of the prize.   This single text may give us a
just notion of the Scriptural doctrine of election and reprobation, and clearly
shows us, that particular persons are not in Holy Writ represented as elected
absolutely and unconditionally to eternal life, or predestinated absolutely and
unconditionally to eternal death : but that believers in general are elected to enjoy the Christian privileges on earth, which, if they abuse, those very elect persons will become reprobate.   St. Paul was certainly an elect person, if ever
there was one.   And yet he declares it was possible he himself might become a
reprobate.   Nay, he actually would have become such, if he had not thus kept
his body under, even though he had been so long an elect person, a Christian,
and an apostle.

X. 1. *Now* that ye may not become reprobates, consider how highly favoured
your fathers were, who were God's elect and peculiar people, and nevertheless
were rejected by him.   They were *all under the cloud*, that eminent token of
God's gracious presence, which screened them from the heat of the sun by day,
and gave them light by night ; *and all passed through the sea*—God opened a way
through the midst of the waters.

2. *And were all* as it were *baptized unto Moses*—Initiated into the religion which
he taught them, *in the cloud and in the sea*—Perhaps sprinkled here and there with
drops of water from the sea or the cloud, by which baptism might be the more
evidently signified.

3. *And all ate the same* manna, termed spiritual meat, as it was typical, 1. Of
Christ and his spiritual benefits ; 2. Of the sacred bread which we eat at his
table.

4. *And all drank the same spiritual drink*, (typical of Christ, and of that cup
which we drink,) *for they drank out of the spiritual* or mysterious rock, the wonderful streams of which followed them in their several journeyings, for many
years, through the wilderness.   And that rock was a manifest type of Christ, the
rock of eternity, from whom his people derive those streams of blessings, which
follow them through all this wilderness.

5. *Yet*—Although they had so many tokens of the Divine presence, *they were
overthrown*—With the most terrible marks of his displeasure.

6. *Now these things were our examples*—Showing what we are to expect, if,
enjoying the like benefits, we commit the like sins.   The benefits are set down in
the same order, as by Moses in Exodus : the sins and punishments in a differ.

* Exod. xiii, 21.   † Exod. xiv, 22.   ‡ Exod. xvi, 15.   § Exod. xvii. ᶠ

7 not desire evil things, * as they desired. Neither be ye idolaters, as *were* some of them, as it is written, † The people sat down to
8 eat and drink, and rose up to play. Neither let us commit fornication; as ‡ some of them committed, and fell in one day three and
9 twenty thousand. Neither let us tempt Christ, as § some of them
10 also tempted, and were destroyed by serpents. ‖ Neither murmur ye, as some of them murmured, and were destroyed by the de-
11 stroyer. Now all these things happened to them for examples, and they were written for our admonition, on whom the ends of the
12 ages are come. Therefore let him that most assuredly standeth,
13 take heed lest he fall. There hath no temptation taken you, but such as is common to man ; and God *is* faithful, who will not suffer you to be tempted above your ability, but will with the temptation make also a way to escape, that ye may be able to bear *it*.
4 Wherefore, my beloved, flee from idolatry. I speak as to wise
5 men ; judge ye what I say. The cup of blessing which we bless,
6 is it not the communion of the blood of Christ ? The bread which

---

ent order : evil desire first, as being the foundation of all ; next idolatry, ver. 7, 14, then fornication, which usually accompanied it, ver. 8, the tempting and murmuring against God, in the following verses. *As they desired*—Flesh, in contempt of manna.

7. *Neither be ye idolaters*—And so, *neither murmur ye*—ver. 10. The other cautions are given in the first person : but these in the second. And with what exquisite propriety does he vary the person ? It would have been improper to say, Neither let *us* be idolaters ; for he was himself in no danger of idolatry ; nor probably of murmuring against Christ, or the Divine Providence. *To play*—That is, to dance, in honour of their idol.

8. *And fell in one day three and twenty thousand*—Beside the princes who were afterward hanged, and those whom the judges slew ; so that there died in all four and twenty thousand.

9. *Neither let us tempt Christ*—By our unbelief. St. Paul enumerates five benefits, ver. 1–4, of which the fourth and fifth were closely connected together ; and five sins, the fourth and fifth of which were likewise closely connected. In speaking of the fifth benefit, he expressly mentions Christ ; and in speaking of the fourth sin, he shows it was committed against Christ. *As some of them tempted* him. This sin of the people was peculiarly against Christ. For when they had so long drunk of that rock, yet they murmured for want of water.

10. *The destroyer*—The destroying angel.

11. *On whom the ends of the ages are come*—The expression has great force. All things meet together, and come to a crisis, under the last, the Gospel dispensation ; both benefits and dangers, punishments and rewards. It remains, that Christ came as an avenger and judge. And even these ends include various periods, succeeding each other.

12. The common translation runs, *let him that thinketh he standeth.* But the word translated thinketh, most certainly strengthens, rather than weakens the sense.

13. *Common to man*—Or, as the Greek word imports, proportioned to human strength. *God is faithful*—In giving the help which he hath promised : *and he will with the temptation*—Provide for your deliverance.

14. *Flee from idolatry*—And from all approaches to it.

16. *The cup which we bless*—By setting it apart to a sacred use, and solemnly nvoking the blessing of God upon it : *is it not the communion of the blood of Christ*—The means of our partaking of those invaluable benefits, which are the purchase of the blood of Christ. *The communion of the body of Christ*—The means of our partaking of those benefits, which were purchased by *the body of Christ*—Offered for us.

* Num. xi, 4.   † Exod. xxxii, 6.   ‡ Num. xxv, 1, 9.   § Num. xxi, 4, &c.
‖ Num. xiv, 1–36.

17 we break, is it not the communion of the body of Christ? For we,
being many, are one bread, and one body; for we are all partakers
18 of the one bread.   Consider Israel after the flesh.   Are not they
19 who eat of the sacrifices, partakers of the altar? What say I then?
That a thing sacrificed to idols is any thing? Or that an idol is any
20 thing?   But that what the heathens sacrifice, they sacrifice to devils, and not to God.   Now I would not that ye should be partakers
21 with devils.   Ye cannot drink the cup of the Lord, and the cup
of devils; ye cannot be partakers of the table of the Lord, and the
22 table of devils.   Do we provoke the Lord to jealousy? are we
23 stronger than he?   All things are lawful for me; but all things are
not expedient; all things are lawful for me; but all things edify
24 not.   Let no one seek his own, but every one another's welfare.
25 Whatever is sold in the shambles eat, asking no questions for
26 conscience' sake.   * For the earth is the Lord's, and the fulness
27 thereof.   And if any of the unbelievers invite you, and ye are disposed to go, eat whatever is set before you, asking no questions for
28 conscience' sake.   But if any one say to you, This hath been sacrificed to an idol, eat not, for his sake that showed thee, and for
29 conscience' sake.   Conscience I say, not thy own, but that of the
other: for why is my liberty judged by another's conscience?
30 For if I by grace am a partaker, why am I blamed for that for
31 which I give thanks?   Therefore whether ye eat or drink, or what-

17. *For* it is this communion which makes us all one. *We being many are* yet
as it were, but different parts of one and the same broken bread, which we receiv
to unite us in one body.
18. *Consider Israel after the flesh*—Christians are the spiritual Israel of God.
Are not they who eat of the sacrifices, partakers of the altar?—Is not this an act
of communion with that God to whom they are offered? And is not the case the
same with those who eat of the sacrifices which have been offered to idols?
19. *What say I then?*—Do I in saying this allow, that an idol is any thing
Divine? I aver, on the contrary, that what the heathens sacrifice they sacrifice
to devils.   Such in reality are the gods of the heathens, and with such only can
you hold communion in those sacrifices.
21. *Ye cannot drink the cup of the Lord, and the cup of devils*—You cannot
have communion with both.
22. *Do we provoke the Lord to jealousy?*—By thus caressing his rivals? *Are
we stronger than he?*—Are we able to resist, or to bear his wrath?
23. Supposing this were *lawful* in itself, yet it is not *expedient;* it is not edifying to my neighbour.
24. *His own* only, *but another's welfare* also.
25. The apostle now applies this principle to the point in question. *Asking
no questions*—Whether it has been sacrificed or not?
26. *For* God, who is the Creator, Proprietor, and Disposer of the earth, and all
that is therein, hath given the produce of it to the children of men, to be used
without scruple.
28. *For his sake that showed thee, and for conscience' sake*—That is, for the
sake of his weak conscience, lest it should be wounded.
29. *Conscience I say, not thy own*—I speak of his conscience, not thine. *For
why is my liberty judged by another's conscience?*—Another's conscience is not
the standard of mine, nor is another's persuasion the measure of my liberty.
30. *If I by grace am a partaker*—If I thankfully use the common blessings of
God.
31. *Therefore*—To close the present point with a general rule, applicable not
only in this, but in all cases, *whatsoever ye do*—In all things whatsoever, who

* Psalm xxiv. 1.

32 soever ye do, do all to the glory of God. Give no offence either
33 to the Jews, or to the Gentiles, or to the Church of God : Even as
I please all men in all things, not seeking my own profit, but that
of many, that they may be saved.

XI. Be ye followers of me, as I also *am* of Christ.

2   Now I praise you, brethren, that ye remember me in all things,
3 and keep the orders, as I delivered *them* to you. But I would
have you know that the head of every man is Christ, and the
head of the woman *is* the man, and the head of Christ *is* God.
4 Every man praying or prophesying with *his* head covered, disho-
5 noureth his head. But every woman praying or prophesying with
her head uncovered, dishonoureth her head ; for it is the same as
6 if she were shaved. Therefore if a woman is not covered, let her
also be shaved : but if it be shameful for a woman to have her
7 hair shaved off, or cut short, let her be covered. A man indeed
ought not to have *his* head covered, being the image and glory of
8 God ; but the woman is the glory of the man. For the man is
9 not of the woman, but the woman of the man. Neither was the
man created for the sake of the woman, but the woman for the
10 sake of the man. For this cause *also* the woman ought to have a

ther of a religious or civil nature, in all the common as well as sacred actions of
life, keep the glory of God in view, and steadily pursue in all this one end of
your being, the planting or advancing the vital knowledge and love of God, first
in your own soul, then in all mankind.

32. *Give no offence*—If, and as far as, it is possible.

33. *Even as I*, as much as lieth in me, please all men.

XI. 2. *I praise you*—The greater part of you.

3. *I would have you know*—He does not seem to have given them any order
before concerning this. The head of every man, particularly every believer,
is Christ, and the head of Christ is God. Christ, as he is Mediator, acts in all
things subordinately to his Father. But we can no more infer, that they are
not of the same Divine nature, because God is said to be the head of Christ, than
that man and woman are not of the same human nature, because the man is said
to be the head of the woman.

4. *Every man praying or prophesying*—Speaking by the immediate power of
God, *with his head*—And face covered, either with a veil or with long hair, *dishonoureth his head*—St. Paul seems to mean, As in those eastern nations, veiling
the head is a badge of subjection, so a man who prays or prophesies with a veil
on his head, reflects a dishonour on Christ, whose representative he is.

5. *But every woman*, who under an immediate impulse of the Spirit, (for then
only was a woman suffered to speak in the Church,) prays or prophesies without
a veil on her face : as it were disclaims subjection, and reflects dishonour on
man, her head. For it is the same, in effect, as if she cut her hair short, and
wore it in the distinguishing form of the men. In those ages, men wore their
hair exceeding short, as appears from the ancient statues and pictures.

6. *Therefore if a woman is not covered*—If she will throw off the badge of subjection, let her appear with her hair cut like a man's : but if it be shameful for a
woman to appear thus in public, especially in a religious assembly, let her for the
same reason keep on her veil.

7. *A man indeed ought not to* veil his head, because he is the image of God, in
the dominion he bears over the creation, representing the supreme dominion of
God, which is his glory. But the woman is only matter of glory to the man,
who has a becoming dominion over her. Therefore she ought not to appear, but
with her head veiled, as a tacit acknowledgment of it.

8. *The man is not*—In the first production of nature.

10. *For this cause also a woman ought to* be veiled in the public assemblies, because of the angels who attend there, and before whom they should be careful
not to do any thing indecent or irregular.

11 veil upon *her* head, because of the angels : Nevertheless, neither is
the man without the woman, nor the woman without the man, in
12 the Lord. And as the woman *was* of the man, so also the man *is*
13 by the woman ; but all things *are* of God. Judge of yourselves :
14 is it decent for a woman to pray to God uncovered ? Doth not
nature itself teach you, that for a man to have long hair, is a
15 disgrace to him ? Whereas for a woman to have long hair, is a
16 glory to her ; for her hair was given her instead of a veil. But if
any one be resolved to be contentious, we have no such custom,
neither the Churches of God.
17 But in this which I declare, I praise *you* not, that ye come
18 together not for the better, but for the worse. For first, when ye
come together in the Church, I hear there are schisms among you,
19 (and I partly believe it. For there must be heresies also among

11. *Nevertheless, in the Lord* Jesus, *there is neither male nor female*—Neither
is excluded ; neither is preferred before the other in his kingdom.
12. *And as the woman was* at first taken out of the man, so also the man is
now in the ordinary course of nature by the woman. But all things are of God,
the man, the woman, and their dependence on each other.
13. *Judge of yourselves*—For what need of more argument in so plain a case ?
Is it decent for a woman to pray to God, the Most High, with that bold and
undaunted air, which she must have, when, contrary to universal custom, she
appears in public with her head uncovered ?
14. *For a man to have long hair*, carefully adjusted, is such a mark of effeminacy as is a disgrace to him.
15. *Given her*—Originally, before the arts of dress were in being.
16. *We have no such custom* here, *nor any of* the other *Churches of God*—The
several Churches that were in the apostle's time had different customs, in things
that were not essential ; and that under one and the same apostle, as circumstances, in different places, made it convenient. And in all things merely
indifferent, the custom of each place was of sufficient weight to determine
prudent and peaceable men. Yet even this cannot overrule a scrupulous conscience, which really doubts whether the thing be indifferent or not. But those
who are referred to here by the apostle, were contentious, not conscientious
persons.
18. *In the Church*—In the public assembly. *I hear there are schisms among
you, and I partly believe it*—That is, I believe it of some of you. It is plain, that
by schisms is not meant any separation from the Church, but uncharitable divisions in it. For the Corinthians continued to be one Church, and notwithstanding all their strife and contention, there was no separation of any one party
from the rest, with regard to external communion. And it is in the same sense
that the word is used, chap. i, 10, and chap. xii, 25, which are the only places in
the New Testament beside this, where Church schisms are mentioned. Therefore the indulging any temper contrary to this tender care of each other, is the
true Scriptural schism. This is therefore a quite different thing from that
orderly separation from corrupt Churches, which later ages have stigmatized as
schism ; and have made a pretence for the vilest cruelties, oppressions, and murders, that have troubled the Christian world. Both heresies and schisms are here
mentioned in very near the same sense ; unless by schisms be meant rather those
inward animosities which occasion heresies ; that is, outward divisions or parties.
So that while one said, I am of Paul, another I am of Apollos, this implied
both schism and heresy. So wonderfully have later ages distorted the words
heresy and schism from their Scriptural meaning. Heresy is not, in all the
Bible, taken for " an error in fundamentals," or in any thing else ; nor schism,
for any separation from the outward communion of others. Therefore both
heresy and schism, in the modern sense of the words, are sins that the Scripture
knows nothing of ; but were invented merely to deprive mankind of the benefit
of private judgment, and liberty of conscience.
19. *There must be heresies*—Divisions, *among you*—In the ordinary course of

20 you, that the approved among you may be manifest.)   Therefore
   when ye come together into one place, it is not eating the Lord's
21 Supper.   For in eating every one taketh before *another* his own
22 supper, and one is hungry, another drinks largely.   What! have
   ye not houses to eat and drink in? or do ye despise the Church of
   God, and shame them that have not?   What shall I say to you?
23 shall I praise you in this? I praise *you* not.   For I received from
   the Lord what I also delivered to you, that the Lord Jesus, the
24 night in which he was betrayed, took bread, And when he had given
   thanks he brake *it*, and said, This is my body, which is broken for
25 you; do this in remembrance of me.   In like manner also *he took*
   the cup after he had supped, saying, This cup is the new covenant
   in my blood: do this as often as ye drink *it*, in remembrance
26 of me.   For as often as ye eat this bread, and drink this cup, ye
27 show forth the Lord's death till he come.   So that whosoever
   eateth the bread and drinketh the cup of the Lord unworthily, shall
28 be guilty of the body and blood of the Lord.   But let a man examine himself, and so let him eat of the bread and drink of the cup.
29 For he that eateth and drinketh unworthily, eateth and drinketh
30 judgment to himself, not distinguishing the Lord's body.   For

---

things; and God permits them, that it may appear who among you are, and who
are not, upright of heart.

20. *Therefore*—That is, in consequence of those schisms, *it is not eating the
Lord's Supper*—That solemn memorial of his death, but quite another thing.

21. *For in eating* what we call the Lord's Supper, instead of all partaking of
one bread, each person brings his own supper, and eats it, without staying for
the rest.   And hereby the poor, who cannot provide for themselves, have nothing,
while the rich eat and drink to the full.   Just as the heathens used to do at the
feasts of their sacrifices.

22. *Have ye not houses to eat and drink* your common meals in?—*Or do ye
despise the Church of God?*—Of which the poor are both the larger and the better part.   Do ye act thus, in designed contempt of them?

23. *I received*—By an immediate revelation.

24. *This is my body which is broken for you*—That is, this broken bread is the
sign of my body, which is even now to be pierced and wounded for your iniquities.   Take then and eat of this bread, in an humble, thankful, obediential
remembrance of my dying love; of the extremity of my sufferings on your
behalf, of the blessings I have thereby procured for you, and of the obligations
to love and duty, which I have by all this laid upon you.

25. *After supper*—Therefore ye ought not to confound this with a common
meal.   *Do this in remembrance of me*—The ancient sacrifices were in remembrance of sin.   This sacrifice once offered is still represented in remembrance of
the remission of sins.

26. *Ye show forth the Lord's death*—Ye proclaim, as it were, and openly avow
it, to God and to all the world, *till he come*—In glory.

27. *Whosoever shall eat this bread unworthily*—That is, in an unworthy, irre-
verent manner, without regarding either him that appointed it, or the design
of its appointment, shall be guilty of profaning that which represents the body
and blood of the Lord.

28. *But let a man examine himself*—Whether he know the nature and the
design of the institution, and whether it be his own desire and purpose thoroughly to comply therewith.

29. *For he that eateth and drinketh* so unworthily as those Corinthians did,
eateth and drinketh judgment to himself—Temporal judgments of various kinds,
(ver. 30,) not distinguishing the sacred tokens of *the Lord's body*—From his
common food.

30. *For this cause*—Which they had not observed, *many sleep*—In death.

CHAPTER XII.

this cause many *are* sick and weak among you, and many sleep.
31 For if we would judge ourselves, we should not be judged. But
32 when we are judged, we are chastened by the Lord, that we may
33 not be condemned with the world. Wherefore, my brethren, when
34 ye come together to eat, wait one for another. And if any one
be hungry, let him eat at home, that ye come not together to condemnation. And the rest I will set in order when I come.

XII. Now concerning spiritual *gifts*, brethren, I would not have you
2 ignorant. Ye know that when ye were heathens, ye were carried
3 away after dumb idols, as ye were led. Therefore I give you to
know, that *as* no one speaking by the Spirit of God, calleth Jesus
accursed; so no one can say, Jesus *is* the Lord, but by the Holy
4 Ghost. Now there are diversities of gifts, but the same Spirit.
5 And there are diversities of ministrations, but the same Lord: And
6 there are diversities of operations, but it is the same God who
worketh all in all.
7 But the manifestation of the Spirit is given to each, to profit
8 withal. For to one is given by the Spirit, the word of wisdom;

---

31. *If we would judge ourselves*—As to our knowledge, and the design with
which we approach the Lord's table, *we should not be thus judged*—That is,
punished by God.

32. *When we are thus judged*, it is with this merciful design, that we may not
be finally condemned with the world.

33. *The rest*—The other circumstances relating to the Lord's Supper.

XII. 1. *Now concerning spiritual gifts*—The abundance of these in the Churches
of Greece strongly refuted the idle learning of the Greek philosophers. But the
Corinthians did not use them wisely, which occasioned St. Paul's writing concerning them. He describes, 1. The unity of the body, ver. 1–27. 2. The variety
of members and offices, ver. 27–30. 3. The way of exercising gifts rightly, namely,
by love, ver. 31, chap. xiii, throughout: and adds, 4. A comparison of several
gifts with each other, in the 14th chapter.

2. *Ye were heathens*—Therefore whatever gifts ye have received, it is from the
free grace of God, *carried away*—By a blind credulity, *after dumb idols*—The
blind to the dumb: idols of wood and stone, unable to speak themselves, and
much more to open your mouths, as God has done; *as ye were led*—By the subtlety of your priests.

3. *Therefore*—Since the heathen idols cannot speak themselves, much less give
spiritual gifts to others, these must necessarily be among Christians only: *as no
one speaking by the Spirit of God, calleth Jesus accursed*—That is, as none who
does this (which all the Jews and heathens did) speaketh by the Spirit of God, is
actuated by that Spirit, so as to speak with tongues, heal diseases, or cast out
devils; *so no one can say, Jesus is the Lord*—None can receive him as such, (for
in the Scripture language to say, or to believe, implies an experimental assurance,) but by the Holy Ghost. The sum is, none have the Holy Spirit but
Christians: all Christians have this Spirit.

4. *There are diversities of gifts, but the same Spirit*—Divers streams, but all
from one fountain. This verse speaks of the Holy Ghost, the next of Christ, the
5th of God the Father. The apostle treats of the Spirit, ver. 7, &c; of Christ,
ver. 12, &c; of God, ver. 28, &c.

5. *Administrations*—Offices. But the same Lord appoints them all.

6. *Operations*—Effects produced. This word is of a larger extent than either
of the former. But it is the same God who worketh all these effects in all the
persons concerned.

7. *The manifestation*—The gift whereby the Spirit manifests itself; *is given
to each* for the profit of the whole body.

8. *The word of wisdom*—A power of understanding and explaining the manifold wisdom of God in the grand scheme of Gospel salvation. *The word of know-*

28

9 to another by the same Spirit, the word of knowledge; To an
other faith by the same Spirit; to another the gift of healing by the
10 same Spirit; To another the working of miracles; to another prophecy; to another the discerning of spirits; to another *divers* kinds
11 of tongues; to another the interpretation of tongues. But one and
the same Spirit worketh all these, dividing to every one severally
as he willeth.

12   For as the body is one, and yet hath many members, but all the
members of the body, many as they are, are one body, so *is*
13 Christ. For we were all baptized by one Spirit into one body,
whether *we are* Jews or Gentiles, whether slaves or freemen; and
14 we have all drank of one Spirit. For the body is not one member,
15 but many. If the foot should say, Because I am not the hand, I
16 am not of the body, is it therefore not of the body? And if the ear
should say, Because I am not the eye, I am not of the body, is it
17 therefore not of the body? If the whole body *were* an eye, where
were the hearing? If the whole *were* hearing, where *were* the smell-
18 ing? But now hath God set the members, every one in the body
19 as it hath pleased him. And if all were one member, where *were*
20 the body? Whereas now there *are* indeed many members, yet
21 but one body. And the eye cannot say to the hand, I have no

---

ledge—Perhaps an extraordinary ability to understand and explain the Old Testament types and prophecies.

9. *Faith* may here mean an extraordinary trust in God under the most difficult or dangerous circumstances. *The gift of healing* need not be wholly confined to the healing diseases with a word or a touch. It may exert itself also,
though in a lower degree, where natural remedies are applied. And it may
often be this, not superior skill, which makes some physicians more successful
than others. And thus it may be with regard to other gifts likewise. As after
the golden shields were lost, the king of Judah put brazen in their place, so after
the pure gifts were lost, the power of God exerts itself in a more covert manner
under human studies and helps : and that the more plentiful, accordingly as there
is the more room given for it.

10. *The working of* other *miracles—prophecy*—Foretelling things to come,
the discerning—Whether men be of an upright spirit or no. Whether they have
natural or supernatural gifts for offices in the Church. And whether they who
profess to speak by inspiration, speak from a Divine, a natural, or a diabolical spirit.

11. *As he willeth*—The Greek word does not so much imply arbitrary pleasure,
as a determination founded on wise counsel.

12. *So is Christ*—That is, the body of Christ, the Church.

13. *For by* that one Spirit which we received in baptism, we are all united in
one body, *whether Jews or Gentiles*—Who are at the greatest distance from each
other by nature ; *whether slaves or freemen*—Who are at the greatest distance by
law and custom : *we have all drank of one Spirit*—In that cup received by faith,
we all imbibed one Spirit, who first inspired and still preserves the life of God in
our souls.

15. *The foot* is elegantly introduced as speaking of the hand, the ear of the
eye, each of a part that has some resemblance to it. So among men, each is
apt to compare himself with those whose gifts someway resemble his own,
rather than with those who are at a distance, either above or beneath him. *Is it
therefore not of the body ?*—Is the inference good ? Perhaps the foot may represent private Christians ; the hand, officers in the Church ; the eye, teachers ; the
ear, hearers.

16. *The ear*—A less noble part : *the eye*—The most noble.

18. *As it hath pleased him*—With the most exquisite wisdom and goodness.

20. *But one body*—And it is a necessary consequence of this unity, that the
several members need one another.

need of thee ; or again, the head to the feet, I have no need of you
22 Yea, the members of the body, which appear to be weaker, are
23 much more necessary. And those which we think to be the less
honourable *parts* of the body, these we surround with more
abundant honour, and our uncomely *parts* have more abundant come-
24 liness. For our comely *parts* have no need ; but God hath tempered the body together, giving more abundant honour to that which
25 lacked : That there might be no schism in the body, but *that* the
26 members might have the same care for each other ; And whether
one member suffer, all the members might suffer with it ; or one
27 member be honoured, all the members might rejoice with it. Now
ye are the body of Christ, and members in particular.
28 And God hath set in the Church, first, apostles, secondly, prophets, thirdly, teachers ; afterward miracles, then gifts of healing,
29 helps, governments, *different* kinds of tongues. *Are* all apostles ?
Are all prophets ? *Are* all teachers ? *Have* all miraculous powers ?
30 Have all the gifts of healing ? do all speak with tongues ? Do all
31 interpret ? Yet covet earnestly the best gifts. But I show unto
you a more excellent way.
XIII.   Though I speak with the tongues of men and of angels, and
have not love, I am become *as* sounding brass, or a tinkling cym-
2 bal.   And though I have the gift of prophecy, and understand all
mysteries and all knowledge, and though I have all faith, so as

---

21. *Nor the head*—The highest part of all, *to the foot*—The very lowest.

22. *The members which appear to be weaker*—Being of a more delicate and
tender structure. Perhaps the brains and bowels ; or the veins, arteries, and
other minute channels in the body.

23. *We surround with more abundant honour*—By so carefully covering them ;
more abundant comeliness—By the help of dress.

24. *Giving more abundant honour to that which lacked*—As being cared for and
served by the noblest parts.

27. *Now ye*—Corinthians, are the body and members of Christ ; part of them,
I mean, not the whole body.

28. *First, apostles*—Who plant the Gospel in the heathen nations ; *Secondly,
prophets*—Who either foretell things to come, or speak by extraordinary inspiration, for the edification of the Church : *Thirdly, teachers,* who precede even those
that work miracles. Under prophets and teachers are comprised evangelists and
pastors, Eph. iv, 11 ; *helps, governments*—It does not appear that these mean distinct offices. Rather any persons might be called helps, from a peculiar dexterity
in helping the distressed ; and governments, from a peculiar talent for governing
or presiding in assemblies.

31. *Yet covet earnestly the best gifts*—And they are worth your pursuit, though
but few of you can attain them. But there is a far more excellent gift than all
these : and one which all may, yea, must attain, or perish.

XIII. The necessity of love is shown, ver. 1–3. The nature and properties,
ver. 4–7. The duration of it, ver. 8–13.

1. *Though I speak with all the tongues* which are upon earth, and with the
eloquence of an angel, *and have not love*—The love of God, and of all mankind
for his sake, I am no better before God than the sounding instruments of brass,
used in the worship of some of the heathen gods. *Or a tinkling cymbal*—This was
made of two pieces of hollow brass, which being struck together, made a tinkling, but with very little variety of sound.

2. *And though I have the gift of prophecy*—Of foretelling future events, and
understanding all the mysteries both of God's word and providence, and all
knowledge of things Divine and human, that ever any mortal attained to : and
though I have the highest degree of miracle-working faith, and have not this love
I am nothing.

3 to remove mountains, and have not love, I am nothing. And
though I give all my goods to feed the poor, and deliver up my
body to be burned, and have not love, it profiteth me nothing.
4 Love suffereth long *and* is kind; love envieth not; love acteth not
5 rashly, is not puffed up : Doth not behave indecently, seeketh not
6 her own, is not provoked, thinketh no evil; Rejoiceth not in ini
7 quity, but rejoiceth in the truth : Covereth all things, believeth all
8 things, hopeth all things, endureth all things. Love never fail
eth : but whether *there be* prophecies, they shall fail; whether
there be tongues, they shall cease ; whether *there be* knowledge,

3 *And though I* deliberately, piece by piece, give all my goods to feed the
poor, yea, though I deliver up my body to be burned, rather than I would renounce my religion, and have not the love hereafter described, it profiteth me
nothing. Without this, whatever I speak, whatever I believe, whatever I know,
whatever I do, whatever I suffer, is nothing.

4. The love of God, and of our neighbour for God's sake, is patient toward all
men. It suffers all the weakness, ignorance, errors, and infirmities of the children of God: all the malice and wickedness of the children of the world ; and
all this, not only for a time, but to the end. And in every step toward overcoming evil with good, it is kind, soft, mild, benign. It inspires the sufferer at once
with the most amiable sweetness, and the most fervent and tender affection. *Love
acteth not rashly*—Does not hastily condemn any one: never passes a severe sentence, on a slight or sudden view of things. Nor does it over act or behave in
a violent, headstrong, or precipitate manner. *Is not puffed up*—Yea, humbles
the soul to the dust.

5. *It doth not behave indecently*—Is not rude, or willingly offensive to any. It
renders to all their due, suitable to time, person, and all other circumstances.
Seeketh not her own—Ease, pleasure, honour, or temporal advantage. Nay, sometimes the lover of mankind seeketh not in some sense even his own spiritual advantage: does not think of himself, so long as a zeal for the glory of God and
the souls of men swallows him up. But though he is all on fire for these ends,
yet he is not provoked to sharpness or unkindness toward any one. Outward
provocations indeed will frequently occur. But he triumphs over all. Love
thinketh no evil—Indeed it cannot but see and hear evil things, and know that
they are so. But it does not willingly think evil of any; neither infer evil
where it does not appear. It tears up, root and branch, all imagining of what
we have not proof. It casts out all jealousies, all evil surmises, all readiness to
believe evil.

6. *Rejoiceth not in iniquity*—Yea, weeps at either the sin or folly of even an
enemy, takes no pleasure in hearing or in repeating it, but desires it may be forgotten for ever. *But rejoiceth in the truth*—Bringing forth its proper fruit, holiness of heart and life. Good in general is its glory and joy, wherever diffused
in all the world.

7. Love *covereth all things*—Whatever evil the lover of mankind sees, hears,
or knows of any one, he mentions it to none ; it never goes out of his lips, unless
where absolute duty constrains to speak. *Believeth all things*—Puts the most
favourable construction on every thing ; and is ever ready to believe whatever
may tend to the advantage of any one's character. And when it can no longer
believe well, it hopes whatever may excuse or extenuate the fault which cannot
be denied. Where it cannot even excuse, it hopes God will at length give repentance unto life. Meantime *it endureth all things*—Whatever the injustice,
the malice, the cruelty of men can inflict. He can not only do, but likewise suffer all things through Christ who strengtheneth him.

8. *Love never faileth*—It accompanies to, and adorns us in eternity : it prepares
us for, and constitutes heaven ; *but whether there be prophecies, they shall fail*—
When all things are fulfilled, and God is all in all: *whether there be tongues, they
shall cease*—One language shall prevail among all the inhabitants of heaven,
and the low and imperfect languages of earth be forgotten. The knowledge likewise which we now so eagerly pursue, shall then vanish away. As starlight is
ost in that of the mid-day sun, so our present knowledge in the light of eternitv.

9 it shall vanish away. For we know in part, and we prophesy in
10 part. And when that which is perfect is come, then that which is
11 in part shall vanish away. When I was a child I talked as a child;
I understood as a child, I reasoned as a child; but when I became
12 a man, I put away childish things. And now we see by means of
a glass obscurely; but then face to face: now I know in part, but
13 then I shall know, even as also I am known. And now abide these
three, faith, hope, love; but the greatest of these is love.
XIV. Follow after love: and desire spiritual *gifts;* but especially
2 that ye may prophesy. For he that speaketh in an *unknown*
tongue, speaketh not to men, but to God; for no one understand-
3 eth *him,* though by the Spirit he speaketh mysteries: Whereas
he that prophesieth, speaketh to men to edification, and exhorta-
4 tion, and comfort. He that speaketh in an *unknown* tongue, edi-
5 fieth himself; but he that prophesieth, edifieth the Church. I
would that ye all spake with tongues, but rather that ye prophesied; for he that prophesieth *is* greater than he that speaketh with
tongues, unless he interpret, that the Church may receive edifica-
6 tion. Now, brethren, if I come to you speaking with tongues,
what shall I profit you, unless I speak to you, either by revelation

9. *For we know in part, and we prophesy in part*—The wisest of men have
here but short, narrow, imperfect conceptions, even of the things round about
them, and much more of the deep things of God. And even the prophecies
which men deliver from God are far from taking in the whole of future events,
or of that wisdom and knowledge of God which is treasured up in the Scripture
revelation.

10. *But when that which is perfect is come*—At death and in the last day, *that
which is in part shall vanish away*—Both that poor, low, imperfect, glimmering
light, which is all the knowledge we now can attain to: and these slow and
unsatisfactory methods of attaining, as well as of imparting it to others.

11. In our present state we are mere infants in point of knowledge, compared
to what we shall be hereafter. *I put away childish things*—Of my own accord,
willingly, without trouble.

12. *Now we see* even the things that surround us, but by means of a glass or
mirror, which reflects only their imperfect forms, in a dim, faint, obscure manner; so that our thoughts about them are puzzling and intricate, and every thing
is a kind of riddle to us. But then we shall see, not a faint reflection, but the
objects themselves *face to face*—Distinctly. *Now I know* but *in part*—Even when
God himself reveals things to me, great part of them is still kept under the veil.
But then shall I know, even as also I am known—In a clear, full, comprehensive
manner; in some measure like God, who penetrates the centre of every object,
and sees at one glance through my soul and all things.

13. *Faith, hope, love,* are the sum of perfection on earth; love alone is the
sum of perfection in heaven.

XIV. 1. *Follow after love*—With zeal, vigour, courage, patience: else you can
neither attain nor keep it. And in their place, as subservient to this, *desire spiritual gifts; but especially that ye may prophesy*—The word here does not mean
foretelling things to come; but rather opening and applying the Scripture.

2. *He that speaketh in an unknown tongue, speaks,* in effect, *not to men, but to
God*—Who alone understands him.

4. *Edifieth himself* only, on the most favourable supposition; *the Church*—
The whole congregation.

5. *Greater*—That is, more useful. By this alone are we to estimate all our
gifts and talents.

6. *Revelation*—of some Gospel mystery. *Knowledge*—Explaining the ancient
types and prophecies. *Prophecy*—Foretelling some future event. *Doctrine*—To
regulate your tempers and lives. Perhaps this may be the sense of these obscure
words.

7 or by knowledge, or by prophecy, or by doctrine? So inanimate things which give a sound, whether pipe or harp, unless they give a distinction in the sounds, how shall it be known what is piped or
8 harped? And if the trumpet give an uncertain sound, who will
9 prepare himself for the battle? So likewise unless ye utter by the tongue words easy to be understood, how shall it be known what is
10 spoken? For ye will speak to the air. Let there be ever so many kinds of languages in the world, and none of them without signi-
11 fication; Yet if I know not the meaning of the language, I shall be a barbarian to him that speaketh, and he that speaketh a barba-
12 rian to me. So ye also, seeing ye desire spiritual gifts, seek to
13 abound *in them*, to the edifying of the Church. Therefore let him that speaketh in an *unknown* tongue, pray that he may interpret.
14 For if I pray in an *unknown* tongue, my spirit prayeth, but my
15 understanding is unfruitful. What then is *my duty?* I will pray with the Spirit; but I will pray with the understanding also : I will sing with the Spirit; but I will sing with the understanding also.
16 Otherwise if thou givest thanks with the Spirit, how shall he that filleth the place of a private person, say Amen to thy thanksgiving,
17 seeing he understandeth not what thou sayest? For thou verily
18 givest thanks well; yet the other is not edified. I thank God,
19 that I speak with tongues more than you all. Yet in the congregation I had rather speak five words with my understanding, that I may teach others also, than ten thousand words in an *unknown*
20 tongue. Brethren, be not children in understanding; in wicked-
21 ness be ye as infants, but in understanding be ye grown men. It

7. *How shall it be known what is piped or harped?*—What music can be made, or what end answered?
8. *Who will prepare himself for the battle?*—Unless he understand what the trumpet sounds? Suppose a retreat or a march?
9. *Unless ye utter by the tongue*—Which is miraculously given you, *words easy to be understood*—By your hearers, *ye will speak to the air*—(a proverbial expression) will utterly lose your labour.
11. *I shall be a barbarian to him*—Shall seem to talk unintelligible gibberish.
13. *That he may be able to interpret*—Which was a distinct gift.
14. *If I pray in an unknown tongue*—The apostle (as he did at the 6th verse) transfers it to himself; *my spirit prayeth*—by the power of the Spirit I understand the words myself, *but my understanding is unfruitful*—The knowledge I have is no benefit to others.
15. *I will pray with the Spirit, but I will pray with the understanding also*—I will use my understanding, as well as the power of the Spirit. I will not act so absurdly, as to utter in a congregation what can edify none but myself.
16. *Otherwise, how shall he that filleth the place of a private person*—That is, any private hearer, *say Amen*—Assenting and confirming your words, as it was even then usual for the whole congregation to do.
19. *With my understanding*—In a rational manner; so as not only to understand myself, but to be understood by others.
20. *Be not children in understanding*—This is an admirable stroke of true oratory! To bring down the height of their spirits, by representing that wherein they prided themselves most, as mere folly and childishness. *In wickedness be ye infants*—Have all the innocence of that tender age, *but in understanding be ye grown men*—Knowing religion was not designed to destroy any of our natural faculties, but to exalt and improve them, our reason in particular.
21. *It is written in the law*—The word here (as frequently) means the Old Testament. *In foreign tongues will I speak to this people*—And so he did. He spake terribly to them by the Babylonians, when they had set at nought what he

ıs written in the law, * In foreign tongues and with foreign lips
will I speak to this people ; and neither so will they hear me, saith
22 the Lord   So that tongues are for a sign, not to believers, but to
unbelievers ; whereas prophecy *is* not for unbelievers, but for
23 believers.   Yet if the whole Church be met together, and all speak
with *unknown* tongues, and there come in ignorant persons, or
24 unbelievers, will they not say that ye are mad ?   Whereas if all
prophesy, and there come in an unbeliever, or an ignorant person,
25 he is convicted by all, he is judged by all : The secrets of his
heart are made manifest, and so falling down on *his* face, he will
worship God, and declare that God is among you of a truth.
26   What a thing is it, brethren, that when ye come together, every
one of you hath a psalm, hath a doctrine, hath a revelation, hath a
tongue, hath an interpretation ?   Let all things be done to edifica-
27 tion.   If any one speak in an *unknown* tongue, le* it be by two or
28 three at most, and that by course, let one interpret.   But if there
be no interpreter, let him be silent in the Church, and let him speak
29 to himself and to God.   Let two or three of the prophets speak,
30 and let the rest judge.   But if *any thing* be revealed to another that
31 sitteth by, let the first be silent.   For ye may all prophesy one by

had spok⸳n to them by the prophets, who used their own language.   These words
received a farther accomplishment on the day of pentecost.
22. *Tongues are* intended *for a sign to unbelievers*—To engage their attention,
and convince them the message is of God.   Whereas prophecy is not so much
for unbelievers, as for the confirmation of them that already believe.
23. *Yet* sometimes prophecy is of more use even to unbelievers than speaking
with tongues.   For instance : *if the whole Church be met together*—On some
extraordinary occasion.   It is probable, in so large a city, they ordinarily met in
several places : *and there come in ignorant persons*—Men of learning might have
understood the tongues in which they spoke.   It is observable St. Paul says here
ignorant persons or unbelievers ; but in the next verse, an unbeliever or an ignorant person.   Several bad men met together hinder each other by evil discourse.
Single persons are more easily gained.
24. *He is convicted by all*—Who speak in their turns, and speak to the heart
of the hearers : *he is judged by all*—Every one says something to which his conscience bears witness.
25. *The secrets of his heart are made manifest*—Laid open, clearly described ;
in a manner which to him is most astonishing and utterly unaccountable.   How
many instances of it are seen at this day ?   So does God still point his word.
26. *What a thing is it, brethren*—This was another disorder among them.
Every one hath a psalm—That is, at the same time one begins to sing a psalm :
another to deliver a doctrine ; another to speak in an unknown tongue ; another
to declare what has been revealed in him ; another to interpret what the former
is speaking : every one probably gathering a little company about him, just as
they did in the schools of the philosophers.   *Let all be done to edification*—So as
to profit the hearers.
27. *By two or three at most*—Let not above two or three speak at one meeting ; *and that by course*—That is, one after another ; *and let one interpret*—
Either himself, ver. 13, or (if he have not the gift) some other, into the vulgar
tongue.   It seems the gift of tongues was an instantaneous knowledge of a
tongue till then unknown, which he that received it could afterward speak when
he thought fit, without any new miracle.
28. *Let him speak* that tongue, if he find it profitable to himself in his private
devotions.
29. *Let two or three of the prophets* (not more at one meeting) speak, one after
another, expounding the Scripture.

* Isaiah xxviii, 11.

32 one, that all may learn, and all may be comforted.   For the spirits
33 of the prophets are subject to the prophets.   For God is not *the
   author* of confusion, but of peace, as in all the Churches of the
34 saints.   Let your women be silent in the Churches; for it is not
   permitted them to speak, but to be in subjection, as * the law also
35 saith.   And if they desire to learn any thing, let them ask their
   own husbands at home ; for it is indecent for a woman to speak
36 in the assembly.   Did the word of God come out from you? or did
37 it come out to you alone?   If any one think himself to be a prophet, or spiritual, let him take knowledge that the things which I
38 write to you are the commandments of the Lord.   But if any one
39 is ignorant, let him be ignorant.   Therefore, brethren, covet to pro-
40 phesy; yet forbid not to speak with tongues.   Let all things be
   done decently and in order.
XV.   Moreover, brethren, I declare to you the Gospel which I
 2 preached to you, which also ye received, and wherein ye stand.   By
   which also ye are saved, if ye hold fast in what manner I preached
 3 to you, unless ye have believed in vain.   For I delivered to you
   first, that which I also received, that Christ died for our sins,
 4 † according to the Scriptures : And that he was buried, and that he
 5 was raised the third day, ‡ according to the Scriptures : And that
 6 he was seen by Cephas, then by the twelve.   Afterward he was

31. *All*—Who have that gift, that all may learn, both by speaking and by
hearing.
32. *For the spirits of the prophets are subject to the prophets*—But what enthu-
siast considers this ?   The impulses of the Holy Spirit, even in men really inspired, so suit themselves to their rational faculties, as not to divest them of the
government of themselves, like the heathen priests under their diabolical possessions.   Evil spirits threw their prophets into such ungovernable ecstacies, as
forced them to speak and act like madmen.   But the Spirit of God left his prophets the clear use of their judgment, when and how long it was fit for them to
speak, and never hurried them into any improprieties, either as to the matter,
manner, or time of their speaking.
34. *Let your women be silent in the Churches*—Unless they are under an extraordinary impulse of the Spirit.   *For* in other cases *it is not permitted them to
speak*—By way of teaching in public assemblies ; *but to be in subjection*—To the
man, whose proper office it is to lead and to instruct the congregation.
35. *And* even *if they desire to learn any thing*, still they are not to speak in
public, but to ask their own husbands at home.   That is the place, and those the
persons to inquire of.
36. *Are ye of Corinth*, either the first or the only Christians?   If not, conform
herein to the custom of all the Churches.
37. *Or spiritual*—Endowed with an extraordinary gift of the Spirit : let him
prove it, by acknowledging that I now write by the Spirit.
38. *Let him be ignorant*—Be it at his own peril.
39. *Therefore*—To sum up the whole.
40. *Decently*—By every individual : *in order*—By the whole Church.
XV. 2. *Ye are saved, if ye hold fast*—Your salvation is begun, and will be perfected, if ye continue in the faith : *unless ye have believed in vain*—Unless indeed
your faith was only a delusion.
3. *I received*—From Christ himself.   It was not a fiction of my own.
4. *According to the Scriptures*—He proves it first from Scripture, then from
the testimony of a cloud of witnesses.
5. *By the twelve*—This was their standing appellation : but their full number
was not then present.

* Gen. iii, 16   † Isa. liii, 8, 9.   ‡ Psa. xvi, 10.

ßeen by above five hundred brethren at once, of whom the greater
7 part remain until now, but some are fallen asleep. After this he
8 was seen by James, then by all the apostles. Last of all he was
9 seen by me also, as an untimely birth. For I am the least of the
apostles, who am not worthy to be called an apostle, because I
10 persecuted the Church of God. But by the grace of God I am
what I am; and his grace toward me was not in vain, but I laboured more abundantly than they all: yet not I, but the grace of God
11 that *was* with me. Whether therefore I or they, so we preach,
12 and so ye believed. But if Christ is preached, that he rose from
the dead, how say some among you that there is no resurrection of
13 the dead? For if there be no resurrection of the dead, neither is
14 Christ raised. And if Christ be not raised, then *is* our preaching
15 vain, and your faith *is* also vain. Yea, and we are found false witnesses of God, because we have testified from God, that he raised
16 up Christ, whom he did not raise, if the dead rise not. For if the
17 dead rise not, neither is Christ raised: And if Christ be not raised,
18 your faith *is* vain; ye are still in your sins. Then also they who
19 sleep in Christ are perished. If in this life only we have hope in
20 Christ, we are more miserable than all men. But now is Christ
21 risen from the dead, the first fruits of them that slept. For since
by man *came* death, by man *came* also the resurrection of the dead.

6. *Above five hundred*—Probably in Galilee: a glorious and incontestable proof!
The greater part remain alive.
7. *Then by all the apostles*—The twelve were mentioned, ver. 5. This title
here therefore seems to include the seventy; if not all those likewise whom God
afterward sent to plant the Gospel in heathen nations.
8. *An untimely birth*—It was impossible to abase himself more than he does by
this single appellation. As an abortion is not worthy the name of a man, so he
affirms himself to be not worthy the name of an apostle.
9. *I persecuted the Church*—True believers are humbled all their lives, even for
the sins they committed before they believed.
10. *I laboured more than they all*—That is, more than any of them, from a deep
sense of a peculiar love God had shown me. Yet, to speak more properly, it is not
I, but the grace of God that is with me. This it is which at first qualified me for
the work, and still excites me to zeal and diligence in it.
11. *Whether I or they, so we preach*—All of us speak the same thing.
12. *How say some*—Who probably had been heathen philosophers.
13. *If there be no resurrection*—If it be a thing flatly impossible.
14. *Then is our preaching*—From a commission supposed to be given after the
resurrection, *vain*—Without any real foundation.
15. *If the dead rise not*—If the very notion of a resurrection be, as they say,
absurd and impossible.
17. *Ye are still in your sins*—That is, under the guilt of them. So that there
needed something more than reformation, (which was plainly wrought,) in order
to their being delivered from the guilt of sin: even that atonement, the sufficiency
of which God attested by raising our great Surety from the grave.
18. *They who sleep in Christ*—Who have died for him, or believing in him, *are
perished*—Have lost their life and being together.
19. *If in this life only we have hope*—If we look for nothing beyond the grave.
But if we have a Divine evidence of things not seen, if we have a hope full of
immortality, if we now taste of the powers of the world to come, and see the crown
that fadeth not away: then, notwithstanding all our present trials, we are more
happy than all men.
20. *But now*—St. Paul declares that Christians have hope, not in this life only.
His proof of the resurrection lies in a narrow compass, ver. 12–19. Almost all
the rest of the chapter is taken up in illustrating, vindicating, and applying '.

442   I. CORINTHIANS

22 For as through Adam all die, even so through Christ shall all be
23 made alive. But every one in his own order: Christ, the first
24 fruits, afterward they who are Christ's at his coming. Then
   cometh the end, when he shall have delivered up the kingdom to
   God, even the Father, when he shall have abolished all rule and
25 all authority and power. For he must reign * till he hath put all
26 enemies under his feet. The last enemy *that* is destroyed *is* death.
27 † For he hath put all things under his feet. But when he saith,
   All things are put under *him, it is* manifest, that he who did put
28 all things under him, is excepted. But when all things shall be
   put under him, then shall the Son himself also be subject to him

The proof is short, but solid and convincing, that which arose from Christ's
resurrection. Now this not only proved a resurrection possible, but as it proved
him to be a Divine teacher, proved the certainty of a general resurrection, which
he so expressly taught. *The first fruits of them that slept*—The earnest pledge
and assurance of their resurrection who slept in him; even of all the righteous.
It is of the resurrection of these, and these only, that the apostle speaks throughout the chapter.

22. *As through Adam all,* even the righteous, *die, so through Christ all* these
shall be made alive—He does not say, shall revive, (as naturally as they die,) but
shall be made alive, by a power not their own.

23. *Afterward*—The whole harvest. At the same time the wicked shall rise
also: but they are not here taken into the account.

24. *Then*—After the resurrection and the general judgment, cometh the end
of the world; the grand period of all those wonderful scenes that have appeared
for so many succeeding generations; when he shall have delivered up the kingdom to the Father, and he (the Father) shall have abolished all adverse rule,
authority, and power. Not that the Father will then begin to reign without the
Son, nor will the Son then cease to reign. For the Divine reign- both of the
Father and Son is from everlasting to everlasting. But this is spoken of the
Son's mediatorial kingdom, which will then be delivered up, and of the immediate kingdom or reign of the Father, which will then commence. Till then the
Son transacts the business which the Father hath given him, for those who are
his, and by them, as well as by the angels, with the Father, and against their
enemies. So far as the Father gave the kingdom to the Son, the Son shall deliver it up to the Father, John xiii, 3. Nor does the Father cease to reign when
he gives it to the Son; neither the Son when he delivers it to the Father : but
the glory which he had before the world began, John xvii, 5; Heb. i, 8, will remain
even after this is delivered up. Nor will he cease to be a King even in his human
nature, Luke i, 33. If the citizens of the New Jerusalem shall reign for ever,
Rev. xxii, 5, how much more shall he ?

25. *He must reign*—Because so it is written, *till he*—The Father, hath put all
his enemies under his feet.

26. *The last enemy that is destroyed is death*—Namely, after Satan, Heb
ii, 14, and sin, ver. 56, are destroyed. In the same ·· rder they prevailed. Satan
brought in sin, and sin brought forth death. And Christ, when he of old
engaged with these enemies, first conquered Satan; then sin, in his death;
and lastly death in his resurrection. In the same order he delivers all the
faithful from them, yea, and destroys these enemies themselves. Death he so
destroys that it shall be no more; sin and Satan, so that they shall no more
hurt his people.

27. *Under him*—Under the Son.

28. *The Son also shall be subject*—Shall deliver up the mediatorial kingdom, that the three-one God may be all in all. All things, (consequently all
persons,) without any interruption, without the intervention of any creature,
without the opposition of any enemy, shall be subordinate to God. All shall
say, "My God, and my all." This is the end. Even an inspired apostle can
see nothing beyond this.

* Psalm cx, 1.   † Psalm viii, 7.

29 that put all things under him, that God may be all in all. Else
what shall they do who are baptized for the dead? If the dead
30 rise not at all, why are they then baptized for them? Why are
31 we also in danger every hour? I protest by your rejoicing, bre-
32 thren, which I have in Christ Jesus our Lord, I die daily. If after
the manner of men I have fought with wild beasts at Ephesus,
what advantageth it me if the dead rise not? Let us eat and drink ;
33 for to-morrow we die. Be not deceived. Evil communications
34 corrupt good manners. Awake to righteousness, and sin not ; for
some have not the knowledge of God. I speak *this* to your
shame.
35   But some one will say, How are the dead raised? And with
36 what kind of body do they come? Thou fool, that which thou
37 sowest is not quickened except it die : And that which thou sowest, thou sowest not the body that shall be, but bare grain per-
38 haps of wheat, or of any other *corn :* But God giveth it a body as

---

29. *Who were baptized for the dead*—Perhaps baptized in hope of blessings to
be received after they are numbered with the dead; or *baptized in the room of the
dead*—Of them that are just fallen in the cause of Christ; like soldiers who advance
in the room of their companions that fell just before their face.

30. *Why are we*—The apostles, *also in danger every hour?*—It is plain we can
expect no amends in this life.

31. *I protest by your rejoicing which I have*—Which love makes my own, *I die
daily*—I am daily in the very jaws of death : beside that I live, as it were, in a
daily martyrdom.

32. *If* to speak *after the manner of men*, that is, to use a proverbial phrase, expressive of the most imminent danger, *I have fought with wild beasts at Ephesus*
—With the savage fury of a lawless multitude, Acts xix, 29, &c. This seems
to have been just before. *Let us eat*, &c.—We might on that supposition as well
say with the Epicureans, Let us make the best of this short life, seeing we have
no other portion.

33. *Be not deceived*—By such pernicious counsels as this. *Evil communications
corrupt good manners*—He opposes to the Epicurean saying a well-known verse
of the poet Menander. *Evil communications*—Discourse contrary to faith, hope,
or love, naturally tends to destroy all holiness.

34. *Awake*—An exclamation full of apostolical majesty. Shake off your
lethargy ! *To righteousness*—Which flows from the true knowledge of God, and
implies that your whole soul be broad awake ; *and sin not*—That is, and ye will
not sin. Sin supposes drowsiness of soul. There is need to press this; for some
among you *have not the knowledge of God*—With all their boasted knowledge they
are totally ignorant of what it most concerns them to know. *I speak this to
your shame*—For nothing is more shameful than sleepy ignorance of God, and
of the word and works of God; in these especially, considering the advantages
they had enjoyed.

35. *But some one* possibly *will say, How are the dead raised up*, after their
whole frame is dissolved ? and with what kind of bodies do they come again, after
these are mouldered into dust ?

36. To the inquiry concerning the manner of rising, and the quality of the
bodies that rise, the apostle answers first by a similitude, ver. 36–42, and then
plainly and directly, ver. 42, 43. *That which thou sowest*, is not quickened into
a new life and verdure, *except it die*—Undergo a dissolution of its parts, a change
analogous to death. Thus St. Paul inverts the objection; as if he had said, Death
is so far from hindering life, that it necessarily goes before it.

37. *Thou sowest not the body that shall be*—Produced from the seed committed
to the ground, but bare naked grain, widely different from that which will afterward rise out of the earth.

38 *But God*—Not thou, O man, not the grain itself, giveth it a body as it
hath pleased him, from the time he distinguished the various species of beings ·

39 it hath pleased him, and to each of the seeds its own body. All
flesh *is* not the same flesh ; but *there is* one *kind of* flesh of men,
40 another of beasts, another of birds, another of fishes. *There are*
also heavenly bodies, and *there are* earthly bodies : but the glory
41 of the heavenly *is* one, and that of the earthly another. *There is*
one glory of the sun, and another glory of the moon, and another
glory of the stars : and *one* star differeth from *another* star in
42 glory. So also *is* the resurrection of the dead : it is sown in cor-
43 ruption ; it is raised in incorruption. It is sown in dishonour ; it is
44 raised in glory : it is sown in weakness ; it is raised in power. It
is sown an animal body ; it is raised a spiritual body. There is
45 an animal body, and there is a spiritual body. And so it is written, * The first Adam was made a living soul ; the last Adam *is* a
46 quickening Spirit. Yet the spiritual *body was* not first, but the
47 animal ; afterward the spiritual. The first man *was* from the
48 earth, earthy ; the second man *is* the Lord from heaven. As *was*

and to each of the seeds, not only of the fruits, but animals also, (to which
the apostle rises in the following verse,) *its own body*—Not only peculiar to
that species, but proper to that individual, and arising out of the substance of
that very grain.

39. *All flesh*—As if he had said, Even earthy bodies differ from earthy, and
heavenly bodies from heavenly. What wonder then if heavenly bodies differ
from earthy ? Or the bodies which rise from those that lay in the grave ?

40. *There are also heavenly bodies*—As the sun, moon, and stars ; *and there
are earthy*—As vegetables and animals. But the brightest lustre which the latter
can have, is widely different from that of the former.

41. Yea, and the heavenly bodies themselves differ from each other.

42. *So also is the resurrection of the dead*—So great is the difference between
the body which fell and that which rises. *It is sown*, (a beautiful word,) committed as seed to the ground, *in corruption*—Just ready to putrefy, and by various
degrees of corruption and decay, to return to the dust from whence it came. *It
is raised in incorruption*—Utterly incapable of dissolution or decay.

43. *It is sown in dishonour*—Shocking to those who loved it best : human
nature in disgrace ! *It is raised in glory*—Clothed with robes of light, fit for
those whom the King of heaven delights to honour. *It is sown in weakness*—
Deprived even of that feeble strength which it once enjoyed : *it is raised in
power*—Endued with vigour, strength, and activity, such as we cannot now
conceive.

44. *It is sown* in this world a merely *animal body*—Maintained by food, sleep,
and air, like the bodies of brutes : but it is raised of a more refined contexture,
needing none of these animal refreshments, and endued with qualities of a spiritual nature, like the angels of God.

45. *The first Adam was made a living soul*—God gave him such life as other
animals enjoy : but *the last Adam*, Christ, *is a quickening Spirit*—As he hath
life in himself, so he quickeneth whom he will ; giving a more refined life to their
very bodies at the resurrection.

47. *The first man was from the earth, earthy ; the second man is the Lord from
heaven*—The first man being from the earth, is subject to corruption and dissolution, like the earth from which he came. *The second man*—St. Paul could not
so well say, " Is from heaven, heavenly ;" because though man owes it to the
earth, that he is earthy, yet the Lord does not owe his glory to heaven. He
himself made the heavens, and by descending from thence showed himself to us
as the Lord. Christ was not the second man in order of time ; but in this re
spect ;—that as Adam was a public person, who acted in the stead of all man
kind, so was Christ. As Adam was the first general representative of men, Christ
was the second and the last. And what they severally did, terminated not in
themselves, but affected all whom they represented.

* Genesis ii, 7.

the earthy, such *are* they also *that are* earthy, and as *was* the
49 heavenly, such *are* they also that are heavenly. And as we have
borne the image of the earthy, we shall also bear the image of the
heavenly.
50　But this I say, brethren, that flesh and blood cannot inherit the
kingdom ⸜of God, neither doth corruption inherit incorruption.
51 Behold, I tell you a mystery; we shall not all sleep, but we shall
52 all be changed, In a moment, in the twinkling of an eye, at the last
trumpet; for the trumpet shall sound, and the dead shall be raised
53 incorruptible, and·we shall be changed. For this corruptible must
54 put on incorruption, and this mortal put on immortality. So when
this corruptible shall have put on incorruption, and this mortal shall
have put on immortality, then shall be brought to pass the saying
55 that is written, * Death is swallowed up in victory. † O death,
56 where *is* thy sting? O hades, where *is* thy victory? The sting of
57 death *is* sin, and the strength of sin *is* the law. But thanks *be* to
God, who hath given us the victory through our Lord Jesus Christ.
58 Therefore, my beloved brethren, be ye steadfast, unmovable, always abounding in the work of the Lord, knowing that your labour
is not in vain in the Lord.
XVI. Concerning the collection for the saints, as I have ordered the

48. *They that are earthy*—Who continue without any higher principle : *they that are heavenly*—Who receive a Divine principle from heaven.
49. *The image of the heavenly*—Holiness and glory.
50. *But* first we must be entirely changed ; *for* such *flesh and blood* as we are clothed with now, *cannot* enter into that kingdom which is wholly spiritual : neither doth this corruptible body inherit that incorruptible kingdom.
51. *A mystery*—A truth hitherto unknown; and not yet fully known to any of the sons of men. *We*—Christians. The apostle considers them all as one, in their succeeding generations : *shall not all die*—Suffer a separation of soul and body ; *but we shall all*—Who do not die, *be changed*—So that this animal body shall become spiritual.
52. *In a moment*—Amazing work of omnipotence ! And cannot the same power now change us into saints in a moment ? *The trumpet shall sound*—To awaken all that sleep in the dust of the earth.
54. *Death is swallowed up in victory*—That is, totally conquered, abolished for ever.
55. *O death, where is thy sting?*—Which once was full of hellish poison. *O hades*, the receptacle of separate souls, *where is thy victory?*—Thou art now rob-bed of all thy spoils : all thy captives are set at liberty. *Hades* literally means the invisible world, and relates to the soul : death to the body. The Greek words are found in the Septuagint translation of Hos. xiii, 14.
56. *The sting of death is sin*—Without which it could have no power. But this sting none can resist by his own strength. *And the strength of sin is the law*—As is largely declared Rom. vii, 7, &c.
57. *But thanks be to God, who hath given us the victory*, over sin, death, and hades.
58. *Be ye steadfast*—In yourselves ; *unmovable*—By others, continually in-creasing in the work of faith and labour of love. *Knowing your labour is not in vain in the Lord*—Whatever ye do for his sake, shall have its full reward in that day.
Let *us* also endeavour, by cultivating holiness in all its branches, to maintain this hope in its full energy : longing for that glorious day, when in the utmost extent of the expression, death shall be swallowed up for ever, and millions of voices, after the long silence of the grave, shall burst out at once into that tri-umphant song, *O death, where is thy sting? O hades, where is thy victory?*
XVI. *The saints*—A more solemn and a more affecting word, than if he had said the poor.

* Isaiah xxv, 8.　† Hosea xiii, 14.

2 Churches of Galatia, so also do ye. On the first *day* of the week, let every one of you lay by him in store according as he hath been
3 prospered, that there may be no collections when I come. And when I am come, whosoever ye shall approve, them will I send
4 with letters, to carry your gift to Jerusalem. And if it be proper
5 that I also should go, they shall go with me. Now I will come to you, when I have passed through Macedonia, (for I pass through
6 Macedonia.) And perhaps I may stay, yea, and winter with you, that ye may bring me forward on my journey, whithersoever I go.
7 For I will not see you now in my way; but hope to stay some
8 time with you, if the Lord permit. But I will stay at Ephesus till
9 pentecost. For a great and effectual door is opened to me, and there *are* many adversaries.
10 But if Timotheus come, see that he be with you without fear,
11 for he worketh the work of the Lord, even as I. Therefore let no man despise him, but conduct ye him forward on his journey in peace, that he may come to me; for I look for him with the
12 brethren. As to *our* brother Apollos, I besought him much to come to you with the brethren; yet he was by no means willing to come
13 now; but he will come when it shall be convenient. Watch ye,
14 stand fast in the faith, acquit yourselves like men; be strong. Let all your affairs be done in love.
15 And I beseech you, brethren, *as* ye know the household of Ste-phanas, that it is the first fruits of Achaia, and that they have de-
16 voted themselves to serve the saints, That ye also submit to such

---

2. *Let every one*—Not the rich only: let him also that hath little, gladly give of that little : *according as he hath been prospered*—Increasing his alms, as God increases his substance. According to this lowest rule of Christian prudence, if a man when he has or gains one pound, give a tenth to God, when he has or gains ten pounds, he will give a tenth to God, when he has or gains a hundred, he will give the tenth of this also. And yet I show unto you a more excellent way. He that hath ears to hear, let him hear. Stint yourselves to no propor-tion at all. But lend to God all you can.

4. *They shall go with me*—To remove any possible suspicion.

5. *I pass through Macedonia*—I purpose going that way.

7. *I will not see you now*—Not till I have been in Macedonia.

8. *I will stay at Ephesus*—Where he was at this time.

9. *A great door*—As to the number of hearers ; *and effectual*—As to the effects wrought upon them : *and there are many adversaries*—As there must always be, where Satan's kingdom shakes. This was another reason for his staying there.

10. *Without fear*—Of any one's despising him for his youth ; *for he worketh the work of the Lord*—The true ground of reverence to pastors. Those who do so, none ought to despise.

11. *I look for him with the brethren*—That accompany him.

12. *I besought him much* to come to you *with the brethren*—Who were then going to Corinth. *Yet he was by no means willing to come now*—Perhaps lest his coming should increase the divisions among them.

13. To conclude. *Watch ye*—Against all your seen and unseen enemies. *Stand fast in the faith*—Seeing and trusting him that is invisible. *Acquit your-selves like men*—With courage and patience. *Be strong*—To do and suffer all his will.

15. *The first fruits of Achaia*—The first converts in that province.

16. *That ye also* in your turn *submit to such*—So repaying their free service *and to every one that worketh with us and laboureth*—That labours in the Gos-pel, either with or without a fellow labourer.

ι7 and to every one that worketh with *us* and laboureth.   I rejoice at
the coming of Stephanas, and Fortunatus, and Achaicus : for they
18 have supplied what was wanting on your part.   For they have re-
19 freshed my spirit and yours ; such therefore acknowledge.   The
Churches of Asia salute you.   Aquila and Priscilla, with the•Church
20 that is in their house, salute you much in the Lord.   All the brethren salute you.   Salute one another with a holy kiss.
21   The salutation of *me* Paul with my own hand.   If any man love
22 not the Lord Jesus Christ, let him be Anathema ; Maran-atha.
23 The grace of our Lord Jesus Christ *be* with you.   My love *be* with
24 you all in Christ Jesus.

17. *I rejoice at the coming of Stephanas, and Fortunatus, and Achaicus*—Who
were now returned to Corinth ; but the joy which their arrival had occasioned
remained still in his heart. *They have supplied what was wanting on your part*
—They have performed the offices of love, which you could not, by reason of
your absence•

18. *For they have refreshed my spirit and yours*—Inasmuch as you share in my
comfort : *such therefore acknowledge*—With suitable love and respect.

19. *Aquila and Priscilla* had formerly made some abode at Corinth, and there
St. Paul's acquaintance with them began, Acts xviii, 1, 2.

21. *With my own hand*—What precedes having been wrote by an amanuensis.

22. *If any man love not the Lord Jesus Christ*—If any be an enemy to his
person, offices, doctrines, or commands, *let him be Anathema ; Maran-atha*—
Anathema signifies a thing devoted to destruction.   It seems to have been customary with the Jews of that age, when they had pronounced any man an Anathema, to add the Syriac expression Maran-atha, that is, the Lord cometh; namely,
to execute vengeance upon him.   This weighty sentence the apostle chose to
write with his own hand : and to insert it between his salutation and solemn
benediction, that it might be the more attentively regarded.

NOTES

ON

ST. PAUL'S SECOND EPISTLE TO THE CORINTHIANS.

In this epistle, written from Macedonia, within a year after the former, St. Paul beautifully displays his tender affection toward the Corinthians, who were greatly moved by the seasonable severity of the former, and repeats several of the admonitions he had there given them. In that he had written concerning the affairs of the Corinthians; in this he writes chiefly concerning his own; but in such a manner, as to direct all he mentions of himself to their spiritual profit. The thread and connection of the whole epistle is historical ; other things are interwoven only by way of digression.

IT CONTAINS,

II. CORINTHIANS.

1 Paul, an apostle of Jesus Christ, by the will of God, and Timotheus our brother, to the Church of God that is in Corinth, with all
2 the saints that are in all Achaia : Grace and peace be to you from God our Father, and from the Lord Jesus Christ.
3 Blessed be the God and Father of our Lord Jesus Christ, the
4 Father of mercies, and God of all comfort, Who comforteth us in

Ver. 2. *Timotheus our brother*—St. Paul writing to Timotheus, styled him his son ; writing of him, his brother.

3. *Blessed be the God and Father of our Lord Jesus Christ*—A solemn and beautiful introduction, highly suitable to the apostolical spirit ; *the Father of mercies, and God of all comfort*—Mercies are the fountain of comfort ; comfort is the outward expression of mercy. God shows his mercy in the affliction itself. He gives comfort both in and after the affliction. Therefore is he termed the God of all comfort. Blessed be this God !

4. *Who comforteth us in all our affliction, that we may be able to comfort them who are in any affliction*—He that has experienced one kind of affliction is able

all our affliction, that we may be able to comfort them who are in any affliction, by the comfort wherewith we ourselves are comforted
5 of God. For as the sufferings of Christ abound in us, so our com-
6 fort also aboundeth through Christ. And whether we are afflicted,
it is for your comfort and salvation ; or whether we are comforted,
it is for your comfort, which is effectual .in the patient enduring
7 the same sufferings which we also suffer. And our hope concerning you is steadfast, knowing that as ye are partakers of the
8 sufferings, so also of the comfort. For we would not have you
ignorant, brethren, of the trouble which befell us in Asia, that we
were exceedingly pressed above *our* strength, so that we despaired
9 even of life. Yea, we had the sentence of death in ourselves, that
we might not trust in ourselves, but in God, who raiseth the dead :
10 Who delivered us from so great a death, and doth deliver : in
11 whom we trust that he will still deliver : You likewise helping
together with us by prayer for us, that for the gift *bestowed* upon
us, by means of many persons, thanks may be given by many on
your behalf.
12 For this is our rejoicing, the testimony of our conscience, that
in simplicity and godly sincerity, not with carnal wisdom, but by
the grace of God, we have had our conversation in the world, and
13 more abundantly toward you. For we write no other things to
you but what ye know and acknowledge, and I trust will acknow-
14 ledge even to the end. As also ye have acknowedged us in part,

to comfort others in that affliction. He that has experienced all kinds of affliction is able to comfort them in all.
5. *For as the sufferings of Christ abound in us*—The sufferings endured on his
account ; *so our comfort also aboundeth through Christ*—The sufferings were
many, the comfort one : and yet not only equal to, but overbalancing them all.
6. *And whether we are afflicted, it is for your comfort and salvation*—For your
present comfort, your present and future salvation : *or whether we are comforted,
it is for your comfort*—That we may be the better able to comfort you ; *which is
effectual in the patient enduring the same sufferings which we also suffer*—
Through the efficacy of which ye patiently endure the same kind of sufferings
with us.
7. *And our hope concerning you*—Grounded on your patience in suffering for
Christ's sake, is steadfast.
8. *We would not have you ignorant, brethren, of the trouble which befell us in
Asia*—Probably the same which is described in the 19th chapter of the Acts.
The Corinthians knew before that he had been in trouble. He now declares the
greatness and the fruit of it. *We were exceedingly pressed, above our strength*—
Above the ordinary strength even of an apostle.
9. *Yea, we had the sentence of death in ourselves*—We ourselves expected
nothing but death.
10. *We trust that he will still deliver*—That we may at length be able to come
to you.
11. *You likewise*—As well as other Churches, *helping with us by prayer, that
for the gift*—Namely, my deliverance, *bestowed upon us by means of many persons*—Praying for it, thanks may be given by many.
12. *For* I am the more emboldened to look for this, because I am conscious of
my integrity : seeing *this is our rejoicing*—Even in the deepest adversity ; *the
testimony of our conscience*—Whatever others think of us, *that in simplicity*—
Having one end in view, aiming singly at the glory of God, *and godly sincerity*—
Without any tincture of guile, dissimulation, or disguise, *not with carnal wisdom,
but by the grace of God*—Not by natural but Divine wisdom, *we have had our conversation in the world*—In the whole world ; in every circumstance.
14. *Ye have acknowledged us in part*—Though not so fully as ye will do, *tha*
29

that we are your rejoicing, as ye also *are* ours in the day of the
15 Lord Jesus. And in this confidence I was minded to come to you
16 before, that ye might have had a second benefit. And to pass by
you into Macedonia, and to come to you again from Macedonia,
17 and to be brought forward by you in my way toward Judea. Now
when I was thus minded, did I use levity?´or the things which I
purpose, do I purpose according to the flesh, so that there should
18 be with me yea and nay? *As* God is faithful, our word to you hath
19 not been yea and nay. For Jesus Christ, the Son of God, who
was preached among you by us, by me, and Sylvanus, and Timo-
20 theus, was not yea and nay; but was yea in him. For all the promises of God *are* yea in him, and amen in him, to the glory of God
21 by us. For he that establisheth us with you in Christ and that
22 hath anointed us *is* God: Who hath also sealed us, and given us
the earnest of the Spirit in our hearts.
23   But I call God for a record on my soul, that to spare you I
24 came not as yet to Corinth. Not that we have dominion over
your faith, but are helpers of your joy; for by faith ye have stood.

---

we are your rejoicing—That ye rejoice in having known us, *as ye also are ours*—
As we also rejoice in the success of our labours among you; and we trust shall
rejoice therein in the day of the Lord Jesus.
    15. *In this confidence*—That is, being confident of this.
    17. *Did I use levity?*—Did I lightly change my purpose? *Do I purpose accord-
ing to the flesh?*—Are my purposes grounded on carnal or worldly considerations? *So that there should be with me yea and nay*—Sometimes one, sometimes
the other: that is, variableness and inconstancy.
    18. *Our word to you*—The whole tenor of our doctrine, *hath not been yea and
nay*—Wavering and uncertain.
    19. *For Jesus Christ who was preached by us*—That is, our preaching con-
cerning him, *was not yea and nay*—Was not variable and inconsistent with itself;
but was yea in him—Always one and the same, centering in him.
    20. *For all the promises of God are yea and amen in him*—Are surely esta-
blished in and through him. They are yea, with respect to God promising:
amen, with respect to men believing: yea, with respect to the apostles: amen,
with respect to their hearers.
    21. I say, *to the glory of God*—For it is God alone that is able to fulfil these
promises; *that establisheth us*—Apostles and teachers, *with you*—All true believers, in the faith of Christ: *and hath anointed us*—With the oil of gladness,
with joy in the Holy Ghost, thereby giving us strength both to do and suffer his
will.
    22. *Who also hath sealed us*—Stamping his image on our hearts, thus marking
and sealing us as his own property: *and giving us the earnest of his Spirit*—
There is a difference between an earnest and a pledge. A pledge is to be restored
when the debt is paid; but an earnest is not taken away, but completed. Such
an earnest is the Spirit. The first fruits of it we have, Rom. viii 23. And we
wait for all the fulness.
    23. *I call God for a record upon my soul*—Was not St. Paul now speaking by
the Spirit? And can a more solemn oath be conceived? Who then can imagine that Christ ever designed to forbid all swearing? *That to spare you I came
not yet to Corinth*—Lest I should be obliged to use severity. He says elegantly,
To Corinth, not to you, when he is intimating his power to punish.
    24. *Not that we have dominion over your faith*—This is the prerogative of God
alone; *but are helpers of your joy*—And faith from which it springs. *For by
faith ye have stood*—To this day.
    We see the light in which ministers should always consider themselves, and
in wh'ch they are to be considered by others: not as having dominion over the
faith of their people, and having a right to dictate, by their own authority, what
they shall believe, or what they shall do, but as helpers of their joy, by helping

11.   But I determined this with myself, not to come to you again in
2 grief.   For if I grieve you, who is he that cheereth me, but he that
3 is grieved by me ?   And I wrote thus to you, that I might not when
I come have grief from those for whom I ought to rejoice ; being
persuaded concerning you all, that my joy is *the joy* of you all.
4 For from much affliction and anguish of heart I wrote to you with
many tears, not that ye might be grieved, but that ye might know
the abundant love which I have toward you.
5   And if any have caused grief, he hath grieved me but in part,
6 that I may not overburden you all.   Sufficient for such a one *is*
7 this punishment *inflicted* by many.   So that on the contrary *ye
should* rather forgive and comfort *him*, lest such a one should be
8 swallowed up with overmuch sorrow.   I beseech you therefore to
9 confirm *your* love toward him.   For to this end also did I write,
that I might know the proof of you, whether ye were obedient in
10 all things.   To whom ye forgive any thing, I *forgive* also ; and
what I have forgiven, if I have forgiven any thing, *it is* for your
11 sakes, in the person of Christ : Lest Satan get an advantage over
us : for we are not ignorant of his devices.
12   Now when I came to Troas, to *preach* the Gospel of Christ, and
13 a door was opened to me by the Lord, I had no rest in my spirit,
because I did not find Titus my brother ; so taking leave of them
I went forth into Macedonia.

them forward in faith and holiness.   In this view, how amiable does their office
appear ?   And how friendly to the happiness of mankind ?   How far then are
they from true benevolence, who would expose it to ridicule and contempt ?
II. 1. *In grief*—Either on account of the particular offender, or of the Church
in general.
2. *For if I grieve you, who is he that cheereth me, but he that is grieved by me ?*
—That is, I cannot be comforted myself till his grief is removed.
3. *And I wrote thus to you*—I wrote to you before in this determination, not
to come to you in grief.
4. *From much anguish I wrote to you*, *not* so much that ye might be grieved,
as that ye might know by my faithful admonition, my abundant love toward
you.
5. *He hath grieved me but in part*—Who still rejoice over the greater part of
you.   Otherwise I might burden you all.
6. *Sufficient for such a one*—With what a remarkable tenderness does St.
Paul treat this offender ?   He never once mentions his name.   Nor does he here
so much as mention his crime.   *By many*—Not only by the rulers of the Church :
the whole congregation acquiesced in the sentence.
10. *To whom ye forgive*—He makes no question of their complying with his
direction, *any thing*—So mildly does he speak even of that heinous sin, after it
was repented of.   *In the person of Christ*—By the authority wherewith he has
invested me.
11. *Lest Satan*—To whom he had been delivered, and who sought to destroy
not only his flesh, but his soul also, *get an advantage over us*—For the loss of
one soul is a common loss.
12. *Now when I came to Troas*—It seems in that passage from Asia to Macedonia, of which a short account is given, Acts xx, 1, 2.   Even though *a door
was opened to me*—That is, there was free liberty to speak, and many were willing to hear ; yet,
13. *I had no rest in my spirit*—From an earnest desire to know how my
letter had been received : *because I did not find Titus*—In his return from you,
so I went forth into Macedonia—Where being much nearer, I might more
easily be informed concerning you.   The apostle resumes the thread of his
discourse, chap. vii, 2, interposing an admirable digression, concerning what he

14	Now thanks *be* to God, who causeth us always to triumph
	through Christ, and manifesteth by us in every place the odour of
15	his knowledge.	For we are to God a sweet odour of Christ, in
16	them that are saved, and in them that perish : To these an odour
	of death unto death, but to those an odour of life unto life.	And
17	who *is* sufficient for these things ?	For we are not as many who
	adulterate the word of God, but as of sincerity, but as from God,
	in the sight of God, speak we in Christ.
III.	Do we again begin to recommend ourselves ?	Unless we need,
	as some *do*, recommendatory letters to you, or recommendatory
2	*letters* from you ?	Ye are our letter, written on our hearts, known
3	and read by all men : Manifestly declared to be the letter of
	Christ ministered by us, written not with ink, but with the Spirit
	of the living God, not in tables of stone, but in the fleshly tables of
4	the heart.	Such trust have we in God through Christ.	Not that
5	we are sufficient of ourselves to think any thing as from ourselves ;
6	but our sufficiency *is* from God : Who also hath made us able

---

had done and suffered elsewhere, the profit of which he by this means derives
to the Corinthians also : and this is a prelude to his apology against the false
apostles.

14. *To triumph* implies not only victory, but an open manifestation of it. And
as in triumphal processions, especially in the east, incense and perfumes were
burnt near the conqueror, the apostle beautifully alludes to the circumstances in
the following verse : as likewise to the different effects which strong perfumes
have upon different persons ; some of whom they revive, while they throw others
into the most violent disorders.

15. *For we*—The preachers of the Gospel, *are to God a sweet odour of Christ*—
God is well pleased with this perfume diffused by us, both in them that believe
and are saved, (treated of chap. iii, 1 ; chap. iv, 2,) and in them that obstinately
disbelieve, and consequently perish, treated of chap. iv, 3–6.

16. *And who is sufficient for these things?*—No man living, but by the power
of God's Spirit.

17. *For we are not as many, who adulterate the word of God*—Like those vint-
ners (so the Greek word implies) who mix their wines with baser liquors : *but as
of sincerity*—Without any mixture : *but as from God*—This rises still higher ;
transmitting his pure word, not our own, *in the sight of God*—Whom we regard
as always present, and noting every word of our tongue, *speak we*—The tongue
is ours, but the power is God's, *in Christ*—Words which he gives, approves, and
blesses.

III. 1. *Do we begin again to recommend ourselves?*—Is it needful ?	Have I
nothing but my own word to recommend me ?	St. Paul chiefly here intends him
self : though not excluding Timotheus, Titus, and Sylvanus.	*Unless we need*—
As if he had said, Do I indeed want such recommendation ?

2. *Ye are our* recommendatory *letter*—More convincing than bare words could
be, *written on our hearts*—Deeply engraven there, and plainly legible to all
around us.

3. *Manifestly declared to be the letter of Christ*—Which he has formed and published to the world ; *ministered by us*—Whom he has used herein as his instruments ; therefore ye are our letter also : *written not in tables of stone*—Like the
ten commandments, but in the tender, living *tables of their hearts ;* God having
taken away the hearts of stone, and given them hearts of flesh.

4. *Such trust have we in God*—That is, we trust in God that this is so.

5. *Not that we are sufficient of ourselves*—So much as to think one good
thought, much less to convert sinners.

.. *Who also hath made us able ministers of the new covenant*—Of the new evan-
gelical dispensation.	Not of the law, fitly called the letter, from God's literally
writing it on the two tables, *but of the Spirit*—Of the Gospel dispensation, which
is written on the tables of our hearts by the Spirit.	*For the letter*—The law, the

mmisteis of the new covenant, not of the letter, but of the Spirit;
7 for the letter killeth, but the Spirit giveth life.   And if the ministration of death engraven in letters of stones was glorious, so that
the children of Israel could not look steadfastly on the face of Mo-
8 ses, because of the glory of his face, which is abolished : Shall not
9 rather the ministration of the Spirit be glorious ? For if the ministration of condemnation was glory, much more doth the ministra-
10 tion of righteousness abound in glory.   For even that which was
made glorious had no glory in this respect, because of the glory
11 that excelleth.   For if that which is abolished *was* glorious, much
12 more that which remaineth *is* glorious.   Having therefore such
13 hope, we use great plainness of speech.   And not as Moses, *who*
put a veil over his face, so that the children of Israel could not
14 look steadfastly to the end of that which is abolished.   But their
understandings were blinded ; and until this day the same veil
remaineth unremoved on the reading of the Old Testament, which
15 is taken away in Christ.   But the veil lieth on their heart when
16 Moses is read until this day.   Nevertheless, when it shall turn to

Mosaic dispensation, *killeth*—Seals in death those who still cleave to it : *but the
Spirit*—The Gospel, conveying the Spirit to those who receive it, *giveth life*—
Both spiritual and eternal. Yea, if we adhere to the literal sense even of the
moral law, if we regard only the precept and the sanction as they stand in themselves, not as they lead us to Christ, they are doubtless a killing ordinance, and
bind us down under the sentence of death.

7. *And if the ministration of death*—That is, the Mosaic dispensation, which
proves such to those who prefer it to the Gospel, the most considerable part of
which was engraven on those two stones, was attended with so great glory.

8. *The ministration of the Spirit*—That is, the Christian dispensation.

9. *The ministration of condemnation*—Such the Mosaic dispensation proved to
all the Jews who rejected the Gospel.   Whereas through the Gospel (hence
called the ministration of righteousness) God both imputed and imparted righteousness to all believers.   But how can the moral law (which alone was engraven on stone) be the ministration of condemnation, if it requires no more
than a sincere obedience, such as is proportioned to our infirm state ? If this is
sufficient to justify us, then the law ceases to be a ministration of condemnation.
It becomes (flatly contrary to the apostle's doctrine) the ministration of righteousness.

10. *It hath no glory in this respect, because of the glory that excelleth*—That
is, none, in comparison of this more excellent glory.   The greater light swallows
up the less.

11. *That which remaineth*—That dispensation which remains to the end of
the world : that Spirit and life which remain for ever.

12. *Having therefore this hope*—Being fully persuaded of this.

13. *And* we do not act *as Moses* did, *who put a veil over his face*—Which is to
be understood with regard to his writings also : so that the children of Israel
could not look steadfastly to the end of that dispensation, which is now abolished.   The end of this was Christ.   The whole Mosaic dispensation tended to, and
terminated in him.   But the Israelites had only a dim, wavering sight of him ;
of whom Moses spake in an obscure, covert manner.

14. *The same veil remaineth* on their understanding *unremoved*—Not so much
as folded back, (so the word implies,) so as to admit a little glimmering light on
the public *reading of the Old Testament*—The veil is not now on the face of Moses or of his writings, but on the reading of them, and on the heart of them that
believe not, *which is taken away in Christ*—That is, from the heart of them that
truly believe in him.

16. *When it*—Their heart, *shall turn to the Lord*—To Christ, by living faith,
the veil is taken away—That very moment, and they see with the utmost clearness, how all the types and prophecies of the law are fully accomplished in him.

17 the Lord, the veil shall be taken away. Now the Lord is that
18 Spirit : and where the Spirit of the Lord *is*, there is liberty. And
we all with unveiled face, beholding as in a glass the glory of the
Lord, are transformed into the same image, from glory to glory, as
by the Spirit of the Lord.

IV. Therefore having this ministry, as we have received mercy, we
2 faint not : But have renounced the hidden things of shame, not
walking in craftiness, nor deceitfully corrupting the word of God,
but by manifestation of the truth commending ourselves to every
3 man's conscience in the sight of God. But if our Gospel also is
4 veiled, it is veiled to them that perish ; Whose unbelieving minds
the god of this world hath blinded, lest the illumination of the glorious Gospel of Christ, who is the image of God, should shine upon
5 them. For we preach not ourselves, but Christ Jesus the Lord,
6 and ourselves your servants for Jesus's sake. For God, who commanded light to shine out of darkness, hath shined in our hearts,
to enlighten *us* with the knowledge of the glory of God in the face
of Jesus Christ.

17. *Now the Lord*—Christ, is that spirit of the law whereof I speak, to which
the letter was intended to lead : *and where the Spirit of the Lord*—Christ, *is, there
is liberty*—Not the veil, the emblem of slavery. There is liberty from servile fear,
liberty from the guilt and from the power of sin, liberty to behold with open face
the glory of the Lord.

18. *And* accordingly *all we* that believe in him, *beholding as in a glass*—In the
mirror of the Gospel, *the glory of the Lord*—His glorious love, *are transformed
into the same image*—Into the same love, from one degree of this glory to another,
in a manner worthy of his almighty Spirit.

What a beautiful contrast is here ! Moses saw the glory of the Lord, and it
rendered his face so bright, that he covered it with a veil, Israel not being able to
bear the reflected light. We behold his glory in the glass of his word, and our
faces shine too. Yet we veil them not, but diffuse the lustre which is continually increasing, as we fix the eye of our mind more and more steadfastly on his
glory displayed in the Gospel.

IV. 1. *Therefore having this ministry*—Spoken of chap. iii, 6, *as we have received mercy*—Have been mercifully supported in all our trials, *we faint not*—We
desist not in any degree from our glorious enterprise.

2. *But have renounced*—Set at open defiance, *the hidden things of shame*—All
things which men need to hide or be ashamed of ; *not walking in craftiness*—
Using no disguise, subtlety, guile ; nor privily corrupting the pure word of God,
by any additions or alterations, or by attempting to accommodate it to the taste
of the hearers.

3. *But if our Gospel also*—As well as the law of Moses.

4. *The god of this world*—What a sublime and horrible description of Satan !
He is indeed the god of all that believe not, and works in them with inconceivable
energy, *hath blinded*—Not only veiled the eye of their understanding. Illumination is properly the reflection or propagation of light, from those who are already
enlightened to others. *Who is the image of God*—Hence also we may understand
how great is the glory of Christ. He that sees the Son, sees the Father in the
face of Christ. The Son exactly exhibits the Father to us.

5. *For* the fault is not in us, neither in the doctrine they hear from us. *We
preach not ourselves*—As able either to enlighten, or pardon, or sanctify you, *but
Jesus Christ*—As your only wisdom, righteousness, sanctification : *and ourselves
your servants*—Ready to do the meanest offices, *for Jesus's sake*—Not for honour,
interest, or pleasure.

6. *For God*—*hath shined in our hearts*—The hearts of all those whom the god
of this world no longer blinds : God, who is himself our light, not only the author of light, but also the fountain of it : *to enlighten us with the knowledge of
the glory of God*—Of his glorious love, and of his glorious image ; *in the face of*

7   But we have this treasure in earthen vessels, that the excellence
8 of the power may be of God, and not of us. *We are* troubled on
9 every side, yet not crushed; perplexed, but not in despair ; Per-
10 secuted, but not forsaken ; thrown down, but not destroyed ; Always
   bearing about in the body the dying of the Lord Jesus, that the
11 life also of Jesus may be manifested in our body. We who live
   are always delivered unto death for the sake of Jesus, that the life
12 also of Jesus may be manifested in our mortal body.   So then
13 death worketh in us, but life in you.   Yet having the same spirit
   of faith, according to what is written, * I believed, and therefore have
14 I spoken, we also believe, and therefore speak : Knowing that he
   who raised up the Lord Jesus, will also raise us up by Jesus, and
15 present *us* with you.   For all things *are* for your sakes, that the
   overflowing grace might through the thanksgiving of many abound
16 to the glory of God.   Therefore we faint not, but even though the
   outward man perish, yet the inward man is renewed day by day.
17 For our light affliction, which is but for a moment, worketh out for
18 us a far more exceeding *and* eternal weight of glory : While we

Jesus Christ—Which reflects his glory in another manner than the face of Moses did.

7. *But we*—Not only the apostles, but all true believers, *have this treasure*—Of
Divine light, love, glory, *in earthen vessels*—In frail, feeble, perishing bodies. He
proceeds to show, that afflictions, yea, death itself, are so far from hindering the
ministration of the Spirit, that they even farther it, sharpen the ministers, and increase the fruit ; that the excellency of the power which works these in us, may
undeniably appear to be of God.

8. *We are troubled*, &c. The four articles in this verse respect inward, the
four in the next, outward affliction. In each clause the former part shows the
earthen vessels, the latter the excellence of the power. *Not crushed*—Not swallowed up in care and anxiety : *perplexed*—What course to take, but never despairing of his power and love to carry us through.

10. *Always*—Wherever we go, *bearing about in the body the dying of the Lord
Jesus*—Continually expecting to lay down our lives like him ; *that the life also
of Jesus might be manifested in our body*—That we may also rise and be glorified
like him.

11. *For we who yet live*—Who are not yet killed for the testimony of *Jesus, are
always delivered unto death*—Are perpetually in the very jaws of destruction ;
which we willingly submit to, that we may obtain a better resurrection.

12. *So then death worketh in us, but life in you*—You live in peace ; we die daily.
Yet living or dying, so long as we believe, we cannot but speak.

13. *Having the same spirit of faith*—Which animated the saints of old ; David
in particular, when he said, I believed, and therefore have I spoken, (that is, I
trusted in God, and therefore he hath put this song of praise in my mouth.) *We
also speak*—We preach the Gospel, even in the midst of affliction and death, because we believe that God will raise us up from the dead, and will *present us*—
Ministers, *with you*—All his members, faultless before his presence with exceeding joy.

15. *For all things*—Whether adverse or prosperous, *are for your sakes*—For the
profit of all that believe, as well as all that preach, *that the overflowing grace*—
Which continues you alive both in soul and body, might abound yet more *through
the thanksgiving of many*—For thanksgiving invites more abundant grace.

16. *Therefore*—Because of his grace, *we faint not. The outward man*—The
body ; *the inward man*—The soul.

17. *Our light affliction*—The beauty and sublimity of St. Paul's expressions
here, as descriptive of heavenly glory, opposed to temporal afflictions, surpass
all imagination, and cannot be preserved in any translation or paraphrase, which
after all must sink infinitely below the astonishing original.

* Psalm cxvi, 10.

aim not at the things that are seen, but at the things that are no
seen ; for the things that are seen *are* temporal, but the things that
are not seen *are* eternal.

V.　　For we know that if our earthly house of *this* tabernacle be dissolved, we have a building from God, a house not made with hands,
2 eternal in the heavens. For in this we groan, earnestly desiring to
3 be clothed upon with our house which is from heaven : If being
4 clothed, we shall not be found naked. For we who are in *this*
tabernacle groan, being burdened : not that we would be unclothed,
but clothed upon, that what is mortal may be swallowed up of
5 life. Now he that hath wrought us to this very thing *is* God,
6 who hath also given us the earnest of the Spirit. Therefore *we*
always behave undauntedly ; knowing that while we are sojourn-
7 ing in the body, we are absent from the Lord : (For we walk by
8 faith, not by sight.) We behave undauntedly, *I say*, and are willing rather to be absent from the body, and present with the Lord.
9 . Therefore we are ambitious, whether present or absent, to be
10 well pleasing to him. For we must all appear before the judgment seat of Christ, that every one may receive according to what

---

18. *The things that are seen*—Men, money, things of earth; *the things that
are not seen*—God, grace, heaven.

V. 1. *Our earthly house*—Which is only a tabernacle or tent, not designed for
a lasting habitation.

2. *Desiring to be clothed upon*—This body (which is now covered with flesh
and blood) with the glorious house which is from heaven. Instead of flesh and
blood, which cannot enter heaven, the rising body will be clothed or covered with
what is analogous thereto, but incorruptible and immortal. Macarius speaks
largely of this.

3. *If being clothed*—As with the image of God while we are in the body, *we
shall not be found naked*—Of the wedding garment.

4. *We groan, being burdened*—The apostle speaks with exact propriety. A
burden naturally expresses groans. And we are burdened with numberless afflictions, infirmities, temptations, sins. *Not that we would be unclothed*—Not that
we desire to remain without a body. Faith does not understand that philosophical contempt of what the wise Creator has given ; *but clothed upon*—With the
glorious, immortal, incorruptible, spiritual body, *that what is mortal*—This present mortal body, *may be swallowed up of life*—Covered with that which lives
for ever.

5. *Now he that hath wrought us to this very thing*—This longing for immortality, is God ; for none but God, none less than the Almighty, could have wrought
this in us.

6. *Therefore we behave undauntedly*—But most of all when we have death in
view ; knowing that our geatest happiness lies beyond the grave.

7. *For* we cannot clearly see him in this life, wherein we walk by faith only :
an evidence indeed that necessarily implies a kind of seeing him who is invisible ;
yet as far beneath what we shall have in eternity, as it is above that of bare, un-
assisted reason.

8. *Present with the Lord*—This demonstrates that the happiness of the saints
is not deferred till the resurrection.

9. *Therefore we are ambitious*—The only ambition which has place in a Christian, *whether present*—In the body, *or absent*—From it.

10. *For we all*—Apostles as well as other men, whether now present in the
body, or absent from it, *must appear*—Openly, without covering, where all hidden
things will be revealed, probably the sins even of the faithful, which were forgiven
long before. For many of their good works (as their repentance, their revenge
against sin) cannot otherwise appear. But this will be done at their own desire,
without grief and without shame. *According to what he hath done in the body,*

11 he hath done in the body, whether good or evil. Knowing therefore the terror of the Lord, we persuade men: but we are made
manifest to God, and I trust we are made manifest in your con-
12 sciences also. We do not again recommend ourselves to you;
but we give you an occasion of glorying on our behalf, that ye may
have something to *answer* them who glory in appearance, and not
13 in heart. For if we are transported beyond ourselves, *it is* to
14 God; if we are sober, *it is* for your sakes. For the love of Christ
constraineth us, while we thus judge, that if one died for all, then
15 were all dead: And *that* he died for all, that they who live should
not henceforth live to themselves, but to him who died for them,
16 and rose again. So that we from this time know no one after the
flesh; yea, if we have known even Christ after the flesh, yet now
17 we know *him so* no more. Therefore if any one *be* in Christ,
there is a new creation: the old things are passed away; behold,
18 all things are become new: And all things *are* from God, who hath

---

whether good or evil—In the body he did either good or evil. In the body he is
recompensed accordingly.

11. *Knowing therefore the terror of the Lord,* we the more earnestly persuade
men to seek his favour: and as God knoweth this, so I trust ye know it in your
own consciences.

12. *We do not* say this, as if we thought there was any need of again recommending ourselves to you, but to give you an occasion of rejoicing and praising
God, and to furnish you with an answer to those false apostles, who glory in
appearance, but not in heart, being condemned by their own consciences.

13. *For if we are transported beyond ourselves*—Or at least appear so to
others, (treated of ver. 15–21,) speaking or writing with uncommon vehemence,
it is to God—He understands (if men do not) the emotion which himself inspires.
If we be sober—(treated of, chap. vi, 1–10,) if I proceed in a more calm, sedate
manner, *it is for your sakes*—Even good men bear this, rather than the other
method in their teachers. But these must obey God, whoever is offended by it.

14. *For the love of Christ* to us, and our love to him, *constraineth us*—Both
to the one and the other, beareth us on with such a strong, steady, prevailing
influence, as winds and tides exert when they waft the vessel to its destined
harbour: *while we thus judge, that if Christ died for all, then were all,* even
the best of men, naturally *dead*—In a state of spiritual death, and liable to death
eternal. For had any man been otherwise, Christ had not needed to have died
for him.

15. *And that he died for all*—That all might be saved, *that they who live*—That
all who live upon the earth, *should not henceforth*—From the moment they know
him, *live unto themselves*—Seek their own honour, profit, pleasure, *but unto him*
—In all righteousness and true holiness.

16. *So that we from this time*—That we know the love of *Christ,* know no
one—Neither ourselves, nor you, neither the rest of the apostles, Gal. ii, 6,
nor any other person, *after the flesh*—According to his former state, country,
descent, nobility, riches, power, wisdom. We fear not the great; we regard
not the rich or wise; we account not the least less than ourselves: we consider
all, only in order to save all. Who is he that thus knows no one after the
flesh? In what land do these Christians live? *Yea, if we have known even
Christ after the flesh*—So as to love him barely with a natural love; so as to
glory in having conversed with him on earth; so as to expect only temporal
benefits from him.

17. *Therefore if any one be in Christ*—A true believer in him, *there is a new
creation*—Only the power that makes a world can make a Christian. And when
he is so created, *the old things are passed away*—Of their own accord, even as
snow in spring. Behold! the present, visible, undeniable change! *All things
are become new*—He has new life, new senses, new faculties, new affections,
new appetites, new ideas and conceptions. His whole tenor of action and con.

reconciled us to himself through Jesus Christ, and hath given to us
19 the ministry of reconciliation: Namely, that God was in Christ
reconciling the world to himself, not imputing their trespasses to
20 them, and hath committed to us the word of reconciliation. Therefore we are ambassadors for Christ, as though God were entreating
by us ; we beseech *you*, in Christ's stead, be ye reconciled to God.
21 For he hath made him, who knew no sin, a sin offering for us, that
we might be made the righteous people of God through him.
VI.   We then, *as* fellow labourers, do also exhort you, not to receive
2 the grace of God in vain.   (For he saith, * I have heard thee in an
acceptable time, and in a day of salvation have I succoured thee ;
behold, now is the accepted time ; behold, now *is* the day of sal-
3 vation.)   Giving no offence in any thing, that the ministry be not
4 blamed : But in all things approving ourselves as the ministers of
God, in much patience, in afflictions, in necessities, in distresses,

---

versation is new, and he lives, as it were, in a new world. God, men, the whole
creation, heaven, earth, and all therein, appear in a new light, and stand related
to him in a new manner, since he was created anew in Christ Jesus.

18. *And all* these new *things are from God*, considered under this very notion,
as *reconciling us*—The world, ver. 39, to himself.

19. *Namely*—The sum of which is, *God*—The whole Godhead, but more eminently God the Father, *was in Christ, reconciling the world*—Which was before
at enmity with God, *to himself*—So taking away that enmity, which could no
otherwise be removed than by the blood of the Son of God.

20. *Therefore we are ambassadors for Christ—we beseech you in Christ's stead*
—Herein the apostle might appear to some transported beyond himself. In ge
neral he uses a more calm, sedate kind of exhortation, as in the beginning of the
next chapter. What unparalleled condescension and divinely tender mercies are
displayed in this verse ?   Did the judge ever beseech a condemned criminal to
accept of pardon ?   Does the creditor ever beseech a ruined debtor to receive an
acquittance in full ?   Yet our almighty Lord, and our eternal Judge, not only
vouchsafes to offer these blessings, but invites us, entreats us, and with the most
tender importunity solicits us not to reject them.

21. *He made him a sin offering, who knew no sin*—A commendation peculiar
to Christ ; *for us*—Who knew no righteousness ; who were inwardly and outwardly nothing but sin ; who must have been consumed by the Divine justice,
had not this atonement been made for our sins, *that we might be made the righteous people of God through him*—Might through him be invested with that righteousness, first imputed to us, then implanted in us, which is in every sense the
righteousness of God.

VI. 1. *We then*—Not only beseech, but as fellow labourers with you, who are
working out your own salvation, do also exhort you, not to receive the grace of
God, which we have been now describing, in vain. We receive it by faith, and
not in vain, if we add to this, persevering holiness.

2. *For he saith*—The sense is, As of old there was a particular time wherein
God was pleased to pour out his particular blessing, so there is now. And this
is the particular time : this is a time of peculiar blessing.

3. *Giving*, as far as in us lies, *no offence, that the ministry be not blamed* on our
account.

4. *But approving ourselves as the ministers of God*—Such as his ministers ought
to be, in much patience , shown, 1. In afflictions, necessities, distresses, (all
which are general terms.) 2. In stripes, imprisonments, tumults, (which are
particular sorts of affliction, necessity, distress.)   3. In labours, watchings, fastings, voluntarily endured.   All these are expressed in the plural number, to
denote a variety of them.   In afflictions, several ways to escape may appear,
though none without difficulty ; in necessities, one only, and that a difficult one
in distresses, none at all appears.

* Isaiah xlix, 8.

5 In stripes, in imprisonments, in tumults, in labours, in watchings,
6 in fastings ; By purity, by prudence, by long suffering, by kindness,
7 by the Holy Ghost, by love unfeigned, By the word of truth, by the
power of God, by the armour of righteousness on the right hand and
8 the left : Through honour and dishonour, through evil report and
9 good report; as deceivers, yet true ; As unknown, yet well known;
10 as dying, yet behold we live ; as chastened, yet not killed ; As sorrowing, yet always rejoicing ; as poor, yet making many rich ; as
having nothing, yet possessing all things.
11 O ye Corinthians, our mouth is open toward you ; our heart is
12 enlarged. Ye are not straitened in us ; but ye are straitened in
13 your own bowels. Now for a recompense of the same, (I speak
14 as to *my* children,) be ye also enlarged. Be not unequally yoked
with unbelievers ; for what fellowship hath righteousness with
unrighteousness ? or what communion hath light with darkness ?
15 And what concord hath Christ with Belial ? Or what part hath a
16 believer with an infidel ? And what agreement hath the temple of

---

5. *In tumults*—The Greek word implies such attacks as a man cannot stand against, but which bear him hither and thither by violence.

6. *By prudence*—Spiritual, Divine; not what the world terms so. Worldly prudence is the practical use of worldly wisdom ; Divine prudence is the due exercise of grace, making spiritual understanding go as far as possible. *By love unfeigned*—The chief fruit of the Spirit.

7. *By the* convincing and converting power of God, accompanying his word, and also attesting it by divers miracles. *By the armour of righteousness on the right hand and the left*—That is, on all sides, the panoply or whole armour of God.

8. *By honour and dishonour*—When we are present; *by evil report and good report*—When we are absent. Who could bear honour and good report, were it not balanced by dishonour? *As deceivers*—Artful, designing men. So the world represents all true ministers of Christ; *yet true*—Upright, sincere in the sight of God.

9. *As unknown*—For *the world knoweth us not, as it knew him not; yet well known*—To God, and to those who are the seals of our ministry. *As dying, yet behold*—Suddenly, unexpectedly! God interposes, and *we live.*

10. *As sorrowing*—For our own manifold imperfections, and for the sins and sufferings of our brethren ; *yet always rejoicing*—In present peace, love, power, and a sure hope of future glory. *As having nothing, yet possessing all things*—For all things are ours, if we are Christ's. What a magnificence of thought is this !

11. From the praise of the Christian ministry, (which he began, chap. ii, 14.) he now draws his affectionate exhortation, *O ye Corinthians*—He seldom uses this appellation; but it has here a peculiar force : *our mouth is open toward you*—With uncommon freedom, because our heart is enlarged in tenderness.

12. *Ye are not straitened in us*—Our heart is wide enough to receive you all : *but ye are straitened in your own bowels*—Your hearts are shut up, and so not capable of the blessings ye might enjoy.

13. *Now for a recompense of the same*—Of my paternal tenderness, (*I speak as to my children*—I ask nothing hard or grievous,) *be ye also enlarged*—Open your hearts, first to God, and then to us : see chap. viii, 5 ; that God may dwell in you, chap. vi, 16; vii, 1; and that ye may receive us, chap. vii, 2.

14. *Be not unequally yoked with unbelievers*—Christians with Jews or heathens. The apostle particularly speaks of marriage : but the reasons he urges equally hold against any needless intimacy with them. Of the five questions that follow, the three former contain the argument ; the two latter the conclusion.

15. *What concord hath Christ*—Whom ye serve, *with Belial*—To whom they belong ?

16. *What agreement hath the temple of God with idols?*—If God would not

God with idols ? Now ye are the temple of the living God, as God hath said, * I will dwell in them, and walk in *them*, and I will

17 be to them a God, and they shall be to me a people. † Therefore come out from among them, and be ye separate, and touch not the

18 unclean person, saith the Lord, and I will receive you, ‡ And will be to you a Father, and ye shall be to me sons and daughters, saith the Lord Almighty.

VII. Having therefore, beloved, these promises, let us cleanse ourselves from all pollution of the flesh and of the spirit, perfecting holiness in the fear of God.

2   Receive us. We have hurt no man, we have corrupted no

3 man, we have defrauded no man. I speak not to condemn *you;* for I have said before, that ye are in our hearts, to live and to die

4 with *you*. Great *is* my freedom of speech toward you ; great *is* my glorying over you : I am filled with comfort, I exceedingly

5 abound with joy over all our affliction. For when we were come into Macedonia, our flesh had no rest, but we were troubled on every side : from without *were* fightings, from within *were* fears.

6 But God, who comforteth them that are brought low, comforted us

---

endure idols in any part of the land wherein he dwelt, how much less under his own roof? He does not say, With the temple of idols. For idols do not dwell in their worshippers. *As God hath said*—To his ancient Church, and in them to all the Israel of God, *I will dwell in them, and walk in them*—The former signifying his perpetual presence ; the latter his operation : *and I will be to them a God, and they shall be to me a people*—The sum of the whole Gospel covenant.

17. *Touch not the unclean person*—Keep at the utmost distance from him ; *and I will receive you*—Into my house and family.

18. *And ye shall be to me for sons and for daughters, saith the Lord Almighty*—The promise made to Solomon, 1 Chron. xxviii, 6, is here applied to all believers ; as the promise made particularly to Joshua is applied to them, Heb. xiii, 5. Who can express the worth, who can conceive the dignity, of this Divine adoption ? Yet it belongs to all who believe the Gospel, who have faith in Christ. They have access to the Almighty ; such free and welcome access as a beloved child to an indulgent father. To him they may fly for aid in every difficulty, and from him obtain a supply in all their wants.

VII. 1. *Let us cleanse ourselves*—This is the latter part of the exhortation, which was proposed, chap. vi, 1, and resumed, ver. 14 ; *from all pollution of the flesh*—All outward sin, *and of the spirit*—All inward. Yet let us not rest in negative religion, but *perfect holiness*—Carrying it to the height in all its branches, and enduring to the end in the loving fear of God, the sure foundation of all holiness.

2. *Receive us*—The sum of what is said in this, as well as in the tenth and following chapters. *We have hurt no man*—In his person ; *we have corrupted no man*—In his principle ; *we have defrauded no man*—Of his property. In this he intimates likewise the good he had done them, but with the utmost modesty, as it were not looking upon it

3. *I speak not to condemn you*—Not as if I accused you of laying this to my charge. I am so far from thinking so unkindly of you, that *ye are in our hearts to live and to die with you*—That is, I could rejoice to spend all my days with you.

4. *I am filled with comfort*—Of this he treats, ver. 6, &c ; of his joy, ver. 7, &c ; of both, ver. 13.

5. *Our flesh*—That is, we ourselves, *had no rest : from without*—From the heathens, *were fightings*—Furious and cruel oppositions : *from within*—From our brethren, *were fears*—Lest they should be seduced.

* Lev. xxvi, 11, &c.   † Isaiah li, 11 ; Zeph. iii, 19, 20.   ‡ Isaiah xliii, 6.

7 by the coming of Titus. And not only by his coming, but also by the comfort wherewith he was comforted over you, when he told us your earnest desire, your grief, your zeal for me, so that I rejoiced
8 the more. For I do not repent that I grieved you by the letter, though I did repent: (for I see that letter grieved you, though
9 but for a season.) Now I rejoice, not that ye were grieved, but that ye grieved to repentance; for ye grieved in a godly manner,
10 so that ye received damage by us in nothing. For godly sorrow worketh repentance unto salvation not to be repented of, whereas
11 the sorrow of the world worketh death. For behold, this very thing, that ye sorrowed after a godly manner, how great diligence it wrought in you, yea, clearing of yourselves, yea, indignation, yea, fear, yea, vehement desire, yea, zeal, yea, revenge? In all things
12 ye have approved yourselves to be pure in this matter. And though I wrote to you, *it was* not for his sake who had done the wrong, nor for his sake who had suffered it, but for the sake of manifesting to you in the sight of God our diligent care over you.
13 Therefore we were comforted in your comfort, and we rejoiced the more exceedingly in the joy of Titus, because his spirit was re-
14 freshed by you all. So that if I had boasted any thing of you to him, I am not ashamed; but as we speak all things to you in truth, so
15 also our boasting to Titus is found a truth. And his tender affection is more abundant toward you, calling to mind the obedience of
16 you all, how ye received him with fear and trembling. I rejoice, therefore, that I have confidence in you in all things.

VIII. Moreover, brethren, we declare to you the grace of God,
2 bestowed on the Churches in Macedonia, That in a great trial of affliction, their overflowing joy and their deep poverty abounded to
3 the riches of their liberality: That to *their* power, I testify, and
4 beyond *their* power, *they* were willing of themselves, Praying us

---

7. *Your earnest desire*—To rectify what had been amiss; *your grief*—For what had offended God, and troubled me.

8. *I did repent*—That is, I felt a tender sorrow for having grieved you, till I saw the happy effect of it.

10. *The sorrow of this world*—Sorrow that arises from worldly considerations, *worketh death*—Naturally tends to work, or occasion death, temporal, spiritual, and eternal.

11. *How great diligence it wrought in you*—Shown in all the following particulars. *Yea, clearing of yourselves*—Some had been more, some less faulty; whence arose these various affections. Hence their apologizing and indignation, with respect to themselves; their fear and desire, with respect to the apostles; their zeal and revenge, with respect to the offender; yea, and themselves also. *Clearing of yourselves*—From either sharing in, or approving of his sin; *indignation*—That ye had not immediately corrected the offender; *fear*—Of God's displeasure, or lest I should come with a rod; *vehement desire*—To see me again; *zeal*—For the glory of God, and the soul of that sinner; *yea, revenge*—Ye took a kind of holy revenge upon yourselves, being scarce able to forgive yourselves. *In all things ye*—As a Church, *have approved yourselves to be pure*—That is, free from blame, since ye received my letter.

12. *It was not* only or chiefly for the sake of the incestuous person, or of his father; but to show my care over you.

VIII. 1. *We declare to you the grace of God*—Which evidently appeared by this happy effect.

2. *In a great trial of affliction*—Being continually persecuted, harassed, and plundered.

II. CORINTHIANS.

with mucn entreaty, to receive the gift and take a part in ministering
5 *it* to the saints. And *this they did* not as we hoped ; but first gave
6 themselves to the Lord, and to us by the will of God : So that we
desired Titus, that as he had begun before, so he would also com-
7 plete this gift among you. Therefore as ye abound in every thing,
in faith, and utterance, and knowledge, and all diligence, and in
8 your love to us, *see* that ye abound in this grace also. I speak not
by way of command, but that by the diligence of others, I may
9 prove the sincerity of your love. For ye know the grace of our
Lord Jesus Christ, that though he was rich, yet for your sake he
10 became poor, that ye through his poverty might be rich. And
herein I give *my* advice : for this is expedient for you, who have
11 begun a year ago, not only to do, but also to do it willingly. Now
therefore complete the work, that as *there was* a ready will, so *there*
12 *may* be also a performance, in proportion to what ye have. For if
there be first a ready mind, a man is accepted according to what
13 he hath, not according to what he hath not. For *I do* not *mean,*
14 that others should be eased, and you burdened ; But by an equality,
let your abundance *be* at this time *a supply* to their want : that
their abundance also may be *a supply* to your want, that there may
15 be an equality, As it is written, * He that *had gathered* the most,
had nothing over ; and he that *had gathered* the least, did not lack.
16 But thanks be to God, who putteth the same diligent care for
17 you into the heart of Titus. For he accepted indeed the exhortation, but being more forward, he went to you of his own accord.
18 And we have sent with him the brother, whose praise in the Gospel

4. *Praying us with much entreaty*—Probably St. Paul had lovingly admonished them not to do beyond their power.
5. *And not as we hoped*—That is, beyond all we could hope ; *they gave themselves to us by the will of God*—In obedience to his will, to be wholly directed by us.
6. *As he had begun*—When he was with you before.
9. *For ye know*—And this knowledge is the true source of love ; *the grace*—The most sincere, most free, and most abundant love. *He became poor*—In becoming man, in all his life ; in his death : *rich*—In the favour and image of God.
12. *A man*—Every believer, *is accepted*—With God, *according to what he hath*—And the same rule holds universally. Whoever acknowledges himself to be a vile, guilty sinner, and in consequence of this acknowledgment flies for refuge to the wounds of a crucified Saviour, and relies on his merits alone for salvation, may, in every circumstance of life, apply this indulgent declaration to himself.
14. *That their abundance*—If need should so require, *may be*—At another time, *a supply to your want, that there may be an equality*—No want on one side, no superfluity on the other. It may likewise have a farther meaning : that as the temporal bounty of the Corinthians did now supply the temporal wants of their poor brethren in Judea ; so the prayers of these might be a means of bringing down many spiritual blessings on their benefactors. So that all the spiritual wants of the one might be amply supplied ; all the temporal of the other.
15. *As it is written, He that had gathered the most, had nothing over ; and he that had gathered the least, did not lack*—That is, in which that scripture is in another sense fulfilled.
17. *Being more forward*—Than to need it, though he received it well.
18. *We*—I and Timothy ; *the brother*—The ancients generally suppose this was St. Luke, *whose praise*—For faithfully dispensing the Gospel, is through all the Churches.

* Exodus xvi, 18.

:9 is through all the Churches : (And not only *so*, but he was alsc appointed by the Churches *to be* a fellow traveller with us, with this gift, which is administered by us, to the glory of the Lord himself,

20 and for *the declaration* of our ready mind.) Avoiding thi's, lest any one should blame us in this abundance, which is administered by

21 us. For we provide things honest, not only before the Lord, but

22 alsc before men. And we have sent with them our brother, whom we have often proved diligent in many things, but now much more

23 diligent, through his great confidence in you. If *any inquire* concerning Titus, *he is* my partner, and fellow labourer with respect to you ; or *concerning* our brethren, *they are* the messengers of the

24 Churches, the glory of Christ. ' Show therefore to them before the Churches, the proof of your love and of our boasting on your behalf.

IX. For concerning the ministering to the saints, it is superfluous

2 for me to write to you. For I know your readiness, which I boast concerning you to the Macedonians, that Achaia was ready a year

3 ago, and your zeal had provoked very many. Yet I have sent the brethren, lest our boasting of you on this head should be made vain,

4 that, as I said, ye may be ready ; Lest if any of the Macedonians come up with me, and find you unprepared, we (not to say you) be

5 ashamed of this confident boasting. Therefore I thought it necessary to desire the brethren to go before to ycu, and complete this your bounty, which had been spoken of before, that it may be

6 ready as a bounty, and not as *a matter* of covetousness. And this *I say*, He that soweth sparingly, shall reap also sparingly ; and he

7 that soweth bountifully, shall reap also bountifully. *Let* every man *do* as he chooseth in his heart, not grudgingly, or of necessity :

8 for * God loveth a cheerful giver. And God is able to make all grace abound toward you, that having always all-sufficiency in all

9 things, ye may abound to every good work : (As it is written, †He

---

19. *He was appointed by the Churches*—Of Macedonia, *with this gift*—Which hey were carrying from Macedonia to Jerusalem : *for the declaration of our ready mind*—That of Paul and his fellow traveller, ready to be the servants of all.

22: *With them*—With Titus and Luke ; *our brother*—Perhaps Apollos.

23. *My partner*—In my cares and labours ; *the glory of Christ*—Signal instruments of advancing his glory.

24. *Before the Churches*—Present by their messengers.

IX. 1. *To write to you*—Largely.

2. *I boast to them at Macedonia*—With whom he then was.

3. *I have sent the* above mentioned brethren before me.

5. *Spoken of before*—By me, to the Macedonians. *Not as a matter of covetousness*—As wrung by importunity from covetous persons.

6. *He that soweth sparingly, shall reap sparingly ; he that soweth bountifully, shall reap bountifully*—A general rule. God will proportion the reward to the work, and the temper whence it proceeds.

7. *Of necessity*—Because he cannot tell how to refuse.

8. How remarkable are these words ! Each is loaded with matter, and in creases all the way it goes. *All grace*—Every kind of blessing, *that ye may abound to every good work*—God gives us every thing, that we may do good therewith, and so receive more blessings. All things in this life, even rewards, are, to the faithful, seeds in order to a future harvest.

9. *He hath scattered abroad*—(A generous word) with a full hand, without any anxious thought, which way each grain falls. *Hi◦ righteousness*—His bene-

* Prov. xxii, 9.   † Psalm cxii, 9.

hath scattered abroad, he hath given to the poor : his righteousness
10 remaineth for ever. * And he who supplieth seed to the sower
and bread for *your* food, will supply and multiply your seed sown,
11 and increase the fruits of your righteousness :) Being enriched
in every thing to all bountifulness, which worketh by us thanks·
12 giving to God. For the administration of this service doth not
only supply the necessities of the saints, but likewise aboundeth
13 by many thanksgivings to God : (Who, by experiment of this
administration, glorify God, for your avowed subjection to the
Gospel of Christ, and for your liberal communication to them and
14 to all men :) And by their prayer for you, who long after you,
15 for the exceeding grace of God which is in you. Thanks *be* to
God for his unspeakable gift.
X.   Now I Paul myself, who when present *am* base among you,
but being absent, am bold toward you, entreat you, by the meek-
2 ness and gentleness of Christ, I beseech, that I may not when I
am present be bold with that confidence wherewith I think to be
3 bold toward some, who think of us as walking after the flesh : For
4 though we walk in the flesh, we do not war after the flesh : (For
the weapons of our warfare *are* not carnal, but mighty through
5 God to the throwing down of strong holds.) Destroying reasonings, and every high thing which exalteth itself against the know

ficence, with the blessed effects of it, *remaineth for ever*—Unexhausted, God still
renewing his store.
10. *And he who supplieth seed*—Opportunity and ability to help others, *and
bread*—All things needful for your own souls and bodies, will continually supply
you with that seed, yea, multiply it to you more and more, *and increase the fruits
of your righteousness*—The happy effects of your love to God and man.
11. *Which worketh by us thanksgiving to God*—Both from us who distribute,
and them who receive your bounty.
13. *Your avowed subjection*—Openly testified by your actions, *to all men*—
Who stand in need of it.
15. *His unspeakable gift*—His outward and inward blessings, the number and
excellence of which cannot be uttered.
X. 1. *Now I Paul myself*—A strongly emphatical expression, *who when present
am base among you*—So probably some of the false teachers affirmed ; copying
after the meekness and gentleness of Christ, *entreat*, though I might command
you.
2. Do not constrain me *when present to be bold*—To exert my apostolical authority, *who think of us as walking after the flesh*—As acting in a cowardly or
crafty manner.
3. *Though we walk in the flesh*—In mortal bodies, and consequently are not
free from human weakness, yet *we do not war*—Against the world and the devil,
after the flesh—By any carnal or worldly methods. Though the apostle here,
and in several other parts of this epistle, speaks in the plural number, for the
sake of modesty and decency, yet he principally means himself. On him were
these reflections thrown, and it is his own authority which he is vindicating.
4. *For the weapons of our warfare*—Those we use in this war, *are not carnal*—
But spiritual, and therefore *mighty to the throwing down of strong holds*—Of all
the difficulties which men or devils can raise in our way. Though faith and
prayer belong also to the Christian armour, Ephes. vi, 15, &c, yet the word of
God seems to be here chiefly intended.
5. *Destroying all vain reasonings, and every high thing which exalteth itself*—
As a wall or rampart, against the knowledge of God, and bringing every thought,
or rather faculty of the mind, *into captivity to the obedience of Christ*—Those
evil reasonings are destroyed. The mind itself, being overcome and taken cap-

* Isaiah lv, 10.

ledge of God, and bringing every thought into captivity to the
6 obedience of Christ, And being in readiness to revenge all disobedience, when your obedience is fulfilled.

7   Do ye look at the outward appearance of things? If any man be
confident that he is Christ's, let him again think this of himself,
8 that as he *is* Christ's, so *are* we also. Yea, if I should boast something more also of the authority which the Lord hath given us for
edification, and not for your destruction, I should not be ashamed.

9 That I may not seem as it were to terrify you by letters. For *his*
10 letters indeed, say they, *are* weighty and strong; but *his* bodily
11 presence *is* weak, and *his* speech contemptible. Let such a one
think this, that such as we are in word by letters, when we are
absent, such *are* we also in deed, when we are present.

12   For we presume not to equal or to compare ourselves with some
of those who recommend themselves: but they among themselves
limiting themselves, and comparing themselves with themselves,
13 are not wise. But we will not boastingly extend ourselves beyond
our measure; but according to the measure of the province which
14 God hath allotted us, a measure to reach even unto you. For we
do not extend ourselves excessively, as not reaching to you; for
15 we are come even to you, in the Gospel of Christ: Not boastingly
extending ourselves beyond *our* measure, in the labours of others;
but having hope, now your faith is increased, to be enlarged by
16 you, *yet still* within our province, abundantly. So as to preach the
Gospel in the regions beyond you, not to boast in another's province
17 of things made ready to our hand. But he that glorieth, let him

tive, lays down all authority of its own, and entirely gives itself up, to perform,
for the time to come, to Christ its conqueror, the obedience of faith.

6. *Being in readiness to revenge all disobedience*—Not only by spiritual censure,
but miraculous punishments: *when your obedience is fulfilled*—When the sound
part of you have given proof of your obedience, so that I am in no danger of
punishing the innocent with the guilty.

7. *Do ye look at the outward appearance of things?*—Does any of you judge
of a minister of Christ by his person, or any outward circumstance? *Let him
again think this of himself*—Let him learn it from his own reflection, before I
convince him by a severer method.

8. *I should not be ashamed*—As having said more than I could make good.

9. I say this, *that I may not seem to terrify you by letters*—Threatening more
than I can perform.

10. *His bodily presence is weak*—His stature (says St. Chrysostom) was low,
his body crooked, and his head bald.

12. *For we presume not*—A strong irony, *to equal ourselves*—As partners of the
same office, *or to compare ourselves*—As partakers of the same labour! *They
among themselves limiting themselves*—Choosing and limiting their provinces according to their own fancy.

13. *But we will not*—Like them, *boastingly extend ourselves beyond our measure,
but according to the measure of the province which God hath allotted to us*—To me
in particular, as the apostle of the Gentiles, a measure which reaches even unto
you. God allotted to each apostle his province, and the measure or bounds
thereof.

14. *We are come even to you*—By a gradual, regular process, having taken the
intermediate places in our way, in preaching the Gospel of Christ.

15. *Having hope, now your faith is increased*—So that you can the better spare
us, *to be enlarged by you abundantly*—That is, enabled by you to go still farther.

16. *In the regions beyond you*—To the west and south, where the Gospel had
not yet been preached.

30

18 glory in the Lord. For not he that commendeth himself is approved, but whom the Lord commendeth.

XI. I wish ye would bear a little with my folly; yea, bear with
2 me. For I am jealous over you with a godly jealousy; for I have
espoused you to one husband, that I may present *you* as a chaste
3 virgin to Christ. But I fear lest as the serpent deceived Eve
through his subtlety, so your minds should be corrupted from the
4 simplicity that is in Christ. If indeed he that cometh preach another Jesus, whom we have not preached, or *if* ye receive another
spirit, which ye have not received, or another Gospel which ye have
5 not accepted, ye might well bear with *him.* But I suppose that
6 I fall nothing short of the very chief apostles. For if *I am* unskilful in speech, yet not in knowledge : but we have been thoroughly
7 made manifest to you in all things. Have I committed an offence
in humbling myself, that ye might be exalted, because I have
8 preached the Gospel of God to you at free cost ? I spoiled other
Churches, taking wages *of them* to serve you : and when I was
9 present with you and wanted, I was chargeable to no man. For
the brethren who came from Macedonia supplied my want; and I
have in all things kept myself from being burdensome, and will
10 keep *myself.* As the truth of Christ is in me, this my boasting
11 shall not be stopped in the regions of Achaia. Wherefore? Be-
12 cause I love you not? God knoweth. But what I do, I will do,
that I may cut off the occasion from them who desire occasion,
13 that wherein they boast, they may be found even as we. For

XI. 1. *I wish ye would bear*—So does he pave the way, for what might otherwise have given offence : *with my folly*—Of commending myself; which to many
may appear folly ; and really would be so, were it not on this occasion absolutely
necessary.

2. *For*—The cause of his seeming folly is expressed in this and the following
verse ; the cause why they should bear with him, ver. 4.

3. *But I fear*—Love is full of these fears ; *lest as the serpent*—A most apposite
comparison, *deceived Eve*—Simple, ignorant of evil, *by his subtlety*—Which is in
the highest degree dangerous to such a disposition ; *so your minds*—We might
therefore be tempted, even if there were no sin in us, *might be corrupted*—Losing
their virginal purity, *from the simplicity that is in Christ*—That simplicity which
is lovingly intent on him alone, seeking no other person or thing.

4. *If indeed*—Any could show another Saviour, a more powerful spirit, a better Gospel, *ye might well bear with him*—But this is impossible.

6. *If I am unskilful in speech*—If I speak in a plain unadorned way, like an
unlearned person. So the Greek word properly signifies.

7. *Have I committed an offence*—Will any turn this into an objection, *in humbling myself*—To work at my trade, *that ye might be exalted*—To be children
of God ?

8. *I spoiled other Churches*—I, as it were, took the spoils of them : it is a military term, *taking wages* (or pay, another military word) *of them*—When I came
to you at first. *And when I was present with you and wanted*—My work not
quite supplying my necessities, *I was chargeable to no man*—Of Corinth.

9. *For*—I chose to receive help from the poor Macedonians, rather than the
rich Corinthians ! Were the poor in all ages more generous than the rich ?

10. *This my boasting shall not be stopped*—For I will receive nothing from you.

11. Do I refuse to receive any thing of you, *because I love you not?*—God
knoweth that is not the case.

12. *Who desire any occasion*—To censure me : *that wherein they boast, they may
be found even as we*—They boasted of being burdensome to no man. But it was
a vain boast in them, though not in the apostle

such *are* false apostles, deceitful workers, transforming themselves
14 into apostles of Christ. And no marvel ; for Satan himself is trans-
15 formed into an angel of light. Therefore it is no great thing, if his
  ministers also be transformed as the ministers of righteousness ;
16 whose end shall be according to their works. I say again, Let no
  man think me a fool ; but if otherwise, yet as a fool receive me,
17 that I also may boast a little. What I speak I speak not after the
  Lord, but as it were foolishly, in this confidence of boasting.
18 Seeing many glory after the flesh, I will glory also. For ye, being
19 wise, suffer fools willingly. For ye suffer, if a man enslave you, if
20 he devour *you*, if he take *from you*, if he exalt himself, if he smite
21 you on the face. I speak with regard to reproach, as though we
  had been weak ; whereas in whatever any is confident, (I speak as
22 a fool,) I am confident also. Are they Hebrews ? so am I. Are
  they Israelites ? so am I. Are they the seed of·Abraham ? so am
23 I. Are they ministers of Christ ? (I speak foolishly) I am more :
  in labours more abundant, in stripes more exceeding, in prisons
24 more abundant, in deaths often. Five times I received from the
25 Jews forty *stripes* save one. Thrice I was beaten with rods,
  once I was stoned, thrice I have been shipwrecked, a day and a
26 night I passed in the deep : In journeyings often, in dangers from
  rivers, in dangers from robbers, in dangers from my own countrymen, in dangers from the heathen, in dangers in the city, in dan-
  gers in the wilderness, in dangers in the sea, in dangers among
27 false brethren ; In labour and toil, in watchings often, in hunger

14. *Satan himself is transformed*—Uses to transform himself; to put on the
fairest appearances.
15. *Therefore it is no great*, no strange *thing*—*whose end*—Notwithstanding all
their disguises, shall be according to their works.
16. *I say again*—He premises a new apology to this new commendation of
himself. *Let no man think me a fool*—Let none think I do this without the
utmost necessity. But if any do think me foolish herein, yet bear with my folly.
17. *I speak not after the Lord*—Not by an express command from him ; though
still under the direction of his Spirit : *but as it were foolishly*—In such a manner
as many may think foolish.
18. *After the flesh*—That is, in external things.
19. *Being wise*—A beautiful irony.
20. *For ye suffer*—Not only the folly, but the gross abuses of those false apostles, *if a man enslave you*—Lord it over you in the most arbitrary manner, *if he
devour you*—By his exorbitant demands, (notwithstanding his boast of not being
burdensome,) *if he take from you*—By open violence, *if he exalt himself*—By the
most unbounded self commendation, *if he smite you on the face*—(A very possible
case,) under pretence of Divine zeal.
21. *I speak with regard to reproach, as though we had been weak*—I say, Bear
with me : even on supposition that the weakness be real, which they reproach
me with.
22. *Are they Hebrews, Israelites, the seed of Abraham*—These were the heads
or which they boasted.
23. *I am more* so than they. *In deaths often*—Surrounding me in the most
dreadful forms.
24. *Five times I received from the Jews forty stripes save one*—Which was the
utmost that the law allowed. With the Romans, he sometimes pleaded his privilege as a Roman. But from the Jews he suffered all things.
25. *Thrice I have been shipwrecked*—Before his voyage to Rome. *In the deep*
—Probably floating on some part of the vessel.
27. *In cold and nakedness*—Having no place where to lay my head : no con

28 and thirst, in fastings often, in cold and nakedness. Beside
the things which are from without, that which rusheth upon me
29 daily, the care of all the Churches. Who is weak, and I am not
30 weak? Who is offended, and I burn not? Since I must glory, I
31 will glory of things that concern my infirmities. The God and
Father of the Lord Jesus Christ, who is blessed for ever, knoweth
32 that I lie not. In Damascus the governor under King Aretas kep
the city of the Damascenes with a guard, being determined to
33 apprehend me. But I was let down through a window in a basket
by the wall, and escaped from his hands.
XII. Surely it is not expedient for me to boast: yet I will come to
2 visions and revelations of the Lord. I knew a man in Christ, above
fourteen years ago, (whether in the body I know not, or out of the
body I know not; God knoweth,) such a one caught up to the
3 third heaven. Yea, I knew such a man, (whether in the body or
4 out of the body I know not, God knoweth.) That he was caught up
into paradise, and heard unspeakable things, which it is not possible

venient raiment to cover me. Yet appearing before noblemen, governors, kings;
and not being ashamed.

28. *Beside the things which are from without*—Which I suffer on the account
of others: namely, *the care of all the Churches*—A more modest expression than
if he had said, *the care of the whole Church.* *All*—Even those he had not seen
in the flesh. St. Peter himself could not have said this in so strong a sense.

29. *Who*—So he had not only the care of the Churches, but of every person
therein, *is weak, and I am not weak*—By sympathy, as well as by condescension.
Who is offended—Hindered in, or turned out of the good way, *and I burn not*—
Being pained as though I had fire in my bosom.

30. *I will glory of the things that concern my infirmities*—Of what shows mv
weakness, rather than my strength.

32. *The governor under Aretas*—King of Arabia and Syria, of which Damascus was a chief city, willing to oblige the Jews, kept the city, setting guards at
all the gates day and night.

33. *Through a window*—Of a house which stood on the city wall.

XII. 1. *It is not expedient*—Unless on so pressing an occasion. Visions are
seen, revelations heard.

2. *I knew a man in Christ*—That is, a Christian. It is plain from ver. 6, 7,
that he means himself, though in modesty he speaks as of a third person ; *whether in the body, or out of the body, I know not*—It is equally possible with God,
to present distant things to the imagination in the body, as if the soul were
absent from it, and present with them; or to transport both soul and body for
what time he pleases to heaven; or to transport the soul only thither for a
season, and in the meantime to preserve the body fit for its re-entrance. But
since the apostle himself did not know, whether his soul was in the body, or
whether one or both were actually in heaven, it would be vain curiosity for us to
attempt determining it. *The third heaven*—Where God is; far above the aerial
and the starry heaven. Some suppose it was here the apostle was let into the
mystery of the future state of the Church: and received his orders to turn from
the Jews and go to the Gentiles.

3. *Yea, I knew such a man*—That at another time.

4. *He was caught up into paradise*—The seat of happy spirits in their separate
state, between death and the resurrection. *Things which it is not possible for
man to utter*—Human language being incapable of expressing them. Here he
anticipated the joyous rest of the righteous that die in the Lord. But this rap-
ture did not precede, but follow after his being caught up to the third heaven.
A strong intimation, that he must first discharge his mission, and then enter into
glory. And beyond all doubt, such a foretaste of it served to strengthen him in
all his after trials, when he could call to mind the very joy that was prepared
for him.

5 for man to utter. Of such a one I will glory; but I will not
6 glory of myself, unless in my infirmities. Yet if I should resolve
to boast, I should not be a fool; for I speak the truth: but I forbear, lest any one should think of me above what he seeth me, or
heareth from me.
7 And lest I should be lifted up with the abundance of the revelations, there was given me a thorn in the flesh, a messenger of
8 Satan, to buffet me, lest I should be lifted up. Concerning this,
9 I besought the Lord thrice, that it might depart from me. But
he said to me, My grace is sufficient for thee; for my strength is
made perfect in weakness. Most gladly therefore will I rather
glory in my weaknesses, that the strength of Christ may rest upon
10 me. Therefore I am well pleased in weaknesses, in reproaches,
in necessities, in persecutions, in distresses for Christ's sake;
11 for when I am weak, then I am strong. I am become a fool in
boasting; *but* ye have compelled me: for I ought to have been
commended by you: for in nothing have I fallen short of the very
chief apostles, though I am nothing.
12 Truly the signs of an apostle were wrought among you, in all
13 patience, in signs, and wonders, and mighty deeds. For wherein
were ye inferior to the other Churches, unless that I myself was
14 not burdensome to you? 'Forgive me this wrong. Behold, the

---

5. *Of such a one I will*—I might, *glory: but I will not glory of myself*—As
considered in myself.

6. *Yet if I should resolve to glory* (referring to, I might glory,) of such a glorious revelation, *I should not be a fool*—That is, it could not justly be accounted
folly to relate the naked truth. *But I forbear*—I speak sparingly of these things,
for fear any one should think too highly *of me*—O where is this fear now to be
found? Who is afraid of this?

7. *There was given me*—By the wise and gracious providence of God, *a thorn
in the flesh*—A visitation more painful than any thorn sticking in the flesh; a
messenger or angel *of Satan to buffet me*—Perhaps both visibly and invisibly:
and the word in the original expresses the present as well as the past time.
All kinds of affliction had befallen the apostle. Yet none of those did he de-
precate. But here he speaks of one, as above all the rest, one that macerated
him with weakness, and by the pain and ignominy of it, prevented his being
lifted up more, or at least not less, than the most vehement headache could
have done; which many of the ancients say he laboured under. St. Paul seems
to have had a fresh fear of these buffetings every moment, when he so frequently
represses himself in his boasting, though it was extorted from him by the utmost
necessity.

8. *Concerning this*—He had now forgot his being lifted up; *I besought the
Lord thrice*—As our Lord besought his Father.

9. *But he said to me*—In answer to the third request, *My grace is sufficient for
thee*—How tender a repulse! We see there may be grace where there is the
quickest sense of pain. My strength is more illustriously displayed by the
weakness of the instrument. Therefore I will glory in my weaknesses, rather
than my revelations, that the strength of Christ may rest upon me. The Greek
word properly means, may cover me all over like a tent. We ought most willingly to accept whatever tends to this end, however contrary to flesh and
blood.

10. *Weaknesses*—Whether proceeding from Satan or men; *for when I am
weak*—Deeply conscious of my weakness, then does the strength of Christ rest
upon me.

11. *Though I am nothing*—Of myself.

14. *The third time*—Having been disappointed twice. *I seek not yours*—
Your goods; *but you*—Your souls.

third time I am ready to come to you: yet I will not be burdensome to you; for I seek not yours, but you; for the children ought
not to lay up treasure for the parents, but the parents for the chil-
15 dren. And I will most gladly spend, and be spent for your souls,
16 though the more abundantly I love you, the less I am loved. But
be it so; I did not burden you: but being crafty, I caught you
17 with guile. Did I make a gain of you by any of them whom I
18 sent to you? I desired Titus, and with him I sent a brother. Did
Titus make a gain of you? Did we not walk in the same spirit?
In the same steps?
19 Think ye that we again excuse ourselves to you? We speak
before God in Christ, and all things, beloved, for your edification.
20 For I fear lest when I come, I should not find you such as I would,
and *lest* I should be found by you such as ye would not: lest
there should be contentions, envyings, wraths, strifes, backbitings,
21 whisperings, swellings, tumults: Lest my God should humble me
when I come to you again, and I should mourn over many of them
who had sinned before, and have not repented of the uncleanness,
and fornication, and lasciviousness, which they have committed.
XIII. I am coming to you this third time: every word shall be esta-
2 blished by the mouth of two or three witnesses. I told *you* before, and do tell you beforehand, (though now absent, as if I were
present the second time,) those who had sinned before, and all the
3 rest, that if I come again, I will not spare: Since ye seek a proof
of Christ speaking in me, who is not weak toward you, but power-
4 ful among you. For though he was crucified through weakness,
yet he liveth by the power of God; and we also are weak with
him; but we shall live with him, by the power of God in you.
5 Examine yourselves whether ye are in the faith: prove yourselves.

---

15. *I will gladly spend*—All I have; *and be spent*—Myself.
16. *But*, some may object, Though I did not burden you, though I did not take
any thing of you myself, yet, *being crafty, I caught you with guile*—I did
secretly by my messengers what I would not do openly, or in person.
17. I answer this lying accusation by appealing to plain fact. *Did I make a
gain of you by Titus*—Or any other of my messengers? You know the contrary.
It should be carefully observed, that St. Paul does not allow, but absolutely
denies, that *he had caught them with guile*—So that the common plea for guile,
which has been often drawn from the text, is utterly without foundation
18. *I desired Titus*—To go to you.
19. *Think ye that we again excuse ourselves?*—That I speak this for my own
sake? No. I speak all this for your sakes.
21. *Who had sinned before*—My last coming to Corinth. *Uncleanness*—Of
married persons: *lasciviousness*—Against nature
XIII. 1. *I am coming this third time*—He had been coming twice before,
though he did not actually come.
2. *All the rest*—Who have since then sinned in any of these kinds. *I will not
spare*—I will severely punish them.
4. *He was crucified through weakness*—Through the impotence of human
nature. *We also are weak with him*—We appear weak and despicable by partaking of the same sufferings for his sake; *but we shall live with him*—Being raised
from the dead; *by the power of God in you*—By that Divine energy which is now
in every believer, ver. 5.
5. *Prove yourselves*—Whether ye are such as can, or such as cannot bear the
best. This is the proper meaning of the word, which we translate reprobates.

Do ye not know yourselves, that Jesus Christ is in you, unless
6 ye are reprobates? And I trust, ye shall know that we are not
7 reprobates. Now I pray God, that ye may do no evil: not that we
may appear approved, but that ye may do that which is good,
8 though we should be as reprobates. For we can do nothing against
9 the truth, but for the truth. For we rejoice, when we are weak
and ye are strong: and this also we wish, *even* your perfection.
10 Therefore I write these things being absent, lest being present I
should use severity, according to the power which the Lord hath
given me for edification, and not for destruction.
11   Finally, brethren, farewell: be perfect, be of good comfort, be
of one mind, live in peace, and the God of love and peace shall
12 be with you. Salute one another with a holy kiss. All the saints
13 salute you. The grace of the Lord Jesus Christ, and the love of
14 God, and the communion of the Holy Ghost, *be* with you all.
Amen.

Know ye not yourselves, that Jesus Christ is in you—All Christian believers know this by the witness and by the fruit of his Spirit. Some translate the words, Jesus Christ is among you, that is, in the Church of Corinth, and understand them of the miraculous gifts, and the power of Christ which attended the censures of the apostle.

6. *And I trust ye shall know*—By proving yourselves, not by putting my authority to the proof.

7. *I pray God that ye may do no evil*—To give me occasion of showing my apostolical power. I do not desire to *appear approved*—By miraculously punishing you; *but that ye may do that which is good, though we should be as reprobates*—Having no occasion to give that proof of our apostleship.

8. *For we can do nothing against the truth*—Neither against that which is just and right, nor against those who walk according to the truth of the Gospel.

9. *For we rejoice when we are weak*—When we appear so, having no occasion to show our apostolic power. *And this we wish, even your perfection*—In the faith that worketh by love.

11. *Be perfect*—Aspire to the highest degree of holiness: *be of good comfort*—Filled with Divine consolation: *be of one mind*—Desire, labour, pray for it, to the utmost degree that is possible.

13. *The grace*—Or favour, *of our Lord Jesus Christ*—By which alone we can come to the Father; *and the love of God*—Manifested to you, and abiding in you; *and the communion*—Or fellowship, *of the Holy Ghost*—In all his gifts and graces.

It is with great reason that this comprehensive and instructive blessing is pronounced at the close of our solemn assemblies. And it is a very indecent thing to see so many quitting them, or getting into postures to remove, before this short sentence can be ended.

How often have we heard this awful benediction pronounced? Let us study it more and more, that we may value it proportionably, that we may either deliver or receive it with a becoming reverence; with eyes and hearts lifted up to God, who giveth the blessing out of Sion, and life for evermore.

NOTES

ST. PAUL'S EPISTLE TO THE GALATIANS.

——

This epistle is not written, as most of St. Paul's are, to the Christians of a particular city, but to those of a whole country in Asia Minor, the metropolis of which was Ancyra. These readily embraced the Gospel; but after St. Paul had left them, certain men came among them, who (like those mentioned, Acts xv,) taught that it was necessary to be circumcised, and to keep the Mosaic law. They affirmed that all the other apostles taught thus: that St. Paul was inferior to them; and that even he sometimes practised and recommended the law, though at other times he opposed it.

The first part therefore of this epistle is spent in vindicating himself and his doctrine, proving, 1. That he had it immediately from Christ himself, and that he was not inferior to the other apostles: 2. That it was the very same which the other apostles preached: and 3. That his practice was consistent with his doctrine.

The second contains proofs drawn from the Old Testament, that the law and all its ceremonies were abolished by Christ.

The third contains practical inferences; closed with his usual benediction. To be a little more distinct,

THIS EPISTLE CONTAINS,

I. The inscription . . . . Chap. i, 1–5
II. The calling the Galatians back to the true Gospel; wherein he
  1. Reproves them for leaving it 6–10
  2. Asserts the authority of the Gospel he had preached, who
    1. Of a persecutor was made an apostle by an immediate call
      from heaven 11–17
    2. Was no way inferior to Peter himself 18–ii, 21
    3. Defends justification by faith, and again reproves the Gala-
      tians . . . . , . . iii, 1–iv, 11
    4. Explains the same thing by an allegory taken out of the
      law itself 12–31
    5. Exhorts them to maintain their liberty . . . . . v, 1–12
    Warns them not to abuse it, and admonishes them to walk
      not after the flesh, but after the Spirit 13–vi, 10
III. The conclusion 11–18

——

GALATIANS.

——

1 PAUL, an apostle, (not of men, neither by man, but by Jesus
2 Christ, and God the Father, who raised him from the dead,) And

Verse 1. *Paul, an apostle*—Here it was necessary for St. Paul to assert his authority. Otherwise he is very modest in the use of this title. He seldom mentions it when he mentions others in the salutations with himself, as in the Epistle to the Philippians and Thessalonians; or when he writes about secular affairs, as in that to Philemon; nor yet in writing to the Hebrews, because he was not pro-

all the brethren who are with me, to the Churches of Galatia;
3 Grace *be* to you, and peace from God the Father, and the Lord
4 Jesus Christ, Who gave himself for our sins, that he might deliver
us from the present evil world, according to the will of our God
5 and Father, To him be glory for ever and ever. Amen.
6 I marvel that ye are so soon removed from him who called you
7 by the grace of Christ to another Gospel. Which is not another;
but there are some that trouble you, and would subvert the Gospel
8 of Christ. But if we, or an angel from heaven, preach to you another Gospel than we have preached to you, let him be accursed.
9 As we have said before, so I say now again, if any one preach to
you another Gospel than that ye received, let him be accursed.
10 For do I now satisfy men, or God? Or do I seek to please men?
For if I still pleased men, I should not be the servant of Christ.
11 But I certify you, brethren, that the Gospel which was preached
12 by me is not according to man. For neither did I receive it from
man, neither was I taught *it*, but by the revelation of Jesus Christ.

---

perly their apostle ; *not of men*—Not commissioned from them ; but from God the
Father ; *neither by man*—Neither by any man as an instrument, but by Jesus
Christ ; *who raised him from the dead*—Of which it was the peculiar business of
an apostle to bear witness.

2. *And all the brethren*—Who agree with me in what I now write.

4. *That he might deliver us from the present evil world*—From the guilt, wickedness, and misery wherein it is involved, and from its vain and foolish customs
and pleasures ; *according to the will of God*—Without any merit of ours. St.
Paul begins most of his epistles with thanksgiving ; but writing to the Galatians,
he alters his style, and first sets down his main proposition, That by the merits
of Christ alone, giving himself for our sins, we are justified : neither does he term
them (as he does others) either saints, elect, or Churches of God.

5. *To whom be glory*—For this his gracious will.

6. *I marvel that ye are so soon removed*—After my leaving you, *from him who
called you by the grace of Christ*—His gracious Gospel, and his gracious power.

7. *Which*—indeed—*is not*—properly—*another* Gospel. For what ye have now
received is no Gospel at all. It is not glad, but heavy tidings ; as setting your
acceptance with God upon terms impossible to be performed ; *but there are
some that trouble you*—The same word occurs, Acts xv, 24 ; *and would*—If they
were able, subvert or overthrow *the Gospel of Christ*—The better to effect which,
they suggest that the other apostles, yea, and I myself, insist upon the observance
of the law.

8. *But if we*—I and all the apostles, *or an angel from heaven*—If it were possible, *preach another Gospel, let him be accursed*—Cut off from Christ and God.

9. *As*—He speaks upon mature deliberation ; after pausing, it seems, between the two verses, *we*—I and the brethren who are with me, *have said
before*—Many times, in effect, if not in terms, *so I say*—All those brethren
knew the truth of the Gospel. St. Paul knew the Galatians had received the
true Gospel.

10. *For*—He adds the reason why he speaks so confidently, *do I now satisfy
men?*—Is this what I aim at in preaching or writing? *if I still*—Since I was an
apostle, *pleased men*—Studied to please them, if this were my motive of action :
nay, if I did in fact please the men who know not God, *I should not be the servant of Christ*—Hear this, all ye who vainly hope to keep in favour both with God
and with the world.

11. *But I certify you, brethren*—He does not till now give them even this appellation ; *that the Gospel which was preached by me*—Among you, *is not according to man*—Not from man, not by man, not suited to the taste of man.

12. *For neither did I receive it*—At once, *nor was I taught it*—Slowly and gradually, by any man ; *but by the revelation of Jesus Christ*—Our Lord revealed to
him at first his resurrection, ascension, and the calling of the Gentiles, and his

13 For ye have heard of my behaviour in time past in the Jewish
religion, that above measure I persecuted the Church of God, and
14 wasted it. And I profited in the Jewish religion above many of
my years among my countrymen, being more abundantly zealous
15 for the traditions of my fathers. But when it pleased God, who
separated me from my mother's womb, and called me by his grace,
16 To reveal his Son in me, that I might preach him among the Gen-
17 tiles, I did not confer with flesh and blood : Neither did I go up
to Jerusalem, to them that were apostles before me ; but I imme-
18 diately went into Arabia, and returned again to Damascus. Then
after three years I-went up to Jerusalem to visit Peter, and abode
19 with him fifteen days. But other of the apostles I saw none, save
20 James, the brother of the Lord. Now the things which I write to
21 you, behold, before God, I lie not. Afterward I came into the
22 regions of Syria and Cilicia ; And I was unknown by face to the
23 Churches of Judea which were in Christ : But only they had heard,
He that persecuted us in time past, now preacheth the faith which
24 once he destroyed. And they glorified God in me.
II.   Then fourteen years after I went up again to Jerusalem with
2 Barnabas, taking Titus also with me. But I went up by revelation,
and laid before them the Gospel which I preach among the Gentiles ;

own apostleship ; and told him then, there were other things for which he would
appear to him.

13. *I persecuted the Church of God*—That is, the believers in Christ.

14. *Being zealous of the* unwritten *traditions*—Over and above those written
in the law.

15. *But when it pleased God*—He ascribes nothing to his own merits, endeavours, or sincerity, *who separated me from my mother's womb*—Set me apart for
an apostle, as he did Jeremiah for a prophet, Jer. i, 5. Such an unconditional
predestination as this may consist both with God's justice and mercy : *and
called me by his grace*—By his free and almighty love, to be both a Christian
and an apostle.

16. *To reveal his Son in me*—By the powerful operation of his Spirit, 2 Cor.
v, 6, as well as to me by the heavenly vision; *that I might preach him to other*s
—Which I should have been ill qualified to do, had I not first known him myself:
I did not confer with flesh and blood—Being fully satisfied of the Divine will, and
determined to obey, I took no counsel with any man, neither with my own reason
or inclinations, which might have raised numberless objections.

17. *Neither did I go up to Jerusalem*—The residence of the apostles, *but I
immediately went into Arabia, and returned again to Damascus*—He presupposes the journey to Damascus, in which he was converted, as being known
to them all.

18. *Then after three years*—Wherein I had given full proof of my apostleship
I went to visit Peter—To converse with him.

19. *But other of the apostles I saw none, save James, the brother* (that is, the
kinsman) *of the Lord*—Therefore when Barnabas is said to have brought him in
to the apostles, Acts ix, 27, only St. Peter and St. James are meant.

22. *I was unknown by face to the Churches of Judea*—Except to that of
Jerusalem.

24. *In me*—That is, on my account.

II. 1. *Then fourteen years after*—My first journey thither, *I went up again to
Jerusalem*—This seems to be the journey mentioned Acts xv ; several passages
here referring to that great council, wherein all the apostles showed that they
were of the same judgment with him.

2. *I went up*—Not by any command from them, but by an express revelation
from God, *and laid before them*—The chief of the Church in Jerusalem, *the
Gospel which I preached among the Gentiles*—Acts xv, 4 ; touching justifica.

but severally to those of eminence, lest by any means I should run.
3 or should have run in vain. (But neither was Titus, who was with
4 me, being a Greek, compelled to be circumcised, Because of false
brethren introduced unawares, who had slipped in, to spy out our
liberty which we have through Christ Jesus, that they might bring
5 us into bondage : To whom we did not yield by submission, no,
not an hour, that the truth of the Gospel might continue with you.)
6 And they who undoubtedly were something, (*but* whatsoever they
were it is no difference to me : God accepteth no man's person,)
7 they who undoubtedly were something, added nothing to me. But
on the contrary, when they saw that I was entrusted with the Gospel
8 of the uncircumcison, as Peter *with that* of the circumcision : (For
he that wrought effectually in Peter for the apostleship of the circumcision, wrought likewise effectually in me toward the Gentiles :)
9 And when James, and Cephas, and John, who undoubtedly were
pillars, knew the grace that was given to me, they gave the right
hands of fellowship to me and Barnabas, that we *should go* to

---

tion by faith alone : not that they might confirm me therein ; but that I might
remove prejudice from them. Yet not publicly at first, *but severally to those of
eminence*—Speaking to them one by one ; *lest I should run, or should have run
in vain*—Lest I should lose the fruit either of my present or past labours. For
they might have greatly hindered this, had they not been fully satisfied both of
his mission and doctrine. The word *run* beautifully expresses the swift progress
of the Gospel.

3. *But neither was Titus, who was with me*—When I conversed with them,
compelled to be circumcised—A clear proof that none of the apostles insisted on
the circumcising Gentile believers. The sense is, and it is true, some of those
false brethren would fain have compelled Titus to be circumcised ; but I utterly
refused it.

4. *Because of false brethren*—Who seem to have urged it, *introduced unawares*—Into some of those private conferences at Jerusalem, *who had slipped in,
to spy out our liberty*—From the ceremonial law, *that they might*—If possible, bring
us into that bondage again.

5. *To whom we did not yield by submission*—Although in love he would have
yielded to any. With such wonderful prudence did the apostle use his Christian
liberty ; circumcising Timothy, Acts xvi, 3, because of weak brethren, but not
Titus, because of false brethren ; *that the truth of the Gospel*—That is, the true
genuine Gospel, *might continue with you*—With you, Gentiles. So we defend, for
your sakes, the privilege which you would give up.

6. *And they who undoubtedly were something*—Above all others, (*what they
were*—How eminent soever, *it is no difference to me*—So that I should alter
either my doctrine or my practice : *God accepteth no man's person*—For any
eminence in gifts or outward prerogatives,) in that conference, *added nothing to
me*—Neither as to doctrine nor mission.

7. *But when they saw*—By the effects which I laid before them, ver. 8 ; Acts
xv. 12, *that I was entrusted with the Gospel of the uncircumcision*—That is, with
the charge of preaching it to the uncircumcised heathens.

8. *For he that wrought effectually in Peter for the apostleship of the circum
cision*—To qualify him for, and support him in, the discharge of that office to the
Jews, wrought likewise effectually in and by me, for and in the discharge of my
office toward the Gentiles.

9. *And when James*—Probably named first, because he was bishop of the
Church in *Jerusalem, and Cephas*—Speaking of him at Jerusalem, he calls him
by his Hebrew name, *and John*—Hence it appears that he also was at the
council, though he is not particularly named in the Acts : *who undoubtedly were
pillars*—The principal supporters and defenders of the Gospel ; *knew*—After they
had heard the account I gave them, *the grace*—Of apostleship, *which was given
me, they*—In the name of all : *gave to me and Barnabas*—My fellow labourer, *the*

10 the Gentiles, and they to the circumcision : Only *they desired* that
    we would be mindful of the poor, which very thing I also was for-
11 ward to do.   But when Cephas came to Antioch, I withstood him
12 to the face, because he was to be blamed.   For before some
    came from James, he ate with the Gentiles · but when they were
    come, he withdrew and separated himself, fearing those of the cir-
13 cumcision.   And the other Jews also dissembled with him, so that
14 even Barnabas was carried away with their dissimulation.   But
    when I saw, that they did not walk uprightly, according to the truth
    of the Gospel, I said to Peter before *them* all, If thou, being a Jew,
    livest after the manner of the Gentiles, and not of the Jews, why
15 compellest thou the Gentiles to Judaize ?   We *who are* Jews by
16 nature, and not sinners of the Gentiles, Even we (knowing that a
    man is not justified by the works of the law, but by the faith of
    Jesus Christ) have believed in Christ Jesus, that we might be jus-

right hands of fellowship—They gave us their hands in token of receiving us as
their fellow labourers, mutually agreeing, *that we*—I and those in union with me,
should go to the Gentiles—Chiefly ; *and they*—With those that were in union with
them, chiefly *to the circumcision*—The Jews.

10. *Of the poor*—The poor Christians in Judea, who had lost all they had for
Christ's sake.

11. *But*—The argument here comes to the height.   Paul reproves Peter himself.   So far was he from receiving his doctrine from man, or from being inferior
to the chief of the apostles, *when Peter*—Afterward, *came to Antioch*—Then the
chief of all the Gentile Churches, *I withstood him to the face, because he was to
be blamed*—For fear of man, ver. 12, for dissimulation, ver. 13, and for not walking uprightly, ver. 14.

13. *And the other* believing *Jews*—Who were at Antioch, *dissembled with him :
so that even Barnabas was carried away with their dissimulation*—Was borne away
as with a torrent, into the same ill practice.

14. *I said to Cephas before them all*—See Paul single against Peter and all the
Jews !   *If thou being a Jew*, yet *livest* in thy ordinary conversation, *after the manner of the Gentiles*—Not observing the ceremonial law, which thou knowest to
be now abolished, *why compellest thou the Gentiles*—By withdrawing thyself, and
all the ministers from them, either to Judaize, to keep the ceremonial law, or to
be excluded from Church communion ?

15. *We*—St. Paul, to spare St. Peter, drops the first person singular, and
speaks in the plural number.   Verse 18, he speaks in the first person singular
again by a figure, and without a figure, ver. 19, &c, *who are Jews by nature*—
By birth, not proselytes only, *and not sinners of the Gentiles*—That is, not sinful
Gentiles ; not such gross, enormous, abandoned sinners, as the heathens generally were.

16. *Knowing that a man is not justified by the works of the law*—Not even of
the moral, much less the ceremonial law, *but by the faith of Jesus Christ*—That
is, by faith in him.   The name Jesus was first known by the Gentiles : the name
Christ by the Jews.   And they are not always placed promiscuously, but generally, in a more solemn way of speaking, the apostle says Christ Jesus, in a more
familiar, Jesus Christ, *even we*—And how much more must the Gentiles, who
have still less pretence to depend on their own works ? *Have believed*—Knowing
there is no other way.   *Because*—Considering the demands of the law, and the
state of human nature, it is evident, that *by the works of the law*—By such an
obedience as it requires, *shall no flesh living*—No human creature, Jew or Gentile, be justified.   Hitherto St. Paul had been considering that single question,
" Are Christians obliged to observe the ceremonial law ?"   But he here insensibly
goes farther, and by citing this scripture shows, that what he spoke directly of
the ceremonial, included also the moral law.   For David undoubtedly did so,
when he said, (Psalm cxliii, 2, the place here referred to.)   In thy sight shall no
man living be justified : which the apostle likewise explains, Rom. iii, 19, 20, in
such a manner as can agree to none but the moral law

tified by the faith of Christ, and not by the works of the law, be-
17 cause by the works of the law no flesh shall be justified. But if
while we seek to be justified by Christ, we ourselves also are found
.18 sinners, *is* Christ therefore the minister of sin? God forbid. For
if I build again the things which I destroyed, I make myself a trans-
19 gressor. For I through the law am dead to the law, that I may
20 live to God. I am crucified with Christ, and I live no longer, but
Christ liveth in me, and the life that I now live in the flesh, I live
by faith in the Son of God, who loved me and delivered up himself
21 for me. I do not make void the grace of God; for if righteousness
is by the law, then Christ died in vain.
III. O thoughtless Galatians, who hath bewitched you, before whose
eyes Jesus Christ hath been evidently set forth, crucified among
2 you? This only would I learn of you, Did ye receive the Spirit
3 by the works of the law, or by the hearing of faith? Are ye so

17. *But if while we seek to 'be justified by Christ, we ourselves are* still *found
sinners*—If we continue in sin, will it therefore follow, that Christ is the minis
ter or countenancer of sin?

18. By no means! *For if I build again*—By sinful practice, *the things which I
destroyed*—By my preaching, I only *make myself*—Or show myself, not Christ,
to be a transgressor: the whole blame lies on me, not him or his Gospel. As if
he had said, the objection were just, if the Gospel promised justification to men
continuing in sin. But it does not. Therefore if any who profess the Gospel
do not live according to it, they are sinners, it is certain; but not justified, and
so the Gospel is clear.

19. *For I through the law*—Applied by the Spirit to my heart, and deeply convincing me of my utter sinfulness and helplessness, *am dead to the law*—To all
hope of justification from it, *that I may live to God*—Not continue in sin. Fo·
this very end am I (in this sense) freed from the law, that I may be freed from
sin.

20. The apostle goes on to describe how he is freed from sin; how far he is
from continuing therein. *I am crucified with Christ*—Made conformable to his
death; *the body of sin is destroyed*, Rom. vi, 6, *and I*—As to my corrupt nature,
live no longer—Being *dead to sin : but Christ liveth within me*—Is a fountain of
life in my inmost soul, from which all my tempers, words, and actions flow.
And the life that I now live in the flesh—Even in this mortal body, *I live by faith
in the Son of God*—I derive every moment that supernatural principle; from a
Divine evidence and conviction, that he loved me, and delivered up himself for me.

21. Meantime, *I do not make void*—In seeking to be justified by my own works;
the grace of God—The free love of God in Christ Jesus. But they do, who seek
justification by the law : *for if righteousness is by the law*—If men might be justified by their obedience to the law, moral or ceremonial, *then Christ died in
vain*—Without any necessity for it, since men might have been saved without
his death; might by our own obedience have been both discharged from condemnation, and entitled to eternal life.

III. 1. *O thoughtless Galatians*—He breaks in upon them with a beautiful abruptness, *who hath bewitched you*—Thus to contradict both your own reason and
experience, *before whose eyes Jesus Christ hath been* as *evidently set forth*—By our
preaching, as if he had been crucified among you.

2. *This only would I learn of you*—That is, this one argument might convince
you. Did ye receive the witness and fruit of the Spirit, by performing the works
of the law, or by hearing of and receiving faith.

3. *Are ye so thoughtless?*—As not to consider what you have yourselves experienced? *Having begun in the Spirit*—Having set out under the light and power
of the Spirit by faith; do ye now, when ye ought to be more spiritual, and
more acquainted with the power of faith, expect to be made perfect by the flesh?
Do you think to complete either your justification or sanctification, by giving up
that faith, and depending on the law, which is a gross and carnal thing, when
opposed to the Gospel?

thoughtless ? Having begun in the Spirit, are ye now made per-
4 fect by the flesh ? Have ye suffered so many things in vain ? If
5 *it be* yet in vain ? Doth he that ministereth the Spirit to you, and
worketh miracles among you, *do it* by the works of the law, or by
6 the hearing of faith ? As Abraham * believed God, and it was im-
7 puted to him for righteousness. Know then that they who are of
8 faith, these are the sons of Abraham. And the Scripture foreseeing that God would justify the Gentiles by faith, declared before
the glad tidings to Abraham, † In thee shall all the nations be
9 blessed. So then they who are of faith are blessed with faithful
10 Abraham. For as many as are of the works of the law are under
a curse ; for it is written, ‡ Cursed *is* every one who continueth
not in all things which are written in the book of the law, to do
11 them. But that none is justified by the law in the sight of God *is*
12 evident ; for § the just shall live by faith. Now the law is not of
13 faith ; but ‖ he that doeth them shall live by them. Christ hath

---

4. *Have ye suffered*—Both from the zealous Jews and from the heathens, *so
many things*—For adhering to the Gospel, *in vain*—So as to lose all the blessings
which ye might have obtained, by enduring to the end, *if it be yet in vain*—As if
he had said, I hope better things, even that ye will endure to the end.

5. And at the present time, doth he that ministereth the gift of the Spirit to
you, and worketh miracles among you, *do it by the works of the law ?*—That is,
in confirmation of his preaching justification by works ? Or of his preaching
justification by faith ?

6. Doubtless in confirmation of that grand doctrine, that we are justified by
faith, even as Abraham was. The apostle, both in this and in the Epistle to the
Romans, makes great use of the instance of Abraham : the rather, because from
Abraham the Jews drew their great argument, (as they do this day,) both for
their own continuance in Judaism, and for denying the Gentiles to be the Church
of God.

7. *Know then*, that they who are partakers of his faith, these, and these only,
are the sons of Abraham : and therefore heirs of the promises made to him.

8. *And the Scripture*—That is, the Holy Spirit, who gave the Scripture, foreseeing that God would justify the Gentiles also by faith, *declared before*—So great
is the excellency and fulness of the Scripture, that all the things which can ever
be controverted, are therein both foreseen and determined, *in* or *through thee*—
As the Father of the Messiah, shall all the nations be blessed.

9. *So then all they*, and they only, *who are of faith*—Who truly believe, *are
blessed with faithful Abraham*—Receive the blessing as he did, namely, by faith.

10. They only receive it : *for as many as are of the works of the law*—As God
deals with on that footing, only on the terms the law proposes, *are under a curse ;
for it is written, Cursed is every one who continueth not in all things which are
written in the law*—*who continueth not in all the things*—So it requires what no
man can perform ; namely, perfect, uninterrupted, and perpetual obedience.

11. *But that none is justified by* his obedience to *the law in the sight of God*—
Whatever may be done in the sight of man, is farther evident from the words of
Habakkuk, *The just shall live by faith*—That is, the man who is accounted just
or righteous before God, shall continue in a state of acceptance, life, and salvation, by faith. This is the way God hath chosen.

12. *And the law is not of faith*—But quite opposite to it. It does not say, *Believe*, but *do*.

13. *Christ*—Christ alone. The abruptness of the sentence shows a holy indignation at those who reject so great a blessing, *hath redeemed us*—Whether
Jews or Gentiles, at a high price, *from the curse of the law*—The curse of God,
which the law denounces against all transgressors of it, *being made a curse for
us*—Taking the curse upon himself, that we might be delivered from it, willingly
submitting to that death, which the law pronounces peculiarly accursed.

* Gen. xv, 6.   † Gen. xiii, 3.   ‡ Deut. xxvii, 26   § Hab. ii. 4   ‖ Lev. xviii, 5

redeemed us from the curse of the law, being made a curse for
us : (for it is written, * Cursed *is* every one that hangeth on a
14 tree.) That the blessing of Abraham might come on the Gentiles through Christ Jesus, that we might receive the promise of
15 the Spirit through faith. I speak after the manner of men : though
it be but a man's covenant, yet if it be confirmed, none disannul-
16 leth or addeth thereto. Now the promises were made to Abraham and his seed. He saith not, And to seeds, as of many ; but
17 as of one, † And to thy seed, which is Christ. And this I say, the
covenant which was before confirmed of God through Christ,
the law, which was four hundred and thirty years after, doth not
18 disannul, so as to make the promise of no effect. And again, if the
inheritance *be* by the law, *it is* no more by promise ; but God gave
19 it to Abraham by promise. Wherefore then *was* the law ? It was
added because of transgressions, till the seed should come to whom
the promise was made : *and it was* ordained by angels, in the
20 hand of a mediator. Now the mediator is not a *mediator* of

14. *That the blessing of Abraham*—The blessing promised to him, *might come
on the Gentiles*—Also that we, who believe, whether Jews or Gentiles, *might receive the promise of the Spirit*—Which includes all the other promises, *through
faith*—Not by works ; for faith looks wholly to the promise.

15. *I speak after the manner of men*—I illustrate this by a familiar instance,
taken from the practice of men. *Though it be but a man's covenant, yet if it be*
once legally *confirmed, none*—No, not the covenanter himself, (unless something
unforeseen occur, which cannot be the case with God,) *disannulleth or addeth
thereto*—Any new conditions.

16. *Now the promises were made to Abraham and his seed*—Several promises
were made to Abraham. But the chief of all, and which was several times repeated, was that of the blessing through Christ. *He*—That is, God, *saith not,
And to seeds, as of many*—As if the promise were made to several kinds of seed ;
but as of one—That is, one kind of seed, one posterity, one kind of sons. And
to all these the blessing belonged by promise, *which is Christ*—Including all that
believe in him.

17. *And this I say*—What I mean is this. *The covenant which was before confirmed of God*—By the promise itself, by the repetition of it, and by a solemn
oath, concerning the blessing all nations *through Christ, the law which was four
hundred and thirty years after*—(Counting from the time when the promise was
first made to Abraham, Gen. xii, 2, 3,) *doth not disannul, so as to make the promise of no effect*—With regard to all nations, if only the Jewish were to receive
it : yea, with regard to them also, if it was by works, so as to supersede it, and
introduce another way of obtaining the blessing.

18. *And again*—This is a new argument. The former was drawn from the
time, this from the nature of the transaction, if the eternal inheritance be obtained by keeping the law, it is no more by virtue of the free *promise*—These being
just opposite to each other. But it is by promise. Therefore it is not by the law.

19. *It* (the ceremonial law) *was added*—To the *promise because of transgressions*—Probably, the yoke of the ceremonial law was inflicted as a punishment
for the national sin of idolatry, Exod. xxxiii, 1 ; at least the more grievous parts
of it ; and the whole of it was a prophetic type of Christ. The moral law was
added to the promise, to discover and to restrain transgressions, to convince men
of their guilt and need of the promise, and give some check to sin. And this
law passeth not away ; but the ceremonial law was only introduced till Christ,
the seed, to, or through *whom the promise was made, should come. And it was
ordained by angels in the hand of a mediator*—It was not given to Israel like the
promise to Abraham, immediately from God himself, but was conveyed by the
ministry of angels to Moses, and delivered into his hand as a mediator between
God and them, to remind them of the great Mediator.

* Deut. xxi, 23.   † Gen. xxii, 18.

21 one; but God is one. *Is* then the law against the promises of
God? God forbid. But if there had been a law given which could
have given life, verily righteousness would have been by the law
22 But the Scripture hath concluded all under sin, that the promise
by faith of Jesus Christ might be given to them that believe
23 But before faith came, we were kept under the law, shut up toge-
24 ther unto the faith which was to be revealed. Wherefore the law
was our schoolmaster unto Christ, that we might be justified by
25 faith. But faith being come, we are no longer under a schoolmaster.
26 For ye are all sons of God by faith in Jesus Christ. For as many
27 of you as have been baptized into Christ, have put on Christ
28 There is neither Jew nor Greek, there is neither bond nor free,
there is neither male nor female; for ye are all one in Christ Jesus
29 And if ye *are* Christ's, then are ye the seed of Abraham, and heirs
according to the promise.
IV.   Now I say, the heir, as long as he is a child, differeth nothing
2 from a servant, though he be lord of all; But is under tutors and

20. *Now the mediator is not a mediator of one*—There must be two parties, or
there can be no mediator between them: but God, who made the free promise to
Abraham, is only one of the parties. The other, Abraham, was not present at
the time of Moses. Therefore in the promise Moses had nothing to do. The
law wherein he was concerned was a transaction of quite another nature.

21. Will it follow from hence, that *the law is against*—Opposite to the promises of God? By no means. They are well consistent. But yet the law cannot give life, as the promise doth. *If there had been a law which could have given
life*—Which could have entitled a sinner to life, God would have spared his own
Son, and righteousness, or justification, with all the blessings consequent upon
it, would have been by that law.

22. *But*, on the contrary, *the Scripture*, wherein that law is written, *hath concluded all under sin*—Hath shut them up together (so the word properly signifies,) as in a prison, under sentence of death, to the end, that all being cut off
from expecting justification by the law, the promise might be freely given to
them that believe.

23. *But before faith*—That is, the Gospel dispensation, *came, we were kept*—
As in close custody, *under the law*—The Mosaic dispensation, *shut up unto the
faith which was to be revealed*—Reserved and prepared for the Gospel dispensation.

24. *Wherefore the law was our schoolmaster unto Christ*—It was designed to
train us up for Christ. And this it did both by its commands, which showed
the need we had of his atonement, and its ceremonies, which all pointed us to
him.

25. *But faith*—That is, the Gospel dispensation, being come, we are no longer
under that schoolmaster, the Mosaic dispensation.

26. *For ye*—Christians, *are all* adult *sons of God*—And so need a schoolmaster
no longer.

27. *For as many of you as have* testified your faith, by being baptized in the
name of Christ, *have put on Christ*—Have received him as your righteousness,
and are therefore sons of God through him.

28. *There is neither Jew nor Greek*—That is, there is no difference between
them; they are equally accepted through faith. *There is neither male nor female*
—Circumcision being laid aside, which was peculiar to males, and was designed
to put a difference, during that dispensation, between Jews and Gentiles.

29. *If ye are Christ's*—That is, believers in him.

IV. 1. *Now*—To illustrate by a plain similitude the pre-eminence of the Chris
tian over the legal dispensation, *the heir as long as he is a child*—As he is under
age, *differeth nothing from a servant*—Not being at liberty either to use or enjoy
his estate, *though he be lord*—Proprietor of it all.

2 *But is under tutors*—As to his person; and *stewards*—As to his substance

3 stewards, till the time appointed by the father. So we also, when
 we were children, were in bondage under the elements of the world.
4 But when the fulness of the time was come, God sent forth his Son,
5 made of a woman, made under the law, To redeem those under the
6 law, that we might receive the adoption of sons.   And because ye
 are sons, God hath sent forth the Spirit of his Son into your hearts,
7 crying, Abba, Father.   Wherefore thou art no more a servant,
 but a son ; and if a son, then an heir of God through Christ.
8 Indeed, then when ye knew not God, ye served them that by nature
9 are not gods.   But now having known God, or rather being known
 of God, how turn ye back to the weak and poor elements, to which
10 ye desire to be in bondage again ?   Ye observe days, and months,
11 and times, and years.   I am afraid for you, lest I have laboured
 among you in vain.
12   Brethren, I beseech you, be ye as I *am ;* for I also *am* as ye
13 *were :* ye have not injured me at all.   Ye know that notwithstand-

---

3. *So we*—The Church of God, *when we were children*—In our minority, under
the legal dispensation, *were in bondage*—In a kind of servile state, *under the
elements of the world*—Under the typical observances of the law, which were like
the first elements of grammar, the A, B, C, of children ; and were of so gross a
nature, as hardly to carry our thoughts beyond this world.

4. *But when the fulness of the time*—Appointed by the Father, ver. 2, *was
come, God sent forth*—From his own bosom, his Son, miraculously made of the
substance *of a woman*—A virgin, without the concurrence of a man ; *made under
the law*—Both under the precept, and under the curse of it.

5. *To redeem those under the law*—From the curse of it, and from that low,
servile state, *that we*—Jews who believe, *might receive the adoption*—All the privileges of adult sons.

6. *And because ye*—Gentiles who believe, are also thus made his adult sons,
God hath sent forth the Spirit of his Son into your hearts likewise, *crying, Abba,
Father*—Enabling you to call upon God both with the confidence, and the tempers of dutiful children.   The Hebrew and Greek words are joined together, to
express the joint cry of the Jews and Gentiles.

7. *Wherefore thou*—Who believest in Christ, *art no more a servant*—Like those
who are under the law, *but a son*—Of mature age ; and if a son, then an heir of
all the promises, and of the all-sufficient God himself.

8. *Indeed, then when ye knew not God, ye served them that by nature*—That is,
in reality, *are no gods*—And so were under a far worse bondage than even that
of the Jews.   For they did serve the true God, though in a low, slavish manner.

9. *But now being known of God*—As his beloved children, *how turn ye back to
the weak and poor elements*—Weak, utterly unable to purge your conscience from
guilt, or to give that filial confidence in God: *poor*—Incapable of enriching the
soul with such holiness and happiness as ye are heirs to.   *Ye desire to be again
in bondage*—Though of another kind : now to these elements, as before to those
idols.

10. *Ye observe days*—Jewish Sabbaths ; *and months*—New moons ; *and times*
—As that of the passover, pentecost, and the feast of tabernacles ; *and years*—
Annual solemnities.   It does not mean sabbatic years.   These were not to be
observed out of the land of Canaan.

11. The apostle here dropping the argument, applies to the affections, ver.
11–20, and humbles himself to the Galatians with an inexpressible tenderness.

12. *Brethren, I beseech you, be as I am*—Meet me in mutual love ; *for I am
as ye were*—I still love you as affectionately as ye once loved me.   Why should
I not ?   *Ye have not injured me at all*—I have received no personal injury from
you.

13. *I preached to you, notwithstanding infirmity of the flesh*—That is, notwithstanding bodily weakness, and under great disadvantage, from the despicable-
ness of my outward appearance

ing infirmity of the flesh, I preached the Gospel to you at first.
14 And ye did not slight or disdain my temptation which was in the
15 flesh, but received me as an angel of God, as Christ Jesus. What
was then the blessedness ye spake of? For I bear you witness,
that, if possible, ye would have plucked out your eyes, and have
16 given them to me. Am I become your enemy because I tell you
17 the truth? They zealously affect you, but not well; yea, they
18 would exclude you, that ye might affect them. Now *it is* good to
be zealous in a good thing always, and not only while I am present
19 with you. My little children, of whom I travail in birth again, till
20 Christ be formed in you, I could wish to be present with you now
and to change my voice; for I stand in doubt of you.
21 Tell me, ye that would be under the law, do ye not hear the law ?
22 For it is written, * Abraham had two sons, one by the bond-
23 woman, another by the free-woman. And he of the bond-woman
was born after the flesh, but he of the free-woman by promise.
24 Which things are an allegory: for these are the two covenants;
one from Mount Sinai, bearing children to bondage, which is Agar.
25 For this is Mount Sinai in Arabia, and answereth to Jerusalem that
26 now is, and is in bondage with her children. But Jerusalem that

14. *And ye did not slight my temptation*—That is, ye did not slight or disdain
me for my temptation, my thorn in the flesh.
15. *What was then the blessedness ye spake of?*—On which ye so congratulated
one another!
17. *They*—The Judaizing teachers who are come among you, *zealously affect
you*—Express an extraordinary regard for you : *but not well*—Their zeal is not
according to knowledge, neither have they a single eye to your spiritual advantage ; yea, *they would exclude you*—From me and from the blessings of the Gospel, that ye might affect, love, and esteem them.
18. *In a good thing*—In what is really worth our zeal. True zeal is only
fervent love.
19. *My little children*—He speaks as a parent, both with authority, and the
most tender sympathy, toward weak and sickly children, *of whom I travail
in birth again*—As I did before, ver. 13, in vehement pain, sorrow, desire,
prayer, *till Christ be formed in you*—Till there be in you all the mind that was
in him.
20. *I could wish to be present with you now*—Particularly in this exigence;
and to change—Variously to attemper *my voice*—He writes with much softness;
but he would speak with more. The voice may more easily be varied according
to the occasion than a letter can ; *for I stand in doubt of you*—So that I am at a
loss how to speak at this distance.
21. *Do ye not hear the law*—Regard what it says ?
23. *Was born after the flesh*—In a natural way ; *by promise*—Through that
supernatural strength which was given Abraham in consequence of the promise.
24. *Which things are an allegory*—An allegory is a figurative speech, wherein
one thing is expressed, and another intended : for those two sons are types of the
two covenants. One covenant is that given *from Mount Sinai, which beareth
children to bondage*—That is, all who are under this, the Jewish covenant, are in
bondage ; which covenant is typified by Agar.
25. *For this is Mount Sinai, in Arabia*—That is, the type of Mount Sinai ; *and
answereth to*—Resembles *Jerusalem that now is, and is in bondage*—Like Agar,
both to the law and to the Romans.
26. But the other covenant is derived *from Jerusalem that is above*, which *is
free*, like *Sarah*—From all inward and outward bondage ; and *is the mother of
us all*—That is, all who believe in Christ, and free citizens of the new Jerusalem.

* Gen xxi, 2, 9.

27 is above is free, which is the mother of us all. (For it is written, * Rejoice, thou barren, that bearest not; break forth and cry, thou that travailest not; for the desolate hath many more children than

28 she that hath a husband.) Now we, brethren, like Isaac, are

29 children of promise. But as then, he that was born after the flesh

30 persecuted him *that was born* after the Spirit, so *it is* now also. But what saith the Scripture? † Cast out the bond-woman and her son; for the son of the bond-woman shall not be heir with the son

31 of the free-woman. So then, brethren, we are not children of the bond-woman, but of the free.

V. Stand fast, therefore, in the liberty wherewith Christ hath made us free, and be not entangled again with the yoke of bondage.

2 Behold, I Paul say unto you, If ye be circumcised, Christ will pro-

3 fit you nothing. For I testify again to every man that is circum-

4 cised, he is a debtor to do the whole law. Christ is become of no effect to you, whosoever of you are justified by the law; ye are

5 fallen from grace. For we through the Spirit wait for the hope of

6 righteousness by faith. For in Christ Jesus, neither circumcision

27. *For it is written*—Those words in the primary sense promise a flourishing state to Judea, after its desolation by the Chaldeans. *Rejoice, thou barren, that bearest not*—Ye heathen nations, who, like a barren woman, were destitute for many ages of a seed to serve the Lord; *break forth, and cry aloud for joy, thou that* in former time *travailest not; for the desolate hath many more children than she that hath a husband*—For ye that were so long utterly desolate, shall at length bear more children than the Jewish Church, which was of old espoused to God.

28. *Now we*—Who believe, whether Jews or Gentiles, *are children of the promise*—Not born in a natural way, but by the supernatural power of God. And as such we are heirs of the promise made to believing Abraham.

29. *But as then he that was born after the flesh persecuted him that was born after the Spirit, so it is now also*—And so it will be in all ages and nations to the end of the world.

30. *But what saith the Scripture?*—Showing the consequence of this. *Cast out the bond-woman and her son*—Who mocked Isaac. In like manner will God cast out all who seek to be justified by the law; especially if they persecute them who are his children by faith.

31. *So then*—To sum up all, *we* who believe *are not children of the bond-woman*—Have nothing to do with the servile Mosaic dispensation; *but of the free*—Being free from the curse and the bond of that law, and from the power of sin and Satan.

V. 1. *Stand fast therefore in the liberty*—From the ceremonial law, *wherewith Christ hath made us*—And all believers, *free;* and be not entangled again with the yoke of legal bondage.

2. *If ye be circumcised*—And seek to be justified thereby, *Christ*—The Christian institution, *will profit you nothing*—For you hereby disclaim Christ, and all the blessings which are through faith in him.

3. *I testify to every man*—Every *Gentile that is circumcised*—He thereby makes himself *a debtor*—Obliges himself, at the peril of his salvation, to do the whole law.

4. Therefore *Christ is become of no effect to you*—Who seek to be justified by the law. *Ye are fallen from grace*—Ye renounce the new covenant. Ye disclaim the benefit of this gracious dispensation.

5. *For we*—Who believe in Christ, who are under the Gospel dispensation, *through the Spirit*—Without any of those carnal ordinances, *wait for*—In sure confidence of attaining, *the hope of righteousness*—The righteousness we hope for, and full reward of it. This righteousness we receive of God through faith; and by faith we shall obtain the reward.

* Isaiah liv. 1.   † Genesis xxi, 1.

availeth any thing, nor uncircumcision, but faith which worketh by
7 love. Ye did run well : who hath hindered you from obeying the
8 truth ? This persuasion *cometh* not from him that called you. A
9 little leaven leaveneth the whole lump. I have confidence in you
10 through the Lord, that ye will be no otherwise minded ; but he
11 that troubleth you shall bear *his* judgment, whosoever he be. But
if I, brethren, still preach circumcision, why do I still suffer per-
12 secution ? Then is the offence of the cross ceased. I wish it :
and they shall be cut off that trouble you.
13   Brethren, ye have been called to liberty ; only *use* not this liberty
14 for an occasion to the flesh, but by love serve one another. For
all the law is fulfilled in one word, in this, * Thou shalt love thy
15 neighbour as thyself. But if ye bite and devour one another, take
heed ye be not consumed one of another.
16   I say then, walk by the Spirit, and fulfil not the desire of the
17 flesh. For the flesh desireth against the Spirit, but the Spirit *de-*

6. *For in Christ Jesus*—According to the institution which he hath established, according to the tenor of the Christian covenant, *neither circumcision*—With the most punctual observance of the law, *nor uncircumcision*—With the most exact heathen morality, *availeth any thing*—Toward present justification, or eternal salvation, *but faith* alone ; even that faith *which worketh by love*—All inward and outward holiness.

7. *Ye did run well*—In the race of faith. *Who hath hindered you*—In your course, that ye should not still obey the truth ?

8. *This*—Your present persuasion, cometh not from God, *who called you*—To his kingdom and glory.

9. *A little leaven leaveneth the whole lump*—One troubler, ver. 10, troubles all.

10. *Yet I have confidence that*—After ye have read this, *ye will be no otherwise minded*—Than I am, and ye were. *But he that troubleth you*—It seems to have been one person chiefly who endeavoured to seduce them, *shall bear his judgment*—A heavy burden already hanging over his head.

11. *But if I still preach circumcision*—As that troubler seems to have affirm ed, probably taking occasion from his having circumcised Timothy, *why do I still suffer persecution ? Then is the offence of the cross ceased*—The grand reason why the Jews were so offended at his preaching Christ crucified, and so bitterly persecuted him for it, was, that it implied the abolition of the law ; yet St. Paul did not condemn the conforming, out of condescension to the weakness of any one, even to the ceremonial law : but he did absolutely condemn those who taught it as necessary to justification.

12. *They shall be cut off*—From your communion, cast out of your Church, that thus trouble you.

13. *Ye have been called to liberty*—From sin and misery, as well as from the ceremonial law. *Only use not liberty for an occasion to the flesh*—Take not occasion from hence to gratify corrupt nature, *but by love serve one another*—And hereby show that Christ has made you free.

14. *For all the law is fulfilled in this, Thou shalt love thy neighbour as thyself* —Inasmuch as none can do this without loving God, 1 John iv, 12, and the love of God and man includes all perfection.

15. *But if*—On the contrary, in consequence of the divisions which those troublers have occasioned among you, *ye bite* one another—By evil speaking, *and devour one another*—By railing and clamour, *take heed ye be not consumed one of another*—By bitterness, strife, and contention, our health and strength both of body and soul are consumed, as well as our substance and reputation.

16. *I say then*—He now explains what he proposed, ver. 13, *walk by the Spirit*—Follow his guidance in all things, *and fulfil not*, in any thing, *the desire of the flesh*—Of corrupt nature.

17. *For the flesh desireth against the Spirit*—Nature desires what is quite con-

* Leviticus xix, 18.

sireth against the flesh, (these are contrary to each other,) that ye
18 may not do the things which ye would.• But if ye are led by the
19 Spirit ye are not under the law. Now the works of the flesh are
   manifest, which are *these*, adultery, fornication, uncleanness, lasci-
20 viousness, Idolatry, witchcraft, enmities, contentions, emulations,
21 wraths, strifes, divisions, heresies, Envyings, murders, drunkenness,
   revellings, and such like : of which I tell you before (as I have also
   told you in time past) that they who practise such things shall not
22 inherit the kingdom of God. But the fruit of the Spirit is love,
23 joy, peace, long suffering, gentleness, goodness, fidelity, Meekness,
24 temperance ; against such there is no law. And they that are
25 Christ's have crucified the flesh with its affections and desires. If
26 we live by the Spirit, let us also walk by the Spirit. Be not desirous of vain glory, provoking one another, envying one another.

trary to the Spirit of God, *but the Spirit against the flesh*—But the Holy Spirit
on his part opposes your evil nature, *(these are contrary to each other*—The flesh
and the Spirit ; there can be no agreement between them,) *that ye may not do the
things which ye would*—That being thus strengthened by the Spirit, ye may not
fulfil the desire of the flesh, as otherwise ye would do.

18. *But if ye are led by the Spirit*—Of liberty and love, into all holiness, *ye
are not under the law*—Not under the curse or bondage of it, not under the guilt
or the power of sin.

19. *Now the works of the flesh*—By which that inward principle is discovered,
are manifest—Plain and undeniable. Works are mentioned in the plural, because they are distinct from, and often inconsistent with each other. But the
fruit of the Spirit is mentioned in the singular, ver. 22, as being all consistent
and connected together, *which are these*—He enumerates those works of the
flesh to which the Galatians were most inclined ; and those parts of the fruit of
the Spirit, of which they stood in the greatest need ; *lasciviousness*—The Greek
word means, any thing inward or outward, that is contrary to chastity, and yet
short of actual uncleanness.

20. *Idolatry, witchcraft*—That this means witchcraft, strictly speaking, (not
poisoning,) appears from its being joined with the worship of devil gods, and
not with murder. This is frequently and solemnly forbidden in the Old Testament. To deny therefore that there is or ever was any such thing, is by plain
consequence to deny the authority both of the Old and New Testament. *Divisions*—In domestic or civil matters ; *heresies*—are divisions in religious com-
munities.

21. *Revellings*—Luxurious entertainments. Some of the works here mentioned are wrought principally, if not entirely, in the mind. And yet they are called *works of the flesh*—Hence it is clear, the apostle does not by the flesh mean
the body, or sensual appetites and inclinations only, but the corruption of human
nature, as it spreads through all the powers of the soul, as well as the members
of the body : *of which I tell you before*—Before the event ; I forewarn you.

22. *Love*—The root of all the rest : *gentleness*—Toward all men ; ignorant and
wicked men in particular : *goodness*—The Greek word means all that is benign,
soft, winning, tender, either in temper or behaviour.

23. *Meekness*—Holding all the affections and passions in even balance.

24. *And they that are Christ's*—True believers in him, have thus *crucified the
flesh*—Nailed it, as it were, to a cross, whence it has no power to break loose,
but is continually weaker and weaker ; *with its affections and desires*—All its
evil passions, appetites, and inclinations.

25. *If we live by the Spirit*—If we are indeed raised from the dead, and are
alive to God, by the operation of his Spirit ; *let us walk by the Spirit*—Let us
follow his guidance, in all our tempers, thoughts, words, and actions.

26. *Be not desirous of vain glory*—Of the praise or esteem of men. They who
do not carefully and closely follow the Spirit, easily slide into this ; the natural
effects of which are, provoking to envy them that are beneath us, and envying
them that are above us.

VI.	Brethren, if a man be overtaken in any fault, ye who are spirit
ua¹ restore such a one in the spirit of meekness; consider
2 ing thyself, lest thou also be tempted.	Bear ye one another's
3 burdens, and so fulfil the law of Christ.	For if any one think him-
self to be something, whereas he is nothing, he deceiveth himself.
4 But let every one try his own work, and then shall he have rejoic-
5 ing in himself alone, and not in another.	For every one shall bear
6 his own burdens.	Let him that is taught in the word impart to him
7 that teacheth in all good things.	Be not deceived; God is not
, mocked; for whatsoever a man soweth, that also shall he reap
8 For he that soweth to his flesh, shall of the flesh reap corruption;
but he that soweth to the Spirit, shall of the Spirit reap life ever-
9 lasting.	But let us not be weary in well doing; for in due season
10 we shall reap, if we faint not.	Therefore as we have opportunity
let us do good unto all men; but especially unto them who are of
the household of faith.

VI. 1. *Brethren, if a man be overtaken in any fault*—By surprise, ignorance,
or stress of temptation, *ye who are spiritual*—Who continue to live and walk by
the Spirit, *restore such a one*—By reproof, instruction, or exhortation. Every one
who can ought to help herein: only in the spirit of meekness. This is essential to a spiritual man. And in this lies the whole force of the cure: *considering
thyself*—The plural is beautifully changed into the singular. Let each take heed
to himself; *lest thou also be tempted*—Temptation easily and swiftly passes from
one to another; especially if a man endeavours to cure another, without preserving his own meekness.
2. *Bear ye one another's burdens*—Sympathize with and assist each other in all
your weaknesses, grievances, trials, *and so fulfil the law of Christ*—The law of
Christ (an uncommon expression) is the law of love: this our Lord peculiarly recommends; this he makes the distinguishing mark of his disciples.
3. *If any one think himself to be something*—Above his brethren; or, by any
strength of his own; *when he is nothing, he deceiveth himself*—He alone will bear
their burdens who knows himself to be nothing.
4. *But let every man try his own work*—Narrowly examine all he is, and all
he doth: *and then he shall have rejoicing in himself*—He will find in himself matter of rejoicing, if his works are right before God; *and not in another*—Not in
glorying over others.
5. *For every one shall bear his own burden*—In that day; shall give an account
of himself to God.
6. *Let* him that is taught impart to him that teacheth all such temporal good
things as he stands in need of.
7. *God is not mocked*—Although they attempt to mock him, who think to reap
otherwise than they sow.
8. *For he that* now *soweth to the flesh*—That follows the desires of corrupt nature, shall hereafter *of the flesh*—Out of this very seed, *reap corruption*—Death
everlasting; *but he that soweth to the Spirit*—That follows his guidance in all
his tempers and conversation, *shall of the Spirit*—By the free grace and power
of God, *reap life everlasting.*
9. *But let us not be weary in well doing*—Let us persevere in sowing to the
Spirit; *for in due season*—When the harvest is come, we shall reap, if we faint
not.
10. *Therefore as we have opportunity*—At whatever time or place, and in whatever manner we can. The opportunity in general is, our lifetime; but there are
also many particular opportunities. Satan is quickened in doing hurt, by the
shortness of the time, Rev. xii, 12. By the same consideration let us be quickened
in doing good. *Let us do good*—In every possible kind, and in every possible
degree; *unto all men*—Neighbours or strangers, good or evil, friends or enemies
but especially to them who are of the household of faith—For all believers are but
one family.

11   Ye see how large a letter I have written to you with my own
12 hand.   As many as desire to make a fair appearance in the flesh,
   these constrain you to be circumcised : only lest they should suffer
13 persecution for the cross of Christ.   For neither they themselves
   who are circumcised keep the law ; but they desire to have you
14 circumcised, that they may glory in your flesh.   But God forbid
   that I should glory, save in the cross of our Lord Jesus Christ, by
15 which the world is crucified to me, and I unto the world.   For
   neither circumcision is any thing, nor uncircumcision, but a new
16 creation.   And as many as shall walk by this rule, peace and mercy
   be upon them, and upon the Israel of God.
17 ˙ From henceforth let none trouble me ; for I bear in my body the
18 marks of the Lord Jesus.   Brethren, the grace of the Lord Jesus
   Christ *be* with your spirit.   Amen.

11. *Ye see how large a letter*—St. Paul had not yet written a larger to any
Church, *I have written with my own hand*—He generally wrote by an amanuensis.

12. *As many as desire to make a fair appearance in the flesh*—To preserve a
fair character, *these constrain you*—Both by their example and importunity, *to
be circumcised*—Not so much from a principle of conscience, as *lest they should
suffer persecution*—From the unbelieving Jews, *for the cross of Christ*—For main
taining that faith in a crucified Saviour is alone sufficient for justification.

13. *For neither they themselves keep the whole law*—So far are they from a zeal
for it.   But yet they desire to have you circumcised, *that they may glory in your
flesh*—That they may boast of you as their proselytes, and make a merit of this
with the other Jews.

14. *But God forbid that I should glory*—Should boast of any thing I have, am,
or do ; or rely on any thing for my acceptance with God, but what Christ hath
done and suffered for me : by means of *which the world is crucified to me*—All
the things and persons in it are to me as nothing ; *and I unto the world*—I am
dead to all worldly pursuits, cares, desires, and enjoyments.

15. *For neither circumcision is any thing, nor uncircumcision*—Neither of these
is of any account, *but a new creation*—Whereby all things in us become new.

16. *And as many as walk according to this rule*—1. Glorying only in the cross
of Christ : 2. Being crucified to the world ; and, 3. Created anew ; *peace and
mercy be upon them, and upon the Israel*—That is, the Church of God ; which
consists of all those, and those only, of every nation and kindred, who walk by
this rule.

17. *From henceforth let none trouble me*—By quarrels and disputes, *for I bear*—
And affliction should not be added to the afflicted ; *in my body the marks of the
Lord Jesus*—The scars, marks, and brands of my sufferings for him.

NOTES

ON

ST. PAUL'S EPISTLE TO THE EPHESIANS

Epʜᴇsᴜs was the chief city of that part of Asia, which was a Roman province Here St. Paul preached for three years, Acts xx, 31, and from hence the Gospel was spread throughout the whole province, Acts xix, 10. At his taking leave of the Church there, he forewarned them both of great persecutions from without, and of divers heresies and schisms, which would arise among themselves. And accordingly he writes this epistle (nearly resembling that to the Colossians, written about the same time) to establish them in the doctrine he had delivered, to arm them against false teachers, and to build them up in love and holiness, both of heart and conversation.

He begins this, as most of his epistles, with thanksgiving to God for their embracing and adhering to the Gospel. He shows the inestimable blessings and advantages they received thereby, as far above all the Jewish privileges, as all the wisdom and philosophy of the heathens. He proves that our Lord is the Head of the whole Church; of angels and spirits, the Church triumphant, and of Jews and Gentiles, now equally members of the Church militant. In the three last chapters he exhorts them to various duties, civil and religious, personal and relative, suitable to their Christian character, privileges, assistances, and obligations.

IN THIS EPISTLE WE MAY OBSERVE,

EPHESIANS.

1   PAUL, an apostle of Jesus Christ by the will of God, to the
saints who are at Ephesus, even to the faithful in Christ Jesus:
2   Grace *be* to you, and peace from God our Father, and the Lord
Jesus Christ.
3   Blessed *be* the God and Father of our Lord Jesus Christ, who
hath blessed us with all spiritual blessings in heavenly *things*
4   through Christ; As he hath chosen us through him before the
foundation of the world, that we might be holy and blameless
5   before him in love: Having predestinated us by Jesus Christ, to
the adoption of sons unto himself, according to the good pleasure
6   of his will, To the praise of the glory of his grace, by which he
7   hath freely accepted us through the Beloved; By whom we have
redemption through his blood, the forgiveness of *our* sins, accord-
8   ing to the riches of his grace: Wherein he hath abounded toward
9   us in all wisdom and prudence; Having made known unto us the
mystery of his will, according to his good pleasure, which he had

---

Verse 1. *By the will of God*—Not by any merit of my own, *to the saints who
are at Ephesus*—And in all the adjacent places. For this epistle is not directed
to the Ephesians only, but likewise to all the other Churches of Asia.

3. *Blessed be the God and Father of our Lord Jesus Christ, who hath blessed
us*—God's blessing us is his bestowing all spiritual and heavenly blessings
upon us. Our blessing God is the paying him our solemn and grateful acknow-
ledgments, both on account of his essential blessedness, and of the blessings
which he bestows upon us. He is the God of our Lord Jesus Christ, as man
and Mediator: he is his Father, primarily with respect to his Divine nature, as
his only-begotten Son; and secondarily with respect to the human nature, as
that is personally united to the Divine: *with all spiritual blessings in heavenly
things*—With all manner of spiritual blessings, which are heavenly in their nature, origin, and tendency, and shall be completed in heaven: far different from
the external privileges of the Jews, and the earthly blessings they expected from
the Messiah.

4. *As he hath chosen us*—Both Jews and Gentiles, whom he foreknew as believing in Christ, 1 Pet. i, 2.

5. *Having predestinated us to the adoption of sons*—Having foreordained that
all who afterward believed should enjoy the dignity of being sons of God, and
joint heirs with Christ, *according to the good pleasure of his will*—According to
his free, fixed, unalterable purpose, to confer this blessing on all those who should
believe in Christ, and those only.

6. *To the praise of the glory of his grace*—His glorious free love, without any
desert on our part.

7. *By whom we*—Who believe, have from the moment we believe, redemption
from the guilt and power of sin, *through his blood*—Through what he hath done
and suffered for us; *according to the riches of his grace*—According to the abundant overflowings of his free mercy and favour.

3. *In all wisdom*—Manifested by God in the whole scheme of our salvation,
and prudence—Which he hath wrought in us, that we may know and do all his
acceptable and perfect will.

9. *Having made known to us*—By his word and by his Spirit, *the mystery of his
will*—The gracious scheme of salvation by faith, which depends on his own sovereign will alone. This was but darkly discovered under the law; is now totally
hid from unbelievers; and has heights and depths which surpass all the knowledge
even of true believers.

10 before purposed in himself, That in the dispensation of the fulness
   of the times, he might gather together into one in Christ, all things
11 which are in heaven, and which are on earth, In him, through
   whom we also having obtained an inheritance, being predestinated
   according to the purpose of him that worketh all things after the
12 counsel of his own will, That we, who first believed in Christ,
13 might be to the praise of his glory: In whom ye likewise *believed,*
   after ye had heard the word of truth, the Gospel of your salvation;
   in whom after ye had believed, ye were also sealed by that holy
14 Spirit of promise, Who js an earnest of our inheritance, till the
   redemption of the purchased possession, to the praise of his glory.
15   Wherefore I also, since I heard of your faith in the Lord Jesus,
16 and love to all saints, Cease not to give thanks for you, making
17 mention of you in my prayers, That the God of our Lord Jesus
   Christ, the Father of glory, may give you the Spirit of wisdom
18 and revelation, through the knowledge of him: The eyes of your

---

10. *That in the dispensation of the fulness of times*—In this last administration of God's fullest grace, which took place when the time appointed was
fully come, *he might gather together into one in Christ*—Might recapitulate,
reunite, and place in order again, under Christ, their common Head, *all things
which are in heaven, and on earth*—All angels and men, whether living or dead
in tne Lord.

11. *Through whom we,* Jews, *also have obtained an inheritance*—The glorious
inheritance of the heavenly Canaan, to which, when believers, we were predestinated, *according to the purpose of him that worketh all things after the counsel
of his own will*—The unalterable decree, he that believeth shall be delivered
which will is not an arbitrary will, but flowing from the rectitude of his nature
else what security would there be that it would be his will to keep his word even
with the elect?

12. *That we*—Jews, *who first believed*—Before the Gentiles. So did some
of them in every place. Here is another branch of the true Gospel predestination: he that believes is not only elected to salvation, (if he endures
to the end,) but is foreappointed of God to walk in holiness, to the praise
of his glory.

13. *In whom ye*—Gentiles, *likewise believed after ye had heard the Gospel*—
Which God made the means of your salvation; *in whom after ye had believed*—Probably some time after their first believing, *ye were sealed with that Holy Spirit
of promise*—Holy both in his nature and in his operations, and promised to all
the children of God. The sealing seems to imply, 1. A full impression of the
image of God on their souls: 2. A full assurance of receiving all the promises,
whether relating to time or eternity.

14. *Who,* thus sealing us, *is an earnest*—Both a pledge and a foretaste of our
inheritance, *till the redemption of the purchased possession*—Till the Church,
which he has purchased with his own blood, shall be fully delivered from all sin
and sorrow, and advanced to everlasting glory, *to the praise of his glory*—Of his
glorious wisdom, power, and mercy.

15. *Since I heard of your faith and love*—That is, of their perseverance and
increase therein.

16. *I cease not*—In all my solemn addresses to God, *to give thanks for you,
making mention of you in my prayers*—So he did of all the Churches, Col. i, 9.

17. *That the Father of* that infinite glory which shines in the face of Christ,
from whom also we receive the glorious inheritance, ver. 18, *may give you the
Spirit of wisdom and revelation*—The same who is the Spirit of promise, is also
in the progress of the faithful the Spirit of wisdom and revelation, making them
wise unto salvation, and revealing to them the deep things of God. He is here
speaking of that wisdom and revelation, which are common to all real Christians.

18. *The eyes of your understanding*—It is with these alone that we discern the

understanding being enlightened, that ye may know what is the hope
of his calling, and what the riches of the glory of his inheritance
19 in the saints, And what the exceeding greatness of his power toward us who believe, according to the energy of his mighty power,
20 Which he exerted in Christ, raising him from the dead: and he
21 hath seated him at his own right hand in heavenly *places*, Far
above all principality, and power, and might, and dominion, and
every name that is named, not only in this world, but also in that
22 which is to come. And he put all things under his feet, and hath
23 given him *to be* head over all things to the Church, Which is his
II. body; *who is* the fulness of him that filleth all in all. And *he hath*
2 *quickened* you, who were dead in trespasses and sins, Wherein ye
formerly walked according to the course of this world, according to

things of God, *being* first opened, and then *enlightened*—By his Spirit, *that ye
may know what is the hope of his calling*—That ye may experimentally and de-
lightfully know, what are the blessings which God has called you to hope for, by
his word and his Spirit, and *what is the riches of the glory of his inheritance in
the saints*—What an immense treasure of blessedness he hath provided as an
inheritance for holy souls.

19. *And what the exceeding greatness of his power toward us who believe*—
Both in quickening our dead souls, and preserving them in spiritual life, *accord
ing to the power which he exerted in Christ, raising him from the dead*—By the
very same almighty power, whereby he raised Christ: for no less would suffice.

20. *And he hath seated him at his own right hand*—That is, he hath exalted
him in his human nature, as a recompense for his sufferings, to a quiet everlasting possession of all possible blessedness, majesty, and glory.

21. *Far above all principality, and power, and might, and dominion*—That is,
God hath invested him with uncontrollable authority over all demons in hell, all
angels in heaven, and all the princes and potentates on earth, *and every name
that is named*—We know the king is above all, though we cannot name all the
officers of his court. So we know that Christ is above all, though we are not
able to name all his subjects; *not only in this world, but also in that which is to
come*—The world to come is so styled, not because it does not exist, but because
it is not yet visible. Principalities and powers are named now. But those also
who are not even named in this world, but shall be revealed in the world to come,
are all subject to Christ.

22. *And he hath given him to be head over all things to the Church*—A head
both of guidance and government, and likewise of life and influence to the whole
and every member of it. All these stand in the nearest union with him, and
have as continual and effectual a communication of activity, growth, and strength
from him, as the natural body from its head.

23. *The fulness of him that filleth all in all*—It is hard to say in what sense
this can be spoken of the Church. But the sense is easy and natural if we refer
it to Christ, who is the fulness of the Father.

II. 1. *And he hath quickened you*—In the 19th and 20th verses of the preceding
chapter, St. Paul spoke of God's working in them by the same almighty power
whereby he raised Christ from the dead. On the mention of this he, in the fulness of his heart, runs into a flow of thought, concerning the glory of Christ's
exaltation, in the three following verses. He here resumes the thread of his
discourse: *who were dead*—Not only diseased, but dead; absolutely void of all
spiritual life; and as incapable of quickening yourselves, as persons literally
dead *in trespasses and sins*—*Sins* seem to be spoken chiefly of the Gentiles who
knew not God. *Trespasses*, of the Jews who had his law, and yet regarded it
not; ver. 5. The latter herein obeyed the flesh, the former the prince of the
power of the air.

2. *According to the course of this world*—The word translated course properly
means a long series of times, wherein one corrupt age follows another, *according to the prince of the power of the air*—The effect of which power all may
perceive, though all do not understand the cause of it: a power unspeakably

the prince of the power of the air, the spirit that now worketh in the
3 sons of disobedience : Among whom also we all formerly had our
conversation, in the desires of the flesh, doing the will of the
flesh and the mind, and were by nature children of wrath, even as
4 the others. But God, being rich in mercy, through his great love
5 wherewith he loved us, Hath quickened even us together with
6 Christ, who were dead in trespasses, (by grace ye are saved,) And
hath raised *us* up together, and made us sit together in heavenly
7 *places* through Christ Jesus : That he might show in the ages to
come the exceeding riches of his grace, in *his* kindness toward us
8 through Christ Jesus. For by grace ye are saved through faith,
9 and this not of yourselves : *it is* the gift of God : Not by works ;
10 lest any one should boast. For we are his workmanship, created
through Christ Jesus unto good works, which God had before prepared, that we might walk in them.

penetrating and widely diffused ; but yet, as to its baneful influences, beneath the
orb of believers. The evil spirits are united under one head, the seat of whose
dominion is in the air. Here he sometimes raises storms, sometimes makes
visionary representations, and is continually roving to and fro : *the spirit that
now worketh*—With mighty power, and so he did and doth in all ages ; *in the
sons of disobedience*—In all who do not believe and obey the Gospel.

3. *Among whom we*—Jews, *also formerly had our conversation: doing the will
of the flesh*—In gross, brutal sins ; *and of the mind*—By spiritual, diabolical
wickedness. In the former clause flesh denotes the whole evil nature ; in the
latter, the body opposed to the soul : *and were by nature*—That is, in our natural
state ; *children of wrath*—Having the wrath of God abiding on us, even as the
Gentiles. This expression, *by nature*, occurs also, Gal. iv, 8 ; Rom. ii, 14 ; and
thrice in the 11th chapter. But in none of these places does it signify by custom, or practice, or customary practice, as a late writer affirms. Nor can it
mean so here. For this would make the apostle guilty of gross tautology ; their
customary sinning having been expressed already, in the former part of the verse.
But all these passages agree in expressing what belongs to the nature of the
persons spoken of.

4. *Mercy* removes misery : *love* confers salvation.

5. *He hath quickened us together with Christ*—In conformity to him, and by
virtue of our union with him. *By grace ye are saved*—Grace is both the beginning and end. The apostle speaks indifferently either in the first or second person, the Jews and Gentiles being in the same circumstance, both by nature and
by grace. This text lays the axe to the very root of spiritual pride, and all glorying in ourselves. Therefore St. Paul, foreseeing the backwardness of mankind
to receive it, yet knowing the absolute necessity of its being received, again
asserts the very same truth, ver. 8, in the very same words.

6. *And hath raised us up together*—Both Jews and Gentiles already in spirit ;
and ere long our bodies too will be raised ; *and made us all sit together in heavenly
places*—This is spoken by way of anticipation. Believers are not yet possessed
of their seats in heaven ; but each of them has a place prepared for him.

7. *The ages to come*—That is, all succeeding ages.

8. *By grace ye are saved through faith*—Grace, without any respect to any
human worthiness, confers the glorious gift ; faith, with an empty hand, and
without any pretence to personal desert, receives the heavenly blessing ; *and this
—Is not of yourselves*. *This*—refers to the whole preceding clause : that ye are
saved through faith, is the gift of God.

9. *Not by works*—Neither this faith nor this salvation is owing to any works
you ever did, will, or can do.

10. *For we are his workmanship*—Which proves both that salvation is by faith,
and that faith is the gift of God : *created unto good works*—That afterward we
might give ourselves to them ; *which God had before prepared*—The occasions
of them : so we must still ascribe the whole to God ; *that we might walk in them*
-Though not be justified by them.

11   Wherefore remember, that ye *being* formerly Gentiles in the
flesh, (who were called the uncircumcision, by that which is called
12 the circumcision performed with hands in the flesh,) Were at
that time without Christ, being aliens from the commonwealth of
Israel, and strangers to the covenants of promise ; having no hope,
13 and without God in the world.   But now through Christ Jesus,
ye who were formerly far off are brought nigh by the blood of
14 Christ.   For he is our peace, he who hath made both one, having
15 broken down the middle wall of partition, Having abolished by his
flesh the enmity, the law of commandments, through *his* decrees,
that he might form the two into one new man in himself, *so* making
16 peace :   And might reconcile both in one body to God through
17 the cross, having slain the enmity thereby.   And he came and
preached peace to you that were afar off, and to them that were
18 nigh.   For through him we both have access by one Spirit to the
19 Father.   Therefore ye are no longer strangers and foreigners, but

11. *Wherefore remember*—Such a remembrance strengthens faith, and increases gratitude ; *that ye being formerly Gentiles in the flesh*—Neither circum
cised in body nor in spirit, who were accordingly *called the uncircumcision*—By
way of reproach ; *by that which is called the circumcision*—By those who call
themselves the circumcised, and think this a proof that they are the people of
God : and who indeed have that outward circumcision, which is performed by
hands in the flesh.

12. *Were at that time without Christ*—Having no faith in, or knowledge of
him ; *being aliens from the commonwealth of Israel*—Both as to their temporal
privileges and spiritual blessings; *and strangers to the covenants of promise*—The
great promise in both the Jewish and Christian covenant was the Messiah ;
having no hope, because they had no promise, whereon to ground their hope,
and being *without God*—Wholly ignorant of the true God, and so in effect
atheists.   Such in truth are, more or less, all men in all ages, till they know
God, by the teaching of his own Spirit ; *in the world*—The wide, vain world,
wherein ye wandered up and down, unholy and unhappy.

13. *Far off*—From God and his people ; *nigh*—Intimately united to both.

14. *For he is our peace*—Not only as he purchased it, but as he is the very
bond and centre of union : he who hath made both, Jews and Gentiles, one
Church.   The apostle describes, 1. The conjunction of the Gentiles with Israel,
ver. 14, 15 ; and 2. The conjunction of both with God, ver. 15–18.   Each description is subdivided into two parts.   And the former part of the one, concerning abolishing the enmity, answers the former part of the other ; the latter part
of the one, concerning the evangelical decrees, the latter part of the other ; *and
hath broken down the middle wall of partition*—Alluding to that wall of old,
which separated the court of Israel from the court of the Gentiles.   Such a wall
was the ceremonial law, which Christ had now taken away.

15. *Having abolished by his* suffering in the flesh the cause of enmity between
the Jews and Gentiles, even the law of ceremonial commandments, through his
decrees, which offer mercy to all ; (see Col. ii, 14 ;) *that he might form the two*
—*Jew* and *Gentile, into one new man*—One mystical body.

16. *In one body*—One Church ; *having slain*—By his own death on the cross,
the enmity—Which had been between sinners and God.

17. *And he came*—After his resurrection ; *and preached peace*—By his minis.
ters and his Spirit ; *to you*—Gentiles ; *that were afar off*—At the utmost distance
from God ; *and to them that were nigh*—To the Jews, who were comparatively
nigh, being his visible Church.

18. *For through him we both*—Jews and Gentiles, *have access*—Liberty of
approaching, by the guidance and aid of one Spirit, to God as our Father.   Christ
the Spirit, and the Father, the three-one God, stand frequently in the same
order.

19. *Therefore ye are no longer strangers, but citizens* of the heavenly Jerusa
lem : no longer foreigners, but received into the very family of God.

20 fellow citizens with the saints, and of the household of God, Built
upon the foundation of the apostles and prophets, Jesus Christ
21 himself being the chief corner stone, On whom all the building,
fitly framed together, groweth into a holy temple in the Lord:
22 On whom ye also are built together, for a habitation of God
through the Spirit.
III.   For this cause I Paul *am* a prisoner of Jesus Christ for you
2 Gentiles; (Seeing ye have heard the dispensation of the grace of
3 God, given me in your behalf.) That by revelation he made
4 known to me the mystery: as I wrote before in few words, By
reading which ye may understand my knowledge in the mystery
5 of Christ: Which in other ages was not made known to the sons
of men, as it hath been now revealed to his holy apostles and pro-
6 phets by the Spirit, That the Gentiles are joint heirs, and of the
same body, and joint partakers of his promise by Christ through
7 the Gospel.   Of which I have been made a minister, according to
the gift of the grace of God given to me by the effectual working
8 of his power.   Unto me, who am less than the least of all saints
hath this grace been given, to preach among the Gentiles the un
9 searchable riches of Christ.   And to make all men see what *is*
the fellowship of the mystery which was hidden from eternity by

20. *And are built upon the foundation of the apostles and prophets*—As the
foundation sustains the building, so the word of God, declared by the apostles
and prophets, sustains the faith of all believers.   God laid the foundation by
them; but Christ himself is the chief corner stone of the foundation.   Elsewhere
he is termed the foundation itself, 1 Cor. iii, 11.
21. *On whom all the building fitly framed together*—The whole fabric of the
universal Church rises up like a large pile of living materials, *into a holy temple
in the Lord*—Dedicated to Christ, and inhabited by him, in which he displays his
presence, and is worshipped and glorified.   What is the temple of Diana of the
Ephesians, whom ye formerly worshipped, to this?
III. 1. *For this cause*—That ye may be so built together; *I am a prisoner for
you Gentiles*—For your advantage, and for asserting your right to these blessings.
That it was which so enraged the Jews against him.
2. *The dispensation of the grace of God given me in your behalf*—That is, the
commission to dispense the gracious Gospel; to you Gentiles in particular.   This
they had heard from his own mouth.
3. *The mystery*—Of salvation by Christ alone, and that both to Jews and Gentiles; *as I wrote before*—Namely, chap. i, 9, 10, the very words of which passage
he here repeats.
5. *Which in other*—In former, *ages was not*—So clearly or fully *made known
to the sons of men*—To any man, no, not to Ezekiel, so often styled son of man,
nor to any of the ancient prophets.   Those here spoken of are New Testament
prophets.
6. *That the Gentiles are joint heirs*—Of God; *and of the same body*—Under
Christ the head; *and joint partakers of his promise*—The communion of the Holy
Ghost.
7. *According to the gift of the grace of God*—That is, the apostleship which
he hath graciously given me; and which he hath qualified me for, *by the effectual working of his power*—In me and by me.
8. *Unto me, who am less than the least of all saints, is this grace given*—Here are
the noblest strains of eloquence to paint the exceeding low opinion the apostle
had of himself, and the fulness of the unfathomable blessings which are treasured
up in Christ.
9. *What is the fellowship of the mystery*—What those mysterious blessings are,
whereof all believers jointly partake, which was in a great measure hidden from
eternity by God, *who*—To make way for the free exercise of his love, *created all
things*—This is the foundation of all his dispensations.

10 God, who created all things by Jesus Christ: That the manifold wisdom of God might now be made known by the Church to the
11 principalities and powers in heavenly *places*, According to the
12 eternal purpose which he purposed in Christ Jesus our Lord, By whom we have boldness and access with confidence through faith
13 in him. Wherefore I entreat you not to faint at my afflictions for
14 you, which is your glory. For this cause I bend my knees to the
15 Father of our Lord Jesus Christ, (Of whom the whole family in
16 heaven and earth is named,) That he would give you according to the riches of his glory, to be strengthened with might by his
17 Spirit in the inner man, That Christ may dwell in your hearts by
18 faith : That being rooted and grounded in love, ye may be able to comprehend with all the saints, what is the breadth, and length,
19 and depth, and height, And to know the love of Christ which surpasseth knowledge, that ye may be filled with all the fulness of God.
20 Now to him that is able to do exceeding abundantly above all that
21 we ask or think, according to the power that worketh in us, To him *be* glory in the Church by Christ Jesus, throughout all 'ages, world without end. Amen.
IV. I, therefore, the prisoner of the Lord, beseech you to walk wor-
2 thy of the calling wherewith ye are called, With all lowliness and

10. *That the manifold wisdom of God might be made known by the Church*—By what is done in the Church, which is the theatre of the Divine wisdom.

12. *By whom we have* free *access*, such as those petitioners have, who are introduced to the royal presence by some distinguished favourite, *and boldness*—Unrestrained liberty of speech, such as children use in addressing an indulgent father, when, without fear of offending, they disclose all their wants, and make known all their requests.

13. The not fainting is your glory.

15. *Of whom*—The Father, the whole family of angels in heaven. Saints in paradise, and believers on earth, is named : being the children of God, (a more honourable title than children of Abraham,) and depending on him as the Father of the family.

16. *The riches of his glory*—The immense fulness of his glorious wisdom, power, and mercy ; *the inner man*—The soul.

17. *Dwell*—That is, constantly and sensibly abide.

18. *That being rooted and grounded*—That is, deeply fixed, and firmly established *in love, ye may comprehend*—So far as a human mind is capable, *what is the breadth of the love of Christ*—Embracing all mankind, *and length*—From everlasting to everlasting, *and depth*—Not to be fathomed by any creature, *and height*—Not to be reached by any enemy.

19. *And to know*—But the apostle corrects himself, and immediately observes, it cannot be fully known. This only we know, that the love of *Christ* surpasses all knowledge, *that ye may be filled*—Which is the sum of all, *with all the fulness of God*—With all his light, love, wisdom, holiness, power, and glory. A perfection far beyond a bare freedom from sin.

20. *Now to him*—This doxology is admirably adapted to strengthen our faith that we may not stagger at the great things the apostle had been praying for, as if they were too much for God to give, or for us to expect from him, *that is able*—Here is a most beautiful gradation. When he has given us exceeding, yea, abundant blessings, still we may ask for more. And he is able to do it. But we may think of more than we have asked. He is able to do this also. Yea, and above all this : above all we ask ; above all we can think ; nay, exceedingly, abundantly above all we can either ask or think.

21. *In the Church*—On earth and in heaven.

IV. 1. *I, therefore, the prisoner of the Lord*—Imprisoned for his sake and for your sakes: for the sake of the Gospel which he had preached among them.

496 EPHESIANS.

3 meekness ; with long suffering forbear one another in love, Endeavouring to keep the unity of the Spirit, by the bond of peace.
4 *There is* one body and one Spirit, as ye are also called in one hope
5 of your calling ; One Lord, one faith, one baptism : One God, and
6 Father of all, who is above all, and through all, and in us all. But
7 to every one of us is given grace, according to the measure of the
8 gift of Christ. Wherefore he saith, * Having ascended on high, he
9 led captivity captive, and gave gifts to men. (Now this expression, He ascended, what is it but that he also descended first to
10 the lower parts of the earth ? He that descended is the same that
ascended also, far above all the heavens, that he might fill all
11 things.) And he gave some apostles, and some prophets, and
12 some evangelists, and some pastors and teachers ; For the perfecting of the saints, for the work of the ministry, to the edifying the

This was therefore a powerful motive to them, to comfort him under it by their obedience.

3. *Endeavouring to keep the unity of the Spirit*—That mutual union and harmony, which is a fruit of the Spirit. The bond of peace is love.

4. *There is one body*—The universal Church, all believers throughout the world, *one Spirit, one Lord, one God, and Father*—The ever-blessed trinity, *one hope*—Of heaven.

5. *One* outward *baptism.*

6. *One God and Father of all*—That believe, *who is above all*—Presiding over all his children, operating through them all by Christ, and dwelling in all by his Spirit.

7. *According to the measure of the gift of Christ*—According as Christ is pleased to give to each.

8. *Wherefore he saith*—That is, in reference to which, God saith by David, *Having ascended on high, he led captivity captive*—He triumphed over all his enemies, Satan, sin, and death, which had before enslaved all the world; allud-ing to the custom of ancient conquerors, who led those they had conquered in chains after them ; and as they also used to give donatives to the people, at their return from victory, so he *gave gifts to men*—Both the ordinary and extraordi-nary gifts of the Spirit.

9. *Now this expression, He ascended, what is it, but that he descended*—That is, does it not imply that he descended first ? Certainly it does, on the supposi-tion of his being God: Otherwise it would not : since all the saints will ascend to heaven, though none of them descended thence, *into the lower parts of the earth* —So the womb is called, Psalm cxxxix, 15. The grave, Psalm lxiii, 9.

10. *He that descended*—That thus amazingly humbled himself, *is the same that ascended*—That was so highly exalted, *that he might fill all things*—The whole Church, with his Spirit, presence, and operations.

11. *And* among other his free gifts, *he gave some apostles*—His chief ministers and special witnesses, as having seen him after his resurrection, and received their commission immediately from him, *and some prophets, and some evangelists* —A prophet testifies of things to come : an evangelist of things past : and that chiefly by preaching the Gospel before or after any of the apostles. All these were extraordinary officers : the ordinary were, *some pastors*—Watching over their several flocks, and some *teachers*—Whether of the same, or a lower order, to assist them as occasion might require.

12. In this verse is noted the office of ministers ; in the next the aim of the saints, in the 14th, 15th, 16th, the way of growing in grace. And each of these have three parts, standing in the same order : *for the perfecting the saints*—The completing them both in number, and their various gifts and graces : *for the work of the ministry*—The serving God and his Church, in their various ministrations, *to the edifying of the body of Christ*—The building up this mystical body in faith, love, holiness.

* Psalm lxviii, 18.

13 body of Christ; Till we all come to the unity of the faith and
knowledge of the Son of Gód, to a perfect man, to the measure of
14 the stature of the fulness of Christ : That we may be no longer
children, fluctuating to and fro, and carried about with every wind
of doctrine, by the sleight of men, by cunning craftiness, whereby
15 they lie in wait to deceive : But speaking the truth in love, may
16 grow up into him in all things, who is the head, *even* Christ : From
whom the whole body fitly joined together and compacted, by that
which every joint supplieth according to the effectual working in
the measure of every member, maketh an increase of the body, to
the edifying of itself in love.
17 This therefore I say and testify in the Lord, that ye no longer
walk as the rest of the Gentiles walk, in the vanity of your mind :
18 Having the understanding darkened, being alienated from the life
of God, by the ignorance that is in them, through the hardness of
19 their hearts : Who being past feeling, have given themselves up
20 to lasciviousness, to work all uncleanness with greediness. But ye
21 have not so learned Christ; Seeing ye have heard him, and been
22 taught by him, (as the truth is in Jesus,) To put off, with respect

---

13. *Till we all*—And every one of us, *come to the unity of the faith and knowledge of the Son of God*—To both an exact agreement in the Christian doctrine,
and an experimental knowledge of Christ as *the Son of God; to a perfect man*—
To a state of spiritual manhood both in understanding and strength, *to the measure of the stature of the fulness of Christ*—To that maturity of age and spiritual
stature wherein we shall be filled with Christ, so that he will be all in all.

14. *Fluctuating to and fro*—From within, even when there is no wind ; *and
carried about with every wind*—From without; when we are assaulted by others,
who are unstable as the wind, *by the sleight of men*—By their cogging the dice ;
so the original word implies.

15. *Into him*—Into his image and Spirit, and into a full union with him.

16. *From whom the whole* mystical *body fitly joined together*—All the parts being fitted for, and adapted to, each other, and most exactly harmonizing with the
whole, *and compacted*—Knit and cemented together with the utmost firmness,
maketh increase by that which every joint supplieth—Or by the mutual help of
every joint, *according to the effectual working in the measure of every member*—
According as every member in its measure effectually works, for the support and
growth of the whole. A beautiful allusion to the human body, composed of different joints and members, knit together by various ligaments, and furnished with
vessels of communication from the head to every part.

17. *This therefore I say*—He returns thither where he begun, ver. 1, *and testify in the Lord*—In the name and by the authority of the *Lord Jesus, in the
vanity of their mind*—Having lost the knowledge of the true God, Rom. i, 21.
This is the root of all evil walking.

18. *Having their understanding darkened, through the ignorance that is in
them*—So that they are totally void of the light of God, neither have they any
knowledge of his will, *being alienated from the life of God*—Utter strangers to
the Divine, the spiritual life, *through the hardness of their hearts*—Callous and
senseless. And where there is no sense, there can be no life.

19. *Who being past feeling*—The original word is peculiarly significant. It
properly means, *past feeling pain.* Pain urges the sick to seek a remedy, which
where there is no pain, is little thought of : *have given themselves up*—Freely,
of their own accord. *Lasciviousness* is but one branch of *uncleanness,* which
implies impurity of *every* kind.

20. *But ye have not so learned Christ*—That is, ye cannot act thus, now ye
know him, since you know the Christian dispensation allows of no sin.

21. *Seeing ye have heard him*—Teaching you inwardly by his Spirit, *as the
truth is in Jesus*—According to his own Gospel.

to the former conversation, the old man, which is corrupt, accord
23 ing to the deceitful desires : But to be renewed in the spirit of your
24 mind ; And to put on the new man, which is created after God in
righteousness and true holiness.
25   Wherefore, putting away lying, speak ye every man truth with
26 his neighbour ; for we are members one of another.   Be ye angry
27 and sin not ; let not the sun go down upon your wrath, Neither
28 give place to the devil.   Let him that stole steal no more, but
rather let him labour, working with his hands the thing which is
29 good, that he may have to give him that needeth.   Let no corrupt
discourse proceed out of your mouth, but that which is good to
the use of edifying, that it may minister grace to the hearers.
30 And grieve not the Holy Spirit of God, whereby ye have been
31 sealed unto the day of redemption.   Let all bitterness, and wrath,
and anger, and clamour, and evil speaking, be put away from
32 you, with all malice.   But be ye kind one to another, tender
hearted : forgiving one another ; as God also for Christ's sake
hath forgiven you.

---

22. *The old man*—That is, the whole body of sin.   All sinful desires are deceitful ; promising the happiness which they cannot give.
23. *The spirit of your mind*—The very ground of your heart.
24. *The new man*—Universal holiness, *after*—In the very image of God.
25. *Wherefore*—Seeing ye are thus created anew, walk accordingly, in every
particular.   *For we are members one of another*—To which intimate union all deceit is quite repugnant.
26. *Be ye angry, and sin not*—That is, if ye are angry, take heed ye sin not.
Anger at sin is not evil ; but we should feel only pity to the sinner.   If we are
angry at the person, as well as the fault, we sin.   And how hardly do we avoid
it ?   *Let not the sun go down upon your wrath*—Reprove your brother, and be reconciled immediately.   Lose not one day.   A clear, express command.   Reader,
do you keep it ?
27. *Neither give place to the devil*—By any delay.
28. *But rather let him labour*—Lest idleness lead him to steal again.   And
whoever has sinned in any kind, ought the more zealously to practise the
opposite virtue ; *that he may have to give*—And so be no longer a burden and
nuisance, but a blessing to his neighbours.
29. *But that which is good*—Profitable to the speaker and hearers, *to the use
of edifying*—To forward them in repentance, faith, or holiness, *that it may minister grace*—Be a means of conveying more grace into their hearts.   Hence we
learn, what discourse is corrupt, as it were stinking in the nostrils of God ;
namely, all that is not profitable, not edifying, not apt to minister grace to the
hearers.
30. *Grieve not the Holy Spirit*—By any disobedience, particularly by corrupt
discourse ; or by any of the following sins.   Do not force him to withdraw
from you, as a friend does whom you grieve by unkind behaviour.   *The day of
redemption*—That is, the day of judgment, in which our redemption will be
completed.
31. *Let all bitterness*—The height of settled anger, opposite to kindness, ve..
32, *and wrath*—Lasting displeasure toward the ignorant, and them that are out
of the way, opposite to *tender heartedness : and anger*—The very first risings
of disgust at those that injure you, opposite to *forgiving one another : and clamour*—Or brawling.   " I am not angry," says one, " but it is my way to speak
so."   Then unlearn that way.   It is the way to hell : *and evil speaking*—Be it in
ever so mild and soft a tone, or with ever such professions of kindness.   Here is
a beautiful retrogradation, beginning with the highest, and descending to the
lowest degree of the want of love.
32. *As God*—Showing himself kind and tender hearted in the highest degree,
hath forgiven you.

CHAPTER V. 499

V   Be ye therefore followers of God, as beloved children; And
2 walk in love, as Christ also hath loved us, and given himself
for us, an offering and a sacrifice to God of a sweet-smelling
3 savour. But let not fornication, or any uncleanness, or ccvet-
4 ousness, be even named among you, as becometh saints: Neither obscenity, nor foolish talking, nor jesting, which are not
5 convenient, but rather thanksgiving. For this ye know, that no
whoremonger, or unclean person, or covetous man, who is an
idolater, hath any inheritance in the kingdom of Christ and of God.
6 Let no one deceive you with vain words; for because of these
things the wrath of God cometh upon the sons of disobedience.
7 Be ye not therefore partakers with them. For ye were once
8 darkness; but now *ye are* light in the Lord: walk as children of
9 light; The fruit of the light *is* in all goodness, and righteousness,
10 and truth: Proving what is acceptable to the Lord. And have no
11 fellowship with the unfruitful works of darkness, but rather reprove
12 them. For it is a shame even to speak the things which are done
13 by them in secret. But all things which are reproved are made
manifest by the light; for whatsoever doth make manifest is light.
14 Wherefore he saith, Awake, thou that sleepest, and arise from the
15 dead, and Christ shall give thee light. See then that ye walk cir-
16 cumspectly, not as fools, but as wise men, Redeeming the time,

V. 1. *Be ye therefore followers*—Imitators, *of God*—In forgiving and loving.
O how much more honourable and more happy to be an imitator of God, than of
Homer, Virgil, or Alexander the Great.
3. *But let not*—Any impure love, be even named or heard of among you.
Keep at the utmost distance from it, as becometh saints.
4. *Nor foolish talking*—Tittle-tattle, talking of nothing, the weather, fashions,
meat and drink; *or jesting*—The word properly means wittiness, facetiousness,
esteemed by the heathens a half virtue. But how frequently even this quenches
the Spirit, those who are tender of conscience know: *which are not convenient*—
For a Christian; as neither increasing his faith nor holiness.
6. *Because of these things*—As innocent as the heathens esteem them, and as
those dealers in vain words would persuade you to think them.
8. *Ye were once darkness*—Total blindness and ignorance. *Walk as children
of light*—Suitably to your present knowledge.
9. *The fruit of the light*—Opposite to the unfruitful works of darkness, ver. 11,
is in—That is, consists in *goodness, and righteousness, and truth*—Opposite to
the sins spoken of, chap. iv, 25, &c.
11. *Reprove them*—To avoid them is not enough.
12. *In secret*—As flying the light.
13. *But all things which are reproved*, are thereby dragged out into the light
and *made manifest*—Shown in their proper colours, by the light; *for whatsoever
doth make manifest is light*—That is, for nothing but light (yea, light from hea
ven) can make any thing manifest.
14. *Wherefore he*—God, *saith*—In the general tenor of his word, to all who
are still in darkness, *Awake, thou that sleepest*—In ignorance of God and thyself,
in stupid insensibility, *and arise from the dead*—From the death of sin, *and Christ
shall give thee light*—Knowledge, holiness, happiness.
15. *Circumspectly*—Exactly, with the utmost accuracy, getting to the highest
pitch of every point of holiness; *not as fools*—Who think not where they are
going, or do not make the best of their way.
16. With all possible care *redeeming the time*—Saving all you can, for the
best purposes: buying every possible moment out of the hands of sin and Satan,
out of the hands of sloth, ease, pleasure, worldly business: the more diligently
because the present are evil days, days of the grossest ignorance, immorality, and
profaneness.

17 because the days are evil. Wherefore be ye not unwise, but un
18 derstanding what is the will of the Lord. And be not drunken
   with wine, wherein is excess; but be ye filled with the Spirit;
19 Speaking to each other in psalms, and hymns, and spiritual songs,
20 singing and making melody with your hearts unto the Lord; Giving
   thanks always for all things to God, even the Father, in the name
21 of our Lord Jesus Christ, Submitting yourselves one to another in
   the fear of God.
22   Wives, submit yourselves to your own husbands as unto the
23 Lord; For the husband is the head of the wife, as Christ also is
24 head of the Church: (and he is the Saviour of the body.) Therefore as he Church is subject to Christ, so also *let* the wives *be*
25 to their own husbands in every thing. Husbands, love your wives,
26 even as Christ loved the Church, and gave up himself for it; That
   he might sanctify it (having cleansed *it* by the washing of water)
27 through the word; That he might present it to himself a glorious
   Church, not having spot or wrinkle, or any such thing, that it
28 may be holy and unblamable. Men ought so to love their wives
29 as their own bodies: he that loveth his wife loveth himself. Now
   no one ever hated his own flesh, but nourisheth and cherisheth

---

17. *What the will of the Lord is*—In every time, place, and circumstance.
18. *Wherein is excess*—That is, which leads to debauchery of every kind; *but be ye filled with the Spirit*—In all his graces, who gives a more noble pleasure than wine can do.
19. *Speaking to each other*—By the Spirit, *in the Psalms*—Of David, *and hymns*—Of praise, *and spiritual songs*—On any divine subject. By there being no inspired songs, peculiarly adapted to the Christian dispensation, as there were to the Jewish, it is evident that the promise of the Holy Ghost to believers in the last days was, by his larger effusion, to supply the lack of it: *singing with your hearts*—As well as your voices, *to the Lord*—Jesus, who searcheth the heart.
20. *Giving thanks*—At all times and places, and for all things, prosperous or adverse, since all work together for good, *in the name of*—Or through *our Lord Jesus Christ*—By whom we receive all good things.
22. In the following directions concerning relative duties, the inferiors are all along placed before the superiors, because the general proposition is concerning submission. And inferiors ought to do their duty, whatever their superiors do. *Wives, submit yourselves to your own husbands*—Unless where God forbids. Otherwise, in all indifferent things, the will of the husband is a law to the wife; *as unto the Lord*—The obedience a wife pays to her husband, is at the same time paid to Christ himself; he being the head of the wife, as Christ is Head of the Church.
23. *The head*—The governor, guide, and guardian of the wife: *and he is the Saviour of the body*—The Church, from all sin and misery.
24. *In every thing*—Which is not contrary to any command of God.
25. *Even as Christ loved the Church*—Here is the true model of conjugal affection. With this degree of it, and to this end, should husbands love their wives.
26. *That he might sanctify it through the word*—The ordinary channel of all blessings; *having cleansed it*—From the guilt and power of sin, *by the washing of water*—In baptism, if with the "outward and visible sign," we receive the inward and spiritual grace.
27. *That he might present it*—Even in this world, *to himself*—As his spouse, *a glorious Church*—All glorious within, *not having spot*—Of impurity from any sin, *or wrinkle*—Of deformity from any decay.
28. *As their own bodies*—That is, as themselves. *He that loveth his wife, loveth himself*—Which is not a sin, but an indisputable duty.

30 it, as also the Lord the Church. For we are members of his
31 body, of his flesh, and of his bones. * For this cause shall a man
leave his father and mother, and shall be joined to his wife, and
32 they two shall be one flesh. This is a great mystery: I mean
33 concerning Christ and the Church. But let every one of you in
particular so love his wife as himself: and let the wife reverence
her husband.
VI. Children, obey your parents in the Lord: for this is right.
2 † Honour thy father and mother, (which is the first commandment
3 with a promise,) That it may be well with thee, and thou mayest
4 live long upon the earth. And, ye fathers, provoke not your
children to wrath, but bring them up in the instruction and dis
cipline of the Lord.
5 Servants, obey *your* masters according to the flesh, with fear and
6 trembling, in singleness of your heart, as unto the Lord: Not with
eye service, as men pleasers, but as servants of Christ, doing the
7 will of God from the soul; With good will doing service as unto
8 the Lord, and not to men: Knowing that whatsoever good each
man doth, the same shall he receive from the Lord, whether *he be*

29. *His own flesh*—That is, himself; *nourisheth and cherisheth*—That is, feeds and clothes it.

30. *For we*—The reason why Christ nourishes and cherisnes the Church, is that close connection between them, which is here expressed in the words of Moses, originally spoken concerning Eve; *are members*—Are as intimately united to Christ, in a spiritual sense, as if we were literally flesh of his flesh, and bone of his bone.

31. *For this cause*—Because of this intimate union.

VI. 1. *Children, obey your parents*—In all things lawful the will of the parent is a law to the child; *in the Lord*—For his sake; *for this is right*—Manifestly just and reasonable.

2. *Honour*—That is, love, reverence, obey, assist in all things. The mother is particularly mentioned, as being more liable to be slighted than the father: *which is the first commandment with a promise*—For the promise implied in the second commandment does not belong to the keeping that command in particular, but the whole law.

3. *That thou mayest live long upon the earth*—This is usually fulfilled to eminently dutiful children. And he who lives long and well has a long seed time for the eternal harvest. But this promise, in the Christian dispensation, is to be understood chiefly in a more exalted and spiritual sense.

4. *And ye fathers*—Mothers are included; but fathers are named, as being more apt to be stern and severe; *provoke not your children to wrath*—Do not needlessly fret or exasperate them; *but bring them up*—With all tenderness and mildness, *in the instruction and discipline of the Lord*—Both in Christian knowledge and practice.

5. *Your masters according to the flesh*—According to the present state of things · afterward, the servant is free from his master: *with fear and trembling*—A proverbial expression, implying the utmost care and diligence; *in singleness of heart*—With a single eye to the providence and will of God.

6. *Not with eye service*—Serving them better when under their eye than at other times; *but doing the will of God from the heart*—Doing whatever you do, as the will of God, and·with your might.

7. *Unto the Lord, and not to men*—That is, rather than to men; and by making every action of common life a sacrifice to God, having an eye to him in all things, ven as if there were no other master.

8. *He shall receive the same*—That is, a full and adequate recompense for it.

* Gen. ii, 34. † Exod. xx, 20.

9 a servant or free   And ye, masters, do the same things to them,
   forbearing threatening, knowing that your own Master is in heaven,
   and there is no respect of persons with him.
10   Finally, brethren, be strong through the Lord, and through the
11 power of his might. Put on the whole armour of God, that ye
12 may be able to stand against the wiles of the devil. For our wrest-
    ling is not against flesh and blood, but against principalities, against
    powers, against the rulers of the world, of the darkness of this age,
13 against wicked spirits in heavenly places. Wherefore, take to you
    the whole armour of God, that ye may be able to withstand in the
14 evil day, and having done all, to stand : Stand, therefore, having
    your loins girt about you with truth, and having put on the breast-
15 plate of righteousness, And having your feet shod with the pre-

9. *Do the same things to them*—That is, act toward them from the same principle ; *forbearing threatening*—Behaving with gentleness and humanity, not in a
harsh or domineering way.
10. *Brethren*—This is the only place in this epistle where he uses this appellation. Soldiers frequently use it to each other in the field : *be strong*—Nothing
'ess will suffice for such a fight. To be weak, and remain so, is the way to perish :
in the power of his might—A very uncommon expression ; plainly denoting what
great assistance we need. As if his might would not do : it must be the powerful
exertion of his might.
11. *Put on the whole armour of God*—The Greek word means a complete suit
of armour. Believers are said to put on the girdle, breastplate, shoes : to take
the shield of faith and sword of the Spirit. *The whole armour*—As if the armour
would scarce do : it must be the whole armour. This is repeated, ver. 13, because
of the strength and subtlety of our adversaries, and because of an evil day of sore
trial being at hand.
12. *For our wrestling*—Is not only, not chiefly, *against flesh and blood*—Weak
men, or fleshly appetites, but against principalities, *against powers*—The mighty
princes of all the infernal legions. And great is their power, and that likewise
of those legions whom they command ; *against the rulers of the world*—Perhaps
these principalities and powers remain mostly in the citadel of their kingdom of
darkness. But there are other evil spirits who range abroad, to whom the provinces of the world are committed ; *of the darkness*—This is chiefly spiritual
darkness ; *of this age*—Which prevails during the present state of things ; *against
wicked spirits*—Who continually oppose faith, love, holiness, either by force or
fraud ; and labour to infuse unbelief, pride, idolatry, malice, envy, anger, hatred ;
in heavenly places—Which were once their abode, and which they still aspire to,
as far as they are permitted.
13. *In the evil day*—The war is perpetual : but the fight is one day less, another more violent. The evil day is either at the approach of death or in life :
may be longer or shorter, and admits of numberless varieties. *And having done
all, to stand*—That ye may still keep on your armour ; still stand upon your
guard ; still watch and pray : and thus ye will be enabled to endure unto the end,
and stand with joy before the face of the Son of man.
14. *Having your loins girt about*—That ye may be ready for every motion,
with truth—Not only with the truths of the Gospel, but with *truth in the inward
parts*—For without this, all our knowledge of Divine truth will prove but a
poor girdle in the evil day. So our Lord is described, Isaiah xi, 5. And as a
girded man is always ready to go on, so this seems to intimate an obedient
heart, a ready will. Our Lord adds to the loins girded, the lights burning, Luke
xii, 35, showing that watching and ready obedience are the inseparable companions of faith and love ; *and having on the breastplate of righteousness*—The
righteousness of a spotless purity, in which Christ will present us faultless before
God, through the merit of his own blood. With this breastplate our Lord is
described, Isaiah lix, 17. In the breast is the seat of conscience, which is
guarded by righteousness. No armour for the back is mentioned. We are
always to face our enemies.

16 paration of the Gospel of peace. Above all, taking the shield of
faith, whereby ye shall be able to quench all the fiery darts of the
17 wicked one. And take the helmet of salvation, and the sword of
18 the Spirit, which is the word of God. Praying always by the
Spirit with all prayer and supplication, and watching thereunto
19 with all perseverance and supplication for all the saints, And
for me, that utterance may be given me, by the opening of my
20 mouth to make known boldly the mystery of the Gospel, For which
I am an ambassador in bonds, that I may speak boldly therein, as
I ought to speak.

15. *And your feet shod with the preparation of the Gospel*—Let this be always
ready to direct and confirm you in every step. This part of the armour for the
feet is needful, considering what a journey we have to go ; what a race to run.
Our feet must be shod, that our footsteps slip not. To order our life and conversation aright, we are prepared by the Gospel blessing, the peace and love of God
ruling in the heart, Col. iii, 14, 15. By this only can we tread the rough ways,
surmount our difficulties, and hold out to the end.

16. *Above*, or over *all*—As a sort of universal covering to every ther part of
the armour itself, continually exercise a strong and lively faith. This you may
use as a shield, which will quench all the fiery darts, the furious temptations,
violent and sudden injections of the devil.

17. *And take for a helmet the hope of salvation*—1 Thess. v, 8. The head is
that part which is most carefully to be defended. One stroke here may prove
fatal. The armour for this is the hope of salvation. The lowest degree of this
hope is a confidence that God will work the whole work of faith in us : the
highest is a full assurance of future glory, added to the experimental knowledge
of pardoning love. Armed with this helmet, (the hope of the joy set before
him,) Christ endured the cross and despised the shame, Heb. xii, 2 : and the
sword of the Spirit, *the word of God*—This Satan cannot withstand, when it is
edged and wielded by faith. Till now our armour has been only defensive. But
we are to attack Satan, as well as secure ourselves : the shield in one hand, and
the sword in the other. Whoever fights with the powers of hell will need both.
He that is covered with armour from head to foot, and neglects this, will be
foiled after all. This whole description shows us how great a thing it is to be a
Christian. The want of any one thing makes him incomplete. Though he has
his loins girt with truth, righteousness for a breastplate, his feet shod with the
preparation of the Gospel, the shield of faith, the helmet of salvation, and
the sword of the Spirit ; yet one thing he wants after all. What is that ? It
follows :—

18. *Praying always*—At all times, and on every occasion, in the midst of all
employments, inwardly praying without ceasing ; *by the Spirit*—Through the
influence of the Holy Spirit ; *with all prayer*—With all sort of prayer, public,
private, mental, vocal. Some are careful in respect of one kind of prayer, and
negligent in others. If we would have the petitions we ask, let us use all.
Some there are who use only mental prayer or ejaculations, and think they are
in a high state of grace, and use a way of worship far superior to any other : but
such only fancy themselves to be above what is really above them ; it requiring
far more grace to be enabled to pour out a fervent and continued prayer, than
to offer up mental aspirations ; *and supplication*—Repeating and urging our
prayer, as Christ did in the garden ; *and watching*—Inwardly attend upon God
to know his will, to gain power to do it, and to attain to the blessings we desire ;
with all perseverance—Continuing to the end in this holy exercise ; *and supplication for all the saints*—Wrestling in fervent, continued intercession for others,
especially for the faithful, that they may do all the will of God, and be steadfast
to the end. Perhaps we receive few answers to prayer, because we do not inter-
cede enough for others.

19. *By the opening my mouth*—Removing every inward and every outward
hinderance.

20. *An ambassador in bonds*—The ambassadors of men usually appear in great
pomp. How differently does the ambassador of Christ appear !

21 But that ye also may know my affairs, how I do, Tychicus, a
beloved brother and faithful minister in the Lord, will make known
22 to you all things : Whom I have sent to you for this very thing,
that ye might know our affairs, and that he might comfort your
23 hearts. Peace *be* to the brethren, and love with faith, from God
24 the Father and the Lord Jesus Christ. Grace *be* with all that love
our Lord Jesus Christ in sincerity. Amen.

21. *Ye also*—As well as others.

22. *That he might comfort your hearts*—By relatir g the supports I find from
God, and the success of the Gospel.

23. *Peace*—This verse recapitulates the whole epi tle.

24. *In sincerity*—Or in incorruption : without co* upting his genuine Gospel,
without any mixture of corrupt affections. And tha* with continuance, till grace
issue in glory.

NOTES

ON

ST. PAUL'S EPISTLE TO THE PHILIPPIANS.

——

PHILIPPI was so called from Philip, king of Macedonia, who much enlarged and beautified it. Afterward it became a Roman colony, and the chief city of that part of Macedonia. Hither St. Paul was sent by a vision to preach: and here, not long after his coming, he was shamefully treated. Nevertheless, many were converted by him during the short time of his abode there : by whose liberality he was more assisted, than by any other Church of his planting. And they had now sent large assistance to him by Epaphroditus; by whom he returns them this epistle.

———

PHILIPPIANS.

——

1 PAUL and Timotheus, servants of Jesus Christ, to all the saints in Christ Jesus who are at Philippi, with the bishops and deacons,
2 Grace *be* unto you, and peace from God our Father and the
3 Lord Jesus Christ. I thank my God upon every mention of you.

Verse 1. *Servants*—St. Paul, writing familiarly to the Philippians, does not style himself an apostle. And under the common title of servants, he tenderly and modestly joins with himself his son Timothy, who had come to Philippi not long after St. Paul had received him, Acts xvi, 3, 12. *To all the saints*—The apostolic epistles were sent more directly to the Churches, than to the pastors of them : *with the bishops and deacons*—The former probably took care of the internal state, the latter of the externals of the Church, 1 Tim. iii, 2–8. Although these were not wholly confined to the one, neither those to the other

4 Always in all my prayers making supplication for you all with
5 joy, For your fellowship in the Gospel from the first day until
6 now : Being persuaded of this very thing, that he who hath begun
   a good work in you, will perfect *it* until the day of Jesus Christ,
7 As it is right for me to think this of you all, because I have you in
   my heart, who are all partakers of my grace, both in my bonds, and
8 in the defence and confirmation of the Gospel. For God is my
   witness, how I long for you all, with the bowels of Jesus Christ.
9 And this I pray, that your love may abound yet more and more, in
10 all knowledge, and *in* all *spiritual* sense, That ye may try the things
   that are excellent, that ye may be sincere and without offence
11 unto the day of Christ. Being filled with the fruits of righteousness, which are through Christ Jesus, to the glory and praise of
   God.

The word bishops here includes all the presbyters at Philippi, as well as the ruling
presbyters ; the names bishop, and presbyter, or elder, being promiscuously used
in the first ages.

4. *With joy*—After the Epistle to the Ephesians, wherein love reigns, follows
this, wherein there is perpetual mention of joy. *The fruit of the Spirit is love,
joy*—And joy peculiarly enlivens prayer. The sum of the whole epistle is, *I
rejoice. Rejoice ye.*

5. The sense is, I thank God for your fellowship with us in all the blessings
of the Gospel, which I have done from the first day of your receiving it until
now.

6. *Being persuaded*—The grounds of which persuasion are set down in the following verse ; *that he who hath begun a good work in you, will perfect it until the
day of Christ*—That he, who having justified hath begun to sanctify you, will
carry on this work till it issue in glory.

7. *As it is right for me to think this of you all*—Why ? He does not say, " Because of an eternal decree ;" or " because a saint must persevere ;" but *because
I have you in my heart, who were all partakers of my grace*—That is, because ye
were all (*for which I have you in my heart*—I bear you the most grateful and
tender affection,) *partakers of my grace*—That is, sharers in the afflictions, which
God vouchsafed me as a grace or favour, ver. 29, 30, both in my bonds, and
when I was called forth to answer for myself, and to confirm the Gospel. It
is not improbable, that after they had endured that great trial of affliction,
God had sealed them unto full victory, of which the apostle had a prophetic
sight.

8. *I long for you all with the bowels of Jesus Christ*—In Paul, not Paul lives,
but Jesus Christ. Therefore he longs for them, with the bowels, the tenderness,
not of Paul, but of Jesus Christ.

9. *And this I pray, that your love*—Which they had already shown, *may
abound yet more and more*—The fire which burnt in the apostle never says, It is
enough ; *in knowledge and in all spiritual sense*—Which is the ground of all
spiritual knowledge. We must be inwardly sensible of Divine peace, joy, love ,
otherwise we cannot know they are.

10. *That ye may try*—By that spiritual sense, *the things that are excellent*—
Not only good, but the very best : the superior excellence of which is hardly discerned, but by the adult Christian : *that ye may be* inwardly *sincere*—Having a
single eye to the very best things ; and a pure heart, and outwardly *without
offence*—Holy, unblamable in all things.

11. *Being filled with the fruits of righteousness, which are through Jesus Christ,
to the glory and praise of God*—Here are three properties of that sincerity which is
acceptable to God. 1. It must bear fruits, the fruits of righteousness, all inward
and outward holiness, all good tempers, words, and works, and that so abun
dantly, that we may be filled with them : 2. The branch and the fruits must derive both their virtue and their very being from the all-supporting, all-supplying
root, Jesus Christ : 3. As all these flow from the grace of Christ, so they must
issue in the glory and praise of God.

12   Now I would have you know, brethren, that the things concerning me have fallen out rather to the furtherance of the Gospel:
13 So that my bonds in Christ have been made manifest in the whole
14 palace, and to all others : And many of the brethren, trusting in the
Lord through my bonds, are more abundantly bold to speak the
word without fear.
15   Some indeed preach Christ even through envy and strife : but
16 some through good will.   The one preach Christ out of contention,
17 not sincerely, supposing to add affliction to my bonds : But the
others out of love, knowing that I am set for the defence of the
18 Gospel.   What then? still every way, whether in pretence or in
truth, Christ is preached : and in this I rejoice, yea, and will re-
19 joice.   For I know that this shall turn to my salvation through
20 your prayer, and the supply of the Spirit of Jesus Christ : According to my earnest expectation and hope, that I shall be ashamed
in nothing, but that with all boldness, as always, *so* now also,
Christ shall be magnified in my body, whether by life or by death.
21   For to me to live *is* Christ, and to die *is* gain.   But if *I am* to
22 live in the flesh, this *is* the fruit of my labour, and what I should
23 choose, I know not.   For I am in a strait between two, having a
24 desire to depart and to be with Christ, *which* is far better.   But to
25 remain in the flesh *is* more needful for you.   And being persuaded
of this, I know that I shall remain and continue with you all, for your

12. *The things concerning me*—My sufferings have fallen out rather to the fur-
.herance than (as you feared) the hinderance of the Gospel.
13. *My bonds in Christ*—Endured for his sake, *have been made manifest*—Much
taken notice of, *in the whole palace*—Of the Roman emperor.
14. *And many*—Who were before afraid, *trusting in the Lord through my
bonds*—When they observed my constancy and safety, notwithstanding are more
bold.
15, 16. *Some indeed preach Christ out of contention*—Envying St. Paul's success, and striving to hurt him thereby ; *not sincerely*—From a real desire to glorify God, *but supposing*—Though they were disappointed, to add more *afflictions
to my bonds*—By enraging the Romans against me.
17. *But the others out of love*—To Christ and me ; *knowing*—Not barely supposing, *that I am set*—Literally, I *lie ;* yet still going forward in his work.   He
remained at Rome as an ambassador in a place were he is employed on an important embassy.
18. *In pretence*—Under colour of propagating the Gospel ; *in truth*—With a
real design so to do.
19. *This shall turn to my salvation*—Shall procure me a higher degree of glory,
through your prayer—Obtaining for me a larger supply of the Spirit.
20. *As always*—Since my call to the apostleship, *in my body*—However it may
be disposed of.   How that might be he did not yet know.   For the apostles did
not know all things : particularly, in things pertaining to themselves, they had
room to exercise faith and patience.
21. *To me to live is Christ*—To know, to love, to follow Christ is my life, my
glory, my joy.
22. Here he begins to treat of the former clause of the preceding verse.   Of
the latter he treats, chap. ii, 17.   *But if I am to live in the flesh, this is the fruit
of my labour*—This is the fruit of my living longer, that I can labour more.   Glorious labour !   Desirable fruit !   In this view, long life is indeed a blessing.   *And
what I should choose, I know not*—That is, if it were left to my own choice.
23. *To depart*—Out of bonds, flesh, the world, *and to be with Christ*—In
a nearer and fuller union.   It is better to depart : it is far better to be with
Christ.
25. *I know*—By a prophetic notice, given him while he was writing this, that

26 furtherance and joy of faith : That your rejoicing for me may abound through Christ Jesus, by my presence with you again.

27 Only let your behaviour be worthy of the Gospel of Christ, that whether I come and see you, or be'absent, I may hear concerning you, that ye stand fast in one spirit, with one soul striving together

28 for the faith of the Gospel, And in nothing terrified by your adversaries, which is to them an evident token of perdition, but to you

29 of salvation. This also *is* of God. For to you it is given with regard to Christ, not only to believe on him, but also to suffer for

30 him : Having the same conflict, which ye saw in me, and now hear *to be* in me.

II. If *there be* then any consolation in Christ, if any comfort of love,

2 if any fellowship of the Spirit, if any bowels of mercies ; Fulfil ye my joy, that ye think the same thing, having the same love, being

3 of one soul, of one mind. *Do* nothing through strife or vain glory, but in lowliness of mind, esteem each the others better than them-

4 selves. Aim not every one at his own things, but every one also

5 at the things of others. Let this mind be in you, which was also

6 in Christ Jesus, Who being in the form of God, counted it no act

7 of robbery to be equal with God ; Yet emptied himself, taking the

---

I shall continue some time longer *with you*—And doubtless he did see them after this confinement.

27. *Only*—Be careful for this, and nothing else, *stand fast in one spirit*—With the most perfect unanimity, *striving together*—With united strength and endeavours, *for the faith of the Gospel*—For all the blessings revealed and promised therein.

28. *Which*—Namely, their being adversaries to the word of God, and to you the messengers of God, *is an evident token*—That they are in the high road to perdition, and you in the way of salvation.

29. *For to you it is given*—As a special token of God's love and of your being in the way of salvation.

30. *Having the same* kind of conflict with your adversaries, *which ye saw in me*—When I was with you, Acts xvi, 12, 19, &c.

II. 1. *If there be therefore any consolation*—In the grace *of Christ, if any comfort*—In the love of God, *if any fellowship of* the Holy Ghost ; *if any bowels of mercies*—Resulting therefrom ; any tender affection toward each other.

2. *Think the same thing*—Seeing Christ is your common head : *having the same love*—To God your common Father : *being of one soul*—Animated with the same affections and tempers, as ye have all drunk into one spirit ; *of one mind*—Tenderly rejoicing and grieving together.

3. *Do nothing through contention*—Which is inconsistent with your thinking the same thing, *or vain glory*—Desire of praise, which is directly opposite to the love of God : *but esteem each the others better than themselves*—(For every one knows more evil of himself than he can of another.) Which is a glorious fruit of the Spirit, and an admirable help to your continuing of one soul.

4. *Aim not every one at his own things*—Only. If so, ye have not bowels of mercies.

6. *Who being in the* essential *form*, the incommunicable nature of God from eternity, (as he was afterward in the form of man, real God, as real man,) *counted it no act of robbery*, (that is the precise meaning of the words,) no invasion of another's prerogative, but his own strict and unquestionable right, *to be equal with God.* The word here translated *equal*, occurs in the adjective form five or six times in the New Testament, Matt. xx, 12 ; Luke vi, 34 ; John v, 18 ; Acts xi, 17 ; Rev. xxi, 16 ; in all which places it expresses not a bare resemblance, but a real and proper equality. It here implies both the fulness and the supreme height of the Godhead ; to which are opposed, *he emptied*, and he *humbled himself.*

7. *Yet*—He was so far from tenaciously insisting upon, that he willingly re-

8 form of a servant, being made in the likeness of men. And being found in fashion as a man, he humbled himself, becoming obedient 9 even unto death, yea, the death of the cross. Wherefore God also hath highly exalted him, and hath given him a name which is 10 above every name, That at the name of Jesus every knee might bow, of those in heaven, and those on earth, and those under the 11 earth; And every tongue might confess, that Jesus Christ is Lord 12 to the glory of God the Father. Wherefore, my beloved, as you have always obeyed, not as in my presence only, but much more now in my absence, work out your own salvation with fear and 13 trembling. For it is God that worketh in you according to his 14 good pleasure, both to will and to do. Do all things without mur- 15 murings and disputings : That ye may be blameless and simple, the sons of God, unrebukable, in the midst of a crooked and perverse

---

linquished his claim. He was content to forego the glories of the Creator, and to appear in the form of a creature : nay, to be made in the likeness of the fallen creatures ; and not only to share the disgrace, but to suffer the punishment due to the meanest and vilest among them all. *He emptied himself*—Of that Divine fulness, which he received again at his exaltation. Though he remained full, John i, 14, yet he appeared as if he had been empty; for he veiled his fulness from the sight of men and angels. Yea, he not only veiled, but in some sense renounced the glory which he had before the world began ; *taking*—And by that very act emptying himself, *the form of a servant*—*The form*, the likeness, the fashion, though not exactly the same, are yet nearly related to each other. The form expresses something absolute ; the likeness refers to other things of the same kind: the fashion respects what appears to sight and sense : *being made in the likeness of men*—A real man, like other men. Hereby he took *the form of a servant.*

8. *And being found in fashion as a man*—A common man, without any pecu- liar excellence or comeliness, *he humbled himself*—To a still greater depth, *becom- ing obedient*—To God, though equal with him, *even unto death*—The greatest instance both of humiliation and obedience, *yea, the death of the cross*—Inflicted on few but servants or slaves.

9. *Wherefore*—Because of his voluntary humiliation and obedience. He hum- bled himself: but *God hath exalted him*—So recompensing his humiliation, *and hath given him*—So recompensing his emptying himself, *a name which is above every name*—Dignity and majesty superior to every creature.

10. *That every knee*—That Divine honour might be paid in every possible man- ner by every creature, *might bow*—Either with love or trembling, *of those in hea- ven, earth, under the earth*—That is, through the whole universe.

11. *And every tongue*—Even of his enemies, *confess that Jesus Christ is Lord* —Jehovah ; not now in the form of a servant, but enthroned in the glory of God the Father.

12. *Wherefore*—Having proposed *Christ's* example, he exhorts them to secure the salvation which *Christ* has purchased ; *as ye have always*—hitherto, *obeyed*— Both God and me his minister ; *now in my absence*—When ye have not me to in- struct, assist, and direct you, *work out your own salvation*—Herein let every man *aim at his own things; with fear and trembling*—With the utmost care and diligence.

13. *For it is God*—God alone, who is with you, though I am not ; *that worketh in you according to his good pleasure*—Not for any merit of yours. Yet his influ- ences are not to supersede, but to encourage our own efforts. *Work out your own salvation*—Here is our duty ; *for it is God that worketh in you*—Here is our encouragement. And O! what a glorious encouragement, to have the arm of Omnipotence stretched out for our support and succour.

14. *Do all things*—Not only without contention, ver. 3, but even *without mur- murings and disputings*—Which are real, though smaller hinderances of love.

15. *That ye may be blameless*—Before men, *and simple*—Before God, aiming at nim alone, *as the sons of God*—The God of love ; acting up to your high charac-

16 generation, among whom ye shine as lights in the world. Holding fast the word of life, that I may glory in the day of Christ, that I have not run in vain, neither laboured in vain.

17 Yea, and if I be offered upon the sacrifice and service of your
18 faith, I rejoice and congratulate you all. For the same cause re-
19 joice ye likewise and congratulate me. Now I trust in the Lord Jesus, to send Timotheus to you shortly, that I also may be en-
20 couraged, when I know your state, For I have none like minded,
21 who will naturally care for what concerneth you. For all seek
22 their own, not the things of Jesus Christ. But ye know the proof of him, that as a son with his father, he hath served with me in
23 the Gospel. Him therefore I hope to send, as soon as ever I
24 know how it will go with me. But I trust in the Lord that I also
25 myself shall come shortly. Yet I thought it necessary to send also to you Epaphroditus, my brother and companion in labour, and fellow soldier, but your messenger, and him that ministered to my
26 need. For he longed after you all, and was full of heaviness, be-
27 cause ye had heard that he was sick. He was indeed sick nigh unto death ; but God had compassion on him ; and not on him only, but on me likewise, lest I should have sorrow upon sorrow.
28 I have sent him therefore the more willingly, that ye seeing him
29 again may rejoice, and that I also may be the less sorrowful. Receive him therefore in the Lord with all gladness, and honour
30 such. Because for the work of Christ he was nigh unto death, not regarding his own life, to supply your deficiency of service toward me.

---

ter, unrebukable in the midst of a crooked, guileful, serpentine, *and perverse generation*—Such as the bulk of mankind always were, *crooked*—By a corrupt nature, and yet more perverse by custom and practice.

17. Here he begins to treat of the latter clause of chap. i, 22. *Yea, and if I be offered*, literally, *if I be poured out upon the sacrifice of your faith*—The *Philippians*, as the other converted heathens, were a sacrifice to God through St. Paul's ministry, Rom. xv, 16. And as in sacrificing, wine was poured at the foot of the altar, so he was willing that his blood should be poured out. The expression well agrees with that kind of martyrdom, by which he was afterward offered up to God.

18. *Congratulate me*—When I am offered up.

19. *When I know*—Upon my return, that ye stand steadfast.

20. *I have none*—Of those who are now with me.

21. *For all*—but *Timotheus, seek their own*—Ease, safety, pleasure, or profit. Amazing ! in that golden age of the Church, could St. Paul thoroughly approve of one only, among all the labourers that were with him ? chap. i, 14, 17. And how many do we think can now approve themselves to God ? *Not the things of Jesus Christ*—They who seek these alone will sadly experience this. They will find few helpers like minded with themselves, willing naked to follow a naked Master !

22. *As a son with his father*—He uses an elegant peculiarity of phrase, speaking partly as of a son, partly as of a fellow labourer.

25. *To send Epaphroditus*—Back immediately, *your messenger*—The Philippians had sent him to St. Paul with their liberal contribution.

26. *He was full of heaviness*—Because he supposed you would be afflicted at hearing he was sick.

27. *God had compassion on him*—Restoring him to health.

28. *That I may be the less sorrowful*—When I know you are rejoicing.

30. *To supply your deficiency of service*—To do what you could not do in person.

III. Finally, my brethren, rejoice in the Lord. To write the same
2 things to you, *is* not tedious to me, and *it is* safe for you. Beware of dogs, beware of evil workers, beware of the concision.
3 For we are the circumcision, who worship God in spirit, and glory
4 in Christ Jesus, and have no confidence in the flesh. Though I
might have confidence even in the flesh. If any other man be
fully persuaded that he may have confidence in the flesh, I more :
5 Circumcised the eighth day, of the stock of Israel, of the tribe
of Benjamin, a Hebrew of Hebrews, touching the law, a Pha
6 risee ; Touching zeal, persecuting the Church, touching the right-
7 eousness which is by the law, blameless. But whatsoever things
8 were gain to me, those I have accounted loss for Christ. Yea,
doubtless, and I account all things to be loss, for the excellency
of the knowledge of Christ Jesus my Lord : for whom I have
suffered the loss of all things, and do account them but dung,
9 that I may gain Christ ; And be found in him, not having my
own righteousness which is of the law, but that which is through
faith in Christ, the righteousness which is from God by faith :

III. 1. *The same things*—Which you have heard before.
2. *Beware of dogs*—Unclean, unholy, rapacious men. The title which the
Jews usually gave the Gentiles, he returns upon themselves *The concision*—
Circumcision being now ceased, the apostle will not call them the circumcision,
but coins a term on purpose, taken from a Greek word used by the seventy, Lev.
xxi, 5, for such a cutting as God had forbidden.
3. *For we*—Christians, *are the* only *true circumcision*—The people now in
covenant with God, *who worship God in spirit*—Not barely in the letter, but with
the spiritual worship of inward holiness ; *and glory in Christ Jesus*—As the only
cause of all our blessings ; *and have no confidence in the flesh*—In any outward
advantage or prerogative.
4. *Though I*—He subjoins this in the singular number, because the Philippians
could not say thus.
5. *Circumcised the eighth day*—Not at ripe age, as a proselyte, *of the tribe
of Benjamin*—Sprung from the wife, not the handmaid ; *a Hebrew of Hebrews*-
By both my parents : in every thing, nation, religion, language ; *touching the law*,
a Pharisee—One of that sect, who most accurately observe it.
6. Having such a zeal for it, as to persecute to the death those who did not
observe it, touching the righteousness which is described and enjoined *by the law*
—That is, external observances, *blameless.*
7. *But* all those *things*, which I then accounted *gain*, which were once my
confidence, my glory, and joy, those, ever since I have believed, *I have accounted
loss*, nothing worth in comparison of *Christ.*
8. *Yea, I* still *account* both all these and *all things* else *to be* mere *loss*, compared to the inward experimental *knowledge of Christ*, as *my Lord*, as my Prophet, Priest, and King, as teaching me wisdom, atoning for my sins, and reigning in my heart. To refer this to justification only, is miserably to pervert the
whole scope of the words. They manifestly relate to sanctification also : yea, to
that chiefly. *For whom I have* actually *suffered the loss of all things*—Which
the world loves, esteems, or admires ; of which I am so far from repenting, that
I still *account them but dung*—The discourse rises. *Loss* is sustained with
patience ; but *dung* is cast away with abhorrence. The *Greek* word signifies any,
the vilest refuse of things, the dross of metals, the dregs of liquors, the excre-
ments of animals, the most worthless scraps of meat, the basest offals, fit only for
dogs ; *that I may gain Christ*—He that loses all things, not excepting himself,
gains Christ, and is gained by Christ. And still there is more ; which even St.
Paul speaks of his having not yet gained !
9. *And be found* by God, ingrafted *in him, not having my own righteousness,
which is of the law*--That merely outward righteousness prescribed by the law,
and performed by my own strength, but that inward righteousness *which is*

10 'That I may know him, and the power of his resurrection, and the fellowship of his sufferings, being made conformable to his
11 death: If by any means I may attain unto the resurrection of
12 the dead. Not that I have already attained, or am already perfected: but I pursue, if I may apprehend that for which I was also
13 apprehended by Christ Jesus. Brethren, I do not account myself to have apprehended: but one thing *I do*, forgetting the things that are behind, and reaching forth unto the things which
14 are before, I press toward the goal, for the prize of the high
15 calling of God in Christ Jesus. Let us therefore, as many as are perfect, be thus minded; and if in any thing ye be otherwise
16 minded. God shall reveal even this unto you; But whereunto we have already attained, let us walk by the same rule, let us mind the same thing.
17   Brethren, be ye followers together of me, and mark them who
18 walk as ye have us for an example. (For many walk, of whom I have told you often, and now tell you even weeping, *that they are*
19 enemies of the cross of Christ. Whose end *is* destruction, whose god *is* their belly, and *whose* glory *is* in their shame; who mind

through faith—Which can flow from no other fountain; *the righteousness which is from God*—From his almighty Spirit, not by my own strength, but by faith alone. Here also the apostle is far from speaking of justification only.

10. The knowledge of Christ mentioned in the 8th verse is here more largely explained. *That I may know him*—As my complete Saviour; *and the power of his resurrection*—Raising me from the death of sin, into all the life of love; *and the fellowship of his sufferings*—Being crucified with him; *and made conformable to his death*—So as to be dead to all things here below.

11. *The resurrection of the dead*—That is, the resurrection to glory.

12. *Not that I have already attained*—The prize. He here enters on a new set of metaphors, taken from a race. But observe how, in the utmost fervour, he retains his sobriety of spirit; *or am already perfected*—There is a difference between one that is perfect, and one that is perfected. The one is fitted for the race, ver. 15; the other, ready to receive the prize. *But I pursue, if I may apprehend that*—Perfect holiness, preparatory to glory; for, in order to *which I was apprehended by Christ Jesus*—Appearing to me in the way, Acts xxvi, 14. The speaking conditionally both here and in the preceding verse, implies no uncertainty, but only the difficulty of attaining.

13. *I do not account myself to have apprehended* this already: to be already possessed of perfect holiness.

14. *Forgetting the things that are behind*—Even that part of the race which is already run; *and reaching forth unto*—Literally, *stretched out over the things that are before*—Pursuing, with the whole bent and vigour of my soul, perfect holiness and eternal glory. *In Christ Jesus*—The author and finisher of every good thing.

15. *Let us—as many as are perfect*—Fit for the race, strong in faith, (so it means here,) *be thus minded*—Apply wholly to this one thing; *and if in any thing ye*—Who are not perfect, who are weak in faith; *be otherwise minded*—pursuing other things, God, if ye desire it, *shall reveal even this unto you*—Will convince you of it.

16. But let us take care not to lose the ground we have already gained. *Let us walk by the same rule* we have done hitherto.

17. *Mark them*—For your imitation.

18. *Weeping*—As he wrote. *Enemies of the cross of Christ*—Such are a... cowardly, all shame-faced, all delicate Christians.

19. *Whose end is destruction*—This is placed in the front, that what follows may be read with the greater horror: *whose god is their belly*—Whose supreme happiness lies in gratifying their sensual appetites; *who mind*—Relish, desire, seek, *earthly things*.

20 earthly things.) For our conversation is in heaven; from whence
21 also we look for the Saviour, the Lord Jesus Christ, Who wil
transform our vile body, that it may be fashioned like unto his
glorious body, according to the mighty working, whereby he is
able even to subject all things to himself.
IV. Therefore, my brethren, beloved and longed for, my joy and
2 crown, so stand fast in the Lord, *my* beloved. I beseech Euodias,
3 and I beseech Syntyche, to be of one mind in the Lord. And I
entreat thee also, true yoke fellow, help those women who laboured
together with me in the Gospel, with both Clement and my other
fellow labourers, whose names *are* in the book of life.
4 Rejoice in the Lord always: again I say, Rejoice. Let your
5 gentleness be known to all men; the Lord *is* at hand. Be care-
6 ful for nothing, but in every thing by prayer and supplication with
7 thanksgiving, let your requests be made known to God: And the

20. *Our conversation*—The Greek word is of a very extensive meaning; our citizenship, our thoughts, our affections, are already in heaven.
21. *Who will transform our vile body*—Into the most perfect state, and the most beauteous form. It will then be purer than the unspotted firmament, brighter than the lustre of the stars: and which exceeds all parallel, which comprehends all perfection; *like unto his glorious body*—Like that wonderfully glorious body which he wears in his heavenly kingdom, and on his triumphant throne.
IV. 1. *So stand*—As ye have done hitherto.
2. *I beseech*—He repeats this twice, as if speaking to each face to face, and that with the utmost tenderness.
3. *And I entreat thee also, true yoke fellow*—St. Paul had many fellow labour ers, but not many yoke fellows. In this number was Barnabas first, and then Silas, whom he probably addresses here. For Silas had been his yoke fellow at the very place, Acts xvi, 19. Help those women who laboured together with me; literally, *who wrestled*—The Greek word doth not imply preaching, or any thing of that kind; but danger and toil endured for the sake of the Gospel: which was also endured at the same time (probably at Philippi) by *Clement and my other fellow labourers*—This is a different word from the former, and does properly imply fellow preachers: *whose names*, although not set down here, *are in* the book of life*—As are those of all believers: an allusion to the wrestlers in the Olympic games, whose names were all enrolled in a book. Reader, is thy name there? Then walk circumspectly, lest the Lord blot thee out of his book.
5. *Let your gentleness*—Yieldingness, sweetness of temper, the result of joy in the Lord; *be known*—By your whole behaviour; *to all men*—Good and bad, gentle and froward. Those of the roughest tempers are good natured to some, (from natural sympathy, and various motives,) a Christian to all. *The Lord*—The Judge, the Rewarder, the Avenger, *is at hand*—Standeth at the door.
6. *Be anxiously careful for nothing*—If men are not gentle toward you, yet neither on this, nor any other account, be careful, but pray. Anxiety and prayer cannot stand together. *In every thing*—Great and small; *let your requests be made known*—They who, by a preposterous shame, or distrustful modesty, cover, stifle, or keep in their desires, as if they were either too small or too great; must be racked with care: from which they are entirely delivered, who pour them out with a free and filial confidence: *to God*—It is not always proper to disclose them to men: *by supplication*—Which is the enlarging upon and press-ng our petition: *with thanksgiving*—The surest mark of a soul free from anxiety, and of prayer, joined with true resignation. This is always followed by peace. Peace and thanksgiving are both coupled together, Col. iii, 15.
7. *And the peace of God*—That calm, heavenly repose, that tranquillity of spirit, which God only can give; *which surpasseth all understanding*—Which none can comprehend, save he that receiveth it; *shall keep*—Shall guard as a garrison does a city; *your hearts*—Your affections; *your minds*—Your understandings, and all

peace of God, which surpasseth all understanding, shall keep your hearts and your minds through Christ Jesus.

8 Finally, brethren, whatsoever things are true, whatsoever things *are* honest, whatsoever things *are* just, whatsoever things *are* pure, whatsoever things *are* lovely, whatsoever things *are* of good report : if *there be* any virtue, and if *there be* any praise, think on these
9 things ; The things which ye have both learned and received and heard and seen in me, these do : and the God of peace shall be with you.
10 I rejoiced in the Lord greatly, that now at last your care of me hath flourished again ; wherein ye were also careful ; but ye
11 wanted opportunity. Not that I speak in respect of want ; for I
12 have learned in whatsoever state I am, to be content. I know how to be abased, and I know how to abound : every where and in every thing I am instructed, both to be full and to be hungry ; both
13 to abound and to want. I can do all things through Christ strength-
14 ening me. Nevertheless ye have done well, that ye did commu-
15 nicate to me in my affliction. And ye know likewise, O Phi-lippians, that in the beginning of the Gospel, when I departed from Macedonia, no Church communicated with me in respect of giving
16 and receiving, but you only For even in Thessalonica ye sent
17 once and again to my necessities. Not that I desire a gift, but I

---

the various workings of them, through the Spirit and power of Christ Jesus, in the knowledge and love of God. Without a guard set on these likewise, the purity and vigour of our affections cannot long be preserved.

8. *Finally*—To sum up all ; *whatsoever things are true*—Here are eight parti-culars placed in two fourfold rows ; the former containing their duty, the latter the commendation of it. The first word in the former row answers the first in the latter, the second word the second, and so on : *true*—In speech : *honest*—In ac-tion : *just*—With regard to others : *pure*—With regard to yourselves : *lovely*—And what more lovely than truth ? *of good report*—As is honesty even where it is not practised. *If there be any virtue*—And all virtues are contained in justice ; *if there be any praise*—In those things which relate rather to ourselves than to our neighbour : *think on these things*—That ye may both practise them your-selves, and recommend them to others.

9. *The things which ye have learned*—As catechumens ; *and received*—By con-tinual instructions, *and heard and seen*—In my life and conversation, *these do, and the God of peace shall be with you*—Not only the peace of God, but God him-self, the fountain of peace.

10. *I rejoice greatly*—St. Paul was no Stoic. He had strong passions, but all devoted to God : *that your care of me hath flourished again*—As a tree blossoms after the winter. *Ye wanted opportunity*—Either ye had not plenty yourselves, or you wanted a proper messenger.

11. *I have learned*—From God. He only can teach this, *in every thing there-with to be content*—Joyfully and thankfully patient. Nothing less is Christian content. We may observe a beautiful gradation in the expressions,—I have learned ; I know ; I am instructed ; I can.

12. *I know how to be abased*—Having scarce what is needful for my body ; *and to abound*—Having wherewith to relieve others also. Presently after the order of the words is inverted, to intimate his frequent transition from scarcity to plenty, and from plenty to scarcity. *I am instructed*—Literally, I am initiated into that mystery, unknown to all but Christians, *both to be full and to be hungry*—For one day ; *both to abound and to want*—For a longer season.

13. *I can do all things*—Even fulfil all the will of God.

15. *In the beginning of the Gospel*—When it was first preached at Philippi, *in respect of giving*—On your part, *and receiving*—On mine.

17. *Not that I desire*—For my own sake, the very gift which I receive of you.

18 desire fruit that may abound to your account. But I have all
   things, and abound; I am filled, having received of Epaphroditus
   the things *which came* from you, an odour of a sweet smell, an
19 acceptable sacrifice, well pleasing to God. And my God shall
   supply all your need, according to his riches in glory through
20 Christ Jesus. Now unto our God and Father *be* glory for ever
   and ever. Amen.
21   Salute every saint in Christ Jesus. The brethren who are
22 with me salute you. All the saints salute you, chiefly they that
23 are of Cesar's household. The grace of the Lord Jesus Christ
   be with you.

---

18. *An odour of a sweet smell*—More pleasing to God than the sweetest perfumes to men.

19. *All your need*—As ye have mine, *according to his riches in glory*—In his
abundant, eternal glory.

NOTES

ON

ST. PAUL'S EPISTLE TO THE COLOSSIANS.

———

COLOSSE was a city of the greater Phrygia, not far from Laodicea and Hierapolis Though St. Paul preached in many parts of Phrygia, yet he never had been at this city. It had received the Gospel by the preaching of Epaphras, who was with St. Paul when he wrote this epistle.

It seems the Colossians were now in danger of being seduced by those who strove to blend Judaism or heathen superstitions with Christianity; pretending that God, because of his great majesty, was not to be approached but by the mediation of angels; and that there were certain rites and observances, chiefly borrowed from the law, whereby these angels might be made our friends.

In opposition to them the apostle, 1. Commends the knowledge of Christ as more excellent than all other, and so entire and perfect, that no other knowledge was necessary for a Christian. He, 2, shows that Christ is above all angels, who are only his servants; and that being reconciled to God through him, we have free access to him in all our necessities.

COLOSSIANS.

1 PAUL, an apostle of Jesus Christ by the will of God, and
2 Timotheus, a brother, To the saints and faithful brethren in
Christ at Colosse, grace *be* unto you, and peace from God our
Father, and the Lord Jesus Christ.
3 We give thanks to the God and Father of our Lord Jesus
4 Christ, (praying always for you, Hearing of your faith in Christ
5 Jesus, and of your love to all the saints.) For the hope which is
laid up for you in heaven, of which ye heard before in the word of
6 truth of the Gospel, Which is come to you, as also *it is* in all the
world, and bringeth forth fruit, as *it hath done* likewise among you,
from the day ye heard *it*, and knew the grace of God in truth:
7 As ye likewise learned of Epaphras, our beloved fellow servant,
8 who is a faithful minister of Christ for you: Who also declared
9 to us your love in the Spirit. For this cause from the day we
heard *it*, we do not cease to pray also for you, and to desire that
ye may be filled with the knowledge of his will, in all wisdom and
10 spiritual understanding; That ye may walk worthy of the Lord,
unto all pleasing, being fruitful in every good work, and increasing
11 in the knowledge of God; Strengthened with all might according
to his glorious power, unto all patience and long suffering with
12 joyfulness: Giving thanks unto the Father, who hath made us
13 meet to partake of the inheritance of the saints in light; Who
hath delivered us from the power of darkness, and hath translated
14 *us* into the kingdom of his beloved Son. In whom we have re-

---

Verse 2. *The saints*—This word expresses their union with God, *and brethren*—
This, their union with their fellow Christians.

3. *We give thanks*—There is a near resemblance between this epistle and those
to the Ephesians and Philippians.

5. *Ye heard before*—I wrote to you; *in the word of truth, of the Gospel*—The
true Gospel preached to you.

6. *It bringeth forth fruit in all the world*—That is, in every place where it is
preached. *Ye knew the grace of God in truth*—Truly experienced the gracious
power of God.

7. *Our fellow servant*—Of Paul and Timotheus.

8. *Your love in the Spirit*—Your love wrought in you by the Spirit.

9. *We pray for you*—This was mentioned in general, ver. 3, but now more
particularly; *that ye may be filled with the knowledge of his will*—Of his revealed
will, *in all wisdom*—With all the wisdom from above, *and spiritual understanding*—To discern by that light whatever agrees with or differs from his will.

10. *That* knowing his whole will, *ye may walk worthy of the Lord unto all
well pleasing*—So as actually to please him in all things, daily increasing in the
living, experimental knowledge of God our Father, Saviour, Sanctifier.

11. *Strengthened unto all patience and long suffering with joyfulness*—This is
the highest point: not only to know, to do, to suffer the whole will of God; but
to suffer it to the end, not barely with patience, but with thankful joy.

12. *Who* by justifying and sanctifying us hath made us meet for glory.

13. *Power* detains reluctant captives. A kingdom cherishes willing subjects.
His beloved Son—This is treated of in the 15th and following verses.

14. *In whom we have redemption*—This is treated of from the middle of the

15 demption through his blood, the forgiveness of sins: Who is the image of the invisible God, the first begotten of every creature.
16 For through him were created all things that are in heaven and that are on earth, visible and invisible; whether *they be* thrones, or dominions, or principalities, or powers; all things were created
17 by him and for him. And he is before all things, and by him
18 all things consist. And he is the head of his body the Church; who is the beginning, the first begotten from the dead, that in all
19 things he might have the pre-eminence. For it pleased *the Father*
20 that all fulness should dwell in him: And by him to reconcile all things to himself, (having made peace by him through the blood of the cross,) whether things on earth, or things in heaven.
21 And you that were once alienated, and enemies in your mind by
22 wicked works, he hath now reconciled, By the body of his flesh,

18th verse. The voluntary passion of our Lord appeased the Father's wrath, obtained pardon and acceptance for us, and consequently dissolved the dominion and power which Satan had over us through our sins. So that forgiveness is the beginning of redemption, as the resurrection is the completion of it.

15. *Who is*—By describing the glory of Christ, and the pre-eminence over the highest angels, the apostle here lays a foundation for the reproof of all worshippers of angels: *the image of the invisible God*—Whom none can represent but his only-begotten Son: in his Divine nature, the invisible image; in his human, the visible image of the Father; *the first begotten of every creature*—That is, begotten before every creature; subsisting before all worlds, before all time, from all eternity.

16. *For*—This explains the latter part of the preceding verses; *through*—implies something prior to the particles *by* and *for;* so denoting the beginning, the progress, and the end: *him*—This word, frequently repeated, signifies his supreme majesty, and excludes every creature: *were created all things that are in heaven*—And heaven itself. But the inhabitants are named, because more noble than the house: *invisible*—The several species of which are subjoined. Thrones are superior to dominions, principalities to powers. Perhaps the two latter may express their office with regard to other creatures: the two former may refer to God, who maketh them his chariots, and, as it were, rideth upon their wings.

17. *And he is before all things*—It is not said, He was: he is from everlasting to everlasting; *and by him all things consist*—The original expression not only implies that he sustains all things in being, but more directly, *all things were and are compacted in him into one system*—He is the cement as well as support of the universe. And is he less than the supreme God?

18. *And*—From the whole, he now descends to the most eminent part, the Church; *he is the head of the Church*—Universal. The supreme and only head both of influence and of government to the whole body of believers, *who is*—The repetition of the expression, see ver. 15, points out the entrance on a new paragraph; *the beginning*—Absolutely the Eternal, *the first begotten from the dead*—From whose resurrection flows all the life, spiritual and eternal, of all his brethren: *that in all things*—Whether of nature or grace, *he might have the preeminence*—Who can sound this depth?

19. *For it pleased the Father that all fulness*—All the fulness of God, *should dwell in him*—Constantly, as in a temple, and always ready for our approach to him.

20. *Through the blood of the cross*—The blood shed thereon: *whether things on earth*—Here the enmity began. Therefore this is mentioned first: *or things in heaven*—Those who are now in paradise; the saints who died before Christ came.

21. *And you that were alienated and enemies*—Actual alienation of affection makes habitual enmity; *in your mind*—Both your understanding and your affections *by wicked works*—Which continually feed and increase inward aliena-

through death, to present you holy, and spotless, and unreprovable
23 in his sight; If ye continue in the faith, grounded, and settled,
and are not removed from the hope of the Gospel which ye have
heard, which is preached to every creature that is under heaven,
24 whereof I Paul am made a minister. Now I rejoice in my sufferings for you, and fill up in my flesh that which is behind of the
25 sufferings of Christ for his body, which is the Church: Of which I
am made a minister, according to the dispensation of God, which
26 is given to me for you, fully to preach the word of God: The
mystery which hath been hid from ages and generations ; but now
27 is manifested to his saints : To whom among the Gentiles it was
the will of God to make known, what is the riches of this glorious
28 mystery, which is Christ in you, the hope of glory ; Whom we
preach, admonishing every man, and teaching every man with all
wisdom, that we may present every man perfect through Christ
29 Jesus. For which also I labour, striving according to his mighty
working, who worketh in me mightily
II.   For I would have you know how great a conflict I have for you
and *for* them at Laodicea, and *for* as many as have not seen my
2 face in the flesh ; That their hearts may be comforted, being knit
together in love, even unto all riches of the full assurance of
understanding unto the acknowledgment of the mystery of God,
3 both the Father and Christ. In whom are hid all the treasures of

tion from and enmity to God; *he hath now reconciled*—From the moment ye
believed.
22. *By the body of his flesh*— (So distinguished from his body, the Church.) The
body here denotes his entire manhood; *through death*—Whereby he purchased
the reconciliation which we receive by faith; *to present you*—The very end of
that reconciliation ; *holy*—Toward God ; *spotless*—In yourselves ; *unreprovable*—
As to your neighbour.
23. *If ye continue in the faith*—Otherwise ye will lose all the blessings which
ye have already begun to enjoy ; *and be not removed from the hope of the Gospel*
—The glorious hope of perfect love ; *which is preached*—Is already begun to be
preached to every creature under heaven.
24. *Now I rejoice in my sufferings for you, and fill up*—That is, whereby I fill
up, *that which is behind of the sufferings of Christ*—That which remains to be
suffered by his members. These are termed the sufferings of Christ ;—1. Because the suffering of any member is the suffering of the whole, and of the head
especially, which supplies strength, spirits, sense, and motion to all. 2. Because they are for his sake, for the testimony of his truth. And these also are
necessary for the Church ; not to reconcile it to God, or satisfy for sin, (for that
Christ did perfectly,) but for example to others, perfecting of the saints, and
increasing their reward.
25. *According to the dispensation of God, which is given me*—Or, the stewardship with which I am intrusted.
26. *The mystery*—Namely, Christ both justifying and sanctifying Gentiles as
well as Jews, which hath been comparatively hid from former ages and past
generations of men.
27. *Christ* dwelling and reigning in you, *the hope of glory*—The ground of
your hope.
28. We *teach* the ignorant, and *admonish* them that are already taught.
II. 1. *How great a conflict*—Of care, desire, prayer. *As many as have not seen
my face*—Therefore, in writing to the Colossians, he refrains from those familiar
appellations, brethren, beloved.
2. *Unto all riches of the full assurance of understanding, unto the acknowledgment of the mystery of God*—That is, unto the fullest and clearest understanding
and knowledge of the Gospel.

4 wisdom and knowledge.   And this I say, that no man may beguile
5 you with enticing words.   For though I am absent from you in the
   flesh, yet I am present with you in spirit, rejoicing to behold your
6 order, and the steadfastness of your faith in Christ.   As ye have
7 therefore received Christ Jesus the Lord, *so* walk in him : Rooted
   and built up in him, and established in the faith, as ye have been
   taught, abounding therein with thanksgiving.
8   Beware lest any man make a prey of you through philosophy
   and empty deceit, after the tradition of men, after the rudiments
9 of the world, and not after Christ.   For in him dwelleth all the ful-
10 ness of the Godhead bodily.   And ye are filled by him, who is the
11 head of all principality and power.   By whom also ye have been circumcised with a circumcision not performed with hands, in putting
   off the body of the sins of the flesh, by the circumcision of Christ :
12 Buried with him in baptism, by which ye are also risen with *him*
   through the faith of the operation of God, who raised him from the
13 dead.   And you, who were dead in trespasses and the uncircumcision of your flesh, hath he quickened together with him, having

---

6. *So walk in him*—In the same faith, love, holiness.
7. *Rooted in him*—As the vine ; *built*—On the sure foundation.
8. *Through philosophy and empty deceit*—That is, through the empty deceit
of philosophy blended with Christianity. This the apostle condemns, 1. Because
it was empty and deceitful, promising happiness, but giving none. 2. Because it
was grounded, not on solid reason, but the traditions of men, Zeno, Epicurus,
and the rest : and, 3. Because it was so shallow and superficial, not advancing
beyond the knowledge of sensible things ; no, not beyond the first rudiments of
them.
9. *For in him dwelleth*—Inhabiteth, continually abideth, *all the fulness of the
Godhead*. Believers are filled with all the fulness of God, Eph. iii, 19. But in
Christ dwelleth all the fulness of the Godhead ; the most full Godhead ; not only
Divine powers, but the Divine nature, chap. i, 19 : *bodily*—Personally, really,
substantially. The very substance of God, if one might so speak, dwells in
Christ, in the most full sense.
10. *And ye*—Who believe, are filled with him, John i, 16. Christ is filled with
God, and ye are filled with Christ. And ye are filled by him. The fulness of
Christ overflows his Church, Psalm cxxxiii, 3. He is originally full. We are
filled by him with wisdom and holiness. *Who is the head of all principality and
power*—Of angels as well as men. Not from angels therefore, but from their
head are we to ask whatever we stand in need of.
11. *By whom also ye have been circumcised*—Ye have received the spiritual
blessings typified of old by circumcision ; *with a circumcision not performed with
hands*—By an inward, spiritual operation in putting off, not a little skin ; but the
whole *body of the sins of the flesh*—All the sins of your evil nature ; *by the circumcision of Christ*—By that spiritual circumcision which Christ works in your
heart.
12. Which he wrought in you, when ye were as it were *buried with him in baptism*—The ancient manner of baptizing by immersion is as manifestly alluded
to here, as the other manner of baptizing by sprinkling or pouring of water is,
Heb. x, 22. But no stress is laid on the age of the baptized, or the manner of
performing it, in one or the other place ; but only on our being risen with Christ,
through the powerful operation of God in the soul ; which we cannot but know
assuredly, if it really is so : and if we do not experience this, our baptism has not
answered the end of its institution ; *by which ye are also risen with him*—From
the death of sin to the life of holiness. It does not appear, that in all this St.
Paul speaks of justification at all, but of sanctification altogether.
13. *And you who were dead*—Doubly dead to God, not only wallowing in
trespasses, outward sins, but also in *the uncircumcision of your flesh*—(A beautiful
expression for original sin,) the inbred corruption 𝚈 ' ʸᵖᵘ ' nature, your uncir

14 forgiven you all trespasses. Having blotted out by *his* decrees the handwriting against us, which was contrary to us ; and having
15 nailed it to his cross, he took it out of the way. *And* having spoiled the principalities and powers, he exposed them openly, triumphing over them in him.
16   Let none therefore judge you in meat, or drink, or in respect of
17 a feast day, or of the new moon, or of Sabbath days : Which are a
18 shadow of things to come ; but the body *is* of Christ. Let none defraud you of your reward by a voluntary humility and worship of angels, intruding into the things which he hath not seen, vainly
19 puffed up by his fleshly mind, And not holding the head, from which all the body being nourished and knit together, by the joints
20 and ligaments, increaseth with the increase of God. Therefore if ye are dead with Christ from the rudiments of the world, why,
21 as living in the world, receive ye ordinances, (Touch not,
22 taste not, handle not : All which are to perish in the using,) after
23 the commandments and doctrines of men ? Which things, (though they have indeed a show of wisdom, in voluntary worship and humility, and not sparing the body,) *yet are* not of any value, *but* are to the satisfying of the flesh.

---

cumcised heart and affections ; *hath he*—God the Father, *quickened together with him*—Making you partakers of the power of his resurrection. It is evident the apostle thus far speaks, not of justification, but of sanctification only.

14. *Having blotted out*—In consequence of his gracious decrees, that Christ should come into the world to save sinners, and that whosoever believeth on him should have everlasting life ; *the handwriting against us*—Where a debt is contracted, it is usually testified by some handwriting. And when the debt is forgiven, the handwriting is destroyed, either by blotting it out, by taking it away, or by tearing it. The apostle expresses in all these three ways God's destroying the handwriting which was contrary to us, or. at enmity with us. This was not properly our sins themselves ; (they were the debt ;) but their guilt and cry before God.

15. *And having spoiled the principalities and powers*—The evil angels of their usurped dominion ; *he*—God the Father ; ·*exposed them openly*—Before all the hosts of hell and heaven ; *triumphing over them in* or *by him*—By Christ. Thus the paragraph begins with Christ, goes on with him, and ends with him.

16. *Therefore*—Seeing these things are so ; *let none judge you*—That is, regard none who judge you ; *in meat or drink*—For not observing the ceremonial law in these or any other particulars, or in respect of a yearly feast, the new moon, or the weekly Jewish sabbaths.

17. *Which are* but a lifeless shadow ; *but the body*, the substance, *is of Christ.*

18. Out of pretended humility they worshipped angels, as not daring to apply immediately to God. Yet this really sprung from their being puffed up, the constant forerunner of a fall ; Prov. xvi, 18. So far was it from being an instance of true humility.

19. *And not holding the head*—He does not hold Christ, who does not trust in him alone. All the members are nourished by faith, and knit together by love and mutual sympathy.

20. *Therefore*—The inference, begun ver. 16, is continued. A new inference follows, chap. iii, 1. *If ye are dead with Christ from the rudiments of the world* —That is, if ye are dead with Christ, and so freed from them, *why receive the ordinances*—Which Christ hath not enjoined ; from which he hath made you free.

21. *Touch not*—An unclean thing ; *taste not*—Any forbidden meat ; *handle not* —Any consecrated vessel.

22. *Perish in the using*—Have no farther use, no influence on the mind.

23. *Not sparing the body*—Denying it many gratifications, and putting it to many inconveniences. Yet they are not of any real value before God, nor do

III.   If ye then are risen with Christ, seek the things above, where
2 Christ sitteth at the right hand of God.   Set your affections on the
3 things above, not the things on the earth.   For ye are dead, and
4 your life is hid with Christ in God.   When Christ our life shall
   appear, then shall ye also appear with him in glory.
5   Mortify therefore your members which are upon the earth, fornication, uncleanness, inordinate affection, evil desire, and covet-
6 ousness, which is idolatry : For which the wrath of God cometh
7 on the children of disobedience : In which ye also once walked,
8 when ye lived in them.   But now put ye likewise all these things
   off, anger, wrath, ill nature, evil speaking, filthy discourse out of
9 your mouth.   Lie not one to another, seeing ye have put off the old
10 man with his deeds, And have put on the new *man*, which is
   renewed in knowledge, after the image of him that created him :
11 Where there is neither Greek nor Jew, circumcision nor uncircumcision ;' barbarian, Scythian, slave *nor* free ; but Christ is all, and
12 in all.   Put on, therefore, as the elect of God, holy and beloved,
   bowels of mercies, kindness, humbleness of mind, meekness, long
13 suffering ; Forbearing one another, and forgiving one another, if any
   have a complaint against any , even as Christ forgave you, so also
14 *do* ye.   And above all these *put on* love, which is the bond of per-
15 fection : And the peace of God shall rule in your hearts, to which

---

they upon the whole mortify, but satisfy the flesh.   They indulge our corrupt
nature, our self will, pride, and desire of being distinguished from others.
   III. 1. *If ye are risen, seek the things above*—As Christ, being risen, immediately went to heaven.
   3. *For ye are dead*—To the things on earth, and your real, spiritual life is hid
from the world, and laid *up in God, with Christ*—Who hath merited, promised,
prepared it for us, and gives us the earnest and foretaste of it in our hearts.
   4. *When Christ*—The abruptness of the sentence surrounds us with sudden
light ; *our life*—The fountain of holiness and glory ; *shall appear*—In the clouds
of heaven.
   5. *Mortify therefore*—Put to death ; slay with a continued stroke ; *your members*—Which together make up the body of sin ; *which are upon the earth*—
Where they find their nourishment ; *uncleanness*—In act, word, or thought ;
inordinate affection—Every passion which does not flow from and lead to the
love of God ; *evil desire*—The desire of the flesh, the desire of the eye, and the
pride of life ; *covetousness*—according to the derivation of the word, means
the desire of having more, or of any thing independent of God ; *which is idolatry*
—Properly and directly : for it is giving the heart to a creature.
   6. *For which*—Though the heathens lightly regarded them.
   7. *Living*—denotes the inward principle ; *walking*—the outward acts.
   8. *Wrath*—is lasting anger ; *filthy discourse*—And was there need to warn
even these saints of God against so gross and palpable a sin as this ?   O what is
man till perfect love casts out both fear and sin !
   10. *In knowledge*—The knowledge of God, his will, his word.
   11. *Where*—In which case, it matters not what a man is externally, whether
Jew or Gentile, circumcised or uncircumcised ; *barbarian*, void of all the advantages of education ; yea, *Scythian*, of all barbarians most barbarous : but
Christ is in all that are thus renewed, and is all things in them, and to them.
   12. All who are thus renewed are elected of God, holy, and therefore the more
beloved of him.   Holiness is the proof of their election, and God's superior love
of their holiness.
   13. *Forbearing one another*—If any thing is now wrong, *and forgiving one another*—What is past.
   14. The love of God contains the whole of Christian perfection, and connects
all the parts of it together.

16 also ye have been called in one body : and be ye thankful. Let
the word of Christ dwell in you richly in all wisdom, teaching and
admonishing one another in psalms, and hymns, and spiritual songs,
17 singing with grace in your heart unto the Lord. And whatsoever
ye do in word or deed, *do* all in the name of the Lord Jesus, giving
thanks unto God and the Father through him.
18   * Wives, submit yourselves to your own husbands (as is fit) in
19 the Lord. Husbands, love. your wives, and be not bitter against
20 them. Children, obey' your parents in all things : for this is well
21 pleasing to the Lord. Fathers, provoke not your children to anger,
22 lest they be discouraged. Servants, obey in all things your masters according to the flesh ; not with eye service as men pleasers,
23 but in singleness of heart fearing God. And whatsoever ye do, do
24 it heartily, as to the Lord, and not to men : Knowing that of the
Lord ye shall receive the reward of the inheritance ; for ye receive
25 the Lord Christ. But he that doth wrong shall receive for the
IV. wrong he hath done ; and there is no respect of persons. Masters, render unto your servants that which is just and equitable,
knowing that ye also have a Master in heaven.
2   Continue in prayer, and watch therein with thanksgiving: Withal,
3 praying likewise for us, that God would open to us a door of utterance, to speak the mystery of Christ : for which I am also in
4 bonds : That I may make it manifest, as I ought to speak. Walk
5 in wisdom toward them that are without, redeeming the time. Let
6 your speech *be* always with grace, seasoned with salt, that ye may
know how ye ought to answer every one.

15. *And* then *the peace of God shall rule in your hearts*—Shall sway every temper, affection, thought, as the reward (so the Greek word implies) of your preceding love and obedience.
16. *Let the word of Christ*—So the apostle calls the whole Scripture, and thereby asserts the Divinity of his Master, *dwell*—Not make a short stay or an occa-
sional visit, but take up its stated residence, *richly*—In the largest measure, and
with the greatest efficacy, so as to fill and govern the whole soul.
17. *In the name*—In the power and spirit of the Lord Jesus, *giving thanks unto
God*—The Holy Ghost, *and the Father through him*—Christ.
18. *Wives, submit*—Or be subject *to*. It is properly a military term, alluding
to that entire submission that soldiers pay to their general.
19. *Be not bitter*—(Which may be without any appearance of anger) either in
word or spirit.
21. *Lest they be discouraged*—Which may occasion their turning either desperate or stupid.
22. *Eye service*—Being more diligent under their eye than at other times,
singleness of heart—A simple intention of doing right, without looking any farther, *fearing God*—That is, acting from this principle.
23. *Heartily*—Cheerfully, diligently. Men pleasers are soon dejected and
made angry ; the single hearted are never displeased or disappointed, because
they have another aim, which the good or evil treatment of those they serve cannot disappoint.
IV. 1. *Just*—According to your contract ; *equitable*—Even beyond the letter
of your contract.
3. *That God would open to us a door of utterance*—That is, give us utterance,
that we may open our mouth boldly, Eph. vi, 19, and give us an opportunity of
speaking so that none may be able to hinder.
6. *Let your speech be always with grace*—Seasoned with the grace of God, as
flesh is with salt.

* Ephesians v, 22, &c.

7   All my concerns will Tychicus declare to you, a beloved brother
8 and a faithful minister and fellow servant in the Lord : Whom I
    have sent to you for this very thing, that he might know your state
9 and comfort your hearts, With Onesimus, a faithful and beloved
    brother, who is one of you : they will make known to you all things
    that *are done* here.
10   Aristarchus, my fellow prisoner, saluteth you, and Marcus, sis-
    ter's son to Barnabas, (touching whom ye have received directions :
11 if he come to you, receive him :) And Jesus, called Justus, who
    are of the circumcision : these *are* the only fellow workers unto
12 the kingdom of God, who have been a comfort to me.   Epaphras,
    who is one of you, a servant of Christ, saluteth you, always labour-
    ing fervently for you in prayers, that ye may stand perfect, and
13 filled with all the will of God.   For I bear him witness, that he
    hath a great zeal for you, and for them in Laodicea, and for them
14 in Hierapolis.   Luke, the beloved physician, and Demas, salute
15 you.   Salute the brethren at Laodicea, and Nymphas, and the
16 Church in his house.   And when this epistle hath been read among
    you, cause it to be read also in the Church of the Laodiceans, and
17 that ye likewise read the epistle from Laodicea.   And say to Ar-
    chippus, Take heed that thou fulfil the ministry which thou hast
18 received in the Lord.   The salutation of Paul by my own hand.
    Be mindful of my bonds.   Grace *be* with you.

---

10. *Aristarchus, my fellow prisoner*—Such was Epaphras likewise for a time,
Philemon, ver. 23.   *Ye have received directions*—Namely, by Tychicus, bringing
.this letter.   The ancients adapted their language to the time of reading the letter ; not (as we do) to the time when it was written.   It is not improbable, they
might have scrupled to receive him, without this fresh direction, after he had left
St. Paul, and departed from the work.
    11. *These*—Three, Aristarchus, Marcus, and Justus, *of* all *the circumcision*,
that is, of all my Jewish fellow labourers, *who are the only fellow workers unto
the kingdom of God*—That is, in preaching the Gospel, *who have been a comfort
to me*—What then can we expect ?   That all our fellow workers should be a
comfort to us ?
    12. *Perfect*—Endued with every Christian grace, *filled*—As no longer being
babes, but grown up to the measure of the stature of Christ, being full of his
light, grace, wisdom, holiness.
    14. *Luke, the physician*—Such he had been at least, if he was not then.
    15. *Nymphas*—Probably an eminent Christian at Laodicea.
    16. *The epistle from Laodicea*—Not to Laodicea.   Perhaps some letter had
been written to St. Paul from thence.
    17. *And say to Archippus*—One of the pastors of that Church, *take heed*—It is
the duty of the flock to try them that say they are apostles, to reject the false,
and to warn, as well as to receive the real ; *the ministry*—Not a lordship, but a
service, a laborious and painful work : an obligation to do and suffer all things ;
to be the least and the servant of all ; *in the Lord*—Christ ; by whom and for
whose sake we receive the various gifts of the Holy Spirit.

NOTES

ON

ST. PAUL'S FIRST EPISTLE TO THE THESSALONIANS

———

This is the first of all the epistles which St. Paul wrote. Thessalonica was one of the chief cities of Macedonia. Hither St. Paul went after the persecution at Philippi. But he had not preached here long, before the unbelieving Jews raised a tumult against him, and Sylvanus, and Timotheus. On this, the brethren sent them away to Berea. Thence St. Paul went by sea to Athens, and sent for Sylvanus and Timotheus to come speedily to him. But being in fear lest the Thessalonian converts should be moved from their steadfastness, after a short time he sends Timotheus to them to know the state of their Church. Timotheus returning, found the apostle at Corinth; from whence he sent them this epistle, about a year after he had been at Thessalonica.

THE PARTS OF IT ARE THESE:

I. The inscription . . . . Chap. i, 1
II. He celebrates the grace of God toward them 2–10
Mentions the sincerity of himself and his fellow labourers ; and ii, 1–12
The teachableness of the Thessalonians 13–16
III. He declares,
1. His desire 17–20
2. His care . . . . iii, 1–5
3. His joy and prayer for them 6–13
IV. He exhorts them to grow,
1. In holiness . . . . iv, 1–8
2. In brotherly love with industry 9–12
V. He teaches and exhorts,
1. Concerning them that sleep 13–18
2. Concerning the times . . . . v, 1–11
VI. He adds miscellany exhortations 12–24
VII. The conclusion 25–28

———

I. THESSALONIANS.

———

1   PAUL, and Sylvanus, and Timotheus, to the Church of the Thessalonians in God the Father and the Lord Jesus Christ, Grace *be* unto you and peace from God our Father, and the Lord Jesus Christ.

2   We give thanks to God always for you all (making mention of

---

Ver. 1. *Paul*—In this epistle St. Paul neither uses the title of an apostle, nor any other, as writing to pious and simple-hearted men, with the utmost familiarity. There is a peculiar sweetness in this epistle, unmixed with any sharpness or reproof: those evils which the apostles afterward reproved, having not yet crept into the Church.

3. *Remembering in the sight of God*—That is, praising him for it : *your work*

3 you in our prayers, Remembering without ceasing your work of
   faith, and labour of love, and patience of hope in our Lord Jesus
4 Christ, in the sight of our God and Father:) Knowing, beloved
5 brethren, your election of God.   For our Gospel came not to you
   in word only, but also with power, and with the Holy Ghost, and
   with much assurance ; as ye know what manner of men we were
6 among you, for your sake.   And ye became imitators of us and
   of the Lord, having received the word in much affliction, with
7 joy of the Holy Ghost.   So that ye became examples to all that
8 believed in Macedonia and Achaia.   For from you the word of
   the Lord sounded forth, not only in Macedonia and Achaia, but
   your faith toward God went abroad in every place also, so that we
9 need not speak any thing.   For they themselves declare concern
   ing us what manner of entrance to you we had, and how ye
10 turned from idols to God, to serve the living and true God, And
   to wait for his Son from heaven, whom he hath raised from the
   dead, *even* Jesus, who delivereth us from the wrath to come.
II.   For yourselves, brethren, know our entrance to you, that it
2 was not in vain : But even after we had suffered before, and had
   been shamefully treated at Philippi, as ye know, we were bold
   through our God to speak to you the Gospel of God with much
3 contention.   For our exhortation *is* not of deceit, nor of unclean-
4 ness, nor in guile.   But as we have been approved of God to be

of faith—Your active, ever-working faith ; *and labour of love*—Love continually
labouring for the bodies or souls of men.   They who do not thus labour, do not
love.   Faith works, love labours, hope patiently suffers all things.

4. Knowing your election (which is through faith) by these plain proofs.

5. *With power*—Piercing the very heart with a sense of sin, and deeply convincing you of your want of a Saviour from guilt, misery, and eternal ruin ;
with the Holy Ghost—Bearing an outward testimony by miracles to the truth of
what we preached, and you felt : also by his descent through laying on of hands;
with much assurance—Literally, with full assurance, and much of it : the Spirit
bearing witness by spreading the love of God abroad in your hearts, which is the
highest testimony that can be given.   And these signs, if not the miraculous gifts,
always attend the preaching of the Gospel, unless it be in vain ; neither are the
extraordinary operations of the Holy Ghost ever wholly withheld where the Gos
pel is preached with power, and men are alive to God : *for your sake*—Seeking
your advantage, not our own.

6. Though *in much affliction*, yet *with* much *joy.*

8. *For from you the word sounded forth*—(Thessalonica being a city of great
commerce,) being echoed, as it were, from you.   And your conversation was
divulged far beyond Macedonia and Achaia ; *so that we need not speak any thing*
—Concerning it.

9. *For they themselves*—The people, wherever we come.

10. *Whom he hath raised from the dead*—In proof of his future coming to judg.
ment ; *who delivereth us*—He hath redeemed us once ; he delivers us continually;
and will deliver all that believe, *from the wrath*, the eternal vengeance which will
then come upon the ungodly.

II. What was proposed, chap. i, 5, 6, is now more largely treated of; concerning Paul and his fellow labourers, ver. 1–12; concerning the Thessalonians,
ver. 13–16.

2. *We had suffered*—In several places; *we are bold*—Notwithstanding, *with
much contention*—Notwithstanding both inward and outward conflicts of all
kinds.

3. *For our exhortation*—That is, our preaching.   A part is put for the whole :
is not, at any time, *of deceit*—We preach not a lie, but the truth of God ; *nor of
uncleanness*—With any unholy or selfish view.   This expression is not always ap.

entrusted with the Gospel, so we speak, not as pleasing men, but
5 God, who trieth our hearts. For neither at any time used we flattering words, as ye know, nor a cloak of covetousness : God
6 is witness : Nor sought we glory of men, neither from you, nor
from others, when we might have been burdensome, as the apos-
7 tles of Christ. But we were gentle in the midst of you, even as
8 a nurse cherisheth her own children. So loving you tenderly,
we were ready to impart to you not only the Gospel of God, but
9 our own souls also, because ye were dear to us. For ye remember, brethren, our labour and toil : working night and day, that
we might not burden any of you, we preached to you the Gospel
10 of God. Ye *are* witnesses, and God, how holily, and justly, and
11 unblamably we behaved among you that believe ; As ye know
how we exhorted and comforted every one of you, as a father his
12 own children, And charged you to walk worthy of God, who hath
13 called you to his kingdom and glory. For this cause also thank
we God without ceasing, *even* because when ye received the word
of God which ye heard from us, ye received *it* not *as* the word of
men, but (as it is in truth) the word of God, who likewise effectually
14 worketh in you that believe. For ye, brethren, became followers
of the Churches of God in Christ Jesus, which are in Judea ; for
ye also suffered the same things from your own countrymen, as
15 they likewise from the Jews : Who both killed the Lord Jesus
and their own prophets, and have persecuted us ; and they please
16 not God, and are contrary to all men ; Forbidding us to speak to
the Gentiles, that they may be saved ; to fill up their sins always :
but wrath is come upon them to the uttermost.

---

propriated to lust, although it is sometimes emphatically applied thereto ; *nor in
guile*—But with great plainness of speech.   .

5. *Flattering words*—This ye know ; *nor a cloak of covetousness*—Of this
God is witness. He calls men to witness an open fact : God the secret inten-
tions of the heart. In a point of a mixed nature, ver. 10, he appeals both to
God and man.

6. *Nor from others*—Who would have honoured us more if we had *been burdensome*—That is, taken state upon ourselves.

7. *But we were gentle*—Mild, tender, *in the midst of you*—Like a hen surrounded with her young ; *even as a nurse cherisheth her own children*—The
offspring of her own womb.

8. *To impart our own souls*—To lay down our lives for your sake.

10. *Holily*—In the things of God ; *justly*—With regard to men ; *unblamably*—
In respect of ourselves, *among you that believe*—Who were the constant observers
of our behaviour.

11. By *exhorting*, we are moved to do a thing willingly ; by *comforting*, to do it
joyfully ; by *charging*, to do it carefully.

12. *To his kingdom* here, and *glory* hereafter

14. *Ye suffered the same things*—The same fruit, the same afflictions, and the
same experience, at all times, and in all places, are an excellent criterion of
evangelical truth ; *as they from the Jews*—Their countrymen.

15. *Us*—Apostles and preachers of the Gospel. *They please not God*—Nor
are they even careful to please him, notwithstanding their fair professions : *and
are contrary to all men*—Are common enemies of all mankind ; not only by their
continual seditions and insurrections, and by their utter contempt of all other
nations ; but in particular by their endeavouring to hinder their hearing or
receiving the Gospel.

16. *To fill up*—The measure of, *their sins always*—As they have ever done :
but—The vengeance of God, *is come upon them*—Hath overtaken them unawares,

17   But we, brethren, being taken from you for a short time in presence, not in heart, laboured with great desire the more abundantly
18 to see your face. Wherefore we would have come to you (even I
19 Paul) once and again, but Satan hindered us. For what is our
20 hope, or joy, or crown of rejoicing? Are not ye also before our
Lord Jesus at his appearing? For ye are our glory and joy.
III.   Therefore, when we could bear no longer, we thought good to
2 be left at Athens alone, And sent Timotheus our brother and a
minister of God, and our fellow worker in the Gospel of Christ, to
3 establish you and to comfort you concerning your faith, That no
one might be moved by these afflictions; for ye yourselves know
4 that we are appointed hereto: For when we were with you we told
you before we should be afflicted; as it came to pass, and ye
5 know. Therefore when I could bear no longer, I sent to know
your faith, lest by any means the tempter should have tempted
6 you, and our labour be in vain. But now when Timotheus was
come to us from you, and had brought us the good tidings of your
faith and love, and that ye have a good remembrance of us always,
7 longing to see us, as we also *to see* you: Therefore, brethren, we
were comforted over you in all our affliction and distress by your
8 faith. For now we live, if ye stand fast in the Lord. For what
9 thanks can we render to God for you, for all the joy wherewith we
10 rejoice for your sake before our God? Night and day praying
exceedingly, that we may see your face, and perfect that which is
11 wanting in your faith. Now our God and Father himself, and our
12 Lord Jesus, direct our way unto you. And the Lord make you to
increase and abound in love toward one another, and toward all
13 men, as we also *do* toward you. That he may establish your

---

while they were seeking to destroy others, and will speedily complete their
destruction.

17. In this verse we have a remarkable instance, not so much of the transient
affections of holy grief, desire, or joy, as of that abiding tenderness, that loving
temper, which is so apparent in all St. Paul's writings toward those he styles his
children in the faith. This is the more carefully to be observed, because the *passions* occasionally exercising themselves, and flowing like a torrent, in the apostle,
are observable to every reader; whereas it requires a nicer attention to discern
those calm standing tempers, that fixed posture of his soul, from whence the others
only flow out, and which more peculiarly distinguish his character.

18. *Satan*—By those persecuting Jews, Acts xvii, 13.

19. *Ye also*—As well as our other children.

III. 1. *We*—*Paul* and *Sylvanus, could bear no longer*—Our desire and fear
for you.

3. *We are appointed hereto*—Are, in every respect, laid in a fit posture for it,
by the very design and contrivance of God himself, for the trial and increase of
our faith, and all other graces. He gives riches to the world; but stores up his
treasure of wholesome afflictions for his children

6. *But now when Timotheus was come to us from you*—Immediately after
his return St. Paul wrote; while his joy was fresh, and his tenderness at
the height.

8. *Now we live*—Indeed. We enjoy life; so great is our affection for you.

10. *And perfect that which is wanting in your faith*—So St. Paul did not know
that they who are once upon the Rock no longer need to be taught by man!

11. *Direct our way*—This prayer is addressed to Christ as well as to the
Father.

13. *With all his*—Christ's, *saints*—Both angels and men.

hearts unblamable in holiness, (before our God and Father, at the appearing of our Lord Jesus Christ,) with all his saints.

IV. It remaineth, then, brethren, that we beseech and exhort you by the Lord Jesus, as ye have received of us how ye ought to walk and to please God, that ye abound *therein* more and more.
2 For ye know what commandments we gave you by the Lord
3 Jesus. For this is the will of God, *even* your sanctification, that
4 ye abstain from fornication ; That every one of you know *how*
5 to possess his vessel in sanctification and honour ; Not in passion-
6 ate desire, as the Gentiles who know not God. That *none* circum-
vent or defraud his brother in this matter, because the Lord is an avenger of all these things, as we have also told you before and
7 testified. For God hath not called us to uncleanness, but to ho-
8 liness. He therefore that despiseth, despiseth not man, but God : who hath also given you his Holy Spirit.
9   Touching brotherly love, we need not write to you : for ye
10 yourselves are taught of God to love one another. And indeed ye do it toward all the brethren that are in all Macedonia ; but we
11 exhort you, brethren, that ye increase more and more, And that ye study to be quiet and do your own business, and to work with your
12 hands, as we commanded you ; That ye may walk decently to-ward them that are without, and may want nothing.
13   Now we would not have you ignorant, brethren, concerning them that are asleep, that ye sorrow not even as others who have no hope.

IV. 1. *More and more*—It is not enough to have faith, even so as to please God, unless we abound more and more therein.
3. *Sanctification*—Entire holiness of heart and life : particular branches of it are subjoined ; *that ye abstain from fornication*—A beautiful transition from sanctification to a single branch of the contrary. And this shows that nothing is so seemingly distant, or below our thoughts, but we have need to guard against it.
4. *That every one know*—For this requires knowledge as well as chastity, *to possess his vessel*—His wife, *in sanctification and honour*—So as neither to dishonour God or himself, nor to obstruct, but farther holiness ; remembering marriage is not designed to inflame, but to conquer natural desires.
5. *Not in passionate desire*—Which had no place in man when in a state of innocence. *Who know not God*—And so may naturally seek happiness in a creature. What seemingly accidental words slide in ; and yet how fine, and how vastly important !
6. *In this matter*—By violating his bed. The things forbidden here are three : fornication, ver. 3 ; the passion of desire, or inordinate affection in the married state, ver. 5 ; and the breach of the marriage contract.
8. *He that despiseth*—The commandments we gave, *despiseth God*—Himself, *who hath also given you his Holy Spirit*—To convince you of the truth, and enable you to be holy. What naked majesty of words ! how oratorical, and yet with what great simplicity ! a simplicity that does not impair, but improve the understanding to the utmost : that, like the rays of heat through a glass, collects all the powers of reason into one orderly point, from being scattered abroad in utter confusion.
9. *We need not write*—Largely ; *for ye are taught of God*—By his Spirit.
11. *That ye study*—Literally, that ye be ambitious ; an ambition worthy a Christian ; *to work with your hands*—Not a needless caution ; for temporal concerns are a cross to them who are newly filled with the love of God.
12. *Decently*—That they may have no pretence to say, (but they will say it still,) " This religion makes men idle, and brings them to beggary ;" *and many want nothing*—Needful for life and godliness. What Christian desires more ?
13. *Now*—Herein the efficacy of Christianity greatly appears, that it neither

14 For if we believe that Jesus died and rose again, so will God bring
15 with him those also that sleep in Jesus. For this we say unto
you by the word of the Lord, that we who are alive, who are left
to the appearing of the Lord, shall not prevent them that are asleep.
16 For the Lord himself shall descend from heaven, with a shout, with
the voice of an archangel, and with the trumpet of God; and the
17 dead in Christ shall rise first. Then we who are alive, vho are
left, shall be caught up together with them in clouds to meet the
Lord in the air; so shall we be ever with the Lord. Wherefore
comfort one another with these words.

V.   But of the times and seasons, brethren, ye have no need that I
2 write to you. For ye yourselves know perfectly, that the day of
3 the Lord so cometh as a thief in the night. When they say, Peace
and safety, then sudden destruction cometh upon them, as travail
4 upon a woman with child, and they shall not escape. But ye, brethren, are not in darkness, that that day should overtake you as a
5 thief. Ye are all children of the light, and children of the day: we
6 are not *children* of the night nor of darkness. Therefore let us
7 not sleep as the others, but let us awake and keep awake. For they
that sleep sleep in the night, and they that are drunken are drunken
8 in the night. But let us who are of the day keep awake, having
put on the breastplate of faith and love, and for a helmet the
9 hope of salvation. For God hath not appointed us to wrath, but
10 to obtain salvation by our Lord Jesus Christ, Who died for us,
that whether we wake or sleep, we may live together with him.
11 Wherefore comfort one another and edify one another, as also
ye do.
12   Now we beseech you, brethren, to know them that labour among

takes away, nor embitters, but sweetly tempers that most refined of all affections,
our desire of, or love to, the dead.

14. *So*—As God raised him; *with him*—With their living head.

15. *By the word of the Lord*—By a particular revelation; *we who are left*—
This intimates the fewness of those who will be then alive, compared to the multitude of the dead. Believers of all ages and nations make up as it were one
body: in consideration of which, the believers of that age might put themselves
in the place, and speak in the person of them, who were to live till the coming
of the Lord. Not that St. Paul hereby asserted (though some seem to have
imagined so) that the day of the Lord was at hand.

16. *With a shout*—Properly a proclamation made to a great multitude: above
this is the voice of an archangel; above both, the trumpet of God! The voice
of God, somewhat analogous to the sound of a trumpet.

17. *Together*—In the same moment; *in the air*—The wicked will remair
beneath, while the righteous, being absolved, shall be assessors with their Lorc
in the judgment; *with the Lord*—In heaven.

V. 1. *But of the* precise *times*, when this shall be.

2. *For* this in general ye do know: that ye can and need know no more.

3. *When they*—The men of the world, say.

4. *Ye are not in darkness*—Sleeping secure in sin.

6. *Awake, and keep awake*—Being awakened, let us have all our spiritua
senses about us.

7. *They* usually *sleep and are drunken in the night*—These things do not lov.
the light.

9. *God hath not appointed us to wrath*—As he hath the obstinately impeniten'.

10. *Whether we wake or sleep*—Be alive or dead, at his coming.

12. *Know them that*, 1. *labour among you;* 2. *are over you in the Lord;* 3.
admonish you. *Know*—See; mark; take knowledge of them and their work.

13 you, and are over you in the Lord, and admonish you. And to
esteem them very highly in love for their works' sake, *and* be at
14 peace among yourselves. And we exhort you, brethren, warn the
disorderly, comfort the feeble minded, support the weak, be long
15 suffering toward all men. See that none render to any man evil
for evil, but ever follow that which is good, both to one another
16, 17 and to all men. Rejoice evermore: Pray without ceasing:
18 In every thing give thanks; for this is the will of God in Christ
19, 20 Jesus concerning you. Quench not the Spirit Despise not
21 prophesyings. Prove all things; hold fast that which is good.
22, 23 Abstain from all appearance of evil. And the God of peace

Sometimes the same person may both labour, that is, preach, be over, or govern, and admonish the flock by particular application to each: sometimes two or more different persons, according as God variously dispenses his gifts. But O! what a misery is it, when a man undertakes this whole work, without either gifts or grace for any part of it! Why then will he undertake it? For pay? What! will he sell both his own soul, and all the souls of the flock? What words can describe such a wretch as this! And yet even this may be an honourable man.

13. *Esteem them very highly*—Literally, *more than abundantly, in love*—The inexpressible sympathy there is between true pastors and their flock, is intimated not only here, but also in divers other places of this epistle, see chap. ii, 7, 8; *for their works' sake*—The principal ground of their vast regard for them. But how are we to esteem them who do not work at all?

14. *Warn the disorderly*—Them that stand, as it were, out of their rank, in the spiritual warfare: some such were even in that Church; *the feeble minded*—Literally, them of little soul, such as have no spiritual courage.

15. *See that none*—Watch over both yourselves and each other; *follow that which is good*—Do it resolutely and perseveringly.

16. *Rejoice evermore*—In uninterrupted happiness in God; *pray without ceasing*—Which is the fruit of always rejoicing in the Lord; *in every thing give thanks*—Which is the fruit of both the former. This is Christian perfection. Farther than this we cannot go; and we need not stop short of it. Our Lord has purchased joy as well as righteousness for us. It is the very design of the Gospel, that, being saved from guilt, we should be happy in the love of Christ. Prayer may be said to be the breath of our spiritual life. He that lives cannot possibly cease breathing. So much as we really enjoy of the presence of God, so much prayer and praise do we offer up without ceasing; else our rejoicing is but delusion. Thanksgiving is inseparable from true prayer. It is almost essentially connected with it. He that always prays, is ever giving praise, whether in ease or pain; both for prosperity and for the greatest adversity. He blesses God for all things, looks on them as coming from him, and receives them only for his sake: not choosing nor refusing, liking nor disliking any thing, but only as it is agreeable or disagreeable to his perfect will.

18. *For this*—That you should thus rejoice, pray, give thanks; *is the will of God*—Always good, always pointing at our salvation.

19. *Quench not the Spirit*—Wherever it is, it burns, it flames in holy love, in joy, prayer, thanksgiving. O quench it not, damp it not, in yourself or others, either by neglecting to do good, or by doing evil.

20. *Despise not prophesyings*—That is, preaching; for the apostle is not here speaking of extraordinary gifts. It seems, one means of grace is put for all. And whoever despises any of these, under whatever pretence, will surely (though perhaps gradually and insensibly) quench the Spirit.

21. Meantime, *prove all things*—Which any preacher recommends. (He speaks of practice, not of doctrines.) Try every advice by the touchstone of Scripture, and *hold fast that which is good*—Zealously, resolutely, diligently, practise it, in spite of all opposition. Observe, those who *heap to themselves teachers having itching ears,* under pretence of *proving all things,* have no countenance or excuse from this scripture.

22. And be equally zealous and careful to *abstain from all appearance of evil.*

himself sanctify you wholly : and may the whole of you, the spirit,
and the soul, and the body, be preserved blameless unto the appear-
24 ing of our Lord Jesus Christ. Faithful is he that calleth you, who
25, 26 also will do *it*. Brethren, pray for us. Salute all the brethren
27 with a holy kiss. I adjure you by the Lord, that this epistle be
28 read to all the holy brethren. The grace of our Lord Jesus Christ
be with you. Amen.

---

23. *And may the God of peace sanctify you*—By the peace he works in you,
which is a great means of sanctification ; *wholly*—The word signifies wholly and
perfectly ; every part, and all that concerns you ; all that is of, or about you ;
and may the whole of you, the spirit, and the soul, and the body—Just before he
said *you*, now he denominates them from their spiritual state, the spirit, Gal. vi,
8 ; wishing that it may be preserved whole and entire ; then from their natural
state, the soul and the body, (for these two make up the whole nature of man,
Matt. x, 28,) wishing it may be preserved blameless till the coming of Christ.
To explain this a little farther ; of the three here mentioned, only the two last
are the natural, constituent parts of man. The first is adventitious, and the
supernatural gift of God, to be found in Christians only. That man cannot possibly consist of three parts appears hence. The soul is either matter or not
matter ; there is no medium. But if it is matter, it is part of the body ; if not
matter, it coincides with the spirit.

24. *Who also will do it*—Unless you quench the Spirit.

27. *I charge you by the Lord*—Christ, to whom proper Divine worship is here
paid ; *that this epistle*—The first he wrote ; *be read to all the brethren*—That is,
in all the Churches. They might have concealed it out of modesty, had not this
been so solemnly enjoined. But what Paul commands under so strong an adju-
ration, Rome forbids under pain of excommunication.

NOTES

ON

ST. PAUL'S SECOND EPISTLE TO THE THESSALONIANS.

THIS epistle seems to have been written soon after the former, chiefly on occasion of some things therein which had been misunderstood. Herein he, 1. Congratulates their constancy in the faith, and exhorts them to advance daily in grace and wisdom. 2. Reforms their mistake concerning the coming of our Lord. And, 3. Recommends several Christian duties.

THE PARTS OF IT ARE FIVE:

II. THESSALONIANS.

---

1 PAUL, and Sylvanus, and Timotheus, to the Church of the Thes
2 salonians in God our Father, and the Lord Jesus Christ; Grace
be unto you and peace from God our Father, and from our Lord
Jesus Christ.
3 We are bound to thank God always for you, brethren, as it is
meet, because your faith groweth exceedingly, and the love of
4 every one of you toward each other aboundeth. So that we ourselves glory of you in the Churches of God, for your patience and
faith in all your persecutions and sufferings which ye endure:
5 A manfest token of the righteous judgment of God, that ye may
be accounted worthy of the kingdom of God; for which ye also
6 suffer. Seeing *it is* a righteous thing with God to recompense
7 affliction to them that afflict you: And to you that are afflicted rest

---

Verse 3. It is highly observable that the apostle wraps up his praise of men in praise to God; giving him the glory. *Your faith groweth*—Probably he had heard from them since his sending the former letter. *Aboundeth*—Like water that overflows its banks, and yet increaseth still.

4. *Which ye endure*—That ye may be accounted worthy of the kingdom.

5. *A manifest token*—This is treated of in the sixth and following verses.

6. *It is a righteous thing with God*—(However men may judge) to transfer the pressure from you to them. And it is remarkable that about this time, at the passover, the Jews raising a tumult, a great number, some say thirty thousand of them, were slain. St. Paul seems to allude to this beginning of sorrows, 1 Thess. ii, 6, which did not end but with their destruction.

with us, at the revelation of the Lord Jesus from heaven with h‧s
8 mighty angels, In flaming fire, taking vengeance on them that
know not God, and who obey not the Gospel of our Lord Jesus.
9 Who shall be punished with everlasting destruction from the pre-
10 sence of the Lord, and from the glory of his power. When he
shall come to be glorified in his saints, and to be admired in all
that believe (for our testimony was believed among you) in that
11 day. To this end we pray always for you, that our God would
make you worthy of *this* calling, and fulfil *in you* all the good plea-
12 sure of *his* goodness, and the work of faith with power ; That the
name of our Lord Jesus may be glorified in you, and ye in him,
according to the grace of our God and the Lord Jesus Christ.
II.   Now I beseech you, brethren, concerning the appearing of our
2 Lord Jesus Christ, and our gathering together unto him, That ye
be not soon shaken in mind or terrified, neither by spirit, nor by
word, nor by letter, as from us, as if the day of the Lord were at
3 hand. Let no man deceive you by any means, for *that day shall
not come*, unless the falling away come first, and the man of sin be
4 revealed, the son of perdition, Who opposeth and exalteth himself
above all that is called God, or that is worshipped, so that he sitteth in the temple of God as God, declaring himself that he is

---

8. *Taking vengeance*—Does God barely permit this ? Or, as the Lord onct
rained brimstone and fire from the Lord, out of heaven, Gen. xix, 24, does a
fiery stream go forth from him for ever ? *Who know not God*—(The root of all
wickedness and misery) who remain in heathen ignorance ; *and who obey not*—
This refers chiefly to the Jews, who had heard the Gospel.

9. *From the glory of his power*—Tremble, ye stout hearted ! *Everlasting destruction*—As there can be no end of their sins, (the same enmity against God
continuing,) so neither of their punishment : sin and its punishment running
parallel throughout eternity itself. They must of necessity therefore be cut off
from all good and all possibility of it ; *from the presence of the Lord*—Wherein
chiefly consists the salvation of the righteous. What unspeakable punishment is
implied even in falling short of this, supposing that nothing more were implied
in his taking vengeance !

10. *To be glorified in his saints*—For the wonderful glory of Christ shall shine
in them.

11. *All the good pleasure of his goodness*—Which is no less than perfect holiness.

12. *That the name*—The love and power, *of our Lord may be glorified*—Gloriously displayed in you.

II. 1. *Our gathering together to him*—In the clouds,

2. *Be not shaken in mind*—In judgment, *or terrified*—As those easily are who
are immoderately fond of knowing future things ; neither by any pretended revelation from the Spirit, nor by pretence of any word spoken by me.

3. *Unless the falling away*—From the pure faith of the Gospel, *come first*—
This began even in the apostolic age. But *the man of sin, the son of perdition*—
Eminently so called, is not yet come. However, in many respects, the pope has
an indisputable claim to those titles. He is, in an emphatical sense, the man of
sin, as he increases all manner of sin above measure. And he is too properly
styled, The son of perdition, as he has caused the death of numberless multitudes,
both of his opposers and followers, destroyed innumerable souls, and will himself perish everlastingly. He it is that opposeth himself to the emperor, once his
rightful sovereign ; and that *exalteth himself above all that is called God, or that
is worshipped*—Commanding angels, and putting kings under his feet, both of
whom are called gods in Scripture : claiming the highest power, the highest
honour ; suffering himself not once only to be styled God or vice-god. Indeed
no less is implied in his ordinary title, Most holy lord or Most holy father. So

5 God. Remember ye not, that I told you these things, when I was
6 *yet* with you? And now ye know that which restraineth, that he
7 may be revealed in his time. For the mystery of iniquity already
worketh; only he that restraineth *will restrain*, till he be taken out
8 of the way. And then will that wicked one be revealed, whom the
Lord will consume with the Spirit of his mouth, and destroy with
9 the brightness of his appearing : Whose appearing is after the
mighty working of Satan, with all power and signs, and lying won-
10 ders, And with all deceivableness of unrighteousness in them that
perish, because they received not the love of the truth, that they
11 might be saved. And therefore God shall send them strong delu-
12 sion, so that they shall believe the lie, That they all may be condemned, who believed not the truth, but had pleasure in unright-
13 eousness. But we ought to give thanks to God always for you,
brethren, beloved of the Lord, because God hath from the beginning chosen you to salvation, through sanctification of the Spirit
14 and belief of the truth : To which he hath called you by our Gos-
15 pel, to the obtaining of the glory of our Lord Jesus Christ. Therefore, brethren, stand fast, and hold the traditions which ye have
16 been taught, whether by word, or by our epistle. Now our Lord
Jesus Christ himself, and God, even our Father, who hath loved

---

that he sitteth—Enthroned, *in the temple of God*—Mentioned Rev. xi, 1, *declaring himself that he is God*—Claiming the prerogatives which belong to God alone.

6. *And now ye know*—By what I told you when I was with you; *that which restraineth*—The power of the Roman emperors, when this is taken away, the wicked one will be revealed. *In his time*—His appointed season, and not before.

7. He will surely be revealed; *for the mystery*—The deep secret power of *iniquity*—Just opposite to the power of godliness, already worketh. It began with the love of honour, and the desire of power; and it is completed in the entire subversion of the Gospel of Christ. This mystery of iniquity is not wholly confined to the Romish Church, but extends itself to others also. It seems to consist of, 1. Human inventions added to the written word. 2. Mere outside perform- ances put in the room of faith and love. 3. Other mediators beside the man Christ Jesus. The two last branches, together with idolatry and bloodshed, are the direct consequence of the former ; namely, the adding to the word of God. *Already worketh*—In the Church. *Only he that restraineth*—That is, the potentate who successively has Rome in his power. The emperors, heathen or Christian : the kings, Goths or Lombards ; the Carolingian or German emperors.

8. *And then*—When every prince and power that restrains is taken away, *will that wicked one*—Emphatically so called, *be revealed : whom the Lord will* soon *consume with the Spirit of his mouth*—His immediate power, *and destroy*—With the very first appearance of his glory.

10. *Because they received not the love of the truth*—Therefore God suffered them to fall into that strong delusion.

11. *Therefore God shall send them*—That is, judicially permit to come upon them, *strong delusion.*

12. *That they all may be condemned*—That is, the consequence of which will be, that they all will be condemned who believed not the truth, *but had pleasure in unrighteousness*—That is, who believed not the truth, because they loved sin.

13. *God hath from the beginning*—Of your hearing the Gospel, *chosen you to salvation*—Taken you out of the world, and placed you in the way to glory.

14. *To which*—Faith and holiness, *he hath called you by our Gospel*—That which we preached, accompanied by the power of his Spirit.

15. *Hold*—Without adding to, or diminishing from, *the traditions which ye have been taught*—The truths which I have delivered to you : *whether by word or by our epistle*—He preached before he wrote. And he had written concerning this, in his former epistle.

us and given us everlasting consolation and good hope througl
17 grace, Comfort your hearts and stablish you in every good word
and work.
III.   Finally, brethren, pray for us, that the word of the Lord may run
2 and be glorified, even as among you: And that we may be delivered from unreasonable and wicked men: for all men have not faith
3 But the Lord is faithful, who will stablish and guard you from the
4 evil one.   And we trust in the Lord concerning you, that ye both
5 do and will do the things which we command you.   And the Lord
direct your hearts into the love of God and into the patience of
Christ.
6   Now we command you, brethren, in the name of our Lord Je
sus Christ, to withdraw yourselves from every brother that walketh disorderly, and not according to the tradition which he received
7 of us.   For yourselves know how ye ought to imitate us: we be-
8 haved not disorderly among you, Neither did we eat any man's
bread for nothing, but wrought with labour and toil, night and day,
9 that we might not burden any of you.   Not because we have not
authority: but that we might make ourselves an example to you,
10 that ye might imitate us.   For when we were with you, this we
11 commanded you, If any will not work, neither let him eat.   For
we hear there are some among you who walk disorderly, doing
12 nothing, but being busy bodies.   Now such we command and exhort by our Lord Jesus Christ, to work quietly, and eat their own
13 bread.   But ye, brethren, be not weary in well doing.   And if any
14 man obey not our word by this epistle, note that man, and have no
15 company with him, that he may be ashamed.   Yet count him not
16 as an enemy, but admonish him as a brother.   Now the Lord of
peace himself give you peace always by all means.   The Lord be
with you all.
17   The salutation of Paul, with my own hand, which is the token
18 in every epistle : So I write.   The grace of our Lord Jesus Christ
be with you all.   Amen.

III. 1. *May run*—Go on swiftly, without any interruption ; *and be glorified*—
Acknowledged as Divine, and bring forth much fruit.
   2. *All men have not faith*—And all who have not are more or less unreasonable and wicked men.
   3. *Who will stablish you*—That cleave to him by faith, *and guard you from
the evil one*—And all his instruments.
   4. *We trust in the Lord concerning you*—Thus only should we trust in any
man.
   5. *Now the Lord*—The Spirit, whose proper work this is, *direct*—Lead you
straight forward, *into the patience of Christ*—Of which he set you a pattern.
   6. *That walketh disorderly*—Particularly by not working; *not according to the
tradition he received of us*—The admonition we gave both by word of mouth, and
in our former epistle.
   10. *Neither let him eat*—Do not maintain him in idleness.
   11. *Doing nothing, but being busy bodies*—To which idleness naturally disposes
   12. *Work quietly*—Letting the concerns of other people alone.
   14. *Have no company with him*—No intimacy, no familiarity, no needless correspondence.
   15. *Admonish him as a brother*—Tell him lovingly of the reason why you
shun him.
   16. *The Lord of peace*—Christ.   *Give you peace by all means*—In every way
and manner.

NOTES

THE FIRST EPISTLE OF ST. PAUL TO TIMOTHY

———

The mother of Timothy was a Jewess, but his father was a Gentile. He was converted to Christianity very early; and while he was yet but a youth, was taken by St. Paul to assist him in the work of the Gospel, chiefly in watering the Churches which he had planted.

He was therefore properly (as was Titus) an itinerant evangelist, a kind of secondary apostle, whose office was to regulate all things in the Churches to which he was sent; and to inspect and reform whatsoever was amiss either in the bishops, deacons, or people.

St. Paul had doubtless largely instructed him in private conversation for the due execution of so weighty an office. Yet to fix things more upon his mind, and to give him an opportunity of having recourse to them afterward, and of communicating them to others, as there might be occasion; as also to leave Divine direction in writing, for the use of the Church and its ministers, in all ages; he sent him this excellent pastoral letter, which contains a great variety of important sentiments for their regulation.

Though St. Paul styles him his own son in the faith, yet he does not appear to have been converted by the apostle; but only to have been exceeding dear to him, who had established him therein; and whom he had diligently and faithfully served, like a son with his father, in the Gospel, Phil. ii, 22.

THE EPISTLE CONTAINS THREE PARTS:

I. TIMOTHY.

1 PAUL, an apostle of Jesus Christ, according to the command-
2 ment of God our Saviour, and Christ Jesus our hope, To Timotheus my own son in the faith, grace, mercy, peace, from God our
Father, and Christ Jesus our Lord.
3 As I exhorted thee when I was going into Macedonia, abide at
Ephesus ; that thou mayest charge some to teach no other doc-
4 trine, Neither to give heed to fables and endless genealogies, that
afford questions, and not godly edifying, which is through faith.
5 Whereas the end of the commandment is love, out of a pure
6 heart, and a good conscience, and faith unfeigned, From which
some, having missed the mark, are turned aside to vain jangling:
7 Desiring to be teachers of the law, understanding neither the
things they say, nor those concerning which they confidently
8 affirm. We know, the law *is* good, if a man use it lawfully,
9 Knowing this, that the law doth not lie against a righteous man ;

Verse 1. *Paul, an apostle*—Familiarity is to be set aside where the things of
God are concerned : *according to the commandment of God*—The authoritative
appointment of God the Father ; *our Saviour*—So styled in many other places
likewise, as being the grand orderer of the whole scheme of our salvation ; *and
Christ our hope*—That is, the author, object, and ground of all our hope.

2. *Grace, mercy, peace*—St. Paul wishes grace and peace in his epistles to the
Churches. To Timotheus he adds mercy, the most tender grace toward those
who stand in need of it. The experience of this prepares a man to be a minister
of the Gospel.

3. *Charge some to teach no other doctrine*—than I have taught. Let them put
nothing in the place of it, add nothing to it.

4. *Neither give heed*—So as either to teach or regard them ; *to fables*—Fabu-
lous Jewish traditions ; *and endless genealogies*—Not those delivered in Scripture, but the long, intricate pedigrees, whereby they strove to prove their descent
from such or such a person ; *which afford questions*—Which lead only to useless
and endless controversies.

5. *Whereas the end of the commandment*—Of the whole Christian institution ;
is love—And this was particularly the end of the commandment which Timotheus was to enforce at Ephesus, ver. 3, 18. The foundation is faith, the end
love. But this can only subsist in a heart purified by faith, and is always attended
with a good conscience.

6. *From which*—Love and a good conscience ; *some are turned aside*—An
affectation of high and extensive knowledge sets a man at the greatest distance
from faith, and all sense of Divine things ; *to vain jangling*—And of all vanities,
none are more vain, than dry, empty disputes on the things of God.

7. *Understanding neither the* very *things they speak*, nor the subject they
speak of.

8. *We* grant *the* whole Mosaic *law is good*—Answers excellent purposes ; *if a
man use it in* a proper manner. Even the ceremonial is good, as it points to
Christ : and the moral law is holy, just, and good in its own nature : and of
admirable use both to convince unbelievers, and to guide believers in all holiness.

9. *The law doth not lie against a righteous man*—Doth not strike or condemn
him : *but against the lawless and disobedient*—They who despise the authority
of the lawgiver, violate the first commandment, which is the foundation of the
law, and the ground of all obedience ; *against the ungodly and sinners*—Who
break the second commandment, worshipping idols, or not worshipping the true

but against the lawless and disobedient, against the ungodly and
sinners, the unholy and profane, against killers of their fathers or
1ᶜ their mothers, against murderers, Against whoremongers, sodomites, man stealers, liars, perjured persons, and if there be any
11 other thing that is contrary to wholesome doctrine. According to
the glorious Gospel of the blessed God, with which I am entrusted
12 And I thank Christ Jesus our Lord, who hath enabled me, in
that he accounted me faithful, having put me into the ministry,
13 Who was before a blasphemer, and a persecutor, and an oppressor ;
but I obtained mercy, because I did *it* ignorantly in unbelief.
14 And the grace of our Lord was exceeding abundant, with faith and
15 love which is in Christ Jesus. This is a faithful saying, and worthy of all acceptation, that Christ Jesus came into the world to
16 save sinners, of whom I am chief. Yet for this cause I obtained
mercy that on me the chief, Jesus Christ might show all long-
suffering, for a pattern to them who should hereafter believe in
17 him to life everlasting. Now to the King of eternity, immortal,
invisible, the only God, *be* honour and glory for ever and ever.
Amen.
18   This charge I commit to thee, son Timotheus, according to the
prophecies which went before concerning thee, that thou mightest
19 by them war the good warfare : Holding fast faith and a good con-

---

God : *the unholy and profane*—Who break the third commandment by taking his
name in vain.

10. *Man stealers*—The worst of all thieves, in comparison of whom high-way-
men and house breakers are innocent ! What then are most traders in negroes,
procurers of servants for America, and all who list soldiers by lies, tricks, or
enticements ?

11. *According to the glorious Gospel*—Which, far from making void, does effectually establish the law.

12. *I thank Christ—who hath enabled me, in that he accounted me faithful,
having put me into the ministry*—The meaning is, I thank him for putting me
into the ministry, and enabling me to be faithful therein.

13. *A blasphemer*—Of Christ ; *a persecutor*—Of his Church ; *a reviler*—Of his
doctrine and people. *But I obtained mercy*—He does not say, because I was
unconditionally elected ; but because he did it in ignorance. Not that his ignorance took away his sin : but it left him capable of mercy : which he would
hardly have been, had he acted thus, contrary to his own conviction.

14. *And the grace*—Whereby I obtained mercy ; *was exceeding abundant, with
faith*—Opposite to my preceding unbelief ; *and love*—Opposite to my blasphemy,
persecution, and oppression.

15. *This is a faithful saying*—A most solemn preface ; *and worthy of all
acceptation*—Well deserving to be accepted, received, embraced, with all the
faculties of our whole soul ; *that Christ*—Promised ; *Jesus*—Exhibited ; *came
into the world to save sinners*—All sinners, without exception.

16. *For this cause* God showed me *mercy*, that all his long suffering might be
shown, and that none might hereafter despair.

17. *The King of eternity*—A phrase frequent with the Hebrews. How unspeakably sweet is the thought of eternity to believers !

18. *This charge I commit to thee*—That thou mayest deliver it to the Church ;
according to the prophecies concerning thee—Uttered when thou wast received as
an evangelist, chap. iv, 14, probably by many persons, chap. iv, 12, that being
encouraged by them, thou mightest war the good warfare.

19. *Holding fast faith*—Which is as a most precious liquor ; *and a good conscience*—Which is as a clean glass ; *which*—Namely, a good conscience ; *some
having thrust away*—It goes away unwillingly. It always says, " Do not hurt
me." And they who retain this, do not make shipwreck of their faith. Indeed

science ; which some having thrust away, have made shipwreck
20 of their faith : Of whom are Hymeneus and Alexander, whom I
have delivered to Satan, that they may learn not to blaspheme.
II.　I exhort therefore, that first of all supplications, prayers, inter-
2 cessions, thanksgivings, be made for all men : For kings and all
that are in authority, that we may lead a quiet and peaceable life,
3 in all godliness and honesty. For this *is* good and acceptable in
4 the sight of God our Saviour, Who willeth all men to be saved and
5 to come to the knowledge of the truth. For *there is* one God, one
6 mediator also between God and men, the man Christ Jesus, Who
gave himself a ransom for all, to be testified of in due season,
7 Whereunto I am ordained a preacher, and an apostle, (I speak the
8 truth, I lie not,) a teacher of the Gentiles in faith and truth. I will

none can make shipwreck of faith who never had it. These therefore were once
true believers. Yet they fell not only foully, but finally. For ships once
wrecked, cannot be afterward saved.
　20. *Whom*—Though absent, *I have delivered to Satan; that they may learn
not to blaspheme*—That by what they suffer they may be in some measure
restrained, if they will not repent.
　II. 1. *I exhort therefore*—Seeing God is so gracious. In this chapter he gives
directions, 1. With regard to public prayers. 2. With regard to doctrine. Supplication is here the imploring help in time of need : prayer is any kind of
offering up our desires to God. But true prayer is the vehemency of holy zeal,
the ardour of Divine love, arising from a calm, undisturbed soul, moved upon
by the Spirit of God. Intercession is prayers for others. We may likewise give
thanks for all men, in the full sense of the word, for that God willeth all men to
be saved, and Christ is the mediator of all.
　2. *For all that are in authority*—Seeing even the lowest country magistrates
frequently do much good or much harm. God supports the power of magistracy
for the sake of his own people, when, in the present state of men, it could not
otherwise be kept in any nation whatever. *Godliness*—Inward religion ; the
true worship of God. *Honesty*—A comprehensive word, taking in the whole
duty we owe to our neighbour.
　3. *For this*—That we pray for all men. Do you ask, Why are not more converted ? We do not pray enough : *is acceptable in the sight of God our Saviour*
—Who has actually saved us that believe, and willeth all men to be saved. It is
strange that any whom he has actually saved, should doubt the universality of
his grace.
　4. *Who willeth* seriously *all men*—Not a part only, much less the smallest part,
to be saved—Eternally. This is treated of ver. 5, 6. And in order thereto, *to
come*—(They are not compelled,) *to the knowledge of the truth*—Which brings
salvation. This is treated of ver. 6, 7.
　5. *For*—The 4th verse is proved by the 5th, the 1st by the 4th. *There is one
God*—And they who have not him, through the one Mediator, have no God ;
one Mediator also—We could not rejoice that there is a God, were there not a
Mediator also ; one who stands between God and men, to reconcile man to God,
and to transact the whole affair of our salvation. This excludes all other mediators, as saints and angels, whom the papists set up, and idolatrously worship as
such ; just as the heathens of old set up many mediators, to pacify their superior
gods ; *the man*—Therefore all men are to apply to this Mediator, who gave himself for all.
　6. *Who gave himself a ransom for all*—Such a ransom the word signifies,
wherein a like or equal is given, as an eye for an eye, or life for life. And this
ransom, from the dignity of the person redeeming, was more than equivalent to
all mankind ; *to be testified of in due season*—Literally, in his own seasons, those
chosen by his own wisdom.
　8. *I will*—A word strongly expressing his apostolical authority ; *therefore*—
This particle connects the eighth with the first verse ; *that men pray in every
place*—Public and private. Wherever men are, there prayer should be ; *lifting*

therefore that men pray in every place, lifting up holy hands, with-
9 out wrath and doubting : Likewise that women adorn themselves
    in decent apparel, with modesty and sobriety, not with curled hair,
10 or gold, or pearls, or costly raiment. But (which becometh wo-
11 men professing godliness) with good works. Let a woman learn
12 in silence with all subjection. For I suffer not a woman to teach,
13 nor to usurp authority over the man, but to be in silence. For Adam
14 was first formed, then Eve. And Adam was not deceived ; but the
15 woman, being deceived, transgressed. Yet she shall be saved in
    child bearing, if they continue in faith, and love, and holiness, with
    sobriety.
III. This *is* a faithful saying, If a man desire the office of a bishop,
 2 he desireth a good work. A bishop therefore must be blameless,
    the husband of one wife, vigilant, prudent, of good behaviour, hos-
 3 pitable, apt to teach ; Not given to wine, no striker, not desirous
 4 of filthy gain, but gentle, patient, not loving money ; Ruling his
    own house well, having his children in subjection with all serious
 5 ness. For if a man know not how to rule his own house, how shall

---

up holy hands—Pure from all known sin, *without wrath*—In any kind, against
any creature. And every temper or motion of our soul, that is not according to
love, is wrath ; *and doubting*—Which is contrary to faith. And wrath, or un
holy actions, or want of faith in him we call upon, are the three grand hinder
ances of God's hearing our petitions. Christianity consists of faith, and love
embracing truth and grace. Therefore the sum of our wishes should be, to pray,
and live, and die, without any wrath or doubt.

9. *With sobriety*—Which (in St. Paul's sense) is the virtue which governs our
whole life according to true wisdom ; *not with curled hair; not with gold*—Worn
ɔy way of ornament ; *not with pearls*—Jewels of any kind, a part is put for the
*ʌ*hole ; *nɔt with costly raiment*—These four are expressly forbidden by name, to
all women, here is no exception, *professing godliness*. And no art of man can
reconcile, with the Christian profession, the wilful violation of an express com.
mand.

12. *To usurp authority over the man*—By public teaching.

13. *First*—So that woman was originally the inferior.

14. *And Adam was not deceived*—The serpent deceived Eve. Eve did not deceive Adam, but persuaded him. Thou hast hearkened unto the voice of thy wife,
Gen. iii, 17. The preceding verse showed why a woman should not usurp authority over the man. This shows why she ought not to teach. She is more easily
deceived, and more easily deceives. *The woman, being deceived, transgressed-—*
The serpent deceived her, Gen. iii, 13, and she transgressed.

15. *Yet she*—That is, women in general, who were all involved with Eve in the
sentence pronounced, Gen. iii, 16, *shall be saved in child bearing*—Carried safe
through the pain and danger which that sentence entails upon them for the
transgression ; yea, and finally saved, if they continue in loving faith and holy
wisdom.

III. 1. *He desireth a good work*—An excellent, but laborious employment.

2. *Therefore*—That he may be capable of it, *a bishop*—Or pastor of a congregation, *must be blameless*—Without fault or just suspicion : *the husband of one
wife*—This neither means that a bishop must be married ; nor that he may not
marry a second wife : which it is just as lawful for him to do as to marry a first,
and may in some cases be his bounden duty. But whereas polygamy and divorce
upon slight occasions were common both among the Jews and heathens, it teaches
us that ministers of all others ought to stand clear of those sins ; *vigilant, prudent*—Lively and zealous, yet calm and wise ; *of good behaviour*—Naturally flowing from that vigilance and prudence.

4. *Having his children in subjection with all seriousness*—For levity undermines
all domestic authority. And this direction, by a parity of reason, belongs to all
parents.

6 he take care of the Church of God? Not a new convert, lest being
7 puffed up, he fall into the condemnation of the devil. He ought
   also to have a good report from them that are without, lest he fall
8 into reproach, and the snare of the devil. Likewise the deacons
   must be serious, not double tongued, not given to much wine, no¹
9 desirous of filthy gain; Holding fast the mystery of the faith in a
10 pure conscience. And let these be proved first, then let them mi
11 nister, being blameless. In like manner their wives *must be* serious,
12 not slanderers, vigilant, faithful in all things. Let the deacons be
   husbands of one wife, ruling their children, and their own houses
13 well. For they that have discharged the office of a deacon well,
   purchase to themselves a good degree, and much boldness in the
14 faith which is in Christ Jesus. These things I write to thee,
15 hoping to come to thee shortly: But if I tarry, that thou mayest
   know how thou oughtest to behave in the house of God, which is
   the Church of the living God.
16   The mystery of godliness is the pillar and ground of the truth,
   and without controversy a great thing: God was manifested in the
   flesh, was justified by the Spirit, seen by angels, preached among
   the Gentiles, believed on in the world, taken up into glory.
IV.   But the Spirit saith expressly, that in the latter times some will

---

6. *Lest being puffed up*—With this new honour, or with the applause which
frequently follows it, *he fall into the condemnation of the devil*—The same into
which the devil fell.

7. *He ought also to have a good report*—To have had a fair character in time
past *from them that are without*—That are not Christians; *lest he fall into reproach*—By their rehearsing his former life, which might discourage and prove a
snare to him.

8. *Likewise the deacons must be serious*—Men of a grave, decent, venerable,
behaviour. But where are presbyters? Were this order essentially distinct from
that of bishops, could the apostle have passed it over in silence? *Not desirous of
filthy gain*—With what abhorrence does he every where speak of this! All that
is gained, (above food and raiment,) by ministering in holy things, is filthy gain
indeed! Far more filthy than what is honestly gained, by raking kennels, or
emptying common sewers.

9. *Holding fast the faith in a pure conscience*—Steadfast in faith, holy in heart
and life.

10. *Let these be proved first*—Let a trial be made, how they behave; *then let
them minister*—Let them be fixed in that office.

11. *Faithful in all things*—Both to God, their husbands, and the poor.

13. *They purchase a good degree*—Or step, toward some high office, *and much
boldness*—From the testimony of a good conscience.

15. *That thou mayest know how to behave*—This is the scope of the epistle, *in
the house of God*—Who is the master of the family, *which is*—As if he had said,
By the house of God, I mean the Church.

16. *The mystery of godliness*—Afterward specified in six articles, which sum
up the whole economy of Christ upon earth; *is the pillar and ground*—The
foundation and support of all the truth, taught in his Church. *God was manifest
in the flesh*—In the form of a servant, the fashion of a man, for three and thirty
years: *justified by the Spirit*—Publicly; *declared to be the Son of God*—By his
resurrection from the dead; *seen*—Chiefly after his resurrection; *by angels*—
Both good and bad; *preached among the Gentiles*—This elegantly follows. The
angels were the least, the Gentiles the farthest removed from him; and the
foundation both of this preaching and of their faith was laid before his assump-
tion: *was believed on in the world*—Opposed to heaven, into which he was taken
up. The first point is, he *was manifested in the flesh*; the last, he was *taken up
into glory.*

depart from the faith, giving heed to seducing spirits and doctrines
2 of devils, By the hypocrisy of them that speak lies, having their
3 own consciences seared as with a hot iron : Forbidding to marry,
and *commanding* to abstain from meats, which God hath created to
be received with thanksgiving by them that believe and know the
4 truth. For every creature of God is good, and nothing to be rejected,
5 being received with thanksgiving ; For it is sanctified by the
6 word of God and prayer. If thou remind the brethren of these
things, thou wilt be a good minister of Jesus Christ, nourishing
them with the words of faith, and of the good doctrine which thou
7 hast accurately traced out. But avoid profane and old wives' fables,
8 and exercise thyself unto godliness. For bodily exercise profiteth
a little ; but godliness is profitable for all things, having the promise
9 of the present life, and of that which is to come. This *is* a faith-
10 ful saying, and worthy of all acceptation. For therefore we both
labour and suffer reproach, because we trust in the living God, who
11 is the Saviour of all men, especially of them that believe. These
12 things command and teach. Let no one despise thy youth ; but
be a pattern to them that believe, in word, in behaviour, in love,
13 in spirit, in faith, in purity. Till I come, give thyself to reading,
14 to exhortation, to teaching. Neglect not the gift that is in thee,

---

IV. 1. *But the Spirit saith*—By St. Paul himself to the Thessalonians, and probably by other cotemporary prophets ; *expressly*—As concerning a thing of great moment, and soon to be fulfilled ; *that in the latter times*—These extend from our Lord's ascension till his coming to judgment ; *some*—Yea, many, and by degrees the far greater part ; *will depart from the faith*—The doctrine once delivered to the saints ; *giving heed to seducing spirits*—Who inspire false prophets.

2. These *will depart from the faith, by the hypocrisy of them that speak lies*, *having their own consciences as senseless* and unfeeling, as flesh that is *seared with a hot iron.*

3. *Forbidding* priests, monks, and nuns to marry, and commanding all men to abstain from such and such meats, at such and such times : *which God hath created to be received by them that know the truth*—That all meats are now clean ; *with thanksgiving*—Which supposes a pure conscience.

5. *It is sanctified by the word of God*—Creating all, and giving it to man for food ; *and by prayer*—The children of God are to pray for the sanctification of all the creatures which they use. And not only the Christians, but even the Jews, yea, the very heathens used to consecrate their table by prayer.

7. Like those who were to contend in the Grecian games, *exercise thyself unto godliness*—Train thyself up in holiness of heart and life with the utmost labour, vigour, and diligence.

8. *Bodily exercise profiteth a little*—Increases the health and strength of the body.

10. *Therefore*—Animated by this promise ; *we both labour and suffer reproach* —We regard neither pleasure, ease, nor honour ; *because we trust*—For this very thing the world will hate us ; *in the living God*—Who will give us the life he has promised ; *who is the Saviour of all men*—Preserving them in this life, and willing to save them eternally ; *but especially*—In a more eminent manner, *of them that believe*—And so are saved everlastingly.

12. *Let no one* have reason to despise thee for thy youth : to prevent this, *be a pattern in word*—Public and private ; *in spirit*—In your whole temper ; *in faith* —When this is placed in the midst of several other Christian graces, it generally means a particular branch of it ; fidelity or faithfulness.

13. *Give thyself to reading*—Both publicly and privately. Enthusiasts, observe tnis ! Expect no end without the means.

14. *Neglect not*—They neglect it who do not exercise it to the full ; *the gift*—

which was given thee by prophecy, with the laying on of the hands
15 of the presbytery. Meditate on these things ; be wholly in them,
16 that thy profiting may appear in all things. Take heed to thyself,
and to *thy* teaching : continue in them, for in so doing thou shalt
save both thyself and them that hear thee

V.   Rebuke not an aged man, but exhort *him* as a father, the younger
2 men as brethren ; The aged women as mothers, the younger as
3 sisters, with all purity. Honour widows that are widows indeed
4 But if any widow have children or grandchildren, let these learn
,first to show piety at home, and to requite their parents ; for this
5 is good and acceptable before God. Now she that is a widow
indeed, and desolate, trusteth in God, and continueth in supplica-
6 tions and prayers, night and day. But she that liveth in pleasure, is
7 dead while she liveth. And enjoin these things, that they may be
8 blameless. But if any provide not for his own, and especially for
those of his own family, he hath denied the faith, and is worse than
9 an infidel. Let not a widow be chosen under threescore years old,
10 having been the wife of one husband, Well reported of for good
works, if she hath brought up children, if she hath lodged strangers, if she hath washed the feet of the saints, if she hath relieved
the afflicted, if she hath diligently followed every good work.

Of feeding the flock, of power, and love, and sobriety ; *which was given thee by prophecy*—By immediate direction from God, by the laying on of my hands, 2 Tim. i, 6, while the elders joined also in the solemnity. This presbytery pro bably consisted of some others, together with Paul and Silas.

15. *Meditate*—The Bible makes no distinction between this and to contem- plate, whatever others do. True meditation is no other than faith, hope, love, joy, melted down together, as it were, by the fire of God's holy Spirit : and offered up to God in secret. He that is wholly in these, will be little in worldly company, in other studies, in collecting books, medals, or butterflies ; wherein many pastors drone away so considerable a part of their lives !

16. *Continue in them*—In all the preceding advices.

V. 1. *Rebuke not*—Considering your own youth, with such a severity as would otherwise be proper.

3. *Honour*—That is, maintain out of the public stock.

4. *Let these learn to requite their parents*—For all their former care, trouble, and expense.

5. *Widows indeed*—Who have no near relations to provide for them ; and who are wholly devoted to God. *Desolate*—Having neither children, nor grand- children to relieve her.

6. *She that liveth in pleasure*—Delicately, voluptuously, in elegant, regular sensuality, though not in the use of any such pleasures as are unlawful in themselves.

7. *That they*—That is, the widows.

8. *If any provide not*—Food and raiment, *for his own*—Mother, and grandmo- ther, being *desolate widows, he hath*, virtually, *denied the faith*—Which does not destroy, but perfect natural duties. What has this to do with heaping up money for our children, for which it is often so impertinently alleged ? But all men have their reasons for laying up money. One will go to hell for fear of want ; another acts like a heathen, lest he should be worse than an infidel.

9. *Let not a widow be chosen*—Into the number of deaconesses, who attend sick women or travelling preachers, *under threescore*—Afterward they were ad- mitted at forty, if they were eminent for holiness ; *having been the wife of one husband*—That is, having lived in lawful marriage, whether with one or more persons successively.

10. *If she hath washed the feet of the saints*—Has been ready to do the meanest offices for them.

11 But the younger widows refuse; for when they are waxed wan-
12 ton against Christ, they want to marry; Having condemnation,
13 because they have rejected their first faith. And withal they
learn *to be* idle, going about from house to house; and not only
idle, but triflers and busy-bodies, speaking what they ought not.
14 I counsel therefore the younger women to marry, bear children,
guide the family, give no occasion of reproach to the adversary.
15 For some are already turned aside after Satan. If any believing
16 man or woman hath widows, let them relieve them; and let not
the Church be burdened, that it may relieve them that are widows
indeed.
17 Let the elders who rule well be counted worthy of double
honour, especially those who labour in the word and teaching.
18 For the Scripture saith, * Thou shalt not muzzle the ox that
treadeth out the corn: and The labourer is worthy of his re-
19 ward. Against an elder receive not an accusation, unless by two
or three witnesses.
20 Those that sin rebuke before all, that the rest also may fear.
21 I charge *thee* before God, and the Lord Jesus Christ, and the
elect angels, that thou observe these things without prejudging,

11. *Refuse*—Do not choose, *for when they are waxed wanton against Christ*—
To whose more immediate service they had devoted themselves, *they want to
marry*—And not with a single eye to the glory of God; and so withdraw themselves from that entire service of the Church, to which they were before engaged.
12. *They have rejected their first faith*—Have deserted their trust in God, and
have acted contrary to the first conviction, namely, that wholly to devote themselves to his service was the most excellent way. When we first receive power
to believe, does not the Spirit of God generally point out what are the most excellent things; and at the same time, give us a holy resolution to walk in the
highest degree of Christian severity? And how unwise are we ever to sink into
any thing below it?
14. *I counsel therefore the younger women*—Widows or virgins, such as are not
disposed to live single, *to marry, to bear children, to guide the family*—Then will
they have sufficient employment of their own: *and give no occasion of reproach
to the adversary*—Whether Jew or heathen.
15. *Some*—Widows, *have turned aside after Satan*—Who has drawn them from
Christ.
17. *Let the elders that rule well*—Who approve themselves faithful stewards of
all that is committed to their charge; *be counted worthy of double honour*—A
more abundant provision, seeing that such will employ it all to the glory of God.
As they were the most laborious and disinterested men who were put into these
offices, so whatever any one had to bestow, in his life or death, was generally
lodged in their hands for the poor. By this means the churchmen became very
rich in after ages. But as the design of the donors was the general good, there
is the highest reason why it should be disposed of according to their pious intent; *especially those*—of them, *who labour*—Diligently and painfully, *in the word
and teaching*—In teaching the word.
19. *Against an elder*—Or presbyter, do not even receive an accusation, *unless
by two or three witnesses*—By the Mosaic law a private person might be cited
(though not condemned) on the testimony of one witness. But St. Paul forbids,
an elder to be even cited on such evidence, his reputation being of more importance than that of others.
20. *Those*—elders, *that sin*—Scandalously, and are duly convicted, *rebuke before all*—The Church.
21. *I charge thee before God*—Referring to the last judgment, in which we shall
stand before God, and Christ with his elect, that is, *holy angels*—Who are the
witnesses of our conversation. The apostle looks through his own labours, and

* Deut. xxv, 4.

22 doing nothing by partiality.   Lay hands suddenly on no man,
23 neither partake of other men's sins; keep thyself pure.   Drink
water no longer, but use a little wine for thy stomach's sake
24 and thy frequent infirmities.   Some men's sins are manifest beforehand, going before to judgment: and some they follow after.
25 In like manner the good works also *of some* are manifest: and
they that are otherwise cannot be hid.
VI.   Let as many servants as are under the yoke, account their
own masters worthy of all honour; lest the name of God and *his*
2 doctrine be blasphemed.   And they that have believing masters,
let them not despise *them*, because they are brethren: but rather
do them service, because they are faithful and beloved, partakers
3 of the benefit.   These things teach and exhort.   If any teach
otherwise, and consent not to sound words, those of our Lord
4 Jesus Christ, and to the doctrine which is after godliness.   He
is puffed up knowing nothing, but being sick of questions and

even through time itself, and seems to stand as one already in eternity—*That
thou observe these things without prejudging*—Passing no sentence till the cause is
fully heard; or *partiality*—For or against any one.
22. *Lay hands suddenly on no man*—That is, appoint no man to Church offices
without full trial and examination.   Else thou wilt be accessary to, and accountable for, his misbehaviour in his office.   *Keep thyself pure*—From the blood of
all men,
24. *Some men's sins are manifest beforehand*—Before any strict inquiry be
made; *going before to judgment*—So that you may immediately judge them unworthy of any spiritual office; *and some they*—Their sins, *follow after*—More
covertly.
25. *They that are otherwise*—Not so manifest, cannot be long *hid*—From thy
knowledge.   On this account also be not hasty in laying on of hands.
VI. 1. *Let servants under the yoke*—Of heathen masters, account them *worthy of
all honour*—All the honour due from a servant to a master; *lest the name of God
and his doctrine be blasphemed*—As it surely will if they do otherwise.
2. *Let them not despise them*—Pay them the less honour and obedience, *because
they are brethren*—And in that respect on a level with them.   They that live in a
religious community know the danger of this, and that greater grace is requisite
to bear with the faults of a brother, than of an infidel, or a man of the world:
but rather do them service—Serve them so much the more diligently, *because they
are* joint *partakers of the great benefit*—Salvation.   *These things*—Paul the aged
gives young Timotheus in charge to dwell upon practical holiness.   Less experienced teachers are apt to neglect the superstructure while they lay the foundation.   But of so great importance did St. Paul see it to enforce obedience to
Christ, as well as to preach faith in his blood, that, after strongly urging the
life of faith on professors, he even adds another charge for the strict observance of it.
3. *If any teach otherwise*—Than strict practical holiness, in all its branches.
and consent not to sound words—Literally, healthful words; words that have no
taint of falsehood, or tendency to encourage sin; *and the doctrine which is after
godliness*—Exquisitely contrived to answer all the ends, and secure every interest of real piety.
4. *He is puffed up*—Which is the cause of his not consenting to the doctrine
which is after inward, practical religion.   By this mark we may know them.
Knowing nothing—As he ought to know; *sick of questions*—Dotingly fond of
dispute.   An evil, but common disease; especially where practice is forgotten.
Such indeed contend earnestly for singular phrases, and favourite points of their
own.   Every thing else, however like the preaching of Christ and his apostles,
is all "Law and bondage and carnal reasoning;" *strifes of words*—Merely ver-
bal controversies; *whereof cometh envy*—Of the gifts and success of others; *contention*—For the pre-eminence.   Such disputants seldom like the prosperity of
others, or to be less esteemed themselves; *evil surmisings*—It not being their
way to think well of those that differ from themselves in opinion.

strifes of words, whereof cometh envy, contentions, evil speak-
5 ings, evil surmisings, Perverse disputings of men of corrupt
minds and destitute of the truth, supposing that gain is godli-
6 ness: From such withdraw thyself. But godliness with content
7 is great gain. For we brought nothing into the world: *it is*
8 manifest that neither can we carry any thing out: Having then
9 food and covering, with these let us be content. But they that
desire to be rich, fall into temptation and a snare, and into many
foolish and hurtful desires, which plunge men into destruction
10 and perdition. For the love of money is the root of all evils;
which some coveting, have erred from the faith, and pierced
11 themselves through with many sorrows. But thou, O man of
God, flee these things; and follow after righteousness, godli-
12 ness, faith, love, patience, meekness. Fight the good fight of
faith, lay hold of eternal life, to which thou hast been called,
and hast confessed the good confession before many witnesses.
13 I charge thee before God, who quickeneth all things, and **Christ
Jesus**, who witnessed the good confession before **Pontius Pilate,**

---

5. *Supposing that gain is godliness*—Thinking the best religion is the getting of money. A far more common case than is usually supposed.

6. *But godliness with content*—The inseparable companion of true vital reli gion, *is great gain*—Brings unspeakable profit in time as well as in eternity.

7. *Neither can we carry any thing out*—To what purpose then do we heap together so many things? O give me one thing; a safe and ready passage to my own country!

8. *Covering*—That is, raiment and a house to cover us. This is all that a Christian needs, and all that his religion allows him to desire.

9. *They that desire to be rich*—To have more than these (for then they would be so far rich, and the very desire banishes content, and exposes them to ruin) *fall, plunge*—A sad gradation! *into temptation.* Miserable food for the soul! *and a snare*—Or trap; dreadful covering! *And into many foolish and hurtful desires*—Which are sown and fed by having more than we need. Then farewell all hope of content! What then remains, but destruction for the body, and perdition for the soul!

10. *Love of money*—Commonly called prudent care, of what a man has, *is the root*—The parent of all manner of evils, *which some coveting have erred*—Lite rally, missed the mark. They aimed not at faith, but at something else, *and pierced themselves with many sorrows*—From a guilty conscience, tormenting pas sions, desires contrary to reason, religion, and one another. How cruel are worldly men to themselves!

11. *But thou, O man of God*—Whatever all the world else do, (*A man of God*— Is either a prophet, or a messenger of God, or a man devoted to God, a man of another world) *flee*—As from a serpent, instead of coveting these things; *follow after righteousness*—The whole image of God; though sometimes this word is used, not in the general, but in the particular acceptation, meaning only that single branch of it which is termed justice; *Faith*—Which is also taken here in the general and full sense: namely, a Divine supernatural sight of God; chiefly in respect of his mercy in Christ. This faith is the foundation of righteousness, the support of godliness, the root of every grace of the Spirit; *Love*—This St. Paul intermixes with every thing that is good; he, as it were, penetrates whatever he treats of with love, the glorious spring of all inward and outward holiness.

12. *Fight the good fight of faith*—Not about words; *lay hold on eternal life*— Just before thee. *Thou hast confessed the good confession*—(Perhaps at his bap tism:) So likewise ver. 13, but with a remarkable variation of the expression; *Thou hast confessed the good confession before many witnesses*—To which they all assented. *He witnessed the good confession;* but Pilate did not assent to it.

13. *I charge thee before God, who quickeneth all things*—Who hath quickened thee, and will quicken thee at the great day.

14 That thou keep the commandment without spot, unrebukable,
15 until the appearing of our Lord Jesus Christ, Which in his own
    times the blessed and only Potentate will show, the King of
16 kings, and Lord of lords: Who only hath immortality, dwelling
    in light unapproachable, whom no man hath seen, neither can
    see; to whom *be* honour and power everlasting. Amen.
17   Charge the rich in this world not to be high-minded, neither
    to trust in uncertain riches, but in the living God, who giveth
18 us richly all things to enjoy: To do good, to be rich in good
19 works, ready to distribute, willing to communicate, Treasuring
    up for themselves a good foundation against the time to come,
    that they may lay hold on eternal life.
20   O Timotheus, keep that which is committed to thy trust,
    avoiding profane, empty babblings, and oppositions of know-
21 ledge, falsely so called: Which some professing have erred from
    the faith. Grace *be* with thee.

15. *Which*—Appearing; *in his own times*—The power, the knowledge and the revelation of which, remain in his eternal mind.

16. *Who only hath*—Underived, independent—*immortality, dwelling in light unapproachable*—To the highest angel; *whom no man hath seen nor can see*—With bodily eyes. Yet we *shall* see him as he is.

17. What follows seems to be a kind of postscript. *Charge the rich in this world*—Rich in such beggarly riches as this world affords, *not to be high-minded* —(O who regards this?) Not to think better of themselves for their money, or any thing it can purchase; *neither to trust in uncertain riches*—(Which they may lose in an hour) either for happiness or defence: *But in the living God*—All the rest is dead clay; *who giveth us*—As it were holding them out to us in his hand, *all things*—Which we have, *richly*—Freely, abundantly, *to enjoy*—As his gift, in him and for him. When we use them thus, we do indeed enjoy all things. Where else is there any notice taken of the rich, in all the apostolic writings, save to denounce woes and vengeance upon them?

18. *To do good*—To make this their daily employ, that they may *be rich*—May abound in all good works; *ready to distribute*—Singly to particular persons; *willing to communicate*—To join in all public works of charity.

19. *Treasuring up for themselves a good foundation*—Of an abundant reward, by the free mercy of God, *that they may lay hold on eternal life*—This cannot be done by alms-deeds: yet they come up for a memorial before God, (Acts x, 4.) And the lack, even of this, may be the cause why God will withhold grace and salvation from us.

20. *Keep that which is committed to thy trust*—The charge I have given thee, ch. i, 18, *avoid profane, empty babblings*—How weary of controversy was this acute disputant! *and knowledge falsely so called*—Most of the ancient heretics were great pretenders to knowledge.

NOTES

ON

THE SECOND EPISTLE OF ST. PAUL TO TIMOTHY.

———

This Epistle was probably written by St. Paul during his second confinement at Rome, not long before his martyrdom. It is, as it were, the swan's dying song. But though it was wrote many years after the former, yet they are both of the same kind, and nearly resemble each other.

———

II. TIMOTHY.

———

1 Paul, an apostle of Jesus Christ, by the will of God accord-
2 ing to the promise of life, which is by Christ Jesus. To Timotheus my beloved son, grace, mercy, peace, from God the Father, and Christ Jesus our Lord.
3 I thank God whom I serve from *my* forefathers with a pure conscience, that I have remembrance of thee in my prayers
4 without ceasing night and day, Longing to see thee, being mind-

———

Verse 3. *Whom I serve from my forefathers*—That is, whom both I and my ancestors served, *with a pure conscience*—He always worshipped God according to his conscience, both before and after his conversion. One who stands on the verge of life, is much refreshed by the remembrance of his predecessors, to whom he is going.
4. *Being mindful of thy tears*—Perhaps frequently shed, as well as at the apostle's last parting with him.

5 ful of thy tears, that I may be filled with joy; Remembering the
unfeigned faith that is in thee, which dwe't first in thy grand-
mother Lois, and thy mother Eunice; I am persuaded in thee
6 also. Wherefore I remind thee of stirring up the gift of God
7 which is in thee, by the laying on of my hands. For God hath
not given us the spirit of fear, but of power, and love, and so-
8 briety. Therefore be not thou ashamed of the testimony of our
Lord, nor of me his prisoner: but be thou partaker of the afflic-
9 tions of the Gospel, according to the power of God, Who hath
saved and called us with a holy calling, not according to our
works, but according to his own purpose and grace, which was
10 given us in Christ Jesus before the world began; But is now
made manifest by the appearing of our Saviour Jesus Christ,
who hath abolished death, and hath brought life and immortality
11 to light through the Gospel: Whereunto I am appointed a
12 preacher, and an apostle, and a teacher of the Gentiles. For
which cause also I suffer these things: yet I am not ashamed,
for I know whom I have trusted, and am persuaded that he is
able to keep that which I have committed to him, until that day.
13 Hold fast the pattern of sound words, which thou hast heard
14 from me, in faith and love which is in Christ Jesus. The good
thing which is committed to thee keep, through the Holy Spirit,
15 who dwelleth in us. This thou knowest, that all who are in Asia

---

5. *Which dwelt*—A word not applied to a transient guest, but only to a settled
inhabitant, *first*—Probably this was before Timothy was born; yet not beyond
St. Paul's memory.

6. *Wherefore*—Because I remember this, *I remind thee of stirring up*—Literally, blowing up the coals into a flame; *the gift of God*—All the spiritual gifts,
which the grace of God has given thee.

7. And let nothing discourage thee; *for God hath not given us*—That is, the
Spirit which God hath given us Christians, is *not the spirit of fear*—Or cowardice, *but of power*—banishing fear; *and love and sobriety*—these animate us in our
duties to God, our brethren, and ourse ves. Power and sobriety are two good
extremes. Love is between, the tie and temperament of both; preventing the
two bad extremes of fearfulness and rashness. More is said concerning power,
ver. 8, concerning love, ch. ii, 14, &c., concerning sobriety, ch. iii, ver. 1, &c.

8. *Therefore be not thou ashamed*—When fear is banished, evil shame also
flees away; *of the testimony of our Lord*—The Gospel, and of testifying the truth
of it to all men; *nor of me*—The cause of the servants of God doing his work,
cannot be separated from the cause of God himself. *But be thou partaker of the
afflictions*—Which I endure for the Gospel's sake, *according to the power of God*
—This which overcomes all things is nervously described in the two next verses.

9. *Who hath saved us*—By faith. The love of the Father, the grace of our
Saviour, and the whole economy of salvation, are here admirably described:
having called us with a holy calling—Which is all from God, and claims us all
for God: *according to his own purpose and grace*—That is, his own gracious purpose, *which was given us*—Fixed for our advantage, before the world began.

10. *By the appearing of our Saviour*—This implies his whole abode upon
earth: *who hath abolished death*—Taken away its sting, and turned it into a blessing, *and hath brought life and immortality to light*—Hath clearly revealed by the
Gospel that immortal life which he hath purchased for us.

12. *That which I have committed to him*—My soul: *until that day*—Of his final
appearing.

13. *The pattern of sound words*—The model of pure, wholesome doctrine.

14. *The good thing*—This wholesome doctrine.

15. *All who are in Asia*—Who had attended me at Rome for a while: *are
turned away from me*—What, from Paul the aged, the faithful soldier, and now

are turned away from me, of whom are Phygellus and Hermo-
16 genes. The Lord give mercy to the family of Onesiphorus; for
he hath often refreshed me, and hath not been ashamed of my
17 chain: But when he was at Rome, he sought me out very dili-
18 gently and found *me*. The Lord grant him to find mercy from
the Lord in that day: and in how many things he served me at
Ephesus, thou knowest very well.

II. Thou therefore, my son, be strong through the grace which is
2 by Christ Jesus. And the things which thou hast heard from
me before many witnesses, these commit to faithful men, who
3 will be able to teach others also. Thou therefore endure afflic-
4 tion as a good soldier of Jesus Christ. No man that warreth entangleth himself in the affairs of *this* life, that he may please him
5 who hath enlisted *him*. And if a man strive, he is not crowned
6 unless he strive lawfully. The husbandman, that laboureth first,
7 must be partaker of the fruit. Consider what I say, and the
8 Lord give thee understanding in all things. Remember Jesus
Christ, of the seed of David, raised from the dead according to
9 my Gospel; For which I endure affliction even unto bonds, as
10 an evil-doer; but the word of God is not bound. Therefore I
suffer all things for the elect's sake, that they also may obtain
the salvation which is through Christ Jesus, with eternal glory.
11 *It is* a faithful saying; if we are dead with *him*, we shall also
12 live with *him*: If we suffer, we shall also reign with *him*: if we
13 deny *him*, he will also deny us: If we believe not, he remaineth
faithful; he cannot deny himself.
14 Remind *them* of these things, charging *them* before the Lord,

---

prisoner of Christ! This was a glorious trial, and wisely reserved for that time,
when he was on the borders of immortality. Perhaps a little measure of the
same spirit might remain with him, under whose picture are those affecting
words: " The true effigy of Francis Xavier, apostle of the Indies, forsaken of all
men, dying in a cottage."

16. *The family of Onesiphorus*—As well as himself; *hath often refreshed me*—
Both at Ephesus and Rome.

II. 2. *The things*—The wholesome doctrine, ch. i, 13. *Commit*—Before thou
leavest Ephesus, *to faithful men, who will be able*—after thou art gone, to teach
others.

4. *No man that warreth entangleth himself*—Any more than is unavoidable, *in
the affairs of this life*—With worldly business or cares, *that*—Minding war only,
he may please his captain. In this and the next verse there is a plain allusion
to the Roman law of arms, and to that of the Grecian games. According to the
former, no soldier was to engage in any civil employment. According to the
latter, none could be crowned as conqueror, who did not keep strictly to the rules
of the game.

6. Unless he *labour first*, he will reap no fruit.

8. *Of the seed of David*—This one genealogy attend to.

9. *Is not bound*—Not hindered in its course.

10. *Therefore*—Encouraged by this, That the word of God is not bound. *I
endure all things*—See the spirit of a real Christian! Who would not wish to be
like minded? Salvation is deliverance from all evil. *Glory*—The enjoyment
of all good.

11. *Dead with him*—Dead to sin, and ready to die for him.

12. *If we deny him*—To escape suffering for him.

13. *If we believe not*—That is, though some believe not, God will make good
all his promises to them that do believe. *He cannot deny himself*—His word
cannot fail.

14. *Remind them*—Who are under thy charge. O how many unnecessary
things are thus unprofitably, nay, hurtfully contended for!

.ot to strive about words to no profit, *but* to the subverting of
15 the hearers. Be diligent to present thyself unto God approved,
a workman that needeth not to be ashamed, rightly dividing the
16 word of truth. But avoid profane, empty babblings; for they
17 will increase to more ungodliness. And their word will eat as a
18 gangrene; of whom are Hymeneus and Philetus, Who have
erred concerning the truth, saying, The resurrection is already
19 past, and overthrow the faith of some. But the foundation of
God standeth firm, having this seal, The Lord knoweth those
that are his: and, Let every one who nameth the name of the
20 Lord depart from iniquity. But in a great house there are not
only vessels of gold and silver, but also of wood and of earth;
21 and some to honour, some to dishonour. If a man therefore
purge himself from these, he shall be a vessel unto honour, consecrated and fit for the Master's use, prepared for every good
22 work. Flee also youthful desires; but follow after righteousness, faith, love, peace with them that call upon the Lord, out of
23 a pure heart. But avoid foolish and unlearned questions, know-
24 ing that they beget strifes: And a servant of the Lord must not
strive, but be gentle toward all men, apt to teach, patient of
25 evil, In meekness instructing those that oppose themselves; if
haply God may give them repentance, to the acknowledging of
26 the truth; And they may awake out of the snare of the devil,
who are taken captive by him at his will.

---

15. *A workman that needeth not to be ashamed*—Either of unfaithfulness or un-
skilfulness; *rightly dividing the word of truth*—Duly explaining and applying
the whole Scripture, so as to give each hearer his due portion. But they that
give one part of the Gospel to all, (the promises and comforts to unawakened,
hardened, scoffing men,) have real need to be ashamed.

16. *They*—Who babble thus will grow worse and worse.

17. *And their word*—If they go on, will be mischievous as well as vain, and
will eat as a gangrene.

18. *Saying, The resurrection is already past*—Perhaps asserting that it is only
the spiritual passing from death unto life.

19. *But the foundation of God*—His truth and faithfulness, *standeth fast*—Can
never be overthrown; being as it were sealed with a seal, which has an inscription on each side: on the one, *The Lord knoweth those that are his;* on the other,
Let every one who nameth the name of the Lord—As his Lord—*depart from iniquity*—Indeed they only are his who depart from iniquity. To all others he will
say, I know you not. Matt. vii, 22, 23.

20. *But in a great house*—Such as the church, it is not strange, that *there are
not only vessels of gold and silver*—Designed for honourable uses, *but also of wood
and of earth*—For less honourable purposes. Yet a vessel even of gold may be
put to the vilest use, though it was not the design of him that made it.

21. *If a man purge himself from these*—Vessels of dishonour, so as to have no
fellowship with them.

22. *Flee youthful desires*—Those peculiarly incident to youth: *Follow peace
with them*—Unity with all true believers, *out of a pure heart*—Youthful desires
destroy this purity: righteousness, faith, love, peace, accompany it.

24. *A servant of the Lord must not*—Eagerly or passionately, *strive*—As do the
vain wranglers spoken of ver. 23, *but be apt to teach*—Chiefly by patience and unwearied assiduity.

25. *In meekness*—He has often need of zeal, always of meekness, *if haply God*
For it is wholly his work, *may give them repentance*—The acknowledging of
the truth would then quickly follow.

26. *Who*—At present, are not only captives, but asleep; utterly insensible of
their captivity.

III. But know this, that in the last days grievous times will come

2 For men will be lovers of themselves, lovers of money, arrogant, proud, evil-speakers, disobedient to parents, ungrateful, unholy.

3 Without natural affection, implacable, slanderers, intemperate,

4 fierce, despisers of good men, Traitors, rash, puffed up, lovers of

5 pleasure more than lovers of God; Having a form of godliness,

6 but denying the power of it. From these also turn away. For of these are they who creep into houses, and captivate silly

7 women, laden with sins, led away by various desires, Ever learn-

8 ing, but never able to come to the knowledge of the truth. Now as Jannes and Jambres withstood Moses, so do these also with-stand the truth; men of corrupt minds, void of judgment as to

9 the faith. But they shall proceed no farther; for their folly

10 shall be manifest to all men, as theirs also was. But thou hast accurately traced my doctrine, manner of life, intention, faith,

11 long-suffering, love, patience, Persecutions, afflictions, which befell me at Antioch, at Iconium, at Lystra; what persecutions

12 I endured; but the Lord delivered me out of all. Yea, and all that are resolved to live godly in Christ Jesus, shall suffer perse-

13 cution. But evil men and impostors will grow worse and worse,

14 deceiving, and being deceived. But continue thou in the things which thou hast learned, and been fully assured of, knowing of

15 whom thou hast learned *them*, And that from an infant thou hast known the Holy Scriptures, which are able to make thee wise

---

III. 1. *In the last days*—The time of the Gospel dispensation, commencing at the time of our Lord's death, is peculiarly styled the *last days: grievous*—Trouble-some and dangerous.

2. *For men*—Even in the Church, *will be*—In great numbers, and to a higher degree than ever, *lovers of themselves*—Only, not their neighbours, the first root of evil: *lovers of money*—The second.

3. *Without natural affection*—To their own children, *intemperate, fierce*—Both too soft and too hard.

4. *Lovers of* sensual *pleasure*—Which naturally extinguishes all love and sense of God.

5. *Having a form*—An appearance of godliness, but not regarding, nay, even denying and blaspheming, the inward power and reality of it. Is not this emi-nently fulfilled at this day?

6. *Of these*—That is, mere formalists.

7. *Ever learning*—New things; but not the truth of God.

8. Several ancient writers speak of *Jannes* and *Jambres*, as the chief of the Egyptian magicians: *men of corrupt minds*—Impure notions and wicked inclina-tions; *void of judgment*—Quite ignorant, as well as careless, of true, spiritual religion.

9. *They shall proceed no farther*—In gaining proselytes.

12. *All that are resolved to live godly*—Therefore count the cost. Art thou re-solved? *in Christ*—Out of Christ there is no godliness; *shall suffer persecution*—More or less. There is no exception. Either the truth of Scripture fails, or those that think they are religious, and are not persecuted, in some shape or other, on that very account, deceive themselves.

13. *Deceiving and being deceived*—He who has once begun to deceive others is both the less likely to recover from his own error, and the more ready to em-brace the errors of other men.

14. *Of whom*—Even from me, a teacher approved of God.

15. *From an infant thou hast known the Holy Scriptures*—Of the Old Testa-ment. These only were extant when Timothy was an infant; *which are able to make thee wise unto salvation through faith*—In the Messiah that was to come. How much more are the Old and New Testament together able, in God's hand,

16 unto salvation, through faith which is in Christ Jesus. All
Scripture *is* inspired of God, and is profitable for doctrine, for
17 reproof, for correction, for instruction in righteousness; That
the man of God may be perfect, thoroughly furnished unto every
good work.

IV.   I charge *thee* therefore before God and the Lord Jesus Christ,
who will judge the living and the dead at his appearing, and
2 his kingdom, Preach the word; be instant in season; convince, rebuke, exhort, with all long-suffering and teaching.
3 For the time will come when they will not endure wholesome
doctrine, but will heap up to themselves teachers, according
4 to their own desires, having itching ears. And they will turn
5 away *their* ears from the truth, and turn aside to fables. But
watch thou in all things, endure affliction, do the work of an
6 evangelist, fulfil thy ministry. For I am now ready to be offered
7 up, and the time of my departure is at hand. I have fought
the good fight, I have finished the course, I have kept the
8 faith; Henceforth there is laid up for me the crown of righteous-

---

to make us more abundantly wise unto salvation? Even such a measure of
present salvation, as was not known before Jesus was glorified.

16. *All Scripture is inspired of God*—The Spirit of God not only once inspired
those who wrote it, but continually inspires, supernaturally assists those that read
it with earnest prayer. Hence it is so profitable for doctrine, for instruction of
the ignorant, for the reproof or conviction of them that are in error or sin: for
the correction or amendment of whatever is amiss, and for instructing or train-
ing up the children of God in all righteousness.

17. *That the man of God*—He that is united to and approved of God; *may be
perfect*—Blameless himself, *and thoroughly furnished*—By the Scripture, either to
teach, reprove, correct, or train up others.

IV. 1. *I charge thee therefore*—This is deduced from the whole preceding chapter, *at his appearing, and his kingdom*—That is, at his appearing in the kingdom
of his glory.

2. *Be instant*—Insist on, urge these things, *in season, out of season*—That is,
continually, at all times and places. It might be translated, *with and without
opportunity*—Not only when a fair occasion is given; even when there is none,
one must be made.

3. *For they will heap up teachers*—Therefore thou hast need of *all long-suffering; according to their own desires*—Smooth as they can wish; *having itching
ear* —Fond of novelty and variety, which the number of new teachers, as well as
their empty, soft, or philosophical discourses pleased. Such teachers, and such
hearers, seldom are much concerned with what is strict or to the purpose: *heap
to themselves*—Not enduring sound doctrine, they will reject the sound preachers,
and gather together all that suit their own taste. Probably they send out one
another as teachers, and so are never at a loss for numbers.

5. *Watch*—An earnest, constant, persevering exercise. The Scripture watching, or waiting, implies steadfast faith, patient hope, labouring love, unceasing
prayer; yea, the mighty exertion of all the affections of the soul that a man is
capable of; *in all things*—Whatever you are doing, yet in that, and it, in all
things, watch: *do the work of an evangelist*—Which was next to that of an
apostle.

6. *The time of my departure is at hand*—So undoubtedly God had shown him;
I am ready to be offered up—Literally, *to be poured out*—as the wine and oil were
on the ancient sacrifices.

8. *The crown of* that *righteousness*—Which God has imputed to me and
wrought in me; *will render to all*—This increases the joy of Paul, and encourages Timotheus. Many of these St. Paul himself had gained: *that have loved
his appearing*—Which only a real Christian can do. I say a real Christian, to
comply with the mode of the times: else they would not understand, although
the word *Christian* necessarily implies whatsoever is holy, as God is holy

ness, which the Lord the righteous Judge will render me in that
day, and not to me only, but to all them likewise that have loved
his appearing.

9 Do thy diligence to come to me shortly, For Demas hath for-
10 saken me, loving the present world, and is gone to Thessalonica,
11 Crescens to Galatia, Titus to Dalmatia. Only Luke is with me.
Take Mark and bring him with thee, for he is profitable to me
12 for *my* ministry. Tychicus I have sent to Ephesus. When thou
13 comest, bring the cloak which I left at Troas with Carpus, and
14 the books, especially the parchments. Alexander the copper-
smith did me much evil; the Lord will reward him according to
15 his works. Of whom be thou also aware; for he hath greatly
16 withstood our words. At my first defence no man appeared
with me, but all forsook me: may it not be laid to their charge!
17 But the Lord stood by me, and strengthened me, that through me
the preaching might be fully known, even that all nations might
18 hear: and I was delivered out of the mouth of the lion. And
the Lord will deliver me from every evil work, and preserve *me*
unto his heavenly kingdom; to whom *be* the glory for ever and
ever. Amen.
19 Salute Priscilla, and Aquila, and the family of Onesiphorus
20 Erastus abode at Corinth; but Trophimus I have left at Miletus
21 sick. Do thy diligence to come before winter. Eubulus saluteth
thee, and Pudens, and Linus, and Claudia, and all the brethren.
22 The Lord Jesus Christ *be* with thy spirit. Grace *be* with you.

Strictly speaking, to join *real* or *sincere* to a word of so complete an import, is
grievously to debase its noble signification, and is like adding *long* to eternity, or
wide to immensity.

9. *Come to me*—Both that he might comfort him, and be strengthened by him.
Timotheus himself is said to have suffered at Ephesus.

10. *Demas*—Once my fellow labourer, Philem. ver. 24, *hath forsaken me*
Crescens—Probably a preacher also, is gone with my consent, to Galatia; *Titus*,
to Dalmatia, having now left Crete. These either went with him to Rome, or
visited him there.

11. *Only Luke*—Of my fellow labourers, *is with me*—But God is with me; and
it is enough. *Take Mark*—Who, though he once departed from the work, is
now again profitable to me.

13. *The cloak*—Either the *Toga*, which belonged to him as a Roman citizen,
or an upper garment, which might be needful as winter came on; *which I left at*
Troas with Carpus—Who was probably his host there; *especially the parchments*
—The books written on parchment.

14. *The Lord will reward him*—This he spoke prophetically.

16. *All*—My friends and companions, *forsook me*—And do we expect to find
such as will not forsake us? *My first defence*—Before the savage emperor, Nero.

17. *The preaching*—The Gospel which we preach.

18. *And the Lord will deliver me from every evil work*—Which is far more than
delivering me from death; yea, and over and above; *preserve me unto his heaven-*
ly kingdom—Far better than that of Nero.

20. When I came on, *Erastus abode at Corinth*—Being chamberlain of the
city; Rom. xvi, 23, *but Trophimus I have left sick*—Not having power (as neither had any of the apostles) to work miracles when he pleased, but only when
God pleased.

NOTES

ON

ST. PAUL'S EPISTLE TO TITUS.

TITUS was converted from heathenism by St. Paul, Gal. ii, 3, and, as it seems, very early, since the apostle accounted him as his brother at his first going into Macedonia. And he managed and settled the Churches there, when St. Paul thought it not good to go thither himself. He had now left him at Crete, to regulate the Churches; to assist him wherein, he wrote this epistle, as is generally believed, after the first, and before the second to Timothy. The tenor and style are much alike in this and in those, and they cast much light on each other; and are worthy the serious attention of all Christian ministers and Churches in all ages.

THIS EPISTLE HAS FOUR PARTS:

cc

TITUS.

---

1 PAUL, a servant of God, and an apostle of Jesus Christ, according to the faith of the elect of God, and the knowledge
2 of the truth which is after godliness, In hope of eternal life, which God, who cannot lie, promised before the world began;
3 And he hath in his own times manifested his word, through the

---

Verse 1. *Paul, a servant of God, and an apostle of Jesus Christ*—Titles suitable to the person of Paul, and the office he was assigning to Titus, *according to the faith*—The propagating of which is the proper business of an apostle. *A servant of God*—According to the faith of the elect. *An apostle of Jesus Christ*—According to the knowledge of the truth. We serve God, according to the measure of our faith: we fulfil our public office according to the measure of our knowledge. *The truth that is after godliness*—Which in every point runs parallel with and supports the vital, spiritual worship of God; and indeed has no other end or scope. These two verses contain the sum of Christianity, which Titus was always to have in his eye, *of the elect of God*—Of all real Christians.

2. *In hope of eternal life*—The grand motive and encouragement of every apostle and every servant of God; *which God promised before the world began*—To Christ our head.

3. *And he hath in his own times*—At sundry times: and *his own times* are fittest for his own work. What creature dares ask, Why no sooner? *manifested his*

preaching wherewith I am entrusted, according to the command-
4 ment of God our Saviour: To Titus, my own son after the common faith, grace, mercy, and peace from God the Father, and the
Lord Jesus Christ our Saviour.
5   For this cause I left thee in Crete, that thou mightest set in
order the things which are wanting, and ordain elders in every
6 city, as I appointed thee: If a man is blameless, the husband of
one wife, having believing children, not accused of luxury, or
7 unruly. For a bishop must be blameless, as the steward of God;
not self-willed, not passionate, not given to wine, not a striker,
8 not desirous of filthy gain: But hospitable, a lover of good men,
9 prudent, just, holy, temperate; Holding fast the faithful word, as
he hath been taught, that he may be mighty by sound doctrine
10 both to exhort and to convince the gainsayers. For there are
many unruly and vain talkers and deceivers, especially they of
11 the circumcision, Whose mouths must be stopped, who overturn
whole families, teaching things which they ought not, for the
12 sake of filthy gain. One of themselves, a prophet of their own,
hath said, The Cretans are always liars, evil wild beasts, lazy
13 gluttons. This witness is true; therefore rebuke them sharply,
14 that they may be sound in the faith; Not giving heed to Jewish
15 fables, and commandments of men, that turn from the truth. To
the pure all things are pure; but to the defiled and unbelieving
nothing is pure; but both their understanding and conscience
16 are defiled. They profess to know God, but by *their* works they

---

word—Containing that promise, and the whole truth which is after godliness; *through the preaching wherewith I am entrusted, according to the commandment of God our Saviour*—And who dares exercise this office on any less authority?
4. *My own son*—Begot in the same image of God, and repaying a paternal with a filial affection. *The common faith*—Common to me and all my spiritual children.
5. *The things which are wanting*—Which I had not time to settle myself; *ordain elders*—Appoint the most faithful, zealous men to watch over the rest. Their character follows, ver. 6–9. These were the *elders*, or *bishops*, that Paul approved of; men that had *living faith*, a *pure conscience*, a *blameless life*.
6. *The husband of one wife*—Surely the Holy Ghost, by repeating this so often, designed to leave the Romanists without excuse.
7. *As the steward of God*—To whom he entrusts immortal souls: *Not self-willed*—Literally, *not pleasing himself;*—but all men for their good to edification: *Not passionate*—But mild, yielding, tender.
9. *As he hath been taught*—Perhaps it might be more literally rendered, *according to the teaching*, or doctrine of the apostles, alluding to Acts ii, 42.
10. *They of the circumcision*—The Jewish converts.
11. *Stopped*—The word properly means, to *put a bit into the mouth* of an unruly horse.
12. *A prophet*—So all poets were anciently called. But besides Diogenes, Laertius says that Epimenides, the Cretan poet, foretold many things. *Evil wild beasts*—Fierce and savage.
14. *Commandments of men*—The *Jewish* or *other teachers*, whoever they were that *turned from the truth*.
15. *To the pure*—Those whose hearts are purified by faith, (this we allow,) *all things are pure*—All kinds of meat; the Mosaic distinction between clean and unclean meats being now taken away; *but to the defiled and unbelieving nothing is pure*—The apostle joins *defiled and unbelieving*, to intimate that nothing can be clean without a true faith. For both the understanding and conscience, those leading powers of the soul, are polluted; consequently so is the man and all he does.

deny *him*, being abominable and disobedient, and void of judg
ment, as to every good work.

II.   But speak thou the things which become wholesome doctrine,
2 That the aged men be vigilant, serious, prudent, sound in faith,
3 love, patience : That the aged women in like manner *be* in behaviour as becometh holiness ; not slanderers, not given to much
4 wine ; teachers of that which is good : That they instruct the
young women to be wise, to love their husbands, to love their
5 children, Discreet, chaste, keepers at home, good, obedient to
their own husbands, that the word of God be not blasphemed.
6 The young men likewise exhort to be discreet, In all things
7 showing thyself a pattern of good works, in doctrine, uncorrupt-
8 ness, seriousness, Wholesome speech, that cannot be reproved ;
that he who is on the contrary part may be ashamed, having no
9 evil thing to say of us. *Exhort* servants to be subject to their
own masters, to please *them* in all things, not answering again,
10 Not stealing, but showing all good fidelity, that they may in all
things adorn the Gospel of God our Saviour.
11   For the saving grace of God hath appeared to all men, In
12 structing us, that having renounced ungodliness and all worldly
desires, we should live soberly, and righteously, and godly, in

---

II. 1. *Wholesome*—Restoring and preserving spiritual health.

2. *Vigilant*—As veteran soldiers, not easily to be surprised: *Patience*—A virtue particularly needful for, and becoming them. *Serious*—Not drolling, or
diverting, on the brink of eternity.

3. *In behaviour*—The particulars whereof follow ; *as becometh holiness*—Literally, observing a holy decorum : *not slanderers*—Or evil speakers ; *not given to
much wine*—If they use a little for their own infirmities. *Teachers*—Age and
experience call them so to be ; let them teach *good* only.

4. *That they instruct the young women*—These Timothy was to instruct himself, Titus by the elder women ; *to love their husbands, their children*—With a
tender, temperate, holy, wise affection. O how hard a lesson !

5. *Discreet*—Particularly in the love of their children ; *Chaste*—Particularly
in the love of their husbands ; *keepers at home*—Whenever they are not called
out by works of necessity, piety, and mercy ; *Good*—Well tempered, sweet, soft,
obliging ; *Obedient to their husbands*—Whose will, in all things lawful, is a rule
to the wife ; *That the word of God be not blasphemed*—Or evil spoken of ; particularly by unbelieving husbands ; who lay all the blame on the *religion* of their
wives.

6. *To be discreet*—A virtue rarely found in youth.

7. *Showing thyself a pattern*—Titus himself was then young ; *in* the *doctrine*
which thou teachest in public : (As to matter, *uncorruptness ;* as to the manner of
delivering it, *Seriousness*—Weightiness, solemnity.)

8. *Wholesome speech*—In private conversation.

9. *Please them in all things*—Wherein it can be done without sin ; *not answering again*—Though blamed unjustly. This honest servants are most apt to do :
not stealing—Not *taking* or *giving* any thing without their masters' leave : this
fair-spoken servants are apt to do.

10. *Showing all good fidelity*—Soft, obliging faithfulness ; *that they may adorn
the doctrine of God our Saviour*—More than St. Paul says of kings. How he
raises the lowness of his subject ! So may they the lowness of their condition.

11. *The saving grace of God*—So it is in its nature, tendency, and design ;
hath appeared to all men—High and low.

12. *Instructing us*—All who do not reject it ; *that having renounced ungodliness*—Whatever is contrary to the fear and love of God ; *and worldly desires*—
Which are opposite to sobriety and righteousness ; *we should live soberly*—In all
purity and holiness. Sobriety, in the Scripture sense, is rather the whole temper of a man, than a single virtue in him. It comprehends all that is opposite to

13 the present world, Looking for the blessed hope and the glorious appearing of the great God, even our Saviour Jesus Christ;
14 Who gave himself for us, that he might redeem us from all iniquity, and purify to himself a peculiar people, zealous of good
15 works. These things speak and exhort, and rebuke with all authority : let no man despise thee.

III. Remind them to be subject to principalities and powers, to
2 obey *magistrates*, to be ready for every good work ; To speak evil of no man, not to be quarrelsome, *to be* gentle, showing all
3 meekness toward all men. For we also were formerly without understanding, disobedient, deceived, enslaved to various desires and pleasures, living in wickedness and envy, hateful, hating
4 one another : But when the kindness and love of God our Sa-
5 viour toward man appeared, Not by works of righteousness which we have done, but according to his own mercy he saved us, by the laver of regeneration, and renewing of the Holy
6 Ghost : Which he poured forth richly upon us, through Jesus
7 Christ our Saviour, That being justified by his grace, we might
8 become heirs, according to the hope of eternal life. *This is* a faithful saying, and these things I will that thou affirm constantly, that they who have believed in God be careful to excel in

---

the drowsiness of sin, the folly of ignorance, the unholiness of disorderly passions. Sobriety is no less than all the powers of the soul, being consistently and constantly awake, duly governed by heavenly prudence, and entirely conformable to holy affections; *and righteously*—Doing to all as we would they should do to us; *and godly*—As those who are consecrated to God both in heart and life.

13. *Looking*—With eager desire for that *glorious appearing*—Which we hope for; *of the great God, even our Saviour Jesus Christ*—So that if there be (according to the Arian scheme) a great God and a little God, Christ is not the little God, but the great one.

14. *Who gave himself for us*—To die in our stead; *that he might redeem us*— Miserable bond slaves, as well from the power and the very being, as from the guilt of all our sins.

15. *Let no man despise thee*—That is, let none have just cause to despise thee. Yet they surely will. Men who know not God will despise a true minister of his word.

III. 1. *Remind them*—All the Cretan Christians, *to be subject*—Passively, not resisting, *to principalities*—Supreme; *and powers*—Subordinate governors; and *to obey*—them actively, so far as conscience permits.

2. *To speak evil*—Neither of them nor any man; *not to be quarrelsome*—To assault none; *to be gentle*—When assaulted; *toward all men*—Even those who are such as we were.

3. *For we*—And as God hath dealt with us, so ought we to deal with our neighbour; *were without understanding*—Wholly ignorant of God; *and disobedient*—When he was declared to us.

4. *When the love of God appeared*—By the light of his Spirit to our inmost soul.

5. *Not by works*—In this important passage the apostle presents us with a delightful view of our redemption. Herein we have, I. The cause of it: not our works or righteousness, but the kindness and love of God our Saviour. II. The effects, which are, 1. Justification, being justified, pardoned, and accepted through the alone merits of Christ, not from any desert in us, but according to his own mercy by his grace, his free, unmerited goodness: 2. Sanctification; expressed by *the laver of regeneration*, (that is, baptism, the thing signified, as well as the outward sign,) and the renewal of the Holy Ghost; which purifies the soul as water cleanses the body, and renews it in the who' : image of God. III. The consummation of all, *that we might become heirs of eternal life*, and live now in the joyful hope of it.

9 good works; these things are good and profitable to men. But avoid foolish questions, and genealogies, and contentions, and
10 strivings about the law; for they are unprofitable and vain. A
11 heretic, after a first and second admonition, reject, Knowing that such a one is perverted and sinneth, being self-condemned.
12 When I shall send Artemas or Tychicus to thee, be diligent to come to me to Nicopolis; for I have determined to winter
13 there. Send forward with diligence Zenas the lawyer, and
14 Apollos, that they may want nothing. And let ours also learn to excel in good works for necessary uses, that they be not unfruit-
15 ful. All that are with me salute thee. Salute them that love us in the faith. Grace be with you all.

8. *Be careful to excel in good works*—Though the apostle does not lay these for the foundation, yet he brings them in at their proper place; and then mentions them, not slightly, but as affairs of great importance. He desires that all believers should *be careful*—Have their thoughts upon them, use their best contrivance, their utmost endeavours, not barely to practise, but *to excel*, to be eminent and distinguished in them: because though they are not the ground of our reconciliation with God, yet they are amiable and honourable to the Christian profession; *and profitable to men*—Means of increasing the everlasting happiness both of ourselves and others.

10. *A heretic, after a first and second admonition, reject*—Avoid, leave to himself. This is the only place in the whole Scripture where this word *heretic* occurs; and here it evidently means a man that obstinately persists in contending about foolish questions, and thereby occasions strifes and animosities, schisms and parties in the Church. This, and this alone, is a *heretic* in the Scripture sense. And his punishment likewise is here fixed. *Shun, avoid him, leave him to himself.* As for the popish sense, "A man that errs in fundamentals," although it crept, with many other things, early into the Church, yet it has no shadow of foundation, either in the Old or New Testament.

11. *Such a one is perverted*—In his heart, at least; *and sinneth, being self-condemned*—Being convinced in his own conscience that he acts wrong.

12. *When I shall send Artemas or Tychicus*—To succeed thee in thy office Titus was properly an evangelist, who, according to the nature of that office, had no fixed residence, but presided over other elders wherever he travelled from place to place, assisting each of the apostles according to the measure of his abilities. *Come to me to Nicopolis*—Very probably not the Nicopolis in Macedonia, as the vulgar subscription asserts: (indeed none of those subscriptions at the end of St. Paul's epistles are of any authority.) Rather, it was a town of the same name, which lay upon the seacoast of Epirus; *for I have determined to winter there*—Hence it appears he was not there yet. If so, he would have said, to winter *here*. Consequently this letter was not written from thence.

13. *Send forward Zenas the lawyer*—Either a Roman lawyer, or an expounder of the Jewish law.

14. *And let ours also*—All our brethren at Crete; *learn*—Both by thy admonition and example. Perhaps they had not before assisted Zenas and Apollos as they ought to have done.

NOTES

ON

ST. PAUL'S EPISTLE TO PHILEMON.

ONESIMUS, servant of Philemon, an eminent person in Colosse, ran away from his master to Rome. Here he was converted to Christianity by St. Paul, who sent him back to his master with this letter. It seems Philemon not only pardoned, but gave him his liberty; seeing Ignatius makes mention of him as succeeding Timotheus, at Ephesus.

THE LETTER HAS THREE PARTS:

PHILEMON.

---

1 PAUL, a prisoner of Christ Jesus, and Timotheus a brother,
2 to Philemon the beloved and our fellow labourer, And to the
beloved Apphia, and Archippus our fellow soldier, and the Church
3 which is in thy house: Grace be unto you, and peace from God
our Father, and the Lord Jesus Christ.
4 I thank my God, making mention of thee always in my
5 prayers, (Hearing of thy faith which thou hast toward the Lord
6 Jesus, and love toward all saints,) That the communication of
thy faith may become effectual, by the acknowledgment of every
7 good thing which is in you toward Christ Jesus. For we have
great joy and consolation in thy love, because the bowels of the
8 saints are refreshed by thee, brother. Wherefore, though I might
9 be very bold in Christ to enjoin thee what is convenient, Yet

---

Verse 1. This single epistle infinitely transcends all the wisdom of the world. And it gives us a specimen, how Christians ought to treat of secular affairs from higher principles. *Paul, a prisoner of Christ*—To whom, as such, Philemon could deny nothing, *and Timotheus*—This was written before the Second Epistle to Timothy, ver, 22.

2. *To Apphia*—His wife, to whom also the business in part belonged; *and the Church in thy house*—The Christians who meet there.

5. *Hearing*—Probably from Onesimus.

6. I pray *that the communication of thy faith may become effectual*—That is, that thy faith may be effectually communicated to others, who see and acknowledge thy piety and charity.

7. *The saints*—To whom Philemon's house was open, ver. 2.

8. *I might be bold in Christ*—Through the authority he hath given me.

36

out of love I rather entreat *thee*, being such a one as Paul the
10 aged, and now also a prisoner of Jesus Christ: I entreat thee
11 for my son, whom I have begotten in my bonds, Onesimus, Who
   was formerly unprofitable to thee, but now profitable to thee and
12 me. Whom I have sent again : thou therefore receive him, that
13 is my own bowels : Whom I was desirous to have retained with
14 me, to serve me in thy stead in the bonds of the Gospel. But I
   would do nothing without thy consent ; that thy benefit might
15 not be, as it were, by constraint, but willingly. And perhaps for
   this end was he separated for a season, that thou mightest have
16 him for ever ; No longer as a servant, but above a servant, a
   brother beloved, especially to me ; and how much more to thee,
17 both in the flesh and in the Lord ? If therefore thou accountest
18 me a partner, receive him as myself. If he hath wronged thee,
19 or oweth *thee* any thing, put that to my account. I Paul have
   written with my own hand ; I will repay *it ;* not to say unto thee
20 that thou owest also thyself to me besides. Yea, brother, let me
   have joy of thee in the Lord ; refresh my bowels in Christ.
21 Having confidence of thy obedience I have written to thee,
22 knowing that thou wilt do even more than I say. Withal prepare me also a lodging ; for I trust I shall be given to you
23 through your prayers. Epaphras, my fellow prisoner in Christ
24 Jesus, saluteth you ; Mark, Aristarchus, Demas, Luke, my fellow
25 labourers. The grace of our Lord Jesus Christ *be* with your
   spirit.

9. *Yet out of love I rather entreat thee*—In how handsome a manner does the
apostle just hint, and immediately drop the consideration of his power to command, and tenderly entreat Philemon, to hearken to his friend, his aged friend,
and now prisoner for Christ! With what endearment, in the next verse, does
he call Onesimus his son, before he names his name! And as soon as he had
mentioned it, with what fine address does he just touch on his former faults, and
instantly pass on to the happy change that was now made upon him! So disposing Philemon to attend to his request, and the motives wherewith he was
going to enforce it.

10. *Whom I have begotten in my bonds*—The son of my age.

11. *Now profitable*—None should be expected to be a good servant, before he
is a good man. He manifestly alludes to his name, Onesimus, which signifies
profitable.

12. *Receive him, that is, my own bowels*—Whom I love as my own soul. Such
is the natural affection of a father in Christ toward his spiritual children.

13. *To serve me in thy stead*—To do those services for me, which thou, if present, wouldst gladly have done thyself.

14. *That thy benefit might not be by constraint*—For Philemon could not have
refused it.

15. God might permit him to be *separated* (a soft word) *for a season, that thou
mightest have him for ever*—Both on earth and in heaven).

16. *In the flesh*—As a dutiful servant, *in the Lord*—As a fellow Christian.

17. *If thou accountest me a partner*—So that thy things are mine, and mine are
thine.

19. *I will repay it*—If thou requirest it, *not to say that thou owest me thyself*—It
cannot be expressed, how great our obligation is to those who have gained our
souls to *Christ ; besides*—Receiving Onesimus.

20. *Refresh my bowels in Christ*—Give me the most exquisite and Christian
pleasure.

22 *Given to you*—Restored to liberty.

NOTES

ON

THE EPISTLE TO THE HEBREWS

It is agreed by the general tenor of antiquity, that this epistle was written by St. Paul; whose other epistles were sent to the Gentile converts; this only to the Hebrews. But this improper inscription was added by some later hand. It was sent to the Jewish Hellenist Christians, dispersed through various countries. St. Paul's method and style are easily observed therein. He places, as usual, the proposition and division before the treatise, chap. ii, 17. He subjoins the exhortatory to the doctrinal part; quotes the same scriptures, chap. i, 6; ii, 8; x, 30, 38; and uses the same expressions as elsewhere. But why does he not prefix his name, which, it is plain from chap. iii, 19, was dear to them to whom he wrote? Because he prefixes no inscription, in which, if at all, the name would have been mentioned. The ardour of his spirit carries him directly upon his subject, (just like St. John in his first epistle,) and throws back his usual salutation and thanksgiving to the conclusion.

This epistle of St. Paul, and both those of St. Peter, (one may add, that of St. James and of St. Jude also,) were written both to the same persons, dispersed through Pontus, Galatia, and other countries, and nearly at the same time. St. Paul suffered at Rome three years before the destruction of Jerusalem. Therefore this epistle likewise was written while the temple was standing. St. Peter wrote a little before his martyrdom, and refers to the epistles of St. Paul, this in particular.

The scope of it is to confirm their faith in Christ. And this he does, by demonstrating his glory. All the parts of it are full of the most earnest and pointed admonitions and exhortations. And they go on, in one tenor, the particle *therefore* everywhere connecting the doctrine and the use.

THE SUM IS,

There are many comparisons in this epistle, which may be nearly reduced to two heads: 1. The prophets, the angels, Moses, Joshua, Aaron, are great; but Jesus Christ is infinitely greater: 2. The ancient believers enjoyed high privileges; but Christian believers enjoy far higher. To illustrate this, examples both of happiness and misery are everywhere interspersed: so that in this epistle there is a kind of recapitulation of the whole Old Testament. In this also Judaism is abrogated, and Christianity carried to its height.

HEBREWS.

1 God, who at sundry times, and in divers manners, spake of old to the fathers by the prophets, hath in these last days spoken 2 to us by *his* Son; Whom he hath appointed heir of all things, by

Verse 1. *God, who at sundry times*—The creation was revealed in the time of Adam, the last judgment in the time of Enoch; and so at various times and in various degrees more explicit knowledge was given, *in divers manners*—In visions, in dreams, and by revelations of various kinds. Both these are opposed to the one entire and perfect revelation which he has made to us by Jesus Christ. The very number of the prophets showed that they prophesied only *in part; of old*—There were no prophets for a large tract of time before Christ came, that the great Prophet might be the more earnestly expected; *spake*—A part is put for the whole, implying every kind of Divine communication, *by the prophets*—The mention of whom is a virtual declaration, that the apostle received the whole Old Testament, and was not about to advance any doctrine in contradiction to it: *hath in these last times*—Intimating that no other revelation is to be expected: *spoken*—All things, and in the most perfect manner, *by his Son*—Alone. The Son spake by the apostles. The majesty of the Son of God is proposed, I, Absolutely, by the very name of Son, ver. 1, and by three glorious predicates, *whom he hath appointed, by whom he made, who sat down;* whereby he is described, from the beginning to the con̄ummation of all things, ver. 2, 3; II, Comparatively to angels, ver. 4. The proof of this proposition immediately follows the name of *Son* being proved, ver. 5. His being heir of all things, ver. 6, 9; his making the worlds, ver. 10, 12; his sitting at God's right hand, ver. 13, &c.

2. *Whom he hath appointed heir of all things*—After the name of Son, his inheritance is mentioned. God appointed him the heir, long before he made the worlds, (Eph. iii, 11; Prov. viii, 22, &c.) The *Son* is the first-born; born before

3 whom he also made the worlds: Who being the brightness of his glory, and the express image of his person, and sustaining all things by the word of his power, when he had by himself purged our sins, sat down on the right hand of the Majesty on 4 high, Being so much higher than the angels, as he hath by in- 5 heritance a more excellent name than they. For to which of the angels did he ever say, * Thou art my Son; this day have I begotten thee? And again, † I will be to him a Father, and he 6 shall be to me a Son? .And again, ‡ When he bringeth in the

---

all things. The *heir* is a term relating to the creation which followed, ver. 6. *By whom he also made the worlds*—Therefore the Son was before all worlds. His glory reaches from everlasting to everlasting, though God spake by him to us only in these last days.

3. *Who sat down*—The third of these glorious predicates, with which three other particulars are interwoven, (which are mentioned likewise, and in the same order, Col. i, 15, 17, 20.) *Who being*—The glory which he received in his exaltation at the right hand of the Father, no angel was capable of; but the Son alone, who likewise enjoyed it long before; *the brightness of his glory*—Glory is the nature of God revealed in its brightness; *the express image* or *stamp*—Whatever the Father is, is exhibited in the Son, as a seal in the stamp on wax; *of his person* or *substance*—The word denotes the unchangeable perpetuity of Divine life and power; *and sustaining all things*—Visible and invisible, in being; *by the word of his power*—That is, by his powerful word; *when he had by himself*— Without any Mosaic rites or ceremonies; *purged our sins*—In order to which it was necessary he should for a time divest himself of his glory. In this chapter St. Paul describes his glory, chiefly as he is the Son of God; afterward, chap. ii, 6, &c., the glory of the man Christ Jesus. He speaks indeed briefly of the former, before his humiliation, but copiously after his exaltation; as from hence the glory he had from eternity began to be evidently seen. Both his purging our sins and sitting on the right hand of God are largely treated of in the seven following chapters; *sat down*—The priests stood while they ministered. Sitting therefore denotes the consummation of his sacrifice. This word, *sat down*, contains the scope, the theme, and the sum of the epistle.

4. This verse has two clauses, the latter of which is treated of ver. 5, the former, ver. 13. Such transpositions are also found in the other epistles of St. Paul, but in none so frequently as in this. The Jewish doctors were peculiarly fond of this figure, and used it much in all their writings. The apostle, therefore, becoming all things to all men, here follows the same method. All the inspired writers were readier in all the figures of speech than the most experienced orators: *Being*—By his exaltation, after he had been lower than them, chap. ii, 9, *so much higher than the angels*—It was extremely proper to observe this, because the Jews gloried in their law, as it was delivered by the ministration of angels. How much more may we glory in the Gospel, which was given, not by the ministry of angels, but of the very Son of God? *As he hath by inheritance a more excellent name*—Because he is the Son of God, he inherits that name, in right whereof he inherits all things. His inheriting that name is more ancient than *all worlds*. His inheriting all things as ancient as *all things: than they*— This denotes an immense pre-eminence. The angels do not inherit all things, but are themselves a portion of the Son's inheritance, whom they worship as their Lord.

5. *Thou art my Son*—God of God, light of light; *this day have I begotten thee*— I have begotten thee from eternity, which, by its unalterable permanency of duration, is one continued unsuccessive day. *I will be to him a Father, and he shall be to me a Son*—I will own myself to be his Father, and him to be my Son, by eminent tokens of my peculiar love. The former clause relates to his natural Sonship, by an eternal, inconceivable generation; the other to his Father's acknowledgment and treatment of him, as his incarnate Son. Indeed this promise related immediately to Solomon, but in a far higher sense to the Messiah.

6. *And again*—That is, in another scripture; *He*—God, *saith, when he bringeth in his first-begotten*—This appellation includes that of son, together with the

* Psa. ii, 7.   † 2 Sam. vii, 14.   ‡ Psa. xcvii, 7.

first-begotten into the world, he saith, And let all the angels of
7 God worship him.   And of the angels he saith, * Who maketh
8 his angels spirits, and his ministers a flame of fire.   But unto
the Son, † Thy throne, O God, *is* for ever and ever : the seep-
9 tre of thy kingdom *is* a sceptre of righteousness : Thou hast
loved righteousness and hated iniquity ; therefore God, *even* thy
God, hath anointed thee with the oil of gladness above thy fel-
10 lows. And, ‡ Thou, Lord, hast in the beginning laid the foundation of the earth, and the heavens are the works of thy hands.
11 They shall perish, but thou endurest ; yea, they all shall grow
12 old as a garment ; And as a mantle shalt thou change them, and
they shall be changed : but thou art the same, and thy years
13 shall not fail.   But to which of the angels did he ever say, § Sit
14 at my right hand, till I make thine enemies thy footstool ?   Are
they not all ministering spirits, sent forth to attend on them
II. who shall inherit salvation ?   Therefore we ought to give the
more earnest heed to the things which we have heard, lest at
2 any time we should let *them* slip.   For if the word spoken by
angels was steadfast, and every transgression and disobedience
3 received a just recompense : How shall we escape, if we neglect
so great a salvation, which, having at its beginning been spoken
by the Lord, was confirmed to us by them that had heard *him ?*

---

right of primogeniture, which the first-begotten Son of God enjoys, in a manner
not communicable to any creature ; *into the world*—Namely, at his incarnation,
He saith, Let all the angels of God worship him—So much higher was he, when in
his lowest estate, than the highest angel !

7. *Who maketh his angels*—This implies, they are only creatures, whereas the
Son is eternal, ver. 8, and the Creator himself, ver. 10. *Spirits and a flame of
fire*—Which intimates not only their office, but also their nature ; which is excellent indeed, the metaphor being taken from the most swift, subtle, and efficacious things on earth ; but nevertheless infinitely below the majesty of the Son.

8. *O God*—God, in the singular number, is never in Scripture, used absolutely
of any but the supreme God : *Thy* reign, of which the sceptre is the ensign, is
full of justice and equity.

9. *Thou hast loved righteousness and hated iniquity*—Thou art infinitely pure
and holy ; *therefore God,* who, as thou art Mediator, is *thy God, hath anointed
thee with the oil of gladness*—With the Holy Ghost, the fountain of joy ; *above thy
fellows*—Above all the children of men.

10. *Thou*—The same to whom the discourse is addressed in the preceding
verse.

12. *As a mantle*—With all ease. *They shall be changed*—Into new heavens
and a new earth ; but thou art eternally the same.

14. *Are they not all*—Though of various orders ; *ministering spirits sent forth*
—Ministering before God, sent forth to men ; *to attend on them*—In numerous
offices of protection, care, and kindness ; *who*—Having patiently continued in
well doing, shall *inherit* everlasting *salvation.*

II. In this and the two following chapters, the apostle subjoins an exhortation,
answering each head of the preceding chapter.

1. *Lest we should let them slip*—As water out of a leaky vessel. So the Greek
word properly signifies.

2. In giving the law, God *spoke by angels*—But in proclaiming the Gospel, by
his Son ; *steadfast*—Firm and valid ; *every transgression*—Commission of sin ;
every disobedience—Omission of duty.

3. *So great a salvation*—A deliverance from so great wickedness and misery,
into so great holiness and happiness. This was first *spoken of* (before he came it
was not known) *by* Him who is *the Lord*—Of angels as well as men ; *and wa*

---

* Psa. civ, 4.   † Psa. xlv. 6, 7.   ‡ Psa. cii, 25, 26, &c.   § Psa. cx, 1.

4 God also bearing witness both by signs, and wonders, and various
miracles, and distributions of the Holy Ghost, according to his
own will.

5 For he hath not subjected to the angels the world to come,
6 whereof we speak. But one in a certain place testified, saying,
*What is man, that thou art mindful of him, or the son of man,
7 that thou visitest him? Thou hast made him a little lower than
the angels, thou hast crowned him with glory and honour, and
hast set him over the works of thy hands. Thou hast put all
8 things in subjection under his feet. Now in putting all things
in subjection under him, he left nothing *that is* not put under
him: but now we do not yet see all things put under him.
9 But we see Jesus crowned with glory and honour, for
the suffering of death, who was made a little lower than the
angels, that by the grace of God he might taste death for every
10 man. For it became him for whom *are* all things, and by whom

confirmed to us—Of this age, even every article of it; *by them that had heard him*
—-And had been themselves also both eye witnesses and ministers of the word.

4. *By signs and wonders*—While he lived; *and various miracles and distributions of the Holy Ghost*—Miraculous gifts, distributed after his exaltation; *according to his own will*—Not theirs who received them.

5. This verse contains a proof of the third; the greater the salvation is, and
the more glorious the Lord whom we despise, the greater will be our punishment. *God hath not subjected the world to come*—That is, the dispensation of the
Messiah; which, being to succeed the Mosaic, was usually styled by the Jews
the world to come—Although it is still, in a great measure, *to come; whereof we
now speak*—Of which I am now speaking. In this last great dispensation the
Son alone presides.

6. *What is man*—To the vast expanse of heaven, to the moon and the stars
which thou hast ordained? This psalm seems to have been composed by David,
in a clear moon-shiny and star-light night, while he was contemplating the wonderful fabric of heaven: because in his magnificent description of its luminaries,
he takes no notice of the sun, the most glorious of them all. The words here
cited concerning dominion were, doubtless, in some sense, applicable to Adam;
although in their complete and highest sense they belong to none but the second
Adam; *or the son of man, that thou visitest him*—The sense rises, we are mindful
of him that is absent; but to visit denotes the care of a present God.

7. *Thou hast made him—Adam; a little lower than the angels*—The Hebrew is,
a little lower than—That is, next to God. Such was man as he came out of the
hands of his Creator: it seems, the highest of all created beings. But these words
are also, in a farther sense, as the apostle here shows, applicable to the Son of
God. It should be remembered that the apostles constantly cited the Septuagint
translation, very frequently without any variation. It was not their business, in
writing to the Jews, who at that time had it in high esteem, to amend or alter
this, which would of consequence have occasioned disputes without end.

8. *Now* this *putting all things under him*, implies that there is nothing that is
not put under him. But it is plain, this is not done now with regard to man in
general.

9. It is done only with regard to Jesus, God-man, who is now *crowned with
glory and honour*—As a reward for his having suffered death. *He was made a
little lower than the angels*—Who cannot either suffer or die; *that by the grace of
God he might taste death*—An expression denoting both the reality of his death,
and the shortness of its continuance; *for every man*—That ever was, or ever will
be born into the world.

10. In this verse the apostle expresses, in his own words, what he expressed
before in those of the psalmist. *It became him*—It was suitable to all his attributes, both to his justice, goodness, and wisdom; *for whom*—As their ultimate
end; *and by whom*—As their first cause, are all things; *in bringing many* adopted

* Psalm viii, 4.

are all things, in bringing many sons to glory, to perfect the cap
11 tain of their salvation by sufferings. For both he that sanctifieth,
and all they that are sanctified, *are* of one ; for which cause he
12 is not ashamed to call them brethren. Saying, *I will declare thy
name to my brethren ; †in the midst of the Church will I sing
13 praise unto thee. And again, ‡I will put my trust in him : And
again, Behold I and the children whom God hath given me.
14 Since then the children partake of flesh and blood, he also himself in like manner took part of the same, that through death he
might destroy him that had the power of death, that is, the devil :
15 And deliver them, as many as through fear of death were all
16 their lifetime subject to bondage. For verily he taketh not hold of

sons to glory—To this very thing, that they are sons, and·are treated as such ; *to
perfect the captain*—Prince, leader, and author of their salvation, by his atoning
sufferings for them. To perfect or consummate implies, the bringing him to a
full and glorious end of all his troubles, chap. v, 9. This consummation by sufferings intimates, 1. The glory of Christ, to whom, being consummated, all
things are made subject : 2. The preceding sufferings. Of these he treats expressly, ver. 11–18 ; having before spoken of his glory, both to give an edge to
his exhortations, and to remove the scandal of sufferings and death. A fuller
consideration of both these points he interweaves with the following discourse on
his priesthood. But what is here said of our Lord's being made perfect through
sufferings has no relation to our being saved or sanctified by sufferings. Even
he himself was perfect, as God and as man, before ever he suffered. By his sufferings, in his life and death, he was made a perfect or complete sin-offering.
But unless *we* were to be made the same sacrifice, and to atone for sin, what is
said of him in this respect is as much out of our sphere as his ascension into
heaven. It is his atonement, and his Spirit carrying on the work of faith with
power in our hearts, that alone can sanctify us. Various afflictions indeed may
be made subservient to this ; and so far as they are blessed to the weaning us
from sin, and causing our affections to be set on things above, so far they do indirectly help on our sanctification.

11. *For*—They are nearly related to each other : *He that sanctifieth*—Christ,
chap. xii, 12 ; *and all they that are sanctified*—That are brought to God, that
draw near, or come to him, (which are synonymous terms,) *are all of one*—Partakers of one nature, from one parent, Adam.

12. *I will declare thy name to my brethren*—Christ declares the name of God,
gracious and merciful, plenteous in goodness and truth, to all who believe, that
they also may praise him : *In the midst of the Church will I sing praise unto thee*
—As the precentor of the choir. This he did literally, in the midst of his apostles, on the night before his passion. And as it means, in a more general sense,
setting forth the praise of God, he has done it in the Church by his word and his
Spirit : he still does, and will do it, throughout all generations.

13. *And again*—As one that has communion with his brethren, in sufferings
as well as in nature, he says, *I will put my trust in him*—To carry me through
them all. *And again*—With a like acknowledgment of his near relation to them,
as younger brethren, who were yet but in their childhood, he presents all believers to God, saying, Behold I and the children whom thou hast given me.

14. *Since then the children partake of flesh and blood*—Of human nature with
all its infirmities, *he also in like manner took part of the same,* that *through his*
own death he *might destroy* the tyranny of *him that had,* by God's permission, the
power of death, with regard to the ungodly. Death is the devil's servant and
sergeant, delivering to him those whom he seizes in sin ; *that is, the devil*—The
power was manifest to all ; but who exerted it they saw not.

15. *And deliver them, as many as through fear of death were all their lifetime,*
till then, *subject to bondage*—Every man who fears death is subject to bondage ; is
in a slavish, uncomfortable state. And every man fears death more or less who
knows not Christ. Death is unwelcome to him, if he knows what death is. But
he delivers all true believers from this bondage.

16. *For verily he taketh not hold of angels*—He does not take their nature upon

* Psa xtii, 22.   † Psa. xii, 22.   ‡ Isa. viii, 17, 18.

17 angels, but he taketh hold of the seed of Abraham. Wherefore it behooved him to be made in all things like his brethren, that he might be a merciful and faithful high priest in things pertaining
18 to God, to expiate the sins of the people. For in that he hath suffered, being tempted himself, he is able to succour them that are tempted.

III. Wherefore, holy brethren, partakers of the heavenly calling, consider the apostle and high priest of our profession, Jesus,
2 Who was faithful to him that appointed him, as *was* also *Moses
3 in all his house. For this person was counted worthy of more glory than Moses, inasmuch as he that builded it hath more
4 honour than the house. Now every house is built by some one:
5 but he that built all things *is* God. And Moses verily was faithful in all his house as a servant, for a testimony of the
6 things which were to be afterward spoken: But Christ as a Son over his own house, whose house we are, if we hold fast the
7 confidence and the glorying of hope firm to the end. Where-
8 fore, (as the Holy Ghost saith,) †To-day, if ye will hear his

him; *but he taketh hold of the seed of Abraham*—He takes human nature upon him. St. Paul says, the seed of Abraham, rather than the seed of Adam, because to Abraham was the promise made.

17. *Wherefore it behooved him*—It was highly fit and proper, yea, necessary, in order to his design of redeeming them, *to be made in all things*—That essentially pertain to human nature, and in all sufferings and temptations, *like his brethren* —This is a recapitulation of all that goes before; the sum of all that follows is added immediately; *that he might be a merciful and faithful high priest*—Merciful toward sinners; faithful toward God. A priest or high priest is one who has a right of approaching God, and of bringing others to him. Faithful is treated of, chap. iii, 2, &c., with its use. Merciful, chap. iv, 14, &c., with the use also. High priest, chap. v, 4, &c.; chap. vii, 1, &c. The use is added from chap. x, 19, in things pertaining to God, *to expiate the sins of the people*—Offering up their sacrifices and prayers to God, deriving God's grace, peace, and blessings upon them.

18. *For in that he hath suffered, being tempted himself, he is able to succour them that are tempted*—That is, he has given a manifest, demonstrative proof, that he is able so to do.

III. 1. *The heavenly calling*—God calls from heaven, and to heaven, by the Gospel: *consider the apostle*—The messenger of God, who pleads the cause of God with us; *and high priest*—Who pleads our cause with God. Both are contained in the one word, Mediator. He compares Christ as an apostle with Moses; as a priest with Aaron. Both these offices, which Moses and Aaron severally bore, he bears together, and far more eminently: *of our profession*— The religion we profess.

2. *His house*—The Church of Israel, then the peculiar family of God.

3. *He that builded it hath more glory than the house*—Than the family itself, or any member of it.

4. *Now* Christ, he that built not only this house, but *all things*, is God; and so infinitely greater than Moses, or any creature.

5. *And Moses verily*—Another proof of the pre-eminence of Christ above Moses; *was faithful in all his house as a servant, for a testimony of the things which were afterward to be spoken*—That is, which was a full confirmation of the things which he afterward spake concerning Christ.

6. *But Christ* was faithful as a Son, *whose house we are*, while we hold fast, and shall be unto the end, if we hold fast our confidence in God, and glorying in his promises; our faith and hope.

7. *Wherefore*—Seeing he is faithful, be not ye unfaithful.

8. *As in the provocation*—When Israel provoked me by their strife and murmurings; *in the day of temptation*—When at the same time they tempted me, by distrusting my power and goodness.

* Num. xii, 7.   † Psa. xcv, 7, &c.

570 HEBREWS.

voice, harden not your hearts as in the provocation, * in the day
9 of temptation in the wilderness, When your fathers tempted
10 me, proved me, and saw my works forty years.   Therefore I
was grieved with that generation, and said, They always err in
11 their hearts, and they have not known my ways.   So I sware
12 in my wrath, They shall not enter into my rest.   Take heed,
brethren, lest there be in any of you an evil heart of unbelief,
13 in departing from the living God : But exhort one another daily,
while it is called to-day, lest any of you be hardened through
14 the deceitfulness of sin : (For we are made partakers of Christ,
if we hold fast the beginning of our confidence firm to the end.)
15 While it is said, To-day, if ye will hear his voice, harden not your
16 hearts, as in the provocation.   For who, when they had heard,
17 provoked *God ?*   *Were* they not all that came out of Egypt by
Moses ?   And with whom was he grieved forty years ?   *Was it*
18 not with them who had sinned?   Whose carcasses fell in the
wilderness.   And to whom sware he that they should not enter
19 into his rest, but to them that believed not?   So we see they
IV. could not enter in because of unbelief.   Let us therefore fear,
lest a promise being left *us* of entering into his rest, any of us
2 should altogether come short *of it.*   For unto us have the good
tidings been declared, as well as unto them ; but the word heard
did not profit them, not being mixed with faith in those that
3 heard *it.*   For we that have believed do enter into the rest ; as

9. *When your fathers*—That hard-hearted and stiff-necked generation. So little
cause had their descendants to glory in them ; *tempted me*—Whether I could and
would help them ; *proved me*—Put my patience to the proof, even while they saw
my glorious works, both of judgment and mercy, and that for forty years.
10. *Wherefore*—To speak after the manner of men, *I was grieved*—Displeased,
offended with that generation ; *and said, They always err in their hearts*—They
are led astray by their stubborn will and vile affections.   *And*—For this reason,
because wickedness has blinded their understanding, *they have not known my
ways*—By which I would have led them, like a flock, *into my rest*—In the promised land.
12. *Take heed lest there be in any of you*—As there was in them, *an evil heart
of unbelief*—Unbelief is the parent of all evil, and the very essence of unbelief
lies in departing from God, as the *living God*—The fountain of all our life, holiness, happiness.
13. *But*—To prevent it, *exhort one another, while it is called to-day*—This to-
day will not last for ever.   The day of life will end soon, and perhaps the day of
grace yet sooner.
14. *For we are made partakers of Christ*—And we shall still partake of him,
and all his benefits, *if we hold fast our faith unto the end.*   *If*—But not else : and
a supposition made by the Holy Ghost is equal to the strongest assertion.   Both
the sentiment and the manner of expression are the same as ver. 6.
16. *Were they not all that came out of Egypt?*—An awful consideration !   The
whole elect people of God (a very few excepted) *provoked God* presently after
their great deliverance; continued to *grieve* his Spirit for forty years, and perished
in their sin !
19. *So we see they could not enter in*—Though afterward they desired it.
IV. 2. *But the word*—Which they heard, *did not profit them*—So far from it,
that it increased their damnation.   It is then only when it is *mixed with faith,*
that it exerts its saving power.
3. *For we only that have believed, enter into the rest*—The proposition is, There
remains a rest for us.   This is proved, ver. 3-11, thus: That psalm mentions a
rest: yet it does not mean, 1. God's rest from creating, for this was long before

* Exod. xvii, 7

he said, I have sworn in my wrath, They shall not enter into
my rest, though the works were finished from the foundation
4 of the world. For he said thus in a certain place of the seventh
day,* And God rested on the seventh day from all his works:
5 And in this again, They shall not enter into my rest. Seeing
6 then it remaineth that some enter into it, and they to whom
the good tidings were declared before entered not in because
7 of unbelief. He again after so long a time fixeth a certain day
saying by David, To-day; as it was said before, To-day, if ye
8 will hear his voice, harden not your hearts. For if Joshua had
given them the rest, he would not have afterward spoken of
9 another day: There remaineth therefore a rest for the people
10 of God. For he that hath entered into his rest hath himself
11 also ceased from his works, as God *did* from his. Let us labour
therefore to enter into that rest, lest any one should fall after
12 the same example of unbelief. For the word of God *is* living
and powerful, and sharper than any two-edged sword, piercing
even to the dividing asunder both of the soul and spirit, both
of the joints and marrow, and *is* a discerner of the thoughts
13 and intentions of the heart. Neither is there any creature that
is not manifest in his sight; but all things *are* naked and opened
to the eyes of him with whom we have to do.
14   Having therefore a great high priest, that is passed through the

the time of Moses. Therefore in his time another rest was expected; of which
they who then heard fell short. Nor is it, 2. The rest which Israel obtained
through Joshua; for the psalmist wrote after him. Therefore it is, 3. The eternal rest in heaven. *As he said*—Clearly showing that there is a farther rest than
that which followed the finishing of the creation; *though the works were finished*
—Before: whence it is plain, God did not speak of resting from them.
4. *For*—Long after he had *rested from his works*—He speaks again.
5. *In this* psalm, of a rest yet to come.
7. *After so long a time*—It was about four hundred years from the time of
Moses and Joshua to David; *as it was said before*—St. Paul here refers to the
text he had just cited.
8. *The rest*—All the rest which God had promised.
9. *Therefore*—Since he still speaks of another day, *there* must *remain* a farther,
even an eternal *rest for the people of God.*
10. For they do not yet so rest. Therefore a fuller rest remains for them.
11. *Lest any one should fall*—Into perdition.
12. *For the word of God*—Preached, ver. 2, and armed with threatenings, ver. 3,
is living and powerful—Attended with the power of the living God, and conveying either life or death to the hearers; *sharper than any two-edged sword*—Penetrating the heart more than this does the body: *piercing*—Quite through, and
laying open, *the soul and spirit, joints and marrow*—The inmost recesses of the
mind, which the apostle beautifully and strongly expresses by this heap of figurative words: *and is a discerner*—Not only of *the thoughts*—But also of the *intentions.*
13. *In his sight*—It is God, whose word is thus *powerful:* it is God, *in* whose
sight every creature is *manifest:* and of this his word working on the conscience
gives the fullest conviction; *but all things are naked and opened*—Plainly alluding to the sacrifices under the law, which were first flayed, and then (as the
Greek word literally means) *cleft asunder through the neck* and back bone: so
that every thing, both without and within, was exposed to open view.
14. *Having therefore a great high priest*—Great indeed, being the eternal Son
of God, *that is passed through the heavens*—As the Jewish high priest passed
through the veil into the holy of holies, carrying with him the blood of the sacrifices, on the yearly day of atonement: so our great High Priest went once for all

* Genesis ii, 2.

heavens, Jesus the Son of God, let us hold fast *our* profession.
15 For we have not a high priest who cannot sympathize with our
infirmities, but one who was in all points tempted like as *we*
16 *are; yet* without sin. Let us therefore come boldly to the throne
of grace, that we may receive mercy, and find grace to help in
time of need.
V.   For every high priest, being taken from among men, is appointed for men in things pertaining to God, that he may offer
2 both gifts and sacrifices for sins : Who can have compassion
on the ignorant and the wandering, seeing he himself also is
3 compassed with infirmity, And because hereof, it behooveth him,
4 as for the people, so also for himself, to offer for sins.   And
no one taketh this honour to himself, but he that is called of
5 God, as *was* Aaron.   So also Christ glorified not himself to be
made a high priest, but he that said to him, * Thou art my Son,
6 this day have I begotten thee.   As he saith also in another
place, † Thou *art* a priest for ever after the order of Melchise-
7 dec : Who in the days of his flesh, having offered up prayers
and supplications, with strong crying and tears unto him that

through he visible heavens, with the virtue of his own blood, into the immediate
presence of God.
  15. *He sympathizes with* us, even in our innocent *infirmities,* wants, weaknesses, miseries, dangers: *yet without sin*—And therefore is indisputably able to
preserve us from it in all our temptations.
  16. *Let us therefore come boldly*—Without any doubt or fear, unto *the throne* of
God, our reconciled Father, even his throne *of grace*—Grace erected it, and
reigns there, and dispenses all blessings, in a way of mere, unmerited favour.
  V. 1. *For every high priest being taken from among men*—Is, till he is taken,
of the same rank with them: *and is appointed*—That is, is wont to be appointed:
in things pertaining to God—To bring God near to men, and men to God: *that
he may offer both gifts*—Out of things inanimate, and animal sacrifices.
  2. *Who can have compassion*—In proportion to the offence: so the Greek word
signifies: *on the ignorant*—Them that are in error: *and the wandering*—Them
that are in sin: *seeing himself also is compassed with infirmity*—Even with sinful
infirmity, and so needs the compassion which he shows to others.
  4. The apostle begins here to treat of the priesthood of Christ. The sum of
what he observes concerning it is, whatever is excellent in the Levitical priesthood is in Christ, and in a more eminent manner. And whatever is wanting in
those priests is in him; *and no one taketh this honour*—The priesthood, *to himself, but he that is called of God, as was Aaron*—And his posterity, who were all
of them called at one and the same time. But it is observable, Aaron did not
preach at all; preaching being no part of the priestly office.
  5. *So also Christ glorified not himself to be a high priest*—That is, did not take
this honour to himself; but received it from him *who said, Thou art my son, this
day have I begotten thee*—Not indeed at the same time: for his generation was
from eternity.
  7. The sum of the things treated of in the 7th and following chapters is contained in ver. 7–10, and in this sum is admirably comprised the process of his
passion with its inmost causes, in the **very** terms used by the evangelists; *who in
the days of his flesh*—Those two days in particular, wherein his sufferings were
at the height, *having offered up prayers and supplications*—Thrice, *with strong
crying and tears*—In the garden, *to him that was able to save him from death*—
Which yet he endured, in obedience to the will of his Father, *and being heard in
that which he* particularly *feared*—When the cup was offered him first, there was
set before him that horrible image of a painful, shameful, accursed death, which
moved him to pray conditionally against it: for if he had desired it, his heavenly
Father would have sent him more than twelve legions of angels to have delivered

* Psalm ii, 7.   † Psalm cx, 1.

was able to save him from death, and being heard in that he
8 feared; Though he was a Son, yet he learned obedience by the
9 things which he suffered, And being perfected, became the
10 author of eternal salvation to all that obey him, Called of God a
high priest after the order of Melchisedec.
11 Concerning whom we have many things to say, and hard to
12 be explained, seeing ye are become dull of hearing, For whereas
for the time ye ought to be teachers, ye have need that one teach
you again, which *are* the first principles of the oracles of God,
and are become such as have need of milk, and not of strong
13 meat. For every one that useth milk *is* unexperienced in the
14 word of righteousness; for he is a babe. But strong meat be-
longeth to them of full age, to them who have *their* senses exer
cised by habit to discern both good and evil.

him. But what he most exceedingly feared was, the weight of infinite justice;
the being bruised and put to grief by the hand of God himself. Compared with
this, every thing else was a mere nothing. And yet, so greatly did he even
thirst to be obedient to the righteous will of his Father, and to lay down even his
life for the sheep, that he vehemently longed to be baptized with this baptism,
Luke xii, 50. Indeed his human nature needed the support of Omnipotence, and
for this he sent up strong crying and tears: but throughout his whole life he
showed that it was not the sufferings he was to undergo, but the dishonour that
sin had done to so holy a God, that grieved his spotless soul. The consideration
of its being the will of God tempered his fear, and afterward swallowed it up.
And he was heard, not so that the cup should pass away, but so that he drank it
without any fear.

8. *Though he were a Son*—This is interposed, lest any should be offended at
all these instances of human weakness. In the garden how frequently did he call
God his Father? Matt. xxvi, 39, &c.; and hence it most evidently appears that
his being the Son of God did not arise merely from his resurrection; *yet learned
he*—The word *learned*, premised to the word *suffered*, elegantly shows how willingly he learned. He *learned obedience* when he began to suffer, when he applied
himself to drink that cup; obedience in suffering and dying.

9. *And being perfected*—By sufferings, chap. ii, 10, brought through all to glory,
he became the author—The procuring and efficient cause, *of eternal salvation to
all that obey him*—By doing and suffering his whole will.

10. *Called*—The Greek word here properly signifies surnamed. His name is,
the Son of God. The Holy Ghost seems to have concealed who Melchisedec
was on purpose that he might be the more eminent type of Christ. This only we
know, that he was a priest, and king of Salem or Jerusalem.

11. *Concerning whom*—The apostle here begins an important digression,
wherein he reproves, admonishes, and exhorts the Hebrews. *We*—Preachers
of the Gospel, *have many things to say and hard to be explained*—Though not so
much from the subject matter, as from your slothfulness in considering, and dul-
ness in apprehending the things of God.

12. *Ye have need that one teach you again which are the first principles of* religion. Accordingly these are enumerated in the first verse of the ensuing chapter. *And have need of milk*—The first and plainest doctrines.

13. *Every one that useth milk*—That neither desires, nor can digest any thing
else, (otherwise strong men use milk; but not milk chiefly, and much less that
only,) *is unexperienced in the word of righteousness*—The sublimer truths of the
Gospel. Such are all who desire, and can digest nothing but the doctrine of justification and imputed righteousness.

14. *But strong meat*—Those sublimer truths relating tc *perfection*, chap. vi, 1,
belong to them of full age who by habit—*Habit* here signifies strength of spiritual
understanding, arising from maturity of spiritual age: by, or in consequence of
this habit, they exercise themselves in these things with ease, readiness, cheerfulness, and profit.

VI.   Therefore leaving the principles of the doctrine of Christ, let
us go on to perfection ; not laying again the foundation of re-
2 pentance from dead works, and of faith in God, Of the doctrine
of baptisms and laying on of hands, and the resurrection of the
3 dead, and eternal judgment.   And this we will do, if God permit.
4 For *it is* impossible for those who were once enlightened, and
have tasted the heavenly gift, and been made partakers of the
5 Holy Ghost, And have tasted the good word of God, and the
6 powers of the world to come, And have fallen away, to renew
them again unto repentance, seeing they crucify to themselves
7 the Son of God afresh, and put *him* to an open shame.   For the
earth which drinketh in the rain that cometh often upon it, and
bringeth forth herbage, meet for them for whom it is tilled, re-
8 ceiveth blessing from God.   But that which beareth thorns and
briers *is* rejected and nigh unto a curse, whose end *is* to be
9 burned.   But, beloved, we are persuaded better things of you,
10 and things that accompany salvation, though we thus speak.   For

VI. 1. *Therefore leaving the principles of the doctrine of Christ*—That is, saying no more of them for the present, *let us go on to perfection ; not laying again
the foundation of repentance from dead works*—From open sins, the very first
thing to be insisted on, and faith in God, the very next point.   So St. Paul in his
very first sermon at Lystra, Acts xiv, 15, Turn from those vanities unto the living God.   And when they believed, they were to be baptized with the baptism
(not of the Jews, or of John, but) of Christ.   The next thing was to *lay hands*
upon them, that they might receive the Holy Ghost; after which they were more
fully instructed, touching *the resurrection*, and the general *judgment*, called *eternal*, because the sentence then pronounced is irreversible, and the effects of it
remain for ever.
3. *And this we will do*—We will *go on to perfection;* and so much the more
diligently, because,
4. *It is impossible for those who were once enlightened*—With the light of the
glorious love of God in Christ, *and have tasted the heavenly gift*—Remission of
sins, sweeter than honey and the honeycomb, *and been made partakers of the
Holy Ghost*—Of the witness and the fruits of the Spirit.
5. *And have tasted the good word of God*—Have had a relish for, and a delight
in it, *and the powers of the world to come*—Which every one tastes who has a
hope full of immortality.   Every child that is *naturally* born first *sees* the light,
then receives and *tastes* proper nourishment, and *partakes* of the things of this
world.   In like manner, the apostle (comparing spiritual with natural things)
speaks of one born of the Spirit, as *seeing* the light, *tasting* the sweetness, and
partaking of the things *of the world to come.*
6. *And have fallen away*—Here is not a supposition, but a plain relation of
fact.   The apostle here describes the case of those who have cast away both the
power and form of godliness; who have lost both their faith, hope, and love,
ver. 10, &c., and that *wilfully*, chap. x, 20.   Of these wilful, total apostates, he
declares it is impossible to *renew them again to repentance*, (though they were
renewed once,) either to the foundation, or any thing built thereon; *seeing they
crucify the Son of God afresh*—They use him with the utmost indignity, *and put
him to an open shame*—Causing his glorious name to be blasphemed.
8. *That which beareth thorns and briers*—Only or chiefly, *is rejected*—No more
labour is bestowed upon it; *whose end is to be burned*—As Jerusalem was shortly
after.
9. *But beloved*—In this one place he calls them so.   He never uses this appellation but in exhorting: *we are persuaded of you things that accompany salvation*
—We are persuaded you are now saved from your sins; and that ye have that
faith, love, and holiness, which lead to final salvation, *though we thus speak*—To
warn you, lest you should fall from your present steadfastness.
10. *For*—Ye give plain proof of your faith and love, which the righteous God
will surely reward.

God *is* not unrighteous, to forget your work and labour of love, which ye have showed toward his name in that ye have minis-
11 tered to the saints, and do minister. But we desire that every one of you may show unto the end the same diligence to the
12 full assurance of hope, That ye be not slothful, but followers of them, who through faith and long suffering inherited the pro-
13 mises. For when God made the promise to Abraham, because
14 he could swear by no greater, he swore by himself, Saying, *Surely blessing I will bless thee, and multiplying I will multi-
15 ply thee. And so, after he had patiently waited, he obtained the
16 promise. For men verily swear by the greater, and an oath for
17 confirmation *is* to them an end of all contradiction. Wherefore God, being willing to show more abundantly to the heirs of the promise the unchangeableness of his counsel, interposed by an
18 oath: That by two unchangeable things, in which *it was* impossible for God to lie, we might have strong consolation, who
19 have fled to lay hold on the hope set before us. Which *hope* we have as an anchor of the soul, both sure and steadfast, and which
20 entereth into the place within the veil, Whither Jesus *our* fore-

11. *But we desire you may show the same diligence unto the end*—And therefore we thus speak, *to the full assurance of hope*—Which you cannot expect, if you abate your diligence. The *full assurance of faith* relates to present pardon; the *full assurance of hope* to future glory. The former is the highest degree of *Divine evidence* that God *is* reconciled to *me* in the Son of his love: the latter is the same degree of *Divine evidence* (wrought in the soul by the same immediate inspiration of the Holy Ghost) of persevering grace, and of eternal glory. So much, and no more, as *faith* every moment *beholds with open face*, so much does *hope* see, to all eternity. But this assurance of faith and hope is not an opinion, not a bare construction of Scripture, but is given immediately by the power of the Holy Ghost; and what none can have for another, but for himself only.
12. *Inherited the promises*—The promised rest; paradise.
13. *For*—Ye have abundant encouragement, seeing no stronger promise could be made, than that great promise which God made to Abraham, and in him to us.
15. *After he had waited*—Thirty years, *he obtained the promise*—*Isaac*, the pledge of all the promises.
16. *Men* generally swear by Him who is infinitely *greater* than themselves, *and an oath for confirmation*, to confirm what is promised or asserted, usually puts *an end to all contradiction.* This shows that an oath taken in a religious manner is lawful even under the Gospel: otherwise the apostle would never have mentioned it with so much honour, as a proper means to confirm the truth.
17. *God interposed by an oath*—Amazing condescension! He who is greatest of all acts as if he were a middle person, as if while he swears, he were less than himself, by whom he swears. Thou that hearest the promise, dost thou not yet believe?
18. *That by two unchangeable things*—His promise and his oath, *in* either, much more in both of which, *it was impossible for God to lie, we might have strong consolation*—Swallowing up all doubt and fear; *who have fled*—After having been tossed by many storms, *to lay hold on the hope set before us*—On Christ the object of our hope, and the glory we hope for through him.
19. *Which hope* in Christ *we have as an anchor of the soul*—Entering into heaven itself, and fixed there, *within the veil*—Thus he slides back to the priesthood of Christ.
20. *A forerunner* uses to be less in dignity than those that are to follow him. But it is not so here; for Christ who is gone before us, is infinitely superior to us. What an honour is it to believers to have so glorious a forerunner, now appearing in the presence of God for them!

* Genesis xxii. 17.

runner is entered for us, who is made a high priest for ever after the order of Melchisedec.

VII. For this Melchisedec, king of Salem, priest of the most high God, * who met Abraham returning from the slaughter of the
2 kings and blessed him, To whom also Abraham divided a tenth part of all *the spoils;* being by interpretation, first, king of righteousness, and then king of Salem also, which is king of
3 peace: Without father, without mother, without pedigree, having neither beginning of days nor end of life, but being made
4 like the Son of God, remaineth a priest continually. Now consider how great this man *was,* to whom even the patriarch
5 Abraham gave the tenth of the spoils, And verily they of the sons of Levi, who receive the priesthood, have a commandment (according to the law) to take tithes of the people, that is, of their brethren, though they come out of the loins of Abraham,
6 But he whose pedigree is not from them, took tithes of Abra-
7 ham, and blessed him who had the promises: And without all
8 contradiction, the less is blessed of the greater. And here men that die receive tithes: but there, he, of whom it is testified that
9 he liveth, And even Levi, who receiveth tithes, paid tithes (so to
10 speak) through Abraham. For he was yet in the loins of his

VII. 1. The sum of this chapter is, Christ, as appears from his type, Melchisedec who was greater than Abraham himself, from whom Levi descended, has a priesthood altogether excellent, new, firm, perpetual.

2. *Being first*—According to the meaning of his own name, *king of righteousness, then*—According to the name of his city, *king of peace*—So in him as in Christ, righteousness and peace were joined. And so they are in all that believe in him.

3. *Without father, without mother, without pedigree*—Recorded, without any account of his descent from any ancestors of the priestly order: *having neither beginning of days nor end of life*—Mentioned by Moses; *but being*—In all these respects, *made like the Son of God*—Who is really *without father*—As to his human nature; *without mother*—As to his Divine; and in this also, *without pedigree*—Neither descended from any ancestors of the priestly order: *remaineth a priest continually*—Nothing is recorded of the death or successor of Melchisedec. But Christ alone does really remain without death and without successor.

4. The greatness of Melchisedec is described in all the preceding and following particulars. But the most manifest proof of it was, that Abraham gave him tithes, as to a priest of God and a superior; though he was himself a patriarch, greater than a king, and a progenitor of many kings.

5. *The sons of Levi take tithes of their brethren*—Sprung from Abraham as well as themselves. The Levites therefore are greater than they; but the priests are greater than the Levites; the patriarch Abraham than the priests, and Melchisedec than him.

6. *He who is not from them*—The Levites; *blessed*—Another proof of his superiority; *even him that had the promises*—That was so highly favoured of God. When St. Paul speaks of Christ, he says, *the promise;* promises refer to other blessings also.

7. *The less is blessed*—Authoritatively *of the greater.*

8. *And here*—In the Levitical priesthood; *but there*—In the case of Melchisedec; *he of whom it is testified that he liveth*—Who is not spoken of, as one that died for another to succeed him: but is represented only as *living,* no mention being made either of his birth or death.

9. *And even Levi, who receiveth tithes*—Not in person, but in his successors, as it were, *paid tithes*—In the person of Abraham.

* Gen. xiv, 18, &c.

11 father, when Melchisedec met him. Now if perfection had been
by the Levitical priesthood, (for under it the people received the
law,) what farther need *was there* that another priest should
rise, after the order of Melchisedec, and not be called after the
12 order of Aaron? For the priesthood being changed, there is
13 also necessarily a change of the law. For he, of whom these
things are spoken, pertaineth to another tribe, of which no man
14 attended on the altar. For *it is* evident, that our Lord sprung
out of Judah, of which tribe Moses spake nothing concerning
15 the priesthood. And it is still far more evident, that another
16 priest is raised up after the likeness of Melchisedec, Who was
made not after the law of a carnal commandment, but after the
17 power of an endless life; For it is testified, Thou *art* a priest
18 for ever, after the order of Melchisedec. For verily there is a
disannulling of the preceding commandment, for the weakness
19 and unprofitableness thereof. For the law made nothing perfect, but the bringing in of a better hope *did*, by which we draw
20 nigh to God. And inasmuch as *he was not made a priest* with-
21 out an oath: (For those *priests* were made without an oath, but
this with an oath, by him that said unto him, The Lord sware,

11. The apostle now demonstrates that the Levitical priesthood must yield to the priesthood of Christ, because Melchisedec, after whose order he is a priest, 1. Is opposed to Aaron, ver. 11, 14. 2. *Hath no end of life*, ver. 15-19, but remaineth a priest continually. *If now perfection were by the Levitical priest-hood*—If this perfectly answered all God's designs, and man's wants; (*for under it the people received the law*—Whence some might infer that perfection was by that priesthood,) *what farther need was there that another priest*—Of a new order, should be set up? From this single consideration it is plain, that both the priesthood and the law, which were inseparably connected, were now to give way to a better priesthood, and more excellent dispensation.

12. *For*—One of these cannot be changed without the other.

13. But the priesthood is manifestly changed from one order to another, and from one tribe to another. *For he of whom these things are spoken*—Namely, Jesus, *pertaineth to another tribe*—That of Judah: of which no man was suffered by the law to attend on, or minister at the altar.

14. *For it is evident that our Lord sprung out of Judah*—Whatever difficulties have arisen since, during so long a tract of time, it was then clear beyond dispute.

15. *And it is far more evident that*—Both the priesthood and the law are changed, because the priest now raised up is not only of another tribe, but of a quite different order.

16. *Who is made*—A priest, *not after the law of a carnal commandment*—Not according to the Mosaic law, which consisted chiefly of commandments, that were carnal, compared to the spirituality of the Gospel; *but after the power of an endless life*—Which he has in himself, as the eternal Son of God.

18. *For there is* implied in this new and everlasting priesthood, and in the new dispensation connected therewith, *a disannulling of the preceding commandment*—An abrogation of the Mosaic law; *for the weakness and unprofitableness there-of*—For its insufficiency either to justify or to sanctify.

19. *For the law*—Taken by itself, separate from the Gospel, *made nothing per-fect*—Could not perfect its votaries, either in faith or love, in happiness or holiness; *but the bringing in of a better hope*—Of the Gospel dispensation, which gives us a better ground of confidence, does: *By which we draw nigh to God*—Yea, so nigh as to be one Spirit with him. And this is true perfection.

20. *And*—The greater solemnity wherewith he was made priest, farther proves the superior excellency of his priesthood.

21. *The Lord sware, and will not repent*—Hence also it appears that his is an unchangeable priesthood.

and will not repent, Thou *art* a priest for ever, after the order
22 of Melchisedec :) Of so much better a covenant was Jesus made
23 a surety. And they truly were many priests, because they were
24 hindered by death from continuing. But this, because he continueth for ever, hath a priesthood that passeth not away.
25 Wherefore he is able also to save them to the uttermost, who
   come to God through him, seeing he ever liveth to make inter-
26 cession for them. For such a high priest suited us, holy, harmless, undefiled, separated from sinners, and made higher than the
27 heavens: Who needeth not daily, as those high priests, to offer
   up sacrifices, first for his own sins, then for those of the people ;
28 for this he did once for all, when he offered up himself. For the
   law maketh men high priests that have infirmity ; but the word
   of the oath which was since the law *maketh* the Son, who is consecrated for evermore.
VIII. The sum of what hath been spoken *is*, We have such a high
   priest, who is set down at the right hand of the throne of the
2 Majesty in the heavens, A minister of the sanctuary, and of the
3 true tabernacle, which the Lord hath fixed, and not man. For
   every high priest is ordained to offer up gifts and sacrifices ;
   whence *it was* necessary that this also should have somewhat
4 to offer. But if he were on earth, he could not be a priest, there

---

22. *Of so much better a covenant*—Unchangeable, eternal, *was Jesus made a
surety*—Or ,Mediator. The word *covenant* frequently occurs in the remaining
part of this epistle. The original word means either a covenant, or a last will
and testament. St. Paul takes it sometimes in the former, sometimes in the
latter sense ; sometimes he includes both.

23. *There were many priests*—One after another.

24. *He continueth for ever*—In life, and his priesthood ; *that passeth not away*
—To any successor.

25. *Wherefore he is able to save to the uttermost*—From all the guilt, power,
root, and consequence of sin, *them who come*—By faith, *to God through him*—As
their priest ; *seeing he ever liveth to make intercession*—That is, he ever lives and
intercedes. He died once. He intercedes perpetually.

26. *For such a high priest suited us*—Unholy, mischievous, defiled sinners ; a
blessed paradox ! *Holy*—With respect to God ; *harmless*—With respect to men ·
undefiled—Without any sin in himself; *separated from sinners*—As well as from
sin. And so he' was, when he left the world ; *and made*—Even in his human
nature, *higher than the heavens*—And all their inhabitants.

27. *Who needeth not to offer up sacrifices daily*—(That is, on every yearly day
of expiation) for he offered *once for all*: not for his own sins; for he then offered
up himself *without spot to God*.

28. *The law maketh men high priests that have infirmity*—That are both weak,
mortal, and sinful: *but the oath which was since the law*—Namely, in the time
of David, *maketh the Son, who is consecrated for ever*—Who' being now free,
both from sin and death, from natural and moral infirmity, remaineth a priest
for ever.

VIII. 1. *We have such a high priest*—Having finished his description of the
type in Melchisedec, the apostle begins to treat directly of the excellency of
Christ's priesthood beyond the Levitical ; *who is set down*—Having finished his
oblation, at the right hand of the majesty of God.

2. *A minister*—Who represents his own sacrifice, as the high priest did the
blood of those sacrifices once a year; *of the sanctuary*—Heaven, typified by the
holy of holies ; *and of the true tabernacle*—Perhaps his human nature, of which
the old tabernacle was a type : *which the Lord hath fixed*—For ever ; *not man*—
As Moses fixed the tabernacle.

4. *But if he were on earth*—If his priesthood terminated here, *he could not be*

5 being priests that offer gifts, according to the law, Who serve after the pattern and shadow of heavenly things, as Moses was admonished of God, when he was about to finish the tabernacle; for, saith he, * See thou make all things according to the model
6 which was shown thee in the mount. But he hath now obtained a more excellent ministry, by how much better a covenant he is
7 a mediator of, which is established upon better promises. For if the first had been faultless, no place would have been sought
8 for a second. But finding fault with them, he saith, † Behold, the days come, saith the Lord, when I will make a new cove-
9 nant with the house of Israel, and with the house of Judah: Not according to the covenant which I made with their fathers, in the day when I took them by the hand, to lead them out of the land of Egypt, because they continued not in my covenant, and I
10 regarded them not, saith the Lord. For this is the covenant which I will make with the house of Israel after those days, saith the Lord: I will put my laws in their minds, and write them on their hearts, and I will be to them a God, and they shall

---

a priest—At all, consistently with the Jewish institutions, *there being*—Other *priests*—To whom alone this office is allotted.

5. *Who serve*—The temple, which was not yet destroyed; *after the pattern and shadow of heavenly things*—Of spiritual, evangelical worship, and of everlasting glory: the pattern, somewhat like the strokes pencilled out upon a piece of fine linen, which exhibit the figures of leaves and flowers, but have not yet received their splendid colours and curious shades: and shadow, or shadowy representation, which gives you some dim and imperfect idea of the body, but not the fine features, not the distinguishing air, none of those living graces which adorn the real person. Yet both the pattern and shadow lead our minds to something nobler than themselves; the pattern to that (holiness and glory) which complete it: the shadow, to that which occasions it.

6. *And now he hath obtained a more excellent ministry*—His priesthood as much excels theirs as the promises of the Gospel (whereof he is a surety) excel those of the law. These better promises are specified, ver. 10, 11. Those in the law were mostly temporal promises.

7. *For if the first had been faultless*—If that dispensation had answered all God's designs and man's wants, if it had not been weak and unprofitable, unable to make any thing perfect, no place would have been for a second.

8. But there is; *for, finding fault with them*—Who were under the old covenant; *he saith, I make a new covenant with the house of Israel*—With all the Israel of God, in all ages and nations. It is new in many respects, (though not as to the substance of it.) 1. Being ratified by the death of Christ. 2. Freed from those burdensome rites and ceremonies. 3. Containing a more full and clear account of spiritual religion. 4. Attended with larger influences of the Spirit. 5. Extended to all men; and 6. Never to be abolished.

9. *When I took them by the hand*—With the care and tenderness of a parent; and just while this was fresh in their memory, they obeyed. But presently after they shook off the yoke, *they continued not in my covenant, and I regarded them not*—So that covenant was soon broken in pieces.

10. *This is the covenant I will make after those days*—After the Mosaic dispensation is abolished: *I will put my laws in their minds*—I will open their eyes and enlighten their understanding to see the true, full, spiritual meaning thereof; *and write them on their hearts*—So that they shall inwardly experience whatever I have commanded: *and I will be to them a God*—Their all-sufficient portion, and exceeding great reward; *and they shall be to me a people*—My treasure, my beloved, loving, and obedient children.

---

* Exod. xxv, 40. † Jer. xxxi, 31, &c.

11 be to me a people: And they shall not teach every one his
neighbour, and every one his brother, saying, Know the Lord ;
for they shall all know me, from the least even to the greatest.
12 For I will be merciful to their unrighteousness, and their sins
13 and their iniquities will I remember no more. In saying a new
covenant, he hath antiquated the first: now that which is antiquated and decayed, is ready to vanish away.
IX. And verily the first *covenant* also had ordinances of worship
2 and a worldly sanctuary. For the first tabernacle was prepared,
in which *was* the candlestick, and the table, and the show bread ;
3 which is called the holy *place*. And beyond the second veil, the
4 tabernacle, which is called The holy of holies, Having the
golden censer, and the ark of the covenant, overlaid round
about with gold, wherein *was* a golden pot having the manna,
and Aaron's rod that blossomed, and the tables of the covenant :
5 And over it *were* the cherubim of glory, shadowing the mercy
6 seat; of which we cannot now speak particularly. Now these
things being thus prepared, the priests go always into the first

---

11. *And they*—Who are under this covenant (though in other respects they
will have need to teach each other to their lives' end, yet) *shall not*—Need to
teach every one his brother, saying, Know the Lord ; for they shall all know me—
All real Christians, *from the least to the greatest*—In this order the saving knowledge of God ever did and ever will proceed, not first to the greatest, and then
to the least. But the Lord will save the tents, the poorest, of Judah first, that
the glory of the house of David, the royal seed, and the glory of the inhabitants of Jerusalem, the nobles and the rich citizens, do not magnify themselves,
Zech. xii, 7.
12. *For I will*—Justify them, which is the root of all true knowledge of God.
This therefore is God's method. First, a sinner is pardoned: then, he knows
God, as gracious and merciful: then God's laws are written on his heart: he is
God's, and God is his.
13. *In saying a new covenant, he hath antiquated the first*—Hath shown that it
is disannulled and out of date : *now that which is antiquated is ready to vanish
away*—As it did quickly after, when the temple was destroyed.
IX. 1. *The first covenant had ordinances of* outward *worship, and a worldly*—
A visible, material sanctuary or tabernacle. Of this sanctuary he treats, ver.
2, 5. Of those ordinances, ver. 6, 10.
2. *The first*—The outward tabernacle, in which was the candlestick, and the
table; the show bread, shown continually before God and all the people, consisting of twelve loaves, according to the number of the tribes, was placed on this
table in two rows, six upon one another in each row. This candlestick and
bread seem to have typified the light and life, which are more largely dispensed
under the Gospel, by him who is the light of the world, and the bread of life.
3. *The second veil*—Divided the holy place from the most holy, as the first veil
did the holy place from the courts.
4. *Having the golden censer*—Used by the high priest only, on the great day
of atonement; *and the ark* or chest *of the covenant*—So called from the tables
of the covenant contained therein ; *wherein was the manna*—The monument of
God's care over Israel; *and Aaron's rod*—The monument of regular priesthood ;
and the tables of the covenant—The two tables of stone, on which the ten commandments were written by the finger of God ; the most venerable monument
of all.
5. *And over it were the cherubim of glory*—Over which the glory of God used
to appear. Some suppose each of these had four faces, and so represented the
Three-one God, with the manhood assumed by the second person ; with out-
spread wings *shadowing the mercy seat*—Which was a lid or plate of gold covering the ark.
6. *Always*—Every day; *accomplishing their services*—Lighting their lamps,

7 tabernacle, accomplishing their services. But into the second,
only the high priest, once a year, not without blood, which he
8 offereth for himself and the errors of the people: The Holy
Ghost evidently showing this, that the way into the holiest was
not yet made manifest, while the first tabernacle was still sub-
9 sisting, Which *is* a figure for the time present, in which are
offered both gifts and sacrifices, which cannot perfect the wor-
10 shipper as to *his* conscience, Only with meats and drinks, and
divers washings, and carnal ordinances, imposed till the time of
11 reformation. But Christ being come, a high priest of good
things to come, through a greater and more perfect tabernacle,
12 not made with hands, that is, not of this creation, And not by
the blood of goats and calves, but by his own blood, entered in
once for all into the holy place, having obtained eternal redemp-
13 tion *for us.* For if the blood of bulls and goats, and the *ashes
of a heifer sprinkling the unclean, sanctifieth to the purifying of
14 the flesh: How much more shall the blood of Christ, who through
the eternal Spirit offered himself without spot to God, purge our
15 conscience from dead works, to serve the living God? And for
this end he is the Mediator of the new covenant, that by means

---

changing the show bread, burning incense, and sprinkling the blood of the sin-
offering.

7. *Errors*—That is, sins of ignorance; to which only those atonements extended.

8. *The Holy Ghost evidently showing*—By this token, *that the way into the
holiest*—Into heaven, *was not made manifest*—Not so clearly revealed, *while
the first tabernacle*—And its service, *were still subsisting*—And remaining in
force.

9. *Which*—Tabernacle, with all its furniture and services, is a figure or type
of good things to come. *Which cannot perfect the worshipper*—Neither the
priest, nor him who brought the offering; *as to his conscience*—So that he should
be no longer conscious of the guilt or power of sin. Observe, the temple was as
yet standing.

10. They could not so perfect him, with all their train of precepts relating to
meats and drinks, and carnal, gross, external ordinances; and were therefore
imposed only *till the time of reformation*—Till Christ came.

11. *A high priest of good things to come*—Described ver. 15; *entered through
a greater*—That is, a more noble *and perfect tabernacle*—Namely, his own body;
not of this creation—Not framed by man as that tabernacle was.

12. *The holy place*—Heaven; *for us*—All that believe.

13. *If the ashes of a heifer*—Consumed by fire as a sin-offering, being sprinkled
on them who were legally *unclean purified the flesh*—Removed that legal uncleanness, and readmitted them to the temple, and the congregation.

14. *How much more shall the blood of Christ*—The merit of all his sufferings;
who through the eternal Spirit—The work of redemption being the work of the
whole Trinity. Neither is the second person alone concerned even in the amazing condescension that was needful to complete it. The Father delivers up the
kingdom to the Son: and the Holy Ghost becomes the gift of the Messiah,
being, as it were, *sent* according to his good pleasure: *offered himself*—Infinitely
more precious than any created victim, and that *without spot to God; purge our
conscience*—Our inmost soul, *from dead works*—From all the inward and outward works of the devil, which spring from spiritual death in the soul, and lead
to death everlasting; *to serve the living God*—In the life of faith, in perfect love,
and spotless holiness!

15. *And for this end he is the Mediator of a new covenant, that they who are
called*—To the engagements and benefits thereof; *might receive the eternal inhe-*

* Num. xix, 17, 18, 19.

of death for the redemption of the transgressors that *were* under
the first covenant, they who are called might receive the promise
16 of the eternal inheritance. For where *such* a covenant *is*, there
must also necessarily be the death of him by whom the covenant
17 is confirmed. For the covenant is of force after he is dead;
whereas it is of no strength while he by whom it is confirmed
18 liveth. Whence neither was the first *covenant* originally trans-
19 acted without blood. For when Moses had spoken all the commandments according to the law, to all the people, he took the
blood of calves and of goats, with water, and scarlet wool, and
hyssop, and the book itself, and sprinkled all the people, saying,
20 *This *is* the blood of the covenant, which God hath enjoined
21 unto you. And in like manner he sprinkled with blood both the
22 tabernacle and all the vessels of the service. And almost all
things are according to the law purified with blood, and without
23 shedding of blood there is no forgiveness. *It was* therefore necessary, that the patterns of things in heaven should be purified
by these, but the heavenly things themselves by better sacrifices

---

ritance, promised to Abraham: not *by means* of legal sacrifices, but of his meritorious *death: for the redemption of the transgressors that were under the first
covenant*—That is, for the redemption of transgressors from the guilt and punishment of those sins which were committed in the time of the old covenant. The
article of his death properly divides the old covenant from the new.

16. I say, *By means of death; for where such a covenant is, there must be the
death of him by whom it is confirmed*—Seeing it is by his death that the benefits of it are purchased. It seems beneath the dignity of the apostle to play
upon the ambiguity of the Greek word, as the common translation supposes him
to do.

17. *After he is dead*—Neither this, nor *after men are dead*, is a literal translation of the words. It is a very perplexed passage.

18. *Whence neither was the first*—The Jewish *covenant, originally transacted
without the blood* of an appointed sacrifice.

19. *He took the blood of calves*—Or heifers, *and of goats, with water, and
scarlet wool, and hyssop*—All these circumstances are not particularly mentioned
in that chapter of Exodus, but are supposed to be already known from other
passages of Moses; *and the book itself*—Which contained all he had said, *and
sprinkled all the people*—Who were near him. The blood was mixed *with water*
to prevent its growing too stiff for sprinkling; perhaps also, to typify that *blood
and water*, John xix, 34.

20. *Saying, This is the blood of the covenant which God hath enjoined* me to
deliver *unto you*—By this it is established.

21. *And in like manner he* ordered *the tabernacle*—When it was made, and all
its vessels to be *sprinkled with blood* once a year.

22. *And almost all things*—(For some were purified by water, or fire) *are,
according to the law, purified with blood*—Offered or sprinkled :. *and* according to
the law, *there is no forgiveness* of sins, *without shedding of blood*—All this pointed
to the blood of Christ, effectually cleansing from all sin, and intimated there can
be no purification from it by any other means.

23. *Therefore*—That is, it plainly appears from what has been said; *it was
necessary*—According to the appointment of God, *that the* tabernacle and all its
utensils, which were *patterns*—Shadowy representations, *of things in heaven
should be purified by these*—Sacrifices and sprinklings; *but the heavenly things
themselves*—Our heaven-born spirits: what more this may mean, we know not
yet; *by better sacrifices than these*—That is, by a better sacrifice, which is here
opposed to all the legal sacrifices, and is expressed plurally, because it includes
the signification of them all, and is of so much more eminent virtue.

24 than these.   For Christ did not enter into the holy place made with hands, the figure of the true; but into heaven itself, now to **25** appear in the presence of God for us.   Nor *did he enter*, that he might offer himself often (as the high priest entered into the **26** holy place every year with the blood of others.)   For then he must often have suffered since the foundation of the world : but now once at the consummation of the ages hath he been mani- **27** fested, to abolish sin by the sacrifice of himself.   And as it is **28** appointed for men once to die, and after this the judgment: So Christ, also, having been once offered to bear the sins of many, will appear the second time, without sin, to them that look for him, unto salvation.

X.   For the law having a shadow of good things to come, not the very image of the things, can never with the same sacrifices which they offer year by year continually, make the comers **2** thereunto perfect.   Otherwise would they not have ceased to be offered?   Because the worshippers, having been once purged, **3** would have had no more consciousness of sins.   But in those **4** *sacrifices there is* a commemoration of sins every year.   For *it is* impossible that the blood of bulls and of goats should take **5** away sins.   Therefore when he cometh into the world, he saith,

---

24. *For Christ did not enter into the holy place made with hands*—He never went into the holy of holies at Jerusalem, *the figure of the true tabernacle* in heaven, chap. viii, 2; *but into heaven itself, to appear in the presence of God for us*—As our glorious high priest, and powerful intercessor.

26. *For then he must often have suffered from the foundation of the world*—This supposes, 1. That by suffering once, he atoned for all the sins which had been committed from the foundation of the world.   2. That he could not have atoned for them without suffering: *at the consummation of the ages*—The sacrifice of Christ divides the whole age or duration of the world into two parts, and extends its virtue backward and forward, from this middle point wherein they meet, to *abolish* both the guilt and power of *sin*.

27. *After this the judgment*—Of the great day : at the moment of death, every man's final state is determined.   But there is not a word in Scripture of a particular judgment immediately after death.

28. *Christ having once* died, *to bear the sins*—The punishment due to them; *of many*—Even as many as are born into the world; *will appear the second time* —When he comes to judgment; *without sin*—Not as he did before, *bearing* on himself *the sins of many*, but to bestow everlasting *salvation*.

X. 1. From all that has been said, it appears that *the law*, the Mosaic dispensation, being a bare, unsubstantial *shadow of good things to come*—Of the Gospel blessings, *and not the* substantial, solid *image of them, can never with the same* kind of *sacrifices*, though continually repeated, *make the comers thereunto perfect* —Either as to justification or sanctification.   How is it possible that any who consider this, should suppose the attainments of David, or any who were under that dispensation, to be the proper measure of Gospel holiness?   And that Christian experience is to rise no higher than Jewish?

2. They who had *been once* perfectly *purged, could have* been no longer *conscious* either of the guilt or power *of* their *sins*.

3. *There is a* public commemoration of the sins both of the last and of all the preceding years: a clear proof that the guilt thereof is not perfectly purged away.

4. *It is impossible the blood of goats should take away sins*—Either the guilt or power of them.

5. *When he cometh into the world*—In the 40th Psalm, the Messiah's coming into the world is represented.   It is said, into the world, not into the tabernacle, chap. ix, 1, because all the world is interested in his sacrifice.   *A body hast thou prepared for me*—That I may offer up myself.

* Sacrifice and offering thou hast not chosen, but a body hast
6 thou prepared for me. Burnt-offerings and *sacrifices* for sin
7 thou hast not delighted in. Then I said, Lo, I come (in the
volume of the book it is written of me) to do thy will, O God.
8 Above, when he said, Sacrifice, and offering, and burnt-offerings,
and *offering* for sin, thou hast not chosen, neither delighted in,
9 which are offered according to the law ; Then, said he, Lo, I
come to do thy will. He taketh away the first that he may
10 establish the second : By which will we are sanctified, through
11 the offering of the body of Jesus Christ once for all. And in
deed every priest standeth daily ministering and offering often
12 the same sacrifices, which can never take away sins : But he,
having offered one sacrifice for sins, for ever sat down at the
13 right hand of God, From thenceforth waiting till his † enemies
14 be made his footstool. For by one offering he hath perfected
15 for ever them that are sanctified. And *this* the Holy Ghost also
16 testifieth to us, after he had said before, ‡ This *is* the covenant
which I will make with them after those days, saith the Lord : I
will put my laws into their hearts, and write them on their
17 minds, And their sins and their iniquities will I remember no
18 more. Now where remission of these *is, there is* no more offering for sin.
19   Having, therefore, brethren, free liberty to enter into the holi-
20 est by the blood of Jesus, By a new and living way, which he
21 hath consecrated for us, through the veil, that is, his flesh, And

---

7. *In the volume of the book*—In this very Psalm, it is written of me. Accordingly *I come to do thy will*—By the sacrifice of myself.
8. *Above when he said, Sacrifice thou hast not chosen*—That is, when the psalmist pronounced those words in his name.
9. *Then said he*—In that very instant he subjoined, *Lo, I come to do thy will*—
To offer a more acceptable sacrifice ; and by this very act he taketh away the
legal, that he may establish the evangelical dispensation.
10. *By which will*—Of God, done and suffered by Christ, *we are sanctified*—
Cleansed from guilt, and consecrated to God.
11. *Every priest standeth*—As a servant in an humble posture.
12. *But he*—The virtue of whose one sacrifice remains, *for ever sat down*—As
a Son in majesty and honour.
14. *He hath perfected for ever them*—That is, has done all that was needful in
order to their full reconciliation with God.
15. In this and the three following verses the apostle winds up his argument,
concerning the excellence and perfection of the priesthood and sacrifice of Christ.
He had proved this before by a quotation from Jeremiah ; which he here repeats,
describing the new covenant as now completely ratified, and all the blessings of
it secured to us by the one offering of Christ, which renders all other expiatory
sacrifices, and any repetition of his own, utterly needless.
19. Having finished the doctrinal part of his epistle, the apostle now proceeds
to exhortation, deduced from what has been treated of from chap. v, 4, which he
begins by a brief recapitulation. *Having therefore liberty to enter*—
20. *By a living way*—The way of faith, whereby we live indeed; *which he
hath consecrated*—Prepared, dedicated, and established, *for us, through the veil*—
That is, *his flesh*--As by rending the veil in the temple, the holy of holies became
visible and accessible, so by wounding the body of Christ, the God of heaven was
manifested, and the way to heaven opened.

* Psa. xl, 7, &c.   † Psa. cx, 1.   ‡ Jer. xxxi, 33, &c.

22 *having* a great high priest over the house of God, Let us draw near with a true heart, in full assurance of faith, having our hearts sprinkled from an evil conscience, and our bodies washed
23 with pure water. Let us hold fast the profession of our hope
24 without wavering, (for he *is* faithful that hath promised.) And let us consider one another, to provoke *one another* to love, and
25 to good works : Not forsaking the assembling of ourselves together, as the manner of some *is ;* but exhorting one *another*, and
26 so much the more, as ye see the day approaching. For when we sin wilfully after having received the knowledge of the truth,
27 there remaineth no more sacrifice for sins, But a certain fearful looking for of judgment, and fiery indignation, which is ready to
28 devour the adversaries. He that despised the law of Moses died
29 without mercy, under two or three witnesses. Of how much sorer punishment suppose ye shall he be thought worthy, who hath trodden under foot the Son of God, and counted the blood of the covenant, by which he hath been sanctified, an unholy
30 thing, and done despite to the Spirit of grace? For we know him that hath said, * Vengeance *is* mine : I will recompense :
31 and again, The Lord will judge his people. *It is* a fearful thing
32 to fall into the hands of the living God. But call ye to mind the former days, in which, after ye were enlightened, ye endured so
33 great a conflict of sufferings : Partly being made a gazing stock, both by reproaches and afflictions ; partly being partakers with
34 them who were so treated. For ye sympathized with my bonds,

22. *Let us draw near*—to God, *with a true heart*—In godly sincerity; *having our hearts sprinkled from an evil conscience*—So as to condemn us no longer ; *and our bodies washed with pure water*—All our conversation spotless and holy, which is far more acceptable to God than all the legal sprinklings and washings.
23. *The profession of our hope*—The hope which we professed at our baptism.
25. *Not forsaking the assembling ourselves*—In public or private worship, *as the manner of some is*—Either through fear of persecution, or from a vain imagination that they were above external ordinances; *but exhorting one another*—To faith, love, and good works ; *and so much the more, as ye see the day approaching* —The great day is ever in your eye.
26. *For when we*—Any of us Christians, *sin wilfully*—By total apostacy from God, termed drawing back, ver. 38, after having received the experimental knowledge of the Gospel truth, *there remaineth no more sacrifice for sins*—None but that which we obstinately reject.
28. *He that*—In capital cases, *despised*—Presumptuously transgressed, *the law of Moses, died without mercy*—Without any delay, or mitigation of his punishment.
29. *Of how much sorer punishment is he worthy, who*—By wilful, total apostacy, (it does not appear that this passage refers to any other sin,) hath, as it were, *trodden under foot the Son of God*—A Lawgiver far more honourable than Moses, and *counted the blood* wherewith the better covenant was established, *an unholy*, a common, worthless thing; *by which he hath been sanctified*—Therefore Christ died for him also, and he was, at least, justified once ; *and done despite to the Spirit of grace*—By rejecting all his motions.
30. *The Lord will judge his people*—Yea, far more rigorously than the heathens, if they rebel against him.
31. *To fall into the hands*—Of his avenging justice.
32. *Enlightened*—With the knowledge of God and of his truth.
34. *For ye sympathized with* all your suffering brethren, and *with me* in particular ; *and received joyfully the* loss of your own goods.

* Deut. xxxii, 35, &c.

and received with joy the spoiling of your goods, knowing that
ye have for yourselves in heaven a better and an enduring sub-
35 stance. Cast not away therefore your confidence, which hath
36 great recompense of reward. For ye have need of patience,
that, having done the will of God, ye may receive the promise.
37 For yet a very little while, and he that cometh will come, and
38 will not tarry. *Now the just shall live by faith; and if he
39 draw back, my soul hath no pleasure in him. But we are not
of them who draw back to perdition, but of them that believe to
the saving of the soul.
XI. Now faith is the subsistence of things hoped for, the evidence
2 of things not seen. And by it the elders obtained a *good* testi-
3 mony. Through faith we understand that the worlds were framed
by the word of God, so that the things which are seen were made

35. *Cast not away therefore* this *your confidence*—Your faith and hope, which
none can deprive you of but yourselves.
36. *The promise*—Perfect love, eternal life.
37. *He that cometh*—To reward every man according to his works.
38. *Now the just*—The justified person, *shall live*—In God's favour, a spiritual
and holy life, *by faith*—As long as he retains that gift of God. *But if he draw
back*—If he make shipwreck of his faith, *my soul hath no pleasure in him*—That
is, I abhor him, I cast him off.
39. *We are not of them that draw back to perdition*—Like him, mentioned
ver. 38; *but of them that believe*—To the end, so as to attain eternal life.
XI. 1. The definition of faith given in this verse, and exemplified in the various
instances following, undoubtedly includes justifying faith; but not directly as
justifying. For faith justifies only as it refers to, and depends on, Christ. But
here is no mention of him as the object of faith; and in several of the instances
that follow, no notice is taken of him or his salvation, but only of temporal blessings obtained by faith. And yet they may all be considered as evidences of the
power of justifying faith in Christ, and of its extensive exercise, in a course
of steady obedience, amid difficulties and dangers of every kind. *Now faith is
the subsistence of things hoped for, the evidence* or *conviction of things not seen*—
Things hoped for are not so extensive as *things not seen*—The former are only
things future, and joyful to us; the latter are either future, past, or present, and
those either good or evil, whether to us or others. *The subsistence of things
hoped for*—Giving a kind of present subsistence to the good things which God has
promised; the Divine, supernatural evidence exhibited to, the conviction hereby
produced in a believer, *of things not seen*—Whether past, future, or spiritual;
particularly of God, and the things of God.
2. *By it the elders*—Our forefathers. This chapter is a kind of summary of
the Old Testament, in which the apostle comprises the designs, labours, sojournings, expectations, temptations, martyrdoms, of the ancients. The former of
them had a long exercise of their patience; the latter suffered shorter, but sharper
trials; *obtained a good testimony*—A most comprehensive word. God gave a
testimony not only of them, but to them; and they received his testimony, as if
it had been the things themselves of which he testified, ver. 4, 5, 39. Hence they
also gave testimony to others, and others testified of them.
3. *By faith we understand that the worlds*—Heaven and earth, and all things
in them, visible and invisible, *were made*—Formed, fashioned, and finished, *by
the word*—The sole command, *of God*—Without any instrument, or preceding
matter. And as creation is the foundation and specimen of the whole Divine
economy, so faith in the Creator is the foundation and specimen of all faith; *so
that things which are seen*—As the sun, earth, stars, *were made of things which do
not appear*—Out of the dark, unapparent chaos, Gen. i, 2; and this very chaos
was created by the Divine power; for before it was thus created, it had no
existence in nature.

* Hab. ii, 3, &c.

4 of things which do not appear. By faith Abel offered unto God
a more excellent sacrifice than Cain, by which he obtained a
testimony that he was righteous, God testifying of his gifts:
5 and by it, being dead, he yet speaketh. By faith Enoch was
translated so as not to see death, and was not found, because
God had translated him; for before his translation he had a
6 testimony that he pleased him. But without faith it is impossible
to please *him:* for he that cometh to God must believe that he
is, and *that* he is a rewarder of them that diligently seek him.
7 By faith Noah, being warned of God of things not seen as yet,
moved with fear, prepared an ark for the saving of his household, by which he condemned the world, and became heir of the
8 righteousness which is by faith. *By faith Abraham, being
called to go out into the place which he was to receive for an
inheritance, obeyed and went out, though he knew not whither
9 he went. †By faith he sojourned in the land of promise as *in*
a strange country, dwelling in tents with Isaac and Jacob, the
10 joint heirs of the same promise. For he looked for the city
11 which hath foundations, whose builder and former *is* God. By
faith ‡Sarah also herself received power to conceive seed, even
when she was past age, because she accounted him faithful who
12 had promised. Therefore there sprang even from one, and him
as it were dead, *a posterity* as the stars in heaven for multitude,

---

4. *By faith*—In the future Redeemer, *Abel offered a more excellent sacrifice*—The firstlings of his flock, implying both a confession of what his own sins deserved, and a desire of sharing in the great atonement: *than Cain*—Whose offering testified no such faith, but a bare acknowledgment of God, the Creator; by which faith he obtained both righteousness and a testimony of it; *God testifying*—Visibly, that his gifts were accepted; probably by sending fire from heaven to consume his sacrifice; a token that justice seized on the sacrifice instead of the sinner who offered it. *And by it*—By this faith, *being dead, he yet speaketh*—That a sinner is accepted only through faith in the great sacrifice.

5. *Enoch was not* any longer *found* among men, though perhaps they sought for him, as they did for Elijah, 2 Kings ii, 17. *He had this testimony*—From God, in his own conscience.

6. *But without faith*—Even some Divine faith in God, *it is impossible to please him: for he that cometh to God*—In prayer, or any other act of worship, must believe that he is.

7. *Noah, being warned of things not seen as yet*—Of the future deluge; *moved with fear, prepared an ark, by which* open testimony *he condemned the world*—Who neither believed nor feared.

9. *By faith he sojourned in the land of promise*—The promise was made before, Gen. xii, 7, *dwelling in tents*—As a sojourner, with *Isaac and Jacob*—Who, by the same manner of living, showed the same faith. Jacob was born fifteen years before the death of Abraham: *the joint heirs of the same promise*—Having all the same interest therein. Isaac did not receive this inheritance from Abraham, nor Jacob from Isaac, but all of them from God.

10. *He looked for a city which hath foundations*—Whereas a tent has none; *whose builder and former is God*—Of which God is the sole contriver, former, and finisher.

11. *Sarah also herself*—Though at first she laughed at the promise, Gen. xviii, 12.

12. *As it were dead*—Till his strength was supernaturally restored, which continued for many years after.

* Gen. xii, 1–4. † Gen. xvii, 8. ‡ Gen. xxi, 2.

13 and as the sand which is on the sea shore innumerable. All these
    died in faith, not having received the promises, but having seen
    them afar off, and embraced *them*, and confessed that they were
14 strangers and sojourners on the earth. For they who speak
15 thus, show plainly that they seek their own country. And truly
    if they had been mindful of that from which they came out, they
16 might have had opportunity to return. But now they desire a
    better *country*, that is, a heavenly : therefore God is not ashamed
    to be called their God ; for he hath prepared a city for them.
17 By faith *Abraham, being tried, offered up Isaac ; yea, he that
18 had received the promises offered up his only begotten *son*, Of
    whom it had been said, † In Isaac shall thy seed be called :
19 Accounting that God was able even to raise *him* from the dead ;
20 from whence also he did receive him in a figure. By faith Isaac
21 blessed Jacob and Esau, concerning things to come. By faith
    Jacob, when dying, ‡ blessed each of the sons of Joseph, and
22 § worshipped, *bowing down* on the top of his staff. By faith
    Joseph, when dying, made mention of the children of Israel,
23 and gave charge concerning his bones. By faith Moses, when
    he was born, was hid three months by his parents, because they
    saw *he was* a beautiful child, and they were not afraid of the
24 king's commandment. By faith Moses, when he was grown up,
25 refused to be called the son of Pharaoh's daughter : Choosing
    rather to suffer affliction with the people of God, than to enjoy
26 the pleasures of sin for a season ; Esteeming the reproach of

---

13. *All these*—Mentioned ver. 7-11, *died in faith*—In 'death faith acts most
vigorously ; *not having received the promises*—The promised blessings. *Embraced*
—As one does a dear friend when he meets him.
   14. *They who speak thus, show plainly that they seek their own country*—That
they keep in view and long for their native home.
   15. *If they had been mindful of*—Their native country, *Ur* of the Chaldeans,
they might have easily returned.
   16. *But they desire a better country, that is, a heavenly*—This is a full, convincing proof that the patriarchs had a revelation and a promise of eternal glory
in heaven. *Therefore God is not ashamed to be called their God ;* seeing *he hath
prepared for them a city*—Worthy of God to give.
   17. *By faith Abraham*—When God made that glorious trial of him, *offered up
Isaac*—The will being accepted, as if he had actually done it ; *yea, he that had
received the promises*—Particularly that grand promise, *In Isaac shall thy seed
be called*, offered up this very son ; the only one he had by Sarah.
   18. *In Isaac shall thy seed be called*—From him shall the blessed seed spring.
   19. *Accounting that God was able even to raise him from the dead*—Though
there had not been any instance of this in the world. *From whence also*—To
speak in a figurative way, *he did receive him*—Afterward, snatched from the
jaws of death.
   20. *Blessed*—Gen. xxvii, 27, 29. Prophetically foretold the particular blessings they should partake of ; *Jacob and Esau*—Preferring the younger before
the elder.
   21. *Jacob when dying*—That is, when near death ; *bowing down on the top of
his staff*—As he sat on the side of his bed.
   22. *Concerning his bones*—To be carried into the land of promise.
   23. *They saw*—Doubtless with a Divine presage of things to come.
   24. *Refused to be called*—Any longer.
   26. *The reproach of Christ*—That which he bore, for believing in the Messiah
to come, and acting accordingly ; *for he looked off*—From all those perishing

   * Gen. xxii, 1, &c.   † Gen. xxi, 12.   ‡ Gen. xlviii, 16·   § Gen. xlvii, 31

Christ greater riches than the treasures of Egypt: for he looked
27 off unto the recompense of reward. *By faith he left Egypt,
not fearing the wrath of the king; for he endured as seeing him
28 that is invisible. By faith †he celebrated the passover, and the
pouring out of the blood, that he who destroyed the first born
29 might not touch them. By faith they passed through the Red
Sea, as by dry land, which the Egyptians trying to do, were
30 drowned. By faith the walls of Jericho, having been encom-
31 passed seven days, fell down. By faith Rahab the harlot perished
not with them that believed not, having received the spies with
32 peace. And what shall I say more? for the time would fail me,
to discourse of Gideon, and Barak, and Samson, and Jephthah,
33 and David, and Samuel, and the prophets: Who by faith ‡sub-
dued kingdoms, § wrought righteousness, obtained promises,
34 ‖ stopped the mouths of lions, **Quenched the violence of fire,
††escaped the edge of the sword, ‡‡out of weakness was made
strong, §§became valiant in fight, ‖‖put to flight armies of the
35 aliens; ***Women received their dead raised to life again:
others were tortured, not accepting deliverance, that they might

treasures, and beyond all those temporal hardships; *unto the recompense of reward*
—Not to an inheritance in Canaan: he had no warrant from God to look for this,
nor did he ever attain it: but what his believing ancestors looked for, a future
state of happiness in heaven.

27. *By faith he left Egypt*—Taking all the Israelites with him; *not then fearing the wrath of the king*—As he did many years before, Exod. ii, 14.

28. *The pouring out of the blood*—Of the paschal lamb, which was sprinkled on
the door posts, lest the destroying angel should touch the Israelites.

29. *They, Moses, Aaron,* and the Israelites, *passed the Red Sea*—It washed
the borders of *Edom*, which signifies *red*. Thus far the examples are cited
from Genesis and Exodus; those that follow are from the former and the latter
prophets.

30. *By* the *faith* of Joshua.

31. *Rahab*—Though formerly one not of the fairest character.

32. After *Samuel, the prophets* are properly mentioned; David also was a prophet: but he was a king too; *the prophets*—Elijah, Elisha, &c., including likewise
the believers who lived with them.

33, 34. *David,* in particular, *subdued kingdoms;* Samuel (not excluding the
rest) *wrought righteousness.* The prophets, in general, *obtained promises,* both
for themselves, and to deliver to others. Prophets also *stopped the mouths of
lions,* as Daniel, and *quenched the violence of fire,* as Shadrach, Meshach, and
Abednego. To these examples, whence the nature of faith clearly appears,
those more ancient ones are subjoined (by a transposition, and in an inverted
order) which receive light from these. Jephthah escaped the edge of the sword:
Samson out of weakness was made strong: Barak became valiant in fight:
Gideon put to flight armies of the aliens. Faith animates to the most heroic
enterprises, both civil and military. Faith overcomes all impediments, effects
the greatest things, attains to the very best, and inverts, by its miraculous power,
the very course of nature.

35. *Women*—Naturally weak, *received their dead* children *raised to life; others
were tortured*—From those who acted great things, the apostle rises higher, to
those who showed the power of faith by suffering, *not accepting deliverance*—
On sinful terms; *that they might obtain a better resurrection*—A higher reward,
seeing the greater their sufferings, the greater would be their glory.

* Exod. xiv, 15.　† Exod. xii, 12–18.　‡ 2 Sam. vii, 1, &c.　§ 1 Sam. viii, 9; xii,
3, &c.　‖ Dan. vii, 22; iii, 27.　** Judg. xii, 3.　†† Judg. xv, 19, &c.; xvi, 28, &c.
‡‡ Judg. iv, 14, &c.　§§ Judg. vii, 21.　‖‖ 1 Kings xvii, 22.　*** 2 Kings iv, 35.

36 obtain a better resurrection. And others had trial of mockings, and scourging, yea, moreover, of bonds and imprisonment.
37 They were stoned, were sawn asunder, were tempted, were slain with the sword : they wandered about in sheep skins, in
38 goat skins, destitute, afflicted, tormented : (Of whom the world was not worthy,) they wandered in deserts, and mountains, and
39 dens, and caves of the earth. And all these having obtained a
40 good testimony through faith, did not receive the promise. God having provided some better thing for us, that they might not be perfected without us.

XII. Wherefore, let us also, being encompassed with so great a cloud of witnesses, lay aside every weight, and the sin which easily besetteth *us*, and run with patience the race that is set
2 before us, Looking to Jesus, the author and finisher of *our* faith ; who, for the joy that was set before him, endured the cross, despising the shame, and is set down at the right hand of the
3 throne of God. For consider him that endured such contradiction from sinners against himself, lest ye be weary and faint in
4 your minds. Ye have not yet resisted unto blood, striving
5 against sin. And yet ye have forgotten the exhortation, which speaketh to you as to sons, * My son, despise not thou the

36. *And others*—The apostle seems here to pass on to recent examples.
37. *They were sawn asunder*—As, according to the tradition of the Jews, Isaiah was by Manasseh ; *were tempted*—(Torments and death are mentioned alternately) every way ; by threatenings, reproaches, tortures, the variety of which cannot be expressed ; and again, by promises and allurements.
38. *Of whom the world was not worthy*—It did not deserve so great a blessing ; *they wandered*—Being driven out from men.
39. *And all these*—Though they obtained a good testimony, ver. 2, yet did not receive the great promise, the heavenly inheritance.
40. *God having provided some better things for us*—Namely, everlasting glory, *that they might not be perfected without us*—That is, that we might all be perfected together in heaven.
XII. 1. *Wherefore, being encompassed with a cloud*—A great multitude tending upward, with a holy swiftness, *of witnesses*—Of the power of faith ; *let us lay aside every weight*—As all who run a race take care to do. Let us throw off whatever weighs us down, or damps the vigour of our soul ; *and the sin which easily besetteth us*—As doth the sin of our constitution, the sin of our education, the sin of our profession.
2. *Looking*—From all other things, *to Jesus*—As the wounded Israelites to the brazen serpent. Our crucified Lord was prefigured by the lifting up of this : our guilt by the stings of the fiery serpents : and our faith, by their looking up to the miraculous remedy ; *the author and finisher of our faith*—Who begins it in us, carries it on, and perfects it ; *who for the joy that was set before him*—Patiently and willingly *endured the cross*—With all the pains annexed thereto ; *and is set down*—Where there is fulness of joy.
3. *Consider*—Draw the comparison, and think : the Lord bore all this : and shall his servants bear nothing ? *him that endured such contradiction from sinners*—Such enmity and opposition of every kind ; *lest ye be weary*—Dull and languid, and so actually faint in your course.
4. *Unto blood*—Unto wounds and death.
5. And *yet ye* seem already to *have forgotten the exhortation*—Wherein God speaketh to you with the utmost tenderness, *despise not thou the chastening of the Lord*—Do not slight, or make little of it, do not impute any affliction to chance, or second causes ; but see and revere the hand of God in it : *neither faint when thou art rebuked of him*—But endure it patiently and fruitfully.

* Prov. iii, 11, &c.

chastening of the Lord, nor faint when thou art rebuked of him.
6 For whom the Lord loveth, he chasteneth, and scourgeth every
7 son whom he receiveth. If ye endure chastening, God dealeth
with you as with sons; for what son is there whom his father
8 chasteneth not? But if ye are without chastening, of which all
9 are partakers, then are ye bastards, and not sons. Now if we
have had fathers of our flesh who corrected us, and we reverenced
them; shall we not much rather be in subjection to the Father
10 of spirits, and live? For they, verily, for a few days chastened
us as they thought good: but he for our profit, that we may be
11 partakers of his holiness. Now all chastening for the present
is assuredly not joyous but grievous; yet afterward it yieldeth
the peaceable fruit of righteousness to them that are exercised
thereby.
12   Wherefore * lift up the hands that hang down, and the feeble
13 knees; And make straight paths for your feet, that the lame be
14 not turned out of the way, but rather healed. Follow peace with
all men, and holiness, without which no man shall see the Lord:
15 Looking diligently, lest any one fall from the grace of God, lest
any root of bitterness springing up trouble *you*, and thereby many
16 be defiled: Lest *there be* any fornicator or profane person, as
17 Esau, who for one meal gave away his birthright: For ye know

---

6. *For* all springs from love. Therefore neither despise nor faint.

7. *Whom his father chasteneth not*—When he offends.

8. *Of which all* sons *are partakers*—More or less.

9. *And we reverenced them*—We neither despised, nor fainted under their correction; *shall we not much rather*—Submit with reverence and meekness to the Father of spirits, that we may *live* with him for ever? The Father of the spirits of all flesh, who is the author, maintainer, and perfecter of our spiritual life and felicity, in time, and in eternity; to accomplish which, all his chastisements tend.

10. *For they verily for a few days*—How few are even all our days on earth! *chastened us as they thought good*—Though frequently they erred therein, by too much either of indulgence or severity; *but he*—Always unquestionably, *for our profit, that we may be partakers of his holiness*—That is, of himself, and his glorious image.

11. *Now all chastening*—Whether from our earthly or heavenly Father, *is for the present grievous, yet it yieldeth the peaceable fruit of righteousness*—Holiness and happiness, *to them that are exercised thereby*—That receive this exercise as from God, and improve it according to his will.

12. *Wherefore lift up the hands*—Whether your own, or your brethren's, *that hang down*—Unable to continue the combat, *and the feeble knees*—Unable to continue the race.

13. *And make straight paths* both *for your* own and for their *feet*—Remove every hinderance, every offence, *that the lame*—They who are weak, scarce able to walk, *be not turned out of the way*—Of faith and holiness.

14. *Follow peace with all men*—This second branch of the exhortation concerns our neighbours; the third, God. *And holiness*—The not following after all holiness, is the direct way to fall into sin of every kind.

15. *Looking diligently, lest any one*—If he do not lift up the hands that hang down, *fall from the grace of God, lest any root of bitterness*—Of envy, anger, suspicion, springing up, destroy the sweet peace: lest any, not following after holiness, fall into fornication or profaneness. In general, any corruption, either in doctrine or practice, is a root of bitterness, and may pollute many.

16. *Esau* was profane, for so slighting the blessing which went along with the birthright.

17. *He was rejected*—He could not obtain it: *for he found no place of repent-*

that afterward, even when he desired to inherit the blessing, he was rejected: for he found no place for repentance, though he sought it diligently with tears.

18 For ye are not come to the mountain that could be touched, and the burning fire, and the thick cloud, and darkness, and
19 tempest, And the sound of a trumpet, and the voice of words; which they that heard entreated, that no more might be spoken
20 to them; For they could not bear that which was commanded,
21 *If even a beast touch the mountain, let it be stoned. And so terrible was the appearance, *that* Moses said, I exceedingly fear
22 and tremble. But ye are come to Mount Sion, and to the city of the living God, the heavenly Jerusalem, and to an innumerable
23 company, To the general assembly of angels, and to the Church of the first born, who are enrolled in heaven, and to God the
24 Judge of all, and to the spirits of just men made perfect. And to Jesus the mediator of the new covenant, and to the blood of

---

ance—There was no room for any such repentance, as would regain what he had lost, *though he sought it*—The blessing of *the birthright, diligently with tears*—He sought too late. Let us use the present time.

18. *For*—A strong reason this, why they ought the more to regard the whole exhortation drawn from the priesthood of Christ; because both salvation and vengeance are now nearer at hand; *ye are not come to the mountain that could be touched*—That was of an earthly, material nature.

19. *The sound of a trumpet*—Formed without doubt by the ministry of angels, and preparatory to the words, that is, the ten commandments, which were uttered with a loud voice, Deut. v, 22.

20. *For they could not bear*—the terror which seized them, when they heard those words proclaimed, If even a beast, &c.

21. Even *Moses*—Though admitted to so near an intercourse with God, who spake to him as a man speaketh to his friend. At other times he acted as a mediator between God and the people. But while the ten commandments were pronounced, he stood as one of the hearers, Exod. xix, 25; xx, 19.

22. *But ye*—Who believe in Christ, *are come*—The apostle does not here speak of their coming to the Church militant, but of that glorious privilege of New Testament believers, their communion with the Church triumphant. But this is far more apparent to the eyes of celestial spirits than to ours which are yet veiled. St. Paul here shows an excellent knowledge of the heavenly economy, worthy of him who had been caught up into the third heaven, *to Mount Sion*—A spiritual mountain, *to the city of the living God, the heavenly Jerusalem*—All these glorious titles belong to the New Testament Church, *and to an innumerable company*—Including all that are afterward mentioned.

23. *To the general assembly*—The word properly signifies a stated convention on some festival occasion; *and Church*—The whole body of true believers, whether on earth or in paradise, *of the first born*—The first born of Israel were enrolled by Moses; but these are enrolled in heaven, as citizens there. It is observable, that in this beautiful gradation these first born are placed nearer to God than the angels: see James i, 18: *and to God the Judge of all*—Propitious to you, adverse to your enemies: *and to the spirits*—The separate souls, *of just men*—It seems to mean of New Testament believers. The number of these being not yet large, is mentioned distinct from the *innumerable company of just men*—Whom their Judge hath acquitted. These are now made perfect in a higher sense than any who are still alive. Accordingly St. Paul, while yet on earth, denies that he was thus made perfect, Phil. iii, 12.

24. *To Jesus the mediator*—Through whom they had been perfected, *and to the blood of sprinkling*—To all the virtue of his precious blood shed for you, whereby ye are sprinkled from an evil conscience. This blood of sprinkling was the foundation of our Lord's mediatorial office. Here the gradation is at the

* Exodus xix, 12, &c.

25 sprinkling, which speaketh better things than *that of* Abel.   See
that ye refuse not him that speaketh: for if they escaped not
who refused him that delivered the oracle on earth, much more
shall not we, who turn away from him *that speaketh* from
26 heaven: Whose voice then shook the earth: but now he has
promised, saying, *Yet once more I will shake, not only the
27 earth, but also the heaven.   And this *word*, Yet once more,
showeth the removal of the things which are shaken, as being
made, that the things which are not shaken may remain.
28 Therefore let us, receiving a kingdom which cannot be
shaken, hold fast the grace whereby we may serve God ac-
29 ceptably, with reverence and godly fear.   For our God *is* a
consuming fire.
XIII.   Let brotherly love continue.   Forget not hospitality, for
2 hereby †some have entertained angels unawares.   Remember
3 them that are in bonds, as being bound with them, *and* them that
4 suffer adversity, as being yourselves also in the body.   Marriage
is honourable in all men, and the bed undefiled: but whore-

highest point.   *Which speaketh better things than that of Abel*—Which cried for
vengeance.
25. *Refuse not*—By unbelief, *him that speaketh*—And whose speaking even
now is a prelude to the final scene.   The same voice which spake both by the
law and in the Gospel, when heard from heaven, will shake heaven and earth:
for if they escaped not—His vengeance, *much more shall not we*—Those of us
who *turn from him that speaketh from heaven*—That is, who came from heaven
to speak to us.
26. *Whose voice then shook the earth*—When he spoke from Mount Sinai: *but
now*—With regard to his next speaking, *he hath promised*—It is a joyful promise
to the saints, though dreadful to the wicked, *yet once more I will shake, not
only the earth, but also the heaven*—These words may refer, in a lower sense, to
the dissolution of the Jewish Church and state.   But in their full sense they
undoubtedly look much farther, even to the end of all things.   This universal
shaking began at the first coming of Christ.   It will be consummated at his
second coming.
27. *The things which are shaken*—Namely, heaven and earth, *as being made*—
And consequently liable to change; *that the things which are not shaken may
remain*—Even the new heavens and the new earth, Rev. xxi, 1.
28. *Therefore let us, receiving*—By willing and joyful faith, *a kingdom*—More
glorious than the present heaven and earth, *hold fast the grace whereby we may
serve God*—In every thought, word, and work, *with reverence*—Literally *with
shame*—Arising from a deep consciousness of our own unworthiness, *and godly
fear*—A tender, jealous fear of offending, arising from a sense of the gracious
majesty of God.
29. *For our God is a consuming fire*—In the strictness of his justice, and purity
of his holiness.
XIII. 1. *Brotherly love*—is explained in the following verses.
2. *Some*—Abraham and Lot, *have entertained angels unawares*—So may an
unknown guest, even now, be of more worth than he appears, and may have
angels attending him, though unseen.
3. *Remember*—In your prayers, and by your help, *them that are in bonds, as
being bound with them*—Seeing ye are members one of another, *and them that
suffer, as being yourselves in the body*—And consequently liable to the same.
4. *Marriage is honourable in*—Or for all sorts of men, clergy as well as laity;
though the Romanists teach otherwise; *and the bed undefiled*—Consistent with
the highest purity; though many spiritual writers, so called, say it is only
licensed whoredom; *but whoremongers and adulterers God will judge*—Though
they frequently escape the sentence of men.

* Haggai ii, 6.   † Genesis xviii, 2; xix, 1.

5 mongers and adulterers God will judge. *Let your* disposition
be without covetousness: *be* content with the things that are
present: for he hath said, *No, I will not leave thee: verily I
6 will not forsake thee. So that we may boldly say, †The Lord
7 is my helper: I will not fear what man can do unto me. Remember them that had the rule over you, who spake to you the
word of God, whose faith follow, considering the end of their
conversation.
8   Jesus Christ is the same yesterday, and to-day, and for ever.
9 Be not carried about with various and strange doctrines; for it
is good that the heart be stablished with grace, not with meats,
10 in which they that have walked have not been profited. We
have an altar, whereof they have no right to eat who serve the
11 tabernacle. For the bodies of those animals, whose blood is
brought into the holy place by the high priest for sin, are burned
12 without the camp. Wherefore Jesus also, that he might sanctify
13 the people by his own blood, suffered without the gate. Let us
then go forth to him without the camp, bearing his reproach.
14 For we have here no continuing city; but we seek one to come.
15 By him therefore let us offer the sacrifice of praise continually
to God, that is, the fruit of *our* lips, giving thanks to his name.
16 But to do good, and to distribute, forget not; for with such
17 sacrifices God is well pleased. Obey them that have the rule
over you, and submit yourselves; for they watch over your

---

5. *He*—God, *hath said*—To all believers, in saying it to Jacob, Joshua, and Solomon.

7. *Remember them*—Who are now with God, *considering the* happy *end of their conversation* on earth.

8. Men may die. But *Jesus Christ* (yea, and his Gospel) *is the same* from everlasting to everlasting.

9. *Be not carried about with various doctrines*—Which differ from that one faith in our one unchangeable Lord; *strange*—to the ears and hearts of all that abide in him; *for it is good*—It is both honourable before God, and pleasant, and profitable, *that the heart be stablished with grace*—Springing from faith in Christ, *not with meats*—Jewish ceremonies, which indeed can never stablish the heart.

10. On the former part of this verse the 15th and 16th depend; on the latter, the intermediate verses. *We have an altar*—The cross of Christ, *whereof they have no right to eat*—To partake of the benefits which we receive therefrom, *who serve the tabernacle*—Who adhere to the Mosaic law.

11. *For*—According to their own law, the sin-offerings were wholly consumed, and no Jew ever ate thereof. But Christ was a sin-offering: therefore they cannot feed upon him, as we do, who are free from the Mosaic law.

12. *Wherefore Jesus also*—Exactly answering those typical sin-offerings, *suffered without the gate*—Of Jerusalem, which answered to the old camp of Israel · *that he might sanctify*—Reconcile and consecrate to God, *the people*—Who believe in him, *by his own blood*—Not those shadowy sacrifices, which are now of no farther use.

13. *Let us then go forth without the camp*—Out of the Jewish dispensation, *bearing his reproach*—All manner of shame, obloquy, and contempt, for his sake.

14. *For we have here*—On earth, *no continuing city*—All things here are but for a moment, and Jerusalem itself was just then on the point of being destroyed.

15. *The sacrifice*—The altar is mentioned, verse 10. Now the sacrifices; 1. Praise, 2. Beneficence: with both of which God is well pleased.

17. *Obey them that have the rule over you*—The word implies, also, that lead or guide you: namely, in truth and holiness: *and submit yourselves*—Give up (not

* Gen. xxviii, 15; Josh. i, 5; 1 Chron. xxviii, 20.   † Psa. cxviii, 6.

souls, as they that shall give account; that they may do this with joy, and not with groans; for that is unprofitable for you.

18 Pray for us; for we trust we have a good conscience, desiring
19 to behave ourselves well in all things. And I beseech you to do this the more earnestly, that I may be restored to you the sooner.

20 Now the God of peace, who brought again from the dead the great Shepherd of the sheep, our Lord Jesus, by the blood of the
21 everlasting covenant, Make you perfect in every good work, to do his will, working in you that which is well pleasing in his sight through Christ Jesus; to whom *be* the glory for ever and ever. Amen.

22 I beseech you, brethren, suffer the word of exhortation; for
23 I have written a letter to you in few words. Know that *our* brother Timotheus is set at liberty, with whom, if he come soon, I will see you.

24 Salute all them that have the rule over you, and all the saints.
25 They of Italy salute you. Grace *be* with you all.

---

your conscience or judgment, but) your own will, in all things purely indifferent: *for they watch over your souls*—With all zeal and diligence, they guard and caution you against all danger, *as they that must give account*—To the great Shepherd for every part of their behaviour toward you. How vigilant then ought every pastor to be! How careful of every soul committed to his charge! *That they may do this*—Watch over you, *with joy, and not with groans*—He is not a good shepherd who does not either rejoice over them, or groan for them. The groans of other creatures are heard: how much more shall these come up in the ears of God! Whoever answers this character of a Christian pastor, may undoubtedly demand this obedience.

20. *The everlasting covenant*—The Christian covenant, which is not temporary, like the Jewish, but designed to remain for ever. By the application of that blood, by which this covenant was established, may he make you in every respect inwardly and outwardly holy!

22. *Suffer the word of exhortation*—Addressed to you in this letter, which, though longer than my usual letters, is yet contained in few words, considering the copiousness of the subject.

23. *If he come*—To me.

25. *Grace be with you all*—St. Paul's usual benediction. God apply it to our hearts.

NOTES

ON

THE GENERAL EPISTLE OF ST. JAMES.

THIS is supposed to have been written by James, the son of Alpheus, the brother (or kinsman) of our Lord. It is called a General Epistle, because written not to a particular person, or Church, but to all the converted Israelites. Herein the apostle reproves that Antinomian spirit which had even then infected many, who had perverted the glorious doctrine of justification by faith into an occasion of licentiousness. He likewise comforts the true believers under their sufferings, and reminds them of the judgments that were approaching.

ST. JAMES.

---

1   JAMES, a servant of God, and of the Lord Jesus Christ, to the twelve tribes which are scattered abroad, greeting.

Verse 1. *A servant of Jesus Christ*—Whose name the apostle mentions but once more in the vhole epistle, chap. ii, 1; and not at all in his whole discourse, Acts xv, 14, &c, or chap. xxi, 20–25. It might have seemed, if he mentioned him often, that he did it out of vanity, as being the brother of the Lord; *to the twelve tribes*—Of Israel; that is, those of them that believe; *which are scattered abroad*—In various countries. Ten of the tribes were scattered ever since the reign of Hosea; and great part of the rest were now dispersed through the Roman empire; as was foretold, Deut. xxviii, 25, &c.; xxx, 4: *greeting*—That is, all blessings, temporal and eternal.

2 My brethren, count it all joy when ye fall into divers tempta-
3 tions, Knowing that the trying of your faith worketh patience.
4 But let patience have its perfect work, that we may be perfect and
5 entire, wanting nothing. If any of you want wisdom, let him ask
  of God, who giveth to all men liberally, and upbraideth not, and
6 it shall be given him. But let him ask in faith, nothing doubting:
  for he that doubteth is like a wave of the sea, driven with the wind
7 and tossed. For let not that man think that he shall receive any
8 thing from the Lord. A double-minded man is unstable in all his
9 ways. Let the brother of low degree rejoice in that he is exalted:
10 But the rich in that he is made low; because as the flower of the
11 grass he shall pass away. For the sun arose with a scorching
  heat, and withered the grass, and the flower fell off, and the beauty
  of its form perished: so also shall the rich man fade away in his
12 ways. Happy *is* the man that endureth temptation: for when he
  hath been proved he shall receive the crown of life, which the
13 Lord hath promised to them that love him. Let no man who is
  tempted say, I am tempted of God; for God cannot be tempted

---

2. *My brethren, count it all joy*—Which is the highest degree of patience, and contains all the rest; *when ye fall into divers temptations*—That is, trials.

4. *Let patience have its perfect work*—Give it full scope, under whatever trials befall you; *that ye may be perfect and entire*—Adorned with every Christian grace; *and wanting nothing*—Which God requires in you.

5. *If any want*—The connection between the first and following verses, both here and in the fourth chapter, will be easily discerned by him who reads them, while he is suffering wrongfully. He will then readily perceive why the apostle mentions all those various affections of the mind; *wisdom*—To understand whence and why temptations come, and how they are to be improved. Patience is in every pious man already. Let him exercise this, and ask for wisdom. The sum of wisdom, both in the temptation of poverty and of riches, is described in the 9th and 10th verses; *who giveth to all*—That ask aright; *and upbraideth not*—Either with their past wickedness, or present unworthiness.

6. *But let him ask in faith*—A firm confidence in God. St. James also both begins and ends with faith, chap. v, 15; the hinderances of which he removes in the middle part of his epistle; *he that doubteth is like a wave of the sea*—Yea, such are all who have not asked and obtained wisdom; *driven with the wind*—From without; *and tossed*—From within, by his own unstableness.

8. *A double-minded man*—Who has, as it were, two souls; whose heart is not simply given up to God; *is unstable*—Being without the true wisdom; perpetually disagrees both with himself and others, chap. iii, 16.

9. *Let the brother*—St. James does not give this appellation to the rich; *of low degree*—Poor and tempted; *rejoice*—The most effectual remedy against double mindedness; *in that he is exalted*—To be a child of God, and an heir of glory.

10. *But the rich in that he is made low*—Is humbled by a deep sense of his true condition; *because as the flower*—Beautiful, but transient; *he shall pass away*—Into eternity.

11. *For the sun arose and withered the grass*—There is an unspeakable beauty and elegance, both in the comparison itself, and in the very manner of expressing it, intimating both the certainty and the suddenness of the event. *So shall the rich fade away in his ways*—In the midst of his various pleasures and employments.

12. *Happy is the man that endureth temptation*—Trials of various kinds; he *shall receive the crown*—That fadeth not away; *which the Lord hath promised to them that love him*—And his enduring proves his love. For it is love only that endureth all things.

13. But *let no man who is tempted*—To sin, say, *I am tempted of God*—God thus tempteth no man.

14 with evil, neither tempteth he any man. But every man is
tempted when he is drawn away by his own desire and enticed.
15 Then desire, having conceived, bringeth forth sin ; and sin, being
perfected, bringeth forth death.
16   Do not err, my beloved brethren. Every good gift, and every
17 perfect gift, is from above, descending from the Father of lights,
18 with whom is no variableness, neither shadow of turning. Of his
own will begat he us by the word of truth, that we might be a
kind of first fruits of his creatures.
19   Wherefore, my beloved brethren, let every man be swift to
20 hear, slow to speak, slow to wrath. For the wrath of man
21 worketh not the righteousness of God. Therefore, laying aside
all the filthiness and superfluity of wickedness, receive with
meekness the ingrafted word, which is able to save your souls.

14. *Every man is tempted when*—In the beginning of the temptation, *he is
drawn away*, drawn out of God, his strong refuge, *by his own desire*—We are
therefore to look for the cause of every sin in (not out of) ourselves. Even the
injections of the devil cannot hurt before we make them our own. And every
one has desires arising from his own constitution, tempers, habits, and way of
life ; *and enticed*—In the progress of the temptation, catching at the bait; so the
original word signifies.
15. *Then desire having conceived*—By our own will joining therewith, *bringeth
forth*—Actual *sin*—It doth not follow that the *desire* itself is not sin. He that
begets a man is himself a man ; *and sin being perfected*—Grown up to maturity,
which it quickly does, *bringeth forth death*—Sin is born pregnant with death.
16. *Do not err*—It is a grievous error to ascribe the evil, and not the good
which we receive, to God.
17. No evil, but *every good gift*—Whatever tends to holiness, *and every perfect
gift*—Whatever tends to glory, *descendeth from the Father of lights*—The appellation of *Father* is here used with peculiar propriety. It follows, *he begat us*—
He is the Father of all light, material or spiritual, in the kingdom of grace and
of glory ; *with whom is no variableness*—No change in his understanding, *or
shadow of turning*—In his will. He infallibly discerns all good and evil, and
invariably loves one and hates the other. There is in both the Greek words a
metaphor taken from the stars, particularly proper where the Father of lights is
mentioned. Both are applicable to any celestial body, which has a daily vicissitude of day and night, and sometimes longer days, sometimes longer nights. In
God is nothing of this kind: he is mere light. If there is any such vicissitude,
it is in ourselves, not in him.
18. *Of his own will*—Most loving, most free, most pure ; just opposite to our
evil desire, ver. 15, *begat he us*—Who believe, *by the word of truth*—The true
word, emphatically so termed: the Gospel ; *that we might be a kind of first fruits
of his creatures*—Christians are the chief and most excellent of his visible creatures, and sanctify the rest. Yet he says *a kind of*—For Christ alone is absolutely the first fruits.
19. *Let every man be swift to hear*—This is treated of from ver. 21 to the end
of the next chapter ; *slow to speak*—Which is treated of in the third chapter;
slow to wrath—Neither murmuring at God, nor angry at his neighbour. This
is treated of in the third, and throughout the fourth and fifth chapters.
20. *The righteousness of God* here includes all duties prescribed by him, and
pleasing to him.
21. *Therefore laying aside*—As a dirty garment, *all the filthiness and superfluity of wickedness*—For however specious or necessary it may appear to worldly
wisdom, all wickedness is both vile, hateful, contemptible, and really superfluous.
Every reasonable end may be effectually answered, without any kind or degree
of it. Lay this, every known sin, aside, or all your hearing is vain ; *with meekness*—Constant evenness and serenity of mind ; *receive*—Into your ears, your
heart, your life: *the word*—Of the Gospel ; *ingrafted*—In believers, by regeneration, ver. 18, and by habit, Heb. v, 14; *which is able to save your souls*—The hope
of salvation nourishes meekness.

22 But be ye doers of the word, and not hearers only, deceiving
23 yourselves. For if any one be a hearer of the word, and not a
24 doer, he is like a man beholding his natural face in a glass. For
he beheld himself, and went away, and immediately forgot what
25 manner of man he was. But he that looketh diligently into the
perfect law, *the law* of liberty, and continueth *therein,* this man
being not a forgetful hearer, but a doer of the work, this man
26 shall be happy in his doing. If any one be ever so religious, and
bridleth not his tongue, but deceiveth his own heart, this man's
27 religion is vain. Pure religion and undefiled before God even
the Father is this, To visit the fatherless and widows in their
affliction, *and* to keep himself unspotted from the world.
II. My brethren, hold not the faith of our Lord Jesus Christ, *the*
2 *Lord* of glory, with respect to persons. For if there come unto
your assembly a man with gold rings, in fine apparel, and there
3 come in also a poor man in dirty raiment, And ye look upon him
that weareth the fine apparel, and say to him, Sit thou here in a
good place, and say to the poor man, Stand thou there, or, Sit thou
4 here under my footstool, Ye distinguish not in yourselves, but are
5 become evil-reasoning judges. Hearken, my beloved brethren,

23. *Beholding his face in the glass*—How exactly does the Scripture glass show a man the face of his soul!

24. *He beheld himself, and went away*—To other business; *and forgot*—But such forgetting does not excuse.

25. *But he that looketh diligently*—Not with a transient glass, but bending down, fixing his eyes, and searching all to the bottom, *into the perfect law*—Of love, as established by faith. St. James here guards us against misunderstanding what St. Paul says concerning the yoke and bondage of the law. He who keeps the law of love is free, John viii, 31, &c. He that does not, is not free, but a slave to sin, and a criminal before God, chap. ii, 10; *and continueth therein*—Not like him who forgot it and went away. *This man*—There is a peculiar force in the repetition of the word; *shall be happy*—Not barely in *hearing,* but *doing* the will of God.

26. *If any one be ever so religious*—Exact in the outward offices of religion; *and bridleth not his tongue*—From backbiting, tale-bearing, evil speaking, he only deceiveth his own heart, if he fancies he has any true religion at all.

27. The only true *religion* in the sight of God *is this, to visit*—With counsel, comfort, and relief, *the fatherless and widows*—Those who need it most, *in their affliction*—In their most helpless and hopeless state; *and to keep himself unspotted from the world*—From the maxims, tempers, and customs of it. But this cannot be done till we have given our hearts to God, and love our neighbour as ourselves.

II. 1. *My brethren*—The equality of Christians, intimated by this name, is the ground of the admonition; *hold not the faith of our* common *Lord, the Lord of glory*—Of which glory all who believe in him partake; *with respect of persons*—That is, honour none, merely for being rich; despise none, merely for being poor.

2. *With gold rings*—Which were not then so common as now.

3. *Ye look upon him*—With respect.

4. *Ye distinguish not*—To which the most respect is due, to the poor or to the rich; *but are become evil-reasoning judges*—You reason ill, and so judge wrong. For fine apparel is no proof of worth in him that wears it.

5. *Hearken*—As if he had said, Stay, consider, ye that judge thus. Does not the presumption lie rather in favour of the poor man? *Hath not God chosen the poor*—That is, are not they whom God hath chosen, generally speaking, poor *in this world;* who yet are *rich in faith, and heirs of the kingdom*—Consequently the most honourable of men? And those whom God so highly honours ought not ye to honour likewise?

Hath not God chosen the poor of this world, rich in faith, and
heirs of the kingdom which he hath promised to them that love
6 him? But ye have disgraced the poor. Do not the rich oppress
7 you, and drag you to the judgment seats? Do they not blas-
8 pheme that worthy name by which ye are called? If ye fulfil
the royal law, (according to the Scripture,) * Thou shalt love thy
9 neighbour as thyself, ye do well. But if ye have respect of persons, ye commit sin, being convicted by the law † as trans-
10 gressors. For whosoever shall keep the whole law, but offend
11 in one point, is become guilty of all; For he that said, Do not
commit adultery, said also, Do not commit murder. If then
thou commit no adultery, yet if thou commit murder, thou art
12 become a transgressor of the law. So speak ye, and so act, as
13 they that shall be judged by the law of liberty. For judgment
without mercy *shall be* to him that hath showed no mercy : but
mercy glorieth over judgment.
14   What doth it profit, my brethren, though a man say he hath
15 faith, and have not works? Can *that* faith save him? If a brother
16 or a sister be naked, and want daily food, And one of you say to

---

6. *Do not the rich* often *oppress you*—By open violence; often *drag you*—
Under colour of law.

7. *Do not they blaspheme that worthy name*—Of God and of Christ. The
apostle speaks chiefly of rich heathens. But are Christians, so called, a whit
behind them?

8. *If ye fulfil the royal law*—The supreme law of the great King, which is
love; and that to every man, poor as well as rich, *ye do well*.

9. *Being convicted*—By that very law.

10. *Whosoever keepeth the whole law*, except *in one point, he is guilty of all*—
Is as liable to condemnation as if he had offended in every point.

11. *For* it is the same authority which establishes every commandment.

12. *So speak and act*—In all things, *as they that shall be judged*—Without
respect of persons, *by the law of liberty*—The Gospel; the law of universal love,
which alone *is* perfect freedom. For their transgression of this, both in word
and deed, the wicked shall be condemned. And according to their works, done
in obedience to this, the righteous will be rewarded.

13. *Judgment without mercy shall be to him*—In that day, *who hath showed no
mercy*—To his poor brethren. But the mercy of God to believers, answering to
that which they have shown, will then glory over judgment.

14. From chap. i, ver. 22, the apostle has been enforcing Christian practice.
He now applies to those who neglect this, under the pretence of faith. St. Paul
had taught that a man is justified by faith without the works of the law. This
some began already to wrest to their own destruction. Wherefore St. James,
purposely repeating (ver. 21, 23, 25) the same phrases, testimonies, and examples
which St. Paul had used, (Rom. iv, 5; Heb. xi, 17, 31,) refutes not the doctrine
of St. Paul, but the error of those who abused it. There is therefore no contradiction between the apostles; they both delivered the truth of God; but in
a different manner, as having to do with different kinds of men. On another
occasion St. James himself plead the cause of faith, Acts xv, 13, 21. And
St. Paul himself strenuously pleads for works, particularly in his latter epistles.
This verse is a summary of what follows. *What profiteth it*, is enlarged on,
ver. 15-17; *though a man say*, ver. 18, 19, *can that faith save him?* ver. 20. It
is not *though he have faith*, but, *though he say he hath faith*. Here, therefore, true,
living faith is meant. But in other parts of the argument, the apostle speaks of
a dead, imaginary faith. He does not therefore teach that true faith *can*, but
that it *cannot*, subsist without works. Nor does he oppose faith to works, but
that empty name of faith, to real faith working by love: *can that faith which is
without works save him?* No more than it can profit his neighbour.

* Lev. xix, 18   † Exod. xxiii, 3.

them, Depart in peace ; be ye warmed and filled, but give them
17 not the things needful for the body, what doth it profit? So like-
18 wise faith, if it hath not works, is dead in itself. But one will
say, Thou hast faith, and I have works. Show me thy faith
without thy works, and I will show thee my faith by my works.
19 Thou believest there is one God: thou dost well: the devils
20 also believe and tremble. But art thou willing to know, O empty
21 man, that the faith which is without works is dead? Was not
Abraham our father justified by works, when he had offered up
22 Isaac his son upon the altar? Thou seest that faith wrought
together with his works, and by works was faith made perfect.
23 And the Scripture was fulfilled which saith, * Abraham believed
God, and it was imputed to him for righteousness; and he was
24 called † The friend of God. Ye see then, that a man is justified

17. *So likowise* that *faith* which *hath not works is a* mere *dead,* empty notion,
of no more profit to him that hath it, than the bidding the naked be clothed is
to him.
18. *But one,* who judges better, *will say*—To such a vain talker, show me, if
thou canst, thy faith without thy works.
19. *Thou believest there is one God*—I allow this. But this proves only, that
thou hast the same faith with the devils. Nay, they not only believe, but *tremble*
—At the dreadful expectation of eternal torments. So far is that faith from
either justifying or saving them that have it.
20. *But art thou willing to know*—Indeed thou art not; thou wouldst fain be
ignorant of it: *O empty man*—Empty of all goodness, *that the faith which is
without works is dead?* And so is not properly faith, as a dead carcass is not
a man.
21. *Was not Abraham justified by works?*—St. Paul says he was justified by
faith, Rom. iv, 2, &c. Yet St. James does not contradict him. For he does
not speak of the same justification. St. Paul speaks of that which Abraham
received many years before Isaac was born, Gen. xv, 6; St. James of that which
he did not receive, till he had offered up Isaac on the altar. He was justified
therefore in St. Paul's sense, that is, accounted righteous, by faith antecedent to
his works. He was justified in St. James' sense, that is, made righteous, by
works subsequent to his faith. So that St. James' justification by works is the
fruit of St. Paul's justification by faith.
22. *Thou seest that faith*—(For by faith Abraham offered up Isaac, Heb. xi, 17,)
wrought together with his works—Therefore faith has one energy and operation,
works another. And the energy and operation of faith are before works, and
together with them. Works do not give life to faith, but faith begets works,
and then is perfected by them. *And by works was faith made perfect*—Here St.
James fixes the sense wherein he uses the word *justified:* so that no shadow of
contradiction remains between his assertion and St. Paul's. Abraham returned
from that sacrifice perfected in faith, and far higher in the favour of God. Faith
hath not its being from works, for it is before them; but its perfection. That
vigour of faith which begets works is then excited and increased thereby: as
the natural heat of the body begets motion, whereby itself is then excited and
increased. See 1 John iii, 22.
23. *And the Scripture*—Which was afterward written, *was* hereby eminently
fulfilled, Abraham believed God, and it was imputed to him for righteousness—
This was twice fulfilled, when Abraham first believed, and when he offered up
Isaac. St. Paul speaks of the former fulfilling, St. James of the latter. *And he
was called the friend of God*—Both by his posterity, 2 Chron. xx, 7, and by God
himself, Isaiah xli, 8. So pleasing to God were the works he wrought in faith.
24. *Ye see then that a man is justified by works, and not by faith only*—St. Paul,
on the other hand, declares, a man is justified by faith, and not by works, Rom.
iii, 28. And yet there is no contradiction between the apostles; because, 1. They

* Gen. xv, 6.   † 2 Chron. xx 7

25 by works, and not by faith only. In like manner, was not Rahab the harlot also justified by works, having received the
26 messengers, and sent them out another way? Therefore, as the body without the spirit is dead, so the faith *which is* without works is dead also.

III. My brethren, be not many teachers, knowing that we shall
2 receive greater condemnation. For in many things we all offend. If any one offend not in word, the same *is* a perfect man, able
3 also to bridle the whole body. Behold, we put bridles into the mouths of horses, that they may obey us, and we turn about their
4 whole body. Behold also the ships, though they are so large, and driven by fierce winds, yet are turned about by a very small
5 helm, whithersoever the steersman listeth. So the tongue also is a little member, yet boasteth great things. Behold how much
6 matter a little fire kindleth. And the tongue *is* a fire, a world of iniquity: so is the tongue among the members, which defileth the whole body, and setteth on fire the course of nature, and is
7 set on fire of hell. Every kind, both of wild beasts and of birds, both of reptiles and things in the sea, is tamed, and hath been
8 tamed by mankind. But the tongue can no man tame: *it is* an
9 unruly evil, full of deadly poison. Therewith bless we God, even the Father, and therewith curse we men, made after the
10 likeness of God. Out of the same mouth proceedeth blessing and cursing. My brethren; these things ought not so to be. Doth a fountain send out of the same opening sweet *water* and
11 bitter? Can a fig tree, my brethren, bear olives, or a vine figs?
12 Neither *can* a fountain yield salt water and fresh.

---

do not speak of the same faith; St. Paul speaking of *living* faith, St. James here of *dead* faith. 2. They do not speak of the same works: St. Paul speaking of works antecedent to faith, St. James of works subsequent to it.

25. After Abraham, the father of the Jews, the apostle cites Rahab, a woman, and a sinner of the Gentiles, to show that in every nation and sex true faith produces works, and is perfected by them; that is, by the grace of God working in the believer, while he is showing his faith by his works.

III. 1. *Be not many teachers*—Let no more of you take this upon you, than God thrusts out: seeing it is so hard not to offend in speaking much; *knowing that we*—That all who thrust themselves into the office; *shall receive greater condemnation*—For more offences. St. James here, as in several of the following verses, by a common figure of speech, includes himself. *We shall receive*—*we offend*—*we put bits*—*we curse*—None of which (as common sense shows) are to be interpreted either of him or of the other apostles.

2. *The same is able to bridle the whole body*—That is, the whole man. And doubtless some are able to do this, and so are in this sense perfect.

3. *We*—That is, *men*.

5. *Boasteth great things*—Hath great influence.

6. *A world of iniquity*—Containing an immense quantity of all manner of wickedness; *it defileth*—As fire by its smoke; *the whole body*—The whole man; *and setteth on fire the course of nature*—All the passions, every *wheel* of his soul.

7. *Every kind*—The expression perhaps is not to be taken strictly. *Reptiles*—That is, creeping things.

8. *But no man can tame the tongue*—Of another; no, nor his own, without peculiar help from God.

9. *Men, made after the likeness of God*—Indeed we have now lost this likeness. Yet there remains from thence an indelible nobleness, which we ought to reverence both in ourselves and others.

13 Who *is* a wise and knowing man among you? Let him show
14 by a good conversation his works with meekness of wisdom. But
if ye have bitter zeal and strife in your hearts, do not glory and
15 lie against the truth. This is not the wisdom which descendeth
16 from above, but *is* earthly, animal, devilish; For where bitter
17 zeal and strife is, there is unquietness and every evil work. But
the wisdom that is from above, is first pure, then peaceable,
gentle, easy to be entreated, full of mercy and good fruits, with-
18 out partiality, and without dissimulation. And the fruit of
righteousness is sown in peace for them that make peace.

IV. From whence *come* wars and fightings among you? *Is it* not
2 hence, from your pleasures that war in your members? Ye desire and have not, ye kill, and envy, and cannot obtain; ye fight
3 and war; yet ye have not, because ye ask not. Ye ask and
receive not, because ye ask amiss, that ye may expend it on your
4 pleasures. Ye adulterers, and adulteresses, know ye not that the
friendship of the world is enmity against God? Whosoever
therefore desireth to be a friend of the world, is an enemy of
5 God. Do ye think that the Scripture saith in vain, The Spirit

13. *Let him show* his wisdom, as well as his faith, *by his works;* not by words only.

14. *If ye have bitter zeal*—True Christian zeal is only the flame of love, even *in your hearts*—Though it went no farther: *do not lie against the truth*—As if such zeal could consist with heavenly wisdom.

15. *This wisdom* which is consistent with *such* zeal, *is earthly*—Not heavenly, not from the Father of lights; *animal*—Not spiritual; not from the Spirit of God: *devilish*—Not the gift of Christ, but such as Satan breathes into the soul.

17. *But the wisdom from above, is first pure*—From all that is earthly, natural, devilish: *then, peaceable*—True peace attending purity, it is quiet, inoffensive: *gentle*—Soft, mild, yielding, not rigid; *easy to be entreated*—To be persuaded or convinced, not stubborn, sour, or morose; *full of good fruits*—Both in the heart and in the life, two of which are immediately specified: *without partiality*—Loving all, without respect of persons: embracing all good things, rejecting all evil; *and without dissimulation*—Frank, open.

18. *And the* principle productive of this righteousness is sown, like good seed, in the peace of a believer's mind, and brings forth a plentiful harvest of happiness (which is the proper fruit of righteousness) *for them that make peace*—That labour to promote this pure and holy peace among all men.

IV. 1. *Fro* *whence come wars and fightings*—Quarrels and jars among you, quite opposit to this peace? *Is it not from your pleasures*?—Your desires of earthly pleasures, *which war*—Against your souls, *in your members?* Here is the first seat of the war. Hence proceeds the war of man with man, king with king, nation with nation.

2. *Ye kill*—In your heart, *for he that hateth his brother is a murderer. Ye fight and war*—That is, furiously strive and contend. *Ye ask not*—And no marvel. For a man full of evil desire, of envy, or hatred, cannot pray.

3. But *if ye do ask, ye receive not, because ye ask amiss*—That is, from a wrong motive.

4. *Ye adulterers and adulteresses*—Who have broken your faith with God, your rightful spouse; *know ye not that the friendship,* or love *of the world*—The desire of the flesh, the desire of the eye, and the pride of life, or courting the favour of worldly men, *is enmity against God?—Whosoever desireth to be a friend of the world*—Whosoever seeks either the happiness or favour of it, does thereby constitute himself *an enemy of God*—And can he expect to obtain any thing of him?

5. *Do ye think that the Scripture saith in vain*—Without good ground. St. James seems to refer to many, not any one particular scripture. The *spirit* of love *that dwelleth in* all believers, *lusteth against envy,* Gal. v, 17, is directly opposite to all those unloving tempers which necessarily flow from the friendship of the world.

6 that dwelleth in us lusteth against envy? But he giveth greater
grace: therefore it saith, * God resisteth the proud, but giveth
7 grace to the humble. Submit yourselves, therefore, to God.
8 resist the devil, and he will flee from you. Draw nigh to God,
and he will draw nigh to you: cleanse *your* hands, ye sinners,
9 and purify *your* hearts, ye double-minded. Be afflicted, and
mourn, and weep; let your laughter be turned into mourning,
10 and *your* joy into heaviness. Humble yourselves before the
Lord, and he will lift you up.
11 Speak not evil one of another, brethren. He that speaketh
evil of his brother, and judgeth his brother, speaketh evil of the
law, and judgeth the law. But if thou judgest the law, thou art
12 not a doer of the law, but a judge. There is one lawgiver that is
able to save and to destroy: Who art thou that judgest another?
13 Come now, ye that say, To-day or to-morrow we will go to
such a city, and continue there a year, and traffic, and get gain:
14 Who know not what *shall be* on the morrow; for what *is* your
life? It is a vapour that appeareth for a little time, and then
15 vanisheth away: instead of your saying, If the Lord will, we
16 shall both live, and do this or that. But now ye glory in your
17 boastings: all such glorying is evil. Therefore to him that
knoweth to do good and doth it not, to him it is sin.
V. Come now, ye rich, weep and howl for your miseries that are
2 coming *upon you.* Your riches are corrupted, and your garments

6. *But he giveth greater grace*—To all who shun those tempers: *therefore it*—
The Scripture, *saith, God resisteth the proud*—And pride is the great root of all
unkind affections.

7. Therefore by humbly *submitting yourselves to God, resist .the devil*—The
father of pride and envy.

8. *Then draw nigh to* God in prayer, *and he will draw nigh unto you,* will hear
you: which that nothing may hinder, *cleanse your hands*—Cease from doing evil,
and purify your hearts—From all spiritual adultery. Be no more double minded,
vainly endeavouring to serve both God and mammon.

9. *Be afflicted*—For your past unfaithfulness to God.

11. *Speak not evil one of another*—This is a grand hinderance of peace. O
who is sufficiently aware of it! He that speaketh evil of another does in effect
speak evil of the law which so strongly prohibits it. *Thou art not a doer of the
law, but a judge*—Of it, thou settest thyself above, and as it were condemnest it.

12. *There is one lawgiver that is able*—To execute the sentence he denounces.
But *who art thou?*—A poor, weak, dying worm.

13. *Come now, ye that say*—As peremptorily as if your life were in your own
hands.

15. *Instead of your saying*—That is, whereas ye ought to say.

17. *Therefore to him that knoweth to do good and doth it not*—That knows
what is right, and does not practise it, *to him it is sin*—His knowledge does not
prevent, but increase his condemnation.

V. 1. *Come now, ye rich*—The apostle does not speak this so much for the sake
of the rich themselves, as of the poor children of God, who were then groaning
under their cruel oppression. *Weep and howl for your miseries which are coming
upon you*—Quickly and unexpectedly. This was written not long before the
siege of Jerusalem; during which, as well as after it, huge calamities came on
the Jewish nation, not only in Judea, but through distant countries. And as
these were an awful prelude of that wrath which was to fall upon them in the
world to come, so this may likewise refer to the final vengeance which will then
be executed on the impenitent.

2. The *riches* of the ancients consisted much in large stores of corn, and of
costly apparel.

* Proverbs iii, 34.

3 are become moth eaten. Your gold and silver is cankered, and
the canker of them will be a testimony against you, and will eat
your flesh as. fire : ye have laid up treasure in the last days.
4 Behold, the hire of your labourers who have reaped your fields,
which is kept back by you, crieth : and the cries of them who
have gathered in your harvest are entered into the ears of the
5 Lord of sabaoth. Ye have lived delicately and luxuriously on
earth ; ye have cherished your hearts, as in a day of sacrifice.
6 Ye have condemned, ye have killed the just : he doth not resist
7 you. Be patient, therefore, brethren, till the coming of the
Lord. Behold, the husbandman waiteth for the. precious fruit
of the earth, and hath patience for it, till he receives the former
8 and the latter rain. Be ye also patient, stablish your hearts : for
9 the coming of the Lord is nigh. Murmur not one against another,
brethren, lest ye be condemned ; Behold, the judge standeth
10 before the door. Take, my brethren, the prophets who spoke
in the name of the Lord, for an example of suffering affliction,
11 and of patience. Behold, we count them happy that endured.
Ye have heard of the patience of Job, and have seen the end of
the Lord ; for the Lord is full of compassion and of tender mercy.
12 But above all things, my brethren, swear not, neither by heaven,
nor by the earth, nor by any other oath ; but let your yea be yea,
and your nay nay, lest ye fall under condemnation.

3. *The canker of them*—Your perishing stores and moth-eaten garments, *will be a testimony against you*—Of your having buried those talents in the earth, instead of improving them according to your Lord's will ; *and will eat your flesh as fire*—Will occasion you as great torment as if fire were consuming your flesh. *Ye have laid up treasure in the last days*—When it is too late; when you have no time to enjoy them.

4. *The hire of your labourers crieth*—Those sins chiefly cry to God, concerning which human laws are silent. Such are luxury, unchastity, and various kinds of injustice. The labourers themselves also cry to God, who is just coming to avenge their cause ; *of sabaoth*—Of hosts or armies.

5. *Ye have cherished your hearts*—Have indulged yourselves to the uttermost, *as in a day of sacrifice*—Which were solemn feast days among the Jews.

6. *Ye have killed the just*—Many just men, in particular *that Just One*, Acts iii, 14. They afterward killed James, surnamed the Just, the writer of this epistle. *He doth not resist you*—And therefore you are secure. But the Lord cometh quickly, ver. 8.

7. *The husbandman waiteth for the precious fruit*—Which will recompense his labour and patience; *till he receive the former rain*—Immediately after sowing, *and the latter*—Before the harvest.

8. *Stablish your hearts*—In faith and patience; *for the coming of the Lord*—To destroy Jerusalem, *is nigh*—And so is his last coming to the eye of a believer.

9. *Murmur not one against another*—Have patience also before each other. *The judge standeth before the door*—Hearing every word, marking every thought.

10. *Take the prophets for an example*—Once persecuted like you, even for *speaking in the name of the Lord*—The very men that gloried in having prophets, yet could not bear their message. Nor did either their holiness or their high commission screen them from suffering.

11. *We count them happy that endured*—That suffered patiently. The more they once suffered, the greater is their present happiness. *Ye have seen the end of the Lord*—The end which the Lord gave him.

12. *Swear not*—However provoked. The Jews were notoriously guilty of common swearing, though not so much by God himself as by some of his creatures. The apostle here particularly forbids these oaths, as well as all swearing in common conversation. It is very observable how solemnly the apostle introduces this command : *above all things, swear not*. As if he had said, Whatever

13 Is any among you afflicted? let him pray. Is any cheerful?
14 let him sing psalms. Is any among you sick? let him call for
the elders of the Church, and let them pray over him, having
15 anointed him with oil in the name of the Lord; And the prayer
of faith shall save the sick, and the Lord shall raise him up, and
16 if he have committed sins, they shall be forgiven him. Confess
your faults one to another, brethren, and pray one for another,
that ye may be healed: the fervent prayer of a righteous man
17 availeth much. Elijah was a man of like passions with us; and
he prayed earnestly that it might not rain; and it rained not on
18 the land for three years and six months. And he prayed again,
and the heaven gave rain, and the land brought forth her fruit.
19 Brethren, if any one among you err from the truth, and one
20 convert him, Let him know that he who converteth a sinner
from the error of his way, shall save a soul from death, and hide
a multitude of sins.

you forget, do not forget this. This abundantly demonstrates the horrible iniquity of the crime. But he does not forbid the taking of a solemn oath before
a magistrate. *Let your yea be yea, and your nay nay*—Use no higher asservera-
tions in common discourse. And let your word stand firm. Whatever ye say,
take care to make it good.

14. *Having anointed him with oil*—This single, conspicuous gift, which Christ
committed to his apostles, Mark vi, 13, remained in the Church long after the
other miraculous gifts were withdrawn. Indeed it seems to have been designed
to remain always, and St. James directs the elders, who were the most, if not the
only gifted men, to administer it. This was the whole process of physic in the
Christian Church, till it was lost through unbelief. That novel invention among
the Romanists, extreme unction, practised not for cure, but where life is despaired
of, bears no manner of resemblance to this.

15. *And the prayer* offered in *faith shall save the sick*—From his sickness, and
if any sin be the occasion of his sickness, *it shall be forgiven him.*

16. *Confess your faults*—Whether ye are sick or in health, *to one another*—He
does not say to the elders: (this may or may not be done; for it is nowhere
commanded.) We may confess them to any one who can pray in faith. He
will then know how to pray for us, and be more stirred up so to do; *and pray
one for another, that ye may be healed*—Of all your spiritual diseases.

17. *Elijah was a man of like passions*—Naturally as weak and sinful as we
are; *and he prayed*—When idolatry covered the land.

18. *He prayed again*—When idolatry was abolished.

19. As if he had said, I have now warned you of those sins to which you are
most liable: and in all these respects watch not only over yourselves, but every
one over his brother also. Labour in particular to recover those that are fallen.
If any one err from the truth—Practically by sin.

20. *He shall save a soul*—Of how much more value than the body! ver. 14;
and hide a multitude of sins—Which shall no more, how many se ever they are,
be remembered to his condemnation.

NOTES

ON

THE FIRST EPISTLE GENERAL OF ST. PETER.

———

THERE is a wonderful weightiness, and yet liveliness and sweetness, in the epistles of St. Peter. His design in both is to stir up the minds of those to whom he writes by way of remembrance, 2 Peter iii, 1; and to guard them not only against error, but also against doubting, chap. v, 12. This he does by reminding them of that glorious grace which God had vouchsafed them through the Gospel, by which believers are inflamed to bring forth the fruits of faith, hope, love, and patience.

I. ST. PETER.

1 PETER, an apostle of Jesus Christ, to the sojourners scattered
2 through Pontus, Galatia, Cappadocia, Asia, and Bithynia, Elect
(according to the foreknowledge of God the Father) through
sanctification of the Spirit unto obedience, and sprinkling of the
blood of Jesus Christ. Grace and peace be multiplied to you.

Verse 1. *To the sojourners*—Upon earth, the Christians, chiefly those of Jewish extraction, *scattered*—Long ago driven out of their own land, (those scattered by the persecution mentioned Acts viii, 1, were scattered only through Judea and Samaria, though afterward some of them travelled to Phenice, Cyprus, and Antioch,) *through Pontus, Galatia, Cappadocia, Asia, and Bithynia*—He names these five provinces in the order wherein they occurred to him, writing from the east. All these countries lie in the lesser Asia. The Asia here distinguished from the other provinces is that which was usually called the proconsular Asia, being a Roman province.

2. *According to the foreknowledge of God*—Speaking after the manner of men. Strictly speaking, there is no foreknowledge, no more than afterknowledge, with God; but all things are known to him as present, from eternity to eternity. This is therefore no other than an instance of the Divine condescension to our low capacities. *Elect*—By the free love and almighty power of God, taken out of, separated from, the world. Election, in the Scripture sense, is God's doing any thing that our merit or power have no part in. The true predestination, or foreappointment of God, is, 1. He that believeth shall be saved from the guilt and power of sin. 2. He that endureth to the end shall be saved eternally. They who receive the precious gift of faith thereby become the sons of God; and being sons, they shall receive the Spirit of holiness, to walk as Christ also walked. Throughout every part of this appointment of God, promise and duty go hand in hand. All is free gift; and yet such is the gift, that the final issue depends on our future obedience to the heavenly call. But other predestination than this, either to life or death eternal, the Scripture knows not of. Moreover it is, 1. Cruel respect of persons; an unjust regard of one, and an unjust disregard of another. It is mere creature partiality, and not infinite justice. 2. It is not plain Scripture doctrine, (if true,) but rather inconsistent with the express written word, that speaks of God's universal offers of grace; his invitations, promises, threatenings, being all general. 3. We are bid to choose life, and reprehended for not doing it. 4. It is inconsistent with a state of probation in those that must be saved or must be lost. 5. It is of fatal consequence; all men being ready on very slight grounds to fancy themselves of the elect number. But the doctrine of predestination is entirely changed from what it formerly was. Now it implies neither faith, peace, nor purity. It is something that will do without them all. Faith is no longer, according to the modern predestinarian scheme, a Divine evidence of things not seen, wrought in the soul by the immediate power of the Holy Ghost: not an evidence at all, but a mere notion. Neither is faith made any longer a means of holiness; but something that will do without it. Christ is no more a Saviour from sin; but a defence, a countenancer of it. He is no more a fountain of spiritual life in the soul of believers, but leaves his elect inwardly dry, and outwardly unfruitful; and is made little more than a refuge from the image of the heavenly; even from righteousness, peace, and joy in the Holy Ghost: *through sanctification of the Spirit*—Through the renewing and purifying influences of his Spirit on their souls; *unto obedience*—To engage and enable them to yield themselves up to all holy obedience, the foundation of all which is, *the sprinkling of the blood of Jesus Christ*—The atoning blood of Christ which was typified by the sprinkling of the blood of sacrifices under the law; in allusion to which it is called the blood of sprinkling.

3 Blessed *be* the God and Father of our Lord Jesus Christ, who, according to his abundant mercy, hath regenerated us to a living
4 hope, by the resurrection of Jesus Christ from the dead, To an inheritance incorruptible and undefiled, and that fadeth not away,
5 reserved in heaven for you, Who are kept by the power of God through faith unto salvation, ready to be revealed in the last time.
6 Wherein ye greatly rejoice, though now for a little while (if need
7 be) ye are in heaviness through manifold temptations: That the trial of your faith, *which is* much more precious than gold, (that perisheth, though it be tried with fire,) may be found unto praise,
8 and honour, and glory, at the revelation of Jesus Christ. Whom having not seen, ye love: in whom though ye see *him* not, yet believing, ye now rejoice with joy unspeakable and full of glory.
9 Receiving the end of your faith, the salvation of your souls. Of
10 which salvation the prophets, who prophesied of the grace *of God*
11 toward you, inquired and searched diligently, Searching what,

3. *Blessed be the God and Father of our Lord Jesus Christ*—His Father with respect to his Divine nature; his God with respect to his human; *who hath regenerated us to a living hope*—A hope which implies true spiritual life, which revives the heart, and makes the soul lively and vigorous; *by the resurrection of Christ*—Which is not only a pledge of ours, but a part of the purchase price. It has also a close connection with our rising from spiritual death, that as he liveth, so shall we live with him. He was acknowledged to be the Christ, but usually called Jesus till his resurrection; then he was also called Christ.

4. *To an inheritance*—For if we are sons, then heirs; *incorruptible*—Not like earthly treasures; *undefiled*—Pure and holy, incapable of being itself defiled, or of being enjoyed by any polluted soul; *and that fadeth not away*—That never decays in its value, sweetness, or beauty, like all the enjoyments of this world, like the garlands of leaves or flowers with which ancient conquerors were wont to be crowned; *reserved in heaven for you*—Who, by patient continuance in well doing, seek for glory, and honour, and immortality.

5. *Who are kept*—The inheritance is reserved; the heirs are kept for it; *by the power of God*—Which worketh all in all; which guards us against all our enemies; *through faith*—Through which alone salvation is both received and retained; *ready to be revealed*—That revelation is made in the last day. It was more and more ready to be revealed ever since Christ came.

6. *Wherein*—That is, in being so kept, *ye* even now *greatly rejoice*, though *now for a little while*—Such is our whole life compared to eternity; *if need be*—(For it is not always needful;) if God sees it to be the best means for your spiritual profit; *ye are in heaviness*—Or sorrow, but not in darkness: for they still retained both faith, ver. 5, hope, and love: yea, at this very time were rejoicing with joy unspeakable, ver. 8.

7. *That the trial of your faith*—That is, your faith which is tried, which is much more precious than gold, (for gold, though it bear the fire, yet will perish with the world,) *may be found*—Though it doth not yet appear, *unto praise*—From God·himself; *and honour*—From men and angels; *and glory*—Assigned by the great Judge.

8. *Having not seen*—In the flesh.

9. *Receiving*—Now already, *salvation*—From all sin into all holiness, which is the qualification for, the forerunner and pledge of, eternal salvation.

10. *Of which salvation*—So far beyond all that was experienced under the Jewish dispensation, the very *prophets who prophesied* long ago *of the grace of God toward you*—Of his abundant, overflowing grace, to be bestowed on believers under the Christian dispensation, *inquired*—Were earnestly inquisitive, and searched diligently, (like miners searching after precious ore,) after the meaning of the prophecies which they delivered.

11. *Searching what time*—What particular period; *and what manner of time*—By what marks to be distinguished; *the glories that were to follow*—His

and what manner of time the Spirit of Christ which was in them
signified, when he testified beforehand the sufferings of Christ
12 and the glories that were to follow. To whom it was revealed,
that not for themselves, but for us they ministered the things
which have been now declared to you by them that have preached
the Gospel to you, with the Holy Ghost sent down from heaven ·
13 which things angels desire to look into. Wherefore gird up the
loins of your mind, be watchful, and hope perfectly for the grace
14 that shall be brought to you at the revelation of Jesus Christ. As
obedient children, conform not yourselves to your former desires
15 in your ignorance : But as he who hath called you is holy, so be
16 ye yourselves also holy in all manner of conversation : For it is
17 written, *Be ye holy; for I am holy. And if ye call on the
Father, who without respect of persons judgeth according to
every man's work, pass the time of your sojourning in fear ;
18 Seeing ye know ye were not redeemed with corruptible things,
as silver and gold, from your vain conversation delivered by
19 tradition from your fathers. But with the precious blood of·
20 Christ, as of a lamb without blemish and without spot, Who
verily was foreknown before the foundation of the world, but
21 was manifested in the last times, for you, Who through him
believe in God that raised him from the dead, and gave him
glory, that your faith and hope might be in God.
22   Having purified your souls by obeying the truth through the

sufferings; namely, the glory of his resurrection, ascension, exaltation, and the
effusion of his Spirit; the glory of the last judgment, and of his eternal kingdom; and also the glories of his grace, in the hearts and lives of Christians.

12. *To whom*—So searching, *it was revealed that not for themselves, but for us
they ministered*—They did not so much by those predictions serve themselves,
or that generation, as they did us, who now enjoy what they saw afar off; *with
the Holy Ghost sent down from heaven*—Confirmed by the inward, powerful testimony of the Holy Ghost, as well as the mighty effusion of his miraculous gifts;
which things angels desire to look into—A beautiful gradation; prophets, righteous
men, kings, desired to see and hear what Christ did and taught. What the Holy
Ghost taught concerning Christ, the very angels long to know.

13. *Wherefore*—Having such encouragement, *gird up the loins of your mind*—
As persons in the eastern countries were wont, in travelling or running, to gird
up their long garments, so gather ye up all your thoughts and affections, and
keep your mind always disencumbered and prepared to run the race which is
set before you; *be watchful*—As servants that wait for their Lord; *and hope to
the end*—Maintain a full expectation of all *the grace*—The blessings flowing
from the free favour of God, which shall be brought to you at the *final* revelation of Jesus Christ; and which are now brought to you, by the revelation of
Christ in you.

14. *Your desires*—Which ye had while ye were ignorant of God.

17. *Who judgeth according to every man's work*—According to the tenor of his
life and conversation; *pass the time of your sojourning*—Your short abode on
earth, *in* humble, loving *fear*—The proper companion and guard of hope.

18. *Your vain conversation*—Your foolish, sinful way of life.

19. *Without blemish*—In himself; *without spot*—From the world.

21. *Who through him believe*—For all our faith and hope proceed from the
power of his resurrection; *in God—that raised* Jesus, *and gave him glory*—A:
his ascension: without Christ we should only dread God; whereas through him
we believe, hope, and love.

22. *Having purified your souls by obeying the truth through the Spirit*—Who

* Lev. xi, 44.

Spirit unto unfeigned love of the brethren, love one another with
23 a pure heart fervently: Being born again, not by corruptible
seed, but incorruptible, through the word of God which liveth
24 and abideth for ever.   * For all flesh is grass, and all the glory
of it as the flower of grass: The grass is withered, and the flower
25 is fallen off: But the word of the Lord endureth for ever.   And
this is the word which is preached to you in the Gospel.
II.   Wherefore laying aside all wickedness, and all guile, and dis-
2 simulation, and envies, and evil speakings, As new-born babes
desire the sincere milk of the word, that ye may grow thereby;
3 Since ye have tasted that the Lord is gracious: To whom coming
4 *as unto* a living stone, rejected indeed by men, but chosen of God
5 *and* precious, Ye also as living stones are built up, a spiritual
house, a holy priesthood, to offer up spiritual sacrifices, accept-
6 able to God through Jesus Christ.   Wherefore also it is contained in the Scripture, † Behold, I lay in Sion a chief corner
stone, elect, precious, and he that believeth on him shall not be
7 confounded.   Therefore to you who believe, *he is* precious;
but as to them who believe not, ‡ The stone which the builders

bestows upon you freely both obedience and purity of heart, and unfeigned love
of the brethren; go on to still higher degrees of love: *love one another fervently*
—With the most strong and tender affection, and yet *with a pure heart*—Pure
from any spot of unholy desire, or inordinate passion.

23. *Which liveth*—Is full of Divine virtue, and abideth the same for ever.

24. *All flesh*—Every human creature is transient and withering as grass; *and
all the glory of it*—His wisdom, strength, wealth, righteousness; *as the flower*—
The most short-lived part of it.   *The grass*—That is, man; *the flower*—That is,
his glory; *is fallen off*—As it were, while we are speaking.

II. 1. *Wherefore laying aside*—As inconsistent with that pure love, *all dissimulation*—Which is the outward expression of guile in the heart.

2. *Desire*—Always, as earnestly *as new-born babes* do, chap. i, 3, *the milk of
the word*—That word of God which nourishes the soul as milk does the body;
and which is *sincere*—Pure from all guile, so that none are deceived who cleave
to it; *that you may grow thereby*—In faith, love, holiness, unto the full stature
of Christ.

3. *Since ye have tasted*—Sweetly and experimentally known.

4. *To whom coming*—By faith; *as unto a living stone*—Living from eternity,
alive from the dead.   There is a wonderful beauty and energy in these expressions, which describe Christ as a spiritual foundation, solid, firm, durable: and
believers as a building erected upon it, in preference to that temple which the
Jews accounted their highest glory.   And St. Peter, speaking of him thus, shows
he did not judge himself, but *Christ*, to be the rock on which the Church was
built; *rejected indeed by men*—Even at this day, not only by Jews, Turks, heathens, infidels; but by all Christians, so called, who live in sin, or who hope to
be saved by their own works; *but chosen of God*—From all eternity to be the
foundation of his Church; *and precious*—In himself, in the sight of God, and in
the eyes of all believers.

5. *Ye*—Believers, *as living stones*—Alive to God through him, *are built up*—
in union with each other; *a spiritual house*—Being spiritual yourselves, and a
habitation of God through the Spirit; *a holy priesthood*—Consecrated to God,
and holy as he is holy; *to offer up*—Your souls and bodies, with all your thoughts,
words, and actions, as spiritual sacrifices to God.

6. *He that believeth shall not be confounded*—In time or in eternity.

7. *To them who believe, he is become the head of the corner*—The chief corner
stone, on which the whole building rests.   Unbelievers too will at length find
him such to their sorrow, Matt. xxi, 44.

* Isa. xl, 6, &c.   † Isa. xxviii, 16.   ‡ Psa. cxviii, 22.

8 rejected is become the head of the corner. And a stone of
 stumbling, and a rock of offence, *to them* who stumble, not be-
9 lieving the word, whereunto *also* they were appointed. But ye
 are a chosen race, a royal priesthood, a holy nation, a purchased
 people, that ye may show forth the virtues of him who hath
10 called you out of darkness into his marvellous light: Who in
 time past *were* not a people, but now *are* the people of God;
 who had not obtained mercy, but now have obtained mercy.
11 Beloved, I beseech *you* as sojourners and pilgrims, abstain
12 from fleshly desires, which war against the soul, Having your
 conversation honest among the Gentiles, that whereas they speak
 against you as evil doers, they may, by your good works which
13 they shall behold, glorify God in the day of visitation. Be subject to every ordinance of man for the Lord's sake, whether it
14 be to the king, as supreme, Or to governors, as sent by him, for
 the punishment of evil doers, and the praise of them that do well.
15 For so is the will of God, that by well doing ye put to silence
16 the ignorance of foolish men: As free, yet not having your
 liberty for a cloak of wickedness, but as the servants of God.
17 Honour all men, Love the brotherhood, Fear God, Honour the
18 king. Servants, be subject to *your* masters with all fear, not

8. *Who stumble, whereunto also they were appointed*—They who believe not, stumble, and fall, and perish for ever. God having appointed from all eternity, *He that believeth not shall be damned.*

9. *But ye*—Who believe in Christ, *are*—In a higher sense than ever the Jews were, *a chosen* or elect *race, a royal priesthood*—Kings and priests unto God, Rev. i, 6. As princes, ye have power with God, and victory over sin, the world, and the devil: as priests, ye are consecrated to God, for offering spiritual sacrifices. Ye Christians are as one *holy nation*—Under Christ your King; *a purchased people*—Who are his peculiar property; *that ye may show forth*—By your whole behaviour to all mankind; *the virtues*—The excellent glory, the mercy, wisdom, and power, *of him*—Christ, *who hath called you out of the darkness*—Of ignorance, error, sin, and misery.

10. *Who in time past were not a people*—(Much less the people of God,) but scattered individuals of many nations. The former part of the verse particularly respects the Gentiles; the latter, the Jews.

11. Here begins the exhortation drawn from the second motive: *Sojourners, pilgrims*—The first word properly means, those who are in a strange house: the second, those who are in a strange country. You sojourn in the body: you are pilgrims in this world: abstain from desires of any thing in this house, or in this country.

12. *Honest*—Not barely unblamable, but virtuous in every respect. But our language sinks under the force, beauty, and copiousness of the original expressions: *that they by your good works which they shall behold*—See with their own eyes, *may glorify God*—By owning his grace in you, and following your example; *in the day of visitation*—The time when he shall give them fresh offers of his mercy.

13. *Submit yourselves to every ordinance of man*—To every secular power. Instrumentally these are ordained by men; but originally all their power is from God.

14. *Or to subordinate governors*, or magistrates.

15. *The ignorance*—Of them who blame you, because they do not know you: a strong motive to pity them.

16. *As free*—Yet obeying governors, for God's sake.

17. *Honour all men*—As being made in the image of God, bought by his Son, and designed for his kingdom; *honour the king*—Pay him all that regard both in affection and action which the laws of God and man require.

18. *Servants*—Literally, household servants; with all fear of offending them

19 only to the good and gentle, but also to the froward. For this
   is thankworthy, if a man for conscience toward God endure
20 grief, though he suffer wrongfully. For what glory *is it*, if when
   ye commit faults and are buffeted, ye take it patiently. But if
   when ye do well and yet suffer, ye take it patiently, this *is* ac-
21 ceptable with God. For even hereunto are ye called; for Christ
   also suffered for us, leaving you an example, that ye might follow
22 his steps: * Who did no sin, neither was guile found in his
23 mouth; Who, when he was reviled, reviled not again; when
   he suffered he threatened not, but committed *himself* to him that
24 judgeth righteously : Who himself bore our sins in his own body
   on the tree, that we being dead to sin might live to righteous-
25 ness: by whose stripes ye were healed. For ye were as sheep
   going astray, but are now returned to the shepherd and bishop
   of your souls.
III. In like manner, ye wives, be subject to your own husbands,
   that if any obey not the word, they also may without the word
2 be won by the deportment of the wives, Beholding your chaste
3 deportment *joined* with fear : Whose adorning let it not be the
   outward *adorning* of curling the hair, and of wearing gold, or
4 of putting on apparel, But the hidden man of the heart, in the
   incorruptible *ornament* of a meek and quiet spirit, which in the

---

or God; *not only to the good*—Tender, kind; *and gentle*—Mild, easily forgiving.
   19. *For conscience toward God*—From a pure desire of pleasing him; *grief*—
Severe treatment.
   21. *Hereunto are ye*—Christians, *called*—To suffer wrongfully; *leaving you an
example*—when he went to God, *that ye might follow his steps*—Of innocence
and patience.
   22, 23. In all these instances the example of Christ is peculiarly adapted to
the state of servants, who easily slide either into sin or guile, reviling their
fellow servants, or threatening them, the natural result of anger without power.
He committed himself to him that judgeth righteously—The only solid ground of
patience in affliction.
   24. *Who himself bore our sins*—That is, the punishment due to them, in his
afflicted, torn, dying *body on the tree*—The cross, whereon chiefly slaves or servants were wont to suffer; *that we being dead to sin*—Wholly delivered both
from the guilt and power of it : (indeed without an atonement first made for the
guilt, we could never have been delivered from the power:) *might live to righteousness*—Which is one only. The sins we had committed, and he bore, were
manifold.
   25. *The bishop*—The kind observer, inspector, or overseer of your souls.
   III. 1. *If any*—He speaks tenderly; *won*—Gained over to Christ.
   2. *Joined with* a loving *fear* of displeasing them.
   3. Three things are here expressly forbidden, curling the hair, wearing gold,
by way of ornament, and putting on costly or gay apparel. These therefore
ought never to be allowed, much less defended, by Christians.
   4. *The hidden man of the heart*—Complete inward holiness, which implies a
meek and quiet spirit. A meek spirit gives no trouble willingly to any : a quiet
spirit bears all wrongs without being troubled: *in the sight of God*—Who looks
at the heart. All superfluity of dress contributes more to pride and anger than
is generally supposed. The apostle seems to have his eye to this by substituting
meekness and quietness in the room of the ornaments he forbids. " I do not regard these things," is often said by those whose hearts are wrapped up in them.
But offer to take them away, and you touch the very idol of their soul. Some
indeed only dress elegantly that they may be looked on; that is, they squander

* Isaiah liii, 4, &c.

5 sight of God is of great price. For thus the holy women also
of old time, who trusted in God, adorned themselves, being
6 subject to their own husbands, As *Sarah obeyed Abraham,
calling him lord, whose children ye are while ye do well, and
7 are not afraid with any amazement: In like manner, ye husbands,
dwell according to knowledge with *the woman,* as the weaker
vessel; giving them honour, as being the joint heirs of the grace
of life, that your prayers be not hindered.
8   Finally, *Be* ye all of one mind, sympathizing with each other;
9 love as brethren, *be* pitiful, *be* courteous: Not rendering evil for
evil, or railing for railing, but contrariwise blessing; knowing
10 that ye are called to this, to inherit a blessing. For †let him
that desireth to love life and to see good days, refrain his tongue
11 from evil, and his lips that they speak no guile   Let him turn
12 from evil and do good; let him seek peace and pursue it. For
the eyes of the Lord *are* over the righteous, and his ears *are*
open to their prayer; but the face of the Lord *is* against them
13 that do evil. And who is he that will harm you, if ye be fol-
14 lowers of that which is good? But even if ye do suffer for
righteousness' sake, happy are ye; and fear ye not their fear,
15 neither be ye troubled, But sanctify the Lord God in your hearts:

---

away their Lord's talent to gain applause; thus making sin to beget sin, and
then plead one in excuse for the other.

5. The adorning of those *holy women, who trusted in God*—And therefore did
not act thus from servile fear, was, 1. Their meek subjection to their husbands;
2. Their quiet spirit, not afraid or amazed; and 3. Their unblamable behaviour,
doing all things well.

6. *Whose children ye are*—In a spiritual as well as natural sense, and entitled
to the same inheritance, while ye discharge your conjugal duties, not out of fear,
but for conscience' sake.

7. *Dwell with the woman according to knowledge*—Knowing they are weak, and
therefore to be used with all tenderness; yet do not despise them for this, but
give them honour—Both in heart, in word, and in action, as those who are called
to be joint heirs of that eternal life which ye and they hope to receive by the free
grace of God: *that your prayers be not hindered*—On the one part or the other.
All sin hinders prayer, particularly anger. Any thing at which we are angry is
never more apt to come into our minds than when we are at prayer. And those
who do not forgive will find no forgiveness from God.

8. *Finally*—This part of the epistle reaches to chap. iv, 11. The apostle seems
to have added the rest afterward. *Sympathizing*—Rejoicing and sorrowing together: *love*—All believers as brethren, *be pitiful*—Toward the afflicted; *be courteous*—To all men. Courtesy is such a behaviour toward equals and inferiors,
as shows respect mixed with love.

9. *Ye are called to inherit a blessing*—Therefore their railing cannot hurt you.
And by blessing them you imitate God who blesses you.

10. *For he that desireth to love life, and to see good days*—That would make
life amiable and desirable.

11. *Let him seek*—To live peaceably with all men, *and pursue it*—Even when
it seems to flee from him.

12. *The eyes of the Lord are over the righteous*—For good: anger appears in
the whole face: love chiefly in the eyes.

13. *Who is he that will harm you?*—None can.

14. *But if ye* should *suffer*—This is no harm to you, but a good: *fear ye not
their fear*—The very words of the Septuagint, Isa. viii, 12, 13. Let not that fear
be in you which the wicked feel.

15. *But sanctify the Lord God in your hearts*—Have a holy fear and a full trus*

* Gen. xviii, 12.   † Psalm xxxiv, 13, &c.

And *be* always ready to give an answer to every one that asketh you a reason of the hope that is in you with meekness and fear:

16 Having a good conscience, that wherein they speak against you as evil doers, they may be ashamed who falsely accuse your good

17 conversation in Christ. For *it is* better, if the will of God be so,

18 to suffer for well doing than for evil doing. For Christ also once suffered for sins, the just for the unjust, that he might bring us to God, being put to death in the flesh, but raised up to life

19 by the Spirit, By which likewise he went and preached to the

20 spirits in prison, Who were disobedient of old, when the long suffering of God waited in the days of Noah, while the ark was preparing, wherein few, that is, eight persons, were carried

21 safely through the water: The antitype whereof, baptism, now saveth us, (not the putting away the filth of the flesh, but the answer of a good conscience toward God,) by the resurrection

22 of Jesus Christ, Who being gone into heaven, is on the right hand of God; angels, and authorities, and powers, being sub-

IV. jected to him. Seeing then Christ hath suffered for us in the flesh, arm yourselves also with the same mind; (for he that hath

2 suffered in the flesh hath ceased from sin;) That *ye* may no longer live the rest of *your* time in the flesh, to the desire of

---

in his wise providence: *the hope*—Of eternal life, *with meekness*—For anger would hurt your cause as well as your soul; *and fear*—A filial fear of offending God, and a jealousy over yourselves, lest ye speak amiss.

16. *Having a good conscience*—So much the more beware of anger, to which the very consciousness of your innocence may betray you. Join with a good conscience, meekness and fear, and you obtain a complete victory; *your good conversation in Christ*—That is, which flows from faith in him.

17. *It is* infinitely better, if it be the will of God, ye should suffer. His permissive will appears from his providence.

18. *For*—This is undoubtedly best, whereby we are most conformed to Christ. *Now Christ suffered once*—To suffer no more, *for sins*—Not his own, but ours; *the just for the unjust*—The word signifies, not only them who have wronged their neighbours, but those who have transgressed any of the commands of God; as the preceding word *just* denotes a person who has fulfilled, not barely social duties, but all kinds of righteousness: *that he might bring us to God*—Now to his gracious favour, hereafter to his blissful presence, by the same steps, of suffering and of glory: *being put to death in the flesh*—As man, *but raised to life by the Spirit*—Both by his own Divine power, and by the power of the Holy Ghost.

19. *By which Spirit he preached*—Through the ministry of Noah, *to the spirits in prison*—The unholy men before the flood; who were then reserved by the justice of God as in a prison, till he executed the sentence upon them all: and are now also reserved to the judgment of the great day.

20. *When the long suffering of God waited*—For a hundred and twenty years, all the time the ark was preparing; during which Noah warned them all to flee from the wrath to come.

21. *The antitype whereof*—The thing typified by the ark, even baptism, *now saveth us*—That is, through the water of baptism we are saved from the sin which overwhelms the world as a flood; not indeed the bare outward sign, but the inward grace; a Divine consciousness, that both our persons and our actions are accepted, through Him who died and rose again for us.

22. *Angels, and authorities, and powers*—That is, all orders both of angels and men.

IV. 1. *Arm yourselves with the same mind*—Which will be armour of proof against all your enemies; *for he that hath suffered in the flesh*—That hath so suffered as to be thereby made inwardly and truly conformable to the sufferings of Christ; *hath ceased from sin*—Is delivered from it.

2. *That ye may live no longer in the flesh*—Even in this mortal body; *to the*

3 men, but to the will of God. For the time of life that is past
  sufficeth to have wrought the will of the Gentiles, when ye
  walked in lasciviousness, evil desires, excess of wine, banquet-
4 ings, revellings, and abominable idolatries. Wherein they think
  it strange, that ye run not with them to the same profusion of
5 riot, speaking evil of *you*, Who shall give account to Him that is
6 ready to judge the living and the dead. For to this end was the
  Gospel preached to them that are dead also, that they might be
  judged according to men in the flesh, but live according to God
7 in the Spirit. But the end of all things is at hand, be ye there-
8 fore sober, and watch unto prayer. And above all things have
  fervent love to each other; for love covereth a multitude of
9 sins.* Use hospitality one to another without murmuring. As
10 every one hath received a gift, *so* minister it one to another, as
11 good stewards of the manifold grace of God. If any man speak,
  let him speak as the oracles of God: if any man minister, *let*
  him minister as of the ability which God supplieth, that God in

---

desires of men—Either your own or those of others. These are various: but the will of God is one.

3. *Banquetings and revellings*—Have these words any meaning now? They had seventeen hundred years ago. Then the former meant, meetings to eat—meetings, the direct end of which was, to please the taste; the latter, meetings to drink; both of which Christians then ranked with abominable idolatries.

4. *The same*—As ye did once; *speaking evil of you*—As proud, singular, silly, wicked, and the like.

5. *Who shall give account*—Of this, as well as all their other ways, *to Him who is ready*—So faith represents him now.

6. *For to this end was the Gospel preached*—Ever since it was given to Adam: *to them that are now dead*—In their several generations, *that they might be judged* —That though they were judged in the flesh according to the manner *of men*— With rash unrighteous judgment, they might live according to the will and word of *God in the Spirit;* the soul renewed after his image.

7. *But the end of all things*—And so of your wrongs and your sufferings, is at hand, *be ye therefore sober, and watch unto prayer*—Temperance helps watchfulness, and both of them help prayer. Watch that ye may pray, and pray that ye may watch.

8. *Love covereth a multitude of sins*—Yea, love covereth all things. He that loves another, covereth his faults, how many soever they be. He turns away his own eyes from them; and, as far as is possible, hides them from others. And he continually prays that all the sinner's iniquities may be forgiven and his sins covered. Meantime the God of love measures to him with the same measure into his bosom.

9. *One to another*—Ye that are of different towns or countries, *without murmuring*—With all cheerfulness.

10. *As every one hath received a gift*—Spiritual or temporal, ordinary or extraordinary, (although the latter seems primarily intended,) *so minister it one to another*—Employ it for the common good; *as good stewards of the manifold grace of God*—The talents wherewith his free love has intrusted you.

11. *If any man speak, let him*—In his whole conversation, public and private, *speak as the oracles of God*—Let all his words be according to this pattern, both as to matter and manner, more especially in public. By this mark we may always know who are, so far, the true or false prophets. The oracles of God teach that men should repent, believe, obey. He that treats of faith and leaves out repentance, or does not enjoin practical holiness to believers, does not speak as the oracles of God: he does not preach Christ, let him think as highly of himself as he will. *If any man minister*—Serve his brother in love, whether in spirituals or temporals, *let him minister as of the ability which God giveth*—That is, humbly and diligently, ascribing all his power to God, and using it with his

* Proverbs x, 12.

all things may be glorified through Jesus Christ, whose is the glory and the might for ever and ever. Amen.

12 Beloved, wonder not at the burning which is among you,
13 which is for your trial, as if a strange thing befell you : But as ye partake of the sufferings of Christ, rejoice, that when his glory shall be revealed, ye may likewise rejoice with exceeding
14 great joy. If ye are reproached for the name of Christ, happy *are ye ;* for the Spirit of glory and of God resteth upon you : on their part he is blasphemed, but on your part he is glorified.
15 But let none of you suffer as a murderer, or a thief, or an evil
16 doer, or as a meddler in other men's matters, Yet if *any suffer* as a Christian, let him not *be* ashamed ; but let him glorify God
17 on this behalf. For the time *is come* for judgment to begin at the house of God : but if it begin at us, what *shall* the end *be*
18 of them that obey not the Gospel of God ? *And if the righteous scarcely be saved, where shall the ungodly and the sinner ap-
19 pear? Wherefore let them also that suffer according to the will of God, commit their souls *to him* in well doing as unto a faithful Creator.
V. The elders that are among you I exhort, who am a fellow

might; *whose is the glory*—Of his wisdom, which teaches us to speak, *and the might*—Which enables us to act.

12. *Wonder not at the burning which is among you*—This is the literal meaning of the expression. It seems to include both martyrdom itself, which so frequently was by fire, and all the other sufferings joined with or previous to it; *which* are permitted by the wisdom of God *for your trial.* Be not surprised at this.

13. *But as ye partake of the sufferings of Christ,* ver. 1, while ye suffer for his sake, rejoice in hope of more abundant glory. For the measure of glory answers the measure of suffering; and much more abundantly.

14. *If ye are reproached for Christ*—Reproachings and cruel mockings were always one part of their sufferings; *the Spirit of glory and of God resteth upon you*—The same Spirit which was upon Christ, Luke iv, 18. He is here termed the Spirit of glory, conquering all reproach and shame, and the Spirit of God, whose Son Jesus Christ is. *On their part he is blasphemed, but on your part he is glorified*—That is, while they are blaspheming Christ, you glorify him in the midst of your sufferings, ver. 16.

15. *Let none of you* deservedly *suffer as an evil doer*—In any kind.

16. *Let him glorify God*—Who giveth him the honour so to suffer, and so great a reward for suffering.

17. *The time is come for judgment to begin at the house of God*—God first visits his Church, and that both in justice and mercy: *what shall the end be of them that obey not the Gospel?*—How terribly will he visit them! The judgments, which are milder at the beginning, grow more and more severe. But good men, having already sustained their part, are only spectators of the miseries of the wicked.

18. *If the righteous scarcely be saved*—Escape with the utmost difficulty, *where shall the ungodly*—The man who knows not God, and the open *sinner appear*—In that day of vengeance? The salvation here primarily spoken of is of a temporal nature; but we may apply the words to eternal things, and then they are still more awful.

19. *Let them that suffer according to the will of God*—Both for a good cause, and in a right spirit, *commit to him their souls*—(Whatever becomes of the body,) as a sacred depositum, *in well doing*—Be this your care, to do and suffer well; he will take care of the rest; *as unto a faithful Creator*—In whose truth, love, and power, ye may safely trust.

V. 1. *I who am a fellow elder*—So the first, though not the head, of the apostles

* Proverbs xi, 31.

elder, and a witness of the sufferings of Christ, and likewise a
2 partaker of the glory which shall be revealed, Feed the flock of
God which is among you, overseeing *it* not by constraint, but
3 willingly, not for filthy gain, but of a ready mind, Neither as
4 lording over the heritage, but being examples to the flock. And
when the chief Shepherd shall appear, ye shall receive the crown
5 of glory that fadeth not away. In like manner, ye younger, be
subject to the elder, yea, being all subject to each other, be
clothed with humility ; * for God resisteth the proud, but giveth
6 grace to the humble. Humble yourselves therefore under the
7 mighty hand of God, that he may exalt you in due time : Casting
8 all your care upon him ; for he careth for you. Watch : be vigilant: for your adversary the devil walketh about as a roaring
9 lion, seeking whom he may devour : Whom resist, steadfast in
the faith, knowing that the same afflictions are accomplished in
your brethren that are in the world.
10   Now the God of all grace, who hath called us by Christ Jesus
to his eternal glory, after ye have suffered awhile, himself shall
11 perfect, stablish, strengthen, settle you. To him *be* the glory and
the might for ever and ever. Amen.
12   By Sylvanus, a faithful brother, as I suppose, I have written

---

appositely and modestly styles himself; *and a witness of the sufferings of Christ*—
Having seen him suffer, and now suffering for him.

2. *Feed the flock*—Both by doctrine and discipline; *not by constraint*—Unwillingly as a burden; *not for filthy gain*—Which, if it be the motive of acting, is
filthy beyond expression. O consider this, ye that leave one flock, and go to
another, merely " because there is more gain, a larger salary !" Is it not astonishing, that men " can see no harm in this ?" That it is not only practised,
but avowed all over the nation.

3. *Neither as lording over the heritage*—Behaving in a haughty, domineering
manner, as though you had dominion over their conscience. The word translated *heritage*, is literally *the portions*. There is one flock, under one chief
Shepherd ; but many portions of this, under many pastors ; *but being examples to
the flock*—This procures the most ready and free obedience.

5. *Ye younger, be subject to the elder*—In years; *and be all*—Elder or younger,
subject to each other—Let every one be ready, upon all occasions, to give up his
own will ; *be clothed with humility*—Bind it on, (so the word signifies,) so that
no force may be able to tear it from you.

6. *The hand of God*—Is in all troubles.

7. *Casting all your care upon him*—In every want or pressure.

8. 'But in the meantime *watch.* There is a close connection between this
and the duly casting our care upon him. How deeply had St. Peter himself
suffered for want of watching ! *Be vigilant*—As if he had said, Awake and
keep awake. Sleep no more ; be this your care. *As a roaring lion*—Full of
rage ; *seeking*—With all subtlety likewise, *whom he may devour* or *swallow up*—
Both soul and body.

9. Be the more *steadfast*—as ye *know the same* kind of *afflictions are accomplished in*—That is, suffered by *your brethren*, till the measure allotted them is
filled up.

10. *Now the God of all grace*—By which alone the whole work is begun, continued, and finished in your soul; *after ye have suffered awhile*—A very little
while compared with eternity; *himself*—Ye have only to watch and resist the
devil: the rest God will perform; *perfect*—That no defect may remain; *stablish*
—That nothing may overthrow you; *strengthen*—That ye may conquer all adverse power; *and settle you*—As a house upon a rock. So the apostle, being
converted, does now strengthen his brethren.

12. *As I suppose*—As I judge, upon good grounds, though not by immediate

* James iv, 6; Prov. iii, 34.

briefly to you, exhorting and adding my testimony, that this is
13 the true grace of God wherein ye stand.   The *Church that is* at
Babylon, elected together with you, saluteth you, and Mark my
14 son.   Salute ye one another with a kiss of charity.   Peace be
with you all that are in Christ.

---

inspiration; *I have written*—That is, sent my letter by him; *adding my testi-mony*—To that which ye before heard from Paul, that this is the true Gospel of the grace of God.

13. *The Church that is at Babylon*—Near which St. Peter probably was, when he wrote this epistle; *elected together with you*—Partaking of the same faith with you.   *Mark*—It seems the evangelist; *my son*—Probably converted by St. Peter. And he had occasionally served him as a son in the Gospel.

NOTES

THE SECOND EPISTLE GENERAL OF ST. PETER.

———

T<small>HE</small> parts of this epistle, wrote not long before St. Peter's death, and the destruction of Jerusalem, with the same design as the former, are likewise three:

———

II. ST. PETER.

———

1 S<small>IMON</small> P<small>ETER</small>, a servant and an apostle of Jesus Christ, to them that have obtained like precious faith with us, through
2 the righteousness of our God and Saviour Jesus Christ, Grace and peace be multiplied unto you, through the knowledge of God,
3 and of Jesus our Lord; As his Divine power hath given us all things that pertain to life and godliness, through the knowledge
4 of him that hath called us by glory and virtue, Through which

Verse 1. *To them that have obtained*—Not by their own works, but by the free grace of God, *like precious faith with us*—The apostles. The faith of those who have not seen, being equally precious with that of those who saw our Lord in the flesh; *through the righteousness*—Both active and passive, *of our God and Saviour*—It is this alone by which the justice of God is satisfied, and for the sake of which he gives this precious faith.

2. *Through the*—Divine, experimental knowledge of God and of Christ.

3. *As his Divine power has given us all things*—There is a wonderful cheerfulness in this exordium, which begins with the exhortation itself; *that pertain to life and godliness*—To the present natural life, and to the continuance and increase of spiritual life, through that Divine *knowledge of him*—Of Christ, *who hath called us by*—His own glorious power, to eternal *glory*—As the end, by Christian *virtue*—Or fortitude, as the means.

4. *Through which*—Glory and fortitude, *he hath given us exceeding great—*

ne hath given us p. ecious and exceeding great promises; that by these, having escaped the corruption which is in the world through desire, ye may become partakers of the Divine nature:

5 For this very reason, giving all diligence, add to your faith
6 courage, and to courage knowledge, And to knowledge temperance, and to temperance patience, and to patience godliness,
7 And to godliness brotherly kindness, and to brotherly kindness'
8 love. For these, being in you and abounding, make *you* neither

and inconceivably *precious promises*—Both the promises and the things promised, which follow in their due season, that, sustained and encouraged by the promises, we may obtain all that he has promised: *that, having escaped the* manifold *corruption which is in the world*—From that fruitful fountain, *evil desire: ye may become partakers of the Divine nature*—Being renewed in the image of God, and having communion with him, so as to dwell in God, and God in you.

5. *For this very reason*—Because God hath given you so great blessings; *giving all diligence*—It is a very uncommon word, which we render *giving*. It literally signifies, *bringing in by the by,* or *over and above;* implying that God works the work; yet not unless we are diligent. Our diligence is to follow the gift of God, and is followed by an increase of all his gifts; *add to*—And *in* all the other gifts of God. Superadd the latter, without losing the former. The Greek word properly means *lead up,* as in a dance, one of these after the other, in a beautiful order. *Your faith,* that *evidence of things not seen,* termed before *the knowledge of God and of Christ*—The root of all Christian graces; *courage* —Whereby ye may conquer all enemies and difficulties, and execute whatever faith dictates. In this most beautiful connection, each preceding grace leads to the following: each following, tempers and perfects the preceding. They are set down in the order of nature, rather than the order of time. For though every grace bears a relation to every other, yet here they are so nicely ranged, that those which have the closest dependence on each other are placed together; *and to your courage knowledge*—Wisdom, teaching how to exercise it on all occasions.

6. *And to your knowledge temperance, and to your temperance patience*—Bear and forbear; sustain and abstain. Deny yourself, and take up your cross daily. The more knowledge you have, the more renounce your own will: indulge yourself the less. *Knowledge puffeth up,* and the great boasters of knowledge (the Gnostics) were those that *turned the grace of God into wantonness.* But see that *your* knowledge be attended with *temperance.* Christian temperance implies the voluntary abstaining from all pleasure which does not lead to God. It extends to all things inward and outward; the due government of every thought, as well as affection. *It is using the world,* so to use all outward, and so to restrain all inward things, that they may become a means of what is spiritual; a scaling ladder to ascend to what is above. Intemperance is to *abuse* the world. He that uses any thing below, looking no higher, and getting no farther, is intemperate. He that uses the creature only so as to attain to more of the Creator, is alone temperate, and walks as Christ himself walked. *And to patience godliness*—Its proper support: a continual sense of God's presence and providence, and a filial fear of, and confidence in him. Otherwise your patience may be pride, surliness, stoicism; but not Christianity.

7. *And to godliness brotherly kindness*—No sullenness, sternness, moroseness: *sour godliness,* so called, is of the devil. Of Christian godliness it may always be said:—

> " Mild, sweet, serene, and tender is her mood,
> Nor grave with sternness, nor with lightness free;
> Against example resolutely good,
> Fervent in zeal, and warm in charity."

And to brotherly kindness love—The pure and perfect love of God, and of al. mankind. The apostle here makes an advance upon the preceding article, *brotherly kindness,* which seems only to relate to the love of Christians toward one another. '

8. *For these being* really *in you*—Added to your faith, *and abounding*—Increasing more and more, otherwise we fall short; *make you neither slothful nor*

slothful nor unfruitful in the knowledge of our Lord Jesus
9 Christ. But he that wanteth these is blind, not able to see afar
off, having forgotten the purification from his former sins.
10 Wherefore, brethren, be the more diligent to make your calling
and election firm ; for if ye do these things ye shall never fall.
11 For so an entrance shall be ministered to you abundantly into
the everlasting kingdom of our Lord and Saviour Jesus Christ.
12 Wherefore I will not neglect always to remind you of these
things, though ye know them, and are established in the present
13 truth ; Yea, I think it right, so long as I am in this tabernacle,
14 to stir you up by reminding *you :* Knowing that shortly I must
put off my tabernacle, even as our Lord Jesus Christ showed
15 me. But I will endeavour that ye may be able after my decease
to have these things always in remembrance.
16 For we have not followed cunningly devised fables, while we
made known to you the power and coming of our Lord Jesus

unfruitful—Do not suffer you to be faint in your minds, or without fruit in
your lives. If there is less faithfulness, less care and watchfulness, since we
were pardoned, than there was before, and less diligence, less outward obedience, than when we were seeking remission of sin, we are both *slothful and
unfruitful in the knowledge of Christ*—That is, in the faith, which then cannot
work by love.

9. *But he that wanteth these*—That does not add them to his faith, *is blind*—
The eyes of his understanding are again closed. He cannot see God or his
pardoning love. He has lost the evidence of things not seen; *not able to see
afar off*—Literally, purblind. He has lost sight of the precious promises; perfect love and heaven are equally out of his sight. Nay, he cannot now see
what himself once enjoyed, *having,* as it were, *forgot the purification from his
former sins*—Scarce knowing what he himself then felt, when his sins were
forgiven.

10. *Wherefore*—Considering the miserable state of these apostates, *brethren*—
St. Peter nowhere uses this appellation in either of his epistles, but in this important exhortation, *be the more diligent*—By courage, knowledge, temperance,
&c., *to make your calling and election firm*—God hath called you by his word
and his Spirit; he hath elected you, separated you from the world, through the
sanctification of the Spirit. O cast not away these inestimable benefits! If ye
are thus diligent to make your election firm, ye shall never finally fall.

11. *For if ye do so, an entrance shall be ministered to you abundantly into the
everlasting kingdom*—Ye shall go in full triumph to glory.

12. *Wherefore*—Since everlasting destruction attends your sloth, everlasting
glory your diligence, *I will not neglect always to remind you of these things*—
Therefore he wrote another so soon after the former epistle; *though ye are established in the present truth*—That truth which I am now declaring.

13. *In this tabernacle*—Or *tent.* How short is our abode in the body! how
easily does a believer pass out of it !

14. *Even as the Lord Jesus showed me*—In the manner which he foretold,
John xxi, 18, &c. It is not improbable he had also showed him that the time
was now drawing nigh.

15. *That ye may be able*—By having this epistle among you.

16. *These things* are worthy to be *always had in remembrance. For* they are
not cunningly devised fables—Like those common among the heathens ; *while we
made known to you the power and coming*—That is, the powerful coming of
Christ in glory. But if what they advanced of Christ was not true, if it was of
their own invention, then to impose such a lie on the world, as it was in the very
nature of things above all human power to defend, and to do this at the expense
of life and all things, only to enrage the whole world, Jews and Gentiles, against
them, was no *cunning,* but was the greatest *folly* that men could have been
guilty of; *but were eye witnesses of his majesty*—At his transfiguration, which
was a specimen of his glory at the last day.

17 Christ; but were eye witnesses of his majesty; For he received honour and glory from God the Father, when there came such a voice to him from the excellent glory; *This is my beloved
18 Son, in whom I delight. And we being with him in the holy
19 mountain, heard this voice coming from heaven. And we have the word of prophecy more confirmed, to which ye do well that ye take heed, as to a lamp that shone in a dark place, till the day
20 should dawn, and the morning star arise in your hearts: Knowing this before, that no Scripture prophecy is of private inter-
21 pretation. For prophecy came not of old by the will of man, but the holy men of God spake, being moved by the Holy Ghost.

II. But there were false prophets also among the people, as there will likewise be false teachers among you, who will privately bring in destructive heresies, even denying the Lord that bought
2 them, and bring upon themselves swift destruction. And many will follow their pernicious ways, by means of whom the way
3 of truth will be evil spoken of. And through covetousness will

17. *For he received* Divine *honour and* inexpressible *glory*—Shining from heaven, above the brightness of the sun, *when there came such a voice from the excellent glory*—That is, from God the Father.

18. *And we*—Peter, James, and John. St. John was still alive; *being with him in the holy mount*—Made so by that glorious manifestation, as Mount Horeb was of old, Exod. iii, 4, 5.

19. *And we*—St. Peter here speaks in the name of all Christians, *have the word of prophecy*— The words of Moses, Isaiah, and all the prophets, are one and the same word, every way consistent with itself. St. Peter does not cite any particular passage, but speaks of their entire testimony; *more confirmed*— By that display of his glorious majesty; *to which* word *ye do well that ye take heed, as to a lamp which shone in a dark place*—Wherein there was neither light nor window. Such anciently was the whole world, except that little spot where this lamp shone; *till the day should dawn*—Till the full light of the Gospel should break through the darkness: as is the difference between the light of a lamp and that of the day, such is that between the light of the Old Testament and of the New; *and the morning star*—Jesus Christ, Rev. xxii, 16, *arise in your hearts*— Be revealed in you.

20. Ye do well, *as knowing this, that no Scripture prophecy is of private interpretation*—It is not any man's own word. It is God, not the prophet himself, who thereby interprets things till then unknown.

21. *For prophecy came not of old by the will of man*—Of any mere man whatever, *but the holy men of God*—Devoted to him, and set apart by him for that purpose, *spake*, and wrote, *being moved*—Literally, carried. They were purely passive therein.

II. 1. *But there were false prophets also*—As well as true, *among the people*— Of Israel. Those that spake even the truth when God had not sent them; and also those that were truly sent of him, and yet corrupted or softened their message, were *false prophets, as there will be false*—As well as true, *teachers among you, who will privately bring in*—Into the Church, *destructive heresies*— They first, by denying the Lord, introduced destructive heresies, that is, divisions; or they occasioned first these divisions; and then were given up to a reprobate mind, even to deny the Lord that bought them. Either the heresies are the effect of denying the Lord, or the denying the Lord was the consequence of the heresies; *even denying*—Both by their doctrine and their works, *the Lord that bought them*—With his own blood. Yet these very men perish everlastingly Therefore Christ bought even them that perish.

2. *The way of truth will be evil spoken of*—By those who blend all false and true Christians together.

3. *They will make merchandise of you*—Only use you to gain by you, as

* Matt. xvii, 5.

they with feigned speeches make merchandise of you, whose judgment now of a long time lingereth not, and their destruction
4 slumbereth not.. For if God spared not the angels that sinned, but having cast them down to hell, delivered them into chains
5 of darkness, to be reserved unto judgment: And spared not the old world, (but he preserved Noah, the eighth *person*, a preacher of righteousness,) bringing a flood on the world of the ungodly;
6 And condemned the cities of Sodom and Gomorrah to destruction, turning *them* into ashes, setting them *as* an example to
7 them that should afterward live ungodly: And delivered right-
8 eous Lot, grieved with the filthy behaviour of the wicked: (For that righteous man dwelling among them, by seeing and hearing, tormented his righteous soul from day to day with *their* unlaw-
9 ful deeds :) The Lord knoweth how to deliver the godly out of temptation, and to reserve the unrighteous to the day of judg-
10 ment to be punished. But chiefly them that walk after the flesh, in the lust of uncleanness, and despise government. Daring,
11 self-willed ; they are not afraid to rail at dignities: Whereas angels, who are greater in strength and power, bring not a
12 railing accusation against them before the Lord. But these men, as natural brute beasts born to be taken and destroyed, speaking evil of the things they understand not, shall perish in
13 their own corruption, Receiving the reward of unrighteousness. They count it pleasure to riot in the day time; spots and blemishes, sporting themselves with their own deceivings, while
14 they feast with you, Having eyes full of adultery, and that cease not from sin ; ensnaring unstable souls, having a heart exercised
15 with covetousness, accursed children: Who have forsaken the

---

merchants do their wares. *Whose judgment now of a long time lingereth not*— Was long ago determined, and will be executed speedily. All sinners are adjudged to destruction; and God's punishing some, proves he will punish the rest.

4. *Cast them down to hell*—The bottomless pit, a place of unknown misery, *delivered them*—Like condemned criminals, to safe custody, as if bound with the strongest chains, in a dungeon *of darkness, to be reserved unto the judgment of the* great day; though still those chains do not hinder their often walking up and down, seeking whom they may devour.

5. *And spared not the old*—The antediluvian world, (*but he preserved Noah, the eighth person*—That is, Noah, and seven others, a preacher as well as a practiser *of righteousness,*) *bringing a flood on the world of the ungodly*—Whose numbers stood them in no stead.

8. It plainly appears from these instances that *the Lord knoweth*—Hath both wisdom, and power, and will, to deliver the godly out of all temptation, and to punish the ungodly.

10. *Chiefly them that walk after the flesh*—Corrupt nature, particularly *in the lust of uncleanness, and despise government*—The authority of their governors; *dignities*—Persons in authority.

11. *Whereas angels*—When they appear before the Lord, Job i, 6; ii, 1, to give an account of what they have seen and done on the earth.

12. Savage *as brute beasts*—Several of which, in the present disordered state of the world, seem born to be taken and destroyed.

13. *They count it pleasure to riot in the day time*—They glory in doing it in the face of the sun. They are spots in themselves, blemishes to any Church; *sporting themselves with their own deceivings*—Making a jest of those whom they deceive, and even jesting while they are deceiving their own souls.

15. *The way of Balaam, the son of Bosor*—(So the Chaldeans pronounced what

right way, and are gone astray, following the way of Balaam, the *son of* Bosor, who loved the reward of unrighteousness.
16 But he had a rebuke for his iniquity: the dumb beast, speaking
17 with man's voice, forbade the madness of the prophet. These are fountains without water, clouds driven by a tempest, to whom
18 the blackness of darkness is reserved for ever. For by speaking swelling *words* of vanity, they ensnare in the desires of the flesh, in wantonness, those that were entirely escaped from them that
19 live in error. While they promise them liberty, themselves are the slaves of corruption; for by whom a man is overcome, by
20 him he is also brought into slavery. For if after they have escaped the pollutions of the world, through the knowledge of the Lord and Saviour Jesus Christ, they are again entangled therein and overcome, their last state is worse than the first.
21 For it had been better for them not to have known the way of righteousness, than having known *it*, to turn from the holy
22 commandment delivered to them. But it has befallen them according to the true proverb, The * dog is turned to his own vomit, and the sow that was washed to her wallowing in the mire.
III. This second epistle, beloved, I now write to you, in *both*
2 which I stir up your pure minds by way of remembrance, That ye may be mindful of the words which were spoken before by the holy prophets, and of the commandments of us, the apostles
3 of the Lord and Saviour: Knowing this first, that there will come scoffers in the last days, walking after their own desires,
4 And saying, Where is the promise of his coming? For ever

the Jews termed Beor,) namely, the way of covetousness; *who loved*—Earnestly desired, though he did not dare to take, *the reward of unrighteousness*—The money which Balak would have given him for cursing Israel.

16. *The beast*—Though naturally dumb.

17. *Fountains* and *clouds* promise water: so do these promise, but do not perform.

18. *They ensnare in the desire of the flesh*—Allowing them to gratify some unholy desire, those who were before entirely escaped from the spirit, custom, and company of *them that live in error*—In sin.

19. *While they promise them liberty*—From needless restraints and scruples, from the bondage of the law, *themselves are the slaves of corruption*—Even sin, the vilest of all bondage.

20. *For if after they*—Who are thus ensnared, *have escaped the pollutions of the world*—The sins which pollute all who know not God, *through the knowledge of Christ*—That is, through faith in him, chap. i, 3, *they are again entangled therein, and overcome, their last state is worse than the first*—More inexcusable, and causing a greater damnation.

21. *The commandment*—The whole law of God, once not only delivered to their ears, but written in their hearts.

22. *The dog, the sow*—Such are all men in the sight of God before they receive his grace, and after they have made shipwreck of the faith.

III. 2. *Be* the more *mindful* thereof, because ye *know scoffers will come first*—Before the Lord comes, *walking after their own evil desires*—Here is the origin of the error, the root of libertinism. Do we not see this eminently fulfilled?

4. Saying, *Where is the promise of his coming*—To judgment? (They do not even deign to name him.) We see no sign of any such thing. *For ever since the fathers*—Our first ancestors, *fell asleep, all things*—Heaven, water, earth, *continue as they were from the beginning of the creation*—Without any such material change as might make us believe they will ever end.

* Proverbs xxvi, 11.

40

since the fathers fell asleep all things continue as *they were* from
5 the beginning of the creation. For this they are willingly ignorant of, that by the word of God the heavens were of old, and
6 the earth standing out of the water and in the water, Through which the world that then was, being overflowed with water,
7 perished. But the heavens and the earth that are now, are by his word treasured up, reserved unto fire, at the day of judgment
8 and destruction of ungodly men. * But, beloved, be not ye ignorant of this one thing, that one day is with the Lord as a thou
9 sand years, and a thousand years as one day. The Lord is not slow concerning his promise (though some men count it slowness) but is long suffering for your sake, not willing that any
10 should perish, but that all should come to repentance. But the day of the Lord will come as a thief, in which the heavens shall

5. *For this they are willingly ignorant of*—They do not care to know or consider, that by the almighty *word of God*—Which bounds the duration of all things, so that it cannot be either longer or shorter; *of old*—Before the flood, the aerial heavens were, *and the earth*—Not as it is now, but *standing out of the water and in the water*—Perhaps the interior globe of earth was fixed in the midst of the great deep, the abyss of water; the shell or exterior globe, standing out of the water, covering the great deep. This, or some other great and manifest difference between the original and present constitution of the terraqueous globe, seems then to have been so generally known, that St. Peter charges their ignorance of it totally upon their wilfulness.

6. *Through which*—Heaven and earth, the windows of heaven being opened, and the fountains of the great deep broken up, *the world that then was*—The whole antediluvian race, *being overflowed with water, perished*—And the heavens and earth themselves, though they did not perish, yet underwent a great change. So little ground have these scoffers for saying, That all things continue as they were from the **creation.**

7. *But the heavens and the earth that are now*—Since the flood, are reserved unto fire, at the day wherein God will judge the world, and punish the ungodly with everlasting destruction.

8. *But be not ye ignorant*—Whatever they are, *of this one thing*—Which casts much light on the point in hand, *that one day is with the Lord as a thousand years, and a thousand years as one day.* Moses had said, Psalm xc, 4, a thousand years are in thy sight as one day, which St. Peter applies with regard to the last day; so as to denote both his eternity, whereby he exceeds all measure of time in his essence and in his operation: his knowledge, to which all things past or to come are present every moment: his power, which needs no long delay in order to bring his work to perfection: and his long suffering, which excludes all impatience of expectation and desire of making haste. *One day is with the Lord as a thousand years*—That is, in one day, in one moment, he can do the work of a thousand years. Therefore he is not slow: he is always equally ready to fulfil his promise; *and a thousand years are as one day*—That is, no delay is long to God. A thousand years are as one day to the eternal God. Therefore he is long suffering; he gives us space for repentance, without any inconvenience to himself. In a word, with God time passes neither slower nor swifter than is suitable to him and his economy. Nor can there be any reason why it should be necessary for him either to delay or hasten the end of all things. How can we comprehend this? If we could comprehend it, St. Peter needed not to have added *with the Lord.*

9. *The Lord is not slow*—As if the time fixed for it were past, *concerning his promise*—Which shall surely be fulfilled in its season; *but is long suffering toward us*—Children of men, *not willing that any*—Soul which he had made, *should perish.*

10. *But the day of the Lord will come as a thief*—Suddenly, unexpectedly, *in which the heavens shall pass away with a great noise*—Surprisingly expressed by

* Psalm xc, 4.

pass away with a great noise, the elements shall melt with fervent heat, and the earth, and the works that are therein, shall be burned
11 up. Seeing then all these things are dissolved, what manner of persons ought ye to be in all holy conversation and godliness,
12 Looking for and hastening on *the* coming of the day of God, wherein the heavens being on fire shall be dissolved, and the
13 elements shall melt with fervent heat? Nevertheless, we look for new heavens and a new earth, according to his * promise, wherein
14 dwelleth righteousness. Wherefore, beloved, seeing ye look for these things, labour to be found of him in peace, without spot
15 and blameless. And account the long suffering of the Lord salvation, as our beloved brother Paul also, according to the
16 wisdom given him, † hath written to you: As also in all his epistles, speaking therein of these things, in which are some

---

the very sound of the original word; *the elements shall melt with fervent heat—* The elements seem to mean, the sun, moon, and stars : not the four, commonly so called : for air and water cannot melt, and the earth is mentioned immediately after, *the earth and all the works—* Whether of nature or art, *that are therein shall be burned up—* And has not God already abundantly provided for this ? 1. By the stores of subterranean fire, which are so frequently bursting out at Etna, Vesuvius, Hecla, and many other burning mountains : 2. By the ethereal (vulgarly called electrical) fire, diffused through the whole globe ; which, if the secret chain that now binds it up were loosed, would immediately dissolve the whole frame of nature. 3. By comets, one of which, if it touched the earth in its course toward the sun, must needs strike it into that abyss of fire. If in its return from the sun, when it is heated (as a great man computes) two thousand times hotter than a red-hot cannon ball, it must destroy all vegetables and animals, long before their contact, and soon after burn it up.

11. *Seeing then that all these things are dissolved—* To the eye of faith it appears as done already. All these things mentioned before : all that are included in that scriptural expression, The heavens and the earth, that is, the universe. On the fourth day God made the stars, Gen. i, 16, which will be dissolved together with the earth. They are deceived, therefore, who restrain either the history of the creation, or this description of the destruction of the world, to the earth and lower heavens, imagining the stars to be more ancient than the earth, and to survive it. Both the dissolution and renovation are ascribed, not to the one heaven which surrounds the earth, but to the heavens in general, ver. 10, 13, without any restriction or limitation. *What persons ought ye to be, in all holy conversation—* With men, *and godliness—* Toward your Creator.

12. *Hastening on—* As it were, by your earnest desires and fervent prayers, *the coming of the day of God—* Many myriads of days he grants to men ; one, the last, is the day of God himself.

13. *We look for new heavens and a new earth—* Raised, as it were, out of the ashes of the old; (we look for an entire new state of things;) *wherein dwelleth righteousness—* Only righteous spirits : how great a mystery !

14. *Labour—* That whenever he cometh, *ye may be found in peace—* May meet him without terror, be sprinkled with his blood, and sanctified by his Spirit, so as to be without spot and blameless.

15. *And account the long suffering of our Lord salvation—* Not only designed to lead men to repentance, but actually conducing thereto; a precious means of saving many more souls; *as our beloved brother Paul also hath written to you—* This refers not only to the single sentence preceding, but to all that went before. St. Paul had written to the same effect concerning the end of the world, in several parts of his epistles, and particularly in the Epistle to the Hebrews.

16. *As also in all his epistles—* St. Peter wrote this a little before his own and St. Paul's martyrdom. St. Paul therefore had now written all his epistles; and even from this expression we may learn that St. Peter had read them all, perhaps sent to him by St. Paul himself. Nor was he at all disgusted by what St. Paul

things hard to be understood, which the unlearned and unstable wrest, as *they do* also the other Scriptures, to their own destruction.

17 Ye, therefore, beloved, knowing *these things* before, beware, lest ye also, being led away by the error of the wicked, fall from

18 your own steadfastness: But grow in grace and *in* the knowledge of our Lord and Saviour Jesus Christ. To him *be* the glory both now and to the day of eternity! Amen.

---

had written concerning him, in the Epistle to the Galatians; *speaking of these things*—Namely, of the coming of our Lord, delayed through his long suffering, and of the circumstances preceding and accompanying it; which things *the unlearned*—They who are not taught of God; *and the unstable*—Wavering, doubleminded, unsettled men, *wrest*—As though Christ would not come, *as they do also the other Scriptures*—Therefore St. Paul's writings were now part of the Scriptures: *to their own destruction*—But that some use the Scriptures ill, is no reason why others should not use them at all.

18. *But grow in grace*—That is, in every Christian temper. There may be, for a time, grace without growth, as there may be natural life without growth. But such sickly life, of soul or body, will end in death, and every day draws nigher to it. Health is the means of both natural and spiritual growth. If the remaining evil of our fallen nature be not daily mortified, it will, like an evil humour in the body, destroy the whole man. But if ye, through the Spirit, do mortify the deeds of the body, (only so far as we do this,) ye shall live the life of faith, holiness, happiness. The end and design of grace being purchased and bestowed on us, is to destroy the image of the earthy, and restore us to that of the heavenly. And so far as it does this, it truly profits us: and also makes way for more of the heavenly gift, that we may at last be filled with all the fulness of God. The strength and well being of a Christian depend on what his soul feeds on, as the health of the body depends on whatever we make our daily food. If we feed on what is according to our nature, we grow; if not, we pine away and die. The soul is of the nature of God, and nothing but what is according to his holiness can agree with it. Sin of every kind starves the soul, and makes it consume away. Let us not try to invert the order of God in his new creation; we shall only deceive ourselves. It is easy to forsake the will of God and follow our own; but this will bring leanness into the soul. It is easy to satisfy ourselves without being possessed of the holiness and happiness of the Gospel. It is easy to call these frames and feelings, and then to oppose faith to one, and Christ to the other. Frames (allowing the expression) are no other than heavenly tempers, the mind that was in Christ: feelings are the Divine consolations of the Holy Ghost, shed abroad in the heart of him that truly believes. And wherever faith is, and wherever Christ is, there are these blessed frames and feelings. If they are not in us, it is a sure sign that though the wilderness became a pool, the pool is become a wilderness again; *and in the knowledge of Christ*—That is, in faith, the root of all: *To him be the glory to the day of eternity*—An expression naturally flowing from that sense which the apostle had felt in his soul throughout this whole chapter. Eternity is a day without night, without interruption, without end.

NOTES

ON

THE FIRST EPISTLE OF ST. JOHN.

——

THE great similitude, or rather sameness, both of spirit and expression, which runs through St. John's Gospel, and all his epistles, is a clear evidence of their being written by the same person. In this epistle he speaks not to any particular Church, but to all the Christians of that age, and in them to the whole Christian Church, in all succeeding ages.

Some have apprehended, that it is not easy to discern the scope and method of this epistle. But if we examine it with simplicity, these may readily be discovered. St. John, in this letter, or rather tract, (for he was present with part of those to whom he wrote,) has this apparent aim, to confirm the happy and holy communion of the faithful with God and Christ, by describing the marks of that blessed state.

THE PARTS OF IT ARE THREE:

I. The preface . . . . Chap. i, 1–4
II. The tract itself 5–v, 1–12
III. The conclusion 13–21

In the preface he shows the authority of his own preaching and writing, and expressly points out (ver. 3) the design of his present writing. To the preface exactly answers the conclusion, more largely explaining the same design, and recapitulating those marks, by *we know* thrice repeated, chap. v, 18, 19, 20.

The tract itself has two parts, treating,

I. Severally,
  1. Of communion with the Father . . . . . . Chap. i, 5–10
  2. Of communion with the Son . . . . ii, 1–2
    With a distinct application to fathers, young men, and little
      children 13–27
    Whereunto is annexed an exhortation to abide in him . 28–iii, 1–24
    That the fruit of his manifestation in the flesh may extend to
      his manifestation in glory.
  3. Of the confirmation and fruit of this abiding through the Spirit . iv, 1–21
II. Conjointly,
  Of the testimony of the Father, and Son, and Spirit; on which
    fai h in Christ, the being born of God, love to God and his
    children, the keeping his commandments, and victory over the
    world are founded . . . . v, 1–12

The parts frequently begin and end alike. Sometimes there is an allusion in a preceding part, and a recapitulation in the subsequent. Each part treats of a benefit from God, and the duty of the faithful derived therefrom by the most natural inferences.

I. ST. JOHN.

1 THAT which was from the beginning, which we have heard, which we have seen with our eyes, which we have beheld, and
2 our hands have handled of the Word of life: (For the life was manifested, and we saw *it*, and testify and declare to you the eternal life which was with the Father, and was manifested to
3 us:) That which we have seen and heard declare we to you, that ye also may have fellowship with us: and truly our fellow-
4 ship *is* with the Father, and with his Son Jesus Christ: And these things write we to you, that your joy may be full.
5 And this is the message which we have heard of him, and declare to you, that God is light, and in him is no darkness at
6 all. If we say we have fellowship with him, and walk in dark-
7 ness, we lie, and do not the truth. But if we walk in the light, as he is in the light, we have fellowship one with another, and

---

Verse 1. *That which was*—here means, he which was the Word himself; afterward it means, that which they had heard from him: *which was*—Namely, with the Father, ver. 2, before he was manifested; *from the beginning*—This phrase is sometimes used in a limited sense. But here it properly means from eternity, being equivalent with *in the beginning*, John i, 1; *that which we*—The apostles have not only heard, but seen with our eyes; *which we have beheld*—Attentively considered on various occasions; *of the word of life*—He is termed the Word, John i, 1; the life, John i, 4, as he is the living Word of God, who, with the Father and the Spirit, is the fountain of life to all creatures, particularly of spiritual and eternal life.

2. *For the life*—The living Word, *was manifested*—In the flesh, to our very senses; *and we testify and declare*—We testify by declaring, by preaching and writing, ver. 3, 4: preaching lays the foundation, ver. 5–10; writing builds thereon: *to you*—Who have not seen; *the eternal life*—Which always was, and afterward appeared to us. This is mentioned in the beginning of the epistle. In the end of it is mentioned the same eternal life, which we shall always enjoy.

3. *That which we have seen and heard*—Of him, and from him, *declare we to you*—For this end, *that ye also may have fellowship with us*—May enjoy the same fellowship which we enjoy: *and truly our fellowship*—Whereby he is in us, and we in him; *is with the Father, and with his Son*—Of the Holy Ghost he speaks afterward.

4. *That your joy may be full*—So our Lord also, John xv, 11; xvi, 22. There is a joy of hope, a joy of faith, and a joy of love. Here the joy of faith is directly intended. It is a concise expression: *your joy*—That is, your faith, and the joy arising from it; but it likewise implies the joy of hope and love.

5. *And this is* the sum of *the message which we have heard of him*—The Son of God; *that God is light*—The light of wisdom, love, holiness, glory. What light is to the natural eye, that God is to the spiritual eye: *and in him is no darkness at all*—No contrary principle. He is pure, unmixed light.

6. *If we say*—Either with our tongue, or in our heart, if we endeavour to persuade either ourselves or others, *we have fellowship with him*—While we walk, either inwardly or outwardly, *in darkness*—In sin of any kind, *we do not the truth*—Our actions prove that the truth is not in us.

7. *But if we walk in the light*—In all holiness, *as God is* (a deeper word than walk, and more worthy of God) *in the light*—Then we may truly say, *we have fellowship one with another*—We who have seen, and you who have not seen, do alike enjoy that fellowship with God: the imitation of God being the only sure

CHAPTER II. 631

8 the blood of Jesus Christ his Son cleanseth us from all sin. If
we say we have no sin, we deceive ourselves, and the truth is
9 not in us. If we confess our sins, he is faithful and just to forgive us our sins, and to cleanse us from all unrighteousness.
10 If we say we have not sinned, we make him a liar, and his word
is not in us.

II. My beloved children, I write these things to you, that ye may
not sin. But if any one sin, we have an Advocate with the
2 Father, Jesus Christ the righteous, And he is the propitiation
for our sins; and not for ours only, but also for *the sins* of the
3 whole world. And hereby we know that we know him, if we
4 keep his commandments. He that saith, I know him, and
keepeth not his commandments, is a liar, and the truth is not
5 in him. But whoso keepeth his word, verily in him the love

proof of our having fellowship with him. *And the blood of Jesus Christ his Son*
—With the grace purchased thereby; *cleanseth us from all sin*—Both original
and actual, taking away all the guilt and all the power.

8. *If we say*—Any child of man, before his blood has cleansed us; *we have no
sin*—To be cleansed from, instead of confessing our sins, ver. 9; *the truth is not
in us*—Neither in our mouth nor in our heart.

9. But if with a penitent and believing heart, *we confess our sins, he is faithful*
—Because he had promised this blessing, by the unanimous voice of all his
prophets. *Just*—Surely then he will punish: no, for this very reason he will
pardon. This may seem strange; but upon the evangelical principle of atonement and redemption, it is undoubtedly true. Because when the debt is paid, or
the purchase made, it is the part of equity to cancel the bond, and consign over
the purchased possession: *both to forgive us our sins*—To take away all the guilt
of them; *and to cleanse us from all unrighteousness*—To purify our souls from
every kind and every degree of it.

10. Yet still we are to retain, even to our lives' end, a deep sense of our past
sins. Still, *if we say we have not sinned, we make him a liar*—Who saith, all
have sinned; *and his word is not in us*—We do not receive it; we give it no
place in our hearts.

II. 1. *My beloved children*—So the apostle frequently addresses the whole body
of Christians. It is a term of tenderness and endearment, used by our Lord himself to his disciples, John xiii, 33. And perhaps many to whom St. John now
wrote were converted by his ministry. It is a different word from that which
is translated *little children* in several parts of the epistle, to distinguish it from
which it is here rendered *beloved children*. *I write these things to you, that ye
may not sin*—Thus he guards them beforehand against abusing the doctrine of
reconciliation. All the words, institutions, and judgments of God are levelled
against sin, either that it may not be committed, or that it may be abolished.
But if any one sin—Let him not lie in sin, despairing of help; *we have an Advocate*—We have for our advocate not a mean person, but him of whom it was
said, This is my beloved Son: not a guilty person, who stands in need of pardon
for himself; but *Jesus Christ the righteous*: not a mere petitioner, who relies
purely upon liberality, but one that has merited, fully merited, whatever he
asks.

2. *And he is the propitiation*—The atoning sacrifice, by which the wrath of
God is appeased; *for our sins*—Who believe: *and not for ours only, but also for
the sins of the whole world*—Just as wide as sin extends, the propitiation extends
also.

3. *And hereby we know that we* truly and savingly *know him*—As the advocate,
the righteous, the propitiation: *if we keep his commandments*—Particularly those
of faith and love.

5. *But whoso keepeth his word*—His commandments, *verily in him the love of
God*—Reconciled to us through Christ, *is perfected*—Is perfectly known: *Hereby*
—By our keeping his word, *we know that we are in him*—So is the tree known
by its fruits. *To know him, to be in him, to abide in him*, are nearly synonymous
terms; only with a gradation: knowledge, communion, constancy.

6 of God is perfected: hereby we know that we are in him. He that saith he abideth in him, ought himself also so to walk, even
7 as he walked. Beloved, I write not a new commandment to you, but the old commandment, which ye have had from the beginning; the old commandment is the word which ye have heard
8 from the beginning. Again, I do write a new commandment to you, which is true in him, and in you: for the darkness is passed
9 away, and the true light now shineth. He that saith he is in the
10 light, and hateth his brother, is in darkness until now. He that loveth his brother, abideth in the light, and there is no occasion
11 of stumbling in him: But he that hateth his brother is in darkness, and walketh in darkness, and knoweth not whither he
12 goeth, because darkness hath blinded his eyes. I have written to you, beloved children, because your sins are forgiven you for
13 his name sake. I write to you, fathers, because ye have known him that is from the beginning. I write to you, young men,

---

6. *He that saith he abideth in him*—Which implies a durable state, a constant, lasting knowledge of, and communion with him: *ought himself*—Otherwise they are vain words, *so to walk even as he walked*—In the world. *As he* are words that frequently occur in this epistle. Believers having their hearts full of him, easily supply his name.

7. When I speak of keeping his word, *I write not a new commandment*—I do not speak of any new one; *but the old commandment which ye had*—Even from your forefathers.

8. *Again, I do write a new commandment to you*—Namely, with regard to loving one another. A commandment, which, though it also was given long ago, yet is truly new in him, and in you. It was exemplified in him, and is now fulfilled by you in such a manner as it never was before. For there is no comparison between the state of the Old Testament believers, and that which ye now enjoy; the darkness of that dispensation is passed away; and Christ, the true light, now shineth in your hearts.

9. *He that saith, he is in the light*—In Christ, united to him, *and hateth his brother*—(The very name shows the love due to him) *is in darkness until now*—Void of Christ, and of all true light.

10. *He that loveth his brother*—For Christ's sake, *abideth in the light*—Of God, *and there is no occasion of stumbling in him*—Whereas he that hates his brother, is an occasion of stumbling to himself. He stumbles against himself, and against all things within and without; while he that loves his brother has a free, disencumbered journey.

11. *He that hateth his brother*—And he must hate, if he does not love him; there is no medium; *is in darkness*—In sin, perplexity, entanglement. He walketh in darkness, and knoweth not that he is in the high road to hell.

12. *I have written to you, beloved children*—Thus St. John bespeaks all to whom he writes. But from the 13th to the 27th verse he divides them particularly into fathers, young men, and little children: *because your sins are forgiven you*—As if he had said, This is the sum of what I have now written. He then proceeds to other things, which are built upon this foundation.

13. The address to spiritual fathers, young men, and little children, is first proposed in this verse, wherein he says, I write to you, fathers; I write to you, young men; I write to you, little children: and then enlarged upon; in doing which he says, I have written to **you**, fathers, ver. 14. I have written to you, young men, ver. 14–17. I have **written** to you, little children, ver. 18–27. Having finished his address to each, he returns to all together, whom he again terms, (as ver. 12,) Beloved children. *Fathers, ye have known him that is from the beginning*—Ye have known the eternal God, in a manner wherein no other, even true believers, know him. *Young men, ye have overcome the wicked one*—In many battles by the power of faith. *Little children, ye have known the Father*—As your Father, (though ye have not yet overcome,) by the Spirit witnessing with your spirit, that ye are the children of God.

because ye have overcome the wicked one. I write to you, little
14 children, because ye have known the Father. I have written to
you, fathers, because ye have known him that is from the beginning. I have written to you, young men, because ye are strong,
and the word of God abideth in you, and ye have overcome the
15 wicked one. Love not the world, neither the things that are in
the world: if any one love the world, the love of the Father is
16 not in him. For all that is in the world, the desire of the flesh,
and the desire of the eye, and the pride of life, is not of the
17 Father, but is of the world. And the world passeth away, and
the desire thereof; but he that doth the will of God abideth for
18 ever. Little children, it is the last time: and as ye have heard
that antichrist cometh, *so* even now there are many antichrists,
19 whereby we know that it is the last time. They went out from
us, but they were not of us: for if they had been of us, they
would have continued with us: but *they went out*, that they
20 might be made manifest that they were not all of us. But ye
have an anointing from the Holy One, and know all things.
21 I have not written to you, because ye know not the truth; but

14. *I have written to you, fathers*—As if he had said, Observe well what I but
now wrote. He speaks very briefly and modestly to these, who needed not much
to be said to them, as having that deep acquaintance with God which comprises
all necessary knowledge. *Young men, ye are strong*—In faith, *and the word of
God abideth in you*—Deeply rooted in your hearts, whereby ye have often foiled
your great adversary.
15. To you all, whether fathers, young men, or little children, I say, *Love not
the world*—Pursue your victory, by overcoming the world. *If any man love the
world*—Seek happiness in visible things, he does not love God.
16. *The desire of the flesh*—Of the pleasure of the outward senses, whether of
the taste, smell, or touch: *the desire of the eye*—Of the pleasures of imagination,
(to which the eye, chiefly, is subservient,) of that internal sense, whereby we
relish whatever is grand, new, or beautiful: *the pride of life*—All that pomp in
clothes, houses, furniture, equipage, manner of living, which generally procure
honour from the bulk of mankind, and so gratify pride and vanity. It therefore
directly includes the desire of praise, and remotely, covetousness. All these
desires are not from God, but from the prince of this world.
17. *The world passeth away, and the desire thereof*—That is, all that can gratify
those desires passeth away with it: *but he that doth the will of God*—That loves
God, not the world, *abideth*—In the enjoyment of what he loves, *for ever*.
18. *Little children, it is the last time*—The last dispensation of grace, that which
is to continue to the end of time, is begun; *ye have heard that antichrist cometh*—
Under the term antichrist, or the spirit of antichrist, he includes all false teachers,
and enemies to the truth, yea, whatever doctrines or men are contrary to Christ.
It seems to have been long after this that the name of *antichrist* was appropriated
to that grand adversary of Christ, the man of sin, 2 Thess. ii, 3. Antichrist, in
St. John's sense, that is, antichristianism, has been spreading from his time till
now; and will do so, till that great adversary arises, and is destroyed by Christ's
coming.
19. *They were not of us*—When they went: their hearts were before departed
from God, otherwise *they would have continued with us: but they went out that
they might be made manifest*—That is, this was made manifest, by their going out.
20. *But ye have an anointing*—A chrism; perhaps so termed in opposition to
the name of antichrist, an inward teaching from the Holy Spirit, whereby *ye
know all things*—Necessary for your preservation from these seducers, and for
your eternal salvation. St. John here but just touches upon the Holy Ghost, of
whom he speaks more largely, chap. iii, 24; iv, 13; v, 6.
21. *I have written*—Namely, ver. 13, *to you, because ye know the truth*—That is,
to confirm you in the knowledge ye have already. *Ye know that no lie is of the
truth*—That all the doctrines of these antichrists are irreconcilable to it.

because ye know it, and that no lie is of the truth. Who is that
22 liar, but he that denieth that Jesus is the Christ? He is anti-
23 christ who denieth the Father and the Son. Whosoever denieth
the Son, he hath not the Father: he that acknowledgeth the Son,
24 hath the Father also. Therefore let that abide in you which ye
heard from the beginning: if that which ye heard from the beginning abide in you, ye also shall abide in the Son, and in the
25 Father. And this is the promise which ye hath promised us,
26 eternal life. These things have I written to you concerning them
27 that seduce you. But the anointing which ye have received of
him abideth in you and ye need not that any should teach you,
save as the same anointing teacheth you of all things, and is true,
and is no lie; and as it has taught you, ye shall abide in him.
28 And now, beloved children, abide in him, that when he shall
appear, we may have confidence, and not be ashamed before him
29 at his coming. Since ye know that he is righteous, ye know that
every one who practiseth righteousness is born of him.
III. Behold what manner of love the Father hath bestowed upon
us, that we should be called the children of God: therefore the
2 world knoweth us not, because it knoweth not him. Beloved,
now are we the children of God, and it doth not yet appear what
we shall be; but we know, when he shall appear, we shall be

22. *Who is that liar*—Who is guilty of that lying, but he who denies that truth
which is the sum of all Christianity: that Jesus is the Christ; that he is the Son
of God; that he came in the flesh, is one undivided truth; and he that denies one
part of this, in effect denies the whole. *He is antichrist*—And the spirit of antichrist, who, in denying the Son, denies the Father also.
23. *Whosoever denieth the* eternal Son of God, *he hath not* communion with
the Father, but he that truly and believingly *acknowledgeth the Son, hath* communion with *the Father also.*
24. *If that*—Truth, concerning the Father and the Son, *which ye have heard
from the beginning, abide*—Fixed and rooted in you, ye also shall abide in that
happy communion with the Son and the Father.
25. *He*—the Son, *hath promised us*—if we abide in him.
26. *These things*—From ver. 21. *I have written to you*—St. John, according
to his custom, begins and ends with the same form, and having finished a kind
of parenthesis, ver. 20-26, continues, ver. 27, what he said in the 20th verse,
Concerning them that would *seduce you.*
27. *Ye need not that any should teach you, save as that anointing teacheth you*—
Which is always the same, always consistent with itself. But this does not exclude our need of being taught by them who partake of the same anointing; *of
all things*—Which it is necessary for you to know; *and is no lie*—Like that
which antichrist teaches. *Ye shall abide in him*—This is added both by way
of comfort and of exhortation. The whole discourse, from ver. 18 to this, is
peculiarly adapted to little children.
28. *And now, beloved children*—Having finished his address to each, he now
returns to all in general: *abide in him, that we*—A modest expression, *may not
be ashamed before him at his coming*—O how will ye, Jews, Socinians, nominal
Christians, be ashamed in that day!
29. *Every one, who practiseth righteousness*—From a believing,
loving heart, *is born of him*—For all his children are like himself.
III. 1. *That we should be called*—That is, should be the children of God, *therefore the world knoweth us not*—They know not what to make of us. We are a
mystery to them.
2. *It doth not yet appear*—Even to ourselves, *what we shall be*—It is something
ineffable, which will raise the children of God to be in a manner as God himself.
But we know—In general, that *when he*—The Son of God, *shall appear, we shall
be like him*—The glory of God penetrating our inmost substance, *for we shall see*

3 like him, for we shall see him as he is. And every one that hath
4 this hope in him purifieth himself even as he is pure. Whosoever
committeth sin transgresseth also the law; for sin is the trans-
5 gression of the law. And ye know that he was manifested to
6 take away our sin, and in him is no sin. Whosoever abideth in
him, sinneth not; whosoever sinneth, seeth him not, neither
7 knoweth him. Beloved children, let no one deceive you. He
that practiseth righteousness is righteous, even as he is righteous.
8 He that committeth sin is of the devil; for the devil sinneth from
the beginning: to this end the Son of God was manifested, to
9 destroy the works of the devil. Whosoever is born of God doth
not commit sin; for his seed abideth in him, and he cannot sin,
10 because he is born of God. Hereby the children of God are
manifested and the children of the devil: whosoever practiseth
not righteousness is not of God; neither he that loveth not his
11 brother. For this is the message which ye have heard from the
12 beginning, that we love one another. Not as Cain, *who* was of
13 the wicked one, and slew his brother. And wherefore slew he
him? Because his own works were evil, and his brother's right-
14 eous. Marvel not, my brethren, if the world hate you. We
know that we are passed from death to life, because we love

him as he is—Manifestly without a veil. And that sight will transform us into
the same likeness.

3. *And every one that hath this hope in him*—In God.

4. *Whosoever committeth sin*—Thereby transgresseth the holy, just, and good
law of God, and so sets his authority at naught: for this is implied in the very
nature of sin.

5. *And ye know that he*—Christ, *was manifested*—That he came into the world
for this very purpose, *to take away our sins*—To destroy them all, root and
branch, and leave none remaining. *And in him is no sin*—So that he could not
suffer on his own account, but to make us as himself.

6. *Whosoever abideth in* communion with *him*—By loving faith, *sinneth not*—
While he so abideth. *Whosoever sinneth* certainly *seeth him not*—The loving eye
of his soul is not then fixed upon God; *neither* doth he then experimentally *know
him*—Whatever he did in time past.

7. *Let no one deceive you*—Let none persuade you, that any man is righteous,
but *he that* uniformly *practiseth righteousness: he* alone *is righteous*—After the
example of his Lord.

8. *He that committeth sin is* a child *of the devil: for the devil sinneth from the
beginning*—That is, was the first sinner in the universe, and has continued to sin
ever since. *The Son of God was manifested to destroy the works of the devil*—
All sin. And will he not perform this in all that trust in him?

9. *Whosoever is born of God*—By living faith, whereby God is continually
breathing spiritual life into his soul, and his soul is continually breathing out
love and prayer to God, *doth not commit sin*. *For* the Divine *seed*—Of loving
faith, *abideth in him: and*—So long as it doth, *he cannot sin, because he is born
of God*—Is inwardly and universally changed.

10. *Neither he that loveth not his brother*—Here is the transition from the general proposition to one particular.

12. *Who was of the wicked one*—Who showed he was a child of the devil, by
killing his brother. *And wherefore slew he him*—For any fault? No, but just the
reverse; for his goodness.

13. *Marvel not if the world hate you*—For the same cause.

14. *We know*—As if he had said, we ourselves could not love our brethren,
unless we were passed from spiritual death to life: that is, born of God. He
that loveth not his brother abideth in death—That is, is not born of God. And
he that is not born of God, cannot love his brother.

the brethren : he that loveth not his brother abideth in death.
15 Whosoever hateth his brother is a murderer, and ye know no
16 murderer hath eternal life abiding in him. Hereby we know the
love *of God*, because he laid down his life for us ; and we ought
17 to lay down our lives for the brethren. But whoso hath this
world's good, and seeth his brother have need, and shutteth up
his bowels of compassion from him, how dwelleth the love of
18 God in him? My beloved children, let us love not in word,
19 neither in tongue, but in deed, and in truth. And hereby we
know that we are of the truth, and shall assure our hearts before
20 him. For if our heart condemn us, God is greater than our
21 heart, and knoweth all things. Beloved, if our heart condemn
22 us not, *then* have we confidence toward God. And whatsoever
we ask, we receive of him, because we keep his commandments,
23 and do those things that are pleasing in his sight. And this is
his commandment, that we should believe on the name of his
Son Jesus Christ, and love one another, as he hath given us

15. He, I say, abideth in spiritual death, is void of the life of God. For *whosoever hateth his brother*—And there is no medium between loving and hating him, *is*, in God's account, *a murderer*—Every degree of hatred being a degree of the same temper which moved Cain to murder his brother. *And no murderer hath eternal life abiding in him.* But every loving believer hath. For love is the beginning of eternal life. It is the same in substance with glory.

16. The word *God* is not in the original. It was omitted by the apostle just as the particular name is omitted by Mary, when she says to the gardener, Sir, if thou hast born him hence : and by the Church, when she says, Let him kiss me with the kisses of his mouth, Sol. Song i, 1, in both which places there is a language, a very emphatical language, even in silence. It declares how totally the thoughts were possessed by the blessed and glorious subject. It expresses also the superlative dignity and amiableness of the person meant; as though he, and he alone, was, or deserved to be, both known and admired by all. *Because he laid down his life*—Not merely for sinners, but for us in particular. From this truth believed, from this blessing enjoyed, the love of our brethren takes its rise, which may very justly be admitted as an evidence that our faith is no delusion.

17. *But whoso hath this world's good*—Worldly substance, far less valuable than life, *and seeth his brother have need*—(The very sight of want knocks at the door of the spectator's heart,) *and shutteth up*—Whether asked or not, *his bowels of compassion from him, how dwelleth the love of God in him?*—Certainly not at all, however he may talk, ver. 18, of loving God.

18. *Not in word*—Only, *but in deed*—In action : not *in tongue*—by empty pro fessions, but *in truth.*

19. *And hereby we know*—We have a farther proof, by this real operative love, *that we are of the truth*—That we have true faith, that we are true children of God, *and shall assure our hearts before him*—Shall enjoy the assurance of his favour, and the testimony of a good conscience toward God. The heart, in St. John's language, is the conscience. The word conscience is not found in his writings.

20. *For if*—we have not this testimony; if in any thing *our heart*—Our own conscience, *condemn us*—Much more does God, who *is greater than our heart*—An infinitely holier, and a more impartial judge; *and knoweth all things*—So that there is no hope of hiding it from him.

21. *If our heart condemn us not*—If our conscience, duly enlightened·by the word and Spirit of God, and comparing all our thoughts, words, and works with that word, pronounce that they agree therewith; *then have we confidence toward God*—Not only our consciousness of his favour continues and increases, but we have a full persuasion, *that whatsoever we ask, we* shall *receive of him.*

23. *And this is his commandment*—All his commandments in one word, *that we should believe and love*—In the manner and degree which he hath taught. This is the greatest and most important command that ever issued from the

24 commandment. And he that keepeth his commandments, abideth
in Him, and He in him; and hereby we know that he abideth in
us, by the Spirit which he hath given us.

IV. Beloved, believe not every spirit, but try the spirits, whether
they are of God, because many false prophets are gone out into
2 the world. Hereby ye know the Spirit of God: every spirit
which confesseth Jesus Christ, who is come in the flesh, is of
3 God. And every spirit which confesseth not Jesus Christ, who
is come in the flesh, is not of God: and this is that *spirit* of
antichrist, whereof ye have heard that it cometh: and now
4 already is it in the world. Ye are of God, beloved children,
and have overcome them; because greater is he that is in you,
5 than he that is in the world. They are of the world; therefore
6 speak they of the world, and the world heareth them. We are
of God: he that knoweth God heareth us: he that is not of God,
heareth not us; hereby know we the Spirit of truth, and the
7 spirit of error. Beloved, let us love one another; for love is of
God, and every one that loveth is born of God, and knoweth
8 God. He that loveth not, knoweth not God; for God is love.
9 Hereby was manifested the love of God toward us, because God
sent his only begotten Son into the world, that we might live
10 through him. Herein is love; not that we loved God, but that
11 he loved us, and sent his Son a propitiation for our sins. Beloved, if God so loved us, we ought also to love one another.
12 No man hath seen God at any time. If we love one another,

---

throne of glory. If this be neglected, no other can be kept: if this be observed,
all others are easy.

24. *And he that keepeth his commandments*—That thus believes and loves,
abideth in him, and God in him. *And hereby we know that he abideth in us, by
the Spirit which he hath given us*—Which witnesses with our spirits, that we are
his children, and brings forth his fruits of peace, love, holiness. This is the
transition to the treating of the Holy Spirit, which immediately follows.

IV. 1. *Believe not every spirit*—Whereby any teacher is actuated; *but try the
spirits*—By the rule which follows. We are to try all spirits by the written
word: to the law and to the testimony! If any man speak not according to these,
the spirit which actuates him is not of God.

2. *Every spirit*—Or teacher, *which confesseth*—Both with heart and voice, *Jesus
Christ, who is come in the flesh, is of God*—This his coming presupposes, contains,
and draws after it the whole doctrine of Christ.

3. *Ye have heard*—From our Lord, and us, that it cometh.

4. *Ye have overcome* these seducers, because greater is the Spirit of Christ that
is in you, than the spirit of antichrist that is in the world.

5. *They*—Those false prophets, *are of the world*—Of the number of those that
know not God: *therefore speak they of the world*—From the same principle,
wisdom, spirit, and of consequence *the world heareth them*—With approbation.

6. *We*—Apostles, *are of God*—Immediately taught and sent by him. *Hereby
we know*—From what is said, ver. 2-6.

7. *Let us love one another*—From the doctrine he has just been defending, he
draws this exhortation—It is by the Spirit that the love of God is shed abroad in
our hearts. Every one that truly loveth God and his neighbour, *is born of God*.

8. *God is love*—This little sentence brought St. John more sweetness, even
in the time he was writing it, than the whole world can bring. God is often
styled holy, righteous, wise: but not holiness, righteousness, or wisdom in the
abstract: as he is said to be love: intimating that this is his darling, his reigning
attribute; the attribute that sheds an amiable glory on all his other perfections.

12. *If we love one another, God abideth in us*—This is treated of, ver. 13-16;
and his love is perfected—Has its full effect, *in us*—This is treated of, ver. 17-19.

13 God abideth in us, and his love is perfected in us. Hereby we
   know that we abide in him, and he in us, because he hath given
14 us of his Spirit. And we have seen and testify, that the Father
15 sent the Son *to be* the Saviour of the world. Whosoever shall
   confess, that Jesus is the Son of God, God abideth in him, and
16 he in God. And we know and believe the love that God hath to
   us. God is love, and he that abideth in love, abideth in God,
17 and God in him. Hereby is our love made perfect, that we may
   have boldness in the day of judgment, because as he is, so are
18 we in this world. *There is no fear in love, but perfect love
   casteth out fear, because fear hath torment. He that feareth is
19 not made perfect in love. We love him, because he first loved
20 us. If any man say, I love God, and hateth his brother, he is a
   liar; for he that loveth not his brother, whom he hath seen,
21 how can he love God, whom he hath not seen? And this commandment have we from him, that he who loveth God, love his
   brother also.
V.   Whosoever believeth that Jesus is the Christ is born of God,
   and every one who loveth him that begat, loveth him also that is
2 begotten of him. Hereby we know that we love the children
3 of God, when we love God, and keep his commandments: For
   this is the love of God, that we keep his commandments; and

14. *And* in consequence of this, *we have seen and testify, that the Father sent
the Son*—These are the foundation and the criteria of our abiding in God, and
God in us, the communion of the Spirit, and the confession of the Son.

15. *Whosoever shall*—From a principle of loving faith, openly *confess*—In the
face of all opposition and danger, *that Jesus is the Son of God, God abideth in him.*

16. *And we know and believe*—By the same Spirit, the love that God hath to us.

17. *Hereby*—That is, by this communion with God, *is our love made perfect;
that we may*—That is, so that we shall *have boldness in the day of judgment*—
When all the stout-hearted shall tremble; *because as he*—Christ, *is*—All love, *so
are we*—Who are fathers in Christ, even *in this world.*

18. *There is no fear in love*—No slavish fear can be where love reigns; *but
perfect*, adult *love casteth out* slavish *fear; because* such *fear hath torment*, and
so is inconsistent with the happiness of love. A natural man has neither fear
nor love: one that is awakened, fear without love; a babe in Christ, love and
fear; a father in Christ, love without fear.

19. *We love him, because he first loved us*—This is the sum of all religion, the
genuine model of Christianity. None can say more. Why should any one say
less? or less intelligibly?

20. *Whom he hath seen*—Who is daily presented to his senses, to raise his
esteem, and move his kindness or compassion toward him.

21. *And this commandment have we from him*—Both God and *Christ; that he
who loveth God, love his brother*—Every one, whatever his opinions or mode of
worship be, purely because he is the child and bears the image of God. Bigotry
is properly the want of this pure and universal love. A bigot only loves those
who embrace his opinions, and receive his way of worship; and he loves them
for that, and not for Christ's sake.

V. The scope and sum of this whole paragraph appears from the conclusion
of it, ver. 13. These things have I written to you who believe, that ye may
know that ye who believe have eternal life. So faith is the first and last point
with St. John also. *Every one who loveth God that begat, loveth him also that is
begotten of him*—Hath a natural affection to all his brethren.

2. *Hereby we know*—This is a plain proof, *that we love the children of God*—
As his children.

3. *For this is the love of God*—The only sure proof of it, that *we keep his
commandments; and his commandments are not grievous*—To any that are born
of God.

4 his commandments are not grievous. For whatsoever is born of God overcometh the world; and this is the victory that over-
5 cometh the world, *even* our faith. Who is he that overcometh the world, but he that believeth that Jesus is the Son of God?
6 This is he that came by water and blood; *even* Jesus Christ; not by the water only, but by the water and the blood; and it is the
7 Spirit who testifieth; because the Spirit is truth. For there are three that testify on earth, the Spirit, and the water, and the
8 blood, and these three agree in one. And there are three that testify in heaven, the Father, the Word, and the Holy Ghost,

---

4. *For whatsoever*—This expression implies the most unlimited universality; *is born of God overcometh the world*—Conquers whatever it can lay in the way, either to allure or fright the children of God from keeping his commandments. *And this is the victory*—The grand means of overcoming, *even our faith*—seeing all things are possible to him that believeth.

5. *Who is he that overcometh the world?*—That is superior to all worldly care, desire, fear? Every believer, and none else. The seventh verse (usually so reckoned) is a brief recapitulation of all which has been before advanced concerning the Father, the Son, and the Spirit. It is cited in conjunction with the sixth and eighth, by Tertullian, Cyprian, and an uninterrupted train of fathers. And indeed what the sun is in the world, what the heart is in a man, what the needle is in the mariner's compass, this verse is in the epistle. By this, the sixth, eighth, and ninth verses are indissolubly connected: as will be evident beyond all contradiction, when they are accurately considered.

6. *This is he*—St. John here shows the immovable foundation of that faith, that Jesus is the Son of God; not only the testimony of man, but the firm, indubitable testimony of God; *who came*—Jesus is he of whom it was promised that he should come: and who accordingly is come. And this the Spirit, and the water, and the blood testify: *Even Jesus*—Who coming by water and blood, is by this very thing demonstrated to be the Christ: *not by the water only*—Wherein he was baptized: *but by the water and the blood*—Which he shed when he had finished the work his Father had given him to do. He not only undertook at his baptism to fulfil all righteousness, but on the cross accomplished what he had undertaken: in token whereof, when all was finished, blood and water came out of his side. *And it is the Spirit who likewise testifieth*—Of Jesus Christ, named by Moses and all the prophets, by John the Baptist, by all the apostles, and in all the writings of the New Testament. And against his testimony there can be no exception, *because the Spirit is truth*—The very God of truth.

7. What Bengelius has advanced both concerning the transposition of these two verses, and the authority of the controverted verse, partly in his Gnomon, and partly in his Apparatus Criticus, will abundantly satisfy any impartial person. *For there are three that testify*—Literally, testifying or bearing witness— The participle is put for the noun witnesses, to intimate that the act of testifying, and the effect of it, are continually present. Properly, persons can only testify; and that three are described testifying on earth, as if they were persons, is elegantly subservient to the three Persons testifying in heaven; *the Spirit*—In the word, confirmed by miracles; *the water*—Of baptism, wherein we are dedicated to the Son, (with the Father and the Spirit,) typifying his spotless purity, and the inward purifying of our nature; *and the blood*—Represented in the Lord's supper, and applied to the consciences of believers. *And these three*— Harmoniously, *agree in one*—In bearing the same testimony, that Jesus Christ is the Divine, the complete, the only Saviour of the world.

8. *And there are three that testify in heaven*—The testimony of the Spirit, the water, and the blood, is by an eminent gradation corroborated by three, who still give a greater testimony; *the Father*—Who clearly testified of the Son, both at his baptism, and at his transfiguration; *the Word*—Who testified of himself, on many occasions, while he was on earth, and again with still greater solemnity, after his ascension into heaven; Rev. i, 5; xix, 13. *And the Spirit*—Whose testimony was added, chiefly after his glorification; chap. ii, 27; John xv, 26; Acts v, 32; Rom. viii, 16. *And these three are one*—Even as those two, the Father and the Son, are one, John x, 30. Nothing can separate the Spirit from the

9 and these three are one. If we receive the testimony of men, the testimony of God is greater; and this is the testimony of
10 God, which he hath testified of his Son. He that believeth on the Son of God, hath the testimony in himself. He that believeth not God, hath made him a liar, because he believeth not the
11 testimony which he hath testified of his Son. And this is the testimony, that God hath given us eternal life, and this life is in
12 his Son. He that hath the Son hath life; and he that hath not the Son of God hath not life.
13   These things have I written to you who believe on the name of the Son of God; that ye may know that ye who believe on
14 the name of the Son of God have eternal life. And this is the

Father and the Son. If he were not one with the Father and the Son, the apostle ought to have said, the Father and the Word (who are one) and the Spirit are two. But this is contrary to the whole tenor of revelation. It remains, that these three are one. They are one in essence, in knowledge, in will, and in their testimony.

It is observable, the three in the one verse are opposed, not conjointly, but severally to the three in the other; as if he had said, not only the Spirit testifies, but also the Father; John v, 37. Not only the water but also the Word; John iii, 11; x, 41. Not only the blood, but also the Holy Ghost, John xv, 26, &c. It must now appear to every reasonable man, how absolutely necessary the eighth verse is. St. John could not think of the testimony of the Spirit, and water, and blood, and subjoin, *the testimony of God is greater*, without thinking also of the testimony of the Son and Holy Ghost, yea, and mentioning it in so solemn an enumeration. Nor can any possible reason be devised, why without *three testifying in heaven*, he should enumerate three, and no more, *who testify on earth*—The testimony of all is given on earth, not in heaven, but they who testify are part on earth, part in heaven; the witnesses who are on earth testify chiefly concerning his abode on earth, though not excluding his state of exaltation. The witnesses who are in heaven testify chiefly concerning his glory at God's right hand, though not excluding his state of humiliation.

The seventh verse therefore, with the sixth, contains a recapitulation of the whole economy of Christ, from his baptism to pentecost: the eighth, the sum of the Divine economy, from the time of his exaltation.

Hence it farther appears, that this position of the seventh and eighth verses, which places those who testify on earth before those who testify in heaven, is abundantly preferable to the other, and affords a gradation admirably suited to the subject.

9. *If we receive the testimony of men*—As we do continually, and must do in a thousand instances; *the testimony of God is greater*—Of higher authority, and much more worthy to be received; namely, this very testimony, which God the Father, together with the Word and the Spirit, hath testified of his Son, as the Saviour of the world.

10. *He that believeth on the Son of God, hath the testimony*—The clear evidence of this, in himself: he that believeth not God in this, hath made him a liar, because he supposes that to be false which God has expressly testified.

11. *And this is the* sum of that testimony, that God hath given us a title to, and the real beginning of, eternal life: and that this is purchased by, and treasured up in his Son, who has all the springs and the fulness of it in himself, to communicate to his body the Church, first in grace, and then in glory.

12. It plainly follows, *He that hath the Son*—Living and reigning in him by faith, hath this life; *he that hath not the Son of God, hath not* this *life*—Hath no part or lot therein. In the former clause the apostle says, simply, the Son; because believers know him: in the latter, the Son of God, that unbelievers may know how great a blessing they fall short of.

13. *These things have I written*—In the introduction, chap. i, 4, he said, I write; now, in the close, I have written; *that ye may know*—With a fuller and stronger assurance, that ye have eternal life.

14. *And we*—Who believe, have this farther *confidence in him, that he heareth*—

confidence which we have in him, that if we ask any thing
15 according to his will, he heareth us. And if we know that he
heareth us, whatsoever we ask, we know that we have the peti-
16 tions which we have asked of him. If any one see his brother
sin a sin *which is* not unto death, let him ask, and he will give
17 him life for them that sin not unto death. There is a sin unto
18 death. I do not say that he shall pray for that. All unrighteous-
19 ness is sin: but there is a sin not unto death. We know that
whosoever is born of God sinneth not; but he that is born of
God keepeth himself, and the wicked one toucheth him not. We
know that we are of God, and the whole world lieth in the wicked
20 one. But we know that the Son of God is come; and he hath
given us an understanding that we may know the true one; and
we are in the true one, *even* in his Son Jesus Christ; this is the
21 true God, and eternal life. Beloved children, keep yourselves
from idols.

—That is, favourably regards, whatever prayer we offer in faith, according to
his revealed will.

15. *We have*—Faith anticipates the blessings, *the petitions which we asked of
him*—Even before the event. And when the event comes, we know it comes in
answer to our prayer.

16. This extends to things of the greatest importance. *If any one see his brother*
—That is, any man, *sin a sin which is not unto death*—That is, any sin, but total
apostacy from both the power and form of godliness, *let him ask, and God will
give him life*—Pardon and spiritual life, for that sinner. *There is a sin unto
death; I do not say that he shall pray for that*—That is, let him not pray for it.
A sin unto death may likewise mean one which God has determined to punish
with death.

17. *All* deviation from perfect holiness *is sin;* but all sin is not unpardonable.

18. Yet this gives us no encouragement to sin. On the contrary, it is an
indisputable truth, *He that is born of God*—That sees and loves God, *sinneth
not*—So long as that loving faith abides in him. He neither speaks nor does
any thing which God hath forbidden. *He keepeth himself*—Watching unto
prayer; *and*—While he does this, *the wicked one toucheth him not*—So as to
hurt him.

19. *We know that we are* children *of God*—By the witness and the fruit of his
Spirit, chap. iii, 24; *but the whole world*—All who have not his Spirit, not only
is touched by him, but by idolatry, fraud, violence, lasciviousness, impiety, all
manner of wickedness; *lieth in the wicked one*—Void of life, void of sense. In
this short expression the horrible state of the world is painted in the most lively
colours; a comment on which we have in the actions, conversations, contracts,
quarrels, and friendships of worldly men.

20. *And we know*—By all these infallible proofs, *that the Son of God is come*—
Into the world. And he hath given us a spiritual understanding, that we may
know him, the true one, the faithful and true witness; *and we are in the true
one*—As branches in the vine, even in Jesus Christ, the eternal Son of God.
This Jesus is the only living and true God, together with the Father and with
the Spirit, and the original fountain of eternal life. So the beginning and the
end of the epistle agree.

21. *Keep yourselves from idols*—From all worship of false gods, from all worship of images or of any creature, and from every inward idol: from loving,
desiring, fearing any thing more than God. Seek all help and defence from
evil, all happiness in the true God alone.

NOTES

THE SECOND EPISTLE OF ST. JOHN.

II. ST. JOHN.

----

1 THE elder unto the elect Kuria and her children, whom I love
in the truth, and not I only, but likewise all who know the truth,
2 For the truth's sake which abideth in us, and shall be with us
3 for ever. Grace be with you, mercy *and* peace from God the
Father, and from Jesus Christ, the Son of the Father, in truth,
and love.
4 I rejoiced greatly that I found of thy children walking in the
5 truth, as we received commandment from the Father. And now
I beseech thee, Kuria, (not as writing a new commandment to
thee, but that which we had from the beginning,) that we may
6 love one another. And this is love, that we walk after his commandments. This is the commandment as ye have heard from

----

Verse 1. *The elder*—An appellation suited to a familiar letter, but upon a
weighty subject; *to the elect*—That is, Christian. *Kuria* is undoubtedly a proper name, both here and in ver. 5. For it was not then usual to apply the title
of *lady* to any but the Roman empress; neither would such a manner of speaking have been suitable to the simplicity and dignity of the apostle; *whom*—Both
her and her children, *I love in the truth*—With unfeigned and holy love.

2. *For the truth's sake, which abideth in us*—As a living principle of faith and
holiness.

3. *Grace*—takes away guilt; *mercy*, misery; *peace* implies the abiding in grace
and mercy. It includes the testimony of God's Spirit, both that we are his
children, and that all our ways are acceptable to him. This is the very foretaste
of heaven itself, where it is perfected; *in truth and love*—Or, faith and love, as
St. Paul speaks. Faith and truth are here synonymous terms.

4. *I found of thy children*—Probably in their aunt's house, ver. 13, *walking in
the truth*—In faith and love.

5. *That which we had from the beginning*—Of our Lord's ministry. Indeed it
was in some sense from the beginning of the world; *that we may love one another*—More abundantly.

6. *And this is* the proof of true love, universal obedience, built on the love of

7 the beginning, that ye may walk in it.   For many seducers are
entered into the world, who confess not Jesus Christ that came
8 in the flesh.   This is the seducer and the antichrist.   Look to
yourselves, that we lose not the things we have wrought, but
9 receive a full reward.   Whosoever transgresseth and abideth not
in the doctrine of Christ, hath not God : he that abideth in the
10 doctrine of Christ, he hath both the Father and the Son.   If any
come to you, and bring not this doctrine, receive him not into
11 your house, neither bid him God speed.   For he that biddeth him
God speed, is a partaker of his evil deeds.
12   Having many things to write to you, I was not minded *to write*
with paper and ink : but I trust to come to you, and speak face
13 to face, that our joy may be full.   The children of thy elect sister
salute thee.

God; *this,* love, *is the* great *commandment which ye have heard from the beginning*
of our preaching.

7. Carefully keep what you have heard from the beginning, *for many seducers
are entered into the world, who confess not Jesus Christ that he came in the flesh*—
Who disbelieve either his prophetic, or priestly, or kingly office.   Whosoever
does this, *is the seducer*—from God, *and the antichrist*—Fighting against Christ.

8. *That we lose not the things which we have wrought*—Which every apostate
does, *but receive a full reward*—Having fully employed all our talents to the
glory of Him that gave them.   Here again the apostle modestly transfers it to
himself.

9. Receive this as a certain rule, *Whosoever transgresseth*—Any law of God,
hath not God—For his Father and his God.   *He that abideth in the doctrine
of Christ*—Believing and obeying it, *he hath both the Father and the Son*—For
his God.

10. *If any come to you*—Either as a teacher or a brother, *and bring not this
doctrine*—That is, advance any thing contrary to it, *receive him not into your
house*—As either a teacher or a brother, *neither bid him God speed*—Give him no
encouragement therein.

11. *For he that biddeth him God speed*—That gives him any encouragement,
is accessary to *his evil deeds.*

12. *Having many things to write, I was not minded to write now*—Only of
these, which were then peculiarly needful.

13. *The children of thy elect* or Christian *sister*—Absent, if not dead, when the
apostle wrote this.

NOTES

ON

THE THIRD EPISTLE OF ST. JOHN.

———

THE THIRD EPISTLE HAS LIKEWISE THREE PARTS:

III. ST. JOHN.

———

1 THE elder unto the beloved Gaius, whom I truly love. Be-
2 loved, I pray that in every respect thou mayest prosper and be
   in health, as thy soul prospereth.
3 For I rejoiced greatly when the brethren came, and testified
4 of the truth that is in thee, as thou walkest in the truth. I have
   no greater joy than this, to hear that my children walk in the
5 truth. Beloved, thou dost faithfully whatsoever thou dost to the
   brethren, and to strangers, who have testified of thy love before
6 the Church; Whom if thou send forward on their journey after
7 a godly sort, thou shalt do well. For they went forth for his
8 sake, taking nothing of the Gentiles. We ought, therefore, to
9 receive such, that we may be fellow helpers to the truth. I wrote
   to the Church; but Diotrephes, who loveth to have the pre-

---

Verse 1. *Gaius* was, probably, that Gaius of Corinth whom St. Paul mentions,
Rom. xvi, 23. If so, either he was removed from Achaia into Asia, or St. John
sent this letter to Corinth.

3. *For*—I know thou usest all thy talents to his glory: *the truth that is in
thee*—The true faith and love.

4. *I have no greater joy than this*—Such is the spirit of every true Christian
pastor: *to hear that my children walk in the truth*—Gaius probably was converted
by St. Paul. Therefore when St. John speaks of him, with other believers, as
his children, it may be considered as the tender style of paternal love, whoever
were the instruments of their conversion. And his using this appellation, when
writing under the character of the elder, has its peculiar beauty.

5. *Faithfully*—Uprightly and sincerely.

6. *Who have testified of thy love before the Church*—The congregation with
whom I now reside: *whom if I send forward on their journey*—Supplied with
what is needful: *thou shalt do well*—How tenderly does the apostle enjoin this

7. *They went forth*—To preach the Gospel.

8. *To receive*—With all kindness, *the truth*—Which they preach.

9. *I wrote to the Church*—Probably that to which they came: *but Diotrephes*
—Perhaps the pastor of it; *who loveth to have the pre-eminence among them*—To

10 eminence among them, receiveth us not. Wherefore, if I come,
I will remember his wicked deeds which he doth, prating against
us with malicious words: and not content therewith, neither doth
he himself receive the brethren, and forbiddeth them that would,
11 and casteth them out of the Church. Beloved, follow not that
which is evil, but that which is good. He that is a doer of good,
12 is of God; he that is a doer of evil, hath not seen God. Demetrius hath a good testimony from all men, and from the truth
itself: yea, we also bear testimony, and ye know that our testimony is true.
13 I had many things to write; but I will not write to thee with
14 ink and pen. But I trust to see thee shortly, and we shall speak
face to face. Peace *be* to thee. Our friends salute thee. Salute
the friends by name.

---

govern all things according to his own will; *receiveth us not*—Neither them nor
me. So did the mystery of iniquity already work!

10. *He prateth against us*—Both them and me, thereby endeavouring to excuse
himself.

11. *Follow not that which is evil*—in Diotrephes, *but that which is good*—in
Demetrius. *He hath not seen God*—Is a stranger to him.

12. *And from the truth itself*—That is, what they testify is the very truth.
Yea, we also bear testimony—I and they that are with me.

14. *Salute the friends by name*—That is, in the same manner as if I had named
them one by one. The word *friend* does not often occur in the New Testament,
being swallowed up in the more endearing one of *brother.*

NOTES

ON

THE GENERAL EPISTLE OF ST. JUDE.

THIS EPISTLE HAS THREE PARTS:

This epistle greatly resembles the second of St. Peter, which St. Jude seems to have had in view while he wrote. That was written but a very little before St. Peter's death; and hence we may gather that St. Jude lived some time after it, and saw that grievous declension in the Church which St. Peter had foretold. But he passes over some things mentioned by St. Peter, repeats some, in different expressions, and with a different view, and adds others; clearly evidencing thereby the wisdom of God which rested upon him. Thus St. Peter cites and confirms St. Paul's writings, and is himself cited and confirmed by St. Jude.

ST. JUDE.

---

1 JUDE, a servant of Jesus Christ, and brother of James, to them that are beloved of God the Father, and preserved through Jesus
2 Christ, and called, Mercy unto you, and peace, and love be multiplied.
3   Beloved, when I gave all diligence to write to you of the com-

---

Verse 1. *Jude, a servant of Jesus Christ*—The highest glory which any, either angel or man, can aspire to. The word *servant*, under the old covenant, was adapted to the spirit of fear and bondage that clave to that dispensation. But when the time appointed of the Father was come, for the sending of his Son to redeem them that were under the law, the word *servant* (used by the apostles concerning themselves and all the children of God) signified one that, having the spirit of adoption, is *made free* by the Son of God. His being a *servant* is the fruit and perfection of his being a son. And whenever the throne of God and of the Lamb shall be in the New Jerusalem, then will it be indeed that *his servants shall serve him*, Rev. xxii. *The brother of James*—St. James was the more eminent, usually styled the brother of the Lord; *to them that are beloved*—The conclusion, ver. 21, exactly answers the introduction: *and preserved through Jesus Christ*—So both the spring and the accomplishment of salvation are pointed out. This is premised, lest any of them should be discouraged by the terrible things which are afterward mentioned: *and called*—To receive the whole blessing of God, in time and eternity.
    3. *When I gave all diligence to write to you of the common salvation*—Designed

mon salvation, it was needful for me to write to you, and exhort you to contend earnestly for the faith which was once delivered
4 to the saints.   For there are certain men crept in unawares, who were of old described before, with regard to this condemnation, ungodly men, turning the grace of our God into lasciviousness,
5 and denying our only Master and Lord, Jesus Christ.   I am therefore willing to remind you, who once knew this, that the Lord, having saved the people out of the land of Egypt, after-
6 ward destroyed them that believed not.   And *the angels, who kept not their first dignity, but left their own habitation, he hath reserved in everlasting chains under darkness to the judgment
7 of the great day.   Even as Sodom and Gomorrah and the cities about them, which, in the same manner with these gave them-selves over to fornication, and went after strange flesh, are set forth for an example, suffering the vengeance of eternal fire.
8 In like manner these dreamers also defile the flesh, † despise
9 authority, rail at dignities.   Yet Michael the archangel, when,

for all, and enjoyed by all believers. Here the design of the epistle is ex-pressed; the end of which exactly answers the beginning; *it was needful to exhort you to contend earnestly*—Yet humbly, meekly, and lovingly; otherwise your contentions will only hurt your cause, if not destroy your soul: *for the faith*—All the fundamental truths, *once delivered*—By God, to remain unvaried for ever.

4. *There are certain men crept in, who were of old described before*—Even as early as Enoch; of whom it was foretold, that by their wilful sins they would incur this condemnation; *turning the grace of God*—Revealed in the Gospel; *into lasciviousness*—Into an occasion of more abandoned wickedness.

5. *He afterward destroyed*—The far greater part of that very *people* whom he had once *saved*. Let no one therefore presume upon *past* mercies, as if he was now out of danger.

6. *And the angels, who kept not their first dignity*—Once assigned them under the Son of God, *but* voluntarily *left their own habitation*—Then properly their own, by the free gift of God: *he reserved*—Delivered to be kept: *in everlasting chains under darkness*—O how unlike their own habitation! When these fallen angels came out of the hands of God they were holy; (else God made that which was evil,) and being holy, they were beloved of God, (else he hated the image of his own spotless purity.) But now he loves them no more: they are doomed to endless destruction: for if he loved them still, he would love what is sinful; and both his former love, and his present righteous and eternal displeasure to-ward the same work of his own hands, are because he changeth not: because he invariably loveth righteousness and hateth iniquity.

7. *The cities who gave themselves over to fornication*—The word here means, *unnatural lust; are set forth as an example, suffering the vengeance of eternal fire* —That is, the vengeance which they suffered is an example or a type of eternal fire.

8. *In like manner these dreamers*—Sleeping and dreaming all their lives, *de-spise authority*—Those that are invested with it by Christ, and made by him the overseers of his flock; *rail at dignities*—The apostle does not seem to speak of worldly dignities. These they had *in admiration for the sake of gain;* verse 16, but these holy men, who for the purity of their lives, the soundness of their doc-trine, and the greatness of their labours in the work of the ministry, were truly honourable before God and all good men: and who were grossly vilified by those who turned the grace of God into lasciviousness. Probably they were the im-pure followers of Simon Magus, the same with the Gnostics and Nicolaitans, Rev. ii, 15.

9. *Yet Michael*—It does not appear whether St. Jude learned this by any revelation, or from ancient tradition. It suffices, that these things were not

contending with the devil, he disputed concerning the body of
Moses, durst not bring against him a railing accusation, but said,
10 The Lord rebuke thee. But these rail at all things which they
know not: and all the things which they know naturally, as the
11 brute beasts, in these they are defiled. Wo to them; for they
have gone in the way of Cain, and ran greedily after the error of
Balaam for reward, and perished in the gainsaying of Korah.
12 These are spots in your feasts of love, while they banquet with
you, feeding themselves without fear: clouds without water,
driven about of winds; trees without leaves, without fruit, twice
13 dead, plucked up by the roots; Raging waves of the sea, foaming out their own shame; wandering stars, for whom is reserved
14 the blackness of darkness for ever. And of these also, Enoch,
the seventh from Adam, prophesied, saying, Behold the Lord
15 cometh with ten thousands of his holy ones, To execute judgment
upon all, and to convict all the ungodly of all their ungodly deeds,
which they have impiously committed, and of all the grievous
things which ungodly sinners have spoken against him.

only true, but acknowledged as such by them to whom he wrote: *the archangel*
—This word occurs but once more in the sacred writings, 1 Thess. iv, 16. So
that whether there be one archangel only, or more, it is not possible for us to
determine; *when he disputed with the devil*—At what time we know not; *concerning the body of Moses*—Possibly the devil would have discovered the place
where it was buried, which God, for wise reasons, had concealed: *durst not
bring* even *against him a railing accusation*—Though so far beneath him in
every respect: *but* simply *said,* (so great was his modesty,) *the Lord rebuke thee*
—I leave thee to the Judge of all.

10. *But these*—Without all shame; *rail at the things* of God *which they know
not*—Neither can know, having no spiritual senses; *and the natural things which
they know*—By their natural senses, they abuse into occasions of sin.

11. *Wo unto them*—Of all the apostles St. Jude alone, and that in this single
place, denounces a wo. St. Peter, to the same effect, pronounces them *cursed
children: for they have gone in the way of Cain*—The murderer, *and ran greedily*
(literally, *have been poured out,* like a torrent without banks) *after the error of
Balaam*—The covetous false prophet; *and perished in the gainsaying of Korah*
—Vengeance has overtaken them as it did Korah, rising up against those whom
God had sent.

12. *These are spots*—Blemishes *in your feasts of love*—Anciently observed in
all the Churches; *feeding themselves without fear*—Without any fear of God, or
jealousy over themselves; *twice dead*—In sin, first by nature, and afterward by
apostacy; *plucked up by the roots*—And so incapable of ever reviving.

13. *Wandering stars*—Literally, *planets*—Which shine for a time, but have no
light in themselves, *and will be soon cast into utter darkness.* Thus the apostle
illustrates their desperate wickedness, by comparisons drawn from the air, earth,
sea, and heavens.

14. *And of these also*—As well as the antediluvian sinners, *Enoch*—So early
was the prophecy referred to, ver. 4, *the seventh from Adam*—There were only
five of the fathers between Adam and Enoch; 1 Chron. i, 1. The first coming
of Christ was revealed to Adam; his second glorious coming to Enoch; and
the seventh from Adam foretold the things which will conclude the seventh
age of the world. St. Jude might know this either from some ancient book,
or tradition, or immediate revelation. *Behold!* As if it were already done, *the
Lord cometh!*

15. *To execute judgment*—Enoch herein looked beyond the flood, *upon all*—
Sinners in general, *and to convict all the ungodly*—In particular, *of all the
grievous things which ungodly sinners* (a sinner is bad; but the ungodly, who sin
without fear, are worse) *have spoken against him,* ver. 8, 10; though they might
not think all those speeches were against him.

16   These are murmurers, complainers, walking after their own
desires, and their mouth speaking great swelling things, having
17 men's persons in admiration for the sake of gain.   But ye, beloved, remember the words which were spoken before by the
18 apostles of our Lord Jesus Christ.   For they told you, In the
last time there will be mockers, walking after their own ungodly desires.
19   These are they who separate themselves, sensual, not having
20 the Spirit.   But ye, beloved, building yourselves up in your most
21 holy faith, praying through the Holy Spirit, Keep yourselves in
the love of God, looking for the mercy of our Lord Jesus Christ
22 unto eternal life.   And some, that are wavering, convince ; Some
23 save, snatching *them* out of the fire ; on others have compassion
with fear, hating even the garment spotted by the flesh.
24   Now to Him *who is* able to keep them from falling, and to
present *you* faultless in the presence of his glory with exceeding
25 joy, To the only God, our Saviour, *be* glory, and majesty, might,
and authority, both now, and to all ages.   Amen.

---

16. *These are murmurers*—Against men ; *complainers*—(Literally, complainers
of their fate) against God ; *walking*, with regard to themselves, *after their own*
foolish ahd mischievous *desires, having men's persons in admiration for the sake
of gain*—Admiring and commending them only for what they can get.

17. *By the apostles*—He does not exempt himself from the number of apostles.
For in the next verse he says, *they told you*, not *us.*

19. *These are they who separate themselves, sensual, not having the Spirit*—
Having natural senses and understanding only, not the Spirit of God : otherwise they could not separate.   For that it is a sin, and a very heinous one, *to
separate from the Church*, is out of all question.   But then it should be observed,
1. That by *the Church*, is meant a body of living Christians, who are *a habitation
of God through the Spirit*.   2. That by *separating* is understood, renouncing all
religious intercourse with them ; no longer joining with them in solemn prayer,
or the other public offices of religion : and, 3. That we have no more authority
from Scripture to call even this *schism*, than to call it *murder.*

20. *But ye, beloved*—Not separating, but *building yourselves up in your most
holy faith*—Than which none can be more holy in itself, or more conducive to
the most refined and exalted holiness : *praying through the Holy Spirit*—Who
alone is able to build you up, as he alone laid the foundation.   In this and the
following verse, St. Jude mentions the Father, Son, and Spirit, together with
faith, love, and hope.

21. By these means, through his grace, *keep yourselves in the love of God*, and
in the confident expectation of that *eternal life*, which is purchased for you, and
conferred upon you through the mere *mercy of our Lord Jesus Christ.*

22. Meantime watch over others, as well as yourselves, and give them such
help as their various needs require.   For instance, 1. *Some that are wavering* in
judgment, staggered by others or by their own evil reasoning, endeavour more
deeply to convince of the whole truth as it is in Jesus.   2. *Some snatch*, with a
swift and strong hand, *out of the fire* of sin and temptation.   3. *On others* show
compassion in a milder and gentler way ; though still *with* a jealous *fear*, lest
yourselves be infected with the disease you endeavour to cure.   See, therefore,
that while you love the sinners, ye retain the utmost abhorrence of their sins,
and of any the least degree of, or approach to them.

24. *Now to Him who* alone *is able to keep them from falling*—Into any of these
errors or sins, *and to present you faultless in the presence of his glory*—That is,
in his own presence, when he shall be revealed in all his glory.'

NOTES

THE REVELATION OF JESUS CHRIST.

———

It is scarce possible for any that either love or fear God, not to feel their hearts extremely affected, in seriously reading either the beginning, or the latter part of the Revelation. These, it is evident, we cannot consider too much: but the intermediate parts I did not study at all for many years: as utterly despairing of understanding them, after the fruitless attempts of so many wise and good men; and perhaps I should have lived and died in this sentiment, had I not seen the works of the great Bengelius. But these revived my hopes of understanding even the prophecies of this book: at least many of them in some good degree; for perhaps some will not be opened but in eternity. Let us, however, bless God for the measure of light we may enjoy, and improve it to his glory.

The following notes are mostly those of that excellent man; a few of which are taken from his *Gnomon Novi Testamenti*, but far more from his *Ekklarte Offenbarung*, which is a full and regular comment on the Revelation. Every part of this I do not undertake to defend. But none should condemn him without reading his proofs at large. It did not suit my design to insert these: they are above the capacity of ordinary readers. Nor had I room to insert the entire translation of a book which contains near twelve hundred pages.

All I can do is, partly to translate, partly abridge the most necessary of his observations; allowing myself the liberty to alter some of them, and to add a few notes where he is not full. His text, it may be observed, I have taken almost throughout, which I apprehend he has abundantly defended both in the *Gnomon* itself, and in his *Apparatus* and *Crisis in Apocalypsin*.

Yet I by no means pretend to understand, or explain all that is contained in this mysterious book. I only offer what help I can to the serious inquirer, and shall rejoice if any be moved thereby more carefully to read, and more deeply to consider the words of this prophecy. Blessed is he that does this with a single eye. His labour shall not be in vain.

———

THE REVELATION.

———

1   The Revelation of Jesus Christ, which God gave unto him to show his servants the things which must shortly come to

==========

Verse 1. *The Revelation*—Properly so called: for things covered before are here revealed or unveiled. No prophecy in the Old Testament has this title: it was reserved for this alone in the New. It is as it were a manifesto, wherein the Heir of all things declares, That all power is given him in heaven and earth, and that he will in the end gloriously exercise that power, maugre all the opposition of all his enemies. *Of Jesus Christ*—Not of John the Divine, a title added in latter ages. Certain it is, that appellation, *the divine*, was not brought into the Church, much less was it affixed to John the apostle, till long after the apostolic age. It was St. John indeed who wrote this book; but the author

CHAPTER I. 651

pass, and he sent and signified *them* by his angel to his servant
2 John, Who hath testified the Word of God and the testimony
3 of Jesus Christ, whatsoever things he saw. Happy is he that
readeth, and they that hear the words of *this* prophecy, and keep
the things which are written therein: for the time *is* near.

---

of it is *Jesus Christ.* *Which God gave unto him*—According to his holy, glorified humanity, as the great prophet of the Church. God gave the revelation tc
Jesus Christ, Jesus Christ made it known to his servants. *To show*—This word
recurs, chap. xxii, 6. And in many places the parts of this book refer to each
other. Indeed the whole structure of it breathes the art of God, comprising in
the most finished compendium things to come, many, various; near, intermediate, remote; the greatest, the least, terrible, comfortable; old, new; long, short;
and these interwoven together, opposite, composite: relative to each other at a
small, at a great distance; and therefore sometimes as it were disappearing,
broken off, suspended, and afterward unexpectedly and most seasonably appearing again. In all its parts it has an admirable variety, with the most exact harmony, beautifully illustrated by those very digressions which seem to interrupt
it. In this manner does it display the manifest wisdom of God shining in the
economy of the Church through so many ages. *His servants*—Much is comprehended in this appellation. It is a great thing to be a servant of Jesus Christ.
This book is dedicated particularly to the servants of Christ in the seven
Churches in Asia: but not exclusive of all his other servants, in all nations and
ages. It is one single revelation, and yet sufficient for them all, from the time
it was written to the end of the world. Serve thou the Lord Jesus Christ in
truth. So shalt thou learn his secret in this book. Yea, and thou shalt feel in
thy heart, whether this book be Divine or not. *The things which must shortly
come to pass*—The things contained in this prophecy did begin to be accomplished
shortly after it was given; and the whole might be said to come to pass shortly,
in the same sense as St. Peter says the end of all things is at hand; and our Lord
himself, Behold, I come quickly. There is in this book a rich treasure of all
the doctrines pertaining to faith and holiness. But these are also delivered in
other parts of holy writ; so that the revelation need not to have been given for
the sake of these. The peculiar design of this is, to show the things which
must come to pass. And this we are especially to have before our eyes, whenever we read or hear it.

It is said afterward, write what thou seest: and again, write what thou hast
seen, and what is, and what shall be hereafter: but here, where the scope of the
book is shown, it is only said, *the things which must come to pass.* Accordingly
the showing things to come, is the great point in view throughout the whole.
And St. John writes what he has seen, and what is, only as it has an influence
on, or gives light to, what shall be. *And he*—Jesus Christ, *sent and signified
them*—Showed them by signs or emblems (so the Greek word properly means)
by his angel—Peculiarly called in the sequel, the angel of God, and particularly
mentioned, chap. xvii, 1; xxi, 9; xxii, 6, 16. *To his servant John*—A title given
to no other single person throughout the book.

2. *Who hath testified*—In the following book, *the word of God*—Given directly
by God, *and the testimony of Jesus Christ*—Which he hath left us, as the faithful
and true witness, *whatsoever things he saw*—In such a manner as was a full confirmation of the Divine original of this book.

3. *Happy is he that readeth, and they that hear the words of this prophecy*—Some
have miserably handled this book. Hence others are afraid to touch it. And
while they desire to know all things else, reject only the knowledge of those
which God hath shown. They inquire after any thing rather than this; as if it
were written, happy is he that doth *not* read this prophecy. Nay, but *happy is
he that readeth, and they that hear* and keep the words thereof: especially at this
time, when so considerable a part of them is on the point of being fulfilled.

Nor are helps wanting whereby any sincere and diligent inquirer may understand what he reads therein. The book itself is written in the most accurate
manner possible: it distinguishes the several things whereof it treats by seven
epistles, seven seals, seven trumpets, seven phials, each of which sevens is
divided into four and three. Many things the book itself explains, as the seven

4   John to the seven Churches which are in Asia : Grace *be* unto
you, and peace, from him who is, and who was, and who cometh,

---

stars; the seven candlesticks; the Lamb, his seven horns and seven eyes; the
incense; the dragon; the heads and horns of the beasts; the fine linen; the
testimony of Jesus.   And much light arises from comparing it with the ancient
prophecies, and the predictions in the other books of the New Testament.
  In this book our Lord has comprised what was wanting in those prophecies,
touching the time which followed his ascension, and the end of the Jewish polity.
Accordingly it reaches from the Old Jerusalem to the New, reducing all things
into one sum in the exactest order, and with a near resemblance to the anci:nt
prophets.   The introduction and conclusion agree with Daniel; the description
of the man-child, and the promises to Sion, with Isaiah; the judgment of Babylon, with Jeremiah: again, the determination of times, with Daniel; the archi-
tecture of the holy city, with Ezekiel; the emblems of the horses, candlesticks,
&c., with Zechariah.   Many things largely described by the prophets are here
summarily repeated: and frequently in the same words.   To them we may,
then, usefully have recourse.   Yet the Revelation suffices for the explaining
itself, even if we do not yet understand those prophecies; yea, it casts much
light upon them.   Frequently, likewise, where there is a resemblance between
them, there is a difference also; the Revelation, as it were, taking a stock from
one of the old prophets, and inserting a new graft into it.   Thus Zechariah
speaks of two olive trees.   And so does St. John: but with a different meaning.
Daniel has a beast with ten horns.   So has St. John : but not quite with the same
signification.   And here the difference of words, emblems, things, times, ought
studiously to be observed.
  Our Lord foretold many things before his passion; but not all things: for it
was not yet seasonable.   Many things, likewise, his Spirit foretold in the
writings of the apostles, so far as the necessities of those times required; now
he comprises them all in one short book : therein presupposing all the other
prophecies, and, at the same time, explaining, continuing, and perfecting them
in one thread.   It is right, therefore, to compare them, but not to measure the
fulness of these by the scantiness of those preceding.
  Christ, when on earth, foretold what would come to pass in a short time;
adding a brief description of the last things.   Here he foretells the intermediate
things; so that both put together, constitute one complete chain of prophecy.
This book is, therefore, not only the sum and the key of all the prophecies which
preceded, but likewise a supplement to all; the seals being closed before.   Of
consequence it contains many particulars not revealed in any other part of Scripture.   They have therefore little gratitude to God for such a revelation, reserved
for the exaltation of Christ, who boldly reject whatever they find here, which
was not revealed, or not so clearly in other parts of Scripture.   *He that readeth,
and they that hear*—St. John probably sent this book by a single person into
Asia, who read it in the Churches, while many heard.   But this, likewise, in a
secondary sense, refers to all that shall duly read or hear it in all ages.   *The
words of this prophecy*—It is a revelation with regard to Christ, who gives it, a
prophecy with regard to John, who delivers it to the Churches.   *And keep the
things which are written therein*—In such a manner as the nature of them requires; namely, with repentance, faith, patience, prayer, obedience, watchfulness, constancy.   It behooves every Christian, at all opportunities, to read what
is written in the oracles of God; and to read this precious book in particular,
frequently, reverently, and attentively.   *For the time*—Of its beginning to be
accomplished, *is near*—Even when St. John wrote.   How much nearer to us is
even the full accomplishment of this weighty prophecy !
  4. *John*—The dedication of this book is contained in the 4th, 5th, and 6th
verses: but the whole Revelation is a kind of letter.   *To the seven Churches which
are in Asia*—That part of the lesser Asia, which was then a Roman province.
There had been several other Churches planted here; but it seems these were
now the most eminent.   And it was among these that St. John had laboured
most during his abode in Asia.   In these cities there were many Jews.   Such of
them as believed in each were joined with the Gentile believers in one Church.
Grace be unto you, and peace—The favour of God with all temporal and eternal
blessings.   *From him who is, and who was, and who cometh*, or *who is to come*—

5 and from the seven Spirits that are before his throne, And from Jesus Christ, the faithful witness, the first begotten from the
6 dead, and the prince of the kings of the earth: To him that loveth us, and hath washed us from our sins with his own blood, and hath made us kings and priests unto his God and Father, to him be the glory and the might for ever.
7   Behold, he cometh with clouds, and every eye shall see him, and they who have pierced him: and all the tribes of the earth

A wonderful translation of the great name Jehovah; he was of old, he is now; he cometh; that is, will be for ever. *And from the seven Spirits which are before his throne—Christ* is he who *hath the seven Spirits of God. The seven lamps which burn before the throne are the seven Spirits of God. The lamb hath seven horns and seven eyes, which are the seven Spirits of God. Seven* was a sacred number in the Jewish Church. But it did not always imply a precise number. It sometimes is to be taken figuratively, to denote completeness or perfection. By these seven Spirits, not seven created angels, but the Holy Ghost, is to be understood: the angels are never termed *Spirits* in this book; and when all the angels stand up, while the four living creatures and the four and twenty elders worship him that sitteth upon the throne and the Lamb, the seven Spirits neither stand up nor worship. To these seven Spirits of God, the seven Churches, to whom the Spirit speaks so many things, are subordinate: as are also their angels, yea, and *the seven angels which stand before God.* He is called *the seven Spirits,* not with regard to his essence, which is one, but with regard to his manifold operations.

5. *And from Jesus Christ, the faithful witness, the first begotten from the dead, and the prince of the kings of the earth*—Three glorious appellations are here given him, and in their proper order. He was the faithful witness of the whole will of God before his death, and in death, and remains such in glory. He rose from the dead, as the first fruits of them that slept; and now hath all power both in heaven and earth. He is here styled a *Prince.* But by and by he bears his title of *King:* yea, *King of kings, and Lord of lords.* This phrase, *the kings of the earth,* signifies their power and multitude, and also the nature of their kingdom. It became the Divine Majesty to call them kings with a limitation; especially in this manifesto from his heavenly kingdom. For no creature, much less a sinful man, can bear the title of king, in an absolute sense, before the eyes of God.

6. *To him that loveth us, and*—Out of that free, abundant love, *hath washed us from*—The guilt and power of, *our sins with his own blood; and hath made us kings*—Partakers of his present, and heirs of his eternal kingdom, *and priests unto his God and Father*—To whom we continually offer ourselves, a holy, living sacrifice: *To him be the glory*—For his love and redemption; *and the might*—Whereby he governs all things.

7. *Behold*—In this and the next verse is the proposition, and the summary of the whole book. *He cometh*—Jesus Christ. Throughout this book, whenever it is said, *He cometh,* it means his glorious coming. The preparation for this began at the destruction of Jerusalem, and more particularly at the time of writing this book, and goes on, without any interruption, till that grand event is accomplished. Therefore it is never said in this book, He will come, but *He cometh.* And yet it is not said, He cometh again. For when he came before, it was not like himself, but in *the form of a servant.* But his appearing in glory is properly his coming, namely, in a manner worthy of the Son of God. *And every eye*—Of the Jews in particular, *shall see him*—But with what different emotions, according as they had received or rejected him! *And they who have pierced him*—They, above all, who pierced his hands, or feet, or side. Thomas saw the prints of these wounds, even after his resurrection. And the same undoubtedly will be seen by all, when he cometh in the clouds of heaven. *And all the tribes of the earth*—The word *tribes,* in the Revelation, always means the Israelites; but where another word, such as *nations* or *people,* is joined with it, it implies likewise (as here) all the rest of mankind. *Shall wail because of him*—For terror and pain, if they did not wail before by true repentance. *Yea. Amen*—This

8 shall wail because of him. Yea. Amen. I am the Alpha and the Omega, saith the Lord God, who is, and who was, and who cometh, the Almighty.

9   I John, your brother and companion in the affliction, and in the kingdom, and patience of Jesus, was in the island Patmos,

10 for the word of God, and for the testimony of Jesus. I was in the Spirit on the Lord's day, and heard behind me a great voice

---

refers to *every eye shall see him.* He that cometh saith, *Yea:* he that testifies it, *Amen.* The word translated *yea,* is Greek; *amen,* is Hebrew: for what is here spoken respects both Jew and Gentile.

8. *I am the Alpha and the Omega, saith the Lord God*—Alpha is the first, Omega the last letter in the Greek alphabet. Let his enemies boast and rage ever so much in the intermediate time, yet the Lord God is both the Alpha or beginning, and the Omega, or end of all things. God is the beginning, as he is the Author and Creator of all things, and as he proposes, declares, and promises so great things. He is the end, as he brings all the things which are here revealed to a complete and glorious conclusion. Again, *the beginning and end of a thing,* is in Scripture styled the whole thing. Therefore God is the Alpha and the Omega, the beginning and the end, that is, one who is all things, and always the same.

9. *I John*—The instruction and preparation of the apostle for the works are described from the 9th to the 20th verse: *your brother*—In the common faith: *and companion in the affliction*—For the same persecution which carried him to Patmos, drove them into Asia. This book peculiarly belongs to those who are under the cross. It was given to a banished man: and men in affliction understand and relish it most. Accordingly it was little esteemed by the Asiatic Church, after the time of Constantine; but highly valued by all the African Churches, as it has been since by all the persecuted children of God. *In the affliction, and kingdom, and patience of Jesus*—The kingdom stands in the midst. It is chiefly under various afflictions that faith obtains its part in the kingdom. And whosoever is a partaker of this kingdom is not afraid to suffer for Jesus, 2 Tim. ii, 12. *I was in the island Patmos*—In the reign of Domitian and of Nerva. And there he saw and wrote all that follows. It was a place peculiarly proper for these visions. He had over against him at a small distance, Asia and the seven Churches; going on eastward, Jerusalem and the land of Canaan, and beyond this Antioch, yea, the whole continent of Asia. To the west he had Rome, Italy, and all Europe, swimming as it were in the sea: to the south, Alexandria and the Nile with its outlets, Egypt and all Africa: and to the north, what was afterward called Constantinople, on the straits between Europe and Asia. So he had all the three parts of the world which were then known, with Christendom as it were before his eyes: a large theatre, for all the various scenes which were to pass before him. As if this island had been made principally for this end, to serve as an observatory for the apostle. *For* preaching *the word of God* he was banished thither, and for the *testimony of Jesus;* for testifying that he is the Christ.

10. *I was in the Spirit*—That is, in a trance, a prophetic vision: so overwhelmed with the power and filled with the light of the Holy Spirit, as to be insensible of outward things, and wholly taken up with spiritual and Divine. What follows is one single connected vision, which St. John saw in one day; and therefore he that would understand it should carry his thoughts straight on through the whole without interruption. The other prophetic books are collections of distinct prophecies, given upon various occasions. But here is one single treatise, whereof all the parts exactly depend on each other. Chap. iv, 1, is connected with chap. i, 29. And what is delivered in the 4th chapter, goes on directly to the 22d. *On the Lord's day*—On this our Lord rose from the dead: on this the ancients believed he would come to judgment. It was therefore with the utmost propriety that St. John *on this day* both saw and described his coming. *And I heard behind me*—St. John had his face to the east: our Lord likewise in this appearance looked eastward toward Asia, whither the apostle was to write; *a great voice as of a trumpet*—Which was peculiarly proper to proclaim the coming of the great King, and his victory over all his enemies.

11 as of a trumpet, Saying, What thou seest write in a book, and
   send to the seven Churches, to Ephesus, and to Smyrna, and to
   Pergamos, and to Thyatira, and to Sardis, and to Philadelphia,
12 and to Laodicea. And I turned to see the voice that spake with
13 me, and being turned, I saw seven golden candlesticks, and in
   the midst of the candlesticks *one* like a Son of man, clothed with
   a garment down to the foot, and girt about at the breast with a
14 golden girdle. His head and hair *were* white as white wool, as
15 snow, and his eyes as a flame of fire, And his feet like fine brass,
   as if they burned in a furnace, and his voice as the voice of many
16 waters. And he had in his right hand seven stars, and out of
   his mouth went a sharp two-edged sword; and his countenance

---

11. *Saying, What thou seest*—And hearest. He both saw and heard. This
command extends to the whole book. All the books of the New Testament
were written by the will of God, but none were so expressly commanded to be
written; *in a book*—So all the revelation is but one book; nor did the letter to
the angel of each belong to him or his Church only; but the whole book was
sent to them all; *to the Churches*—Hereafter named; and through them to all
Churches, in all ages and nations. *To Ephesus*—Mr. Thomas Smith, who in
the year 1671 travelled through all these cities, observes, that from Ephesus to
Smyrna is forty-six English miles; from Smyrna to Pergamos, sixty-four; from
Pergamos to Thyatira, forty-eight; from Thyatira to Sardis, thirty-three; from
Sardis to Philadelphia, twenty-seven; from Philadelphia to Laodicea, about
forty-two miles.
12, 13. *And I turned to see the voice*—That is, to see him whose voice it was;
and being turned, I saw—It seems the vision presented itself gradually. First
he heard a voice, and upon looking behind he saw the *golden candlesticks*, and
then in the midst of the candlesticks, which were placed in a circle, he saw
one like a Son of man—That is, in a human form. As a man likewise our
Lord doubtless appears in heaven, though not exactly in this symbolical man
ner, wherein he presents himself as the head of his Church. He next observed
that our Lord was *clothed with a garment down to the foot, and girt with a golden
girdle*—Such the Jewish high priests wore. But both of them are here marks
of royal dignity likewise; *girt about at the breast*—He that is on a journey girds
his loins. Girding the breast was an emblem of solemn rest. It seems that
the apostle, having seen all this, looked up to behold the face of our Lord;
but was beat back by the appearance of his *flaming eyes*, which occasioned his
more particularly observing his feet. Receiving strength to raise his eyes
again, he saw the stars in his right hand, and the sword coming out of his
mouth: but upon beholding the brightness of his glorious countenance, (which
probably was much increased since the first glance the apostle had of it,) he *fell
at his feet as dead*—During the time that St. John was discovering these several
particulars, our Lord seems to have been speaking. And doubtless even his
voice at the very first bespoke the God; though not so insupportably as his
glorious appearance.
14. *His head and* his *hair*—That is, the hair of his head, not his whole head,
were white as white wool—Like the Ancient of days, represented in Daniel's
vision, chap. vi, 6. Wool is commonly supposed to be an emblem of eternity; *as
snow*—Betokening his spotless purity. *And his eyes as a flame of fire*—Piercing
through all things; a token of his omniscience.
15. *And his feet like fine brass*—Denoting his stability and strength; *as if
they burned in a furnace*—As if having been melted and refined they were still
red hot; *and his voice*—To the comfort of his friends and the terror of his
enemies, *as the voice of many waters*—Roaring aloud, and bearing down all
before them.
16. *And he had in his right hand seven stars*—In token of his favour and powerful protection; *and out of his mouth went a sharp two-edged sword*—Signifying
his justice and righteous anger, continually pointed against his enemies as a
sword, *sharp*, to stab; *two-edged*, to hew; *and his countenance was as the sun
shineth in his strength*—Without any mist or cloud.

17 was as the sun shineth in his strength. And when I saw him I
   fell at his feet as dead: and he laid his right hand upon me,
18 saying, Fear not, I am the First and the Last, And he that liveth
   and was dead, and behold I am alive for evermore, and have
19 the keys of death and of hades. Write the things which thou
20 hast seen, and which are, and which shall be hereafter: The
   mystery of the seven stars which thou sawest in my right hand,
   and *of* the seven golden candlesticks. The seven stars are'
   angels of the seven Churches; and the seven candlesticks are
   seven Churches.

17. *And I fell at his feet as dead*—Human nature not being able to sustain so
glorious an appearance. Thus was he prepared (like Daniel of old, whom he
particularly resembles) for receiving so weighty a prophecy. A great sinking
of nature usually precedes a large communication of heavenly things. St. John,
before our Lord suffered, was so intimate with him as to lean on his breast,
to lie in his bosom. Yet now, near seventy years after, the aged apostle is by
one glance struck to the ground. What a glory must this be! Ye sinners, be
afraid; cleanse your hands; purify your hearts. Ye saints, be humble; prepare; rejoice; but rejoice unto him with reverence. An increase of reverence
toward this awful majesty can be no prejudice to your faith. Let all petulancy, with all vain curiosity, be far away, while you are thinking or reading
of these things. *And he laid his right hand upon me*—The same wherein
he held the seven stars. What did St. John then feel in himself? *Saying,
Fear not*—His look terrifies, his speech strengthens. He does not call John
by name, (as the angels did Zacharias and others,) but speaks as his well
known master. What follows is also spoken to strengthen and encourage
him. *I am*—When in his state of humiliation he spoke of his glory, he
frequently spoke in the third person, as Matt. xxvi, 65. But he now speaks
of his own glory, without any veil, in plain and direct terms. *The first and
the last*—That is, the one, eternal God, who is from everlasting to everlasting,
Isa. xli, 4.
   18. *And he that liveth*—Another peculiar title of God; *and I have the keys of
death and of hades*—That is, the invisible world in the intermediate state: the
body abides in death, the soul in hades. Christ hath the keys of, that is, the
power over both, killing or quickening of the body, and disposing of the soul,
as it pleaseth him. He gave St. Peter the keys of the kingdom of heaven; but
not the keys of death or hades. How comes then his supposed successor at
Rome by the keys of purgatory?
   From the preceding description mostly are taken the titles given Christ in the
following letters, particularly the first four.
   19. *Write the things which thou hast seen*—This day: which accordingly are
written, chap. i, 11-18; *and which are*—The instructions relating to the present
state of the seven Churches. These are written, chap. i, 20; chap. iii, 22; *and
which shall be hereafter*—To the end of the world; written chap. iv. 1, &c.
   20. Write first *the mystery*—The mysterious meaning *of the seven stars*—St.
John knew better than we do, in how many respects these stars were a proper
emblem of those angels; how nearly they resembled each other, and how far
they differed in magnitude, brightness, and other circumstances. *The seven stars
are angels of the seven Churches*—Mentioned in the 11th verse. In each Church
there was one pastor or ruling minister, to whom all the rest were subordinate
This pastor, bishop, or overseer, had the peculiar care over that flock; on him
the prosperity of that congregation in a great measure depended; and he was,
to answer for all those souls at the judgment seat of *Christ*. *And the seven
candlesticks are seven Churches*—How significant an emblem is this! For a
candlestick, though of gold, has no light of itself; neither has any Church or
child of man. But they receive from *Christ* the light of truth, holiness, comfort,
that it may shine to all around them.
   As soon as this was spoken St. John wrote it down, even all that is contained
in this first chapter. Afterward what was contained in the second and thir
chapters was dictated to him in like manner.

II. To the angel of the Church at Ephesus write, These things saith he that holdeth the seven stars in his right hand, that 2 walketh in the midst of the seven golden candlesticks. I know thy works, and thy labour, and thy patience, that thou canst not bear evil men; and thou hast tried those who say they are

---

II. Of the following letters to the angels of the seven Churches it may be necessary to speak first in general, then particularly.

In general we may observe, when the *Israelites* were to receive the law at Mount *Sinai* they were first to be purified. And when the kingdom of God was at hand John the Baptist prepared men for it by repentance. In like manner we are prepared by these letters for the worthy reception of this glorious *Revelation.* By following the directions given herein, by expelling incorrigibly wicked men, and putting away all wickedness, those Churches were prepared to receive the precious depositum. And whoever, in any age, would profitably read or hear it, must observe the same admonitions.

These letters are a kind of sevenfold preface to the book. *Christ* now appears in the form of a man, (not yet under the emblem of a lamp,) and speaks mostly in proper, not in figurative words. It is not till chap. iv, 1, that St. John enters upon that grand vision which takes up the residue of the book.

There is in each of these letters,

1. A command to write to the angel of the Church.
2. A glorious title of Christ.
3. An address to the angel of that Church, containing
   A testimony of his mixed, or good, or bad state:
   An exhortation to repentance or steadfastness:
   A declaration of what will be; generally, of the Lord's coming.
4. A promise to him that overcometh, together with the exhortation, *He that hath an ear to hear, let him hear.*

The address in each letter is expressed in plain words; the promise in figurative. In the address our Lord speaks to the angel of each Church which then was, and to the members thereof directly: whereas in the promise he speaks of all that should overcome, in whatever Church or age, and deals out to them one of the precious promises (by way of anticipation) from the last chapters of the book.

II. 1. *Write*—So Christ dictated to him every word. *These things saith he who holdeth the seven stars in his right hand*—Such is his mighty power! Such his favour to them, and care over them, that they may indeed shine as stars, both by purity of doctrine and holiness of life! *Who walketh*—According to his promise, *I am with you always, even to the end of the world; in the midst of the golden candlesticks*—Beholding all their works and thoughts, and ready to *remove the candlestick out of its place*—If any being warned, will not repent. Perhaps here is likewise an allusion to the office of the priests in dressing the lamps, which was to keep them always burning before the Lord.

2. *I know*—Jesus knows all the good and all the evil which his servants and his enemies suffer and do. Weighty word, I know! How dreadful will it one day sound to the wicked, how sweet to the righteous! The Churches and their angels must have been astonished to find their several states so exactly described, even in the absence of the apostle; and could not but acknowledge the all-seeing eye of Christ and of his Spirit. With regard to us, to every one of us, also he saith, *I know thy works!* Happy is he that conceives less good of himself than Christ knows concerning him! *And thy labour*—After the general, three particulars are named, and then more largely described in an inverted order:

1. Thy labour.
2. Thy patience.
3. Thou canst not bear evil men.

6. Thou hast borne for my name's sake, and hast not fainted.
5. Thou hast patience.
4. Thou hast tried those who say they are apostles, and are not, and hast found them liars.

And thy patience—Notwithstanding which *thou canst not bear* that incorrigibly *wicked men* should remain in the flock of Christ. *And thou hast tried those who say they are apostles, and are not*—For the Lord hath not sent them.

42

3 apostles, and are not, and hast found them liars: And hast patience, and hast borne for my name's sake, and hast not fainted.
4 But I have against thee, that thou hast left thy first love. Re-
5 member therefore from whence thou art fallen, and repent, and
do the first works: if not, I come to thee, and will remove thy
6 candlestick out of its place, unless thou repent. But thou hast
this, that thou hatest the works of the Nicolaitans, which I also
hate. He that hath an ear let him hear what the Spirit saith to
7 the Churches. To him that overcometh will I give to eat of the
tree of life, which is in the paradise of my God.

4. *But I have against thee, that thou hast left thy first love*—That love for which
all that Church was so eminent when St. Paul wrote his epistle to them. He
need not have left this: he might have retained it entire to the end; and he did
retain it in part, or there could not have remained so much of what was com-
mendable in him. But he had not kept (as he might have done) the first tender
love in its vigour and warmth. Reader, hast thou?
5. It is not possible for any to recover the first love but by taking these three
steps: 1. *Remember;* 2. *Repent;* 3. *Do the first works. Remember from whence
thou art fallen*—From what degree of faith, love, holiness, though perhaps insensibly; *and repent*—Which in the very lowest sense implies a deep and lively
conviction of thy fall. Of the seven angels, two, at Ephesus and at Pergamos,
were in a mixed state; two, at Sardis and at Laodicea, were greatly corrupted.
All these are exhorted to *repent;* as are the followers of Jezebel at Thyatira.
Two, at Smyrna and Philadelphia, were in a flourishing state, and are therefore
only exhorted to steadfastness.
There can be no state, either of any pastor, Church, or single person, which
has not here suitable instructions. All, whether ministers or hearers, together
with their secret or open enemies, in all places and all ages, may draw hence
necessary self-knowledge, reproof, commendation, warning, or confirmation.
Whether any be as dead as the angel at Sardis, or as much alive as the angel
at Philadelphia, this book is sent to him, and the Lord Jesus hath something
to say to him therein. For the seven Churches with their angels represent the
whole Christian Church, dispersed throughout the whole world, as it subsists
not (as some have imagined) in one age after another, but in every age. This
is a point of deep importance, and always necessary to be remembered; that
these seven Churches are, as it were, a sample of the whole Church of Christ,
as it was then, as it is now, and as it will be in all ages. *Do the first works*—
Outwardly and inwardly, or thou canst never regain the first love: *But if not*—
By this word is the warning sharpened to those five Churches which are called
to repent; (for if Ephesus was threatened, how much more shall Sardis and
Laodicea be afraid,) and according as they obey the call or not, there is a promise or a threatening, chap. ii, 5, 16, 22; iii, 3, 20. But even in the threatening
the promise is implied, in case of true repentance. *I come to thee, and will
remove thy candlestick out of its place*—I will remove, unless thou repent, the
flock now under thy care to another place, where they shall be better taken care
of. But, from the flourishing state of the Church of Ephesus after this, there
is reason to believe he did repent.
6. *But thou hast this*—Divine grace seeks whatever may help him that is
fallen to recover his standing; *that thou hatest the works of the Nicolaitans*—
Probably so called from Nicolas, one of the seven deacons, Acts vi, 5. Their
doctrines and lives were equally corrupt. They allowed the most abominable
lewdness and adulteries, as well as sacrificing to idols; all which they placed
among things indifferent, and plead for as branches of Christian liberty.
7. *He that hath an ear, let him hear*—Every man, whoever can hear at all,
ought carefully to hear this. *What the Spirit saith*—In these great and precious
promises, *to the Churches*—And in them to every one that overcometh; that
goeth on from faith to faith, and by faith to full victory over the world, and the
flesh, and the devil.
In these seven letters twelve promises are contained, which are an extract of
all the promises of God. Some of them are not expressly mentioned again in

8   And to the angel of the Church at Smyrna write, These things
9   saith the First and the Last, who was dead and is alive; I know
thy works, and thy affliction and poverty, (but thou art rich,)
and the reviling of those who say they are Jews, and are not,
10 but a synagogue of Satan. Fear none of those things which
thou art about to suffer; behold the devil is about to cast some
of you into prison, that ye may be tried, and ye shall have affliction ten days: Be thou faithful unto death, and I will give thee
11 the crown of life. He that hath an ear, let him hear what the
Spirit saith to the Churches: He that overcometh shall not be
hurt by the second death.

this book, as *the hidden manna*, the inscription of *the name of the New Jerusalem*, the *sitting upon the throne*. Some resemble what is afterward mentioned,
as *the hidden name*, chap. xix, 12; *the ruling the nations*, chap. xix, 15; *the
morning star*, chap. xxii, 16. And some are expressly mentioned, as *the tree of
life*, chap. xxii, 2. Freedom from *the second death*, chap. xx, 6; the name in *the
book of life*, chap. xx, 16; xxi, 27; the remaining *in the temple of God*, chap. vii,
15; the inscription of *the name of God and of the Lamb*, chap. xiv, 1; xxii, 4.
In these promises sometimes the enjoyment of the highest goods, sometimes
deliverance from the greatest evils, is mentioned. And each implies the other,
so that where either part is expressed, the whole is to be understood. That
part is expressed which has most resemblance to the virtues or works of him
that was spoken to in the letter preceding. *To eat of the tree of life*—The first
thing promised in these letters, is the last, and the highest in the accomplish
ment, chap. xxii, 2, 14, 19. *The tree of life*, and *the water of life*, go together,
chap. xxii, 1, 2; both implying the living with God eternally: *in the paradise
of my God*—The word *paradise* means a garden of pleasure. In the .earthly
paradise there was one tree of life: there are no other trees in the paradise
of God.

8. *These things saith the First and the Last, who was dead and is alive*—How
directly does this description tend to confirm him against the fear of death! ver.
10, 11. Even with the comfort wherewith St. John himself was comforted,
chap. i, 17, 18, shall the angel of this Church be comforted.

9. *I know thy affliction and poverty*—A poor prerogative in the eyes of the
world! The angel at Philadelphia likewise had in their sight but a *little strength*.
And yet these two were the most honourable of all in the eyes of the Lord.
But thou art rich—In faith and love, of more value than all the kingdoms of the
earth. *Who say they are Jews*—God's own people; *and are not*—They are not
Jews inwardly, not circumcised in heart: *but a synagogue of Satan*—Who, like
them, was a liar and a murderer, from the beginning.

10. The first and last words of this verse are particularly directed to the
minister; whence we may gather, that his suffering and the affliction of the
Church were at the same time, and of the same continuance. *Fear none of those
things which thou art about to suffer*—Probably by means of the false Jews. *Behold*—This intimates the nearness of the affliction. Perhaps the *ten* days began
on the very day that the Revelation was read at Smyrna, or at least very soon
after. *The devil*—Who sets all persecutors to work; and these more particularly: *is about to cast some of you*—Christians at Smyrna; where, in the first
ages, the blood of many martyrs was shed: *into prison, that ye may be tried*—
To your unspeakable advantage, 1 Pet. iv, 12–14: *and ye shall have affliction*—
Either in your own persons, or by sympathizing with your brethren: *ten days*
—(Literally taken) in the end of Domitian's persecution, which was stopped by
the edict of the Emperor Nerva. *Be thou faithful*—Our Lord does not say, *till
I come*, as in the other letters, but *unto death*—Signifying that the angel of
this Church should quickly after seal his testimony with his blood; fifty years
before the martyrdom of Polycarp, for whom some have mistaken him: *and I
will give thee the crown of life*—The peculiar reward of them who are *faithful
unto death*.

11. *The second death—The lake of fire*, the portion of the *fearful,* who do not
overcome, chap. **xxi**, 8.

12   And to the angel of the Church at Pergamos write, These
13 things saith he who hath the sharp two-edged sword. I know
thy works, and where thou dwellest, where the throne of Satan
is; and thou holdest fast my name, and hast not denied my faith,
in the days wherein Antipas *was* my faithful witness, who was
14 slain among you where Satan dwelleth. But I have a few things
against thee, that thou hast there them that hold the doctrine of
Balaam, who taught Balak to cast a stumbling block before the
sons of Israel, to eat things sacrificed to idols, and to commit
15 fornication. In like manner thou also hast them that hold the
16 doctrine of the Nicolaitans, which I hate. Repent therefore; if
not, I come to thee, and will fight against them with the sword
17 of my mouth. He that hath an ear, let him hear what the
Spirit saith to the Churches. To him that overcometh will I
give of the hidden manna, and will give him a white stone,
and on the stone a new name written, which none knoweth, but
he that receiveth it.
18·   And to the angel of the Church at Thyatira write, These
things saith the Son of God, who hath eyes as a flame of fire,

---

12. *The sword*—With which I will cut off the impenitent, ver. 16.

13. *Where the throne of Satan is*—Pergamos was above measure given to
idolatry: so Satan had his throne and full residence there   *Thou holdest fast my
name*—Openly and resolutely confessing me before men : *in the days wherein
Antipas*—Martyred under Domitian; *was my faithful witness*—Happy is he to
whom Jesus, the faithful and true witness, giveth such a testimony !

14. *But thou hast there*—Whom thou oughtest immediately to have cast out
from the flock: *them that hold the doctrine of Balaam*—Doctrine nearly resembling his: *who taught Balak*—And the rest of the Moabites, *to cast a stumbling
block before the sons of Israel*—They are generally termed *the children,* but here
the sons of Israel, in opposition to the daughters of Moab, by whom Balaam
enticed them to fornication and idolatry: *to eat things sacrificed to idols*—
Which, in so idolatrous a city as Pergamos, was in the highest degree hurtful
to Christianity: *and to commit fornication*—Which was constantly joined with
the idol worship of the heathens.

15. *In like manner thou also*—As well as the angel at Ephesus; *hast them
that hold the doctrine of the Nicolaitans*—And thou sufferest them to remain in
the flock.

16. *If not, I come to thee*—Who wilt not wholly escape when I punish them .
and will fight with them—Not with the Nicolaitans, who are mentioned only by
the by; but the followers of Balaam; *with the sword of my mouth*—With my just
and fierce displeasure. Balaam himself was first withstood by the angel of the
Lord *with his sword* drawn, Num. xxii, 23, and afterward *slain with the sword,*
Num. xxxi, 8.

17. *To him that overcometh*—And eateth not of those sacrifices; *will I give
of the hidden manna*—Described John vi. The new name answers to this: it is
now *hid with Christ in God.* The Jewish manna was kept in the ancient ark
of the covenant. The heavenly ark of the covenant appears under the trumpet
of the seventh angel, chap. xi, 19, where also *the hidden manna* is mentioned
again. It seems properly to mean the full, glorious, everlasting fruition of God.
And I will give him a white stone—The ancients, on many occasions, gave their
votes on judgment by small stones: by black they condemned; by white ones
they acquitted. Sometimes also they wrote on small, smooth stones. Here may
be an allusion to both. *And a new name*—So Jacob, after his victory, gained the
new name of Israel. Wouldst thou know what thy *new name* will be: the way
to this is plain; *overcome.* Till then all thy inquiries are vain. Thou wilt then
read it on the *white stone.*

18. *And to the angel of the Church at Thyatira*—Where the faithful were but
a little flock; *these things saith the Son of God*—See how great he is, who

19 and his feet like fine brass. I know thy love and faith, and thy
service and patience, and thy last works more than the first.
20 But I have against thee, that thou sufferest that woman Jezebel,
who calleth herself a prophetess, and teacheth and seduceth my
servants to commit fornication, and to eat things sacrificed to
21 idols : And I gave her time to repent of her fornication ; but she
22 will not repent. Behold, I will cast her into a bed, and them
that commit adultery with her, into great affliction, unless they
23 repent of her works. And I will kill her children with death ;
and all the Churches shall know that I am he who searcheth the
reins and hearts ; and I will give you, every one, according to
24 your works. But I say to you, the rest that are at Thyatira, As
many as do not hold this doctrine, who have not known the

---

appeared *like a Son of man!* chap. i, 12. *Who hath eyes as a flame of fire—
Searching the reins and the heart,* ver. 23 ; *and his feet like fine brass*—Denoting
his immense *strength.* Job comprises both these, his wisdom to discern whatever is amiss, and his power to avenge it, in one sentence, chap. xlii, 2. *No
thought is hidden from him, and he can do all things.*

19. *I know thy love*—How different a character is this from that of the angel
of the Church at Ephesus? The latter could not bear the wicked, and hated
the works of the Nicolaitans ; but had left his first love and first works. The
former retained his first love, and had more and more works, but did bear the
wicked, did not withstand them with becoming vehemence. Mixed characters
both ; yet the latter, not the former, is reproved for his fall, and commanded
to repent : *and faith, and thy service, and patience—Love* is shown, exercised,
and improved, by serving God and our neighbour ; so is faith by patience and
good works.

20. *But thou sufferest that woman Jezebel*—Who ought not to teach at all,
1 Tim. ii, 12, *to teach and seduce my servants*—At Pergamos were many followers of Balaam ; at Thyatira, one grand deceiver. Many of the ancients have
delivered, that this was the wife of the pastor himself. Jezebel of old led the
people of God to open idolatry. This Jezebel (fitly called by her name from
the resemblance between their works) led them to partake in the idolatry of the
heathens. This she seems to have done by first enticing them to fornication,
just as Balaam did ; whereas at Pergamos they were first enticed to idolatry,
and afterward to fornication.

21. *And I gave her time to repent*—So great is the power of Christ : *but she
will not repent*—So, though repentance is the gift of God, man may refuse it :
God will not compel.

22. *I will cast her into a bed—into great affliction, and them that commit* either
carnal or spiritual *adultery with her, unless they repent*—She had her time before :
of her works—Those to which she had enticed them, and which she had committed with them.

It is observable, the angel of the Church at Thyatira was only blamed for
suffering her. This fault ceased when God took vengeance on her. Therefore
he is not expressly exhorted to repent, though it is implied.

23. *And I will kill her children*—Those which she hath borne in adultery, and
them whom she hath seduced ; *with death*—This expression denotes death by the
plague, or by some manifest stroke of God's hand. Probably the remarkable
vengeance taken on her children was the token of the certainty of all the rest :
and all the Churches—To which thou now writest, *shall know that I search the
reins*—The desires, *and hearts*—Thoughts.

24. *But I say to you,* who *do not hold this doctrine*—Of Jezebel ; *who have
not known the depths of Satan*—O happy ignorance ! *as they speak*—That were
continually boasting of the *deep things* which they taught. Our Lord owns
they were *deep,* even deep as hell ; for they were the very depths of Satan.
Were these the same of which Martin Luther speaks ? 'Tis well if there are
not some of his countrymen, now in England, who know them too well : *I will
lay upon you no other burden*—Than that you have already suffered from Jezebel
and her adherents.

depths of Satan, as they speak, I will lay upon you no other
25 burden. But what ye have, hold fast till I come. And he that
26 overcometh, and keepeth my works unto the end, to him will I
27 give power over the nations, (And he shall rule them with a rod
of iron; they shall be dashed in pieces like a potter's vessel,) as
28 I also have received from my Father. And I will give him the
29 morning star. He that hath an ear, let him hear what the Spirit
saith to the Churches.

III. And to the angel of the Church at Sardis write, These things
saith he that hath the seven spirits of God, and the seven stars,
I know thy works, that thou hast a name that thou livest, but art
2 dead. Be watchful, and strengthen the things which remain,
which are ready to die; for I have not found thy works com-
3 plete before my God. Remember therefore how thou hast received and heard, and hold fast, and repent. If thou watch not
I will come as a thief, and thou shalt not know at what hour I
will come upon thee. Yet thou hast a few names in Sardis, who
have not defiled their garments; and they shall walk with me in
5 white: they are worthy. He that overcometh, he shall be clothed
in white raiment; and I will not blot his name out of the book
of life, and I will confess his name, before my Father and before
6 his angels. He that hath an ear, let him hear what the Spirit
saith to the Churches.

25. *What ye*—Both the angel and the Church have.

26. *My works*—Those which I have commanded; *to him will I give power over the nations*—That is, I will give him to share with me in that glorious victory which the Father hath promised me over all the nations who as yet resist me, Psalm ii, 8, 9.

27. *And he shall rule them*—That is, shall share with me when I do this; *with a rod of iron*—With irresistible power, employed on those only who will not otherwise submit; who will hereby *be dashed in pieces*—Totally conquered.

28. *I will give him the morning star*—Thou, O Jesus, art the morning star. O give thyself to me! Then will I desire no sun, only thee, who art the sun also. He whom this star enlightens, has always morning and no evening. The duties and promises here answer each other. The valiant conqueror has power over the stubborn nations. And he that, after having conquered his enemies, keeps the words of Christ to the end, shall *have the morning star*—An unspeakable brightness and peaceful dominion in him.

III. 1. *The seven spirits of God*—The Holy Spirit, from whom alone all spiritual life and strength proceed: *and the seven stars*—Which are subordinate to him: *thou hast a name that thou livest*—A fair reputation, a goodly outside appearance. But that Spirit seeth through all things, and every empty appearance vanishes before him.

2. *The things which remain*—In thy soul; knowledge of the truth, good desires, and convictions: *which are ready to die*—Wherever pride, indolence, or levity revives, all the fruits of the Spirit are ready to die.

3. *Remember how*—Humbly, zealously, seriously, thou didst receive the grace of God once, *and hear*—His word; *and hold fast*—The grace thou hast received; *and repent*—According to the word thou hast heard.

4. *Yet thou hast a few names*—That is, persons. But though few, they had not separated themselves from the rest; otherwise the angel of Sardis would not have had them. Yet it was no virtue of his, that they were unspotted; whereas it was his fault that they were but few: *who have not defiled their garments*—Either by spotting themselves, or by partaking of other men's sins: *they shall walk with me in white*—In joy, in perfect holiness; in glory; *they are worthy*—A few good among many bad, are doubly acceptable to God. O how much happier is this worthiness than that mentioned, chap. xvi, 6.

5. *He shall be clothed in white raiment*—The colour of victory, joy, and triumph

7 And to the angel of the Church at Philadelphia write, These things saith the Holy One, the True One, he that hath the key of David, he that openeth, and none shutteth, and shutteth, and
8 none openeth · I know thy works, (behold, I have given before thee an opened door, none can shut it,) that thou hast a little strength, and hast kept my word, and hast not denied my name.
9 Behold, I bring them of the synagogue of Satan, who say they are Jews, and are not, but lie; behold, I will make them come and bow down before thy feet, and know that I have loved thee:
10 Because thou hast kept the word of my patience, I also will keep thee from the hour of temptation, which shall come upon the
11 whole world, to try them that dwell upon the earth. I come quickly. Hold fast what thou hast, that none take thy crown.
12 He that overcometh, I will make him a pillar in the temple of my God, and he shall go out no more: and I will write upon him the name of my God and the name of the city of my God, the New Jerusalem, which cometh down out of heaven from my
13 God, and my new name. He that hath an ear, let him hear what the Spirit saith to the Churches.

and I will not blot his name out of the book of life—Like that of the angel of the Church at Sardis, but he shall live for ever. *I will confess his name*—As one of my faithful servants and soldiers.

7. *The Holy One, the True One*—Two great and glorious names. *He that hath the key of David*—A master of a family, or a prince, has one or more keys wherewith he can open and shut all the doors of his house or palace. So had David a key, (a token of right and sovereignty,) which was afterward adjudged to Eliakim, Isaiah xxii, 22. Much more has Christ, the Son of David, the key of the spiritual city of David, the New Jerusalem: the supreme right, power, and authority, as in his own house. He openeth this to all that overcome, *and none shutteth*—He shutteth it against all the fearful; *and none openeth*—Likewise, when he openeth a door on earth for his work or his servants, none can shut; and when he shutteth against whatever would hurt or defile, none can open.

8. *I have given before thee an open door*—To enter into the joy of thy Lord, and meantime to go on unhindered in every good work. *Thou hast a little strength*—But little outward human strength: a little, poor, mean, despicable company. Yet thou *hast kept my word*—Both in judgment and practice.

9. *Behold I*—Who have all power; and they must then comply; *I will make them come and bow down before thy feet*—Pay thee the lowest homage, *and know*—At length, that all depends on my love, and that thou hast a place therein. O how often does the judgment of the people turn quite around, when the Lord looketh upon them! Job xlii, 7.

10. *Because thou hast kept the word of my patience*—The word of Christ is indeed a word of patience; *I also will keep thee*—O happy exemption from that spreading calamity! *from the hour of temptation*—So that thou shalt not enter into temptation, but it shall pass over thee. The hour denotes the short time of its continuance, that is, at any one place. At every one it was very sharp, though short, wherein the great tempter was not idle, chap. ii, 10, which hour *shall come upon the whole earth*—The whole Roman empire. It went over the Christians and over the Jews and heathens; though in a very different manner. This was the time of the persecution under the seemingly virtuous Emperor Trajan. The two preceding persecutions were under those monsters, Nero and Domitian. But Trajan was so admired for his goodness, and his persecution was of such a nature that it was a temptation indeed, and did thoroughly try them that dwelt upon the earth.

11. *Thy crown*—Which is ready for thee if thou endure to the end.

12. *I will make him a pillar in the temple of my God*—I will fix him as beautiful, as useful, and as immovable as a pillar in the Church of God; *and he shall go out no more*—But shall be holy and happy for ever. *And I will write upon him the name of my God*—So that the nature and image of God shall appear

14 And to the angel of the Church at Laodicea write, These things saith the Amen, the faithful and true witness, the begin-
15 ning of the creation of God. I know thy works, that thou art
16 neither cold nor hot; O that thou wert cold or hot! So because thou art lukewarm, and neither cold nor hot, I will spue thee
17 out of my mouth. Because thou sayest, I am rich, and have enriched myself, and have need of nothing, and knowest not that thou art wretched, and pitiable, and poor, and blind, and naked.
18 I counsel thee to buy of me gold purified in the fire, that thou mayest be rich; and white raiment, that thou mayest be clothed, and the shame of thy nakedness may not appéar: and eye salve
19 to anoint thiné eyes, that thou mayest see. Whomsoever I love,
20 I rebuke and chasten: be zealous and repent. Behold, I stand at the door and knock: if any man hear my voice and open the door, I will come in to him, and sup with him, and he with me.
21 He that overcometh, I will give him to sit with me on my throne, as, I also have overcome, and sat down with my Father on his
22 throne. He that hath an ear, let him hear what the Spirit saith to the Churches.

visibly upon him. *And the name of the city of my God*—Giving him a title to dwell in the New Jerusalem; *and my new name*—A share in that joy which I entered into, after overcoming all my enemies.

14. *To the angel of the Church at Laodicea*—For these St. Paul had had a great concern, Col. ii, 1. *These things saith the Amen* -That is the true One, the God of truth; *the beginning*—The author, prince, and ruler *of the creation of God*—Of all creatures; the beginning, or author, by whom God made them all.

1 . *I know thy works*—Thy disposition and behaviour, though thou knowest it not thyself; *that thou art neither cold*—An utter stranger to the things of God, having no care or thought about them; *nor hot*—As boiling water: so ought we to be penetrated and heated by the fire of love. *O that thou wert*—This wish of our Lord plainly implies that he does not work on us irresistibly, as the fire does on the water which it heats; *cold or hot*—Even if thou wert cold, without any thought or profession of religion, there would be more hope of thy recovery.

16. *So because thou art lukewarm*—The effect of lukewarm water is well known; *I will spue thee out of my mouth*—I will utterly cast thee from me; that is, unless thou repent.

17. *Because thou sayest*—Therefore *I counsel thee*, &c. *I am rich*—In gifts and grace, as well as worldly goods. *And knowest not that thou art*—In God's account, *wretched and pitiable*.

18. *I counsel thee*—Who art *poor, and blind, and naked, to buy of me*—Without money or price, *gold purified in the fire*—True living faith, which is purified in the furnace of affliction; *and white raiment*—True holiness, *and eye salve*—Spiritual illumination; the unction of the Holy One, which teacheth all things.

19. *Whomsoever I love*—Even thee, thou poor Laodicean! O how much has his unwearied love to do? *I rebuke*—For what is past: *and chasten*—That they may amend for the time to come.

20. *I stand at the door and knock*—Even at this instant; while he is speaking this word; *If any man open*—Willingly receive me : *I will sup with him*—Refreshing him with my graces and gifts, and delighting myself in what I have given; *and he with me*—In life everlasting.

21. *I will give him to sit with me on my throne*—In unspeakable happiness and glory. Elsewhere heaven itself is termed the throne of God. But this throne is in heaven.

22. *He that hath an ear, let him hear*, &c. This stands in the three former letters before the promise; in the four latter, after it: clearly dividing the seven into two parts, the first containing three, the last four letters. The titles given our Lord in the three former letters peculiarly respect his power after his resur-

IV. After these things I saw, and behold, a door opened in heaven, and the first voice which I had heard, as of a trumpet talking with me, said, Come up hither, and I will show thee things 2 which must be hereafter. And immediately I was in the Spirit, and behold a throne was set in heaven, and one sitting on the

rection and ascension, particularly over his Church; those in the four latter his Divine glory, and unity with the Father and the Holy Spirit. Again, this word being placed before the promises in the three former letters, excludes the false apostles at Ephesus, the false Jews at Smyrna, and the partakers with the heathens at Pergamos, from having any share therein. In the four latter being placed after them, it leaves the promises immediately joined with Christ's address to the angel of the Church: to show that the fulfilling of these was near; whereas the others reach beyond the end of the world. It should be observed that the *overcoming* or victory, (to which alone these *peculiar* promises are annexed,) is not the ordinary victory obtained by every believer, but a special victory over great and peculiar temptations, by those that are strong in faith.

Chap. iv. We are now entering on the main prophecy: the whole Revelation may be divided thus:

The 1st, 2d, and 3d chapters contain the introduction;
The 4th and 5th, the proposition;
The 6th, 7th, 8th, and 9th, describe things which are already fulfilled;
The 10th–14th, things which are now fulfilling;
The 15th–19th, things which will be fulfilled shortly;
The 20th, 21st, 22d, things at a greater distance.

IV. 1. *After these things*—As if he had said, after I had written these letters from the mouth of the Lord. By the particle *and*, the several parts of this prophecy are usually connected: by the expression *after these things*, they are distinguished from each other, chap. vii, 9; xix, 1, by that expression, *and after these things* they are distinguished and yet connected, chap. vii, 1; xv, 5; xviii, 1. St. John always saw and heard, and then immediately wrote down, one part after another. And one part is constantly divided from another by some one of these expressions. *I saw*—Here begins the relation of the main vision, which is connected throughout, as it appears from the throne and him that sitteth thereon, the Lamb, (who hitherto hath appeared in the form of a man,) *the four living creatures* and *the four and twenty elders*, represented from this place to the end. From this place it is absolutely necessary to keep in mind the genuine order of the text, as it stands in the preceding table. *A door opened in heaven*—Several of these openings are successively mentioned. Here *a door is opened*, afterward *the temple of God in heaven*, chap. xi, 19; xv, 5: and at last *heaven* itself, chap. xix, 11: by each of these St. John gains a new and more extended prospect: *and the first voice which I had heard*—Namely, that of Christ, (afterward he heard the voices of many others,) *said, Come up hither*—Not in body, but in spirit; which was immediately done.

2. *And immediately I was in the Spirit*—Even in a higher degree than before, chap. i, 10, *and behold a throne was set in heaven*—St. John is to write *things which shall be*. And in order thereto he is here shown, after a heavenly manner, how whatever shall be, whether good or bad, flows out of invisible fountains: and how after it is done on the visible theatre of the world and the Church, it flows back again into the invisible world, as its proper and final scope. Here commentators divide: some proceed theologically, others historically; whereas the right way is to join both together.

The court of heaven is here laid open: and the throne of God is as it were the centre, from which every thing in the visible world goes forth, and to which every thing returns. Here also the kingdom of Satan is disclosed; and hence we may extract the most important things out of the most comprehensive, and at the same time the most secret history of the kingdom of hell and heaven. But herein we must be content to know only what is expressly revealed in this book. This describes not barely what good or evil is successively transacted on earth, but how each springs from the kingdom of light or darkness, and continually tends to the source whence it sprung. So that no man can explain all that is contained therein, from the history of the Church militant only.

And yet the histories of past ages have their use, as this book is properly

3 throne. And he that sat was in appearance like a jasper and
  a sardine stone; and a rainbow *was* round about the throne, in
4 appearance like an emerald. And round about the throne *are*
  four and twenty thrones, and on the thrones four and twenty
  elders sitting, clothed in white raiment, and upon their heads
5 crowns of gold. And out of the throne go forth lightnings, and
  voices, and thunders, and seven lamps of fire burn before the
6 throne, which are the seven spirits of God. And before the
  throne *is* a sea as of glass, like crystal; and in the midst of the

prophetical. The more therefore we observe the accomplishment of it, so much
the more may we praise God, in his truth, wisdom, justice, and almighty power,
and learn to suit ourselves to the time according to the remarkable directions
contained in the prophecy. *And one sat on the throne*—As a king, governor, and
judge. Here is described God, the Almighty, the Father of heaven, in his
majesty, glory, and dominion.

3. *And he that sat was in appearance*—Shone with a visible lustre, like that
of sparkling precious stones, such as those which were of old on the high
priest's breastplate, and those placed as the foundations of the New Jerusalem,
chap. xxi, 19, 20. If there is any thing emblematical in the colours of these
stones, possibly the *jasper*, which is transparent and of a glittering white, with
an intermixture of beautiful colours, may be a symbol of God's purity with
various other perfections, which shine in all his dispensations. The *sardine
stone*, of blood-red colour, may be an emblem of his justice, and the vengeance
he was about to execute on his enemies. *An emerald*, being green, may betoken
favour to the good; *a rainbow*, the everlasting covenant: see Gen. ix, 9. And
this being *round about* the whole breadth of the *throne*, fixed the distance of those
who stood or sat round it.

4. *And round about the throne*—In a circle, *are four and twenty thrones, and
on the thrones four and twenty elders*—The most holy of all former ages, (Isa.
xxiv, 23; Heb. xii, 1,) representing the whole body of the saints: *sitting*—In
general; but falling down when they worship: *clothed in white raiment*—This
and their *golden crowns* show that they had already finished their course, and
taken their places among the citizens of heaven. They are never termed souls,
and hence it is probable that they had glorified bodies already. Compare Matt.
xxvii, 52.

5. *And out of the throne go forth lightnings*—Which affect the sight; *voices*—
Which affect the hearing; *thunderings*—Which cause the whole body to tremble.—
Weak men account all this terrible; but to the inhabitants of heaven it is a mere
source of joy and pleasure, mixed with reverence to the Divine Majesty. Even
to the saints on earth these convey light and protection, but to their enemies
terror and destruction.

6. *And before the throne is a sea as of glass, like crystal*—Wide and deep, pure
and clear, transparent and still. Both the seven lamps of fire and this sea are
before the throne: and both may mean the seven spirits of God, the Holy Ghost;
whose powers and operations are frequently represented both under the emblem
of fire and of water. We read again, chap. xv, 2, of *a sea as of glass:* where
there is no mention of the seven lamps of fire; but, on the contrary, the sea
itself is mingled with fire. We read also, chap. xxii, 1, of a stream of water
of life, clear as crystal. Now the *sea* which was *before the throne*, and the
stream which goes out of the throne, may both mean the same, namely, the
Spirit of God. *And in the midst of the throne*—With respect to its height:
round about the throne—That is, toward the four quarters, east, west, north, and
south; *were four living creatures*—(Not beasts, any more than birds.) These
seem to be taken from the cherubim in the visions of Isaiah and Ezekiel, and in
the holy of holies. They are doubtless some of the principal powers of heaven;
but of what order it is not easy to determine. It is very probable that the
twenty-four elders may represent the Jewish Church. Their harps seem to
intimate their having belonged to the ancient tabernacle service, where they
were wont to be used. If so, the *living creatures* may represent the Christian
Church. Their number is also symbolical of universality, and agrees with the
dispensation of the Gospel, which extended to all nations under heaven, and the

throne and round about the throne four living creatures, full of
7 eyes before and behind. And the first living creature *is* like a
lion, and the second living creature *is* like a calf, and the third
living creature hath a face as a man, and the fourth *is* like a
8 flying eagle. And the four living creatures hath each of them

---

new song which they all sing, saying, Thou hast redeemed us out of every
kindred, and tongue, and people, and nation, (chap. v, 9,) could not possibly suit
the Jewish without the Christian Church. The first *living creature was like a
lion*—To signify undaunted courage: the second *like a calf* or *ox*—Ezek. i, 10,
to signify unwearied patience: *the third with the face of a man*—To signify
prudence and compassion: the fourth *like an eagle*—To signify activity and
vigour; *full of eyes*—To betoken wisdom and knowledge: *before*—To see the
face of Him that sitteth on the throne; *and behind*—To see what is done among
the creatures.

7. *And the first*—Just such were the four cherubim in Ezekiel, who supported the moving throne of God: whereas each of those that overshadowed
the mercy seat in the holy of holies, had all these four faces: whence a late
great man supposes them to have been emblematical of the Trinity, and the
incarnation of the second Person. *A flying eagle*—That is, with wings ex-
panded.

8. *Each of them had six wings*—As had each of the seraphim in Isaiah's
vision. *Two covered his face*—In token of humility and reverence: *two his
feet*—Perhaps in token of readiness and diligence for executing Divine com-
missions: *round about and within they are full of eyes*—Round about, to see every
thing which is farther off from the throne than they are themselves: *and within*
—On the inner part of the circle which they make with one another. First,
they look from the centre to the circumference, then from the circumference to
the centre. *And they rest not*—O happy unrest! *Day and night*—As we speak
on earth. But there is no night in heaven; *and say, Holy, holy, holy*—Is the
Three-one God.

There are two words in the original very different from each other, both which
we translate holy. The one means properly merciful; but the other, which
occurs here, implies much more. This holiness is the sum of all praise, which
is given to the almighty Creator, for all that he does and reveals concerning
himself, till the new song brings with it new matter of glory.

This word properly signifies separated, both in Hebrew and other languages.
And when God is termed holy, it denotes that excellence which is altogether
peculiar to himself; and the glory flowing from all his attributes conjoined,
shining forth from all his works, and darkening all things beside itself, whereby he is, and eternally remains, in an incomprehensible manner, separate and
at a distance, not only from all that is impure, but likewise from all that is
created.

God is separate from all things. He is, and works from himself, out of
himself, in himself, through himself, for himself. Therefore, He is the first
and the last, the only One and the Eternal, living and happy, endless and unchangeable, almighty, omniscient, wise and true, just and faithful, gracious and
merciful.

Hence it is, that holy and holiness mean the same as God and Godhead: and.
as we say of a king, his majesty; so the Scripture says of God, his holiness,
Heb. xii, 10. The Holy Spirit is the Spirit of God. When God is spoken of,
he is often named The Holy One. And as God swears by his name, so he does
also by his holiness, that is, by himself.

This holiness is often styled glory: often his holiness and glory are celebrated
together, Lev. x, 3; Isa. vi, 3; for holiness is covered glory, and glory is uncovered holiness. The Scripture speaks abundantly of the holiness and glory
of the Father, the Son, and the Holy Ghost. And hereby is the mystery of the
Holy Trinity eminently confirmed.

That is also termed holy which is consecrated to Him, and to that end separated from other things. And so is that wherein we may be like God, or united
to him.

In the hymn resembling this, recorded by Isaiah, chap. vi, 3, is added, *The*

six wings; round about and within they are full of eyes: and they rest not day and night, saying, Holy, holy, holy is the Lord God, the Almighty, who was, and who is, and who cometh

9 And when the living creatures give glory, and honour, and thanks to him that sitteth upon the throne, that liveth for ever

10 and ever, The four and twenty elders fall down before him that sitteth upon the thrône, and worship him that liveth for ever and

11 ever, and cast their crowns before the throne, saying, Worthy art thou, O Lord our God, to receive the glory, and the honour, and the power: for thou hast created all things, and through thy will they were, and are created.

V. And I saw in the right hand of him that sat upon the throne

---

whole earth is full of his glory. But this is deferred in the Revelation, till the glory of the Lord (his enemies being destroyed) fills the earth.

10. *And when the living creatures give glory—the elders fall down*—That is, as often as the living creatures give glory, immediately the elders fall down. The expression implies, that they did so at the same instant, and that they both did this frequently. The living creatures do not say directly, *Holy, holy, holy art thou:* but only bend a little out of deep reverence, and say, *Holy, holy, holy is the Lord.* But the elders, when they are *fallen down,* may say, *Worthy art thou, O Lord our God.*

11. *Worthy art thou to receive*—This he receives not only when he is thus praised, but also when he destroys his enemies and glorifies himself anew; *the glory, and the honour, and the power*—Answering the thrice holy of the living creatures, ver. 9. *For thou hast created all things*—Creation is the ground of all the works of God. Therefore for this, as well as for all his other works, will he be praised to all eternity: *and through thy will they were*—They began to be. It is to the free, gracious, and powerfully working will of Him who cannot possibly need any thing, that all things owe their first existence: *and are created*—That is, continue in being ever since they were created.

V. 1. *And I saw*—This is a continuation of the same narrative: *in the right hand*—The emblem of his all-ruling power. He held it openly, in order to give it to him that was worthy. It is scarce needful to observe, that there is not in heaven any real book of parchment or paper, or that Christ does really stand there, in the shape of a lion or of a lamb. Neither is there on earth any monstrous beast, with seven heads and ten horns. But as there is upon earth something which, in its kind, answers such a representation, so there are in heaven Divine counsels and transactions answerable to these figurative expressions. All this was represented to St. John at Patmos in one day, by way of vision. But the accomplishment of it extends from that time throughout all ages. Writings serve to inform us of distant and of future things. And hence things which are yet to come are figuratively said to be *written in* God's *book:* so were at that time the contents of this weighty prophecy. But the book was sealed. Now comes the opening and accomplishing also of the great things that are, as it were, the letters of it. *A book written within and without*—That is, no part of it blank, full of matter; *sealed with seven seals*—According to the seven principal parts contained in it, one on the outside of each. The usual books of the ancients were not like ours, but were volumes, or long pieces of parchment, rolled upon a long stick, as we frequently roll silks. Such was this represented, which was sealed with seven seals. Not as if the apostle saw all the seals at once: for there were seven volumes wrapped up one within another, each of which was sealed: so that upon opening and unrolling the first, the second appeared to be sealed up, till that was opened, and so on to the seventh. The book and its seals represent all power both in heaven and earth given to Christ. A copy of this book is contained in the following chapters. By the trumpets, contained under the seventh seal, the kingdom of the world is shaken, that it may at length become the kingdom of Christ. By the phials, under the seventh trumpet, the power of the beast, and whatsoever is connected with it, is broken. This sum of all we should have continually before our eyes: so the whole revelation flows in its natural order.

2 a book written within and without, sealed with seven seals. And
  I saw a strong angel proclaiming with a loud voice, Who *is*
3 worthy to open the book, and to loose the seals thereof? And
  none in heaven, or in earth, neither under the earth, was able to
4 open the book, neither to look thereon. And I wept much that
  none was found worthy to open the book, neither to look thereon.
5 And one of the elders saith to me, Weep not; behold, the Lion
  of the tribe of Judah, the root of David, hath prevailed to open
6 the book and the seals thereof. And I beheld, in the midst of
  the throne, and of the four living creatures, and in the midst of
  the elders, a Lamb standing as if he had been slain, having seven
  horns and seven eyes, which are the seven Spirits of God, sent
7 forth into all the earth. And he came and took the book out of

---

2. *And I saw a strong angel*—This proclamation to every creature was too
great for a man to make, and yet not unbecoming the Lamb himself. It was therefore made by an angel, and one of uncommon eminence.

3. *And none*—No creature; no, not Mary herself; *in heaven, or in earth, nei-*
ther under the earth—That is, none in the universe. For these are the three
great regions into which the whole creation is divided; *was able to open the book*
—To declare the counsels of God; *nor to look thereon*—So as to understand any
part of it.

4. *And I wept much*—A weeping which sprung from greatness of mind. The
tenderness of heart which he always had, appeared more clearly, now he was
out of his own power. The Revelation was not written without tears; neither
without tears will it be understood. How far are they from the temper of
St. John, who inquire after any thing rather than the contents of this book?
yea, who applaud their own clemency, if they excuse those that do inquire into
them?

5. *And one of the elders*—Probably one of those who rose with Christ, and
afterward ascended into heaven; perhaps one of the patriarchs; some think it
was Jacob, from whose prophecy the name of Lion is given him, Gen. xlix, 9.
The Lion of the tribe of Judah—The victorious Prince who is, like a lion,
able to tear all his enemies in pieces; *the root of David*—As God, the root and
source of David's family, Isa. xi, 1, 10; *hath prevailed to open the book*—Hath
overcome all obstructions, and obtained the honour to disclose the Divine
counsels.

6. *And I saw*—First, Christ in or on the midst of the throne; secondly, the
four living creatures making the inner circle round him; and thirdly, the four
and twenty elders, making a larger circle round him and them: *standing*—He
lieth no more; he no more falls on his face; the days of his weakness and
mourning are ended. He is now in a posture of readiness to execute all his
offices of prophet, priest, and king; *as if he had been slain*—Doubtless with the
prints of the wounds which he once received. And because he was slain, he is
worthy to open the book, ver. 9, to the joy of his own people, and the terror of
his enemies. *Having seven horns*—As a king, the emblem of perfect strength;
and seven eyes—The emblem of perfect knowledge and wisdom. By these he
accomplishes what is contained in the book, namely, by his almighty and all-
wise Spirit. To these seven horns and seven eyes answer the seven seals and
the sevenfold song of praise, ver. 12. In Zechariah likewise, chap. iii, 9; iv, 10,
mention is made of *the seven eyes of the Lord which go forth over all the earth;*
which—Both the horns and the eyes, *are the seven Spirits of God, sent forth into*
all the earth—For the effectual working of the Spirit of God goes through the
whole creation; and that in the natural, as well as spiritual world. For could
mere matter act or move? Could it gravitate or attract? Just as much as it can
think or speak.

7. *And he came*—Here was, *Ask of me*, Psalm ii, 8, fulfilled in the most glorious manner, *and took*—It is one state of exaltation that reaches from our Lord's
ascension to his coming in glory. Yet this state admits of various degrees. At
his ascension, angels, and principalities, and powers, were subject to him. Ten
days after, he received from the Father, and sent the Holy Ghost. And now he

8 the right hand of him that sat upon the throne. And when he took the book, the four living creatures and the four and twenty elders fell down before the Lamb, having every one a harp, and golden phials full of incense, which are the prayers of the saints.
9 And they sing a new song, saying, Worthy art thou to take the book, and to open the seals thereof; for thou wast slain, and hast redeemed us to God by thy blood out of every tribe, and
10 tongue, and people, and nation, And hast made them unto our
11 God kings and priests, and they shall reign over the earth. And I saw and heard a voice of many angels, round about the throne, and the living creatures and the elders; and the number of them was ten thousand times ten thousand, and thousands of thousands,
12 saying with a loud voice, Worthy is the Lamb that was slain to receive the power, and riches, and wisdom, and strength, and
13 honour, and glory, and blessing. And every creature which is in the heaven, and on the earth, and under the earth, and on the

took the book out of the right hand of him that sat upon the throne—Who gave it him as a signal of his delivering to him all power in heaven and earth. He received it, in token of his being both able and willing to fulfil al. that was written therein.

8. *And when he took the book, the four living creatures fell down*—Now is homage done to the Lamb by every creature. These, together with the elders, make the beginning, and afterward, ver. 14, the conclusion. They are together surrounded with a multitude of angels, ver. 11, and together sing the new song, as they had before praised God together, chap. iv, 8, &c. *Having every one—* The elders, not the living creatures, *a harp*—Which was one of the chief instruments used for thanksgiving in the temple service: a fit emblem of the melody of their hearts, *and golden phials*—Cups or censers, *full of incense, which are the prayers of the saints*—Not of the elders themselves, but of the other saints still upon earth, whose prayers were thus emblematically represented in heaven.

9. *And they sing a new song*—One which neither they nor any other had sung before, *Thou hast redeemed us*—So the living creatures also were of the number of the redeemed; this does not so much refer to the act of redemption, which was long before, as to the fruit of it; and so more directly to those who had finished their course, *who were redeemed from the earth,* chap. xiv, 1, *out of every tribe, and tongue, and people, and nation*—That is, out of all mankind

10. *And hast made them*—The redeemed. So they speak of themselves, also in the third person, out of deep self abasement. *They shall reign over the earth—* The new earth: herewith agree the golden crowns of the elders. The reign of the saints in general follows, under the trumpet of the seventh angei: particularly after the first resurrection, as also in eternity, chap. xi, 18; xv, 7; xx, 4; xxii, 5; Dan. vii, 27; Psalm xlix, 15.

11. *And I saw*—The many angels, *and heard*—The voice and the number of them, *round about the elders*—So forming the third circle. It is remarkable, that men are represented through this whole vision as nearer to God than any of the angels. *And the number of them was*—At least two hundred millions, and two millions over. And yet these were but a part of the holy angels; afterward, chap. vii, 11, St. John heard them all.

12. *Worthy is the Lamb*—The elders said, ver. 9, *Worthy art thou.* They were more nearly allied to him than the aigels. *To receive the power,* &c. This sevenfold applause answers the seven seals, of which the four former describe all visible, the latter all invisible things, made subject to the Lamb. And every one of these seven words bears a resemblance to the seal which it answers. •

13. *And every creature*—In the whole universe, good or bad, *in the heaven, on the earth, under the earth, on the sea*—With these four regions of the world, agrees the fourfold word of praise. What is *in heaven* says *blessing;* what is *on earth, honour;* what is *under the earth, glory;* what is *on the sea, strength; is unto him.* This praise from all creatures begins before the opening of the first seal; but it continues from that time to eternity, according to the capacity of

sea, and all that are in them, I heard them all saying, To him
that sitteth on the throne, and to the Lamb, *is* the blessing, and
the honour, and the glory, and the strength, for ever and ever.
14 And the four living creatures said, Amen : and the elders fell
down and worshipped.

VI.   And I saw when the Lamb opened one of the seven seals, and

---

each. His enemies must acknowledge his glory; but those in heaven say,
Blessed be God and the Lamb.

This royal manifesto is, as it were, a proclamation, showing how Christ fulfils
all things, *and every knee bows to him*, not only *on earth*, but also *in heaven and
under the earth*. This book exhausts all things, 1 Cor. xv, 27, 28, and is suitable
to a heart enlarged as the sand of the sea. It inspires the attentive and intelligent reader with such a magnanimity, that he accounts nothing in this world
great, no, not the whole frame of visible nature, compared to the immense greatness of what he is here called to behold, yea, and in part to inherit.

St. John has in view, through the whole following vision, what he has been
now describing, namely, the four living creatures, the elders, the angels, and all
creatures, looking together at the opening of the seven seals.

Chap. VI. The seven seals are not distinguished from each other, by specify-
ing the time of them. They swiftly follow the letters to the seven Churches,
and all begin almost at the same time. By the four former is shown, that all the
public occurrences of all ages and nations, as empire, war, provision, calamities,
are made subject to Christ. And instances are intimated of the first in the east,
the second in the west, the third in the south, the fourth in the north, and the
whole world.

The contents, as of the phials and trumpets, so of the seals, are shown by the
songs of praise and thanksgiving annexed to them. They contain therefore *the
power, and riches, and wisdom, and strength, and honour, and glory, and blessing,*
which the Lamb received. The four former have a peculiar connection with
each other : and *so have the three latter seals. The former relate to visible
things, toward the four quarters to which the four living creatures look.

Before we proceed, it may be observed, 1. No man should constrain either
himself or another to explain every thing in this book. It is sufficient for every
one to speak, just so far as he understands. 2. We should remember that although the ancient prophets wrote the occurrences of those kingdoms only with
which Israel had to do, yet the revelation contains what relates to the whole
world through which the Christian Church is extended. Yet, 3. We should not
prescribe to this prophecy, as if it must needs admit or exclude this or that history, according as we judge one or the other to be of great or small importance.
God *seeth not as man seeth.* Therefore what we think great is often omitted,
what we think little, inserted, in Scripture history or prophecy. 4. We must
take care not to overlook what is already fulfilled; and not to describe s fulfilled
what is still to come.

We are to look into history for the fulfilling of. he four first seals, quickly
after the date of the prophecy. In each of these appears a different horseman.
In each we are to consider, first, the horseman himself; secondly, what he does.

The horseman himself, by an emblematical Prosopopeia, represents *a swift
power*, bringing with it either, 1. A flourishing state; or, 2. Bloodshed; or, 3.
Scarcity of provisions; or, 4. Public calamities. With the qualities of each of
these riders, the colour of his horse agrees. The fourth horseman is expressly
termed *death;* the first, with his bow and crown, a conqueror. The second,
with his great sword, is a warrior, or, as the Romans termed him, *Mars:* the
third, with the scales, has power over the produce of the land. Particular incidents under this or that Roman emperor are not extensive enough to answer
any of these horsemen.

The action of every horseman intimates farther, 1. Toward the east, wide-
spread empire, and victory upon victory; 2. Toward the west, much bloodshed;
3. Toward the south, scarcity of provisions; 4. Toward the north, the plague
and various calamities.

VI. 1. *I heard one*—That is, the first, *of the living creatures*—Who looks for
ward toward the east.

I heard one of the four living creatures saying as the voice of
2 thunder, Come *and* see. And I saw, and behold a white horse,
and he that sat on him had a bow, and a crown was given him,
and he went forth conquering and to conquer.
3 And when he opened the second seal, I heard the second living
4 creature saying, Come. And there went forth another horse *that
was* red ; and to him that sat thereon it was given to take peace
from the earth, that they should kill one another ; and there was
given him a great sword.
5 And when he opened the third seal, I heard the third living crea-

---

2. *And I saw, and behold a white horse, and he that sat on him had a bow*—This
colour, and the bow shooting arrows afar off, betoken victory, triumph, prosperity, enlargement of empire, and dominion over many people.
  Another horseman indeed, and of quite another kind, appears on a white
horse, chapter xix, 11. But he that is spoken of under the first seal must be so
understood as to bear a proportion to the horseman in the second, third, and
fourth seals.
  Nerva succeeded the emperor Domitian at the very time when the Revelation
was written, in the year of our Lord 96. He reigned scarce a year alone: and
three months before his death, he named Trajan for his colleague and successor,
and died in the year 98. Trajan's accession to the empire seems to be the
dawning of the seven seals. *And a crown was given him*—This, considering his
descent, Trajan could have no hope of attaining. But God gave it him by the
hand of Nerva ; and then the east soon felt his power. *And he went forth conquering and to conquer*—That is, from one victory to another. In the year 108,
the already victorious Trajan went forth toward the east, to conquer not only
Armenia, Assyria, and Mesopotamia, but also the countries beyond the Tigris,
carrying the bounds of the Roman empire to a greater extent than ever. We
find no emperor like him for making conquests. He aimed at nothing else: he
lived only to conquer. Meantime in him was eminently fulfilled, what had been
prophesied of the fourth empire, Dan. ii, 40 ; vii, 23, That he should devour,
tread down, and break in pieces the whole earth.
  3. *And when he had opened the second seal, I heard the second living
creature*—Who looked toward the west, *saying, Come*—At each seal it was
necessary to turn toward that quarter of the world which it more immediately
concerned.
  4. *There went forth another horse that was red*—A colour suitable to bloodshed
And to him that sat thereon it was given, to take peace from the earth—Vespasian,
in the year 75, had dedicated a temple to peace. But after a time, we hear no
more of peace. All is full of war and bloodshed, chiefly in the western world,
where the main business of men seemed to be to kill one another.
  To this horseman *there was given a great sword*—And he had much to do with
it. For as soon as Trajan ascended the throne, *peace was taken from the earth*.
Decebalus, king of Dacia, which lies westward from Patmos, put the Romans to
no small trouble. The war lasted five years, and consumed abundance of men
on both sides ; yet was only a prelude to much other bloodshed which followed
for a long season. All this was signified by *the great sword*, which strikes those
who are near, as the bow does those who are at a distance.
  5. *And when he had opened the third seal, I heard the third living creature*
toward the south, *saying, Come*—And behold a black horse, a fit emblem of mourning and distress ; particularly of *black famine*, as the ancient poets term it—*And
he that sat on him had a pair of scales in his hand*—When there is great plenty,
men scarce think it worth their while to weigh and measure every thing, Gen.
xli, 49, but when there is scarcity, they are obliged to deliver them out by measure and weight, Ezek. iv, 16. Accordingly these scales signify scarcity. They
serve also for a token, that all the fruits of the earth, and consequently the whole
heavens, with their courses and influences,—that all the seasons of the year, with
whatsoever they produce, in nature or states, are subject to Christ. Accordingly
his hand is wonderful, not only in wars and victories, but likewise in the whole
course of nature.

ture say, Come. And I saw, and behold a black horse, and he
6 that sat on him had a pair of scales in his hand. And I heard a
voice in the midst of the four living creatures saying, A measure
of wheat for a penny, and three measures of barley for a penny;
and hurt not the oil and the wine.
7 And when he opened the fourth seal, I heard the voice of the
8 fourth living creature saying, Come. And I saw, and behold a
pale horse, and he that sat on him, his name is Death, (and Hades
followeth even with him,) and power was given him over the
fourth part of the earth, to kill with the scimetar, and with famine,
and with death, and by the wild beasts of the earth.

6. *And I heard a voice*—It seems from God himself, *saying-* To the horsemen,
hitherto shalt thou come, and no farther. Let there *be a measure of wheat for a
penny*—The word translated *measure*, was a Grecian measure, nearly equal to
our quart. This was the daily allowance of a slave. The Roman penny (as
much as a labourer then earned in a day) was about sevenpence half-penny
English. According to this, wheat would be near twenty shillings per bushel.
This must have been fulfilled, while the Grecian measure and the Roman penny
were still in use: as also, where that measure was the common measure, and
this money the current coin. It was so in Egypt under Trajan. *And three measures of barley for a penny*—Either barley was, in common, far cheaper among
the ancients than wheat; or the prophecy mentions this as something peculiar.
And hurt not the oil and the wine—Let there not be a scarcity of every thing. Let
there be some provision left to supply the want of the rest.
This was also fulfilled in the reign of Trajan, especially in Egypt, which lay
southward from Patmos. In this country, which used to be the granary of the
empire, there was an uncommon dearth at the very beginning of his reign; so
that he was obliged to supply Egypt itself with corn from other countries. The
same scarcity there was in the thirteenth year of his reign, the harvest failing
for want of the rising of the Nile: and that not only in Egypt, but in all those
other parts of Africa where the Nile uses to overflow.
7. *I heard the voice of the fourth living creature*—Toward the north.
8. *And I saw, and behold a pale horse*—Suitable to pale *Death*, his rider: *and
hades*—The representative of the state of separate souls, *followeth even with
him*—The four first seals concern living men. Death therefore is properly introduced here. Hades is only occasionally mentioned as a companion of death.
So the fourth seal reaches to the borders of things invisible, which are comprised in the three last seals. *And power was given to him over the fourth part
of the earth*—What came single and in a low degree before, comes now together,
and much more severely. The first seal brought victory with it: in the second
was a great sword; but here a scimetar. In the third was moderate dearth;
here famine, and plague, and wild beasts beside. And it may well be, that
from the time of Trajan downward, the fourth part of men upon the earth,
that is, within the Roman empire, died by sword, famine, pestilence, and
wild beasts. "At that time," says Aurelius Victor, "the Tiber overflowed
much more fatally than under Nerva, with a great destruction of houses; and
there was a dreadful earthquake through many provinces, and a terrible plague
and famine, and many places consumed by fire. *By death*—That is, by pestilence. Wild beasts have, at several times, destroyed abundance of men. And
undoubtedly there was given them, at this time, an uncommon fierceness and
strength. It is observable that war brings on scarcity, and scarcity pestilence,
through want of wholesome sustenance. And pestilence, by depopulating the
country, leaves the few survivors an easier prey to the wild beasts. And thus
these judgments make way for one another, in the order wherein they are here
represented.
What has been already observed may be a fourfold proof that the four
horsemen, as with their first entrance in the reign of Trajan, which does by no
means exhaust the contents of the four first seals, so with all their entrances
in succeeding ages, and with the whole course of the world, and of visible

9　And when he opened the fifth seal, I saw under the altar the souls of them that had been slain for the word of God, and for the
10　testimony which they held : And they cried with a loud voice, saying, How long, O Lord, thou Holy One and true, dost thou not judge and avenge our blood upon them that dwell upon the
11　earth ? And there was given to them, to every one, a white robe : and it was said to them, that they should rest yet for a time, till their fellow servants also and their brethren should be fulfilled, who should be killed even as they *were*.

---

nature, are in all ages subject to Christ, subsisting by his power, and serving his will, against the wicked, and in defence of the righteous. Herewith likewise a way is paved for the trumpets, which regularly succeed each other. And the whole prophecy, as to what is future, is confirmed by the clear accomplishment of this part of it.

9. *And when he opened the fifth seal*—As the four former seals, so the three latter have a close connection with each other. These all refer to the invisible world; the fifth to the happy dead, particularly the martyrs; the sixth to the unhappy; the seventh to the angels, especially those to whom the trumpets are given. *And I saw*—Not only the Church warring under Christ, and the world warring under Satan, but also the invisible hosts both of heaven and hell are described in this book. And it not only describes the actions of both these armies upon earth, but their respective removals from earth into a more happy or more miserable state, succeeding each other at several times, distinguished by various degrees, celebrated by various thanksgivings; and also the gradual increase of expectation and triumph in heaven, and of terror and misery in hell; *under the altar*—That is, at the foot of it. Two altars are mentioned in the Revelation; the golden altar of incense, chap. ix, 13, and the altar of burnt offerings, mentioned here, and chap. viii, 5; xiv, 18; xvi, 7. At this the souls of the martyrs now prostrate themselves. By and by their blood shall be avenged upon Babylon; but not yet: whence it appears that the plagues in the fourth seal do not concern Rome in particular.

10. *And they cried*—This cry did not begin now, but under the first Roman persecution. The Romans themselves had already avenged the martyrs slain by the Jews on that whole nation; *how long*—They knew their blood would be avenged; but not immediately, as is now shown them; *O Lord*—The Greek word properly signifies the master of a family. It is therefore beautifully used by those who are peculiarly of the household of God. *Thou Holy One and true*— Both the holiness and truth of God require him to execute judgment and vengeance; *dost thou not judge and avenge our blood ?*—There is no impure affection in heaven. Therefore this desire of theirs is pure and suitable to the will of God. The martyrs are concerned for the praise of their Master, of his holiness and truth : and the praise is given him, chap. xix, 2, where the prayer of the martyrs is changed into a thanksgiving.

Thou Holy One and true:	True and right are thy judgments:
How long dost thou not judge,	He hath judged the great whore, and hath
and avenge our blood ?	avenged the blood of his servants:

11. *And there was given to every one a white robe*—An emblem of innocence, joy, and victory, in token of honour and favourable acceptance. *And it was said to them*—They were told how long. They were not left in that uncertainty, *that they should rest*—Should cease from crying. They rested from pain before; *a time*—This word has a peculiar meaning in this book; to denote which we may retain the original word *chronos*. Here are two classes of martyrs specified, the former killed under heathen Rome, the latter under papal Rome. The former are commanded to rest till the latter are added to them. There were many of the former in the days of John: the first fruits of the latter died in the thirteenth century. Now a *time* or *chronos* is 1111 years. This *chronos* began A. C. 98, and continued to the year 1209; or from Trajan's persecution to the first crusade against the Waldenses. *Till*—It is not said, Immediately after this time is expired vengeance shall be executed: but only, that immediately

12   And I saw when he opened the sixth seal, and there was a
great earthquake, and the sun became black as sackcloth of hair,
13 and the moon became as blood; And the stars of heaven fell to
the earth, as a fig tree casteth its untimely figs, when it is shaken
14 by a mighty wind: And the heavens departed as a book that is
rolled together, and every mountain and island were moved out
15 of their places.   And the kings of the earth, and the great men,
and the chief captains, and the rich and the mighty, and every
slave, and every free man, hid themselves in the caves, and in the
16 rocks of the mountains : And said to the mountains and to the rocks,
Fall on us, and hide us from the face of him that sitteth on the
17 throne, and from the wrath of the Lamb; For the great day of his
wrath is come; and who is able to stand?
VII.   And after these things I saw four angels standing on the four
corners of the earth, holding the four winds, that the wind should

after this time their brethren and fellow servants will come to them. This event
will precede the other, and there will be some space between.
    12. *And I saw*—This sixth seal seems particularly to point out God's judgment
on the wicked departed. St. John saw how the end of the world was even set
before those unhappy spirits. This representation might be made to them without any thing of it being perceived upon earth. The like representation is made
in heaven, chap. xi, 11. And there was a great earthquake or shaking, not of the
earth only, but the heavens. This is a farther description of the representation
made to those unhappy souls.
    13. *And the stars fell to* or toward *the earth*—Yea, and so they surely will, let
astronomers fix their magnitude as they please; *as a fig tree casteth its untimely
figs when it is shaken by a mighty wind*—How sublimely is the violence of that
shaking expressed by this comparison !
    14. *And the heavens departed as a book that is rolled together*—When the
Scripture compares some very great with a little thing, the majesty and omnipotence of God, before whom great things are little, are highly exalted. *Every
mountain and island*—What a mountain is to the land, that an island is to
the sea.
    15. *And the kings of the earth*—They who had been so in their day, *and the
great men and the chief captains*—The generals and nobles, *hid themselves*—So
far as in them lay, *in the rocks of the mountains*—There are also rocks on the
plains; but they were rocks on high which they besought to fall upon them.
    16. *To the mountains and the rocks*—Which were tottering already, ver. 12;
hide us from the face of him—Which *is against the ungodly.*
    VII. 1. *And after these things*—What follows is a preparation for the seventh
seal, which is the weightiest of all. It is connected with the sixth by the particle *and :* whereas what is added, ver. 9, stands free and unconnected; *I saw
four angels*—Probably evil ones. They have their employ with the four first
trumpets, as have other evil angels with the three last, namely, the angel of the
abyss, the four bound in the Euphrates, and Satan himself. These four angels
would willingly have brought on all the calamities that follow without delay;
but they were restrained till the servants of God were sealed, and till the seven
angels were ready to sound : even as the angel of the abyss was not let loose,
nor the angels in the Euphrates unbound, neither Satan cast to the earth, till
the fifth, sixth, and seventh angels severally sounded, *standing on the four corners of the earth*—East, west, south, north. In this order proceed the four
first trumpets; *holding the four winds*—Which else might have softened the
fiery heat under the first, second, and third trumpet ; *that the wind should not
blow upon the earth, nor on the sea, nor on any tree*—It seems that these expressions betoken the several quarters of the world : that *the earth* signifies that to
the east of Patmos, Asia ; which was nearest to St. John, and where the trumpet
of the first angel had its accomplishment. Europe swims in *the sea* over against
this : and is accordingly termed by the prophets *the islands.* The third part,

2 not blow upon the earth, nor on the sea, nor on any tree. And I saw another angel ascending from the *rising of the sun*, having the seal of the living God : and he cried with a loud, voice to the

3 four angels to whom it was given to hurt the earth and the sea, Saying, Hurt ye not the earth, neither the sea, neither the trees, till we

4 have sealed the servants of our God on their foreheads. And I heard the number of them that were sealed ; a hundred forty-four thou-

5 sand were sealed out of all the tribes of the children of Israel. Of the tribe of Judah *were* sealed twelve thousand ; of the tribe of Reuben *were* sealed twelve thousand ; of the tribe of Gad *were*

6 sealed twelve thousand ; Of the tribe of Asher *were* sealed twelve thousand ; of the tribe of Naphtali *were* sealed twelve thousand ;

7 of the tribe of Manasseh *were* sealed twelve thousand ; Of the tribe of Simeon *were* sealed twelve thousand ; of the tribe of Levi *were* sealed twelve thousand ; of the tribe of Issachar *were* sealed

8 twelve thousand ; Of the tribe of Zebulon *were* sealed twelve thousand ; of the tribe of Joseph *were* sealed twelve thousand ; of the tribe of Benjamin *were* sealed twelve thousand.

9 After these things I saw, and behold a great multitude, which no man could number, of all nations, and tribes, and people, and

---

Africa, seems to be meant, chap. viii, 7, 8, 10, by *the streams of water*, or *the trees*, which grow plentifully by them.

2. *And I saw another*—A good *angel, ascending from the east*—The plagues begin in the east ; so does the sealing ; *having the seal of* the only *living* and true *God ; and he cried with a loud voice to the four angels*—Who were hastening to execute their charge ; *to whom it was given to hurt the earth and the sea*—First, and afterward *the trees*.

3. *Hurt not the earth, till we*—Other angels were joined in commission with him ; *have sealed the servants of our God on their foreheads*—Secured the servants of God of the twelve tribes from the impending calamities ; whereby they shall be as clearly distinguished from the rest as if they were visibly marked on their foreheads.

4. *Of the children of Israel*—To these will afterward be joined a multitude out of all nations. But it may be observed, this is not the number of all the Israelites who are saved from Abraham or Moses to the end of all things ; but only of those who were secured from the plagues which were then ready to fall on the earth. It seems as if this book had, in many places, a special view to the people of Israel.

5. Judah is mentioned first, in respect of the kingdom, and of the Messiah sprung therefrom.

7. After the Levitical ceremonies were abolished, Levi was again on a level with his brethren.

8. *Of the tribe of Joseph*—Or Ephraim ; perhaps not mentioned by name, as having been, with Dan, the most idolatrous of all the tribes. It is farther observable of Dan, that it was very early reduced to a single family ; which family itself seems to have been cut off in war before the time of Ezra. For in the Chronicles, where the posterity of the patriarchs is recited, Dan is wholly omitted.

9. *A great multitude*—Of those who had happily finished their course. Such multitudes are afterward described, and still higher degrees of glory which they attain, after a sharp fight and magnificent victory, chap. xiv, 1 ; xv, 2 ; xix, 1 ; xx, 4. There is an inconceivable variety in the degrees of reward in the other world. Let not any slothful one say, If I get to heaven at all, I will be content such a one may let heaven go altogether. In worldly things men are ambitious to get as high as they can. Christians have a far more noble ambition. The difference between the very highest and the lowest state in the world, is nothing to the smallest difference between the degrees of glory. But who has time to think

tongues, standing before the throne, and before the Lamb, clothed
10 with white robes and palms in their hands.   And they cry with a
loud voice, saying, Salvation to our God who sitteth on the throne,
11 and to the Lamb.   And all the angels stood round about the throne,
and the elders, and the four living creatures ; and they fell before
12 the throne on their faces, and worshipped God, Saying, Amen:
the blessing, and the glory, and the wisdom, and the thanksgiving,
and the honour, and the power, and the strength, *be* to our God for
13 ever and ever.   And one of the elders answered, saying to me,
Who are these that are clothed in white robes ? and whence are
14 they come ?   And I said to him, My lord, thou knowest.   And he
said to me, These are they who come out of great affliction, and
they have washed their robes and made them white in the blood
15 of the Lamb, Therefore are they before the throne of God, and
serve him day and night in his temple, and he that sitteth upon the
16 throne shall have his tent over them :   They shall hunger no more,
neither thirst any more ; neither shall the sun light on them, nor
17 any heat.   For the Lamb who is in the midst of the throne will

of this ?   Who is at all concerned about it ?   *Standing before the throne*—In the
full vision of God, and *palms in their hands*—Tokens of joy and victory.

10. *Salvation to our God*—Who hath saved us from all evil into all the
happiness of heaven.   The salvation for which they praise God is described,
ver. 15; that for which they praise the Lamb, ver. 14; and both in the 16th
and 17th verses.

11. *And all the angels stood*—In waiting, *round about the throne, and the
elders, and the four living creatures*—That is, the living creatures next the
throne, the elders round these, and the angels round them both ; *and they fell on
their faces*—So do the elders, once only, chap. xi, 16.   The heavenly ceremonial
has its fixed order and measure.

12. *Amen*—With this word all the angels confirm the words of the great multitude.   But they likewise carry the praise much higher ; *the blessing, and the
glory, and the wisdom, and the thanksgiving, and the honour, and the power, and
the strength, be unto our God for ever and ever*—Before the Lamb began to open the
seven seals, a seven-fold hymn of praise was brought him by *many angels*, chap.
v, 12.   Now he is upon opening the last seal, and the seven angels are going to
receive seven trumpets, in order to make the kingdoms of the world subject to
God, all the angels give seven-fold praise to God.

13. *And one of the elders*—What stands, ver. 13–17, might have immediately
followed the 10th verse : but that the praise of the angels which was at the same
time with that of the great multitude, came in between ; *answered*—He answered
St. John's desire to know, not any words that he spoke.

14. *My lord*—Or *my master*—A common term of respect.   So Zechariah
likewise bespeaks the angel ; chap. i, 9 ; iv, 4 ; vi, 4 : *thou knowest*—That is, I
know not ; but thou dost.   *These are they*—Not martyrs ; for these are not such
a multitude as no man can number.   But as all the angels appear here, so do all
the souls of the righteous, who had lived from the beginning of the world ; who
come—He does not say, Who did come.   But who come now also ; to whom
li' ewise pertain all who will come hereafter ; *out of great affliction*—Of various
kinds, wisely and graciously allotted by God to all his children ; *and have washed
their robes*—From all guilt, *and made them white*—In all holiness, *by the blood
of the Lamb*—Which not only cleanses, but adorns us also.

15. *Therefore*—Because they *come out of great affliction, and have washed their
robes in his blood, are they before the throne*—It seems, even nearer than the
angels ; *and serve him day and night*—Speaking after the manner of men, that
is, continually ; *in his temple*—Which is in heaven ; *and he shall have his tent
over them*—Shall spread his glory over them as a covering.

16. *Neither shall the sun light on them*—For God is their sun ; *nor any*—painful heat, or inclemency of seasons.

feed them, and will lead ·them to living fountains of water : and
God will wipe away all tears from their eyes.
VIII.　And when he had opened the seventh seal, there was silence
2 in heaven about half an hour.　And I saw the seven angels who
3 stood before God, and seven trumpets were given them.　And

17. *For the Lamb will feed them*—With eternal peace and joy, so that they
shall hunger no more ; *and will lead them to living fountains of water*—The
comforts of the Holy Spirit, so that they shall thirst no more.　Neither shall
they suffer or grieve any more: *for God will wipe away all tears from their
eyes.*

VIII. 1. *And when he had opened the seventh seal, there was silence in heaven*—
Such a silence is mentioned but in this one place.　It was uncommon and highly
observable.　For praise is sounding in heaven day and night.　In particular,
immediately before this silence, all the angels, and before them the innumerable
multitude, had been crying with a loud voice: and now, all is still at once
there is a universal pause.　Hereby the seventh seal is very remarkably distinguished from the six preceding.　This silence before God shows that those
who were round about him were expecting, with the deepest reverence, the great
things which the Divine Majesty would farther open and order.　Immediately
after the seven trumpets are heard, and a sound more august than ever.　Silence
is only a preparation : the grand point is, the sounding the trumpets to the
praise of God.　*About half an hour*—To St. John in the vision it might seem a
common half hour.

2. *And I saw*—The seven trumpets belong to the seventh seal, as do the
seven phials to the seventh trumpet.　This should be carefully remembered, that
we may not confound together the times which follow each other.　And yet it
may be observed in general, concerning the times of the incidents mentioned in
this book, it is not a certain rule, that every part of the text is fully accomplished, before the completion of the following part begins.　All things mentioned in the epistles are not fully accomplished before the seals are opened ;
neither are all things mentioned under the seals fulfilled, before the trumpets
begin.　Nor yet is the seventh trumpet wholly past before the phials are poured
out.　Only the beginning of each part goes before the beginning of the following.　Thus the epistles begin before the seals, the seals before the trumpets, the
trumpets before the phials.　One epistle begins before another, one seal before
another, one trumpet especially before another, one phial before another.　Yea,
sometimes what begins later than another thing, ends sooner ; and what begins
earlier than another thing, ends later.　So the seventh trumpet begins earlier
than the phials, and yet extends beyond them all.　*The seven angels which stood
before God*—A character of the highest eminence ; *and seven trumpets were
given them*—When men desire to make known openly a thing of public concern,
they give a token that may be seen or heard far and wide : and among such none
are more ancient than trumpets, Lev. xxv, 9 ; Numb. x, 2 ; Amos iii, 6.　The
Israelites in particular used them, both in the worship of God and in war, therewith openly praising the power of God, before, after, and in the battle, Josh. vi,
4 ; 2 Chron. xiii, 14, &c.　And the angels here made known by these trumpets
the wonderful works of God, whereby all opposing powers are successively
shaken, till the kingdom of the world becomes the kingdom of God and his
anointed.

These trumpets reach nearly from the time of St. John to the end of the world ;
and they are distinguished by manifest tokens.　The place of the four first is
specified, namely, east, west, south, and north successively.　In the three last,
immediately after the time of each, the place likewise is pointed out.

The seventh angel did not begin to sound till after the going forth of th
second wo : but the trumpets were given to him and the other six together, (as
were afterward the phials to the seven angels,) and it is accordingly said of all
the seven together, that they prepared themselves to sound.　These therefore
were not men, as some have thought, but angels properly so called.

3. *And*—In the 2d verse the trumpets were given to the seven angels, and in
the sixth they prepared to sound.　But between these the incense of this angel
and the prayers of the saints are mentioned : the interposing of which shows

another angel came and stood at the altar, having a golden censer, and much incense was given him, that he might place it with the prayers of all the saints upon the golden altar which is before
4 the throne. And the smoke of the incense ascended before God
5 out of the angel's hand with the prayers of the saints. And the angel took the censer and filled it with the fire of the altar, and threw it upon the earth, and there were thunderings, and lightnings, and voices, and an earthquake.
6 And the seven angels, who had the seven trumpets, prepared
7 themselves to sound. And the first sounded, and there was hail, and fire mingled with blood, and they were cast upon the earth; and the third part of the earth was burnt up, and the third part of the trees was burnt up, and all the green grass was burnt up.

that the prayers of the saints, and the trumpets of the angels go together. And these prayers, with the effects of them, may well be supposed to extend through all the seven. *Another angel*—Another created angel. Such are all that are here spoken of. In this part of the Revelation, Christ is never termed an angel, but the Lamb; *came and stood at the altar*—Of burnt offerings; *and there was given him a golden censer*—A censer was a cup on a plate or saucer. This was the token and the business of the office. *And much incense was given*—Incense generally signifies prayer. Here it signifies the longing desires of the angels that the holy counsel of God might be fulfilled. And there was *much incense* for as the prayers of all the saints in heaven and earth are here joined together, so are the desires of all the angels, which are brought by this angel; *that he might place it*—It is not said offer it; for he was discharging the office of an angel, not a priest: *with the prayers of all the saints*—At the same time; but not for the saints. The angels are fellow servants with the saints, not mediators for them.

4. *And the smoke of the incense came up before God, with the prayers of the saints*—A token that both were accepted.

5. *And there were thunderings, and lightnings, and voices, and an earthquake*—These, especially when attended with fire, are emblems of God's dreadful judgments, which are immediately to follow.

6. *And the seven angels prepared themselves to sound*—That each when it should come to his turn might sound without delay. But while they do sound, they still stand before God.

7. *And the first sounded*—And every angel continued to sound till all which his trumpet brought was fulfilled, and till the next began. There are intervals between the three woes, but not between the four first trumpets. *And there was hail, and fire mingled with blood, and they were cast upon the earth*—The earth seems to mean Asia; Palestine in particular. Quickly after the Revelation was given, the Jewish calamities under Adrian began; yea, before the reign of Trajan was ended: and here the trumpets begin. Even under Trajan, in the year 114, the Jews made an insurrection with a most dreadful fury; and in the parts about Cyrene in Egypt, and in Cyprus, destroyed four hundred and sixty thousand persons. But they were repressed by the victorious power of Trajan, and afterward slaughtered themselves in vast multitudes. The alarm spread itself also into Mesopotamia, where Lucius Quintius slew a great number of them. They rose in Judea again in the second year of Adrian; but were presently quelled. In the year 133 they broke out more violent than ever, under their false Messiah, Barcochab: and the war continued till the year 135, when almost all Judea was desolated. In the Egyptian plague also hail and fire were together. But here hail is to be taken figuratively, as also blood, for a vehement, sudden, powerful, hurtful invasion; and fire betokens the revenge of an enraged enemy, with the desolation therefrom. *And they were cast upon the earth*—That is, the fire, and hail, and blood. But they existed before they were cast upon the earth. The storm fell, the blood flowed, and the flames raged round Cyrene, and in Egypt, and Cyprus, before they reached Mesopotamia and Judea. *And the third part of the earth was burnt up*—Fifty well-fortified cities,

THE REVELATION.

8 And the second angel sounded, and as it were a great mountain, burning with fire, was cast into the sea; and the third part of the 9 sea became blood. And the third part of the creatures that were in the sea, which had life, died, and the third part of the ships were destroyed.

10 And the third angel sounded, and there fell from heaven a great star, burning as a torch, and it fell on the third part of the rivers, and on the fountains of waters.

---

and nine hundred and eighty-five well-inhabited towns of the Jews, were wholly destroyed in this war. Vast tracts of land were likewise left desolate and without inhabitants; *and the third part of the trees was burnt up, and all the green grass was burnt up*—Some understand by the trees, men of eminence among the Jews; by the grass the common people. The Romans spared many of the former. The latter were almost all destroyed.

Thus vengeance began at the Jewish enemies of Christ's kingdom; though even then the Romans did not quite escape. But afterward it came upon them more and more violently: the second trumpet affects the Roman heathens in particular; the third, the dead, unholy Christians; the fourth, the empire itself.

8. *And the second angel sounded, and as it were a great mountain burning with fire, was cast into the sea*—By the sea, particularly as it is here opposed to the earth, we may understand the west, or Europe; and chiefly the middle parts of it, the vast Roman empire. A mountain here seems to signify a great force and multitude of people, Jer. li, 25. So this may point at the irruption of the barbarous nations into the Roman empire. The warlike Goths broke in upon it about the year 250. And from that time the irruption of one nation after another never ceased, till the very form of the Roman empire, and all but the name was lost. The fire may mean the fire of war, and the rage of those savage nations. *And the third part of the sea became blood*—This need not imply, that just a third part of the Romans were slain. But it is certain an inconceivable deal of blood was shed in all these invasions.

9. *And the third part of the creatures that were in the sea*—That is, of all sorts of men of every nation and degree, *died*—By these merciless invaders. *And the third part of the ships were destroyed*—It is a frequent thing to resemble a state or republic to a ship, wherein many people are embarked together, and share in the same dangers. And how many states were utterly destroyed by those inhuman conquerors? Much likewise of this was literally fulfilled. How often was the sea tinged with blood? How many of those who dwelt mostly upon it were killed? And what number of ships destroyed?

10. *And the third angel sounded, and there fell from heaven a great star, and it fell on the third part of the rivers*—It seems Africa is meant by the rivers, with which this burning part of the world abounds in an especial manner. Egypt, in particular, which the Nile overflows every year far and wide. In the whole African history, between the irruption of the barbarous nations into the Roman empire, and the ruin of the western empire, after the death of Valentinian the Third, there is nothing more momentous than the Arian calamity, which sprung up in the year 315. It is not possible to tell how many persons, particularly at Alexandria, in all Egypt, and in the neighbouring countries, were destroyed by the rage of the Arians. Yet Africa fared better than other parts of the empire with regard to the barbarous nations, till the governor of it, whose wife was a zealous Arian, and aunt to Genseric king of the Vandals, was under that pretence unjustly accused before the Empress Placidia. He was then prevailed upon to invite the Vandals into Africa; who, under Genseric, in the year 428, founded there a kingdom of their own, which continued till the year 533. Under these Vandal kings the true believers endured all manner of afflictions and persecutions. And thus Arianism was the inlet to all heresies and calamities, and at length to Mahommedanism itself.

This great star was not an angel, (angels are not the agents in the two preceding or the following trumpet,) but a teacher of the Church, one of *the stars in the right hand of Christ*. Such was Arius. He fell from on high, as it were

11 And the name of the star is called Wormwood, and the third part of the waters became wormwood, and many men died of the
12 waters, because they were made bitter. And the fourth angel sounded, and the third part of the sun was smitten, and the third part of the moon, and the third part of the stars ; so that·the third part of them was darkened, and the day shone not for the third part thereof, and the night likewise.
13 And I saw and heard an angel flying in the midst of heaven, saying with a loud voice, Wo, wo, wo to the inhabitants of the

from heaven, into the most pernicious doctrines ; and made in his fall a blazing on all sides, being *great*, and now *burning as a torch*. He *fell on the third part of the rivers;* his doctrines spread far and wide, particularly in Egypt; *and on the fountains of waters*—Wherewith Africa abounds.

11. *And the name of the star was called Wormwood*—The unparalleled bitter. ness both of Arius himself and of his followers, shows the exact propriety of his title ; *and the third part of the waters became wormwood*—A very considerable part of Africa was infected with the same bitter doctrine and spirit ; *and many men* (though not a third part of them) *died*—By the cruelty of the Arians.

12. *And the fourth angel sounded, and the third part of the sun was smitten* (or *struck*)—After the emperor Thodosius died, and the empire was divided into the eastern and the western, the barbarous nations poured in as a flood. The Goths and Huns in the years 403 and 405 fell upon Italy itself with an impe. tuous force ; and the former in the year 410 took Rome by storm, and plundered it without mercy. In the year 452 Attila treated the upper part of Italy in the same manner. In 455 Valentinian the Third was killed, and Genseric invited from Africa. He plundered Rome for fourteen days together. Recimer plun dered it again in 472. During all these commotions, one province was lost after another, till in the year 476, Odoacer seized upon Rome, deposed the emperor, and put an end to the empire itself.

An eclipse of the sun or moon is termed by the Hebrews a stroke. Now, as such a darkness does not come all at once, but by degrees, so likewise did the darkness which fell on the Roman, particularly the western empire : for the stroke began long before Odoacer, namely, when the barbarians first conquered the capital city. *And the third part of the moon, and the third part of the stars; so that the third part of them was darkened*—As under the first, second, and third trumpets, by the earth, sea, and rivers, are to be understood the men that inhabit them, so here by the sun, moon, and stars, may be understood the men that live under them, who are so overwhelmed with calamities in those days of darkness, that they can no longer enjoy the light of heaven, unless it may be thought to imply their being killed, so that the sun, moon, and stars shine to them no longer. The very same expression we find in Ezekiel, chapter xxxii, 8. *I will darken all the lights of heaven over them*—As then the fourth seal tran. scends the three preceding seals, so does the fourth trumpet the three preceding trumpets. For in this, not the third part of the eartn, or sea, or rivers only, but of all who are under the sun are affected, *and the day shone not for a third part thereof*—That is, shone with only a third part of its usual brightness, and the night likewise, the moon and the stars having lost a third part of their lustre, either with regard to those who being dead, saw them no longer, or those who saw them with no satisfaction.

The three last trumpets have the time of their continuance fixed, and between each of them there is a remarkable pause : whereas between the four former there is no pause, nor is the time of their continuance mentioned ; but all together the four seem to take up a little less than four hundred years.

13. *And I saw and heard an angel flying*, *in the midst of heaven*—Between the trumpets of the fourth and fifth angel, *in the midst of heaven*—The three woes (as we shall see) stretch themselves over the earth from Persia eastward, beyond Italy westward, all which space had been filled with the Gospel by the apostles. In the midst of this lies Patmos, where St. John saw this angel, *Saying, Wo, wo, wo*—Toward the end of the fifth century, there were many presages of approaching calamities; *to the inhabitants of the earth*—All without exception. Heavy trials were coming

earth, by reason of the other voices of the trumpets of the three
angels, who are yet to sound.

IX. And the fifth angel sounded, and I saw a star falling from heaven to the earth, and to him was given the key of the bottomless
2 pit. And he opened the bottomless pit, and there ascended a
smoke out of the pit, as the smoke of a great furnace, and the sun
3 and the air were darkened by the smoke of the pit. And out of
the smoke there came forth locusts upon the earth, and power was
4 given them, as the scorpions of the earth have power : And it was
commanded them, not to hurt the grass of the earth, neither any
green thing, neither any tree, but only the men who have not the
5 seal of God on their foreheads. And it was given them, not to kill
them, but that they should be tormented five months ; and the tor-

---

on them all. Even while the angel was proclaiming this, the preludes of these
three woes were already in motion. These fell more especially on the Jews. As
to the prelude of the first wo in Persia, Isdegard II. in 454, was resolved to abolish the Sabbath, till he was by Rabbi Mar diverted from his purpose. Likewise
in the year 474, Phiruz afflicted the Jews much, and compelled many of them to
apostatize. A prelude of the second wo was the rise of the Saracens, who in
510 fell upon Arabia and Palestine To prepare for the third wo, Innocent I.,
and his successors, not only endeavoured to enlarge their episcopal jurisdiction
beyond all bounds, but also their worldly power, by taking every opportunity of
encroaching upon the empire, which as yet stood in the way of their unlimited
monarchy.

IX. 1. *And the fifth angel sounded, and I saw a star*—Far different from that
mentioned, chap. viii, 11. This star belongs to the invisible world. The third wo
is occasioned by the dragon cast out of heaven ; the second takes place at the
loosing of the four angels who were bound in the Euphrates. The first is here
brought by the angel of the abyss, which is opened by this star, or holy angel,
falling to the earth—Coming swiftly and with great force, *and to him was given*
—When he was come, *the key of the bottomless pit*—A deep and hideous prison,
but different from the lake of fire.

2. *And there ascended a smoke out of the pit*—The locusts who afterward rise
out of it, seem to be (as we shall afterward see) the Persians ; agreeably to which
this smoke is their detestable idolatrous doctrine, and false zeal for it, which now
broke out in an uncommon paroxysm, *as the smoke of a great furnace*—Where
the clouds of it rise thicker and thicker, spread far and wide, and press one upon
another, so that the darkness increases continually. *And the sun and the air were
darkened*—A figurative expression denoting heavy affliction. This smoke occasioned more and more such darkness over the Jews in Persia.

3. *And out of the smoke*—Not out of the bottomless pit, but from the smoke
which issued thence, *there went forth locusts*—A known emblem of a numerous,
hostile, hurtful people. Such were the Persians, from whom the Jews in the
sixth century suffered beyond expression. In the year 540, their academies were
stopped, nor were they permitted to have a president for nearly fifty years. In
589 this affliction ended ; but it began long before 540. The prelude of it was
about the year 455 and 474. The main storm came on in the reign of Cabades,
and lasted from 483 to 532. Toward the beginning of the sixth century, Mar
Rab Isaac, president of the academy, was put to death. Hereupon followed an
insurrection of the Jews, which lasted seven years before they were conquered by
the Persians. Some of them were then put to death, but not many ; the rest
were closely imprisoned. And from this time the nation of the Jews were
hated and persecuted by the Persians, till they had well nigh rooted them out.
The scorpions of the earth—The most hurtful kind. The scorpions of the air
have wings.

4. *And it was commanded them*—By the secret power of God, *not to hurt the
grass, neither any green thing, nor any tree*—Neither those of low, middling, or
high degree, but only such of them as were *not sealed*—Principally the unbelieving Israelites. But many who were called Christians suffered with them.

ment of them *is* as the torment of a scorpion, when he stingeth a
6 man. And in those days the men shall seek death, but not find
7 it; and shall desire to die, but death will flee from them. And the
appearances of the locusts *are* like horses made ready for battle :
and on their heads *are* as it were crowns like gold, and their faces
8 *are* as the faces of men. And they had hair as the hair of women,
9 and their teeth were as *the teeth* of lions. And they had breastplates, as it were breastplates of iron, and the noise of their wings
was as the noise of chariots of many horses running to battle.
10 And they have tails like scorpions, and stings were in their tails;
11 their power *is* to hurt men five months. And they have over them
a king, the angel of the bottomless pit ; his name in the Hebrew
12 is Abaddon, but in the Greek he hath the name Apollyon. One
wo is past ; behold there come yet two woes after these things.
13 And the sixth angel sounded, and I heard a voice from the
14 four corners of the golden altar which is before God, Saying to
the sixth angel, who had the trumpet, Loose the four angels who

---

5. *Not to kill them*—Very few of them were killed; in general, they were imprisoned and variously tormented.
6. *The men*—That is, the men who are so tormented.
7. *And the appearances*—This description suits a people neither thoroughly
civilized, nor entirely savage. And such were the Persians of that age ; *of the
locusts are like horses*—With their riders. The Persians excelled in horseman-
ship, *and on their heads are as it were crowns*—Turbans, *and their faces are as
the faces of men*—Friendly and agreeable.
8. *And they had hair as the hair of women*—All the Persians of old gloried in
long hair ; *and their teeth were as the teeth of lions*—Breaking and tearing all
things in pieces.
9. *And the noise of their wings was as the noise of chariots of many horses*—
With their war chariots drawn by many horses, they, as it were, flew to and fro
10. *And they have tails like scorpions*—That is, each tail is like a scorpion, not
like the tail of a scorpion, *to hurt the* unsealed *men five months*—Five prophetic
months, that is, seventy-nine common years. So long did these calamities last.
11. *And they have over them a king*—One by whom they are peculiarly directed and governed. *His name is Abaddon*—Both this and Apollyon signify a
destroyer. By this he is distinguished*from the dragon, whose proper name is
Satan.
12. *One wo is past: behold there come yet two woes after these things*—The
Persian power, under which was the first wo, was now broken by the Saracens ;
from this time the first pause made a wide way for the two succeeding woes. In
589, when the first wo ended, Mohammed was twenty years old, and the contentions of the Christians with each other were exceeding great. In 591 Chosroes
II. reigned in Persia, who after the death of the emperor made dreadful distur-
bances in the east. Hence Mohammed found an open door for his new religion
and empire. And when the usurper Phocas had, in the year 606, not only declared the bishop of Rome, Boniface III. universal bishop, but also the Church
of Rome the head of all Churches ; this was a sure step to advance the papacy to
its utmost height. Thus, after the passing away of the first wo, the second, yea,
and the third, quickly followed : as indeed they were both on the way together
with it, before the first effectually began.
13. *And the sixth angel sounded*—Under this angel goes forth the second wo;
and I heard a voice from the four corners of the golden altar—This golden altar
is the heavenly pattern of the Levitical altar of incense. This voice signified,
that the execution of the wrath of God, (mentioned ver. 20, 21,) should, at no
intercession, be delayed any longer.
14. *Loose the four angels*—To go every way to the four quarters : these were
evil angels, or they would not have been bound. Why, or how long they were
bound, we know not.

15 are bound in the great river Euphrates. And the four angels
were loosed, who were prepared for the hour, and day, and
16 month, and year, to kill the third part of men. And the number
of the army of horsemen *was* two hundred millions ; I heard their
17 number. And thus I saw the horses in the vision and them that
sat on them, having breastplates of fire, and hyacinth, and brimstone : and the heads of the horses *are* as the heads of lions, and
18 out of their mouths goeth fire, and smoke, and brimstone. By these
three plagues were the third part of men killed, by the fire, and
the smoke, and the brimstone, which went out of their mouths.

---

15. *And the four angels were loosed, who were prepared*—By loosing them, as
well as by their strength and rage, *to kill the third part of men*—That is, an immense number of them, *for the hour, and day, and month, and year*—All this
agrees with the slaughter which the Saracens made, for a long time after Mohammed's death. And with the number of angels let loose agrees the number
of their first and most eminent Caliphs. These were Ali, Abubeker, Omar, and
Osman. Mohammed named Ali, his cousin and son-in-law, for his successor.
But he was soon worked out by the rest, till they severally died, and so made room
for him. They succeeded each other, and each destroyed innumerable multitudes
of men. There are in a prophetic

	Common years :		Common days :	
Hour		Eight		} in all 212
Day		& 196		years.
Month fifteen		& 318		
Year 196		& 117		

Now the second wo (as also the beginning of the third) has its place, between
the ceasing of the locusts, and the rising of the beast out of the sea ; even at
the time that the Saracens (who were chiefly cavalry) were in the height of their
carnage ; from the first Caliph Abubeker, till they were repulsed from Rome,
under Leo IV. These 212 years may therefore be reckoned from the year 634
to 847. The gradation in reckoning the time, beginning with the hour, and
ending with a year, corresponds with their small beginning and vast increase.
Before and after Mohammed's death, they had enough to do to settle their affairs
at home. Afterward Abubeker went farther, and in the year 634 gained great
advantage over the Persians and Romans in Syria. Under Omar was the con-
quest of Mesopotamia, Palestine, and Egypt made. Under Osman, that of Africa,
(with the total suppression of the Roman government in the year 647,) of Cyprus, and of all Persia, in 651. After Ali was dead, his son Ali Hasen, a peaceable prince, was driven out by Muavio ; under whom and his successors the
power of the Saracens so increased, that within fourscore years after Mohammed's death, they had extended their conquests farther than the warlike Romans
did in four hundred years.

16. *And the number of the horsemen was two hundred millions*—Not that so
many were ever brought into the field at once, but (if we understand the expression literally) in the course of *the hour, and day, and month, and year*. So
neither were *the third part of men killed* at once ; but during that course of
years.

17. *And thus I saw the horses and them that sat on them in the vision*—St.
John seems to add these words, *in the vision*, to intimate that we are not to take
this description just according to the letter ; *having breastplates of fire*—Fiery
red, *and hyacinth*—Dun-blue, *and brimstone*—A faint yellow. Of the same colour
with the *fire, and smoke, and brimstone*—which *go out of the mouths of their
horses, and the heads of their horses are as the heads of lions*—That is, fierce and
terrible, *and out of their mouths goeth fire, and smoke, and brimstone*—This figurative expression may denote the consuming, blinding, all-piercing rage, fierceness, and force of these horsemen.

18. *By these three*—Which were inseparably joined, *were the third part of
men* in the countries they overran, *killed*—Omar alone in eleven years and a
half took thirty-six thousand cities or forts. How many men must be killed
therein !

19 For the power of the horses is in their mouths and in their tails : for their tails *are* like serpents having heads, and with them they

20 do hurt. And the rest of the men, who were not killed by these plagues, yet repented not of the works of their hands, that they should not worship devils, and idols of gold, and silver, and brass, and stone, and wood, which can neither see, nor hear, nor walk :

* 21 Neither repented they of their murders, nor of their sorceries, nor of their fornications, nor of their thefts.

X. And I saw another mighty angel coming down from heaven, clothed with a cloud, and a rainbow upon his head, and his face

---

19. *For the power of these horses is in their mouths and in their tails*—Their riders fight retreating as well as advancing ; so that their rear is as terrible as their front ; *for their tails are like serpents, having heads*—Not like the tails of serpents only. They may be fitly compared to the amphisbena, a kind of serpent which has a short tail, not unlike a head ; from which it throws out its poison, as if it had two heads.

20. *And the rest of the men who were not killed*—Whom the Saracens did not destroy. It is observable, the countries they overran were mostly those where the Gospel had been planted ; *by these plagues*—Here the description of the second wo ends ; *yet repented not*—Though they were *called* Christians, *of the works of their hands*—Presently specified ; *that they should not worship devils*—The invocation of departed saints, whether true, or false, or doubtful, or forged, crept early into the Christian Church, and was carried farther and farther ; and who knows how many who are invoked as saints, are among evil, not good angels ? Or how far devils have mingled with such blind worship, and with the wonders wrought on those occasions ? *And idols*—About the year 590 men began to venerate images ; and though upright men zealously opposed it, yet by little and little images grew into manifest idols. For after much contention both in the east and west, in the year 787 the worship of images was established by the second council of Nice. Yet was image worship sharply opposed some time after by the Emperor Theophilus ; but when he died, in 842, his widow, Theodora, established it again ; as did the council at Constantinople, in the year 863, and again in 871.

21. *Neither repented they of their murders, nor of their sorceries*—Whoever reads the histories of the seventh, eighth, and ninth centuries, will find numberless instances of all these in every part of the Christian world. But though God cut off so many of these scandals to the Christian name, yet the rest went on in the same course. Some of them, however, might repent under the plagues which follow.

Chap. x. From the first verse of this chapter to chap. xi, 13, preparation is made for the important trumpet of the seventh angel. It consists of two parts, which run parallel to each other. The former reaches from the first to the seventh verse of this chapter : the latter from the eighth of this to the thirteenth verse of the eleventh chapter : whence, also, the sixth verse of this chapter is parallel to the eleventh verse. The period to which both these refer begins during the second wo, as appears, chap. xi, 14 ; but being once begun, it extends in a continued course far into the trumpet of the seventh angel. Hence many things are represented here which are not fulfilled till long after. So the joyful consummation of the mystery of God is spoken of in the seventh verse of this chapter, which yet is not till after the consummation of the wrath of God, chap. xv, 1. So the ascent of the beast out of the bottomless pit is mentioned chap. xi, 7, which nevertheless is still to come, chap. xvii, 8. And so the earthquake, by which a *tenth part of the city falls, and the rest are converted*, chap. xi, 13, is really later than that by which the same city is split into three parts, chap. xvi, 19. This is a most necessary observation, whereby we may escape many and great mistakes.

X. 1. *And I saw another mighty angel*—Another from that mighty angel mentioned chap. v, 2 ; yet he was a created angel ; for he did not swear by himself, ver. 6 ; *clothed with a cloud*—In token of his high dignity, *and a rainbow upon his head*—A lovely token of the Divine favour. And yet it is not too glorious

2 as the sun, and his feet as pillars of fire. And he had in his hand
a little book opened; and he set his right foot upon the sea, and
3 his left upon the earth. And he cried with a loud voice, as a lion
roareth; and while he cried seven thunders uttered their voices.
4 And when the seven thunders had uttered their voices, I was
about to write: and I heard a voice from heaven, saying, Seal up
the things whicn the seven thunders have uttered, and write them
5 not. And the angel whom I saw standing upon the sea and upon
6 the earth, lifted up his right hand toward heaven, And sware
by him that liveth for ever and ever, who created the heaven,
and the things that are therein; and the earth, and the things that
are therein; and the sea, and the things that are therein, There

for a creature. The woman, chap. xii, 1, is described more glorious still; *and
his face as the sun*—Nor is this too much for a creature, for all the righteous
shall shine forth as the sun, Matt. xiii, 43; *and his feet as pillars of fire*—Bright
as flame.
2. *And he had in his hand*—His left hand : he swore with his right. He stood
with his right foot on the sea, toward the west : his left on the land, toward the
east; so that he looked southward. And so St. John (as Patmos lies near Asia)
could conveniently take the book out of his left hand. This sealed book was
first in the right hand of him that sat on the throne. Thence the Lamb took it
and opened the seals. And now this *little book*, containing the remainder of the
other, is given, *opened* as it was, to St. John. From this place the Revelation
speaks more clearly and less figuratively than before. *And he set his right foot
upon the sea*—Out of which the first beast was to come, *and his left foot upon the
earth*—Out of which was to come the second. The sea may betoken Europe ;
the earth Asia ; the chief theatres of these great things.
3. *And he cried*—Uttering the words set down, ver. 6 ; *and while he cried*—Or
was crying, at the same instant *seven thunders uttered their voices*—In distinct
words, each after the other. Those who spoke these words were glorious heavenly powers, whose voice was as the loudest thunder.
4. *And I heard a voice from heaven*—Doubtless from him who had at first
commanded him to write, and who presently commands him to take the book,
namely, Jesus Christ. *Seal up those things which the seven thunders have uttered, and write them not*—These are the only things of all which he heard, that
he is commanded to keep secret. So some things peculiarly secret were revealed
to the beloved John, beside all the secrets that are written in this book. At the
same time we are prevented from inquiring what it was which these thunders
uttered. Suffice that we may know all the contents of the opened book, and of
the oath of the angel.
5. *And the angel*—This manifestation of things to come under the trumpet
of the seventh angel, hath a twofold introduction. First, the angel speaks for
God, ver. 7. Then Christ speaks for himself, chap. xi, 3. The angel appeals
to the prophets of former times ; Christ to his own two witnesses. *Whom I
saw standing upon the earth and upon the sea, lifted up his right hand towara
heaven*—As yet the dragon was in heaven. When he is cast thence, he brings
the third and most dreadful wo on the earth and the sea : so that it seems as if
there would be no end of calamities. Therefore the angel comprises in his pos
ture and in his oath both heaven, sea, and earth, and makes on the part of the
eternal God and almighty Creator a solemn protestation that he will assert his
kingly authority against all his enemies. *He lifted up his right hand toward
heaven*—The angel in Daniel, chap. xii, 7, (not improbably the same angel,`
lifted up both his hands.
6. *And sware*—The six preceding trumpets pass without any such solemnity.
It is the trumpet of the seventh angel alone which is confirmed by so high an
oath, *by him that liveth for ever and ever*—Before whom a thousand years are
but a day; *who created the heaven, the earth, the sea, and the things that are
therein*—And consequently has the sovereign power over all : therefore all his
enemies, though they rage awhile in heaven, on the sea, and on the earth, yet

7 shall be no more a time. But in the days of the voice of the seventh angel, while he shall sound, the mystery of God shall be fulfilled, as he hath declared to his servants the prophets.

8 And the voice which I heard from heaven spake with me again, and said, Go, take the book which is open in the hand of the an

9 gel, who standeth on the sea and on the earth. And I went to the angel, saying to him, Give me the book. And he saith to me, Take and eat it up, and it will make thy belly bitter, but it will

10 be sweet as honey in thy mouth. And I took the book out of the angel's hand, and ate it up, and it was in my mouth sweet as ho-

11 ney, but when I had eaten it my belly was bitter. And he saith to me, Thou must prophesy again concerning the people, and na-

---

must give place to him; *that there shall be no more a time, but in the days of the voice of the seventh angel the mystery of God shall be fulfilled*—That is, a time, a chronos, shall not expire before that mystery is fulfilled. A chronos (1111 years) will nearly pass before then, but not quite. The period then which we may term a non-chronos, (not a whole time,) must be a little, and not much shorter than this. The non-chronos here mentioned seems to begin in the year 800, (when Charles the Great instituted in the west a new line of emperors or of many kings,) to end in the year 1836; and to contain, among other things, the short time of the third wo, the three times and a half of the woman in the wilderness, and the duration of the beast.

7. *But in the days of the voice of the seventh angel*—Who sounded not only at the beginning of those days, but from the beginning to the end, *the mystery of God shall be fulfilled*—It is said, chap. xvii, 17, The word of God shall be fulfilled. The word of God is fulfilled by the destruction of the beast, the mystery by the removal of the dragon. But these great events are so near together, that they are here mentioned as one. The beginning of them is in heaven, as soon as the seventh trumpet sounds; the end is on the earth and the sea. So long as the third wo remains on the earth and the sea the mystery of God is not fulfilled. And the angel's swearing is peculiarly for the comfort of holy men who are afflicted under that wo. Indeed the wrath of God must be first fulfilled by the pouring out of the phials; and then comes the joyful fulfilling of the mystery of God. *As he hath declared to his servants the prophets*—The accomplishment exactly answering the prediction. The ancient prophecies relate partly to that grand period, from the birth of Christ to the destruction of Jerusalem; partly to the time of the seventh angel, wherein they will be fully accomplished. To the seventh trumpet belongs all that occurs from chap. xi, 15, to chap. xxii, 5. And the third wo, which takes place under the same, properly stands, chap. xii, 12; chap. xiii, 1–18.

8. *And*—What follows from this verse to chap. xi, 13, runs parallel with the oath of the angel, and with the fulfilling of the mystery of God, as it follows under the trumpet of the seventh angel. What is said, ver. 11, concerning St. John's prophesying again, is unfolded immediately after; what is said, ver. 7, concerning the fulfilment of the mystery of God, is unfolded, chap. xi, 15–19, and in the following chapters.

9. *Eat it up*—The like was commanded to Ezekiel. This was an emblem of thoroughly considering and digesting it. *And it will make thy belly bitter, but it will be sweet as honey in thy mouth*—The sweetness betokens the many good things which follow, chap. xi, 1, 15, &c; the bitterness, the evils which succeed under the third wo.

11. *Thou must prophesy again*—Of the mystery of God; of which the ancient prophets had prophesied before. And he did prophesy, by measuring the temple, chap. xi, 1. As a prophecy may be delivered either by words or actions, *concerning people, and nations, and tongues, and many kings*—The people, nations, and tongues are cotemporary; but the kings, being many, succeed one another These kings are not mentioned for their own sake, but with a view to the holy city, chap. xi, 2. Here is a reference to the great kingdoms in Spain, England, Italy, &c, which arose from the eighth century, or at least underwent a con-

XI. tions, and tongues, and many kings. And there was given me a reed, like a measuring rod; and he said, Arise, and measure the temple of God, and the altar, and them that worship therein.
2 But the court which is without the temple cast out, and measure it not: for it is given to the Gentiles; and they shall tread
3 the holy city forty-two months. And I will give to my two witnesses to prophesy twelve hundred *and* sixty days, clothed in sack-
4 cloth. These are the two olive trees and the two candlesticks,
5 standing before the Lord of the earth. And if any one would hurt them, fire proceedeth out of their mouths, and devoureth their
6 enemies; and if any would kill them, he must thus be killed. These

---

siderable change, as France and Germany in particular, to the Christian, afterward Turkish, empire in the east; and especially to the various potentates who have successively reigned at or over Jerusalem, and do now, at least titu larly, reign over it.

Chap. xi. In this chapter is shown how it will fare with the holy city till the mystery of God is fulfilled: in the twelfth, what will befall the woman, who is delivered of the man child: in the thirteenth, how it will be with the kingdom of Christ while the two beasts are in the height of their power. *And there was given me*—By Christ, as appears from the third verse, *and he said, Arise*—Probably he was sitting to write, *and measure the temple of* God—At Jerusalem, where he was placed in the vision. Of this we have a large description by Eze kiel, chap. xl-xlviii, concerning which we may observe,

1. Ezekiel's prophecy was not fulfilled at the return from the Babylonish captivity.

2. Yet it does not refer to the New Jerusalem, which is far more gloriously described.

3. It must infallibly be fulfilled even then when they are ashamed of all that they have done, chap. xliii, 11.

4. Ezekiel speaks of the same temple which is treated of here.

5. As all things are there so largely described, St. John is shorter, and refers thereto.

XI. 2. *But the court which is without the temple*—The old temple had a court in the open air for the heathens who worshipped the God of Israel, *cast out*—Of thy account, *and measure it not*—As not being holy in so high a degree; *and they shall tread*—Inhabit the holy city, Jerusalem, Matt. iv, 5. So they began to do before St. John wrote. And it has been trodden almost ever since, by the Romans, Persians, Saracens, and Turks. But that severe kind of treading which is here peculiarly spoken of, will not be till under the trumpet of the seventh angel, and toward the end of the troublous times. This will continue but forty-two common months, or twelve hundred and sixty common days; being but a small part of the non-chronos.

3. *And I*, Christ, *will give to my two witnesses*—These seem to be two prophets, two select, eminent instruments. Some have supposed (though without founda tion) that they are Moses and Elijah, whom they resemble in several respects, *to prophesy twelve hundred and sixty days*—Common days, that is, a hundred and eighty weeks. So long will they prophesy, (even while that last, and sharp treading of the holy city continues,) both by word and deed, witnessing that Jesus is the Son of God, the heir of all things, and exhorting all men to repent, and fear, and glorify God; *clothed in sackcloth*—The habit of the deepest mourn. ers, out of sorrow and concern for the people.

4. *These are the two olive trees*—That is, as Zerubbabel, and Joshua, the two olive trees spoken of by Zechariah, chap. iii, 9; iv, 10, were then the two chosen instruments in God's hand, even so shall these be in their season. Being them. selves full of the unction of the Holy One, they shall continually transmit the same to others also; *and the two candlesticks*, burning and shining lights, *stand. ing before the Lord of the earth*—Always waiting on God, without the help of man, and asserting his right over the earth and all things therein.

5. *If any would kill them*—As the Israelites would have done Moses and Aaron, Numb. xvi, 41; *he must thus be killed*—By that devouring fire.

nave power to shut heaven, that it rain not in the aays of their
prophesying, and have power over the waters, to turn them into
blood, and to smite the earth with all plagues as often as they
7 will.   And when they shall have finished their testimony, the
wild beast that ascendeth out of the bottomless pit shall make
8 war with them, and conquer them, and kill them.   And their
dead bodies *shall be* in the street of the great city, which is called
spiritually Sodom and Egypt, where also their Lord was cruci-
9 fied.   And *some* of the people, and tribes, and tongues, and nations, beheld their dead bodies three days and a half, and they
10 shall not suffer their dead bodies to be put in a grave.   And they
that dwell upon the earth rejoice over them, and they shall make
merry and send gifts to one another ; because these two prophets
11 tormented them that dwelt upon the earth.   And after the three
days and a half, the Spirit of life from God came into them, and
they stood upon their feet; and great fear fell upon them that
12 saw them.   And I heard a great voice saying from heaven to
them, Come up hither.   And they went up to heaven in a cloud,
and their enemies beheld them.

6. *These have power*—And they use that power, (see ver. 10,) *to shut heaven
that it rain not in the days of their prophesying*—During these twelve hundred
and sixty days ; *and have power over the waters*—In and near Jerusalem, *to turn
them into blood*—As Moses did those in Egypt ; *and to smite the earth with all
plagues as often as they will*—This is not said of Moses or Elijah, or any mere
man beside.   And how is it possible to understand this otherwise than of two
individual persons ?
7. *And when they shall have finished their testimony*—Till then they are in-
vincible; *the wild beast*—Hereafter to be described; *that ascendeth*—First out of
the sea, chap. xiii, 1, and then *out of the bottomless pit*, chap. xvii, 8, *shall make
war with them*—It is at his last ascent, not out of the sea, but the bottomless pit,
that the beast makes war upon the two witnesses.   And even hereby is fixed the
time of treading the holy city and of the two witnesses.   That time ends after
the ascent of the beast out of the abyss, and yet before the fulfilling of the
mystery ; *and shall conquer them*—The fire no longer proceeding out of their
mouth when they have finished their work; *and kill them*—These will be among
the last martyrs, though not the last of all.
8. *And their bodies shall be*—Perhaps hanging on a cross, *in the street of the
great city*—Of Jerusalem, a far greater city than any other in those parts.   This
is described both spiritually and historically: spiritually as it is called Sodom,
(Isa. i,) and Egypt, on account of the same abominations abounding there at the
time of the witnesses, as did once in Egypt and Sodom: historically, *where also
their Lord was crucified*—This possibly refers to the very ground where his cross
stood.   Constantine the Great enclosed this within the walls of the city.   Perhaps
on that very spot will their bodies be exposed.
9. *Three days and a half*—So exactly are the times set down in this prophecy.
If we suppose this time began in the evening, and ended in the morning, and
included (which is no way impossible) Friday, Saturday, and Sunday, the weekly
festival of the Turkish people, the Jewish tribes, and the Christian tongues ;
then all these together, with the heathen nations, would have full leisure to gaze
upon and rejoice over them.
10. *And they that dwell upon the earth*—Perhaps this expression may peculiarly denote earthly-minded men ; *shall make merry*—As did the Philistines over
Samson ; *and send gifts to one another*—Both Turks, and Jews, and heathens,
and false Christians.
11. *And great fear fell upon them that saw them*—And now knew that God was
on their side.
12. *And I heard a great voice*—Designed for all to hear.   *And they went up to
heaven, and their enemies beheld them*—Who had not taken notice of their rising
again ; by which some had been convinced before.

13   And in that hour there was a great earthqʻıake, and the tenth
part of the city fell, and there were slain in the earthquake seven
thousand men, and the rest were terrified, and gave glory to the
14   God of heaven. The second wo is past: behold, the third wo
cometh quickly.
15   And the seventh angel sounded ; and there were great voices ın

---

13. *And there was a great earthquake, and the tenth part of the city fell*—We
have here an unanswerable proof that this city is not Babylon, or Rome, but
Jerusalem. For Babylon shall be wholly burnt before the fulfilling of the mystery of God. But this city is not burnt at all ; on the contrary, at the fulfilling
of that mystery, a tenth part of it is destroyed by an earthquake, and the other
nine parts converted. *And there were slain in the earthquake seven thousand men*
—Being a tenth part of the inhabitants, who therefore were seventy thousand
in all ; *and the rest*—The remaining sixty-three thousand, were converted : a
grand step toward the fulfilling of the mystery of God. Such a conversion we
no where else read of. So there shall be a larger as well as holier Church at
Jerusalem than ever was yet : *were terrified*—Blessed terror ! *And gave glory*—
The character of true conversion, Jer. xiii, 16, *to the God of heaven*—He is
styled the Lord of the earth, ver. 4, when he declares his right over the earth by
the two witnesses ; but the God of heaven, when he not only gives rain from
heaven, after the most afflicting drought, but also declares his majesty from heaven, by taking his witnesses up into it. When the whole multitude gives glory
to the God of heaven, then that treading of the holy city ceases. This is the
point so long aimed at, the desired fulfilling of the mystery of God, when the
Divine promises are so richly fulfilled on those who have gone through so great
afflictions. All this is here related together, that whereas the first and second
wo went forth in the east, the rest of the eastern affairs being added at once, the
description of the western might afterward remain unbroken.
It may be useful here to see how the things here spoken of, and those hereafter
described, follow each other in their order.
1. The angel swears : the non-chronos begins : John eats the book : the many
kings arise.
2. The non-chronos and the many kings being on the decline, that treading
begins, and the two witnesses appear.
3. The beast (after he has with the ten kings destroyed Babylon) wars with
them, and kills them. After three days and a half they revive and ascend to
heaven. There is a great earthquake in the holy city. Seven thousand perish,
and the rest are converted. The treading of the city by the Gentiles ends.
4. The beast and the kings of the earth, and their armies are assembled to
fight against the great King.
5. Multitudes of his enemies are killed, and the beast and the false prophet
cast alive into the lake of fire.
6. While John measures the temple of God and the altar with the worshippers,
the true worship of God is set up. The nations, who had trodden the holy city,
are converted. Hereby the mystery of God is fulfilled.
7. Satan is imprisoned. Being released for a time, he, with Gog and Magog,
makes his last assault upon Jerusalem.
14. *The second wo is past*—The butchery made by the Saracens ceased about
the year 847, when their power was so broken by Charles the Great, that they
never recovered it. *Behold, the third wo cometh quickly*—Its prelude came while
the Roman see took all opportunities of laying claim to its beloved universality,
and enlarging its power and grandeur. And in the year 755 the bishop of Rome
became a secular prince, by King Pepin's giving him the exarchate of Lombardy.
The beginning of the third wo itself stands, chap. xii, 12.
15. *And the seventh angel sounded*—This trumpet contains the most important and joyful events, and renders all the former trumpets matter of joy to all
the inhabitants of heaven. The allusion therefore in this and all the trumpets
is to those used in festal solemnities. All the seven trumpets were heard in
heaven. Perhaps the seventh shall once be heard on earth also, 1 Thess. iv, 16.
And there were great voices—From the several citizens of heaven. At the open
ing of the seventh seal, there was silence in heaven ; at the sounding of the

heaven, saying, The kingdom of the world is become *the kingdom* of our Lord and of his Christ, and he shall reign for ever and
16 ever. And the four and twenty elders, who sat before God on
17 their thrones, fell on their faces and worshipped God, Saying, We give thee thanks, O Lord God, the Almighty, who is, and who was, because thou hast taken thy great power, and hast reigned.
18 And the nations were wroth; and thy wrath is come, and the time of the dead, that they be judged, and to give a reward to thy servants the prophets, and the saints, and to them that fear thy name, small and great, and to destroy them that destroyed the earth.

seventh trumpet, great voices. This alone is sufficient to show, that the seven seals and seven trumpets do not run parallel to each other. As soon as the seventh angel sounds, the kingdom falls to God and his Christ. This immediately appears in heaven, and is there celebrated with joyful praise. But on earth several dreadful occurrences are to appear first. This trumpet comprises all that follows from these voices to chap. xxii, 5. *The kingdom of the world*— That is, the royal government over the whole world and all its kingdoms, Zech. xiv, 9, *is become the kingdom of our Lord*—This province has been in the enemy's hands: it now returns to its rightful Master. In the Old Testament, from Moses to Samuel, God himself was the king of his own people. And the same will be in the New Testament: he will himself reign over the Israel of God: *and of his Christ*—This appellation is now first given him (since the introduction of the book) on the mention of the kingdom devolving upon him, under the seventh trumpet. Prophets and priests were anointed, but more especially kings; whence that term, *the anointed*, is applied only to a king. Accordingly, whenever the Messiah is mentioned in Scripture, his kingdom is implied: *is become*—In reality all things (and so the kingdom of the world) are God's in all ages. Yet Satan and the present world, with its kings and lords, are risen against the Lord and against his Anointed. God now puts an end to this monstrous rebellion, and maintains his right to all things. And this appears in an entirely new manner, as soon as the seventh angel sounds.

16. *And the four and twenty elders*—These shall reign over the earth, chap. v, 10; *who sit before God on their thrones*—Which we do not read of any angel.

17. *The Almighty*—He who hath all things in his power as the only Governor of them; *who is, and who was*—God is frequently styled, He who is, and who was, and who is to come. But now he is actually come, the words, *who is to come*, are, as it were, swallowed up. When it is said, We thank thee that thou hast taken thy great power, it is all one as, We thank thee that thou art come. This whole thanksgiving is partly an enlargement on the two great points mentioned in the 15th verse; partly a summary of what is hereafter more distinctly related. Here it is mentioned how the kingdom is the Lord's; afterward how it is the kingdom of his Christ. *Thou hast taken thy great power*—This is the beginning of what is done under the trumpet of the seventh angel. God has never ceased to use his power: but he has suffered his enemies to oppose it, which he will now suffer no more.

18. *And the* heathen *nations were wroth*—At the breaking out of the power and kingdom of God. This wrath of the heathens now rises to the highest pitch; but it meets the wrath of the Almighty, and melts away. In this verse is described both the going forth and the end of God's wrath, which together take up several ages. *And the time of the dead is come*—Both of the quick and dead, of whom those already dead are far the more numerous part; *that they be judged*—This, being infallibly certain, they speak of as already present; *and to give a reward*—At the coming of Christ, chap. xxii, 12; but of free grace, not of debt: 1. To his servants the prophets; 2. To his saints, to them who were eminently holy; 3. To them that fear his name. These are the lowest class. Those who do not even fear God will have no reward from him: *small and great*—All universally, young and old, high and low, rich and poor; *and to destroy them that destroyed the earth*—The earth was destroyed by the great whore in particular, chap. xvii, 2, 5; xix, 2. But likewise in general by the open rage and hate of wicked men against all that is good: by wars, and the various

19   And the temple of God was opened in heaven, and the ark of
the covenant was seen in the temple, and there were lightnings,
and voices, and thunders, and an earthquake, and great hail.

XII.   And a great sign was seen in heaven, a woman clothed with
the sun, and the moon under her feet, and on her head a crown
2 of twelve stars.   And being with child, she crieth, travailing in

---

destruction and desolation naturally flowing therefrom ; by such laws and con-
stitutions as hinder much good, and occasion many offences and calamities ; by
public scandals, whereby a door is opened for all dissoluteness and unrighteousness ; by abuse of secular and spiritual powers ; by evil doctrines, maxims, and
counsels ; by open violence and persecution, and by sins crying to God to send
plagues upon the earth.

This great work of God, destroying the destroyers, under the trumpet of the
seventh angel, is not the third wo, but matter of joy, for which the elders solemnly give thanks.   All the woes, and particularly the third, go forth over those
who dwell upon the earth, but this destruction over those who destroy *the earth*,
and were also instruments of that wo.

19. *And the temple of God*—The inmost part of it, *was opened in heaven*—
And hereby is opened a new scene of the most momentous things ; that we may
see how the contents of the seventh trumpet are executed, and notwithstanding
the greatest opposition, particularly by the third wo, brought to a glorious con
clusion.   *And the ark of the covenant was seen in his temple*—The ark of the
covenant, which was made by Moses, was not in the second temple, being probably burnt with the first temple by the Chaldeans.   But here is the heavenly
ark of the everlasting covenant, the shadow of which was under the Old Testament, Heb. ix, 4.   The inhabitants of heaven saw the ark before.   St. John also
saw it now : for a testimony that what God had promised should be fulfilled
to the uttermost.   *And there were lightnings, and voices, and thunders, and an
earthquake, and great hail*—The very same there are, and in the same order,
when the seventh angel has poured out his phial, chap. xvi, 17–21.   One place
answers the other.   What the trumpet here denounces in heaven, is there executed by the phial upon earth.   First, it is shown what will be done, and afterward it is done.

Chap. xii. The great vision of this book goes straight forward, from the fourth
to the twenty-second chapter.   Only the tenth, with part of the eleventh chapter, was a kind of introduction to the trumpet of the seventh angel : after which it
is said, *The second wo is past : behold the third wo cometh quickly.*   Immediately
the seventh angel sounds, under whom the third wo goes forth.   And to this trumpet belongs all that is related to the end of the book.

XII. *And a great sign was seen in heaven*—Not only by St. John, but many
heavenly spectators represented in the vision.   A sign means something that
has an uncommon appearance, and from which we infer, that some unusual thing
will follow.   *A woman*—The emblem of the Church of Christ, as she is originally
of Israel, though built and enlarged on all sides by the addition of heathen converts : and as she will hereafter appear, when all her natural branches are again
grafted in.   She is at present on earth, and yet with regard to her union with
Christ, may be said to be in heaven, Eph. ii, 6.   Accordingly she is described as
both assaulted and defended in heaven, ver. 4, 7.   *Clothed with the sun, and the
moon under her feet, and on her head a crown of twelve stars*—These figurative
expressions must be so interpreted, as to preserve a due proportion between them.
So in Joseph's dream the sun betokened his father, the moon his mother, the
stars their children.   There may be some such resemblance here.   And as the
prophecy points out the power over all nations, perhaps the sun may betoken the
Christian world, the moon the Mohammedans, (who also carried the moon in
their ensigns,) and the crown of twelve stars the twelve tribes of Israel ; which
are smaller than the sun and moon.   The whole of this chapter answers the state
of the Church, from the ninth century to this time.

2. *And being with child, she cried, travailing in birth*—The very pain, without any outward opposition, would constrain a woman in travail to cry out.
These cries, throes, and pains to be delivered, were the painful longings, the
sighs and prayers of the saints for the coming of the kingdom of God   The wo-

3 birth, and pained to be delivered. And another sign was seen in heaven; and behold a great red dragon, having seven heads and 4 ten horns, and seven diadems on his heads. And his tail draweth the third part of the stars of heaven, and casteth them to the earth. And the dragon stood before the woman who was ready to be delivered, that when she had brought forth, he might devour the 5 child. And she brought forth a man child, who was to rule all the nations with a rod of iron; and her child was caught up to God 6 and to his throne. And the woman fled into the wilderness, where she hath a place prepared by God, that they may feed her there twelve hundred *and* sixty days.

7 And there was war in heaven; Michael and his angels warred

---

man groaned and travailed in spirit, that Christ might appear, as the shepherd and king of all nations.

3. *And behold a great red dragon*—His fiery red colour denoting his disposition, *having seven heads*—Implying vast wisdom, *and ten horns*—Perhaps on the seventh head : emblems of mighty power and strength, which he still retained, and *seven diadems on his heads*—Not properly crowns, but costly bindings, such as kings anciently wore. For though fallen, he was a great potentate still, even *the prince of this world.*

4. *And his tail*—His falsehood and subtlety, *draweth*—As a train, *the third part*, a very large number, *of the stars of heaven*—The Christians and their teachers, who before sat in heavenly places with Christ Jesus, *and casteth them to the earth*—Utterly deprives them of all those heavenly blessings. This is properly a part of the description of the dragon, who was not yet himself on earth, but in heaven. · Consequently this casting them down was between the beginning of the seventh trumpet and the beginning of the third wo : or between the year 847, and the year 947 : at which time pestilent doctrines, particularly that of the Manichees in the east, drew abundance of people from the truth. *And the dragon stood before the woman, that, when she had brought forth, he might devour the child*—That he might hinder the kingdom of Christ from spreading abroad as it does under this trumpet.

5. *And she brought forth a man-child*—Even Christ, considered not in his person, but in his kingdom. In the ninth age many nations with their princes were added to the Christian Church, *who was to rule all nations*—When his time is come, *and her child*—Which was already in heaven, as were the woman and the dragon, *was caught up to God*—Taken utterly out of his reach.

6. *And the woman fled into the wilderness*—This wilderness is undoubtedly on earth, where the woman also herself is now supposed to be. It betokens that part of the earth, where, after having brought forth, she found a new abode. And this must be in Europe, as Asia and Africa were wholly in the hands of the Turks and Saracens : and in a part of it where the woman had not been before. In this wilderness God had already prepared a place, that is, made it safe and convenient for her. The wilderness is, those countries of Europe which lie on this side the Danube : for the countries which lie beyond it had received Christianity before, *that they may feed her*—That the people of that place may provide all things needful for her, *twelve hundred and sixty days*—So many prophetic days; which are not, (as some have supposed,) twelve hundred and sixty, but seven hundred and seventy-seven common years. (This Bengelius has shown at large in his German Introduction.) These we may compute from the year 847 to 1524. So long the woman enjoyed a safe and convenient place, in Europe, which was chiefly Bohemia ; where she was fed, till God provided for her more plentifully at the Reformation.

7. *And there was war in heaven*—Here Satan makes his grand opposition to the kingdom of God. But an end is now put to his accusing the saints before God. The cause goes against him, ver. 10, 11, and Michael executes the sentence. That Michael is a created angel, appears from his not daring, in disputing with Satan, Jude 9, to bring a railing accusation, but only saying, *The Lord rebuke thee.* And this modesty is implied in his very name : for Michael signi-

8 with the dragon, and the dragon warred and his angels : But he
prevailed not, neither was his place found any more in heaven
9 And the great dragon was cast out, the ancient serpent who is
called the devil and Satan, who deceiveth the whole world : he was
cast out unto the earth, and his angels were cast out with him.
10 And I heard a loud voice saying in heaven, Now is come the salvation, and the might, and the kingdom of our God, and the power of
his Christ, for the accuser of our brethren is cast out, who accused
11 them before our God day and night.　And they have overcome
him by the blood of the Lamb, and by the word of their testimony ;
12 and they loved not their lives unto the death.　Therefore rejoice

fies, Who is like God? Which implies also his deep reverence toward God, and
distance from all self exaltation. Satan would be like God. The very name
of Michael asks, who is like God? Not Satan : not the highest archangel. It
is he likewise, that is afterward employed to seize, bind, and imprison that proud
spirit.

8. *And he prevailed not*—The dragon himself is principally mentioned; but his
angels likewise are to be understood. *Neither was his place found any more in
heaven*—So till now he had a place in heaven. How deep a mystery is this?
One may compare this with Luke x, 18 ; Eph. ii, 2; iv, 3 ; vi, 12.

9. *And the great dragon was cast out*—It is not yet said unto the earth. He
was cast out of heaven. And at this the inhabitants of heaven rejoice. He is
termed *the great dragon*—As appearing here in that shape, to intimate his poi-
sonous and cruel disposition ; *the ancient serpent*—In allusion to his deceiving
Eve in that form. Dragons are a kind of large serpents : *who is called the devil
and Satan*—These are words of exactly the same meaning, only the former is
Greek, the latter Hebrew, denoting the grand adversary of all the saints, whether Jews or Gentiles ; he has *deceived the whole world*—Not only in their first
parents, but through all ages and in all countries, into unbelief and all wickedness, into the hating and persecuting faith and all goodness. *He was cast out
unto the earth*—He was cast out of heaven : and being cast out thence, himself
came to the earth. Nor had he been unemployed on the earth before, although
his ordinary abode was in heaven.

10. *Now is come*—Hence it is evident, that all this chapter belongs to the
trumpet of the seventh angel. In the eleventh chapter, from the fifteenth to the
eighteenth verse, are proposed the contents of this extensive trumpet : the execution of which is copiously described in this and the following chapters : *the
salvation*—Of the saints, *the might*—Whereby the enemy is cast out, *the kingdom*
—Here the majesty of God is shown, *and the power of his Christ*—Which he will
exert against the beast. And when he also is taken away, then will the kingdom
be ascribed to Christ himself, chap. xix, 16 ; xx, 4, *the accuser of our brethren*—
So long as they remained on earth. This great voice therefore was the voice of
men only, *who accused them before our God day and night*—Amazing malice of
Satan and patience of God !

11. *And they have overcome him*—Carried the cause against him, *by the blood
of the Lamb*—Which cleanses the soul from all sin, and so leaves no room for
accusing, *and by the word of their testimony*—The word of God, which they believed and testified even unto death. So, for instance, did Olam, king of Sweden, in the year 900, whom his own subjects would have compelled to idolatry :
and upon his refusal, slew him as a sacrifice to the idol which he would not worship. So did multitudes of Bohemian Christians, in the year 916, when Queen
Drahomire raised a severe persecution, wherein many loved not their lives unto
the death.

12. *Wo to the earth and to the sea*—This is the fourth and last denunciation of
the third wo, the most grievous of all. The first was only, the second chiefly, *on
the earth*, Asia ; the third both on the *earth and the sea*, Europe. The earth is
mentioned first, because it began in Asia, before the beast brought it on Europe
He knoweth he hath but a little time—Which extends from his casting out of
heaven to his being cast into the abyss.

yc heavens, and ye that dwell in them : Wo to the earth and the sea; for the devil is come down to you having great wrath; because he knoweth he hath but a little time.

13 And when the dragon saw that he was cast to the earth, he persecuted the woman that had brought forth the male child.

14 And there were given to the woman the two wings of the· great

---

We are now come to a most important period of time. The non-chronos hastens to an end. We live in the little time wherein Satan hath great wrath · and this little time is now upon the decline. We are in the time, times, and half a time, wherein the woman is fed in the wilderness ; yea, the last part of it, the half time, is begun. We are (as will be shown) toward the close of the for- ty-two months of the beast ; and when his number is fulfilled, grievous things will be.

Let him who does not regard the being seized by the wrath of the devil, the falling unawares into the general temptation ; the being borne away by the most dreadful violence into the worship of the beast and his image, and consequently drinking the unmixed wine of the wrath of God, and being tormented day and night for ever and ever in the lake of fire and brimstone ; let him also, who is confident that he can make his way through all these, by his own wisdom and strength, without need of any such peculiar preservative as the word of this pro- phecy affords : let him, I say, go hence. But let him who does not take these warnings for senseless outcries and blind alarms, beg of God with all possible earnestness, to give him his heavenly light herein.

God has not given this prophecy in so solemn a manner, only to show his pro- vidence over his Church ; but also that his servants may know at all times in what particular period they are. And the more dangerous any period of time is, the greater is the help which it affords. But where may we fix the beginning and end of the little time ? which is probably four-fifths of a chronos, or some- what above eight hundred and eighty-eight years. This, which is the time of the third wo, may reach from 947 to the year 1836. For 1. The short interval of the second wo, which wo ended in the year 840, and the seven hundred and seventy- seven years of the woman, which began about the year 847, quickly after which fol- lowed the war in heaven, fix the beginning not long after 864. And thus the third wo falls in the tenth century, extending from 900 to 1000, called the dark, the iron, the unhappy age. 2. If we compare the length of the third wo, with the period of time which succeeds it in the twentieth chapter, it is but a little time to that vast space which reaches from the beginning of the non-chronos to the end of the world.

13. *And when the dragon saw*—That he could no longer accuse the saints in heaven, he turned his wrath to do all possible mischief on earth, *he persecuted the woman*—The ancient persecutions of the Church were mentioned, chap. i, 9 ; ii, 10; vii, 14. But this persecution came after her flight, ver. 6, just at the beginning of the third wo. Accordingly in the tenth and eleventh centuries, the Church was furiously persecuted by several heathen powers. In Prussia, King Adelbert was killed in the year 997, King Brunus in 1008. And when King Stephen encouraged Christianity in Hungary he met with violent oppo- sition. After his death, the heathens in Hungary set themselves to root it out, and prevailed for several years. About the same time the army of the emperor, Henry the Third, was totally overthrown by the Vandals. These, and all the accounts of those times show, with what fury the dragon then persecuted the woman.

14. *And there were given to the woman the two wings of the great eagle, that she might fly into the wilderness to her place*—Eagles are the usual symbols of great potentates. So Ezekiel xvii, 3, by a great eagle means the king of Baby- lon. Here the great eagle is the Roman empire : ·the two wings, the eastern and western branches of it. , A place in the wilderness was mentioned in the sixth verse also. But it is not the same which is mentioned here. In the text there follow one after the other ;

1. The dragon's waiting to devour the child.
2. The birth of the child, which is caught up to God.
3. The fleeing of the woman into the wilderness.

eagle, that she might fly into the wilderness to her place, where she is fed for a time, and times, and half a time, from the face of
15 the serpent. And the serpent cast out of his mouth after the woman, water, as a river, that he might cause her to be carried away
16 by the stream. But the earth helped the woman, and opened her

---

4. The war in heaven, and the casting out of the dragon.
5. The beginning of the third wo.
6. The persecution raised by the dragon against the woman.
7. The woman's flying away upon the eagle's wings.
In like manner there follow one after the other ;
1. The beginning of the twelve hundred and sixty days.
2. The beginning of the *little times.*
3. The beginning of the time, times, and half a time. This third period partly coincides, both with the first and the second. After the beginning of the 1260 days, or rather of the third wo, Christianity was exceedingly propagated, in the midst of various persecutions. About the year 948 it was again settled in Denmark : in 965 in Poland and Silesia : in 980 through all Russia. In 997 it was brought into Hungary ; into Sweden and Norway, both before and after. Transylvania received it about 1000, and soon after, other parts of Dacia.
Now all the countries in which Christianity was settled between the beginning of the 1260 days, and the imprisonment of the dragon, may be understood by the wilderness, and by her place in particular. This place contained many countries ; so that Christianity now reached an uninterrupted tract from the eastern to the western empire. And both the emperors now lent their wings to the woman, and provided a safe abode for her ; *where she is fed*—By God rather than man, having little human help ; *for a time, and times, and half a time*—The length of the several periods here mentioned, seems to be nearly this :—

1. The non-chronos contains less than   1111 years.
2. The little time   888
3. The time, times, and half a time   777
4. The time of the beast   666

And comparing the prophecy and history together, they seem to begin and end nearly thus :—

1. The non-chronos extends from about   800 to 1836.
2. The 1260 days of the woman   from 847 to 1524.
3. The little time   from 947 to 1836.
4. The time, times, and half a time   from 1058 to 1836.

5. The time of the beast is between the beginning and end of the three times and a half. In the year 1058, the empires had a good understanding with each other, and both protected the woman : the bishops of Rome likewise, particularly Victor II., were duly subordinate to the emperor. We may observe, the 1260 days of the woman, from 847 to 1524, and the three times and a half, refer to the same wilderness. But in the former part of the 1260 days, before the three times and a half began, namely, from the year 847 to 1058, she was fed by others, being little able to help herself: whereas, from 1058 to 1524, she is both fed by others, and has food herself. To this the sciences, transplanted into the west from the eastern countries, much contributed ; the Scriptures in the original tongues, brought into the west of Europe by the Jews and Greeks, much more ; and most of all, the reformation grounded on those Scriptures.

15. Water is an emblem of a great people ; this water of the Turks in particular. About the year 1060, they overran the Christian part of Asia. Afterward they poured into Europe, and spread farther and farther till they had overflowed many nations.

16. *But the earth helped the woman*—The powers of the earth ; and, indeed, she needed help through this whole period. The *time* was from 1058 to 1280 ; during which the Turkish flood ran higher and higher, though frequently repressed by the emperors, or their generals, *helping the woman.* The (two) *times* were from 1280 to 1725. During these, likewise, the Turkish power flowed far and wide. But still, from time to time, the princes of the earth helped the woman, that she was not carried away by it. The *half time* is from 1725 to 1836 In the beginning of this period, the Turks began to meddle with the affairs of

mouth, and swallowed up the river which the dragon had cast
17 out of his mouth. And the dragon was wroth with the woman
and went forth to make war with the rest of her seed, who
keep the commandments of GOD, and retain the testimony of
Jesus.

XIII. And I stood on the sand of the sea, and saw a wild beast coming up out of the sea, having seven heads and ten horns, and upon
his horns ten diadems, and upon his heads a name of blasphemy.

Persia, wherein they have so entangled themselves, as to be the less able to prevail against the two remaining Christian empires. Yet this flood still reaches
the woman in her place; and will till near the end of the half time; itself will
then be swallowed up, perhaps by means of Russia, which is risen in the room of
the eastern empire.

17. *And the dragon was wroth*—Anew, because he could not cause her to be
carried away by the stream; *and he went forth*—Into other lands, *to make war
with the rest of her seed*—Real Christians, living under heathen or Turkish
governors.

XIII. 1. *And I stood on the sand of the sea*—This also was in the vision.
And I saw—Soon after the woman fled away, *a wild beast coming up*—He comes
up twice, first from the sea, then from the abyss. He comes from the sea, before
the seven phials; the great whore comes after them.

O reader! this is a subject wherein we also are deeply concerned: and which
must be treated, not as a point of curiosity, but as a solemn warning from God.
The danger is near. Be armed, both against force and fraud, even with the
whole armour of God. *Out of the sea*—That is, Europe. So the three woes
(the first being in Persia, the second about the Euphrates,) move in a line from
east to west. This beast is the Romish papacy, as it came to a point six hundred years since, stands now, and will for some time longer. To this, and no
other power on earth, agrees the whole text, and every part of it, in every point,
as we may see with the utmost evidence, from the propositions following:—

Prop. 1. It is one and the same beast, having seven heads, and ten horns,
which is described in this and in the 17th chapter. Of consequence his heads
are the same, and his horns also.

Prop. 2. This beast is a spiritually secular power, opposite to the kingdom of
Christ. A power not merely spiritual or ecclesiastical, not merely secular or
political; but a mixture of both. He is a secular prince; for a crown, yea, and
a kingdom are ascribed to him. And yet he is not merely secular; for he is also
a false prophet.

Prop. 3. The beast has a strict connection with the city of Rome. This
clearly appears from the 17th chapter.

Prop. 4. The beast is now existing. He is not past; for Rome is now exist
ing: and it is not till after the destruction of Rome that the beast is thrown into
the lake. He is not altogether to come. For the second wo is long since past,
after which the third came quickly. And presently after it began the beast rose
out of the sea. Therefore, whatever he is, he is now existing.

Prop. 5. The beast is the Romish papacy. This manifestly follows from the
third and fourth propositions: the beast has a strict connection with the city of
Rome; and the beast is now existing. Therefore either there is some other
power more strictly connected with that city, or the pope is the beast.

Prop. 6. The papacy or papal kingdom began long ago.

The most remarkable particulars relating to this are here subjoined; taken
so high as abundantly to show the rise of the beast, and brought down as low
as our own time, in order to throw a light on the following part of the prophecy:—

A. D. 1033. Benedict the Ninth, a child of eleven years old, is bishop of Rome,
and occasions grievous disorder for above twenty years.

A. D. 1048. Damascus II. introduces the use of the triple crown.

A. D. 1058. The Church of Milan is, after long opposition, subjected to the
Roman.

A. D. 1073. Hildebrand, or Gregory VII., comes to the throne.

A. D. 1076. He deposes and excommunicates the emperor.
A. D. 1077. He uses him shamefully, and absolves him.
A. D. 1080. He excommunicates him again, and sends a crown to Rodolph, his
        competitor.
A. D. 1083. Rome is taken. Gregory flees. Clement is made pope, and crowns
        the emperor.
A. D. 1085. Gregory VII. dies at Salarno.
A. D. 1095. Urban II. holds the first popish council, (at Clermont,) and gives
        rise to the crusades.
A. D. 1111. Paschal II. quarrels furiously with the emperor.
A. D. 1123. The first western general council in the Lateran. The marriage of
        priests is forbidden.
A. D. 1132. Innocent II. declares the emperor to be the pope's liege man or
        vassal.
A. D. 1143. The Romans set up a government of their own, independent of In-
        nocent II. He excommunicates them and dies. Celestine II. is by an
        important innovation chosen to the popedom, without the suffrage of
        the people : the right of choosing the pope is taken from the people,
        and afterward from the clergy, and lodged in the cardinals alone.
A. D. 1152. Eugene II. assumes the power of canonizing saints.
A. D. 1155. Adrian IV. puts Arnold of Brixia to death for speaking against the
        secular power of the papacy.
A. D. 1159. Victor IV. is elected and crowned. But Alexander III. conquers
        him and his successor.
A. D. 1168. Alexander III. excommunicates the emperor, and brings him so
        low, that
A. D. 1177. He submits to the pope's setting his foot on his neck.
A. D. 1204. Innocent III. sets up the Inquisition against the Vaudois.
A. D. 1208. He proclaims a crusade against them.
A. D. 1300. Boniface VIII. introduces the year of Jubilee.
A. D. 1305. The pope's residence is removed to Avignon.
A. D. 1377. It is removed back to Rome.
A. D. 1378. The fifty years' schism begins.
A. D. 1449. Felix V., the last antipope, submits to Nicholas V.
A. D. 1517. The Reformation begins.
A. D. 1527. Rome is taken and plundered.
A. D. 1557. Charles V. resigns the empire; Ferdinand I. thinks the being
        crowned by the pope superfluous.
A. D. 1564. Pius IV. confirms the council of Trent.
A. D. 1682. Doctrines highly derogatory to the papal authority are openly
        taught in France.
A. D. 1713. The constitution Unigenitus.
A. D. 1721. Pope Gregory VII. canonized anew.

He who compares this short table with what will be observed, ver. 3, and chap.
xvii, 10, will see that the ascent of the beast out of the sea, must needs be fixed
toward the beginning of it; and not higher than Gregory VII., nor lower than
Alexander III.

The secular princes now favoured the kingdom of Christ; but the bishops of
Rome vehemently opposed it. These at first were plain ministers or pastors of
the Christian congregation at Rome, but by degrees they rose to an eminence
of honour and power over all their brethren : till about the time of Gregory VII.
(and so ever since) they assumed all the ensigns of royal majesty; yea, of a
majesty and power far superior to that of all other potentates on earth.

We are not here considering their false doctrines, but their unbounded power.
When we think of those, we are to look at the false prophet, who is also termed
a wild beast, at his ascent out of the earth. But the first beast then properly
arose, when, after several preludes thereto, the pope raised himself above the
emperor.

Prop. 7. Hildebrand, or Gregory VII., is the proper founder of the papal kingdom. All the patrons of the papacy allow that he made many considerable
additions to it : and this very thing constituted the beast, by completing the
spiritual kingdom; the new maxims, and the new actions of Gregory, all proclaim this. Some of his maxims are,

1. That the bishop of Rome alone is universal bishop.
2. That he alone can depose bishops, or receive them again.
3. That he alone has power to make new laws in the Church.
4. That he alone ought to use the ensigns of royalty.
5. That all princes ought to kiss his foot.
6. That the name of Pope is the only name under heaven; and that his name alone should be recited in the Churches.
7. That he has a power to depose emperors.
8. That no general synod can be convened but by him.
9. That no book is canonical without his authority.
10. That none upon earth can repeal his sentence, but he alone can repeal any sentence.
11. That he is subject to no human judgment.
12. That no power dare to pass sentence on one who appeals to the pope.
13. That all weighty causes every where ought to be referred to him.
14. That the Roman Church never did, nor ever can err.
15. That the Roman bishop, canonically ordained, is immediately made holy, by the merits of St. Peter.
16. That he can absolve subjects from their allegiance.

These the most eminent Romish writers own to be his genuine sayings. And his actions agree with his words. Hitherto the popes had been subject to the emperors, though often unwillingly. But now the pope began himself, under a spiritual pretext, to act the emperor of the whole Christian world: the immediate dispute was about the investiture of bishops, the right of which each claimed to himself. And now was the time for the pope either to give up or establish his empire for ever. To decide which Gregory excommunicated the emperor, Henry IV., "having first," says Platina, "deprived him of all his dignities." The sentence ran in these terms:—" Blessed Peter, prince of the apostles, incline, I beseech thee, thine ears, and hear me thy servant—In the name of the Omnipotent God, Father, Son, and Holy Ghost, I cast down the Emperor Henry from all imperial and regal authority, and absolve all Christians that were his subjects, from the oath whereby they used to swear allegiance to true kings. And moreover, because he had disputed mine, yea, thy admonitions, I bind him with the bond of an anathema."

The same sentence he repeated at Rome in these terms:—" Blessed Peter, prince of the apostles, and thou Paul, teacher of the Gentiles, incline, I beseech you, your ears to me, and graciously hear me—Henry, whom they call emperor, hath proudly lifted up his horns, and his head against the Church of God—who came to me, humbly imploring to be absolved from his excommunication. I restored him to communion, but not to his kingdom—neither did I allow his subjects to return to their allegiance. Several bishops and princes of Germany, taking this opportunity, in the room of Henry, justly deposed, chose Rodolph emperor: who immediately sent ambassadors to me, informing me—That he would rather obey me than accept of a kingdom; and that he should always remain at the disposal of God and us. Henry then began to be angry, and at first entreated us to hinder Rodolph from seizing his kingdom. I said, I would see to whom the right belonged—and give sentence which should be preferred. Henry forbade this—Therefore I bind Henry and all his favourers with the bond of an anathema, and again take from him all regal power. I absolve all Christians from their oath of allegiance, forbid them to obey Henry in any thing, and command them to receive Rodolph as their king. Confirm this therefore by your authority, ye most holy princes of the apostles, that all may now at length know, as ye have power to bind and loose in heaven, so we have power to give and take away on earth, empires, kingdoms, principalities, and whatsoever men can have."

When Henry submitted, then Gregory began to reign without control. In the same year, 1077, on September 1, he fixed a new era of time, called the indiction, used at Rome to this day.

Thus did the pope claim to himself the whole authority over all Christian princes. Thus did he take away or confer kingdoms and empires, as a king of kings. Neither did his successors fail to tread in his steps. It is well known the following popes have not been wanting to exercise the same power, both over kings and emperors. And this the later popes have been so far from disclaiming, that three of them have sainted this very Gregory, namely, Clement VIII., Paul V., and Benedict XIII. Here is then the beast, that is, the king; in fact such, though not in name : according to that remarkable observation of Cardinal Bellarmine, " Antichrist will govern the Roman empire, yet without the name of Roman Emperor." His spiritual title prevented his taking the name, while he exerciseth all the power. Now Gregory was at the head of this novelty. So Aventine himself, " Gregory VII. was the first founder of the Pontifical Empire."

Thus the time of the ascent of the beast is clear. The apostasy and mystery of iniquity gradually increased, till he arose who opposeth and exalteth himself above all, 2 Thess. ii, 3. Before the seventh trumpet, the adversary wrought more secretly. But soon after the beginning of this, the beast openly opposes his kingdom to the kingdom of Christ.

Prop. 8. The empire of Hildebrand properly began in the year 1077. Then it was, that upon the emperor's leaving Italy, Gregory exercised his power to the full. And on the first of September, in this year, he began his famous epoch.

This may be farther established and explained by the following observations.

Obs. 1. The beast is the Romish Papacy, which has now reigned for some ages.

Obs. 2. The beast has seven heads and ten horns.

Obs. 3. The seven heads are seven hills, and also seven kings. One of the heads could not have been as it were mortally wounded, had it been only a hill.

Obs. 4. The ascent of the beast out of the sea is different from his ascent out of the abyss: the Revelation often mentions both the sea and the abyss : but never uses the terms promiscuously.

Obs. 5. The heads of the beast do not begin before his rise out of the sea, but with it.

Obs. 6. These heads, as kings, succeed each other.

Obs. 7. The time which they take up in this succession is divided into three parts. Five of the kings signified thereby are fallen : one is : the other is not yet come.

Obs. 8. One is ; namely, while the angel was speaking this.

He places himself and St. John in the middlemost time : that he might the more commodiously point out the first time as past, the second as present, the third as future.

Obs. 9. The continuance of the beast is divided in the same manner. The beast was, is not : will ascend out of the abyss, chap. xvii, ver. 8 and 11. Between these two verses, that is, interposed as parallel with them, Five are fallen : one is, the other is not yet come.

Obs. 10. Babylon is Rome. All things which the Revelation says of Babylon, agree to Rome, and Rome only. It commenced Babylon when it commenced the Great. When Babylon sunk in the east it arose in the west. And it existed n the time of the apostles, whose judgment is said to be avenged on her.

Obs. 11. The beast reigns both before and after the reign of Babylon. First, .he beast reigns, chap. xiii, 1, &c, then Babylon, chap. xvii, 1, &c, and then the beast again, chap. xvii, 8, &c.

Obs. 12. The heads are of the substance of the beast : the horns are not. The wound of one of the heads is called the wound of the beast itself, ver. 3, but the horns or kings, receive the kingdom with the beast, chap. xvii, 12. That word alone, The horns and the beast, chap. xvii, 16, sufficiently shows them to be something added to him.

Obs. 13. The forty-two months of the beast fall within the first of the three periods. The beast rose out of the sea in the year 1077. A little after, power was given him for forty-two months. This power is still in being.

Obs. 14. The time when the beast is not, and the reign of Babylon, are together. The beast, when risen out of the sea, raged violently, till his kingdom was darkened by the fifth phial. But it was a kingdom still, and the beast having a kingdom, though darkened, was the beast still. But it was afterward said, the beast was, (was the beast, that is, reigned,) and is not: is not the beast; does not reign, having lost his kingdom. Why ? because the woman sits upon the beast, who sits a queen, reigning over the kings of the earth ; till the beast rising out of the abyss, and taking with him the ten kings, suddenly destroys her.

Obs. 15. The difference there is between Rome and the pope, which has always subsisted, will then be most apparent. Rome, distinct from the pope, bears three meanings, the city itself, the Roman Church, and the people of Rome. In the last sense of the word, Rome with its dutchy, which contained part of Tus-many and Campania, revolted from the Greek emperor in 726, and became a free state, governed by its senate. From this time the senate, and not the pope, enjoyed the supreme civil power. But in 796, Leo III. being chosen pope, sent to Charles the Great, desiring him to come and subdue the senate and people of Rome, and constrain them to swear allegiance to him. Hence arose a sharp contention between the pope and the Roman people, who seized and thrust him into a monastery. He escaped and fled to the emperor, who quickly sent him back in great state. In the year 800 the emperor came to Rome, and shortly after, the Roman people, who had hitherto chosen their own bishops, and looked upon themselves and their senate, as having the same rights with the ancient senate and people of Rome, chose Charles for their emperor, and subjected themselves to him in the same manner as the ancient Romans did to their emperors. The pope crowned him and paid him homage on his knees, as was formerly done to the Roman emperors : and the emperor took an oath "to defend the holy Roman Church in all its emoluments." He was also created consul, and styled himself thenceforward Augustus, emperor of the Romans. Afterward he gave the government of the city and dutchy of Rome to the pope, yet still subject to himself.

What the Roman Church is, as distinct from the pope, appears, 1. When a council is held before the pope's confirmation ; 2. When upon a competition, judgment is given which is the true pope ; 3. When the see is vacant ; 4. When the pope himself is suspected by the inquisition.

How Rome, as it is a city, differs from the pope, there is no need to show.

Obs. 16. In the first and second period of his duration, the beast is a body of men, in the third, an individual. The beast with seven heads is the papacy of many ages : the seventh head is the man of sin, antichrist. He is a body of men, from chap. xiii, 1, to xvii, 7. He is a body of men and an individual, chap. xvii, from the eighth to the eleventh verse. He is an individual, from chap. xvii, 12, to xix, 20.

Obs. 17. That individual is the seventh head of the beast, or the other king after the five and one, himself being the eighth, though one of the seven. As he is a pope, he is one of the seven heads. But he is the eighth, or not a head, but the beast himself, not as he is a pope, but as he bears a new and singular character at his coming from the abyss. To illustrate this by a comparison : suppose a tree of seven branches, one of which is much larger than the rest. If those six are cut away, and the seventh remain, that is the tree.

Obs. 18. He is the wicked one, the man of sin, the son of perdition, usually termed antichrist.

Obs. 19. The ten horns, or kings, *receive power as kings with the wild beast one hour*, chap. xvi., 12. With the individual beast *who was not*. But he receives his power again, and the kings with it, who quickly give their new power to nim.

Obs. 20. The whole power of the Roman monarchy, divided into ten kingdoms, will be conferred on the beast, chap. xvii, 13, 16, 17.

Obs. 21. The ten horns and the beast will destroy the whore, ver. 16.

Obs. 22. At length the beast, the ten horns, and the other kings of the earth, will fall in that great slaughter, chap. xix, 19.

Obs. 23. Daniel's fourth beast is the Roman monarchy, from the beginning of it till the thrones are set. This therefore comprises both the Apocalyptic beast, and the woman, and many other things. This monarchy is like a river which runs from its fountain in one channel, but in its course sometimes takes in other rivers, sometimes is itself parted into several streams, yet is still one continued river. The Roman power was at first undivided. But it was afterward divided into various channels, till the grand division into the eastern and western empires, which likewise underwent various changes. Afterward the kings of the Heruli, Goths, Lombards, the Exarchs of Ravena, the Romans themselves ; the emperors, French and German, beside other kings, seized several parts of the Roman power. Now, whatever power the Romans had before Gregory VII, that Daniel's beast contains. Whatever power the papacy has had from Gregory VII., this the Apocalyptic beast represents. But this very beast (and so Rome

2 And the wild beast which 1 saw *was* like a leopard, and his **feet** *were* as *the feet* of a bear, and his mouth as the mouth of a lion, and the dragon gave him his power, and his throne, and great au-
3 thority.   And *I saw* one of his heads as it were wounded to death; and his deadly wound was healed; and the whole earth wondered

---

with its last authority) is comprehended under that of Daniel.   *And upon his heads a name of blasphemy*—To ascribe to a man what belongs to God alone is blasphemy.   Such a name the beast has, not on his horns, nor on one head, but on all.   The beast himself bears that name, and, indeed, through his whole du-ration.   This is the name of *papa* or *pope;* not in the innocent sense wherein it was formerly given to all bishops, but in that high and peculiar sense wherein it is now given to the bishop of Rome, by himself and his followers : a name which comprises the whole pre-eminence of the highest and most holy father upon earth.   Accordingly, among the above-cited sayings of Gregory, these two stand together, that his name alone should be recited in the churches : and that it is the only name in the world.   So both the Church and the world were to name no other father on the face of the earth.

2. The three first beasts in Daniel are like a leopard, a bear, and a lion.   In all parts, except his feet and mouth, this beast was like a leopard, or female pan-ther ; which is fierce as a lion, or bear, and is also swift and subtle.   Such is the papacy, which has, partly by subtlety, partly by force, gained power over so many nations.   The extremely various usages, manners, and ways of the pope, may likewise be compared to the spots of the leopard.   *And his feet were as the feet of a bear*—Which are very strong, and armed with sharp claws.   And as clumsy as they seem, he can therewith walk, stand upright, climb, or seize any thing. So does this beast seize and take for his prey whatever comes within the reach of his claws ; *and his mouth was as the mouth of a lion*—To roar, and to devour. *And the dragon*—Whose vassal and vicegerent he is, *gave him his power*—His own strength and innumerable forces, *and his throne*—So that he might command whatever he would, having great, absolute authority.   The dragon had his throne in heathen Rome, so long as idolatry and persecution reigned there.   And after he was disturbed in his possession, yet would he never wholly resign, till he gave it to the beast in Christian Rome, so called.

.3. *And I saw one*—Or the first, *of his heads as it were wounded*—So it ap-peared as soon as ever it rose.   The beast is first described more generally, then more particularly, both in this and in the 17th chapter.   The particular de-scription here, respects the former parts : there, the latter parts of his duration : only that some circumstances relating to the former are repeated in the 17th chapter.

This deadly wound was given him on his first head by the sword, ver. 14, that is, by the bloody resistance of the secular potentates, particularly the German emperors.   These, for a long season, had the city of Rome, with her bishop un-der their jurisdiction.   Gregory determined to cast off this yoke from his own, and to lay it on the emperor's shoulders.   He broke loose and excommunicated the emperor, who maintained his right by force, and gave the pope such a blow, that one would have thought the beast must have been killed thereby, immedi-ately after his coming up.   But he recovered, and grew stronger than before. The first head of the beast extends from Gregory VII. at least to Innocent III. In that tract of time the beast was much wounded by the emperors.   But not.withstanding, the wound was healed.

Two deadly symptoms attended this wound : 1. Schisms and open ruptures in he Church.   For while the emperors asserted their right, there were, from the ear 1080 to the year 1176 only, five open divisions, and at least as many anti-popes ; some of whom were, indeed, the rightful popes.   This was highly dan-gerous to the papal kingdom.   But a still more dangerous symptom was, 2. The rising of the nobility at Rome, who would not suffer their bishop to be a secular prince, particularly over themselves.   Under Innocent II., they carried their point, re-established the ancient commonwealth, took away from the pope the government of the city, and left him only his episcopal authority.   " At this, says the historian, " Innocent II. and Celestine II. fretted themselves to death · Lucius II., as he attacked the capitol wherein the senate was, sword in hand

4 after the wild beast, And worshipped the dragon, because he gave the authority to the wild beast; and worshipped the wild beast. saying, Who *is* like the wild beast; and who can war with him?
5 And there was given him a mouth speaking great things and blas-
6 phemy; and authority was given him forty and two months. And he opened his mouth in blasphemy against God, to blaspheme his
7 name and his tabernacle, even them that dwell in heaven. And it was given him to make war with the saints, and to overcome then., and authority was given him over every tribe, and people, and
8 tongue, and nation. And all that dwell upon the earth will worship him, whose name is not written in the book of life of the Lamb,

---

was struck with a stone, and died in a few days: Eugenius III., Alexander III., and Lucius III. were driven out of the city : Urban III. and Gregory VIII. spent their days in banishment. At length they came to an agreement with Clement III., who was himself a Roman." *And the whole earth*—The whole western world, *wondered after the wild beast*—That is, followed him with wonder in his councils, his crusades, and his jubilees. This refers not only to the first head, but also to the four following.

4. *And they worshipped the dragon*—Even in worshipping the beast, although they knew it not, *and worshipped the wild beast*—Paying him such honour as was not paid to any merely secular potentate. That very title, " Our most holy Lord," was never given to any other monarch on earth, *saying, Who is like the wild beast?*—*Who is like him?* is a peculiar attribute of God. But that this is constantly attributed to the beast, the books of all his adherents show.

5. *And there was given him*—By the dragon, through the permission of God, *a mouth speaking great things and blasphemy*—The same is said of the little horn on the fourth beast in Daniel. Nothing greater, nothing more blasphemous can be conceived, than what the popes have said of themselves, especially before the reformation. *And authority was given him forty-two months*—The beginning of these is not to be dated immediately from his ascent out of the sea, but at some distance from it.

6. *To blaspheme his name*—Which many of the popes have done explicitly, and in the most dreadful manner, *and his tabernacle, even them that dwell in heaven*— (For God himself dwelleth in the inhabitants of heaven :) digging up the bones of many of them, and cursing them with the deepest execrations.

7. *And it was given him*—That is, God permitted him, *to make war with the saints*—With the Waldenses and Albigenses. It is a vulgar mistake, that the Waldenses were so called from Peter Waldo, of Lyons. They were much more ancient than him; and their true name was Vallenses, or Vaudois, from their inhabiting the valleys of Lucerne and Angrogne. This name, Vallenses, after Waldo appeared, about the year 1160, was changed by the Papists into Waldenses, on purpose to represent them as of modern original. The Albigenses were originally people of Albigeois, part of Upper Languedoc, where they considerably prevailed, and possessed several towns in the year 1200. Against these, many of the popes made open war. Till now the blood of Christians had been shed only by the heathens or Arians : from this time by scarce any but the papacy. In the year 1208 Innocent III. proclaimed a crusade against them. In June, 1209, the army assembled at Thoulouse ; from which time abundance of blood was shed, and the second army of martyrs began to be added to the first, who had cried from beneath the altar. And ever since the beast has been warring against the saints, and shedding their blood like water. *And authority was given him over every tribe and people*—Particularly in Europe. And when a way was found by sea into the East Indies and the West, these also were brought under his authority.

8. *And all that dwell upon the earth will worship him*—All will be carried away by the torrent but the little flock of true believers. The name of these only is written in the Lamb's book of life. And if any even of these make ship-wreck of the faith, he will blot them out of his book ; although they were written therein from (that is, before) the foundation of the world, chap. xvii, 8.

9 who was slain from the foundation of the world. If any man have
10 an ear, let him hear. If any leadeth into captivity, he goeth into
captivity; if any man kill with the sword, he must be killed with
the sword. Here is the patience and the faithfulness of the
saints.
11 And I saw another wild beast coming up out of the earth, and he
12 had two horns like a lamb, but he spake like a dragon: And he
exerciseth all the authority of the first wild beast before him; and
he causeth the earth, and them that dwell therein, to worship the
13 first wild beast, whose deadly wound was healed. And he doth
great wonders, so that he even maketh fire to come down out of
14 heaven to the earth in the sight of men. And he deceiveth them
that dwell on the earth by the wonders which it is given him to
do before the wild beast: saying to them that dwell on the earth,
to make an image to the wild beast which had the wound by the
15 sword, and yet lived. And it was given him to give breath to the
image of the wild beast: so that the image of the wild beast
should speak: and he will cause that as many as will not wor-
16 ship the image of the wild beast shall be killed. And he causeth

9. *If any man have an ear, let him hear*—It was said before, He that hath an ear, let him hear. This expression, *if any*, seems to imply that scarce will any that hath an ear be found. *Let him hear*—With all attention, the following warning, and the whole description of the beast.

10. *If any man leadeth into captivity*—God will in due time repay the followers of the beast in their own kind. Meanwhile *here is the patience and faithfulness of the saints*—Exercised: their patience, by enduring captivity or imprisonment: their faithfulness, by resisting unto blood.

11. *And I saw another wild beast*—So he is once termed, to show his fierceness and strength; but in all other places, The false prophet. He comes to confirm the kingdom of the first beast, *coming up*—After the other had long exercised his authority, *out of the earth*—Out of Asia. But he is not yet come, though he cannot be far off. For he is to appear at the end of the forty-two months of the first beast. *And he had two horns like a lamb*—A mild, innocent appearance, *but he spake like a dragon*—Venomous, fiery, dreadful: so do those who are zealous for the beast.

12. *And he exerciseth all the authority of the first wild beast*—Described in the 2d, 4th, 5th, and 7th verses, *before him*—For they are both together; *whose deadly wound was healed*—More thoroughly healed by means of the second beast.

13. *He maketh fire*—Real fire, *to come down*—By the power of the devil.

14. *Before the wild beast*—Whose usurped majesty is confirmed by these wonders; *saying to them*—As if it were from God, *to make an image to the wild beast*—Like that of Nebuchadnezzar, whether of gold, silver, or stone. The original image will be set up where the beast himself shall appoint. But abundance of copies will be taken, which may be carried into all parts, like those of Diana of Ephesus.

15. *So that the image of the wild beast should speak*—Many instances of this kind have been already among the papists as well as the heathens; *and as many as will not worship*—When it is required of them; as it will be of all that buy or sell, *shall be killed*—By this the pope manifests that he is antichrist, directly contrary to Christ. It is Christ who shed his own blood. It is antichrist who sheds the blood of others. And yet it seems his last and most cruel persecution is to come. This persecution, the reverse of all that preceded, will, as we may gather from many scriptures, fall chiefly on the outward court worshippers, the formal Christians. It is probable that few real, inward Christians, shall perish by it; on the contrary, those who watch and pray always, shall be accounted worthy to escape all these things, and to stand before the Son of man, Luke xxi, 36.

all, both small and great, both rich and poor, both free and slaves,
17 to receive a mark on the right hand or on the forehead; That
no man might buy or sell but he that had the mark, the name of
18 the wild beast, or the number of his name. Here is the wisdom.
Let him that hath understanding count the number of the wild
beast: for it is the number of a man; and his number is six
hundred sixty-six.
XIV. And I looked, and behold the Lamb standing on Mount Sion,
and with him a hundred forty-four thousand, having his name and
2 the name of his Father written on their foreheads. And I heard
a sound out of heaven, as a sound of many waters, and as a sound
of a great thunder; and the sound which I heard *was* as of harpers
3 harping on their harps. And they sing a new song before the
throne, and before the four living creatures, and the elders : and

---

16. *On their forehead*—The most zealous of his followers will probably choose
this. Others may receive it on their hand.
17. *That no man might buy or sell*—Such edicts have been published long
since against the poor Vaudois; *but he that had the mark*, namely, *the name
of the first beast, or the number of his name*—The name of the beast is that
which he bears through his whole duration, viz. that of *papa* or *pope*. The
number of his name is the whole time during which he bears this name. Whosoever therefore receives the mark of the beast, does as much as if he said
expressly, "I acknowledge the present papacy as proceeding from God:" or,
"I acknowledge that what St. Gregory VII. has done according to his legend,
(authorized from Benedict XIII.,) and what has been maintained in virtue
thereof, by his successors to this day, is from God." By the former, a man
hath the name of the beast, as a mark; by the latter, the number of his name.
In a word, to have the name of the beast is to acknowledge his papal holiness: to have the number of his name is to acknowledge the papal succession.
The second beast will enforce the receiving this mark, under the severest
penalties.
18. *Here is the wisdom*—To be exercised. *The patience of the saints* availed
against the power of the first beast: the wisdom God giveth them will avail
against the subtlety of the second. *Let him that hath understanding*—Which
is a gift of God, subservient to that wisdom, *count the number of the wild
beast*—Surely none can be blamed for attempting to obey this command, *for
it is the number of a man*—A number of such years as are common among
men, *and his number is six hundred sixty-six* years. So long shall he endure
from his first appearing.
XIV. 1. *And I* saw *on Mount Sion*, the heavenly Sion, *a hundred forty-four
thousand*—Either those out of all mankind who had been the most eminently
holy, or the most holy out of the twelve tribes of Israel, the same that were
mentioned, chap. vii, 4, and perhaps also, chap. xv, 2. But they were then
in the world, and were sealed in their foreheads, to preserve them from the
plagues that were to follow. They are now in safety, and have the name of
the Lamb and of his Father written on their foreheads—As being the redeemed
of God and of the Lamb, his now unalienable property. This prophecy often
introduces the inhabitants of heaven as a kind of chorus with great propriety
and elegance. The Church above making suitable reflections on the grand
events which are foretold in this book, greatly serves to raise the attention of
real Christians, and to teach the high concern they have in them. Thus is the
Church on earth instructed, animated, and encouraged, by the sentiments, temper
and devotion of the Church in heaven.
2. *And I heard a sound out of heaven*—Sounding clearer and clearer: first, at
a distance, as the sound of many waters or thunders; and afterward, being
nearer, it was as of harpers harping on their harps. It sounded vocally an
instrumentally at once.
3. *And they*—The hundred forty-four thousand, *sing a new song; and none
could learn that song*—To sing and play it in the same manner, *but the hundred*

45

none could learn the song but the hundred forty-four thousand,
4 who were redeemed from the earth. These are they who had
not been defiled with women; for they are virgins: these are
they who follow the Lamb whithersoever he goeth. These were
redeemed from among men: first fruits to God and the Lamb.
5 And in their mouth there was found no guile: they are without
fault.
6   And I saw another angel flying in the midst of heaven, having
an everlasting Gospel to preach to them that dwell on the earth,
7 and to every nation, and tribe, and tongue, and people: Saying
with a loud voice, Fear God, and give glory to him; for the hour
of his judgment is come: and worship him that made the heaven,
and the earth, and the sea, and fountains of water.
8   And another angel followed, saying, Babylon the great is fallen,
is fallen; she that hath made all nations drink of the wine of her
fornication.

forty-four thousand who were redeemed from the earth—From among men: from
all sin.
    4. *These are they who had not been defiled with women*—It seems that the
deepest defilement, and the most alluring temptation, is put for every other.
They are virgins—Unspotted souls; such as have preserved universal purity.
These are they who follow the Lamb—Who are nearest to him. This is not
their character, but their reward. *First fruits*—Of the glorified spirits. Who is
ambitious to be of this number?
    5. *And in their mouth there was found no guile*—(Part for the whole,) nothing
untrue, unkind, unholy. *They are without fault*—Having preserved inviolate a
virgin purity, both of soul and body.
    6. *And I saw another angel*—A second is mentioned, ver. 8; a third, ver. 9
These three denote great messengers of God, with their assistants, three men who
bring messages from God to men. The first exhorts to the fear and worship of
God; the second proclaims the fall of Babylon; the third gives warning concerning the beast. Happy are they who make the right use of these Divine messages!
Flying—Going on swiftly, *in the midst of heaven*—Breadthwise, *having an everlasting Gospel*—Not the Gospel properly so called; but a gospel, or joyful message,
which was to have an influence on all ages, *to ˌpreach to every nation, and tribe,
and tongue, and people*—Both to Jew and Gentile, even as far as the authority of
the beast had extended.
    7. *Fear God, and give glory to him; for the hour of his judgment is come*—The
joyful message is properly this, that the hour of God's judgment is come.
And hence is that admonition drawn, *Fear God, and give glory to him:* they
who do this will not worship the beast, neither any image or idol whatsoever:
and worship him that made—Whereby he is absolutely distinguished from idols
of every kind, *the heaven, and the earth, and the sea, and fountains of water*—
And they who worship him shall be delivered when the angels pour out their
phials on the earth, sea, fountains of water, on the sun, and in the air.
    8. *And another angel followed, saying, Babylon is fallen*—With the overthrow
of Babylon, that of all the enemies of Christ, and consequently happier times are
connected. *Babylon the great*—So the city of Rome is called upon many accounts. Babylon was magnificent, strong, proud, powerful. So is Rome also.
Babylon was first, Rome afterward, the residence of the emperors of the world.
What Babylon was to Israel of old, Rome hath been both to the literal and spiritual Israel of God. Hence the liberty of the ancient Jews was connected with
the overthrow of the Babylonish empire. And when Rome is finally overthrown.
then the people of God will be at liberty.
    Whenever Babylon is mentioned in this book, *the great* is added; to teach us
that Rome then commenced Babylon, when it commenced the great city: when
it swallowed up the Grecian monarchy and its fragments, in Syria in particular,
and in consequence of this obtained dominion over Jerusalem about sixty years
before the birth of Christ. Then it began, but it will not cease to be Babylon

9   And a third angel followed them; saying with a loud voice, If any one worship the wild beast and his image, and receive *his* mark
10   on his forehead or on his hand, He shall also drink of the wine of the wrath of God, which is poured unmixed into the cup of his indignation, and shall be tormented with fire and brimstone, in the
11   presence of the angels, and in the presence of the Lamb. And the smoke of their torment ascendeth for ever and ever, and they have no rest day or night, who worshipped the wild beast and his
12   image, and whosoever receiveth the mark of his name. Here is the patience of the saints, who keep the commandments of God, and the faith of Jesus.
13   And I heard a voice out of heaven, saying, Write: From hence forth happy are the dead who die in the Lord: Yea, (saith the Spirit,) that they may rest from their labours. Their works follow them.

till it is finally destroyed. Its spiritual greatness began in the fifth century, and increased from age to age. It seems it will come to its utmost height just before its final overthrow.

Her fornication is her idolatry, invocation of saints and angels, worship of images, human traditions, with all that outward pomp, yea, and that fierce and bloody zeal wherewith she pretends to serve God. But with spiritual fornication, as elsewhere, so in Rome, fleshly fornication is joined abundantly. Witness the stews there, licensed by the pope, which are no inconsiderable branch of his revenue. This is fitly compared to wine, because of its intoxicating nature.

Of this *wine she hath* indeed *made all nations drink,* more especially by her later missions. We may observe, this *making them drink* is not ascribed to the beast, but to Babylon. For Rome itself, the Roman inquisitions, congregations, and Jesuits, continually propagate their idolatrous doctrines and practices, with or without the consent of this or that pope, who himself is not secure from their censure.

9. *And a third angel followed*—At no great distance of time, *saying, If any one worship the wild beast*—This worship consists, partly in an inward submission, a persuasion that all who are subject to Christ must be subject to the beast, or they cannot receive the influences of Divine grace; or, as their expression is, "There is no salvation out of the Church." Partly in a suitable outward reverence to the beast himself, and consequently to his image.

10. *He shall drink*—With Babylon, chap. xvi, 19, *and shall be torn, nted*—With the beast, chap. xx, 10. In all the Scripture there is not another so terrible threatening as this. And God by this greater fear arms his servants against the fear of the beast. *The wrath of God which is poured unmixed*—Without any mixture of mercy, without hope, *into the cup of his indignation*—And is no real anger implied in all this? O what will not even wise men assert to serve a hypothesis!

11. *And the smoke*—From the fire and brimstone, wherein they are tormented —*ascendeth for ever and ever*—God grant thou and I may never try the strict, literal eternity of this torment!

12. *Here is the patience of the saints*—Seen; in suffering all things rather than receive this mark; *who keep the commandments of God*—The character of all true saints, and particularly the great command to believe in Jesus.

13. *And I heard a voice*—This is most seasonably heard, when the beast is in his highest power and fury; *out of heaven*—Probably from a departed saint; *Write*—He was at first commanded to write the whole book. Whenever this is repeated, it denotes something peculiarly observable. *Happy are the dead (from henceforth* particularly)—1. Because they escape the approaching calamities; 2. Because they already enjoy so near an approach to glory; *who die in the Lord*— In the faith of the Lord Jesus: *for they rest*—No pain, no purgatory follows; but pure, unmixed happiness: *from their labours*—And the more laborious their life was, the sweeter is their rest. How different this state from that of those

14 And I looked, and behold a white cloud, and on the cloud one sitting like a son of man, having a golden crown on his head, and
15 a sharp sickle in his hand. And another angel came out of the temple, crying with a loud voice to him that sat on the cloud, Thrust in thy sickle and reap; for the time to reap is come: for
16 the harvest of the earth is ripe. And he that sat on the cloud thrust in his sickle upon the earth, and the earth was reaped.
17 And another angel came out of the temple which is in heaven;
18 and he also had a sharp sickle. And another angel came out from the altar, who had power over fire, and cried with a loud cry to him that had the sharp sickle, saying, Thrust in thy sickle, and lop off the clusters of the vine of the earth; for her grapes are fully
19 ripe. And the angel thrust in his sickle upon the earth, and lopped off the vine of the earth, and cast it into the great wine press
20 of the wrath of God. And the wine press was trodden without the city, and blood came out of the wine press, even to the horses' bridles, one thousand six hundred furlongs.
XV. And I saw another sign in heaven great and wonderful, seven angels having the seven last plagues: for by them the wrath of
2 God is fulfilled. And I saw as it were a sea of glass mingled with

ver. 11, *who have no rest day or night!* Reader, which wilt thou choose? *Their works*—Each one's peculiar works; *follow*—Or accompany them: that is, the fruit of their works. Their works do not go before, to procure them admittance into the mansions of joy; but they follow them when admitted.

14. In the following verses, under the emblem of a harvest and a vintage, are signified two general visitations: First, many good men are taken from the earth by the harvest; then many sinners during the vintage. The latter is altogether a penal visitation; the former seems to be altogether gracious. Here is no reference in either to the day of judgment, but to a season which cannot be far off. *And I saw a white cloud*—An emblem of mercy; *and on the cloud sat one like a son of man*—An angel in a human shape, sent by Christ, the Lord both of the vintage and the harvest; *having a golden crown on his head*—In token of his high dignity; *and a sharp sickle in his hand*—The sharper, the welcomer to the righteous.

15. *And another angel came out of the temple,* (which is in heaven,) ver. 17. Out of which came the judgments of God in the appointed seasons. *Crying*—By the command of God, *Thrust in thy sickle for the harvest is ripe*—This implies a high degree of holiness in those good men, and an earnest desire to be with God.

18. *And another angel from the altar*—Of burnt offerings; from whence the martyrs had cried for vengeance; *who had power over fire*—As *the angel of the waters,* chap. xvi, 5, had over water; *cried, saying, Lop off the clusters of the vine of the earth*—All the wicked are considered as constituting one body.

20. *And the wine press was trodden*—By the Son of God, chap. xix, 15, *without the city of Jerusalem.* They to whom St. John writes, when a man said, The city, immediately understood this; *and blood came out of the wine press, even to the horses' bridles*—So deep, at its first flowing from the wine press; *one thousand six hundred furlongs*—So far: at least two hundred miles through the whole land of Palestine.

XV. 1. *And I saw seven holy angels, having the seven last plagues*—Before they had the phials, which were as instruments whereby those plagues were to be conveyed. They are termed *the last,* because by them the wrath of God is fulfilled. Hitherto God had borne his enemies with much long-suffering, but now his wrath goes forth to the uttermost, pouring plagues on the earth from one end to the other, and around its whole circumference. But even after these plagues, the holy wrath of God against his other enemies does not cease, chap. xx, 15.

2. The song was sung, while the angels were coming out with their plagues

fire and them that gained the victory over the wild beast, and over his image, and over the number of his name, standing at the sea
3 of glass, and having the harps of God. And they sing the song of Moses, the servant of God, and the song of the Lamb, saying, Great and wonderful *are* thy works, Lord God Almighty ; righteous
4 and true are thy ways, O King of the nations ! Who would not fear thee, O Lord, and glorify thy name ? For thou only *art* gracious : for all the nations shall come and worship before thee : for thy judgments are made manifest.
5 And after these things I looked, and the temple of the taber-
6 nacle of the testimony was open in heaven : And the seven angels that had the seven plagues came out of the temple clothed in pure, white linen, and having their breasts girt with golden girdles.

---

who are therefore mentioned both before and after it, ver. 1, 6. *And I saw as it were a sea of glass, mingled with fire*—It was before *clear as crystal*, chap. iv, 6 ; but now *mingled with fire*—Which devours the adversaries, *and them that gained*, or *were gaining, the victory over the wild beast*—More of whom were yet to come. The mark of the beast, the mark of his name, and the number of his name, seem to mean here nearly the same thing ; *standing at the sea of glass*— Which was before the throne ; *having the harps of God*—Given by him, and appropriated to his praise.

3. *And they sing the song of Moses*—So called, partly from its near agreement with the words of that song, which he sung after passing the Red Sea, Exod. xv, 11 ; and of that which he taught the children of Israel a little before his death, Deut. xxxii, 3, 4. But chiefly because Moses was the minister and representative of the Jewish Church, as Christ is of the Church universal. Therefore it is also termed *The song of the Lamb.* It consists of six parts, which answer each other :—

1. Great and wonderful are thy works, Lord God Almighty ;
2. For thou only art gracious :
3. Just and true are thy ways, O King of the nations ;
4. For all the nations shall come and worship before thee :
5. Who would not fear thee, O Lord, and glorify thy name ?
6. For thy judgments are made manifest.

We know and acknowledge, that all thy works in and toward all thy creatures are great and wonderful : that thy ways with all the children of men, good and evil, are just and true. *For thou only art gracious*—And this grace is the spring of all those wonderful works, even of his destroying the enemies of his people. Accordingly in the 136th Psalm, that clause, *for his mercy endureth for ever*, is subjoined to the thanksgiving for his works of vengeance, as well as for his delivering the righteous : *for all the nations shall come and worship before thee*— They shall serve thee as their King with joyful reverence. This is a glorious testimony of the future conversion of all the heathens. The Christians are now a little flock ; they who do not worship God an immense multitude. But all the nations shall come from all parts of the earth to worship him, and glorify his name : *for thy judgments are made manifest*—And then the inhabitants of the earth will at length learn to fear him.

5. *After these things the temple of the tabernacle of the testimony*—The holiest of all, *was opened*—Disclosing a new theatre, for the coming forth of the judgments of God, now made manifest.

6. *And the seven angels came out of the temple*—As having received their instructions from the oracle of God himself. St. John saw them in heaven, (ver. 1,) before they went into the temple. They appeared in habits like those the high priest wore, when he went into the most holy place to consult the oracle. In this was the visible testimony of God's presence ; *clothed in pure, white linen* —Linen is the habit of service and attendance ; *pure*—Unspotted, unsullied ; *white*—Or bright and shining, which implies much more than bare innocence *and having their breasts girt with golden girdles*—In token of their high dignity and glorious rest.

7 And one of the four living creatures gave the seven angels **seven**
8 golden phials full of the wrath of God, who liveth for ever. And
the temple was filled with smoke from the glory of God, and from
his power: and none could go into the temple, till the seven
plagues of the seven angels were fulfilled.
XVI. And I heard a loud voice out of the temple, saying to the
seven angels, Go, pour out the seven phials of the wrath of God
2 upon the earth. And the first went and poured out his phial upon
the earth, and there came a grievous ulcer on the men that had
3 the mark of the wild beast, and that worshipped his image. And
the second poured out his phial upon the sea, and it became blood,
as *the blood* of a dead man, and every living soul in the sea died.
4 And the third poured out his phial on the rivers and fountains
5 of water, and they became blood. And I heard the angel of the
waters saying, Righteous art thou, who art, and who wast, the
6 Gracious One; because thou hast judged thus. For they have

---

7. *And one of the four living creatures gave the seven angels*—After they were
come out of the temple, *seven golden phials*—Or bowls. The Greek word signifies vessels broader at the top than at the bottom; *full of the wrath of God, who
liveth for ever and ever*—A circumstance which adds greatly to the dreadfulness
of his wrath.

8. *And the temple was filled with smoke*—The cloud of glory was the visible
manifestation of God's presence in the tabernacle and temple. It was a sign of
protection at erecting the tabernacle and at the dedication of the temple. But
in the judgment of Korah, the glory of the Lord appeared, when he and his companions were swallowed up by the earth. So proper is the emblem of smoke
from the glory of God, or from the cloud of glory, to express the execution of
judgment, as well as to be a sign of favour. Both proceed from the power of
God, and in both he is glorified; *and none*—Not even of those who ordinarily
stood before God, *could go into the temple*—That is, into the inmost part of it,
till the seven plagues of the seven angels were fulfilled—Which did not take up
a long time, like the seven trumpets, but swiftly followed each other.

XVI. 1. *Pour out the seven phials*—The epistles to the seven Churches are
divided into three and four: the seven seals, and so the trumpets and phials, into
four and three. The trumpets gradually, and in a long tract of time, overthrow
the kingdoms of the world; the phials destroy chiefly the beast and his followers,
with a swift and impetuous force. The four first affect the earth, the sea, the
rivers, the sun; the rest fall elsewhere, and are much more terrible.

2. *And the first went*—So *the second, third, &c,* without adding *angel,* to
denote the utmost swiftness: of which this also is a token, that there is no period
of time mentioned in the pouring out of each phial. They have a great resemblance to the plagues of Egypt, which the Hebrews generally suppose to have
been a month distant from each other. Perhaps so may the phials; but they are
all yet to come: *and poured out his phial upon the earth*—Literally taken, *and
there came a grievous ulcer*—As in Egypt, Exod. ix, 10, 11; *on the men who had
the mark of the wild beast*—All of them, and them only. All these plagues seem
to be described in proper, not figurative words.

3. *The second poured out his phial upon the sea*—As opposed to the dry land;
and it became blood as of a dead man—Thick, congealed, and putrid; *and every
living soul*—Men, beasts, and fishes, whether on or in the sea, *died.*

4. *The third poured out his phial on the rivers and fountains of water*—Which
were all over the earth; *and they became blood*—So that none could drink
thereof.

5. *The Gracious One*—So he is styled when his judgments are abroad: and
that with a peculiar propriety. In the beginning of the book he is termed *the
Almighty.* In the time of his patience he is praised for his power, which otherwise might then be less regarded. In the time of his taking vengeance, for his
mercy. Of his power there could then be no doubt

shed the blood of saints and prophets, and thou hast given them
7 blood to drink. They are worthy. And I heard *another* from
the altar, saying, Yea, Lord God Almighty ; true and righteous
8 *are* thy judgments. And the fourth poured out his phial upon
9 the sun ; and it was given him to scorch the men with fire. And
the men were scorched exceedingly, and blasphemed the name
of God, who had power over these plagues : but they repented
10 not to give him glory. And the fifth poured out his phial upon
the throne of the wild beast : and his kingdom was darkened.
11 And they gnawed their tongues for pain, and blasphemed the God
of heaven, because of their pains, and because of their ulcers, and
12 repented not of their works. And the sixth poured out his phial
upon the great river Euphrates, and the water of it was dried up,
13 that the way of the kings from the east might be prepared. And
I saw out of the mouth of the dragon, and out of the mouth of the

---

6. *Thou hast given them blood to drink*—Men do not drink out of the sea, but out of fountains and rivers. Therefore this is fitly added here. *They are worthy* —Is subjoined with a beautiful abruptness.

7. *Yea*—Answering the angel of the waters, and affirming of God's judgments in general what he had said of one particular judgment.

8. *The fourth poured out his phial upon the sun*—Which was likewise affected by the fourth trumpet. There is also a plain resemblance between the first, second, and third phials, and the first, second, and third trumpets ; *and it was given him*—The angel, *to scorch the men*—Who had the mark of the beast, *with fire*—As well as with the beams of the sun. So these four phials affected earth, water, fire, and air.

9. *And the men blasphemed God, who had power over these plagues*—They could not but acknowledge the hand of God, yet did they harden themselves against him.

10. The first four phials are closely connected together, the fifth concerns the throne of the beast, the sixth the Mohammedans, the seventh chiefly the heathens. The four first phials and the four first trumpets go round the whole earth ; the three last phials and the three last trumpets go lengthwise over the earth in a straight line.
The fifth poured out his phial upon the throne of the wild beast—It is not said, on the beast and his throne. Perhaps the sea will then be vacant, *and his kingdom was darkened*—With a lasting, not a transient darkness. However, the beast, as yet, has his kingdom. Afterward the woman sits upon the beast, and then it is said, *The wild beast is not*, chap. xvii, 3, 7, 8.

11. *And they*—His followers, *gnawed their tongues*—Out of furious impatience, *because of their pains, and because of their ulcers*—Now mentioned together, and in the plural number, to signify that they were greatly heightened and multiplied.

12. *And the sixth poured out his phial upon the great river Euphrates*—Affected also by the sixth trumpet, *and the water of it*—And of all the rivers that flow into it, *was dried up*—The far greater part of the Turkish empire lies on this side the Euphrates. The Romish and Mohammedan affairs ran nearly parallel to each other for several ages. In the seventh century was Mohammed himself, and a little before him Boniface III. with his universal bishopric. In the eleventh, both the Turks and Gregory VII. carried all before them. In the year 1300, Boniface appeared with his two swords at the newly erected jubilee. In the self-same year arose the Ottoman Porte ; yea, and on the same day. And here the phial, poured out on the throne of the beast, is immediately followed by that poured out on the Euphrates, *that the way for the kings from the east might be prepared*—Those who lie east from the Euphrates, in Persia, India, &c, who will rush blindfold upon the plagues which are ready for them, toward the holy land, which lies west of the Euphrates.

13. *Out of the mouth of the dragon, the wild beast, and the false prophet*—It seems the dragon fights chiefly against God—the beast against Christ—the false

wild beast, and out of the mouth of the false prophet, three unclean
14 spirits like frogs, go forth, (They are spirits of devils, working
miracles,) to the kings of the whole world, to gather them unto the
15 battle of the great day of GOD, the Almighty. (Behold, I come as
a th·ef. Happy is he that watcheth and keepeth his garments, lest
16 he walk naked, and they see his shame.) And they gathered them
together to the place which is called in the Hebrew Armageddon.
17 And the seventh poured out his phial upon the air, and there went
forth a loud voice out of the temple from the throne, saying, It is
18 done. And there were lightnings, and voices, and thunders, and a
great earthquake; such as had not been since men were upon the
19 earth, such an earthquake so great. And the great city was *splt*
into three parts, and the cities of the nations fell, and Babylon the
Great was remembered before GOD, to give her the cup of the wine
20 of the fierceness of his wrath. And every island fled away, and
21 the mountains were not found. And a great hail, every hailstone
about the weight of a talent, falleth out of heaven upon the men,
and the men blasphemed GOD, because of the plague of the hail;
for the plague thereof is exceeding great.

prophet against the spirit of truth; and that the three unclean spirits which come
from them, and exactly resemble them, endeavour to blacken the works of creation, of redemption, and of sanctificatior. *The false prophet*—So is the second
beast frequently named, after the kingdom of the first is darkened.
For he can then no longer prevail by main strength, and so works by lies and
deceit. Mohammed was first a false prophet, and afterward a powerful prince.
But this beast was first powerful, as a prince: afterward a false prophet, a teacher
of lies· *like frogs*—Whose abode is in fens, marshes, and other unclean places,
to the kings of the whole world—Both Mohammedan and Pagan, *to gather them*—
To the assistance of their three principals.
15. *Behold, I come as a thief*—Suddenly, unexpectedly. Observe the beautiful
abruptness. *I*—Jesus Christ. Hear him! *Happy is he that watcheth*—Looking
continually for him that *cometh quickly, and keepeth* on *his garments*—Which
men use to put off when they sleep, *lest he walk naked, and they see his shame*—
Lest he lose the graces, which he takes no care to keep, and others see his sin
and punishment.
16. *And they gathered them together to Armageddon*—Mageddon, or Megiddo,
is frequently mentioned in the Old Testament. Armageddon signifies the city or
the mountain of Megiddo, to which the valley of Megiddo adjoined. This was a
place well known in ancient times, for many memorable occurrences, in particular, the slaughter of the kings of Canaan, related, Judg. v. 19. Here the narrative breaks off. It is resumed, chap. xix, 19.
17. *And the seventh poured out his phial upon the air*—Which encompasses the
whole earth. This is the most weighty phial of all, and seems to take up more
time than any of the preceding. *It is done* -What was commanded, ver. 1. The
phials are poured out.
18. *And a great earthquake, such as had not been since men were upon the earth*
—It was therefore a literal, not a figurative earthquake.
19. *And the great city*—Namely, Jerusalem, here opposed to the heathen
cities in general, and particularly to Rome; *and the cities of the nations fell*—
Were utterly overthrown, *and Babylon was remembered before God*—He did not
forget the vengeance which was due to her, though the execution of it was delayed.
20. Every island and mountain was moved out of its place, chap. vi, 14, but
here they all flee away. What a change must this make in the face of this terraqueous globe! And yet the end of the world is not come.
21. *And a great hail falleth out of heaven*—From which there was no defence.
From the earthquake men would flee into the fields. But here also they are met
by the hail. Nor were they secure if they returned into their houses, when each
hailstone weighed sixty pounds.

XVII.   And there came one of the seven angels who had the seven
phials, and talked with me, saying, Come hither, I will show thee
the judgment of the great whore, that sitteth upon many waters :
2 With whom the kings of the earth have committed fornication, and
the inhabitants of the earth have been made drunk with the wine
3 of her fornication.   And he carried me away in the Spirit, into a
wilderness, and I saw a woman sitting upon a scarlet wild beast,
4 full of names of blasphemy, having seven heads and ten horns.   And
the woman was arrayed in purple and scarlet, and adorned with
gold, and precious stones, and pearls, having in her hand a golden
5 cup, full of abomination and filthiness of her fornication : And on
her forehead, a name written, Mystery ; Babylon the great, the

XVII. 1. *And there came one of the seven angels saying, Come hither*—This
relation concerning the great whore, and that concerning the wife of the Lamb,
chap. xxi, 9, 10, have the same introduction in token of the exact opposition between them.   *I will show thee the judgment of the great whore*—Which is now
circumstantially described, *that sitteth as a queen*—In pomp, power, ease, and
luxury, *upon many waters*—Many people and nations, ver. 15.

2. *With whom the kings of the earth*—Both ancient and modern, for many
ages, *have committed fornication*—By partaking of her idolatry and various
wickedness, *and the inhabitants of the earth*, *have been
made drunk with the wine of her fornication*—No wine can more thoroughly in-
toxicate those who drink it, than false zeal does the followers of the great whore.

3. *And he carried me away*—In the vision, *into a wilderness*—The Compagna
di Roma, the country round about Rome, is now a wilderness, compared to what
it was once, *and I saw a woman*—Both the Scripture and other writers frequently
represent a city under this emblem, *sitting upon a scarlet wild beast*—The same
which is described in the thirteenth chapter.   But he was there described, as
he carried on his own designs only : here, as he is connected with the whore.
There is indeed a very close connection between them, the seven heads of the
beast being seven hills on which the woman sitteth.   And yet there is a very
remarkable difference between them : between the papal power and the city of
Rome.   This woman is the city of Rome, with its buildings and inhabitants,
especially the nobles.   The beast which is now scarlet-coloured, (bearing the
bloody livery, as well as the person of the woman,) appears very different from
before.   Therefore St. John says at first sight, I saw *a beast*, not *the beast full
of names of blasphemy*—He had before *a name of blasphemy upon his head*, chap.
xiii, 1, now he has many.   From the time of Hildebrand, the blasphemous titles
of the pope have been abundantly multiplied, *having seven heads*—Which reach
in a succession from his ascent out of the sea, to his being cast into the lake
of fire, *and ten horns*—Which are cotemporary with each other, and belong to
his last period.

4. *And the woman was arrayed*—With the utmost pomp and magnificence, *in
purple and scarlet*—These were the colours of the imperial habit ; the purple in
times of peace ; and the scarlet in times of war, *having in her hand a golden
cup*—Like the ancient Babylon, Jer. li, 7, *full of abominations*—The most abominable doctrines as well as practices.

5. *And on her forehead a name written*—Whereas the saints have the name of
God and the Lamb on their foreheads, *Mystery*—This very word was inscribed
on the front of the pope's mitre, till some of the reformers took public notice of
it.   *Babylon the great*—Benedict XIII., in his proclamation of the jubilee, A. D.
1725, explains this sufficiently.   His words are, " To this holy city, famous for
the memory of so many holy martyrs, run with religious alacrity.   Hasten to
the place which the Lord hath chose.   Ascend to this new Jerusalem, whence
the law of the Lord and the light of evangelical truth hath flowed forth into all
nations, from the very first beginning of the Church ; the city most rightfully
called the palace, placed for the pride of all ages, the city of the Lord, the Sion
of the Holy One of Israel : this catholic and apostolical Roman Church is the
head of the world the mother of all believers, the faithful interpreter of God,

6 mother of harlots, and abominations of the earth.   And I saw the woman drunk with the blood of the saints, and with the blood of the witnesses of Jesus.   And when I saw, I wondered exceedingly.

7   And the angel said to me, Wherefore didst thou wonder?   I will tell thee the mystery of the woman, and of the wild beast that

8 carrieth her, which hath the seven heads and the ten horns.   The wild beast which thou sawest was, and is not, and shall ascend out of the bottomless pit, and go into perdition; and they that dwell on the earth, (whose names are not written in the book of life from the foundation of the world,) shall wonder when they behold the

9 wild beast, that he was, and is not, and yet will be.   Here is the

10 mind that hath wisdom.   The seven heads are seven hills, on which

---

and mistress of all Churches." But God somewhat varies the style, *the mother of harlots*—The parent, ringleader, patroness, and nourisher of many daughters that closely copy after her, and *abominations*—Of every kind, spiritual and fleshly, *of the earth*—In all lands.   In this respect she is indeed catholic or universal.

6. *And I saw the woman drunk with the blood of the saints*—So that Rome may well be called, *The slaughter house of the martyrs.*   She hath shed much Christian blood in every age; but at length she is even drunk with it, at the time to which this vision refers.   *The witnesses of Jesus*—The preachers of his word; *and I wondered exceedingly*—At her cruelty and the patience of God.

7. *I will tell thee the mystery*—The hidden meaning of this.

8. *The beast which thou sawest,* (namely, ver. 3,) *was,* &c.   This is a very observable and punctual description of the beast, ver. 8, 10, 11.   His whole du ration is here divided into three periods, which are expressed in a fourfold manner.

I. He, 1. was, 2. and is not, 3. and will ascend out of the bottomless pit, and go into perdition.

II. He, 1. was, 2. and is not, 3. and will be again.

III. The seven heads are seven hills and seven kings. 1. Five are fallen, 2. One is, 3. The other is not come: and when he cometh, he must continue a short space.

IV. He, 1. was, 2. and is not, 3. even he is the eighth, and is one of the seven, and goeth into perdition.

The first of these three is described in the thirteenth chapter.   This was past when the angel spoke to St. John.   The second was then in its course; the third was to 'come, *and is not*—The fifth phial brought darkness upon his kingdom: the woman took this advantage to seat herself upon him.   Then it might be said, *He is not.*   Yet shall he afterward *ascend out of the bottomless pit*—Arise again with a diabolical strength and fury.   But he will not reign long.   Soon after his ascent he goeth into perdition for ever.

9. *Here is the mind that hath wisdom*—Only those who are wise will under-stand this.   The seven heads are seven hills.

10. *And they are seven kings*—Anciently there were royal palaces on all the seven Roman hills.   These were the Palatine, Capitoline, Cælian, Exquiline, Viminal, Quirinal, Aventine hills.   But the prophecy respects the seven hills at the time of the beast, when the Palatine was deserted, and the Vatican in use. Not that the seven heads mean hills distinct from kings; but they have a com-pound meaning, implying both together.

Perhaps the first head of the beast is the Cælian hill, and on it the Lateran with Gregory VII. and his successors: the second, the Vatican with the Church of St. Peter, chosen by Boniface VIII.   The third, the Quirinal, with the Church of St. Mark, and the Quirinal palace built by Paul II., and the fourth, the Ex-quiline hill, with the temple of St. Maria Maggiore, where Paul V. reigned. (The fifth will be added hereafter.)   Accordingly in the papal register, four pe-riods are observable since Gregory VII.   In the first, almost all the bulls made in the city, are dated in the Lateran; in the second at St. Peter's; in the third at St. Mark's or in the Quirinal; in the fourth, at St. Maria Maggiore.   But no fifth, sixth, or seventh hill, has yet been the residence of any pope.   Not that one

the woman sitteth, and they are seven kings ; five are fallen : one
is, the other is not yet come ; when he cometh, he must continue a
11 short space.   And the wild beast that was, and is not, even he is
12 the eighth, and is of the seven, and goeth into perdition.   And the
ten horns which thou sawest are ten kings, who have not received
the kingdom, but receive authority as kings one hour with the
13 wild beast.   These have one mind, and give their power and
14 authority to the wild beast.   These shall make war with the Lamb,
and the Lamb shall overcome them : for he is Lord of lords, and
King of kings ; and they that *are* with him *are* called, and chosen,
and faithful.

---

hill was deserted, when another was made the papal residence ; but a new one
was added to the other sacred palaces.
    Perhaps the times hitherto mentioned might be fixed thus.
          1058 Wings are given to the woman.
          1077 The beast ascends out of the sea.
          1143 The forty-two months begin.
          1810 The forty-two months end.
          1832 The beast ascends out of the bottomless pit.
          1836 The beast finally overthrown.
    The fall of those five kings seems to imply not only the death of the popes, whc
reigned on those hills, but also such a disannulling of all they had done there,
that it will be said, The beast is not : the royal power, which had so long been
lodged in the pope, being then transferred to the city.   *One is, the other is not
yet come*—These two are remarkably distinguished from the five preceding, whom
they succeed in their turns.   The former of them will continue not a short space,
as may be gathered from what is said of the latter ; the former is under the go
vernment of Babylon ; the latter is with the beast.
    In this second period.   One is, at the same time that the beast is not.   Even
then there will be a pope ; though not with the power which his predecessors
had.   And he will reside on one of the remaining hills, leaving the seventh for
his successor.
    11. *And the wild beast that was, and is not, even he is the eighth*—When the
time of his not being is over.   The beast consists as it were of eight parts.
The seven heads are seven of them ; and the eighth is his whole body, or the
beast himself.   Yet the beast himself, though he is in a sense termed the eighth,
is of the seven, yea, contains them all.   The whole succession of popes from
Gregory VII. are undoubtedly antichrist.   Yet this hinders not, but that the last
pope in this succession will be more eminently the antichrist, the man of sin ;
adding to that of his predecessors a peculiar degree of wickedness from the bottomless pit.   This individual person, as a pope, is the seventh head of the beast ;
as the man of sin, he is the eighth, or the beast himself.
    12. *The ten horns are ten kings*—It is no where said, that these horns are on
the beast, or on his heads.   And he is said to have them, not as he is one of the
seven, but as he is the eighth.   They are ten secular potentates, cotemporary
with, not succeeding each other, who receive authority as kings with the beast,
probably in some convention, which, after a very short space, they will deliver
up to the beast.   Because of their short continuance, only authority as kings,
not a kingdom, is ascribed to them.   While they retain this authority together
with the beast, he will be stronger than ever before ; but far stronger still when
their power is also transferred to him.
    13. In the 13th and 14th verses is summed up what is afterward mentioned
concerning the horns and the beast, in this and the two following chapters.
These have one mind, and give—They all, with one consent, give their warlike
power and royal authority to the wild beast.
    14. *These* kings with the beast, *shall make war with the Lamb. He is Lord
of lords*—Rightful Sovereign of all, and ruling all things well ; *and King of
kings*—As a King he fights with, and conquers all his enemies.   *And they that
are with him*—Beholding his victory. are such as were, while in the body, called

15   And he saith to me, The waters which thou sawest, where the
     whore sitteth, are people, and multitudes, and nations, and tongues,
16 And the ten horns which thou sawest, and the wild beast, these.
     shall hate the whore, and shall make her desolate and naked, and
17 shall eat her flesh, and burn her with fire.   For God hath put *it*
     into their hearts, to execute his sentence, and to agree, and to give
     their kingdom to the wild beast, till the words of God shall be ful-
18 filled.   And the woman whom thou sawest is the great city, which
     reigned over the kings of the earth. •
XVIII.   And after these things I saw another angel coming down
     out of heaven, having great power, and the earth was enlightened
 2 with his glory.   And he cried mightily with a loud voice, saying,
     Babylon the great is fallen, is fallen, and is become a habitation
     of devils, and a hold of every unclean spirit, and a cage of every
 3 unclean and hateful bird.   For all nations have drunk of the wine
     of her fornication, and the kings of the earth have committed forni-
     cation with her, and the merchants of the earth are waxed rich,
     through the abundance of her delicacies.
 4   And I heard another voice out of heaven saying, Come out of
     her, my people, that ye be not partakers of her sins, and that ye
 5 receive not of her plagues.   For her sins have reached even to
 6 heaven, and God hath remembered her iniquities.   Reward her even
     as she hath rewarded, and give her double according to her works

by his word and Spirit ; *and chosen*—Taken out of the world, when they were
enabled to believe in him ; *and faithful*—Unto death.
     15. *People, and multitudes, and nations, and tongues*—It is not said *tribes ;* for
Israel hath nothing to do with Rome in particular.
     16. *And shall eat her flesh*—Devour her immense riches.
     17. *For God hath put it into their hearts*—Which indeed no less than Almighty
power could have effected, *to execute his sentence till the words of God*—Touch.
ing the overthrow of his enemies, *should be fulfilled.*
     18. *The woman is the great city which reigned*—Namely, while the beast is
not, and the woman sitteth upon him.
     XVIII. 1. *And I saw another angel coming down out of heaven*—Termed ano.
ther, with respect to him who *came down out of heaven,* chap. x, 1 ; *and the earth
was enlightened with his glory*—To make his coming more conspicuous. If such
be the lustre of the servant, what images can display the majesty of the Lord,
who has thousand thousands of those glorious attendants ministering to him,
and ten thousand times ten thousand standing before him ?
     2. *And he cried, Babylon is fallen*—This fall was mentioned before, chap. xiv,
8, but is now declared at large ; and is become a habitation, a free abode of
devils ; *and a hold,* a prison, *of every unclean spirit*—Perhaps confined there,
where they had once practised all uncleanness, till the judgment of the great
day. How many horrid inhabitants hath desolate Babylon ? Of invisible beings,
devils, and unclean spirits ; of visible, every unclean beast, every filthy and hate.
ful bird.   Suppose then Babylon to mean heathen Rome. What have the
Romanists gained ? Seeing from the time of that destruction, which they say
is past, these are to be its only inhabitants for ever.
     4. *And I heard another voice*—Of Christ, whose people, secretly scattered even
there, are warned of her approaching destruction ; *that ye be not partakers of her
sins*—That is, of the fruits of them.
     What a remarkable providence it was, that the Revelation was printed in the
midst of Spain, in the Great Polyglott Bible, before the reformation ? Else how
much easier had it been for the papists to reject the whole book, than it is to
evade these striking parts of it ?
     5. *Even to heaven*—An expression which implies the highest guilt.
     6. *Reward her*—This God speaks to the executioners of his vengeance, even

7 in the cup which she mingled, mingle to her dou'le.   As much as
she hath glorified herself and lived deliciously so much torment
and sorrow give her: because she hath said in her heart, I sit as
8 a queen, and am no widow, and shall see no sorrow.   Therefore
shall her plagues come in one day, death, and sorrow, and famine ;
and she shall be burnt with fire ; for strong *is* the Lord God who
9 judgeth her.   And the kings of the earth, who had committed fornication and lived deliciously with her, shall weep and mourn over
10 her, when they see the smoke of her burning, Standing afar off
for fear of her torment, saying, Alas, alas ! Thou great city Baby-
11 lon, thou strong city !   In one hour is thy judgment come.   And
the merchants of the earth weep and mourn over her ; for none
12 buyeth their merchandise any more :   Merchandise of gold, and silver, and precious stone, and pearl, and fine linen, and purple, and
silk, and scarlet, and all sorts of thyine wood, and all sorts of vessels of ivory, and all sorts of vessels of most precious wood, and of
13 brass, and iron, and marble ;   And cinnamon, and amomum, and
odours, and ointment, and frankincense, and wine, and oil, and fine
flour, and wheat, and beasts, and sheep ; and *merchandise* of horses,
14 and of chariots, and of bodies and souls of men.   And the fruits which
thy soul desireth are departed from thee, and all things that were

---

as she hath rewarded others : in particular, the saints of God ; *and give her
double*—This, according to the Hebrew idiom, implies only a full retaliation.

7. *As much as she hath glorified herself*—By pride and pomp, and arrogant
boasting ; *and lived deliciously*—In all kinds of elegance, luxury, and wantonness ; *so much torment give her*—Proportioning the punishment to the sin.   *Because she saith in her heart*—As did ancient Babylon, (Isaiah xlvii, 8, 9,) *I sit*—
Her usual style.   Hence those expressions, " The Chair, the See of Rome."
She sat so many years, *as a queen*—Over many kings, " Mistress of all Churches :
the supreme ; the infallible ; the only spouse of Christ ; out of which there is no
salvation :" *and am no widow*—But the spouse of Christ ; *and shall see no sorrow*
—From the death of my children, or any other calamity ; for God himself will
defend " the Church."

8. Therefore, as both the natural and judicial consequence of this proud
security, *shall her plagues come*—The death of her children, with an incapacity
of bearing more ; sorrow of every kind : *and famine*—In the room of luxurious
plenty ; the very things from which she imagined herself to be most safe : *for
strong is the Lord God who judgeth her*—Against whom therefore all her strength,
great as it is, will not avail.

10. *Thou strong city*—Rome was anciently termed by its inhabitants, Valentia,
that is, strong.   And the word Rome itself in Greek signifies strength.   This
name was given it by the Greek strangers.

12. *Merchandise of gold*, &c.—Almost all these are still in use at Rome, both
in their idolatrous service, and in common life ; *fine linen*—The sort of it mentioned in the original is exceeding costly ; *Thyine wood*—A sweet-smelling
wood, not unlike citron, used in adorning magnificent palaces ; *vessels of most
precious wood*—Ebony in particular, which is often mentioned with ivory : the
one excelling in whiteness, the other in blackness, and both in uncommon
smoothness

13. *Amomum*—A shrub whose wood is a fine perfume ; *and beasts*—Cows and
oxen ; *and of chariots*—A purely Latin word is here inserted in the Greek.   This
St. John undoubtedly used on purpose, in describing the luxury of Rome ; *and
of bodies*—A common term for slaves ; *and souls of men*—For these also are
continually bought and sold at Rome.   And this of all others is the most gainful
merchandise to the Roman traffickers.

14. *And the fruits*—From what was imported they proceed to the domestic
delicacies of Rome : none of which are in greater request there than the par
ticular sort which is here mentioned   The word properly signifies, pears

dainty and splendid are perished from thee, and thou shalt find
15 them no more. The merchants of these things, who became rich
by her, shall stand afar off, for fear of her torment, weeping and
16 mourning, Saying, Alas, alas ! The great city that was clothed
in fine linen, and purple, and scarlet, and adorned with gold, and
precious stone, and pearl : in one hour so great riches are become
17 desolate. And every shipmaster, and all the company belonging
18 to ships, and sailors, and all who trade by sea, stood afar off, And
cried when they saw the smoke of her burning, saying, What *city*
19 *was* like the great city ? And they cast dust on their heads, and
cried, weeping and mourning, saying, Alas, alas ! The great city,
wherein were made rich all that had ships in the sea, by reason
20 of her magnificence, for in one hour she is made desolate. Rejoice
over her, thou heaven, and ye saints, and apostles, and prophets ;
for God hath avenged you on her.
21 And a mighty angel took up a stone like a great mill stone,
and threw *it* into the sea, saying, Thus with violence shall Babylon, the great city, be thrown down, and shall be found no more at
22 all. And the voice of harpers, and musicians, and pipers, and trumpeters, shall be heard no more at all in thee, and no artificer of any
kind shall be found any more in thee, and the sound of a mill stone
23 shall be heard no more at all in thee. And the light of a candle
shall shine no more at all in thee ; and the voice of the bridegroom and the bride shall be heard no more in thee : for thy
merchants were the great men of the earth : for by thy sorceries

---

peaches, nectarines, and all of the apple and plum kinds ; *and all things that
are dainty*—To the taste ; *and splendid*—To the sight ; as clothes, buildings,
furniture.

19. *And they cast dust on their heads*—As mourners. Most of the expressions
here used in describing the downfall of Babylon, are taken from Ezekiel's description of the downfall of Tyre, chap. xxvi, and xxvii.

20. *Rejoice over her, thou heaven*—That is, all the inhabitants of it ; *and* more
especially, *ye saints :* and among the saints still more eminently, *ye apostles and
prophets.*

21. *And a mighty angel took up a stone and threw it into the sea*—By a like
emblem Jeremiah foreshowed the fall of the Chaldean Babylon, chap. li, 63, 64.

22. *And the voice of harpers*—Players on stringed instruments ; *and musicians*
—Skilful singers in particular ; *and pipers*—Who played on flutes, chiefly on
mournful, whereas trumpeters played on joyful, occasions ; *shall be heard no
more in thee ; and no artificer*—Arts of every kind, particularly music, sculpture,
painting, and statuary, were there carried to their greatest height. No, nor even
the sound of a mill stone shall be heard any more in thee—Not only the arts that
adorned life, but even those employments without which it cannot subsist, will
cease from thee for ever. All these expressions denote absolute and eternal
desolation. *The voice of harpers*—Music was the entertainment of the rich
and great ; trade, the business of men of middle rank : preparing bread and the
necessaries of life, the employment of the lowest people : marriages, in which
lamps and songs were known ceremonies, are the means of peopling cities, as
new births supply the place of those that die. The desolation of Rome is there
fore described in such a manner, as to show that neither rich nor poor, neither
persons of middle rank, nor those of the lowest condition, should be able to live
there any more. Neither shall it be repeopled by new marriages, but remain
desolate and uninhabited for ever.

23. *For thy merchants were the great men of the earth*—A circumstance which
was in itself indifferent, and yet led them into pride, luxury, and numberless
other sins.

24 were all nations deceived. And in her was found the blood of prophets, and saints, and of all that had been slain upon the earth.

XIX. After these things I heard a loud voice of a great multitude in heaven, saying, Hallelujah! The salvation, and the glory,
2 and the power to our God. For true and righteous *are* his judgments : for he hath judged the great whore, who corrupted th. earth with her fornications, and hath avenged the blood of his
3 servants at her hand. (And again they said, Hallelujah ;) and her
4 smoke ascended for ever and ever. And the four and twenty elders, and the four living creatures, fell down, and worshipped
5 God that sat on the throne, saying, Amen, Hallelujah. And a voice came forth from the throne, saying, Praise our God, all

---

24. *And in her was found the blood of the prophets and saints*—The same angel speaks still, yet he does not say *in thee*, but *in her*, now so sunk as not to hear these last words ; *and of all that had been slain*—Even before she was built ; see Matt. xxiii, 35. There is no city under the sun which has so clear a title to Catholic blood-guiltiness as Rome. The guilt of the blood shed under the heathen emperors has not been removed under the popes, but hugely multiplied. Nor is Rome accountable only for that which hath been shed in the city, but for that shed in all the earth. For at Rome, under the pope, as well as under the heathen emperors, were the bloody orders and edicts given : and wherever the blood of holy men was shed, there were the grand rejoicings for it. And what immense quantities of blood have been shed by her agents! Charles IX. of France, in his letter to Gregory XIII., boasts, that in, and not long after, the massacre of Paris, he had destroyed seventy thousand Hugonots. Some have computed, that from the year 1518 to 1548, fifteen millions of Protestants have perished by war and the inquisition ! This may be overcharged ; but certainly the number of them in those thirty years, as well as since, is almost incredible. To these we may add innumerable martyrs, in ancient, middle, and late ages, in Bohemia, Germany, Holland, France, England, Ireland, and many other parts of Europe, Africa, and Asia.

XIX. 1. *I heard a loud voice of a great multitude*—Whose blood the great whore had shed, *saying, Hallelujah*—This Hebrew word signifies, Praise ye Jah, or Him that is. God named himself to Moses, EHEIEH, that is, I will be, Exod. ii, 14, and at the same time Jehovah, that is, He that is, and was, and is to come. During the trumpet of the seventh angel he is styled, He that is, and was, chap. xvi, 5, and not He that is to come : because his long-expected coming is, under this trumpet, actually present. At length he is styled Jah, He that is ; the past, together with the future, being swallowed up in the present ; the former things being no more mentioned, for the greatness of those that now are. This title is, of all others, the most peculiar to the everlasting God. The salvation is opposed to the destruction which the great whore had brought upon the earth. His power and glory appear from the judgment executed on her, and from the setting up his kingdom to endure through all ages.

2. *For true and righteous are his judgments*—This is the cry of the souls under the altar, changed into a song of praise.

4. *And the four and twenty elders, and the four living creatures, fell down*— The living creatures are nearer the throne than the elders. Accordingly they are mentioned before them, with the praise they render to God, chap. iv, 9, 10 ; chap. viii, 14 ; inasmuch as there the praise moves from the centre to the circumference. But here, when God's judgments are fulfilled, it moves back from the circumference to the centre. Here therefore the four and twenty elders are named before the living creatures.

5. *And a voice came forth from the throne*—Probably from the four living creatures, *saying, Praise our God*—The occasion and matter of this song of praise follow immediately after, ver. 6, &c. God was praised before for his

6 ye his servants, and ye that fear him, small and great. And I
heard, as it were, a voice of a great multitude, and as a voice
of many waters, and as a voice of mighty thunders, saying, Halle-
7 lujah : for the Lord God, the Almighty, reigneth. Let us be glad,
and rejoice, and give the glory to him; for the marriage of the Lamb
8 is come, and his wife hath made herself ready. And it was given
to her to be arrayed in fine linen, white and clean : the fine linen
is the righteousness of the saints.
9 And he saith to me, Write : Happy *are* they who are invited to
the marriage supper of the Lamb. ·And he saith to me, These are
10 the true sayings of God. And I fell before his feet to worship him ;
but he saith to me, *See thou do it not :* I am thy fellow servant, and
of thy brethren that keep the testimony of Jesus. Worship God.
The testimony of Jesus is the Spirit of prophecy.
11 And I saw the heaven opened, and behold a white horse, and
he that sitteth on him, called Faithful and True : and in righteous-
12 ness he judgeth and maketh war. His eyes *are* a flame of fire,
and upon his head *are* many diadems ; and he hath a name writ-

---

judgment of the great whore, ver. 1–4; now for that which follows it; for
the Lord God, the Almighty, takes the kingdom to himself, and avenges himself
on the rest of his enemies. Were all the inhabitants of heaven mistaken ? If
not, there is real, yea, and terrible anger in God.

6. *And I heard the voice of a great multitude*—So all his servants did praise
him, *The Almighty reigneth*—More eminently and gloriously than ever before.

7. *The marriage of the Lamb is come*—Is near at hand, to be solemnized
speedily. What this implies, none of the spirits of just men, even in paradise,
yet know. O what things are those which are yet behind ! And what purity of
heart should there be to meditate upon them ! *And his wife hath made herself
ready*—Even upon earth; but in a far higher sense, in that world. After a time
allowed for this, the New Jerusalem comes down, both made ready and adorned,
chap. xxi, 2.

8. *And it is given to her*—By God. The bride is, all holy men, the whole
invisible Church; *to be arrayed in fine linen, white and clean*—This is an
emblem of *the righteousness of the saints*—Both of their justification and
sanctification.

9. *And he*—The angel, *saith to me, Write*—St. John seems to have been so
amazed at these glorious sights, that he needed to be reminded of this, *Happy are
they who are invited to the marriage supper of the Lamb*—Called to glory; *and
he saith*—After a little pause.

10. *And I fell before his feet to worship him*—It seems, mistaking him for
the Angel of the covenant ; *but he saith, See thou do it not*—In the original it
is only *See not*, with a beautiful abruptness. To pray to, or worship the
highest creature, is flat idolatry. *I am thy fellow servant, and of thy brethren
that have the testimony of Jesus*—I am now employed as your fellow servant
to testify of the Lord Jesus, by the same Spirit which inspired the prophets
of old.

11. *And I saw the heaven opened*—This is a new and peculiar opening of it,
in order to show the magnificent expedition of Christ and his attendants
against his great adversary; *and behold a white horse*—Many little regarded
Christ when he came meek, riding upon an ass. But what will they say when
he goes forth upon his white horse, with the sword of his mouth ? *White*—
Such as generals use in solemn triumphs—*And he that sitteth on him, called
Faithful*—In performing all his promises, *and True*—In executing all his threatenings ; *and in righteousness*—With the utmost justice, *he judgeth and maketh
war*—Often the sentence and execution go together.

12. *And his eyes are a flame of fire*—They were said to be *as* or *like* a
flame of fire before, chap. i, 14; an emblem of his omniscience ; *and upon his
head are many diadems*—For he is King of all nations; *and he hath a name*

13 ten, which none knoweth but himself.   And he *is* clothed in a
vesture dipt in blood, and his name is called, The Word of God.
14 And the armies which were in heaven followed him on white
15 horses, clothed in clean fine linen.   And out of his mouth goeth
forth a sharp two-edged sword, that with it he might smite the
nations.   And he shall rule them with a rod of iron ; and he treadeth the winepress of the fierceness of the wrath of God, the Al-
16 mighty.   And he hath on his vesture and on his thigh a name
17 written, King of kings, and Lord of lords.   And I saw an angel
standing in the sun ; and he cried with a loud voice, saying to all
the birds that fly in the midst of heaven, Come, and gather your-
18 selves together to the great supper of God : That ye may eat the
flesh of kings, and the flesh of chief captains, and the flesh of
mighty men, and the flesh of horses, and of those that sit on them,
and the flesh of all men, both freemen and slaves, both small and
19 great.   And I saw the wild beast, and the kings of the earth and
their armies gathered together, to make war with him that sat on
20 the horse and with his army.   And the wild beast was taken, and
with him the false prophet, who had wrought the miracles before
him, with which he had deceived them who had the mark of the
wild beast, and them who had worshipped his image. These two

written, which none knoweth but himself—As God, he is incomprehensible to every
creature.
13. *And he is clothed in a vesture dipt in blood*—The blood of the enemies he
hath already conquered, Isa. lxiii, 1, &c.
15. *And he shall rule them*—Who are not slain by his sword, *with a rod of
iron*—That is, if they will not submit to his golden sceptre. *And he treadeth
the winepress of the wrath of God*—That is, he executes his judgments on the
ungodly.
This Ruler of the nations was born (or appeared as such) immediately after
the seventh angel began to sound. He now appears, not as a child, but as a
victorious warrior. The nations have long ago felt his iron rod, partly while
the heathen Romans, after their savage persecution of the Christians, themselves groaned under numberless plagues and calamities, by his righteous vengeance : partly while other heathens have been broken in pieces by those who
bore the Christian name. For although the cruelty, for example, of the Span-
iards in America was unrighteous and detestable, yet did God therein execute
his righteous judgment on the unbelieving nations. But they shall experience his
iron rod as they never did yet. And then will they all return to their rightful
Lord.
16. *And he hath on his vesture and on his thigh*—That is, on the part of his
vesture which is upon his thigh, *a name written*—It was usual of old for great
personages in the eastern countries to have magnificent titles affixed to their
garments.
17. *Gather yourselves together to the great supper of God*—As to a great
feast which the vengeance of God will soon provide : a strongly figurative expression, (taken from Ezekiel, chap. xxxix, 17,) denoting the vastness of the ensuing slaughter.
19. *And I saw the kings of the earth*—The ten kings mentioned, chap. xvii,
12, who had now drawn the other kings of the earth to them, whether popish,
Mohammedan, or pagan, *gathered together to make war with him that sat on the
horse*—All beings, good and evil, visible and invisible, will be concerned in this grand
contest : see Zech. xiv, 2, &c.
20. *The false prophet who had wrought the miracles before him*—And therefore shared in his punishment ; *these two* ungodly men *were cast alive*—Without
undergoing bodily death, *into the lake of fire*—And that before the devil himself, chap. xx, 10. Here is the last of the beast. After several repeated strokes

21 were cast alive into the lake of fire burning with brimstone. And the rest were slain by the sword of him that sat upon the horse, which went forth out of his mouth, and all the birds were satisfied with their flesh.

XX.   And I saw an angel descending out of heaven, having the 2 key of the bottomless pit, and a great chain in his hand. And he laid hold on the dragon, the old serpent, who is the devil and Sa-

of Omnipotence, he is gone alive into hell. There were *two* that went alive into heaven; perhaps there are two that go alive into hell. It may be, Enoch and Elijah went at once into glory, without first waiting in paradise. The beast and the false prophet plunge at once into the extremest degree of torment, without being reserved in chains of darkness till the judgment of the great day. Surely none but the beast of Rome would have hardened himself thus against the God he pretended to adore, or refused to have repented under such dreadful, repeated visitations! Well is he styled a beast, for his carnal and vile affections; a wild beast, for his savage and cruel spirit! *The rest were slain—* A like difference is afterward made between the devil and Gog and Magog, chap. xx, 9, 10.

21. Here is a most magnificent description of the overthrow of the beast and his adherents. It has, in particular, one exquisite beauty; that after exhibiting the two opposite armies, and all the apparatus for a battle, ver. 12-19, then follows immediately, ver. 20, the account of the victory, without one word of an engagement or fighting. Here is the most exact propriety; for what struggle can there be between Omnipotence and the power of all the creation united against it! Every description must have fallen short of this admirable silence.

XX. 1. *And I saw an angel descending out of heaven*—Coming down with a commission from God. Jesus Christ himself overthrew the beast: the proud dragon shall be bound by an angel; even as he and his angels were cast out of heaven by Michael and his angels; *having the key of the bottomless pit*—Mentioned before, chap. ix, 1; *and a great chain in his hand*—The angel of the bottomless pit was shut up therein before the beginning of the first wo. But it is now first, that Satan, after he had occasioned the third wo, is both chained and shut up.

2. *And he laid hold on the dragon*—With whom undoubtedly his angels were now cast into the bottomless pit, as well as finally into everlasting fire, Matt xxv, 41. *And bound him a thousand years*—That these thousand do not precede or run parallel with, but wholly follow the times of the beast, may manifestly appear, 1. From the series of the whole book, representing one continued chain of events: 2. From the circumstances which precede. The woman's bringing forth is followed by the casting of the dragon out of heaven to the earth. With this is connected the third wo, whereby the dragon through, and with the beast rages horribly. At the conclusion of the third wo the beast is overthrown, and cast into the lake of fire. At the same time the other grand enemy, the dragon, shall be bound and shut up. 3. These thousand years bring a new, full, and lasting immunity from all outward and inward evils, (the authors of which are now removed,) and an affluence of all blessings. But such a time the Church has never yet seen. Therefore it is still to come. 4. These thousand years are followed by the last times of the world, the letting loose of Satan, who gathers together Gog and Magog, and is thrown to the beast and false prophet in the lake of fire. Now Satan's accusing the saints in heaven, his rage on earth, his imprisonment in the abyss, his seducing Gog and Magog, and being cast into the lake of fire, evidently succeed each other. 5. What occurs from chap. xx, 11, to chap. xxii, 5, manifestly follows the things related in the 19th chapter. The thousand years came between; whereas if they were past, neither the beginning nor the end of them would fall within this period. In a short time, those who assert that they are now at hand, will appear to have spoken the truth. Meantime let every man consider, what kind of happiness he expects therein. The danger does not lie in maintaining that the thousand years are yet to come, but in interpreting them, whether past or to come, in a gross and car-

3 tan, and bound him a thousand years. And cast him into the bottomless pit, and shut *him* up, and set a seal upon him, that he might deceive the nations no more, till the thousand years should be fulfilled. After this he must be loosed for a small time.

4 And I saw thrones, and they that sat on them, and judgment was given to them: and *I saw* the souls of them who had been beheaded for the testimony of Jesus, and for the word of God, and those who had not worshipped the wild beast nor his image, neither had received the mark on their forehead or on their hand ; and

---

ual sense. The doctrine of the Son of God is a mystery. So is his cross; and so is his glory. In all these he is a sign that is spoken against. Happy they who believe and confess him in all.

3. *And set a seal upon him*—How far these expressions are to be taken literally, how far figuratively only, who can tell ? *That he might deceive the nations no more*—One benefit only is here expressed, as resulting from the confinement of Satan. But how many and great blessings are implied ? For the grand enemy being removed, the kingdom of God holds on its uninterrupted course among the nations, and the great mystery of God, so long foretold, is at length fulfilled: namely, when the beast is destroyed and Satan bound. This fulfilment approaches nearer and nearer, and contains things of the utmost importance, the knowledge of which becomes every day more distinct and easy. In the meantime it is highly necessary to guard against the present rage and subtlety of the devil. Quickly he will be bound : when he is loosed again, the martys will live and reign with Christ. Then follow his coming in glory, the new heaven, new earth, and new Jerusalem. The bottomless pit is properly the devil's prison: afterward he is cast into the lake of fire. He can deceive the nations no more, till the thousand years mentioned before, ver. 2, are fulfilled. *Then he must be loosed*—So does the mysterious wisdom of God permit, *for a small time*—Small comparatively : though upon the whole it cannot be very short, because the things to be transacted therein, ver. 8, 9, must take up a considerable space. We are very shortly to expect, one after another, the calamities occasioned by the second beast, the harvest and the vintage ; the pouring out of the phials, the judgment of Babylon ; the last raging of the beast, and his destruction ; the imprisonment of Satan. How great things these ! And how short the time ! What is needful for us ? Wisdom, patience, faithfulness, watchfulness. It is no time to settle upon our lees. This is not, if it be rightly understood, an acceptable message to the wise, the mighty, the honourable of this world. Yet that which is to be done, shall be done. There is no counsel against the Lord.

4. *And I saw thrones*—Such as are promised the apostles, Matt. xix, 28 ; Luke xxii, 30, *and they*—Namely, the saints whom St. John saw at the same time. Dan. vii, 22, sat upon them ; and judgment was given to them, 1 Cor. vi, 2 Who and how many these are, is not said. But they are distinguished from the souls or persons mentioned immediately after ; and from the saints already raised. *And I saw the souls of them who had been beheaded with the axe*—So the original word signifies. One kind of death, which was particularly inflicted at Rome, is mentioned for all ; *for the testimony of Jesus, and for the word of God*—The martyrs were sometimes killed for the word of God in general, sometimes particularly for the testimony of Jesus : the one, while they refused to worship idols ; the other while they confessed the name of Christ, *and those who had not worshipped the wild beast nor his image*—These seem to be a company distinct from those who appeared, chap. xv, 2. Those overcame, probably, in such contests as these had not. Before the number of the beast was expired, the people were compelled to worship him, by the most dreadful violence. But when the beast was not, they were only seduced into it by the craft of the false prophet, *and they lived*—Their souls and bodies being reunited, *and reigned with Christ* —Not on earth, but in heaven. *The reigning on earth*, mentioned, chap. xi, 15, is quite different from this, *a thousand years*—It must be observed, that two distinct thousand years are mentioned throughout this whole passage. Each is mentioned thrice ; the thousand wherein Satan is bound, ver. 2, 3, 7, the thousand wherein the saints shall reign, ver. 4, 5, 6. The former end before the end

5 they lived and reigned with Christ a thousand years. The rest
　 of the dead lived not again till the thousand years were ended
6 This *is* the first resurrection. Happy and holy *is* he that hath a
　 part in the first resurrection : over these the second death hath no
　 power ; but they shall be priests of God and of Christ, and shall
　 reign with him a thousand years.
7　 And when the thousand years are fulfilled, Satan shall be loosed
8 out of his prison. And shall go forth to deceive the nations, which
　 are in the four corners of the earth, Gog and Magog, to gather
　 them together to battle, whose number is as the sand of the sea.
9 And they went up on the breadth of the earth, and surrounded the
　 camp of the saints, and the beloved city : and fire came down from
10 God out of heaven, and devoured them. And the devil that deceived
　 them was cast into the lake of fire and brimstone, where both the

of the world : the latter reach to the general resurrection. So that the beginning
and end of the former thousand is before the beginning and end of the latter.
Therefore as in the second verse, at the first mention of the former, so in the
fourth verse, at the first mention of the latter, it is only said a thousand years ;
in the other places, the thousand, ver. 3, 5, 7, that is, the thousand mentioned
before. During the former, the promises concerning the flourishing state of the
Church, chap. x. 7, shall be fulfilled. During the latter, while the saints reign
with Christ in heaven, men on earth will be careless and secure.

5. *The rest of the dead lived not till the thousand years*—Mentioned ver. 4,
were ended. The thousand years in which Satan is bound, both begin and end
much sooner.

The small time, and the second thousand years, begin at the same point, immediately after the first thousand. But neither the beginning of the first, nor of the
second thousand, will be known to the men upon earth, as both the imprisonment
of Satan and his loosing are transacted in the invisible world.

By observing these two distinct thousand years, many difficulties are avoided.
There is room enough for the fulfilling of all the prophecies, and those which before seemed to clash are reconciled : particularly those which speak on the one
hand, of a most flourishing state of the Church as yet to come ; and on the other,
of the fatal security of men in the last days of the world.

6. *They shall be priests of God and of Christ*—Therefore Christ is God, *and
shall reign with him*—With Christ, *a thousand years.*

7. *And when the* former *thousand years are fulfilled, Satan shall be loosed out
of his prison*—At the same time that the first resurrection begins. There is a great
resemblance between this passage and chap. xxii, 12. At the casting out of the
dragon, there was joy in heaven : but there was wo upon earth. So at the loosing of Satan, the saints begin to reign with Christ ; but the nations on earth are
deceived.

8. *And shall go forth to deceive the nations in the four corners of the earth*—
(That is, in all the earth,) the more diligently, as he hath been so long restrained, and knoweth he hath but a small time, *Gog and Magog*—Magog, the second
son of Japhet, is the father of the innumerable northern nations toward the east.
The prince of these nations, of which the bulk of that army will consist, is termed
Gog by Ezekiel also, chap. xxxviii, 2. Both Gog and Magog signify high, or
lifted up, a name well suiting both the prince and people. When the fierce
leader of many nations shall appear then will his own name be known ; *to gather
them*—Both Gog and his armies. Of Gog little more is said, as being soon mingled with the rest in the common slaughter. The Revelation speaks of this the
more briefly, because it had been so particularly described by Ezekiel. *Whose
number is as the sand of the sea*—Immensely numerous, a proverbial expression.

9. *And they went up on the breadth of the earth,* or *the land,* filling the whole
breadth of it, *and surrounded the camp of the saints*—Perhaps the Gentile Church,
dwelling round about Jerusalem, and *the beloved city*—So termed likewise Eccl.
xxiv, 11.

10. *And they*—All these, *shall be tormented day and night*—That is, without

wild beast and the false prophet *are :* and they shall be tormented day and night for ever and ever.

11 And I saw a great white throne, and him that sat thereon, from whose face the earth and the heaven fled away ; and there was no

12 place found for them. And I saw the dead, great and small, stand ing before the throne ; and the books were opened ; and another book was opened, which is *the book* of life :* and the dead were judged out of the things that were written in the books, according

13 to their works. And the sea gave up the dead that were therein : and death and hades gave up the dead that were in them, and they

14 were judged every one according to their works. And death and hades were cast into the lake of fire : this is the second death

15 And whosoever was not found written in the book of life was cast into the lake of fire.

XXI. And I saw a new heaven and a new earth ; for the first hea- ven and the first earth were passed away : and there was no more

---

any intermission. Strictly speaking, there is only night there. No day, no sun, no hope !

11. *And I saw*—A representation of that great day of the Lord, *a great white throne*—How great, who can say ? White with the glory of God, of Him that sat upon it, Jesus Christ. The apostle does not attempt to describe him here, only adds that circumstance, far above all description. *From whose face the earth and the heaven fled away*—Probably both the aerial and the starry heaven ; which *shall pass away with a great noise : and there was found no place for them* —But they were wholly dissolved, the very elements melting with fervent heat. It is not said, they were thrown into violent commotion, but they fled entirely away ; not, they started from their foundations, but they fell into dissolution ; not, they removed to a distant place, *but there was found no place for them;* they ceased to exist ; they were no more. And all this, not at the strict command of the Lord Jesus ; not at his awful presence, or before his fiery indignation, but at the bare presence of his majesty, sitting with severe, but adorable dignity on his throne.

12. *And I saw the dead great and small*—Of every age and condition. This includes all those who undergo a change equivalent to death, 1 Cor. xv, 51. *And the books*—Human judges have their books written with pen and ink. How different is the nature of these books ! *were opened*—O how many hidden things will then come to light ! And how many will have quite another appearance, than they had before, in the sight of men ? With the book of God's omniscience, that of conscience will then exactly tally. The book of natural law, as well as of revealed, will then also be displayed. It is not said the books will be read : the light of that day will make them visible to all. Then particularly shall every man know himself, and that with the utmost exactness. This will be the first true, full, impartial, universal history. *And another book*—Wherein are enrolled all that are accepted through the beloved : all who lived and died in the faith that worketh by love, *which is the book of life, was opened*—What manner of expectation will then be, with regard to the issue of the whole ?

13. *Death and hades gave up the dead that were in them*—Death gave up all the bodies of men, and hades, the receptacle of separate souls, gave them up to be reunited to their bodies.

14. *And death and hades were cast into the lake of fire*—That is, were abolished for ever. For neither the righteous nor the wicked were to die any more : their souls and bodies were no more to be separated. Consequently neither death nor hades could any more have a being.

XXI. 1. *And I saw*—So it runs, chap. xix, 11 ; chap. xx, 1, 4, 11, in a succes sion. All these several representations follow one another in order. So the vision reaches into eternity, *a new heaven and a new earth*—After the resurrec- tion and general judgment. St. John is not now describing a flourishing state of the Church, but a new and eternal state of all things : *for the first heaven*

2 sea. And I saw the holy city, the new Jerusalem, coming down
from God out of heaven, prepared as a bride adorned for her hus-
3 band. And I heard a loud voice out of heaven saying, Behold the
tabernacle of God with men, and he will pitch his tent with them ;
and they shall be his people, and God himself *shall be* with them,
4 *and be* their God. And he shall wipe away all tears from their
eyes, and death shall be no more, neither shall sorrow, or crying,
or pain be any more ; because the former things are gone away.
5 And he that sat upon the throne said, Behold, I make all things
new. And he saith to me, Write : these sayings are faithful and
6 true. And he said to me, It is done. I am the Alpha and the
Omega, the beginning and the end. I will give to him that thirsteth
7 of the fountain of the water of life freely. He that overcometh
shall inherit these things ; and I will be to him a God, and he
8 shall be to me a son. But the fearful, and unbelieving, and abominable, and murderers, and whoremongers, and sorcerers, and

and the first earth—Not only the lowest part of heaven, not only the solar system, but the whole ethereal heaven, with all its hosts, whether of planets or
fixed stars, Isa. xxxiv, 4 ; Matt. xxiv, 29. All the former things will be done
away, that all may become new, ver. 4, 5 ; 2 Pet. iii, 10, 12, *are passed away*—
But in the fourth verse it is said, are gone away. There the stronger word is used ;
for death, mourning, and sorrow, go away together ; the former heaven and earth
only pass away, giving place to the new heaven and the new earth.
2. *And I saw the holy city*—The new heaven, the new earth, and the new
Jerusalem, are closely connected. This city is wholly new, belonging not to
this world, not to the millennium, but to eternity. This appears from the series
of the vision, the magnificence of the description, and the opposition of this city
to the second death, chap. xx, 11, 12 ; xxi, 1, 2, 5, 8, 9 ; xxii, 5. *Coming down*
—In the very act of descending.
3. *They shall be his people, and God himself shall be with them, and be their
God*—So shall the covenant between God and his people be executed in the most
glorious manner.
4. *And death shall be no more*—This is a full proof that this whole description belongs not to time, but eternity : *neither shall sorrow, or crying, or pain be
any more ; for the former things are gone away*—Under the former heaven and
upon the former earth, there was death and sorrow, crying and pain, all which
occasioned many tears. But now pain and sorrow are fled away, and the saints
have everlasting life and joy.
5. *And he that sat upon the throne said*—Not to St. John only From the
first mention of him that sat upon the throne, chap. iv, 2, this is the first speech
which is expressly ascribed to him. *And he*—The angel, *saith to me, Write*—
As follows, *these sayings are faithful and true*—This includes all that wen,
before. The apostle seems again to have ceased writing, being overcome with
ecstasy at the voice of him that spake.
6. *And he*—That sat upon the throne, *said to me, It is done*—All that the
prophets had spoken ; all that was spoken, chap. iv, 1. We read this expression
twice in this prophecy : first (chap. xvi, 17,) at the fulfilling of the wrath of God,
and here at the making all things new. *I am the Alpha and the Omega, the be
ginning and the end*—The latter explains the former, the everlasting. *I will
give to him that thirsteth*—The Lamb saith the same, chap. xxii, 17.
7. *He that overcometh*—Which is more than he that thirsteth ; *shall inherit
these things*—Which I have made new. *I will be his God, and he shall be my
son*—Both in the Hebrew and Greek language, in which the Scriptures were
written : what we translate *shall* and *will* are one and the same word. The only
difference consists in an English translation, or in the want of knowledge in him
that interprets what he does not understand.
8. *But the fearful and unbelieving*—Who, through want of courage and faith,
do not overcome ; *and abominable*—That is, Sodomites ; *and whoremongers, and*

ıdolaters, and all liars, their part *is* in the lake that burneth with
fire and brimstone, which is the second death.

9   And there came one of the seven angels that had the seven
phials full of the seven last plagues, and talked with me, saying,
10 Come hither, I will show thee the bride, the Lamb's wife. And
he carried me away in the Spirit to a great and high mountain, and
showed me the holy city Jerusalem, descending out of heaven from
11 God, Having the glory of God: her window was like the most
12 precious stone, like a jasper stone, clear as crystal, Having a wall
great and high, having twelve gates, and at the gates twelve angels,
and the names written thereon, which are *the names* of the twelve
13 tribes of the children of Israel: On the east three gates, and on the
north three gates, and on the south three gates, and on the west
14 three gates. And the wall of the city had twelve foundations, and
15 upon them the names of the twelve apostles of the Lamb. And
he that talked with me had a measure, a golden reed to measure the
16 city, and the gates thereof, and the wall thereof. And the city
lieth four-square, and the length is as large as the breadth. And
he measured the city with the reed twelve thousand furlongs: the
17 length, and the breadth, and the height of it, are equal. And he

sorcerers, and idolaters—These three sins generally went together : their part is
in the lake.

9. *And there came one of the seven angels that had the seven phials*—Whereby
room had been made for the kingdom of God; *saying, Come, I will show thee
the bride*—The same angel had before showed him Babylon, chap. xvii, 1, which
is directly opposed to the New Jerusalem.

10. *And he carried me away in the Spirit*—The same expression as before,
chap. xvi, 3 ; *and showed me the holy city Jerusalem*—The old city is now forgotten, so that this is no longer termed the new, but absolutely Jerusalem. O
how did St. John long to enter in ! But the time was not yet come. Ezekiel
also describes the holy city, and what pertains thereto, chap. xl–xlviii; but a
city quite different from the old Jerusalem, as it was either before or after the
Babylonish captivity. The descriptions of the prophet and of the apostle agree
in many particulars. But in many more they differ. Ezekiel expressly describes the temple, and the worship of God therein, closely alluding to the
Levitical service. But St. John saw no temple, and describes the city far more
large, glorious, and heavenly than the prophet. Yet that which he describes
is the same city ; but as it subsisted soon after the destruction of the beast.
This being observed, both the prophecies agree together, and one may explain
the other.

11. *Having the glory of God*—For her light, ver. 23; Isa. lx, 1, 2 ; Zech. ii, 5.
Her window—There was only one which ran all around the city. The light did
not come in from without through this. For the glory of God is within the city.
But it shines out from within to a great distance, ver. 23, 24.

12. *Twelve angels*—Still waiting upon the heirs of salvation.

14. *And the wall of the city had twelve foundations, and on them the names
of the twelve apostles of the Lamb*—Figuratively showing, that the inhabitants
of the city had built only on that faith which the apostles once delivered to the
saints.

15. *And he measured the city twelve thousand furlongs*—Not in circumference,
but on each of the four sides. Jerusalem was thirty-three furlongs in circumference ; Alexandria thirty in length, ten in breadth. Nineveh is reported to
have been four hundred furlongs round; Babylon four hundred and eighty.
But what inconsiderable villages were all these compared to the new Jerusalem ? By this measure is understood the greatness of the city, with the exact
order and just proportion of every part of it: to show figuratively that this
city was prepared for a great number of inhabitants, how small soever the
number of real Christians may sometimes appear to be : and that every thing

measured the wall thereof, a hundred and forty-four *reeds*, the
18 measure of a man, that is, of an angel.   And the building of the
wall thereof was jasper, and the city *was* of pure gold, like clear
19 glass.   And the foundations of the wall of the city were adorned
with all manner of precious stones.   The first foundation *was* a
jasper, the second a sapphire, the third a chalcedony, the fourth an
20 emerald, The fifth a sardonyx, the sixth a sardius, the seventh a
chrysolite, the eighth a beryl, the ninth a topaz, the tenth a chry-
21 sophrase, the eleventh a jacinth, the twelfth an amethyst.   And
the twelve gates *were* twelve pearls, each of the gates was of one
pearl: and the street of the city *was* pure gold, transparent as
22 glass.   And I saw no temple therein: for the LORD GOD Almighty
23 and the Lamb are the temple of it.   And the city hath no need of
the sun, neither of the moon, to shine on it; for the glory of God
24 hath enlightened it, and the Lamb *is* the lamp thereof.   And the
nations shall walk by the light thereof, and the kings of the earth
25 bring their glory into it.   And the gates of it shall not be shut

---

relating to the happiness of that state was prepared with the greatest order and
exactness.

The city is twelve thousand furlongs high; the wall a hundred and forty-four
reeds.   This is exactly the same height, only expressed in a different manner.
The twelve thousand furlongs being spoken absolutely, without any explanation,
are common human furlongs: the hundred forty-four reeds are not of common
human length; but of angelic, abundantly larger than human.   It is said the
measure of a man, that is, of an angel, because St. John saw the measuring
angel in a human shape.   The reed therefore was as great as was the stature of
that human form in which the angel appeared.   In treating of all these things,
a deep reverence is necessary, and so is a measure of spiritual wisdom; that we
may neither understand them too literally and grossly, nor go too far from the
natural force of the words.   The gold, the pearls, the precious stones, the walls,
foundations, gates, are undoubtedly figurative expressions: seeing the city itself
is in glory, and the inhabitants of it have spiritual bodies; yet these spiritual
bodies are also real bodies, and the city is an abode distinct from its inhabitants;
and proportionate to them who take up a finite and a determinate space.   The
measures therefore above-mentioned are real and determinate.

18. *And the building of the wall was jasper*—That is, the wall was built of
jasper; *and the city*—The houses, was *of pure gold.*

19. *And the foundations were adorned with precious stones*—That is, beauti
fully made of them.   The precious stones on the high priest's breastplate of
judgment were a proper emblem to express the happiness of God's Church, in his
presence with them, and in the blessing of his protection.   The like ornaments
on the foundations of the walls of this city, may express the perfect glory and
happiness of all the inhabitants of it, from the most glorious presence and pro
tection of God.   Each precious stone was not the ornament of the foundation,
but the foundation itself.   The colours of these are remarkably mixed.   A jasper
is of the colour of white marble, with a light shade of green and of red; a sapphire is of a sky-blue speckled with gold; a chalcedony, or carbuncle, of the
colour of red hot iron; an emerald, of a grass-green.

20. A sardonyx is red, streaked with white; a sardius, of a deep red; a chry
solite, of a deep yellow; a beryl, sea-green; topaz, a pale yellow.   A chrysophrase
is greenish and transparent, with gold specks; a jacinth, of a red purple; an
amethyst, violet-purple.

22. *The Lord God and the Lamb are the temple of it*—He fills the new heaven
and the new earth.   He surrounds the city and sanctifies it, and all that are
therein.   He is all in all.

23. *The glory of God*—Infinitely brighter than the shining of the sun.

24. *And the nations*—The whole verse is taken from Isa. lx, 3; *shall walk by
the light thereof*—Which throws itself outward from the city far and near; *and
the kings of the earth*—'Those of them who have a part there; *bring their glory*

26 by day : and there shall be no night there. And they shall bring
27 the glory and the honour of the nations into it. But there shall in
no wise enter into it any thing common, or that worketh abomination, or *maketh* a lie, but they who are written in the Lamb's book
of life.

XXII. And he showed me a river of the water of life clear as crys-
2 tal, proceeding out of the throne of God and of the Lamb. In the
midst of the street of it, and on either side of the river, *is* the tree
of life, bearing twelve sorts of fruits, yielding its fruit every month :
3 and the leaves of the tree *are* for the healing of the nations. And
there shall be no more curse : but the throne of God and of the
4 Lamb shall be in it : and his servants shall worship him, And
5 shall see his face, and his name *shall be* on their foreheads. And
there shall be no night there, neither is there need of a lamp, or
of the light of the sun ; for the Lord God will enlighten them, and
they shall reign for ever.

---

into it—Not their old glory, which is now abolished ; but such as becomes the
new earth, and receives an immense addition by their entrance into the city.

26. *And they shall bring the glory of the nations into it*—It seems a select part
of each nation ; that is, all which can contribute to make this city honourable
and glorious shall be found in it ; as if all that was rich and precious throughout
the world was brought into one city.

27. *Common*—That is, unholy ; *but those who are written in the Lamb's book
of life*—Truly, holy, persevering believers. This blessedness is enjoyed by those
only, and as such they are registered among them who are to inherit eternal
life.

XXII. 1. *And he showed me a river of the water of life*—The ever fresh and
fruitful effluence of the Holy Ghost. See Ezek. xlvii, 1-12, where also the
trees are mentioned which bear fruit every month, that is, perpetually, *proceeding out of the throne of God and of the Lamb. All that the Father hath*, saith the
Son of God, *is mine*—Even the throne of his glory.

2. *In the midst of the street*—Here is the paradise of God, mentioned chap.
ii, 7 ; *is the tree of life*—Not one tree only, but many ; *every month*—That is, in
inexpressible abundance. The variety likewise, as well as the abundance of the
fruits of the Spirit, may be intimated thereby : *and the leaves are for the healing
of the nations*—For the continuing their health, not the restoring it ; for no
sickness is there.

3. *And there shall be no more curse*—But pure life and blessing. Every effect
of the displeasure of God for sin being now totally removed ; *but the throne of God
and the Lamb shall be in it*—That is, the glorious presence and reign of God :
and his servants—The highest honour in the universe, *shall worship him*—The
noblest employment.

4. *And shall see his face*—Which was not granted to Moses. They shall
have the nearest access to, and thence the highest resemblance of him. This is
the highest expression, in the language of Scripture, to denote the most perfect
happiness of the heavenly state, 1 John iii, 2. *And his name shall be on their
foreheads*—Each of them shall be openly acknowledged as God's own property :
and his glorious nature most visibly shine forth in them : *and they shall reign*—
But who are the subjects of these kings ? The other inhabitants of the new
earth. For there must needs be an everlasting difference between those who
when on earth excelled in virtue, and those comparatively slothful and unprofit
able servants, who were just saved as by fire. The kingdom of God is taken by
force. But the prize is worth all the labour. Whatever is high, lovely, or excellent in all the monarchies of the earth, is, all together, not a grain of dust,
compared to the glory of the children of God. God is not ashamed to be called
their God, for whom he hath prepared this city. But who shall come up into this
holy place ? They who keep his commandments, ver. 14.

5. *And they shall reign for ever and ever*—What encouragement is this to the
patience and faithfulness of the saints ? That whatever their sufferings are they

6   And he said to me, These sayings *are* faithful and true: the
Lord, the God of the spirits of the prophets, hath sent his angel
7 to show his servants the things which must be done shortly. Behold I come quickly: happy *is* he that keepeth the words of the
8 prophecy of this book. And *it was* I John who heard and saw
these things ; and when I had heard and seen, I fell down to wor
9 ship at the feet of the angel who showed me these things. But
he saith to me, See *thou do it* not ; I am thy fellow servant, and
of thy brethren the prophets, and of them who keep the sayings
10 of this book : worship God. And he saith to me, Seal not the
11 sayings of the prophecy of this book : the time is nigh. He that
is unrighteous, let him be unrighteous still ; and he that is filthy
let him be filthy still ; and he that is righteous, let him be righteous
12 still ; and he that is holy, let him be holy still. ' Behold, I come
quickly, and my reward *is* with me, to render to every one as his
13 work shall be.   I am the Alpha and the Omega, the first and the
last, the beginning and the end.
14   Happy *are* they that do his commandments, that they may have

will work out for them an eternal weight of glory. Thus ends the doctrine of
this revelation, in the everlasting happiness of all the faithful. The mysterious
ways of Providence are cleared up, and all things issue in an eternal Sabbath,
an everlasting state of perfect peace and happiness, reserved for all who endure
to the end.

6. *And he said to me*—Here begins the conclusion of the book, exactly agreeing with the introduction, (particularly verses 6, 7, 10, with chapter i, 1, 3,) and
giving light to the whole book, as this book does to the whole Scripture. *These
sayings are faithful and true*—All the things which you have heard and seen shall
be faithfully accomplished in their order, and are infallibly true. *The Lord, the
God of the holy prophets*—who inspired and authorized them of old, *hath* now *sent
me his angel, to show his servants*—By thee, *the things which must be done shortly*—Which will begin to be performed immediately.

7. *Behold, I come quickly*—Saith our Lord himself; to accomplish these things,
Happy is he that keepeth—Without adding or diminishing, ver. 18, 19, the words
of this book.

8. *I fell down to worship at the feet of the angel*—The very same words which
occur, chap. xix, 10. The reproof of the angel likewise, *See* thou do it *not ; for
I am thy fellow servant*, is expressed in the very same terms as before. May it
not be the very same incident which is here related again ? Is not this far more
probable, than that the apostle should commit a fault again, of which he had been
so solemnly warned before ?

9. *See* thou do it *not*—The expression in the original is short and elliptical, as
is usual in showing vehement aversion.

10. *And he saith to me*—After a little pause, *Seal not the sayings of this book*—
Conceal them not, like the things that are sealed up. *The time is nigh*—wherein they shall begin to take place.

11. *He that is unrighteous*—As if he had said, the final judgment is at hand ·
after which the condition of all mankind will admit of no change for ever. *Unrighteous*—Unjustified, *filthy*—Unsanctified, unholy.

12. *I*, Jesus Christ, *come quickly*—To judge the world, *and my reward is with
me*—The rewards which I assign both to the righteous and the wicked are given
at my coming, *to give to every man according as his work*—His whole inward and
outward behaviour, *shall be.*

13. *I am the Alpha and the Omega, the first and the last*—Who exist from
everlasting to everlasting. How clear, incontestable a proof does our Lord nere
give of his Divine glory !

14. *Happy are they that do his commandments*—His who saith, *I come* He
speaks of himself; *that they may have right*—Through his gracious covenant, *to
the tree of life*—To all the blessings signified by it   When Adam broke his con

right to the tree of life, and may enter in by the gates into the city
15 Without *are* dogs, and sorcerers, and whoremongers, and murderers, and idolaters, and every one that loveth and maketh a lie.
16 I Jesus have sent my angel to testify to you, to the Churches, these things. I am the root and offspring of David, the bright, the
17 morning star. And the Spirit and the bride say, Come. And let him that heareth say, Come. And let him that thirsteth come ; let him that willeth take the water of life freely.
18 I testify to every one that heareth the words of the prophecy of this book, if any man add to them, GOD shall add to him the
19 plagues that are written in this book. And if any man shall take away from the words of the book of this prophecy, GOD shall take away his part of the tree of life, and the holy city, which are written in this book.
20 He that testifieth these things saith, Yea, I come quickly. Amen : Come, Lord Jesus.
21 The grace of the Lord Jesus *be* with all.

---

mandment he was driven from the tree of life. They who keep his commandments shall eat thereof.

15. *Without are dogs*—The sentence in the original is abrupt, as expressing abhorrence. The gates are ever open; but not for dogs; fierce and rapacious men.

16. *I Jesus have sent my angel to testify these things*—Primarily to you, the seven angels of the Churches; then to those Churches, and afterward to all other Churches in succeeding ages. I, as God, am the root and source of David's family and kingdom ; as man, am descended from his loins. I am the star out of Jacob, Num. xxiv, 16, like the bright morning star, who put an end to the night of ignorance, sin, and sorrow, and usher in an eternal day of light, purity, and joy.

17. *The Spirit and the bride*—The Spirit of adoption in the bride, in the heart of every true believer, says with earnest desire and expectation, *Come*, and accomplish all the words of this prophecy ; *and let him that thirsteth, come*—Here they also who are farther off are invited ; *and whosoever will, let him take the water of life*—He may partake of my spiritual and unspeakable blessings as freely as he makes use of the most common refreshments; as freely as he drinks of the running stream.

18, 19. *I testify to every one*, &c—From the fulness of his heart the apostle utters this testimony, this weighty admonition, not only to the Churches of Asia, but to all who should ever hear this book. He that *adds*, all the plagues shall be added to him : he that *takes from* it, all the blessings shall be taken from him. And doubtless this guilt is incurred by all those who lay hinderances in the way of the faithful, which prevent them from hearing their Lord's *I come*, and answering, *Come, Lord Jesus*. This may likewise be considered as an awful sanction given to the whole New Testament ; in like manner as Moses guarded the law, Deut. iv, 2, and xii, 32, and as God himself did, Mal. iv, 4, in closing the canon of the Old Testament.

20. *He that testifieth these things*—Even all that is contained in this book, *saith*, for the encouragement of the Church in all her afflictions, *Yea*—Answering the call of the Spirit and the bride. *I come quickly*—to destroy all her enemies, and establish her in a state of perfect and everlasting happiness. The apostle expresses his earnest desire and hope of this, by answering, *Amen ; Come, Lord Jesus !*

21. *The grace*—The free love of the Lord Jesus, and all its fruits, be with all who thus long for his appearing.

IT MAY BE PROPER TO SUBJOIN HERE A SHORT VIEW OF THE WHOLE CONTENTS OF THIS BOOK.

In the year of the world

3940. Jesus Christ is born, three years before the common computation. In that which is vulgarly called the thirtieth year of our Lord, Jesus Christ dies, rises; ascends.

A. D. 96. The Revelation is given; the coming of our Lord is declared to the seven Churches in Asia, and their angels, Rev. i, ii, iii.

97, 98. The seven seals are opened, and under the fifth the Chronos is declared, chap. iv–vi.

Seven trumpets are given to the seven angels, chap. vii, viii.

Century 2d, 3d, 4th, 5th, the trumpets of the 1st, 2d, 3d, 4th, angel, chap. viii.

510–589. The first wo

589–634. The interval after the first wo } chap. ix.

634–840. The second wo

800. The beginning of the non-chronos: many kings

840–947. The interval after the second wo } chap. ix, x.

847–1521. The 1260 days of the woman, after she had brought forth the man child, chap. xii, 6.

947–1836. The third wo, ver. 12.

1058–1836. The time, times, and half a time, and within that period, the beast his forty-two months, his number 666, to chap xiii, 5.

1209. War with the saints : the end of the Chronos, ver. 7.

1614. An everlasting Gospel promulged, chap. xiv, 6.

1810. The end of the forty-two months of the beast; after which, and the pouring out of the phials, he is not, and Babylon reigns queen chap. xv, xvi.

1832. The beast ascends from the bottomless pit, chap. xvii, xviii.

1836. The end of the non-chronos, and of the many kings: the fulfilling of the word, and of the mystery of God: the repentance of the survivors in the great city : and the end of the little time, and of the three times and a half: the destruction of the beast : the imprisonment of Satan, chap. xix, xx.

After-   The loosing of Satan for a small time ; the beginning of the 1000
ward   years' reign of the saints ; the end of the small time, chap. xx.

The end of the world ; all things new, chap. xx–xxii.

The several ages, from the time of St. John's being in Patmos, down to the present time, may, according to the chief incidents mentioned in the Revelation, be distinguished thus :

Age II. The destruction of the Jews by Adrian, chap. viii, ver. 7.

III. The inroads of the barbarous nations, ver. 8

IV. The Arian bitterness, ver. 10.

V. The end of the western empire, ver. 12.

VI. The Jews tormented in Persia, chap. ix, 1.

VII. The Saracen cavalry, ver. 13.

VIII. Many kings, chap. x, 11.

IX. The ruler of the nations born, chap xii, 5.

X. The third wo, ver. 12.

XI. The ascent of the beast out of the sea, chap. xiii, 1.

XII. Power given to the beast, ver. 5.

XIII. War with the saints, ver. 7.

XIV. The middle of the third wo.

XV. The beast in the midst of his strength.

XVI. The reformation ; the woman better fed.

XVII. An everlasting Gospel promulged, chap. xiv, 6.

XVIII. The worship of the beast and of his image, ver. 9.

O God, whatsoever stands or falls, stands or falls by thy judgment. Defend thy own truth. Have mercy on me and my readers ! To thee be glory for ever·

INDEX

WORDS EXPLAINED IN THE PRECEDING COMMENT.